ASCETICISM

ASCETICISM

Edited by

Vincent L. Wimbush

Richard Valantasis

With the assistance of

Gay L. Byron

William S. Love

OXFORD
UNIVERSITY PRESS

OXFORD
UNIVERSITY PRESS

Oxford New York
Auckland Bangkok Buenos Aires Cape Town Chennai
Dar es Salaam Delhi Hong Kong Istanbul Karachi Kolkata
Kuala Lumpur Madrid Melbourne Mexico City Mumbai Nairobi
São Paulo Shanghai Singapore Taipei Tokyo Toronto

and an associated company in Berlin

First published in 1998 by Oxford University Press, Inc.
198 Madison Avenue, New York, New York 10016

www.oup.com

First issued as an Oxford University Press paperback, 2002

Oxford is a registered trademark of Oxford University Press

Library of Congress Cataloging-in-Publication Data
Asceticism / edited by Vincent L. Wimbush, Richard Valantasis.
p. cm.
Essays originally presented at an international conference on the
Ascetic dimension in religious life and culture, held at Union
Theological Seminary in New York, Aug. 25–29, 1993.
Includes bibliographical references and index.
ISBN 0-19-508535-3; 0-19-515138-0 (pbk.)
1. Asceticism—Congresses. I. Wimbush, Vincent L.
II. Valantasis, Richard, 1946—
BL625.A836 1995
291.4'47—dc20 94-17642 CIP

1 3 5 7 9 8 6 4 2

Printed in the United States of America
on acid-free paper

CONTENTS

FOREWORD

If we make a preliminary distinction between religion as social institution and religion as personal inner transformation, asceticism in its most general sense is close to the heart of the latter. (This preliminary distinction tends, however, to break down as we note the important role of the ascetic—the shaman, the renunciant, the anchorite, the monastic—in certain societies.) Asceticism occurs either in the search for or in response to a believed-in sacred reality—whether found "above" us or through the depths of our own being—in relation to which, or in unity with which, is thought to be our highest good. For it is probably a universal religious intuition that "true religion" is to be found within the wide spectrum that begins with commitment, dedication, singleness of mind, purity of heart, and self-discipline in prayer or meditation; that extends into practices of pilgrimage, fasting, vigils, celibacy, poverty, and obedience; and that may go on to further and sometimes extreme austerities, which border in the end upon clearly pathological excesses. In various religious traditions, asceticism ranges, for example, from the mild self-denials of Christians during Lent to the more demanding self-denial of Muslims during Ramadan to the yet more rigorous and complete renunciation of worldly things by *saṃnyāsin*s in the Brahmanic tradition and the Hindu sectarian traditions of South Asia. It embraces the whole realm of spiritual method and discipline, including the solitude, silence, and devotions of monastics, the austerities of shamans, and the severe practices of ascetics seeking special insights and visions.

It is the tremendous width of this spectrum that makes the subject of asceticism so vast and so difficult to encompass. But what makes it important is a virtually universal and spontaneous respect for those in whose lives we can see a renunciation of purely personal satisfactions in order to serve God/Truth/Dharma. This is true both at the level of such world-shaping figures as Jesus and Gautama and at that of such lesser but enormously influential figures as Francis of Assisi and Mahatma Gandhi. And it is true again in endlessly varying degrees of innumerable men and women in every part of the world who have inspired their neighbors by self-mastery in their dedication to a higher claim. In contrast, there is a natural tendency for people to "see through" religious figures who are manifestly interested in wealth, fame, power, or personal gratification.

The subject of asceticism functions as a window on to the history of religions through the ages and across the centuries. No one volume, however broad in scope, can cover everything; there will always be more work to do, more topics to study and examine. The present collection of essays concentrates primarily on the Christian tradition, but it also includes accounts of the ascetic impulse in the ancient Mediterranean world, in Judaism, in Tibetan Buddhism, in Islam, and in certain religious traditions in South Asia and Africa. In its interdisciplinary approach to asceticism, it provides a fresh view of a vast field; in so doing it will be an important stimulus to new research and to further interdisciplinary and cross-cultural collaboration.

John Hick

EDITORS' NOTE: John Hick is a Fellow of the Institute for Advanced Research in the Humanities, University of Birmingham, and Danforth Professor Emeritus, The Claremont Graduate School.

ACKNOWLEDGMENTS

The publication of this volume has been a massive and complicated project. The two major stages in the project—the convening of an international conference at Union Thological Seminary in New York City in April 1993 and the research and editorial work that transformed the conference proceedings into the published form now before the reader—have involved the support of a great number of persons and institutions.

We should like to offer words of sincere gratitude first to those who made possible the convening of the international conference.

We extend thanks to an extraordinary group of students at Union Theological Seminary and Columbia University—William S. Love, who as assistant director of the conference was the one person who could be counted on at all times to get things done, to smooth out difficulties, to take the heat and so little credit; Ricardo (Rick) Carson, Gay Byron, and Jeffrey Jones, who were with us from beginning to end; Daniele (Fabri) Di Piazzi, Tammy Ison, Michelle Lim, Judy Stevens, Richard Carter, John Hindsman and Victor Mavi, who were consistently supportive in many different areas. These all volunteered an enormous amount of time to the planning, coordination and staffing of all aspects of the conference. (We pulled it off!)

Thanks are due to the administrators at the two institutions with which we are affiliated. At Union, we thank especially President Holland Hendrix and Academic Dean Peter Van Ness, for consistent financial support and for encouragement of new academic ventures for a new academic era at Union. At Saint Louis University, we thank William M. Shea, chair of the Department of Theological Studies; Donald G. Brennan, dean of the Graduate School of Arts and Sciences; and Donald P. Sprengel, Research Services of the Graduate School of Arts and Sciences, for financial support and for believing in Richard Valantasis and his long-distance exploits.

We express our gratitude to the staff at Union for supporting the effort in so many different ways. Burke Library staff members Milton McGatch, Drew Kadel, and Seth Kasten are to be commended for the work they did in putting together an excellent display on Ascetica, and for general support. Associate Dean James Hayes and the Academic Office staff, including Assistant James Nally and faculty secretaries Julia Galas and Vera Balma; Sandra Jones, then director of communications; Awilda Fosse, Michael Orzechowski, and the Facilities Office staff; Karen Barsness and the catering staff; colleagues in the Biblical Field; Rafael Hejduk in Media

Services; Jack Saviano and the bookstore staff; Pat Laws and James Wilkinson of the Finance Office; and Susan Blain and Harry Huff of the Worship Office all made a great difference to the cause.

For the most generous financial support received we extend a hearty thanks to Professor Steven S. Rockefeller, Middlebury College; the Louisville Institute, Louisville, Kentucky; and the Reverent Basil S. Gregory and John S. Latsuis, U.S.A. Inc.

Several other institutions and colleagues aided the conference with financial, in-kind, and moral support—Chancellor Ismar Schorsch, Provost Ivan Marcus and the Jewish Theological Seminary of America; Dean Robert McCaughey, Professor Jack Hawley, and Barnard College; Dean Roger Bagnall and the Columbia University Graduate School of Arts and Sciences; Philemon Sevastiades; Dean Harold Trulear and New York Theological Seminary; Dean John Koenig, Professor Deirdre Good, and General Theological Seminary; President Barbara Wheeler and Auburn Theological Seminary; the departments of religion, classics, and history at Columbia University. To these institutions and colleagues we are most grateful for their collegiality, friendship, and support.

The conference was held together, moved along in timely fashion, and was even made quite exciting in general discussion by several moderators. We should like to thank the following colleagues for their general practical wisdom and for their friendly yet firm hands at the head table: Alan Cameron, Richard Norris, William V. Harris, Anitra Kolenkow, James E. Goehring, Suzanne Said, Burton Visotzky, Robert Somerville, Caroline Walker Bynum, Celia Deutsch, Ivan Marcus, Deirdre Good, and Larry Rasmussen.

We should like to give special thanks to colleague Virginia Burrus for pinch-hitting at the last minute. She read convincingly and with clarity a paper not her own, written originally in a language other than English.

Words of gratitude are also due those who helped prepare the conference papers for publication.

We express thanks to Union students Tammy Ison, Daniele (Fabri) Di Piazzi, William S. Love, and Ricardo (Rick) Carson, for their proofreading and translation work. Union faculty secretaries Julia Galas and Vera Balma are to be thanked for their assistance with typing, photocopying, and general correspondence.

Colleagues Elizabeth Castelli (California), Burton Visotzky (Jewish Theological Seminary), Walter O. Kaelber (Wagner College), and Kosuke Koyama (Union) we thank for their expert and critical reading in certain areas of difficulty for the editors. And Sharon Krengle (New Jersey) we thank for her expert translation of a manuscript written in Italian.

To Union research librarians Drew Kadel and Seth Kasten we express our gratitude for their assistance with knotty footnote and bibliographic references. And Kristine Veldheer of the library staff we thank for assistance with some technical computer challenges.

Zachary Maxey, a former student of Vincent Wimbush at Claremont, is thanked for his preliminary work done on bibliography; and the staff of the Institute for Antiquity and Christianity in Claremont is thanked for some technical assistance in connection with the preliminary bibliography. For research work in connection with particular sections of the bibliography William S. Love, a Ph.D. candidate at Columbia, is due another expression of thanks.

For the extensive proofreading we express our gratitude to Janet F. Carlson, spouse of Richard Valantasis, and to Stephen Hoskins and Kevin O'Connor, graduate students at Saint Louis University.

Gay L. Byron, a Ph.D. candidate at Union, is due many expressions of thanks for the outstanding work—translation, editorial, bibliographic, general research—she did in helping to shape the entire manuscript into the volume that it has become.

To our families—Janet; Linda and Lauren—for the support they gave that sustained us through challenging times, we say thanks, even though we know it is not an adequate expression of our debt to you.

To Claude Conyers and Scott Lenz at Oxford University Press, for their support and enthusiasm for this project, and for the professional wisdom and energy that they brought to it, we express our thanks.

There is absolutely no way the two stages in this massive project could have been completed as successfully and as quickly as they have been without the great assistance of Ph.D. candidates Gay Byron and William Love. We hope that they will accept our heartfelt gratitude, a partial expression of which is found on the title page.

Vincent L. Wimbush
Richard Valantasis

CONTRIBUTORS

Peter J. Awn
Professor of Religion, Columbia University

Dianne M. Bazell
Assistant Professor, Department of Humanities, Syracuse University

Jason Beduhn
Department of Religious Studies, Indiana University

Daniel Boyarin
Hermann P. and Sophia Taubman Professor of Near Eastern Studies, University of California, Berkeley

William C. Bushell
Visiting Scholar, Anthropology Program, Massachusetts Institute of Technology

Averil Cameron, FBA
Warden of Keble College, University of Oxford

Elizabeth A. Castelli
Assistant Professor of Religion, Barnard College

Elizabeth A. Clark
John Carlisle Kilgo Professor of Religion, Duke University

Gillian Clark
Professor of Ancient History, University of Bristol

Gregory Collins, OSB
Glenstal Abbey, County of Limerick, Ireland

Gail P. Corrington-Streete
Associate Professor of Religious Studies, Rhodes College

William E. Deal
Severance Associate Professor of the History of Religion, Case Western Reserve University

J. Duncan M. Derrett
Half Way House, Blockley, Gloucestershire, England

John M. Dillon
Regius Professor of Greek, Trinity College, University of Dublin

Sidney H. Griffith
Professor of Semitic and Egyptian Languages and Literatures, Institute of Christian Oriental Research, Catholic University of America

Geoffrey Gait Harpham
Professor of English, Tulane University

Verna E. F. Harrison
Independent scholar, Berkeley, California

John Stratton Hawley
Professor of Religion, Barnard College

Yizhar Hirschfeld
Field Archaeologist, The Israel Museum, Jerusalem

Ephraim Isaac
Director, Institute of Semitic Studies, Princeton University

Paul Julian
Solitary monastic, New York, New York

Walter O. Kaelber
Professor of Religion, Wagner College

Charles Kannengiesser
Professor of Theology, Concordia University

Gillian Lindt
Dean, Graduate School of Arts and Sciences, Columbia University

Bruce J. Malina
Professor of Theology, Creighton University

Fedwa Malti-Douglas
Martha C. Kraft Professor of Humanities, Indiana University

Bernard McGinn
Naomi Shenstone Donnelly Professor of Historical Theology and of the History of Christianity, Divinity School, University of Chicago

J. Giles Milhaven
Professor of Religious Studies, Brown University

Patricia Cox Miller
Associate Professor of Religion, Syracuse University

Vasudha Narayanan
Professor of Religion, University of Florida

Patrick Olivelle
Alma Cowden Madden Professor in the Humanities, University of Texas at Austin

Elaine H. Pagels
Harrington Spear Paine Professor of Religion, Princeton University

John Pinsent
Honorary Senior Fellow, School of Classics and Ancient History, University of Liverpool

Ann W. Ramsey
Assistant Professor of History, University of Texas at Austin

Samuel Rubenson
Professor of Theology, University of Lund

Michael L. Satlow
Associate Professor of Religious Studies, University of Virginia

Giulia Sfameni Gasparro
Istituto di Studi Storico—Religiosi, Università di Messina

Teresa M. Shaw
Religion Program Coordinator, Adjunct Lecturer in Religion, Claremont Graduate School

Robert A. F. Thurman
Jey Tsong Khapa Professor of Indo-Tibetan Studies, Columbia University

Leif E. Vaage
Assistant Professor of New Testament, Emmanuel College, Toronto School of Theology

Richard Valantasis
Professor of New Testament and Christian Origins, Iliff School of Theology

Peter H. Van Ness
Lecturer in Chronic Disease Epidemiology, Yale University

Kallistos Ware
Lecturer in Eastern Orthodox Studies and Fellow of Pembroke College, University of Oxford

Robert L. Wilken
William R. Kenan, Jr., Professor of the History of Christianity, University of Virginia

Vincent L. Wimbush
Professor of New Testament and Christian Origins, Union Theological Seminary

Edith Wyschogrod
J. Newton Rayzor Professor of Philosophical and Religious Thought, Rice University

Ehsan Yarshater
Director, Center for Iranian Studies, and Hagop Kevorkian Professor Emeritus of Iranian Studies, Columbia University

INTRODUCTION

Vincent L. Wimbush and Richard Valantasis

Historical Sketch of the Study of Asceticism

Because it is a universal phenomenon, in evidence in ancient as well as modern societies, and because it is often a dramatic, even controversial, part of religions and cultures, asceticism has long been the subject of popular and intellectual interest. In antiquity, various cultures usually registered such interest in homilies, philosophical or theological treatises, popular meditations, rituals, ecclesiastical canons, diatribes, letters, revelations, panegyrics, vitae.[1] Numerous discussions about the importance of asceticism and debates about the superiority and imperative of different forms of renunciation can be found in these and other genres of literature of Eastern and Western religious traditions.

As is the case with most complex phenomena, however, the detailed description and sustained criticism of asceticism began in the modern period, in particular in the nineteenth century. Histories (often a part of the history of the ethics or theologies or ethos of a particular religious or cultural tradition), exegetical studies (many texts belonging to the genres mentioned above); ethnographic studies; systematic theologies; dictionary and encyclopedia articles; philosophical and cultural critical essays, even primitive psychological and psychiatric studies—these are among the types of scholarly writings appearing in the modern period in the West that have had asceticism as their subject.

What is striking about the scholarship from the modern period, including even recent writings from the 1980s, is its tendency to be neither comprehensive in historical development nor cross-cultural in scope and methodology. Few works have had as their aim and focus the origins and development of the whole complex and range of phenomena that fall under the rubric "asceticism." Even fewer works have had as their focus the cross-cultural framework essential for a sustained critical perspective. Most works on asceticism have focused upon particular religious traditions, particular cultural systems, particular historical periods, exemplary individuals and texts, or particular behaviors. Most works—especially, but not limited to, those of Western theology—have also tended to reflect strong, not very subtle biases either in favor of or against a particular tradition or set of practices.

Others have tended to reflect modernity's "secular" intellectual and popular understandings of, and prejudices against, the ascetic impulse as expressive of the irrationality, traditionalism, or fanaticism of the religious life. Examples are too numerous to detail; a selective summary treatment follows, in order to establish the general thrust of modern Western scholarly treatment of asceticism.[2]

In nineteenth-century England and Germany works appeared that focused upon asceticism as a legacy of pathology, especially regarding sexuality *(perversio vitae sexualis),* that had to be addressed and overcome if a healthy social order were to be sustained. Johannes Baptista Friedrich's *System der gerichtliche Psychologie* (1852), Henry Maudsley's *The Pathology of the Mind* (3d ed., 1879), Richard von Krafft-Ebing's *Lehrbuch der Psychiatrie* (1879) and *Psychopathia Sexualis* (1887) are examples of such works. Friedrich Nietzsche's better-known works (especially *Beyond Good and Evil,* and *On the Genealogy of Morals*), although they were in nature more historical-interpretive and philosophical than proto-social-scientific, were better known because they squared with the sensibilities among many self-styled "secular intellectuals" of the times.

If usage in the Protestant, English-speaking world is any indicator, popular understandings of asceticism in the beginnings of modernity in the West were rather negative. *The Oxford English Dictionary*—no insignificant index of popular cultural sentiment in the English-speaking world—defines "asceticism" as "extreme" and "severe" abstinence: as "austerity." And the earliest English usage it cites—"Doomed to a life of celibacy by the asceticism which had corrupted the simplicity of Christianity" (Sir Thomas Browne, 1646)—reflects little restraint in its bias.

Whether in direct response to popular understandings and usages, to the tone and tenor of some of the scholarly works listed above, or to the larger and more complex world that was being discovered, a number of scholarly works in the late nineteenth and early twentieth centuries focused upon the histories of asceticism in particular religious and cultural traditions. Theodor Waitz's *Anthropologie der Naturvölker* (6 vols., 1859–1872) focused upon primitive practices and sensibilities; Sir Monier M. Williams's *Buddhism in Its Connexion with Brahmanism and Hinduism in Its Contrast with Christianity* (1889), Isidor Silbernagl's *Der Buddhismus nach seiner Enstehung, Forbildung und Verbreitung* (1891), Thomas Ebenezer Slater's *The Higher Hinduism in Relation to Christianity* (1903), and Caroline A. Rhys Davids's *Buddhism* (1912), among others, began to shed light—however patronizing and refracted through Western traditions and sensibilities—upon Eastern traditions.

The literature on Judaism and Christianity from this period is voluminous. Among the many works that focused upon Judaism, Wilhelm Bousset's *Die Religion des Judentums* (2d ed.; 1906) was significant. So were Adolf von Harnack's *Das Mönchtum* (1881; trans. *Monasticism*) and Otto Zoeckler's *Askese und Mönchtum* (2d ed.; 1897), which traced the history of asceticism (more precisely monasticism), in Christianity. John Mason Neale's *History of the Eastern Church* (5 vols., 1850–1873), J. Mayer's *Die christliche Askese: Ihre Wesen und ihre historische Entfaltung* (1894), Christoph Ernst Luthardt's *Die Ethik Luthers in ihren Grundzeugen* (2d ed., 1875), and Newman Smythe's *Christian Ethics* (1892) prefigured the interpretive histories of Christian asceticism in the modern period of scholarly investigation.

In the late twentieth century, many more sophisticated histories and critical interpretations of particular traditions and practices appeared. Peter Brown's *Body and Society: Men, Women and Sexual Renunciation in Early Christianity* (1987) has clearly become the standard historical-interpretive work on early Christianity. It represents the apex of that tradition of Western scholarship that emphasizes the command of primary sources. English professor Geoffrey Harpham's *The Ascetic Imperative in Culture and Criticism* (1987) and philosopher-theologian Edith Wyschogrod's *Saints and Postmodernism: Revisioning Moral Philosophy* (1990) are provocative examples of the heightened interest in asceticism among postmodernist critics. Although they are not strictly works of history, their treatments of ancient texts have enormous historical-interpretive implications.

The names and works above are highlighted not only because they are better known by the editors but also because they can show how scholarship focused on the ascetic impulse crosses disciplines, fields, and religious traditions. Scholarship on asceticism reflects the late twentieth-century humanist emphasis on comprehensiveness of scope and sophisticated engagement of a number of methods and approaches.

A number of such treatments on the ascetic in particular traditions beyond Christianity have appeared recently: the works of Ross Kraemer, Stephen Fraade, and Daniel Boyarin on Judaism; Patrick Olivelle, Vasudha Narayanan, Walter Kaelber, and Wendy Doniger on Hinduism; Robert Thurman, Steven Collins, and Stanley Tambiah on Buddhism; Fedwa Malti-Douglas on Islamic traditions.

These lists are of course not exhaustive, even of the category created for purposes of the argument. And many other works on asceticism have appeared during the second half of this century that have tended to reflect the same basic scholarly skills in philology and historical interpretation—if not always the cultural critical perspectives and the profundity—represented in the works of the exemplars referred to above. Yet for all the comprehensiveness of scope and sophisticated analysis in their works, scholars interested in asceticism still generally do not talk to each other across disciplinary and field boundaries or across religious and cultural traditions.

The works of some female scholars whose focus is on women and the ascetic in particular cultural traditions may hold the promise of more cross-fertilization and daring methodological experimentation. Averil Cameron, Elizabeth Clark, Fedwa Malti-Douglas, Vasudha Narayanan, and other women scholars who share this focus have challenged longstanding assumptions, including the single-issue, single-motive interpretations of asceticism, that have focused primarily on males. Ultimately, perhaps, the acceptance of more complex phenomenological explanations will inspire conversation about the ascetic across the lines of gender, religious traditions, and academic disciplines.

We are clearly not yet at the point, however, at which such interpretation is common. There have been very few works that have argued for or provided a model for a consistently comparative, multicultural or multitraditional perspective in the study of asceticism. Many of the histories and critical treatments—especially those written before the late twentieth century—have, it appears, assumed that the ascetic within a particular religious or cultural tradition was simple in character, and most have respected the artificially designated boundaries between particular religions or cultures (e.g., "Christian," "Jewish," or "Greek" asceticism and so forth). Even Peter Brown's magisterial work refers often to "Christian asceticism," as though it always clearly entailed something quite different in essence from other contemporary expressions. There is a striking lack of consistent comparative focus in historical-interpretive treatments on asceticism in the modern period in works both popular and scholarly. The collection of essays edited by Austin Creel and Vasudha Narayanan entitled *Monastic Life in the Christian and Hindu Traditions* (1990) is the only recent work to represent a truly comparative focus. And it should be noted—as the title itself indicates—that even this work limits itself to comparison between two traditions, and then only to a discussion of one manifestation or type of ascetic behavior within those two traditions.

Perhaps the popularity of a particular genre of scholarly writing, the "Lone Ranger project," that is, the monograph or text by a single author, has influenced the lack of progress in the cross-disciplinary study of asceticism. Who, having spent a lifetime digging deeply into one text, historical personality, or tradition, would want to venture across those lines? But the early twentieth-century popularity of other types of scholarly writing suggested a move in a different direction. As a reflection of the transformation of many European and American colleges into complex comprehensive research universities, signaling the Western cultural quest for comprehensive knowledge about all phenomena, other genres of scholarly or "scientific" writing that have much relevance for the study of asceticism appeared in the twentieth century—the encyclopedia or dictionary article and the sourcebook.

Relevant examples are numerous. A fourteen-part entry—a general introduction followed by thirteen articles on various religious traditions—appears under the headword "asceticism" in James Hastings's comprehensive *Encyclopaedia of Religion and Ethics* (1909). *The Dictionnaire de spiritualité* (1937) contains an extensive treatment covering almost as many traditions under "ascète, ascétisme." The *Reallexikon für Antike und Christentum* (1950) and *Die Religion in Geschichte und Gegenwart: Handwörterbuch für Theologie und Religionswissenschaft* (1957), both including extensive entries under "Askese," have represented the highest level of scholarship in international circles among scholars of religion for more than three decades.

Sourcebooks have also emerged containing documents that exemplify the wide range of types of ascetic pieties within specific cultural traditions. Owen Chadwick's *Western Asceticism* (1958; rev. ed., 1979) and *Ascetic Behavior in Greco-Roman Antiquity: A Sourcebook,* edited by Vincent L. Wimbush (1990), include texts exemplifying types of ascetic piety within traditions and currents that have become Western culture. Patrick Olivelle's *Samnyasa Upanishad: Hindu Scriptures on Asceticism and Renunciation* (1992); Yoshoko Kurata Dykstra's *Miraculous Tales of the Lotus Sutra from Ancient Japan: The "Dainihonkoku hokekyo kenki" of the Priest Chingen* (1983) and *Bhagavati aradhana* (Jainist; 1978) provide access to other traditions. And, of course, there are other such texts.

Although each of the above-named works is obviously valuable in its own right in providing greater access to the sources, none is comprehensive or representative of asceticism in all its diversity. There is no sourcebook on the ascetic that crosses major divisions in religious and cultural traditions. The degree of advancement in comprehensiveness and complexity within the particular tradition represented in each collection of texts only highlights the larger continuing problem that has plagued the study of the ascetic. But the complexity that now seems to be acknowledged in almost all recent studies of the ascetic has yet to result in extensive collaboration and conversation across traditions.

The most recent summary/encyclopedic treatment on asceticism, Walter O. Kaelber's article by the same title in *The Encyclopedia of Religion,* edited by Mircea Eliade (1987), brings the problem into sharp focus. Kaelber's article makes an attempt to describe late twentieth-century scholarly consensus about asceticism. Of course, it registers mainly frustration about the lack of such consensus, and ultimately it does not provide a full explication either of problems and shortcomings or of their answers and resolutions. Yet Kaelber does argue—mostly in the glosses in the bibliography section—that the most serious shortcoming in the treatments of asceticism in the different types of writings, especially the encyclopedic treatments surveyed above, lies in the tendency to discuss the phenomenon without a cross-cultural theoretical framework.

This shortcoming and its consequences are dramatically displayed in the entry in the Hastings volume, still the most comprehensive, if flawed, treatment. Despite the numerous articles on different types of asceticism within different cultures throughout world history (Buddhist, Celtic, Christian, Egyptian, Greek, Hindu, Japanese, Jewish, Muhammadan, Persian, Roman, Semitic and Egyptian, Vedic), it is striking that there is no overarching theoretical framework in evidence. It is as though the contributors of the different parts never conferred with one another, did not know one another's works or working presuppositions, or were not focusing at all upon the same phenomenon or phenomena. Thomas C. Hall, author of Hastings's general introduction (and former professor at Union Theological Seminary in the City of New York), did not provide such a framework for the articles to follow. His introductory essay nevertheless reflects a bias; it is simply not a bias that can provide a springboard for significant cross-cultural learning. He subtly advances something of a bipolar typology: "disciplinary" (with the goal of training the body, will, and spirit) and "dualistic" (with the goal of escaping the evil body and all things associated with it). His bias toward the "disciplinary" type—which happens to resemble the modernist progressive Protestant ethos—is quite evident. The limited usefulness of such a perspective is obvious.

But the need for such an elaborate framework has rarely been discussed in theology and religio-critical works. There have been very few theoretical and comparative works that have had as their focus the interpretation of asceticism. Oscar Hardman's *The Ideals of Asceticism: An Essay in the Comparative Study of Religion* (1924) is one of the very few extant examples of the advancement of a fully formulated theoretical typology. It respects the comparative method that was emerging in the study of religion in the first third of the twentieth century, taking into account ascetic practices in the Hindu, Buddhist, Jainist, Christian, and Islamic traditions as well as in the "pre-Christian" cultures around the Mediterranean.

Hardman typifies asceticism according to ideals or goals. The three types are (1) "the mystical ideal—fellowship," (2) "the disciplinary ideal—righteousness," and (3) "the sacrificial ideal—reparation." The mystical ideal has as its goal both divine "possession" and community ("sympathetic association"). The disciplinary ideal seeks "conformity" with, or consistent observance of, divine laws and order. The third ideal, the sacrificial, has as its goal the removal of all forms of pollution and evil through the sacrifical offerings of certain ethical behaviors.

Hardman's proposal, although an improvement upon all other treatments of asceticism at the time, is nonetheless fraught with difficulties. It clearly reflects a bias toward Christianity, even to the point of arguing for an evolutionary or developmental schema in the history of asceticism. Christianity is seen as the highest and purest manifestation of asceticism because of its "social utility," namely, its worldliness. All other types are inferior. It is not that Hardman lost sight of his bias; he clearly wanted to advance "Christian asceticism" as the "touchstone" for all asceticisms because of his understanding of what should be the social utility of religion and the shape of the social order. That his understanding of such things was influenced, even determined, by a type of Christian socialization is, of course, quite obvious; and it severely limits the usefulness of his typology.

The only other fully articulated proposal for a typology of asceticism that has been advanced is by German sociologist Max Weber.[3] In his *Protestant Ethic and the Spirit of Capitalism* and *Sociology of Religion,* especially, but also in other works, Weber advances four "ideal-types" of orientation—"innerworldly asceticism," "innerworldly mysticism," "otherworldly asceticism," and "otherworldly mysticism." The types represent different religious orientations to the world. The rather chiastic character of the typology collapses easily into bipolar opposites—otherworldly mysticism, representing the extreme of exercising the least influence upon the sociopolitical order, and innerworldly asceticism, representing the other extreme, that of exercising the most influence upon the sociopolitical order. (The other opposites are seen as being of little importance to Weber's agenda.) In the latter type, the world is seen as opponent, but there is no attempt to escape from it; with the former type, an attempt is made to seek the divine in solitude, away from the challenges and responsibilities and pollution of the world.

Although Weber's typology would seem to have great potential for sustained cross-cultural study of ascetic responses, under closer scrutiny it proves to be problematic and of limited usefulness. Quite evident is Weber's bias toward "innerworldly asceticism," on account of its ethos that encourages positive orientation to the world. Because Weber's major concern was to account for the emergence of "bourgeois capitalism," because his categories are advanced as "ideal-typical constructions," and because only the ethos of "innerworldly asceticism" is argued to have been capable of giving birth to "bourgeois capitalism," the other types are seen as derivative. This raises the question about whether the typology has general usefulness beyond explaining the origins and historio-evolutionary development of Western Protestant social and political sensibilities and orientations.

Weber's students have made use of his typology for a number of arguments and theories. But there has been little advancement upon the typology itself, certainly not for the purpose of providing a framework for a more cross-cultural perspective in the exploration of the phenomenon of asceticism. Weber's contribution, therefore, remains provocative, but flawed and problematic.[4]

There are, of course, other theoretical, cross-cultural works that are relevant for the interpretation of asceticism but do not focus upon it. Emile Durkheim, William James, Gerardus van der Leeuw, and, more recently, Shmuel Eisenstadt and Louis Dumont, among others, provide provocative theses and frameworks for the interpretation of religion itself that also have great potential for the interpretation of asceticism. But in every case it is necessary to qualify arguments and suppositions with reference to asceticism because of limitation of scope or conceptualization.

Problems in the Study of Asceticism

So we are left in the late twentieth century with a long history of scholarly exploration of asceticism that is as frustrating and confusing, as naive and limiting, as it is impressive in scope, productivity, diversity, and depth. We are still without a comprehensive theoretical framework for the comparative study of asceticism. We are left not only with a legacy of academic and popular culture-specific biases and prejudices regarding the origins, essence, and value of asceticism but also without a sharp delineation of the problematic issues that are behind the reference to "asceticism." Is it, can it be, a reference to one thing, one sentiment, worldview, set of behaviors? If multiple meanings and functions are granted, with what are we left as a common thread? Is another rubric needed? Is "asceticism" as a rubric, too loaded? Does it point too quickly to closure on a certain conceptual front?

It is most difficult for serious students of the phenomenon to engage in high-level conversation with one another across religious and cultural divisions, so as to learn about the different aspects and nuances of asceticism registered in different cultures and historical periods. The stumbling blocks are strong. In the current academic/intellectual climate—as the arguments above suggest—asceticism is studied quite intensely, to be sure, but, for the most part, only within particular academic guilds and with a view to the limitations of their presuppositions, and without the benefit of a broad cross-cultural view. In Western popular culture there is much evidence that asceticism has been rediscovered as a positive phenomenon (see Geoffrey Harpham, *Semeia* 58, 1992). An explosion of different manifestations and meanings rechanneled from traditional religious communities is evident. The many different forms and aspects of contemporary modern and postmodern existence are now often expressed through preoccupations with diet control (non-fat, low-calorie foods); with fitness; with vacations turned into retreats, monastery style; and with moderation—sometimes even abstinence—in sexual relations. But how are these responses to be interpreted, or to be accounted for? How do they square with the supposedly secular cultures of the late twentieth century? With what critical perspectives can we come to understand the sensibilities, the *mentalité,* behind these responses? What is it about particular religions, societies, and cultures that makes certain ascetic impulses so important today? What is it about religious life in general, and about every historical cultural formation, that makes asceticism so significant? Was Durkheim *(Elementary Forms of Religious Life)* correct in arguing that asceticism is a "necessary" part of every religion and culture? Is Geoffrey Harpham *(The Ascetic Imperative in Culture and Criticism)* more than just provocative in arguing that asceticism is "subideological," "a primary transcultural structuring force," a kind of "MS-DOS" of cultures because, given the tension it always creates within a culture, it "raises the issue" of culture?

No one individual, no one field or discipline can grasp the totality and complexity of these and other historical, philosophical, phenomenological, theological, culture-critical questions and issues. These provocative questions and arguments cannot be addressed except by sustained collaborative effort, supported by a broad historical and comparative perspective. As the foregoing has indicated, the few modern attempts to understand the ascetic impulse in religious life and culture in general are dated; and they have been neither comprehensive nor based directly upon a significant degree of comprehensive historical and comparative work. This remains a significant weakness in the history of the study of asceticism.

The International Conference on Asceticism that provided the impetus for the essays collected in this volume was designed as a forum for scholarly exchange about asceticism as a complex, universal phenomenon in the histories of religion and culture. Given the narrowness and biases in the history of scholarship on asceticism, given the current general diffusion but academic disciplinary compartmentalization of scholarship, and given the need to understand more about the functions of the ascetic impulse in religious life throughout history and across worlds and cultures, it was deemed important to facilitate direct, face-to-face exchange on the topic between scholars of different disciplines and fields.

Arising out of conversations and debates among scholars of early Christianity and late antique religions in particular, the objective of the conference was to encourage and model a significant degree of interdisciplinary and cross-cultural discussion that could provide broader, critical perspectives from which many different types of questions about the ascetic in religious life and culture could be pursued. It was thought that the conference, if successfully convened, would neither begin nor conclude with the new definition or conceptualization or meaning of the ascetic; rather, it would seek to explode all simple notions about asceticism, including the notion that it has to do simply with the negative and simply with the distant past. The conference in fact began and ended with strategic possibilities or models for the reconceptualization of the ascetic, first in particular religious and cultural formations, and then in religious life and culture in general. In short, we wanted to experiment, to try something that had not been done before. We wanted to test whether and to what degree it would be possible to have among scholars of various persuasions and predilections and disciplinary camps sustained discussions about "asceticism"; or whether we would need to conclude that the term "asceticism" has no significant referent, having come to mean too many things to too many for too long a period of time to be meaningful and to warrant comparative study in the present. The whole effort was understood to be something of a gamble; we knew that it would leave us vulnerable on many different fronts—not enough of some emphases here, too much of other emphases there, not enough of the scope or depth or accuracy that an expert in any area would demand. Yet the possibility, however remote, that the discussion of a phenomenon so complex could traverse the usual boundaries was too tempting to let go. Because we think that in the engagement and analysis of the ascetic we are not far from approaching a higher (viz., truly comparativist, multidisciplinary) understanding about the religious life itself, we could not restrain ourselves; we had to begin somewhere; we had to proceed with the experiment, no matter how many difficulties and questions remained.

Vision and Structure of the Conversation

The conference papers were explicitly structured so as to model and provide impetus for such experimentation. The four types of presentations from the conference that are included in this volume are (1) plenary addresses, (2) major papers, (3) responses to major papers, and (4) in appendix, short papers and a panel discussion.

The two general addresses set the stage for the dialogue to follow. They are very persuasive arguments for the scholarly reconsideration of asceticism in an effort to understand religious life and cultural formation, as well as their reformation. The major papers, twenty-four in number, were the focal point of the conference, and they assume the same importance in this volume: they model the interdisciplinary dialogue that was the original impetus for the conference. The papers are arranged according to four broad cross-cultural themes:

1. origins and meanmgs of asceticism, with focus on the motivations, impulses, ideals, socio-cultural matrices and explanations, for different asceticisms,
2. politics of asceticism, with focus on the sociopolitical locations, functions and ramifications (for different genders, classes, and ethnic groups) of asceticism,
3. hermeneutics of asceticism, with focus on the different types of sources—textual, material—and their representations, and presuppositions, methodological challenges, and possibilities for the interpretations of asceticism, and
4. aesthetics of asceticism, with focus on the different types of emotions that are ascetic practices, and on the responses evoked by the different practices themselves, or by different (literary, material, and other) representations or expressions of asceticism.

The papers herein are evidence that high-level dialogue about asceticism was very much facilitated by the four themes, in combination with the two general addresses, mentioned above.

Implications and Future Directions for Asceticism

The conference's most significant contribution rests in its modality: conversation. In order to demonstrate the power of this contribution it is important for the reader to keep in mind the history behind the conference. For over seven years, a small group of scholars of late antique religion had been meeting to discuss the social functions of asceticism. Their discussions had been intense, their production great (a collection of Greco-Roman ascetical texts and a collection of essays on the discursive practices of asceticism), and the quality of their communication significant. This small group modeled the potential depth and breadth of scholarly discourse, in an amicable tone, sometimes with great difference of opinion but always with grace and respect. The international asceticism conference itself was the culmination of these earlier conversations. At the conference, scholars and practitioners representing widely divergent, multicultural, transhistorical, world-religious perspectives presented papers, responded to the papers, and discussed the implications of the formal presentations. It was often difficult to traverse the solid, clearly defined boundaries of disciplines, orientations, religions, cultures, and languages, but the conference participants persisted throughout in attending to the perspectives of others. For a brief time, the alterity in world religions became a meeting ground of scholars. The study of asceticism will never again be the same, because the conversation and mutual striving for understanding, knowledge, and appreciation of the "other" set the stage for continued, transformative, and collegial scholarly pursuit.

In addition to the quality of conversation and the collegiality of investigation inherent in the conference's modality, the substance of the conference has opened a number of future directions for the study of asceticism that revolve about the following topics: the categories of investigation, ethics, and the retrieval of the ancient ascetical arts from among the world's religious traditions.

Categories of investigation

Usually asceticism has been studied as site-specific, that is, as part of the structure of a particular culture, at a particular time in history, in a particular religion. The two plenary speakers generally, and the other papers more specifically, directed future studies toward a reassessment and revision of those specific categories of ascetical study. Kallistos Ware argued that the cultural construction of "asceticism" as purely negative must be discarded as lacking in nuance and as nonrepresentative of ascetical discourse itself. Withdrawal and self-denial were not thoroughly negative categories to those who practiced them, and, therefore, their positive and life-giving aspects must be discovered and articulated. The study of asceticism must, Ware insisted, also direct particular attention to the stated subject of asceticism, the theological and spiritual content of ascetic texts. It must be taken seriously, especially by scholars who value their objectivity and secularity, because without a thoroughgoing study of such categories as demons, the reality of God, and the efficacy of prayer the ascetics themselves remain invisible. The study of asceticism, crossing as it does the boundaries of culture, religion, and chronology, opens the proper subjects of ascetical practice and theorizing to academic and public scrutiny first, on their own terms and then later as part of other discursive practices.

Edith Wyschogrod directed attention toward the epistemic and semiotic systems within ascetical practice. Her postmodern retrieval of asceticism, refracted through the classical and Christian systems constitutive of ascetical ethics, points toward a reapportionment of categories, to which Kallistos Ware would direct attention. The categories important to the society coeval with the ascetics under study cannot become the categories our contemporary society adopts for its own ascetical theory and practice. The postmodern retrieval particularizes and universalizes, in that it looks to site-specific and fully embodied ascetical expressions while simultaneously looking beyond the limitations and boundaries imposed by traditions of interpretation, chronological sequence, academic disciplines, cultural hegemonies, or religious divisions. This is not a contradiction. The assumptions of the historical ascetical texts to which Ware directs attention may be interpreted within the epistemic systems of their own historical periods and within the systems of analysis of a site-specific ascetical religion, but, knowing that that perspective does not exhaust our analysis or the retrievability of asceticism, the postmodern retrieval must re[de]construct the episteme within a world far more inclusive than the original site-specific asceticism. This world has vastly different problems and understandings and no longer readily coheres within traditional boundaries of discipline, religion, or human agency. Modernist, historicist, and postmodernist perspectives mutually inhabit the site-specific arena of asceticism and the postmodern world.

Pluralist ethics

The same situation that scholars addressed in an international conference appears as a practical problem in postmodern living. Ethics, the modern and secular term that usurped the place of historical asceticism, functions in a similar traditionalist and pluralist polarity. The root of asceticism remains ethical formation (as Wyschogrod indicates) and ethics cannot function without addressing personal formation. By severing ethics from its ascetical roots, postmodern society loses its memory about personal and corporate development, finds itself incapable of molding people who live ethically, and remains paralyzed in addressing questions of violence, hatred, bigotry, and abuse. The ancient Western ascetical interest in developing an ethics of behavior, beginning in the classical Greek period, revolved around the personal development of particular virtues, and the personal strategies for the avoidance of vice constitute the primary focus of ascetical practice. Ascetical practice not only developed the theory of virtue and vice but trained societies in their practice. In historically isolated and geographically separated cultures (that is, in modern and premodern societies), this ethical formation appeared to be universal, in that the ascetical systems operative both in the dominant culture and in subcultures emerged from a particular symbolic universe and anthropology. The discussions at the conference, however, established that ascetical formation, like ethical formation, cannot be postulated in a monolithic, universalist fashion without reference to other systems in other religious environments, other historical periods, and other world cultures. Ethics (as asceticism) cannot remain in its premodern incarnation as a set of rules imposed upon social beings to perpetuate a dominant and hierarchically imposed morality. Ethics must develop the rhetorical art of persuading groups of people of the ethical imperatives of contemporary living and the ascetical art of teaching social beings the means of developing and nurturing a particular moral and ethical modality. Critical ascetical study may provide a fulcrum for lifting ethics from its monolithic foundationalist bedrock to the mountains of discursive interactions. It may be that one direction for developing an ethics reflective of the pluralist world of nations, cultures, and religions can emerge from the comparative study of asceticism; for asceticism, in its pluralist orientation, informs ethics and guides ethical discourse toward a polyvalent, multicultural, and simultaneously site-specific and universally conversant discourse.

The immediate import of such an ascetical orientation toward ethical formation is nowhere more evident than among the youth in our urban centers. Cities have become centers for formation in violence, as the member of any gang in the United States or racial supremacist group in Europe will attest, so that any young person willing to submit to the intense formative experience of entering a gang or a racist group will easily become capable of inflicting violence and acting out hatred. This constitutes an asceticism of violence, an ethics of destruction. Since most prior generations have matured with at least the common guiding illusion of a monolithic system of reality, social organizations have never really been forced to develop ethics in a pluralist environment, nor have participants been instructed in the formative practices of their ethical behaviors. The refusal of a pluralist, ascetical ethics has simply ignored the formative aspect of ethics and morals, leaving the primary formation to others. Ethical and moral formation happens consistently in every society, and yet that formation has not been scrutinized, analyzed, or questioned in any significant way. The cities throughout the world have become armed camps of youths alienated from each other, from other social organizations, and from the political and religious institutions around them, and yet fully capable of a formation toward violence and hatred. Without intensive study of ethics, of personal formation in a pluralist society, this trend will only continue. The categories of ethical formation, however, must not simply invoke one system (whether Christian, secular, Hindu, Buddhist, animist, or whatever), but must emerge from a comparative study of cultures and religions in dialogue, that is, from the postmodern realities of contemporary living.

Renewal of the *ars ascetica*

The final area of redirection that emerged from the conference is the ancient theological discipline of asceticism, the *ars ascetica,* the study of the ascetical systems within world religions, in ancient societies, and in Eastern, Western, and world Christianity. The renewal of these ascetical arts, however, emerges from the refraction of asceticism through the postmodern prism: it is not simply the clothing of ancient practices in modern garb, but the refashioning of probably the most ancient of all the arts and the designing of new systems for global human development. This renewal would be advantageous from three perspectives: those of anthropology, spirituality, and interfaith dialogue.

Anthropology. An issue that has plagued modern academic study in many disciplines is the question of social construction versus essentialism. How are human beings essentially the same (across cultures and across historical periods), and how are they primarily socially constructed? These questions cannot be answered without diachronic, synchronic, and cross-cultural studies focused, as is most ascetical teaching, on the regulation, meaning, and significance of the body within its specific social and cultural location. Asceticism looks at the body enmeshed in physiology, theology, regulatory practices, social environments, and the other semiotic systems that reflect social and cultural meaning. In the process of comparing asceticisms through historical progressions, in cultures different from the one in which one lives, in religions with widely divergent understandings of subjectivity, social relations, and the symbolic universe, aspects illuminating what perdures through human existence and what changes emerge more carefully. The myopia of the discussion is corrected by the lens of comparative study, and the human being—indeed, humanity—may emerge from the nexus of embodied particularity as a subject more easily understood in essence and in social construction. Asceticism, however, must also take up within its anthropology the categories of gender, race, and class. Human beings, implicated in the structures of their society, their architecture of race and gender, and their social complexes of power (or weakness) and wealth (or poverty), cannot be naively constructed; even the most optimistic of ascetic masters would question such naiveté. The development of sophisticated anthropological theories including gender, race, and class becomes, therefore, essential.

Spirituality. The question of "spiritual formation" emerges as a corollary to this conversation about anthropology and ethics. The modern interest in "spirituality," like that in ethics, must involve postmodern discourse about asceticism. In attempting to move to a place within the human being where "spirit" and "body" cohere, studies in spirituality perpetuate the body/spirit dichotomy that they attempt to transcend. In addition to its dualist propensities, spirituality ignores the particular characteristics of people of different ages, different cultures, and different religious sensibilities in its construction of a "humanity" that trascends all difference and that attempts to circumvent religious traditions in order to arrive at the "authentic" religious experience undergirding all human religious expression. In the conversation about asceticism, however, such constructions appeared as uninformed, ingenuously triumphant, and universalist in orientation. Although it is not impossible to reach across barriers and to traverse boundaries, such bridging and crossings require the careful articulation of differences as well as similarities; congruences as well as incongruities; and inappropriate comparisons as well as suitable correlations. In other words, in the comparative study of asceticism, the common tradition, the common spiritual goals and methods, rest firmly on a foundation of critical, comparative, historical, and cross-cultural difference. This difference cannot be established without beginning free of the assumption of prior polarities. One should start not with language contingent upon spirit/body but with language and constructions expressive of the practices, relationships, and symbolic constructions of the full human. Asceticism opens the study of spirituality to the unitive function it seeks.

Interfaith dialogue. The postmodern religious world paints reality with the most wildly diverse colors. Moving from the confines of university religious studies to the religious experience of people throughout the world, a religious practitioner or theorist discovers the complex of differences lurking behind geographical, historical, cultural, and religious boundaries. The sheer complexity of diversity makes clarity elusive; the sheer volume of religious experience makes commonality seem impossible. And yet, after digging about for a few days in the teeming richness of diversity in a scholarly setting, familiar patterns of behavior emerge (fasting, social withdrawal, continual prayer), similar metaphoric patterns develop (marriage to the divinity, distrust of the body, valuation of the intellect), and correlative theological formulations appear (ascent to the divine, avoidance of evil, regeneration). Asceticism, as a system of formation for religious behavior and thought, lays out the potential for communication about the heart of religious differences from within the center of the religious experience. Comparative asceticism assists in laying out the terms, modalities, structures, and practices of religious experience so that others, from another era of history and in another part of the world, may look in and begin to understand. For the postmodern religious discourse, the study of asceticism may provide the space and method for discussing religious differences without needing to discount them in order to find commonality.

Suggestions for Reading These Proceedings

The greatest asceticism for scholars, however, is what we call the "asceticism of appreciation." It is a frustrating and difficult conversation when the conversants gather from widely divergent places, all speak a different language, all employ disparate categories and systems of analysis, and all find the discourse of outsiders baffling. To gather essays written by scholars of religion, as well as by anthropologists, philosophers, ethicists, and literary critics and at the same time to represent many of the world's religions and explore the development of religion through the whole history of human existence, is to gather a Babel of viewpoints and to court frustration. Disciplined, appreciative reading of such diverse submissions itself constitutes an asceticism. This asceticism of appreciation seeks out the expression of difference as fruitful ground for understanding, while holding in abeyance (resisting the desire, to use the Western formulation) the need to find one's own categories and perceptions mirrored in the other. By the end of the conference, scholars who had never been exposed to such differences began to find, ever so hesitatingly at first, a common ground for their study.

The essays that follow reflect rich and frightening diversity. For the purposes of this volume, the responses to the papers reflect the forging of a common language and common categories. They should be read first, as the initial guide through the individual essays, and they will stimulate other directions when reread after the individual essays. Since the matrix of the conference was a specific quality of conversation amid a wide range of scholars and fields, and since it is our desire to stimulate further conversation within the academic study and religious practice of asceticism, the editors have included all of the formal papers of the conference: these papers reflect the state of ascetical studies with all its attendant strengths and weaknesses, and they provide the foundation for further study and debate by presenting the wealth of perspectives on the subject. By working through the essays with an asceticism of appreciation, we hope to advance significantly the study of asceticism and the ascetic dimension in religious life and culture.

NOTES

1. In addition to the range of literary expressions, non-literary types of evidence must also be considered as sources for asceticism. See Yizhar Hirschfeld's essay (#19) in this volume. And see also his "Life of Chariton: In Light of Archaeological Research," pp. 425–447; and Robert F. Boughner and James E. Goehring, "Egyptian Monasticism (Selected Papyri)," pp. 456–463, in *Ascetic Behavior in Greco-Roman Antiquity: A Sourcebook*, edited by Vincent L. Wimbush (Minneapolis: Fortress, 1990). Goehring's article entitled "Through a Glass Darkly: Diverse Images of the APOTAKTIKOI(AI) of Early Egyptian Monasticism" (*Semeia* 58 [1992]: 25–45) speaks directly to the larger interpretive challenges.
2. See the extensive and still very useful entry on "Asceticism" in Hastings's *Encyclopaedia of Religion and Ethics* (1909). Although dated in many respects, it contains information about valuable contributions from the nineteenth century.
3. We are indebted to our friend and colleague Walter Kaelber for insights and suggestions from formal papers read and from many informal conversations about Max Weber and asceticism in general, asceticism and typologies in particular. See his response-essay below (#22); and his paper entitled "Understanding Asceticism: Methodological Issues and the Construction of Typologies," read at the American Academy of Religion / Society of Biblical Literature Annual Meeting, held in Boston, December 1987.
4. See the advancement upon Weber especially regarding socio-religious problems in the works of S. N. Eisenstadt, ed., *Origins and Diversity of Axial Age Civilizations* (Albany: State University of New York Press, 1986); and Hans G. Kippenberg, *Die vorderasiatischen Erloesunreligionen in ihrem Zusammenhang mit der antiken Stadtherrschaft: Heidelberg Max-Weber-Vorlesungen 1988* (Frankfurt am Main: Suhrkamp, 1991).

PART ONE

General Challenges and Reconsiderations

1

The Way of the Ascetics: Negative or Affirmative?

Kallistos Ware

An Entry into Freedom?

"Asceticism means the liberation of the human person," states the Russian Orthodox philosopher Nicolas Berdyaev (1873–1948). He defines asceticism as "a concentration of inner forces and command of oneself," and he insists: "Our human dignity is related to this."[1] Asceticism, that is to say, leads us to self-mastery and enables us to fulfill the purpose that we have set for ourselves, whatever that may be. A certain measure of ascetic self-denial is thus a necessary element in all that we undertake, whether in athletics or in politics, in scholarly research or in prayer. Without this ascetic concentration of effort we are at the mercy of exterior forces, or of our own emotions and moods; we are reacting rather than acting. Only the ascetic is inwardly free.

The Roman Catholic Raimundo Pannikar adds that asceticism frees us in particular from fear: "True asceticism begins by eliminating the fear of losing what can be lost. The ascetic is the one who has no fear."[2] The prisoner Bobynin, in Alexander Solzhenitsyn's novel *The First Circle,* expresses a genuinely ascetic attitude when he says to Abakumov, the Minister of State Security, "I've got nothing, see? Nothing! . . . You only have power over people so long as you don't take *everything* away from them. But when you've robbed a man of *everything* he's no longer in your power—he's free again."[3] How much more free is the one who has not been robbed of everything but with ascetic freedom has given it up by his own choice!

While Berdyaev regards asceticism as an entry into freedom, another Russian Orthodox thinker, Father Paul Florensky (1882–1943), links it with beauty: "Asceticism produces not a *good* but a *beautiful* personality."[4] He would surely have welcomed the fact that our conference is devoting two of its sessions to the "aesthetics of asceticism." In the eyes of Jacob of Serug (c.449–521), the asceticism of Symeon the Stylite—altogether horrifying by our standards—made possible a revelation of the saint's beauty: "Good gold entered the crucible and manifested its beauty." Even Symeon's gangrenous foot was from the spiritual point of view an object full of beauty: "He watched his foot as it rotted and its flesh decayed. And the foot stood bare like a tree beautiful with branches. He saw that there was nothing on it but tendons and bones."[5]

In Greco-Roman antiquity, ascetic practice was regarded equally as the pathway to happiness and joy. The Cynics saw rigorous self-denial as "part of *askēsis* (training) for happiness."[6] Philo's Therapeutai assembled at great festivals "clad in snow white raiment, joyous but with the height of solemnity,"[7] and celebrated the feast by dancing together. The same joyful note re-echoes in the *mīmrā* attributed to St. Ephrem the Syrian (c.306–373), *On Hermits and Desert Dwellers:*

> There is no weeping in their wanderings and no grieving in their gatherings;
> the praises of the angels above surround them on every side.
>
> There is no distress in their death, nor wailing at their departing;
> for their death is the victory with which they conquer the adversary.[8]

Freedom, beauty, joy: that is what asceticism meant to Berdyaev, Florensky, and the Syrian monks. But most people in our present-day world have a radically different perception of what asceticism implies: to them it signifies not freedom but submission to irksome rules; not beauty but harsh rigor; not joy but gloomy austerity. Where does the truth lie? The case against asceticism is often stated, and is thoroughly familiar to all of us. Rather than restate it once again, let us try to discover what can be said in defense of the ascetic life. This we can best do by considering two basic components in ascetic practice—*anachōrēsis* (withdrawal) and *enkrateia* (self-control). Our primary questions will be:

1. Does *anachōrēsis* mean simply a flight in order to escape, or can it sometimes signify a flight followed by a return? What if, in fact, there is no return?
2. Does *enkrateia* mean the repression or the redirection of our instinctive urges? Does it involve "violence to our natural appetites" (Durkheim) or their transfiguration?

Obviously these are not the only questions to be asked about asceticism, and in seeking to respond to them I make no claim to provide any overarching cross-cultural framework. My answers will be given, not as a sociologist, but as a theologian and church historian, specializing in Greek Christianity. But the questions themselves have a wider scope, for they are applicable to the Christian West as well as the Christian East, and to non-Christian as well as Christian traditions.

A Flight Followed by a Return?

In itself *anachōrēsis* can be either negative or positive, either world-denying or world-affirming. Often it is the world-denying aspect that seems to be dominant. When Abba Arsenius asks, "Lord, guide me so that I may be saved," he is told: "Flee from humans, and you will be saved."[9] Arsenius's motive here seems to be exclusively his own salvation, and this involves an avoidance of all contact with his fellow humans; he does not appear to be interested in trying to help them. When a high-ranking Roman lady comes to visit him and asks him to remember her in his prayers, Arsenius answers brusquely: "I pray to God that he will wipe out the memory of you from my heart." Not surprisingly, she departs much distressed.[10] When asked by Abba Mark, "Why do you flee from us?," Arsenius gives an answer that is only slightly more conciliatory: "God knows that I love you, but I cannot be both with God and with humans."[11] There still seems to be no suggestion that he has any responsibility to assist others and to lead them to salvation. Abba Macarius of Egypt is equally inexorable. "Flee from humans," he says; and, when asked what that means, he replies: "It is to sit in your cell and weep for your sins."[12] A monk, so it appears, has no duty toward his neighbor; he must simply think about himself and repent his own offenses. Texts such as these, taken in isolation, certainly suggest that monastic *anachōrēsis* is something introspective and selfish. When Paul the First Hermit withdraws into total and lifelong seclusion, what possible benefit did this confer on society around him?[13]

Yet this is not the whole story. In other cases the ascetic undertakes, not simply a flight in order to escape, but a flight followed by a return. This pattern can be seen in particular in the immensely influential *Life* of St. Antony of Egypt (231–356), attributed (perhaps correctly) to St. Athanasius of Alexandria.[14] At the outset Antony withdraws gradually into an ever increasing solitude, which reaches its extreme point when he encloses himself for two decades in a ruined fort, refusing to speak or meet with anyone. But when he is fifty-five there comes a crucial turning point. His friends break down the door and he comes out from the fortress. During the remaining half-century of his long life, Antony still continues to live in the desert, apart from two brief visits to Alexandria. Yet, even though he does not go back to the world in an outward and topographical sense, on the spiritual level he does indeed "return." He makes himself freely available to others, he accepts disciples under his care, and he offers guidance to a constant stream of visitors, serving "as a physician given by God to Egypt," in the words of his biographer.[15] Palladius, recounting the story of Eulogius and the cripple, provides a vivid picture of how in practice Antony exercised this ministry of spiritual direction.[16] His description is strikingly similar to the account—written fifteen centuries later—of the Russian *staretz* Zosima surrounded by the pilgrims, in Dostoevsky's novel *The Brothers Karamazov*.[17]

Here, then, in St. Antony's case, there is a flight into the desert which turns out to be not world-denying but world-affirming. Although he begins by avoiding all contact with his fellow humans, he ends by accepting great numbers of them under his pastoral care. If the portrait of him given in the *Apophthegmata* is to be trusted, Antony felt an intense compassion for others, a direct sense of responsibility. "From our neighbor is life and death," he said; "if we gain our brother, we gain God, but if we cause our brother to stumble, we sin against Christ."[18] Such is the pattern of Antony's life: silence gives place to speech, seclusion leads him to involvement.

This same pattern—of a flight followed by a return—recurs repeatedly in the course of monastic history. It marks the life of St. Basil of Caesarea in fourth-century

Cappadocia, of St. Benedict of Nursia in sixth-century Italy, of St. Gregory Palamas (1296–1359) in Palaeologan Byzantium, and of St. Sergius of Radonezh (c.1314–1392) and St. Seraphim of Sarov (1759–1833) in Russia. In all of these instances, the ascetic starts by withdrawing into seclusion and ends by becoming the guide and leader of others, a spiritual father[19] or "soul friend."[20] What is more, these two stages—solitude, followed by leadership—are not merely juxtaposed in time but are integrally connected with each other. It is precisely because they first withdrew into solitude that these ascetics were afterwards able to act as spiritual guides. Without the ascetic preparation that they underwent in the silence of the wilderness, St. Antony, St. Benedict, or St. Seraphim would never have been able to bring light and healing to others in the way that they did. Not that they withdrew in order to become guides and spiritual masters to their generation; for they fled, not in order to prepare themselves for any other task, but simply in order to be alone with God. When St. Benedict hid himself in a cave near Subiaco, he wanted simply to save his own soul, and had not the slightest intention of saving Western civilization. But his solitary quest for personal salvation did in fact exercise in the long term a profoundly creative effect on European culture. Often it is precisely the men and women of inner stillness—not the activists but the contemplatives, fired by a consuming passion for solitude—who in practice bring about the most far-reaching alterations in the society around them.

In the case of saints such as Antony, Benedict, or Seraphim, the flight was followed by a return. Yet what is to be said of the many ascetics who, after the model of the legendary Paul the First Hermit, never actually "returned" but remained to the end in solitary isolation? Were their lives entirely wasted? Was their *anachōrēsis* simply negative? Not necessarily so; it all depends on our criteria. In speaking earlier about Arsenius I was careful to use the words "seems" and "appears." When Arsenius flees from his fellow humans, it may indeed seem to the modern reader that he is doing nothing to help them. But, in the eyes of many of his contemporaries, he was in fact doing something extremely positive in the solitude of the desert: he was praying. Significantly, Arsenius, the Desert Father who represents *anachōrēsis* in its most uncompromising form, is depicted in the *Apophthegmata* as, above all, a person of unceasing, fiery prayer:

> A certain brother went to the cell of Abba Arsenius in Scetis and looked through the window, and he beheld the old man as if completely on fire; for the brother was worthy to see this. . . . They also said about him, that late on Saturday evening he turned his back on the setting sun, and stretched out his arms towards heaven in prayer; and so he remained until the rising sun shone on his face. And then he sat down.[21]

Such, then, is the service which the solitary ascetic renders to society around him. He helps others not through active works of charity, not through writings and scholarly research, nor yet primarily through giving spiritual counsel, but simply through his continual prayer. His *anachōrēsis* is in itself a way of serving others, because the motive behind his withdrawal is to seek union with God; and this prayerful union supports and strengthens his fellow humans, even though he knows nothing about them; and they, on their part, are unaware of his very existence.

The point is effectively summed up by Palladius in the phrase "guarding the walls." In his chapter on Abba Macarius of Alexandria, whom he met around 391 CE during his early years in Cellia, he recounts: "Once, when I was suffering from listlessness *(akēdia)*, I went to him and said: 'Abba, what shall I do? For my thoughts afflict me, saying: You are making no progress; go away from here.' And he replied to me, 'Tell them: For Christ's sake I am guarding the walls.' "[22] The monks keep watch like sentries on the walls of the spiritual city, thus enabling the other members of the church inside the walls to carry on their daily activities in safety. Guarding the walls against whom? The early Christian ascetics would have had a clear and specific answer: against the demons. Guarding the walls by what means? With the weapon of prayer. In the words of the *Historia monachorum:* "There is not a village or city in Egypt and the Thebaid that is not surrounded by hermitages as if by walls, and the people are supported by their prayers as though by God himself."[23]

The positive value of flight into the desert is evident when we take into account the meaning that the desert possessed for these early Christian ascetics. It had a twofold significance. It was both the place where God is to be found—here the classic prototype was Moses, who met God face to face in the desert of Sinai—and at the same time it was the place where the demons dwell. The second meaning is vividly emphasized in the *Life of Antony:* as Antony withdraws into the deep desert, he hears the demons shouting, "Depart from our territory. What business have you here in the desert?"[24] So the solitary, in withdrawing into the desert, has a double aim: to meet God and to fight the demons. In both cases he is not being selfish, and his purpose is not to escape but to encounter. He goes out to discover God and to achieve union with him through prayer; and this is something that helps others. Equally he goes out to confront the demons, not running away from danger but advancing to meet it; and this also is a way of helping others. For the devil with whom he enters into combat is the common enemy of all humankind. Thus there is nothing self-centered in his act of *anachōrēsis*. Every prayer that he offers protects his fellow Christians, and every victory that he wins over the devil is a victory won on behalf of the human family as a whole. Such, therefore, is the positive value of *anachōrēsis,* even when it is not followed in any visible or explicit fashion by a movement of "return." Of course, many twentieth-century students of early Christian literature do not believe in the existence of demons or in the efficacy of prayer; but such persons need to recognize that the authors of the literature that they are studying believed keenly and intensely in both of these things.

According to the early Christian worldview, then, the solitaries were assisting others simply by offering prayer—not just through prayer of intercession, but through any kind of prayer:

> Civilization, where lawlessness prevails, is sustained by their prayers,
> and the world, buried in sin, is preserved by their prayers.[25]

In the words of an Orthodox writer in Finland, Tito Colliander:

> Prayer is action; to pray is to be highly effective. . . . Prayer is the science of scientists and the art of artists. The artist works in clay or colours, in word or tones; according to his ability he gives them pregnancy and beauty. The working material of the praying person is living humanity. By his prayer he shapes it, gives it pregnancy and beauty: first himself and thereby many others.[26]

The ascetic in the desert, that is to say, helps his fellow humans not so much by anything that he does, but rather by what he is. "First himself and thereby many others": he serves society by transforming himself through prayer, and by virtue of his own self-transfiguration he also transfigures the world around him. By weeping for his own sins, the recluse is in fact altering the spiritual situation of many others.

The rationale of ascetic *anachōrēsis* is concisely summed up by St. Seraphim of Sarov: "Acquire the spirit of peace, and then thousands around you will be saved."[27] Perhaps the more a monk thinks about converting himself, and the less he thinks about converting others, the more likely it is that others will in fact be converted. St. Isaac the Syrian (seventh century) goes so far as to maintain that it is better to become a solitary than to win over "a multitude of heathen" to the Christian faith: "Love the idleness of stillness above providing for the world's starving and the conversion of a multitude of heathen to the worship of God. . . . Better is he who builds his own soul than he who builds the world."[28] That is to put the point in a deliberately provocative way; but in fact he who "builds his own soul" is at the same time building the world, and until we have ourselves been in some measure "converted" it is improbable that we shall ever convert anyone else to anything at all. Actually, solitaries did on occasion prove quite effective as missionaries, as is shown, for example by the story of St. Euthymius (377–473) and the Bedouin tribe,[29] but this is exceptional.

In this way the solitaries, through their ascetic *anachōrēsis,* are indeed cooperating in the salvation of the world; but they do this not actively or intentionally but existentially—not through outward works but through inner perfection. In the words of Father Irénée Hausherr: "All progress in sanctity realized by one member benefits everyone; every ascent to God establishes a new bond between him and humanity as such; every oasis of spirituality renders the desert of this world less savage and less uninhabitable."[30]

Repression or Transfiguration?

Anachōrēsis, then, can be world-affirming as well as world-denying. The flight of the solitary from the world may be followed by a "return," in which he or she acts as a spiritual guide, as a "soul friend"; and, even when there is no such return, the hermits are helping others by the very fact of their existence, through their hidden holiness and prayer. What then of *enkrateia?* Often in Eastern Christian sources this seems to imply an attitude toward material things, toward the human body, and toward members of the other sex, that is little short of dualist. But is this invariably the case? Cannot ascetic *enkrateia* be likewise affirmative rather than negative?

First of all, early Christian ascetic texts insist repeatedly on the need for moderation in all forms of abstinence and self-restraint. Doubtless this was necessary precisely because so many ascetics were immoderate; yet it is nonetheless significant how often the best and most respected authorities issue firm warnings against excess. What distinguishes true from demonic fasting, states Amma Syncletica, is specifically its moderate character: "There is also an excessive asceticism *(askēsis)* that comes from the enemy, and this is practised by his disciples. How then are we to distinguish the divine and royal asceticism from that which is tyrannical and demonic? Clearly, by its moderation."[31] As regards food, the *Apophthegmata* and other early sources regularly discourage prolonged fasting, and state that the best course is to eat something every day.[32] If we want to fast in the right way, affirms John of Lycopolis, the golden rule is never to eat to satiety, never to stuff one's belly.[33] According to St. Barsanuphius of Gaza, we should always rise from the meal feeling that we should have liked to eat a little more.[34] The same principle applies to the drinking of water: we should restrict our intake, stopping well short of the point where we feel that we cannot possibly drink any more.[35] Sober advice of this kind serves to counterbalance the stories of spectacular and inhuman fasting.[36]

"Moderation," however, is a vague term. To render our evaluation of *enkrateia* more exact, let us take up a distinction that is made by Dom Cuthbert Butler between natural and unnatural asceticism:

> The mortifications recorded of the Egyptian solitaries, extraordinary and appalling as they were, were all of a kind that may be called natural, consisting in privation of food, of drink, of sleep, of clothing; in exposure to heat and cold; in rigorous enclosure in cell or cave or tomb; in prolonged silence and vigils and prayer; in arduous labour, in wandering through the desert, in bodily fatigue; but of the self-inflicted scourgings, the spikes and chains, and other artificial penances of a later time, I do not recollect any instances among the Egyptian monks of the fourth century.[37]

What basically distinguishes natural from unnatural asceticism is its attitude toward the body. Natural asceticism reduces material life to the utmost simplicity, restricting our physical needs to a minimum, but not maiming the body or otherwise deliberately causing it to suffer. Unnatural asceticism, on the other hand, seeks out special forms of mortification that torment the body and gratuitously inflict pain upon it. Thus it is a form of natural asceticism to wear cheap and plain clothing, whereas it is unnatural to wear fetters with iron spikes piercing the flesh. It is a form of natural asceticism to sleep on the ground, whereas it is unnatural to sleep on a bed of nails. It is a form of natural asceticism to live in a hut or a cave, instead of a well-appointed house, whereas it is unnatural to chain oneself to a rock or to stand permanently on top of a pillar. To refrain from marriage and sexual activity is natural asceticism; to castrate oneself is unnatural. To choose to eat only vegetables, not meat, and to drink only water, not wine, is natural asceticism; but it is unnatural intentionally to make our food and drink repulsive, as was done by Isaac the Priest, who after the Eucharist emptied the ashes from the censer over his food, and by Joseph of Panepho, who added sea water to the river water that he drank.[38] Incidentally, such actions surely display a curious disrespect to God as creator; for we are not to disfigure the gifts that God confers on us.

Unnatural asceticism, in other words, evinces either explicitly or implicitly a distinct hatred for God's creation, and particularly for the body; natural asceticism may do this, but on the whole it does not. The official attitude of the church, especially from the fourth century onwards, has been entirely clear. Voluntary abstinence for ascetic reasons is entirely legitimate; but to abstain out of a loathing for the material creation is heretical. The point is firmly made in the *Apostolic Canons* (Syria, c.400 CE):

> If any bishop, presbyter or deacon, or any other member of the clergy, abstains from marriage, or from meat and wine, not by way of asceticism *(askēsis)* but out of abhorrence for these things, forgetting that God made "all things altogether good and beautiful" (Gen. 1:31), and that he "created humankind male and female" (Gen. 1:27), and so blaspheming the work of creation, let him be corrected, or else be deposed and cast out of the Church. The same applies also to a lay person.[39]

The Council of Gangra (Asia Minor, c.355 CE) likewise anathematizes those who censure marriage and meat eating as essentially sinful. The motive for asceticism must be positive, not negative: "If anyone practices virginity or self-control *(enkrateia),* withdrawing from marriage as if it were a loathsome thing and not because of the inherent beauty and sanctity of virginity, let such a one be anathema."[40] When we fast, so Diadochus of Photice (mid-fifth century) insists, "we must never feel loathing for any kind of food, for to do so is abominable and utterly demonic. It is emphatically not because any kind of food is bad in itself that we refrain from it." We fast, not out of hatred for God's creation, but so as to control the body; also fasting enables us to help the poor, for the food that we ourselves refrain from eating can be given to others who are in need.[41]

Natural asceticism, it can be argued, is warfare not against the body but for the body. When asked by some children, "What is asceticism?," the Russian priest Alexander Elchaninov (1881–1934) replied, "A system of exercises which submits the body to the spirit"; and when they inquired what was the first exercise of all, he told them, "Breathe through the nose."[42] Our ascetic aim is not to impede our breathing through some forced technique, but simply to breathe correctly and so to let the body function in a natural way. "The important element in fasting," Father Alexander added, "is not the fact of *abstaining* from this or that, or of *depriving* oneself of something by way of punishment"; rather its purpose is the "refinement" of our physicality, so that we are more accessible to "the influence of higher forces" and thus approach closer to God.[43] Refinement, not destruction: that is the aim.

In contrast, then, to the unnatural variety, natural asceticism has a positive objective: it seeks not to undermine but to transform the body, rendering it a willing instrument of the spirit, a partner instead of an opponent. For this reason another

Russian priest, Sergius Bulgakov (1871–1944), used to say (employing the word "flesh" in its Pauline sense, to signify not our physicality but our fallen and sinful self): "Kill the flesh, so as to acquire a body."[44] As for the body, so far from killing it we are to hold it in honor and to offer it to God as a "living sacrifice" (*Rom.* 12.1). The Desert Father Dorotheus was surely wrong to say of his body, "It kills me, I kill it";[45] and he was tacitly corrected by another Desert Father, Poemen, who affirmed: "We were taught, not to kill the body, but to kill the passions."[46] There is an eloquent assertion of the intrinsic goodness of the body in the *mīmrā* already quoted, *On Hermits and Desert Dwellers:*

> Their bodies are temples of the Spirit, their minds are churches;
> their prayer is pure incense, and their tears are fragrant smoke. . .
>
> They greatly afflict their bodies, not because they do not love their bodies,
> rather, they want to bring their bodies to Eden in glory.[47]

It is reassuring in this connection to find that the earliest and most influential of all Greek monastic texts, the *Life of Antony,* adopts a markedly positive attitude towards the body. When Antony emerged after twenty years of enclosure within a fort, his friends "were amazed to see that his body had maintained its former condition, neither fat from lack of exercise, nor emaciated from fasting and combat with demons, but he was just as they had known him before his withdrawal. . . . He was altogether balanced, as one guided by reason and abiding in a natural state."[48] There is no dualistic hatred of the body here; asceticism has not subverted Antony's physicality but restored it to its "natural state," that is to say, to its true and proper condition as intended by God. This natural state of the body continues up to the end of Antony's long life. Although he lived to be more than a hundred, "his eyes were undimmed and quite sound, and he saw clearly; he lost none of his teeth—they had simply become worn down to the gums because of the old man's great age. He remained strong in both feet and hands."[49] So according to the texts, *enkrateia* enhanced rather than impaired Antony's bodily health.

"We were taught, not to kill the body, but to kill the passions," says Abba Poemen. But is he right? Cannot even the passions be redirected and used in God's service? Our answer will depend in part on the meaning that we attach to the word *pathos* (passion). Are we to regard it in a Stoic sense, as something fundamentally diseased and disordered, a morbid and pathological condition, or should we rather follow the Aristotelian standpoint and treat it as something neutral, capable of being put either to evil or to good use?[50] The manner in which we understand *pathos* will also influence the sense that we give to the term *apatheia* (dispassion, passionlessness). But this is not simply a linguistic issue; for the way in which we employ words influences the way in which we think about things. It makes a considerable difference what we say to others and, indeed, to ourselves: do we enjoin "mortify" or "redirect," "eradicate" or "educate," "eliminate" or "transfigure"?

Philo adopts the Stoic view of *pathos,* and many Greek Christian fathers follow him in this, regarding the passions as "contrary to nature" and even directly sinful. This is the position of Clement of Alexandria, Nemesius of Emesa, Gregory of

Nyssa, Evagrius of Pontus, and John Climacus, to mention only a few. But there are significant exceptions, and both Theodoret of Cyrus and Abba Isaias of Scetis adopt a more positive attitude. Desire and anger, says Theodoret, are "necessary and useful to nature": without desire we would experience no longing for divine things, no appetite for food and drink, no impulse towards "lawful procreation," and so the human race would perish. Anger in its turn has a positive function, he says, for it prevents our desire from passing beyond due limits.[51] Isaias likewise argues that the different passions can all be put to a positive use that is "in accordance with nature." Desire, employed aright, impels us to love God; jealousy (or *zēlos* [zeal]) spurs us on to make greater efforts in the spiritual life (cf. *1 Cor.* 12.31); anger and hatred prove beneficial, if directed against sin and the demons; even pride can be used in a constructive way, when we employ it to counteract self-depreciation and despondency. The aim of the ascetic, then, is not to suppress these passions but to reorient them.[52] St. Maximus the Confessor (c.580–662) follows the same approach when he describes love for God as a "holy passion."[53] In similar terms St. Gregory Palamas speaks of "divine and blessed passions"; our objective is not the *nekrōsis* (mortification) of the passions but their *metathesis* (transposition).[54]

Even in those authors, such as Evagrius, who speak of *pathos* (passion) in pejorative terms, the notion of *apatheia* (dispassion) is by no means unduly negative. Evagrius himself links it closely with *agapē*.[55] It is not an attitude of passive indifference and insensibility, still less a condition in which sinning is impossible, but it is on the contrary a state of inner freedom and integration, in which we are no longer under the domination of sinful impulses, and so are capable of genuine love; "apathy" is thus a particularly misleading translation. Adapting Evagrius's teaching to a Western audience, St. John Cassian wisely rendered *apatheia* as *puritas cordis* (purity of heart) a phrase that has the double advantage of being both scriptural in content and positive in form.[56] To denote its dynamic character, Diadochus employs the expressive phrase "the fire of *apatheia*."[57] It is no mere mortification of the passions, but a state of soul in which a burning love for God and for our fellow humans leaves no room for sensual and selfish impulses.

From all this it is evident that *enkrateia*, although often understood in a negative manner—as hatred of the body, as the destruction of our instinctive urges—can also be interpreted in more affirmative terms, as the reintegration of the body and the transformation of the passions into their true and natural condition. Again and again, when the patristic texts are carefully analyzed, the Greek fathers turn out to be advocating not repression but transfiguration.

A Vocation for All

Our explanation of the terms *anachōrēsis* and *enkrateia* has made clear that *askēsis* signifies not simply a selfish quest for individual salvation but a service rendered to the total human family; not simply the cutting off or destroying of the lower but, much more profoundly, the refinement and illumination of the lower and its transfiguration into something higher. The same conclusion could be drawn from an examination of other key ascetic terms, such as *hēsȳchia* (stillness, tranquillity, quietude). This too is affirmative rather than negative, a state of plenitude rather than emptiness, a sense of presence rather than absence. It is not just a cessation of speech, a pause between words, but an attitude of attentive listening, of openness and communion with the eternal: in the words of John Climacus, "*Hēsȳchia* is to worship God unceasingly and to wait on him. . . . The Hesychast is one who says, 'I sleep, but my heart is awake'" (*Song* 5.2).[58]

Interpreted in this positive way, as transfiguration rather than mortification, *askēsis* is universal in its scope—not an élite enterprise but a vocation for all. It is not a curious aberration, distorting our personhood, but it reveals to us our own true nature. As Father Alexander Elchaninov observes, "Asceticism is necessary first of all for creative action of any kind, for prayer, for love: in other words, it is needed by each of us throughout our entire life. . . . *Every Christian is an ascetic.*"[59] Without asceticism none of us is authentically human.

NOTES

1. In Donald A. Lowrie, *Christian Existentialism: A Berdyaev Anthology* (London, 1965), pp. 86–87 (translation altered).
2. *The Trinity and the Religious Experience of Man* (New York/London, 1973), p. 66.
3. *The First Circle,* trans. Michael Guybon (London: Fontana Books, 1970), pp. 106–107.
4. See Nicholas O. Lossky, *History of Russian Philosophy* (New York, 1951), p. 182; cf. Paul Florensky, *Salt of the Earth: Or a Narrative on the Life of the Elder of Gethsemane Skete Hieromonk Abba Isidore,* trans. Richard Betts, edited by the St. Herman of Alaska Brotherhood (Platina, 1987), p. 11.
5. Jacob of Serug, *Homily on Simeon the Stylite,* trans. Susan Ashbrook Harvey, in Vincent L. Wimbush, ed., *Ascetic Behavior in Greco-Roman Antiquity: A Sourcebook,* Studies in Antiquity and Christianity (Minneapolis, 1990), pp. 21–22.
6. Leif A. Vaage, in Wimbush, *Ascetic Behavior,* p. 117.
7. Philo, *On the Contemplative Life* 8.66, trans. Gail Paterson Corrington, in Wimbush, *Ascetic Behavior,* p. 149.
8. *On Hermits and Desert Dwellers,* lines 329ff., trans. Joseph P. Amar, in Wimbush, *Ascetic Behavior,* p. 75.
9. Arsenius 1, in *The Desert Christian: Sayings of the Desert Fathers, The Alphabetical Collection.* trans. B. Ward (New York, 1975); also in J. P. Migne, ed., *Patrologiae cursus completus: Series Graeca,* 65 vols. (Paris, 1857–1866).
10. Arsenius 28.
11. Arsenius 13.
12. *Desert Christian . . . Alphabetical Collection,* Macarius 27: cf. Macarius 41.
13. See the *Vita* by Jerome, trans. Paul B. Harvey, in Wimbush, *Ascetic Behavior,* pp. 357–369. Paul himself may be legendary, but his story is typical; there must have been many historical figures who fled like him into the desert, permanently breaking off their contacts with other humans.
14. For bibliography on the authorship of the *Life of Antony,* see Alvyn Pettersen, *Athanasius and the Human Body* (Bristol, 1990), p. 33, note 69.
15. *Life of Antony* 87 (*PG* 26.965A).
16. *The Lausiac History of Palladius,* ed. Cuthbert Butler (Cambridge, 1898), 21:63–68.
17. *The Brothers Karamazov,* book 2., chapter 3, "Devout Peasant Women." Dostoevsky was not simply inventing an imaginary scene but reproducing what he had actually seen in the Optina hermitage; cf. John B. Dunlop, *Staretz Amvrosy: Model for Dostoevsky's Staretz Zossima* (Belmont, Mass., 1972).

18. *Desert Christian,* Antony 9. Similar statements can be found in the (perhaps authentic) Letters attributed to Antony (trans. Derwas J. Chitty, Fairacres Publication 50 [Oxford, 1975]); cf. Samuel Rubenson, *The Letters of St. Antony: Origenist Theology, Monastic Tradition and the Making of a Saint* (Lund, 1990).
19. There can of course be "spiritual mothers" as well as "spiritual fathers": the Alphabetical Collection of *Apophthegmata* contains 3 *ammas* alongside 117 *abbas,* so women are certainly represented, although in a minority. Cf. Sister Benedicta Ward, "Apophthegmata Matrum," in *Studia Patristica* 16 (Berlin, 1985), pp. 63–66; reprinted in Ward, *Signs and Wonders: Saints, Miracles, and Prayers from the 4th Century to the 14th,* Variorum Collected Studies Series, CS 361 (Brookfield, 1992), section I.
20. *Anmchara* (soul friend) is a term found in Celtic Christianity. Cf. Kenneth Leech, *Soul Friend: A Study of Spirituality* (London, 1977), p. 50.
21. Arsenius 27 and 30.
22. *The Lausiac History* 18:58.
23. *Historia monachorum in Aegypto,* prologue 10; cf. Norman Russell, trans., *The Lives of the Desert Fathers* (London/Oxford, 1980), p. 50.
24. *Life of Antony* 13 (*PG* 26.861C).
25. *On Hermits and Desert Dwellers,* lines 509ff., trans. Amar, in Wimbush, *Ascetic Behavior,* p. 79.
26. *The Way of the Ascetics,* new ed. (London/Oxford, 1983), pp. 57, 59.
27. Ivan Kologrivof, *Essai sur la sainteté en Russie* (Bruges, 1953), p. 430.
28. *Mystic Treatises by Isaac of Nineveh,* trans. A. J. Wensinck (Amsterdam, 1923), pp. 32, 298; *The Ascetical Homilies of Saint Isaac the Syrian,* trans. Dana Miller (Boston: Holy Transfiguration Monastery, 1984), pp. 32, 306 (translation altered).
29. Cyril of Scythopolis, *Life of Euthymius* 10 and 15, in R. M. Price, trans., *Lives of the Monks of Palestine,* Cistercian Studies 114 (Kalamazoo, 1991), pp. 14–17, 20–21.
30. "L'hésychasme: Étude de spiritualité," in Hausherr, *Hésychasme et prière,* Orientalia Christiana Analecta 176 (Rome, 1966), p. 181.

    In the discussion above, *anachōrēsis* has been understood in its exterior sense, as a physical withdrawal into solitude. The term can also denote an inner, spiritual state, as when Abba Isaias of Scetis (died 489 CE) states: "The ancients who were our fathers said that *anachōrēsis* is flight from the body and meditation upon death," in *Logos* 26.3, ed. Monk Avgoustinos of the Jordan (Jerusalem, 1911), p. 184. Compare John Climacus: "Withdrawal *(anachōrēsis)* from the world is a willing hatred of all that is materially prized, a denial of nature for the sake of what is above nature," in *The Ladder of Divine Ascent,* Step 1, trans. Colm Luibheid and Norman Russell, The Classics of Western Spirituality (New York, 1982), p. 74.
31. Alphabetical Collection, Syncletica 15. Now see translation by Elizabeth Castelli, "The Life and Activity of the Blessed Teacher Syncletica," in Wimbush, ed., *Ascetic Behavior,* pp. 265–311. On the dangers of excessive asceticism and the need for relaxation, see ibid., Antony 8 and 13.
32. See, for example, ibid., Ammonas 4 and Poemen 31.
33. *Historia monachorum in Aegypto* 1.29, p. 56.
34. *Questions and Answers,* ed. Sotirios N. Schoinas (Volos, 1960), §84; trans. Lucien Regnault and Philippe Lemaire (Solesmes, 1972), §158; cf. §511.
35. See Evagrius, *Practicus* 18, eds. Antoine Guillaumont and Claire Guillaumont, Sources chrétiennes 171 (Paris, 1971), p. 542; cf. *Historia monachorum in Aegypto* 20.16, p. 107.
36. See, for example, the story of Macarius of Alexandria at Tabennisi in *The Lausiac History* 18:52–53.

37. *The Lausiac History* 1:188. The wearing of chains is, however, occasionally found in Egypt, as with the body of Sarapion, discovered at Antinoe: see Derwas J. Chitty, *The Desert a City* (Oxford, 1966), p. 17, note 36. It is, however, far more common in Syria: cf. Theodoret of Cyrus, *Historia religiosa* 10.1, 15.2, 23.1, eds. Pierre Canivet and Alice Leroy-Molinghen, Sources chrétiennes 234, 257 (Paris, 1977–1979), 1:438; 2:18, 134. But initially ascetic practices in Syria were relatively moderate; severe feats of mortification only begin to appear in the late fourth and early fifth centuries (cf. Amar, in Wimbush, *Ascetic Behavior,* p. 67).
38. *Apophthegmata,* Isaac the Priest 6, Eulogius the Priest 1.
39. Apostolic Canon 51, in Périclès-Pierre Joannou, *Discipline générale antique (IVe–IXes.),* 1.2, *Les canons des Synodes Particuliers* (Grottaferrata, 1962), pp. 35–36; trans. Henry R. Percival, *The Seven Ecumenical Councils of the Undivided Church: Their Canons and Dogmatic Decrees,* A Select Library of Nicene and Post-Nicene Fathers of the Christian Church, 2d series, vol. 14 (Oxford/New York, 1900), p. 597.
40. Canon 9; cf. Canons 1–2, 4, 10, 14, in Joannou, op. cit., pp. 89–95; trans. O. Larry Yarbrough, in Wimbush, *Ascetic Behavior,* pp. 451–453. The Council of Gangra also forbids women to wear men's clothing (Canon 13).
41. *On Spiritual Knowledge and Discrimination* 43, trans. G.E.H. Palmer, Philip Sherrard, and Kallistos Ware, *The Philokalia: The Complete Text,* vol. 1 (London/Boston, 1979), p. 266.
42. *The Diary of a Russian Priest* (London, 1967), p. 213.
43. Ibid., pp. 129, 187.
44. Cf. Metropolitan Anthony (Bloom), "Body and Matter in Spiritual Life," in A. M. Allchin, ed., *Sacrament and Image: Essays in the Christian Understanding of Man,* The Fellowship of St. Alban and St. Sergius (London, 1967), p. 41.
45. *The Lausiac History* 2:17.
46. *Apophthegmata,* Poemen 184.
47. *On Hermits and Desert Dwellers,* lines 97ff., 189ff., trans. Amar, in Wimbush, *Ascetic Behavior,* pp. 70, 72.
48. *Life of Antony* 14 (*PG* 26. 864C–865A). On the significance of this passage, see Chitty, *The Desert a City,* p. 4.
49. *Life of Antony* 93 (*PG* 26. 973AB).
50. See Kallistos Ware, "The Meaning of 'Pathos' in Abba Isaias and Theodoret of Cyrus," in *Studia Patristica* 20 (Leuven, 1989), pp. 315–322.
51. Theodoret, *The Healing of Hellenic Maladies* 5.76–79, ed. Pierre Canivet, Sources chrétiennes 57 (Paris, 1958), pp. 251–252.
52. *Logos* 2.1–2, ed. Avgoustinos, p. 5.
53. *On Love* 3.67, trans. Palmer, Sherrard, and Ware, *The Philokalia: The Complete Text,* vol. 2 (London/Boston, 1981), p. 93.
54. *Triads in Defence of the Holy Hesychasts* 2.2.22; 3.3.15, ed. Jean Meyendorff, *Spicilegium Sacrum Lovaniense* 30–31 (Louvain, 1959), pp. 367, 723.
55. *Practicus* 81, ed. Guillaumont, p. 670: "Love is the offspring of *apatheia.*"
56. Cf. Owen Chadwick, *John Cassian,* 2nd ed. (Cambridge, 1968), p. 102.
57. *On Spiritual Knowledge and Discrimination* 17, trans. Palmer et al., vol. 2, p. 258.
58. *Ladder* 27, trans. Luibheid and Russell, pp. 263, 269–270.
59. *The Diary of a Russian Priest,* pp. 177, 188 (translation altered).

2

The Howl of Oedipus, the Cry of Héloïse: From Asceticism to Postmodern Ethics

Edith Wyschogrod

Asceticism is a complex of widely varying practices, beliefs and motives that have appeared in particular historical and cultural contexts. It is, to use the language of art criticism, site-specific. If the historical and phenomenological integrity of asceticism's many manifestations is to be preserved, it is beyond dispute that ascetic phenomena must be allowed to emerge in discrete material and psycho-social meaning constellations.[1]

Yet, I want to argue, there is also for every psycho-social practice an episteme, a cluster of ideas often invisible, that is both the conceptual backdrop and the enabling mechanism for the emergence of ascetic life *in situ*. Thus, I shall allow myself to speak in more sweeping terms of Western asceticism and a Western episteme with the understanding that neither term implies theoretical or practical unity, but that both point to a loosely linked, open-ended chain of mythemes and philosophemes. These are the narrative and conceptual units that acquire meaning through their relation with one another and that, taken together, constitute a tradition. I sometimes refer to the linkage of these units as a chain of signifiers. Concrete practices do not lie outside a tradition but feed back into it in a loop that may overturn a formation or render it more supple. Within this episteme, there are discernible discursive formations—lesser patterns of signification. Thus, no essence of asceticism will be specified; I shall argue that the discursive formations within the episteme of asceticism are bound up with the self-imposition of corporeal and psychic pain or privation; but I shall also argue that not all pain and privation, even when self-generated, is ascetic.

In what follows four interrelated claims are considered: first, in order to understand the cluster of notions that enter into asceticism as an episteme, two prior and competing discourses, that of *erōs* (love) and of *dikē* (justice), especially as Plato interprets them, must be distinguished. The body concepts associated with each need to be sorted out, as well as the way in which these views of body are taken up or rejected in ascetic discourse. Second, Western asceticism demands the devaluing of the world, the turning of the world into vanity. In order to see this, the type of negation involved in world negation will be analyzed. Third, within the structure of asceticism, gaps or fissures appear in its understanding of love, pleasure, and pain in the form of an eroticism that asserts and denies itself. This is especially evident in the correspondence of Héloïse and Abelard. The view of the body that emerges presages a new postmodern understanding of asceticism and its relation to ethics. Finally, this new conception of body will allow asceticism, love and justice to intersect without integrating them heuristically or dialectically.

The Howl of Oedipus

In one of Greek tragedy's most powerful passages, a messenger recounts the cry of Oedipus upon discovering Jocasta hanged, a cry that gathers into itself the cumulative pain of incest and patricide.

> And with a dread shriek, as though someone beckoned him on, he sprang at the double doors, and from their sockets forced the bending bolts and rushed into the room.
>
> There beheld we the woman hanging by the neck in a twisted noose of swinging cords. But he, when he saw her, with a dread deep cry of misery, loosed the halter whereby she hung. . . . Then was the sequel dread to see. For he tore from her raiment the golden brooches wherewith she was decked and lifted them, and smote full on his own eye-balls.[2]

The howl of Oedipus is followed by a remarkable act of automutilation: Oedipus tears out his eyes. Why, it might be asked, is it so unthinkable, so counterintuitive to consider this self-infliction of pain and deprivation an ascetic practice? Perhaps Oedipus's cry of pain is simply the spontaneous response to powerful emotions, whereas asceticism involves a nexus of beliefs and practices that must be consciously set in place and should have a specific aim. I want to argue that the howl of Oedipus, far from being akin to the scream uttered in response to physical injury, a biological reflex as it were, is a distillate of a certain *telos* (purpose) and of a complex discursive formation, one that is different from asceticism.

A clue may be derived from Claude Lévi-Strauss's interpretation, not of the Oedipus story itself, upon which he has commented copiously, but of the incest taboo. The incest prohibition, he contends, occurs at the intersection of culture and nature and provides the link between them: "Before it, culture is still non-existent, with it nature's sovereignty over man is ended."[3] Although its universality has been contested by anthropologists, what is crucial for Lévi-Strauss and germane to my argument is his contention that, "The *fact of being a rule,* completely independent of its modalities, is indeed the very essence of the incest prohibition."[4] To be sure, nature alone already operates lawfully, in that living things reproduce their own kind and not some other. Nevertheless, it is culture and not nature that regulates allowable degrees of consanguinity in human societies. The aberrations of nature recorded in Sophocles' *Oedipus,* the inability of animals and humans to bring forth their young, are responses by nature to the violation of a social prohibition. What I want to focus on is the regulative character of the taboo in order to bring to the fore the episteme from which it arises. By regulative I mean the establishment of culture's suzerainty over nature as reflecting a reapportionment of power, a reallocation that is essentially a juridical process belonging to a classical episteme, that of justice.

Missing in the explanation of Lévi-Strauss is a grasp of the juridical character of the discursive formation to which the Oedipus myth belongs. Early Greek philosophy's understanding of nature as cosmos and cosmos as a juridical *topos* (theme) belong to this conceptual formation. Beginning with the biologism of Aristotle, the cosmological genealogy of justice, in which the ideals of retributive and distributive justice and of punishment and equity can be traced, has been obscured. It is not at the level of genera and species, or even at the plane of the laws of motion as Aristotle formulates them, that nature is first understood, but rather as a moral field. Plato and Aristotle fabricate a new context for the interpretation of justice, subordinating its cosmic character to a psychological and political discourse. The terms of this discourse are those of the internal relations of the soul's constituent parts and of citizens' relations to one another and to their rulers. When the cosmological dimension of justice is reinstated in Stoicism, it is too late: the political subreption of the cosmic model is now a *fait accompli.*

Cosmic justice, the episteme in which the order of things is perceived in terms of apportionment or measure, is first brought to the fore in the pre-Socratic fragment of Anaximander:

> The Unlimited is the first-principle of things that are. It is that from which the coming-to-be of things and qualities take place and it is that into which they return when they perish by moral necessity, giving satisfaction to one another and making reparation for their injustice, according to the order of time.[5]

The *apeiron* (boundless) is an "ontological storehouse,"[6] the venue of physical change out of which things come to be and into which they pass away. I want, however, to resist Heidegger's rejection of the axiological or moral dimension of this text: his view that the fragment points to an overcoming of negativity in the coming-to-be or "presencing" of things. Instead the text describes a moral balance sheet: things make reparations for their injustice. The *aperion* is always already configured as a moral *topos* against which wrongs are redressed by reimbursing it for the gift of being. Things and qualities "know" the order of time; they cannot not know when and how to make restitution.

Reparation is also an issue in establishing the boundary between nature and culture. The misreadings of consanguinity that characterize Oedipus's relation to his mother and father is a failure of knowledge about the social order, which requires the intervention of nature's power if equilibrium is to be restored. Divine punishment is meted out for Oedipus's inability to recognize not the precept—Oedipus knows the incest and patricide proscriptions well enough—but the placeholders to whom the proscriptions apply. Thus Oedipus cries out that he has "failed in knowledge of those whom [he] yearned to know [and that] henceforth [he] would be dark."[7] Oedipus's transgression (whatever Freud may have made of it later) does not belong within the framework of a classical definition of erotics but within one of justice, transgression, and punishment. (Much the same case could be made for

King Lear, with madness substituting for blindness in the chain of signifiers, and consanguine daughterly obligation for primal sexual transgression.)

What is the function of Oedipus's physical pain within the terrain I have mapped out, the terrain of deficit and expenditure governed by the episteme of justice? (I shall defer for the moment the question of how this pain differs from that of asceticism.) In the realm of justice pain becomes both the instrument and the sign for power's redistribution. When justice becomes a political discourse in classical philosophy, pain is the agent of a punishment that is both pedagogic and retributive. Knowing how much pain is required, no more and no less, demands knowledge of both fact and value: knowledge of justice, the ideal, and of the angle of declination from that ideal reflected in particular cases. Methods for entering the storehouse of truths and applying them form the nub of the Platonic and Aristotelian discourses of justice.

Within the episteme of justice, Oedipus's failure to know his mother lies at the dividing line between nature and culture. The incest taboo is a crossover signifier, belonging to two intertwined chains of meaning: the cosmic and the political dimensions of justice. Violating the rule that is always already in place if any other rule is to follow, he "makes reparation for [this] injustice according to the order of time" through an act of ocular self-mutilation.

The Body of the Just

In praise of the past, first-century Stoic Seneca writes:

> In that age which was called golden, Poseidonius maintains that rule was in the hands of the wise. They restrained aggression, protected the weaker from the stronger, advised and dissuaded and indicated what was advantageous and what was not. Their prudence saw to it that their people lacked for nothing, their courage averted dangers and their generosity enabled their subjects to . . . flourish.[8]

This Stoic distillate of the classical view of the philosopher depicts the just man as having knowledge, being prudent enough to apply this knowledge, and sufficiently courageous to act upon it.

In considering this account of the Stoic sage, the question is not simply how justice is reflected in the conception of the wise man or of the things done in the body, but what that body must be in order for there to be wisdom. Plato's radical answer is that the body is a disturbance. Thus, for example, in *Phaedo,* the most negative of the discourses on body, Socrates maintains:

> The body is a source of endless trouble to us by reason of the mere requirement of food; and is liable also to diseases; . . . it fills us full of loves and lusts and fears and fancies of all kinds . . . even if we are at leisure and betake ourselves to some speculation, the body is always breaking in on us.[9]

The body as a whole, with its auxiliary organs of sensation, obstructs the knowledge of an absolute justice attainable by the rational soul.

For the Socratic just man no genuine decontamination of the body is possible short of the complete "separation of the soul from the body," a separation achieved in death. Only then is "the release of the soul from the chains of the body" fully consummated.[10] But if the soul alone has access to the world of ideal forms, the body, severed from the soul, is cut off from that which is "in the likeness of the divine."[11] Whereas other material things imitate the forms, the disengaged body is not just another thing, but a thing bereft of soul. Denied access to forms, it can only imitate an absence. Thus the wise man's body is an imitation of the presence of an absence, of a formless form: death. This imitation cannot have suicide for its object, as for Socrates (if not for the Stoics) man is the property of the gods and as such cannot dispose of his own life. If Socratic discourse is to remain coherent, the wise man can only continue to exist in a deathlike suspension of pain and pleasure.

This view is consistent with the irrelevance attributed to gender in allocating guardianship in the ideal state: "The same education which makes a man a good guardian will make a woman a good guardian for their original nature is the same."[12] In theory at least the body of the just is genderless, unhindered by pain or pleasure, the distractions of sensation or the stirrings of desire. With the "biologism" of Aristotle, this view of body and soul would seem to collapse. For Aristotle, after all, soul is the principle of life in the animal body and as such inseparable from the body. Yet it is not in mere life that the relation of the human soul to its body is determined but, as with Plato, in rational life. Even when this claim is reconfigured by the Stoics, so that reason along with impression and impulse, becomes a faculty, there is no question as to pride of place. Thus Epictetus:

> What then is a philosopher's matter? Not a ragged coat surely? No it is reason. What is his end? Surely it is not wearing a ragged coat? No it is keeping his reason right. What kind of theorems? Surely not ones with how to grow a large beard or long hair? No, but rather what Zeno says: to understand the elements of reason, what sort of thing each of them is, how they fit together and what their consequences are.[13]

The sage attends not only to the order of state and cosmos, but to the examination of reason itself. Although it belongs to the same moral *topos,* the same episteme of justice as the howl of Oedipus, classical philosophy transposes the death of the body into the body of death, indifferent to the pain of Oedipus because it is indifferent to death.

In sum, within the episteme of justice, reason alone can determine what counts as "reparation for injustice." Traces of the older notion of cosmic justice persist in later classical discourse so that justice does not assume the dryly computational form that the idea of reparation appears to imply. Pain remains an expression of compensatory power or, as in the case of Oedipus, the ideogram or sign of crime and its aftermath, while pleasure inheres in the ratiocinative process itself. By contrast, in the discursive formations of Western asceticism, pain will become a driving force, both instrument and end.

Three discursive strands will enter into the meaning constellation of Western asceticism: first, an erotics, a term defined by Foucault as "the purposeful art of love"[14] which constitutes the focus of the *Symposium* and the first section of the

Phaedrus and is linked to several fragments of Heraclitus; second, a cosmic heuristics, the subject of the *Timaeus;* and third an axiology implicit in the biblical text of *Ecclesiastes.*

The Fire of *Erōs*

> This universe which is the same for all, has not been made by any god or man, but it always has been, is, and will be—an ever-living fire, kindling itself by regular measures and going out by regular measures.[15]

In this fragment of Heraclitus, fire is not to be envisaged as an element like the water or air of Miletian physics. It is not a material substratum of the world, for Heraclitus adds, "The phases of fire are craving and satiety."[16] Cosmic fire burns with an erotic glow, that "throws apart and then brings together."[17] The cosmos as a *topos* of desire will recur in Plato's cosmology, but Heraclitean fire will be downgraded to one among several elements even if it burns, as Plato claims, with the brightness and beauty of the divine form.

Fire as an explicit erotic motif is absent in the *Symposium* and *Phaedrus,* perhaps because of fire's frequent association in classical discourse not with lust but, honorifically, with light. For an understanding of this terrain, we need only examine Foucault's admirable treatment of these dialogues. He argues as follows: The groundwork for the Socratic discussion of *erōs* is laid in culturally accepted views of love that are retained in radically transformed fashion by Socrates. The *Symposium* sets forth the uses and abuses of pleasure, especially with regard to the love of boys, with an eye to explaining the relation of pleasure to truth.[18] Its early speeches, like those of the *Phaedrus,* are psychological set pieces about the dishonorable games lovers play and are largely concerned with how to distinguish noble from base love. Aristophanes' speech posits the bisecting of primal human beings who will continue to seek their lost counterparts. As halves of a symmetrical whole they are equals, but this parity of the lovers does not change the basic character of their bond. No issue of proper relations within the erotic can be resolved until love's essential nature is uncovered.[19]

Through the discourse on love of the crone Diotima, Socrates shows that love is by nature an intermediate state born of deficiency and plenty, of ignorance and knowledge. The genuine lover lacks that which he desires, not the beloved's body but truth or beauty itself. For Socrates "it is not exclusion of the body that . . . is fundamental [but] rather that, beyond the appearances of the object, love is a relation to truth," Foucault writes.[20] The one who has access to truth is the master of love, indifferent to seduction and to the fires of lust. Unlike the other speakers, Socrates does not produce an etiquette of sexual reticence but an account of the soul's resistance to its appetites through the knowledge of its relation to its own desires and to their objects.

This resistance, Foucault alleges, is important for "the transformation of ethics into a morality of renunciation and for the constitution of a hermeneutics of Desire,"[21] in short, into asceticism. I shall not enter here into the matter of Foucault's much disputed account of asceticism's relation to the Greco-Roman understanding of the self in his late work.[22] In the present context I take Foucault to be partly right when he suggests Western asceticism is an outcome of indifference to the body's appetites. Yet this indifference cannot, as he claims, be a transformation of ethics, as Foucault understands this term, for it belongs within the episteme of justice in which body and soul are severed. By contrast, the body of classical erotics cannot be cordoned off. Love cannot escape the bodily because insofar as it is lack, it cannot be taken up into the rational soul. Even when love's objects are truth and beauty, love will continue to bear the imprint of a body it cannot jettison. When the transcendent becomes love's object, love will continue to be marked by an ineradicable corporeality that will necessitate a transfiguring *askēsis*. It is just this persistence of the body, I shall argue that allows for the transferring of ethics in the postmodern sense from the terrain of the classical *dikē* to that of *erōs*.

It is not surprising that the two-tiered ontology of ideal forms and physical objects that governs Plato's account of human love also dominates his cosmology. In the great cosmogonic drama of the *Timaeus*, "that which always is and never becomes" is distinguished from "that which is always becoming but never is."[23] It is also not surprising that, because the creator is benevolent and wants all things to be as like himself as possible, that the divine craftsman transforms a preexistent chaos in accordance with ideal goodness and beauty. What *is* striking is that the resulting artifact is a living thing, so that the body comes to function as a heuristic device for understanding the cosmos. Because the intelligent is superior to the non-intelligent and intelligence is impossible without soul, Timaeus argues, the creator "implanted reason in soul and soul in body . . . [so that] this world came to be, through God's providence, a living being with soul and intelligence."[24] Thus cosmos and body mirror one another.

Plotinus, eager to protect the beauty of the cosmos against its gnostic depreciation,[25] refuses to link bodily *erōs*, the earthly Aphrodite, with cosmos. Thus, Plotinus inquires, when "love is represented as homeless, bedless, and bare-footed: would not that be a shabby description of the Cosmos and quite out of the truth?"[26] By contrast, the cosmos of the *Timaeus* might be read as longing for its eternal counterpart. Such a cosmos must be stilled just as bodily desire must be stilled if the soul is to turn towards beauty and truth. Thus, speaking of the Valentinian *gnōsis*, Peter Brown refers to the calming of human sexual agitation as "the outward visible sign of a mighty subsidence that takes place in the spiritual reaches of the universe."[27]

Hebhel: The Nothingness of the All

> I the Preacher have been king over Israel in Jerusalem . . . I have seen everything that is done under the sun; and behold all is vanity and a striving after wind.[28]

The discursive formations of Western asceticism cannot fall into place until the world is reduced to vanity, to *hebhel*, a mere breath of air. The devaluing of all that is in *Ecclesiastes* is a far more profound depreciation of the world than Stoic detachment. The Stoic sage is one who classifies things as good or indifferent, who can distinguish vice from virtue. By contrast, the narrator of *Ecclesiastes* declares, "I applied my mind to know wisdom and to know madness and folly. I perceive that this also is a striving after wind. For in much wisdom is much vexation, and he who increases knowledge increases sorrow."[29] When all is vanity, the all that is *hebhel* refers both to the totality of the world and to the maximum intensity of the worthlessness attributed to the world.

Hebhel, mere wind, can be viewed as the obverse of *ruaḥ,* wind or breath in the honorific sense of spirit. Thus it is said "you do not know how the spirit *(ruaḥ)* comes to the bones in the womb of a woman with child."[30] This infusion of *ruaḥ* or vital breath into the child is compared in the same verse with the mysterious work of God: "so [too] you do not know the work of God who makes everything."[31]

It is here that the site of vanity must be distinguished from both the moral *topos* of justice and the lack that characterizes classical erotics as I have described them: the totality that is devalued by vanity is God's creation. In his brilliant account of vanity, Jean Luc Marion suggests that two possible standpoints can be taken towards this totality: first, the ontological standpoint, the view from inside which posits the world as the sum of beings. From this perspective, the difference between being and not being, suffering and enjoying, knowing and not knowing, looms large. But there is another standpoint from outside the world such that the world appears as "stricken with vanity."[32]

I would, however, take issue with Marion's Heideggerian reading of the innerworldly perspective as the domain of Being and the beings. Despite its veneer of classical philosophy, *Ecclesiastes* stands under the aegis of the biblical doctrine of creation, of the world as God's work. Missing from Marion's otherwise extraordinary account is a hermeneutic of work. The word for work in *Ecclesiastes,* as in the "work of God" mentioned earlier, is *maaseh,* the same root as the word for story or narrative. The account of creation in the *Timaeus* is governed by the eternal patterns so that when it is referred to as "merely probable" the truth of the account is measured by the forms. By contrast, God's creation or work is plotted, is narrated. Thus, to strike the world with vanity is to cease to be one of the characters in the story and to assume the standpoint of narrator. The demiurge of the *Timaeus* is the fashioner of a divine artifact; the God of *Ecclesiastes,* the artisan of history, the controller of event-filled time. Sheer temporal passing must end in worldweariness: "All things are full of weariness; a man cannot utter it."[33] When everything that has been repeats itself, when there is nothing new under the sun, as Marion observes, something like the French *ennui* permeates earthly existence.

Vanity is not simply another discursive formation alongside of classical erotics. Rather, it operates upon Plato's psychology and cosmology to denegate them. Denegation is a denial that denies itself.[34] By denying the world, vanity institutes a negativity; but at the same time it brings the world that is being denied to the fore. It can be argued that classical erotics already reflects an effort to negate at least the corporeality of the world. But vanity in denying the "all" also denies the denial of the classical world. The body that is negated in classical erotics, a body from which nevertheless there is no dispensation, is transformed in asceticism into the body of temptation. In the new episteme of asceticism, vanity's denegation of classical erotics is reflected in one of asceticism's most powerful opening moves, Paul's declaration: "Creation was subjected to vanity *(mataiotēti).*"[35]

Classical erotics and its denegation as vanity merge into a single *topos,* that of an asceticism that tries to manage the eruption of materiality into the chain of signifiers, a materiality that manifests itself in the body's unsurpassability. Ascetics across cultural and historical lines force pain and pleasure into new meaning constellations, so that through practices of self-mortification and deprivation the body is made transparent, a conduit for transcendence. At the same time, the transformed body also becomes an ideogram for this process. Thus when after twenty years of "pursuing the ascetic life" St. Antony emerged from his fortress, his friends "were amazed to see that his body maintained its former condition, neither fat from lack of exercise, nor emaciated from fasting and combat with demons, but was just as they had known him prior to his withdrawal."[36] The flesh is shown as polysemic: resplendent with higher meaning when disciplined, but always ready to erupt into temptation.

Héloïse's Cry

It is now time to revisit the meaning constellations considered earlier, classical erotics and justice, in order to determine how they emerge in postmodernity and to inquire into the prospects for a postmodern retrieval of asceticism. It would appear that the classical discourse of justice with its attendant notions of reason would provide the conceptual site for postmodern moral deliberation. By contrast, it could be assumed that classical erotics with its linking of sexual desire to truth would be superseded by the pansexuality of contemporary Western culture. Divested of its previous presuppositions, classical erotics would now be reshaped into new conceptual and corporeal practices.

With respect to the Platonic *erōs,* Foucault contends that, far from liberating a new sphere of pleasure, contemporary psychology has converted sex into discourse. The ruses that modernity has used to turn sex into a language of power, "to make us love sex, to make the knowledge of it desirable and everything said about it precious,"[37] are comparable to the strategies Christianity once employed to render the body suspect. If sex is discourse, what has become of the ineradicable corporeality of classical erotics? Where are the spoors or traces of a body whose putrescence has been refined away in Christian asceticism by a self-imposed regimen of pain so that it may become the pure receptacle of transcendence?

Let us pursue these questions by considering Ander Nygren's famous account of the distinction between *erōs* and *agapē.* Nygren argues that the Platonic *erōs* is "acquisitive desire and longing" and expresses the lover's drive to satisfy a need. Although it may be determined by the worth and beauty of its object, *erōs* remains egocentric. By contrast, Christian *agapē* is unselfish, a love originating in plenitude. Patterned on divine love, "*agapē* loves and creates value in its object."[38] What is more, Nygren attributes a Platonic-erotic thrust to many early Christian accounts of Pauline *agapē,* such that love of the other subserves a beatitude that remains personal.

Despite difficulties both scholarly and philosophical that I shall not rehearse here,[39] Nygren's account is useful from a postmodern perspective in that it captures the powerful sense of need and the penumbra of sensuality that clings to *erōs.* When directed towards an object to which value is attributed, need—what the body requires to remain alive—turns into desire, and desires spawn one another. "Desire for something different [becomes] a different desire,"[40] George Simmel affirms. An *erōs* expressing need and desire attests to human destitution, a bodily indigence that asceticism will cast into high relief by the corporeal mimicry of it: hunger by fasting; sexual desire by chastity; bodily ease by self-mortification. Asceticism denegates corporeality: pain and privation deny the visceral body, but at the same time bring it to the fore, in that only the nonidealized body that ascetic practice hopes to perfect can become the terrain of the physical suffering necessary to purify it. It is this version of corporeality, the tenacious residue of the classical *erōs,* that postmodernity will reconfigure in a new asceticism that will join the *erōs* of need to the terrain of ethics.

Before this new asceticism can become evident, we must show the relation of the classical *erōs* to generosity and compassion—to the *Other.* In a response to Nygren, A. Hilary Armstrong contends that although the primary meaning of *erōs* in ancient Greek society was sexual passion from its heights to animal lust, Nygren has failed to see that *erōs* is also a god. For Armstrong, love is not only a desire for possession but for a union of lover and beloved in order to create beauty.[41] Thus, it can be argued, within the same *erōs,* the element of generosity is always already present in that a gift—beauty—is created in the interest of another.

The corporeal content of the classical *erōs* (the body reminding itself of itself endlessly) and the theme of generosity are nowhere more closely intertwined than in the twelfth-century reconfiguration of these philosophemes in the letters of Héloïse to Abelard, a text that, even if spurious, remains a *locus classicus* for bringing these themes to light.[42] A penumbra of sensuality shadows her renunciation of its physical expression:

> The pleasures of lovers which we shared have been too sweet. . . . Wherever I turn they are always before my eyes, bringing with them awakened longings and fantasies which will not even let me sleep. Even during the celebration of the Mass . . . my thoughts are on their wantonness instead of on prayers."[43]

The giving of self at first concentrated in her love for Abelard becomes disseminated, distributed, as it were, to the nuns under her care for whose weaknesses she pleads: "Certainly those who laid down rules for monks were not only completely silent about women but also prescribed regulations which they know to be quite unsuitable for them."[44]

It could be asserted that, both in Abelard's *Historia calamitatum* and in the exchange of letters between Abelard and Héloïse, romantic motifs have infiltrated the discourse of a more traditional asceticism.[45] Thus Abelard writes, "We were united first under one roof, then in heart. . . . [W]ith our books open before us, more words of love than of our reading passed between us, and more kissing than teaching."[46] In the present context we need only note that in Héloïse is concentrated not merely the motif of generosity but also that of a pain that fissures the discursive formations of asceticism with a cry of desire and longing that presages the postmodern body of ethics.

Héloïse's desire is articulated not only in terms of the recognized vices—greed, anger, pride and the like—but as a cry for help issuing from a sensual nature only half disowned. Héloïse's love is doomed not because Abelard "was deprived of those organs with which he practiced [his lechery],"[47] nor even because the life of a religious person had been foisted upon her, but because, within the discursive formation of asceticism, no rule of distributive justice could compensate her for a desire that sought not an object but another desire. This is not to say that issues of gender bound up with the reallocation of ecclesial power are lacking. Far from it. Yet, unlike the howl of Oedipus, the primordial cry of the juridical person whose pain is weighed on the scales of justice, the discourse of Héloïse "like nails that cannot touch wounds gently, but only pierce through them"[48] enters the chain of signifiers as insatiable need. Thus she entreats:

> Do not suppose me healthy and so withdraw the grace of your healing. Do not believe I want for nothing and delay helping me in my hour of need. Do not think me strong, lest I fall before you can sustain me.[49]

The Postmodern Body of Ethics

The pain expressed in Héloïse's lament opens the discursive space of a postmodern ethic in which corporeality emerges as a fundamental datum. Consider, first, the way in which postmodernism reconfigures corporeality as a focus of interpretation. On the one hand, the body is seen as a text; on the other, the pain and death to which bodies are subject remain an *hors texte,* an insurpassable negation that slips both inside and outside the field of textuality. The body as text, as a chain of signifiers that convey multiple messages decodable by the astute reader, is a narrative body. Such a body tells its story, one of gender, social position, physical appearance, and the like. When actual or potential pain and death break into this sphere of narration, they introduce proscriptive and prescriptive meaning. No longer does the body serve the purpose of self-description; instead its vulnerability to pain calls the observer to responsibility. When seen in this way the body is not the body of an other but of the Other. Its vulnerability is not made explicit but is given prereflectively, instantaneously, as it were, in an act of immediate awareness. The lament of Héloïse gives verbal utterance to this prereflective aperçu.

What must bodies be if the Other can disturb one's world, come crashing into one's self-satisfaction? Or, put otherwise, how is the body's vulnerability expressed within the discursive sphere of ethics? Recognition of the body's vulnerability comes from an unlikely quarter. In the *Ego and the Id,* Freud interrupts his account of ego structure with a crucial aside:

> A person's own body, and above all its surface, is a place from which both external and internal perceptions may spring. It is seen like any other object, but to the touch it yields two different kinds of sensations, one of which may be equivalent to an internal perception. . . . Pain too seems to play a part in the process, and the way in which we gain new knowledge of our organs during painful illnesses is perhaps the model of the way by which, in general, we arrive at the idea of our body.
>
> The ego is first and foremost a bodily ego; it is not merely a surface entity but is itself the projection of a surface.[50]

In a note for the English edition, Freud adds: "The ego is ultimately derived from bodily sensations, chiefly from those springing from the surface of the body. It may thus be regarded as a mental projection of the surface of the body."[51]

The new and fruitful notions Freud introduces here are the receptive character of the body; the pedagogy of pain through which the body comes to know itself as vulnerability; and, finally, the dispersion that enables primordial meanings to arise as differences between the *quanta* and *qualia* of local sensation. These discoveries are nevertheless harnessed by Freud to the notion of a unitary subject. Such a subject is consciousness insofar as it reduces what is specifically Other about other persons to a content of consciousness. Viewed in terms of corporeality, the Other slips back into the chain of signifiers that constitute the narrative body. To use the language of Emmanuel Levinas's philosophy of the otherness, the Other is reduced to the same.

To avoid such reduction and to conform to the spirit of Maurice Blanchot's remark that one should learn to think with pain, Levinas goes on to envisage pain as the "non-ground" of thought. The intertwining of thinking and pain follows from his interpretation of sensation as dependent upon two distinct functions of bodily existence: first, vulnerability and susceptibility, sensation's passive side; and second, aesthetic (in the etymological sense) articulation, its active dimension. On the one hand, sensation leads into language and thought; on the other, it is lived as a field of receptivity. The body of ethics is identified with the passivity of sensation, with the body's defenselessness.[52]

Why, it might be asked, is ethics linked to receptivity and the passivity of corporeality? Is ethics not regularly identified with moral action and the deliberation that precedes it? In terms of my earlier analysis, does ethics not fall within the episteme of justice, the plane of discourse reflected in the howl of Oedipus? Levinas's analysis must be taken a step further: "Corporeality is susceptible to pain . . . exposed to outrage and wounding, to sickness and aging,"[53] he maintains. Pain penetrates to the heart of the self that wills and thinks and calls it to order. Thus the body of ethics is a brake or restraint upon the active self prior to action, even to deliberation. Pain challenges self-righteousness. The sphere of moral deliberation, the possibility for the discourse of justice, supervenes upon the primordial level of sheer exposure to the Other, where neither reciprocity nor deliberation is possible.

Moral rules and juridical principles are necessary, following from the fact that there is a social order (internalized if not actually in evidence) requiring the allocation of material and nonmaterial goods. But before there can be justice there must be an Other.

It is now possible to discern the *topos* of postmodern asceticism. The fragility of the Other may lead not only to refraining from harmful action but to undertaking meliorative action on behalf of the Other, to placing the Other higher than the self. When such deeds occur repeatedly they begin to form a pattern of altruistic behavior. Such a pattern begins to take shape when the vulnerability of the Other shatters one's ego, turning it into vanity, thus giving vanity a new meaning. Preparation for this new social space requires a new *askēsis,* one that will respond to the cry of Héloïse.

NOTES

1. This point is stressed in Vincent L. Wimbush, "Rhetorics of Restraint: Discursive Strategies, Ascetic Piety and the Interpretation of Religious Literature," *Semeia* 57 (1992):1–9. In the two volumes *Semeia* 57 and 58, entitled *Discursive Formations, Ascetic Piety and the Interpretation of Early Christian Literature* (1992), devoted to social, cultural, historical, and literary manifestations of asceticism, this diversity is exemplified.
2. Sophocles, *Oedipus the King,* trans. R. C. Jebb, in *The Complete Greek Drama,* eds. Whitney J. Oates and Eugene O'Neill, Jr. (New York: Random House, 1938), 1:410.
3. Claude Lévi-Strauss, *The Elementary Structures of Kinship,* trans. James Harle Bell, John Richard von Sturmer, and Rodney Needham (Boston: Beacon Press, 1969), p. 25.
4. Ibid., p. 32.
5. Anaximander, frag. 1, in Philip Wheelwright, *The Pre-Socratics* (New York: Odyssey Press, 1966), p. 34.
6. The term is Wheelwright's. See *The Pre-Socratics,* p. 5.
7. Ibid.
8. *The Hellenistic Philosophers,* 2 vols., eds. and trans. A. A. Long and D. N. Sedley (Cambridge: Cambridge University Press, 1987), p. 434.
9. Plato, *Phaedo* 66 in *The Dialogues of Plato,* ed. Benjamin Jowett (New York: Random House, 1920), 1:450.
10. Plato, *Phaedo* 67 in *Dialogues of Plato,* 1:450.
11. *Phaedo* 80 in *Dialogues of Plato,* 1:465.
12. Plato, *Republic* V, 456, in *Dialogues of Plato,* 1:717.
13. *The Hellenistic Philosophers,* 1:185–186.
14. Michel Foucault, *The Use of Pleasure,* vol. 2, *The History of Sexuality,* trans. Robert Hurley (New York: Vintage Books, 1990), p. 229.
15. Heraclitus, frag. 29, in *The Pre-Socratics,* p. 71.
16. Ibid., frag. 30.
17. Ibid., frag. 31.
18. Michel Foucault, *The Use of Pleasure,* p. 229.
19. Ibid., pp. 232–233.
20. Ibid., p. 240.
21. Ibid., p. 230.
22. For an excellent account of this controversy see Marilyn Nagy, "Translocation of Parental Images in Fourth Century Ascetic Texts: Motifs and Techniques of Identity," in *Semeia* 58 (1992):3–23.

23. Plato, *Timaeus* 27 in *Timaeus and Critias*, trans. Desmond Lee (London: Penguin Books, 1977), p. 40.
24. Plato, *Timaeus* 30, p. 43.
25. Plotinus, *Ennead* 2.9.1–18, in *The Enneads*, trans. Stephen MacKenna (New York: Pantheon Books, n.d.), pp. 132–152.
26. Plotinus, *Ennead* 3.5.5, in ibid., pp. 195–196.
27. Peter Brown, *The Body and Society: Men, Women and Sexual Renunciation in Early Christianity* (Chicago: University of Chicago Press, 1988), p. 111.
28. *Ecclesiastes* 1.12–14 in *The Oxford Annotated Bible, Revised Standard Version* (New York: Oxford University Press, 1962), pp. 805–806.
29. *Ecclesiastes* 1.17–18, in ibid., p. 806.
30. *Ecclesiastes* 11.5, in ibid., p. 813.
31. Ibid.
32. Jean Luc Marion, *God without Being*, trans. Thomas A. Carlson (Chicago: University of Chicago Press, 1991), p. 127.
33. *Ecclesiastes* 1.8, in *The Oxford Annotated Bible*, p. 805.
34. The term "denegation" is used by Jacques Derrida to describe the meaning of the term secret: that which "denies itself because it appears to itself in order to be itself." See "How to Avoid Speaking: Denials," trans. Ken Frieden, in *Derrida and Negative Theology*, eds. Harold Coward and Toby Foshay (Albany: SUNY Press, 1989), p. 95.
35. This is Jean Luc Marion's translation of *Romans* 8.20 in *God without Being*, p. 122. *The Oxford Annotated Bible* renders the verse: "For the creation was subjected to futility" (p. 1368).
36. Athanasius, *The Life of Antony and the Letter to Marcellinus*, trans. Robert C. Gregg (New York: Paulist Press, 1980), p. 42.
37. Michel Foucault, *History of Sexuality: An Introduction*, vol. 1, trans. Robert Hurley (New York: Vintage Books, 1980), p. 159.
38. Anders Nygren, *Agape and Eros*, trans. Philip S. Watson (London: S.P.C.K., 1953), p. 210.
39. For a concise account of the debate initiated by Nygren's account of *erōs* and *agapē* in a contemporary psychological context, see Paul Rigby and Paul O'Grady, "Agape and Altruism: Debates in Theology and Social Psychology," *Journal of the American Academy of Religion*, 57.4 (Winter 1989):719–737.
40. Simmel is cited in Anders Nygren, *Eros and Agape*, p. 177.
41. A. Hilary Armstrong, "Platonic Eros and Christian Agape," in *The Downside Review* 82 (1964):268. Reprinted in his *Plotinian and Christian Studies* (London: Variorum Reprints, 1979), 9:106–107.
42. The authenticity of the letters is contested by a number of scholars. See Jean Leclerq, *Monks and Love in Twelfth Century France* (Oxford: Clarendon Press, 1979), p. 119. For the purpose of my argument it is the textually constructed Héloïse that is significant.
43. *The Letters of Abelard and Héloïse*, trans. Betty Radice (London: Penguin Books, 1974), p. 133.
44. Ibid., p. 162.
45. Jean Leclerq in *Monks and Love in Twelfth Century France* notes the strong sexual imagery of St. Bernard of Clairvaux in his commentary on the *Song of Songs* and elsewhere. Bernard's adversarial relations with Abelard brought them into contact and Bernard is cited as having been in touch with Héloïse when he visited the monastery of the Paraclete. For Abelard and Héloïse "it is quite natural that in such an environment the language of chivalry and the court, and the love literature which flowed from them

should be familiar to all. It was part of the very air of the province" (p. 99). The literature on the personal relation of the lovers, of Abelard to Bernard, and ecclesiastical authorities of the day is vast. A recent relatively brief bibliography can be found in Enid McLeod, *Héloïse* (London, Chatto and Windus, 1971), pp. 305ff. As romance, the tale of Héloïse and Abelard has found its way into Western literature from Petrarch and Pope to the present.

46. Ibid., p. 67.
47. Ibid., p. 65.
48. Ibid., p. 135.
49. Ibid., p. 134.
50. Sigmund Freud, *The Ego and the Id,* trans. Joan Rivière (New York: W. W. Norton and Co.), pp. 15–16.
51. Ibid., p. 16, note 1.
52. Emmanuel Levinas, *Otherwise than Being or Beyond Essence,* trans. Alphonso Lingis (The Hague: Martinus Nijhoff, 1981), p. 53.
53. Ibid., p. 56.

PART TWO

Origins and Meanings of Asceticism

3

Women and Asceticism in Late Antiquity: The Refusal of Status and Gender

Gillian Clark

This paper takes one kind of historical approach to the question of origins and meanings: it seeks to consider late antique asceticism in relation to a social context which in recent years, thanks to some brilliant and persuasive writing,[1] has become more clearly visible. It asks what ascetics were reacting against or refusing, what signals their lifestyles sent within a particular cultural range, whether late antique asceticism was an intensification of familiar practices, or a radical break from them. Christian ascetics in the fourth and fifth centuries were pioneers in working out what must be done by people who find the ordinary human concerns of household and city an intolerable distraction from their commitment to God. They experimented with styles and structures; tried out and competed with each other's techniques for strengthening the soul against harmful desires and demonic attack; and shared and analyzed their experience. Writers of the period—Athanasius, Jerome, Augustine, Basil—present the ascetic as hero or heroine, as the standard of true Christian commitment in an age when commitment was no longer tested by martyrdom. They suggest, and their writings also helped to create, an intense and widespread interest in ascetic practice.[2]

The source material is (in comparison with most aspects of Greco-Roman antiquity) unusually rich. There is a wide range of fourth- and fifth-century texts concerned with ascetic life and practices: exhortation; sermons; correspondence; rules for communities; lives of ascetics and collections of their sayings; and detailed spiritual guidance. Nevertheless, it is often unclear why exactly ascetics chose to do what they did, either in terms of individual motives for leading an ascetic life or in terms of invented or imitated ascetic practice. Some texts (for instance, the *Life and Teachings of Syncletica*) explain the purpose of fasting, discarding fine clothes, renouncing wealth; others merely admire or give an instruction. This is particularly true for women ascetics, since, as is almost always the case in Greco-Roman antiquity, women's voices are heard only indirectly. If women wrote any of the treatises and lives, their authorship is unacknowledged. They certainly wrote to spiritual advisers, but their letters are lost, whereas those of their male correspondents are preserved. Consequently, some of the most startling and most highly publicized ascetic practices of late antiquity are also the most difficult to interpret.

Women's asceticism, as practiced in late antiquity, is startling now because it is so extreme a rejection of family ties and female identity; and it was startling then simply because women did it. Christianity inherited standard Greco-Roman assumptions about women: that women in general are both physically and morally weaker than men; more dominated by the needs and desires of the body; and therefore less able to understand what is good and to hold fast what they know to be good. It also inherited the assumption which Greco-Roman philosophers made on the few occasions when they actually thought about the women they knew: that some women, at least, are capable of understanding and living by moral principles, and of being the moral equals, or even superiors, of men.[3] This point was often made by praising an admirable woman for masculine courage or intelligence (a habit which persisted at least until the 1950s). Christianity transformed the lives of women by offering support for a wholly new option, the rejection of marriage and childbearing. It made individual women a subject for biography, because spiritual triumphs had become (for some readers) as interesting as military or political triumphs. But the lives of women celibates were still constrained by traditional beliefs about women—in particular, that women are responsible for the desire which men feel for them. So the asceticism practiced by women should provide one route into the origin and meanings of late antique asceticism. If the asceticism of women differed from the asceticism of men, why and how did it differ? Did it mean the same for a woman to be poor and a man to be poor, for a woman to be celibate and a man to be celibate? What aspects of their ordinary social lives did women refuse, and what was their vision of what life should be?

The fifth-century biographer of Melania the Younger begins with a standard acknowledgment that his *Life* does not tell the full story:

> For who would be able to recount in a clear and worthy manner the manly deeds of this blessed woman? I mean of course her utter renunciation of worldly things, her ardor for the orthodox faith (an ardor hotter than fire), her unsurpassable beneficence, her intense vigils, her persistence in lying on the ground, her ill-treatment and ceaseless ascetic discipline of her soul as well as of her body, her gentleness and temperance that vie with the incorporeal powers, the cheapness of her clothing, and even more than these, her humility, the mother of all good things.[4]

This paragraph, and the *Life* as a whole, present a mixture of characteristics which, on first reading, range from the admirable to the baffling. Melania, the reader discovers, dressed in dark coarse cloth; it probably irritated her skin even when she did not wear a haircloth shirt underneath. She avoided washing. Once she stayed for the whole of Lent in her convent cell, sitting on a piece of sackcloth: when she emerged, and the sackcloth was shaken out, enormous lice fell out of it. She fasted for five days at a time, and went without sleep to read the Bible and all the theology she could lay her hands on—millions of lines of it, in Latin and Greek. She was heir to one of the greatest fortunes of Rome and married at thirteen to the heir of another. She asked him to live in chastity with her, and he was sympathetic, but refused to do so until they had produced heirs in their turn. A girl, dedicated at birth to a life of celibacy, died in infancy; a boy died in a birth which nearly killed the mother too—very likely because she had kept vigil for a martyr's feast day the night before she went into labor. Her husband, fearing she would die, vowed chastity. They gave away their fortune in charity and in founding monasteries, fighting the protests of their city, their families, and the slaves on their many estates. At last, triumphantly destitute, they considered signing up on the welfare list of the Bishop of Jerusalem. A member of the community Melania founded once asked if she were not tempted to spiritual pride in her achievement. She said that she had not achieved much; but if she were tempted, she would think of those who fasted and slept rough, not from choice but from necessity. Why, then, had she made this choice and forced it upon her husband?[5] What was the merit of poverty, hunger and dirt, the rejection of family claims and social responsibilities?

Voluntary poverty can be said to be required by the teachings of Jesus. "If you want to be perfect, sell all you have, and give to the poor, and come, follow me" (*Mt.* 19.21). This is the verse which, according to the *Life of Antony,* inspired St. Antony, around 270 CE, to pioneer the ascetic lifestyle in the Egyptian desert. But "sell all you have and give to the poor" is a much clearer instruction than "come, follow me." When Jesus said it to the rich young ruler, it meant "come with me now." Antony, according to the *Life,* took "follow me" to mean "devote your life to prayer and study of the Bible" but found that he could not do so unless he withdrew entirely from the distractions of village life and human contact. So he went away from the valley to the desert, where he could learn from the survival techniques of others who had gone "up country," *anachōritae.* These techniques necessarily included fasting and self-neglect.[6] Antony's experience was publicized in the *Life of Antony* ascribed to Athanasius, and Egyptian ascetic practice was publicized by Athanasius during his exiles in the Western Empire; from c.370 CE on the *Life* was more widely available in a Latin translation by Evagrius. This is a simple historical sequence, but much more is needed to explain why Antony became the model for ascetic practice. The question is not just whether solitary asceticism is more or less beneficial than the communal model developed by Pachomius, though this was intensively discussed.[7] The question is why Antony interpreted "following Christ" as solitary prayer and study rather than as evangelism or as help for his fellow villagers, and why his example was so impressive that people in very different circumstances withdrew to the desert, or tried to create their own.[8]

Not all Christians wanted to be perfect, or thought that perfection always requires renunciation of wealth. Some reassuring arguments have a long history: that Jesus was speaking to an individual who had a particular spiritual need, not necessarily to all Christians; and that, for most Christians, responsible use of money may well be more helpful. Clement of Alexandria, early in the second century, had reasonably asked what would happen if there were no Christians left who were able to give to the poor.[9] Augustine's renunciation of a promising public career was triggered, according to the *Confessions,* by the story of Antony; but he was a bishop by the time he met Melania, early in the fifth century, and he tried to persuade her that monasteries were a better long-term investment than charitable donations. He wrote to another Christian who was worried by the story of the rich young ruler, arguing that what matters is to give up not riches but attachment to riches: the church needs its supertax payers.[10]

Poverty, then, was not a necessary choice for a committed Christian, but it was a choice that some Christians felt they must make. It was also the most obvious message conveyed by ascetic dress and lifestyle. "Changing one's clothes" became an immediately recognizable metaphor for "adopting the ascetic life" or for "entering a community." There was not yet a monastic habit, a uniform that declared adherence to a specific order (these too were still in the experimental stage), but there was a common ascetic style that signaled renunciation: maybe not total renunciation of property, but at least renunciation of the lifestyle that went with it. Rich people—men and women both—wore fine wools and silks, brightly colored and enriched with gold. Men's formal clothes declared their social status and also functioned as uniforms, advertising their public offices in embroidered or woven panels. Women held no public office, but their clothes declared social status and demanded attention for wealth and beauty. Working people wore dark, coarse cloth: the Latin word *pullati* (dark-clad) functioned like "blue-collar." Really poor people could not vary their clothes for winter and summer but were lucky to have one all-purpose garment.[11]

Other aspects of the ascetic life could also be interpreted as consequences of the choice of poverty: hunger, dirt, extremes of heat and cold. Poor people often went hungry: famine and crop failure were endemic, and when crops failed and taxation stripped the countryside, the country people drifted into town and starved in the streets. Welfare schemes and private charity were patchy at best, and the Roman government accepted no overall responsibility for welfare.[12] Some benefactors provided subsidized public baths, but really poor and shabby people were unlikely to get past the doorman. Dirt, bad smells, and infestation were part of their lives. They slept rough, in public places, improvised huts, or tombs. Fourth- and fifth-century writings often make the point that ascetic practices are much more difficult for those who had been used to comfort.

Voluntary poverty rejected a social identity defined by status, in a society where status entailed not just inherited social obligations, but financial commitments to the local community which were imposed by law. Emperors found it necessary to legislate on whether men who were ordained as Christian clergy could stop being *decuriones*, members of local councils who were responsible for the local budget and had to meet any shortfalls. Escape was allowed only if they renounced their property in favor of another relative, who would inherit the obligation. This release might be welcome, but there were worse consequences of being poor. The Christian virtue of humility needs to be understood in relation to the treatment the ascetic might receive by looking like one of the *humiles*, the lower orders. They had always been socially liable to neglect and contempt, but since the second century CE the *humiles* had been legally liable to beating and even torture, treatment formerly reserved for slaves. Such penalties were ordered by local magistrates: a political career usually required the infliction of violence, and renunciation of wealth made it possible for some people to avoid being part of the structures of violent oppression.[13]

But voluntary poverty, and an appearance proclaiming poverty, did not mean that ascetics renounced their wealth and status as an act of solidarity and identification with the poor. Antony made himself poor, but did not live among the poor of his village. Poor people often believed that ascetics could do them good, because their prayers could defeat the demons who were held to cause illness and crop failure; but ascetics often avoided human contact, seeking refuge in the desert or in monasteries from people who wanted them to use their spiritual strength to fight illness or to give advice.[14] Some Christians chose to work among the poor in addition to giving alms. Jerome praised his friend Fabiola for her readiness to give nursing care to the sick; and this should not be underestimated, because the people who needed nursing care were those who had no home to provide it, and whose physical condition was often revolting. But, in fourth- and fifth-century texts, the focus is more often on the self-denial and endurance of the ascetic hero than on her or his good works. Ministering to the sick attracted less praise than patient endurance of one's own, perhaps revolting, illness.[15] Ascetics were praised, not blamed, for seeking solitude and rejecting even their close family, for human company was a distraction from the life of prayer.

For male ascetics, female company, even the presence of a woman, was held to be particularly distracting. Years of hard spiritual struggle could be thrown away in a brief encounter, and even old and experienced monks were afraid. John of Lycopolis had not seen a woman for forty years when he said: "it is not in our interest to have our dwellings near inhabited places, or to associate with women. For meetings of this kind give rise to an inexpungeable memory, which we draw from what we have seen and from what we have heard in conversation." Similarly, a young monk said to his aged mentor, "Father, you are growing old. Let us now move back nearer to inhabited places." The old man said to him, "Let us go to a place where there are no women." His disciple replied, "Where is there a place where there are no women except in the desert?" So the old man said, "Take me to the desert."[16]

The construct of woman as sexual temptress, as desire personified, was apparently so powerful that even men committed to a life of prayer could not think of women as fellow human beings with the same commitment. An abbess once said to the monk who had carefully avoided her sisters, "If you were a perfect monk you would not have looked at us, and you would not have seen that we were women."[17] She meant not that he would have gone beyond awareness of gender, but that he would not have paid any attention to the world around him. The downcast gaze expected of both monks and nuns avoided all distractions, especially sexual distractions. It was acknowledged that women ascetics also experienced desire for men, and that a man's look was dangerous to them.[18]

There was no general consensus that sexual desire is always dangerous or disgusting. Some fourth-century Christians argued that desire is God-given for procreation, and that married people can achieve a Christian life which is just as valuable as the life of a celibate; some believed that a celibate Christian woman and man can share a house without risk to their chastity, though this was generally held to be overly optimistic.[19] But it seems to have been common ascetic experience that sexual desire was both exceptionally strong and exceptionally persistent, a clear indication especially for men, who experienced involuntary erections and seminal emissions, that the body was still not reclaimed from its fallen state. Since the perceived danger to ascetics was so great, the precautions were only sensible. Even mothers were a hazard to be avoided, because (according to John Cassian) first you think about your mother or your sister; then about some religious woman you have met; then about some other woman.[20] The problem was not just sexual temptation. Women signified human contact and the ties of family and householding, the life from which the ascetic sought to escape into the desert, because women had no recognized role in life except to keep house and bear children—or to resist that role.

In such a context, it is not surprising that women ascetics made a drastic renunciation of identity as women, or rather of identity with the construct of women as sexual and domestic beings. The first step was not to look desirable. Preaching to women standardly denounced their concern for how they looked, and this was not just a preacher's cliché: it was the area of major temptation for women. They could not openly exercise political power, so it was their dress and hairstyle and makeup which proclaimed wealth and status, demanded attention, and thereby stimulated desire. So "changing one's clothes" had even greater significance for women than for men. The ascetic woman's clothing was a refusal of status, but it also refused all power of sexual attraction. It did not correspond to the poor woman's rags—unless, that is, it is described by Jerome, who claims to have seen strategically placed "designer rips" and hair straggling out from under provocative veils.[21] The cloth was dark or undyed, like the clothing of the poor, but the body had to be concealed, the hair hidden, and the head veiled. The hair might be cut short, provided that gender was not denied by uncovered head and cross-dressing. Male and female dress was similar, but cross-dressing perhaps seemed provocative, or presented dangers to men who would not realize they were associating with a woman.[22]

A woman who led the ascetic life would not wish to provoke desire in men (especially not in ascetic men who were fighting the same battle as she was) or to stimulate her own desires. She had to suppress her own awareness of her body as attractive, so she was urged not to take care of it, to make it less obviously a female body, even to make it repellent.[23] Bathing was suspect, not because poor people could not afford it, but because it is an activity in which the body is on view and receiving attention. It was still predominantly a communal activity, often but not always single-sex. Great houses of the time sometimes had private baths, but even in them women would not be alone, and would also be aware of their own bodies. Melania, when still subject to her parents, bathed only her eyes, and bribed her attendants not to tell; Olympias went to the baths only on doctor's orders, and never bathed naked. Clothes too were not always clean. Augustine's rule says that the superior should decide when clean clothes are handed out, so that people (monks or nuns) do not become too concerned about clean clothes, but he did also require "proper hygienic care" of the body, including baths when necessary.

Jerome's friend Paula declared more bluntly that a clean dress is the sign of a dirty mind.[24]

The refusal to look attractive or to attend to the body signified the refusal of sexual activity. Late twentieth-century interpreters may seem unduly preoccupied with the renunciation of sexuality by these ascetic women, but it was also a major concern for the fourth century. Women were confronted with one fundamental choice in life: to marry or to reject marriage, whether as virgin or as widow. The refusal to bear children in pain, to a husband who was a master, was at once an attempt to reverse the effects of the Fall as described in *Genesis* 3.16 and a rejection of a life socially determined by gender. Once the choice was made, there were established techniques for reducing sexual desire. Medical theory made the reasonable assumption that the body has available for reproduction the surplus which it does not use for maintenance. Men generally burned off much of the surplus in hard physical exercise or manual work: ascetics combined hard work with reduced food intake. Women were generally less active, and were trained to moderate their food intake: ascetics used extremes of fasting. The perceived connection between food intake and sexual feeling was reinforced by the story of the Fall, in which greed for the apple led to sexual awareness. Extreme fasting made the female body less female in appearance and probably, though this point is not made explicit, caused amenorrhea, so that the woman was not tied to a reminder of fertility and desire: menstruation was associated with desire on the analogy of estrus in other mammals.[25] If the aim is to refuse a female identity which is constructed in terms of weakness, negative qualities and unwelcome desire, it makes sense to become physically unattractive—dirty and smelly—or at least unnoticeable, an "old woman" even in youth.[26] Fasting to the point of anorexia and amenorrhea is still a survival strategy, though a self-destructive strategy, in adolescents who wish to deny their sexuality; making oneself repellent is still a strategy against rape.

But more positive interpretations are possible. It can be argued that Christian ascetics, far from wishing to negate the body, especially the female body, as being hostile to the soul, took embodiment with complete seriousness. They interpreted sexual feeling as the characteristic desire of fallen human beings to possess something which distracts them from good, and therefore hoped to replace sexual with nonsexual relationships. They recognized that it was extremely difficult for men and women to meet without any sexual awareness, and that sexual feeling was the most obvious and persistent sign of fallenness. But they thought it possible to transform the body together with the soul, freeing it from the constraints of life after the Fall and causing it to function differently.[27]

For women as for men, renouncing sexual activity implied (except in some cases of postmarital chastity) renouncing the life of a parent and householder, and thereby renouncing a clear social identity determined by status and gender. The household, as Aristotle said, was the building block of society. The woman's role in the household, and in society, was defined by gender: her task was to marry, provide children, keep house, be faithful. But it was not immediately obvious what, having rejected this role, she should do instead. Modest women were expected to live within the protection of a house, and only a few ascetic women are reported to have risked the solitary life in the desert. The lifestyle of some ascetic women has continuities with the lives of nonascetic women who were not sexually active. The as yet unmarried daughter living at home supplies a model for the dedicated virgin, living in seclusion and close to her mother, modestly dressed, weaving fabric for the poor rather than for the family. The poor widow supplies another model for the more independent celibate: dressed in black, free to visit other households or to trade in the marketplace, because she is socially invisible as a woman.

But there was no need for an ascetic woman to live in a traditional household. Fourth-century experiments included a range of possibilities. There was the individual ascetic living a restricted life within, or on the fringes of, a predominantly female household, like Asella and Lea in the household of Marcella, or Domnina in a hut in her mother's garden.[28] There was the all-female household of ladies and their women slaves, in which the social hierarchy was modified to the extent that the ladies shared the chores. There was the celibate household of man and woman, both committed to the ascetic life, which tended to be pulled back into traditional patterns of male/female pairing, both in sexuality and in structure.[29] There was the female community taking over a house or living in accommodation built for the purpose. In all of these, there was no reason for the lifestyle of women to be determined by gender or to differ from the lifestyle of men. Male ascetics had to learn to cope with domestic chores; only a few tasks, like heavy digging and building work, were deemed to be beyond the physical strength of women ascetics. Rules of life could apply both to male and to female communities—though there is a tendency to say that women will need more of whatever virtue is in question.

> Now since communities are not only of men but also of virgins, everything that has been said will be common to both. But one thing must be known: the way of life among women demands more and greater decorum, and correct use of poverty, quiet, submissiveness and community feeling, and care about access, and watchfulness over meetings, and conduct towards each other, and not having particular friendships. In all these aspects the way of life of virgins must be regulated with greater zeal.[30]

It will simply be more difficult for them to live in stability, celibacy and harmony.

Once again, the lifestyles of late antique asceticism can be read negatively, as a fierce rejection of sexuality, marriage, childbearing, housekeeping, a life determined by gender and status. They can also be read positively, as an attempted return to paradise, living in friendship and dependence on God, undisturbed by greed or desire.[31] The negative interpretation depends in part on a bleak picture of late antique social relationships. Twentieth-century interpreters have suggested that spouses were resentful of arranged marriages, and that both men and women were encouraged by medical and philosophical discourse to think of sexual activity as dangerous and depleting. Mothers, it has been said, were in any case indifferent to the children conceived against their wishes and cared for by household slaves, or else were eager to help their daughters escape their own fate by choosing virginity. People wanted to reclaim themselves from the relentless purposes of society.[32] These explanations are offered because it is so difficult to understand why late antique ascetics found it necessary, and right, to cut themselves off from family and society and to impose on themselves pain and deprivation. This is not a purely twentieth-century reaction: it was shared by fourth-century Christians and non-Christians, and something like it was presented to the elderly Augustine by the young Julian of Eclanum.[33] Why is all this rejection felt to be necessary? Why not live a moderate, self-disciplined life, giving generously to the poor, producing children in youth and abstaining when your family is complete, meeting your social obligations but making time for your religious commitment?

There was a recognizable and long-established lifestyle for doing just that. It was acknowledged that the philosopher, the lover of wisdom, should be able to cope with heat and cold and hard physical activity, should need little sleep and food, and should abstain altogether from luxuries including elaborate food, wine and non procreative sex. Philosophers must be tough, or how can they concentrate on wisdom without being distracted by minor discomforts? The traditional philosopher's cloak, ideally a single garment worn in both winter and summer, was a symbol that its wearer was committed to these ideals rather than to the advertisement of status and wealth; the Cynic philosopher, instantly identifiable by cloak, bag and stick, offered a dramatic role model for stripping down needs to the minimum. But, as Epictetus pointed out, the Cynic lifestyle is not suitable for babies. The philosophically trained Greek or Roman man was exhorted not to abandon his family duties; he might prefer to devote himself to philosophy without distraction, but he had an obligation to provide grandchildren for his parents, citizens for his city and worshippers for the gods. The choice of the philosophically minded Greek or Roman woman was taken for granted.

The first-century CE teaching of Epictetus neatly demonstrates the contrast between traditional philosopher and Christian ascetic. Epictetus had been a slave, and used his experience to point out to his audience of well-fed young Romans that if slaves can endure hunger, loneliness, hard labor, beatings, life as fugitives with every person's hand against them, those who are slaves to the comfortable life should be ashamed of themselves when they complain about a disciplined lifestyle and the hard intellectual work required by living as one ought. But he did not suggest that they should try to share the experience of a slave. The fourth-century Christian ascetic, by contrast, is praised for deliberately seeking deprivation. He, or she, triumphs over the needs of the ordinary human being for food, drink, warmth, comfort, sleep, company; and he or she may carry this triumph to the point of self-inflicted wounds, or of fasting so as to cause permanent illness—though several ascetics thought it wrong actually to damage the body.[34]

The dominant philosophy of late antiquity was Platonism, and Platonism is often blamed for negative Christian attitudes to the body (as also for complex theological doctrines). But these attitudes were not shared by Platonists. Plato does seem to have distrusted, or feared, the needs of the body, and he does seem to be responsible for the discourse of body as opposed to spirit.[35] But late Platonist philosophers did not see any need to torment their bodies or to seek out suffering.

They aimed at the spiritual strength and discipline which would allow them to be unaffected, in their essential selves, not just by passing discomfort but by the loss of home and country and people they loved (even their children), or by suffering such as the philosopher Plotinus underwent in his final illness. This is the ideal of *apatheia*. It is not, of course, apathy or indifference, but something much closer to the conviction that nothing can separate us from the love of God: our reasoning souls, the part of us which is closest to God, can retain their link with God whatever happens in this transitory world.

There are two late Platonist texts, both (probably) from the fourth century, which offer examples of the admirable philosopher. Iamblichus, in his *On the Pythagorean Life,* presents Pythagoras as remarkable from birth: he has an exceptional intellect; his lifestyle is austere; he can become wholly absorbed in the pursuit and contemplation of wisdom; and his spiritual gifts include discernment, influence over nonrational animals, and even bilocation (two seminars on the same day on both sides of the Straits of Messina). His followers will not abandon his teaching even when their lives are threatened by a tyrant; one woman, in her last month of pregnancy, is told she will be tortured and bites off her tongue so that she will be unable to betray secrets even if torture overcomes her physical resistance. There is a case for saying that Iamblichus, in describing the communities Pythagoras (allegedly) founded, sets out to challenge comparison with Christian monasticism.[36] If so, he was aware of some very early manifestations of monasticism, since his book can hardly be dated even as late as the reign of Constantine. But whether or not he set out to make it, the contrast is there. The Pythagorean communities, as he describes them, include family groups and involve themselves in local government. Their lifestyle is temperate, and their diet is both moderate and restricted, but they show no signs of deprivation or of any need to work for a living. Ideally, their property is held in common, but it is undoubtedly there. They wear clean white linen, which demonstrates that they are ritually pure (dirt or bloodstains would show up at once) and ready at any time to make offering to the gods. Linen was expensive and is troublesome to clean, but Iamblichus is assuming that the slaves will do that. His Pythagoreans are a self-aware, self-disciplined spiritual and social élite.

Iamblichus himself became an example in Eunapius's *Lives of the Philosophers.* The subjects of Eunapius's brief biographies usually married into other philosophical families—like Christian ascetics, they tended to be interrelated anyway—and met the obligations of a prosperous household while adopting a disciplined lifestyle of temperance and study. They did not overeat, oversleep or indulge in nonprocreative sex. They could withdraw into contemplation without going off into the desert. The women of such households were themselves philosophers in that they lived by philosophic principles. They dressed modestly and declined to advertise wealth or to attract lustful attention. Like all well-brought-up women, they were trained to control their physical appetites: to eat in moderation, to drink little or no wine, not to take sexual initiatives. But they did not fast, or neglect the ordinary care of the body. Marriage partners were taught that sex should be used only for procreation, but they did expect to produce children. This applied even to the amazing Sosipatra, whom Eunapius found worthy of inclusion in a book about men. As a child, she had acquired remarkable spiritual gifts from two mysterious strangers. She instantly recognized the only man worthy to marry her, and told him that they would have three sons. Marriage and childbearing did not interfere at all with her practice and teaching of philosophy. Eunapius said of her son Antoninus, "He made very rapid progress towards kinship with the divine. He took no account of the body and was liberated from its pleasures; he practiced a wisdom unknown to the many . . . everyone admired his perseverance, his unswerving and constant character."[37] But he did not engage in self-torment. The philosophical tradition of austerity and continence provides a context for late antique asceticism, but Christian ascetic practice cannot simply be located further along a continuum, as an intensification of philosophical *askēsis*.[38] It was a radical break, puzzling and repellent to non-Christians and also to some Christians.

So why do it? Why subject the body to brutal regimes of near starvation, sleep deprivation, pain, loneliness, and neglect—tactics which are more often associated with agents of terror, not with holiness? There is a link here which was also recognized in the fourth century: a sharing of suffering not so much with the poor as with Christ and the martyrs. Jesus died as a victim of Roman judicial torture, having experienced hunger and solitude in the desert and dereliction on the cross. The ascetics of the late fourth century were only half a century away from victims of persecution under Diocletian. Victricius of Rouen, welcoming relics of martyrs late in the fourth century, points out the contrast: "We have seen no executioners, we have not known swords drawn against us, yet we set up altars of Divinity. No bloody enemy assails us today, yet we are enriched by the Passion of the Saints. No torturer has stretched us on the rack, yet we bear the Martyrs' trophies."[39] The legal penalties suffered by pre-Constantinian martyrs were not ancient history, but were still current in late Roman law codes: burning, condemnation to wild beasts, tearing with hooks. The Theodosian Code, compiled by the most Christian emperor Theodosius II and promulgated in 438, is notorious for its use of cruel and unusual punishments, including torture and specific mutilation. Some historians prefer to think that these are menaces rather than practices; but there is evidence that extremes of violence were still inflicted, in public and by lawfully constituted authority, in the fourth and fifth centuries. According to one Pelagian tract, they were ordered by magistrates who called themselves Christian.[40]

The stories of martyrs were read to the crowds who came to their shrines on their feast days. Another interpretation of late antique asceticism invokes the wish to be a hero, fighting and dying gloriously for the faith. The wish might be particularly strong in women, since Christian women had died as martyrs, in public and on display, like an athlete or a gladiator. There were few opportunities for a woman to be a hero. The denial of gender can be read as a simple refusal to believe that femaleness has anything going for it. As a bishop once said to his deacon, who had asked about the remarkable woman Olympias, "Do not say 'woman': say 'what a remarkable human being,' for she is a man despite her outward appearance."[41] If you live in a culture which has no role models for women except the virtuous wife and the temptress, it is not surprising for you to reject identity as a woman and to aim for identity as a hero.

The culmination of the martyr's story is the *passio,* the long accounts of what they suffered and how they continued to praise God in the midst of their torment, unshaken by the pain. It is difficult, now, to know how to read *passiones,* because it seems impossible that human beings endured such things undismayed, or even that other human beings could believe they had done so. But the stories should not be read as a simple report of what happened. The *passiones* are a declaration, a performance, of the Christian claim that extremes of human suffering, and all manifestations of evil, can be overcome by acceptance of God's love.[42] Similarly, asceticism is the "long martyrdom," and the ascetic's constant prayer to God, from the midst of pain, dereliction and demonic assault, is an acting out of the central truth and thus advances the fight against evil.[43] So there was a reason for ascetics to seek out suffering. They could express in physical terms the condition of the human soul: chafed by sin as the ascetic was chafed by haircloth and lice, and assaulted by demonic forces of evil which worked through physical illness as they had once worked through Roman torturers, it is still able to cry out in praise of God.

This paper has offered a range of suggested meanings for late antique asceticism. They are all linked to a particular historical context; not surprisingly, they overlap and are inconsistent. If the voice most often heard sounds like that of a puzzled pagan, this too belongs to the context in which late antique asceticism developed. Christians of the fourth and fifth centuries included those who (perhaps) came too close to philosophical overconfidence in human ability to cope, and, perhaps, were also too ready to assume that ordinary human commitments must be respected. Pelagius, himself an ascetic, was not impressed by a woman who said that family life gave her no time to pray: all you have to do, he said, is set aside time each day. Syncletica's warning, "It is dangerous for someone who has not been trained in the practical life to teach," applies to all interpreters of asceticism.[44]

NOTES

1. As the editors requested, this paper is only slightly revised from the conference version, but I have profited very much from the other papers and responses and from informal discussion. I should particularly like to thank Dianne Bazell, Averil Cameron, Elizabeth Castelli and Teresa Shaw. I am also indebted to Aline Rousselle, Peter Brown, Robert Markus and, of course, to Elizabeth Clark.
2. "Written *Lives* were mimetic; real ascetic discipline in turn imitated the written *Lives.*" In Averil Cameron, *Christianity and the Rhetoric of Empire* (Berkeley: University of California Press, 1991), p. 57.
3. There is an unusually positive statement of this position in G. Gould, "Women in the Writings of the Fathers." In *Women and the Church,* eds. Sheils and Wood. Studies in Church History 27 (Oxford: Blackwell, 1990), pp. 1–13.
4. Trans. E. A. Clark (1984), pp. 25–26.
5. "It is the powerful who express imitation of Christ as (voluntary) poverty, (voluntary) nudity and (voluntary) weakness." C. W. Bynum, *Fragmentation and Redemption* (New York: Zone Books, 1992), p. 34.
6. A. Rousselle, *Porneia* (Oxford: Blackwell, 1988), pp. 141–147, 160–178.
7. For Pachomius, see N. Russell, *Lives of the Desert Fathers* (Oxford and London: Mowbray, 1980); H. Chadwick, "Pachomios and the Ideal of Sanctity." In *History and*

Thought of the Early Church (London: Variorum, 1982), paper 14; P. Rousseau, *Ascetics, Authority, and the Church in the age of Jerome and Cassian* (Oxford: Oxford University Press, 1978).

8. For the impact of the desert, as opposed to the world and as an alternative world, see Brown 1989:216–217; see also Meredith 1976; Ward 1987; Gould 1993.
9. *The Rich Man's Salvation* 11–13, in Countryman 1980.
10. Advice to Melania, *Life of Melania* 20. The letter is to Hilarius, *Epistulae* 157. Antony's role in Augustine's conversion, *Confessiones* 8.6.14.
11. See, for instance, Paulinus of Nola, Letter 45.3 in Migne, *PL* 61.393. On ascetic dress generally, G. Clark 1993:113–118.
12. On provision (or lack of it) for the poor, see Brown 1992:91–103.
13. Cf. G. Clark 1991.
14. Cf. Brown 1971 for a nuanced account.
15. For vivid examples of illness, see Venantius Fortunatus, *Life of Radegund* 17 (McNamara 1992:77) on nursing the sick, and the *Life of Syncletica* 105–111 (Castelli 1990:307–310).
16. Russell 1980:36; Ward 1975:Sisoes 3.
17. Ward 1975:4.62. For the construct of femaleness, cf. Cameron 1991:72–73; for the perceived impossibility of friendship between the sexes, E. A. Clark 1979.
18. The frankest acknowledgment came from Basil of Ancyra, who (like many educated men) had medical as well as philosophical training. Migne, *PG* 30.669–810.
19. On cohabitants, see E. A. Clark 1979; see also Hunter 1987, 1989, and 1992 for the debate in fourth-century Italy on marriage and virginity. Cooper 1992 assesses praise of the married or celibate Christian woman.
20. Cassian, *Collationes Patrum* (CSEL 13)
21. Letters 117.7 (*PL* 22.957), 130.18 (*PL* 22.1122).
22. Anson 1974; Patlagean 1981. On masculine and feminine appearance, see further Gleason 1990.
23. The London *Independent* of 12 February 1993 reported on a community of nuns who had sought advice from a color consultant. The motive was to make their individual personalities an advertisement for God, and perhaps also to be free from any concern about how they looked, because they knew they looked right. It is a striking instance of social and religious transformation.
24. For baths, see G. Clark 1993:92–93; and see now R. Ward 1992 with Delaine 1993.
25. Medical background in Rousselle 1988 and 1991; on attitudes to menstruation, see G. Clark 1993:76–80; on the varied significance of fasting, Bynum 1987.
26. "If you do not dress in youthful clothes, you will not be called 'young woman': you will be called 'old lady' and treated with respect as an older woman." pseudo-Athanasius, *On Virginity* (*PG* 28.264).
27. Brown 1989, esp. pp. 222–224; Markus 1991:81–82. On the physical effects of fasting, see Musurillo 1956, but his findings may need to be modified by recent work on endorphins. See William Bushell's paper in this collection.
28. Jerome, Letter 127 (*PL* 22.1089); Theodoret, *History of the Monks of Syria* 30 (*PG* 82.1492). For the home-based virgin, see Shaw 1990.
29. On these experiments, see E. A. Clark 1986.
30. *Eiusdem sermo asceticus,* ascribed to Basil, *PG* 31.888A, trans. G. Clark; on rules applicable to male and female communities, see Elm 1991, Lawless 1987.
31. Cf. Elliott 1987.
32. Rousselle 1988; Brown 1989.

33. See on this debate E. A. Clark 1986.
34. The most famous case of self-destruction is Blesilla, Jerome Letter 39.6 (*PL* 22.472); Basil of Caesarea and John Chrysostom permanently damaged their health, Martin of Tours was forbidden by his bishop to continue fasting. For advice against damaging the body, see, e.g., the treatise ascribed to Athanasius (*PG* 28.264–265) in G. Clark 1993:93; and Basil of Ancyra, *On Virginity* 9–11 (*PG* 30.669–689).
35. These problems are discussed further in John Dillon's paper. For a wider perspective on dualism and the body, see Castelli 1992.
36. On the life of Pythagoras, see G. Clark 1989; Dillon and Hershbell 1991. On the continuities between philosophical and Christian asceticism, see Bremmer 1992.
37. Eunapius, *Vitae sophistarum,* 471.
38. Cp. Rousselle 1988:131, and cf. Bremmer 1992.
39. *Praise of the Saints* 1, translated by Hillgarth 1986:23. Bibliography on asceticism and martyrdom in Gould 1993:2, note 8.
40. *On Riches* 6 (*PL* supplement 1.1385–1386). On torture in late Roman law codes, see further Grodszynski 1984.
41. Palladius, *Dialogue on the Life of St. John Chrysostom* (*PG* 47.56). For recent discussions of the "honorary man" and female inferiority, see G. Clark 1993:120–130; Harrison 1990; Hunter 1992.
42. I should like to thank the members of the Cambridge Classics Interdisciplinary Seminar, especially John Henderson, for their response to a paper on Prudentius that explored some of these questions; and to thank Elizabeth Castelli for her own explorations in her unpublished paper of 1992.
43. Cf. Jacob of Serug on Simeon. Harvey 1990.
44. Pelagius, *To Celantia* 24 (*PL* 22.1216) (ascribed to Jerome); Syncletica's warning: Syncletica 12 (*PG* 65.425). On the fourth-century debate, especially concerning women's asceticism, see Hunter 1992.

BIBLIOGRAPHY

Anson, J. 1974. "The Female Transvestite in Early Monasticism: The Origin and Development of a Motif," *Viator* 5.

Bremmer, J. 1992. "Symbols of Marginality from Early Pythagoreans to Late Antique Monks," *Greece and Rome,* n.s. 39.

Brock, S. and S. Harvey. 1987. *Holy Women of the Syrian Orient.* Berkeley: University of California Press.

Brown, P. 1971. "The Rise and Function of the Holy Man in Late Antiquity," *Journal of Roman Studies* 61.

Brown, P. 1989. *The Body and Society: Men, Women and Sexual Renunciation in Early Christianity.* London: Faber.

Brown, P. 1992. *Power and Persuasion in Late Antiquity: Towards a Christian Empire.* Madison: University of Wisconsin Press.

Bynum, C. W. 1987. *Holy Feast and Holy Fast: The Religious Significance of Food to Medieval Women.* Berkeley: University of California Press.

Bynum, C. W. 1992. *Fragmentation and Redemption: Essays on Gender and the Human Body in Medieval Religion.* New York: Zone Books.

Cameron, Averil. 1989. "Virginity as Metaphor." In *History as Text,* ed. A. Cameron. London: Duckworth.

Cameron, Averil. 1991. *Christianity and the Rhetoric of Empire.* Berkeley: University of California Press.

Castelli, E. 1990. "The Life and Activity of the Blessed Teacher Syncletica." Translated in V. L. Wimbush, ed., *Ascetic Behavior in Greco-Roman Antiquity: A Sourcebook*. Minneapolis: Fortress Press.

Castelli, E. 1992. "Mortifying the Body, Curing the Soul: Beyond Ascetic Dualism in *The Life of Saint Syncletica*." *Differences* 4.2.

Chadwick, H. 1982. "Pachomios and the Ideal of Sanctity." In *History and Thought of the Early Church*. London: Variorum.

Chadwick, H. 1985. "The Ascetic Ideal in the History of the Church." In W. J. Sheils, ed., *Monks, Hermits and the Ascetic Tradition*. Studies in Church History, vol. 22. Oxford: Blackwell.

Clark, E. A. 1979. *Jerome, Chrysostom and Friends*. New York: Edwin Mellen.

Clark, E. A. 1983. *Women in the Early Church*. Wilmington, Del.: Michael Glazier.

Clark, E. A. 1984. *The Life of Melania the Younger*. New York: Edwin Mellen.

Clark, E. A. 1986. *Ascetic Piety and Women's Faith*. New York: Edwin Mellen.

Clark, G. 1989. *Iamblichus: On the Pythagorean Life*. Translated Texts for Historians. Liverpool: Liverpool University Press.

Clark, G. 1991. "Let Every Soul Be Subject: The Fathers and the Empire." In *Images of Empire*, ed. L. Alexander. Sheffield: Sheffield Academic Press.

Clark, G. 1993. *Women in Late Antiquity: Pagan and Christian Lifestyles*. Oxford: Clarendon Press.

Cooper, K. 1992. "Insinuations of Worldly Influence: An Aspect of the Christianization of the Roman Aristocracy." *Journal of Roman Studies* 82.

Countryman, L. 1980. *The Rich Christian in the Church of the Early Empire*. New York: Edwin Mellen.

Delaine, J. 1993. "Roman Baths and Bathing." *Journal of Roman Archaeology* 6.

Dillon, J., and J. Hershbell. 1991. *Iamblichus: On the Pythagorean Way of Life*. Atlanta: Scholars Press.

Elliott, A. 1987. *Roads to Paradise: Reading the Lives of the Early Saints*. Hanover: University Press of New England.

Elm, S. 1991. "Evagrius Ponticus' *Sententiae ad Virginem*." *Dumbarton Oaks Papers* 45.

Gleason, M. 1990. "The Semiotics of Gender: Physiognomy and Self-Fashioning in the Second Century CE." In *Before Sexuality: the Construction of Erotic Experience in the Ancient Greek World*, eds. D. Halperin, J. Winkler, and F. Zeitlin. Princeton: Princeton University Press.

Gould, G. 1990. "Women in the Writings of the Fathers: Language, Belief and Reality." In W. J. Sheils and D. Wood, eds., *Women and the Church*. Studies in Church History, vol. 27. Oxford: Blackwell.

Gould, G. 1993. *The Desert Fathers on Monastic Community*. Oxford: Oxford University Press.

Grodszynski, D. 1984. "Tortures mortelles et catégories sociales. Les *summa supplicia* dans le droit romain aux IIIe et IVe siècles." In *Du châtiment dans la cité: Supplices corporels et peine de mort dans le monde antique*. Collections de l'école française de Rome 79.

Harrison, V. 1990. "Male and Female in Cappadocian Theology." *Journal of Theological Studies* 41.

Harvey, S. A. 1990a. *Asceticism and Society in Crisis: John of Ephesus and the Lives of the Eastern Saints*. Berkeley: University of California Press.

Harvey, S. A. 1990b. "Jacob of Serug, Homily on Symeon the Stylite." Translated in V. L. Wimbush, ed., *Ascetic Behavior in Greco-Roman Antiquity: A Sourcebook*. Minneapolis: Fortress Press.

Hillgarth, J. 1986. *Christianity and Paganism, 350–750.* Philadelphia: University of Pennsylvania Press.

Hunter, D. G. 1987. "Resistance to the Virginal Ideal in Late Fourth-Century Rome: The Case of Jovinian." *Journal of Theological Studies* 48.

Hunter, D. G. 1989. "*On the Sin of Adam and Eve:* A Little Known Defense of Marriage and Childbearing by Ambrosiaster." *Harvard Theological Review* 82.

Hunter, D. G. 1992. "The Paradise of Patriarchy: Ambrosiaster on Women As [not] in God's Image." *Journal of Theological Studies* 43.

Lawless, G., 1987. *Augustine of Hippo and His Monastic Rule.* Oxford: Oxford University Press.

Lienhard, J.T.H. 1977. *Paulinus of Nola and Early Western Monasticism.* Bonn: Peter Hanstein.

Markus, R. 1991. *The End of Ancient Christianity.* Oxford: Oxford University Press.

McNamara, J., ed. 1992. *Sainted Women of the Dark Ages,* trans. with J. E. Halborg and G. Whatley. Durham: Duke University Press.

Meredith, A. 1976. "Asceticism—Christian and Greek." *Journal of Theological Studies,* n.s. 27.

Musurillo, H. 1956. "The Problem of Ascetical Fasting in the Greek Patristic Fathers." *Traditio* 12.

O'Donnell, J. J. 1992. *Augustine: Confessions.* Oxford: Clarendon Press.

Patlagean, E. 1981. "L'histoire de la femme déguisée en moine." In *Structure sociale, famille, chrétienté à Byzance IVe–XIe siècles.* London: Variorum.

Rousseau, P. 1978. *Ascetics, Authority and the Church in the Age of Jerome and Cassian.* Oxford: Oxford University Press.

Rousseau, P. 1985. *Pachomius: The Making of a Community in Fourth-Century Egypt.* Berkeley: University of California Press.

Rousselle, A. 1988. *Porneia: On Desire and the Body in Antiquity.* Oxford: Blackwell.

Rousselle, A. 1991. "La politique des corps." In P. S. Pantel, ed., *Histoire des Femmes I: L'Antiquité.* Paris: Plon.

Russell, N. 1980. *The Lives of the Desert Fathers.* Oxford and London: Mowbray.

Shaw, T. 1990. "Homily: On Virginity." Translated in V. L. Wimbush, ed., *Ascetic Behavior in Greco-Roman Antiquity: A Sourcebook.* Minneapolis: Fortress Press.

Ward, B. 1975. *The Sayings of the Desert Fathers.* Oxford and London: Mowbray.

Ward, B. 1987. *Harlots of the Desert: A Study of Repentance in Early Monastic Sources.* Oxford and London: Mowbray.

Ward, R. B. 1992. "Women in Roman Baths." *Harvard Theological Review* 85.

White, C. 1992. *Christian Friendship in the Fourth Century.* Cambridge: Cambridge University Press.

4

Christian Asceticism and the Emergence of the Monastic Tradition

Samuel Rubenson

Christian asceticism has, since the fourth century, been closely linked to the monastic tradition. Ascetic practice is at the roots of monasticism, and most of the ascetic writings in Christian traditions stem from monks or nuns and have been produced, copied and read primarily in monasteries. At the same time, it is obvious that Christian asceticism does not originate in the monastic setting: it preceded it and goes back to a tradition older than the New Testament. It has its roots in a common heritage of the Hellenistic world, a heritage christianized in the first centuries. Tertullian and Origen, the most famous advocates of ascetic practice in the early church, both died decades before the first known monks established themselves in the desert.

Monasticism thus inherited an earlier tradition of ascetic theology and practice. A few decades into the fourth century, this heritage was developed and made the cornerstone of monastic tradition. While we have only scant evidence for monastic practice earlier than the 320s, it is obvious that the monastic theology and the sets of rules shaped before the 380s has remained the foundation of monasticism until today.[1] By the year 400 CE, monasticism was already firmly established throughout the Christian world; and, within the monastic setting, the theory as well as practice of asceticism in Christianity was provided with a place to develop. From the fourth century onward, Christian asceticism cannot be studied separately from monasticism.

For the understanding of the *Christian* ascetic traditions the rise of monasticism—namely, monastic theology as well as monastic practice—is of utmost importance. It is primarily in the making of monastic tradition in fourth-century Egypt that the forms and concepts of later Christian ascetic practices and theories are formulated for the first time. It is also here that the experiences of the first monks of the desert, negative as well as positive, are developed into a tradition of spiritual guidance. Behind the great systematicians of monastic thinking—John Cassian in the West and Evagrius of Pontus in the East—there is the tradition and experiences of the Desert Fathers.[2] The unrivaled head of that school is (according to tradition) St. Antony of Egypt.

St. Antony and the Elusive Origins of Monasticism

The precise origins and earliest development of monasticism, here defined as the creation of a community permanently separated from ordinary society, is still a matter of scholarly dispute. The roots of Christian monasticism have been sought in Egyptian religion, Judaism, Greek philosophical schools, and Manichaeism, in relation to gnosticism; in social and political circumstances (taxation, repression, national protest); in ecclesiastical developments (as a protest against the secularization of the church); etc.[3]

The choice among different factors behind the rise of monasticism is naturally influenced by the image of the earliest monastic tradition, an image partly shaped by theories about its origins and partly by sources emanating from a later stage in its development. In order to avoid both circular reasoning and dependence upon later sources, we have to study the historical setting and intellectual environment of the first monks and review later material critically. We cannot take for granted that the image given of the first monks in writings produced in the late fourth century describes the actual situation, motives and thoughts of the first decades of that century.[4]

Although it was Pachomius, and not Antony, who created the first monasteries in the sense of walled centers of communal living, it is Antony who stands out as the author of monasticism, even in the Pachomian sources.[5] In the *Apophthegmata,* the collection of sayings of, and anecdotes about, the Desert Fathers, he is the most prominent authority. In the main sources about Egyptian monasticism from the end of the century, the *Historia monachorum in Aegypto* (Rufinus) and the *Historia Lausiaca* (Palladius), as well as in the historical works of Socrates and Sozomenos, he is the "father" of the tradition.[6] Although his importance was greatly enhanced by the biography allegedly written by St. Athanasius, the *Vita Antonii,* it is clear that his fame was not the result of the *Vita* but rather its cause.[7]

The main sources for St. Antony are the *Vita Antonii,* the sayings attributed to or mentioning him in the *Apophthegmata,* and the *Letters of St. Antony.* Of these the *Vita* has been the most prominent through the centuries and shaped the image of Antony and of monasticism in general. At the end of the last century, the historicity of the *Vita* was, however, strongly challenged by Helmut Weingarten; and, although the most far-reaching criticism was rejected, the *Vita* has never regained its credibility as the true story of Antony's life, thoughts, speeches, and deeds. The *Vita* is today generally seen as a literary composition presenting an ideal of monastic life in the shape of an historical person whose image is reworked according to the interests of the author, whether Athanasius or someone else.[8] The credibility of various parts of the *Vita* must thus be checked with help from other sources.

With the work of Wilhelm Bousset (1923), the *Apophthegmata* emerged as a major historical source for the desert fathers. His faith in the credibility of the sayings was widely accepted and to many scholars the sayings remain the primary source, almost the genuine reproduction of what the first monks thought, said and did.[9] In his major study on St. Antony, Hermann Dörries made the sayings on St. Antony the basis of his investigation into the *Vita* as an historical source.[10] Dörries's conclusions and his critique of the traditional image of St. Antony based on the *Vita* has generally been accepted. Thus, the image of an hero of the church fighting demons, philosophers and heretics has given way to the image of a penitent monk fleeing into the desert.

Common to both these sources is the image of Antony as a simple, uneducated, even illiterate, man. The *Vita* repeatedly states that he had no education; he was taught by God alone. He is said to have gone directly from his seclusion in his home into the seclusion of his monastic cell; to have spoken only in Coptic; and to have rejected all contact with worldly rulers and with Greek philosophy.[11] This fits well into the general picture of the fathers in the *Apophthegmata* and is strengthened by their rejection of worldly education and theological speculation. The fact that the *Vita* actually presents Antony as engaged in discussing philosophical concepts and writing letters is either overlooked or regarded as unhistorical.[12]

The third source, the letters, has not received the same amount of attention. The reason is partly the difficult and unsatisfactory transmission of the text and partly the fact that the letters can hardly have been written by the person emerging from the *Vita* and the *Apophthegmata*. Thus they have either been overlooked or regarded as spurious. The credibility of the attribution of the letters to Antony should, however, not be compared to that of the *Life* or the *Sayings*, since the presentation they make of Antony is open to doubt. In the first major study of the letters, I was able to show that they must be regarded as genuine and as the main source for the teachings of St. Antony; and I will not repeat here my arguments based on the manuscripts, numerous other sources and internal evidence.[13]

The main problem with the authenticity of the letters and the image of St. Antony presented by them is that they challenge much of what has generally been said about the nature of early Egyptian monasticism. This is also the main argument put forward against an attribution of the letters to Antony. They cannot have been written by a simple illiterate Coptic peasant fleeing into the desert with only a rudimentary and fanatic biblical faith. In order to reject the arguments against the authenticity of the letters it has been necessary not only to show that the later sources, the *Vita* and the *Apophthegmata*, have their reasons for presenting Antony and the early monks as uneducated, but also that there is positive evidence for a rather different view of the setting of early monastic tradition.

Asceticism and Theology in Egypt, c.300 CE

Egypt was at the beginning of the fourth century a land characterized by a variety of religious forms and experiences. Besides the traditional cult, largely merged with Greek and to some degree Roman cults, there was the cult of the emperors, the so called mystery religions, the Greek philosophical schools, Manichaeism and various forms of Judaism, Christianity, and gnosticism. Egypt was also the place of far-reaching cultural exchange, a bilingual society in which Greek and Coptic culture had long lived together. The third century brought a deep economic crisis affecting the entire society and restructuring social life by creating a new mobility and driving numerous peasants from their land.[14]

In this social upheaval, this mixture of traditional cults and new ideas, this contact with various cultural traditions, Christianity, gnosticism and Manichaeism spread rapidly. The papyri show beyond doubt that this spread of ideas and writings was not confined to the larger cities, nor to the Greek population. Religious writings, like parts of the Bible, Manichaean hymns, and gnostic apocrypha found their way into the countryside. In the second part of the third century the need for Coptic translations becomes evident. Literacy was not something restricted to those who went through the Greek gymnasia and fulfilled the standards of Greek education; many would have been able to understand and even read simple Greek, though not able to converse fluently or write literary Greek.[15]

Christianity spread in this society primarily as a philosophy, a taught way of life based on a special interpretation of sacred texts. The earliest pieces of evidence for Egyptian Christianity give numerous references to schools, to reading, interpreting, and working with texts—even to what must be termed scholarly work.[16] Although there is no proof for, and little credibility in the opinion that, Egyptian Christianity was thoroughly heterodox until the fourth century, it is evident that there was no strict form of orthodoxy applied everywhere. In the papyri from the third and fourth century the gnostic and other heretic texts are very few compared to the ones accepted as orthodox. Besides the biblical texts the most common writings seem to have been the *Shepherd of Hermas,* the *Paschal Homily* of Melito of Sardis, the *Acts of Paul,* and the homilies of Origen.[17] It is within this tradition that one could expect to find the heritage that shaped a young Christian seeking spiritual guidance.

There is, furthermore, no evidence that Christianity primarily attracted the lowest level in society. From the papyri and other evidence it seems that the literate middle classes of the towns constituted the majority in the church. There is also ample evidence of Christians from the upper class. By the early fourth century, the church had accumulated considerable wealth and was deeply engaged in trade and cultivation of land. The office of bishop, and thus governor of this wealth, soon became very attractive, as evinced by the warnings uttered by Origen and Athanasius, and the fact that the church soon decided to appoint monks as bishops.[18] From this background in society and church, it becomes more difficult to imagine that the leading monks of the first generation were illiterate peasants; they were, rather, educated and prosperous leaders of a certain social standing. Their motive for leaving society behind and settling in isolation was not flight from oppression or fanaticism, but the result of a philosophical or religious quest combined with an aversion to the disruption occasioned by the worldly concerns of property, social obligation, and the material side of the emerging church. Even on a theoretical level, it is hard to imagine that a movement with such a rapid growth and permanent effects should have come out of a number of insignificant and illiterate individuals' simply fleeing society.

The Monastic Interpretation of Ascetic Tradition

St. Antony as a spiritual teacher handing down his teaching in a series of seven letters, written in Coptic and full of biblical quotations marked by the exegetical and theological tradition of Origen of Alexandria, is no unlikely figure in the 330s. The earliest archives of Egyptian monasteries show that the monks had some education and were deeply involved in studies and correspondence.[19] The lists from and recoveries of early monastic libraries show that Origen played an important role in the shaping of the minds of the first monks. The opponents of Origen, like Epiphanius, Theophilos of Alexandria and Jerome, as well as his followers, like Palladius and Rufinus, attest to the impact Origen's writings had made on some of the leading monks of the fourth century and to the existence of an "Origenist network" of Nitria.[20] Most probably it is even the Origenism of the tradition rooted in St. Antony that lies behind the attempts of the author of the *Vita* and the *Apophthegmata* to rework the image of St. Antony, making it to a large degree incompatible with the letters.

The seven letters of St. Antony are important not only as the major source for St. Antony himself. They are also, together with the strange letters of Pachomius, the first major writings of Egyptian monasticism and most probably the first original writings in Coptic, although preserved only in Arabic, Georgian, and Latin.[21] Given the significance of Antony for the monastic tradition, they can be regarded as a major source for the later development of monastic theology. A comparison of Antony's letters with the letters of Ammonas, Macarius and the writings of Evagrius will also show a common tradition.[22] It thus seems safe to regard the letters as our main source for what can be termed the School of St. Antony, shaping lower Egyptian monastic theology.

Probably the most striking feature of the letters is their emphasis on *gnōsis* (knowledge). Exhortations to know and understand recur throughout the letters and are clearly rooted in a theology for which knowledge is at the center. Knowledge is necessary in order to be saved—that is, to return to God. This knowledge is primarily self-knowledge: one must come to know the self in order to know God; one must return to self in order to return to God. Knowledge of God is possible since humans participate in God, a participation found in a person's *ousia noera* (intellectual substance). The body must be cleansed and made subject to the spirit so that it does not tie one to what is material and passing. The redemption brought by Christ is the granting of the power to return and become again a spiritual unity. Behind these notions lie, no doubt, a Platonic understanding of the human being and as is evident in some passages an Origenistic interpretation of Christianity.[23]

Asceticism in Antony's letters is a necessary first step in the human being's return to God. The human being is torn apart by passions attacking through the senses and ideas attacking through the mind. He or she has no power over self, but has become a seat of unclean motions and demons. The latter must be driven out and the body and the soul cleansed. Ascetic practice is the method of cutting short the influences of the motions and demons. There is, however, no specific teaching about various ascetic practices in the letters, only an emphasis on the need to purify each member of the body, and the need to be guided and strengthened by the spirit. A very important aspect of Antony's teaching is his emphasis on the natural condition of human beings.[24] Virtue is nothing foreign to human nature; on the contrary, salvation is the return of the human being to a natural state. Nature is not fallen and should not be rejected. God thus calls human beings primarily through the natural law laid down in their hearts. The written (scriptural) law, and the teaching of the Holy Spirit, those other ways in which God calls human beings, do not contain anything new. The coming of Jesus, his presence, reveals what is already laid down in creation—it reestablishes the unity that once existed. It is worth noting that the same emphasis on the natural goodness of human beings reappears in the sermon attributed to Antony in the *Vita*. (Actually, there are numerous similarities between the letters and the teachings put forward in the *Vita*.[25])

In the letters of Ammonas, his disciple, we find very little of Antony's emphasis on God's calling and his dispensations and on what the human being is expected to give in return. There is also no specific teaching on ascetic practice. But it is clear that Ammonas shared Antony's philosophical background of strong dualism between matter, division, and temporality on the one hand and spirit, unity, and eternity on the other. Ammonas is, however, more concerned with mystical experience, with what God grants everyone who puts aside this world. He describes the joy, power, and revelations that come to anyone who endures the ascetical struggle. Asceticism is not a goal in itself, not a merit, not a punishment or suffering; it is a way to open oneself to what God wants to give. While Antony put his stress on God's wrath and the struggle to be liberated from the demons and return to oneself, Ammonas has added an important dimension to monastic tradition: the longing for God and the pleasures of a communion with God.[26]

After Antony and Ammonas, the tradition settles in Nitria and Scetis, where some of the disciples of Antony, such as Macarius and Pambo and their disciples, create the setting of the *Apophthegmata patrum*. Rufinus, who visited Nitria in the 370s, and Palladius, who lived there in the 380s and 390s, both attest to the role Antony played as the authority of the past and the importance of Origen's writings for the monastic community. The latter is also confirmed by Epiphanius, who accuses the monks of Nitria of being followers of Origen. From Palladius we even gain an image of the leading monks as highly literate and engaged in philosophical problems.[27] Although the *Sayings* tends to downplay this aspect of the monks, there are also here numerous examples of books being read, copied, or written, and even of highly allegorical interpretations of biblical texts being discussed.[28]

It is thus clear that Evagrius did not settle in the desert as the great philosopher in the midst of illiterate peasants. He emerges from his own writings as a pupil of the masters of the desert.[29] What he did was to collect the wisdom and to systematize the teaching of his own masters. He is the first writer to incorporate a collection of sayings in his own writings, and his later works are generally written as series of aphorisms, or *kephalaia* (chapters).[30] This is not the place to speak about Evagrius's teachings on asceticism, but it seems obvious to me that the tradition of the desert played as great a role as did his reading of Origen. It was probably his own experiences of desert asceticism, however, practicing what he was taught by his masters, that formed his writings and made them valuable for others. In them the results of monastic asceticism are made available for any person who starts to wrestle with self.

The contribution of the early monastic tradition to ascetic theology is, perhaps, primarily the realization of the need for separation from ordinary life and the creation of an autonomous "city" (*polis*). According to the *Vita,* what Antony realized was that it is impossible to live a fully ascetic life—that is, a life marked by spiritual warfare—within the context of ordinary social obligations. What monasticism adds to ascetic theology is the establishment of a milieu in which ascetic practice can flourish and in which its fruits can be handed down in spiritual teaching through the writings of the monks. It is this creation of a "Sonderwelt," this creation of a *polis* out of the desert, that marks the beginning of monasticism. It should probably also be regarded as the basic condition necessary for asceticism to flourish in Christian tradition. Asceticism needs to be linked to the idea of a citizenship of heaven, not of worldly society, if it is not to remain a mere physical practice, comparable to sports.[31]

A secondary contribution of the early monks is what could be called the christianization of Hellenic ascetic traditions. Through the popularization of Origen's synthesis of Platonic philosophy and the teachings of the New Testament, Antony and his followers provided a Christian interpretation of popular philosophy and a philosophical understanding of popular piety. This interpretation was, moreover, practiced in front of the people and personified in the monk, "the holy man." In him and the tradition formed through his disciples, a canon of Christianity was created, a canon probably as influential as the biblical writings. The fact that the monk was independent of ordinary society, even almost independent of bodily needs, meant that he could be trusted as a mediator not only of God, but also of other human beings.[32] As an ascetic and a man without civil obligations, the monk was freer than most. The success of Christianity could hardly have come about without the devotion of the ascetics combined with the Platonic interpretation of Christianity that developed in the monasteries of Egypt and Palestine.

NOTES

1. The date of origin and the earliest developments of monasticism have been a matter of dispute for more than a century. The position taken in 1877 by Helmut Weingarten—based on the silence of such sources as Eusebius and Athanasius (the *Life of Antony* he considered to be spurious)—that monasticism emerged only after Constantine has been refuted mainly on the basis of papyri. See, for example, E. A. Judge, "The Earliest Use of Monachos for 'Monk' and the Origins of Monasticism," *Jahrbuch für Antike und Christentum* 20 (1977):72–89; James Goehring, "The Origins of Monasticism," *Eusebius, Christianity and Judaism,* Studia Post-Biblica 42, eds. H. W. Attridge and C. Hato (Leiden: Brill 1992), pp. 235–255, and others. For early material see the archives of Paphnutios, published in H. I. Bell, *Jews and Christians in Egypt: The Jewish Troubles in Alexandria and the Athanasian Controversy* (London, 1924), and Nephoros, published in Barbel Kramer and John C. Shelton, *Das Archiv des Nephoros und verwandte Texte* (Mainz, 1987). Texts like the *Life of Antony,* the Pachomian material, the

Apophthegmata patrum, the *Historia monachorum in Aegypto*, and the *Historia Lausiaca* all look back on a tradition of one or two generations. For a survey see Samuel Rubenson, *The Letters of St. Antony: Origenist Theology, Monastic Tradition and the Making of a Saint* (Lund, 1990), pp. 116–119.

2. Cassian's dependence on the Egyptian fathers is documented in H.-O. Weber, *Die Stellung des Johannes Cassianus zur asuserpachomianischen Mönchstradition* (Münster, 1961). Evagrius's dependence is discussed in Gabriel Bunge, "Évagre de Pontique et les deux Macaire," *Irénikon* 56 (1983):215–227, 322–360; and S. Rubenson, "Evagrios Pontikos and die Theologie der Wuste," in *Festschrift Louise Abramowski* (Berlin: Walter de Gruyter, 1993).
3. The different theories were collected by Karl Heussi in his important but outdated *Der Ursprung des Mönchtums* (Tübingen, 1936), pp. 280–304. Recent discussions, albeit rather different, are found in Armand Veilleux, "Monasticism and Gnosis in Egypt," Birger A. Pearson and James E. Goehring, eds., *The Roots of Egyptian Christianity* (Philadelphia, 1986), pp. 271–306; Goehring, in "Origins," and Douglas Burton-Christie, *The Word in the Desert: Scripture and the Quest for Holiness in Early Christian Monasticism* (Oxford, 1993), pp. 36–39. The latter seems to me too apologetical and too negative on the influence of Hellenic philosophy. Cf. Rubenson, *The Letters*, pp. 119–125.
4. The difficulty in using the *Vita Antonii* as a historical source is discussed in H. Dörries, *Die Vita Antonii als Geschichtsquelle* (Göttingen, 1949); revised edition in *idem*, *Wort und Stunde*, Erster Band, *Gesammelte Studien zur Kirchengeschichte des vierten Jahrhunderts* (Göttingen, 1966), and with critical remarks on Dörries in Rubenson, *The Letters*, pp. 126–144. For the Pachomian material see P. Rousseau, *Pachomius: The Making of a Community in Fourth-Century Egypt* (Berkeley, 1986), pp. 37–55. For the *Apophthegmata* see Rubenson, *The Letters*, pp. 145–162, and its caution against the general reliance on the sayings as "the authentic voice of the desert fathers."
5. *Vita Pachomii Graeca*, chapters 2, 22, 99, 120, 136 and parallels in Coptic. See Rousseau, *Pachomius*, pp. 45–48, 60, and 179; and, for a full discussion, Rubenson, *The Letters*, pp. 165–172.
6. For a discussion of all references to Antony see Rubenson, *The Letters*, pp. 172–184.
7. See Michael A. Williams, "The *Life of Antony* and the Domestication of Charismatic Wisdom," *Charisma and Sacred Biography, Journal of the American Academy of Religion* (1982), Thematic Studies 48.3–4.
8. The literature on the *Vita Antonii* is vast. For a list of editions and for recent summaries see *Clavis patrum graecorum* 2101, ed. M. Geerard, 5 vols. (Brepols, 1974–1987) and G.J.M. Bartelink, "Die literarische Gattung der Vita Antonii: Struktur und Motive," *Vigiliae Christianae* 36 (1982) and Rubenson, *The Letters*, pp. 126–132.
9. W. Bousset, *Apophthegmata: Studien zur Geschichte des ältesten Mönchtums* (Tübingen, 1923). A recent example of a similar reliance on the sayings is Burton-Christie, *The Word in the Desert*.
10. See above, note 4.
11. *Vita Antonii* 1, 16, 66, 72–74, 81.
12. For a discussion see Rubenson, *The Letters*, pp. 141–144.
13. Ibid., pp. 35–47.
14. For descriptions of Egypt in this period see Alan K. Bowman, *Egypt after the Pharaohs* (London, 1986) and Naphtali Lewis, *Life in Egypt under Roman Rule* (Oxford, 1983). The results of papyrological and historical research bearing on the setting of early mo-

nasticism is discussed in Rousseau, *Pachomius*, pp. 1–36, and Rubenson, *The Letters*, pp. 89–125.

15. Evidence from the papyri in Rubenson, *The Letters*, pp. 95–99, 109–115, 119–125.
16. See Colin Roberts, *Manuscript, Society and Belief in Early Christian Egypt* (London, 1979).
17. Roberts, *Manuscript*, pp. 60–65.
18. Rubenson, *The Letters*, p. 107, quoting Athanasius, *Historia Arianorum* 78.1.3 and Origen, *Commentarii in Mattheam* 15.26.
19. See the editions of monastic archives mentioned in note 1 and the discussion on a Pachomian origin of the Nag-Hammadi codices summarized and developed in Clemens Scholten, "Die Nag-Hammadi-Texte als Buchbesitz der Pachomianer," *JAC* 31 (1988). Cf. Rubenson, *The Letters*, pp. 119–125.
20. Epiphanius, *Panarion* 64.4.1; Jerome, *Epistulae* 86–92; Palladius, *Historia Lausiaca* 3, 4, 11, 38, 47, 55; *idem, Dialogus de vita Iohannis Chrysostomi* 17; Rufinus, *Historia ecclesiastica* 2.4.8. See also Jon F. Dechow, *Dogma and Mysticism in Early Christianity: Epiphanius of Cyprus and the Legacy of Origen* (Mercer University Press, 1988) and Elizabeth Clark, *The Origenist Controversy: The Cultural Construction of an Early Christian Debate* (Princeton, 1992).
21. See S. Rubenson, "St. Antony, 'The First Real Coptic Author'?" *Actes du IVe congrés copte* (Louvain, 1992), pp. 16–27.
22. See Rubenson, "Evagrios Pontikos als Erbe der Wüste."
23. Rubenson, *The Letters*, pp. 59–88.
24. *Epistulae Antonii* 4.13; 7.11, pp. 49–51.
25. See Rubenson, *The Letters*, p. 73, note 2, and more general ibid., pp. 132–141.
26. The literature on the letters of Ammonas is very meager. Except for the editions listed in *CPG* 2380 and Franz Klejna, "Antonius und Ammonas: Eine Untersuchung über Herkunft und Eigenart der altesten Mönchsbriefe," *Zeitschrift für Katholische Theologie* 62 (1938), the only study is S. Rubenson, "Ammonas—en bortglomd gestalt i den kristna mystikens tidiga historia," *Florilegium Patristicum: En Festskrift till Per Beskow* (Delsbo: Åsak, 1991), pp. 168–185.
27. See above, note 20.
28. See Burton-Christie, *The Word in the Desert*, pp. 111–114 and Rubenson, *The Letters*, p. 119ff.
29. See Bunge, "Évagre le Pontique et les deux Macaires."
30. For Evagrios, see Gabriel Bunge, *Evagrios Pontikos, Briefe aus der Wüste* (Trier, 1986).
31. In the *Vita Antonii*, the first attempt to interpret nascent monasticism in the Christian tradition, Athanasius makes this his "Leitmotif." See *Vita Antonii* 14.
32. This theme is developed in Peter Brown, "The Rise and Function of the Holy Man in Late Antiquity," *Journal of Roman Studies* 61 (1971). Antony's role as mediator is borne out in *Vita Antonii* 84–87.

5

Asceticism and Mysticism in Late Antiquity and the Early Middle Ages

Bernard McGinn

In 1752, the Italian Jesuit Giovanni Battista Scaramelli issued his *Direttorio ascetico* designed "to teach the manner of leading souls through the ordinary ways of grace to Christian perfection." This was followed, in 1754, with his posthumous *Direttorio mistico* "aimed at the directors of those souls which God leads through the way of contemplation."[1] Scaramelli's works were probably the most influential proponents in designating "asceticism" and "mysticism," or ascetical and mystical theology, as the received terms for the basic divisions in the Christian path to perfection over the past two centuries, at least in the Catholic tradition. The publication of the *Direttorio mistico* was itself a minor miracle. Scaramelli had presented it for ecclesiastical judgment in 1743, and in the antimystical atmosphere of the reaction to Quietism and the condemnations not only of the questionable Madame Guyon, but also of the well-established Archbishop Fénélon, it is not surprising that it took over a decade and considerable willingness on the author's part to respond to the censors that allowed the document finally to see the light and to enjoy its subsequent success.[2] The *Direttorio ascetico* encountered no such problems and was even more popular.

Scaramelli's two-stage view of Christian perfection remained normative down to living memory in Roman Catholicism. Among its last great monuments was the *Preçis de théologie ascetique et mystique* of the Sulpician Adolph Tanquerey, who taught for fifteen years in the United States, before retiring to France, where his *magnum opus* appeared in 1923–1924. It went through nine French editions, was translated into at least ten languages, and remained a basic textbook in Catholic seminaries down to Vatican II.

I mention Scaramelli and Tanquerey not because they were responsible for creating the connection between asceticism and mysticism, but because they transmitted what they conceived the traditional relationship between these terms to have been to the modern era. Doubtless both the Italian Jesuit and the French Sulpician would have been amazed at a conference devoted to the study of asceticism, rather than its practice. They might well have insisted that any such conference would be incomplete without some consideration being accorded to the second stage of their itinerary to God, the mystical one. My purpose is to ask why and how asceticism and mysticism came to be so intimately linked in the Christian tradition. Although asking the question may seem to be merely otiose (asceticism has always been linked to mysticism, correct?), what has so often been taken as a mere given is actually the product of a complex history which deserves further study.

To be sure, the very act of asking questions about the relation between "asceticism" and "mysticism" would have made little sense to Christian thinkers before the seventeenth century. "Mysticism" is a relatively recent term, and Michel de Certeau has persuasively argued that the creation of the substantive "la mystique" in French in the early seventeenth century (better translated as "mystics" in comparison with mathematics) marks a decisive shift in Western perceptions of that element in its religious history. Moderns attempt to circumscribe this when they use the term "mysticism."[3] The adjectival and adverbial forms (*mystikos, mystikōs* in Greek; *mysticus, mystice* in Latin), of course, have a long history in Christianity, one intimately connected with what modern scholars call mysticism, but also with a wider penumbra of signification. Even "asceticism" as a technical term may be more modern than we usually think.[4] The Greek substantives *askēsis* and *askētēs* are as old as Homer (*Iliad* 10.438 and 23.743; *Odyssey* 23.198); but the terms do not occur in the New Testament (though the verb *askeō* is used in *Acts* 24.16). Early Christian adaptations of *askēsis* were often broader and more diffuse than the modern term "asceticism," which in English at least appears to be a seventeenth-century creation.[5] Full semantic studies of the evolution of both terms are still lacking.

My purpose here is not to try to give any history, even a sketchy one, of how Christianity adopted, adapted and perhaps even abused *askēsis* in its formative centuries, but to reflect on some—by no means all—stages in how Christians came to see ascetical practice and mystical contemplation as integral parts of one path, the road to God. My remarks are meant to be provocative rather than probative, designed to open up avenues for discussion and debate. I shall suggest a thesis, but a tentative one, still open to qualification and revision.

In my book *The Foundations of Mysticism* I argued that the struggle over the true meaning of *gnōsis,* or saving knowledge, during the second and early third centuries was formative in the history of Christian mysticism. The development of Christian mysticism, like Christian orthodoxy, must be understood in the light of this debate.[6] The mystical elements that were of importance for many gnostic groups—such as the ascent of the soul, the awakening to the immanence of God, the role of visions, the relation of faith and love to *gnōsis,* and the necessity for a spiritual reading of the scriptures—were to remain of central significance in later Christian mysticism.[7] But on several crucial issues the debate over *gnōsis* produced significant reactions against views held by those we today call Gnostics. These involve not only the dogmatic foundations of later Christian mysticism: that is, teachings like the goodness of material creation, the unity of the Creator and Redeemer, and the real enfleshment of redeeming Logos, but also issues more directly involved in what came to be called mystical theology.

Most Gnostics, like the mystics of the pagan Platonic tradition, taught that the "spark of the soul" was innately divine, needing only to be awakened to its true self in order to be saved. Anti-Gnostics like Justin, Irenaeus, Clement and Origen insisted that the soul was created, even its "spark" being something only divinizable rather than inherently divine. The spokesmen for the orthodox party also gave *pistis* (faith) a saving role, though they believed that among the "true Gnostics" *pistis* should flower into a higher stage marked by both *gnōsis* and *agapē*. To paraphrase Clement of Alexandria, "All the elect are good, but some are more elect than others."[8] Finally, the orthodox came to insist that visionary experience and even the spiritual interpretation of scripture, which was of central importance for patristic mysticism, was to be tested not by its ability to facilitate contact with God for the few through the revelation of gnostic mythology as a deeper and more real message about salvation. Rather, it should be evaluated according to its conformity to the exoteric *paradosis* (framework) of the Christian community enshrined in the teaching of the bishops, and therefore open to all.[9] Although Christianity included an esoteric element from the beginning, the gnostic crisis effected a decisive shift in the forms of modified esotericism that were considered legitimate. Since the time of the great debate over *gnōsis*, any forms of esotericism founded upon diversity of message and not merely upon different modes of transmission or levels of reception have always been suspect, and often condemned, in the Christian tradition.

Professor Gedaliahu Stroumsa of Hebrew University has suggested a similar dialectical relation between gnostic and orthodox views of asceticism. In a paper comparing the roles of asceticism in gnosticism and in early monasticism, Stroumsa argues that despite many initial similarities and overlaps, there is a fundamental difference between the two. "The Gnostic is essentially a stranger to the world; his asceticism only makes it possible to confirm this inherent situation. In the case of the monk, on the other hand, the long effort of asceticism is absolutely necessary to enable him to detach himself from the world."[10] The root of this, according to Stroumsa, is in the lack of a concept of human personality in gnosticism, which is a corollary to the gnostic insistence on the innate spark of divinity discussed above. Long ago, Plotinus, who shared the Gnostics' view about the innate divinity of the soul, also detected another significant root of the difference between his own philosophical understanding of asceticism and that which he found in the Gnostics, when he upbraided them for neglecting the study of virtue.[11]

Gnostic asceticism and mysticism presented a major challenge to those Christians—the not-so-silent majority—who eventually won the day. Important elements of the "orthodox" Christian view of the relation of asceticism and mysticism began to take shape in the debate over *gnōsis*. The orthodox party (if I may be permitted to describe something so amorphous in shorthand fashion) certainly based its view of what constitutes acceptable ascetical and mystical practice on what we can call "internal" components of Christian beliefs, such doctrines as the goodness of creation and the created nature of the soul; but the task of putting asceticism and mysticism together into a coherent program was to be accomplished only with tools taken from Hellenistic philosophy, as a brief look at Clement of Alexandria and Origen will suggest.[12] The real work of making this program of Christian *paideia* (ideals of culture) a central element in the history of Christianity, however, was accomplished by monasticism. Monastic asceticism was not founded on the carefully structured educative pattern envisaged by Origen, though Origenist influence on the early monks, such as Antony, cannot be excluded.[13] It was the "Origenist wave" of the late fourth century, culminating in the writings of Evagrius of Pontus, which brought the practice of the desert and the speculative genius of Origen together into a program that was to prove decisive in the history of Christian spirituality, both in the East and the West.

Clement of Alexandria was deeply concerned with the limits of Christian self-denial, as we can see from his treatise *Quis dives salvetur?*, as well as from his reflections on martyrdom and on the role of *apatheia*. He is one of the first Christians to use the term *askēsis*, describing "gnostic *askēsis*" as an important Christian ideal in the *Stromateis*.[14] Clement was no less concerned with the role of direct forms of contact with the unknown God present in Jesus Christ through prayer and contemplation; indeed, it was he who first domesticated the term *theōria* (theory) in Christianity (he uses it eighty-four times). In this Alexandrian teacher we can find many of the core elements relating to the later history of both Christian asceticism and Christian mysticism; but, given the eclectic nature of his thought, they have not yet been placed into any comprehensive or articulated structure.

One area in Clement's thought, however, deserves special notice for an understanding of later treatments of the connection between asceticism and mysticism. Asceticism's relation to mysticism was often to be expressed in terms of *praxis* and *theōria*, or what the Western Christian tradition came to call the *vita activa* and the *vita contemplativa*.[15] Clement initiated the domestication of these terms taken from classical philosophy into Christianity. *Praxis* (doing) and *theōria* (originally, gazing or watching) first signified two kinds of activity at the basis of two discrete forms of life, the political and the philosophical. Later they came to be viewed as two aspects of the life of any thinking person, aspects that also gave rise to two specific kinds of knowledge. Plato, in his *Statesman* (258E) divided "all *epistēmē* (science) into two parts, calling the one *praktikēn* (practical) the other *monon gnōstikēn* (purely gnostic)." Aristotle, in the *Nicomachean Ethics* 10.7 (1177A–1178A) adapted the terms "practical" and "theoretical" for these forms of knowledge, arguing that the theoretical or contemplative activity was better, insofar as it is based upon "something divine" in humanity. In later Greek philosophy, and especially in Christianity, these root meanings shifted. Among both pagans and Christians *theōria* came to be taken not just for any form of philosophical observation, but only for contemplative vision of the divine; *praxis*, among Christians like Clement, came to signify active love for neighbor, the *agapē* enjoined in the New Testament, not the public life of the citizen.

In the *Stromateis*, Clement notes the three things necessary for the true Gnostic—"These three things our philosopher attaches to himself: first, *theōria;* second, the fulfillment of the commandments; third, the forming of virtuous persons. . . ."[16] It seems reasonable to take the latter two as comprising the realm of *praxis*, so that while Clement neither identifies *praxis* with *askēsis*, nor provides any clear account of how *praxis* and *theōria* are to be related in the life of the "true Gnostic," by insisting that both elements are necessary he nevertheless laid the seeds for much to come—especially when monastic authors explicitly identified *praxis* and *askēsis*.

Clement was a precursor, Origen a direct source for many subsequent Christian attempts to bring together self-denial in the name of the gospel and mystical contemplation of God. The question as to whether Origen's thought constitutes a "system" or not, in this case regarding the question of the relation of asceticism and mysticism, seems to me misplaced.[17] The great Alexandrian was not unlike Plato in this respect. He was not interested in "systems" in the modern sense, but everything he wrote sprang from a unified perspective based on deep and careful thought. Nowhere is this more true than in his thoughts about Christian *paideia,* that is, the lifelong training necessary to achieve the goal of human existence. Here his contributions were both original and epochal.

Origen himself was a noted ascetic. Whatever we are to make of his famous self-castration, Eusebius's description of how "He went to the limit in practicing a life given up to philosophy,"—that is, strict asceticism—is evidence enough.[18] Even today, an academic who sold off all his books and restricted himself to an income less than that of a day laborer (four *obols,* says Eusebius) would be a source of surprise, if not of emulation, to his colleagues. Origen provides the earliest Christian spiritual itineraries that describe the progress of the soul from its present fallen state through the various stages of self-denial, practice of virtue, and finally encounter with the saving Logos. The most famous of these occurs in *Homily 27 on Numbers,* entitled "De mansionibus filiorum Istrahel" in the surviving Latin translation.[19]

In the exegetical treatise that closes the *De principiis,* Origen had advanced the key hermeneutical principle that "the prophecies which are uttered concerning the various nations ought rather to be referred to souls and the different heavenly dwelling places occupied by them" (*De prin.* 4.3.10). This is applied to the forty-two stations or camps of the wanderings of the children of Israel in the desert described in *The Book of Numbers,* chapter 33. Spiritually interpreted, the account reveals a "double exodus": first, of those who pass from a "Gentile" life to one lived under knowledge of the divine law; and second, the exodus of the soul's leaving the body. ". . . Let us strive to go forward," says Origen the preacher, "and to ascend one by one each of the steps of faith and the virtues. If we persist in them until we come to perfection, we shall be said to have made a stage at each of the steps of the virtues . . ." (*Hom.* 27.3). The rather tiresome, if consistently ingenious, way in which Origen interprets each of the forty-two waystops mingles ascetic struggle and the attainment of virtues with contemplative experience. The struggle to attain virtues by self-denial is a warfare against demons ("There is not a sin accomplished without them," says Origen [*Hom.* 27.8])—an important point for subsequent monastic appropriation of the Alexandrian's thought. The second stage, for example, is *Buthan* or "valley": "For in valleys and in low places the struggle against the devil and the opposing powers takes place" (*Hom.* 27.9). The actual mystical aspects of the journey are not clearly delineated, as, for example, stage twenty-three, *Thara,* which is interpreted as "contemplation of amazement" (*contemplatio stuporis;* Greek *exstasis*), and is briefly described as "a time when the mind is struck with amazement by the knowledge of great and marvelous things" (*Hom.* 27.12).[20] It would be difficult to make a coherent itinerary from this homily alone, but Origen is clearly attempting to provide some structure for the process by which the soul advances in the spiritual life.

The beginning and the end of *Homily 27 on Numbers* hint at another, more coherent model of the soul's progress, which was to be one of Origen's major contributions to the history of spirituality. The Alexandrian introduces the homily by describing three kinds of food that nourish the Christian's advance to perfection—the milk of simple souls, which is identified with moral instruction; then the *olera* (vegetables) and lastly the *fortis cibus* (strong meat) which is suitable for the more advanced. Unfortunately, he does not stop to tell us more about the latter two. At the very end of the piece, however, he tellingly defends a homily he knows that some will think contrived by a comparison with the progress that students make in school:

> In our analogy the students appear to linger in each different topic for public speaking and to make, as it were, stages in them; and they set out from one to the next, and again from it to another. In the same way why should not the names of the stages and the setting out from one to the next and from it to another be believed to indicate the progress of the mind and the acquisition of virtues? *Hom. 27.13*

This paidetic analogy illuminates the significance of Origen's most influential presentation of an integrated picture of the pilgrim soul's progress, the stages of development achieved through the instruction given in the three books of the true Solomon, that is, Christ the Teacher.

The well-known prologue to the *Commentary on the Song of Songs* likens the teaching found in the Song with the "strong food" (*Heb.* 5.14) also mentioned in the Numbers homily.[21] Subsequently, Origen identifies Solomon's three books, *Proverbs, Ecclesiastes* and the *Song of Songs,* with the "three general disciplines by which one attains knowledge of the universe," going on to say "The Greeks call them ethics, physics, and epoptics; and we can give them the terms moral, natural, and contemplative."[22] The *disciplina moralis* teaches the "habits conducive to virtue." *Disciplina naturalis* shows how "each individual thing is assigned those uses for which it has been brought forth by the Creator," and *disciplina contemplativa* enables the mind to "transcend visible things and contemplate something of the divine and heavenly things."[23]

As Pierre Hadot has shown, what Origen is doing here is appropriating the paidetic program of classical philosophy in the service of Christianity.[24] We often forget how far the ancient view of philosophy was from the modern one.[25] The classical concept of leading the philosophic life had nothing to do with a comfortable academic position and everything to do with a way of life that broke with the normal *bios* of the politically engaged citizen. Philosophy was a way of life more than a mode of discourse—a spiritual exercise founded upon *askēsis* and *theōria theou* (vision of the divine). The philosopher was, by definition, *atopos* (unclassifiable), that is, outside the ordinary social and political categories. In this sense, later Christian identification of the monks as true philosophers was far more appropriate than our modern linking of the Greek notion of philosophy with contemporary teachers of what we call philosophy. (By the way, just to be fair to all, modern theologians would have an equally difficult time fulfilling the job description of ancient theology, at least as Evagrius of Pontius put it—"If you are a theologian you truly pray. If you truly pray you are a theologian."[26]) In the ancient world, philosophers had already begun to create a form of life that attempted to join what Scaramelli and Tanquerey, almost two millennia later, called asceticism and mysticism.

Origen's pioneering efforts to integrate the ascetical and mystical elements in Christianity into a coherent program was achieved on the basis of transmutation of the categories created in ancient philosophy. Whether this is to be condemned as a Greek invasion of authentic gospel purity, or to be applauded by closet Platonists, is not mine to judge. But even the closet Platonist should be attentive to the changes that the Alexandrian introduced into the classical philosophical paradigm in adapting it for Christian purposes. Plato, of course, had wanted philosophers to study reality, specifically the cosmos, to arrive at *epistēmē.* Later philosophers insisted that their students study books, especially the books of Plato. While the best and brightest, such as Plotinus, used the classical texts to advance their own thought, most philosophical education, even good philosophy, was conducted on the basis of the exegesis of received texts. However important these written authorities were in their respective textual communities, an importance that often rested on their connection with *palaios logos* (ancient revelation) they could not equal the power of the Christian scriptures as sources both of group cohesiveness and of personal spiritual growth.

Origen's identification of Solomon Christ's three books of instruction as mapping out a new educational curriculum fused the classical view of textbooks as manuals for the "atopic" lifestyle of the philosopher with Christian emphasis that truth was really available only through the "divine oracles," the books of the Old and New Testaments. For Origen, the transformative process by which the fallen soul is trained in virtue in order to come to contemplative experience takes place in the very act of reading and appropriating the scriptural text. The homology that he established between the three components of the human person (body, soul, and spirit) and three levels of deepening penetration into the scripture (see *De prin.* 4.2.4) was only a shorthand way of presenting the complex process by which the believer is to place him- or herself *within* the text to inscribe its real meaning on the soul.[27] The trichotomic scheme, which expresses the inner unity of Origen's view of scripture, of *paideia,* and of human nature, controls his total ascetical and mystical teaching.

Origen's program was a great intellectual achievement. Its survival and subsequent influence, however, cannot be understood apart from its institutionalization in monasticism. But if Origen needed monasticism, monasticism also needed Origen. If it is legitimate to see monasticism, among other things, as the last great "philosophical school" of antiquity—as the monks themselves later claimed—then we have to admit that it was the Origenist view of Christian *paideia* that enabled them to create a full philosophical program, that is, one that not only lived an "atopic" life of the spiritual exercises of *askēsis* and *theōria,* but that also could express this in philosophical discourse. Here I will speak primarily of the discourse itself in relation to its major creator, Evagrius of Pontus.[28]

Evagrius had a background and training rather different from that of most of the monks of his time. An educated Greek courtier, he arrived in the Egyptian desert in 382 CE after spending some time among the Origenists in Palestine. But his training under Macarius and others gave him a real reputation for *askēsis*. Palladius records his saying, "I did not touch lettuce or any vegetable greens, or fruit, or grapes, nor did I even take a bath, since the time I have come to the desert."[29] He was especially abstemious in drinking water, an element that he considered a particular instrument of diabolic temptations. But this "most learned man," as Rufinus describes him in the additions he made in his translation of the *Historia monachorum in Aegypto,* was especially noted for his "grace in the discernment of spirits and the purging of thoughts," which were so great that "it was thought that no other brother had ever achieved such subtle and spiritual knowledge."[30] Evagrius's impeccable credentials as a monastic ascetic and the profundity of his theology created what Louis Bouyer has justly called "the first complete system of Christian spirituality."[31]

The beginning of Evagrius's *Praktikos* summarizes this system in three stages that are based on Origen's three sciences. "Christianity is the teaching of Christ our Savior. It is composed of *praktikē* (practice) of the *theōria* (contemplation) of the physical world, and of the contemplation of God."[32] This ternary division, however, does not rule out binary forms of expression: "The *praktikoi* understand the practical reasons, but the *gnōstikoi* see gnostic realities," as we are told at the beginning of the *Gnostikos*.[33] Several things are immediately evident in these programatic statements: the adaption of Origen's threefold *paideia* to describe Christianity itself (something Origen would certainly have agreed with); the substitution of *praktikē* for *disciplina moralis;* and the use of the Platonic and Clementine vocabulary of *gnōstikos* along with the more usual *theōretikos* as contrasting terms with *praktikos*. Evagrius's structuring of the inherited terminology into a flexible program of a fundamentally binary character—that is, one based on *praktikē,* or asceticism, and *gnōstikē,* or mysticism—which program could also be expressed in more mediational language of a ternary kind (*praktikē, physikē, theologikē,* the ancestor of the later categories of purgation-illumination-union) was the *Magna Carta* of the main tradition of itineraries of Christian spirituality in both the East and the West.

Evagrius's contributions to subsequent programs of spirituality based on the inner relation of asceticism and mysticism went far beyond merely setting up the theoretical structure. His thought marks a new stage in the history of both asceticism and mysticism, though, because of his condemnation for Origenism in the sixth century he was to be more directly influential in the ascetical tradition. The three stages (*praktikē, physikē, theologikē*), the latter two constituting *gnōstikē* (which might be as easily called *mystikē*),[34] are specified by their aims according to Evagrius. At the end of the *Gnostikos* he summarizes: "The goal of *praktikē* is to purify the intellect and to render it impassible; that of the *physikē* is to reveal the truth hidden in all beings; but to remove the intellect from all material things and to turn it toward the First Cause is a gift of *theologikē*."[35] The monk's major theoretical works, all expressed in the chapter form which he appears to have adopted from the ethical-ascetical *Sentences of Sextus* and the desert tradition of *dicta*,[36] or sayings of the respected abbas and ammas, formed a systematic, if gnomical, trilogy he called the *Monachikos*. The *Praktikos* consists of a hundred chapters on the ascetical life and can be supplemented by several other ascetical works, especially the popular *Antirrheticus*.[37] The *Gnostikos* contains fifty chapters dealing with how the contemplative teaches spiritual knowledge. Both these works of a more practical character are based upon the speculative Origenist systematics found in the *Kephalaia gnostica*, six centuries of ninety chapters each.[38] Evagrius's teaching on *proseuchē* (prayer) a term that he used almost interchangably with *theōria* and *gnōsis*, was so essential to his mysticism that he devoted a separate treatise of 153 chapters to it. This work forms a useful supplement to the *Kephalaia*.[39]

Although Evagrius, as we have seen, was known for his asceticism, the *Praktikos* and the *Antirrheticus* are not manuals or rules detailing external practices, but rather speculative considerations and advice about the more important internal asceticism by which the monk learns to master the *logismoi* (the evil tendencies within) that are the work of the demonic forces and the main obstacles to the return of *nous* (soul, spirit) to its true goal of perfect union with the Trinity.[40] Evagrius's subtle teaching about the eight *logismoi (gastrimargia, porneia, philargyria, lypē, orgē, akēdia, xenodoxia, hyperphania)*, the ancestors of the "Seven Deadly Sins" of the later Western tradition,[41] make up the bulk of his ascetical writings. Even his ascetical treatises, however, always keep the mystical goal of the vision of the Trinity in mind, as the prologue to the *Antirrheticus* shows:

> We take pains that what will stand before the judgment seat of Christ is not a solitary man, but a solitary *nous*. For a solitary man is one who has turned from sin through his substantive deeds and actions, but a solitary *nous* is one who has turned from that sin that springs from the thoughts that reside in it and that sees the light of the Holy Trinity at the time of prayer.[42]

"Reading, vigils and prayer. . . . Hunger, toil and solitude" (*Praktikos* 15), as well as the characteristically Evagrian "Limiting one's intake of water" (*Praktikos* 17) all play their part in acquiring the science of *praktikē*, but the fundamental training occurs within, by keeping careful watch over one's thoughts. "Let him [the monk] note well the complexity of his thoughts, their periodicity, the demons which cause them, with the order of their succession and the nature of their associations. Then let him ask from Christ the explanations of these data he has observed" (*Praktikos* 50).

This monk's mystical teaching, while based upon Origen's view of the fall and return of the *nous* (also described as the *logikos*), was both original and controversial. Evagrius went well beyond Origen in a number of ways, especially his use of apophatic language and his notion of what can be called an absorptive concept of union with God, perhaps the earliest in the history of Christian mysticism. By making contemplative prayer, or "pure prayer" in his terms,[43] the goal of the monastic life Evagrius made explicit a marriage between the developing forms of monasticism, in which the early rules generally say little about contemplation, and the rich tradition of Greek speculation about *theōria*.[44] For the theme under consideration, it is also important to take a brief look at the ways in which Evagrius drew out the inner connections between the ascetical and the mystical parts of his spiritual program through his treatment of *apatheia* and *agapē*.

Apatheia, the "health of the soul" as Evagrius called it (*Prak.* 56), was a key term in his spiritual vocabulary.[45] Perfect *apatheia,* which "develops in the soul after the victory over all the demons whose function it is to offer opposition to the ascetic life" (*Prak.* 60), has been well described by John Eudes Bamberger as "deep calm arising from the full and harmonious integration of the emotional life."[46] An important passage in the "Letter to Anatolius" that prefaces the *Praktikos* describes the relation between *apatheia* and *agapē* as the two forces whose dynamic relation binds together the ascetical and the mystical stages of the Evagrian spiritual itinerary:

> The fear of God strengthens faith, my son, and continence in turn strengthens this fear. Patience and hope make the latter virtue solid beyond all shaking and they also give birth to *apatheia*. Now this *apatheia* has a child called *agapē* who keeps the door to deep knowledge of the created universe [that is, *physikē*]. Finally, to this knowledge succeed theology and the supreme beatitude.[47]

A more complete investigation than can be given here would reveal that *apatheia* and *agapē* can be considered as two sides of the same *katastasis* (state of soul) the goal of all ascetic effort and the necessary precondition for the pure prayer, the two stages of which lead to "essential *gnōsis* of the Trinity."[48]

Greek Christian speculation about the relation of asceticism to mysticism became available to Latin Christianity in the fourth and the fifth centuries. Origen's analysis of the three kinds of teaching—the moral, the natural and the mystical—that lead to loving union with the Word was adopted by Ambrose of Milan in his treatise *De Isaac,* which despite its title is really a mystical commentary on the *Song of Songs*.[49] The bishop describes this triple pattern of the soul's progress as *institutio, profectus,* and *perfectio* (*De Isaac* 8.68–70), language that already hints at the standard three stages that were to prove so popular later, especially through the influence of the Dionysian texts. Augustine of Hippo, on the other hand, was little touched by Origen, in this area at least, and did not see the *Song of Songs* as a mystical text in the sense of containing the deepest message about the soul's erotic relation to God. Augustine's adoption of Plotinian motifs in describing the soul's ascent to the divine realm, both in the *Confessions* and in later works actually stands on the margin of the mainstream of subsequent attempts at structuring the spiritual journey.[50] More important for our theme (and I must stress that I am considering only one element of a complex picture here) was the North African's teaching on the relation of the active and the contemplative lives. Augustine, building on earlier philosophical accounts,[51] as well as on the Christian transformation of the meaning of the *vita activa* already noted, taught that contemplation of divine things was superior to action conceived of as loving service to neighbor, but that the highest ideal was the interaction of action and contemplation in what he called the *vita composita.* "No one should be so contemplative that in his contemplation he does not think of his neighbor's need; no one so active that he does not seek the contemplation of God."[52]

The system of Evagrius,[53] especially as disseminated by his student, John Cassian, the third of the founders of Western Christian mysticism,[54] was as important in the West as it was in the East, particularly because of its role in the institutionalization of an integrated program of asceticism and mysticism within the monastic life. Cassian, a monk trained in both Palestine and Egypt, fled the East at the time of the first Origenist controversy about 400 CE, eventually settling in southern Gaul. His writings, the *Institutiones,* which described the external practices of the Eastern coenobites, and the *Conlationes,* the teachings of the Desert Fathers about the interior life, were the most important link between early monasticism and the monks of the West.

Cassian was neither so original nor so systematic a thinker as Evagrius; but his somewhat simplified and practical version of the Evagrian understanding of the relation of asceticism and mysticism set the mold within which early medieval spirituality, largely monastic in character, appropriated this theme. *Conlatio* 14, put in the mouth of Abba Nestorius, divides *spiritalis scientia* (spiritual knowledge) into two parts: "First there is practical, that is, active science, which is perfected in correcting moral actions and purging vices; and second, the theoretical science, which consists in the contemplation of divine things and the grasp of the most sacred meanings [of Scripture]."[55] *Scientia actualis,* what Scaramelli would later call ascetical theology, has both a negative and a positive side. Negatively, the monk strives to overcome the eight principal vices, Evagrius's *logismoi* that Cassian introduced to the West; positively, asceticism acquires and orders the virtues under the direction of *puritas cordis* (purity of heart), which was Cassian's more biblically oriented term for Evagrius's *apatheia.* Purity of heart is described as the *scopos,* or *destinatio,* of the monastic life, that is, the proper aim or intention which makes the ultimate goal of the enjoyment of heaven possible (*Conl.* 1.4). In a sense, Cassian integrated both parts of his ascetico-mystical itinerary even more closely than Evagrius. Purity of heart is at one and the same time tranquil avoidance of vice (*Conl.* 1.6) and "the perfection of apostolic charity."[56] The *Gospel of Matthew* 5.8 had promised the vision of God to the pure of heart, so that Cassian saw the *puritas cordis* gained through constant repetition of the formula of "unceasing prayer" (*Deus in adiutorium meum intende: Domine ad adiuvandum me festina,* cf. *Psalms* 69.2, in the Septuagint) as leading to *theoriae* (invisible and celestial contemplations) and to that inexpressible fire of prayer experienced by very few" (*Conl.* 10.10).

Cassian's description of *scientia theoretikē* differs from that of Evagrius in being directly tied to the Bible, its two parts being described as "historical interpretation" and "spiritual understanding, which consists in tropology, allegory and anagogy" (*Conl.* 14.8). Thus, like Origen, the whole program of monastic education for him was explicitly biblical; he even cites the Origenist identification of Solomon's three books with three ascending stages of the soul's progress, though tying them in, with a typically monastic twist, to three forms of renunciation. The *Book of Proverbs* teaches the renunciation of the flesh and earthly things; the *Book of Ecclesiastes* teaches the vanity of the world, while the *Song of Songs* instructs the soul in the renunciation of "every present visible thing" so that "the mind transcending everything visible is joined to God's Word by the contemplation of heavenly things" (*Conl.* 3.6).

Cassian also discussed the relation of action and contemplation, but only in a monastic vein. *Conlatio* 19 identifies the *vita activa* with the coenobitic life of the community, while the *vita contemplativa* is primarily associated with hermits. But things are not quite that simple. The heights of *scientia theologikē* can be reached by coenobites too (see *Conl.* 9.25–27); and Cassian appears to think that some mixing of action and contemplation is found in both kinds of monasticism, although his thoughts on this topic are not notably clear. His monastic reading of the two forms of life, however, was to be modified by his early medieval successors, notably Julianus Pomerius and Gregory the Great.

Julianus was a late fifth-century Gallic church leader, poised between the dying world of bishops like Sidonius Apollinaris, who could still think of themselves as Roman gentlemen, albeit of Christian persuasion, and the Western episcopate of the seventh century—educators, missionaries and functionaries who could only dream of belonging to a world that no longer existed. His popular work called *De vita contemplativa* was a handbook for bishops describing how to relate the active life (of restraining the passions and performing works of charity) to the contemplative life (of the vision of God, which can only be fully enjoyed in heaven, but to whose foretaste not just monks, but even bishops are called), ". . . Who will be such a stranger to faith as to doubt that such men are sharers in the contemplative virtue, by whose words as well as example many become coheirs of the kingdom of heaven?"[57]

It was Gregory the Great, pope from 590 to 604 CE, who gave the most thought to the question of the proper relation between action and contemplation, and whose views on this subject were to become normative for almost the entire medieval period. This is not the place to go into the details of the pope's understanding of either asceticism or mysticism; but, in order to complete this sketch of the pre-Dionysian development of our theme, at least in the West, we can highlight four major contributions that he made to the later history. First, Gregory recognized an important ascetic element present in all the charitable activities of the *vita activa.* For him there were two ways of carrying the cross in imitation of the Redeemer—"*aut per abstinentiam in corpore . . . aut per compassionem in corde*" (either through abstinence in the body, or through compassion in the heart).[58] Gregory's broad and deeply interiorized conception of asceticism is still in need of further study.[59] Second, the pope taught that contemplation could not be restricted to the monastic life, or even to bishops. As a text in his *Homilies on Ezekiel* puts it:

> For it is not that the grace of contemplation is given to the highest [the clergy] and not to the least, but frequently the highest, frequently the least, more frequently "those set apart" [*remoti,* that is, the monks], and sometimes even the married receive it. Therefore, there is no Christian state from which the grace of contemplation can

be excluded. Whoever has an interior heart can be illuminated by the light of contemplation. . . .[60]

Third, Gregory furthered the movement away from the purely monastic understanding of action and contemplation found in Cassian. His teaching was fundamentally Augustinian in that it accepted both modes of life as good and saw contemplation as the superior life, but insisted that contemplation must yield to the demands of active love when necessary. Fourth, and perhaps most important, Gregory went beyond both Augustine and Julianus in his discussion of the conditions under which contemplation must yield to action and the reasons why an oscillation between the two is necessary in the Christian life. Fuller development of this dimension, however, would lead us away from the issue of the fundamental structural relations between asceticism and mysticism that has been our main concern.

Asceticism and mysticism are modern terms and the legitimacy of applying them throughout almost twenty centuries of Christian history is not without its dangers. Nevertheless, I have suggested that the effort of placing what later ages came to call asceticism and mysticism into a coherent and integrated program of spiritual training that has a succession down almost to the present era is rooted in the encounter between Christianity and Hellenism between c.200 and 400 CE. Clement and Origen were the initiators, and Origen's adaptation of the classical threefold program of *paideia* in the service of Christian biblical culture marked the first great stage. The second stage came with monasticism and is evident in writers such as Evagrius and Cassian who can—paradoxically for some—be seen as the last ancient philosophers: that is, writers who used their experience of the atopic life to create a philosophical discourse fusing ascetic self-denial with contemplative vision of God. A complicating factor, one viewed in different ways by the participants, was how far the categories of *praktikē* and *theoretikē,* that is, *actio* and *contemplatio,* were to be used to express these stages on the road to Christian perfection.

NOTES

1. For an introduction to Scaramelli, see Giuseppe Mellinato, "Scaramelli (Jean-Baptiste)," *Dictionnaire de spiritualité,* eds. M. Viller, S.J., et al., 14:396–402.
2. Thirteen Italian editions during the seventeenth and eighteenth centuries, two editions of the Latin translation, and translations into Spanish, German, French, Polish, and English.
3. See Michel de Certeau, "'Mystique' au XVIIe siècle: Le problème du langage 'mystique,'" *L'Homme devant Dieu: Mélanges offerts au Pere Henri de Lubac* (Paris: Aubier, 1963), 2:267–291; and *The Mystic Fable,* volume 1, *The Sixteenth and Seventeenth Centuries* (Chicago: University of Chicago, 1992), pp. x, 3–13.
4. On the early evolution of the term, see "Ascèse, Ascétisme," *DS* 1:939–941.
5. The early appearances of both terms cited in the *Oxford English Dictionary* were often pejorative ones. In 1646, Sir Thomas Browne in his *Pseudegraphia Epigrapha* spoke of those who were ". . . doomed to a life a celibacy by the asceticism which had corrupted the simplicity of Christianity." In 1763 John Wesley's *Journal* spoke of the "poison of mysticism" that has "extinguished every spark of life."
6. Bernard McGinn, *The Foundations of Mysticism: Origins to the Fifth Century* (New York: Crossroad, 1991), pp. 89–99.

7. For a recent interpretation of gnostic mysticism, see Bentley Layton, *The Gnostic Scriptures* (Garden City: Doubleday, 1987). A summary of "Gnostic Spirituality" by R. M. Grant can be found in *Christian Spirituality I: Origins to the Twelfth Century* (New York: Crossroad, 1985), pp. 44–60.
8. *Quis dives salvetur* 36 (ed. O. Stählin, *Die griechischen christlichen Schriftsteller der ersten drei Jahrhunderte* [Leipzig, 1897–1941; Berlin and Leipzig, 1953; Berlin 1954ff.], 3:183); cf. *Stromateis* 5.14.141 (*GCS* 2:421).
9. This is not to deny the modified esotericism found in thinkers like Clement and Origen, which is part of an important trajectory in early Christian thought. Clement, with his teaching on the *gnostikē paradosis* (*Strom.* 1.1.15), is the clearest example; but Origen's *Contra Celsum* also witnesses to this motif (e.g., 1.7, 3.60, 4.6). See Gedaliahu Stroumsa, "*Paradosis:* traditions ésoteriques dans le christianisme des premiers siècles," *Savoir et salut* (Paris: Cerf, 1992), pp. 127–143. Others were more radically opposed, for example, Irenaeus, *Libros quinque adversus haereses,* 3.3.1.
10. Gedaliahu Stroumsa, "Ascèse et gnose: Aux origines de la spiritualité monastique," *Revue Thomiste* 81 (1981):557–573 (quote on 570). This paper is also reprinted in *Savoir et salut,* pp. 145–162.
11. See Plotinus, *Enneads* 2.9.15.
12. On the relation between Christianity and classical education, see especially Henry Chadwick, *Early Christian Thought and the Classical Tradition* (New York: Oxford University Press, 1966); and Werner Jaeger, *Early Christianity and Greek Paideia* (New York: Oxford University Press, 1969).
13. See Samuel Rubenson, *The Letters of St. Antony: Origenist Theology, Monastic Tradition and the Making of a Saint* (Lund: Lund University Press, 1990).
14. For example, *Strom.* 4.21.132 and 7.7.46 (*GCS* 2:306.33, 3:35.10) Clement uses *askēsis* twenty-seven times and *askētēs* six times.
15. For a useful overview, see Nicholas Lobkowicz, *Theory and Practice: History of a Concept from Aristotle to Marx* (Notre Dame: University of Notre Dame Press, 1967). For Christian uses, see P. T. Camelot, "Action et contemplation dans la tradition chrétienne," *La Vie Spirituelle* 78 (1948):272–301; and Aime Solignac, "Vie active, vie contemplative, vie mixte," in *DS* 16:592–623.
16. "*Strom.* 2.10.46 (*GCS* 2:137.14–16); cf. 7.1.4.
17. Henri Crouzel, in his *Origen* (San Francisco: Harper and Row, 1989), pp. 167–169, 266, insists that he did not; but Crouzel's understanding of "system" seems unduly rigid; and his denial of system in Origen is also tinged by the desire to maintain Origen's orthodoxy at all costs.
18. Eusebius, *Church History* 6.3.6–9.
19. The Latin text can be found in the *GCS, Origenes Werke VII,* ed. W. A. Baehrens, pp. 255–280. I will cite from the translation of Rowan A. Greer, *Origen* (New York: Paulist Press, 1979), pp. 245–269.
20. Other stages that seem to indicate what we can call mystical aspects of the journey include number 35 (*Selmona,* or "shadow of the portion" of Christ and the Holy Spirit) and number 326 (*Phinon,* or the "frugality of mouth" that follows contemplation of Christ and the Holy Spirit).
21. The text of the *Commentary* has been edited by Baehrens in *GCS, Origenes Werke VIII* (the *prologus* appears on pp. 61–88). I will use the translation of Greer in *Origen,* pp. 217–244.
22. The correct name for the third science is *epoptics,* not *enoptics* as Greer, following some versions, reads. As in so much else, Origen's program was foreshadowed in Clement,

who, in *Strom.* 1.28.176 (*GCS* 2:108–109) fits the four divisions of "Mosaic philosophy" into the three branches of philosophy—the historic and the legislative belong to ethics; the sacrificial to physics; "and the fourth, above all the department of theology, *epopteia,* which Plato predicates of the truly great mysteries."

23. On the importance of the three sciences in Origen's thought, see Andrew Louth, *The Origins of the Christian Mystical Tradition* (Oxford: Clarendon Press, 1981), pp. 56–62; and Karl Rahner, "The 'Spiritual Senses' according to Origen," *Theological Investigations* (New York: Seabury, 1979), 16:92–94.
24. Pierre Hadot, "Les divisions des parties de la philosophie dans l'antiquité," *Museum Helveticum* 36 (1979):218–231. Cf. the same author's "Théologie, exégèse, révelation, écriture, dans la philosophie grecque," *Centre d'études des religions du livre: Les règles de l'interprétation,* ed. Michel Tardieu (Paris: Cerf, 1987), pp. 13–34; and "Forms of Life and Forms of Discourse in Ancient Philosophy," *Critical Inquiry* 16 (1990):218–231.
25. On this question, see the studies collected in Pierre Hadot, *Exercises spirituels et philosophie antique,* 2d ed. (Paris, 1987); as well as Peter Brown, *The Philosopher and Society in Late Antiquity. The Center for Hermeneutical Studies: Protocol of the Thirty-Fourth Colloquium,* eds. E. C. Hobbs and W. Weullner (Berkeley: University of California Press, 1978).
26. Evagrius Ponticus, *Praktikos. Chapters on Prayer,* ed. and trans. John Eudes Bamberger (Spencer, Mass.: Cistercian Publications, 1970); see especially *Chapters on Prayer* 60 (p. 65).
27. See Karen Jo Torjesen, *Hermeneutical Procedure and Theological Method in Origen's Exegesis* (Berlin: de Gruyter, 1986), pp. 39–41, 130–138. Cf. Marguerite Harl, "Le langage de l'expérience religieuse chez les pères grecs," *Rivista di storia e letteratura religiosa* 15 (1977):5–34.
28. For the account of Evagrius that follows, as well as for comments on the literature, see *Foundations of Mysticism,* pp. 144–157.
29. *Palladius: The Lausiac History,* translated and annotated by Robert T. Meyer (Westminster: Newman, 1965), 38.12 (p. 114). Most of what we know of Evagrius's life comes from this chapter of the *Historia Lausiaca.*
30. See *The Lives of the Desert Fathers,* trans. Norman Russell (London: Mowbray, 1981), 20.15, with "Additions of Rufinus" (p. 150).
31. Louis Bouyer, *The Spirituality of the New Testament and the Fathers* (New York: Seabury, 1982), p. 381.
32. *Praktikos,* eds. Antoine and Claire Guillaumont, 2 vols. (Paris: Cerf, 1971). I will generally use the translation of John Eudes Bamberger, *The Praktikos. Chapters on Prayer* 15 (here adapted).
33. *Évagre le Pontique. Le Gnostique,* eds. Antoine and Claire Guillaumont (Paris: Cerf, 1989), p. 88.
34. The term, to my knowledge, does not occur in the surviving Greek texts of Evagrius, but it is found in his master Origen. See *Commentary on Lamentations,* fragment 14, in *GCS, Origenes Werke* 3:241.3f.
35. *Gnostikos,* ed. Guillaumont, 49.191.
36. On the second-century *Sentences of Sextus,* see the edition of Henry Chadwick (Cambridge: Cambridge University Press, 1959), pp. 161–162 for the influence on Evagrius.
37. For a partial translation and discussion, see *Ascetic Behavior in Greco-Roman Antiquity: A Sourcebook,* ed. Vincent L. Wimbush (Minneapolis: Fortress, 1990), pp. 243–262.

38. This survives in two Syriac versions, S1 and S2, of which the latter is more authentic. See the edition of Antoine Guillaumont, *Les six centuries des "Kephalaia Gnostica" d'Évagre le Pontique* (Paris: Firmin-Didot, 1958). There is a translation of the first century in Wimbush, *Ascetic Behavior,* pp. 175–186. The threefold division appears in numerous chapters of the *Kephalaia,* for example, 1.10 and 5.65.
39. The *De oratione* may be found in *PG* 79:1165–1200.
40. Though the struggle against the demons is most evident on the level of *praktikē,* their opposition is also experienced in *physikē* and *theologikē.* See *KG* 1.10: "Among the demons, certain oppose the practice of the commandments, others oppose thoughts of nature, and others oppose words *(logoi)* about divinity because the knowledge of our salvation is constituted from these three" (*Ascetic Behavior,* p. 178).
41. For an overview of the development, see A. Solignac, "Péchés capitaux," *DS* 12:853–862.
42. Evagrius Ponticus, *Antirrheticus,* prologue (*Ascetic Behavior,* p. 248).
43. For Evagrius's teaching on pure prayer, see, for example, *Chapters on Prayer* 30, 53, 55, 60, 67, 70, 72, 75, 80, 97, 113, 153. For the broader doctrine, see David A. Ousley, "Evagrius's Theology of Prayer and the Spiritual Life," Ph.D. diss., University of Chicago, 1979.
44. See John Eudes Bamberger's introduction to the *Chapters on Prayer* in *Praktikos,* pp. 45–46.
45. On *apatheia,* see especially *Praktikos* 57–89. For background, see Bamberger, *Praktikos,* pp. 82–87; and "Apatheia," *DS* 1:734–736.
46. Bamberger, *Praktikos,* p. 84.
47. Bamberger, *Praktikos* 14. Cf. *Prak.* 81 and 84 for other expressions of this inner relationship.
48. On the role of *apatheia* in pure prayer, see, for example, *KG* 1.27 and 81, 2.4, and 5.75; for the knowledge of the Trinity, see *KG* 2.2–3, 3.42 and 5.40.
49. For example, Ambrose, *De Isaac* 4.17–32 (ed. C. Schenkl, Corpus scriptorum ecclesiasticorum latinorum [Vienna, 1866ff.], 32.1:655–661). See the discussion in *Foundations of Mysticism,* p. 210; and especially, Solange Sagot, "Le triple sagesse dans le *De Isaac vel anima:* Essai sur les procédés de composition de saint Ambroise," *Ambroise de Milan: XVI*[e] *centenaire de son élection épiscopale* (Paris: Etudes Augustiniennes, 1974), pp. 67–114.
50. For this aspect of Augustine's thought, see *Foundations of Mysticism,* pp. 232–243. More extensive discussions can be found in Paul Henry, *The Path to Transcendence: From Philosophy to Mysticism in St. Augustine* (Philadelphia: Pickwick Press, 1981); and Suzanne Poque, "L'expression de l'anabase plotinienne dans la prédication de saint Augustin et ses sources," *Recherches augustiniennes* 10 (1977):187–215.
51. A number of earlier Latin authors had taught the superiority of the mixed form of life that combined action and contemplation, that is, at least as understood in philosophy. For example, Cicero, *De finibus* 2.13.40; and Seneca, *De otio* 5.1, 5.8.
52. Augustine, *De civitate Dei* 19.19, where he also criticizes Varro's understanding of the three forms of life (cf. *De civitate Dei* 8.4). There is a brief discussion in *Foundations of Mysticism,* pp. 256–257.
53. Some of Evagrius's own writings were available in Latin. The *Antirrheticus* and the *Gnostikos* were both translated by Gennadius, but these have been lost. Two Latin versions of the *Mirror for Monks and Nuns* survive.
54. What follows is based in part on *Foundations of Mysticism,* pp. 218–227. On the relations between Evagrius and Cassian, the best study remains that of Salvatore Marsili,

Giovanni Cassiano ed Evagrio Pontico: Dottrına sulla carıta e contemplazione (Rome: Herder, 1936).

55. *Conlationes* 14.1, ed. E. Pichéry, 3 vols. This text can be found ın 2:184.

56. *Instıtutes* 4.43: "Purıty of heart is acquired by the flowering of the virtues, and the perfectıon of apostolic charity is possessed by means of purity of heart" (ed. J. -C. Guy in Sources chrétiennes [Paris, 1940ff.], 109.184.16–17).

57. *De vıta contemplativa* 1.25 (*PL* 59.410B). See the translatıon and study by Sister Mary Josephine Suelzer, *Julıanus Pomerıus: The Contemplative Life* (New York: Paulist Press, 1947).

58. Gregory, *Homılıa ın Evangelia* 32.3 (*PL* 76.1234BC). Cf. *Hom.* 37.5 (1277AB).

59. There are, of course, a number of useful studies. See especıally, Carole Straw, *Gregory the Great: Perfection in Imperfection* (Berkeley: University of California Press, 1988), chapter 6; Robert Gıllet, "Spiritualıté et place du moine dans l'église selon Grégoire le Grand," *Théologıe de la vie monastıque* (Parıs: Aubier, 1961), pp. 323–351; and Jean Laporte, "Une théologie systematique chez Grégoire?" in *Grégoire le Grand*, eds. Jacques Fontaine, Robert Gillet, and Stan Pellıstrandi (Parıs: Centre Natıonale de la Recherche Scıentifique, 1986), pp. 235–244.

60. Gregory the Great, *Homilia in Ezechıelem* 2.5.19 (SC 360.264.2–10).

6

Practical, Theoretical, and Cultural Tracings in Late Ancient Asceticism

RESPONSE TO THE THREE PRECEDING PAPERS

Teresa M. Shaw

Our three papers, which share some points of interest on the general landscape of ancient ascetic behavior, suggest directions or trajectories for a broad discussion of the origins and meaning of ascetic behavior and interpretation in religion and culture. They raise questions of particular interest for those of us studying the Greco-Roman religious world of late antiquity. Clark's paper, especially, raises the question of the social and cultural meanings of ascetic behaviors. What does the renunciation of marriage, a meager diet, simple clothing, or communal living communicate to the dominant culture? How do these behaviors critique or validate existing social and power structures? How do physical techniques and practical lifestyles represent theological formulations? To borrow Clark's terms, does the "negative" act of renunciation allow both negative and positive formulations of its religious and social meaning? Rubenson has challenged our assumptions about class, education, and literary production among early desert monastics and illustrated the ways in which those assumptions have shaped our understanding of the formation of Egyptian ascetic theology.

In tracing the influence of the Greek philosophical treatments of *praxis* or *askēsis* and *theōria* on early Christian ascetic theory and the development of a Christian *paideia,* McGinn throws light on two crucial issues: the ties between pagan philosophical asceticism and its early Christian counterpart; and the relationship between physical renunciation and psychological or contemplative discipline. The same issues concern Clark, and also Rubenson, for the standard view of Antony which he rejects depends on a split between "high" philosophical or contemplative asceticism and "low" physical asceticism. For this response I will take up three general themes that have especially intrigued me: the role of physical and contemplative disciplines in the spiritual life; the relationship between pagan philosophical and Christian asceticism (I will discuss these two issues in light of Evagrius of Pontus); and the interpretation of ascetic behavior in culture and society. Here I will briefly consider female asceticism.

It is interesting to me that McGinn draws connections between philosophical and Christian asceticism by demonstrating the Christian use of the earlier delineation of *praxis* and *theōria*. This more philosophical or theoretical strain in Christian asceticism is the focus of McGinn's paper. For Clark, on the other hand, whatever direct or indirect influence of classical and Hellenistic philosophical *askēsis* on Christian ascetic theory may be demonstrated, the evidence that some ascetic masters and writers advocated self-inflicted bodily suffering (rather than mere endurance of hardship) constitutes Christianity's "radical break" with the earlier traditions. Further, Clark is not surprised that Christian ascetic practices were "puzzling and repellent to non-Christians." In these particular discussions in their respective papers, at least, one might guess that McGinn and Clark are examining two different groups, both answering to the name of Christian ascetics.

Of course neither Clark nor McGinn would paint this small a picture; but the contrasting sketches found here and the sources each author uses remind us of a basic tension in early Christian ascetic literature. Hagiographical accounts of rigorous, even extreme, ascetic mortifications exist alongside treatises and other more theoretical ascetic writings which emphasize the need for moderation. To some extent, this distinction may be accounted for by the functions of literary genres: hagiography tends to incorporate more bizarre details and wondrous events and persons. Very often, however, both emphases are in the same text. Stated more broadly, the practical and the theoretical are tightly interwoven in the ascetic life. The physical discipline and the philosophical or contemplative process, while distinguishable both by ancient writers and modern scholars, are rarely separable in an individual's life as it unfolds.

Evagrius of Pontus, mentioned by all three of the papers under consideration, is a useful and challenging example of this tension. Well educated, trained by the premier philosopher-theologians of his day as well as by the ascetic heroes of the Egyptian desert, Evagrius's writings and career show the influence not only of Clement, Origen, the Cappadocian fathers, and Melania the Elder, but also of Macarius the Great and Macarius of Alexandria, and, if Rubenson is correct, of Antony himself. As McGinn has noted, in his time Evagrius was famous not only for his superior theoretical understanding and ability to discern thoughts, but also for his "incredible" abstinence.[1] Palladius records Evagrius as saying, "Since I arrived in the desert I have not eaten lettuce or any other green vegetable, nor fruit, nor grapes, nor meat, nor [have I taken] baths." At the end of his life, Palladius notes, Evagrius evaluated his own success in the desert by his endurance in fasting, and by the fact that he had not suffered from sexual desire for the three years before his death.[2]

This Evagrius—tested and shaped by the harshness of the desert—seems different from the Evagrius we encounter in the esoteric cosmological and eschatological reflections of the *Kephalaia gnostica* and the *Letter to Melania*. Because of the very different types of texts attributed to Evagrius, as well as the different strands of influence on his thought, we face the danger of making a fragmented assessment. It is easy, for example, to attribute Evagrius's practical teachings and his own ascetic rigors to his relationship with the masters of the Egyptian desert; and to attribute his more speculative theological notions to philosophical training outside of the desert. In this assessment, we risk oversimplification not only of Evagrius the philosopher-ascetic, but also the personalities of his teachers. Rubenson has similarly shown, in his discussion of the scholarly assessment of Antony, how the tendency to "fit" ancient personalities into modern analytic molds may actually prevent us from seeing the larger historical picture—in this case, the development of ascetic thought and practice from Antony to Evagrius.

Further, the complex relationship between the practical and the contemplative—the *praktikē* and the *gnōstikē*—in the ascetic journey cannot be delineated with bold strokes. As McGinn has illustrated, it is clear that Evagrius distinguishes between, and establishes a hierarchy of, these two phases in the spiritual life. Physical ascetic exercise, the battle against thoughts, and the pursuit of virtue lead one toward the goal of *apatheia,* which is by no means the high goal, but only the entry into the next level—*gnōstikē*—at which the goal is spiritual knowledge or theology, the contemplation of God. But in our efforts to understand the Evagrian system it is a mistake to *separate* the *praktikē* from the *gnōstikē;* both are integral to the process of salvation and return to original unity. Physical training, including fasting, vigils, chastity, and withdrawal, is fundamental in order to battle successfully against thoughts. And the one who has already progressed to the level of *gnōstikē* does not abandon bodily *askēsis.* In the *Gnostikos,* for example, Evagrius warns: "Do not soften the dietary regimen of your life and do not insult the *apatheia* by degrading it with a fat body."[3]

Evagrius understood what Clement of Alexandria and other Christian and pagan theorists, philosophers, and physicians knew: that the state of one's body affected the state of one's soul. Thus, for example, Galen writes, "the character of the soul is corrupted by bad habits in food, drink, exercise, sights, sounds, and music."[4]

Further, scholarly distinctions between practical or physical and contemplative or mystical exercise—while useful categories for analysis which were certainly articulated by the ancients themselves—must not disguise the fact that often one and the same person is ascetic and mystic, wonder worker, and teacher. This may be said of both pagan philosophers and Christian ascetics. In the same way, it seems to me, we should be careful about our characterizations of and comparisons between ancient and Hellenistic philosophical *askēsis* and Christian ascetic practice and theology. Of course there are clear and significant differences between Macarius of Alexandria's standing naked in a mosquito-ridden swamp for six months[5] and the philosopher in contemplative withdrawal to the household garden. Nevertheless Christian and pagan philosophical asceticism cannot simply be divided according to degree of physical deprivation or degree of support for the dominant culture, civic life, or social order.

In fact, James A. Francis argues that an examination of this watershed period indicates that pagan ascetics such as Peregrinus Proteus and Apollonius of Tyana were suspect for many of the same reasons that Christian ascetics would later be problematic for ecclesiastical authorities in the fourth century: their behaviors and the individual charismatic authority they enjoyed threatened traditional societal norms and the status quo. Francis thus persuasively delineates the potentially subversive character of pagan asceticism and argues that the hostility of pagan writers and authorities toward Christian asceticism can only be understood in the context of their own familiarity with the power expressed and claimed by ascetic behavior.[6]

This issue of the relationship of ascetic behavior and theory to society takes us back to Gillian Clark's question—what signals are sent to a particular society by ascetic lifestyle and renunciations—and to the broader question of asceticism and culture. Clark has suggested that early Christian ascetic behaviors can be interpreted "negatively" as rejections of marriage, sexual relations, procreation, and traditional gender and social relations—all born out of a basic rejection of the body; or, more "positively," as efforts to return—body and soul—to the condition of paradise before the Fall. These interpretations are in some sense two sides of the same coin. The denigration of marriage and sexuality may be the negative expression of the desire to return to the original blessings of paradise and the original, blessed condition of humanity and body. (And, of course, early Christian ascetic theorists understood both the similarities and differences between these two notions, and went to great lengths to distinguish the "orthodox" affirmation of the value of chastity, fasting, and other ascetic disciplines from the "heretical"—namely Manichaean, Encratite—condemnation of marriage and meat eating.)

The fourth-century ascetic interpretation of the *Book of Genesis* account of creation and the Fall typically saw marriage, procreation through sexual intercourse, physical labor, agriculture, cooking, meat eating, gender hierarchy (or gender differentiation itself), and, in general, the human obsession with meeting the needs and desires of the body, as results of the Fall. Indeed, these are enterprises of humanity's fall into *culture;* and they will be eliminated in the Kingdom. The notion of an earlier, superior condition of humanity, free from cultural pursuits and technologies, is also found in the myth of the golden age, which Porphyry uses to argue for the value of a vegetarian diet. Thus what Geoffrey Harpham calls the "yearning for the precultural, postcultural, anticultural, or extracultural"[7] is, here in early Christian and philosophical asceticism, played out not only in bodily behaviors which identify the individual with the earlier ideal, but also in the protological and theological constructs which interpret that behavior. I would be interested to know if ascetic disciplines in cultures and religious traditions outside of these Greco-Roman and early Christian settings are similarly interpreted through the lens of protological myth.

In any event, we should not separate the theological formulations of ancient and modern "spin doctors" of ascetic theory from the physical discipline. At least in the case of the fourth-century East, one does not make sense without the other. I have found this to be most evident in the example of female asceticism. In order to make sense of treatises and hagiographies that praise, if not advocate, the mortification of the female body to the point of its being no longer recognizable or socially functional as female (even, in some cases, to the point of amenorrhea), scholars must take account not only of ancient medical models and physiology, but also of theological interpretations of creation, embodiment, the Fall, and the cycle of procreation and death (a cycle perpetuated through the fertile female body).[8]

Finally, there are issues we have not discussed directly, but which seem important. One is how texts are used in the process of institutionalization and in the domestication of radical elements in asceticism. For example, although John Cassian was clearly influenced by Evagrian practice and theology, he does not mention his teacher's name, and Evagrius's system is cleaned up and repackaged for presentation to the West in Cassian's writings. Thus, the Evagrian goal of *apatheia* becomes *puritas cordis* (purity of heart). Similarly, hagiographical texts not only establish models for imitation in the spiritual life, but can also serve to rein in the spiritual authority attached to individual ascetic heroes like Antony. I would be interested in Rubenson's views on this regarding the *Life of Antony*.

Second, Clark has argued that ascetic renunciation for women often involved a rejection of social status. It seems to me, however, that in many of our sources the ascetic life enhanced or at least did not significantly diminish status. Melania the Elder and Melania the Younger are particularly good examples. After taking up the ascetic life, their élite social networks, standing, financial resources, and influence remained key factors in their fame as renouncers and founders of ascetic communities. Further, their friends and enemies alike were powerful and prominent ecclesiastical and political figures. In the two Melanias we meet not anonymous withdrawal and rejection of status but visible and public wielding of influence and power.

Third, I am curious as to what McGinn thinks is the usefulness of the distinction between asceticism and mysticism. How does the distinction enhance the scholarly discussion, and what are its dangers?

NOTES

1. *Historia monachorum in Aegypto* (Latin) 27 (*PL* 21.449A).
2. Palladius, *Historia Lausiaca* 38, ed. Cuthbert Butler, *The Lausiac History of Palladius*, 2 vols. (Cambridge: Cambridge University Press, 1898, 1904), 2:122.
3. Evagrius of Pontus, *Gnostikos* 37, eds. Antoine and Claire Guillaumont, *Évagre le Pontique: Le gnostique*, Sources chrétiennes 356 (Paris: Éditions du Cerf, 1989), p. 158.
4. Galen, *De sanitate tuenda* 1.8, ed. C. G. Kuhn, *Galeni Opera Omnia* (Leipzig: K. Knobloch, 1823–1833; reprint, Hildesheim: George Olms, 1965), 6:40.
5. Palladius, *Historia Lausiaca* 18 (Butler, 2:48–49).
6. James A. Francis, *Subversive Virtue: Asceticism and Authority in the Pagan World of the Second Century* CE (University Park: Pennsylvania State University Press, 1994), chapter 6.
7. Geoffrey Galt Harpham, *The Ascetic Imperative in Culture and Criticism* (Chicago: University of Chicago Press, 1987), p. xii.
8. I address these topics in *The Burden of the Flesh: Fasting and the Female Body in Early Christian Ascetic Theory* (Minneapolis: Fortress Press, forthcoming).

7

Rejecting the Body, Refining the Body: Some Remarks on the Development of Platonist Asceticism

John M. Dillon

It will be my purpose in this paper to examine the Platonist contribution to the European tradition of asceticism,[1] with a view to elucidating what seem to me to be two significant strands in that tradition, both stemming from Plato himself, but developing separate histories in later times: that of straightforward rejection of the body, or at least of the soul's association with it, which involves what I would identify as a negative attitude to the world; and that of the disciplining and refining of the body, to make it a worthy, or at least noninjurious receptacle of the soul, which might be seen, I think, as essentially world-affirming. Both of these objectives involve practices that might fairly be termed ascetic—and, indeed largely the very same practices—but it will become evident, I think, that the perspectives on the body are distinct.[2]

Both attitudes, however, could be seen to derive from Plato himself, and it is with Plato that I wish to begin. Plato's most notable expression of rejection of the body occurs in the *Phaedo*. The fact that Socrates is here about to depart this life provides a suitable context for Plato's expression of these attitudes in this work. He was not, after all, compelled to compose a dialogue portraying Socrates on the evening of his death. He chose to do this because he had something definite that he wanted to say, in particular about the soul's relation to the body.

The topic is first developed at 63e8ff., where Socrates sets out to defend the claim that the philosopher's life is essentially a preparation for death, that is, the separation of the soul from the body. The argument involves portraying the body as the element in our makeup that gets in the way of the soul's pursuit of its true concern, which is the attainment of truth. At 64D, eating, drinking, and sex are identified as the cardinal distractions presented by the body, all others arising from those. At 66C he develops this theme further:

> The body affords us countless distractions, owing to the nurture it must have; and again, if any illnesses befall it, they hamper our pursuit of that which is. Besides, it fills us up with lusts and desires, with fears and fantasies of every kind, and with any amount of trash, so that really and truly we are, as the saying goes, never able to

> think of anything at all because of it. Thus, it's nothing but the body and its desires that brings wars and factions and fighting; because it's over the gaining of wealth that all wars take place, and we're compelled to gain wealth because of the body, enslaved as we are to its service; so for all these reasons it leaves us no leisure for philosophy [translated by Gallop].

We must therefore be rid of it, if we want to attain to wisdom and truth, and, pending any such happy release, we shall do best "if we consort with the body as little as possible, and do not commune with it, except in so far as we must, and do not infect ourselves with its nature, but remain pure from it, until God himself shall release us" (67A).

We have here, then, in this section of the *Phaedo*, a pretty comprehensive manifesto for what I would identify as the world-negating tradition of asceticism. Whether or not Plato really intended to be so negative, however, one cannot be quite sure, particularly in virtue of the ambiguity of one notable remark back at 62b3, where Socrates, under prodding from Cebes, gives as a reason for not committing suicide (even though life without the body is so much more attractive for the soul than life within it), that "we men are *en tini phrourai* and one ought not to release oneself from this or run away."

I do not translate this central phrase, because it is precisely about the correct rendering of such that controversy has raged ever since antiquity. The problem is that *phroura* can mean either "prison" or "guard post," and the connotations of each meaning would be significantly different. The former carriers with it overtones of punishment for some "original" sin; while the latter bears the implication that we are entrusted with some honorable duty in this world that we must perform to the best of our ability. In either case, certainly, the implication is that the soul would be better off, and would prefer to be, somewhere else, but otherwise the distinction is, it seems to me, precisely between basically world-negating and world-affirming attitudes to human life.

The weight of ancient opinion is in favor of the former interpretation: we are here as in a kind of prison. Already Plato's pupil and second successor Xenocrates[3] had provided, somewhere, a comprehensive exegesis of the controversial phrase, explaining it by reference to the Orphic myth about Dionysus and the Titans. The Titans treacherously killed and ate the child Dionysus (all but his heart, which was saved by Athena, and from which he was reconstituted); and they were punished by being incinerated by Zeus's thunderbolt. But from their ashes arose human beings, who are therefore tainted in their origins, and are condemned to imprisonment in mortal bodies on this earth, but who may free themselves and attain happiness after death by the practice of strict ascetic practices, including abstention from meat. We find this story elaborated further by Dio Chrysostom in one of his orations,[4] but he has probably derived it ultimately from Xenocrates.

This Orphic conception is tied in with a famous Pythagorean dictum, also known to Plato (cf. *Cratylus* 400B), that for the soul, *sōma* (the body) is a *sēma* (tomb). Indeed, the present image of our life as a *phroura* is attributed to Pythagoras by Cicero, in the *Cato Maior* (20)—though, to complicate our picture, he understands *phroura* as guard duty rather than as prison.[5]

Most modern translators and commentators, following Cicero, in fact opt for "guard duty," but there is not much support for this in the Platonic tradition. On the other hand, in later Neoplatonism,[6] we find a remarkably positive interpretation (again, Damascius *In Phaedrum* 1.2), according to which the *phroura* (interpreted now as "protective custody," or something such) is either that of the Good itself—the supreme principle of the *Republic*—or else that of the Demiurge of the *Timaeus,* with the implication that the motivation behind our detention in this life is entirely benevolent.

I am in danger, however, of wandering from the track. My belief is that the sense intended by Plato here is actually guard post rather than prison, and thus that the tone of the *Phaedo* is somewhat more world-affirming than it was generally taken to be in antiquity. In the immediately subsequent passage, after all, he speaks of "freeing oneself" and of "running away," which is easier to do from a guard post than from a prison. Socrates may well be intended here to make some reference to his own position, in which he refused his friend Crito's insistent pleas to allow himself to be "sprung" from the Athens jail; but we must bear in mind that Socrates refuses to do this precisely because he regards himself as being, in a way, on guard duty—as being in honor bound to the laws of Athens not to the desert the post to which they have assigned him.

We see, then, emanating from the Orphic and Pythagorean traditions, and adopted at least by Xenocrates—if not by Plato himself—a complex of beliefs that should not be too unfamiliar to those of us coming from the Christian tradition. Here I am referring to a notion of the physical world as a sort of prison camp, or Vale of Tears, to which humans have been condemned because of some original sin, and from which it is only possible to escape by means of the complete rejection of all its works and pomps. But if that is one strand of asceticism deriving from the Platonic tradition, it is not the only one, nor, I would maintain, the most important.

The other strand is one which has no particular quarrel with the body or the world, but which sees the ensouled body as an organism that gains greatly by being finely tuned. Soul should dominate body, and rational soul should dominate irrational soul, and the whole organism should dominate—or, rather, transcend as far as possible—its environment. This is all not so much because the body and the physical environment are irremediably evil (though no Platonist regarded the physical world with any great degree of enthusiasm), as because it behooves us in this environment to lose no opportunity to refine and fine-tune both our bodies and our irrational impulses, so that both may become ever more perfectly subordinated to our ruling reason. Many of the same ascetic practices may be observed, but their purpose now is not the rejection of the world so much as its utilization for the purpose of self-perfection.

In the case of Plato, I think, the distinction between the two types of asceticism is best observed by contrasting his attitude to the human personality in the *Phaedo* with that which he reveals in the *Republic.*[7] In the *Phaedo,* all irrational and passionate impulses come to the soul from the body, not from any irrational element in itself. By the time Plato comes to write the *Republic,* however, he has come to realize that irrational impulses, though they may indeed originate in bodily needs, are unequivocally psychic phenomena and must be accommodated in any theory of the nature of the soul. The nature of the task before the philosopher, or the aspirant to virtue, becomes rather different.

In Book IV, as we know, three elements, or "parts," of the soul are discerned, and their correct relationship worked out, in the interests of defining the true nature of justice. For our purposes, the essential concept is *sōphrosynē,* usually translated "moderation" or "self-control." At 430E–431A, we find it described as follows:

> Moderation is a certain orderliness and mastery over certain pleasures and appetites, as people somehow indicate by using the phrase "self-control" and other expressions which give a clue to its nature. . . . The expression seems to want to indicate that in the soul of the man himself there is a better and a worse part; whenever what is by nature the better part is in control of the worse, this is expressed by saying that the man is "self-controlled" or master of himself, and this is a term of praise. When, on the other hand, the smaller and better part, because of poor upbringing or bad company, is overpowered by the larger and worse, this is made a reproach, and is called being defeated by oneself, and a man in that situation is called uncontrolled [translated by Grube].

We see here a situation in which a whole section of the soul, and in some sense its "largest" part, is considered to be irrational and a prey to passions. It is not, however, to be eliminated. It is rather to be controlled and disciplined. The two higher elements in the soul which have been identified, the rational and the spirited, band together to achieve this. I quote further from a little later in the book (442AB):

> These two parts, then, thus nurtured and having truly learned their own role and being educated in it, will exercise authority over the appetitive part, which is the largest part in any man's soul and is insatiable for possessions. They will watch over it to see that it is not filled with the so-called pleasures of the body, and by becoming enlarged and strong thereby no longer does its own job but attempts to enslave and rule over those over whom it is not fitted to rule, and so upsets everyone's whole life.

This acceptance of the problem of purification or refinement as lying within the soul is, one might say, an advance on the attitude of the *Phaedo.* But does it betoken a positive attitude to the world? Not very much. The physical world is still represented by such an image as the cave at the beginning of Book VII, which is certainly profoundly negative. The positive aspect, however, is that once the prisoner has escaped from the cave, he is expected to go back down, enriched by the vision of true reality, and see what he can do for his fellow prisoners. The world is not to be simply rejected; it is to be worked on, and worked through, in order to attain one's own perfection.

The *Republic* does, however, end on a fairly thoroughly world-negating note, when Socrates in Book X (611B–612A) comes to speak of the nature and fate of the soul when freed from the body. Here, remarkably, we are presented with a picture of the soul rather more like that of the *Phaedo,* a unitary rather than a triadic entity which must be pried loose from the accretions that have grown upon it by reason of its association with the body, accretions that seem to include its own irrational part. It is compared to the sea god Glaucus, who is almost unrecognizable through being twisted and distorted and encrusted with barnacles. Only when all of these are scraped off will its true beauty be recognized.

Socrates continues, using language very reminiscent of the argument from affinity in the *Phaedo* (78B–84B):

> We must note the things of which it has apprehensions, and the associations for which it yearns, as being itself akin to the divine and the immortal and to eternal being, and to consider what it might be if it followed the gleam unreservedly and were raised by this impulse out of the depths of this sea in which it is now sunk, and were cleansed and scraped free of the rocks and barnacles which, because it now feasts on earth, cling to it in wild profusion of earthy and stony accretion by reason of these feastings that are accounted happy. And then one might see whether in its real nature it is manifold or single in its simplicity, or what is the truth about it and how [611E–612A, translated by Shorey].

This is all pretty austere stuff, it must be admitted, and the same may be said for the great central myth of the *Phaedrus,* with its pessimistic portrayal of the inevitable periodic fall of the soul, by reason of the unruliness of its irrational element, portrayed graphically as the rough and shaggy horse of a pair controlled by a charioteer, who is the rational element. The tripartition of the *Republic* is maintained, but it is subsumed into a basic bipartition (rational charioteer as against irrational horses) that remains the basic Platonist division in later times. One's time in the world is to be used in disciplining this unruly horse and thereby refining the soul as a whole, through the correct contemplation of physical beauty. But basically the soul's entry into the world is a fall, a mistake which must be recovered from, and this makes the *Phaedrus* on the whole nearer to the *Phaedo* in its attitude to the world than to the *Republic.*

It is not before the *Timaeus,* I think, that we find a really positive attitude to the physical world, insofar as that world is recognized both as necessitated, and as good as it can possibly be. In a famous passage, *Timaeus* 30A, Plato declares of the Demiurge, "He was good, and the good can never have any jealousy of anything. And being free from jealousy, he desired that all things should be as like himself as they could be." The world is "a blessed god," as we are told somewhat later (34B).

The soul, furthermore, is presented as inevitably involved with the material world, so that there is no longer any question of its "falling" or being constrained (34C–37C). Of course, the process of birth is still a profound trauma, which causes severe distortions in its structure (43A–44A). But our duty is to bring the circuits in the soul back to their proper state through the philosophical contemplation of the order of the heavens and other physical beauties (44B–46C).

It may seem that this is something of an exception in the Platonic corpus; but we must bear in mind that the *Timaeus* was in later antiquity perhaps the single most influential dialogue of Plato, so that the views expressed in it would carry very considerable weight. Plato is still emphatic that our true kingdom is not of this world, but the difference is now that our presence in this world is not a mistake or a disaster (though it is a challenge), and salvation lies not in rejecting the body, but rather in refining it, to make it a suitable vehicle for the soul.

A most significant passage occurs near the end of the dialogue, at the culmination of a lengthy and detailed discourse on human biology, which is itself significant as betokening a much more positive attitude to the body. It is worth, I think, quoting in full (90A–90D):

> And we should consider that God gave the sovereign part of the human soul to be the divinity [*daimōn*] of each one, being that part which, as we say, dwells at the top of the body, and inasmuch as we are a plant not of an earthly but of a heavenly growth, raises us from earth to our kindred who are in heaven. And in this we say truly, for the divine power suspends the head and root of us from that place where the generation of the soul first began, and thus makes the whole body upright.
>
> When a man is always occupied with the cravings of desire and ambition, and is eagerly striving to satisfy them, all his thoughts must be mortal, and, as far as it is possible altogether to become such, he must be mortal every whit because he has cherished his mortal part. But he who has been earnest in the love of knowledge and of true wisdom, and has exercised his intellect more than any other part of him, must have thoughts immortal and divine, if he attain truth, and in so far as human nature is capable of sharing in immortality, he must altogether be immortal, and since he is ever cherishing the divine power and has the divinity within him in perfect order, he will be singularly happy.
>
> Now there is only one way of taking care of things, and that is to give each the food and motion which are natural to it. And the motions which are naturally akin to the divine principle within us are the thoughts and revolutions of the universe. These each man should follow, and by learning the harmonies and revolutions of the universe, should correct the courses of the head which were corrupted at our birth, and should assimilate the thinking being to the thought, renewing his original nature, so that having assimilated them, he may attain to that best life which the gods have set before mankind, both for the present and the future [translated by Jowett].

This may reasonably, I think, be taken as Plato's final word on this subject, and it is, clearly, essentially world-affirming.[8] Plotinus, we may note, devotes the beginning of his essay on *The Descent of the Soul into Bodies* (*Ennead* 4.8.1) to a discussion of whether or not Plato views the descent of the soul into the physical world negatively or positively. After reviewing the accounts in the *Phaedo*, the *Republic* and the *Phaedrus* which I have mentioned, and accounting them on the whole negative, he turns finally to the *Timaeus* and declares it positive. Moreover, he declares it to be Plato's real view (since for Plotinus the divine Plato could not be in two minds on any subject):

> And, though in all these passages he disapproves of the soul's coming to body, in the *Timaeus* when speaking about this universe he praises the world and calls it a blessed god, and says that the soul was given by the goodness of the Demiurge, so that this universe might be intelligent, and this could not be without soul. The Soul of the Universe, then, was sent into it for this reason by the god, and the soul of each one of us was sent that the universe might be perfect; since it was necessary that all

> the very same kinds of living things which were in the intelligible world should also exist in the world perceived by the senses [translated by Armstrong, slightly altered].

Plotinus has analyzed the situation most acutely, except perhaps in concluding that there can be only one true Platonic view of the matter.[9] In fact, I think, Plato's ambivalence can be traced back to the personality of his master Socrates. Socrates was certainly an ascetic of a sort, but he was not one in any world-negating or neurotic sense. Socrates seems to have been truly indifferent to the pleasures of the body and the goods of the external world. He did not reject them, however. He was quite prepared to sit down and eat and drink with the best of them, and indeed, as we see in the *Symposium,* drink everyone else under the table, if the occasion warranted. But he was supremely indifferent to such pleasures, and indeed, it would seem, to the ordinary conveniences of life, such as shoes or warm clothing (cf. *Symp.* 220AB). He did not reject his body. Instead, he had refined it to the point where it was the willing instrument of his soul, giving him as little trouble as possible. His true heir in asceticism is not in fact Plato, I should say, but rather Antisthenes (of whom Plato did not approve) and the Cynic tradition, exemplified by Crates and Diogenes of Sinope, who traced their ancestry to him. Plato himself is, if anything, more world-negating than Socrates. Socrates, for instance, married and had a family (though he was a sore trial to his wife, and does not seem to have been a very good father). Plato, on the other hand, did not marry, and does not seem to have much respect for the institution; nor do his views on even homosexual love and its possible sublimation, as set out in the *Symposium* and the *Phaedrus,* strike one as either humane or realistic. If one may make a distinction between the world-affirming and world-negating types of asceticism manifested in the Platonic corpus, it may after all be most accurate to attribute the former to Socrates (and see the Cynic tradition as his heirs in that), and the latter to Plato himself, despite the important evidence of the *Timaeus.* If Plato takes up a basically word-affirming position there, that is attributable to metaphysical considerations which do not necessarily betoken a change of heart on the ethical front.

NOTES

1. It may be noted that the term *askēsis* has a role in Greek philosophical discourse, though not quite the one which it occupies in early Christian thought. It was generally held in later times (first laid down, so far as we can see, by Aristotle, in *Eudemian Ethics* 1.1.1214a16ff. and in *Nicomachean Ethics* 10.9.1179b20ff.) that three elements were required for successful philosophizing: *physis* (natural ability, or disposition), *mathēsis* (study), and *askēsis* (practice of what one has learned). This last can equally well refer to going over one's irregular verbs, if one is learning a language, or doing one's training, if one is learning how to throw the javelin; but in the context of ancient philosophy, which was, after all, a *bios,* or "way of life," as well as a body of doctrines, *askēsis* could fairly be seen to refer to practices that might be regarded as "ascetic."
2. I have been greatly influenced in composing this paper by the magnificent study of Peter Brown, *The Body and Society* (Princeton, 1988), though he is dealing with late antiquity rather than with Plato himself. On p. 223 of that work he remarks: "The ascetics of late antiquity tended to view the human body as an 'autarkic' system. In ideal conditions, it was thought capable of running on its own 'heat'; it would need only enough nourishment

to keep that heat alive. In its 'natural' state—a state with which the ascetics tended to identify the bodies of Adam and Eve—the body had acted like a finely tuned engine, capable of 'idling' indefinitely. It was only the twisted will of fallen men that had crammed the body with unnecessary food, thereby generating in it the dire surplus of energy that showed itself in physical appetite, in anger, and in the sexual urge. In reducing the intake to which he had become accustomed, the ascetic slowly remade his body. He turned it into an exactly calibrated instrument." This is an excellent description of the second of the two types of Platonist asceticism that I am seeking to identify, which I would see as the position of Socrates himself.

3. Apud Damascius, *In Phaed.* 12=Fr. 20 in R. Heinze, *Xenokrates; Darstellung der Lehre und Sammlung der Fragmenten* (Leipzig, 1892).
4. *Orationes* 30.10–11.
5. "Vetatque Pythagoras iniussu imperatoris, id est dei, de praesidio et statione vitae decedere"—"Pythagoras forbids us to depart from our guard-post and station in life without the permission of our commander, that is, God."
6. Later than Plotinus, certainly, who adopts the meaning "prison" at *Enneads* 4.8.1, 32, and regards the passage as representing a thoroughly world-negating point of view.
7. For good discussions of the development in Plato's doctrine of the soul, see T. M. Robinson, *Plato's Psychology* (Toronto, 1970) and G.M.A. Grube, *Plato's Thought* (London, 1935), chapter 4.
8. I do not here discuss the description of the ascent to spiritual enlightenment through love in the *Symposium* (210A–212A), though it does have some relevance to the theme of asceticism, as was noted repeatedly during the conference (cf. in particular the paper of J. G. Milhaven elsewhere in this volume). However, Plato's theory of love seems to me to be a separate topic. Correct Platonic eroticism is certainly a disciplined activity, and thus "ascetic" in the broad sense, but I do not see that it is ascetic in the more technical sense.
9. Plotinus's own position, though thoroughly ascetic, is on the whole world-affirming to a greater degree than was that of Plato, mainly for the reason that becomes plain in his analysis of Plato's position, which I have quoted. He holds that the world is a necessary development, and in fact "the best of all possible worlds." He is also concerned, as becomes obvious from his polemic *Against the Gnostics* (*Enn.* 2.9), to combat the world-negating tendencies of contemporary Christian Gnostics, some of whom seem to have had some contact with his philosophical circle.

   The essentially ascetic nature of Plotinus's own lifestyle, and that which he encouraged in his followers, is nicely illustrated by the story of the senator Rogatianus (told by Porphyry, *Life of Plotinus,* chapter 7), who gave up all the privileges and luxuries to which he had been accustomed, including even his own house, and instead "spent his time here and there at his friends' and acquaintances', sleeping and eating with them, and taking, at that only one meal every other day"—almost, in fact, like a Manichaean holy man.

8

Primitive Christianity as an Ascetic Movement

J. Duncan M. Derrett

How far was primitive Christianity ascetic? What input secured its supersubstantial promises? I approve the approach of Marsilius (c.1275–1342)[1] and here contrast my own *Ascetic Discourse* (1989) with A. E. Harvey's well-wrought *Strenuous Commands* (1990) and with other "obstructive erudition" (so named by Albert Schweitzer).[2]

Definitions

Primitive Christianity refers to Jesus, his disciples, and Paul. The fourth Gospel and the non-Pauline New Testament epistles mark early Christianity. Righteousness is a subjective condition, "blamelessness" (Gr. *dikaiosynē;* Heb. *zᵉkût* rather than *sᵉdāqāh*). Blame would arise from breach of God's will, learned from prophets like Paul. To be righteous is to be like God.

Askein (practice) appears in the New Testament (note *Acts of the Apostles* 24.16). It is voluntary discipline of the self to benefit the soul. It has no codified abstentions (*1 Cor.* 10.12). Hebrew *pᵉrîšût* implies renunciation, and *sîgup* voluntary privation; *askein* is broader. Asceticism does not imply propitiation of a deity. Contemplation is not a requirement. Ascetics can be married (*1 Cor.* 7.29–34); and to stay married can be ascetical. Ascetical programs do not require celibacy. Even dietary restraint is not essential (according to Paul). Neurotic or obsessional behavior, being involuntary, is not ascetic. Imitation will not make an ascetic, though Paul urged it (via exhortatory compositions).[3] An alternative Greek expression *diatribē peri eusebeian* means "a religious program," while a constant pursuit of something is *ep-askein* (from a third century inscription).

Through asceticism, morality is conducted as an athlete conducts his or her physical life.[4] Conduct, including speech, is trimmed to produce predetermined behavior. Like athleticism, asceticism is a way of life. *Askēsis* means training,[5] pursuing a course of instruction; asceticism is training for righteousness without despising a material return.[6] Ascetics and their disciples may be symbiotic, the latter maintaining the former.[7] Asceticism is an internal exchange: a rigorous training exchanges short-term enjoyment for long-term gains. The trainer offers an advantage to the public at a price it will pay. An investment is sunk, and current returns finance development.

One claims the benefits of Christianity (for example, eternal life) can be realized (1) by chiseling scripture to diminish the cost of the input, and (2) by reducing its ascetic precepts in conformity with its (irresponsible) apocalyptic revelations; while (3) taking all indications regarding input as recommendatory, and therefore optional. Harvey's thesis finds no imperatives in even strenuous commands.

Sources and Objections

Do we believe our sources? The weight of ascetic precepts remains to be assessed. Primitive and early Christianity were ascetical. As a feature of those religions, asceticism was their partial characteristic, but nonetheless an essential one. It fails to describe later Christianity, which mocks monastic and puritan lifestyles.[8]

The early Christians were neither exclusively nor totally ascetical. Our sources are paraenetics, essentially trainers' handbooks, which seldom congratulated Christians on their success.[9] Evidences of their undergoing training can indeed presage success, but that is pedagogic technique.

There is a pervasive disposition to attain maximum output with minimum input. Hymns (naturally), sermons, lectures, broadcasts, and journals devote much less space to Jesus' teaching than to his glory. Startling verses such as *John* 14.15, "If you love me, you will keep my commandments"; and *John* 15.10, "If you keep my commandments, you shall abide in my love," are seldom heard, as if he issued no commandments, or obedience to them were optional. Objectors are eloquent:

1. Was not Jesus' parent religion nonascetical? If the Baptist's movement was ascetical, it faded.[10] But ascetical features exist in Judaism.[11] *Ḥasîdîm,* the ultra-pious, have included ascetics.

2. Did Jesus teach asceticism or rather (*Mk.* 2.18) an unascetic natural intercourse with the world (K. G. Kuhn)? What of Cana (*Jn.* 2.1–11); Jesus' "eating and drinking" (*Mt.* 11.18–19; *Lk.* 5.33); the "bag" (*Mt.* 14.17–18; *Jn.* 12.6, 13.29); Peter's marriage (*Mk.* 1.30); households with incomes (*Lk.* 10.40; *Acts* 12.12–13); the disciples' married or industrial life (*1 Cor.* 9.5); Zacchaeus's unsold house (*Lk.* 19.8–9); Simon's tanning (*Acts* 10.6, 9, 17)? Ananias and Sapphira died of shock.[12] If sharing a virtue the community did not seek to have nothing to share.[13] Disinclination to work and parasitism developed,[14] for the Way was misunderstood.[15] Such instances prove the character of the asceticism, as well as its failures. Evangelistic homelessness[16] illustrated asceticism, but, while consistent with primitive Christianity, it did not provide it with a global definition.

3. Are some ascetical precepts impracticable?[17] Not knowing, one can suspect the Sermon on the Mount would breed a feeble and enslaved race.[18] Tolstoy insisted on the literal application of certain commandments (he did not exemplify them himself), in particular nonresistance to evil.[19] As he was contradicted in his lifetime,[20] societies named for him did not survive long. But the texts relied on were

misunderstood; and asceticism need not be bad for business if scrupulousness can be shown to increase profits.[21]

4. The play of the gifts of *homo sapiens,* recognized by Paul,[22] demands the maximizing of potentialities. But humanity lacks automatic control of appetites. Culture requires restraint of instincts. And asceticism was not proffered on speculation; it was a rational means to the goal. Opponents admit the rationality of a minimum of restraint. But trainers make contracts with trainees. Jesus expected only 25 percent of hearers to accept an offer,[23] allegedly lucrative relative to the input (*Is.* 48.17; *Lk.* 19.42), a trainer's formula in ethics as in athletics.[24]

5. Ascetics can be power seekers; but not all power is bad. Bogus ascetics give the word a bad name.[25] Outward appearances are not enough (*Rom.* 2.28–29). Human approbation is fallacious (*Mt.* 6.2; *Jn.* 12.43). But asceticism did not imply fatuity; nor is it ascetical to encourage corruption,[26] sinning vicariously.[27] To be ready to be abused or cheated[28] is not the same as tolerating cheating in others.[29]

6. Paul was an ascetic-mystic,[30] a follower of Christ.[31] Targets of his mission included unregenerates, whose performance disappointed him.[32] Compromises existed even by c.60 CE, toward a relaxed, and away from a rigorous, formula.[33] Too much input was demanded of them. Will not an ascetical Christianity empty churches? Religion also is a business, and even the word "ascetical" drives business away.

7. Asceticism is historically and psychologically a response to dualism. If God and Satan are coordinate forces, a righteous hatred of the flesh[34] restrains natural appetites. Unrestricted hedonism and opportunism suit devotees of Satan.[35] Small wonder the wicked are happier than the just![36] These alternatives impress neurotics.

8. Supersubstantial benefits have been sought at minimal cost by the relaxed over centuries. Christianity boasts of its fringe benefits.[37] Asceticism attracts persecution. Yet persecution of the church arose not because of perversity, but because the Way threatened the surrounding society, which customarily functioned differently, on other hypotheses.

9. The virtues and vices listed in the New Testament[38] are like those known to Stoics and Cynics, comparable with a Christian *askēsis.* The philosophical heirs of Greece and Rome admired, but did not practice, a naive or rigorous asceticism; nor need we, it is said. But Cynic and Stoic animadversions do not equal the Christian package,[39] and if Paul was all things to all men (*1 Cor.* 9.19–23), he did not deny the selfishness of pagan philosophy or abandon the Christian hope.

10. Jesus died for the remission of past sins (*Mk.* 10.45), and disciples were authorized to forgive future sins (*Mt.* 18.18; *Jn.* 20.23). Rigorist demands hardly fit this flexibility. Were the sins of the rich not condoned easily (*Is.* 5.23)? Therefore Jesus' requirements were recommendations. Supersubstantial benefits would not be forfeited if absolution was readily available. The rigorist position asserted in *Hebrews* 6.4–8 ("It is impossible for those who were once enlightened . . . if they shall fall away, to renew them again unto repentance"), and reiterated in 10.26–31, is hardly typical. But the package fails if an article is neglected. The burden, however "light" (*Mt.* 11.30), must be shouldered entire. To urge otherwise is hypocrisy, against which Christ inveighed.[40]

11. "Commandment" really means "tendency." The fine parody by Arthur Hugh Clough (1819–1861) in "The Latest Decalogue" (*Poems,* ed. A.L.P. Norrington [Oxford, 1986], Shorter Poems, No. 13) is inimitable. "Thou shalt not kill," except in war, in judicial executions, during public disorder, under mental provocation, or euthanasia. "Thou shalt not commit adultery," except when the other gender is willing. "Thou shalt not steal," except when the owner is absent, negligent, or rich. "Thou shalt not lie," except when personal or national interest suggest it. Artful definitions confuse moral imperatives with social and legal convenience. In fact, primitive and early Christianity did not look to law for moral guidance: at best it could be neutral (*Rom.* 13.3–5; *Gal.* 4.23). One sought to control inclinations in the furtherance of a subjective condition, more easily described than defined. The positive requirements of the Way were far weightier than the negative.

12. Ascetics make bad leaders, rude, unable to compromise. Poor administrators (*Acts* 6.1), they are unaware of being manipulated. Enthusiasm for them can easily be hypocritical or a surrogate for righteousness (*Lk.* 11.27). But who suggested an ascetic should be a political leader? Catherine of Siena did play diplomatic and political roles without compromising her asceticism, but she was a catalyst. Admittedly, since self-sacrifice is seldom found in youth, youthful interest in ascetics can be shallow and brief.

13. Overachievement foments abuses and arouses jealousy. In mutual competition ascetics may tender their respective constituencies some sets of observances. Some ascetics, ignoring fashion, may repudiate all observances; the public, however, sees in observances high visibility coupled with low cost. Moral achievement is another matter. There are indeed unedifying conflicts over observances,[41] and emphasis on formality of behavior can well be psychically damaging, fatal to flexibility.

Another trap is vicarious holiness. Almsgiving diminishes censure and confers precedence (*Prv.* 18.16). One may be ascetic by deputy, maintaining holy beggars to share in their merits. The early church seems sadly to have stumbled into this abuse.[42]

All thirteen objections form a Berlin Wall of skepticism of the texts. Who indicates to our spiritual athletes how to surmount it? Meanwhile, it is an attractive argument that modern Christianity is a different religion from those of the early phases of the church. But it is inconsistent that those who want the merit of continuity should fail to attend to history. *Luke* 6.46 ("Why do you call me 'Lord, Lord,' and omit to do what I say?") is a standing reproach.

The Thesis

The Way was fortified by the notion it attempted to convey of Jesus' biography. Its apocalyptic mode attempted to inculcate the imitative lifestyle as urgent. It appealed only to those who heard Jesus' voice (*Jn.* 10.3, 16, 27, 18.37). Attainment of righteousness was indispensable to the rebirth or conversion of the remnant, whose effort would purchase (inherit) the promised Kingdom. Jewish theology was stretched to accommodate gentiles, whose input was debated (*Acts* 15.1–35). Objectors to asceticism tend to overlook the remnant.[43]

The Way also assumed the will of God to have been authoritatively revealed. Jews would recognize a standard of moral rectitude equally authentic with the righteous gentiles' discoveries (*Rom.* 2.6–29). Inspiration apart (the work of the Paraclete), the Way did not seek ɩo be practical in economic and political terms. The purposes of God can be presumed seldom to coincide with the short-term projects of God's untrained creatures.

Skepticism emerged when, regardless of flexibility, the Way refused the rewards and punishments that held civilized society together. What worked in the unregenerate world, even if badly, was safer than a search for unworldly righteousness, the value of which could not be verified. The Way was not merely religious. God's will took priority over Caesar's.[44] Partisans of temporal expediency obtain no grip upon ascetical packages.

The Way can be depicted in summary form:

1. God's will is to be served; bliss is impossible without knowledge of and obedience to it.[45]

2. Every human specimen is created[46] the potential beneficiary of the concern that a servant of God should feel for a fellow creature,[47] an argument suited to a collective society. The shepherd looks after his sheep,[48] for such is the image of the believer, incongruous in the modern West.

3. Humility before God, and fostering of fellow beings, are therefore requisite.[49] Likewise, it is necessary to place a fellow creature's interests on an equal plane with one's own.[50]

4. To treat illness is one of a shepherd's functions.[51] Faith expedites a cure. Cure is a proper concern of Christians; whereas the world treats healing as a commodity, and self-explanatory at that.

5. The world, not reborn, unaware of dependence on God, is to be handled warily.[52] It rejects a morality it cannot monitor, or reward.

6. Candidates for a credible alternative society, the reborn, must demonstrate endurance,[53] as already understood by the world at its best. They endure in the Way.

7. Appetites placing one individual in a position superior to another, except in the context of training, belong to the flesh, the world's program; the work of Satan, its controller (*Lk.* 4.5–7; *Jn.* 12.31, 14.30, 16.11). One must abandon (1) a search for status at the expense of others[54] (except in a competition of righteousness),[55] (2) greed (Gk. *pleonexia,* the desire to have more than others have), and (3) all possessions that hinder one's obedience to God.[56] Except for the gifted (*Mt.* 19.12), the sexual urge, too, must be used so as not to imperil religious duties (*1 Cor.* 7.29–35). Paul only *prefers* abstention (*1 Cor.* 7.7–8). Ascetics may, in principle, be of either gender, widows having greater opportunities (*Lk.* 2.37; *1 Tm.* 5.5,9). Sexual options such as lusting after women, adultery (*Mt.* 5.28, 32) and homosexuality (*Rom.* 1.26–27) will be disallowed.[57] To "love one's neighbor as oneself" one must foresee harm impending on others.[58]

8. This Christian asceticism was impressive from the first, and taxing. The Way

could be called rigorous, if athletic training is rigorous. It is either rigorous or it is not training. It automatically, like a boxer's camp, required severance from the unregenerate family or other inhibiting ties. A new notional family was to be joined, serving as a support group.[59] As a sign of their ascetic belonging, each kisses the others in public as a greeting (*Rom.* 16.16; *1 Cor.* 16.20), as a proof that there is neither slave nor free male or female in this family (*Gal.* 3.28; *Col.* 3.11)—an exhibition which, in context, was truly ascetic.

Paul shows how ascetic his version of Christianity was: "The mind that is set on the flesh is hostile to God; it does not submit to God's law . . . those who are in the flesh cannot please God" (*Rom.* 8.7–8; cf. *1 Jn.* 2.15–17). "Put on the Lord Jesus Christ and make no provision for the flesh to gratify desires" (*Rom.* 13.14). "We hunger and thirst, we are ill-clad, buffeted and homeless, and we work with our own hands. When reviled we bless; when persecuted we endure; when slandered we conciliate; we are the refuse of the world, as it were scapegoats for all" (*1 Cor.* 4.11–13). "Every athlete uses overall self-control: he does it for a perishable wreath, we for an imperishable one" (*1 Cor.* 9.25). "I bruise my body and subdue it (like a professional pugilist), lest after preaching to others I myself turn out to be sub-standard" (*1 Cor.* 27). "Observe, the spiritual does not come first; the physical body comes first, and then the spiritual. The first man is from earth, made of dust; the second man is from heaven. The man made of dust is the pattern of all who are made of dust, and the heavenly man is the pattern of all the heavenly. As we have worn the likeness of the man of dust, so we shall wear the likeness of the heavenly man" (*1 Cor.* 15.46–49). "Let us cleanse ourself of every defilement of body and spirit and attain perfect holiness in fear of God" (2 *Cor.* 7.1). "Those who belong to Christ Jesus have crucified the flesh with its passion and desires . . . Do not be deceived; God is not mocked, for whatever a man sows, that he will also reap. For he who sows from his own flesh will reap from it corruption; but he who sows to the Spirit will from the Spirit reap eternal life. And let us not grow weary in doing good, for in due time we shall reap, if we do not lose heart" (*Gal.* 6.7–9). "I glory . . . in the Cross . . . by which the world has been crucified to me and I to the world" (*Gal.* 5.24, 6.14). "I know how to be humiliated, and to be well-off; I am thoroughly initiated in the arts of satiety and hunger, superfluity and destitution" (*Phil.* 4.12). "I do not account my life of any value . . . if only I may accomplish my course and the ministry which I received from the Lord Jesus (*Acts* 20.24)."[60] Asceticism was not the object of the Way, it was the Way; it was a route to its goal.

Antithesis

In my *Ascetic Discourse* I argue from Matthew's approach that Christianity must be ascetical. A decline soon set in[61] and progressed[62] for the early Christians. The rigorous and the relaxed competed inside the church for many centuries. Councils tended to brand the rigorous (for example, Tatian, Montanus, Novatian, Donatus) as heretics, in favor of the view of a majority of their constituents. A heresy hunter like Augustine interpreted the Sermon on the Mount in a relaxed manner,[63] and so decline was confirmed.

Anthony Harvey's *Strenous Commands*[64] takes a different view. He does not deny that Jesus issued commands, but he denies them imperative and literal content.[65] One can accept specific commands that one is free to adapt, to take as guidelines as if the Kingdom were upon us (which it manifestly is not).[66] All summaries are unfair; and Harvey's attractive work is thoroughly documented; but I trust what follows is not a caricature.

Primitive Christianity (according to Harvey) cannot have been ascetical, since Paul does not claim a distinctive moral code derived from Jesus, whose commands figure in three institutional contexts.[67] Did itinerant preachers function as ascetics?[68] Some of the disciples were oriented toward asceticism, but that style may have penetrated Palestine from the East.[69] The church came to terms with that element. Paul's teaching coincides with traditional wisdom;[70] if loving everyone was a distinctive ethic of Jesus, Paul was no example of it.[71]

Jesus never legislated, though he required Moses' commandments to be observed.[72] Pithy aphoristic sentences appealed to him; and, like the writer of *Ecclesiastes,* he diverged from prudence at times for dramatic effect.[73] His ethic cannot be judged authoritative or impracticable, since it was not a set of rules, but challenged prevailing presuppositions, as did the Cynics.[74] He did not argue his conclusions.[75] He offered hope to the poor, emphasizing Jewish benevolence toward the underdog. His moral injunctions aped legal propositions (a mock-casuistic).[76] Even on divorce, he was not preparing a code of practice. Divorce was as bad as adultery if that were the intention behind it. "He that devises to do evil shall be called a mischievous person" (*Prv.* 24.8).[77]

Utopian promises were consistent with Jewish exhortations (*Dt.* 15); the Pentateuch itself conveys moral precepts (e.g., not to covet) as if they were divine statutes.[78] Everyone was favorable to enlightened common sense. He reformulated the Golden Rule (*Lk.* 6.31, an ascetical proposition), going beyond other moralists' maxims without discarding their idiom or their aim.[79] Selfless behavior could be based on wisdom, if not prudence.[80] Even Matthew does not treat radical pronouncements on forgiveness seriously while he organizes church discipline (*Mt.* 18.18).[81] Unlike *Luke* 17.3–4 ("If your brother trespasses against you . . . you shall forgive him"), Jesus wants only a readiness to forgive.[82] Jesus' teaching on wealth aims at the individual impulse, not any social contrivance.[83] Axioms of the wisdom tradition soon take the place of his exaggerated exhortations to be generous.[84] Selling everything (*Mt.* 19.21) is a moralist's hyperbole.[85]

Advocacy of Jesus' approach was not confined to enthusiasts. Tolerant of his audacious exaggerations,[86] they did not mind a scheme challenging commonplace assumptions and calculations. Total renunciation (*Lk.* 14.33) was not seriously demanded.[87] The strenuous commands radicalize what was in the established moral tradition.[88] Jesus intensified the sense of obligation toward God and neighbor.[89] He spoke as if the standards he propounded were imperatives since the coming of the Kingdom of Heaven created a state of emergency.[90] Jesus did not behave strictly in accordance with his own standards,[91] the ethic being contingent. His life and death constitute an example, not his individual acts. He was not a model of *agapē* (identifying with others' interests).[92] Or so the sources suggest.

Moral teaching is seldom systematic; maxims have various meanings. Using a wisdom style, eschewing a sectarian code of conduct, hinting at a divinely enhanced human motivation, by taking the extreme case, with a pungency that came from an artistic talent for delicate exaggeration, Jesus enabled those who sought to follow his teaching and example to see the extent to which he challenged their assumptions and preferences.[93]

Was that his policy and his practice, from which his followers soon began to decline? Little declination seems necessary. The gospels that reflect his teaching place him close to God; and John visualizes him as like God, with a continuing supernatural existence. What justified this? Paul takes Jesus to be (not to have been) divine. How is this explained?

Was it for the sake of such a program as Harvey describes that Jesus was spied upon,[94] challenged,[95] betrayed, abused, arrested, and handed over to a foreign power, flogged, crucified, and mocked, and has left, apparently deliberately,[96] a legacy of persecution and hatred to all his followers? Something seems wrong with Harvey's thesis. Jesus' actual friends were endangered; patients he cured were persecuted;[97] his brothers did not believe in him (*Jn.* 7.5), yet when one was converted (*Gal.* 1.19, 2.9; *Acts* 12.17), the Jewish authorities stoned him to death (Josephus, *Antiquitates judaicae* 20.200). Jesus often escaped arrest and went into hiding. His upper-class supporters sedulously concealed their faith.[98] "For fear of the Jews" explains much evasive behavior.[99]

So a comical, allegedly well-intentioned, perhaps rather irresponsible moralist, anticipated by Stoics and Cynics, in a territory, like most Asian lands, where self-appointed sages moralize morning, noon, and night, has been a continuous irritant from his own day onwards! Even diluted, his teaching was a real threat. It must have been successful (*Jn.* 11.48, 12.19). Can it have been a rhetorical version of wisdom, even of Torah teaching? Was it a joke at the expense of the complacent, or an enhancement of Jewish scriptural traditions like the Baptist of *Luke* 3.10–14? Or was it something civilization cannot stomach? Harvey says the gospel, including the Sermon on the Mount, is subject to the judgment of the church.[100] So William Shakespeare was once subject to Thomas Bowdler. Fortunately the church does not monopolize studies of Jesus any more.

Stoic and Cynic teachings were never persecuted: if occasionally indiscreet, then reward was no comment on their doctrines. Jewish piety, if sometimes ridiculed, was a part of Judaism. Pagans attempted to make people free at a time when political and economic freedom was impossible. Jewish piety extended the study of exact obedience to Yahweh's will. Neither aimed at the rebirth of the individual. Nicodemus's ignorance (*Jn.* 3.10–11) illustrates the unfamiliarity of the idea. There were not myriad seekers for the promise given to Abraham, Isaac, and Jacob, building up an individual treasure in heaven.[101] The Holy Spirit, which Jews saw as the spirit of prophecy, for the common good, was actually offered by Jesus to the individual trainee.[102] This was altogether novel.

Synthesis

The Way was an offer. No failure, after initial acceptance, can diminish its character. The various types of "Christianity on the cheap" which parody the Way prove how high it aimed. One who is not bound by its precepts is not a (Christian) religious person. Enthusiasm does not imply a want of reason. Unenthusiastic commitment is no commitment. The Way expects a rebirth, an opting out of the standards of the world into which one is born with biological urges. Hence, in times of persecution, survival comes second to righteousness.[103] Self-defense is not excluded (as opposed to combativeness), not merely to give biology its due, but to preserve an arena in which to achieve righteousness. When self-defense spills over into aggression, one has driven off the road.

The Way has its logic, not based on smart maxims or alleged wisdom. Like evolution, it aims at a lifestyle adapted to survival. It places cooperation before competition. Survival requires neither status nor wealth, which need to be escaped, not merely ridiculed (as by the Cynics). The world suspects beginnings, but it respects perseverance and its rewards. Meanwhile, even physical and mental competitions have their drawbacks.

Most interesting for comparison are the Hasidic sects, led by charismatic rebbes, which have cultivated purity of observant Jewish life for about three centuries against both the protests of *mitnagdîm* (non-Hasidic orthodox Jews) and the indifference of gentiles. Observing their inward-looking commitment to a messianic style of Torah observance, and noticing their refusal to be bound by the standards of any courts but their own,[104] one finds points of similarity with primitive Christianity, and turns to the study of the *ḥasîdîm* of the centuries before the Talmuds were compiled. Recognized to be at a degree higher than those who feared sin, they illustrate the maxim of the miracle worker R. Pinhas ben Yair, that fear of sin leads to *ḥasîdût,* (usually translated "saintliness"), which leads to the (receipt of) holiness.[105] These old pious men (Mishnah, *Berakhot* 5.1) built a fence around the law (Mishnah, *Avot* 1.1, 3.14), not (as Harvey suggests) by creating additional commandments, but by ensuring that their inclinations never put others to loss, so that love of humanity and love of God coincided. *Ḥasîdût* was the most highly esteemed quality of religiosity (Talmud Bavli, '*Avodah Zarah*' 20b, *Arakhin* 16b, *Niddah* 17a), and it could be said that their (hypothetical) Mishnah (which was never compiled) would satisfy the prophet Elijah when the strictly legal requirements of the *halakhah* (sections of rabbinic literature that deal with Jewish law) fell short of saintliness.[106]

A *baraita* (teaching or tradition of the Tannaim excluded from the Mishnah and incorporated in a later collection) (*Shabbat* 88b; *Yoma* 23a; *Gittin* 36b) identifies those who love God, or those whom God loves (Mekhilta, *Nezîqîn* 18.13–16), with those who: do not return abuse (cf. *1 Pt.* 2.23; *1 Cor.* 4.12); do not reply to calumny; act habitually out of love of God; and rejoice in chastisement. These, obviously *ḥasîdîm,* are "like the Sun when he goes forth in his might" (*Jgs.* 5.31). Nevertheless, some fought on the side of the Maccabees against Syria, and a "Fortress of the Ḥasîdîm" was known as late as the second century CE.

The scrupulosity of the *ḥasîd* is a kind of supererogation. Some say he must live right up to the standards of *Nezîqîn* (the order of the Talmud that deals with legal damages), some that he must embody the principles of *Avot* (the ethics of the fathers), some say those of *Berakhot* (the benedictions).[107] Accepting the normative provisions of the Torah, the *ḥasîd* can be characterized as one who, when he forgot from which of two men he bought something, would pay both; or when he forgot from which of five men he appropriated something, would restore to all.[108] In the order of acquisitiveness, he says, "What is mine is yours and what is yours is your own." He not only gives alms, but wishes that everyone else should (he evinces no jealousy); and he is hard to provoke and easy to appease—in short he is the dead opposite of the wicked.[109] *Ḥasîdîm* were prepared to forfeit their rights (cf. *1 Cor.* 6.7), they eschewed *pleonexia* (covetousness) in all spheres, and so took to their logical conclusions well-known principles of the Torah, as demonstrated by Paul in *Romans* 2.17–26. The Torah is holy, but its spirit (as divined by the gifted rebbes) is higher. The *ḥasîd* studies *Micah* 6.8: "What does the Lord require of you, but to do justly, and to love mercy, and to walk humbly with your God?" He judges both custom and *halakhah* by this yardstick (cf. *Mt.* 15.5, 10, 14–20).

Such a program is certainly ascetic. It uses *anachōrēsis* (seclusion)[110] as a means to an end. Its scrupulosity is not of the type ridiculed in *Matthew* 23.23–24 and *Luke* 11.42, where details of the Torah are concentrated upon as observances, while the spirit of it is overlooked, and a proper balance is not achieved.[111] Hasidic observance is a form of training and a moral athleticism. No amount of individual failure diminishes its authenticity. That phenomenon should be taken up in the sphere of comparative religion, in order to illuminate the varieties of New Testament asceticism.[112]

The question why primitive and early Christians suffered so much hostility; they had to suffer for righteousness' sake (*1 Pt.* 3.14–16). They down-graded the Sabbath, the laws of purity, and the dietary laws. "Chosen" meant the converted, not the Jewish people (cf. *Mt.* 8.11–12, 15.28). Circumcision itself became optional (*Acts* 16.3). Torah principles were relativized in the light of *Hosea* 6.6, "I desire mercy, not sacrifice." This was not what *ḥasîdîm* considered doing. Jesus' attack on the temple system (*Mt.* 21.13 and parallels) did not, indeed, set the Torah aside. On the other hand, a form of Judaism that claimed a special illumination (*Mt.* 13.10–17) and could unpredictably issue commandments (*Mt.* 22.35–40 and parallels; *Lk.* 10.25–28); should consider several of them to be of allegorical significance (cf. *Mt.* 2.25–26, 3.4); could decide on the degree of intensity appropriate to any accepted obligation (cf. *Lk.* 11.52); and could allow individuals to forgive sins (*Mk.* 2.6–7; *Jn.* 20.23; *Acts* 10.43, 26.18; cf. *2 Kgs.* 5.18–19) on a basis professedly derogatory to the Torah (*Acts* 13.38–39),[113] must undermine any Jewish community and any Jewish state. A teacher who undertook that risk and was unable to establish his *bona fides* over time made matters worse by exalting the wisdom of uneducated children (*Mt.* 21.15–16; *Mt.* 11.20 / *Lk.* 10.21; cf. *Lk.* 18.17) and doubting what the authorized builders (that is scholars) were building (*Mk.* 12.10–12). He was concerned only for the spiritual welfare of his sheep.[114] His skepticism of the observances of the pious could be gravely embarrassing to the pseudo-pious.[115] Since primitive Christianity far from coincided with traditional wisdom, Jesus and his followers could ridicule normal behavior patterns[116] and call for no less than the reduction of the population (*Mt.* 12.43–45). Early Christianity shows an awkward skepticism of intellectual activity (*1 Tm.* 6.3–5; *2 Tm.* 2.17–18, 23), a fact that would justify the establishment's doubts as to even its honesty.

Meanwhile, citizens who can neither be threatened nor bribed are a threat—to any known polity. Small wonder asceticism, whatever its degree of achievement, remains unpopular.

NOTES

1. Marsilius, *Defensor Pacis,* trans. Alan Gewirth (New York: Columbia University, 1956), chapters 11, §2–3; 12, §27–31; and 13, was inspired (1324) by the controversy raised by the Spiritual Franciscans (see *Oxford Dictionary of the Christian Church,* 2d ed. [Oxford: Oxford University Press, 1977], p. 1301). Evangelical (voluntary) poverty is consistent with present enjoyment of unowned goods. Vows to the contrary are void: *DP,* chapter 13, §§5, 17, 22, 23, 34. It is an open door to all the virtues (§26). Thought must be given to the present (*Mt.* 6.26, 31, 32, 34). Objections and their refutations in *DP,* chapter 14 (ownership not essential to enjoyment or transfer).
2. Canon Anthony E. Harvey, *Strenuous Commands: The Ethic of Jesus* (Philadelphia: Trinity Press International, 1990) was published soon after my *Ascetic Discourse: An Explanation of the Sermon on the Mount* (Eilsbrunn: Ko'amar, 1989). Harvey claims (letter of 25 February 1993) to have given Jesus' teaching "high marks for distinctiveness, originality, and the power to endure though setting almost (but not quite) unattainable objectives . . . in the idiom of a cosmopolitan tradition."
3. *1 Cor.* 4.16, 11.1; *Phil.* 3.17, 4.9; cf. *Lk.* 6.39–45; *Mt.* 23.16, 24. Autonomy is powerfully attractive, and autonomous persons are imitated: Sarah Lloyd, *An Indian Attachment* (London: Collins, 1984), p. 237 (a Sikh *Dehra*).
4. Aristophanes, *Plutus* 585; Plato, *Republic* 430E–404A; Philo, *De praemiis et poenis* 1–6; *Testamentum Jobi* 4.10; Epictetus, *Dissertationes* 3.12.7, 15.3; Dio Chrysostom, *Orationes* 28.10, 12 (cf. 29.9. 31.21); Lucian, *Anacharsis* 15; Plutarch, *Moralia* 561A, 1105C. *1 Cor.* 9.24–26; *1 Tm.* 4.7–10; *2 Tm.* 2.5; *Heb.* 12.1–2. Ignatius of Antioch *To Polycarp* 1.3, cf. 2.3, 3.1. *Idem, To Diognetus* 6.9. V. C. Pfitzner, *Paul and the Agon Motif* (Leiden: Brill, 1967). *Enkratēs, enkrateia* (disciplined, self-control) are shared by athletes and ascetics. Xenophon, *Memorabilia* 1.5, 6; 4.8, 11. This virtue is at *Acts* 24.25; *1 Cor.* 7.9, 9.25; *Gal.* 5.23; *Ti.* 1.8; *2 Pt.* 1.6, and twenty-three times in Hermas's *The Shepherd.*
5. See last note, also *Sibylline Oracles* 4.170; Pseudo-Phocylides 76, 123; *Epistle of Aristeas* 168, 225, 285; *Second Letter of Clement* 20.4; Ignatius of Antioch, *Letter to the Philadelphians* 9.1; *To Diognetus* 5.2, 12.5; *Hermas,* mandate 8.10. In Philo *askēsis* is the practice of piety; in Josephus the exercise of virtue (*Antiquitates judaicae* 1.6) or practical moral exercise (*Against Apion* 2.171, 173).
6. Alfred Braunthal, *Salvation and the Perfect Society* (Amherst: University of Massachusetts Press, 1979), pp. 2–3. *Mk.* 10.30 is realistic. T. E. Schmidt, "Mark 10:29–30; Matthew 19:29: 'Leave house . . . and region'?" *New Testament Studies* 38 (1992):605–616, would remove "fields" (wrongly). *2 Cor.* 8.6–15. *1 Tm.* 6.5–6. Marsilius, *DP,* chapter 14, §14 (assets to be made available to the needy). Fourth-century ascetics kept servants and needed the police (St. Basil, Letters, 1.28–29 [No. 3]).

7. *Mt.* 10.9–19, 19.27–30; *Mk.* 6.8–9; *Lk.* 8.1–3, 10.38–41, 19.5, 34; *Acts* 11.26, 20.10–11; *Rom.* 9.5 (cf. 18), 15.25–28, 16.1–2; *1 Cor.* 9.9; *1 Tm.* 5.18 (cf. *Dt.* 25.4); 2 *Cor.* 8.1–15, 9.11–14. Note the cashlessness at *Acts* 3.6. Paul's exposulations: *Acts* 18.3, 20.33–35; *Rom.* 9.6–15, 18; *2 Cor.* 11.7–8; *1 Thes.* 2.9; *2 Thes.* 2.7–8. Does the symbiosis diminish the ascetic's power? Bryan S. Turner, *Religion and Social Theory: A Materialist Perspective* (New Jersey: Humanities Press, 1983) brings out the aspect of exploitation.
8. Erasmus, *Praise of Folly* (1509. Various editions); Robert Burton, *The Anatomy of Melancholy* (1621) (London and Toronto: Dent, 1972), 3.319, 341–343; John Earle, *Microcosmographia* (1928) in Arthur Quiller-Couch, ed., *The Oxford Book of English Prose* (Oxford: Clarendon, 1930), no. 138 ("A She-Precise Hypocrite"). Samuel Butler, *Hudibras* (1663–1668, revised 1674. Various editions), satirizes hypocrisy in Puritanism (see part 3, canto 1). Unnatural repressions bear evil fruits: James Orr, "Asceticism," in Charles H. H. Wright and Charles Neil, eds., *A Protestant Dictionary* (London: Hodder & Stoughton, 1904), pp. 50–51. Fair resolutions have a predictable end: William Shakespeare, *Love's Labours Lost,* I.1.29–32, 36–49 (*Riverside Shakespeare*). The exemplary, ascetical and pacifist bishop E. W. Barnes decried "verminous asceticism": John Barnes, *Ahead of His Age* (London: Collins, 1979), pp. 105, 137, 212. The ascetic Albert Schweitzer had no time for "asceticism."
9. *Col.* 2.5–9; *1 Thes.* 4.9. Contrast the admonitions of *Ti.* 2.1–10. The pastoral epistles possibly contain reused Pauline material: E. Earle Ellis, "The Pastorals and Paul," *Expository Times* 104 (1992–1993):45–47.
10. *Mk.* 1.5–6; *Mt.* 11.7; *Lk.* 5.33, 7.33. Cf. *Mk* 6.34–37, 8.4. K. G. Kuhn, "Askese," in Kurt Galling, ed., *Die Religion in Geschichte und Gegenwart* 1 (Tubingen: Mohr, 1957), pp. 642–643. As a disciple of John, Jesus may have renounced possessions and marriage. He did not impose this on his disciples. On the reasons for John's withdrawal and fasts: Hartwig Thyen, "Babtisma metanoias eis aphesin hamartion," in *Zeit und Geschichte: Dankesgabe an Rudolf Bultmann zum 80. Geburtstag,* ed. Erich Dinkler (Tübingen: Mohr, 1964), pp. 97–125, especially pp. 111–112.
11. The Sabbath, tithes, fasts, etc., are programmatically ascetical. Philo said the sabbatical year was an ascetic program (*Special Laws* 2.87–88). Within Judaism historical examples of asceticism, such as the Nazarite, can be pointed to. Abstentions from women: *Qiddushin* 70a; Targum Ps. Jon. *Nm.* 12.8. Kuhn, "Askese" (op. cit.), pp. 641–642. M. Simon, "Asceticism in Jewish sects," in *La tradizione dell' enkrateia. Motivazioni ontologiche e protologiche. Atti del Colloquio Internazionale, Milano 20–23 aprile 1982,* ed. U. Bianchi (Rome: Ateneo, 1985), pp. 393–431. S. D. Fraade, "Ascetical aspects of ancient Judaism," *Jewish Spirituality: From the Bible to the Middle Ages,* vol. 13, *World Spirituality,* ed. A. Green (New York: Crossroad, 1986), pp. 253–288. A. Lazaroff, "Bahyā's asceticism against its rabbinic and Islamic background," *Journal of Jewish Studies* 21 (1970):11–38. Hans Peter Ruger, *Die Weischeitschrift aus der Kairöer Geniza: Text, Ubersetzung, und philologischer Kommentar,* Wissenschaftliche Untersuchunger zum Neuen Testament 53 (Tubingen: Mohr, 1991). Daniël Meijers, *Ascetic Hasidism in Jerusalem,* Studies in Judaism in Modern Times 10 (Leiden: Brill, 1992). David Landau, *Piety and Power: The World of Jewish Fundamentalism* (London: Secker and Warberg, 1992). An ascetic, R. Hanina: *Ber.* 17b, *Ḥul.* 86a. An ascetic outlook: Josephus, *Against Apion* 2.189. Derrett, *Ascetic Discourse,* p. 97. W. Schoedel, "Jewish Wisdom and the Formation of the Christian Ascetic," in *Aspects of Wisdom in Judaism and Early Christianity,* ed. R. C. Wilken (Notre Dame University Press, 1975), pp. 143–168.

12. J.D.M. Derrett, *Studies in the New Testament*, 5 vols. (Leiden, Brill, 1977–1989), 1:193–201; Daniel Marguerat, "La mort d'Ananias et Saphvia," *NTS* 39 (1993):209–226.
13. *Acts* 4.32–35, 5.11; *Rom.* 12.10, 15.26; *2 Cor.* 8.1–2, 13–15 (*Ex.* 16.18); *Heb.* 13.2–16; *1 Pt.* 4.9. Work in fields (*Mk.* 13.15); business (*1 Cor.* 5.9–10, 7.31); earning presupposed (*Lk.* 16.19–31; *Mk.* 12.13–17; *Acts* 20.35.)
14. *Acts* 11.26. 18.3, 20.33–35; *1 Cor.* 9.5–18; *2 Cor.* 11.7–8; *1 Thes.* 2.9, 4.11–12, 5.14; *2 Thes.* 2.6–12. M.J.J. Menken, "Paradise Regained or Still Lost?" *NTS* 38 (1992):271–289. Gautama Buddha denied he was a parasite: *Sutta-nipāta,* Kasibhār-advājasutts (1.4) in Lord Chalmers, ed. and trans., *Buddha's Teachings,* Harvard Oriental Series 37 (Cambridge: Harvard University Press, 1932), pp. 20–25. Cf. *Mt.* 10.10 and *Lk.* 10.7. *Didache* 11.8–13.
15. See last note. *Acts* 22.4, 24.22 ("Way," Heb. *derek* [Mishnah, *Avot* 2.9]). Diversity of styles was admitted by Jesus: *Mt.* 11.18–19 and *Lk.* 7.33–34; cf. *Lk.* 10.8. Adaptability: *Lk.* 5.39 (texts); *Rom.* 13.2–23 (taboos). Baḥyā ben Joseph Ibn Paquda, *Ḥôvôt ha-levāvôt (Duties of the Heart),* Treatise 9, chapter 5, trans. Moses Hyamson, 2 vols. (Jerusalem & New York: Feldheim, 1970), 2:323. "The beginning of abstinence (*pᵉrîšût*) is to concentrate the mind on making proper arrangements for one's livelihood." See *Prv.* 10.16.
16. *Mt.* 8.19–22 and *Lk.* 9.57–58, but cf. 4.13 (*katoikēsen,* "dwelt"). Cf. *2 Sm.* 15.20? Marsilius, *DP,* chapter 3, §33 (Christ the poor wayfarer: *Lk.* 18.22). J.D.M. Derrett, "The Homelessness of the Religious Leader," *Brahmavidyā,* Adyar Library Bulletin 50 (1986), pp. 198–217. Julian, *Letter to Themistius* 256D. A Cynic ascetic may teach: Pseudo-Lucian, *Cynicus* 19. C. Wolff, "Niedrigkeit und Verzicht," *NTS* 34 (1988):183–196, at p. 184. J. D. Kingsbury, "On Following Jesus: The 'Eager' Scribe and the 'Reluctant' Disciple (*Matthew* 8.18–22)," *NTS* 34 (1988):45–59. The nature miracle at *John* 2.1–11 (Cana) has no bearing on Jesus' lifestyle (J.D.M. Derrett, "Intoxication, Joy, and Wrath: 1 Cor. 11:21 and Jn. 2:10," *Filología Neotestamentaria* 2 (1989):41–56.
17. Statements referred to by Derrett, *Ascetic Discourse,* p. 100. Add: A. N. Wilson, *Tolstoy* (London: Hamish Hamilton, 1988), pp. 300–301. Alfred Reynalds, *Jesus versus Christianity* (London: Cambridge International, 1988), pp. 216–217.
18. Julian, *Against the Galileans* 229E–235A. Arguments for and against pacifism: Barnes, *Ahead of His Age,* p. 361.
19. Leo Tolstoy, *A Confession: The Gospel in Brief, and What I Believe,* trans. Aylmer Maude (London: Oxford University Press, 1971); *The Kingdom of God and Peace Essays* (London: Oxford University Press, 1974); *Essays and Letters* (London: Oxford University Press, 1911).
20. Aylmer Maude, *What I Believe,* p. 324, note 1 (See Maude, *Life of Tolstoy,* 2 vols. [London: Constable, 1908–1910], 2 [3d ed., 1911]:36–55); 331, note 1; 343, note 1; 391, note 1; 480, note 1. Also see his *Leo Tolstoy* (London: Methuen, 1918), chapter 12 (nonresistance) and chapter 13 (a criticism). Cf. Leo Tolstoy, *Tolstoy's Writings on Civil Disobedience and Non-Violence* (New York: Bergman, 1967). A positive approach in R. V. Sampson, *Tolstoy: Discovery of Peace* (London: Heinemann, 1973) is criticized by E. B. Greenwood, "Tolstoy and Religion" in *New Essays on Tolstoy,* ed. Malcolm Jones (Cambridge: Cambridge University Press, 1978), pp. 149–174, esp. pp. 168–171.
21. *Mk.* 10.29–30 and *Lk.* 18.29b–30. One thinks of Jains, Quakers, Mennonites. Pretence of piety to prosper in trade, and reluctance to offend rich members: Christopher Hill,

A Tinker and a Poor Man (New York: Knopf, 1989), p. 237. John A. Hostetler, *Amish Society* (Baltimore and London: Johns Hopkins University Press, 1968). Gillian L. Gollin, *Moravians in Two Worlds* (New York and London: Columbia University Press, 1967).

22. *Rom.* 12.6–8; *1 Cor.* 12.4–11, 28–31. The philosopher in Pseudo-Lucian (*Cynicus: Lucian* 8.380–411) denies he rejects God's bounty, admiring Hercules, ascetic but powerful.
23. *Mk.* 4.8, 20; *Mt.* 13.3–8, 23. *Mt.* 11.28–30 (cf. *Is.* 55.3); *Gospel of Thomas* 90. Meek as Moses (*Nm.* 12.3), speaking as heavenly Wisdom, Jesus offers rest (*Is.* 11.10, 28.12; *Jer.* 6.16) to those that assume the yoke, which, while it implies obligation and work (*1 Kgs.* 12.4; *Lam.* 3.27; Mishnah, *Avot* 3.5), is gracious (*Ps.* 34.8, 116.7), leading to repentance (*Rom.* 2.4), a necessary (*Mt.* 11.20–24) alternative to the plan which failed under the Old Covenant (*Psalm of Solomon* 7.9; *Acts* 15.10). The pattern for this pronouncement is in *Sirach* 6.18–37, 24.19–22, 40.1, 51.26–30. Celia Deutsch, *Hidden Wisdom and the Easy Yoke* (Sheffield: Journal for the Study of the Old Testament Press, 1987) seems not (pp. 133–135) to explain "easy." Diogenes Laertius, in W. R. Paton, ed., *Greek Anthology,* 5 vols. (Cambridge: Harvard University Press), vol. 2, no. 87.4, p. 52, claims the legislator Solon lightened the compatriots' burdens by good laws, including a general release from secured debts.
24. Marsilius, *DP,* chapter 13, §39. The narrow gate: *Mt.* 7.13–14 and *Lk.* 13.24. J.D.M. Derrett, *Studies* 4:147–156. M. J. Suggs, "The Christian Two Ways tradition: Its Antiquity, Form, and Function," in D. E. Aune, ed., *Studies in the New Testament and Early Christian Literature: Essays in honor of A. P. Wikgren* (Leiden: Brill, 1972), pp. 60–74.
25. *Mt.* 13.22, 24.26; *Lk.* 6.26; *2 Cor.* 11.9; *2 Tm.* 3.12; *1 Jn.* 2.18; *2 Jn.* 7; *Didache* 11.5–6. *Piers Plowman,* B. version, prologue 53–57 (George Kane and E. Talbot Donaldson, eds., *Piers Plowman: The B. Version* [London: Athlone, 1975], p. 230). Marsilius, *DP,* chapter 12, §32. Enthusiasm for ascetics: *Lk.* 9.17, 11.27–28; *Jn.* 12.19, 21–22. His name: *Lk.* 9.49–50, 10.17. Power to be renounced: *Lk.* 7.15, 9.42. Honor contrary to ascetic principles: *Mt.* 26.8–9; *Lk.* 7.39 (more tactful).
26. See note 14, above.
27. Jesus' teaching on marriage (for example, *Mt.* 5.32). Hillel, in Mishnah, *Avot* 2.7. *Mt.* 18.6–7 (causing others to "stumble"), cf. 13.41.
28. Litigation being prohibited. *Mt.* 5.39–40; *Didache* 1.4; *1 Cor.* 6.7.
29. *2 Cor.* 11.20. Do not relax vigilance (*1 Pt.* 5.8) to allow others to deceive you.
30. Albert Schweitzer, *The Mysticism of Paul the Apostle,* trans. William Montgomery (London: A. & C. Black, 1931); (Paul is not an "ascetic zealot"—he is free from the things of the world: p. 332); Alfred Wikenhauser, *Pauline Mysticism: Christ in the Mystical Teaching of St. Paul* (Edinburgh and London: Nelson, 1960).
31. See last note. *1 Cor.* 11.1.
32. *Rom.* 7.18–25, 8.13, 13.13; *1 Cor.* 5; *2 Cor.* 12.20, 26; cf. *1 Pt.* 2.1.
33. The eucharist controversy at *1 Cor.* 11.18–22 may illustrate this. *Heb.* 3.16–4.1, 4.11–13, 6.4, 12.3–4, 7–11, 13.13 (cf. *Jas.* 1.3–4) represent a return to rigor. Sinners held the form of religion but denied the power of it (*2 Tm.* 3.1–9). See below, note 111. Dale Goldsmith, "Toward Writing the History of a Logion" *NTS* 35 (1989):254–265 (the fate of *Mt.* 7.7–11).
34. *Gal.* 5.16, 19–21; *Col.* 2.11; *1 Pt.* 2.11, 4.2; *1 Jn.* 2.16. "Flesh" is opposed to "spirit"; it can never possess the Kingdom (*1 Cor.* 15.50). At home in the body we are exiles from the Lord (*2 Cor.* 5.7).

35. Braunthal, *Salvation*, pp. 101–102. Baḥyā says the evil inclination furthers attachment to the "world" (Treatise 9, chapter 2).
36. Braunthal, *Salvation*, pp. 15–18. *Ps.* 94.3–7; *Eccl.* 4.1; *Jer.* 12.1. Mishnah, *Avot* 4.15. The observation is universal: cf. Seneca, *On Benefits* 2.28, 2–3.
37. François René, Vicomte de Chateaubriant, *Le Génie du Christianisme* (1802, 1828), many editions and translations. The business of religion (*1 Tm.* 6.5–9) does not preclude a self-interested clergy (Adam Smith, *An Inquiry into the Nature and Causes of the Wealth of Nations* [1812. Various editions], book 5, chapter 1, part 3, articles 2 and 3), as the bourgeois society sets its own standards: Hill, *Tinker*, pp. 21–11. Mysticism does not require misery: Robin L. Fox, *Pagans and Christians* (Harmondsworth: Penguin, 1986), p. 125.
38. Vices: *Mt.* 15.19; *Rom.* 1.29–32; *1 Cor.* 6.9–10; *Gal.* 5.19–21; cf. 1QS IV.9–11; *Didache* 5.1–2. Cf. *Ti.* 2.1–10; *1 Pt.* 2.13, 17. Harvey, *Strenuous*, pp. 195–201, suggests Jesus was one of an international community of moral educators, plus "something more" (*Mt.* 19.20). Rational advice: *Col.* 3.18–4.1. Roy Yates, "The Christian Way of Life: The Paraenetic Material in Colossians 3.1–4.6," *Evangelical Quarterly* 63 (1991):241–251 (the ethical texts have antecedents in Hellenistic as well as Jewish religious life).
39. F. Gerald Downing, *Christ and the Cynics: Jesus and Other Radical Preachers in First Century Tradition* (Sheffield: JSOT Press, 1988). Cynics taught abstinence and restraint (Pseudo-Lucian, *Cynicus*); Jesus the avoidance of vices fueled by greed. Repentance, law, merit, grace, miracles, demonology, eschatology, Christology, *talio*, and a systematic theology are missing from Stoic-Cynic teaching, but especially the commandment of "mutual service" (*Gal.* 5.13).
40. For the yoke, see note 23, above. Hypocrisy: *Mt.* 23.2–4, 5–12, 27–28. Hearing alone is useless: *Mt.* 7.26 (cf. *Lk.* 10.42). Lip-service: *Mt.* 21.28–32. Cf. *Jas.* 2.10.
41. *Mt.* 3.1, 15.2–3; *Lk.* 5.33–38; *Jn.* 15.1, 28–29; *Acts* 18.18, 21.23–26. Peter: *Gal.* 2.11–14. Apollos: *Acts* 18.22–28; *1 Cor.* 1.12, 3.4–6, 21–23, 4.6, 16.12. Cf. *2 Cor.* 11.2–5, 10–15. On occasional celibacy see R. E. Oster, "Use, Misuse, and Neglect of Archaeological Evidence in Some Modern Works on 1 Corinthians," *Zeitschrift für die neutestamentliche Wissenschaft* 82 (1992):52–73. In a Buddhist metaphor, those that have crossed a river by means of a raft need not carry it thereafter on their backs. What observances have a continuous value?
42. Vicarious achievement: *Mt.* 7.22; vicarious merit, patronage: *1 Cor.* 15.29; *Mt.* 10.41–42; vicarious merit denied: *Mt.* 25.12; charity: *Mt.* 25.34–46. Value of alms: *Jn.* 12.8; *Mk.* 14.7. Abuses: *1 Tm.* 5.3–16.
43. *Is.* 4.2, 10.21, 65.8–12, 66.19. *Ez.* 34.26; *Hos.* 2.23; *Zec.* 8.11, 9.7. *Damascus Document (CD)* 1.4, 2.5, 9–10. *Mt.* 3.9, 22.14; *Rom.* 11.1–7, 25–26; cf. *Jn.* 1.11–13, 47; *Gal.* 6.16. The chosen: *Mt.* 22.14. Recorded names: *Lk.* 10.20 (*Ex.* 32.32–33; *Ps.* 56.8, 69.28); *Phil.* 4.3; *Rv.* 5.3. Xavier Léon-Dufour, ed., *Dictionary of Biblical Theology*, trans. P. Joseph Cahill (London: Geoffrey Chapman, 1970), article called "Remnant."
44. *Mk.* 12.13–17; *Rom.* 13.1–7; *1 Cor.* 2.6; *1 Pt.* 2.13–17. *Martyrdom of Polycarp* 10.2. Note *Jn.* 19.11. *Acts* 5.29, *Gal.* 1.10; *1 Thes.* 2.4. *Jn.* 19.12, 15 criticize Jewry.
45. *Mt.* 7.21, 12.50, 21.31; *Mk.* 3.35; *Lk.* 11.28; *Jn.* 4.34, 5.30; *Rv.* 22.14. Righteousness above prudence: *Mt.* 6.24–34; wisdom over comity: *Mt.* 11.16–19; true aims: *Mt.* 6.25–34 and *Lk.* 12.22–32. Positive requirements not to be codified (*Lk.* 18.14); talents must be employed (*Lk.* 19.11–27). Human standards worthless: *Mt.* 6.1–4, 5–7, 6.16–18; nonresponders threatened: *Mt.* 10.15, 11.20–24. Effort required: *Lk.* 6.46–49 (cf.

Septuagint, *Ps.* 47.9, 86.5), *Lk.* 14.29, 9.62. The daily cross: *Lk.* 9.23, 14.27. Non-ascetic lifestyle heedless: *Lk.* 17.27–28.

46. Cf. Mishnah, *Avot* 3.14. *Mk.* 13.19, 16.15; *Ps.* 8.4–6; *Rom.* 1.25; *1 Cor.* 11.9; *Col.* 1.16, 23, 3.10. Concern for the cosmos in John. Strangers must not be made to stumble: *Mt.* 17.27.
47. The powerful: *Phil.* 2.4–8; *1 Cor.* 12.31–13.13. Forgive utterly: (*Mt.* 6.14, 18.22). No aggression: *Mt.* 5.22, 25, 39. Even beggars not to be repulsed: *Mt.* 5.42. "Loving one another" (*Jn.* 13.34–35) is weaker. "Love your enemies" (*Mt.* 5.38–48; *Lk.* 6.27–36) drops from the paraenetic tradition since that (*Rom.* 12.14, 17–20; *1 Thes.* 5.15; *1 Pt.* 3.9; *1 Cor.* 4.12) aims at domestic success and public reputation. Paul did not love persecuting Jews. Jewish precepts carry more weight than Jesus' boldness: John Piper, *Love Your Enemies: Jesus' Love Command in the Synoptic Gospels and in the Early Christian Paraenesis,* Society for New Testament Studies Monograph Series 38 (Cambridge: Cambridge University Press, 1979). Anthony E. Harvey, "The Testament of Simeon Peter," in *A Testament to Geza Vermes,* eds. Philip R. Davies and Richard T. White, (Sheffield: JSOT Press, 1990), pp. 335–354. *Didache* 1.3: "Love those that hate you and you will have no enemy."
48. *Mt.* 9.36; *Jn.* 10.3–4, 11, 14 (cf. *Mk.* 8.32–33). *Is.* 40.11; *Jer.* 3.15, 23.3–4. Xavier Léon-Dufour, "Jesus le bon pasteur," chapter 18 in *Les paraboles évangéliques: Perspectives nouvelles,* ed. J. Delorme; (Paris, 1989); also F. Genuyt, "La Porte et le pasteur," chapter 19 in the same volume. The shepherd knows the sheep's merits: *Mk.* 12.43; he is a fair judge: *Mt.* 16.19, 18.18–19. J.D.M. Derrett, *New Resolutions of Old Conundrums* (Shipston-on-Stour, Warwickshire, Drinkwater, 1986), pp. 38–49.
49. *Dt.* 6.5 and *Lv.* 19.18 as projected at *Mt.* 22.37–40. *Mt.* 7.11–12, 10.8, 18.23–35; *Jn.* 14.15, 15.14, 13.34 (15.12, 17; *1 Jn.* 3.23). The Samaritan (*Lk.* 10.33–35) was an ascetic. J.D.M. Derrett, *Law in the New Testament* (London: Darton, Longman & Todd, 1970), chapter 9. Baḥyā, *Duties,* Treatise 9, chapters 4–5, delineates the humility of the "abstainer" and his care for his fellow men. Klaus Wengst, *Humility: Solidarity of the Humiliated* (London: S.C.M., 1988).
50. Cf. Mishnah, *Avot* 2.10, 12. *Mt.* 5.45; *2 Cor.* 8.13–15. Generosity rather than commerce: *Mt.* 20.12–13; almsgiving: *Lk.* 12.33–34. Reciprocity is not enough: *Lk.* 6.34–35. Compassion (see last note). Contributions to the poor: *Acts* 11.29, 24.17.
51. *Mt.* 4.23, 9.35, 10.1, 15.31; 10.8 (gratuitously). *Mt.* 23.37 (solicitude). *Mk.* 16.18; *Lk.* 16.27–28. The healer-exegete wins: *Lk.* 13.7. Cf. *Jn.* 11.4 (what sickness?); *Mt.* 8.17 (savior). *Jas.* 5.14–15. Baḥyā, *Duties,* Treatise 9, chapter 2, says the "abstainer" visits the sick and gives them his superfluities. Cf. 4Q521 II.12.
52. Whereas Seneca, *Moral Epistles* 7.7, says one should loathe the crowd, and St. Augustine, *Confessions* 1.16, condemns human custom, Christian renouncers are not supramundane. But see *Rom.* 12.2 (this "age"); *Jn.* 7.7, 15.18–19, 16.33, 17.14; *1 Jn.* 4.5. The arena of the enemy: *Lk.* 4.5–6; its mammon (*Lk.* 16.13), and the use of the latter (*Lk.* 16.23, 16.4, 9). The world must be enlightened: *Mt.* 5.13–16. It hates Christians because they oppose its pleasures: Ignatius of Antioch, *To Diognetus* 6.5. "The world is distinguished from the holy," Baḥyā, *Duties,* Treatise 9, chapter 7.
53. *Mt.* 10.22, 24.13; *1 Cor.* 13.7; *2 Cor.* 6.4; *Phil.* 4.5; *Eph.* 4.2; *Col.* 3.13; *Jas.* 1.34, 5.11; *1 Pt.* 2.19. If truly reborn (*Jn.* 3.3; *2 Cor.* 5.17; *Col.* 3.9; *1 Pt.* 1.3, 23) *hypomonē* (*Lk.* 8.15, 21.9; *Rom.* 12.12; *Heb.* 10.32–33—a word occurring eight times in Old Testament pseudepigrapha) would hardly be called for. *Heb.* 12.7: suffering is part of your training. Rational objections brushed aside: *Mt.* 16.21–23; cf. *1 Pt.* 3.14–16. A slave should not try to mitigate the degradation of his slavery: John M. G. Barclay,

"Paul, Philemon, and the Dilemma of Christian Slave-Ownership," *NTS* 37 (1991):161–186.

54. *Mt.* 20.20–27, 23.5–12; *Lk.* 9.46–50 (cf. *Mk.* 9.35, servant of all), 11.43, 14.8–11, 20.45–47, 22.24–26; *Jn.* 13.12–17. The child: *Mt.* 18.1–4; cf. 19.14). First last: *Mt.* 19.27–30, 20.8, 16; *Mk.* 10.31; *Lk.* 13.30. In respect of merit status cannot be claimed: *Mt.* 19.30, 20.8, 16; 25.21, 23—an idea absent from John. *Mk.* 10.37 (sons of Zebedee). *Rom.* 12.16; *1 Cor.* 4.10. Hence humility: *Phil.* 2.3, *1 Tm.* 6.17.
55. *Rom.* 12.10. Though not incompatible with love, it conflicts with Jesus' teaching that no one can estimate merit (see last note).
56. *Ps.* 119.36; *1 Thes.* 2.5; *2 Pt.* 2.14–15. Poverty praised: *Mt.* 5.3. Subsistence enough: *Mt.* 10.9–10. Needs will be met: *Mt.* 6.28, 17.24–27. Rich, possessing nothing: *2 Cor.* 6.10 (*Prv.* 13.7), 8.9. *Lk.* 12.13–15, 21; 8.14; 16.9. Ignore reciprocity: *Lk.* 14.12–14. Appetites to be watched: *Mt.* 14.20–21. Against *pleonexia: Lk.* 12.15; *Col.* 3.5; *1 Tm.* 6.9–10; *Heb.* 13.2; *Jas.* 4.2; Pseudo-Lucian, *Cynicus* 15. Material goods are to be abandoned: *1 Cor.* 13.3; but *Lk.* 12.15, 18–20 militates against hoarding. Thomas E. Schmidt, *Hostility to Wealth in the Synoptic Gospels*, (Sheffield: JSOT Press, 1987): Jesus taught dependence on God. Kuhn, "Askese," p. 643, §2: possessions inconsistent with discipleship of the Kingdom, Luke retaining ascetic touches. Martin Hengel, *Property and Riches in the Early Church* (London: S.C.M., 1974): primitive Christianity contained a radical criticism of riches, demanding detachment, but early Christian ethics led to a "healthy detachment from external goods" (ibid., pp. 84–88) by way of compromises rather than "love communism." Marsilius, *DP*, chapter 13, §29, contends a vow to accept nothing for distribution to the poor would be void. James Alison, *Knowing Jesus* (London: Society for the Preservation of Christian Knowledge, 1993), pp. 56–57: human desire must be moved out of the pattern of rivalry, a relationship based on death, to a relationship based on the pacific imitation of Jesus, a relationship with others and gratuity, service—for one has received life gratuitously.
57. *Mt.* 5.28, 32; *Rom.* 1.26–27. Marriage allowed: *1 Cor.* 7.1–40; *1 Thes.* 4.3–7; *Heb.* 13.4. In *ḥasîdût* (saintliness) chastity is prized; and the "uplifted eye," sinful: Adolph Büchler, *Types of Jewish-Palestinian Piety from 70 B.C.E. to 70 C.E.: The Ancient Pious Men* (London: Jews' College Press, 1922; reprinted, New York, 1968), pp. 42–55.
58. See *Phil.* 2.4. Note *Mt.* 17.27, 18.6. *Lk.* 16.21–22. One protects oneself against burglars in the latter's interest (*Mt.* 24.43). J.D.M. Derrett, *Studies* 2:124–129.
59. Jesus' parents were models of conventional piety, yet see *Lk.* 2.49. *Mt.* 12.46–50, 13.55–58; *Lk.* 8.20–25, 12.51–53; *Mt.* 10.37–38; *Lk.* 14.26; *Gosp. Thom.* 101. James H. Charlesworth, *Jesus within Judaism* (London: S.P.C.K., 1989), pp. 84–87. The "world" (note 52, above), like Sodom, does not bury its dead: *Mt.* 8.22 (Derrett, *Studies* 5:74–80). Fellow-villagers will be nonsupportive: *Mk.* 6.2–3.
60. See also the goal-centered *2 Cor.* 6.5, 11.27. If all this is not enough evidence, what is enough? The ascetic tone is heard at *Col.* 2.5, 11, 3.5–9; *Heb.* 13.14; *Jas.* 1.27. *Ephesians* has a rational approach, as *Col.* 3.18–25, 4.1. *1* and *2 Thes.* are not ascetical; *2 Thes.* 4 is antiascetical. The rigorous tone of *Heb.* 3.16–4.1, 4.11–13, 12.3–4, 12.13 sounds apologetic; likewise, *1 Pt.* 2.11, 3.16, 4.13 (neurotic), 5.8. C. Wolff, "Niedrigkeit und Verzicht in Wort und Weg Jesu und in der apostolischen Existenz des Paulus," *NTS* 34/2 (1988):183–196 (Paul the renouncer proves his discipleship of Jesus).
61. *Mt.* 5.32 ("save for . . ."); *Lk.* 17.4 (cf. *Mt.* 18.21–22) ("I repent"); *Mt.* 24.45–51 (corruption); *Lk.* 12.15 (surplus); *Lk.* 12.41–48 (degrees); *Acts* 6.1–4 (neglect). Good works are a judaizing feature: *Mt.* 5.16 (so *Epistle of James* and Dead Sea Scrolls). *Mt.*

5.44 (pray for persecutors is a decline from *Lk.* 6.27–28 (benefit those that hate you, cf. *Rom.* 12.14). Schmidt (note 56, above) shows that the decline from Jesus' standard was rapid. Notional dispossession became enough (*1 Cor.* 7.30), and compromise was inevitable (Schmidt, op. cit., pp. 166–167).

62. Aland, *Synopse,* §230, p. 312 (the injured are at fault). *Mt.* 5.22 variant reading *eikē,* "without ground." *Jas.* 4.11–12 (against slander) dilutes *Mt.* 7.1 (judgment). *Didache* 1.4, 1.3, 6.4; *2 Clement* 10.2. Harvey, *Strenuous,* p. 144. Even in the diluted form brethren needed to be "strengthened": *Acts* 14.22, 15.32, 41, 18.23, 20.2. Christians were oppressed by rich coreligionists: *Jas.* 5.6–7. Harvey, op. cit., p. 11, is frank: *Col* 3.18–20 (slaves); *1 Cor.* 16. 15–16 (leadership). God's word is peddled: *2 Cor.* 2.17; *Ti.* 1.11; *2 Pt.* 2.2–3.4. Decline is actually discussed: *2 Tm.* 4.3–4. See note 33, above.
63. Augustine, *De Sermone Domini in Monte,* in Richard C. Trench, *Exposition of the Sermon on the Mount Drawn from the Writings of St. Augustine,* 2d ed. (London: J. W. Parker, 1851). Derrett, *Ascetic discourse,* chapter 12. Religion must not be spiritualized so far as to place it beyond the reach of ordinary mortals; it must not endanger ecclesiastical wealth and pomp: A. D. Howell Smith, *Thou Art Peter* (London: Watts & Co., 1950), p. 696.
64. Note 2, above.
65. Harvey, *Strenuous,* pp. 132–133. *Entolē, entellomai* are used in the Synoptic Gospels of God's commands (cf. *Acts* 13.47), except at *Mt.* 17.9, which proves the rule. *Jn.* 13.34, 14.15, 21, 15.10, 12, 14, 17 insinuates Jesus' precepts are God's. Ignatius of Antioch found the Lord and the Apostles issued decrees *(dogmata, diatagmata)*: *Ad Magnesios* 13.1, *Ad Tralcianos* 7.1; cf. *Eph.* 9.2.
66. Harvey, *Strenuous,* pp. 168, 207–209. Bruce Chilton and J.I.H. McDonald, *Jesus and the Ethics of the Kingdom,* Biblical Foundation in Theology 2 (London: S.P.C.K., 1987), pp. 119, 123–124 (positive responses never become principles in themselves). *1 Cor.* 7.29–31 (cf. *Ez.* 7.12; *Is.* 24.2) supports Harvey so far as it goes. R. Minnerath, *Les Chrétiens et le Monde* (Paris: Gabalda, 1973), pp. 332–333. *2 Clem.* 12.6: the coming of the Kingdom depends on perfect restraint.
67. Harvey, *Strenuous* pp. 13, 24; cf. 190.
68. Ibid., pp. 15, 27, 129.
69. Ibid., pp. 190, 202; cf. 16, 128. This idea disparaged asceticism as "negative": Ernst von Dobschulz, *Christian Life in the Primitive Church* (New York: Putnam, 1904), pp. 377–378.
70. Harvey, *Strenuous,* pp. 23; cf. 2.
71. Ibid., pp. 35–36. Curses: *Acts* 13.10, 23.3; *Gal.* 1.8–9. Yet the teacher loves the taught. Christian morality corresponds with thoughtful people's standards. See Harvey, *Strenuous,* pp. 22–32.
72. Harvey, *Strenuous,* pp. 40, 92; cf. 139. Moses: *Mt.* 5.19, 19.17–21, 23.2; *Mk.* 10.19; *Lk.* 18.20; cf. *Lk.* 1.6. *1 Cor.* 7.19.
73. Harvey, *Strenuous,* pp. 49–60, 83, 203; cf. 142–143, 148. Jesus' commands cannot be commended as enlightened good sense. At p. 184 Harvey admits *1 Cor.* 13 goes beyond the norms of moral conduct based on prudence. Did *Ecclesiastes* diverge from wisdom?
74. Harvey, *Strenuous,* pp. 62–64, 195–197, 202.
75. Ibid., p. 66.
76. Ibid., pp. 78, 88. Jesus was not interested in law reform.
77. Ibid., pp. 85–86. In fact this was an Hasidic position.
78. Ibid., pp. 147–148, 165–166.
79. Ibid., p. 107; cf. 141, Harvey will not explain (p. 104) "love your enemies."

80. Ibid., p. 110.
81. Ibid., p. 114.
82. Ibid., pp. 113–114.
83. Ibid., pp. 119–120.
84. Ibid., p. 122. See note 47, above.
85. Ibid., pp. 124–127.
86. Ibid., pp. 130, 133; cf. p. 8. Mishnah, *Avot* (Ethics of the Fathers) contains many "exaggerated" admonitions, typical of Jewish moralist style.
87. Ibid., pp. 127, 135.
88. Ibid., pp. 136, 148.
89. Ibid., p. 157.
90. Ibid., p. 160. One gets rid of entanglements.
91. Ibid., p. 179. Seneca, *Moral Epistles* 98, §17, in Loeb Classical Library 79, *Seneca* 6:128–129. Marsilius, *DP*, chapter 13, §37.
92. Harvey, *Strenuous*, pp. 181–183, 185–186. But his motives are obscure, except in John. I doubt Jesus' alleged want of compassion. At pp. 187 and 189 Harvey points to *1 Cor.* 10.24, 13.5 as having no anchorage in any recorded teaching of Jesus. But Paul's is an Hasidic position.
93. Ibid., pp. 130, 137, 183, 206.
94. *Mt.* 15.2, 22.34–36 (and parallels); *Lk.* 20.20; *Jn.* 7.32, 45–46.
95. *Mt.* 12.2, 16.1, 19.3, 22.35 (all with parallels).
96. *Mt.* 10.11–15, 16.23, 23.34 (and parallels), 24.9; *Mk.* 3.6, 10.30; *Lk.* 6.23, 11.49, 21.16; *Jn.* 15.19–20, 16.2–4; *Acts* 6.10–8.1–3, 9.24, 29. Hence fearlessness was required: *Lk.* 12.4.
97. *Jn.* 5.10–13, 9.24, 34, 11.8, 16, 12.11–12.
98. *Jn.* 3.2, 19.38.
99. *Jn.* 7.13, 20.19; *Acts* 8.1. How justified this was *Acts* 6.10, 7.57–58, 9.24, 29, 13.50, 14.19; *Rom.* 8.35.
100. Harvey, *Strenuous*, p. 194.
101. *Lk.* 12.21. *Mt.* 6.20, 11.27, 19.27–30. Mishnah, *Avot* 3.17, 5.19, 6.11.
102. *Mt.* 21.31–32. *Jn.* 7.39, 20.22; *Acts* 2.4, 5.32; *Rom.* 8.2, 4; *2 Cor.* 1.22; *Gal.* 5.16–17. Its autonomy: *Jn.* 3.8; *1 Cor.* 2.15–16, 4.4. Cf. *Ex.* 31.3, 35.31; *Nm.* 11.26–29.
103. *Mt.* 10.28, 16.24–26; *Lk.* 9.24–25; *Jn.* 12.25; *Acts* 20.24, 21.13. *Martyrdom of Polycarp* 11.2. Derrett, *New Resolutions*, chapter 4. G. Schwarz, "Der Nachfolgespruch Markus 8.34b.c. Parr. Emendation un Ruckubersetzung," *NTS* 33 (1987):255–265. *Mt.* 3.7–10; *Jn.* 14.6: "input" turns an offer into a contract. Cf. *Job* 2.4–5.
104. An ancient principle, known in Qumran; cf. b. *B.Q.* 113b–114a. Maimonides, *Mishneh Torah (Code)* 14.1.26, 7, trans. Abraham M. Hershman, *The Code of Maimonides*, Book 14, *The Book of Judges*, Yale Jewish Studies 3 (New Haven: Yale University Press, 1949), p. 80. *Sunday Telegraph* (London), 4 August 1991, p. 3.
105. Mishnah, *Soṭah* 9 (end). Buchler, *Types*, p. 42. On the *ḥasîdîm*, their "sin-fearing" and standards, see *idem*, pp. 29–32 and, generally, also S. Safrai, "Teaching of pietists in Mishnaic literature," *Journal of Jewish Studies* 16 (1965):15–33. Maimonides, *Moreh Nevûkîm* 3.37, trans. S. Pines, *The Guide for the Perplexed*, 2 vols. (Chicago and London, University of Chicago Press, 1963), 2:545. The avoidance of temptation at *Mt.* 18.7–9 is obviously Hasidic. Placing others above oneself is Jewish piety: Josephus, *Against Apion* 2.196. A work by a *ḥasîd* is quoted by Bahyā ben Joseph ibn Paquda, *Duties of the Heart*, Hebrew and English version by Moses Hyamson (New York: Feldheim, 1970), 2:335–337.

106. R. Joshua ben Levi betrays Ulla: *Terumot* 8, 46b50; Midrash, *Gen. Rabbah* 94 (end). Büchler, *Types,* p. 38, note 1.
107. b. *B.Q.* 30a. They bury dangerous objects: j. *B.Q.* 3, 3c44. Büchler, *Types,* pp. 37–38. Maimonides, *Code,* 11.1.13, 22.
108. And so on. See b. *B.Q.* 103b; Buchler, *Types,* p. 36. An *ḥasîd* will not wash in water heated with straw gathered in the seventh year: Mishnah, *Sevi'it* 8.11.
109. Mishnah, *Avot* 5.10–11, 13–14.
110. *Mt.* 4.2, *Jn.* 6.15; *Mt.* 9.24; *Mk.* 1.35, 45; *Mk.* 6.30–32, 7.24. Ralph W. Emerson "Self-reliance," *Works* (London: Routledge, n.d.) no. 12, col. 2. Did the Qumran sect actually set up (notional) camps in the Desert? Robert H. Eisenman and Michael Wise, *The Dead Sea Scrolls Uncovered* (Shaftesbury, Dorset: Element, 1992) take a positive position on this.
111. See note 40, above. Hypocrites often cover their real enmity against the power of godliness with a pretended zeal for the form of it: Matthew Henry, *Exposition of the New Testament,* 10 vols. (London: Thomas C. Jack, William Mackenzie, 1886–1888), 4:253 (on *Jn.* 5.16).
112. Martin Buber said (1948), "I consider Hasidic truth vitally important for Jews, Christians, and others; and at this particular hour more important than ever before. For now is the hour when we are in danger of forgetting for what purpose we are on earth, and I know of no other that reminds us of this so forcibly." Quoted by Samuel H. Dresner, *The Zaddik* (London: Abelard-Schuman, n.d.), pp. 13–14. Dresner was a powerful defender of Hasidism.
113. Juan Mateos, "Algunas notas sobre el evangelio de Marcos (IV)," *Filología Neotestamentaria* 5 (1992):61–68; pp. 64–65 show how the seated scribes in *Mk.* 2.6 imply simply the mute resistance of the Torah as presented in Galilee to Jesus' proceedings and their implications.
114. *Mt.* 5.22, 29–30, 10.28, 16.18, 18.6–9; *Jn.* 5.14, 8.11. Cf. 4Q521 II.13.
115. *Mk.* 2.18, 7.4, 12.33; *Lk.* 5.33–38, 11.38–41. For the "Lord, Lord" syndrome, see *Lk.* 6.46. Skepticism on alms: *Jn.* 12.8; *Mk.* 14.7. A collapse of observances alarmed Catholics at the Reformation: John Bossy, *The English Catholic Community 1570–1850* (London: Darton, Longman and Todd, 1975), pp. 157–158; therefore the rapid recovery under Queen Mary I: Eamon Duffy, *The Stripping of the Altars* (New Haven: Yale University Press, 1992). See note 111, above.
116. *Lk.* 16.14–15; *Jn.* 5.44; cf. 41; cf. 7.18. *Jn.* 12.43; *Acts* 19.28, 34, 28.30(?). Rational objections to suffering are brushed aside: *Mt.* 16.21–23.

9

Tibetan Buddhist Perspectives on Asceticism

Robert A. F. Thurman

The Greek *askēsis* relates to "exercise" and "training," according to Walter O. Kaelber's stimulating article in Macmillan's *Encyclopedia of Religion.*[1] The example is given of the Greek athlete "subjecting himself to systematic exercise or training in order to attain a goal of physical fitness." Later the idea emerges that one can train the will, mind, or soul "systematically and rigorously . . . so as to attain a more virtuous life or a higher spiritual state."

What is missing here and should be included with mention of the athlete is mention of the warrior. It seems evident that an important source of asceticism is warrior training, as the life-and-death context of battle is what makes the heroic self-overcomings involved in asceticism realistic. Spiritual asceticism definitionally or essentially must be understood in parallel and contrast with military asceticism, tracing this polarity all the way back into the archaic to the complementary and yet rival figures of shaman and war chief.[2]

In recent millennia at least, India seems to be the primary land of organized spiritual athleticism, spiritual militancy, or asceticism (I think primarily for economic reasons). Within India, Buddhism was the ascetical movement that promoted asceticism to a new level, through the significant institutional innovation of the cenobitic monastery, some five to seven centuries before such institutions began to develop in western and eastern Asia. Therefore, Indian and Buddhist perspectives on questions of asceticism, from origins to forms to meanings, should cast useful light on the general subject.

In what follows, I will (1) attempt a provisional definition of asceticism as an evolutionary phenomenon; (2) describe the early Buddhist attitude to this phenomenon, illustrated in Buddhist narratives and instructions, against the background attitudes emerging in the contemporary cultures of the Indian subcontinent; and (3) go on to an account of Tibetan Buddhist developments in asceticism.

Definitions. Essences, Origins, and Forms

It seems that asceticism can be defined as the evolutionary impulse in human beings to attempt consciously to improve control over their habitual life processes, with a view to bettering their situation at least in a relative, and, if possible, an ultimate, way. This involves purposively withdrawing energy invested in these habitual processes and conditioning the self to channel those recovered energies into newly, consciously designed and improved processes. Asceticism thus involves (1) conscious reflective awareness of one's activities as habitually governed; (2) ability to imagine more complete awareness and more effective activity; and (3) ambition or enthusiasm to develop higher awareness and effective activity. Asceticism so defined can be divided into two types, relative and ultimate, and each of these having mundane and spiritual varieties.

Relative asceticism means asceticism that uses self-development toward relative goals, such as success, wealth, pleasure, status, virtue, or righteousness. These relative goals can be mundane: that is, winning battles, up to even world conquest; accumulating treasure; having more exotic sense pleasures; rising in class status; feeling righteous in terms of a secular system of law. Or they can be spiritual: winning a struggle with an evil spirit; accumulating merit; enjoying religious ceremonies; rising in a spiritual hierarchy; feelıng pure or holy or enlightened.

Ultimate asceticism uses ascetical developmental methods to achieve ultimate goals. Mundane ultimate asceticism would be asceticism aspiring to states of extreme and permanent pleasure and calm, some form of a state of permanent oblivion. Spiritual ultimate asceticism works methodically to achieve the highest goal of the spiritual system: which might be self-absorption in an all-powerful god or goddess as in Christıan mysticism, Islam, Kabbala, Shaivism, Vaishnavism, or Shaktism; self-extinction in a dualistic form of liberation such as some kinds of Buddhist nirvanas; realization of identity with an absolute godhead, such as Brahman; or the Mahayana nondual realization of perfect Buddhahood. These types can be schematized accordingly:

		asceticism	
	relative		ultimate
mundane	spiritual	mundane	spiritual

If this definitional scheme is in any way serviceable, then the origıns of asceticism are not mysterious. Any animal that tries to improve its success or pleasure by controlling an instinctive reaction is practicing asceticism—for example, a prey animal that hides immobile or plays dead, controlling ıts abject terror and instinct to flee heedlessly in order to elude capture; or a predator that controls its first impulse to spring, while waiting for a better position.

In archaic societies, asceticism is practiced by warriors in many ways, in order to develop greater strength and prowess to assure survival and victory, buildıng on the skills developed by hunters in the battle with prey animals. And asceticism is practiced by women in all societies in many ways, in order to improve the knowledge of and control over the environment in order to sustain their children. In a sense, the ordeal of self-denial, extra effort, and struggle involved in bearing children—that is, sharing your bloodstream and inner nutrıents; going through the agonies of labor; sharing your inner vital essence through milk; and sharing your time and constant attention while rearing—is perhaps the prımal ascetical act, as the common example of self-sacrifice of a mammalian mother for her offspring is the primal ascetical heroism.

In the spiritual realm, archaic societies are highly reliant upon the ascetical activities of both male and female shamans, who practice systematic withdrawal from habitual energy routines in order to achieve improved awareness and prowess in dealing with the unseen and subtle realms and beings of the spiritual environment. Sickness, madness and death are the special concerns of these ascetics, and they are dedicated to helping themselves and their fellows deal with those most profound of challenges. Their highest asceticism involves the systematic simulation of all of these states, including death, in order to explore them and bring back guidelines for their fellows who will themselves have to face the real things. In their journeyings they encounter spiritual beings, benevolent and malevolent, so they naturally become the special mediators between the human, and superhuman, and subhuman realms.

The methods of ascetics are quite naturally based upon the necessities of normal or habitual (instinct-driven) life, since the ascetic learns to withdraw concern for them. Human beings need air, food and water; sleep; sexuality; such equipment as clothing and shelter; companionship and status; communication; sense-pleasure; and a sense of identity. Thus, withdrawal of energies habitually invested in these things involves the practices, respectively, of trance (breath retention); fasting; vigil; continence; poverty including nakedness and homelessness; isolation; silence; endurance of pain; and self-transcendence. Archaic mothers, hunter/warriors, and shamans all practiced these methods to accomplish their various goals, relative and ultimate, mundane and spiritual. They are the originals for the ascetics of the modern nations and world religions.

Buddhism and Asceticism

The Buddha's story should be known by everyone. He grew up a pampered prince, knowing only pleasure, according to the myth (that must be a myth!). Somehow he also learned the skills of a warrior, the military and organizational training princes received in his day, at least sufficiently to win the rather violent tournament necessary to secure a bride in his culture. After having his first child, and on the eve of being crowned on his father's abdication, he decided his awareness and prowess were inadequate for his situation. He renounced status, property, relationships, pleasures, and even his identity, and turned to the severe asceticism that was widely practiced by determined individual males at that time, who called themselves *shramanas* (wanderers). He fasted to an extreme degree, eating but a grain of sesame a day, withering to skin and bones. He stayed naked out in the elements, sat in freezing rivers in winter, and meditated in summer in the blazing sun surrounded by four fires. He sat sleepless in contorted postures. He did not speak for years. His only companions were others just as isolated and self-afflicting. He mastered the entire range of self-expanding and self-annihilating trances, including the severe breath retention of cataleptic trance.

He then decided one day that this severe asceticism was not useful in itself, as the austerities were too extreme. The focus on mental and physical discomfort was just as deluded, obsessive, binding, and unliberating as had been his princely focus on mental and physical comfort. It is usually said that he abandoned asceticism at this point, but that is not accurate in our present context. Rather, we should say he abandoned extreme asceticism.

He took food, bathed, clothed himself after a fashion, and then sat under a special tree, proclaiming his determination not to move from that spot until all things were known to him—until the mysteries of life and death had become clear. According to the tradition, in the early morning of that night's vigil, he became a perfectly enlightened Buddha. He achieved complete insight into the ultimate identitylessness that Buddhists reason is the source of acceptance of relative embodiedness, this being the full commitment to universal selfless love and compassion. That is, according to the standard definition of a Buddha, he attained perfect awareness of all realities, both transcendent and mundane, and so could exercise unimpeded prowess in compassion's task of sharing that awareness with all other beings in order to free them and enlighten them.

His problem in this regard was special, something unusual at that time in the world. That is, he did not experience the ultimate by dissolving permanently into some absolute that was absolutely outside the relative universe; nor did he emerge from his enlightenment experience with a sacred authority conferred by the god or gods of his nation. He did not emerge with a command or creed that people should do this or that, or believe this or that, and thereby be saved by the powers that be. He emerged with the rather worrisome news that the powers that be were just as much in need of being saved as were the people—gods were simply higher animals, much more knowledgeable and powerful, but just as bound by their evolutionary history as were humans.

Thus, the Buddha emerged with the unsettling insight that salvation could not be gained by following commands or by accepting creeds. His good news was that humans did not need all-powerful gods, all-certain commands, all-saving creeds. The human understanding was already very highly evolved, very close to full awareness of the real situation of life and death. And such full awareness conferred upon the human both the freedom from bondage and suffering and the ability to share that freedom and happiness with others.

The question was, how to move the human understanding that last little evolutionary bit. His answer was that it was a matter of *adhishiksha* (spiritual education), of *vinaya* (discipline), and *shila* (ethics); *bhāvanā/samādhi* (training or cultivation); and, finally, *prajñā* (insight or wisdom). This answer forced the Buddha to establish an educational institution. He could have returned to his own kingdom, accepted his throne, and then turned his country into a school for spiritual ascetics, imposing the enlightenment curriculum on his countrymen by royal decree. Or he could have remained in the forest to instruct other ascetics who already had the discipline and relative freedom to live outside the norms of society, helping them with the final inner asceticism of achieving detachment from ascetical prowess itself and gaining the wisdom of ultimate identitylessness and universal compassion. The first option he rejected, possibly because it would have identified his movement with the Shakya nation and made it unacceptable to the rulers and people of the many other city states of the region; or else because it was simply discordant with the ascetical ethos, by nature voluntary, to order people to participate in it. The second option he also rejected, probably because it would excessively limit the number of people he could assist through his liberating curriculum, since only those already determined to commit themselves to asceticism—all males, mostly from the Brahmin priest and warrior classes—would be able to avail themselves of the teachings.

He invented a third way, a middle way between the regulated pattern of normal social life and the extremely deregulated practice of extranormal ascetical life. He gradually but systematically established the Buddhist monastic community *(saṃgha),* a cenobitic ascetical community located midway between city and forest—in the suburbs, that is—with four kinds of members: the fully ordained monks and nuns who pursued full-time advanced studies; and the more moderately ordained lay men and women (eventually including many of the wealthiest merchants and the most powerful kings of the time), who studied more preliminary teachings, performed more preliminary practices, and served as the main practical support for the community. He located the monastic *saṃgha* in the suburbs by ruling that the cenobites should beg their food each day, for that day, before noon. He made it possible for the laity to practice on an appropriate level as well, by ruling that the monks and nuns should be prepared to lecture to the donors upon receiving their food, as well as at other designated times. He thus created an alternative, symbiotic community that preserved the educationally necessary aspects of asceticism while making the discipline accessible to historically unprecedented numbers of people.

Following Toynbee,[3] it must be pointed out that none of the other axial age teachers contemporary with the Buddha—the pre-Socratics, Zoroastrian masters, Confucius, and so on—came anywhere close to exercising such a widespread influence in their respective societies as the Buddha did in India through this unique institutional innovation.

The rule that developed for this *saṃgha* was based on the cardinal practices of asceticism. The four cardinal rules—transgression meant expulsion—were sexual continence, non-killing, poverty, and non-pretension to spiritual attainment. Monks and nuns were allowed only one main meal a day, making fasting mandatory from noon to dawn the following day. Night vigils were routine, with sophisticated contemplative exercises taught to all. Hair was shorn; dress was standardized in neatly sewn-together death-shroud pieces; names were changed; home was abandoned; family ties and class affiliations abolished; casual conversation was severely restricted; and bodily deportment was strictly controlled, with disciplines like keeping the gazc downcast one cartwheel diameter ahead when walking through town to beg lunch. Most important, the main business of these moderate ascetics was to learn the method of investigating the self to discover its metaphysical lack of fixity and rigid identity, and then to practice the method in sophisticated contemplations, ranging from systematic self-observation of the body and breath, sensations, thought flow, and experiential processes, leading up to the breakthrough contemplations that penetrated the core of the self, reaching the liberating insight of identitylessness.

In short, motivated by his new level of insight and the unprecedented universalism it dictated, the Buddha organized the highly individualistic ascetical traditions of his time into a mass educational institution, with a monastic core, an ethical foundation in a larger counter-cultural community, and an open-ended intellectual culture to provide the curriculum. Here, the old dichotomy between shaman and warrior resonated on the mass level in the modernizing or urbanizing climate of the axial age. For another equal and opposite institution was just developing at the same time—namely, the institution of universalistic militarism. The technology of iron in agriculture and warfare had enabled city states to develop the surplus needed to maintain year-round professional armies; and the intermittent warfare between city states now became more protracted and much more devastating. Naturally, individual city states, the Indian Spartas and Athenses, began to desire empires. The training of the necessary professional soldiers was expanded from the old *kṣatriya* traditions and systematized by mobilizing the mundane relative asceticism of the warrior in a mass educational method aimed at goals opposite to the liberation intended in the Buddhist community. The professional soldier also renounced home; shaved hair; wore a uniform; gave up identity to the unit; lived ascetically; submitted to painful training; and steeled himself to face and embrace, if necessary, death, in the service of his nation. Only here the asceticism was not aimed at liberation, unless indirectly it was liberation of the nation from the clutches of the enemy. And the asceticism was mundane and relative, not spiritual and ultimate.

As the two institutions—universalizing monasticism and universalizing militarism—were developing in the same period throughout Eurafroasia, it is interesting that both in the West (Egypt, Palestine, Iran, Mesopotamia, Syria) and East (Central Asia, the Chinese city states) the monastic ascetical institution was not able to get started for another seven hundred years, in spite of the no doubt profound and intense efforts of many an individual seeker, many a martyred shaman, many a warrior ascetic who tired of incessant violence and sought the solace of the desert or the mountains. That it was able to start in the fifth century BCE in India indicates the greater wealth of that ecoregion and the greater surpluses of food, resources, and manpower available to its monarchical military authorities. Indeed, one suspects that the kings of the time were less impressed with the Buddha's wisdom and charisma than they were appreciative of the potential of his monastic communities to keep some of the surplus freedom seekers off the streets, battling the devil for spiritual liberation rather than battling the authorities for social liberation.

Tibetan Buddhist Developments

The Buddhist mass-ascetical monastic institutions flourished throughout India for fifteen hundred years, effecting considerable changes in that civilization, which had developed into a normally unified empire from a century or two after the Buddha's time. By the Gupta and later Gupta ages from the fourth and fifth centuries, the monasteries had become universities, teaching all applicants a wide range of subjects beyond the core curriculum of what were called *adhyatmavidya* (spiritual sciences). Scholars came from all over continental Asia, from Iran to China, returning with their learning to spread the new culture in their home region. The change from monastery to university grounded an expansion of the Buddhist impact on Indian civilization, adding to the foundational contribution of a monastically organized mass asceticism *(Shravakayana)* both a universal social ethic of love and compassion, complete with Bodhisattva intercessor and savior figures and deified, omnicompassionate Buddhas *(Mahāyāna),* and a vast and sophisticated priestcraft of ritual, blessing, and healing *(Tantrayana).*[4] Thus, after a thousand years, Buddhism was a mainstream force in Indian civilization, the balancing universalistic complement of the particularistic Hinduism that actually mirrored many of Buddhism's developments while preserving the national gods, the caste system, and ever more sanitized forms of the ancestral blood sacrifices that Buddhism rejected.

From the early seventh century, the Tibetan warrior society, having gone through the process of unifying all the peoples on the plateau, one million square miles, into a warrior empire that routinely conquered lowland kingdoms in all directions—including silk route states, Nepal, Indian kingdoms, and Chinese states—reached its maximum viable expansion and began to tire of the warrior ethic. Its rulers recognized that a shamanistic imperial cult—an ethic of violence based on the worship of mountain war gods and a feudal system based on loyalties that could shift with the fortunes of war or the devastating vacuum of lack of war—was not an ideology sufficient to keep a nation together over the long haul. Looking around the civilized world, especially at the archenemy T'ang China and the admired neighbor post-Gupta India, they saw that Buddhism, with its monastic universities and universalistic social myth and ethic, provided the institutional curriculum and the ideological glue to weave and hold together the diverse peoples of those vast empires in relatively stable and prosperous societies. So the emperors of Tibet began a process of importing Buddhism, mainly from India, since that was its homeland and a subcontinent full of empires that they rarely fought with. They sent scholars to learn Sanskrit, funded massive translation projects, brought in historic icons of the Buddha, and built a network of temples to create an imperial Buddhist cult. It took them five generations and two centuries to construct one properly mass-ascetical monastery, and another two centuries before the Tibetan people themselves really developed a grass-roots appreciation of the monasticized lifestyle.

The Tibetan experiment with the Buddhist ascetical educational movement was different from the Indian one, since it inherited a culture that had already accumulated a thousand years of experience in educating the many Indian nations. It imported monastic, messianic, and apocalyptic vehicles in one unified whole. And so the transformative process for Tibet was relatively accelerated. A result of this—most interesting in our context of comparative asceticism studies—is the preservation of the forms of the archaic level of Tibetan spirituality, though their content is quite transvalued. Before Buddhism, shamanism was highly developed in Tibet, complementing its violent warrior culture. These shamans were expert thaumaturges, adept in out-of-body journeyings, spirit fighting, underworld exploring, with regular oracular visitations up the world axis, mountain and tree, to discern the wills of the national gods and see to the offering of proper, regular, and bountiful sacrifices to them.[5] To develop their knowledge and abilities, they were certainly adept ascetics, masters of the fast, the vigil, the vision quest, the cataleptic trance—and thus could perform all manner of magical feats with elegance and ease. The following colorful Tibetan legend illustrates the interaction of Buddhism and shamanism in Tibet.

The building of the first monastery was constantly unsuccessful, and the eighth-century emperor, Trisong Detsen, was in danger of emptying his treasury, since these shamans and the spirits they controlled did not want a Buddhist monastery on their sacred land. A Buddhist "super-shaman" had to be invited from India to deal with the magicians and the gods on their own level. A *mahāsiddha* (great adept) called Padma Sambhava arrived on the scene, fresh from many centuries (this is a myth!) of missions to the various peoples of the Indian subcontinent, who all had to be "tamed" on the spirit level before the educational curriculum could be implemented. After all the majority was illiterate and most could not have read a Buddhist scripture written in another language even if they wanted to. Therefore, they required teaching on the level they understood. The Buddhist masters had to demonstrate their experiential awareness of the problems of the spirit world—of sickness, of madness, and of the worlds of death and the dangers of a bad rebirth—and had to show their effectiveness in helping people deal with those realities they faced. So Padma Sambhava, after a cursory conversation with the emperor and his courtiers, retired to a mountain cave and entered into spiritual struggle with the national deity and his retinue of fierce war gods. After a mighty battle, with hailstones and lightning bolts flying around for weeks on end, the god surrendered in defeat, and pledged to respect the Buddhist teaching and support its institutions, as long as its adepts maintained the sincerity, true depth of understanding, and total compassion that had given Padma Sambhava the power to triumph over him.

Then, with the blessing of the national god, the monastery could easily be completed, translation projects mounted, and the national mass-ascetical education begun. After all, the Buddhist "taming" requires an abstaining from blood violence, starting with the national blood sacrifices that provides the customary tribal deity diet; a controlling of the sexual impulse in complete continence for monks and nuns and strict observation of family ethics for laity; an acceptance of poverty for the monk and a restrained minimalism, except in giving charity, for the laity; and a commitment to the quest for truth, a national dedication to the ascetical spiritual education. An unfortunate byproduct of the mass asceticism that Buddhism implements in any nation is eventually a kind of unilateral disarmament that has led to the physical downfall of many a Buddhist nation, or of Buddhist institutions within a nation, of which Tibet is a recent example of the former, and India an ancient example of the latter.

In the modern forms of Tibetan Buddhism, there are a wide variety of practices, comfortably supported in a unique country (at least until the Chinese invasion, occupation, and genocidal oppression of the last forty-four years), home of a unique civilization centered around what I call mass monasticism, with over 10 percent of the population being monastics. It was, until the takeover, governed by a monastically generated and maintained government, ruled by the ultimate shaman ascetics who had attained such a degree of adeptness in traversing the spirit ways that they were believed to have the ability to return from death and consciously take rebirth in a chosen womb. Tibetan ascetical practices are manifold and sophisticated. They range from the monk-for-a-day vow or the afternoon fast all the way to thirty-year-long dark and silent meditation retreats; from the common assumption of a national identity—a sense of belonging to a nation chosen by a messianic Bodhisattva who keeps a special covenant so long as the identity remains open to identitylessness—all the way to the refined understanding of the advanced insight contemplative who attains visceral experience of his or her absolute identitylessness; from the social practice of renouncing a national defense force all the way to the allocation of 85 percent of the national budget for the education of spiritual practitioners. They are practiced by lay persons as well as monastics. The entire population of the country lives in a relatively timeless cosmos, where the imminent reality of future lives is as real to them as the miles of trails leading over the vast steppes that spread between high mountain ranges. Therefore, there is a general awareness that the human life form should be used for spiritual evolution. Acceleration of the development of the human life form itself toward liberation and encompassment of a larger happiness is seen as the purpose of the human life itself.

Therefore, people commonly spend years in physical, verbal, and mental development. For example, the body is developed by performing millions of full-body prostrations, which take years to perform and require special equipment: sliding boards, knee pads, mittens, head pads, and counting mechanisms. Sometimes the prostrator will do all the prostrations at one holy site, sometimes he or she will go on a thousand mile pilgrimage, prostrating every second step. Prostration involves both aspects of ascetical training: withdrawal of energy from habit patterns, and reinvestment of that energy in new patterns of ritual design. Energy is withdrawn from self-aggrandizing or even self-maintaining patterns of behavior, such as goal-oriented travel, productive labor, aggressive sport, or libidinal release; and invested in cultivating an attitude of selfless abnegation, purificative self-abasement, trustful dependence on benevolent higher beings to whom one bows again and again, putting oneself at the mercy of the powers that be. Of course, such practice is not performed by the body alone, but is accompanied by the recitation of magical and holy speech, reciting mantras such as OM MANI PADME HUM, the invocation of the Seraphic Bodhisattva, Avalokiteshvara, the very incarnation of universal love and mercy. Energy is withdrawn from habitual speech and disciplined into the incessant flow of the mantra by repeating it millions of times. The mind is not allowed to wander, but is linked to patterns of visualization of the presence of the divine being who receives one's repeated gestures of submission and contemplation of the devout and steady attitude of faith, love, and self-transcendence.

This brief description of the typical ascetical practice of multiple prostrations, not three or five at certain times of day, but millions year in and year out, gives the flavor of Tibetan civilization as both mass-monastic and mass-ascetical. And there is no doubt that this culture developed without any belief in a monotheistic creator god. The key component of its cosmos was rather the universal belief in karmic evolution, the reality sense that life is beginningless and endless, and that a single human life experience is a crucial opportunity to ensure the positive direction of that evolution; to win freedom from any compulsive momentum toward suffering; and to gain the ability to transform the universe into realms of happiness for others as well as self.

If prostration is a most basic form of asceticism in Tibetan practice, then the advanced philosophical and meditational techniques of realizing voidness—the systematic critical penetration of the felt subjectivities and perceived objectivities, structures and substances, of apparent reality—is the most subtle and sophisticated. The educated Buddhist monastic studies the ancient tradition of Centrist philosophy (*Mādhyamika*).[6] This discipline provides a highly developed methodology of overcoming naive realism about self and world, offering a curriculum of thought experiments and mind disciplines gradually enabling the practitioner to withdraw the deepest kind of habit energy, that which is invested in the sense of having a fixed core self, a permanent identity of soul invariably buttressed by a habitual perception of core self and soul in other things and beings. The Centrist philosophic and contemplative process enables the practitioner to become a psychological ascetic, actually experiencing the dissolution of self and objective world, withdrawing all energies habitually invested in maintaining such fictional constructions. The resultant insight, usually called "the wisdom that realizes identitylessness," avoids becoming a nihilistic trap by also seeing through anything real or substantial in the state of voidness, recognizing the voidness or selflessness of the state of freedom itself. The experienced freedom thus does not itself become a trap, and the practitioner is free to reinvest the withdrawn and recovered core life energies in new forms of relative, fluid selfhood; free to make the artist's creative investment in making life beautiful for self and others; and inspired to do so by the discovery of the happiness of freedom.

Time and space do not allow me to describe more fully the extraordinary heights and exotic extremes of the many forms of Tibetan asceticism. I am highly conscious of having just scratched the surface. Nevertheless, I hope I have given a new perspective on the phenomenon of asceticism itself, drawn impressionastically from the vast literature on the subject that exists in Indian and Tibetan Buddhist sources. And I hope that the community of religion scholars that studies asceticism will begin to work more systematically in a cross cultural way. My Oxford colleague Richard Gombrich mentions that the total number of Greek and Latin codices on which our sense of ancient Mediterranean civilization is based is around thirty thousand, while the number of ancient Sanskrit manuscripts (excluding multiple copies of the same work) is over two million! This relatively huge figure does not count the numerous works lost in Sanskrit (many thousands of which are preserved in Tibetan), or the many millions of classical works in other ancient Asian languages. The ancient Indian civilization was perhaps excessively preoccupied with spiritual, psychological, and philosophical matters, and therefore the records of its civilizations vastly expand the database within which the scholar of asceticism can profitably wander. Tibetan literature itself can usefully be approached as a multi-century tradition of devoted monastic secondary scholarship.

NOTES

1. M. Eliade, J. Kitagawa, et al., *Encyclopedia of Religion* (New York: Macmillan, 1987), 1.441–445.
2. See W. I. Thompson, At the *Edge of History* (New York: Harper & Row, 1971).
3. A. J. Toynbee, *Mankind and Mother Earth* (New York: Oxford University Press, 1976).
4. This describes the development of the "three vehicles" of Indian Buddhism, individual, universal, and apocalyptic vehicles, as I call them.
5. This description of shamanic prowess relies on Mircea Eliade's classic compendium, *Shamanism; Archaic Techniques of Ecstasy,* trans. Willard R. Tvask (New York: Bollingen Foundation [Pantheon Books], 1964).
6. See R.A.F. Thurman, *Central Philosophy of Tibet* (Princeton: Princeton University Press, 1988).

10

Trajectories of Ascetic Behavior

Response to the Three Preceding Papers

Gail P. Corrington-Streete

To those who work with the trajectories of ascetic behavior, West and East, attempts to define (that is, put limits around) or to describe (that is, write concerning) asceticism as a phenomenon or series of phenomena are decidedly frustrating. But these attempts—according to what Geoffrey Galt Harpham has termed "the ascetic imperative"—seem to be compulsory and inevitable.[1] When such attempts are attempted (the redundancy is deliberate), it appears that we are always confronted with layers of meaning. When we attempt to peel away these layers, the presumed inner core eludes us, is perhaps itself an illusion. Hence, the conclusion we come to is that there is no essential asceticism: the best we can do is allude to it, to "play" at it, in the root meaning of the term *ludere,* while it "plays away" *(e-ludere)* from us. Such word play (I almost said "world-play") may seem a sight too clever for a serious discussion of asceticism, which after all involves discipline in the sense of both learning and training, but the "sporting" root of our term asceticism is never far from us, and thus is one of the concepts underlying my response. *Askēsis* is serious play, or even at times "a play," a dramatic performance, live theatre. To complicate the matter further, this response of mine is yet a response to three responses to responses.

For, as Walter Kaelber has observed, asceticism, whether Eastern or Western, "represents a range of responses to the social, political, and physical worlds."[2] Ascetic behavior, in whatever context it is clothed, is a response,—a challenge, a rejoinder—to world. Further, this response is one that is lived or enacted. In philosophical terms, this enactment is known as a *bios,* way of life, as delineated in J. M. Dillon's paper on Platonist asceticism. In early Christian terms, it is known as *hodos,* simply way or pathway, as set forth in J.D.M. Derrett's excursus on primitive Christianity. R.A.F. Thurman offers a somewhat broader definition of ascetic behavior: a kind of victory over instinct and habitual response, even over the instinct for personal survival. Thus, we might conclude that two factors operative in the discourse of asceticism are response and world.

Further, the arena in which the responses to the world distinct to ascetic behavior appear to operate is the body: it is the arena (or, if we employ Thurman's terminology, the battleground) in which the world is accepted, rejected, refined, transcended, transformed, or defeated. In Western traditions of asceticism, the body itself appears to function as a metaphor for the world: the microcosm reflects, and, in a sense, replicates, the macrocosm. By examining the microcosm, the macrocosm can be interpreted, defined (have its boundaries drawn), or even refined (have undesirable boundaries redrawn) and consequently controlled to a degree. Platonist and early Christian interpretations of "body" therefore seem analogous to their respective and often interwoven interpretations of "world." Can the world be perceived in terms of cosmic dualism (as in Plato's division into visible and corruptible versus invisible and eternal)? Then the body as human person will also be perceived as divisible into these two realms. Can the world be perceived in terms of historical dualism (as in the apocalyptic perspective of earliest Christianity), divided into "this present [evil] age," "this present world," or, in the Johannine phrase, simply "this world," and "the age to come," "the world to come," "the Kingdom of God or of Heaven"? Then the body itself is capable, like the world, of moving towards "the world to come," perhaps, as in some gnostic Christian ways of experiencing the world, of already having realized it in the present through persistent denial of the fleshly realm. Or, as Derrett has remarked of the Hasidic program (if I understand him correctly) withdrawal *(anachōrēsis)* itself helps to create a type of spatial realm of bodily observance that assists in realizing the world to come. The Buddhist program, as Thurman delineates it, also needs to address the world: indeed, it may derive from the mundane or worldly relative asceticism of the warrior, which seeks the victory that is liberation or release (*mokṣa*) from continued existence, or being-in-the-world.

I would at this point like to raise two questions that I hope will provoke a wider discussion. First, is it true that the Western ascetic traditions Dillon and Derrett discuss have such a close connection between body and world? Second, is it true that these traditions also are dualistic in the sense that the spirit is opposed to the body, the ascetic opposed to the world? Indeed, as Derrett claims in the case of early Christianity, "Asceticism is historically and psychologically a response to dualism." We might therefore ask whether dualism is a necessary component of asceticism. One might also ask these questions of Thurman's paper: Is the relationship between body and world in the Tibetan Buddhist tradition similar to that of the Platonist and Christian? Is Eastern asceticism, as it here appears, less dualistic than that of the West, or is that an artificial and not especially helpful distinction? In asking this I have in mind a statement by Huston Smith in his book *World Religions,* (formerly known as *The Religions of Man*).[3] In dealing with the various emphases of major world religions, he observes that those of the West (under which he includes Judaism, Christianity, and Islam) emphasize the material: for good or ill, matter, which includes space (location) and time (history) as well as the created or material world, matters. In contrast, he observes that religious traditions arising in the subcontinent of India (Buddhism, Hinduism) have a psychological emphasis and thus are not as concerned with materiality and history. Thurman's paper suggests a refinement of this basically simplistic but perhaps heuristically useful schema, the idea of ultimate identitylessness of Buddhism as the source of full acceptance of relative embodiedness. Hence, the body and the world are not problems for

Buddhism, to be solved (or "dissolved"). A further complication of this difference appears to be over the question of ultimacy: Theravada Buddhism at least cannot talk about a deity or even a transcendent being or state of being as ultimate.

J. M. Dillon's intriguing remarks on the development of Platonic asceticism demonstrate two significant strands or responses to the perceived problem of being-in-the-world (and therefore the body, which occupies space in the world). The first is straightforward rejection. According to Dillon, this rejection is of the body, the microcosmic reflection of the macrocosm as visible realm. For Plato, bodily existence that is a constant reminder of worldliness, or the realm of appearances, change, flux, and appetite, is the focus of the problem. The only remedy is not "to infect ourselves with" the nature of the body, and hence to be free of its compulsions (*Phaedo* 67A). I wish to focus on one aspect of this world-denying or body-denying stance—interpretation of the body as a *phroura,* a word that may be interpreted either as a prison, the tomb of the soul, in which sense most pupils and interpreters of Plato have understood it, or as guard post. I think that Dillon is correct in emphasizing its ambiguity, in the sense that Plato himself appears to be ambivalent over whether the soul is intended to stand guard over the passions and desires of the unruly body; or to find itself inexplicably located in a corruptible prison from which it longs to escape, or at least resist as its limit. This military metaphor is found elsewhere, in Plato's *Apology,* in which Socrates claims that his philosophical activities result from his having, as a good soldier should, to remain in the post, or *taxis* (station) where the god of Delphi had placed him, although running the risk of death (*Apol.* 28D–28E).

Thurman's analysis of Tibetan Buddhist asceticism may cast some light here. If this asceticism has as its source warrior training as well as athletic discipline, namely the language of running risks (so that an ultimate goal may be achieved), it can be understood not simply as world-denying but as world (or environment-) controlling. This distinction may help to explain Plato's apparent ambivalence.

Ambivalent attitude and ambiguous language somewhat similar to those of Plato can be found in the apostle Paul's *Letter to the Philippians,* written from an actual imprisonment which, like that of Socrates in the *Phaedo,* leads Paul to consider release from the flesh, perhaps through death: "I am hard pressed between the two: my desire is to depart and be with Christ, for that is far better; but to remain in the flesh is more necessary for you" (*Phil.* 1.23–24, New Revised Standard Version). Nevertheless, despite this similarity, I would hesitate to designate this sentiment as "Christian," or to suggest a concept of the physical world as a sort of prison camp, or Vale of Tears, to which humans are condemned because of some original sin (Dillon, p. 82). But Christianity, as Derrett indicates, also has forms of world affirmation, or, at the very least, world transformation, as well as world denial. In this sense, as Derrett observes, the world is rather a boxer's training camp. So I do not believe, *pace* Dillon, that for Christianity, at least in its earlier forms, even this apparent denial of the world entails a complete rejection of the physical world, with all its works and pomps, as satanic. Indeed, I believe Derrett reads early Christianity aright in seeing asceticism of either kind—world affirming or world denying—as a partial, albeit essential, component of its *ēthos.* As he also notes, asceticism as a training for righteousness in early Hasidic Judaism, as well as in primitive Christian piety, does not necessarily despise a material return or reject a tangible result.

Both Platonism and Christianity therefore present a second form of asceticism, a stance that, as Dillon depicts it, is essentially world affirming, one that accepts the material world as it accepts the material body, in the belief and hope of its transformation, accepting the soul's involvement with the world, but attempting the transformation of the world by means of a transformed soul. One may thus discipline and refine the body as a vessel, to make it a worthy or at least a noninjurious one for the soul or spirit. In Buddhist terms, this might be viewed as an acceptance of relative embodiment, committed to the quest for truth. In just such a way, as Peter Brown has observed of late antique Christianity in *The Body and Society,* the human body is destined to be transformed into an awesome model, a resplendent vehicle, a temple of God.[4] Transformation of the microcosm, the body, thus will entail experience of the transformed macrocosm, the world. In the world-affirming ascetic mode, for Platonic thought as for Christian, the physical world is essentially good, and thus the physical body is essentially good. In both ways of thinking, however, the physical needs are not to be neglected, but to be directed by and oriented toward the divine power or spirit, which has the capability of transforming the human person in the direction of the divine. In Buddhist thinking, as Thurman observes, this transformation may even extend to the divine.

It is undeniable that this transformation is an expression of power and of control. In Platonic and early Christian thought, God or the Demiurge may have created the physical body, but the divine within has the potential to re-create it. In this sense, the world that is perceived by the early Christians as not being reborn, according to Derrett, can be replaced by the "credible alternative society," the "reborn." The appetites that belong to the flesh (in the body, the microcosm) and thus also to the world's (macrocosm's) program, may thus be controlled or abandoned. Derrett locates Paul within this ascetic Christianity by quoting from *Romans* 8.7–8: "The mind that is set on the flesh is hostile to God. . . ."

Did this spiritual athletic training of Paul and other early Christians take a world-denying or world-affirming shape? In short, can we determine whether early Christianity (or, more properly speaking, following Jacob Neusner's example, "Christianities") was ascetic?

If I interpret him correctly, Derrett says both yes and no, and the answer also depends on whether we are talking about "The Way" as that followed by Jesus' disciples, the Pauline churches, or the seesaw between the rigorists (outside of normative orthodoxy) or the relaxed (the ultimately orthodox). Certainly it would seem that if Jesus and his followers preached a voluntary, if rigorous, control of inclination as a means to the goal of righteousness, then by that definition The Way was ascetic. So, also, Paul's asceticism tends to urge, if not demand, control of the appetites. Nevertheless, neither stance rejects the body, but sees it as the realm in which the spirit operates, and one that can be transformed by the spirit, much as the Holy Spirit was to transform the world, which could not be entirely rejected either. Derrett points out that it was the microcosm, the individual, in Jesus' teaching, which was transformed first by the offer of the Holy Spirit. Hence, we might say that early Christianity exhibited a form of "worldly asceticism," behaving as if, in terms of Jesus' teaching, the Kingdom of God had already begun (according to Derrett); as if, in Paul's understanding, the schema of this world had already passed away (according to Vincent Wimbush, acting *hōs mē* (as if it were not).[5] It did not appear to despise the world so much as to feel the need to overcome it, much as Jesus himself was seen to have overcome the world, or at least its restrictions. In this sense, then, we could say that early Christianity was mainly of the world-affirming variety: it did not deny the reality of bodily existence, however much it might have "pushed the envelope."

I would like to make some concluding remarks about Dillon's and Derrett's papers on what are essentially Western or at least Mediterranean worldviews, before turning East to Thurman's paper on Tibetan Buddhist asceticism. It might be suggested, first of all, that an essential difference between Platonist asceticism and early Christian asceticism is the social status and social location of its practitioners. Greek and Roman philosophy was largely the province of aristocratic males, and thus its responses to the world are tempered by issues of social control and the availability of power. (Parenthetically, I might take issue with Derrett's contention that Stoic and Cynic teachings were never persecuted. It is certainly the case that one cannot persecute teachings, only teachers and those who follow them. Nevertheless, while individual Stoics and Cynics were not so actively or so gruesomely persecuted as individual Christians, there were executions and expulsions of prominent adherents to Stoic and Cynic teachings during the reigns of the emperors Vespasian and Domitian. These occurred because of their opposition to the usurpation of senatorial authority by the imperial office. These philosophers were not persecuted as severely as the Christians, probably because of their rank.) I would agree with Derrett, however, that ascetics can be power seekers; but not all power is bad. Perhaps asceticism is, indeed, a form of taking power, power over the microcosm (the body) when power over the macrocosm is denied or restricted. This point of view, if I am not mistaken, appears to be utterly alien to Buddhist ideas or practices of asceticism, even though they may have ultimately derived from the warrior caste.

Finally, I am not a little intrigued, as well as somewhat disturbed, by the occurrence of the term "neurotic" in connection with ascetic behavior in both Dillon's and Derrett's papers. Dillon claims that Plato's Socrates is an ascetic of a sort, but not in any world-negating or neurotic sense. Derrett asserts that neurotic or obsessional behavior is not ascetic. I do not mean to imply that either author deliberately labels ascetic behavior as neurotic; nonetheless, I would be interested in knowing why discussions of asceticism require an *apologia* against charges of neurosis. Perhaps neurosis is just a modern term for heresy, since ascetic behavior, either of the world-affirming or world-denying sort, appears to be a significant departure from the modern term for orthodoxy: "the norm."

The language of neurosis does not seem to have entered Thurman's paper, perhaps because he is not speaking from a Western standpoint. Certainly, by Western psychological standards, the Buddha's behavior after the Great Renunciation verged on, if it did not actually enter, the realm of the neurotic. Such actions are depicted as extreme, and eventually led the Buddha to abandon such extreme asceticism for the "Middle Way," which also represents a middle ground between regulated normal social life and deregulated extranormal ascetic life. Perhaps an analogue to the early Christian Way can be found in that the Buddha's Way, like the Christian *hodos,* created an alternative, symbiotic community. Therein may lie Buddhism's difference from the philosophy of Plato, who never succeeds in creating—and perhaps never tried to create—anything other than the idea of an alternative community, the ideal *polis,* which, after all, is only imagined in order to show how an individual soul might realize justice in an imperfect world. Having tried to indicate some ways of looking at difference in similarity, I would like to invite further discussion.

NOTES

1. Geoffrey Galt Harpham, *The Ascetic Imperative in Culture and Criticism* (Chicago: University of Chicago Press, 1987).
2. Walter Kaelber, "Asceticism," *Encyclopedia of Religion,* edited by Mircea Eliade (New York: Macmillan, 1987), 1:441–445.
3. Huston Smith, *The Religions of Man* (New York: Harper & Row, 1958).
4. Peter Brown, *The Body and Society* (New York: Columbia University Press, 1988), p. 171.
5. Vincent L. Wimbush, *Paul, The Worldly Ascetic* (Macon, Ga.: Mercer University Press, 1987), pp. 73–93.

PART THREE

Hermeneutics of Asceticism

11

Asceticism and Anthropology: *Enkrateia* and "Double Creation" in Early Christianity

Giulia Sfameni Gasparro

The correspondence between Dionysius, the bishop of Corinth (166–175 CE), and Pinytus of Knossus, which was briefly but plainly referred to by Eusebius of Caesarea,[1] effectively presented a series of problems central to early Christian life during the first few centuries after Christ. Since these problems addressed the existential condition of humanity, they necessarily involved the ethical sphere of behavior and the theoretical realm of anthropology defined in light of Christian salvation.

The correspondents discussed *hagneia* or "purity," by which was meant sexual continence as an alternative to *gamos* (marriage), rather than chastity in the broader sense. Since the two writers were bishops, their respective positions on the issue were not merely theoretical, but would have had immediate, decisive repercussions on community life and on commitments and choices made by the faithful.

Indeed, Dionysius attempted to use his authority to change a situation he considered overly oppressive for the Christians of Knossus. In his opinion, it was wrong to impose the heavy burden of continence as a requirement. Thus, it seems clear that Pinytus's church presented *hagneia* as an intrinsic part of the perfect Christian life. In fact, the bishop of Knossus's response, while cloaked in respectfully diplomatic language, could not mask his unswerving defense of his own strict position. By clearly adopting Paul's language and reasoning,[2] Pinytus compared Dionysius's moderate teachings, which were also inspired by Paul's appeal concerning human *astheneia* (lack of strength)[3] to the kind of nourishment suited only to youngsters. This he countered with his more solid food for adults: that is, those Christians who chose to obey fully the imperatives of salvation. Therefore, Pinytus saw continence as a necessary response to the gospel call for conversion.

The correspondence between the two bishops testifies to the existence of a situation that was fairly common in second-century Christianity. In fact, around the year 170, extremely different, at times conflicting, positions on the issue of sexual conduct coexisted and struggled for primacy within the church. Each side used the apostle Paul to support and justify its claims. It is also significant that two centuries later the historian Eusebius praised both bishops, while stressing the perfect orthodoxy espoused by the radical Pinytus in terms of both his belief in and solicitude for the faithful.[4]

It may be concluded, therefore, that the heavy burden of continence, which the bishop of Knossus considered necessary to a perfect Christian life, was not seen as an absolute ban on, or condemnation of, marriage. Indeed, at that time representatives of the Great Church considered both positions to be incompatible with the teachings of the Bible and rejected them as a serious deviation from the apostles' teachings.

Eusebius's position, however, shows that in the fourth century the two sides represented by Dionysius and Pinytus no longer seemed irreconcilable and, more important, that continence had remained central to Christianity, while actually determining other, equally important aspects of the religion. Indeed, numerous treatises on virginity[5] appeared during that century, and the earliest, most crucial experiments with monasticism in its eremitic and cenobitic forms also took place at that time.

The widest rifts in the Christian community resulting from the problem of *enkrateia* (self-control) occurred during the second century, however. The situation became quite complex, and authoritative figures sharply debated individuals and groups that counseled complete continence as a condition for attaining the ideal preached by the gospel. In addition, these same groups explicitly and systematically condemned marriage.

While Eusebius only briefly mentioned Musanus, who flourished under Marcus Aurelius and hence was a contemporary of Dionysius and Pinytus, as the author of "Against the Heresy of the So-Called Encratites" (*Historia ecclesiae* 4.28), Irenaeus made lively arguments against a group of heretics, also known as Encratites, who were inspired by their predecessor, the Syrian Tatian. In his *Discourse to the Greeks,* Tatian, who was a disciple of Justin Martyr, proved to be a skillful defender of the Christian faith against prevailing paganism. After his mentor's death, Tatian became known for his definition of matrimony as "fornication and corruption," as well as for his doctrine on Adam's damnation. He left Rome because of strong opposition to his radical positions and returned to his homeland; it was there that he wrote his famous evangelic "harmony," the *Diatessaron,* which continued to be used in the Syrian church until at least the end of the fifth century.[6]

At the same time, Clement of Alexandria devoted a considerable part of his *Stromateis* to an explanation and refutation of two opposing trends, one libertine and the other rigorist, which coexisted within the Christian community in Alexandria.[7] In each case, the element that characterized the so-called encratic position was a radical rejection of marriage. Their goal was not so much to extol the virtues of sexual continence as to denounce the sinful nature of *gamos,* which was thus incompatible with the teachings of the Christian faith.

This position, perceived to be inspired by deceitful spirits and a sign of the coming of the eschatological era, had already been condemned in *1 Timothy* 4.1–5, which stated that, in the decisive crisis that would precede the *parousia* (second coming of Christ) false leaders would appear in Christian communities and "forbid marriage and enforce abstinence from the food that God had created" for the faithful to accept with thanksgiving. This vivid glimpse of the conflict within churches during the early decades of the second century, as reflected in the epistle under discussion, demonstrates that the prohibition on marriage was associated with the ban on meat eating. According to later sources, this double abstention frequently appeared in encratic circles.

A correct historio-religious evaluation of these positions, including complete sexual abstinence as both a sign and consequence of acceptance of the Christian message, requires identification of the motivations behind each individual, historical context. The same behavior in practice can be based on very different theoretical assumptions, while similar principles sometimes result in conduct differing sharply on ethical and practical levels. The result is a nonhomogeneous, anthropological plan that emerges on the encratic horizon. This complex phenomenon, which is conventionally and legitimately called encratism, includes the position espoused by those individuals in early Christianity who prohibited the faithful from marrying and procreating. On the other hand, the overall anthropological picture is highly diversified in terms of the justifications (with varying degrees of theoretical complexity) that were made in support of such a radical espousal of *enkrateia*.[8] Therefore, it is necessary to identify each position's point of ideological reference when calling for Christians' total abstinence from sexual activity and hence procreation.

At the same time, while it is legitimate to place the numerous forms of encratism under a single heading—that is, the common denominator of unswerving condemnation of sexual activity and procreation—its various forms must be viewed against the broader background of theoretical and practical attitudes towards marriage and procreation within the Christian community at that time.[9]

The heresiological design that pits heresy against orthodoxy, which is an inappropriate tool for critical investigation, also proves to be unsuited to the historical reality of early Christianity, which is more complex and more diverse than originally thought. Therefore, an overall view of *enkrateia* within the framework of the early Christian tradition is required in order to place it specifically within its own historical context, with its Jewish and pagan *facies* (character). Indeed, the practice is deeply rooted—and gradually developed—within a dialectical relationship of comparison and conflict, of assimilation and convergence. This method should make it possible to understand all of the variations on this theme; its continuity with positions found in the New Testament or the extent of its sometimes radical divergence from them; and possible relationships or conflicts with Judaic and Greco-Roman culture.

The anthropological dimension assumes particular importance in this case since it proves to be one of the specific features of what may be defined as the "tradition of *enkrateia*." This tradition should be understood as a broad, though broken, line that runs through early Christianity, thereby cohering various experiences regarding questions of sex and procreation.

From a historical and typological point of view, it is valid to distinguish between two large and varied currents into which Christian attitudes on the sexual question may be grouped. On the one hand, we find Christians who praised *enkrateia* for its doctrine of sexual abstinence and went so far as to suggest it as a condition of becoming the perfect Christian (as in the case of Pinytus of Knossus). These same people did not condemn marriage, however, which remained an alternative for ordinary believers. On the other hand, we have another group of Christians, who, like Tatian, considered total abstinence to be an unavoidable precept for every Christian; they completely rejected sexual union with the consequent procreation, considering this to be fornication and corruption. Therefore, *enkrateia* can be divided into a moderate camp, which itself had a wide range of interpretations, and a radical camp, which eventually became known as encratism, which was followed by "Encratites," using a term taken from old heresiological sources used in a historical context without any sort of value judgment applied.

Another important distinction must be made within the radical camp. Its rejection of all sexual activity and procreation was shared by both nonditheist Encratites and the numerous followers of gnosticism, who were attracted by well-defined, dualistic positions on the theological, cosmological and anthropological level. Thus, while the practical considerations of gnostic *enkrateia* were similar to the radical abstinence preached by a broad group of early Christians, the gnostic version was also characterized by its unusual connection with the idea of the intrinsic ontological negativity of matter, the human body, and its creator (or creators). Within the framework of the gnostic dualism of principles and natures, marriage and procreation were detested as activities that were necessarily connected with the second, evil, level of reality, represented in various ways in different systems. The complete continence proclaimed to be an undeniable corollary of redemptive knowledge in many gnostic contexts thus rested on specific ontological foundations, dualistic, anticosmic and antisomatic.[10]

Within the broad framework of this proposed classification, critical analysis should proceed with the greatest caution and flexibility to make it possible to identify a wide range of positions and their respective motivations. Besides the wide gulf that separates the two camps in question, and often places them in bitter opposition, there is a series of shared issues, language, images, and, most important, an *ēthos* that ensures substantial homogeneity in the perception of humanity's sexual dimension and sexual activity. It is seen as the focus, or at least one of the main reference points, upon which religious identity and soteriological perspectives are based.

The image *ad extra* proposed in the middle of the second century by the apologists not only emphasized the severity of certain Christian customs, as noted by Aristides,[11] but also called into question the refusal of many of the faithful (male and female alike) to marry, a position taken by Justin Martyr.[12] This refusal was characterized in Athenagoras's *Supplication for the Christians* as "the hope of being closer to God."[13] What appeared to pagans of that era as unusual behavior when adopted by a mass of people and not just an élite group of individual wise men (something with which pagans were somewhat familiar), Christians considered, by contrast, to be a purely religious choice. This fact accentuated the radical nature and value of this break with traditional parameters, since it was closely bound up with a strong desire to heed the new message in all its forms.

In pointing out this distinctive aspect of the Christian *ēthos*, the apologists were careful to note that this strictness, which was basically alien to the contemporary Greco-Roman environment (except in unusual cases),[14] did not entirely exclude the practice of marriage and procreation. In fact, procreation was usually presented as the only reason for marriage.[15] In this way, Christian ethics basically conformed with the fundamental canons of accepted morality within pagan society at that time, since it used marriage to ensure the continuity of the race and its communities.

Therefore, while this justification for sexuality within marriage was formulated (and would later become the backbone of the Great Church's matrimonial doctrine as it developed up through Augustine[16]), the presence of this reasoning in second-century apologetic writings confirmed the centrality of *enkrateia* in the spiritual life of early Christianity.

The controversial nature of this problem, which clearly emerged from the passage cited in the *First Letter to Timothy,* was implicit in the only two mentions of *hagneia/enkrateia* found in the Apostolic Fathers. Indeed, Clement of Rome, in his *Letter to the Corinthians,* considered *enkrateia en hagiasmoi* ("holy continence") to be one of God's gifts to the faithful and advised his readers that "he who is chaste in the flesh must not boast about it, but rather understand that it is another who grants him temperance."[17] Ignatius, addressing himself to Polycarp of Smyrna, was equally cautious: "If one can remain chaste in honor of the flesh of the Lord, he must do so with humility. If one boasts about it, he is lost, and if one is recognized by someone other than his bishop, he is corrupt."[18]

In emphasizing the purposes and religious bases of *enkrateia* (a divine gift practiced as a sign of respect for the uncontaminated *sarx* of the Savior), both authors proved to be aware of the risks associated with it. Their insistence on the boastfulness and pride to which the temperate person was subject clearly indicated actual ruptures within the community, with the consequent formation of a class of perfect Christians who, in choosing continence, proclaimed their superior religious status over those believers who married. The bishops of Rome and Antioch, who were concerned with preserving cohesion and the correct hierarchical order within their churches (while nonetheless recognizing the unique virtues of chastity), did not fail to understand the discriminatory impact that chastity would have had on the community, if viewed as a mark of distinction of a privileged, charismatic minority.

Chapter 7 of Paul's first letter to the church of Corinth was the earliest example of the controversy that quickly broke out within Christianity on the question of sexuality. Paul's text, a sort of *magna carta* of the tradition of *enkrateia,* would later be the subject of exegeses as well as a necessary point of reference for any discussion of this issue. The numerous and as yet unresolved problems encountered when trying to identify the Corinthian Christians' religious and ideological beliefs are well documented and the subject of extensive scientific debate beyond the scope of this paper.[19] In fact, interpretation of *1 Corinthians* 7, which cannot be separated from the general context of this debate, is open to question.[20]

Paul's argument was so highly significant that a partial approach runs the risk of unduly emphasizing certain aspects. Furthermore, its decisive role in any investigation of the tradition of *enkrateia* makes it impossible to ignore because of Paul's authority as an apostle and the influence of his teachings on future generations of

Christians, as well as the light shed by his address to the Corinthians upon the broader historical context.

The complexity of the religious situation tackled by Paul's address is confirmed (if confirmation is truly necessary) by a comparison between the rigorist position revealed in chapter 7 and the libertine approach, which is reflected in the notion of an acquired spiritual freedom denounced by Paul in *1 Corinthians* 5.3–5. On the one hand, the apostle seems to agree with the rigorist position, while, on the other, he introduces certain moderating elements to ensure the social and moral balance that a radical choice of *enkrateia* would put at risk. "Concerning the matters about which you wrote me, it is well for a man not to touch a woman," Paul confirms, "but because of the temptation of fornication, each man should have his own wife and each woman her own husband" (*1 Cor.* 7.1).

The recommendation "not to touch a woman" appeared to have expressed the opinion of at least some of the faithful of Corinth, and the apostle states his substantial agreement with this assumption, but with all-important distinctions and, more to the point, the reasoning behind them. Thus, his clear view of *enkrateia* as a distinguishing aspect of the Christian religion is tempered by his considerable flexibility, which shows him to be capable of balancing this radical principle and its religious and eschatological motivations with the reality of individual situations, viewed from a religious and psychological point of view. Paul counsels married couples not to engage in a rash, unilateral renunciation of sexuality; with his extraordinary and almost revolutionary open-mindedness, he views sexuality as an equal right and duty of both men and women. In line with this principle, a bride and groom had to make a *symphōnia* (prior agreement) to abstain from sex; and the agreement had to note that this temporary state was devoted to prayer "lest Satan tempt you because of your intemperance" (*1 Cor.* 7.5).

It is impossible to analyze all the nuances of Paul's address, since every word and every image was destined to influence later tradition. Indeed, it would lend itself to rigorist, Tatian-like exegesis in encratic circles as well as to more moderate positions within patristic ones. It is important to note, however, that the address tackled some issues of late Judaism, including ascetic tendencies and a suspicion of, if not outright contempt for, sexuality as part of humanity's lustful nature. More specifically, in these circles sexual activity took on ambiguous connotations because of its connection with an *epithymia* (desire) rooted in sin and sometimes considered to be a powerful agent of humanity's moral decadence, as biblically portrayed in the story of Eden.[21]

The mention of *porneia,* which to Jews was synonymous with sins against the basic ethic rules governing sexuality (fornication, adultery, etc.), as well as the more detailed, specific aspects of Mosaic law on matrimony,[22] leads us to a subject clearly illustrated by the *Testament of Ruben.* This text considered the spirit of *porneia* to be the first and most dangerous of the seven spirits of error, which could cause the ruin of humanity in general and of devout Hebrews in particular.[23]

The need to abstain from the nuptial *homilia* (lecture, sermon) in order to devote oneself to divine worship, which was affirmed by Philo of Alexandria[24] and also found in rabbinical tradition,[25] was described in the *Testament of Naphtali* in terms similar to those used by Paul. In this writing, the author distinguished between "a time for union with woman and a time for *enkrateia,* for prayer" (8.7–8).

Paul's perspective clearly emphasized the link between sexuality and *akrasia* (abandonment of principles), while nonetheless admitting the legitimacy of sexual activity within marriage. Both its indissoluble nature and the concomitant ban on new marriages (*1 Cor.* 7.10–11) were reiterated in accordance with the well-known gospel pericopes of *Matthew* 19.1–11, *Mark* 10.2–12, and *Luke* 16.18. Indeed, *porneia,* incontinence, and temptation by Satan, all weighed heavily on marriage as practiced by a large number of early Christians and would lead to fairly serious constraints on it, as well as harsh condemnation by Encratites.

Naturally, a distinction must be made between encratism, with its own motivations and consequences, and Paul's position in favor of a Christian's freedom of choice, since the option of celibacy (whether virginal or created by widowhood) was a personal decision based on careful evaluation of one's ability to follow through. It is impossible to ignore one final, decisive aspect of Paul's address: the wholly religious and eschatological purpose of Paul's exhortation to embrace *enkrateia* and the particular tension between spiritual and worldly situations which it implied. The bond of marriage was in fact viewed as a typical instrument of the subjugation of humanity to earthly necessities; one who married did not sin, but would nonetheless experience the tribulation of the flesh (*1 Cor.* 7.28). A married couple was driven by the need to please each other and thus pursue worldly things, while a celibate, a virgin or a widow would have only to think of God. Their only worry was how best to follow him and thereby (while awaiting the *parousia*) enjoy a complete, undivided spiritual freedom in which all of their energies were concentrated on religious practice.

The Pauline perspective, with its significant eschatological tension, not only demonstrated one important aspect of Christian spirituality during the time of the apostle, but also represented the essence of ascetic trends that would be highly pervasive in later Christian circles. The eschatological choices of virginity and continence outlined in the apostle's address would find expression (to varying degrees) both within what has been labeled the moderate trend of *enkrateia,*—essentially represented by the Church Fathers and susceptible to change based on the times, places and various authors consulted—and within encratism itself.

Tertullian is a useful example of the patristic approach; his often fiery, radical imagery and language, which mirror his lively personality and literary style, are the direct result of the acute eschatological tension of his religious vision.[26] Similarly, expectation of the approaching end had a decisive impact on the encratic environment surrounding Clement of Alexandria, who rebukes those who refused to marry and procreate because they consider themselves already resurrected, that is, among the saved.[27] The apocryphal *Acts of Paul,* which defines the apostle's message as an "address on *enkrateia* and the resurrection," thereby considering the former to be a necessary condition of the latter, were closer to Paul's position, although they were more radically encratic than the original.[28]

There is no disputing the encratic *ēthos* of this work, which Tertullian considered to have been written by an Asian presbyter. This text, and much of the rich, similarly inspired apocryphal literature,[29] bore witness to the enormous appeal of radical continence to early Christians, apart from the heresiological gulf between orthodoxy and heresy.

The boundaries of the positions adopted by the two sides of *enkrateia* during the earliest Christian period were fluid, and it was possible to switch from one to the other simply by emphasizing or minimizing certain nuances and characteristics on the basis of a shared religious tension. This is confirmed by a noteworthy analogy between an early scene in the apocryphal *Acts of Paul* and a curious episode from the canonical *Acts of the Apostles.* In the latter case, Paul, who is being held prisoner, illustrates to the Roman procurator, Felix, and his Jewish wife, Drusilla, the essential aspects of belief in Jesus Christ. The apostle talks about three basic subjects: justice and continence and future judgment (*Acts* 24.24–25).

Paul's teachings, which *Acts* had already shown to include belief in resurrection of the dead as an essential part thereof (cf. *Acts* 24.14–20), are emblematically summarized into the three main points *dikaiosynē, enkrateia,* and *krima.* Thus, there was ample material for people (including the presbyter who wrote the apocryphal *Acts* mentioned above) to view *enkrateia,* and, indeed, the entire spectrum of ethical and religious observance bound up in the notion of justice, as a condition for approaching the last judgment, which was a prelude to resurrection or unfailing salvation.

The Encratites familiar to Clement of Alexandria and similar circles favored, instead, a scenario of realized eschatology, in which they viewed total *enkrateia* as an inescapable duty of all Christians. They considered themselves to have been resurrected already, that is, fully assimilated through baptism into Christ's experience of death and resurrection. This view, which seems to suggest the encratic approach condemned in *1 Timothy,*[30] often attempted to link itself implicitly or explicitly to both Paul's teachings and Luke's pericope (*Lk.* 20.27–40), as well as the synoptic parallels (*Mt.* 22.23–33; *Mk.* 12.18–27). Together with *1 Corinthians* 7, the pericope presented reflections and exegeses that played a decisive role in defining the ascetic and abstentionist *ēthos* of early Christianity.

In addition to some portions of *Luke* where Christ exhorted his followers to break all family ties including those of marriage,[31] Matthew's famous text (without synoptic parallels) on the three types of eunuchs was also very important in creation of this *ēthos.* In this case, only the third type of eunuch, or those people "who became eunuchs for the sake of the kingdom of heaven" (*Mt.* 19.21), had any religious significance.

Without entering into a complex debate on the meaning of these statements and their relationship to Jesus' confrontation with the Pharisees initially and with his disciples later concerning the indissoluble bond of marriage,[32] it is nonetheless interesting to note that the gospel approach to *eunouchia* (condition of being a eunuch) fueled broad sectors of early Christian spirituality, both its moderate and radical forms. This approach was seen as an alternative to marriage in the individual pursuit of the religious ideal.

In any case, the text *Luke* 20.27–40 on the condition of the resurrected was more meaningful, and had greater impact on the tradition of *enkrateia,* in terms of its ethical and anthropological aspects. When this text is compared with the treatment of similar subjects in *Matthew* 22.29–30 and *Mark* 12.18–27, which simply states that "in resurrection, one takes neither wife nor husband, but is like the angels in heaven," it appears to be richer in significance than the others. It was based on the antithesis between the "children of this eon (time/world)" who took husbands and wives and "those that have been judged to be worthy of another eon and of resurrection of the dead. Those who take neither wives nor husbands; indeed, they can no longer die, they are *isangeloi* (like the angels) and are children of God, since they are children of the resurrection."

Luke's reasoning, the deep significance of which cannot be adequately analyzed here, emphasized the profound difference (if not outright conflict) between the children of this eon and those who were worthy of *anastasis* (resurrection) and thus called "children of God" and "children of the resurrection." Their condition, which was defined in terms of *isangelia* (angelhood), was different from that of the children of this eon for two, interrelated reasons: they did not marry and they could no longer die, since the latter was the cause and basis of the former.

Although this discussion actually concerned the eschatological perspective and the situation of the resurrected, it nonetheless established a bond between marriage and death, which was defined further in a textual variant of Luke's pericope in the *Codex Bezae*. The variant introduced the subject of giving birth and being born as a connotation of children of this eon.[33]

Without overburdening Luke's text with the deep meanings that would be attributed to it by later exegesis, it may still be noted here that it discussed similarities between the angels and the saved in relation to humanity's sexual dimension and sexual activity. Sexuality was identified as an essential element of earthly life, but one which was extraneous to eschatological existence.

The idea that the just would take on an angelic dimension is most fruitfully compared with later Jewish apocalyptic writings, which probably shared the same historical roots.[34] This angelic condition was best expressed when used to define the situation of virgins and continent men who, like the angels, did not marry. The situation of the first virgin creatures in Paradise before the sin was characterized by their similarity to the angels.

The two possibilities mentioned above were sometimes distinct so that, depending on the emphasis placed on the values of *enkrateia* in Christian conduct, the existential status of virgins and continent men was, to varying degrees, likened to that of the angels. It was seen as an earthly sign and foretaste of the blessed state of the resurrected. Throughout the various approaches to *enkrateia* under examination here, the definition of virgins and continent men in terms of their similarity to angels was such a widespread practice as to seem almost banal.[35] Starting in the fourth century, this theme would find one of its most typical expressions in the figure of the monk as *bios angelikos* and would recur again and again in ascetically inspired patristic literature and numerous encratic texts without undergoing substantial variation.[36]

The choice of the angelic model as a parameter for the situation of male or female Christians who gave up sexual activity reduced that model to just one of its components—the lack of sexual differentiation—while viewing this lack as the primary, if not unique, goal of the religious tension felt by the faithful. In other words, it was both a condition and an effect of eschatological salvation.

The anthropology emerging from a perspective identifying human sexuality as an element that was not only eschatologically ineffective, but could also be eliminated in this lifetime through realization of the religious ideal (both as a result of free choice and the inexorable obligation to surmount this obstacle), sometimes had another connotation. This occurred when the eschatological *isangelia* that virgins and continent men experienced in this world was perceived at the same time as restoration of the prelapsarian human condition.

The notion of the angelic quality of Adam's original situation was often found in the tradition of *enkrateia*. Adam's condition provided another basis for the practice of continence in both the moderate and radical approaches. This basis sometimes coexisted with the ascetic approach—rejection of sexuality in order to attain spiritual perfection—as well as with the eschatological approach, thereby covering the wide range of possibilities inherent in these sometimes convergent and sometimes divergent justifications for *enkrateia*.

The anthropological framework is important to all contexts favoring either or both of the ascetic and eschatological approaches to virginity and continence, whether viewed as the result of free choice or as an obligation imposed on Christians as a necessary condition for creating their own religious identities. Indeed, definition of the anthropological framework involves all the approaches according to which the sexual component was seen in terms of its ontological foundation and function. A series of levels, as well as times, clearly constitute the anthropological structure. The idea that marriage and procreation were extraneous to the original, perfect condition of humanity as planned and carried out by the creator, but that they later came into being as a result of Adam's sin (both the object of his sin and its necessary consequence), implies that sexual practice, and sometimes even the physical differences between men and women, were considered to be a second level of reality and secondary to the original divine plan for humankind. They were the result of a sin that thus gained a typical effectiveness.

The idea of a single, divine, demiurgic act firmly prevailed among currents within the Great Church favoring *enkrateia,* as well as within nongnostic encratism itself, expressed by the teachings of Tatian, Julius Cassian, and numerous groups mentioned by heresiological and anonymous sources (largely made up of apocryphal writings similar to the Gospels and the *Acts of the Apostles*). Similarly, there was substantial continuity between the Old and New Testaments, since they recognized one God, the creator of humanity and its savior through the mediation of Christ.

When the complex network of reasoning that convinced a Christian to choose *enkrateia*—whether in the form of virginity or of continence during marriage or widowhood—was influenced by the idea that sexuality, or even sexual differentiation (extraneous to humanity's original nature as planned or carried out by the creator), was the result or cause of original sin, the consequence was an anthropological plan with fairly specific connotations. This plan no longer coincided with the biblical perspective that considered marriage and "going forth and multiplying" to be the primary goal of the creation of man and woman. Instead, this anthropological vision was greatly influenced by the idea of previous sin and modeled on the basis of double creation.[37] Indeed, an essential aspect of humanity's present state (sexuality and its practice with consequent procreation) was perceived to be the result of original sin, which, while being attributed to the first human couple, created a second level of reality for their descendants that was extraneous to that couple to whom God had given life in his first creative act.

The formulations of this concept were so diverse that it would be impossible to analyze them in detail here. Tatian's doctrine of the damnation of Adam,[38] which certainly included the first creature's unforgivable responsibility for the process of fornication and corruption (as the encratic teacher classified marriage), was linked with framework that contextually contemplated early humanity's having dwelt in a heavenly paradise, followed by its fall to earth after the first sin and the harmonious union of the spiritual couple made up of the *pneuma* (breath, spirit) and the soul. Once the soul had been separated from the divine spirit because of its sin, it lost its wings and plunged into a condition of innate mortality, from which it could be saved only by the intervention of a higher spirit.[39]

These principles, set out in the *Discourse to the Greeks,* which did not specifically emphasize abstinence, were the basis for a profound encratite formulation contained in *Perfection According to the Savior,* which was familiar to Clement of Alexandria.[40] In this work, Tatian contrasted the practice of marriage, which he considered to be devoted to incontinence and Satan, with the harmonious accord that instead made it possible to be in perfect agreement with the Lord. This *symphōnia,* which clearly echoed Paul's language in *1 Corinthians* 7, was both an agreement on continence, in favor of prayer, made by newlyweds and the redeeming reunion of the two members of the spiritual *syzygia* (opposition or conjunction) that were separated in the beginning by a dramatic occurrence. This occurrence brought together the biblical themes of the first creatures' ruinous sin and the soul's loss of wings, which demonstrated a decidedly Platonic anthropology, and the breaking apart of the two components that existed prior to humanity's earthly descent. The result was the idea of previous sin and double creation, which represents the specifics of the anthropological framework as well as the motivation for *enkrateia.*

An anthropology of clearly Platonic influence supported Julius Cassianus's encratic postulates, which, though connected to Valentinian gnosticism by Clement of Alexandria, appear to be part of nonditheist encratism. This conclusion is corroborated both by his thinking (as briefly summarized by Clement[41]) and his eagerness, in his lost work, *exegetica*[42] to prove Moses to have been a forerunner of the Greek philosophers, and them to have depended upon him. This eagerness seemed hardly justifiable in a gnostic, for whom the God of the Old Testament, seen as an inferior demiurge, played a complementary role to a higher, transcendent divinity.

Julius's anthropology envisioned a preexisting soul of divine nature and origin which fell to an earthly level because of the desire *(epithymia)* for procreation and death.[43] Sexual union, which the creator did not intend for human bodies (identifiable by the biblical "tunic of skin"), was in its turn the result of a diabolical trick. This framework, which was based on the story of the Creation and the Fall in *Genesis,* gave rise to an anthropology divided into two levels and two moments in time. Marriage, which was the result of a double decline (that of the soul effeminized by desire and that of Adam and Eve enticed by the serpent to imitate savage beasts), took on the obscure connotations of extreme corruption of the human *facies* and the principal tool of their separation from divine life. Therefore, the Lord's action proved its revolutionary effectiveness by overturning this sinful situation. According to Julius Cassianus, he "has transformed and freed us from error and from the relationship of the sexual organs and from these shameful appendages."[44]

This statement expresses one of the basic postulates of nonditheistic encratism, which, by recognizing the oneness of God the creator and savior, ascribed marriage and procreation to the Old Testament, according to which these activities were carried out under the sign of sin and were granted by God himself to indulge human frailty. In this way, the novelty of Jesus' redeeming message was identified with the call to radical *enkrateia.*

This postulate is most clearly expressed in the teachings of the Egyptian ascetic Hierakas, whose considerable biblical knowledge and irreproachable ethics were greatly appreciated by Epiphanius.[45] Hierakas reconciled his own encratite postulates with recognition (denied by the Gnostics) of a unique, divine, demiurgic act and continuity between the Old and New Testaments. He stated that marriage and procreation, which were conceded by God to sinful humanity, were prohibited by the new plan for salvation ushered in by Christ.

The fusion of *archē* (beginning) and *telos* (end) in the name of angelic similarity was basically, if not exclusively, perceived as the absence of sexual activity and, at times, even of sexual differentiation. This fusion also had a profound effect on the broad segments of *enkrateia* that have been defined as moderate because of their acceptance of the legitimacy of marriage even under Christ's new plan for salvation. Authors as important as Tertullian, Ambrose, Jerome and, among the Latin fathers, Augustine in the early phase of his career,[46] as well as Origen, Eusebius of Caesarea, Athanasius, Didymus the Blind, Methodius of Olympus, Eusebius of Emesa, Basil of Ancyra, Gregory of Nyssa, Gregory of Nazianzus, John Chrysostom and numerous other fathers writing in Greek, praised continence in its various forms (especially virginity) and connected its ethical motivations with ascetic ones.[47]

The idea that marriage and procreation were not part of Adam's sin, except in rare cases,[48] but rather were introduced into humanity's existence as a result of this sin (without which they would not have been useful or necessary) was the backbone of the two-tiered anthropology of these authors, as mentioned previously. In fact, marriage and procreation, which were at the heart of the human condition at that time, were not contemplated in the original, divine plan for humanity, although they were later granted by the one God, creator and savior. The determinant cause of these activities was the sin of the first humans; therefore, they were seen as later, secondary realities within humanity's condition and a sign of humanity's painful fall and loss of angelic, original perfection and integrity.

In conclusion, sexual activity, even in the institutionalized, legitimate form of Christian marriage, was seen as a serious obstacle to the achievement of salvation to which God had destined his creatures.

Much of patristic literature emphasized the irrational, animal side of the sexual sphere and its activities, thereby greatly increasing the division between the perfect *archē* of human creation by God and humanity's actual condition. Humanity was burdened not only by ethical degradation, but also by the ontologically effective assumption of elements of quality and nature that were extraneous to humanity's existential structure.[49]

If we now shift our attention from theory and principle to the actual life of the early Christians, a question arises as to the impact the theoretical plane had on these people. In this case, it is essential to examine the diversity of the various sociocultural contexts of Christian communities in relation to geography and history. This type of research, which should make use of sociological as well as historio-religious analysis, has not yet been completed, although useful approaches designed to identify specific aspects of the local Christian *facies* based on studies of culturally and religiously homogeneous regions and areas, are not lacking.[50]

It is a well-known fact that Alexandrian Christianity has been rightfully identified as one of the hubs of that form of *enkrateia* concerned with anthropological questions.[51] The Syrian context, on the other hand, was one of the most fertile grounds for asceticism and its more widespread and profound establishment within the social fabric, thereby involving large segments of believers.[52]

The Syrian church appears to have continued through the time of Aphrahat the practice of baptizing only those who pledged themselves to continence.[53] The Syrian context, which was deeply pervaded by encratic tendencies, encouraged the production and circulation of apocryphal writings that praised (often very warmly) the Christian commitment to celibacy and continence as the only way to heed the Gospels' message.[54]

In any case, ascetic demands, particularly the tendency to emphasize *enkrateia* over all other religious values, to some degree permeated the entire early Christian world. The strain and controversy that grew up between the moderates and radicals would become quite serious. The result was deep rifts in the various communities, with the gradual marginalization and exclusion from the Great Church of those who fell within the heresiological definition of "Encratites." Nonetheless, those values were one of the main parameters of the entire Christian *facies,* thus distinguishing it from the contemporaneous context of Greco-Roman society and the Jewish tradition.

One component of religious and social importance in early Christian encratism, with its various approaches resulting in both combination and conflict, was the role played by women. The female dimension took on a specific anthropological function, since the conditions by which it was understood (in terms of its essential structure and its approach to the male dimension) were an essential part of the overall vision of humanity accepted by early Christianity.

There is no need to emphasize the scientific community's interest in the history of women from antiquity to the present day.[55] An extensively documented bibliography, which sheds light on much of the subject under examination, has already been put together with regard to the early centuries of Christianity.[56] It would be impossible to present a detailed analysis of the many questions involved. Therefore, we will confine ourselves to noting that within the tradition of *enkrateia* the value and role of women was discussed on two levels, that is, on the theoretical and ideological, and the practical and sociological, level. In fact, given the fairly strong connection between marriage and procreation on the one hand and passion and desire on the other (the latter judged from a purely male point of view), an unbreakable bond was formed between passion and desire and the female role. Marriage, and especially procreation, were thus placed entirely within the female sphere and came to define it as an inextricable compromise with the cycle of corruption and death that is created and fed by those activities. "To abstain from the works of woman" is the Lord's command to Salomē in the *Gospel According to the Egyptians,* which was used by the Encratites. When she asked him when death would disappear, he replied that that would occur "when you women cease to procreate."[57]

The link between femininity and sexual activity, with the ambiguous, often negative, connotations of the latter having an impact on the former, became stronger and practically unbreakable when the practice of *enkrateia* was forced to find justification and basis. Indeed, given its specific biblical connotations, this situation placed the blame for sin on Eve. In encratic terms, sin was identified with the practice of marriage. In the patristic tradition, original sin was considered to have unleashed sexual activity, which was required by a fallen, mortal humanity as a tool for survival through procreation. In both cases, therefore, Eve's primary responsibility for what happened in Paradise (the first humans' violation of the rule, leading to humanity's connection with death and corruption, depicted as marriage and procreation) led to further deterioration of the already precarious position of the female *facies.*[58]

It would be incorrect to overestimate the significance of Tertullian's well-known epistrophe defining women as *ianua diaboli* (entrances of the devil) since it was an example of the rhetorical emphasis typical of his style.[59] It cannot be denied, however, that the unique connection between Eve and original sin operated at various levels within the anthropological vision of early Christianity. This strong bond helped to establish the subordinate role of women by providing it with the seal of religious approval.[60] When this situation was linked with *enkrateia,* femininity was seen as a highly risky, if not inherently negative, condition. This perspective provided a background for the metaphor about "becoming male" as a way of gaining access to a state of perfection and completeness.[61] This metaphor, which was widely cited in different contexts with varying degrees of significance, had already been used in several works by Philo of Alexandria.[62]

Since this metaphor was used to express the possibility of woman's spiritual transformation, with simultaneous rejection of the worst aspects of her femininity, it introduced the second, essential dimension of the female question within the context of the tradition under examination here. The practice of continence, particularly of virginity, made it possible for women to adhere fully to the religious ideal proposed to every Christian and thereby reach substantial parity with men in a situation characterized by complete dignity and spiritual freedom.

The example of the removal of the veil of shame by the young bride who, in complete agreement with her husband, abstains from marital relations because of the Lord's entreaty is presented in the *Acts of Thomas* and is particularly useful to our discussion.[63] This situation effectively expressed the sense of freedom inspiring all Christians, and especially women, who chose continence. In this way, they would experience liberation from original sin, which, ever since Eden, had had an impact on all of humanity in the form of sexual activity. In fact, the connection between the bride in question and the garment of shame resulting from Adam's sin[64] once again confirmed the enormous significance of the protological motivation in defining the *ēthos* and anthropological structure of *enkrateia.*

Without overestimating the importance of this ideological framework and its sociological impact on the liberation of women from the many forms of sociocultural conditioning in effect at that time, it is clear that women played a fairly extensive and active role in the acceptance of *enkrateia,* which was presented as the ultimate goal of each Christian.

In my opinion, there is not enough evidence to support the recently advanced theory about female authorship of some portions of the apocryphal literature.[65] There is no question, however, that this literature made a point of praising the exceptional commitment of various heroines and their strict adherence to the apostles' call for continence, as well as their influence (with varying degrees of effectiveness) on their male partners, who often were averse or even hostile to the idea.

There is also ample documentation available on numerous women who completely and enthusiastically embraced the ideal of virginity and continence. As noted above, this devotion appeared in different forms ranging from the earliest examples of domestic asceticism to the later monastic or anchoritic organizations that followed male models and the phenomenon of *virgines subintroductae* common in much of early Christianity. This last case, which is of particular religious interest, appeared to be connected to spiritual marriage among ascetics, with its complicated religious and social implications.[66]

Therefore, from this perspective as well, the tradition of *enkrateia* presented innovative, though fairly unusual, anthropological models. Indeed, the choice of continence (whether more radical or more moderate), which was unique to early Christian circles, challenged established ideological and social institutions, thereby provoking opposition and criticism by those who saw it as a threat to the social order and the very fate of humanity. At the same time, this choice affected the delicate and intricate network of male–female relationships. It offered women options that differed from the traditional roles of wife and mother. This new existential situation, based on the ascetic and abstentionist model, provided women with an opportunity to explore other, essential aspects of their personal identities, though under particular conditions and within a specific religious framework.

NOTES

1. Eusebius, *Historia ecclesiae* 4.23.7–8. Among Dionysius's "Catholic" letters (*Hist. eccl.* 4.23.1–13), the one addressed to the Churches of Amastris and Pontus also deals with themes pertaining to marriage and chastity *(hagneia)* (*Hist. eccl.* 4.23.6).
2. Cf. *1 Cor.* 3.1–2; *Heb.* 5.12–14.
3. Cf. *1 Cor.* 7.1–11.
4. In fact, Eusebius concludes: "In this letter the orthodoxy of Pinytus in the faith, his care for those under him, his learning and theological understanding are shown as in a most accurate image" (*Hist. eccl.* 4.23.8).
5. On this subject, see Giulia Sfameni Gasparro, *Enkrateia e antropologia: Le motivazioni protologiche della continenza e della verginità nel cristianesimo dei primi secoli e nello gnosticismo* (Rome: Institutum Patristicum "Augustinianum," 1984), pp. 221–253.
6. Cf. Sfameni Gasparro, *Enkrateia e antropologia,* pp. 23–56.
7. Sfameni Gasparro, *Enkrateia e antropologia,* pp. 56–79.
8. On this question, see Ugo Bianchi, ed., *La tradizione dell' enkrateia: Motivazioni ontologiche e protologiche,* Atti del Colloquio internazionale, Milano 20–23 aprile 1982 (Rome: Edizioni dell'Ateneo, 1985).
9. There is an extensive bibliography on this subject (the most important titles of which are mentioned in my *Enkrateia e antropologia,* cited in note 5 above), but here I would simply like to draw attention to the recent work by Elaine Pagels, *Adam, Eve, and the Serpent* (New York: Random House, 1988) and, most important, the thorough summary by Peter Brown, *The Body and Society: Men, Women, and Sexual Renunciation in Early Christianity* (New York: Columbia University Press, 1988). Brown's book examines the problem within the framework of contemporary Judaism and Greco-Roman paganism. See also my introduction, with updated bibliography, in Giulia Sfameni Gasparro, C. Magazzù, and C. Aloe Spada, *La coppia nei Padri* (Milano, 1991), pp. 11–170.
10. On gnostic rejection of sexual activity and procreation, consult Sfameni Gasparro, *Enkrateia e antropologia,* pp. 115–166, and, in Bianchi, *La tradizione dell'enkrateia* (note 8 above), the following essays: A. Boehlig, "Einheit und Zweiheit als metaphysische Vorraussetzung fur das Enkratieverständnis in der Gnosis" (pp. 109–131); S. Giversen, "Some Instances of Encratism with Protological Motivations in Gnostic Texts" (pp. 135–142); H.-M. Schenke, "Radikale sexuelle Enthaltsamkeit als hellenistisch-judisches Vollkommenbeitsideal im Thomas-Buch (*NHC* II. 7)" (pp. 263–292); R. McL. Wilson, "Alimentary and Sexual Encratism in the Nag Hammadi Tractates" (pp. 317–332); J. Ries, "L'enkrateia et ses motivations dans les Kephalaia coptes de Medînet Mâdi" (pp. 369–383); G. Mantovani, "La tradizione dell'enkrateia nei testi di Nag Hammadi e nell'ambiente monastico egiziano del IVe secolo" (pp. 561–599); and C. Giuffrè Scibona, "Le motivazioni ontologiche e protologiche dell'enkrateia nel manicheismo occidentale" (pp. 679–686). For Manichean *enkrateia,* one of the more radical expressions of gnostic revulsion against all sexual activities and procreation, see Giulia Sfameni Gasparro, "Enkrateia e dualismo: alle radici della gnosi manichea," in *Agathe Elpis: Studi storico-religiosi in onore di Ugo Bianchi* (Rome, 1993).
11. Aristides, *Apology* 15.4.
12. Justin Martyr, *First Apology* 15.1–7.
13. Athenagoras, *Supplication for the Christians,* 33.
14. Cf. Brown, *Body and Society,* pp. 5–31. Other pertinent comments may be found in

A. Meredith, "Asceticism, Christian and Greek," *Journal of Theological Studies* n.s. 27 (1976):313–332.

15. This type of motivation recurs throughout the patristic tradition. This is clear from the collection of texts in Ch. Munier, *Mariage et Virginité dans l'Eglise ancienne (I^{e}–IIIe siècles)* (Bern and New York: Peter Lang, 1987); and from Sfameni Gasparro, Magazzù, and Aloe Spada, *La coppia nei Padri* (note 9, above).
16. Cf. Sfameni Gasparro, *Enkrateia e antropologia,* pp. 167–322.
17. Clement of Rome, *First Epistle to the Corinthians* 1.38.2.
18. Ignatius of Antioch, *Letter to Polycarp, Bishop of Smyrna* 5.2; cf. Giulia Sfameni Gasparro, "I Padri Apostolici di fronte ai movimenti eretıcali di tipo encratita e gnostico," *Parola Spirito e Vita* 12 (1985):228–244.
19. For a direct approach to this problem on the basis of recent interpretations, cf. Pier Franco Beatrice, "Gli avversari di Paolo e il problema della gnosi a Corinto," *Cristianesimo nella Storia* 6 (1985):1–25.
20. The account of the *status quaestionis* in Benedetto Prete, *Matrimonio e continenza nel cristianesimo delle origini: Studio su I Cor. 7. 1–40* (Brescia: Paideia, 1979) is still helpful, though it needs to be updated to include subsequent contributions.
21. For an extensive discussion and documentation of this theme in ancient Judaism, consult Sfameni Gasparro, *Enkrateia e antropologia,* pp. 323–365. See also V. Cerutti, *Antropologia e apocalittica* (Rome, 1990).
22. L. Rosso Ubigli, "Alcuni aspetti della concezione della porneia nel tardo giudaismo," *Henoch* 1 (1979):201–245.
23. Cf. Paolo Sacchi, "Da Qohelet al tempo di Gesù: Alcune linee del pensiero giudaico," in *Aufstieg und Niedergang der römischen Welt* 2.19.1, eds. Hildegard Temporini and Wolfgang Haase (Berlin and New York: de Gruyter, 1979), pp. 3–32, especially, pp. 27–29.
24. Cf. *De vita Mosaica,* 2.68–69.
25. Adolf Buchler, *Types of Jewish-Palestinian Piety from 70 BCE to 70 CE: The Ancient Pious Men* (New York: Ktav, 1968), pp. 50–52.
26. In addition to Sfameni Gasparro, *Enkrateia e antropologia,* pp. 174–184, see also Pier Angelo Gramaglia's well-documented introductions to some of Tertullian's treatises on this subject: *Tertulliano. De virginibus velandis. La condizione femminile nelle prime communità cristiane* (Rome: Borla, 1984); *Tertulliano. Il matrimonio nel cristianesimo pre-niceno. Ad uxorem. De exhortatione castitatis. De monogamia* (Rome: Borla, 1988).
27. Clement of Alexandria, *Stromateis* 3.6.48.1.
28. *Acta Pauli et Teclae* 5. On the relationship between faith in resurrection and the practice of chastity, cf. Ton H. C. van Eijk, "Marriage, and Virginity, Death and Immortality," in *Epektasis: Mélanges patristiques offerts au Cardinal Jean Daniélou,* eds. Jean Fontaine and Charles Kannengiesser (Paris: Beauchesne, 1972), pp. 209–235. Also cf. B. Lang, "No Sex in Heaven: The Logic of Procreation, Death and Eternal Life in Judaeo-Christian Tradition," *Alten Orient und altes Testament* 215 (1985):237–253.
29. See in Giulia Sfameni Gasparro, "Gli Atti apocrifi degli Apostoli e la tradizione dell'enkrateia. Discussione di una recente formula interpretativa," *Augustinianum* 23 (1983): 287–307, an analysis of some positions taken in the essays collected in François Bovon et al., eds., *Les Actes apocryphes des Apôtres: Christianisme et monde païen* (Paris: Labor et fides, 1981). See Sfameni Gasparro, *Enkrateia e antropologia,* pp. 87–101, and Giulia Sfameni Gasparro, "L'epistula Titi de disposizione sanctimonii e la tradizione

dell'enkrateia," in *ANRW* 2.25.6, eds. Wolfgang Haase and Hildegard Temporini (Berlin and New York: de Gruyter, 1988), pp. 4551–4664.

30. This is the interpretation of *1 Tm.* 4 in W. L. Lane, "*I Tm.* 4.1–3: An Early Instance of Over-Realized Eschatology?" *New Testament Studies* 11 (1966):164–167.
31. *Lk.* 14.25–26, 18.29–30; cf. *Mt.* 19.29.
32. Of the numerous exegeses proposed, we need mention only one by Quentin Quesnell, "'Made Themselves Eunuchs for the Kingdom of Heaven' (*Mt.* 19.12)," *Catholic Biblical Quarterly* 30 (1968):335–358, which interprets the gospel pericope not as an appeal to virginity but as a definitive and irrevocable commitment within matrimony. Pier Franco Beatrice, "Continenza e matrimonio nel cristianesimo primitivo," in *Etica sessuale e matrimonio nel cristianesimo delle origini,* ed. R. Cantalamessa (Milano: Vita e pensiero, 1976), p. 59, on the other hand, views it as an invitation to complete continence within matrimony. Cf. Sfameni Gasparro, *Enkrateia e antropologia,* pp. 16–18.
33. F. H. Schrivener, *Codex Bezae Cantabrigiensis* (Cantabrigiae: Sumptibus Academiae phototypice repraesentatus, 1899), fol. 266b. As we know, this variant has a parallel in the ancient Syrian translation of the gospel: cf. F. C. Burkitt, *Evangelion Da-Mepharreshe: The Curetonian Version of the Four Gospels with the Readings of the Sinai Palimpsest and the Early Syriac Patristic Evidence,* 2 vols. (Cambridge: Cambridge University Press, 1904), 1:386–387 and 2:299. Cf. Gilles Quispel, *Makarius, das Thomasevangelium und des Lied von der Perle* (Leiden: Brill, 1967), pp. 82ff.
34. See note 21, above.
35. Sfameni Gasparro, *Enkrateia e antropologia.*
36. Cf. Peter Nagel, *Die Motivierung der Askese in der alten Kirche und die Ursprung des Mönchtums,* Texte und Untersuchungen 95 (Berlin: Akademie-Verlag, 1966), pp. 34–48; Karl Suso Frank, *Angelikos Bios: Begriffsanalytische und Begriffsgeschichtliche Untersuchung zum "Engelgleichen Leben" im frühen Mönchtum* (Münster: Aschendorffsche Verlagsbuchhandlung, 1964).
37. On "double creation" as indicated above, consult Ugo Bianchi, "La 'doppia creazione' dell'uomo come oggestto di ricerca storico-religiosa," in *La 'doppia creazione' dell'uomo negli Alessandrinim, nei Cappadoci e nella gnosi,* ed. Ugo Bianchi (Rome: Edizioni dell'Ateneo & Bizzarri, 1978), pp. 1–23.
38. Irenaeus, *Adversus Haereses* 1.28.1; cf. 3.23.8.
39. *Discourse to the Greeks* 7.13–20.
40. *Strom.* 3.12.81.
41. *Strom.* 3.13.91.
42. *Strom.* 1.21.101.
43. *Strom.* 1.13.93.
44. *Strom.* 3.13.92.
45. Epiphanius, *Panarion, haer.* 47 *sive* 67. Cf. Karl Heussi, *Der Ursprung des Mönchtums* (Tubingen: Mohr, 1936).
46. Augustine, after initially accepting—under Ambrosian influence—the postlapsarian characterization of marriage and procreation, later has difficulty choosing among various solutions. Finally, he rejects the postlapsarian formula and argues that man and woman were originally destined to sexual intercourse and procreation in accordance with the original plan of creation. Nonetheless, in the complex Augustinian doctrine on the connection between marriage and lust there are elements of the tradition under discussion. Cf. Pier Franco Beatrice, *Tradux peccati. Alle fonti della dottrina agostiniana del peccato originale* (Milano: Vita e pensiero, 1978) and Sfameni Gasparro, *Enkrateia e antropologia,* pp. 300–322; Giulia Sfameni Gasparro, "Il tema della concupiscenza in

Agostino e la tradizione dell'enkrateia," *Augustinianum* 25 (1985):155–183; Giulia Sfameni Gasparro, "Concupiscenza e generazione: aspetti antropologici della dottrina agostiniana del peccato originale," in *Atti del Congresso Internazionale su S. Agostino nel XVI anniversario della conversione Roma 15–20 settembre 1986* (Rome: Institutum Patristicum "Augustinianum," 1987), 2:225–255. See also J. van Oort, "Augustine and Mani on Concupiscentia Sexualis," in *Augustiniana Traiectina. Communications présentées au Collogue International d'Utrecht 13–14 novembre 1986,* eds. J. van den Boef and J. van Oort (Paris: Études Augustiniennes, 1987), pp. 137–152.

47. Cf. Sfameni Gasparro, *Enkrateia e antropologia,* pp. 167–300.

48. Clement of Alexandria expressed this opinion, including the idea that marriage was a part of the Lord's plan, but that it had been entered into too early by the first humans (*Strom.* 3.14.94.3; cf. *Protrepticus* 11.111.1). Of the Latin Fathers, Zeno of Verona identifies marriage with Adam's sin (Liber 1, tractatus 2.8).

49. On the relationship between this idea and that of man "in the image of God," see Giulia Sfameni Gasparro, "Image of God and Sexual Differentiation in the Tradition of Enkrateia: Protological Motivations," in *Image of God and Gender Models in Judaeo-Christian Tradition,* ed. Kari E. Børresen (Oslo: Solum Forlag, 1991), pp. 138–171.

50. Walter Bauer's summary treatment, in *Rechglaubigkeit und Ketzerei im altesten Christentum* (Tubingen: Mohr/Siebeck, 1934, 1964), translated by the Philadelphia Seminar on Christian Origins in *Orthodoxy and Heresy in Earliest Christianity,* eds. Robert Kraft and Gerhard Krodel (Philadelphia: Fortress Press, 1971), builds upon the comprehensive and provocative work done by A. von Harnack. *Die Mission und Ausbreitung des Christentum in den ersten drei Jahrhunderten,* 2 vols. (Leipzig: J. C. Hinrichs, 1902, 1924), and it suggests new perspectives in the analysis of the varied *facies* of early Christianity. But it needs to be investigated further, with significant changes made in the conclusions. In this respect, see G. Strecker's appendix to the 1964 reprint and, more recently, Stephen Gero, "With Walter Bauer on the Tigris: Encratite Orthodoxy and Libertine Heresy in Syro-Mesopotamian Christianity," in *Nag Hammadi, Gnosticism, and Early Christianity,* eds. Charles W. Hedrick and Robert Hodgson, Jr. (Peabody, Mass.: Hendrickson, 1986), pp. 287–307. In addition to Brown, *Body and Society,* consult the well-documented volume by Robin Lane Fox, *Pagans and Christians* (London: Viking, 1986), containing elements that may be useful in defining the spiritual environment of the time. The historical, cultural and religious background to New Testament writings is clearly explained by Helmut Koester, *Introduction to the New Testament: History, Culture, and Religion of the Hellenistic Age* (Philadelphia: Fortress Press, 1982).

51. See G. Quispel, *Makarius* (note 33 above), and Jean Daniélou's review of this work in *Vigilae Christianae* 22 (1968):301–304. On the specificity of the facies in Egyptian Christianity, consult Birger A. Pearson and James E. Goehring, eds., *The Roots of Egyptian Christianity* (Philadelphia: Fortress Press, 1986); and C. W. Griggs, *Early Egyptian Christianity from its Origins to 451 CE* (Leiden: Brill, 1990).

52. Arthur Voobus, *History of Asceticism in the Syrian Orient,* 2 vols. (Louvain, 1958–1960); A.F.J. Klijn, *Edessa, die Stadt des Apostels Thomas. Das alteste Christentum in Syrien* (Neukirchen-Vluyn: Verlag des Erziehungsvereins, 1965). Of the many contributions on this subject, we mention Hans W. Drijvers, "Facts and Problems in Early Syriac Speaking Christianity," *Second Century* 2 (1982):157–175.

53. Arthur Vöobus, *Celibacy, a Requirement for Admission to Baptism in the Early Syrian Church* (Stockholm: Estonian Theological Society in Exile, 1961) and further documentation in Giulia Sfameni Gasparro, "L'epistula Titi," pp. 4607–4612.

54. The Syrian situation is connected with encratite-inspired literature on the apostle

Thomas and his deeds, found in both the *Acts* and the Coptic *Gospel* contained in the Nag Hammadi manuscripts, the interpretation of which is still a subject for discussion (cf. Sfameni Gasparro, *Enkrateia e antropologia,* pp. 79–87). On the complex issue of the composition of the *Acts of Thomas,* cf. A.F.J. Klijn, *The Acts of Thomas* (Leiden: Brill, 1968) and Y. Tissot, "Les Actes de Thomas, example de recueil composite," in Bovon et al. (note 29 above), pp. 223–232.

55. See especially P. Grimal, ed., *Histoire mondiale de la femme,* 4 vols. (Paris: Nouvelle Librairie de France, 1965–1967) and the more recent *Storia delle donne in Occidente,* 4 vols., ed. Georges Duby and Michèle Perrot (Bari, 1990–1992), spanning all of history from antiquity through the present day. Two volumes of this history have appeared in English translation. See *A History of Women,* vols. 1 and 2, trans. Arthur Goldhammer (Cambridge: Harvard University Press, 1992–1993).
56. Work on this subject is so extensive and the bibliography so complete that it is impossible to list the principal titles. We mention only the recent work by A. M. Vérilhac, C. Vial, and L. Darmezin, *La femme dans le monde méditerranéen,* 2, *La femme grecque et romaine: Bibliographie* (Lyon: Maison de l'Orient, 1990). Cf. our introduction to Sfameni Gasparro, Magazzù, and Aloe Spada, pp. 42–74.
57. Clement of Alexandria, *Strom.* 3.6.45; cf. 3.9.64.
58. Cf. Sfameni Gasparro, "Enkrateia e dualismo."
59. Tertullian, *De cultu feminarum* 1.1.2.
60. Cf. Sfameni Gasparro, Magazzù, and Aloe Spada, pp. 17–41.
61. Relevant comments in Marvin W. Meyer, "Making Mary Male: The Categories of 'Male' and 'Female' in the Gospel of Thomas," *New Testament Studies* 31 (1985):554–570; K. Vogt, "'Becoming Male': One Aspect of an Early Christian Anthropology," *Concilium* (1985):95–107. This metaphor is often combined with the motif of female "weakness" as opposed to "virility." Cf. U. Mattioli, *Astheneia e andreia: Aspetti della femminilità nella letteratura classica, biblica, e cristiana* (Parma: Università di Parma, Istituto di lingua e letteratura latina, 1983).
62. Richard A. Baer, Jr., *Philo's Use of the Categories Male and Female* (Leiden: Brill, 1970).
63. *Acta Thomas* 14.
64. Giulia Sfameni Gasparro, "La vergogna di Adamo e di Eva nella riflessione dei Padri," *Parola Spirito e Vita* 20 (1989):253–270.
65. Virginia Burrus, "Chastity as Autonomy: Women in the Stories of the Apocryphal Acts," *Semeia* 38 (1986):101–117. On the female role in the apocryphal literature, cf. also Ross Shepard Kraemer, "The Conversion of Women to Ascetic Forms of Christianity," *Signs* 6 (1980):298–307; Gail Paterson Corrington, "The Divine Woman? Propaganda and the Power of Chastity in the New Testament Apocrypha," *Helios* 13.2 (1986):151–162. Discussion of these exegetic formulations can be found in Jean-Daniel Kaestli, "Fiction littéraire et réalité sociale: que peut-on savoir de la place des femmes dans le milieu de production des Actes apocryphes des Apôtres?" in *La fable apocryphe* (Brepolds, 1990), 1:279–302.
66. On this question, cf. Sfameni Gasparro, "L'epistula Titi."

12

Ascetic Closure and the End of Antiquity

Averil Cameron

I wish to explore in this paper the idea of an "ascetic closure"—in historical terms, the notion of a closing in of possibilities, a contraction of horizons, somehow to be connected with the predominance of asceticism. Four recent books, in all of which early Christian asceticism plays a large role, have each emphasized this notion of closing in, of a narrowing of the horizons of society at large. Thus, the complex of ideas and practices labeled "asceticism" can be transferred to considerations of broader historical change.[1] The language used is instructive: "silence"; "icy overtones"; "frailty"; "bizarre, postclassical shapes." Ascetic thought and practice is, it seems, identified as dominating the movement from antiquity to the Middle Ages, from an open society to a closed one. Peter Brown uses such expressions as "the draining away of secularity" and writes of a very different world; Robert Markus speaks of epistemological excision.[2] The concept of closure is contained in the title of his book, *The End of Ancient Christianity,* and, as if to reinforce the point, the last chapter is itself entitled "Within Sight of the End." Markus further associates this closure with the pervasion of lay society (he writes mainly of the West) by the image of the monastic community and the ascetic ideal. Brown, too, agreeing with Jacques Le Goff, writes of a very different sense of community and of the human person within it, which he locates in the late fifth and sixth centuries and identifies with the end of the ancient world and the beginning of the Middle Ages.

We are thus presented with a major challenge of historical explanation. Is asceticism itself to be regarded as a constituting a major factor in such broad processes of historical change? Peter Brown's most recent judgment is that an unequivocally Christian empire, which he identifies with Byzantium, was already in existence in the later fifth century.[3] That this narrowing process is somehow related to Christianization is apparent in both books. Indeed, Brown aligns it with what he sees as a simultaneous retreat of possible alternatives; according to this view, pagans, or "Hellenes," as the Christians called them, were demoralized, left only with the possibility of quiet courage, not real resistance; resigned to an old-fashioned and studiously nonabrasive world and able to hope for no more than a moral survival-kit,[4] in contrast to the strident and aggressive attitudes taken up by some contemporary Christians. It is equally clear that both Brown and Markus believe that the process also had something to do with asceticism. Markus's penultimate chapter is entitled "The Ascetic Invasion"; the chapter before it ends with the following claim about the diffusion of ascetic ideals:

> The boundary between desert and City was being blurred, and the distance between the monastic life and the life of the parishes diminished. The image of the monastic community was becoming adapted to serving as a model for the Christian community in the world, while the ascetic ideal it proposed to its members was becoming adapted to serve as the model for bishops and clergymen.[5]

At the end of *The Body and Society,* Peter Brown, too, explicitly links changing historical periods with the advance of asceticism:

> When in the course of the late fifth and sixth centuries profound changes sapped the political and economic structure of the cities of the Mediterranean, the Christian notions we have just described came to the fore. They ratified a very different sense of the community and of the human person within it from that current in the age of Marcus Aurelius. They made plain what Jacques le Goff has described, in a memorable phrase, as *la déroute du corporel,* the definitive "rout of the body," that marked the end of the ancient world and the beginning of the Middle Ages.[6]

This formulation juxtaposes the influence of asceticism with other kinds of historical change, rather than ascribing transition directly to it. But *Power and Persuasion* is, if anything, more explicit in its association of ascetic ideals with historical change, and just as uncomplimentary about their effects. By the use of such words as "melodramatic"; "deadly"; "confrontational"; "overpowering"; and "vertiginous";[7] Brown suggests both an immense vertical stratification of society and a narrow and uncompromising quality in the Christian messages coming from the ascetic literature and from Christians ascetics in action.[8] The fifth-century Egyptian abbot, Shenoute of Atripe, not perhaps the most typical representative of Christian ascetic thought, though indeed a great leader, can be made to stand here for the contemporary recognition of actual "crushing asymmetries of power"; "townsmen and peasants alike learned to approach the great on bended knee. . . . before the emperor, as before God, all subjects were poor."[9]

I shall do no more than suggest here that the question of date remains open. More central to my present purpose is to give further examination to the contention that the growth of asceticism can itself be a dynamic factor in historical change.

In order to establish the thesis, it would be necessary to argue that ascetic thought, expressed in ascetic language, was not simply the domain of the few, but rather the experience of society at large. Such seepage from the theological and the ascetic spheres was a central theme of my book *Christianity and the Rhetoric of Empire.* And, while it is not so easy to demonstrate for the fourth century, it does, I think, become progressively more apparent in the succeeding period. Nevertheless, it is worth returning to the issue.

My own recent approach has been through cognitive change and now focuses upon the use of language in particular. The last chapter of *Christianity and the Rhetoric of Empire* may itself seem to point to closure, ending as it does with the reign of Justinian and its well-known attempts at state regimentation. Indeed, the discourses of authority and resistance are very prominent in early Byzantine literature, not least in its major historian, Procopius, just as they are also embedded in the emperor's own official pronouncements.[10] At first sight asceticism does not seem to fit well into this context, for, as has often been pointed out, the ascetic discourse of hagiography is itself implicated in a dynamic of resistance to social norms: the ascetic rejects conventional authority in his dress, behavior and rejection of culture, the holy fool representing the furthermost step in this direction. But even the latter rejects culture only in order to prescribe higher rules; in its broader sense, ascetic discourse, too, is predicated on regulation; and is thus also in its very nature authoritarian.[11] The tension between the model of the ascetic as "holy man" and that of the ascetic as monastic leader, bishop or patriarch is an interesting product of this duality. In addition, when considering the relation between asceticism and authority, one needs to recognize the inherently hierarchical and inclusive aspects of Christian discourse, the impulse towards coherence,[12] pushed to logical conclusions by the official rhetoric of Justinian and others.

But such coherence is not hierarchical only in the political sense. Nor is all Christian discourse ascetic, at any rate in the commonly accepted sense. A more inclusive discourse can embrace an altogether more humane way of thinking, from Mary miracles to the piety of icons. Nor was the transference of the undoubtedly hierarchical and coherence-seeking side of Christian discourse to the political sphere unambiguously successful in historical terms. Rather, as I now want to stress, it both gave rise to, and in a sense even depended on, the other side of Christian thought, which in my book I term "paradox," but which also stands for resistance to—and escape from—its more "public" and integrated aspects. The concluding paragraph of the chapter on the sixth century hints at future tensions without spelling them out (for this is not a book about Byzantium).[13] We are left, therefore, to question both the nature of the Byzantine dark ages and the actual degree of continuance thereafter—and, indeed, throughout Byzantine history—of this official thrust toward orthodoxy.

Those attempts were in practice exposed to continual challenge. Despite appearances, despite the repeated claims of emperors, patriarchs, and councils given expression in official policy; in the liturgy; and in the material culture of church and state; and despite the substantial elements of historical continuity in its cultural tradition, Byzantium was far from being the stable and unchanging society it has sometimes seemed.[14] More particularly, it was subject to a long series of divisive struggles, as whoever was in power attempted to enforce views (far from always consistent) of what was to be considered orthodox.[15] The long and bitter struggle of images in the eighth and ninth centuries, the condemnation of John Italus in the late eleventh century, and the hesychast crisis in the fourteenth, are merely high spots in a long history of repeated moves to define heresy, in a society where church and state were as often in conflict as they were in harmony, and where both "church" and "state" are terms which disguise dramatic fluctuations of interest, personnel, and politics. One of the most striking products of this tendency is the so-called Synodikon of Orthodoxy, a lengthy statement of condemnation of error which gradually evolved, with many later additions, after the formal ending of the iconoclastic controversy in 843 CE. As an unequivocal demonstration of that closing of intellectual horizons to which I have referred, it was read out each year on the Sunday of Orthodoxy, a feast still observed today. It formally condemns not just Christian heresies, but also Platonism, Hellenic philosophy, and all dangerous doctrines leading to pluralism and secular thinking.[16] It is thus a symbolic statement of closure of the clearest possible kind. In the last phase of this development, represented by the vindication of Gregory Palamas against his opponents in the fourteenth century, official Byzantium also resoundingly vindicated the ascetic legacy of early Christianity.[17] But the Synodikon is simultaneously a demonstration of the possibility and the actuality of division. The unity it proclaims was more actual than real. For all its proclamations of order and harmony,[18] official Byzantium did not hesitate, when driven by adversity, to resort to whatever ideological or political steps seemed expedient, including that of seeking reunion with Rome; indeed, the emperor was still officially in union with Rome when the city fell to Mehmet II in 1453 CE.[19] Can it be possible that apparent systematization did not merely conceal, but also consistently provoked, dissonance?

What has this to do with asceticism? We must return to the role of language in determining culture. In the rest of this paper I want to examine more closely the question of what an ascetic discourse might have been, in the context of the transition from late antique to Byzantine society, how such a discourse might affect society at large, and whether it necessarily implied a closure in the sense which seems to be suggested in the works mentioned above. In view of the questions of divisions of historical period which have been raised, and since the early Byzantine period is my current area of concern, most of my examples will be taken from that chronological range, and from the Greek East. Nevertheless, I am interested here in methodology and principles more than in the specifics of place or period; as I hope to demonstrate, this may be one of the areas in which history can benefit from the methods and questions of literary criticism. Should that prove to be the case, an important result, I believe, will have been established.

What Is Ascetic Discourse?

By "discourse"[20] I mean the typical ways of expressing ascetic ideas, including the vocabulary used; the discourse may be oral or written, and, if the latter, literary or nonliterary. It may seem odd to suggest that the term can also refer to visual material,[21] though the related term "rhetoric" has become accepted in its broader sense with this application; as it happens, however, my remarks here relate more to the former categories.[22] It is less easy to decide where ascetic discourse stops: certain genres, such as that of the *Apophthegmata patrum* and related collections like the *Pratum spirituale* of John Moschus, clearly fall squarely within the definition, as do works specifically written to advocate ascetic practice, such as the *Ladder of Divine Ascent* of John Climacus. Such non-Christian works as Porphyry's *De abstinentia* must naturally also be included. It is somewhat less clear, however, whether all hagiography constitutes ascetic discourse by its very definition—still less so whether all theological writing is necessarily ascetic, and less so again what other kinds of text can be brought into this category.

First, then, let us address the limited sense of the term. An ascetic discourse is one which explicitly advocates asceticism. Much monastic literature, and much hagiography, falls into this category, as do those non-Christian texts of our period which deal with similar issues—for example Iamblichus's *On the Pythagorean Life,* Porphyry's *Letter to Marcella* and *Life of Plotinus,* Marinus's *Life of Proclus.* The *Life of Antony* has long been rightly regarded as a work of seminal importance, both for the pattern which it lays down, including its typology of demonic temptation, and its agenda of physical privation; and for its diffusion and subsequent influence. In the Greek Christian East in later periods, works such as John Climacus's *Ladder of Divine Ascent* are central, as are the monastic-ascetic collections of extracts made by individual monasteries for their own use right through the Byzantine period and thereafter. The eleventh-century monastery of the Evergetis in Constantinople, now the subject of study by an interdisciplinary group of specialists,[23] was only one of many such establishments that possessed its own such collection—a handbook of extracts from earlier ascetic writers for use within the monastery itself. Certain works and writers are favorites, among them the *Apophthegmata patrum,* Ephrem the Syrian in Greek translation, Isaac the Syrian, Maximus Confessor, Diadochos of Photikē, and others. Likewise, manuscript traditions from the ninth century onwards attest to the wide and complex diffusion of a whole range of ascetic tales from the earlier period throughout the Byzantine world.[24] We are dealing with a living and persistent tradition which managed to gain a strong hold over orthodox thinking and spirituality and to retain it until modern times. It is clearly a mistake to regard this tradition as historically marginal. One instance in which the connection is demonstrable is that of the controversy surrounding Gregory Palamas in the fourteenth century: for, while the spirituality of Palamas was deeply dependent upon the ascetic tradition established in late antiquity, the controversy surrounding hesychast teaching in the fourteenth century, in the course of which Palamas emerged triumphant, had all the aspects of deep intellectual, political, and social division; it was no simple matter of a marginalized dispute between monks and clerics.

An ascetic discourse, in early Christian terms, can also evidently be identified where certain key terms and concepts are present, even where the text as a whole may not be concerned with advocating asceticism directly. Thus, the complex of ideas clustering round the themes of renunciation, temptation, denial, spiritual progress or ascent in the spiritual life, and the specialized use of Greek terms such as *porneia, erōs, logismoi, aktēmosynē* would be a fair indicator. The many commentaries on the *Song of Songs* by Christian writers, especially from Origen onwards, can fairly be assigned to the genre of ascetic discourse.[25] Similarly, the theory of demons, worked out, for instance, by Evagrius of Pontus or in the Macarian homilies, is an integral part of the ascetic complex as it finds expression in the early monastic literature; and the presence of similar ideas about demons elsewhere is another indicator of ascetic thinking. It ought to be possible to define an ascetic vocabulary in Greek (as presumably also in Syriac), and then to see how often and in what contexts it is used by writers outside of explicitly ascetic writings, or to what extent it is used in their other writings by writers who combine, as many did in late antiquity, ascetic writings with a wide range of other types of works. Writers like Basil or John Chrysostom, for example, or Augustine, Ambrose, or Jerome, in Latin, are remarkable as much for the range of their works as for their quantity, a feature which continues to impress in the case of such later figures as Maximus Confessor or John of Damascus.[26] Peter Brown has studied in great detail ideas of ascetic renunciation in late antique society at large up to the time of Augustine; now, I believe, we must carry the search further chronologically, and look specifically at language use as an indicator of diffusion. How far were Greek terms carried over into Latin, for example? But in broader terms as well, ascetic terminology and ascetic ideas were not confined to a specialized discourse. Many of their most prominent exponents were deeply involved in lay society at large, whether locally or centrally, and often at very high levels. Emperors were drawn in, whether as writers, like Justinian, or as participants and protagonists in religious controversy.

Thus, a closer definition of ascetic discourse is essential before we can really begin to assess its influence. Yet the prominence of ascetic literature and ascetic themes in my own book, and in that of Robert Markus, neither of which is ostensibly about asceticism as such, prompts one to ask more directly about the role played by ascetic discourse both in Christianization and in broader historical developments in late antiquity.

Asceticism and Christianization

In assessing the effects and extent of Christianization, some scholars have looked for signs of improvement in moral behavior, only to find them wanting.[27] Such changes would, in any case be hard to trace, given the nature of our evidence. But the project itself seems misguided. A different approach starts from the investigation of the actual discourses by which late antique society may have been shaped. A good case can be made for thinking that the ascetic strand was one of the most important; however, we soon come up against the question of whether the theme of asceticism should be disentangled from that of Christianization. There is certainly a danger of falling into the trap of too easily equating the two, especially as we are ourselves so much conditioned to assume the eventual triumph of Christianity. Yet just as Byzantium, as I have already suggested, was, in practice, far from being the monolithically Christian society it is usually assumed to have been, so also the culture of late antiquity was a shifting mix of many different elements, not merely the Christian ones. Indeed, recent scholarship lays emphasis on the continued vitality and variety of non-Christian traditions and practice.[28] Seen against this background, study of the process of Christianization has to be put into more subtle perspective. We can save the contention that ascetic discourses had a profound effect on late antique and Byzantine society by incorporating into that view the ascetic discourses which lay outside Christianity. If this paper focuses mainly on Christian ascetic discourse, therefore, that leaves open a further and perhaps equally important area of investigation; namely, whether Peter Brown is right in suggesting that pagan ascetics from Eunapius onwards were saddened and in retreat and therefore, by definition, without major influence. Perhaps we should still be looking, as in earlier periods, for the influence of asceticism in a much broader sense, drawing not only on Christian examples, but on pagan, Jewish, Manichaean, or other components.

Asceticism and Literary Expression

In his book *The Ascetic Imperative,* still in press when I was writing *Christianity and the Rhetoric of Empire,* Geoffrey Harpham made the interesting move of extending the term "ascetic" into the fields of literary criticism and iconography.[29] The book moves from the late antique classics of asceticism—the *Life of Antony* and Augustine's *Confessions*—to much later works of art inspired by the early ascetic ideal, the so-called Thebaid paintings of the Reformation period, depicting ascetics and hermits in the Egyptian desert, and the well-known Isenheim Altarpiece attributed to Grunewald. No doubt for similar reasons, though as it happens independently of Harpham's book, some of the same images also found their way into the illustrations of *Christianity and the Rhetoric of Empire.* As his introduction makes clear, Harpham is concerned with the legacy of ascetic ideals to the medieval and postmedieval West. Indeed, he terms the *Life of Antony* "the master text of Western asceticism."[30] Instead of focusing on other works of art as examples of borrowing, namely the use of this model by the French writers and painters of the nineteenth century, not least by Flaubert,[31] he turns instead to the ascetic imperative of modern literary criticism and argues for the practice of hermeneutics and criticism as essentially a modern ascetic activity. Asceticism has become not merely a force in history but a universal impulse.

This broadening of the term asceticism is extremely interesting, and obviously merits further discussion. I should like, however, to stress some features of late antique ascetic discourse that Harpham has singled out for particular comment. He points first to the integral and self-conscious connection between asceticism and texts: the ascetic drive is closely, indeed, explicitly, bound to linguistic expression. I draw attention in my book to the ways in which the (deeply ascetic) *Apocryphal Acts,* for instance, frequently halt the narrative in order to discuss words, writing and speech. The self-consciousness of asceticism itself embodies an act of self-creation that possesses its own aesthetics; it transcends the natural and resembles an act of literary or artistic creation.[32] The internal contradictions of such a strategy are apparent: while Antony is the figure who rejects culture for the desert, he is also the embodiment of *logos;* and while the secular learning of Evagrius of Pontus is to be discounted once he enters the desert, his talents are nevertheless utilized in symbolic debates with pagan philosophers. Augustine, the most self-conscious of the ascetics, was also the greatest linguistic philosopher since Plato. Not only the writings which deal directly with words and meanings, such as the *De doctrina christiana* and the *De magistro,* but also the *Confessions* (in Harpham's phrase "an ascetic's success story") are permeated by Augustine's heightened awareness of words, and of God as the Word.[33]

Harpham also points to the exploitation by late antique asceticism of the concept of desire, one of the features which makes it highly congenial to modern critics. As late antique asceticism defined itself by means of the notion of temptation, it also focused on desire, in such a way that the ascetic was said to transcend desire while at the same time exercising the freest form of desire in his or her individual relation with God.[34] Christian asceticism was not merely self-conscious, but deeply implicated in textual hermeneutics; it is therefore doubly close to modern criticism, which sees itself as an activity characterized by desire and proceeding through exegesis.[35]

Ascetic discourse in late antiquity frequently implied narrative, very often in the form of biography.[36] To that extent it imposed limits, implied an ending, and imposed closure on the way in which life was to be lived and understood. These biographies, embedded, as the Christian examples were, in the broader scheme of Christian creation and salvation history, also implied a sense of narrative time.[37] Moreover, the biographies implied a relation between the texts and real life. Real lives, it was hinted, should follow the pattern set in the texts, themselves accounts of exemplary lives.[38] Thus, this kind of late antique ascetic discourse was profoundly mimetic. Integral to it is the implication that texts and real life—social behavior—are in fact closely linked.[39] While appearing to be the discourse of retreat, and thus of the marginalized, it calls for an audience. Its object and its *raison d'être* are in fact advertisement, even pleasure.[40] The late antique ascetic discourse was, paradoxically, predicated on being known by the outside world; in just this way, the power of the stylite saint, the ascetic star, displayed itself most fully exactly at the point when he stepped down from his column and confronted his audience.

The Impact of Ascetic Discourse

The notion of ascetic closure, in the sense described at the beginning of this paper, presupposes the diffusion of ascetic values and ideas to the public at large. Clearly we are not talking about a modern society, where ideas, fashions, and the like can spread with real speed. Many, indeed most, of the means of such communication were lacking; not only had no basic changes taken place in technology or communication, but the political and territorial disturbances of the period must, in some cases, have actually made such communication more difficult. It is all the more striking, therefore, when we do find widespread evidence of the transport of ideas, social practice, or literary and artistic themes and styles. A few brief examples must suffice. Ramsay MacMullen has argued that the audiences of preachers such as John Chrysostom were less socially mixed than is sometimes assumed, and consisted primarily of the middle class and the well-to-do.[41] But we would not necessarily have expected anything different. And, in this highly stratified society, they were the ones who had the opportunity and the influence.

I turn now to dissemination. The social range of this ascetic discourse was wide. Elizabeth Clark's recent study of the Origenist controversy illustrates one way in which upper-class social networks could spread ideas and arguments with great speed over distances which, in view of the difficulty of travel in the ancient world, can now only seem surprising.[42] Letter writing flourished among groups of ascetics and individuals. Bishops also crossed social and intellectual boundaries. Still largely drawn from the well-to-do who could afford a standard classical education, they might well have sat in mixed classes with pagans, but once they became bishops they had to deal not only with the local governors, but also with the ordinary people in their dioceses, or on the poor registers—not to mention the rather ordinary clergy beneath them. Pilgrims, too, have left their traces all over the late antique world; they ranged from very ordinary people to those who came from the highest strata in the empire. Thousands of pilgrim tokens were manufactured for them to take home as souvenirs,[43] and elaborate buildings constructed to house them near this or that shrine. As nearly as one can use the term in this period, pilgrimage became big business. Somehow, people knew where to go, just as they knew, apparently, where monasteries were, and what they were for.

A certain minimizing tendency is observable in some recent scholarship as to the spread of Christian art, or the evidence for social diffusion of Christian ideas, and clearly one must not be tempted to overstate the case. But the stories of urban disturbances over religious grievances are very frequent; there is a considerable volume of saints' lives, homiletic, and miracle stories being produced by, say, the sixth century (and a number and variety of translations of popular works, especially of apocrypha). In addition, there is good evidence for the pilgrim trade and the spread of monastic sites (over sixty in the Judaean desert on the most recent figures). All of the foregoing indicate diffusion of ascetic discourse at social levels other than that of the literate upper classes. It should be noted that literacy, as such, is not necessarily a requirement for such diffusion in a society in which oral communication and visual influences are equally important. Finally, the religious and political history of the period, especially in its later phases, demonstrates the actual contact and involvement between secular and ecclesiastical leaders, and between political and religious issues. When emperors and courtiers implicated themselves in doctrinal controversy; participated in councils; dealt with bishops; listened to homilies; and sponsored public religious debate, it would be hard to maintain that ascetic discourse was confined only to the strictly ascetic/monastic sphere.

Ascetic discourse affected society at large in multiple ways: through personal contact; through oral communication; by example; through travel and contact with travelers; through exposure to visual images; as well as—no doubt in a much more limited way—by the actual reading of texts. Late antique society was not like the modern world; yet a case can be made for regarding it as a time when social juxtaposition became possible on a wider scale than before, and when the crossing of social boundaries in unexpected ways was even at times elevated to the realm of the desirable. Indeed, part of the very attraction of asceticism lay precisely in this overturning of social norms. Through the influence of this very ascetic discourse, the poor became for the first time an object of intense interest and attention among the more favored members of society.[44] Women, another problematic group in Greco-Roman culture, did not of course achieve anything approximating liberation or equality. Yet they, too, gained from the spread of ascetic discourse; for while on the one hand they tended to be assigned the symbolic role of temptress and were tainted with the inheritance of Eve, they, too, could become ascetics, retiring to the desert, or practicing the religious life at home. They could go on pilgrimage, found monasteries, read and commission religious books, learn Hebrew, reject arranged marriage, dress as they liked, and debate with men; ascetic friendships might replace human desire.[45]

Constantine the Great put Christianity onto the public agenda, and licensed the entry of himself and his successors into the politics of the Christian church. This much is clear; in addition, he opened even the imperial court to ascetic influence, personally preaching, sending letters to St. Antony in Egypt (if we can believe the *Life of Antony*), and ordering copies of the scriptures for Constantinople.[46] By the fifth century, Theodosius II's court was allegedly run like a religious house; by the sixth, Justinian and Theodora had a whole flock of Eastern monks and clergy living in the palace. There was little sense of a separation of church and state, and despite the persistence of classicizing education, much less of a practical division between secular and religious discourse than one might imagine. Ascetics and others did not live in the separate worlds that the literature leads us to expect.

Implications for Historical Change

All of this seems to suggest a degree of novelty and variety of choice. Yet the books I mentioned at the beginning of this paper emphasize a narrowing down of ascetic discourse and Harpham's view presents it as the discourse of negation, of limit, of denial. We must, therefore, now ask what the broader implications may have been of the permutation of contemporaneous textuality by the ascetic discourse.

Interesting things were happening in late antiquity in relation to textual politics. The rise to prominence of the highly self-conscious narratives of asceticism; the intense preoccupation with words and meaning and the resort to metaphor; the constant (indeed relentless) attempts to define the essentially indefinable; the obsession with hermeneutics; the technologizing of error in the form of condemnation of heresy—all made late antiquity a questing, restless, and energetic period.

Certain of these characteristics are also exactly the same mechanisms to which other societies have resorted in order to construct new systems of knowledge—that process which is the very opposite of what Markus sees happening in late antiquity. Metaphor, imagination, narrative and categorization (here seen in the systematized lists of heresies and the schematization of correct belief around approved texts and authorities) are all key methodologies in such a process.[47] What was taking place in late antiquity in intellectual and imaginative terms was surely a competitive process of system construction, a persistent impulse towards definition. The ascetic discourse was very much part of that process.

The Ascetic State?

Many elements in Christian discourse as it developed during late antiquity pointed in the direction of hierarchy and systematization. It was more comforting to have a sense of completeness, of all-enveloping explanation: a theory of everything.[48] The arm of authority, as represented by the state or the official church, did its best to enforce uniformity. Words and actions went together; sanctions were imposed for wrong belief. The ascetic discourse was well suited to such a trend, since its very nature implied discipline as well as certainty; it allowed no overt challenge, no possibility of tolerance, no uncertainty. Refusal to conform could only be condemned: it is no surprise, therefore, that a sophisticated heresiology ran parallel with asceticism; or that the monks themselves were often claimed (by their apologists) to have been particularly violently opposed to the slightest whiff of error, while clearly being powerfully drawn to it in practice. The construction of the ascetic body also had implications for the body politic. We can now begin to see, perhaps, why Christian ascetic discourse had a so much better chance of prevailing than other kinds, furthered as it was both by a powerful machinery of enforcement and by much more enveloping discourse of inclusion and exclusion. Its boundaries were indeed clearly, even luridly, drawn. Peter Brown is right to draw attention to the confrontational quality of Christian hagiography, a feature still more overtly expressed in Christian heresiology.[49]

The authoritarian stance continued into Byzantium, where it was essential to the official *personae* of the Byzantine emperors. The preoccupation of the early Byzantine state with heresy, including the intensification of its polemics against Jews and its prolonged internal struggle over the authority of religious images, moved the debate from the individual ascetic to the state. Iconoclastic emperors attacked monks as well as images. Yet the effect of the imperial stance of authoritarianism may have been precisely the opposite of what was intended. Instead of calming and stabilizing society, the much vaunted serenity of the Christian emperors, often expressing itself in practice in bloodthirsty religious intolerance, in actuality stimulated division. The constant and public search for certainty generated its own resistance. Heresy was never successfully suppressed. It reappeared incessantly in different forms, only to be formally condemned yet again. In structural terms, the orthodox emperor required resistance in order to be able to assert his orthodoxy, just as he required enemies on whom to trample in endless triumphal iconography in order to assert his eternal victory.[50]

In the same way ascetic discourse required an audience, just as it required its demons.[51] Without an audience, the self-consciousness of the ascetic would lead only to silence. Like Christian authoritarianism, asceticism is of its nature combative; it defines itself through negation and exclusion. Similarly, Christian imperial authority implied not tranquillity but resistance, whether defined as heresy or in the form of the less tractable kinds of religious understanding.[52] The canons of the Quinisext Council in 691–692 CE; the long struggle of the iconoclasts; and the successive stages of the Byzantine Synodikon of Orthodoxy show us an ever-present tension between authority and resistance. It is hard at times to know how far this is symbolic, at the level of the text, and how far it represents real diversity.[53] Yet the level of the text is enough; the symbolism was all. By a seemingly paradoxical, though in fact predictable, turn, Byzantine monasteries themselves became another of the players in the game of power and authority, even while retaining their hold on the ascetic ideals of renunciation from which they originally grew.

The story of ascetic closure is thus both an interesting and a complex one. In late antiquity, I would like to suggest, Christian ascetic discourse lent itself well to the broader ecclesiastical discourse of authority and exclusion, to which it contributed the primary notions of limit, hierarchy, and struggle against opponents. In time, the very practice of asceticism became identified with the politics of the Byzantine state. In its puritanism, its insistence on strong boundaries and its polemical stance, it led in due course to the dialectic of iconoclasm.[54] And, just as the ascetic discourse called for a developed demonology against which to define itself and over which to assert its repeated victories, so the discourse of religious and state authority required a perpetual supply of real or alleged opponents in order to be able to maintain its continued credibility. Heretics and secularists (those tempted by Hellenic wisdom) are the state's demons, and heresiology the state's ascetic discourse.

The nature of "the unambiguously Christian empire that we associate with Byzantium"[55] is still largely to be assessed. Perhaps the phrase denotes the hopes of the Byzantine emperors themselves rather than their actual achievement. I would suggest that their enterprise very much resembled that of the ascetics of late antiquity. They too—the imperial authorities—needed an audience; their role was as much symbolic as practical. They needed an audience in order to maintain credibility in what they represented, their place within the world order, and their capacity to overcome resistance. Doubtless they also needed an audience in order to convince themselves. Both of the discourses—the ascetic and the imperial—were self-perpetuating and self-sustaining. The objective of asceticism, and of ascetic discourse, is necessarily mastery, and thus is highly likely to be intolerant.[56] Yet that mastery is achievable only if there is resistance to be overcome. The same is true in regard to the authoritarian Christian state. The Byzantine state itself replicated the ascetic subject.

NOTES

1. Peter Brown, *The Body and Society. Men, Women and Sexual Renunciation in Early Christianity* (New York, 1988); *idem, Power and Persuasion in Late Antiquity* (Madison, Wisconsin, 1992); Robert A. Markus, *The End of Ancient Christianity* (Cambridge, 1990); Averil Cameron, *Christianity and the Rhetoric of Empire* (Berkeley and Los Angeles, 1991).
2. Markus, *End of Ancient Christianity,* pp. 224–225.
3. Brown, *Power and Persuasion,* pp. 134, 142, 143f., 157.
4. Ibid., pp. 142–146.
5. Markus, *End of Ancient Christianity,* p. 197.
6. Brown, *The Body and Society,* p. 441.
7. Brown, *Power and Persuasion,* pp. 156, 144, 154, 153. The whole section from p. 142 to p. 158, the end of the book, illustrates the importance of such metaphorical language

in the historian's own technique of persuasion; the careful choice of such terms is, of course, itself a major element in Peter Brown's methodology.

8. Though not, significantly, from their pagan counterparts, who are presented instead, as we have already observed, in terms of melancholy resignation.
9. Ibid., p. 154; a slightly different view at pp. 140f.
10. See, for example, Tony Honoré, *Tribonian* (London, 1978); Averil Cameron, *Procopius and the Sixth Century* (London, 1985); Michael Maas, *John Lydus and the Roman Past* (London, 1992).
11. As is implied by P. Rousseau's study *Ascetics, Authority and the Church in the Age of Jerome and Cassian* (Oxford, 1978); for this aspect, exemplified in conciliar acta, see also V. Burrus, "Ascesis, Authority and Text: the *Acts of the Council of Saragossa,*" *Semeia* 58 (1992):85–108.
12. For cognitive dissonance, and for the systematizing aspect of early Christian thought, see H. Versnel, *Inconsistencies in Greek and Roman Religion* 1–2 (Leiden, 1990, 1993).
13. Cameron, *Christianity and the Rhetoric of Empire,* p. 221.
14. A. Kazhdan and G. Constable, *People and Power in Byzantium* (Washington, D.C., 1982).
15. A. Ducellier, *L'église byzantine: Entre pouvoir et esprit, 313–1204* (Paris, 1990).
16. Ed. J. Gouillard, "Le Synodikon de l'Orthodoxie. Édition et commentaire," *Travaux et Mémoires* 2 (1967):1–316; see also Averil Cameron, "Texts as Weapons: Polemic in the Byzantine Dark Ages," in Alan Bowman and Greg Woolf, eds., *Literacy and Power in the Ancient World* (Cambridge, 1994).
17. See especially Jean Meyendorff, *A Study of Gregory Palamas,* trans. George Lawrence (London, 1964).
18. See Averil Cameron, "The Construction of Court Ritual: The Byzantine *Book of Ceremonies,*" in S.R.F. Price and D. Cannadine, eds., *Rituals of Royalty: Power and Ceremonial in Traditional Societies* (Cambridge, 1987), pp. 106–136.
19. See D. Nicol, *The Immortal Emperor* (Cambridge, 1992).
20. I am mainly confining myself here to ascetic discourses within Christianity; the ascetic discourse of contemporary Neoplatonists and others is different in degree and diffusion, but presumably had its share in any wider effects.
21. Some ways of reading Byzantine religious art, especially icons, in this way are given in my article "The Language of Images: Icons and Christian Representation," in Diana Wood, ed., *The Church and the Arts,* Studies in Church History 28 (Oxford, 1992), pp. 1–42; the approach can certainly be extended.
22. "Rhetoric" is used in this broad sense of linguistic expression (rather than, say, discourse), for example, by Paul de Man and others.
23. Led by Dr. M. E. Mullett of The Queen's University of Belfast. The ascetic collection of this monastery is known in more than fifty manuscripts; its continuing influence can be judged from the fact that it has been reprinted seven times since publication in the eighteenth century.
24. For an idea of the wide diffusion of this material, see J. R. Wortley, "Paul of Monembasia and His Stories," in J. Chrysostomides, ed., *Kathegetria. Essays Presented to Joan Hussey for her 80th Birthday* (Camberley, 1988), pp. 303–316.
25. On the early ascetic literature, see Andrew Louth, *The Origins of the Christian Mystical Tradition: From Plato to Denys* (New York, 1981).
26. On the question of the range and volume of writings by such authors such as Maximus and John, see Averil Cameron, "Byzantium and the Past in the Seventh Century: The

Search for Redefinition," in J. N. Hillgarth and J. Fontaine, eds., *The Seventh Century: Change and Continuity* (London, 1992), pp. 250–276.

27. R. MacMullen, "What Difference Did Christianity Make?" *Historia* 35 (1986):322–343.
28. See, for example, G. W. Bowersock, *Hellenism in Late Antiquity* (Cambridge, 1990); P. Chuvin, *Chronique des derniers paiens* (Paris, 1991), abridged Eng. trans., *A Chronicle of the Last Pagans* (Cambridge, Mass., 1990); M. Tardieu, *Les paysages reliques* (Paris, 1992); F. R. Trombley, *Hellenic Religion and Christianization, c.370–529* 1–2 (Leiden, 1993).
29. Harpham, *The Ascetic Imperative in Culture and Criticism* (Chicago, 1987).
30. Ibid., p. 3.
31. See my Inaugural Lecture, *"The Use and Abuse of Byzantium"* (King's College, London, 1992).
32. Ibid., pp. 24f.
33. Ibid., pp. 91ff., and for what follows see p. 130; Cameron, *Christianity and the Rhetoric of Empire,* p. 157.
34. Ibid., pp. 51ff.; I explore this theme further in two forthcoming papers.
35. See E. Wyschogrod's essay included above in this volume, and cf. R. Boyne and A. Rattansi, eds., *Postmodernism and Society* (London, 1990).
36. Cameron, *Christianity and the Rhetoric of Empire,* pp. 72ff.; further aspects of the biographical model are explored by N. Kelsey, "The Body as Desert in the *Life of St. Anthony,*" *Semeia* 57 (1992):131–151.
37. See, for example, P. Ricoeur, "Narrative Time," in W.J.T. Mitchell, ed., *On Narrative* (Chicago, 1981), pp. 165–186. In the same volume, Frank Kermode brings out the intimate relation of narrative with secrets, or, to put it differently, with unfolding or disclosure ("Secrets and Narrative Sequence," ibid., pp. 79–97). In relation to this we should point also to the metaphorical or figural quality of Christian discourse emphasised in Cameron, *Christianity and the Rhetoric of Empire,* especially chapter 2, and its exegetical focus on surprise.
38. Cameron, *Christianity and the Rhetoric of Empire,* chapter 3; see also Peter Brown, "The Saint as Exemplar in Late Antiquity," in *Representations* 1 (1983):1–25. These issues are discussed in more general terms in E. Wyschogrod, *Saints and Postmodernism: Revisioning Moral Philosophy* (Chicago, 1990), especially in chapter 1, a book that proposes saints' lives as the basis for a postmodern moral philosophy. It also sees Christian saints' lives as essentially demonstrative of altruism, saintly dissolution of self-interest; this may be a modernizing view. Presumably all saints are ascetics, but not all ascetics are saints. What are the distinguishing factors?
39. See Harpham, *The Ascetic Imperative,* p. 24, citing Peter Brown, "The Rise and Function of the Holy Man in Late Antiquity," in *Journal of Religious Studies* 61 (1971):93.
40. See G. G. Harpham, "Old Water in New Bottles: The Contemporary Prospects for the Study of Asceticism," in *Semeia* 58 (1992):134–148, at 144f.
41. Ramsay MacMullen, "The Preacher's Audience (AD 350–400)," in *Journal of Theological Studies* 40 (1989):503–511.
42. Elizabeth A. Clark, *The Origenist Controversy: The Cultural Construction of an Early Christian Debate* (Princeton, 1992), chapter 1.
43. See the excellent introduction by Gary Vikan, *Byzantine Pilgrimage Art* (Washington, D.C., 1982).
44. And, one may say, the object of new forms of exploitation by them; see Brown, *Power and Persuasion,* chapter 3.

45. See C. Militello, "Amicizia tra asceti e ascete," in U. Mattaioli, ed., *La donna nel pensiero cristiano antico* (Genoa, 1992), pp. 279–304 (but on male–female friendship, see Gillian Clark, in this volume); and see, generally, Gillian Clark, *Women in Late Antiquity: Pagan and Christian Lifestyles* (Oxford, 1993), with earlier bibliography.
46. Preaching: Eusebius, *Vita Constantine,* 4.9; scriptures for Constantinople: ibid., 4.36–37; letter to Antony: *Vita Antonii* 81. Even if Eusebius's various other claims for Constantine go too far, the symbolic precedent still holds.
47. M. Johnson, *The Body in the Mind* (Chicago, 1987), pp. 171ff.; some of these models are also used by Neal Kelsey, "The Body as Desert in the *Life of St. Anthony*" *Semeia* 57 (1992):131–151 (note 36).
48. See also Averil Cameron, "Divine Providence in Late Antiquity," in Leo Howe and Alan Wain, eds., *Predicting the Future,* the Darwin College Lectures (Cambridge, 1993), pp. 118–143.
49. Brown, *Power and Persuasion,* p. 144. The tendency is all the more striking in view of John North's argument for religious pluralism in the context in which Christianity first took shape: John North, "The Development of Religious Pluralism," in J. Lieu, J. North, and T. Rajak, eds., *The Jews among Pagans and Christians in the Roman Empire* (London, 1992), pp. 174–193.
50. For imperial triumph at Byzantium, see M. McCormick, *Eternal Victory* (Cambridge, 1986). The case of Basil II (d. 1025 CE) is wonderfully instructive in this regard: the fully armed and victorious emperor is depicted trampling his enemies beneath a bust of Christ, but the medium is the miniatures of an illuminated Psalter. Likewise visual art depicted the politics of orthodoxy: see particularly L. Brubaker, "Byzantine Art in the Ninth Century: Theory, Practice and Culture," in *Byzantine and Modern Greek Studies* 13 (1989):23–93; Brubaker, "Perception and Conception: Art, Theory and Culture in Ninth-Century Byzantium," in *Word and Image* 5 (1989):19–32; K. Corrigan, *Visual Polemics in Ninth-Century Psalters* (Cambridge, 1992).
51. Harpham, *The Ascetic Imperative,* p. 54.
52. See Cameron, *Christianity and the Rhetoric of Empire,* chapter 5.
53. See J. Gouillard, "L'hérésie dans l'empire byzantin des origines au XIIe siècle," in *Travaux et Mémoires* 1 (1965):299–324.
54. See W. J. Thomas Mitchell, *Iconology: Image, Text and Ideology* (Chicago, 1986), esp. pp. 160–208.
55. Brown, *Power and Persuasion,* p. 142.
56. That is, Brown's "confrontation" rather than Wyschogrod's "altruism."

13

Pain, Power, and Personhood: Ascetic Behavior in the Ancient Mediterranean

Bruce J. Malina

When I began to prepare this essay, my first step was to read through the splendid collection of documents, as well as the perceptive and insightful essays, prepared by Professor Vincent Wimbush and his colleagues in the Society of Biblical Literature Group on Ascetic Behavior in Greco-Roman Antiquity (Wimbush 1990, 1992). A distinctive feature of these presentations is the lack of a specific definition of the subject to which the group has dedicated its efforts. After so much reading about behaviors which Neal Kelsey (1992:146, note 6) would label as "ascetical"—"dieting, vegetarianism, fasting, sexual abstinence, sexual control, sexual continence, virginity, physical retreat from society, general dissipation of the body, wearing of rough clothing, flagellation, political quietism, prayer, night vigils, martyrdom, and abstinence from bathing"—I gave in to the temptation and asked: what do all these behaviors have in common? I asked this question first from the viewpoint of modern psychology; then from the viewpoint of social psychology; and, finally, from the viewpoint of cultural anthropology. My presentation will set forth the answers I uncovered to these questions, although cultural anthropology will be my principal concern.

Ascetic Behavior: Common Psychological Features

Apart from prayer (for which see Malina 1980), the common feature in the behaviors listed by Kelsey, usually called ascetic behaviors, is that all entail shrinking the self, in the modern psychological sense of the term (see Mitchell 1988; Harré 1980, 1989). Because of this, I initially define asceticism as the shrinkage of the self motivated by avoidance or attainment goals. All of the listed behaviors diminish the self by centering on the physical dimensions of the human being, that is, the physical self, the body (see Synnott and Howes 1992). Other behaviors work to this end as well, for example: alcoholism, suicide, binge eating, sexual masochism, anorexia, drug addiction, hysteria, workaholism, dedicated jogging, world class sports competition, and the like. Hence these, likewise, belong among ascetical practices covered by the foregoing definition, since they shrink the self.[1]

The self here refers to the unfolded or developed human self to whom adults can and do apply the word "I." This self is simultaneously an individual and social self. The individual person is socialized from birth when sensory and motor activity are at the forefront of behavior. This sensory and motor self is often called the self as body, the psychophysical self, the self as conscious physical entity. In socialization, this individual conscious entity unfolds and develops in the direction of socialized self-awareness in terms of social identity, roles, statuses, skills, and attributes. Concretely but inaccurately speaking, the individual psychophysical self and the psychological socialized self together form the adult self. The self can then be understood as a socialized individual psychophysical entity intertwined with culturally specific meanings. The culturally specific meanings typical of a self include: social identity, social roles (rights and obligations), social statuses, and individual goals, aspirations, possibilities. Self-shrinkage involves the dissociation and elimination of the social self, with its identity, roles, statuses, skills and attributes, from individual self-awareness. What is left (apart from the case of successful suicide), is the self as a living psychophysical entity, conscious or unconscious.

Now a self is always a culturally defined member of a human group. While the self can reflect upon its individual psychophysical being and upon the meanings attributed to it, for all that, its awarenesses remain culturally moored and socially coproduced. From this perspective, the self is an individualized socially meaningful interpretation of human experience (that is, affixed to a psychophysical being known intuitively to be human). This perspective is of fundamental importance in understanding who can practice asceticism and why. For it would seem that not everyone has ready social legitimation to shrink the self or deny the self. In antiquity, for example, the ascetic life was open only to the worthy, that is those of adequate social status.

As an individual psychophysical being endowed with social meaning, each one of us has a fundamental drive to convey meaning to other selves (especially by control, namely, by taking charge and showing initiative) and to impart meaning to the self as well (via individual and group self-esteem, by displaying qualities desirable, attractive and useful to others). The drive to mean, to make sense, underlies all the so-called needs that pop psychology has ascribed to the self. People do not simply seek food, sleep, warmth, comfort and sex, but seek to mean while realizing such nurture, and by means of such nurture (see Douglas and Isherwood 1979).

The meaningful self is always linked with emotional sets, based on those encouraged by the social group: anxiety and acceptance, shame and honor, pride and guilt (see Augsburger 1986:111–143). And there are many other emotions associated with group/self control and esteem.[2] Finally, the self shares images of what it would like to be (values, goals, norms, aspirations), as well as assessments of what it is actually like—along with social roles and statuses. In sum, to shrink the self means to rid the self of all social accretions with a view to reducing the self to its psycho-physical components, even to its primordial sensory and motor condition if possible. Or, as Baumeister puts it:

> Escaping the self is not a matter of removing the self entirely, but rather of shrinking it down to its bare minimum. In particular one gets rid of many of the definitions of self that are causing trouble. The minimum self that a person can have is the body. There is no way to avoid having a body. But if one's self is reduced to only being a body, that is quite a feat, and many sources of distress, worry, concern and threat are removed. Escaping from the self is, more precisely, an escape from identity into body. *Baumeister 1991:17*

It seems that people are motivated to shrink the self either by the desire to avoid something negative, such as awareness of calamity, failure, stress and the like, as in preparation for torture (Tilley 1991); to attain something positive, such as cosmic insight and ecstasy (see Goodman 1988b, 1990); or to achieve some limit or "flow" experience (see Csikszentmihalyi 1975, 1981; for sports, see Macho 1985). In all such goals, the social self must be shrunk because it seems to be a paramount and overwhelming impediment, hindrance, and obstacle to the task at hand. In sum, in the social system that endows this usage with meaning and feeling, the "I," the self, could be said to consist of an individual body and a set of socially meaningful definitions (after Baumeister 1991).

It is well known that the history of the concept of self in the Mediterranean world began by equating self with physical being. People assessed themselves and others in nonintrospective and nonpsychological ways. Demons and spirits made do for internal impulses, insights, drives and the like. It was only gradually that the nonphysical dimensions emerged (see Malina 1989, 1992; Valantasis 1992). Recent history, on the other hand, has witnessed an escalation and expansion of inner, nonphysical attributes of the self. Modern Western psychology, popular and professional, has come to regard the inner self as vast, stable, unique, important, and difficult to know; and we presume that it contains thoughts, feelings, intentions, personality traits, latent talents and capabilities, wellsprings of creativity, key ingredients to personal fulfillment, and the solutions to many of life's problems. The very notion that a person can look inside the self to find the solution to a dilemma would be regarded as absurd in cultures that do not share our perception of the inner self (see Baumeister 1991:3–4). In fact, what was typical of the ancient Mediterranean was that it was anti-introspective, not psychologically minded at all. What sort of self, then, was available for asceticism in antiquity?

Ascetic Behavior in Antiquity: Common Social Psychological Features

Anyone considering asceticism in antiquity quickly discovers a different sort of self, closer to the self as physical being than to the contemporary inner self. The reason for this is that the self of the past was, for the most part, a socially embedded or group enmeshed self, perhaps through all the stages of its development (see Geertz 1976).

Historically, the group always had precedence over the self; however, in the last century or so, especially in the West, the self began to take precedence over the group. In the United States, this trend has simply accelerated; people place a higher emphasis on the self than on marriage and the family, than on job or education. Whatever supports self is to be embraced; whatever constraints self is to be avoided. Baumeister talks of the overgrown, overemphasized self: the article of faith that each person is different, special and unique, with an obligation to cultivate inner potential in order to achieve his or her specially assigned destiny. Each person is thus given the burden of maintaining the self. And the self individuals seek to maintain is an overgrown, overemphasized, bloated self. Self-shrinkage in this context is the process of easing this burden or totally escaping from it.[3]

Prior to modern individualism and its individualistic thrust, emphasis fell upon the group. Here we might speak of the overgrown, overemphasized group self: the article of faith that each group is different, special and unique, with a demand to cultivate potential within the group in order to achieve its specially assigned destiny. Each group is thus given the burden to maintain the group self. And the group self that individuals are urged to maintain is an overgrown, overemphasized, bloated group self. Now what in the social system is available to individuals for them to learn about the existence of a recalcitrant individual self, as well as about options for dealing with a recalcitrant self that did not wish to comply with group demands? Clearly it is the family of antiquity, the preindustrial kinship groups in their limited range of forms that revealed each self to the groups' individual members. And it was traditional childrearing that provided instruction in those basic practices for dealing with the self that emerge as ascetical practices (see Todd 1985).

To begin with, the traditional, preindustrial families, regardless of their modes of settlement and inheritance, were typically strong group, collectivistic, enmeshed families (see Triandis 1989; Schwartz 1990). Members learned to blur the boundaries of each other's psychic unity. They intruded on each other's psychological privacy and attempts at autonomy. Everyone was responsible for the well being of the others, and each was taught to be exquisitely alert and responsive to the implicit demands of others. As we learn from modern forms of such families, a growing child becomes precociously responsive to the needs of others and is fearful of expressing or even experiencing independent desires. Spontaneity and true self-gratification are submerged beneath a desire to please and gain approval from needed others. What developed in preindustrial society was a group-oriented self. By U.S. standards, that was a false self with a peaceful and compliant façade. The group-oriented self gradually eroded the vitality of the true self that was hidden and, eventually, forgotten. As the child became more embedded in the family myth and more dependent on affirmation from family members, he or she did not create an autonomous or secure self that might later function satisfactorily in the extrafamilial world apart from the family. When apart from the family, the individual was not expected to cope with the changes brought about by the individuation appropriate to adolescence and young adult life. The condition produced by such family behavior is a condition of being enmeshed—embedded—encysted (see Bemporad et al. 1988).[4]

What kept the individual enmeshed and embedded in the family were childrearing techniques that sought to avoid spoiling the child, specifically by crushing self-will and pride. Spoiling the child invariably meant allowing the child to behave in a way in which the child stood out apart from the group, as something special or distinctive. Implicit here was the belief that no child had a right to anything more than everyone else in the group. The child was a miniature adult seeking expanded gratification of desires and motivated by self-interest, taking it beyond the group. These desires had to be nipped in the bud; and self-interest had to be transformed into group interest. Note that the usual monastic lists of vices or sins are those that damage harmony within a group. These are already naturally manifest in childhood: gluttony, lust, greed, sadness, anger, listlessness, vainglory, and pride (from Evagrius of Pontus, cited by O'Laughlin, 1990:244).

The approach to childrearing, then, was distrustful and directive rather than trusting and cooperative. A fundamental reason for such an attitude lay in the total unawareness of any sort of biological givens influencing the needs and behavior of the developing human being. Parents perceived the infant as being selfish and demanding, and wanting as much gratification and indulgence as he or she could get (usually too much). Any gratification of the infant would lead to the danger of spoiling it if more than the right amount were given. Thus adults perceived the infant as attempting to obtain gratification, behaving in ways that were self-willed, demanding, manipulative, cunning (thus confirming belief in inherent potential for badness).

In other words, it seemed that a child's emerging self-awareness was pride; the self was pride. (Perhaps the reason for this was—and is—that the practical, experiential self is the self-interested self. And self-interest entails animosity, prejudice, disharmony, divisiveness, claims to honor and status, aggressive acts, aversive emotions, and the like. The self is self only over against and at the expense of the group.) The parents' goal and obligation was to control and direct the child's behavior and to produce a "good" child (who will be obedient and conform).

The ideal was to mold the child to a predetermined pattern; to secure control by regulating habits, and to train it in accepting authority and discipline. Of course, the child had to be taught right from wrong and to meet the demands of obedience. To this end, parents were compelled to extinguish self-will, and other bad behavior and to insist on and reinforce good behavior. Parents felt it right to ignore the child's point of view and to disregard its feelings and capacities. The child was to conform to the requirements of the adult world. In these circumstances, as the child's hostility and negativism became aggravated (unless they are repressed), parents felt justified in applying force to control the child. Parental disapproval was rather frequent and often reinforced by threats, punishment, and sometimes violence or inculcation of shame (see Cook 1978).[5]

Of course, any childrearing of this sort would be labeled abusive by contemporary standards. Abuse may be defined as any behavior directed to another that coerces the other "to surrender one's feeling, knowing, functioning self" (Furman 1986:47). Such behavior includes teasing, confusing, falsely blaming, as well as physically wounding, disabling or injuring another. Abusive behavior attempts to reduce the helpless self of a child into a compliant nothing. This culturally approved mode of parenting was (and is) essentially destructive of the individual self, undoubtedly for the benefit of some authority, either some individual or the group as a whole. For while family dynamics in this period were significant, they would not have proved effective unless replicated by other social institutions. Just as the family sought to extinguish self-will and not to spoil the child, so too, social norms in other institutions sought to limit the female role to that of an objectified and passive nurturer, and the male role to that of an objectified and passive obeyer of paternal (and imperial) wishes.

Consequently, since the primary sphere of self awareness in the ancient Mediterranean context was the group, self-denial is denial of the group self; self-shrinkage is shrinkage of the group self. Self shrinkage in a strong group context is the process of dissociating oneself and one's limited self-awareness from the group or totally escaping from the group. Ancient asceticism involved escaping group anonymity and its collective orientation, especially by standing out as an individual against the group and its demands for total loyalty and conformity. In other words, self-denial meant to deny one's collective self, to deny one's group, to leave one's group, to distance oneself from one's group![6] From a political perspective, the individual would appear superior to others in the group, while from a kinship perspective, the individual would be seen to have moved his or her loyalties elsewhere. Now this perceived superiority and switch of loyalties had to be dealt with socially (for example, with a label like "deviant" or "prominent"). Without group restraints a person was left with heightened awareness of urges for the gratification of self-serving desire and self-interest. Without group restraints, a female became either a slut or a nun,[7] a male either a rake or a monk. The slut and the rake were considered without restraint, the nun and the monk beyond group restraint. Thus, among the outcomes of asceticism, the ascetic (like the slut and the rake) may be perceived to be beyond all groups, but, instead, in a positive way. The group self has been shrunk to such an extent that in the perception of others it simply ceases to be (see Malina and Neyrey 1986). In such cases as those of the martyrs[8] described by Tilley (1991) and the holy men described by Brown (1971), individuals could not be affected by isolation or indoctrination (partisan influence); socially they were available for mediation, arbitration or whatever else anyone may have sought from a person who was not embedded in a group.

The Self Available in the Ascetic Behavior in Antiquity

If persons in the ancient world were group-enmeshed persons, then self-shrinking entailed disembedding the self from the group. It was the shrinkage of group self that marked self-denial in the ancient Mediterranean. Such self-shrinkage was not available to all selves. Rather, it was available only to a self that was aware enough to shrink in the face of the group in which it was initially embedded. In other words, self-shrinkage was available only to a person socially aware of his or her ability to disengage from the group of origin. Such persons included converts to fictive kin groups, such as Christian groups before Constantine; and, afterward, persons with appropriate social status, whether aristocratic or inheriting family member (head of the family, inheriting son, widow) who perceived the sense of taking such a step.

Here my focus will be on ascetics who were not in preparation for the tortures of political witnessing in the pre-Constantinian Mediterranean basin. In this context, self-shrinkage or self-denial was an escape from concern for group esteem and group honor.[9] The ascetic ceased to be concerned with a proper self or group image. He or she rejected gaining prestigious civic credentials, lost concern for making a good impression (by dint of new and fashionable clothing; self-serving explanations for group failures and mishaps; need to make others take the blame for group misfortune; or need to mask group foibles). There was no more concern to have information about others for purposes of comparison, or interest in fighting with others who impugned the ascetic's respectability or superiority, for the group's sake. Ceasing to grope for rationalizations, the ascetic also ceased to be embarrassed or to brood in the face of humiliation. In sum, he or she gave up the usual full-time job of maintaining both group esteem and self-esteem within, and on behalf of the group.

In instances of ascetism, to shrink the self is to free it from the struggle to maintain a certain image, to give up prevailing motivations; that is, quest for honor, with its concomitant esteem and control. The ascetic is able to dodge the pressures, demands, obligations, responsibilities, and other factors that plague males and females in the kin group. Choosing the life of the ascetic marked the end of the emotional roller coaster of prevailing group reputation. Forgotten are all the grand, complex, abstract, wide-ranging definitions of one's ethnic group, one's family and one's family roles. Thus reduced to simple humanity symbolized by the body shorn of social concerns, one can live in radical *communitas,* with the sole task of keeping the body in check.

Asceticism, then, is about what people did and do to get away from the self, whatever type of self existed or exists in a given society. To understand ascetic behavior, one must appreciate how such behavior is related to the self in question, and how much it allows a person to escape from awareness of the self. In antiquity, this meant essentially no more ethnic boundaries or kinship boundaries to define the prevailing social self. But there is more to the social self.

Comparing Social Features of Ascetic Behavior in Antiquity and Now

The goals pursued by self-shrinkers are necessarily skewed and nuanced by the social institutions within which these goals are pursued. The modern individual is socialized into a society in which kinship, politics, religion and economics are perceived and treated as free-standing social institutions. Thus individuals are said to have a family life, a political life, a religious life and an economic life, among others. We moderns have been taught to believe that there are four basic social institutions—church, state, kinship, and politics—quite separate and distinct from each other. This separation is in most instances seen as quite desirable.

Persons can undergo self-shrinkage in a manner specific to each institution. Consider the following examples of self-shrinkage motivated by the attainment of goals, and generally evaluated as very positive. The mother of a large family might dedicate herself totally to the nurture and well-being of that family. Should all time and energy be confined to the family, such family (or kinship) rooted self-shrinkage, the self shrunk to family concerns, would yield honor and family acclaim of her worth. The reason for this is that honor is the "currency" of solidarity and belonging. Group members acclaim the worth of those who devote themselves to the well-being of the group.

Similarly, a politician or government official who works assiduously and competently at tasks within the hierarchical structure of the government would be rewarded for selfless dedication with more significant roles in the government, with increasing access to the power typical of the institution. Again, the reason for this is that power is the currency of the political institution.

Third, dedicated religious persons in specialized religious groups, devoted to meditation and contemplation, presumably arrive at significant insights and wisdom by devoting their total selves, their total time and energy, to grasping and being grasped by the All, by God. Influence, in the form of insight, advice and reasons, is the currency of the religious or ideological institution and its manifold surrogates.

None of these three institutions, however, holds the central focus in U.S. experience. Rather, economics, which deal with provisioning persons in society, is the focal social institution. In our context, security means economic security; success means economic success. To this end, all members of our society are expected to lead a disciplined life, with adequate preparatory self-discipline and cognitive awareness. This discipline requires a prolonged adolescence to develop skills such as abstract thinking ability, in order to deal with time and schedule; delayed gratification; thrift; insight into the market system; endurance at tasks; problem solving; and the like. Of course the currency marking success and security in this institution is money and what it can procure. Since every person in society is expected to restrain the self in pursuit of profit (a living, wealth), we will find among the truly devoted many nonélite as well as élite forms of ascetics in this domain.

It would seem that the heroic ideal of such asceticism in the United States is the ascetic business person in the economic institution, motivated by the profit motive and the profit ethic of traditional capitalism (= Calvinism). Such persons are the American worthies who can and do control the society in its power, kinship and religious system. They largely appoint the "civil religion" clergy (political office holders); ultimately decide how the kinship system will work; are prominent on boards of schools and churches; and surely have the most powerful military in the world at their disposal (consider the new world order evinced in Iraq).

I would suggest that the devoted business person of today holds the same focal social position as did the prominent ascetic in the post-Constantinian Christianity of antiquity. The largest difference between the two, however, is the quality of the self and the arrangement of social institutions involved. Today, our arrangements include the individualistic self behaving in a society in which economics is central.

In the past there was the group-embedded self behaving in a society in which politics or kinship were central. Modern economic ascetics are blessed with rewards truly incommensurable with the rewards available to ordinary humans; they earn a salary in the millions, a truly supernatural outcome for their limited dedication and devotion. Ancient ascetics were rewarded, likewise, in a way incommensurable with the rewards available to ordinary humans. Theirs was favor from the divine Patron, with ability to control the forces of social and cosmic nature, and the like.

One of the main reasons for this difference between modern and ancient heroic ascetics is the fact that, in antiquity, only two social institutions were considered to encompass all of human life: that is, the kinship institution and the political institution (Malina 1986b). There existed a domestic economy and domestic religion as well as a political economy and political religion, singly or in combination. Perhaps for most people, the focus was on the kinship institution alone, with the political simply being the property of another family that could be recruited in patronage. In such a context, it was honor rooted in kinship, and power rooted in politics, that counted in the task of meaningful living.

Turning Pain into Power

Pain was often applied in ancient exercises of self-shrinkage. Of course this comes as no surprise. For it seems that the ancient Mediterranean was a sadistic world, with people ever prepared to apply pain to those outside their group, both as control and as sport (cf. crucifixions, impalements, gladiatorial contests, gratuitous beating of and killing of persons and animals).[10] Parents, likewise, applied pain to put a halt to and to divert a child's self-interested quest for gratification. How did the endurance of pain produce socially acknowledged power? Obviously, institutional arrangements and values were at issue. The efficacy of nonviolence depends upon which institutional arrangements and values are held by opposing parties; and so, too, does the efficacy of pain to work an effect upon others. For example, nonviolence worked in India against the British and their cultural values, but nothing of the sort worked against the Soviets, the Nazis, or the Israelis and their respective values.

Pain, however, can be turned to power. By power here I mean the social recognition of a person's ability to control the behavior of others based on the implied sanction of force. People recognize a person's power because behind it they sense the presence of force, especially should they prove recalcitrant to the control of the power wielder (Malina 1986a:92–95). Power in this sense is a symbol. It is the central symbol of the political institution, the task of which is effective collective action. Now if a power wielder attempts to control another to no avail, that other person in fact makes the claim that the power wielder really has no power. The public message is that power is inflated—lots of symbolic huff and puff, but no teeth, no force. The power wielder must apply the sanctions of force in order to prove his or her power. Now when force is applied to another, that other person is expected to comply with the wishes of the power wielder.

Yet if the other person still does not comply, even in face of force, then the value of force is viewed as inflated in the eyes of the public. In a limited good society, one person's inflated force is another person's inflated power (see Malina 1993). Thus, the endurance of force, usually in the form of pain, yields power to the one enduring it.

Similarly, humiliation can to be turned to honor. Humiliation is the process by means of which a person is publicly shamed and dishonored by someone considered competent in evaluating his or her worth. Parents, for example, can irrevocably shame children by insisting, in specific instances, that they are worthless human beings. Thus, certain persons who can endow another with honor (a claim to worth) and can equally control the behavior of others by threat of shame (a claim of nonworth). What is required for this sanction to be operative is that the persons involved must somehow believe that they belong together, for example, as family members, group members, and the like.

A person is expected to comply under threat of shame with the wishes of the one shaming. If, however, the person does not comply, even in the face of shame and utter humiliation, then the position of the one attempting to humiliate is open to question in the eyes of the public. In a limited good society, one person's inflated ability to get another to comply under threat of being shamed is another person's inflated honor. Humiliation endured can thus produce an increase of honor and a sense of solidarity in the eyes of an observing public.

Thus, the defiant endurance of force can produce power, just as the defiant endurance of humiliation can produce honor along with a sense of loyalty and solidarity. What is significant, then, is the role of enduring pain and humiliation in the process of shrinkage of self. When politics and kinship were the central institutions, pain and humiliation were the prevalent sanctions to be dealt with.

But how did a person's willing selection of pain (e.g. self-flagellation) or humiliation (e.g. begging) gain power and honor? How does self-induced suffering produce power and self-humiliation produce honor? The endurance of self-induced pain, of freely chosen suffering, is the endurance of the sanction of power. To endure pain is to signify that one has no fear of power, that one is impervious to power, and that power wielders can have no effect. Since power wielders are normally those of superior status in society, freely chosen suffering is a claim to superiority over persons of superior status, if not a claim to their power. If this claim is recognized by compliance on the part of others, then power claims become real power.

Similarly, the endurance of self-humiliation is the endurance of the sanction of those who can shame and humiliate a person, the superiors in one's group. To endure self-humiliation is to signify that one has no fear of these group superiors, that one is impervious to claims of loyalty and solidarity, and that commitment wielders can have no effect. Since group superiors are normally ascribed superior status in society, freely chosen humiliation is a claim to superiority over superior status persons, a claim to their honor. If this claim is recognized by compliance on the part of others, then claims to honor become real honor.

In conclusion, asceticism is self-shrinkage for purposes of avoidance or attainment. A comparison of modern and ancient forms of asceticism indicates that both the kind of self involved, as well as the dimensions of purpose, have changed. Modern purposes are rooted in social arrangements (institutions) that differ radically from those of the past. Furthermore, childrearing behavior that prepared ancients for their life of asceticism is considered criminal in U.S. society, while the application of pain today is considered sadistic. Yet asceticism lives on, this time motivated by the socially defined need for security through economic success or the need to escape the self.

NOTES

1. Modern psychologists are more interested in this latter listing of self-shrinking behavior than in the conventional ascetical variety (for the latter, see the classical textbook in the Roman Catholic tradition by Tanquerey 1932, and the attempted update by a group of French Dominicans, anonymously edited 1950). It has been by reading through the contemporary literature dealing with contemporary self-shrinking or self-escape or self-depreciation, however, that I learned about ancient self-denial and self-renunciation. In all such negations of the self, the adult self is taken at a given point of its unfolding story and shrunk. The story comes to an abrupt halt. A new story then opens, looking to new outcomes. On such self-shrinkage, see Baumeister 1988, 1991; Bemporad et al. 1988; Glickauf-Hughes 1991; Pestrak 1991.
2. Emotions, too, depend on meaning. Emotion is bodily arousal in addition to an interpretive label based on the situation (see Schachter and Singer 1962; Schachter 1971). Emotions are transitory roles based on cultural interpretations of experiences (see Averill 1980). Since people feel emotional reactions to events defined in terms of cultural values, or to nonphysical stimuli such as reading a book or a letter, emotions are not simply natural responses to physical stimuli, but rather are culturally induced. Anger, for example, depends on complex evaluations of the situation against a set of norms and expectations (see Averill 1982).
3. Of course, self-shrinkage may occur in deviant or prominent form. Deviant self-shrinkage includes forms of asceticism that are considered contrary to social norms. If the life goal of the U.S. citizenry is (economic) achievement, then any form of asceticism hindering a person from competing to achieve would be deviant. For example, alcoholism, anorexia, suicide, binge eating, sexual masochism, hoboism, lonerism, and the like are all indicative of dropping out rather than of striving to achieve. On the other hand, prominent forms of asceticism include vigils (working extra long hours), exercise and dieting to stay in shape (to work), thrift, abstemiousness, meditation, etc. One can speak in public about having participated in any or in all of these behaviors.
4. Considering the behavior of Thecla in *The Acts of Paul and Thecla* along with all sorts of asides in the lives of the Desert Fathers, it would seem that these ancient ascetics shared the following traits with modern hysterics (of the nineteenth century) and with anorexics (of today):

   Ascetics come from families that, on the surface at least, are orderly, respectable and conventional; in Mediterranean terms, they are "good" families of some social status.

   Yet, under the surface these families are full of secret obligations, stifling prohibitions, mutually ignored dishonesty; these conditions are typical of "good" families of some social status in the Mediterranean (hence the need for arbitrators, mediators, etc. when dealing with other families).

Those initially choosing self-shrinkage as a way of life are adolescent males and females.

All eventually reveal an almost psychotic indifference to gross bodily dysfunction.

On the milder end of the spectrum, ascetics reveal themselves as exemplars of what is considered the normal male and female standard for the era: courageous, bold, persevering, etc.

Ascetics often attract other conflicted individuals in a sort of social contagion, thus a rash of persons join the virgin or ascetic male.

The lines of conduct are exaggerations, perhaps perversions or sublimations, of an esteemed ideal (for example, premarital chastity as a lifelong state; courage in the face of adversity as a permanent condition); in the United States the behavior becomes pathological only when blatantly irrational, however religion(s) may have provided rationales in antiquity.

Any attempt to treat ascetical conditions by having the ascetic return to some original condition only stirs up a sense of frustration and futility in those dealing with the ascetic (family members, future husband, friends); the ascetics steadfastly (stubbornly) refuse to cooperate.

Even if ascetical individuals agree to return to the family, they invariably continue to follow their own secret agenda, hence betraying an elusive quality.

In these conditions, psychological problems are often displaced onto the body, the hallmark of the ascetical life.

Obviously, some unacknowledged gratification must be obtained from the ascetical lifestyle; for instance, the repression of an intolerable idea or wish while simultaneously expressing the idea or satisfying the wish in a disguised form, or a sense of mastery and control that ascetical practice affords.

5. Modern psychologists consider such child-rearing techniques as contributing to increased risk of conflict, frustration and stress in unsatisfying relationships. A child's sensitivity may be blunted; externally imposed discipline may break down sooner or later in rebelliousness. Finally, with emotional maturation at risk, maladjustment and psychopathology are likely.
6. Macho (1985) presents an interesting, if brief, comparison of ancient and modern sports theory. Relative to asceticism and sports, he notes that behavior related to modern competitive sports is not unlike boundary experiences in traditional cultures in that it requires "(1) social isolation, (2) physical asceticism and (3) confrontation with death." Compare this with Tilley's (1991) description of torture techniques. The "individualization" of modern competitive sports and asceticism have this quality in common with traditional boundary experiences of status elevation or restoration. "The quality of all boundary experiences, necessarily directed against the body, consists in radical individualization. For the body is from the start a social medium: as body, the human being is not an individual person, but rather a *zōon politikon*. Hence the body must be made subordinate through asceticism. It is discipline that allows for ecstasy and 'enlightenment.'"
7. To understand who is a prostitute, one must begin with the social institution in which this role is considered deviance.

When kinship is the focal social institution, and the structure of the male world is the topside organizing structure, then the behavior of the unbounded female is the most significant form of deviance.

When economics is the focal social institution, and the structures of the profit-making capitalist world is the topside organizing structure, then the possession of undeclared wealth is the most significant form of deviance.

When politics is the focal social institution, and the structure of the power controlling or determining the world is the topside organizing structure, then the wielding of uncontrolled arms is the most significant form of deviance.

When religion is the focal social institution, and the structure of the meaning determining the world is the topside organizing structure, then the proclamation of untested visions is the most significant form of deviance.

The family in the ancient Mediterranean world was an enduring group of male and female relatives standing apart from other families, yet connected to other groups by its women. Women must always be bounded by males; they are like fields, always fenced in (hence embedded, encysted). Just as an unfenced field is simply land, an anomalous space in organized society, so too, an unfenced female is simply a female, an anomalous person in organized society.

Since in the first-century Mediterranean (and earlier) kinship was the focal social institution, and the structure of the male world was the topside organizing structure, *porneia* would refer to the behavior of a female who does not serve to connect two male groups. Men form boundaries, women are the bounded. When the bounded move beyond the boundaries, there is defilement of the boundaries. Thus men are defiled, women are defilers. Indication of such defiling behavior is the social existence of a female unbounded by a male; this is the *pornē,* anyone committing typically women's sins.

1. These are typically woman's proper behaviors:

   She may not connect two male worlds, yet remain always bounded, since she is living in fenced in, chaperoned, controlled conditions. Examples are the sacred virgin, the unmarried daughter, the never married.

   She may connect by marriage and be bounded by her husband.

   She may cease to connect. An example would be the widowed, free to act "like a man."

2. These are typically women's sins:

   She may misconnect via elopement, unbounded by her father or brothers (if marriage follows, children are legitimate).

   She may disconnect via adultery, unbounded by her husband, to his detriment (children are illegitimate).

   She may not connect two male worlds, yet come from a (Israelite) priestly family, hence living in a divinely fenced in, divinely chaperoned and divinely controlled family. An example would be the prostitute daughter of a priest (children are illegitimate).

   She may not connect two male worlds, hence be unbounded by anyone, since she is living in unfenced, unchaperoned and uncontrolled conditions. Examples are the prostitute and the witch (children presumed illegitimate).

3. These are borderline cases:

   She may not connect two male worlds, yet be unbounded by humans, since she is living in divinely fenced in, divinely chaperoned and divinely controlled conditions. An example would be the *hierodule* (sacred prostitute); forbidden in Israel as idolatry.

   She may connect more than two male worlds should her husband permit her to have sexual relations with others: the pimp husband, the tavern keeper. Here, she is abnormally bounded, living in porously fenced and anomalously controlled conditions: the (permissible) prostitute (children are legitimate).

8. Tilley has excellently described the positive function of asceticism in the social contexts of the pre-Constantinian world in which Christians were summoned as witnesses. Asceticism was preparation for "taking the stand" as witness. The usual method of interro-

gating witnesses well into modern times was by torture (Tilley cites the United Nations definition: "any act by which severe pain or suffering, whether physical or mental, is intentionally inflicted on a person by agents of the state." And she continues, citing Stover and Nightingale: "Although infliction of . . . pain is integral . . . the purpose of torture is to break the will of the victim and ultimately to destroy his or her humanity." Finally, citing psychologist Peter Suedfeld, Tilley lists the five goals of torture: information, incrimination of friends and associates, intimidation of other members of the community, isolation, and indoctrination. These last two features underscore the true purpose of torture: "to control people who hold as true a vision of reality contrary to that of the torturers," thus to get victims to "affirm as true what they previously denied" (Tilley 1991:468–469). She notes how torture sought to deconstruct the mind through deconstructing the body. Witness preparation produces this deconstruction of the mind by deconstructing the body through: (1) ascetical practices (fasting, vigils, celibacy, etc.), (2) hysterical fugue (an altered state of consciousness and compensatory mechanism in which language about realities and the realities represented are decoupled; this often happens when persons cannot control intolerable situations—as compensatory mechanism, disabling, disintegrating pain is often not felt), (3) reconfiguring the meaning of pain so that torture pains reinforce that meaning (for example, suffering with Christ).

9. How does the ascetic life affect a person's actions and feelings? According to Baumeister, the following features are involved: passivity and impulsivity; suppression of emotions; removal of inhibitions; instability of mental narrowing states; and irrationality, fantasy, and inconsistency (1991:67–80). In his listing of the consequences of spiritual exercises, his conclusions are similar. Outcomes include: passivity; escape from emotion; irrationality, yet with transitory ecstatic/meditative states; and new perspectives, knowledge, and understanding (1991:194–200). Perhaps there is overlap in both lists. In his description of Cynics, Vaage (1992) underscores the removal of inhibitions typical of these ascetics.
10. There is definite proof that cruelty to animals replicates in cruelty to fellow humans—see Brenman 1985 and Felthouse et al. 1987; for pain tolerance see Zatzick et al. 1990.

BIBLIOGRAPHY

(Anonymous ed.). 1955. *Christian Asceticism and Modern Man,* trans. Walter Mitchell. New York: Philosophical Library.

Augsburger, David. 1986. *Pastoral Counseling Across Cultures.* Philadelphia: Westminster.

Averill, James. 1980. "A Constructivist View of Emotion." In *Theories of Emotion,* eds. R. Plutchik and H. Kellerman. Orlando: Academic Press.

Averill, James. 1982. *Anger and Aggression: An Essay on Emotion.* New York: Springer Verlag.

Baumeister, Roy F. 1988. "Masochism as Escape from Self." *Journal of Sex Research* 25.

Baumeister, Roy F. 1991. *The Escaping Self: Alcoholism, Spirituality, Masochism and Other Flights from the Burden of Selfhood.* New York: Basic Books.

Bemporad, Jules R., John J. Ratey, Gillian O'Driscoll, and Maria L. Daehler. 1988. "Hysteria, Anorexia and the Culture of Self Denial." *Psychiatry* 51.

Brenman, Eric. 1985. "Cruelty and Narrowmindedness." *International Journal of Psycho-Analysis* 66.

Brown, Peter. 1971. "The Rise and Function of the Holy Man in Late Antiquity." *Journal of Roman Studies* 61.

Cook, Peter S. 1978. "Childrearing, Culture and Mental Health: Exploring an Ethological-Evolutionary Perspective in Child Psychiatry and Preventive Mental Health with Particular Reference to Two Contrasting Approaches to Early Childrearing." *Medical Journal of Australia Special Supplement* 2.

Csikszentmihalyi, Mihalyi. 1975. *Beyond Boredom and Anxiety.* San Francisco: Jossey-Bass.

Csikszentmihalyi, Mihalyi. 1981. "Some Paradoxes in the Definition of Play." In A. T. Cheska, ed., *Play as Context: 1979 Proceedings of the Association for the Anthropological Study of Play.* Westpoint, N.Y.: Leisure Press.

Douglas, Mary, and Baron Isherwood. 1979. *The World of Goods.* New York: Basic Books.

Dubarle, D. 1955. "Anthropological Factors Conditioning Acts of Penance." In *Christian Asceticism and Modern Man,* trans. Walter Mitchell. New York: Philosophical Library.

Felthous, Alan R., and Stephen R. Kellert. 1987. "Childhood Cruelty to Animals and Later Aggression against People: A Review." *American Journal of Psychiatry* 144.

Furman, Erna. 1986. "Aggressively Abused Children." *Journal of Child Psychotherapy* 12.1.

Geertz, Clifford. 1976. "'From the Native's Point of View': On the Nature of Anthropological Understanding." In Keith H. Basso and Henry A. Selby, eds., *Meaning and Anthropology.* Albuquerque: University of New Mexico Press.

Glickauf-Hughes, Cheryl, and Marolyn Wells. 1991. "Current Conceptualizations on Masochism: Genesis and Object Relations." *American Journal of Psychotherapy* 45.

Goleman, Daniel. 1988. *The Meditative Mind: The Varieties of Meditative Experience.* New York: St. Martin's Press.

Goodman, Felicitas D. 1988a. *How About Demons? Possession and Exorcism in the Modern World.* Bloomington: University of Indiana Press.

Goodman, Felicitas D. 1988b. *Ecstasy, Ritual and Alternative Reality: Religion in a Pluralistic World.* Bloomington: University of Indiana Press.

Goodman, Felicitas D. 1990. *Where the Spirits Ride the Wind: Trance Journeys and Other Ecstatic Experiences.* Bloomington: University of Indiana Press.

Harré, Rome. 1980. *Social Being: A Theory for Social Psychology.* Totowa, N.J.: Rowman and Littlefield.

Harré, Rome. 1984. *Personal Being: A Theory for Individual Psychology.* Cambridge, Mass.: Harvard University Press.

Harré, Rome. 1989. "The 'Self' as a Theoretical Concept." In Michael Krausz, ed., *Relativism, Interpretation and Confrontation.* Notre Dame: University of Notre Dame Press.

Kelsey, Neal. 1992. "The Body as Desert in *The Life of Saint Anthony.*" *Semeia* 57 (*Discursive Formations, Ascetic Piety and the Interpretation of Early Christian Literature, Part 1,* ed. Vincent L. Wimbush).

Macho, Thomas H. 1985. "In corpore sano: Spekulationen uber Gesundheitsideale des Sports." *Gruppendynamik* 16.

Malina, Bruce J. 1980. "What is Prayer?" *The Bible Today* 18.

Malina, Bruce J. 1986a. *Christian Origins and Cultural Anthropology.* Atlanta: John Knox.

Malina, Bruce J. 1986b. "Religion in the World of Paul: A Preliminary Sketch." *Biblical Theology Bulletin* 16.

Malina, Bruce J. 1989. "Dealing with Biblical (Mediterranean) Characters: A Guide for U.S. Consumers." *Biblical Theology Bulletin* 19.

Malina, Bruce J. 1990. "Mother and Son." *Biblical Theology Bulletin* 20.

Malina, Bruce J. 1992. "Is There a Circum-Mediterranean Person? Looking for Stereotypes." *Biblical Theology Bulletin* 22.

Malina, Bruce J. 1993. *The New Testament World: Insights from Cultural Anthropology.* Rev. ed. Louisville: Westminster/John Knox.

Malina, Bruce J., and Jerome H. Neyrey. 1988. *Calling Jesus Names: The Social Value of Labels in Matthew.* Sonoma, Calif.: Polebridge Press.

Mitchell, Stephen A. 1988. *Relational Concepts in Psychoanalysis: An Integration.* Cambridge, Mass.: Harvard University Press.

Nagy, Marilyn, 1992. "Translocation of Parental Images in Fourth-Century Ascetic Texts: Motifs and Techniques of Identity." *Semeia* 58 (*Discursive Formations, Ascetic Piety and the Interpretation of Early Christian Literature, Part 2,* ed. Vincent L. Wimbush).

O'Laughlin, Michael, trans., ed. 1990. "Evagrius Ponticus: Antirrheticus (Selections)." In Vincent L. Wimbush, ed., *Ascetic Behavior in Greco-Roman Antiquity: A Sourcebook.* Minneapolis: Fortress/Augsburg Press.

Pestrak, Victor A. 1991. "The Masochistic Personality Organization: Dynamic, Etiological, and Psychotherapeutic Factors." *Journal of Contemporary Psychotherapy* 21.

Sabom, W. Stephen. 1985. "The Gnostic World of Anorexia Nervosa." *Journal of Psychology and Theology* 13.

Schachter, S. 1971. *Emotion, Obesity and Crime.* New York, Academic Press.

Schachter, S., and J. E. Singer. 1962. "Cognitive, Social and Physiological Determinants of Emotional States." *Psychological Review* 69.

Schwartz, Shalom H. 1990. "Individualism / Collectivism: Critique and Proposed Refinements." *Journal of Cross Cultural Psychology* 21.

Synnott, Anthony, and David Howes. 1992. "From Measurement to Meaning: Anthropologies of the Body." *Anthropos* 87.

Tanquerey, Adolphe. 1932. *The Spiritual Life: A Treatise on Ascetical and Mystical Theology,* trans. H. Branderis. 2d ed. Tournai: Desclee.

Tilley, Maureen A. 1991. "The Ascetic Body and the (Un)Making of the World of the Martyr." *Journal of the American Academy of Religion* 59.

Todd, Emmanuel. 1985. *The Explanation of Ideology: Family Structures and Social Systems,* trans. David Garrioch. Oxford: Basil Blackwell.

Triandis, Harry C. 1989. "Cross-Cultural Studies of Individualism and Collectivism." In Richard A. Dienstbier et al., eds., *Nebraska Symposium on Motivation 1989.* Lincoln: University of Nebraska Press.

Vaage, Leif E. 1992. "Like Dogs Barking: Cynic Parrēsia and Shameless Asceticism." In *Semeia* 57 (*Discursive Formations, Ascetic Piety and the Interpretation of Early Christian Literature, Part 1,* ed. Vincent L. Wimbush).

Valantasis, Richard. 1992. "Demons and the Perfecting of the Monk's Body: Monastic Anthropology, Daemonology and Asceticism." In *Semeia* 58 (*Discursive Formations, Ascetic Piety and the Interpretation of Early Christian Literature, Part 2,* ed. Vincent L. Wimbush).

Wimbush, Vincent L., ed. 1990. *Ascetic Behavior in Greco-Roman Antiquity: A Sourcebook.* Minneapolis: Fortress/Augsburg Press.

Zatzick, Douglas F., and Joel E. Dimsdale. 1990. "Cultural Variations in Response to Painful Stimuli." *Psychosomatic Medicine* 52.

14

Asceticism—Audience and Resistance

Response to the Three Preceding Papers

Elizabeth A. Castelli

First of all, I would like to thank Professors Sfameni Gasparro, Cameron, and Malina for their very engaging papers, which collectively demonstrate the evocative possibilities of the overarching theme, the hermeneutics of asceticism. Indeed, although each essay in its own way addresses early Christian asceticism, each pursues the task so differently from the others that I found myself, initially, wondering what, in fact, these essays had in common, beyond their broad subject matter. Several rereadings produced a list of themes and concerns that the papers share; and so my response is largely an attempt to explore these shared interests, although I also have some questions for the presenters.

Let me begin with the most obvious shared theme: each of these papers, in its own way, is concerned with the hermeneutics of asceticism, though two of them are primarily concerned with ascetical hermeneutics (that is, how producers of ascetical discourses interpreted earlier texts), while one brings a social-psychological hermeneutic to the subject matter of asceticism. Professors Sfameni Gasparro and Cameron focus on the matter of how texts, discourses, and ideologies on the one hand, and lived realities, on the other, intersect in the world of asceticism; Professor Malina concerns himself with the question of how asceticism itself can be read or interpreted. Professor Sfameni Gasparro, indeed, emphasizes the diverse relations between ideas and activities early in her paper, when she states:

> The same behavior in practice can be based on very different theoretical assumptions, while similar principles sometimes result in conduct differing sharply on ethical and practical levels (p. 129).

Moreover, she demonstrates that the so-called Encratites (a name itself charged with hermeneutical resonances) embrace a hermeneutic that articulates a continuity between their own ideological stance and certain biblical traditions; but that their hermeneutic involves both a radicalization and literalization of those earlier texts. She is particularly concerned with the Encratites' use of the biblical story of human origins and of Paul's writings, and their elaboration, through the lens of Christian understanding, of Christ's transformative effect on human history—an elaboration which produces the theological idea of double creation.

While Sfameni Gasparro emphasizes the hermeneutical maneuvers of early church fathers in relation to specific biblical texts which will become fundamental for many ascetic movements within early Christianity, Cameron takes a different tack. Following Geoffrey Harpham's intriguing study, she emphasizes more broadly the textual dimension of early Christian asceticism—a textual dimension involved both in the reading of texts imbued with ascetic discourse and in the production of new, self-conscious, ascetical texts. The biographies and autobiographies that constituted the major narrative formulation of early Christian asceticism were texts which transformed their subjects into texts themselves, exemplars with whom readers were called into mimetic relation. Indeed, Cameron and Harpham both argue that the ascetic life became like a text itself, one shaped by the shared aesthetics of its participants, one produced for others to read. As Cameron puts it, "The self-consciousness of asceticism itself embodied an act of self-creation with its own aesthetics; it transcended the natural and resembled an act of literary or artistic creation." Cameron argues that the textual and hermeneutical bent of early Christian asceticism contributed to broader Christian discourse, where the direction was toward systematization, totality, completeness, and all-enveloping explanation.

Both Sfameni Gasparro and Cameron use language as a register for determining who belongs within the framework of encratism or asceticism. Indeed, shared language, imagery, and literary themes constitute for Sfameni Gasparro the ground upon which she will maintain that, in spite of discernible and significant differences between moderate and radical Encratites, there remains a substantial homogeneity among those whose ideas and practices fall under the term, "encratic." Cameron also argues that an ascetic discourse can be identified where certain central terms and concepts are present (renunciation, temptation, denial, spiritual progress or ascent, theories of demons, and technical uses of words like *porneia, erōs, logismoi,* and *aktēmosynē*); moreover, she posits the possibility of the existence of an ascetic vocabulary whose appearance across temporal and geographical boundaries might serve as a good measure of the degree of diffusion of ascetic discourses and practices.

It is interesting, then, that Bruce Malina's hermeneutic of asceticism does not engage textuality or discourse, but focuses rather on the social effects of a large range of behaviors that he would classify as "ascetic." Malina's ascetics are not readers and interpreters; indeed, they appear as people who absent themselves not only from social discourse, but indeed, perhaps from discourse altogether. I wonder whether there is not something worth exploring further here—in this methodological difference between Sfameni Gasparro and Cameron on the one hand, and Malina on the other. To put it as a question: how does attention to the uses and character of discourse within asceticism focus the discussion and produce certain results? How does a method which does not examine discourse produce a different kind of reading of the phenomenon of asceticism? And perhaps a further question for Malina: why, in using the method of contemporary psychology, is discourse not an object of analysis? Certainly psychoanalysis, social psychology's daunting older sibling, particularly in its postmodern manifestations, attends with great detail to the role of discourse in the production of subjectivity. Given that this social-psychological hermeneutic of asceticism so emphasizes the subject (or the self), why so little attention to discursive influences? Given, moreover, that the sources for our knowledge about ancient subjects are largely textual sources—that is, what we know about ancient people derives in some significant measure from what ancient people (granted, privileged and élite ancient people) wrote about themselves and others—how do we escape from the need to analyze that discourse carefully, even when we are equally concerned with the limits of the textual record to tell us everything we might be able to know about antiquity? How, in short, can we study ancient Christian asceticism without recourse to its textual and discursive traces?

So much for the obvious. A second theme is raised explicitly only in Professor Cameron's paper, but I believe that it is relevant in both of the other papers, though once again in rather different ways: it is the theme of closure. For Professor Cameron, along with other historians of late antiquity she discusses, ascetic discourse contributes to the broader Christian movement toward historical and social closure—that through its emphases on limit, hierarchy, and resistance, ascetic discourse lent itself to the totalizing structures that have been identified traditionally with the Byzantine empire. Toward the end of her paper, Cameron argues that ascetic discourse provided analogies for the operations of the Byzantine state, in effect, that

> in time the very practice of asceticism became identified with the politics of the Byzantine state. . . . [But] just as ascetic discourse called for developed demonology against which to define itself and over which to assert its repeated victories, so the discourse of religious and state authority required a perpetual supply of real or alleged opponents in order to be able to maintain its continued credibility. Heretics and secularists . . . are the state's demons, and heresiology the state's ascetic discourse. . . . The Byzantine state itself replicated the ascetic subject (p. 158).

I found myself persuaded by Cameron's suggestions that asceticism, through its affinity for hierarchical and exclusionary discourses, lent itself to historical movements toward cultural and ideological closure. At the same time, I found myself wondering how this view intersects with the closing argument of Geoffrey Harpham's book, *The Ascetic Imperative in Culture and Criticism,* a book which (as I have already noted) is clearly important for Cameron's reading of the textual and discursive in the ascetic. In the last chapter—indeed, on the last page—of Harpham's book, he contrasts ethics and asceticism (in the context of a discussion of the unresolved character of debates within contemporary literary theory) by suggesting that an "ascetics of interpretation" might be preferable to an "ethics of interpretation." Why? Harpham suggests, first of all, that an "ascetics of interpretation" is desirable because its "extension is indeterminate." Moreover, he suggests, it might usefully supplant ethics because:

> Ethics implies closure and decision, an end to temptation; asceticism repudiates such a possibility. Ethics honors the distinction between "being tempted" and "resisting"; asceticism acknowledges no such distinction. Ethics worries the differences between *what* you might resist; asceticism demands only *that* you resist. Asceticism, then, is the resistance to ethics as well as the basis for ethics (p. 269).

While, obviously, Harpham is not here talking about the historical context of early Christian asceticism, but rather about asceticism as a trope for interpretation, I wonder whether his characterization of asceticism as the repudiation of the possibility of closure is not worthy of some further discussion on a theoretical level.

I would argue that Professor Sfameni Gasparro's paper implies the presence within encratic anthropology and theology of a movement toward closure. When Encratites focused on the *Genesis* story of the origins of humanity and sexuality in the past, on the one hand, and on the possibility for the achievement of the *bios angelikos* in the future, on the other, they enclosed human history within a kind of ideological and mythical parenthesis. By their hermeneutical linking of protological and eschatological concerns (Sfameni Gasparro's language), the Encratites certainly presuppose a kind of historical closure, whereby human existence is always oriented towards both its mythical origin and its culmination. The ideological privilege accorded to the framing mythical narratives of creation and resurrection, mediated through sexual renunciation, suggests an encratic emphasis on closure. By Sfameni Gasparro's reading, the Encratites sought to embody the singular and unified story of the beginning and end of human history, producing a kind of enacted discourse not at all unlike the ascetic discourse which Cameron describes through recourse to terms like closure, limit, hierarchy, and exclusion. The theme of historical closure, discerned explicitly by Cameron (and, with different language, by Brown and Markus), appears implicitly also among the Encratites, though there seem to be two very different conceptualities of history at work among Cameron's ascetics and Sfameni Gasparro's Encratites.

Malina's paper also seems to suggest the importance of closure for his view of asceticism, though his version of closure is personal and subject-oriented, rather than historical. Malina's foundational category—self-shrinkage—seems to imply some understanding of asceticism as limit, reduction, refusal of ambiguity. While I will want to take issue with this definition of asceticism a bit later on, for the moment I would simply point out that some dimension of closure is also present in Malina's approach to ascetic practices.

A general question which occurs to me in relation to this theme of closure is whether ascetic discourse need necessarily always lend itself to historical closure, or whether this tendency is peculiar to ascetic discourse in the realm of Christianity. I am thinking particularly about forms of ascetic behavior and discourse which involve some explicit form of cultural critique (a theme I will discuss below), rather than those which seem to contribute to the eventual hegemony of the Christian state. That is, there are many examples in modern history where ascetic discourse and behavior are used, for example, against the state. These include the preparatory practices involved in Gandhian civil disobedience; the hunger strikes of imprisoned Irish Republican Army members fifteen years ago; the fasts of United Farm Workers leader César Chavez, whose death was accelerated by a constitution weakened by repeated and extended fasts; the hunger strikes of HIV-infected Haitian refugees in Guantanamo Bay, and of their supporters on college and university campuses across the United States. Does this asceticism contribute to something like historical closure, or rather the opening up of history toward some other kind of reality? Does asceticism always promote a reduction of historical options, as its alliance with limitation and hierarchy might seem to suggest? Or can it also operate, in an appropriation of Harpham's terms, simply as resistance?

Related to this theme of closure is the question of history as it emerges in these three papers. Here I was interested to observe real differences between Sfameni Gasparro's and Cameron's essays. As I have just mentioned, Sfameni Gasparro's Encratites seem to focus their sights primarily on protological and eschatological concerns—their *archē,* where they have come from, and their *telos,* where they are going. What is interesting about this focus, however, is that their asceticism, their sexual renunciation which embodies both the purity of the first creation and the immortality of the angelic life, actually brings the idyllic past and the religious ideal of the eschaton into the present. By focusing on eschatological and protological realities, these ascetics make radically contingent all of the lived human reality that occupies the space in between; they deny the entirety of social, political, and cultural realities; and, thereby, I would suggest, they deny history itself in favor of asserting the priority and privilege of the mythic past and future. Everything in between the moment of pure origin and the moment of salvational fulfillment is reduced to an unmediated present, caught simply between beginning and end. By enacting these protological and eschatological concerns through recourse to sexual renunciation, the Encratites embody a denial not only of generation, but also of genealogy, erasing any sense from the historical categories of continuity and change.

Meanwhile, Cameron's ascetics appear, rather than to be denying history, to be crafting it through self-conscious recourse to narrative and, particularly, (auto)biography. Moreover, if Cameron's conclusions are correct—that ascetic discourse provided a kind of ideological model for the Byzantine state—then her ascetics cannot be reduced to the otherworldly focused Encratites of Sfameni Gasparro's essay nor to the self-shrinkers and world deniers of Malina's (whether late ancient Christian renouncers of sexuality or the United States's late twentieth-century capitalists). In general, I would be interested in hearing the panelists discuss the tensions they see among the papers on the question of history. One explanation which occurs to me to account for the difference between Sfameni Gasparro's Encratites and Cameron's ascetics is, indeed, a historical difference; their different takes on the problematic of history may itself reflect different historical realities, as the Encratites occupy a rather radical marginality in an embryonic and embattled church, whereas the later ascetics occupy a privileged center in a hegemonic church. Once one has power, perhaps the contingency of history needs be renegotiated.

The fourth idea which is given expression in each of these essays is the interaction between asceticism and the self. Here, once again, there seem to be significant differences between the first two papers and the last one. I understood both Sfameni Gasparro and Cameron to be taking a position alongside others, such as Peter Brown, who would characterize asceticism as a highly self-conscious process of self-formation. Indeed, the anthropology of Sfameni Gasparro's Encratites, who seek to escape the limitations of the second creation through a bodily process of sexual renunciation, and their hermeneutics, which seek to literalize scriptural meanings through physical restraint, both imply a self cast in molds created by the intersections of theology and literary understanding. Moreover, Cameron's ascetics—who are constituted through narrative framings, through interrogations of desire, and through the unresolvable tensions between temptation and resistance—are agents in the production of a new self, the ascetic subject. Rather than being a subject reduced, the ascetic subject appears here as a carefully crafted reformulation of what constitutes the human.

Therefore, I found myself raising a number of questions about Professor Malina's definitions of asceticism and the self. Although thoroughly interwoven, they struck me as quite out of keeping with this other realm of discussion (associated with Cameron's essay). Malina begins his discussion with a definition of asceticism as self-shrinkage. I should say that it is with a certain degree of both humility and irony that I call this definition into question, insofar as I am a member of the group sponsoring this conference, a group that has been meeting for seven years without coming to anything resembling a consensus on such a definition! Indeed, Malina points to this absence of consensus in the opening of his essay. As the debates continue among the theoreticians, the systematizers, and the we-know-it-when-we-see-it people, Malina has diagnosed an interesting paradox of our group's work: we have published three volumes about something we have yet to define. Indeed, part of our asceticism seems to have been to resist what Averil Cameron calls "the persistent impulse towards definition," and it may have been one of our more sustained and successful endeavors! Nevertheless, I will take the risk of asking some questions about Malina's definitions, because I think they will open up some important theoretical and methodological issues.

"Asceticism is the shrinkage of the self motivated by avoidance or attainment goals," says Malina. He elaborates this definition in a couple of important ways, notably, first, in explaining that self-shrinkage refers to a diminishing of the self by centering on the physical dimensions of human being, the physical self, the body; and second, by defining the self as "the unfolded human self to whom adults can and do apply the word, 'I.' " He goes on to discuss the ways that such a self was produced through childrearing practices in antiquity, and suggests that traditional childrearing offered the models for practices that became ascetic practices.

Despite the clear attempt to draw careful distinctions between ancient Mediterranean cultures and contemporary, postmodern culture in the United States, Malina's characterization of the self and subjectivity in his discussion of asceticism nevertheless struck me as troublingly unhistoricized, on the one hand, and grounded in some problematic generalizations on the other. The self in Malina's discussion appears as a transhistorical reality, in spite of the claim that self-awareness is situated culturally and produced socially. There are a number of difficulties as I see them: Malina argues that ancient Mediterranean peoples do not share the contemporary American fixation on individuality. Fair enough. Yet, pressed to its most absolute formulation, such a claim requires that Malina virtually abandon his initial definition of a self as an individual, an "I," in order to reorient his definition: the ancient Mediterranean self was not an individual, an "I," at all, but what Malina comes to call a group self. Moreover, he argues that this ancient self was reducible to physical being because, "In fact, what was typical of the ancient Mediterranean self was that it was anti-introspective, not psychologically minded at all." Now I am completely willing to concede that ancient Mediterranean people did not engage in activities in any way approximating the kinds of indulgent—and indeed paradoxically public—introspection (from confessional television talk shows to "I'm dysfunctional/you're dysfunctional" recovery groups) to which American culture seems thoroughly oversubscribed. At the same time, I can easily think of any number of examples from philosophers, especially the Stoics whose views had an important influence on early Christian ascetics, where careful observance of one's own appetites, drives, and desires could help to produce a remade individual self. This is no simple new age self-improvement project, but it is about individual transformation, and it is about self-consciousness. Moreover, I found myself wondering, from a methodological point of view, how—if "the ancient Mediterranean self was . . . not psychologically minded at all"—an approach which makes use of categories drawn from modern psychology is appropriate to the subject matter.

The ahistorical character of subject formation and subjectivity appears in the claims made about childrearing practices and also in the claims made about the pressures placed upon the group self that would cause it to undertake an ascetic life in order to escape. I would want to hear more about the sources for our information about childrearing practices, and whether Professor Malina thinks it makes any difference that children in the upper classes (with which he largely concerns himself in this discussion) were reared predominantly by slaves (nurses and pedagogues) and not by their parents. I am also interested in the claim made in the paper that one of the impacts of these childrearing practices is that the psychic unity of the subject was dangerously blurred. Such a claim, of course, presupposes a preexisting psychic unity which, on my reading of psychoanalysis, is not easily presumed. Psychoanalysis posits not a psychic unity of infant subjects, but rather a subjectivity characterized by pre-Oedipal fusion with the mother: the problem is not that an original psychic self-recognition and unity exists and is blurred through processes of socialization, but rather the reverse: that the original fusion of the child with the mother must be broken through socializing processes that establish psychic differentiation. I understand that Professor Malina is not making use of psychoanalytic sources in his own psychological model, but I wonder exactly where in ancient sources we might find evidence that such a problem of subject formation indeed existed.

I am also interested in the claim toward the end of the paper that asceticism, as an escape from the demands of family identity, functioned as a kind of liberation. Malina writes:

> Choosing the life of the ascetic marked the end of the emotional roller coaster of prevailing group reputation. Forgotten are all the grand, complex, abstract, wide-ranging definitions of one's ethnic group, one's family, and one's family roles. Thus reduced to simple humanity symbolized by the body shorn of social concerns, one can live in radical *communitas,* with the sole task of keeping the body in check (p. 168).

A number of questions present themselves to me at this point: first of all, how do we know that the obligations and connections that constituted family life in antiquity were intrinsically burdensome, rather than simply being constructed as such by rhetoricians whose interests lay in promoting the ascetic life? (Of course, there is a degree to which rhetoric is effective when it appeals to the sensibilities of its audience, yet there is also a large measure of persuasion involved in any rhetorical act, that is, an attempt to offer a new interpretation of reality which the audience explicitly does not embrace.) If we are to be allowed to psychologize in interpreting ancient Christian ascetics' experiences, then cannot one argue equally persuasively that the family's conferral of identity and status provided a kind of access to psychological reassurance so compelling that, even when people left their natal or marriage families to become Christian ascetics, they entered into a community which provided them with immediate access to identity through the idiom of kinship that characterized early Christian communities? In other words, they left one family, but they immediately entered into another one. Secondly, I wonder whether the historical record bears out this kind of characterization of asceticism in all of its manifestations. When, for example, aristocratic Roman women like Melania the Elder undertook to pursue ascetic lives in their extensive and influential households, they hardly reduced themselves to simple humanity, but rather retained their social networks, simply reorienting their influence toward the ascetic life. The kind of disruption which Malina's characterization implies may not be so thorough as it initially appears.

In general, I wonder whether asceticism is better defined, not as an escape from self-awareness, but rather as an intensification of self-awareness. Given the many warnings on the parts of spiritual fathers and mothers against the sin of pride, one has the definite sense that the ascetic does not abandon awareness of self, but rather escalates it, and that such a magnification of the focus on the self can produce two contradictory results: more careful management of the self, or self-aggrandizement grounded in one's overzealous success at such self-surveillance.

In addition to the themes I have discussed so far—the hermeneutical and discursive; the concerns over closure, the problematics of history; and the character and nature of the self—there remain some other issues raised in common by these writers which deserve at least some brief discussion.

Each of these writers has, in different ways, raised the question of the importance of the audience for the hermeneutics of asceticism. Professor Sfameni Gasparro has discussed, for example, the ways in which the early apologists framed *enkrateia* for a skeptical non-Christian public, and how central concerns over boastfulness were in relation to discussions of *enkrateia* in the Church Fathers. In different ways, both of these examples suggest that how others view asceticism is in some way crucial to the discussion. In the first case, among the apologists, how Christian Encratites looked to the encircling culture mattered; in the second case, the self-presentation of ascetic behavior—how ascetic behavior was to be seen by people besides the practitioner—is crucial. I would suggest that the ongoing discourses of asceticism, with their continual concern over the problem of boastfulness and sins of pride among ascetics, simply continue this early concern over asceticism and its audiences.

Professor Malina's whole hermeneutical model, drawing upon social psychology, implicitly invokes the importance of an audience for asceticism. Towards the end of his paper, in his discussion of the dynamics of pain and power, shame and honor, this concern becomes explicit. Spectators are required in a situation described by language like: "then the position of the one attempting to humiliate is open to question in the eyes of the *public*," and "Humiliation endured can thus produce an increase of honor and a sense of solidarity in the eyes of *an observing public*" (p. 171, emphasis Castelli).

Professor Cameron also raises the necessity of the audience for asceticism, particularly in her focus on the textual character of ascetic discourses in which narratives and biographies became the privileged genres. The very production of such texts presupposes that someone will read them, and as Professor Cameron puts it, "even discourses of retreat call for an audience."

I wonder whether there is something endemic to asceticism that requires an audience, and whether asceticism can possibly ever be a private affair removed from the realm in which it is displayed, understood, given meaning. The necessity for an audience would, of course, be complicated by the efficacy of total *anachōrēsis*, which Kallistos Ware has characterized (chapter 1) as flight without return; yet one wonders whether even such a complete withdrawal is ever completely without an audience, if only the small group of family and acquaintances one has left behind. If the audience is a necessary component of the ascetic dimension of religious culture, are there broader conclusions that we can draw concerning the relationship between asceticism and, for example, spectacle? Must an ascetic be seen (either literally or metaphorically) by others in order for there to be asceticism? Does the term "asceticism" signify outside of the reach of an audience? (I realize that this question is a bit like the one about the proverbial tree falling in the forest when there is no one there to hear it, yet I think that this question of audience may be an important one for thinking generically about asceticism.)

Another area I think might be worth some discussion is how the different authors address the question of asceticism's role in a broader agenda of cultural critique. Professor Sfameni Gasparro's reading of the Encratites, in their attempts to bring both the mythic past and the promised future into the present, suggests that encratism was, at heart, a counter-cultural movement. In rejecting the practices of generation and the valuation of genealogy within the broader culture, its adherents challenged the ideological and practical contours of their cultural environment. Professor Cameron's rendering suggests a tension between cultural critique and the prospects for asceticism's underwriting some modes of social change, on the one hand, and the contributions of asceticism to the broader historical movement toward Christian hegemony in the Byzantine state, on the other. Meanwhile, Professor Malina seems to argue that asceticism in late antiquity was a form of resistance to the dominant (that is, familial) culture's demands upon and expectations of the individual, whereas in late twentieth-century capitalist U.S. culture, asceticism provides a powerful basis for the maintenance of the cultural status quo, and is downright institutional in its effects. Leaving aside the fact that I would probably interpret U.S. capitalism as more gluttonous than ascetic, I wonder, nevertheless, what the differences are between different moments in which asceticism comes into contact with culture. Why is it that asceticism can sometimes underwrite critique, whereas at other times it rationalizes existing relations? Does it ultimately and necessarily tend toward the open-endedness of resistance for its own sake, as Harpham argues, or are there moments when it contributes to hegemony, as Cameron suggests? Is asceticism, then, an ultimately malleable strategy, one which can shape itself differently in relation to different sets of social and historical circumstances? If so, how does this characteristic malleability fit into an emerging definition of asceticism?

My comments here certainly in no way exhaust the possibilities for discussion offered by these rich essays. I would be interested, for example, in pursuing the theories of power that undergird the different papers, as well as the tensions presented by papers which emphasize very differently the intersections of ascetic behavior and discourses with ancient structures of gender. Nevertheless, it seems equally crucial that I engage in a form of asceticism suited to this kind of academic forum, and resist the temptation to talk beyond my allotted time. Therefore, I will stop here, hoping that these initial reflections on the panelists' papers will provide some useful framework for the discussion ahead of us.

15

Deconstruction of the Body in Indian Asceticism

Patrick Olivelle

Asceticism, modern scholarship has often argued, is a cornerstone of Indian religions. It was fashionable not too long ago to contrast Indian religions, with their life-and-world-negating tendencies, to the life-affirming religions of the West.[1] Louis Dumont's (1960) seminal study, "World Renunciation in Indian Religions," pointed out the inadequacy of that generalization by showing what Heesterman (1985) has called "the inner conflict of the tradition," that is, the conflict between world-renouncing and world-affirming ideologies within the history of Indian religious traditions. Dumont's own emphasis on world renunciation as the dominant and creative force within Indian religious history has been recently subjected to review and correction (Madan 1987). Indeed, Dumont's structural dichotomy between the renouncer and the man in the world is tenable only at the level of ideal types: the lived reality of both the ascetics and people living in society was much more complex and much less tidy.

The more significant point of Dumont's analysis, in my view, is the dialectical and creative relationship and tension in which the ascetic and the societal dimensions of Indian religions existed and developed both ideologically and in their institutions and practices. This relationship is the point of departure for this paper, which examines the ascetic creation of the human body. But, like most aspects of Indian ascetic ideology and practice, the ascetic creation of the body can be understood adequately only within its structural relationship to the human body as social creation. Thus, at least for heuristic purposes, I think it is useful to consider the ascetic creation as a deconstruction[2] of the socially created body. This approach is justified also by the native theological understanding of renunciatory asceticism at least with the Brāhmaṇical tradition, which views asceticism as an antithetical category defined more by its negation of social structures than by any internal structure or property of its own (Olivelle 1975).

Given recent scholarship in widely different disciplines, it is unnecessary to belabor the major assumption of this paper: the human body as culturally created and perceived stands as the primary symbol of the social body, the body politic. Bodily appearance, movements, and functions—from dress, hair, food, and toilet to excrement, sexual fluids, and menstrual discharge—are culturally and socially determined meanings (Mauss 1973; Turner 1984). The ascetic deconstruction of the body has to be located, therefore, within the socially constructed correspondence between the two bodies—the physical and the social—well expressed by Mary Douglas:

> The social body constrains the way the physical body is perceived. The physical experience of the body, always modified by the social categories through which it is known, sustains a particular view of society. There is a continual exchange of meanings between the two kinds of bodily experience so that each reinforces the categories of the other. As a result of this interaction the body itself is a highly restricted medium of expression. The forms it adopts in movement and repose express social pressures in manifold ways. The care that is given to it, in grooming, feeding and therapy, the theories about what it needs in the way of sleep and exercise, about the stages it should go through, the pains it can stand, its span of life, all the cultural categories in which it is perceived, must correlate closely with the categories in which society is seen in so far as these also draw upon the same culturally processed idea of the body.[3]

One of the arguments of this paper will be that the ascetic deconstruction of the body also carries implicit meanings with regard to society and socially sanctioned roles and values.

I will focus here on four major themes in the ascetic deconstruction of the body: (1) the physical body; (2) sexuality; (3) food; and (4) hair.

Body without Boundaries

If, with Mary Douglas (1984), we define dirt as matter out of place, then it seems that, at least as far as the social perception of the human body is concerned, dirt gathers predominantly on its margins and in a special way at the openings that lets the inside of the body meet the outside both by letting bodily excreta and fluids flow out and by permitting outside elements—especially food and water—to come inside. The protection of these boundaries has been a major preoccupation of most traditional religions, and the Indian are no exception. Especially within the Brāhmaṇical tradition, maintaining the purity of the body was and continues to be a major element of ritual and morality. Mary Douglas (1982) again has argued, convincingly I believe, that anxiety about bodily margins and the preoccupation with keeping them clean express anxieties about social integrity and concern for maintaining social order. This anxiety and the resultant preoccupation with bodily purity increase with the increase in the perceived threat to the integrity of the social body. As throughout their history the Israelites were a minority threatened with the loss of group identity, so each Hindu caste—especially the Brahmins—was a minority vis-à-vis the larger society. Both the Jews and the Brahmins show a similar anxiety about the body and bodily fluids. The Brahmin anxiety has to varying degrees pervaded other castes of Indian society.[4] It is, nevertheless, the Brahmin ideology and practice that is the counterpoint for much of ascetic rhetoric and behavior.

In Brāhmaṇical ideology, then, the body is by definition a pure structure constantly threatened at its boundaries with impurity, both through the discharge of bodily fluids and excrement and from contact with impure substances and individuals. There are thus minute prescriptions regarding the maintenance of bodily purity: when and how to bathe; how to purify after eating, defecating, and urinating, sexual intercourse and menstruation, touching anything or anybody impure; what to eat; from whom to accept food; with whom one can have sexual, social, or physical contact; and so on.

The ascetic deconstruction begins with the body itself. Far from being something intrinsically pure that is under the constant threat of impurity, ascetic discourse presents the body as impure in its very essence, the source indeed of all pollution. Here, for example, is a tongue-in-cheek parody of the Brāhmaṇical effort at maintaining purity by constant bathing:

> Made with its mother's and father's filth, this body dies soon after it is born. It is a filthy house of joy and grief. When it is touched a bath is ordained.
>
> By its very nature, foul secretions continuously ooze out from its nine openings. It smells foul and it contains awful filth. When it is touched a bath is ordained.
>
> Through its mother the body is impure at birth; in birth-impurity it is born. It is impure also through death. When it is touched a bath is ordained.[5]

Society itself views the sexual act as impure and requires the couple to bathe after it to restore purity to their bodies. The ascetic deconstruction shows the futility of this, since the body itself is created from that impure act. The body is thus intrinsically and at its very source impure, molded out of its parents' filthy sexual fluids. The birth of a child in Brāhmaṇical practice, likewise, results in impurity and requires a bath. So does death. But the body cannot be purified from those events, argues the ascetic, because they are not events external to the body, but constitute its very essence. The ascetic author concludes that after touching the body one must surely bathe. But of course that is impossible, because one is constantly in touch with one's body. That is the dilemma of an embodied being. The deconstruction thus begins with familiar concepts, but subverts their meanings and demonstrates their inadequacy.

> Lord, this body is produced just by sexual intercourse and is devoid of consciousness; it is a veritable hell. Born through the urinary canal, it is built with bones, plastered with flesh, and covered with skin. It is filled with feces, urine, wind, bile, phlegm, marrow, fat, serum, and many other kinds of filth. In such a body do I live.[6]

This prayer of an ascetic points out several significant aspects of the ascetic deconstruction. The body is impure in its very creation, produced, as it is, by sexual intercourse and born through the urinary canal. Note the constant association of the body with excrement and bodily discharges. The body is also dissociated from consciousness, the familiar dichotomy between body and spirit. Detached from the spirit, the body—and, I believe, the society of which it is the symbol—is devalued as worthless. Indeed, we find this separation of consciousness from the body in several Indian theologies with deep ascetic roots, such as Sāṃkhya, Yoga, Jainism, and Advaita Vedānta. Even in Buddhism, which regards consciousness as one of the five elements that constitute an individual in *saṃsāric* existence (cycle of matter, thoughts, and events), that consciousness, together with the other bodily properties, is carefully separated from the ultimate dimension of nirvāṇa, however that may be defined.

Further, in the above passage the body is compared implicitly to a house, an image we encounter frequently and more explicitly in ascetic literature. The most significant aspect of this analogy is the contents of this house: feces, urine, phlegm, fat, and the like—the very substances that Brāhmaṇical practice regards as causing bodily impurity. If the body itself consists of these substances, how can it be made pure? What can purify the very source of impurity? These impurities do not exist at the boundaries of the body but at its very heart. What purpose is there in protecting the boundaries when the danger is present within?

A medieval work compares the body explicitly to a house full of filth. The purpose of this comparison is to instill a sense of loathing towards the body and a desire to be rid of it.

> Let him abandon this impermanent dwelling place of the elements. It has beams of bones tied with tendons. It is plastered with flesh and blood and thatched with skin. It is foul-smelling, filled with feces and urine, and infested with old-age and grief. Covered with dust and harassed by pain, it is the abode of disease.
>
> If a man finds joy in the body—a heap of flesh, blood, pus, feces, urine, tendons, marrow, and bones—that fool will find joy even in hell.[7]
>
> Those who take delight in this collection of skin, flesh, blood, tendons, marrow, fat, and bones, stinking with feces and urine—what difference is there between them and worms?[8]

These passages invite the listener to look upon the body not as a whole—an illusory perspective that presents the body as beautiful and pure—but as it truly is when it is dissolved into its constituent parts. When they are found separately, society considers them to be impure. People are polluted when they touch human bones, flesh, blood, pus, and excrement. How, then, can the body be pure or beautiful when it contains and consists of these very substances? The body is thus likened to a rubbish heap or to a putrefying corpse inhabited by worms. People who find delight in their own bodies and those of others are thus likened to worms; both revel in putrid matter and excrement.

The very boundary of the body that people take such great care in keeping pure consists of skin. Now dead skin is an extremely polluting substance; tanners and leather workers in India belong to a very low caste, and their very touch pollutes a person of an upper caste. But, the ascetic argues, our body is covered with precisely that skin, which should make us even more impure than an untouchable tanner!

The parallel between body and house is interesting as much for its deconstruction of the body and the house, both nearly universal symbols of society, as for its resonance with the ascetic practice of leaving home and family and leading a homeless and wandering life. The conception of the house as a body and the body as a house is not confined to the Hindu ascetic traditions. The Buddhist text *Visuddhimagga,* for example, states:

> Just as when a space is enclosed by timbers, creepers, grass and clay, it is called a "house," so when a space is enclosed by bones, sinews, flesh and skin, it comes to be called "body."[9]

This correlation between the images of house and body is not the invention, however, of the ascetic traditions. Indian culture in general has conceived of the building of a temple or a house not as a construction project but as a conception leading to a birth (Beck 1976). Daniels (1984) has described how in modern South India a house is conceived as a body, with the mouth and face in the front, the belly (kitchen) at the center, and the excretory openings at the back. Indians attend meticulously to maintaining the purity of both their bodies and their houses.[10] This well-established correlation permits the ascetic to deconstruct both: the body is like a house full of filth and the house itself contains filthy bodies and hides filthy activities, especially sex. The same Sanskrit word, *gṛha,* means both home and house. It conveys the same sense of warmth and security to Indian listeners as it does to the western, a sense admirably captured by Gaston Bachelard in *The Poetics of Space:*

> A house constitutes a body of images that give mankind proofs or illusions of stability. We are constantly re-imagining its reality: to distinguish all these images would be to describe the soul of the house; it would mean developing a veritable psychology of the house. *Bachelard 1964:17*

Ascetic discourse attempts to reverse this feeling by focusing on the possibility that this very womb of comfort, security, and stability may become the source of fear, danger, and death, as when a house is on fire or harbors a snake.

I will examine in the third section of this paper a Buddhist myth of origins that has counterparts also in the Hindu mythological complex (Olivelle 1991), a myth that depicts the gradual deterioration of the world set in motion by, of all things, eating food. Food causes, among other things, the differentiation of sexes. When men and women emerged as sexually distinct individuals, some began to engage in sexual intercourse. Seeing this, others were scandalized and threw dirt at those depraved beings. The latter then built houses to hide their sexual activities! Sexually differentiated bodies, the lust arising out of that differentiation, the sexual acts resulting from lust, and houses where those acts take place are neatly brought together here. From the ascetic perspective, therefore, all of them have negative connotations.

A house carried a deeply negative value in the Indian ascetic tradition of wandering mendicants. Departure from home to the homeless state was the defining element of this form of asceticism within Brāhmaṇical, Buddhist, and Jain traditions. "He leaves home for the homeless state" *(agārasmā anagāriyaṃ pabbajati)* is a stock phrase in the Pāli canon. The words *pravrajati* (he goes forth or he departs) and *pravrajyā* (going forth) are used in all these traditions as technical terms for the rite for becoming an ascetic. These terms refer to the ascetic's initial departure from home to the homeless state. The absence of a permanent residence has remained—at least in theory, ritual, and legal fiction, but occasionally also in practice—a defining element of mendicant asceticism throughout its history, even after many of these ascetic traditions had adopted monastic forms of life. So when the ascetic traditions compare a body to a house, it is a telling comparison. The stability and security of a house is just as illusory as that of a body. A house represents all that is evil in social living: lust, sex, attachment, and prolongation of *saṃsāric* life. An ascetic has rejected it and freed himself from home. But he carries a second home with him, and that is his own body. It is this more intimate "house" toward which the rhetoric of deconstruction is directed so as to elicit in the ascetic a sense of repugnance toward the body, and implicitly towards society of which it is a symbol.

We saw how ascetic literature dwells on bodily components to illustrate the radical impurity of the body. Another strategy is to contemplate the body as bereft of the conscious life-giving spirit. Brāhmaṇical ascetics are frequently encouraged to contemplate their body as a corpse.[11] Buddhist meditative practice also adopts the technique of deconstructing the body by mentally dissecting it and by seeing it as a lifeless corpse. The *Visuddhimagga* (chapter 6) advises Buddhist monks to meditate on a corpse in various stages of dismemberment and putrefaction: swollen, discolored, festering, cut up, mangled, dismembered, bloody, filled with worms, and finally a skeleton. In the meditative technique of *satipaṭṭhāna* (mindfulness), one contemplates, among other things, one's own body. "This contemplation opens," Nyanaponika Thera (1962:65) comments,

> as it were with a scalpel, the skin of this body of ours, and exposes to view what is hidden under it. This mental dissection dissolves the vaguely held notion of the oneness of the body, by pointing to its various parts; it removes the delusion of the body's beauty, by revealing its impurity. When visualizing the body as a walking skeleton loosely covered by flesh and skin, or seeing it as a conglomeration of its various strangely-shaped parts, one will feel little inclination to identify oneself with one's so-called "own" body, or to desire that of another being.

The *Mahāsatipaṭṭhāna Sutta* of the Pāli canon, the basic text on which the Theravāda meditative practice is based, echoes the Brāhmaṇical texts in explaining the reality of the human body.

> And again, monks, a monk reflects upon this very body, from the soles of his feet up and from the crown of his head down, enclosed by the skin and full of impurities, thinking thus: "There are in this body: hair of the head, hair of the body, nails, teeth, skin, flesh, sinews, bones, marrow, kidneys, heart, liver, pleura, spleen, lungs, intestines, mesentery, gorge, faeces, bile, phlegm, pus, blood, sweat, solid fat, liquid fat, saliva, mucus, synovic fluid, urine."[12]

The body, therefore, is not a single bounded reality, whose boundaries are threatened with contamination and need to be carefully protected. In reality, it is simply an aggregate of substances that are in themselves impure and loathsome. These substances are contained in a bag of skin with nine openings out of which they continuously ooze out. And we call it our body! Only one kind of attitude and feeling is appropriate with regard to such a thing: a feeling of disgust accompanied by a desire to be rid of it.

Sexuality and Procreation

Two activities constitute the very heart of Vedic theology and religion: sacrifice and procreation (Olivelle 1993:35–55). Only a married man accompanied by his lawful wife could legitimately undertake either of these activities. Marriage and family constituted, therefore, the foundation as much of Vedic religion as of Vedic society. Creation itself is often depicted as an act of procreation by the creator god Prajāpati, and the working of the sacrifice is likened to the procreative process. Sacrifice, creation and procreation are all intertwined in the images and thought of Vedic theology.

Immortality itself, Vedic texts argue, is dependent on procreation. A Ṛgvedic verse (5.4.10) contains this prayer: "Through offspring, O Agni, may we attain immortality." The *Taittirīya Brāhmaṇa* (1.5.5.6) puts it in a nutshell: "In your offspring you are born again; that, O mortal, is your immortality." The importance of marriage and the obligation to father a son are central and recurrent themes of Brāhmaṇical theology.

> A full half of one's self is one's wife. As long as one does not obtain a wife, therefore, for so long one is not reborn and remains incomplete. As soon as he obtains a wife, however, he is reborn and becomes complete. *Satapatha Brāhmaṇa, 5.2.1.10*

A man is reborn in the wife when he deposits his semen in her and she conceives a son. One of the most eloquent statements on the importance of offspring in general and of sons in particular is found in the *Aitareya Brāhmana* (7.13):

> A debt[13] he pays in him,
> and immortality he gains;
> The father who sees the face
> of his son born and alive.
>
> Greater than the delights
> that earth, fire, and water
> bring to living beings,
> is a father's delight in his son.
>
> By means of sons have fathers ever
> crossed over the mighty darkness;
> For one is born from oneself
> a ferry laden with food.
>
> What is the use of dirt and deer skin?
> What profit in beard and austerity?[14]
> Seek a son, O Brahmin;
> He is the world free of blame.

Food is life, clothes protect.
Gold is for beauty, cattle for marriage.
The wife is a friend, a daughter brings grief.
  But a son is a light in the highest heaven.

The husband enters the wife;
  becoming an embryo he enters the mother.
Becoming in her a new man again,
  he is born in the tenth month.

A wife is called wife,[15]
  because in her he is born again.
He is productive, she's productive,
  for the seed is placed in her.

The gods and the seers
  brought to her great luster.
The gods said to men:
  "She is your mother again."

"A sonless man has no world";
  all the beasts know this.
Therefore a son mounts
  even his mother and sister.

This is the broad and easy path
  along which travel men with sons, free from sorrow;
Beasts and birds see it;
  so they copulate even with their mothers.

The son, therefore, is the father reborn; in him and his descendants the father continues to live, and through them he attains immortality. A classical Indian law book puts it this way:

> Through a son one wins the worlds, through a grandson one attains eternal life, and through one's son's grandson one ascends the very summit of heaven. A man saves himself by begetting a virtuous son. A man who obtains a virtuous son saves from the fear of sin seven generations—that is, six others with himself as the seventh—both before him and after him. . . . Therefore, he should assiduously beget offspring.[16]

In sharp contrast to this construction of human sexuality stands the ideal of celibacy in Indian asceticism. I want to focus here on just two aspects of the ascetic deconstruction of sexuality: the son and the female body. The first is the central element of the Vedic theology of sexuality. The second is the object of male desire, and the subject of poetic imagination.

Within the ideology of rebirth, karmic retribution, and *mokṣa* (final liberation) which emerged as the Vedic period came to a close (around the fifth century BCE), the son is not viewed either as assuring bliss after death or securing immortality for the father. The son and the sexual lust inherent in fathering offspring are regarded instead as two of the main sources of desire and attachment that keep people bound to the rounds of birth and death. An early Upaniṣadic passage states that the wise give up all desires, including the desire for a son, and live a life of celibacy as wandering mendicants.[17] Sons and sacrifices may secure heavenly worlds. But these are temporary joys that will come to an end. The world that the ascetic seeks is his own *ātman* (self), and no person other than himself can secure it for him.

The ascetic deconstruction of the son also depicts him as a source of constant pain and headaches for the father rather than a source of solace here and hereafter. An early Buddhist text presents Māra, the god of death and evil, as upholding the traditional values. "A *puttimā* [father: lit. "a man with sons"] rejoices in his sons," says Māra. To which the Buddha replies: "A father grieves on account of his sons."[18] The Buddha does not spell out how a son brings grief to his father. One sure way, however, is the attachment a father feels towards his son, an attachment that will prolong his saṃsāric life of suffering. Ascetic literature identifies this attachment as one of the primary links to the world that an ascetic must sever in order to seek personal liberation.

Verses cited in several medieval works from the Brāhmaṇical tradition give other and more immediate reasons for avoiding marriage and sons.

> A son, when he is not conceived, long torments the parents. When conceived, he causes pain by miscarriage or in delivery. When he is born one has to contend with the influence of evil planets, illnesses, and the like. When he is young he takes to mischief. Even after he has undergone Vedic initiation, he may not learn, and should he become learned he may not get married. As a young man he may commit adultery and the like. When he has a family he may become penniless. If he is rich then he may die. There is no end to the suffering caused by a son.[19]

Apart from the ideological battle regarding the religious importance of a son, the ascetic traditions had a more immediate concern regarding human sexuality: sexual instincts do not die merely because a man has cut his family ties and become an ascetic. In the fantasy world of the ascetic, the female body must have occupied a prominent place, judging from the frequent allusions to the loathsome nature of a woman's body and to the dangers that women pose. Misogynous attitudes and statements, of course, are not limited to ascetic literature; they are found in most Brāhmaṇical texts. In ascetic works, however, the tone is harsher and the intent is not just mistrust but total abhorrence of the female species. "A man becomes intoxicated," one ascetic text declares, "by seeing a young woman just as much as by drinking liquor. Therefore, a man should avoid from afar a woman, the mere sight of whom is poison."[20] The perfect ascetic may be like an eunuch, "who remains the same when he sees a sixteen-year-old young lady, as when he sees a newborn girl or a hundred-year-old woman,"[21] but most ascetics are undoubtedly moved by the youthful female body. This internal attraction is often externalized and projected onto the object of desire in ascetic texts: women are depicted as evil temptresses who want to entrap the hapless ascetic.

> With stylish hair and painted eyes, hard to touch but pleasing to the eye, women are like the flame of sin and burn a man like straw.

> Burning from afar, sweet yet bitter, women indeed are the fuel of hellfire, both lovely and cruel. Foolish women are the nets spread out by the fowler called Kāma,[22] binding the limbs of men as if they were birds.
>
> A woman is the bait on the fishhook tied to the line of evil tendencies for men who are like fish in the pond of birth, wading in the mud of the mind.[23]

Liquor intoxicates when it is drunk, fire burns when it is touched, snakes kill when they bite, but women do all that by their mere sight!

India may be the land of ascetics, but it is also home to some of the best and most explicit erotic sculpture, art, and literature the world has known. Cultured courtesans occupied a place of honor in ancient Indian society. Erotic love and sexual techniques became the subject of specialized inquiry in texts such as the *Kāmasūtra* long before the advent of Masters and Johnson. This "worldly" tradition of artistic expression saw the female body as the epitome of beauty and the source of both erotic and aesthetic joy. Sanskrit belles-lettres dwell on the beauty of the female body, describing tenderly the charm of a woman's eyes, lips, hair, breasts, hips, and so forth. The poet Bilhāna reminisces longingly on the beauty of his lover.

> Even now,
> if I see her again,
> her full moon face, lush new youth,
> swollen breasts, passion's glow,
> body burned by fire from love's arrows—
> I'll quickly cool her limbs!
>
> Even now,
> if I see her again,
> a lotus-eyed girl
> weary from bearing her own heavy breasts—
> I'll crush her in my arms
> and drink her mouth like a madman,
> a bee insatiably drinking a lotus!
>
> Even now,
> I remember her in love—
> her body weak with fatigue,
> swarms of curling hair
> falling on pale cheeks,
> trying to hide
> the secret of her guilt.
> Her soft arms
> clung
> like vines on my neck.[24]

And the greatest of Indian poets, Kālidāsa, paints this picture of Śakuntalā, the forest girl of heavenly beauty:

With rounded breasts concealed by cloth of bark
fastened at the shoulder in a fine knot,
her youthful form enfolded like a flower
in its pale leafy sheath unfolds not its glory.

Her lower lip has the rich sheen of young shoots,
her arms the very grace of tender twining stems;
her limbs enchanting as a lovely flower
glow with the radiance of magical youth.[25]

Even Bhartṛhari, in his ode to renunciation, admits:

Renunciation of worldly attachments
is only the talk of scholars,
whose mouths are wordy with wisdom.

Who can really forsake the hips
of beautiful women bound
with girdles of ruby jewels?[26]

Ascetic deconstruction seeks to dispel this male fascination with and fantasy about the female body by analyzing what it regards as the reality behind its imagined beauty.

> What, pray, is the beauty of a woman, who is a puppet of flesh furnished with tendons, bones, and joints, within a cage of limbs moved by a machine?
>
> Examine her eyes after separating the skin, the flesh, the blood, the tears, and the fluid, and see if there is any charm. Why are you bewitched in vain?
>
> The same breast of a girl, on which we see the brilliant splendor of a pearl necklace comparable to the swift waters of the Ganges rippling down the slopes of mount Meru, is in time eaten with relish by dogs in remote cemeteries as if it were a little morsel of food.[27]

The author here resorts to surgical dissection to uncover the hidden beauty of the female eye, so lovingly described by poets, and finds only blood, skin, veins, and other impurities. Of beauty there is none. Another text focuses directly on the final object of sexual passion: the vagina. Why, the author wonders, are people enamored by this opening of flesh that is foul smelling and resembles a festering wound?

> Even though a woman's private parts are not different from a deep and festering ulcer, men generally deceive themselves by imagining them to be different.
>
> I salute those who take delight in a piece of skin split in two scented by the breaking of the wind! What could be more rash?[28]

A significant aspect of the ascetic deconstruction of the body in general and of the female body in particular is the association of the body or of particular parts of the body, such as the vagina, with urine and excrement. Within the context of Brāhmaṇical culture which considered bodily excreta as extremely defiling, this association evokes feelings of disgust, precisely the feelings that ascetics are expected to have with regard to the body.

Such attitudes with regard to the female body is not confined to Brāhmaṇical asceticism. I want to mention just one example from the Jain ascetic tradition. Padmanabh Jaini (1991) has recently studied a long-standing Jain controversy regarding the possibility of women achieving *strīmokṣa* (liberation). One argument against such a possibility is of interest to our study. The Digambara Jains who reject the possibility of female liberation present two reasons. First, ascetic nudity is essential for liberation, but women cannot go naked. Second, women cannot be ordained ascetics, because women's bodies produce small creatures. These creatures are killed when women purify themselves. Thus it is impossible for women to observe the fundamental Jain vow of *ahiṃsā* (noninjury).

> [A nun] eats only one meal a day and wears a single piece of cloth. According to the Teaching of the Jina, a person wearing clothes cannot attain mokṣa even if he be a Tīrthaṅkara. The path of mokṣa consists of nudity; all other paths are wrong paths.
>
> In the genital organs of women, in between their breasts, in their navels, and in the armpits, it is said [in the scriptures that] there are very subtle living beings. How can there be the mendicant ordination for them [since they must violate the vow of ahiṃsā]?
>
> Women have no purity of mind; they are by nature fickle-minded. They have menstrual flows. [Therefore] there is no meditation for them free from anxiety.[29]

Although this conception of women relates to a theological debate, it parallels the Brāhmaṇical conceptions examined earlier. The reason for the inferiority of women is the very constitution of their bodies which are subject to menstrual flows, which harbor living creatures, and which cannot be revealed naked in public.

Food

Because I have written a longer article on this topic recently (Olivelle 1991), I will here summarize some of the observations I made there. In few other cultures does food play as central a role in cosmological speculations, ritual practice, and social transactions as in India (Khare 1976; Marriott 1968). Not only is the creative act closely associated with the creation of food in Brāhmaṇical myths and theology, but even the creator god Prajāpati is often depicted as food. The whole of creation consists of food and eaters of food; but because food is food only when it is eaten, and the eater in its turn become the eaten, one can equate reality with food. The centrality of food in ancient Indian cosmology is highlighted in the speculations regarding the cycle of beings. Food when eaten becomes semen, and from semen arises a person. Indeed, in some Upaniṣadic speculations food itself is a dead person transformed: when he is cremated, the dead person becomes smoke, rises to the sky and through a complicated process, the details of which we do not have the time to investigate, returns as rain, which is transformed into plants, food, and finally into semen and a new birth.[30]

The continued existence of the universe depends, moreover, on ritual food transactions between gods and humans. It is well known that every Indian ritual from the earliest Vedic sacrifices to the recent devotional liturgies involves offering food to the gods (Khare 1992). The law book of *Manu* (3.76) puts it plainly:

> An oblation duly offered in the fire reaches the sun; from the sun comes rain, and from rain food, and thereby living creatures derive their sustenance.

This then is the ritual food chain: sacrifice, rain, plants, food, procreation.

The ritual use of food underscores both its centrality at the cosmic and social levels and its inherently transactional nature. Food is the central element of a cosmic transaction that maintains both the social and the physical cosmos. Food becomes plentiful only when it is shared. The didactic literature admonishes people not to cook for themselves alone; such food becomes poison.[31] Indian food transactions include all known beings: gods, ancestors, various divine and demonic beings, and human guests and beggars. The interdependence of all beings within the cosmic chain is expressed in this socio-ritual-cosmic food transaction. The cosmos, indeed, is a giant food cycle (Khare 1976).

The regulation and restriction of food transactions between humans, moreover, is at the root of social stratification and caste distinctions (Marriott 1968).

> Historical and textual studies as well as substantial ethnographic research show that Hindu culture in India has preserved, throughout its history, a set of core cultural assumptions concerning the link between human society, food transactions, and divinity. These assumptions are: that the interdependence of men and gods depends on ritual transactions of food between them; that the distinctiveness of various groups in Hindu society as well as the relationship between such groups is *ritually constructed* in such food transactions with the gods; and lastly, that the ritual concentration and redistribution of food is a critical mechanism for the formation of social groups and the articulation of leadership [original italics].
>
> *Breckenridge 1986:24*

Food, therefore, plays a central role in the socio-cultural construction of reality in India. Rules of proper and improper food provide a clear cultural definition of food. Rules regarding food transactions constitute a social code that strengthens the hierarchical organization of castes and demarcates the boundaries of purity. The rules that surround all aspects of food in Indian society can thus be seen as constituting an elaborate food code.

Ascetic ideology and practice, however, presents an interesting counterpoint to the socially constructed reality of food. The ascetic attitude towards food can be broadly described as one of fear and ambivalence. On the one hand, one has to eat and is therefore dependent on food. On the other hand, food is what keeps *saṃsāra* going and is, therefore, inimical to the whole ascetic enterprise. This ambivalence has created what I would characterize as an obsession with food within Indian ascetic traditions.

Indeed, the relationship to food—how one procures it, how long one stores it, and how and whether one eats it—is a defining characteristic of Indian asceticism in general as well as of individual ascetic orders and sects. A common name for wandering ascetics—*bhikṣu* or beggar—points to this relationship. Mendicant ascetics do not own or produce food and are totally dependent on the generosity of others for their sustenance. Forest hermits show a different relationship to food: they are food gatherers. Their food is not mediated by culture and consists of wild and uncultivated fruits, leaves, roots, and the like. Most Brāhmaṇical classifications of ascetics, moreover, are based on the way ascetics procure, store, and consume food.

There are four areas of the human relationship to food that play significant roles in ascetic food practices: production or procurement, storage, preparation, and consumption. In each of these areas, people expend enormous effort and energy, which I will call the human food effort. The major pattern that emerges from ascetic food practices is the minimization and, at some levels, even the elimination of the human food effort in each of these four areas. At the level of production, ascetic behavior demonstrates a progressive lessening of effort. All Indian ascetics abandon cultural mediation in procuring/producing their food. This, indeed, appears to be a hallmark of Indian asceticism. Both the mendicant and the hermit are, each in his own way, food gatherers. Hermits gather from the forest, renouncers gather or beg from people. In several Brāhmaṇical classifications of mendicants, the highest type does not direct any effort at all toward procuring food and are said to observe the "python vow:" they remain still like a python awaiting what they may receive by chance.

The length of food storage is the most frequent criterion for the classification of hermits; the highest do not store at all, eating what they gather each day. All mendicants follow the same rule of not storing anything for the morrow. They are, moreover, forbidden to cook, the absence of fire being a hallmark of mendicant ascetics.

When the minimization of the food effort is taken to its logical conclusion, an ascetic would not even make the effort to take food into his mouth or to swallow it. This is religious suicide by fasting, a well-known and respected way of ending life in numerous Hindu and non-Hindu traditions, especially the Jain (Dundas 1985; Settar 1986, 1990).

The ascetic attitude toward food is the very antithesis of the boast recorded in the *Taittirīya Upaniṣad* (3.10.6):

> Wonderful! Wonderful! Wonderful!
> I am food! I am food! I am food!
> I am the eater of food! Eater of food! Eater of food!

and of the value placed on having plenty of food:

> According to the Veda, one's diet was overdetermined. Eating was simultaneously an act of nourishment, a display of wealth and status, and a demonstration of domination over that which was eaten. In all cases, to eat one's proper food was to participate in a natural and cosmic order of things. *Smith 1990:178*

The minimization of the food effort, which is a major principle behind ascetic food practices, is based on the ascetic ideology that sees creation as something deeply flawed and from which one must seek liberation. The Vedic tradition's close association between food and creation would generate positive attitudes with regard to food if creation and human life are considered positively as things of value. If, however, creation is regarded as a fall from a more perfect state, then the same cosmic role of food would necessarily impart a negative value to food. This is what appears to have happened within the context of the *saṃsāric* view of creation shared by all ascetic traditions.

An interesting confirmation of this comes from a Buddhist myth found in the *Aggañña Sutta* of the *Dīgha Nikāya.*[32] In the beginning, before the appearance of the sun and the moon, there existed beings without sexual or other distinctions. This is presented as a paradisiacal state. Then on the primordial cosmic water there appeared a sort of scum tasting like honey. The beings made the fatal mistake of eating this scum. This first eating of food set in motion a series of events that gave rise to the world as it is. All the significant moments of this process involved eating, which made the beings more coarse and food more scarce. As the eating progressed the early forms of spontaneous food was replaced by rice. This primordial rice was without the husk or brown powder that today covers the grain. It did not have to be cultivated, and it could be eaten as it was picked. As they continued to eat that rice sexual differentiation emerged among those beings: men and women appeared. Lust and passion entered their hearts and they began to have sexual intercourse with each other. The origin of houses, as we have seen, is traced to these depraved acts; they built them to hide their acts from others!

The event that finally destroyed the early paradisiacal state was the act of food storage. Until then rice had grown spontaneously in a form that needed no preparation and was ready to be eaten. When one crop was gathered, another appeared the next day. Some of those people, however, were lazy and did not want to go out each morning and evening to gather rice. They began to fetch rice sufficient for more than one day. As they hoarded rice, powder and husk began to envelop the grain, and when reaped the rice plants did not spontaneously grow back. Rice had to be cultivated. Cultivation led to private property, theft, and the institution of social and governmental structures. All because those primordial beings had started to eat!

In the ideal world nature provides everything humans need. So long as they take only what they need each day, this condition continues. Taking more than one needs, hoarding for the future, creation of ownership: these results of greed are the basic causes of the world's deterioration.

The food code of ascetics has both a cosmological and a soteriological dimension and meaning. The progression of the ascetic withdrawal from the food effort is a mirror image of the progression of cosmic evolution, an evolution produced by the human involvement in the food effort. At one level it signifies the ascetic evaluation of the cosmos and society as negative realities from which the ascetic flees. His very withdrawal from food is an expression of his withdrawal from social and cosmic engagement. He stands outside the food cycle, because he only eats food but never offers it to others, thus inverting the admonition, often repeated, that food must be shared. The food of the ascetic is thus unlike the food of other humans.

The ascetic deconstruction of food transforms its ritual and social meanings. Many sources, for example, ask ascetics to regard food as medicine—something to be taken because of necessity and not for enjoyment, something whose taking lacks the meanings ascribed to it within society and underscores the ascetic perception of the body as a disease in search of a cure.

Hair

In the three decades since the publication of Leach's seminal essay "Magical Hair" (1958), which was itself a response to the naive psychoanalytic work of Berg (1951), the social and anthropological significance of the cultural manipulation of head hair has received long overdue scholarly attention (Hallpike 1969, 1987; Cooper 1971; Firth 1973; Hershman 1974; Lincoln 1977). This is not the place to discuss the controversies between the socio-anthropological and the psychoanalytic interpretations of hair symbolism. I believe, however, that the recent work of Obeyesekere (1981, 1990) has provided us a way of combining the best of both disciplines, an approach I will follow in this study.

There appears, however, to be a scholarly consensus that, cross-culturally, control of head hair marks a person's association with society and his or her participation in social structures (Hallpike 1969, 1987; Douglas 1982:72). Shaving, on the other hand, represents a moment of separation from society. Such separations in India occur during periods of mourning and prior to a life-cycle ritual (van Gennep 1960). Some forms of separation and social marginality (Douglas 1982:85), moreover, are signified by loose and unkempt hair. In the case of women in India, this occurs also during periods of mourning and menstruation, when their hair is left unbraided and unwashed (Hershman 1974). These are the social and what Leach (1958:153) calls the publicly recognized meanings of hair.

Leach (1958) himself acknowledges, however, that much of the ethnographic evidence supports an unconscious association of hair with sexuality: "In ritual situations: long hair = unrestrained sexuality; short hair or partially shaved hair or tightly bound hair = restricted sexuality; close shaven hair = celibacy" (p. 154). Leach, however, separates the unconscious sphere from the social, the former dealing with individual deep motivations and the latter with socially accepted meanings and public means of communication. Obeyesekere objects, rightly I believe, both to Leach's watertight division between private and public symbols and to the psychoanalyst assumption that all symbols must have deep motivational significance. He makes a useful distinction between personal symbols involving deep motivational significance and what he calls psychogenetic symbols, which originate in the unconscious but acquire conventional and publicly available meanings. "Symbols originating from unconscious sources," Obeyesekere (1981) observes, "are used to give expression to meanings that have nothing to do with their origin" (pp. 13–14). These operational meanings of symbols such as hair should be analytically distinguished from their deep motivational genesis. In his recent work *The Work of Culture* (1990), Obeyesekere calls this distinction symbolic remove. A symbol may operate at different levels of symbolic remove from its genesis in deep motivation "producing different levels of symbolization, some closer to, some more distant from the motivations that initially (psychogenetically) triggered the symbolic formation" (Obeyesekere 1990:57).

The public meaning of separation from society as well as the unconscious sexual associations of shaven and unkempt hair are operative in the symbolic complex of the hair of Indian ascetics.[33] Ascetic hair in India comes in two forms: it may be completely shaved or it may be left unkempt and thus become matted. The former is associated with wandering mendicants, including Hindu *saṃnyāsins* as well as Buddhist and Jain monks, who are ritually separated from society but return to it to beg their food and who operate within it as holy men and teachers. The latter is obligatory for forest hermits who are physically separated from society.

Let us take up first the case of matted-haired ascetics. To understand adequately the symbolism of matted hair it is necessary to locate it within the larger grammar of the symbols associated with the physical withdrawal from society. Besides long and matted hair, bodily symbols include long and uncut beard in the case of males, long and uncut nails, eating only uncultivated forest produce, clothes of tree bark or animal skin, and frequently also bodily uncleanliness. People with matted hair are required to live in the forest and not to enter a village; they are repeatedly admonished not to step on plowed land,[34] the prime symbol of civilized geography. They are said to imitate the habits of wild animals. One can decipher from this symbolic grammar the following statement: a matted-haired individual renounces all culturally mediated products and institutions and all culturally demarcated geographical areas. He or she leaves social structures and return to the state of nature and to the way of life of wild animals. Not grooming the hair, not controlling it in any way, letting it grow naturally into a matted condition—all this symbolizes a person's total and absolute withdrawal from social space, structures, and controls.

Mary Douglas (1982) has drawn attention to the correspondence between social control and bodily control:

> If there is no concern to preserve social boundaries, I would not expect to find concern with bodily boundaries. The relation of head to feet, of brain and sexual organs, of mouth and anus are commonly treated so that they express the relevant patterns of hierarchy. Consequently I now advance the hypothesis that bodily control is an expression of social control—abandonment of bodily control in ritual responds to the requirements of a social experience which is being expressed.[35]

Matted-haired ascetics of India are a prime example of total neglect of bodily boundaries resulting in the utter lack of control of those boundaries. Nails, beard, hair—they are all left uncontrolled. This lack of concern for bodily boundaries, as Mary Douglas's hypothesis predicts, is accompanied by total withdrawal from society and socially defined space.

Leach and others consider long and uncontrolled hair as equivalent to sexual license. While in a given case this may be true, in a publicly available symbol such as the Indian matted hair there is a considerable symbolic remove between its operational meaning and its possible unconscious sexual associations. It is clear that sexual license was not a characteristic of Indian matted-haired ascetics. Here the primary public meaning of matted hair appears to be the total physical separation from society and social boundaries. Thus the matted hair and other outward insignia of a forest hermit are employed even when a person is sent into political exile, the most prominent case of which is that of Rāma and his wife Sītā. The unconscious associations, however, have some relevance, because the sexuality of the matted-haired ascetic has always remained ambiguous, in stark contrast to the universally accepted celibacy of the shaven-haired ascetic. In any case, celibacy is not a hallmark of matted-haired hermits of India.

Let us now turn to the shaven-headed ascetics. A central feature of the rites of initiation into the ascetic life in all traditions—Hindu, Buddhist, and Jain—is the removal of the hair of the head and, for males, of the face. Although, as we shall see, there are clear sexual implications in shaving the head, I believe that its central social message is not that of castration, as many have argued, but the ritual (as opposed to the physical) separation from society of the shaven ascetic. The message of ascetic shaving cannot be totally different from the message inherent in the spectrum of Indian rites involving shaving. And that message is not principally about sex but about society, or, more accurately, about the ritual separation from society. The shaven head of an ascetic, just as much as the shaven head of an initiated student, a widow, or a criminal, proclaims that the individual is not part of society and has no social role or status.

Sexual symbolism, however, is not lacking. All people ritually shaven, not just ascetics, are forbidden to engage in sex. For most this is a temporary condition required by a rite of passage or necessitated by ritual pollution, but for the ascetic it is permanent, and therein lies the difference between ascetic and other forms of ritual shaving. Social control is primarily sexual control, and the controlled hair of social individuals symbolizes their participation in the socially sanctioned structures for sexual expression, especially marriage. Removal of hair separates the individual from that structure and from the legitimate exercise of sexual activity. Shaving for the ascetic, I believe, indicates his or her removal from socially sanctioned sexual structures and also from other types of social structures and roles. In the Indian context, this implies loss of caste, inability to own property, and lack of legal standing in a court of law.

Elements of the ascetic initiatory ritual indicate, furthermore, that shaving symbolizes the return to the sexually and socially undifferentiated status of an infant. During the Hindu ritual, for example, the shaven ascetic takes off all his clothes. The naked renouncer is significantly called *jātarūpadhara,* which literally means "one who bears the form one had at birth." The ascetic is not just naked; he is reduced to the condition in which he was born, to the state of a new-born infant. I believe that shaving is part of the symbolic complex that signifies his return to the form he had at birth. The absence of hair, just as much as nakedness, takes the initiate back to the prepubertal state of infancy.

The sexual symbolism of hair also helps explain some interesting features of ascetic behavior toward hair. It is well known that Jain monks at their initiation and periodically throughout their life remove the hair of their head by the painful procedure of plucking them from their roots. That this custom was not limited to the Jains is demonstrated by its presence in a somewhat abbreviated form in the Hindu ritual of ascetic initiation. Here the ascetic's hair is first shaved, but five or seven hairs at the crown are left uncut. At the conclusion of the rite the ascetic plucks these few hairs from the roots. Now, one may attribute this practice to the common ascetic propensity to bodily torture and pain. But I think that this literal eradication of hair can be viewed as a symbolic uprooting of sexual drives and attachments, a ritual castration.

That shaving is the opposite of sexual engagement is also brought out in the way Hindu ascetics shave their heads during the annual liturgical cycle. They are not allowed to shave any time they want to. Rather the prescribed time for shaving is at the junctures between the five Indian seasons: spring, summer, rains, autumn, and winter. Now the Sanskrit term for season is *ṛtu,* the same term that is used to indicate the monthly menstrual cycle of a woman. A husband is required to have sexual intercourse with his wife in the *ṛtu,* that is soon after the end of her menstrual period when a new season begins for his wife. I think it is not farfetched to see a correspondence between the husband approaching his wife at the beginning of her season, and the ascetic shaving his head at the beginning of a season. This shaving appears to symbolize an ascetic's renunciation of sex precisely at the time when the ethics of society requires a man to engage in it.

Mary Douglas (1982) has argued, convincingly I believe, that there is a direct correspondence between social experience and bodily expression. Ecstatic states, spirit possessions, and lack of bodily control depend not as much on psychological maladjustment or economic deprivation as on the experience of weak social constraints. Social marginality is thus expressed through the medium of the body by the slackening of bodily control.

Even within societies with a high degree of control, where, in Douglas's terminology, the group and the grid are strong, there are bound to be individuals and groups that are alienated from or ideologically opposed to the social and religious mainstream. These subsystems also express their alienation through the restricted code of bodily symbols. In such subsystems,

> we can see another restricted code taking over. The body is still the image of society but somewhere inside it someone is not accepting its rule. I am suggesting that the symbolic medium of the body has its restricted code to express and sustain alienation of a sub-category from the wider society. In this code the claims of the body and of the wider society are not highly credited: bodily grooming, diet, pathology, these subjects attract less interest than other non-bodily claims. The body is despised and disregarded, consciousness is conceptually separated from its vehicle and accorded independent honour. Experimenting with consciousness becomes the most personal form of experience, contributing least to the widest social system, and therefore most approved.[36]

Many of the features that Mary Douglas identifies in the subsystems of alienation are precisely those we have seen within the ideology and practice of Indian ascetic traditions. These include antiritualism, neglect of the body, withdrawal from society, an ethic of internal motive, techniques for gaining altered states of consciousness, lack of community, and the lonely quest for personal salvation. The deconstruction of the body we have examined can thus be seen as the expression of an antisocial and individualist ideology through the medium of the body. We can see in this type of religion the rejection of a religious view based on strong social constraints, such as we find in the early Vedic and the later Brāhmaṇical traditions. The rejection of social structures implicit in the deconstruction of the body is also expressed in the ascetic imitation of the life and habits of wild beasts, what may be called the ascetic's adoption of an animal body. Animal symbolism is present in much of Indian ascetic literature, especially in connection with forest hermits. The ascetic impulse to leave society and culturally mediated structures, tools, and geography is nicely captured in this verse:

Moving about with wild beasts,
    and dwelling with them alone;
Living a life just like theirs—
    clearly that's the way to heaven.[37]

But what sort of a social experience creates the ascetic alienation and underlies the ascetic bodily expressions? This is a question to which we cannot provide an adequate answer, because we have so little information about Indian society during the time when many of these ascetic traditions started, although ascetic movements in India appear around the same time as the formation of city-states.[38]

The ascetic deconstruction of the body throughout the history of Indian religions, however, has remained in lively tension with the socially approved expressions of bodily control. At many points the two attitudes and expressions influenced and modified each other. A good example of this is the controversies regarding bodily purity and the observance of the Brāhmaṇical code within medieval ascetic sects (Olivelle 1986–1987). Over time, moreover, ascetic traditions themselves became monastic institutions with powerful social, economic, and political roles within society. The social experience of individuals in such institutions was clearly not marginal, alienated, or revolutionary; their society was, to use Douglas's terms, strong in terms of both group and grid. The changes such changing social experiences caused in the ascetic perception of the body are an interesting and important subject of inquiry, but outside the scope of this essay.

NOTES

1. Contrasting the Indian forms of asceticism to the Hellenistic, which according to him originated within specific historical circumstances, Albert Schweitzer (1960:19) echoes a commonly held, though clearly erroneous, perception: "In the thought of India, on the other hand, world and life negation does not originate in a similar experience. It is there from the very beginning, self-originated, born as it were in a cloudless sky."
2. I do not attach an overly technical meaning to this term, such as that found in literary theory. My use of the term in intended to show that the ascetic construction of the body can be understood adequately only in its negative and thus deconstructing relationship to the socially constructed body.

3. M. Douglas, 1982:65.
4. Even though modern scholarship has shown that Brāhmaṇical perceptions and attitudes, especially in matters of ritual purity, do not necessarily reflect those of Indian society as a whole (Carman and Marglin 1985), nevertheless Brahmin customs and ideas, especially when codified in "sacred" texts, became often the standard for others to imitate and emulate.
5. *Maitreya Upaniṣad*, pp. 113–114.
6. Ibid., p. 108.
7. *Nāradaparivrājaka Upaniṣad*, p. 144. The first passage also occurs in *Manu Smṛti* 6.76–77.
8. *Nāradaparivrājaka Upaniṣad*, p. 160.
9. *Visuddhimagga* 18.28, cited from Collins 1982:167. For a detailed discussion of "house imagery" in the Buddhist tradition, see Collins 1982:165–176.
10. Mary Douglas (1982:158) has described a similar conception of the home in working-class British families.
11. *Paramahaṃsa Upaniṣad*, p. 48; *Nāradaparivrājaka Upaniṣad*, pp. 153, 175, 201.
12. Cited from the translation of Nyanaponika Thera (1962:119).
13. This refers to the Vedic doctrine of debts with which humans are born and which they must pay during their lifetime. The classical doctrine of debts is spelled out in the *Taittirīya Saṃhitā* 6.3.10.5: "A Brahmin, at his very birth, is born with a triple debt—of studentship to the seers, of sacrifice to the gods, of offspring to the fathers. He is, indeed, free from debt, who has a son, is a sacrificer, and who has lived as a student."
14. This appears to be a reference to the ascetics who rejected marriage and procreation and lived celibate lives in the forest.
15. This is a play on *jāyā*, the Sanskrit word for wife, which is derived from a verbal root meaning "to beget." So, a wife's "wifehood" consists in begetting a son for her husband.
16. *Baudhāyana Dharmasūtra* 2.16.6, 8, 9, 11.
17. *Bṛhadāraṇyaka Upaniṣad* 3.5.1; 4.4.22.
18. *Suttanipāta*, pp. 33–34.
19. Vidyāraṇya, *Pañcadaśi* 12.65–67; *Yājñavalkya Upaniṣad*, p. 317.
20. *Nāradaparivrājaka Upaniṣad*, p. 196.
21. Ibid., p. 147.
22. The term means both lust and the god of love.
23. *Yogavāsiṣṭha* 1.21.11, 12, 18, 20; *Yājñavalkya Upaniṣad*, pp. 315–316.
24. Bilhāṇa's *Caurpañcaśikā*. From the translation of Barbara Stoler Miller, *The Hermit and the Love-Thief* (Harmondsworth: Penguin, 1990), pp. 105–106.
25. Translation from Chandra Rajan, *Kālidāsa: The Loom of Time* (Harmondsworth: Penguin, 1989), p. 177.
26. Barbara Stoler Miller, op. cit., p. 82.
27. *Yogavāsiṣṭha*, 1.21.1–2, 5–6. This chapter of the *Yogavāsiṣṭha* contains a detailed deconstruction of the female body. See also *Yājñavalkya Upaniṣad*, p. 315.
28. *Nāradaparivrājaka Upaniṣad*, p. 160.
29. The *Sūtraprābhṛta* of Digambara Ācārya Kundakunda (c.150 CE), pp. 5–8. Translation taken from Jaini 1991:35.
30. See *Bṛhadāraṇyaka Upaniṣad*, 6.2.15–16; *Chāndogya Upaniṣad* 5.10. For perhaps the most eloquent praise of food as the primary cosmological principle, see the *Taittirīya Upaniṣad*, 2.1–2; 3.7–10.
31. *Baudhāyana Dharmasūtra*, 2.5.18.
32. For a longer discussion see Olivelle 1991. The nature of this myth has been the subject of some controversy: see Olivelle 1991: note 8; Gombrich 1992; Collins (unpublished

ms.) has noted the resonance in terminology and images between this myth and the Buddhist monastic code. Gombrich has argued that this is not a creation myth but a satirical parody of the Brāhmaṇical obsession with food. For my purposes it does not matter whether it is a myth or a parody. In either case the story presents a view that is antithetical to the Brāhmaṇical ideology of food. For a similar myth from the Hindu tradition, see *Liṅga Purāṇa* 1.39.

33. I refer the reader to my forthcoming longer study of hair symbolism in India in general and among Indian ascetics in particular: "Hair and Society: Social Significance of Hair in Indian Religions."
34. *Gautama Dharmasūtra* 3.32.
35. M. Douglas op.cit., pp. 70–71.
36. Ibid., pp. 160–161.
37. This verse concludes and encapsulates the sections dealing with holy householders (3.2.19) and forest hermits (3.3.22) in the *Baudhāyana Dharmasūtra.*
38. For a longer discussion about the possible connection between urbanism and the rise of asceticism, see Olivelle 1993:55–58. The psychoanalytic attempts to imagine the social experiences (Masson 1976) underlying Indian asceticism are mere scholarly guesses, not historical evidence.

BIBLIOGRAPHY

Bachelard, Gaston. 1964. *The Poetics of Space,* trans. Maria Jolas. New York: Orion Press.

Beck, E. F. Brenda. 1976. "The Symbolic Merger of Body, Space and Cosmos in Hindu Tamil Nadu." *Contributions to Indian Sociology* n.s. 10.2.

Berg, C. 1951. *The Unconscious Significance of Hair.* London: George Allen & Unwin.

Breckenridge, C. A. 1986. "Food, Politics and Pilgrimage in South India, 1350–1650." In *Food, Society and Culture: Aspects in South Asian Food Systems.* Durham N.C.: Carolina Academic Press.

Carman, J. B., and F. A. Marglin, eds. 1985. *Purity and Auspiciousness in Indian Society.* Leiden: E. J. Brill.

Collins, Steven. 1982. *Selfless Persons: Imagery and Thought in* Theravāda *Buddhism.* Cambridge: Cambridge University Press.

Collins, Steven. "The Discourse on What Is Primary (Aggañña-sutta): An Annotated Translation." Unpublished manuscript.

Cooper, W. 1971. *Hair: Sex Society Symbolism.* New York: Stein and Day.

Daniels, E. Valentine. 1984. *Fluid Signs: Being a Person the Tamil Way.* Berkeley: University of California Press.

Douglas, Mary. 1982. *Natural Symbols: Explorations in Cosmology.* New York: Pantheon Books.

Douglas, Mary. 1984. *Purity and Danger: An Analysis of the Concepts of Pollution and Taboo.* London: ARK Paperbacks.

Dumont, Louis. 1960. "World Renunciation in Indian Religions." *Contributions to Indian Sociology* 4.

Dundas, Paul. 1985. "Food and Freedom: The Jaina Sectarian Debate on the Nature of the Kevalin." *Religion* 15.

Firth, R. 1973. *Symbols: Public and Private.* London: George Allen & Unwin.

Gennep, Arnold van. 1960. *The Rites of Passage,* trans. M. B. Vizedom and G. L. Caffee. Chicago: University of Chicago Press.

Gombrich, Richard. 1992. "The Buddha's Book of Genesis," *Indo-Iranian Journal* 35.

Hallpike, Christopher R. 1969. "Social Hair." *Man* n.s. 4.

Hallpike, Christopher R. 1987. "Hair." *The Encyclopedia of Religion,* ed. M. Eliade et al. New York: Macmillan.

Heesterman, J. C. 1985. *The Inner Conflict of Tradition: Essays in Indian Ritual, Kingship, and Society.* Chicago: University of Chicago Press.

Hershman, P. 1974. "Hair, Sex and Dirt." *Man* n.s. 9.

Jaini, Padmanabh S. 1991. *Gender and Salvation: Jaina Debates on the Spiritual Liberation of Women.* Berkeley: University of California Press.

Khare, R. S. 1976. *Culture and Reality: Essays on the Hindu System of Managing Foods.* Simla: Indian Institute of Advanced Studies.

Khare, R. S., ed. 1992. *The Eternal Food: Gastronomic Ideas and Experiences of Hindus and Buddhists.* Albany: SUNY Press.

Leach, E. R. 1958. "Magical Hair." *Journal of the Royal Anthropological Institute* 88.

Lincoln, Bruce. 1977. "Treatment of Hair and Fingernails among the Indo-Europeans." *History of Religions* 16.

Madan, T. N. 1987. *Non-Renunciation: Themes and Interpretations of Hindu Culture.* Delhi: Oxford University Press.

Maitreya Upaniṣad. Trans. in *Saṃnyāsa Upaniṣads.*

Marriott, McKim. 1968. "Caste Ranking and Food Transactions: A Matrix Analysis." In *Structure and Change in Indian Society,* eds. Milton Singer and Bernard S. Cohn. Chicago: Aldine Publishing Company.

Masson, J. Moussaieff. 1976. "The Psychology of the Ascetic." *The Journal of Asian Studies* 35.

Mauss, Marcel. 1973. "Techniques of the Body," trans. Ben Brewster. *Economy and Society* 2.1.

Nāradaparivrājaka Upaniṣad. Trans. in *Saṃnyāsa Upaniṣads.*

Nyanaponika Thera. 1962. *The Heart of Buddhist Meditation: A Handbook of Mental Training Based on the Buddha's Way of Mindfulness.* London: Rider & Company.

Obeyesekere, G. 1981. *Medusa's Hair: An Essay on Personal Symbols and Religious Experience.* Chicago: University of Chicago Press.

Obeyesekere G. 1990. *The World of Culture: Symbolic Transformation in Psychoanalysis and Anthropology.* Chicago: University of Chicago Press.

Olivelle, Patrick. 1975. "A Definition of World Renunciation." *Wiener Zeitschrift für die Kunde Südasiens* 19.

Olivelle, Patrick. 1986–1987. *Renunciation in Hinduism: A Medieval Debate.* 2 vols. Vienna: University of Vienna Institute for Indology.

Olivelle, Patrick. 1991. "From Feast to Fast: Food and the Indian Ascetic." In *Rules and Remedies in Classical Hindu Law,* ed. Julia Leslie. Leiden: E. J. Brill.

Olivelle, Patrick. 1993. *The* Āśrama *System: The History and Hermeneutics of a Religious Institution.* New York: Oxford University Press.

Saṃnyāsa Upaniṣads, trans. Patrick Olivelle. New York: Oxford University Press, 1992.

Settar, S. 1986. *Inviting Death: Historical Experiments on Sepulchral Hill.* Dharwad, India: Karnatak University, Institute of Indian Art History.

Settar, S. 1990. *Pursuing Death: Philosophy and Practice of Voluntary Termination of Life.* Dharwad, India: Karnatak University, Institute of Indian Art History.

Smith, Bryan K. 1990. "Eaters, Food, and Social Hierarchy in Ancient India: A Dietary Guide to a Revolution in Values." *Journal of the American Academy of Religion* 58.

Schweitzer, Albert. 1960. *Kultur und Ethik.* Munich: Beck.

Turner, Bryan S. 1984. *The Body and Society.* Oxford: Basil Blackwell.

Yājñavalkya Upaniṣad. Trans. in *Saṃnyāsa Upaniṣads.*

16

Ascetic Moods in Greek and Latin Literature

John Pinsent

It has been said that there is no word in French for "home" and none in British English for the American "home town." Similarly, there is no word in Greek for "asceticism," even though the word itself is derived from the Greek. The explanation is the same in all three cases: that the concept is in each case peculiar to the culture in which the word belongs. In our case, "asceticism" is a concept peculiar to the Christian culture of late antiquity. Since its history and development in this and other less closely related cultures will be the business of other contributors to this conference, I shall hope only to give some indication of how that use of the word derived from its earlier use in classical Greek literature.

The word ἄσκησις, the abstract noun from ἀσκέω, means "practice" in the two senses of that word; the practice of an art, craft or profession (πολεμική ἄσκησις, Xenophon, *Cyropedia*—but this may mean "practice for war"); or the process by which this former is acquired and improved, as in the phrase "practice makes perfect." The word is coupled in the Hippocratic treatise *Vetera medicina* with γυμγασίαι (exercises), nicely establishing an athletic connotation never entirely lost.

From this mundane use the word was applied to the more important sphere of the acquisition of desirable traits of character, and, more broadly, of the acquisition of virtue. From Democritus comes the phrase ἐξ ἀσκησίος ἀγαθοι γίνονται (from practice good men are made). For Plato, virtue is οὐ δίδακτον ἀλλ' ἀσκητικόν, and this applies also to a particular virtue, one important for this study, σωφροσύνη (temperance) (*Gorgias,* 487C, 507D).

The concept of ἄσκησις (practice) has thus moved over into the sphere of moral education and moral philosophy. In its systematized form the Spartan ἀγώγη can be regarded as an ἄσκησις, a regimen and discipline designed, like that of an old-fashioned English public school, to inculcate certain approved habits of behavior.

So far, religion has made no appearance in this account, although philosophy has, and philosophy in the ancient world filled some of the cultural niches that are now occupied by religions, religions that, unlike most Greek and Roman religion, enjoin upon their practitioners certain standards of behavior. Some philosophers, rather like mendicant friars or traveling missionaries, were recognized by their idiosyncratic way of life, which could also be called an ἄσκησις. Thus Lucian in

Toxaris 27 talks of ἡ κυνικὴ ἄσκησις (Cynic practice), and Strabo uses the term of the Brahmins (15.1.61) and of the people of Heliopolis (17.1.29), identifying them as a kind of sect without referring exclusively to what the editors of the ninth edition of Liddell and Scott's *Greek Lexicon* call their "asceticism."

From this summary account of the history of the word in classical Greek, we may turn to consideration of the implications of the practice of virtue in antiquity: to what extent, for what reasons, and with what justification it involved what we might call ascetic practices.

Virtue in the ancient world was mostly self-centered. The aim of the good person was self-improvement, even if this goal might have as a by-product a concern for other people. However, we may distinguish between pragmatic self-centeredness and otherworldly self-centeredness. The aim of the former is to become a first-rate specimen of humanity in this world, given that moral virtue is the true end of human beings. The latter pursues virtue in the interests of an immortal soul that is harmed by the practice of injustice. For both types of self-centeredness the cardinal virtues of temperance, courage, wisdom, and justice are important; and the good person will practice them all. But for Plato, a type of otherworldly philosopher, they represent states of the different parts of a tripartite soul, with justice mediating the proper relation among the other three. His philosophy displays to this world, and to the material body, an attitude which may properly be called "ascetic."

The virtue of temperance may be traced as far back as the Homeric poems. A passage in the *Odyssey* (19.23–304) is devoted to the evils of the demon drink, when Antinous chides the disguised Odysseus for wanting to try the bow, saying that he must be drunk. (The maid servant Melantho had given the same explanation regarding Odysseus's challenge to Irus [18.331 ἦ ῥά σε οἶνος ἔχει φρένας: her words are later repeated by Eurymachus, 18.391]). Antinous says:

> οἶνος σε τρώει μελιηδής, ὅς τε καὶ ἄλλον βλάπτει, ὅς ἄν μιν χανδὸν ἕλῃ μηδ' αἴσιμα πίνῃ.
> Wine wounds you, honeysweet, which harms another also, whoever does not take it eagerly and does not drink appropriately [author's trans.].

and goes on to cite the mythological paradigm of the centaur Eurytion,

> οἶνος καὶ Κένταυρον, ἀγακλυτὸν Εὐρυτίωνα, ἄασ' ἐνὶ μεγάροις μεγαθύμου Πειριθόοιο, ἐς Λαπίθας ἐλθόνθ'· ὁ δ' ἐπεὶ φρένας ἄασεν οἴνῳ, μαινόμενος κάκ' ἔρεξε δόμον κάτα Πειριθόοιο.
> Wine also a Centaur, very famous Eurytion, infatuated in the halls of great-spirited Perithous, to the Lapiths when he came; and he, when he had infatuated his mind with wine being mad did evil things in the house of Perithous [author's trans.].

The poem says no more than κάκ' ἔρεξε without specifying Eurytion's offence, which was to try and carry off Peirithous's bride. In view of this passage, we should perhaps interpret the metopes of the Parthenon as a temperance tract.

Wine, however, only destroys the wits of ὅς ἄν μιν χᾶνδὸγ ἕλῃ μηδ' αἴσιμα πίνῃ. The recommendation is not total abstinence, only moderation, the epic equivalent of σωφροσύνη (temperance). Poems in Theognis's corpus similarly counsel moderation in drinking.

Temperance, then, is one of the characteristics of the ἀνὴρ τετράγωνος (men foursquare), the cultural ideal of archaic and classical Greece, to be paralleled perhaps by the Roman ideal of the *prisci Romani* (old Romans): Cincinnatus summoned from the plough, Curius Dentatus refusing the Samnite bribe. Temperance is not asceticism, rather a part simply of a cultural ideal of sobriety and solemnity.

Temperance only moves over toward asceticism in the philosophy of Plato, in whom we discover, most notably in the *Phaedo,* the idea that the body cuts us off from reality. So the philosopher must, as far as possible, be detached from it. The philosophic life will be a preparation for the death that will at last liberate the soul and translate it to the metaphysical world of the Forms, its true home. Plato could have endorsed the sentiments of Wordsworth in his ode on "Intimations of Immortality from Recollections of Early Childhood":

Our birth is but a sleep and a forgetting:
The Soul that rises with us, our Life's Star,
Hath had elsewhere its setting,
And cometh from afar:
Not in entire forgetfulness,
And not in utter nakedness,
But trailing clouds of glory do we come
From God, who is our home.

or those of Shelley, in "Adonais":

Life, like a dome of many-coloured glass,
Stains the white radiance of Eternity
Until Death tramples it to fragments. Die,
If thou wouldst be with that which thou dost seek!

For Plato, however, the philosopher must, once he has attained knowledge by the arduous path of the dialectic, return from time to time to the world he has rejected and live a kind of monastic life. He has a duty to try to instruct those who can accept this hard and inhumane doctrine; only he must be careful not to spend too long at this activity lest he be corrupted; for "Evil communications corrupt good manners." In Plato's *Republic* temperance is the virtue of the lowest part of the soul, τὸ ἐπιθυμητικόν (that which desires), and of the lowest class in the city; and it is a purely negative virtue that consists in not indulging the physical desires of the body. Indeed it is never entirely clear whether Plato (despite the myth of the *Phaedrus*) regards τὸ ἐπιθυμητικόν, or even τὸ Θυμῶδες (that which is spirited) as part of the immortal soul. Rather the one is an inevitable impediment, the result of incarnation, the other an auxiliary that assists, as best it can, τὸ λογιστικόν (that which reasons) in its attempts to control τὸ ἐπιθυμητικόν, or as we would say, to help it practice self-denial. The pagan martyr Socrates is depicted as one impervious alike to the seductions of sex (personified as Alcibiades, whom indeed he can drink under the table without being intoxicated himself), and to the pain of cold (meditating all night at Potidaea in icy weather).

In Plato, then, as nowhere else in Greek thinking, temperance gives place to asceticism, an asceticism that is practiced because only by that means can the soul free itself from the chains of the body in which it is imprisoned. It seems questionable whether Plato believed that the good life could ever be lived in the world, unless by an exceptional character, such as Socrates. Certainly, in the perhaps Pythagorean simile of the Olympic Games, the βίος θεωρητικός (life of the spectator) is superior to the ἀγωνιστικός (competitive life) and certainly to the ἀπολανστικός (life of enjoyment) of the βαναῦσοι (artisans) who have no interest in the Games, except as an opportunity for huckstering and enjoyment. Plato rejects the βίος ἀπολαυστικός as completely as he does the ἀνεξήταστος (unexamined). In Plato, then, we may discover the purest and, I think, the only real example of asceticism in the ancient world.

Yet Plato's asceticism cannot be seen as religious, unless indeed the aim of the soul is to contemplate the Beatific Vision, which that virtuous pagan could envisage only as the Form of the Good, the final answer to the question "Why?": "Because it is good." He was unable in his lifetime to know the supreme condescension of goodness in the (Christian) Incarnation and Redemption, and retains something of the Hellenic belief that moral excellence is a thing worth pursuing for itself alone, the true end of humans.

Before Plato, however, we encounter in literature an example of a certain fastidiousness leading its possessor to a life of purity that gives him access to a divinity. In the *Hippolytus* of Euripides, the innocence of its eponymous hero has kept him from sexual knowledge even in pictures (such as we know from those erotic Greek vases now more frequently published than they once were). His innocence and moral fastidiousness (despite his insistence, when tricked into an oath from which full knowledge of the circumstances would have saved him) lead him in the end to death and consequent desertion by the divinity to whom his despairing farewell is "μάκραν σὺ λείπεις ῥᾳδίως ὁμιλίαν" ("how easily you leave a long association"). Hippolytus's behavior is described as σεμνότης (pride), and it is generally taken that Euripides disapproved of it as much as he does that of Pentheus's refusal in the *Bacchae* to acknowledge the power of Dionysus.

The character of Hippolytus, a natural ascetic, is drawn, however, with great sympathy, if not approval, and may conceivably have been taken from life. It is interesting that Thucydides, another Athenian aristocrat, was prudish enough to state that the Herms were mutilated τὰ πρόσωπα (the bits in front) when the truth is easily to be seen from existing Herms and from Aristophanes. Although Euripides may have recognized the power of Aphrodite as he does that of Dionysus, he may not have approved of it, even while accepting that divine justice is not necessarily human justice. The despairing cry at the end of the *Bacchae*—"gods' tempers should not be as humans'"—implying that we expect from gods a higher standard of morality, is met by Dionysus's stark assertion of his divinity. For Euripides, as for the tragedians in general, the gods are inaccessible and capricious, beings whose ways can only be accepted and never understood, let alone approved, by mortals.

The temperamental asceticism of Hippolytus is simply sexual. We may contrast Thetis's advice to Achilles, who is still mourning the dead and buried Patroclus (*Illiad* 24.128–132):

> τέκνον ἐμόν, τέο μέχρις ὀδυρόμενος καὶ ἀχεύων σὴν ἔδεαι κραδίην, μεμνημένος οὔτε τι σίτου οὔτ' εὐνῆς; ἀγαθὸν δὲ γυναικί περ ἐν φιλότητι μίσγεσθ'. οὐ γάρ μοι δηρὸν βέῃ, ἀλλά τοι ἤδη ἄγχι πατέστηεν θάνατος καὶ μοῖρα κραταιή.
> My child, up to what point lamenting and grieving will you eat out your heart, mindful neither at all of food nor of the bed? It is good even with a woman in friendship to be involved: for not for me long will you live, but for you already near has stood death and powerful fate [author's trans.].

For Thetis, even if she seems almost to be recommending the philosophy "Eat, drink and be merry, for tomorrow we die," and recognizing that for Achilles a woman is only second best to Patroclus (if that be the force of περ), the appetite for sex is something as natural as that for food. Agamemnon says, in the oath he is ready to take before Achilles, that he has laid no hands on Briseis: οὔτ' εὐνῆς πρόφασιν κεχρημένος οὔτε τευ ἄλλου (neither wanting pretext of the bed, nor of anything else) (19.262); so also in Book 9: ἣ θέμις ἀνθρώπων Πέλει, ἀνδρῶν ἠδὲ γυναικῶν (which is the customary right of humankind, of men and of women) (134; cf.276: ἣ θέμις ἐστίν, ἄναξ, ἤ τ' ἀνδρῶν ἤ τε γυναικῶν, [which is the customary right, lord, both of men and of women]).

For the attitude to sex and women exemplified by Hippolytus, to which the repressed sexuality of Pentheus is not dissimilar, possible psychological explanations have been given by Philip Slater in *The Glory of Hera.* He links it to the series of terrible women in tragedy and with an etiology of Hellenic homosexuality: the boy, like a prepubertal girl, is felt as less threatening than the mature woman. A chorus in the *Choephori* of Aeschylus provides a mythological list of such women, and Deianeira in the *Trachiniae* of Sophocles is another such, a Medea *manquée* who does not admit to herself her desire to kill Heracles. It is possible to regard the Gorgoneion as a schematic representation of the female genitalia, exposure of which, in European folklore, will drive away the devil.

It is a further manifestation of Hippolytus's attitude when he wishes that children might be obtained for money at the temples, without the need for women, though this speech conforms to a general Hellenic pattern of misogyny (with overtones also of the concern that sons are not always satisfactory replicas of their fathers). But the attitude is not confined to Hellenic culture. Sir Thomas Browne, the seventeenth-century English doctor, in his *Religio Medici,* boasts that he "was never yet married once, and commend their resolution who never marry twice," going on to express the wish that we might reproduce like trees "without that trivial and vulgar act of coition." "It is," he continues, "the foolishest thing a man does in his life."

It is necessary to consider these psychological attitudes toward sex, because they are an important component of the culture of classical antiquity; and one that made it possible for that culture to provide a medium in which Christian asceticism could later grow. In an earlier essay on Roman spirituality (in A. H. Armstrong, ed.,

Ancient Mediterranean Spirituality, a volume in the *Encyclopedia of World Spirituality*), I have revealed the manifestation of a similar attitude in a poet more generally considered a supreme exponent of love. Catullus expressed, both in some of his elegiac epigrams and also most powerfully and significantly in his epyllion *Attis,* his reaction to what he saw as the unfaithfulness of Lesbia. This seems to be a revulsion that might well have found its expression in asceticism.

Avoidance of sexual love, regarded as common in Hellenic and Roman literature, is also a factor in the two major philosophies of the Hellenistic world, Stoicism and Epicureanism. The confident theodicy of Aeschylus gives way to the puzzled faith of Sophocles and the equally puzzled agnosticism of Euripides, all three still working in and protected by the tightly knit organization of the city-state. Deprived of this security, the individual in the world of the Successor Kingdoms, with the opportunities it provided for geographical as well as social mobility downward as well as upward, felt increasingly at the mercy of a capricious fortune, which might treat him or her, in life as in literature, as it does characters in the *Satyricon* of Petronius and the *Golden Ass* of Apuleius.

The two major and contrasting philosophies of Stoicism and Epicureanism can be seen as a reaction to this insecurity. Confronted by the apparently random operation of Fortune, the philosophers asked why one event happened rather than another (a concern already apparent in the fourth century: witness Xenophon's ending to his *Hellenica*). They reacted, usually in one of two ways. They either accepted that fate was indeed random, the result of chance collisions of swerving atoms in the void (according to the philosophy of Epicurus); or they stoically decided that all was fated. Both Stoics and Epicureans had to decide what behavior to adopt in order to cope with the uncertainties of life; the one counsels avoidance, the other acceptance.

Epicurus and his disciples in their garden led a life that may properly be described as ascetic, almost monastic. For them the desire for ἀταραξία (being undisturbed) led them to avoid all powerful and disturbing stimuli, among which was the passion of love, long regarded in Hellenic culture as a dangerous disease capable of upsetting the social order as well as the individual. "Never may Cypris for her seat select my dappled liver." So A. E. Housman parodied the language, but not the sentiment. The Epicurean whose writings most strongly express this distrust of sexual passion is, of course, Lucretius: his revulsion (4.1058–1120) surely owes as much to his own psychological composition as to his ardent embrace of a philosophy that promised deliverance from fear.

The Stoic, on the other hand, entrusts himself to the dictates of fate, confident that he is acting in harmony with the divine will. His life will be ascetic because he believes in divesting himself as far as possible of all hostages to fortune, and he will commit himself as little as possible to what may make it hard for him to accept that will. "I have grown rich," said one of them, "I have learned to do without something." Xenophon predates the philosophy of Zeno, but his response to the news of his sons' death was stoical: "For I did not suppose that I had begotten immortals."

Stoicism appealed to the Roman ruling class because it was readily compatible with their ideology and sense of duty. For both reasons they disapproved of *luxus*, a word that has some of the connotations of "self-indulgence." Both Epictetus and Marcus Aurelius, slave and emperor, were content to do their duty, without complaint, in that state of life to which it had pleased fate to call them. A famous Victorian painting in the Walker Art Gallery at Liverpool depicts a Roman soldier sturdily apprehensive in the murk of Pompeii: it is called *Faithful unto Death* and is a truly stoic picture, even if the title does rather suggest a hound guarding the body of his dead master. Suicide, therefore, is not approved of in Stoicism, because we should not relinquish the post to which fate has assigned us before it calls us to do so in death.

It has been said that Stoicism was the true religion of the Romans, just as it was for the English of my generation and that of Rudyard Kipling before me. It is true that both Stoicism and Epicureanism perform the cultural role that religion does in some other cultures. Stoicism does so particularly because of its belief in God, a word that could be substituted for fate in all the instances that I have given, and which is combined with it in the first of the iambic lines of Cleanthes, ἄγου δὲ μ' ὦ Ζεῦ καὶ σύ γ' ἡ πεπρωμένη (Lead me, O Zeus, and you my fated portion). Both philosophies, however, had an explanation for everything; and both recommended a lifestyle that can justly be called temperate, if not ascetic.

The question of the influence of the moralities of the ancient world upon Christian asceticism has generated some discussion, unfortunately not accessible to me. I note especially J. W. Swain's Columbia dessertation of 1916, "The Hellenic Origins of Christian Asceticism," and V. Bullough's *Sexual Variance in Society and History* (New York, 1971). I owe both these references to Eva Cantarella's *Bisexuality in the Ancient World* (Yale University Press, 1972), p. 263, note 13. She pays particular attention to the views on marriage of Musonius Rufus and of Seneca, and, following Aline Rousselle, *Porneia: On Desire and the Body in Antiquity* (Oxford, 1988), to those of medical writers.

These views on marriage, like those of Hippolytus noted above, may more properly belong to a discussion of Hellenic misogyny (as expressed, for example, by Hesiod and Semonides) than to one on asceticism; but the views of the medical writers, that sexual intercourse, like cigarettes and alcohol today, may affect the health, serve to point to a particular form of asceticism, not unknown today, closely related to the etymology of the word.

This is the view that there is almost a duty to maintain oneself in training, not so much for its own sake, though such practices may become addictive, as to prepare oneself for demands that may be made and hardships to be endured. There is perhaps something of this in Stoicism, but I should like to adduce evidence from an unexpected quarter, the English writer of adventure stories, John Buchan, perhaps better known on this side of the Atlantic as Lord Tweedsmuir, a governor general of Canada, or as the author of *The Thirty-nine Steps*. His upper-middle-class heroes often complain of a condition of *accidie*, which they overcome by a program of strenuous physical exercise (such as deer stalking on the Scottish hills) that turns out to have prepared them for an equally strenuous adventure.

I find something of the same attitude in the "new Puritanism," which seems to regard physical fitness as in some way a moral matter and obesity, smoking, and drinking alcoholic beverages (the latter especially by pregnant women) as immoral acts against which there ought to be laws. This attitude can be extended by a comparison between the rich Western states and the poorer countries of the world, the former consuming more than their share of the planet's produce. Such countries can also provide arguments for vegetarianism—that animals bred and kept to provide meat for human consumption are an inefficient as well as an immoral way of obtaining protein.

The asumption made here is that an ascetic, or a more ascetic, lifestyle is healthier. Therefore, it is part of one's duty to oneself to make the self at all times ready for duty. Also, for the same reason, fitness is part of one's duty to others, because persons whose unfitness or illness is induced by self-indulgence place an unfair burden upon medical resources. It should be said, however, that Sir David Ross, a stern moralist, was once heard to say that those who speak of their duty to themselves are dishonest in other ways as well.

The word "self-indulgence" suggests a different form of asceticism, to be found in Plato. This is based on the belief that the body, if not in itself evil, at least requires constantly to be kept on a tight rein, like the black horse in the myth of the *Phaedrus,* against its continuous tendency to return to so-called bodily pleasure. Sweet indeed are the intellectual pleasures of scholarship and philosophy; sweeter still, no doubt, the comforts or the ecstasies of religion; but the pleasures of the world, the flesh, and the devil are considerably more attractive and persuasive. Moralists do their case no good by insisting that the latter are not really pleasant, even if there are good reasons for the practice of self-denial.

This Platonic mode of asceticism has a metaphysical basis. It regards the practice of asceticism as a means to an end: the body gets in the way of our perception of the real world of the intellect. It has much, therefore, in common with the first type that I have defined; but differs in that it is based upon the premise that there is an intellectual world superior to, and Plato would say more real than, the illusory way of the senses.

Of Christian asceticism I am not qualified to speak. As a newly confirmed and impressionable adolescent I was given a book of devotions that told me to ask of any activity, however apparently innocent, "Does it bring you nearer Christ?" If the answer was, as expected, "No," the activity was to be abjured. Some may maintain that self-denial, the opposite of self-indulgence, is a good in itself, but I would suppose that Christian asceticism is to be regarded rather as a means to an end, a help on the way to, or in, the religious life, whether active or contemplative—possibly even a necessary means, but not an end in itself.

Asceticism can only be an end in itself if the body be itself evil, the flesh to be mortified—a prison not merely a temporary tomb from which the soul must escape. This view is close to gnosticism, paradoxically part of the Hellenic rather than of the Judaic inheritance of Christianity. The Incarnation, in this view, is a willing degradation of divinity rather than a sanctification of the human. I am no theologian, but here I smell heresy.

I have deliberately extended my purview beyond the simple exposition of ascetic moods to be discerned in the literatures of the ancient world. Instead, I have used these moods as the basis for a brief analysis of what I deem to be various modes of asceticism, and I leave it to others to approve or to condemn my definitions.

Claudite jam rivos, pueri, sat prata biberunt.

17

Asceticism in the Church of Syria: The Hermeneutics of Early Syrian Monasticism

Sidney H. Griffith

Many commentators on the history of asceticism in the Syrian Orient in the early Christian period have highlighted what they often call its encratic features. They cite the harsh and seemingly bizarre forms of ascetic life that flourished there. And everyone who knows anything at all about asceticism in Syria knows that it was home to that peculiar ascetical institution, the stylite—the holy man or woman who passed his or her life elevated above the cares of contemporaries, dwelling on a platform secured to the top of a pillar, and served by a monastic community gathered below.[1] One might borrow a phrase from Peter Brown to say that in the popular scholarly imagination the Syrian tradition of asceticism "admitted more vivid gestures than it did in the Greek world."[2] Indeed, Brown goes on to characterize the Syrian conception of monasticism, or of the "angelic life," as its practitioners would call it, as a "freedom that resembled that of the beasts, wandering up the mountainsides to graze, with the sheep, on the natural grasses."[3] He calls attention to the Syria-based "Messalians," who "provoked genuine alarm in the late fourth and fifth centuries."[4] Brown concedes that "the world East of Antioch was no spiritual 'Wild West'";[5] but, nevertheless, he speaks of drastic measures and deep pessimism as characteristic of Syrian asceticism. This general impression of the severity, or at least of the peculiarity, of asceticism in the Syrian Orient has become almost a stereotype, comparable to the stereotype of Egyptian asceticism in the fourth century as unrelievedly that of the Antonian hermit or the Pachomian cenobite, with no finer distinctions required to understand what was, in fact, a more complicated social phonomenon.[6]

The history of the earliest forms of asceticism in the Syriac-speaking world is inevitably bound up with the study of such foundational documents as the *Odes of Solomon* and the *Acts of Judas Thomas*. The interpretation of these texts necessarily involves a further inquiry into the much discussed issue of the styles of Christianity that first flourished in the Syrian milieu. There is no doubt that the followers of Marcion, Mani, and Bar Daysan, for example, were major players in the drama that saw the unfolding of Christian intellectual and cultural life in the environs of Nisibis and Edessa, the two cities that became the foci of the Syriac-speaking world—the one always open to Persia, and the other, at least from the second century onward, a stalwart champion of the Roman empire.[7] But, by the early fourth century, those forces prevailed in the church in Syria, which brought it ever more intimately into the socio-political life of the "Church of the Empire."[8] It is during this period that one begins to find the appearance in inner Syria of institutions typical of the "Great Church," including one that would uniquely mark Christian life for centuries to come, the institution of monasticism. This institution was easily as powerful and significant at the time as the institution of the hierarchical episcopacy, which also appeared in Syria in the fourth century.

The history of monasticism as a style of the ascetical life in Syria needs renewed scholarly attention. In recent years, it has become increasingly clear that the hitherto prevailing view rests, at least in part, upon mistaken assumptions from two sources about its origins. One is the traditional, monastic hagiography deriving from the Greco-Syrian milieu itself. The other is a modern scholarly mistake about the date and the authorship of certain texts crucial to the case as documentary evidence.

The first problem that one encounters in attempting to write the history of the forms of monasticism in the Syriac-speaking communities is that the past has almost always been read through lenses supplied by such essentially Byzantine texts as Theodoret of Cyrrhus's *History of the Monks of Syria,* Palladius's *Historia Lausiaca,* and Sozomen's *Church History.* These texts, and others of their ilk, rather than native Syriac ones, have set the parameters within which commentators have long discussed the biographies of such principal figures as Jacob of Nisibis (fl. 303–338 CE) and Ephraem the Syrian (306–373 CE).[9] They present verbal icons of these saints that conform to an hagiographic profile much esteemed in fifth and sixth century Syro-Byzantine monastic circles. But they have nothing much to do with the historical portraits of these figures that more indigenous Syriac materials allow one to draw. The result has been that the origins of monasticism in the Syriac-speaking world were considered to be part of the general flowering of the monastic phenomenon—which is supposed to have begun in the deserts of Egypt in the days of Antony. This errant view found a currency even in native Syriac milieus, in the accounts of St. Awgin, which, in later centuries enjoyed a considerable popularity in Syria.[10]

The modern scholarly mistake regarding Syrian monasticism has been the attribution of five Syriac texts, which describe the exploits and present the thinking of Syriac-speaking ascetics who withdrew into the deserts and mountains of Syria in pursuit of the anchoritic ideal, to St. Ephraem. The texts have such titles as the "Letter to the Mountaineers"; "On the Solitary Life of the Anchorites"; "On Anchorites, Hermits and Mourners"; another work similarly titled, "On Anchorites, Hermits and Mourners"; and "On Solitaries."[11] The problem is that in his influential book *History of Asceticism in the Syrian Orient,* and elsewhere, Arthur Vööbus vigorously defends the authenticity of these texts as works of St. Ephraem.[12] The result has been that subsequent historians have, accordingly, thought of them as documents indicative of the ascetical and monastic theory current in Syria in St. Ephraem's time and earlier. They abound in descriptions of the vivid gestures of asceticism of which Peter Brown speaks in the passages from his book already quoted (p. 220). But, in fact, these works, some of which are in the manuscript tradition sometimes attributed to Isaac of Antioch (fifth century), date from well after the time of Ephraem.[13] They tell us next to nothing about the origins of monasticism within Syrian asceticism. Rather, they reflect developments of the anchoritic idea which come from a later time, no real traces of which appear in Ephraem's certainly genuine works.

When one reads the texts of the native Syriac writers of the formative fourth century without the presuppositions imposed by either the Byzantine icon of the monastic holy man leading the hermit life, or the *idée fixe* supplied by what one might call the Vööbus hypothesis, a portrait of the emerging monastic, or premonastic, life in Syria emerges that bears the stamp of originality. On the one hand, as we shall see, the outward style of life that the sources describe is very similar to what recent scholars find elsewhere, in Egypt, for instance.[14] On the other hand, in the Syriac-speaking world the terms of burgeoning monastic life have their own resonances and nuances which impart a distinctive conceptual flavor that they never completely lose throughout the course of later developments.

Briefly put, crucial texts by Aphrahat, "the Persian Sage" (died c.345 CE) and Ephraem the Syrian allow one a glimpse of the lifestyle within the church of Syria of communities of "singles" in God's service, whose way of life is parallel to that of the biblical widows and virgins and with whom the men and women "singles" will be bracketed in later canonical legislation.[15] Within the first quarter of the fourth century, however, the anchoritic life also makes its appearance in Syria in the person of Julian Saba (died c.367 CE), whose experience Ephraem the Syrian, among others, would celebrate in hymns that in Syria functioned literarily in much the same way that Athanasius's *Life of Antony* would function in Egypt and elsewhere. They present Julian's exploits in a religious vocabulary that had already become traditional, while at the same time they indicate a paradigm shift in the forms of asceticism that, in an uncanny way, transmutes traditional ascetical terminology.[16]

In the late fourth century, and throughout the fifth century, the church in Syria both eagerly adopted monasticism, the new ascetical fashion that went together with the hierarchical features of Eusebius's Constantinian "Great Church"; and at the same time developed the institution in accordance with its own temperament. That temperament manifests itself in the *Liber graduum,* a late fourth- or early fifth-century text that in many ways echoes traditional Syrian ascetical vocabulary, already long familiar from Manichaean as well as more mainstream Christian discourse.[17] The stylites, too, were expressions of the Syrian temperament, as were the "mourners," "solitaries," and "mountaineers" whose "vivid gestures" Peter Brown mentions. Later Syrians took eagerly to the monastic thought of Evagrius of Pontus: so much so that his thinking, and that of commentators under his influence, such as Palladius and even Theodoret of Cyrrhus, eventually came to dominate the theory of asceticism in the Syriac-speaking milieu.[18] The important point in connection with all of these figures is that they were not the original Syrian ascetics. Rather, their enthusiasms were the product of the change in ascetical fashion which began in the fourth century after the Constantinian peace of the church. "Monasticism" is the term which has come functionally to designate the new fashion, the hallmark of which, from a phenomenological point of view, was what the Greeks called *anachōrēsis,* the departure of individuals or groups of individuals from the life of the city's church community to an environment more suited to the practice of asceticism seemingly for its own sake, or at least free of the entanglements of day-to-day ecclesiastical life. But the church of Syria long preserved adepts of the old ways, who continued to live in the general community and to use the traditional ascetical vocabulary, although much of it was also adopted by the new enthusiasts.[19]

The purpose of the present essay is to look again at several key terms in the traditional Syriac vocabulary of asceticism and monasticism, with the intention of highlighting their denotations and connotations within the Syrian hermeneutical horizon. The focus of attention will be on two expressions, the term *îḥîdāyâ,* and the phrase *bnay* (or *bnāt*) *qyāmâ,* especially in the works of Aphrahat and Ephraem, the two classical writers of Syriac in the fourth century. And there will be a brief discussion of the uniquely Syriac ascetical term, *abîlâ.* The assumption is that Aphrahat and Ephraem used these expressions in their traditional Syrian senses and that their works made them more readily available for those writers coming after them. It is hoped that the study will contrast and compare these typically Syrian conceptions with parallel Greek modes of expression that became increasingly important to the Syrians, especially in the fifth and sixth centuries. The final section of this essay returns to the discussion of the history and the forms of asceticism in Syria, in the light of the foregoing investigations.

Îḥîdāyâ

In the tradition of the Syriac-speaking churches, the term *îḥîdāyê* regularly appears in the earliest texts together with the terms *bnay qyāmâ, btûlê/btûlātâ,* and *qaddîšê* to designate a class of people in the believing community who occupied a special status in the church.[20] They were not ministers properly so-called, such as the *šammōšê, mšammšānê* (deacons) or the *qaššîšê* (presbyters) or the *rāʿawwātâ* (shepherd-bishops); although, as we shall see, *îḥîdāyê* were sometimes to be found in the pastoral ministry among the minor officials, or *ʿallānê* (herdsmen), as they were sometimes called, in the service of a local bishop.[21] Rather, the *îḥîdāyê* occupied a position comparable to that assigned to widows and virgins already in the New Testament and in early ecclesiastical books of canons.[22] In fact, the term *îḥîdāyê,* in general came to include both male and female virgins, as well as persons who may once have been married, but who subsequently consecrated themselves in a special way and who then lived as consecrated celibates in the Christian community under the name *qaddîšê* (saints or holy ones).[23]

The earliest texts in Syriac to which one may turn for help in the effort to explore the meaning of the term *îḥîdāyâ* in this sense are from the fourth century, the *Demonstrations* of Aphrahat, the Persian Sage (died c. 345 CE), and the hymns and

[Some of the material in this section appeared in an earlier form in S. H. Griffith, "Singles in God's Service: Thoughts on the *Iḥîdāyê* from the Works of Aphrahat and Ephraem the Syrian," *The Harp* 4 (1991):145–159.]

homilies of Ephraem the Syrian (d. 373 CE). By the fourth century, one supposes, the term was already current in ecclesiastical circles. Were it not for what one can learn of its connotations in the writings of Aphrahat and Ephraem, one would be poorly prepared to understand it in the few places where it appears in the yet earlier texts that have survived.

Scholarly essays dedicated to exploring the denotation and the connotations of the term *îḥîdāyâ* have not been lacking, and during the twenty years between 1953 and 1973 there was a mini-debate on the subject in the periodical literature. The discussion began with the publication in 1953 and 1954 of Alfred Adam's influential article, "Grundbegriffe des Mönchtums in sprachlicher Sicht,"[24] and it achieved something approaching closure, at least for the time being, in 1974 and 1975, when Robert Murray reviewed the whole matter in summary fashion in another influential article, "The Exhortation to Candidates for Ascetical Vows at Baptism in the Ancient Syriac Church."[25] In the meantime, additional important contributions to the discussion came from such notable scholars as Dom Edmund Beck O.S.B.,[26] Gilles Quispel,[27] and Antoine Guillaumont,[28] all of whom have called attention to important aspects of the definition of the term *îḥîdāyâ.*

For a while, the discussion was complicated by the inability of scholars to decide whether the employment of the Syriac term in the earliest texts presumed the currency, and distinctively Christian sense, of the Greek word *monachos,* or vice versa. Arthur Vööbus, and to some extent even Edmund Beck, presumed that the Greek word was in fact primary, with its emphasis on the solitariness of the person described, to the effect that such a one lives alone, and is single, or celibate, that is to say unmarried and sexually continent.[29] Alfred Adam and Antoine Guillaumont, on the other hand, insisted that in the Syriac-speaking world the word *îḥîdāyâ* has a deeper primary sense than simply what the adjective "single" implies about the human lifestyle—married or single—even in the basic denotation of the word. To support their position, they appealed to Semitic philology, and to the use of the term *îḥîdāyâ* in the works of the classic writers of Syriac: Aphrahat, and particularly Ephraem. For in Syriac religious texts the term is not simply a designation for a Christian ascetic of some sort, but is first of all a title of Christ with biblical authority; and this is its primary point of reference for many Syriac writers.[30]

Robert Murray has summarized the meanings of the term *îḥîdāyâ* in reference to a Christian ascetic, as these meanings have become clear from the two decades and more of scholarly controversy on the subject. Murray sees three senses for the term: *monachos* (single from wife or family); *monotropos, monozōnos* (single in heart), not *dipsuchos* (doubleminded, as in *Jas.* 1.8); and *monogenēs* (united to the Only Begotten).[31] These three senses are, in fact, among the connotations of the term *monachos* that Eusebius of Caesarea had mentioned in connection with his discussion of the word *monotropous* as it occurs in *Psalm* 68.7 (LXX).[32] And Murray, following Guillaumont, was able to show that in Syriac and, particularly, in the writings of St. Ephraem these senses of the Greek term are also senses of the word *îḥîdāyâ* and are fundamental to the comprehension of the definition of the word as the Syriac fathers used it.

The practical corollary to this is, therefore, that in Syriac ascetical texts the denotation of the term *îḥîdāyâ* is not limited to the notion of singleness that bespeaks celibacy or religious bachelorhood. Rather, it includes the element of singleness of purpose (*monotropos*), along with the clear claim that a person called single for ascetical reasons is thereby also said to be in a special relationship with Jesus the Christ, the "Single One," the single son of God the Father (*John* 1.14, 18, 3.16, 18). This latter sense of the term may have been the primary one for the Syrians.

One must concede that in the Peshitta New Testament the adjective *îḥîdāyâ* appears to describe the single son not only of God the Father, but also the single son of the widow of Naim (*Luke* 7.12), the single son of the man whose boy was possessed (*Luke* 9.38), and the single daughter of Jairus (*Luke* 8.42). Nevertheless, the occurrence of the adjective five times to describe Jesus as God's "single son" was enough to ensure its currency in the Syriac-speaking world as a special Christological title.[33] In those texts in which Aphrahat and Ephraem speak of the "singles" in God's service in the church, they seldom fail to make this connection explicitly.

Aphrahat is the author most often quoted in discussions of the *îḥîdāyê*. Among his *Demonstrations,* one is in fact exclusively devoted to them, entitled *bnay qyāmâ,* the name for the *îḥîdāyê* that, in Aphrahat's day, was used to signify their position in the social organization of the church, as we shall see.[34] For Aphrahat, it is clear, the *îḥîdāyê* were certainly celibates. He says, "It is just, right and good for me to give this advice to myself, and to my beloved *îḥîdāyê:* they should not take wives."[35] And, just a few lines later, he describes the religious significance he attributes to this celibacy:

> For those who do not take wives will be served by the Watchers of heaven; the observers of consecrated holiness (*qaddîšûtâ*) will come to rest at the sanctuary of the Exalted One. The *îḥîdāyâ* who is from the bosom of the Father [*John* 1.14, 18] will gladden the *îḥîdāyê*. There will be there neither male nor female, neither slave nor free, but all are sons of the Most High [see *Galatians* 3.28].[36]

Finally, at the conclusion of that section of *Demonstration 6,* which some commentators call "Aphrahat's Rule," he writes:

> These things are fitting for the *îḥîdāyê,* those who take on the heavenly yoke, to become disciples to Christ. For so is it fitting for Christ's disciples to emulate Christ their Lord.[37]

Aphrahat's so-called rule stipulates for the *îḥîdāyê* such standard religious practices as faith, fasting, prayer, humility, simplicity; and the avoidance of hilarity, fancy dress, deceitful contention, avarice, and scorn. These are the practices that he calls suitable for the *îḥîdāyê,* the sons of the covenant, the virgins, and the *qaddîšê* (consecrated holy ones).[38] But what is of particular interest in the present discussion is Aphrahat's sense of the term *îḥîdāyâ* itself; it bespeaks the "one who is from the bosom of the Father," who "will gladden the *îḥîdāyê.*" Clearly, for Aphrahat, Christ's title is of determining significance for the self-understanding of the *îḥîdāyê.* To become single after the image of the Father's only son, as Marie-Joseph Pierre has recently reminded readers of Aphrahat, had constituted the eschatological ideal for earlier writers in the Syrian milieu, such as the author of the *Gospel of Thomas.*[39]

Ephraem the Syrian's remarks are even more to the point. For him, of course, as for Aphrahat, the *îḥîdāyâ* is celibate. In the *Hymns of Paradise,* for example, Ephraem says of the ascetical person:

> Whoever sensibly
>   abstains from wine,
> For him the grapevines of Paradise
>   are eagerly awaiting.
> Each one stretches out
>   to offer him its cluster.
> And if he is also a virgin,
>   they draw him in,
> Well within their embrace,
>   because being an *îḥîdāyâ*
> He had not lain within an embrace,
>   nor on a bed of marriage.[40]

Clearly, for Ephraem, the *îḥîdāyâ* is a celibate person, and one need not adduce any further evidence here to make the point.[41] But it is also true that Ephraem invested the term *îḥîdāyâ* with an even deeper significance, given the fact that for him it not only describes someone living an ascetical, celibate life in the church, but it is also a title of Christ in the Syriac scriptures.[42] And for Ephraem, as for Aphrahat, an important element in the understanding of the ascetical *îḥîdāyâ* in the church here below is his relationship to the *îḥîdāyâ* from the bosom of the Father in heaven.

It has become clear during recent decades of scholarship that the occasion of the baptism of adults was also the occasion when prospective virgins and *qaddîšê* in the churches of Aphrahat and Ephraem entered the ranks of the *îḥîdāyê.*[43] Accordingly, it is not surprising that some of Ephraem's clearest language about the relationship between the earthly *îḥîdāyê* and the heavenly *Îḥîdāyâ* occurs in the metrical hymns he composed for the feast of the baptism of our Lord, the Epiphany. The clearest and most often quoted passages evoking this theme are the following lines:

> Here they are, coming to be baptized
>   and to become Virgins and Holy Ones.
> They step down, are baptized,
>   and they put on [*lbešw*] the one *Îḥîdāyâ*
>
> For whoever is baptized and puts on [*lābeš*]
> the *Îḥîdāyâ,* the Lord of the many,
> has come to fill for Him the place of the many,
> and Christ becomes for him the greatest
>   treasure.[44]

In another Epiphany hymn Ephraem returns to the same theme:

> You to be baptized, who have found the kingdom
>   in the very bosom of Baptism,

Step down, put on [*lûbšûhy*] the *Îḥîdāyâ*
  who is the Lord of the kingdom.
Blessed are you who have been crowned.[45]

It may well be the case that St. Ephraem envisions here not only ascetics, but every baptized person as one who has put on the heavenly *Îḥîdāyâ*.[46] Nevertheless, the fact remains that the very synonymy of the titles for the only begotten Son of God and the celibate ascetics in Ephraem's ecclesial community bespeaks a special relationship between Christ and the celibate ascetic that is inherent in the very term designating them. For this reason, Dom Edmund Beck has now revised an earlier *dictum* that the two uses of the term *îḥîdāyâ* have nothing to do with one another,[47] in favor of the suggestion that there is an indirect relationship between the two applications of the same term. The indirect connection, Beck suggests, bespeaks a higher rank in the community of the baptized for the ascetic, because "Christ becomes for him the greatest treasure," and the ascetic in turn comes "to fill the place of the many," as St. Ephraem says, in the presence of Christ, the heavenly *Îḥîdāyâ*.[48]

It is interesting to observe the language St. Ephraem uses to express the inauguration of the special relationship between Christ the *Îḥîdāyâ* and the ascetic *îḥîdāyâ* at the sacrament of baptism. He speaks of the candidate putting on Christ the *Îḥîdāyâ* in a way that reminds one of the clothing metaphor St. Ephraem and other Syriac writers so often used to express the doctrine of the Incarnation; they customarily spoke of the Word of God as "having put on the body (*lbeš pagrâ*)" of humanity for the sake of our salvation.[49] Further, it was a commonplace in baptismal contexts to speak of the baptized as putting on the robes of glory and light that Christ had left behind for them in the water at his own baptism in the Jordan.[50] Accordingly, when the divine *Îḥîdāyâ* was put on at baptism, the ascetic was, in Ephraem's view, putting on divinity, in the name of the many in Christ the *Îḥîdāyâ,* just as the "Word" of God had put on humanity in Christ at the Incarnation. In this view, the ascetic *îḥîdāyâ* came to anticipate symbolically, almost in an iconic fashion, the situation of paradise restored;[51] he represented publicly and liturgically humanity's response to the salvation offered to them in the Incarnation (Passion, death, Resurrection) of God's only son.

There are yet further dimensions of meaning in the term *îḥîdāyâ*. Scholars studying the history of the forms of asceticism in the early Christian communities have made reference in this connection to the parlance of the Jewish communitarians at Qumran, where the Hebrew word *yaḥad* described the community whose sometimes celibate members were described by the adjective *yaḥîd*.[52] Furthermore, this Hebrew term, especially in the biblical narratives where it occurs independently of any influence of Qumran, means not only "sole" or "single," to designate, for example, a single or only son or daughter. It also bespeaks an affective relationship that Greek translators of the Bible sometimes reflected by translating the Hebrew term *yaḥîd* with the Greek word *agapētos*. Greek translators also employed the word *monogenēs* to render the Hebrew word *yaḥîd*.[53] And so the multiple connotations of the term *îḥîdāyâ* in Syriac versions of the Bible which can be used to translate all of these expressions, must be taken into account if one wants to hear how it echoes when describing an ascetical person in the Syriac-speaking early Christian community. Such a person is not only single in the sense of a celibate, but also singleminded, and has a special relationship with the beloved only son of the Father, which is assumed at baptism.[54] Baptism was thus not only the inauguration of a full life as a Christian, but of special status as *îḥîdāyâ*. All of these senses of the term have been discussed by earlier scholars; and Robert Murray has summarized them in his now classic article, "The Exhortation to Candidates for Ascetical Vows at Baptism in the Ancient Syriac Church."[55]

Yet another nuance in the meaning of the term *îḥîdāyâ* has come to light. In a study of the Christological title, *monogenēs unigenitus*, in the earliest patristic literature, Francesca Cocchini has shown that the scriptural passages that underlie this title most often employ the terms *yaḥîd/monogenēs/îḥîdāyâ, îḥîdāyûtâ* (Old Testament) and *monogenēs/îḥîdāyâ* (New Testament) in contexts that in the Old Testament involve the notion of sacrifice and in the New Testament describe an individual who experiences both death and resurrection: either Christ himself (*Jn.* 1.14, 18) or people whom Christ raised from the dead (*Lk.* 7.12, 8.42, 9.38).[56] So the title both fulfils a typological function (e.g. Isaac/Christ, those whom Christ raised/the resurrected Christ); and, with its sacrificial aura, it suggests that the Only One takes the place of the many, be he the Christ who saved the many by his Passion, death, and Resurrection, or be he the ascetic *îḥîdāyâ* who takes the place of the many as a *rāzâ* (token) of humanity restored to its pristine state in Paradise.

The conclusion to which the preceding discussion leads is that the Syriac term *îḥîdāyâ,* unlike the Greek term *monachos,* which shares part of its range of meaning, is a scriptural term[57] that in Christian usage applies first of all to Christ, with the full set of connotations that only the several Greek words used to interpret it will allow the non-Syriac speaker to discern.[58] Secondly, in Syriac this term is also used by writers such as Aphrahat and Ephraem to designate the so-called ascetics in the community, precisely because the intention of these ascetic celibates was publicly to put on the *persona* of the *Îḥîdāyâ* from the bosom of the Father. Their purpose was to imitate Christ. Aphrahat is perfectly clear on this point. At the end of his rule for the *îḥîdāyê* he says of them, "For so is it fitting for the disciples of Christ to imitate Christ, their Lord."[59]

With his accustomed poet's objectivity, St. Ephraem puts the same point well in the verses he composed in praise of a notable *îḥîdāyâ* of his own day, St. Julian Saba (d.367 CE). Of him Ephraem said,

> In his lifestyle, Jesus was ever depicted.
> Because he had seen the glory of the *îḥîdāyâ,*
> He too became an *îḥîdāyâ*. . . .
> In humility he showed a "type" to his own people.[60]

The senses of the term *îḥîdāyâ* as applied to holy men and women thus come before us in the works of two classical authors of the fourth century. The presumption is that, by their day, such ideas were already traditional in the Syriac-speaking world. The term *îḥîdāyâ* does not occur in the allegedly second-century

Odes of Solomon, nor in the *Acts of Judas Thomas,* where, nevertheless, themes closely associated with the institution of the *îḥîdāyûtâ* do occur.[61] But a number of scholars do think that the term *îḥîdāyâ* did appear among the *logia* (sayings) of Jesus in the presumably originally Syriac *Gospel of Thomas* that now survives only in Coptic.[62] There are at least seven *logia* in which the expression "single one" appears in Coptic, in some of which the Coptic translator actually used the Greek word *monachos* to render the original expression. For example, "Blessed are the solitary (*monachos*) and elect, for you shall find the kingdom" (*logion* 49), and "Many are standing at the door, but the solitary (*monachos*) are the ones who will enter the bridal chamber" (*logion* 75).[63] If the Syriac term *îḥîdāyâ* does in fact lie behind the term *monachos* in such passages as these, its occurrence would be the only remaining documentary evidence of the word *îḥîdāyâ* in a nonbiblical text from earlier than the fourth century to describe a celibate ascetic, or a spiritually elect person among the Christians. It is this presumption that has prompted some scholars to propose, further, that the Greek word *monachos,* which is first found in a papyrus fragment dated 6 June 324 to designate a Christian devotee, could have come into the Christian vocabulary in this sense as a calque on the Syriac word *îḥîdāyâ.*[64] If this proposal has any plausibility, it goes a long way toward explaining why Greek writers like Eusebius had to use so many different Greek words to summon up the several dimensions of meaning in the single Syriac word. Few of these dimensions leap readily to mind at the simple sight of the nonscriptural Greek word *monachos;* many of them are already evident in the senses of the Syriac word *îḥîdāyâ,* when it is read in the light of the traditional usages we have described.

Bnay Qyāmâ

Within the Syriac-speaking Christian communities of the fourth century, and presumably earlier, the *îḥîdāyê,* be they *btûlê* (virgins) or *qaddîšê* (consecrated holy ones), belonged to a somewhat informal class of believers in the church whom the early writers called *bnay* (or *bnāt*) *qyāmâ.*[65] It has become customary to render this phrase as "sons (or daughters) of the covenant," or simply as "covenanters." Scholars are increasingly aware, however, of the limitations of the customary translations of the phrase.[66] In fact, as we shall see, the term *qyāmâ* has connotations in Syriac that go far beyond what the word "covenant" alone suggests. These connotations are decisive for an understanding of the social standing of the *îḥîdāyê* in the church.

Aphrahat's *Demonstration 6,* devoted entirely to the concerns of the *bnay qyāmâ,* is the earliest and the most basic document we have even to mention the phrase. And here it is perfectly clear that for Aphrahat the *îḥîdāyê* are the *bnay qyāmâ.*[67] Furthermore, later in his book, in *Demonstration 8,* the author refers to *Demonstration 6,* "*Bnay Qyāmâ,*" as a discourse on the *îḥîdāyê,*[68] so there can be no doubt that, for Aphrahat, the two terms designate the same people in the community. What differentiates them, then, is their point of reference in regard to these same people. The term *îḥîdāyâ* bespeaks both the single, celibate condition of the individual so described, and the special relationship one assumes at baptism with the Son, the *Îḥîdāyâ* "from the bosom of the Father." The point of reference for the term *bar qyāmâ* turns on the senses of the word *qyāmâ* in Syriac, a noun derived from the verbal root *q-y-m,* which basically means "to rise," "to stand."[69]

The basic study of the significance of the expression *bar qyāmâ* is the influential article, "The Covenanters of the Early Syriac-Speaking Church," by George Nedungatt, S.J.[70] Here the author studies the seventy-seven occurrences of the word *qyāmâ* in the *Demonstrations* of Aphrahat, in nine basic usages. He notices that in almost half of its occurrences (thirty-five times), the term *qyāmâ* means "any religious covenant in the history of salvation."[71] And Nedungatt suggests that this is the basic sense of the term: that is, "pact" or "covenant." Accordingly, he understands the expression *bnay qyāmâ* to mean sons of the covenant or covenanters. His conclusion regarding the significance of this expression in the present context is as follows:

> In a typological or theological sense the whole Church was the *Qyāmâ* of God, but in the language of everyday life the *bnay qyāmâ* and the *bnāt qyāmâ* represented an inner circle of élite Christians.[72]

Nedungatt goes on to say that "consecrated virgins are partners in a *qyāmâ* with Christ,"[73] and that, in Aphrahat's day, "the *qyāmâ* of the Covenanters was the equivalent of a perpetual vow of chastity, by which they knew to be freely entering upon a higher state of life in the Church, regulated by its pastors."[74] Finally, he says, "their *qyāmâ* therefore, can be rightly called the covenant of celibacy."[75]

Having come to the conclusion that *qyāmâ* means covenant or pact, even when it is used to signify the state of the *îḥîdāyê* in the Syriac-speaking church, Nedungatt makes the connection between this Syriac usage and the parlance of the Greek and Latin speakers on the same subject. He says,

> The *qyāmâ* of the Covenanters does not differ from the *synthēke* and *pactum virginitatis* of the *monádzontes* in the Greco-Roman world of the early fourth century.[76]

With this allegation, Nedungatt expresses both what had become the conventional wisdom regarding the significance of the term *bnay qyāmâ,* and also brings it within the range of the familiar Western (Greek and Latin) frames of reference employed by most scholars of early Christianity. By doing so, however, he leaves unexplored the further connotations of the expression in Syriac—connotations that are equally significant for understanding what authors like Aphrahat and Ephraem actually have to say about the role in the life of the church of the *îḥîdāyê.*

The verbal root *q-w-m* means basically "to rise" and "to stand," and the noun derived from it, *qyāmâ,* means not only "covenant," but, depending on the context, it means "stand," or "status," "state," "station," (as in station in life); and even "resurrection," as in "standing up" from among the dead—although for the latter phenomenon the related noun *qyamtâ* is generally employed.[77] Accordingly, a number of scholars have now called attention to the further dimensions of meaning in the term, all the while abiding by the convention of translating it with the word "covenant."[78]

Scholars have been intrigued by the translated expression "sons of the covenant" because it is clear that in some passages Aphrahat used the word *qyāmâ* in the sense of covenant, to designate the church as a whole.[79] And to historically minded researchers this usage recalled the Hebrew term *bᵉrît* (covenant), as the Qumran covenanters used it to designate their own somewhat ascetically oriented community.[80] Once this Jewish/Christian connection was made, the way was open to the suggestion that comparably in the early Syriac-speaking Christian community, baptism, and consequently, full membership in the church/covenant, was open only to the celibate. Arthur Vööbus was the scholar whose works have most recently put this view into wide circulation, when he proposed that passages from Aphrahat's *Demonstrations* have preserved liturgical strains from earlier times in the Syriac milieu.[81] Vööbus's studies did much to highlight the baptismal setting of the initiation of an individual into the *îḥîdāyûtâ*. But for the understanding of the ecclesial institution, the *bnay qyāmâ,* this line of inquiry proved to be something of a "red herring." For the attention of scholars was distracted from the investigation of the conditions and of the symbolic value of the station in life of those professing *îḥîdāyûtâ,* to combat the notion that, in the early days in the Syriac-speaking community, only the celibate might receive the sacrament of baptism.[82]

As for the connotations of the Syriac term *qyāmâ,* once one gets beyond the implications of the translation word "covenant," one is free to follow the guidance of the senses of the word in the various contexts in which it appears. In the works of Aphrahat and Ephraem, there are two senses of the term that seem to be particularly significant. First there is the resurrection idea that is never far below the surface when the root *q-w-m* is deployed. Then there is the fact that a number of nouns derived from this root straightforwardly bespeak one's status or station in life in the church—exactly the nuance one wants to interpret the expression *bnay qyāmâ.*

A number of passages in Aphrahat's *Demonstrations* and elsewhere speak of the *îḥîdāyê* or the *bnay qyāmâ* as human beings who have "taken on the likeness of the angels,"[83] for whom virginity is a "communion with the Watchers of heaven."[84] When one conjoins this idea with the gospel passage that speaks of those who have risen from the dead as being "equal to the angels, being the children of God, the children of the resurrection" (*Luke* 20.36), it is a short step to the suggestion that the phrase *bnay qyāmâ* means simply "sons of the resurrection." While one knows of no text in the works of Aphrahat or Ephraem that explicitly makes this connection, there are scholars who posit the connection on the grounds of its internal logic.[85] Peter Nagel, for example, says,

> To me the conclusion seems to be unavoidable, that by the designation *Bnay Qyāmâ,* the Syrian ascetics understood themselves as "Sons of the Resurrection," since in their *Askēsis* they realized the *Vita Angelica.*[86]

Only one scholar, Michael Breydy, has straightforwardly followed Nagel's suggestion that the phrase *bnay qyāmâ* means simply "sons of the resurrection."[87] Others have argued against the proposal, citing Aphrahat's failure to make such an understanding explicit, even when his context would seem to demand it.[88] Therefore it seems highly unlikely that the expression "sons of the resurrection" is itself an apt rendering of the phrase *bnay qyāmâ;* even though it might, strictly speaking, be lexically possible.

While "resurrection" is not by itself an apt translation of the word *qyāmâ* in the contexts we have been discussing, it is nevertheless unlikely that the resurrection concept was entirely absent from Aphrahat's mind in his discussion of the *bnay qyāmâ.* It is the nature of Semitic languages and their semantics to employ polyvalent terms. Given the presumption that all forms derive from a particular set of root consonants, they carry a reference to all the other lexical possibilities implicit in their shared roots.[89] Indeed, this feature of a language like Syriac is one of the means at the disposal of its writers to compose artful speech—*Kunstprosa,* one might call it. In this enterprise, Aphrahat the writer was a master, as more than one scholar has observed.[90] Accordingly, one cannot claim that no notion of resurrection lies behind the phrase *bnay qyāmâ.* Rather, one might most plausibly say that it is always present, at least by implication, and that sometimes, as in the following quotation from the *Demonstrations* on the *bnay qyāmâ,* the polyvalent possibilities of the root *q-w-m* are the very focus of the writer's artistry. The passage comes near the end of the *Demonstration* in question; and, in terms of Aphrahat's distinctive eschatology, it describes the final resurrection of the *îḥîdāyâ.* Aphrahat says,

> As for the one who keeps the Spirit of Christ in purity, when it comes into the presence of Christ, it will say to Him, the body into which I came, and which clothed me with the waters of Baptism, kept me in consecrated holiness *(qadîšûtâ).* And this Spirit of holiness will exhort Christ at the resurrection *(qyāmteh)* of the body which kept it in purity, and the Spirit will pray that it will be added to that body to rise *(danqūm)* in glory. . . . When the end time of completion comes, and the time of the resurrection *(qyāmtâ)* draws near, the Spirit of holiness which was kept in purity will hearken to the great power of its own nature, and it will come ahead of Christ, and it will stand *(qyāmâ)* at the gate of the cemetery, the location of the buried men who kept it in purity, and it will await the cry. And when the Watchers open the gates of heaven before the King, then the horn will call and the trumpets will blare, and the Spirit that is awaiting the cry will hear and rapidly it will open the graves and raise up *(wamqîmâ)* the bodies and everything concealed in them, and it will clothe in glory the one that will accompany it, and it will be within for the resurrection *(qyāmteh)* of the body, and the glory will be without for the ornamentation of the body.[91]

In this relatively short passage, three of the six occurrences of the root *q-w-m* are the customary word for "resurrection," *qyāmtâ.* The assemblage of six occurrences of the root in so abbreviated a space is obviously a stylistic feature of the artistry of the passage, given its subject matter. It would hardly escape the notice of the practiced reader of such a piece that it is part of a discourse on the eschatological future of the *bnay qyāmâ.* The connection between the words *qyāmtâ* and *qyāmâ* would, therefore, be implicit here and allusive. But they could in no way be declared to be utterly distinct from, and completely irrelevant to, one another.

In another passage, toward the beginning of *Demonstration 6,* the manuscripts themselves give variant readings, and it is unclear whether one is to read *qyāmtâ* or *qyāmâ* in a sentence which it seems best to translate, "Let us be partakers in his (i.e., Christ's) passion, so that we might live in his resurrection."[92] So one may plausibly say that the resurrection idea is inevitably implied in the term *qyāmâ* in the phrase *bnay qyāmâ,* without being the best choice, or even, by itself, the correct one for rendering the term in a Western language.

In addition to the valid translation word "covenant" for the Syriac term *qyāmâ* in the phrase *bnay qyāmâ,* and in addition, as well, to any allusion to resurrection, there is the rendering "status" or "station in life." There are a number of passages in which this sense of the word seems most plausible. Perhaps for the present purpose a single stanza from St. Ephraem's *Nisibene Hymns* will serve best to illustrate the point. Here Ephraem is praising Bishop Abraham of Nisibis (361–363 CE); and the stanza is rich for our understanding of the role of the *bnay qyāmâ* in Ephraem's conception of the ecclesiastical polity. He says to the bishop,

You are the crown of the priesthood;
  in you the ministry shines.
You are a brother to the presbyters,
  a superintendent to the deacons.
You are a master for the youth,
  a staff and a helping hand for the aged.
You are a protective wall for the chaste women;
  in the status you assume, the people of
  station achieve glory.
The church is adorned with your beauty;
  blest is the One who elected you
  to fill the office of priest.[93]

The interesting line here is the one that reads, "in the status you assume *(qawmāk),* the people of station *(qyāmâ)* achieve glory." In the immediate context, Ephraem is speaking both of the bishop's own status in the church and that of the chaste women, presumably *bnāt qyāmâ,* whose station *(qyāmâ)* and that of others, presumably *bnay qyāmâ,* is enhanced by their relationship to the bishop's status. The status he assumes, and the station the others have, seems to be that of participants in the *îḥîdāyûtâ.* For earlier in the same collection of hymns, Ephraem said of the same bishop Abraham that he was:

Single *(îḥîdāyâ)* in his everyday life,
  being within his own body "holy" *(qadîšâ);*
Single *(îḥîdāyâ)* in his house,
  inwardly and outwardly chaste *(nakpâ).*[94]

Accordingly, the expression *bnay qyāmâ* may be understood to express the station in life the *îḥîdāyê* assume, by the extra step they take at baptism to put on the heavenly *Îḥîdāyâ,* "the Lord of the many"—whereby they come, as St. Ephraem said in the Epiphany Hymn quoted earlier, "to fill for Him the place of the many, and Christ becomes [for them], the greatest treasure."[95] On this reading the status or the station in life the *îḥîdāyê* take, by contract or covenant, is much more than just a pact of virginity or celibacy, as Nedungatt would have it. For the many, they stand for Christ, and for Christ they stand for the many, as Ephraem says. If this is their station in life, it may also be why they are called people of status in the community. It seems to have been not so much a matter of a spiritual élite, as Dom Edmund Beck would have it,[96] or a matter of a church within the church, as Robert Murray has suggested[97]; although neither of these characterizations is false. Rather, the active stance that the *îḥîdāyâ* was expected to take in the community consisted principally in serving as a type for his own people. This, as St. Ephraem said, was the accomplishment of Julian Saba in the passage quoted earlier.[98] This was the role of the *îḥîdāyâ* as a living icon of paradise restored. It determined his status within the ecclesial community.

Abîlâ

In one stanza of the third hymn in praise of Syria's first hermit/monk of record, St. Ephraem characterizes him in very traditional ascetical terms. He says,

> Saba is the champion, the virgin, the holy one,
> Who preserved chastity, virginity, without injury;
> Mournfulness without outrage;
> Humility without pride;
> And leadership without the troublesomeness of boasting.[99]

The only term not yet discussed in this string of traditional terms, or their abstract expressions, in which Ephraem customarily characterized the *îḥîdāyê* is "mournfulness." As St. Ephraem uses it, the term refers to that sorrow or compunction for sin that, in his day, led some ascetic Christians into the desert in mournful penitence, most likely in response to the Beatitude: "Blessed are they who mourn, for they shall be comforted" (*Mt.* 5.4). The term *abîlâ,* or "mourner," thus became one of the technical expressions which Ephraem and others used to describe a person who in another milieu might be called an anchorite.[100] In Syriac, however, the term accents the attitude of the penitent rather than the outward circumstances in which he lived out his compunction. Ephraem put the phrase in context in one of his hymns *On Virginity,* in which he speaks of the biblical town of Ephraim, "the neighbor of the desert," as he calls it, where, according to *John* 11.54, Jesus and his disciples took refuge from the Jews during the time before the Passion. Ephraem says in a verse of praise addressed to the town of Ephraim,

> In you is the type [God] depicted for the
> mourners *(abîlê)* who love
> The all-freeing desert waste.[101]

He means that the penitential mourners in the Christian communities he knew were liable to seek the solitude of the desert for the exercise of their penitence. And there they were likely to neglect the amenities of civilized life, as a passage in one of Ephraem's hymns *On Paradise* suggests. He says in words addressed to such mourners,

Bear up, O life of mourning,
so that you might attain to Paradise;
Its dew will wash off your squalor,
while what it exudes will render you fragrant;
Its support will afford rest after your toil,
its crown will give you comfort.[102]

The squalor spoken of in this verse is, of course, the squalor of sin; but given a desert setting for the life of penitent mourning, the squalor may just as well also be that actual dirt that attaches to one who lives in the desert among the animals after the model of the penitent king Nebuchadnezzar (*Dn.* 4.33–37), as St. Ephraem depicts in the thirteenth hymn *On Paradise.*[103]

For St. Ephraem, the term *abîlâ* (mourner) suggests a penitent ascetic with a penchant for living alone for a time in the desert. *Abîlûthâ* (mourning) and the *îḥîdāyûthâ* (single lifestyle) for him unite to make up the profile of the ascetical life, as people in his milieu were inclined to live it. Julian Saba's principal difference from the traditional singles consisted in his role as the founding father of a community of hermits, whose style of life required a permanent withdrawal in a body from town and village ecclesiastical society. Later in the fourth and fifth centuries, the Syriac poets who sang the praises of the burgeoning movement of hermits in the church used the traditional ascetic term *abîlâ* as almost the equivalent of the word "hermit." In this sense it was a term unique to the Syrians, and it played no small role in presenting the tableau of vivid gestures that Peter Brown found to be characteristic of asceticism in the Syriac-speaking milieu. But in its traditional meaning, as St. Ephraem used it, it had nothing to do with anchoritic monks, and everything to do with the expression of ascetic penitence.

History and the Forms of Asceticism

For all practical purposes, the works of Aphrahat and St. Ephraem are the only documentary sources available to the modern scholar who wants to inquire into the history of the early organized forms of asceticism in the Syriac-speaking world. They both flourished in the fourth century. Even when earlier texts like the *Odes of Solomon* or the *Acts of Judas Thomas*[104] afford one some insight into the ascetical thinking of an earlier age, one almost always has to recast the scene in reference to what is learned from Aphrahat and Ephraem, who are primary witnesses to the institutions of their own day in Syria. By the fourth century, these institutions were already well enough established that certain abuses had crept into them, and currents of change and reform in the ascetical establishment were already afoot, prompted perhaps by the Peace of Constantine, which effectively removed one earlier form of complete self-giving, namely martyrdom.

Both Aphrahat and Ephraem addressed themselves to abuses among the *îḥîdāyê* and the *bnay qyāmâ*. In *Demonstration* 6 Aphrahat was forceful in his exhortation to both men and women celibates against their cohabitation. He said,

> Any man, a *bar qyāmâ,* or a consecrated holy one who loves *îḥîdāyûtâ,* but wants a woman, a *bat qyāmâ* like himself, to live with him, it were better for him to take a woman openly and not be captivated in lust. And a woman too, it is also fitting for her, if she cannot separate from the man, the *îḥîdāyâ,* to belong to the man openly.[105]

Aphrahat goes on later in the *Demonstration* to give explicit advice to single, consecrated women who have received invitations of cohabitation from single men. It is worth translating the advice in full, because the terms Aphrahat uses fairly express his estimation of the values involved. He says,

> O virgins, who have espoused yourselves to Christ, if one of the *bnay qyāmâ* should say to one of you, "May I live with you, and you serve me." You say to him, "I am betrothed to a man, the King, and him I serve. If I leave his service and come to serve you, my betrothed will be angry at me and he will write me a letter of divorce and he will dismiss me from his house. If you want to be held in honor by me, and if I am to be held in honor by you, so that no harm might reach me or you, do not put a fire in your bosom, lest you set your own clothes to burning. Rather, you stay honorably alone, and I will be honorably alone. Such things as the Bridegroom prepared for the eternities of his banquet get for yourself for a wedding gift and prepare yourself to meet Him. And I shall get oil ready for myself to enter with the wise ones, and not be left outside with the foolish virgins."[106]

Clearly there were abuses among the celibate men and women singles in the church in Aphrahat's day. And St. Ephraem, at a slightly later date, registered a similar complaint in similar language. In his *Letter to Publius* Ephraem contrasted the hypocrisy of publicly proclaimed virgins with the manifest virtue of those who did not bear the formal title of virginity. He made the comparison in the description of a vision of the next life. He said,

> I saw there pure virgins whose virginity had been rejected because it had not been adorned with the good oil of excellent works. . . . I also saw there those who did not have the title of virginity, but who were crowned with victorious deeds, their conduct having filled the place of virginity. . . . Let no man any longer trust in the chaste reputation alone of virginity when it is deprived of the works which constitute the oil of the lamps.[107]

The evidences of a decline in the morals of some of the professional celibates in the fourth century are clear. Commentators generally suppose that both Aphrahat and Ephraem preserve the ideals of an earlier age, while they address the problems that had crept into the institution of the *bnay qyāmâ* in their own day. According to this reading, one might suppose that earlier (perhaps even as remote as the second century) enthusiastic, single Christians had led lives of consecrated virginity along the lines recommended in the *Acts of Judas Thomas.* One might further suppose that they had consecrated their virginity to God at baptism, along the lines suggested by Arthur Vööbus, and that their consecration was encouraged by the homiletic themes so evocatively studied by Robert Murray.[108] One also supposes that these singles were called *îḥîdāyê.* But these suppositions are all extrapolations from the fourth-century evidence we actually have in hand, which immediately testifies to a more easily imaginable set of human circumstances.

From the evidence we have in hand it seems that, at the dawn of the fourth century at least, both the men and the women celibates were free to choose their own living arrangements within their local communities. One does not yet hear of withdrawn individuals or communities of singles in desert or mountain areas in the Syriac-speaking world. This ascetical fashion appears in texts from Syria toward the end of St. Ephraem's lifetime. But St. Ephraem does offer evidence of some formal ecclesiastical organization among the *îḥîdāyê* of his day. He says that Bishop Abraham of Nisibis, for example, was the protector of the *bnay qyāmâ* of his diocese.[109] The bishop himself was an *îḥîdāyâ,*[110] so this status was not incompatible with formal office in the church. Moreover, he governed his diocese as the chief *rā'yâ* (shepherd) of the *mar'îtâ* (flock), with the help of what St. Ephraem called a *dayrâ d'allānê* (fold of herdsmen);[111] of which group he was himself a member, on his own testimony.[112] St. Ephraem says, further, that in his day there were daughter churches in every direction from Nisibis, each with their own *dayrôtô* (sheep folds)[113] and, one supposes, resident *îḥîdāyê,* in whose number would be the priests and deacons who were the *'allānê* (herdsmen) of the chief shepherd's larger flock.

One notices that St. Ephraem's vocabulary here includes traditional terms such as *îḥîdāyâ, qyāmâ,* and *dayrâ* that in Syriac would become the standard terms for "monk," monastic "status," and "monastery" in a later parlance. But modern scholars prefer to speak of the period of St. Ephraem's own Nisibene ministry, and of earlier times, as the period of premonasticism or protomonasticism.[114] The reason for this preference seems to be that in modern discourse the words "monk," "monastery," and "monasticism" bespeak the more organized forms of religious life that emerged in the course of the fourth century and that were based on an individual or collective physical withdrawal from the society of the baptized community as a whole, that is, *anachōrēsis* as a condition of a new form of ascetical life. St. Ephraem himself noticed and praised this development in the Syriac-speaking world in the accolades he penned in praise of the anchorite outside Edessa, St. Julian Saba. But it is noteworthy that the terms of St. Ephraem's praise are the traditional terms appropriate to the *bnay qyāmâ.* Thus, in the Syriac-speaking church the old and new forms of ascetical, celibate life lived on together.[115] Occasionally one even finds the traditional terms used to evoke an earlier day, to which the writer looks back with nostalgia. The sixth century writer of the *Doctrina Addai,* for example, portrays the early Syriac-speaking Christians of Mesopotamia as one and all worthy *îḥîdāyê,* members of the *qyāmâ.* The *Doctrina* says of the ministry of Aggai, the apostle Addai's successor:

> In the souls of the believers he enriched Christ's church. For the whole *qyāmâ* of men and women were chaste and resplendent. They were consecrated holy *(qadîšê)* and pure, and they were living singly *(îḥîdā'ît)* and chastely without defilement.[116]

Of such language are ecclesiastical legends made—and of such suggestions are some, now legendary, scholarly theories constituted—about the origins of monastic asceticism in the Syriac-speaking orient. But the word studies presented here enable one to discern some of the most important ascetic, and, eventually, monastic vocabulary arising, in their traditional meanings, in the works of the classic writers of fourth-century Syria.

Bnay qyāmâ designated a group of celibate people belonging to a certain station in life in the community that in the early period of the history of the church in the Syriac-speaking world they assumed by covenant, or solemn pledge, at baptism. Such persons took their stand with an anticipatory view to the Resurrection, the goal of all Christians. Their status in the community served as a type for the expectations of all the baptized.

In the fourth century, and presumably earlier, *îḥîdāyâ* designated an individual member of the *bnay qyāmâ* in such a way that the term first of all invoked the person's special investiture in Christ Jesus, the Son of God, "God the *Îḥîdāyâ* in the bosom of the Father" (*John* 1.18)—to the effect that he stood out from the many sacrificially, and filled their place for the Lord of the many, as St. Ephraem put it.[117] Secondly, the *îḥîdāyâ*'s emulation of Jesus Christ meant that, like Christ, he was single as a celibate, and single in his lifestyle. It was neither right nor fitting, as Aphrahat would put it, for men or women *îḥîdāyê* even to take house companions of the opposite sex.[118] Later in the Syriac-speaking world the term *îḥîdāyâ* came to have the same range of meanings as did the Greek term *monachos,* the very Greek term that, if some modern scholars are correct in their surmises, writers in the early fourth century had first used in a Christian context to render the Syriac term *îḥîdāyâ!*[119] Jacob of Serug (d. 521 CE), for an example of the later Syriac usage, in his metric homilies "To the *îḥîdāyê,*" was clearly addressing people whom no modern scholar would hesitate to call monks.[120]

So the final question is whether, in what they had to say about the *îḥîdāyê,* or about the *bnay qyāmâ,* to use their institutional designation, Aphrahat and St. Ephraem were talking about monasticism, properly so called. Some modern scholars think that some such term as "protomonasticism" or "premonasticism" would be more appropriate.[121] But what we call monasticism in our Western languages is what grew out of the anchoritic and cenobitic experiences of many Christians in Egypt and Palestine in the fourth century. When these usages reached the Syriac-speaking world in the days of St. Ephraem, in the person of Julian Saba and his followers they assumed the proportions of a reform movement among the *bnay qyāmâ,* and eventually they all but supplanted the old ways. As for the term "monk," it is an etymologically correct term to render the Syriac *îḥîdāyâ* in Western languages. But like many translation words, it is essentially misleading, given the inevitable overtones of fourth-century Egypt that accompany the words "monk" and "monasticism" as we now actually use them. The *bnay qyāmâ* and the *abîlê* were not properly speaking monks, but their institutions and their traditional vocabulary were ready to contribute to the growth of monasticism when it appeared in Syria, together with the other institutions of the Great Church. And, as in many other instances, so in this one, while Ephraem the Syrian was not himself a monk, his life and his work did everything to provide for the success of monasticism in Syria in the fourth century—in its own distinctive style.

NOTES

1. See I. Peña et al., *Les stylites syriens* (Milan: Franciscan Printing Press, 1975); H.J.W. Drijvers, "Spätantike Parallelen zur altchristlichen Heiligenverehrung unter besonderer Berücksichtigung des syrischen Stylitenkultes," in *Aspekte frühchristlicher Heiligenverehrung,* Oikonomia 6 (Erlangen: University of Erlangen, 1977), pp. 54–76; Susan Ashbrook Harvey, "The Sense of a Stylite: Perspectives on Simeon the Elder," *Vigiliae Christianae* 42 (1988):376–394. See now Robert Doran, *The Lives of Simeon Stylites,* Cistercian Studies 112 (Kalamazoo, Mich.: Cistercian Publications, 1992).
2. Peter Brown, *The Body and Society; Men, Women and Sexual Renunciation in Early Christianity* (New York: Columbia University Press, 1988), p. 330.
3. Ibid., p. 332.
4. Ibid., p. 333.
5. Ibid., p. 334.
6. On this subject see E. A. Judge, "The Earliest Use of Monachos for 'Monk' (P. Coll. Youtie 77) and the Origins of Monasticism," *Jahrbuch für Antike und Christentum* 20 (1977):72–89; *idem,* "Fourth-Century Monasticism in the Papyri," in Roger S. Bagnall, ed., *Proceedings of the Sixteenth International Congress of Papyrology; New York, 24–31 July 1980,* American Studies in Papyrology 23 (Chico, Calif.: Scholars Press, 1981), pp. 613–620. See also James E. Goehring, "The World Engaged; the Social and Economic World of Early Egyptian Monasticism," in J. E. Goehring et al., eds., *Gnosticism and the Early Christian World; in Honor of James M. Robinson* (Sonoma, Calif.: Polebridge Press, 1990), pp. 134–144.
7. See particularly the studies of Han J. W. Drijvers, "The 19th Ode of Solomon: Its Interpretation and Place in Syrian Christianity," *Journal of Theological Studies* 31 (1980):337–355; *idem,* "Odes of Solomon and Psalms of Mani; Christians and Manichaeans in Third-Century Syria," in *Studies in Gnosticism and Hellenistic Religions: Festschrift G. Quispel* (Leiden: E. J. Brill, 1981), pp. 117–130; *idem,* "Die Legende des heiligen Alexius und der Typus des Gottesmannes im syrischen Christentum," in M. Schmidt, ed., *Typus, Symbol, Allegorie bei den östlichen Vätern und ihren Parallelen im Mittelalter,* Eichstatter Beiträge 4 (Regensburg: Pustet, 1981), pp. 187–217.
8. See S. H. Griffith, "Ephraem, the Deacon of Edessa, and the Church of the Empire," in T. Halton and J. P. Williman, eds., *Diakonia: Studies in Honor of Robert T. Meyer* (Washington: Catholic University of America Press, 1986), pp. 22–52; *idem,* "Ephraem the Syrian's Hymns 'Against Julian'; Meditations on History and Imperial Power," *Vigiliae Christianae* 41 (1987):238–266; *idem,* "Setting Right the Church of Syria; Ephraem's Hymns against Heresies," *Journal of Eastern Christian Studies,* to appear.
9. See P. Peeters, "La legende de saint Jacques de Nisibe," *Analecta Bollandiana* 38 (1920):285–373; David Bundy, "Jacob of Nisibis as a Model for the Episcopacy," *Le Muséon* 104 (1991):235–249; E. Mathews, "The *Vita* Tradition of Ephrem the Syrian," *Diakonia* 22 (1988–1989):15–42; S. H. Griffith, "Images of Ephraem: the Syrian Holy Man and his Church," *Traditio* 45 (1989–1990):7–33; Joseph P. Amar, "Byzantine Ascetic Monachism and Greek Bias in the *Vita* Tradition of Ephrem the Syrian," *Orientalia Christiana Periodica* 58 (1992):123–156.
10. See J.-M. Fiey, "Aonès, Awun et Awgin (Eugène) aux origines du monachisme mésopotamien," *Analecta Bollandiana* 80 (1962):52–81.
11. The "Letter to the Mountaineers" is most recently published in Edmund Beck, *Des heiligen Ephraem des Syrers Sermones IV,* Corpus scriptorum christianorum orientalium, vol. 334 (Louvain, 1973), pp. 28–43. The second text, too, is most recently edited

in Beck, *Sermones IV*, pp. 1–16, as well as the third text, pp. 16–28. The fourth text is most recently re-presented, with an English translation, in E. Mathews, "Isaac of Antioch: A Homily on Solitaries, Hermits, and Mourners," master's thesis, The Catholic University of America, Washington, D.C., 1987.

12. See Arthur Vööbus, "Beitrage zur kritischen Sichtung der asketischen Schriften, die unter dem Namen Ephraem des Syrers uberliefert sind," *Oriens Christianus* 39 (1955):48–55; *idem, History of Asceticism in the Syrian Orient,* CSCO, vol. 197 (Louvain, 1960), 2:1–11; *idem, Literary Critical and Historical Studies in Ephraem the Syrian* (Stockholm, 1958), pp. 59–65, 69–86.
13. See the case presented with full bibliographical citations of earlier studies in E. Mathews, "'On Solitaries': Ephraem or Isaac?" *Le Muséon* 103 (1990):91–110.
14. See the studies cited in note 6 above, and Samuel Rubenson, *The Letters of St. Anthony; Origenist Theology, Monastic Tradition and the Making of a Saint* (Lund: Lund University Press, 1990).
15. One thinks in particular of the legislation attributed to Rabbula, the famous fifth-century bishop of Edessa. See Arthur Vööbus, *Syriac and Arabic Documents Regarding Legislation Relative to Syrian Asceticism,* Papers of the Estonian Theological Society in Exile (Stockholm, 1960), 11:24–50, 78–86; *idem, History of Asceticism in the Syrian Orient,* CSCO, vol. 500 (Louvain, 1988), 3:68–77. See also Susan Ashbrook Harvey, "Bishop Rabbula: Ascetic Tradition and Change in Fifth Century Edessa," to appear in a forthcoming issue of the *Journal of Eastern Christian Studies.*
16. See Sidney H. Griffith, "Hymns to Julian Saba; the Hermit/Monk of Syria," a forthcoming study of texts (already published in Edmund Beck, *Des heiligen Ephraem des Syrers: Hymnen auf Abraham Kidunaya und Julianos Saba,* CSCO, vols. 322 and 323 [Louvain, 1972]).
17. See Antoine Guillaumont, "Situation et signification du 'Liber Graduum' dans la spiritualité syriaque," in *Symposium Syriacum 1972,* Orientalia Christiana Analecta 197 (Rome, 1974), pp. 311–322; Aleksander Kowalski, *Perfezione e Giustizia di Adamo nel Liber Graduum,* Orientalia Christiana Analecta 232 (Rome, 1989); Columba Stewart, *'Working the Earth of the Heart'; The Messalian Controversy in History, Texts, and Language to AD 431* (Oxford, 1991).
18. See Antoine Guillaumont, *Les 'Kephalaia Gnostica' d'Evagre le Pontique et l'histoire de l'Origénisme chez les grecs et les syriens* (Paris, 1962); Pierre Canivet, *Le monachisme syrien sélon Theodoret de Cyr,* Théologie historique 42 (Paris, 1977). A still masterly study is that of Stephan Schiwietz, *Das morgenlandische Mönchtum,* vol. 3, *Das Mönchtum in Syrien und Mesopotamien und das Asketentum in Persien* (Mödling bei Wien, 1938).
19. The old ways persisted particularly in that segment of the Syriac-speaking world that would later be called the Syrian Orthodox church. See Arthur Vööbus, "The Institution of the *Benai Qeiama* and *Benat Qeiama* in the Ancient Syriac Church," *Church History* 30 (1961):19–27; Susan Ashbrook Harvey, *Asceticism and Society in Crisis; John of Ephesus and the Lives of the Eastern Saints* (Berkeley, Calif.: University of California Press, 1990).
20. See, for example, I. Parisot, ed., *Aphraatis Sapientis Persae Demonstrationes,* Patrologia Syriaca (Paris, 1894, 1907), 1.6.260, 272.
21. See below, and E. Beck, *Des heiligen Ephraem des Syrers Carmina Nisibena,* erster Teil, CSCO, vol. 218 (Louvain, 1961), 17.3–4, p. 46.
22. See, for example, *1 Timothy* 5.3–16; *1 Corinthians* 7.25–35; and I. E. Rahmani, ed., *Testamentum Domini Nostri Jesu Christi* (Moguntiae, 1899), pp. 104–109.

23. See A. Vööbus, *History of Asceticism in the Syrian Orient* 1:104–106; Marie-Joseph Pierre, trans., *Aphraate le Sage Persan, les Exposés,* Sources chrétiennes, vols. 349, 350 (Paris, 1988), 1:376, note 38.
24. A. Adam, "Grundbegriffe des Mönchtums in sprachlicher Sicht," *Zeitschrift fur Kirchengeschichte* 64 (1953/54):209–239.
25. R. Murray, "The Exhortation to Candidates for Ascetical Vows at Baptism in the Ancient Syriac Church," *New Testament Studies* 21 (1974–1975):59–80.
26. E. Beck, "Ein Beitrag zur Terminologie des altesten syrischen Mönchtums," in *Antonius Magnus Eremita,* Studia Anselmiana 38 (Rome, 1956), pp. 254–267; "Asketentum und Monchtum bei Ephraem," in *Il Monachesimo Orientale,* Orientalia Christiana Analecta 153 (Rome, 1958), pp. 341–362. French translation in *L'Orient Syrien* 3 (1958):273–298.
27. G. Quispel, "L'Évangile selon Thomas et les origines de l'ascèse chrétienne," in *Gnostic Studies II* (Istanbul, 1975), pp. 98–112.
28. A. Guillaumont, "Monachisme et éthique judéo-chrétienne," *Recherches de science religieuse* 60 (1972):199–218; "Le nom des 'Agapètes,'" *Vigiliae Christianae* 23 (1969):30–37. Both articles appear in Guillaumont's collection of separately published pieces, *Aux origines du monachisme chrétien,* Spiritualité orientale 30 (Bégrolles en Mauges, 1979).
29. See Vööbus, *History of Asceticism* 1:6–8; Beck, "Ein Beitrag zur Terminologie," written expressly against the ideas advanced by Alfred Adam in "Grundbegriffe des Monchtums." Adam replied in "Der Monachos Gedanke innerhalb der Spiritualitat der alten Kirche," in *Glaube, Geist, Geschichte; Festschrift E. Benz* (Leiden, 1967), pp. 259–265.
30. See the articles cited in notes 24 and 28 above.
31. Murray, "Exhortation to Candidates," p. 67.
32. Eusebius of Caesarea, "Commentaria in Psalmos," *PG* 23.689.
33. R. Murray, *Symbols of Church and Kingdom: A Study in Early Syriac Tradition* (Cambridge, 1975), p. 355.
34. I. Parisot, *Aphraatis Sapientis Persae Demonstrationes,* Patrologia Syriaca (Paris, 1884), cols. 239–312. See A. J. Van der Aalst, "A l'origine du monachisme syrien; les 'ihidaye' chez Aphrahat," in A.A.R. Bastiaensen et al., eds., *Fructus Centesimus; Mélanges offerts à Gerard J. M. Bartelink,* Instrumenta Patristica 19 (Steenburg, 1989); pp. 315–324.
35. Parisot, *Aphraatis Demonstrationes,* col. 261.
36. Ibid., col. 269.
37. Ibid., col. 276.
38. Ibid., col. 272.
39. Pierre, *Aphraate, les exposés* 1:383, note 51.
40. E. Beck, *Des heiligen Ephraem des Syrers Hymnen de Paradiso und Contra Julianum,* CSCO, vol. 174 (Louvain, 1957), 7.18, p. 29. See now the English version of the Paradise hymns by Sebastian Brock, *St. Ephraem the Syrian: Hymns on Paradise* (Crestwood, N.Y., 1990), p. 125 for a slightly different translation.
41. Other Ephraem texts are discussed by Edmund Beck, O.S.B., in the articles cited in note 27 above.
42. In *John* 1.18, the term is *Îḥîdāyâ* in the Peshitta; in the *Diatessaron,* as Ephraem commented on it, the term is *Yaḥîdâ.* See L. Leloir, *Saint Ephrem, Commentaire de l'Evangile concordant* (Dublin, 1963), p. 2. See also L. Leloir, *Le Temoignage d'Ephrem sur le Diatessaron,* CSCO, vol. 227 (Louvain, 1962), p. 100.

43. See Murray, "The Exhortation to Candidates," for bibliography regarding the earlier controversy over celibacy as a requirement for baptism in the Syriac-speaking church, and A. Vööbus, *Celibacy, a Requirement for Admission to Baptism in the Early Syrian Church* (Stockholm, 1951). See now Edmund Beck, *Dōrea und Charis, die Taufe,* CSCO, vol. 457 (Louvain, 1984), pp. 56–185.
44. Edmund Beck, *Des heiligen Ephraem des Syrers Hymnen de Nativitate (Epiphania),* CSCO, vol. 186 (Louvain, 1959), p. 173.
45. Beck, *Des heiligen Ephraem Hymnen de Nativitate (Epiphania),* p. 191.
46. Such is the interpretation of Beck, *Dōrea und Charis,* pp. 162–163.
47. See the earlier statement in Beck, "Asketentum und Mönchtum," p. 344.
48. See Beck, *Dōrea und Charis,* p. 157, note 78; and pp. 160–161.
49. See Sebastian Brock, "Clothing Metaphors as a Means of Theological Expression in Syriac Tradition," in M. Schmidt, ed., *Typus, Symbol, Allegorie bei den östlichen Vätern und ihren Parallelen im Mittelalter,* Eichstatter Beitrage, vol. 4 (Regensburg, 1981), pp. 15–16, 25–26. See, too, the fascinating study of an earlier use of clothing imagery in the Semitic world by N. M. Waldman, "The Imagery of Clothing, Covering and Overpowering," *The Journal of the Ancient Near Eastern Society* 19 (1989):161–170; also M. E. Vogelzang and W. J. van Bekkum, "Meaning and Symbolism of Clothing in Ancient Near Eastern Texts," in H.L.J. Vanstiphout et al., eds., *Scripta Signa Vocis: Studies about Scripts, Scriptures, Scribes and Languages in the Near East, Presented to J. H. Hospers by His Pupils, Colleagues and Friends* (Groningen: Egbert Forsten, 1986), pp. 265–284.
50. Brock, "Clothing Metaphors." See also Sebastian Brock, *The Luminous Eye: The Spiritual World Vision of St. Ephrem* (Rome, 1985), pp. 65–76; revised ed., Cistercian Studies 124 (Kalamazoo, Mich., 1992), pp. 85–94.
51. See A. de Halleux, "Saint Éphrem le Syrien," *Revue théologique de Louvain* 14 (1983):353, for a discussion of Ephraem's idea of the church as the sacramental situation of Paradise restored.
52. See Françoise-E. Morard, "Monachos, moine; histoire du terme grec jusqu'au 4e siècle," *Freiburger Zeitschrift für Philosophie und Theologie* 20 (1973):354–357; H. Fabry, "*Yāḥad,*" in G. J. Botterweck and H. Ringgren, *Theologisches Wörterbuch zum alten Testament,* Band 3 (Stuttgart, 1982), cols. 595–603.
53. See A. Guillaumont, "Le nom des 'Agapètes,'" *Vigiliae Christianae* 23 (1969):30–37.
54. See A. Guillaumont, "Monachisme et éthique Judéo-Chrétienne," *Recherches de science religieuse* 60 (1972):199–218.
55. See note 5 above.
56. Francesca Cocchini, "Il Figlio Unigenito Sacrificato e Amato," *Studi Storico-Religiose* 1 (1977):201–323.
57. It is notable in this connection that in North Africa St. Augustine had to defend the use of the term *monachos/monachus* against the Donatist charge that the word is unscriptural. See St. Augustine's "Exposition of Psalm 132" in English translation in A. Zumkeller, *Augustine's Ideal of the Religious Life,* trans. E. Colledge (New York, 1986), pp. 398–401.
58. *Monogenēs, monotropos, monozōnos,* etc. See Murray, "Exhortation to Candidates"; and Guillaumont, "Monachisme et éthique."
59. Parisot, *Aphraatis Demonstrationes,* col. 276.
60. E. Beck, *Des heiligen Ephraem des Syrers: Hymnen auf Abraham Kidunaya und Julianus Saba,* CSCO, vol. 322 (Louvain, 1972), 2.13, p. 41.
61. See Murray, "Exhortation to Candidates."

62. See A. Guillaumont, "Sémitismes dans les Logia de Jesus retrouvés à Nag-Hamâdi," *Journal asiatique* 246 (1958):113–123; M. Harl, "A propos des *Logia* de Jésus: le sens du mot *MONAXOS*," *Revue des Études Grecques* 73 (1960):464–474; A.F.J. Klijn, "Das Thomasevangelium und das altsyrische Christentum," *Vigiliae Christianae* 15 (1961):146–159; *idem*, "The 'Single One' in the Gospel of Thomas," *Journal of Biblical Literature* 81 (1962):271–278; G. Quispel, "L'Evangile selon Thomas et les origines de l'ascese chrétienne," in G. Quispel, *Gnostic Studies II* (Istanbul, 1975), pp. 98–112; W. Vycichl, *Dictionnaire étymologique de la langue copte* (Leuven, 1983), pp. 173–174.
63. Klijn, "The 'Single One,'" p. 271.
64. See E. A. Judge, "The Earliest Use of Monachos," pp. 72, 86–87; F. E. Morard, "Monachos: Une importation sémitique en Égypte?' *Studia Patristica* 12 (1975):242–246; *idem*, "Encore quelques reflexions sur Monachos," *Vigiliae Christianae* 34 (1980):395–401.
65. The remarks that follow on this subject appear in an inchoate form in S. H. Griffith, "'Singles' and the 'Sons of the Covenant'; Reflections on Syriac Ascetic Terminology," in E. Carr et al., eds., *Eulogêma: Studies in Honor of Robert Taft, S.J.* (Rome: Pontificio Ateneo S. Anselmo, 1993).
66. See Murray, *Symbols of Church*, pp. 13–15; De Halleux, "Saint Éphrem le Syrien," p. 331. Pierre translates it "membres de l'Ordre." See the explanation in Pierre, *Aphraate, Exposés* 1:98, note 81.
67. See Parisot, *Aphraatis Demonstrationes*, 1.260, 272.
68. Ibid., col. 404.
69. R. Payne Smith, *Thesaurus Syriacus*, 2 vols. (Oxford, 1879–1883), pp. 3522–3538.
70. George Nedungatt, "The Covenanters of the Early Syriac-Speaking Church," *Orientalia Christiana Periodica* 39 (1973):191–215, 419–444.
71. Ibid., p. 195.
72. Ibid., p. 203.
73. Ibid., p. 433.
74. Ibid., p. 437.
75. Ibid., p. 438.
76. Ibid., p. 443.
77. Payne Smith, *Thesaurus Syriacus* 2:3533–3535.
78. See Murray, *Symbols of Church*, p. 13, note 5.
79. Nedungatt, "The Covenanters," pp. 196–199.
80. See Murray, *Symbols of Church*, p. 15, note 1.
81. See A. Vööbus, *Celibacy, a Requirement for Admission to Baptism in the Early Syrian Church* (Stockholm, 1951); *idem*, *History of Asceticism* 1:93–95, 175–178. The idea that Aphrahat's *Demonstrations* showed that the *bnay qyāmâ* were the baptized laity of the early Syriac-speaking church was put forward first by F. C. Burkitt, *Early Eastern Christianity* (London, 1904), pp. 129, 137–138.
82. Already, in 1905, R. H. Connolly reacted to Burkitt's proposals in his article, "Aphraates and Monasticism," *Journal of Theological Studies* 6 (1905):522–539. For an early review of Vööbus's proposals see J. Gribomont, "Le monachisme au sein de l'église en Syrie et en Cappadoce," *Studia Monastica* 7 (1965):7–24. Now Robert Murray's article, "Exhortation to Candidates" gives the best summary of the discussion and broadens the inquiry into the baptismal and liturgical circumstances of the inauguration of a prospective *bar gyāmâ*. Other studies not mentioned earlier that touch on the issues of the controversy are the following: A. Baker, "Syriac and the Origins of Monasti-

cism," *Downside Review* 86 (1968):342–353; *idem,* "Early Syriac Asceticism," *Downside Review* 88 (1970):393–409; S. Jargy, "Les 'fils et filles du pacte' dans la littérature monastique syriaque," *Orientalia Christiana Periodica* 17 (1951):304–320; *idem,* "Les origines du monachisme en Syrie et en Mésopotamie," *Proche-Orient Chrétien* 2 (1952):110–124; *idem,* "Les premiers instituts monastiques et les principaux representants du monachisme syrien au ive siècle," *Proche-Orient Chrétien* 4 (1954):106–117; M. M. Maude, "Who were the B^{e}nai Q^{e}yama?" *Journal of Theological Studies* 36 (1935):13–21.

83. Parisot, *Aphraatis Demonstrationes* 1.248.
84. Ibid., col. 309. See R. Murray, "Some Themes and Problems of Early Syriac Angelology," in *V Symposium Syriacum,* Orientalia Christiana Analecta 236 (Rome, 1990), pp. 143–153.
85. See Pierre, *Aphraate, les Exposés* 1:361, note 7.
86. P. Nagel, *Die Motivierung der Askese in der alten Kirche und der Ursprung des Mönchtums,* Texte und Untersuchungen 95 (Berlin, 1966), p. 43. See also the author's earlier article, "Zum Problem der 'Bundessohne' bei Afrahat," *Forschungen und Fortschritte* 36 (1962):152–154.
87. See Michael Breydy, "Les laics et les Bnay Qyomo dans l'ancienne tradition de l'église syrienne," *Kanon* 3 (1977):60–62.
88. See Nedungatt, "The Covenanters," p. 438, note 2.
89. See Louis Massignon, *Parole Donnée* (Paris, 1962), pp. 361–385.
90. See, for example, L. Hafeli, *Stilmittel bei Afrahat dem persischen Weisen* (Leipzig, 1932); M. Maude, "Rhythmic Patterns in the Homilies of Aphrahat," *Anglican Theological Review* 17 (1935):225–233.
91. Parisot, *Aphraatis Demonstrationes* 1.293–296. For the theological context of this passage see F. Gavin, "The Sleep of the Soul in the Early Syriac Church," *Journal of the American Oriental Society* 40 (1920):103–120.
92. Parisot, *Aphraatis Demonstrationes* 1.241. (See note for line 23.) See also Pierre, *Aphraate, les Exposés* 1:361, note 7.
93. E. Beck, *Des heiligen Ephraem des Syrers Carmina Nisibena, erster Teil,* CSCO, vol. 218 (Louvain, 1961), 21.5, pp. 55–56.
94. Beck, *Carmina Nisibena I* 15.9, p. 41.
95. Beck, *Hymnen de Nativitate (Epiphania)* 186:173.
96. See E. Beck, *Dōrea und Charis, die Taufe,* CSCO, vol. 457 (Louvain, 1984), p. 161.
97. See Murray, *Symbols of Church,* p. 13.
98. E. Beck, *Des heiligen Ephraem des Syrers: Hymnen auf Abraham Kidunaya und Julianus Saba,* CSCO, vol. 322 (Louvain, 1972), 2.13, p. 41.
99. Beck, *Hymnen auf Julianos Saba* 322.3.2, pp. 42–43.
100. See Beck, "Ein Beitrag zur Terminologie," pp. 262–263.
101. Edmund Beck, *Des heiligen Ephraem des Syrers Hymnen de Virginitate,* CSCO, vol. 223 (Louvain, 1962), 21.2, p. 71.
102. Edmund Beck, *Des heiligen Ephraem des Syrers: Hymnen de Paradiso und contra Julianum,* CSCO, vol. 174 (Louvain, 1957), 7.3, p. 26. The English translation here is that of Sebastian Brock, *Saint Ephrem; Hymns on Paradise* (Crestwood, N.Y., 1990), p. 119.
103. See Beck, *Hymnen de Paradiso* 174 esp. 13.2, 3, 4, 5, 6, 7, 8, 9, 10, 11, pp. 55–57. For a very insightful discussion of these stanzas in light of this theme, see the forthcoming study by Gary A. Anderson, "The Penitence of Adam in Early Judaism and Christianity."

104. See J. H. Charlesworth, ed., *Odes of Solomon* (Missoula, Montana, 1977); A.F.J. Klijn, *Acts of Thomas,* Novum Testamentum Supplements 5 (Leiden, 1962). In the present writer's opinion, the earlier currents of ascetical thought in the Syriac-speaking world can best be studied in the history of the origins of Manichaeism. See Han J. W. Drijvers, "Odes of Solomon and Psalms of Mani: Christians and Manichaeans in Third-Century Syria," in R. van den Broek and M. I. Vermaseren, eds., *Studies in Gnosticism and Hellenistic Religions Presented to Gilles Quispel* (Leiden, 1981), pp. 117–130; *idem,* "Conflict and Alliance in Manichaeism," in H. G. Kippenberg, ed., *Struggles of Gods* (Berlin, 1984), pp. 99–124; S.N.C. Lieu, *Manichaeism in the Later Roman Empire and Medieval China* (Manchester, 1985).
105. Parisot, *Aphraatis Demonstrationes* 1.260.
106. Ibid., col. 272.
107. S. Brock, "Ephrem's Letter to Publius," *Le Muséon* 89 (1976):286–287.
108. See Murray, "The Exhortation to Candidates" and *Symbols of Church.*
109. See Beck, *Carmina Nisibena,* CSCO, 218.21.5, pp. 55–56.
110. Ibid., 15.9, p. 41.
111. Ibid., 17.3, p. 46.
112. See E. Beck, *Des heiligen Ephraem des Syrers Hymnen contra Haereses* CSCO, vol. 169 (Louvain, 1957), 56.10, pp. 211–212.
113. See Beck, *Carmina Nisibena,* CSCO, 218.14.1, p. 37. See, also, Sidney H. Griffith, "Setting Right the Church of Syria: Saint Ephraem's Hymns against Heresies," forthcoming in *Middle Eastern Christian Studies* 1.
114. Some scholars, however, speak anachronistically of a monasticism in St. Ephraem's milieu, and of the saint himself as a monk. See the articles of S. Jargy in note 83 above, and L. Leloir, "Saint Éphrem, moine et pasteur," in *Théologie de la vie monastique* (Paris, 1961), pp. 85–97; *idem,* "La pensée monastique d'Éphrem et Martyrus," in *Symposium Syriacum 1972,* Orientalia Christiana Analecta 197 (Rome, 1974), pp. 105–134.
115. See the survey of Nedungatt, "The Covenanters," pp. 200–215.
116. G. Phillips, *The Doctrine of Addai, the Apostle* (London, 1876), p. 50 (Syriac).
117. See note 44 above.
118. See Parisot, *Aphraatis Demonstrationes* 1.260–272.
119. See E. A. Judge, "The Earliest Use of *Monachos,*" pp. 72, 86–87; E. Morard, "Monachos: une importation sémitique en Égypte?" *Studia Patristica* 12 (1975):242–246.
120. See P. Bedjan, *Homiliae Selectae Mar-Jacobi Sarugensis* (Paris, 1908), 4:818–871.
121. See A. Guillaumont, "Perspectives actuelles sur les origines du monachisme," in T. T. Segerstedt, ed., *The Frontiers of Human Knowledge* (Uppsala, 1978), pp. 111–123. Reprinted in the author's *Aux origines du monachisme chrétien* (Bégrolles en Mauges, 1979), pp. 215–227; *idem,* "Esquisse d'une phénomenologie du monachisme," *Numen* 25 (1978):40–51. Reprinted in *Aux origines,* pp. 228–239. On Aphrahat and his thought see the following works of Peter Bruns: *Das Christusbild Aphrahats des Persischen Weisen,* Studien zur alten Kirchengeschichte 4 (Bonn: Borengasser, 1990), which originally appeared as the author's 1988 doctoral dissertation, Katholisch-Theologischen Fakultat zu Bochum; and *Aphrahat, Unterweisungen; aus dem Syrischen übersetzt und eingeleitet,* Fontes Christiani 5/1 (Freiburg im Breisgau: Herder, 1991).

18

Ascetic Moods, Hermeneutics, and Bodily Deconstruction

Response to the Three Preceding Papers

Leif E. Vaage

As increasingly happens of late, I have again been asked to speak out of my ignorance. It is at least something I enjoy doing, and may even do better than I think. All of us who are interested in understanding the ascetic dimension in human life and culture beyond the confines of a certain area of technical expertise will undoubtedly share this experience to some degree. I hope that you will also share my growing sense of intrigue and fascination with the theme taken up by the three papers under consideration, despite the fact that most of what I have to say is patently awash in an unfinished process of reflection.

The papers before us are diverse, to say the least. One of them, by John Pinsent, discusses ascetic moods in classical Greek and Latin literature, ranging roughly from the epic narratives of Homer in the eighth century BCE to the social satires of Lucian of Samosata in the second century CE, with occasional leaps forward into the poetry, art, and social values of Victorian England. A second paper, by Sidney Griffith, focuses much more narrowly on three particular words and the type of persons whom they referred to in the third and fourth-century CE Christian church of eastern Syria. Meanwhile, the third, by Patrick Olivelle, reviews a broadly based set of ascetical writings regarding the physical body and its socially significant re/con/disfiguration in India up through the mediaeval period (fifteenth and sixteenth centuries CE).

I am not in a position to dispute these papers' specific interpretations of their exemplary texts and the judgments that they make about them. I will, rather, concentrate upon the conflict and convergence among their renderings of these texts and social practices as ascetic, hoping in this way to contribute further to our joint reflection at this conference on the possibility of something like a general theory of asceticism.

There are certain theoretical assumptions or "axes to grind" that are of obvious importance for the task at hand, which I shall not belabor in my response, except to mention them now. These include the dialectical relationship between the ascetic de/construction of the human body and the social body in which the same activity and artifact are both immersed—hence, "culturally created"—and to the ongoing "reproduction" of which they simultaneously contribute. Everything done to the body is thus always a political statement. As Patrick Olivelle puts it: "the human body as culturally created and perceived stands as the primary symbol of the social body, the body politic."[1]

This fundamental intuition, well expressed by Mary Douglas in her book on *Natural Symbols: Explorations in Cosmology,* continues to be exceedingly productive of inquiry and telling observation.[2] I would only caution us to remember that, like other heuristic equations, its truth is based not on evidence, namely, self-evidence; but, rather, on the degree to which it succeeds in sponsoring further investigation and thought. Mary Douglas herself provides no obvious proof for this intuition beyond the general integrity of her own presentation of it.[3]

John Pinsent's paper begins by discussing what otherwise might be termed the origins of acesticism in Western civilization, at least as a specific form of human (religious) cultural activity. Pinsent believes that there is no word in Greek for asceticism, even though the word itself is derived from the Greek. Only in Plato, he says, "we may discover the purest and I think the only real example of asceticism in the ancient world." Pinsent understands asceticism, like the English term "home" and the French "patrie," to designate a social institution (the word is his) peculiar to the culture to which the word belongs. Pinsent also says that asceticism is a concept peculiar to the Christian culture of late antiquity.

The suggestion by Pinsent that Plato is probably the only real example of asceticism in the ancient world makes clear that, for Pinsent, asceticism, as such, refers to a narrowly defined type of spiritual quest whose ultimate object is properly otherwordly. Indeed, in what I find the most questionable paragraph of his paper, Pinsent states immediately thereafter concerning the asceticism of Plato:

> Yet Plato's asceticism cannot be seen as religious, unless indeed the aim of the soul is to contemplate the Beatific Vision, which that virtuous pagan could envisage only as the Form of the Good, the final answer to the question "Why?," "Because it is good." He was unable in his lifetime to know the supreme condescension of goodness in the (Christian) Incarnation and Redemption, and retains something of the Hellenic belief that moral excellence is a thing worth pursuing for itself alone, the true end of humans.[4]

Asceticism seems to be, for Pinsent, one of the distinctive innovations wrought by Christianity on the occasionally inclined but essentially un(der) developed transcendent sensibility of the classical Greek and Roman world. This understanding, however, of asceticism as a concept peculiar to the Christian culture of late antiquity, if accepted by *Webster's Unabridged Dictionary of the English Language* or the *Encyclopedia of Religion,* would make it extremely difficult to ascertain what we should name the otherwise not dissimilar religious traditions of the Indian subcontinent, as described by Olivelle in his paper.

At the same time, the instinctive sense, perhaps struggling for expression in Pinsent's definition of asceticism, that what we may colloquially refer to as Christian asceticism—namely, the stark separatist spirituality epitomized by the stylites of Syria and their eremitic and cenobitic counterparts in Egypt—represents a notable shift, if not a decided break, in the traditional social patterns of ancient Mediterranean civilization. This shift is worthy of consideration, insofar as it helps to raise, at least for the traditions descended from this particular social matrix, the question of ascetic discourse and practice as a mode of cultural invention. Do we have in the rhetoric and rituals of Christian asceticism something essentially new vis-à-vis classical Greek and Latin literature? If so, what exactly does "new" mean?

Are the origins, however, of Christian asceticism in fact as *sui generis* as Pinsent's presentation of ascetic moods in Greek and Latin literature seems to suggest? Are we really still to assume, with Eusebius, that Christian asceticism somehow constituted a—if not *the*—great (spiritual) leap forward after the classical world's *praeparatio evangelii?* More fairly stated, if we were to admit that Christian asceticism was, in some strong sense, a different enterprise from its affective antecedents in the pre-Christian Greek and Roman world, what is it precisely that constitutes the break with them? And what would it mean, if we were to agree in principle on the fact of this difference, but were then quite unable at the level of description to isolate the critical feature(s) that account for it?

On the other hand, if we disagree with Pinsent's basic perspective and suggest that Christian asceticism is in fact no more than an extension—namely, exaggeration—of certain features of the classical Greek and Roman world that Pinsent inadequately represents, how do we then account for the perception that the ascetic literature produced in fourth-century CE Egypt and Syria breathes a different air from the spirit animating most of the texts surveyed by Pinsent? If the original break with classical Greek and Roman civilization embodied by subsequent Christian asceticism is not so clean and sharp as Pinsent seems to imply, how instrumental or symbolic was the specific practice of asceticism in producing the shift that did occur?

At the other end of the spectrum from Pinsent's paper stands, python-like (though still not observing the "python vow"), the essay by Olivelle on the "Deconstruction of the Body in Indian Asceticism." Olivelle begins his study with the modern scholarly assumption that "Asceticism . . . is a cornerstone of Indian religions," only to untidy the social meaning of that fact a little further, but never to question its basic factuality.[5] What for Pinsent in classical Greek and Latin literature was finally only an intimation à la Wordsworth of the renunciative Christian glory yet to come, is for Olivelle in classical Indian religion an established institutional praxis going back beyond historical memory. The question of origins, namely, "what sort of a social experience creates the ascetic alienation and underlies the ascetic bodily expressions" typical of Indian religion and rehearsed by Olivelle in terms of the physical body, sexuality, food, and hair, is said to be a question we cannot answer, "because we have so little information about Indian society during the time when many of these ascetic traditions started."[6] However lively the interactive tension may have been between the ascetic deconstruction of the body and other socially approved expressions of bodily control throughout Indian history, the impression given by Olivelle is that, for all intents and purposes, asceticism in this civilization has always just been there.

An interesting contrast thus emerges. In Pinsent's paper, we have a view of (Christian) asceticism that sees it as an identifiable cultural innovation, belonging to a particular stage, in the (literary) history of Western (classical Greek and Roman) civilization. In Olivelle's paper, on the other hand, we have a view of (renunciatory) asceticism that sees it as a discernible constant, belonging in shifting ways to the ongoing elaboration of Indian culture as such: one part of "the dialectical and creative relationship and tension in which the ascetic and the societal dimensions of Indian religions existed and developed both ideologically and in their institutions and practices."[7] Does the apparent contrast stem from fundamental differences in the specific natures of ancient Mediterranean and Indian civilizations; or do the imputed emergence—and perennial character—of the same phenomenon belong to the constitutive antinomies of asceticism itself?

The paper by Sidney Griffith presents a point of view different from that of both Pinsent and Olivelle. Griffith neither ponders the origin of Syrian asceticism *per se*[8] nor takes the presence of this type of religious practice within late antique Syrian culture as simply a standard feature of the social landscape. Instead, Griffith's inquiry is situated methodologically at a moment of perceived change and intersection between two divergent styles of asceticism before and after the establishment of the Constantinian "Great Church" in Syria. It claims to discern and to recover signs of a certain modulation and transformation within the single, namely, singular, ascetic tradition of this region. Asceticism in Syria is thus not just one type of activity. In this respect it would seem to compare rather nicely to the similarly diverse but equally ascetic traditions of the Indian subcontinent.

The second of Griffith's two types of ancient Syrian asceticism is the better known, more flamboyant, severe exuberance of "the harsh, and seemingly bizarre forms of ascetic life that flourished there,"[9] epitomized especially by the stylites; who, however, according to Griffith, "were not the original Syrian ascetics. Rather, their enthusiasms were the product of the change in ascetical fashion which began in the fourth century after the Constantinian peace of the church."[10] The first type—the original form—of Syrian asceticism was rather to be realized in the general community, constituting a "lifestyle within the church of Syria of communities of singles in God's service, whose way of life is parallel to that of the biblical widows and virgins and with whom the men and women singles will be bracketed in later canonical legislation."[11]

If Pinsent is correct that asceticism is a concept peculiar to the Christian culture of late antiquity, it seems that Griffith would at least want to insist that, first, there were different Christian cultures of Late Antiquity—take Syria, for example, where the way Christianity was practiced was not the same as it was in other regions of the ancient Mediterranean. Secondly, even within the one culture of Syrian Christianity, there were at least two different modes or manners of being an ascetic. Though sequential in their dominance, these were, furthermore, not mutually exclusive, insofar as they appear to have coexisted during much of the fourth century. A cross-cultural understanding of asceticism must thus recognize that even within the single Christian culture of late antiquity, there was more than one way to be a genuine ascetic. We might then wish, at this point in the discussion, to go one step further and to inquire: What is it about the nature of genuine asceticism that allows it to be more than one thing at a time?

The first part of my response has had as one of its primary objectives to raise, on the basis of the papers by Pinsent, Olivelle, and Griffith, the question, much larger than their immediate concerns, of asceticism itself; namely, the need for a working definition of the phenomenon of which all three authors imply an understanding—insofar as they each use the term "ascetic" in their respective works—but the general definition of which is not the specific goal of any of these inquiries. Their colloquy, however, makes the effort to ignite some sort of categorical fire beneath them irresistible—even if it consists only in rubbing each paper's flinty surface against that of the others, in order to determine whether some coherence can be found among them.

In keeping, therefore, with this incendiary view of our immediate undertaking, let me propose a(nother) definition of asceticism, if only as (further) tinder for your own more substantive contributions to the ensuing conflagration. Actually, I offer here not a proper definition, but merely a series of leading questions.

If asceticism is not to be understood as itself the goal of its own practice, as though self-mortification, personal deprivation, lack of pleasure, and an accelerated death were simply the main point of it all—that is, if one agrees with Olivelle in rejecting the false generalization he refers to as the once customary Western scholarly characterization of Indian religions as being simply life and world negating;

if the term asceticism were, instead, to be considered properly to refer to the privileged use of a certain type of self-disciplinary means, for the sake of achieving a separate purpose;

if, that is, asceticism were to be seen as essentially an intermediate activity undertaken toward enjoyment of some other end—as Pinsent puts it regarding Christian asceticism: "a means to an end, a help on the way to, or in, the religious life, whether active or contemplative—possibly even a necessary means, but not an end in itself," versus those who "may maintain that self-denial, the opposite of self-indulgence, is a good in itself";[12]

Then how would such an understanding of the thoroughly middling nature of asceticism enable us better to appreciate what the various Greek, Roman, Syrian, and Indian styles of asceticism described in the three papers before us all have in common—without requiring us at the same time to suggest that somehow these plainly different social practices are nonetheless finally really about the same thing?[13]

What the various forms of asceticism described by Pinsent, Olivelle, and Griffith all share to some degree—and the question of degree becomes thereby (one of) the critical consideration(s) regarding the identification of different types of asceticism—is the same technical preference. All display the same option for a certain disciplinary *technē* of the body as the specific means deemed most likely to permit the achievement of a stipulated end. All share, in other words, the same general form of cultural "engineering,"[14] a discernable and distinct style of "crafting" the social self:[15] Thus, the pragmatic and theoretical wager that, through "asceticism," one can enjoy a still unrealized, but progressively anticipated, greater sense of personal well-being.[16]

For such an affirmation, however, to serve in any way as a useful definition of asceticism, it will be necessary meaningfully to distinguish between certain core characteristics of asceticism as such, versus the considerable variety, and seemingly arbitrary (or contextually highly sensitive) selection of the actual concrete gestures employed. Is this, in fact, possible?

What would the critical features of asceticism be as a sort of social (religious/cultural) share-ware, its varied practices being simply the predictable diverse applications of a basic body technology? Any one of us, for example, could describe both the surface similarities and the deep differences among (the many varieties of) a typewriter and (the even greater range of options in) a personal computer. What by analogy, are the salient features that would permit us to identify in any given culture the presence and practice of asceticism, including ascetic moods, as distinct from these superficially similar activities: the military formation of character in recruits; or the creation of a certain class consciousness through inculcated codes of dress and conduct by established aristocracies such as successful businessmen and women, academic scholarly guilds, and others of the professional rank?

Rather than proceed at this point to make a specific proposal myself, I invite suggestions as to what are perceived to be the salient points of contact, or the *Anknüpfungspunkte,* in soteriological methodology between the different ascetic traditions that have been examined separately.[17]

What are the specific goals of the distinct forms of asceticism described by Pinsent, Griffith, and Olivelle in their respective papers, if the purpose of these different undertakings is not simply to be equated with the particular pleasures and pains of each one's peculiar round of rigors?[18] In the case of Pinsent, the question might be better phrased as follows: What made the adoption or creation of ascetic moods in Greek and Latin literature the desirable or indicated thing to do? The answer appears to be (apart perhaps from Plato) the rather modest, even mundane goal of enhancing the experience of certain customary virtues, taken as equivalent to a more complete embodiment of the perceived finer features of the ancient Mediterranean human being. By indulging less and less in a given set of specified activities or substances, determined aspects of an imagined ideal social self were thought to be encouraged to be(come) more and more apparent, present, dominant, secure.

In this regard, Greek and Roman ascetic practices, or moods, were simply derivative of a number of conventional social disciplines. They belong to the standard educational activity of classical antiquity, a fact which may account for why Greek and Roman asceticism never became so radically dissociative a discourse, or so plainly differentiated a praxis, as did other forms of asceticism, both subsequently in the Mediterranean basin and elsewhere in other cultures.

All such personal training belonged for its Greek and Roman practitioners—or more precisely the literary depictions of them as described by Pinsent—to the widespread pursuit in classical antiquity of both a better understanding and fuller experience of the good life.[19] Such a life was sought after to be lived here and now, even if the continuing need for its pursuit implied, in fact, that its realization remained postponed and, depending upon the refinement of one's analytical evaluation, to some degree always out of reach.

Thus, Aristotle's dictum, "Call no one happy before their death," would be of a piece with Plato's unwillingness to rely on the knowledge of immediate, even mediated, sensible reality as a sufficient basis for enduring contentment. Though neither Plato nor Aristotle—and here I beg to differ with Pinsent regarding his interpretation of Plato's otherworldliness—posited another self or world different from those of the inquiring subjects of their discourse where the projected fulfillment of their directed development would occur.

Pinsent's description of ascetic moods in Greek and Latin literature seems to be based upon an assumption that, whatever else asceticism may be, it is principally a matter of denial. In so doing, he fails to consider adequately what his own summary account of the history of the word in classical Greek makes clear, namely, that asceticism as a certain type of practice means the acquisition hereby of a certain skill or ability: the first of "the two senses of that word: the practice of an art, craft, or profession (πολεμικὴ ἄσκησις, Xenophon, *Cyropedia*)."[20]

Whatever renunciation may be required in order to exercise a given ascetic regimen, the point of the process is basically constructive, insofar as the ascetic thereby expects to be able to do something (e.g., live) well, or at least better than before. In this regard, Plato is hardly the only real example of asceticism in the ancient world, even if, in some other sense, he may be the purest instance of the Greek ethical ideal taken to one logical extreme.

For example, except for Lucian's reference to *he kynikē askēsis* in *Toxaris* 27, Pinsent ignores the Cynics as another—more sullied than Plato's pure—example of asceticism in Greco-Roman antiquity. I mention the Cynics, in part because, unlike the Stoics and the Epicureans, whom Pinsent discusses at some length and characterizes, regarding the Epicureans, as "properly . . . ascetic, almost monastic" and in both instances "justly . . . called 'temperate' if not 'ascetic,'" the Cynics did not "have an explanation for everything," but emphasized, like many of the later superstars of Christian asceticism and numerous Indian ascetics, the importance of "just doing it."[21]

Indeed, were it not for the historically successful ideological interventions of Athanasius's *Life of Antony,* Ephraem the Syrian's hymns in celebration of the life of Julian Saba, and other such efforts (like modern academic scholarship) to elaborate upon, and thereby to persuade, generations of readers of the deeper meaning of these persons' plainly odd and sometimes sick behavior,[22] the Cynics' equally blatant and demonstrative departure from the dominant culture of their day, embodied and performed for public consumption and personal appropriation, could hardly be overlooked or ignored as a clear analogy to the supposedly peculiar concept of the Christian culture of late antiquity.

The same frontal assault on standard values of the local culture is equally a fundamental feature of the renunciatory type of Indian asceticism described by Olivelle. According to Olivelle, "the Brāhmaṇical tradition . . . views asceticism as an antithetical category defined more by its negation of social structures than by any internal structure or property of its own." Thus, the ascetic creation of a certain type of bodily existence is nothing more and nothing less than a deconstruction of the socially created body.[23] In the conclusion to his paper, Olivelle states: "The deconstruction of the body we have examined can thus be seen as the expression of an antisocial and individualist ideology through the medium of the body."[24] Versus the implicit confidence of Greek and Latin literature as surveyed by Pinsent—that, even in an ascetic mood, the good life, however defined, could only be realized in the context of (ancient) human society—the type of renunciatory asceticism described by Olivelle appears to be predicated on the decisive negation of any such possibility. For this form of ascetic practice, it seems, the good that is sought in such a fashion requires precisely a radical separation from all current social orders, structures, arrangements, if not life itself.

Whereas Greek and Roman asceticism, as described by Pinsent, might be said to register a refinement—or, more fittingly perhaps regarding Plato—a distillation of the perceptible, albeit shadowy good in contemporary society, Indian asceticism, as Olivelle presents it, is, at the level of the problem to be solved, like the abused child, beaten woman, or victim of torture just wanting this to be over, finding, it seems, in the present circumstances of human society only overwhelming grief. At the level of its solution to this problem, Indian asceticism, as Olivelle presents it, is, then, to continue the previous comparison, certainly an unambiguous way of simply saying no to it all, not unlike the Arctic wolf that, rather than remain alive a little longer trapped in the iron jaws of an alien human economy, prefers instead to chew its own leg off and limp away to die elsewhere, alone. Unlike these analogies, however, Indian asceticism, as Olivelle presents it, is hardly rash or desperate, however extreme its methods may appear. A better comparison at the level of the solution might be the pronounced aspiration of Christian apophatic mysticism, which finally cannot say directly what it wants to achieve, but, via thoroughgoing negation, progresses steadily toward its goal of unspeakable transcendence, namely, immanence.

If the preceding statements are at all true, it is then difficult to understand the precise meaning of what Olivelle calls in the conclusion to his paper "the [Indian] ascetic's adoption of an animal body."

> The rejection of social structures implicit in the deconstruction of the body is also expressed in the ascetic imitation of the life and habits of wild beasts, what may be called the ascetic's adoption of an animal body. Animal symbolism is present in much of Indian ascetic literature, especially in connection with forest hermits. The ascetic impulse to leave society and culturally mediated structures, tools, and geography is nicely captured in this verse:
>
> Moving about with wild beasts,
>   and dwelling with them alone;

Living a life just like theirs—
clearly that's the way to heaven.[25]

Such a discourse, used both to critique the mores of conventional society, and to promote in their place a contrary lifestyle, would typically be referred to in Greek and Latin literature as the call to *physis* (following nature). It is ultimately viewed as something positive by its adherents in classical society, although it deviates from the ideal model of the social order then current. The same imitation of nature by Indian ascetics is rather more negative, to the degree that wild beasts and all they represent are not imagined to embody in any constructive fashion the desired end state of human (non-)being. Yet both types of asceticism similarly, if not equally, derive the concrete gestures whereby they express discrepancy with the existing social construction of reality by recourse to the inhuman realm of nature. How significant is this fact?

To what extent is asceticism, however practiced, always imagined or practically conducted as a return to nature? When viewed in contrast to the unnatural adventure and evident errors of human civilization, is not asceticism, with its sharp social critique and its pursuit of a (radically) different frame of existential reference, nonetheless (by virtue of this recurring identification with the state of nature) finally far more earthbound, and more conservative and reactionary, than is sometimes thought?[26]

Or is Pinsent now suddenly correct, as he argues that the ascetic moods of Greek and Latin literature do not, in fact, anticipate subsequent Christian asceticism—for the Christian ascetic's dream of realizing through such a practice the higher life form of an angelic or androgynous existence is ultimately in deep discontinuity with the biblical tradition's affirmation of the good in life as that which coincides with nature, namely, "male and female created he them" (*Genesis* 5.1)?

In such a case, however, we would then need to conclude that the statement by Peter Brown quoted at the beginning of Griffith's paper, that the angelic life embodied by later Syrian ascetics pursued a "freedom that resembled that of the beasts, wandering up the mountainsides to graze, with the sheep, on the natural grasses," is basically incorrect, or at least not true for the original Syrian ascetics.[27] Or is the angelic life later pursued by the more infamous representatives of asceticism in Syria essentially equivalent to what Griffith otherwise calls the situation of paradise restored that was anticipated almost in iconic fashion in the body of the earlier Syrian ascetic *îḥîdāyâ*? Does the situation of paradise restored amount as well, for all intents and purposes, to a return to nature, namely, the pristine condition of the primal person in the *paradeisos* (garden) of Eden?

Returning to Olivelle's paper, once the socially created body has been deconstructed through asceticism, with the adoption of an animal body serving as the (primary?) vehicle for this process of genetic dismantling—are there, by the way, other types of bodies in addition to the animal one that the Indian ascetic may adopt (imitate) to bring about the desired state of personal decomposition—is there, then, in Indian asceticism, as in Christian asceticism, yet another type of body whose eventual enjoyment the ascetic is pursuing?

In Griffith's discussion, for example, of the multiple senses of the term *îḥîdāyâ* in Syrian Christianity, reference is made to "the language St. Ephraem uses to express the inauguration of the special relationship between Christ the *Îḥîdāyâ* and the ascetic *îḥîdāyâ* at the sacrament of baptism. He speaks of the candidate putting on Christ the *Îḥîdāyâ* in a way that reminds one of the clothing metaphor St. Ephraem and other Syriac writers so often used to express the doctrine of the Incarnation."[28] One also speaks of the aspiration "publicly to put on the *persona* of the *Îḥîdāyâ* from the bosom of the Father."[29] The goal, in other words, is to be(come) as fully as possible a concrete and complete manifestation of the body of Christ.

Or is deconstruction in the case of Indian asceticism just deconstruction: the hoped-for realization of a total death wish? Successful deconstruction of the socially created body in Indian asceticism would thus essentially refer to the vanishing point of a progressive series of Hegelian-like acts of inner alienation whose alternating logic of ongoing participation in, and deepening dissociation from, society has as its governing objective a projected eschatological moment in which, to mix thoroughly the cultural metaphors at our disposal, "my boomerang won't come back"; hence, for example, the practice of inner and outer nakedness by some Indian ascetics, to be further discussed below.[30]

If deconstruction is just deconstruction, how, then, if at all, does such a thoroughly negative self-understanding of their place (actually, displacement) in human society by Indian ascetics significantly alter their practice of asceticism, beyond heightening perhaps the severity of their endeavored dissociation? How does this compare with the innerworldly ascetic moods of Greek and Latin literature and the shifting social styles of Syrian asceticism? Does the Indian ascetic's thoroughly negative self-understanding, in other words, have any appreciable practical effect at the level of performance? Or is the concrete result simply a certain rise in metaphorical bodily temperature: the heat is turned up just a little higher in the furnace of the Indian ascetic's body and the self-consuming flame thus flares all the more intensely in this particular type of asceticism than at the less-than-white-hot forges of otherwise similar ascetic practices? Or is there a significant difference of a qualitative kind regarding the deconstructive energy that burns within the breast and through the flesh of the Indian ascetic approaching nirvana?

How is the successful Indian ascetic's prolonged penance for accumulated karma performatively or sociologically different from the saintly Syrian ascetic's extended *abîlâ* (mourning, sorrow, compunction for sin)? And how much does the serious Greek philosopher's traditional *skythropos* (long face) owe to the ongoing stupidity of human beings?

Regarding Syrian asceticism, what is it that the original ascetics in Syria imagined that they were accomplishing, or were supposed to have accomplished, through their brand of spiritual/social training? Griffith is at pains to demonstrate that contrary to the later histrionics (my term, not his) of the better-known ascetic superstars of the Syrian church, the earlier ascetic *îḥîdāyâ*, as already noted, "came to anticipate symbolically, almost in an iconic fashion, the situation of paradise restored."[31] These persons were, in other words, essentially a role model, masters in the Western medieval sense of the term, showing others less advanced in the craft of Christian living how exactly it was to be done and what the end result of the religious labor at hand was supposed to look like.

From this perspective, Syrian asceticism suddenly seems strangely similar in its original *raison d'être,* if not in its concrete gestures, to the primary purpose of the ascetic moods in Greek and Latin literature; namely, to emphasize and undergird the social values held to be foundational, that is, the ideal virtues of the culture in question. In the case of Syrian Christianity, such values were specifically those of the new, restored, angelic community constituted especially through the rite of baptism by the company of believers in Christ.

Both Pinsent and Olivelle mention suicide in connection with the practice of asceticism. They do so, admittedly, in rather incidental fashion, but, like most Freudian slips, all such coincidences are the bread and butter of every analyst's response. And, in the case of Olivelle, even though he does not speak at length in these precise terms, his general theme of the deconstruction of the body in Indian asceticism might suggest that his brief reference to religious suicide[32] is, in fact, but the tip of the renunciatory iceberg. It is the burden of his paper to describe the more socially submerged and lifebound practices of ascetism.

Regarding Stoicism, Pinsent simply remarks that suicide was not approved, not being in accordance with this philosophy's resigned form of virtue, insofar as such an act might suggest that one had ceased to be in agreement with the course of almighty destiny: "we should not relinquish the post to which fate has assigned us before it calls us to do so in death."[33]

Conversely, Olivelle speaks of suicide by fasting as the proper manner in which to bring to completion a successful ascetic career in more than one Indian religion: it is "a well-known and respected way of ending life in numerous Hindu and non-Hindu traditions, especially the Jain."[34] Reference is made to Paul Dundas's "Food and Freedom: The Jaina Sectarian Debate on the Nature of the Kevalin,"[35] and to Shadakshari Settar's *Inviting Death: Historical Experiments on Sepulchral Hill* (= *Inviting Death: Indian Attitude towards the Ritual Death*) and *Pursuing Death: Philosophy and Practice of Voluntary Termination of Life.*[36]

The apparent contrast, however, between the ritual practice of voluntary death in Indian religion and the Stoic view of suicide, as Pinsent has described it, is much less than it might first appear to be. The recurring refrain of the well-known Stoic teacher, Epictetus, to whom Pinsent himself symbolically refers, that "the door is always open," represents, in fact, an affirmation of the possible role of suicide in the philosopher's general effort to achieve liberation from every false constraint and longing.

Indeed, the suggestion that suicide was not a part of the Stoic and, by extension, ancient Mediterranean ascetic philosophical tradition, seems incorrect. The recent book, for example, by Arthur J. Droge and James D. Tabor, entitled *A Noble Death: Suicide and Martyrdom Among Christians and Jews in Antiquity,* is able to devote an entire (second) chapter to the theme of suicide in Greek and Roman antiquity, describing "The Death of Socrates and Its Legacy."[37] The Stoics, including Epictetus and Marcus Aurelius, are all said to have "recognized the right of an individual to take his own life, but what concerned them more than the act itself was the context and manner in which it might be performed."[38]

Other traditions include the Cynics. The death of Diogenes of Sinope is discussed, who, according to one version of the story, committed *Selbstmord* by holding his breath, in a manner not unlike the enlightened Indian sage's final self-induced meditative withdrawal from the present round of *saṃsāra*. It would be interesting, for me at least, to compare at greater length the description by Droge and his sources of the noble deaths of the philosophers with the ritual deaths of the Indian ascetics represented by Settar.

What about Syria? Though we all must finally die alone—the effort to do so well, or properly, being (one of) the primary purpose(s) of both Greco-Roman moral philosophy and Indian religion—the ascetic singles of Syrian Christianity before the time of Constantine's Great Church are said by Griffith to have understood themselves in their ascetic practice to be acting primarily as members of the general community, or, I take it, in a way that was perceived by them and others to enhance the social project shared by all. Though these singles had presumably dissociated themselves in specific ways from certain of the usual habits of social life in ancient Syria, it is difficult to imagine how in this case, at least as described by Griffith, a given person's ritual or self-induced death could ever have been conceived as serving any meaningful purpose.

Not even the later more flamboyant stylites and their adepts, to my knowledge, made gestures in the direction of suicide as part of the fulfillment of their role as heroes of abnegation. If this is true, what was it, then, in Syrian asceticism that, unlike its parallels in Greco-Roman and Indian ascetic traditions, excluded from the self-understanding of this tradition any mention of voluntary death as either desirable or an option?

Griffith does make one very interesting—if again tangential—observation:

> By the fourth century these institutions [i.e., the early organized forms of asceticism in the Syriac-speaking world] were already well enough established that certain abuses had crept into them, and currents of change and reform in the ascetical establishment were already afoot, prompted perhaps by the Peace of Constantine, which effectively removed one earlier form of complete self-giving, namely, martyrdom.[39]

If asceticism in Syria thus served, both theologically and sociologically, to replace the finally *passé* practice of martyrdom, to what extent did Syrian asceticism, likewise, continue the tendency of the earlier martyrs to invite and provoke the deadly use of alien force upon themselves, as the privileged means of testifying to the hope that was in them? What would prevent us from concluding that, as the martyr, so the ascetic in ancient Syria pursued with similar intentionality a self-conscious death, through which both hoped to display in frail but tempered flesh the glorious presence of the divine life each sought to enjoy?

Whatever the precise place of suicide may be in the differing worlds of Greek, Roman, Syrian, and Indian asceticism, in none of them is the practice of asceticism itself its simple equivalent. Let me now state more precisely the specific theoretical question which I have been trying to tease out of the papers before us. What is it that makes of the practice of any type of asceticism not simply a slow, delayed, protracted and deliberate(d) form of suicide? If politics is just war by a different name, why and how is asceticism not merely another term for self-determined auto-destruction?

That asceticism is, in fact, not simply a curious means of prolonged dying at one's own hand seems clear to me from the fact that, however rigorous and extreme the disciplinary endeavors brought to bear upon the body by the ascetic practitioner; and however much the ascetic may lament his or her continuing incorporation within the cycle of needs and desires that constitute this world, simply to cut oneself loose, as soon as possible, from every conceivable threat of implication in the same predicament is never imagined or seen as an acceptable solution.

Olivelle remarks, for example, in his comment on religious suicide, part of which I have already cited:

> When the minimization of the food effort is taken to its logical conclusion, an ascetic would not even make the effort to take food into his mouth or to swallow it. This is religious suicide by fasting, a well-known and respected way of ending life in numerous Hindu and non-Hindu traditions, especially the Jain.[40]

Lest you think, however, that such an act could be performed wherever and whenever one might feel so inclined, the rules for effectively conducting the indicated ritual death are extremely demanding and require multiple obstacles to be surmounted. Taking the minimization of the food effort to its logical conclusion is thus neither simply a *reductio ad absurdum* nor the logic of Indian asceticism *in extremis*. It represents instead quite literally the culmination of a strenuous series of progressive abstractions whereby the ascetic finally succeeds in working through everything that stands between him or her and the desired state of eventual complete release from the perceived human predicament.

As Settar writes in *Pursuing Death:*

> Lest any kind of termination of life be mistaken for liberation, elaborate rules have been evolved to regulate the spiritual journey of the aspirant. No one is allowed to attempt liberation without first severing his links with all kinds of attachment: nudity is the outward symbol of this detachment. But mere nakedness, without purity of mind, is meaningless; hence, Kundakundacarya lays down, in the *Bhava Pahuda,* that a monk "should become naked from inside, by giving up false faith and flaws, and then he becomes automatically a naked monk according to the command of the Jina."[41]

Likewise, in Stoicism, according to Droge, the actual decision when finally to die was typically seen as one of the privileges reserved for the truly wise person, who alone was thought to be able to make the reasoned judgment necessary as to when circumstances no longer permitted a given individual's life to be lived in accordance with nature or virtue and, therefore, not to be worth living. Even then, an integral feature of such wisdom was being able, on the basis of prior training, to recognize when the sign from God had come for the same person's prescribed departure.

According to Droge, Seneca is rather unique in his exaltation of the act of suicide at any moment as the gesture *par excellence* of the free man or woman; though Seneca's reasoning in support of this position remains completely within the standard Stoic logic of perfect freedom as full identification with the will of the universal Logos: for Seneca, "it is by no means contrary to the will of God if at any time an individual chooses to end his life. It is precisely because of the divine order of things that one is at all times free to die," given that God, according to Seneca, has "set life on a downward slope."[42]

Both Epictetus and Marcus Aurelius are said by Droge on occasion to approach the Cynic position, described earlier by the same author as "at all times free to take their own lives,"[43] indeed, appearing "in contrast to Plato . . . prepared to recommend voluntary death on the slightest provocation." Epictetus, otherwise, emphasized that "an individual ought not to give up on life irrationally or for frivolous reasons," awaiting instead (as advised by Zeno and Cleanthes, Chrysippus and Cicero) "the sign [that God provides] indicating that an individual should remove himself."[44]

Thus, suicide, while permitted, required that its agent exercise powers of discernment and manifest a clear understanding of the reasons why the act was now to be performed, so as not merely to display once more the contemptible weakness of moral blindness and general stupidity. Thus, Droge writes:

> Cicero argues that in similar circumstances [as those attending the death of Cato of Utica (95–46 BCE), the famous opponent of Julius Caesar] one man (in this case, Cato) ought to kill himself, whereas another ought not. Cato's circumstances after the triumph of Caesar were the same as those of other men [i.e., Cato's allies and followers], but it was Cato's character that set him apart. Cicero's description of Cato—his austerity, constant resolve, and manner of life—fits the model of the ideal Stoic [ascetic] sage. If this is the case, then Cicero appears to be justifying Cato's death solely on the ground that he was a wise man.[45]

Even the Cynics, whose discourse on suicide might seem, as already noted, to suggest a much looser approach to the practice of voluntary death, did not, in fact, actually advocate such a demise too early in the life of the philosopher. Although they generally rejected all of the customary disciplines of learning, their primary goal was precisely to discover and display how best to be happy, no matter what the concrete circumstances of the moment might be. Only when a person could no longer live such a carefree life—that is, when old age or some other bodily weakness made living in this fashion (freely, self-sufficiently, and in accordance with nature) impossible to achieve—owing to physical and psychological demands imposed on the human frame by lack of care for it, was one to be free no longer to suffer the indignity and compulsion of such a state.

To what extent, therefore, is asceticism of any sort quintessentially a means of learning how to die, a certain rehearsal or cultivation of the act of death (much as Michel de Certeau speaks of the discipline of writing history as, in my words, the discourse of oblivion)[46]—and, thus, for its practitioners, also the best way of learning how to live, by coming to know what life finally, fully, truly is, through first achieving (via self-conscious embodiment) an understanding of its passing nature?[47] For this reason, at least, in none of the ascetic traditions that we have been discussing can suicide properly occur too soon or without adequate preparation. It must be plainly evident at the moment when death occurs, at least for the death in question to be seen as somehow salvific or noble, that the person whose life thus ends has also thereby brought to its logical conclusion a previous process of continued clarification (variously known as enlightenment, purification, or the construction of a noble character) that the practice of asceticism has created and displayed.

I have responded to the papers by Pinsent, Griffith, and Olivelle at essentially four different levels of commentary: (1) by examining the variations in the historical manifestation of asceticism as delineated by these authors; (2) by seeking a nonreductive definition of asceticism able to integrate the three authors' work without suggesting thereby that the different subjects of their separate studies are really about the same thing; (3) by observing both differences and similarities in the apparent goals of the three distinct ascetic traditions; and (4) by inquiring as to the relationship in general between the practice of asceticism and suicide.

I wish to conclude by posing one final question. It has, in fact, been implicit at every level of the preceding response. It concerns the relationship between the practice of asceticism and the overall human enterprise of education or, if you prefer, the cultural fabrication of human life.[48] To what extent is all ascetic activity, whether Greek, Latin, Syrian, Indian, or any other, finally just one more instance of human social formation, another of the variable strategies devised and deployed by *homo faber* for the education of his or her desire? This formation holds out to all prospective practitioners (as with every other type of human *technē*) the promise of achieving in this fashion a mode of existence—perhaps extinction—experienced as somehow higher or at least better than one's antecedent (original/natural/fallen) state of being.

What exactly does one finally learn as an ascetic, whether Platonic, Stoic, Epicurean, *îḥîdāyâ*, Brāhmaṇical, *Svetambara, Digambara?* What makes this type of strenuous learning more desirable for its adherents than any other type of *Ausbildung?* Can what is learned ascetically only be learned in this fashion? And once acquired, what is ascetic knowledge—Greek, Latin, Syrian, Indian—ultimately good for?[49]

NOTES

1. See Olivelle, p. 188.
2. Ibid., Mary Douglas, *Natural Symbols: Explorations in Cosmology* (New York: Random House/Vintage Books, 1973; originally published in 1970), pp. 93–112.
3. Olivelle refers as well to the oft-noted essay by Marcel Mauss, "Body Techniques," in *Sociology and Psychology,* Ben Brewster, trans. (London, Boston, and Henley: Routledge & Kegan Paul, 1979), pp. 97–123, or *Economy and Society* 2/1 (1973):70–88

(originally a presentation to the Société de psychologie, 17 May 1934, first published as "Les techniques du corps," *Journal de psychologie normale et pathologique* 32 [1935]:271–293; reprinted as Part 6 of *Sociologie et anthropologie* [Paris: Presses Universitaires de France, 1950], pp. 365–386); and Bryan S. Turner, *The Body and Society* (Oxford/New York: Basil Blackwell, 1984). Neither of these works, however, seeks to establish as such the homology of "body" and "society" that Douglas proposes and Olivelle assumes.

4. Cf. Pinsent, p. 214. Pinsent concludes, "Asceticism can only be an end in itself if the body be itself evil, the flesh to be mortified—a prison not merely a temporary tomb from which the soul must escape. This view is close to gnosticism, paradoxically part of the Hellenic rather than of the Judaic inheritance of Christianity. The Incarnation, in this view, is a willing degradation of divinity rather than a sanctification of the human. I am no theologian, but here I smell heresy" (p. 218).
5. Olivelle, p. 188.
6. Ibid., p. 207.
7. Ibid., p. 188.
8. See, however, Griffith, p. 245, note 104: "In the present writer's opinion, the earlier currents of ascetical thought in the Syriac-speaking world can best be studied in the history of the origins of Manichaeism."
9. Ibid., p. 220.
10. Ibid., p. 222.
11. Ibid., p. 222.
12. Pinsent, p. 218.
13. Cf. Margaret R. Miles, *Fullness of Life: Historical Foundations for a New Asceticism* (Philadelphia: Westminster, 1981), p. 161: "Finally, we have seen that the Christian authors who described the ascetic life of the fourth and fifth centuries were aware that fascination with the 'tools' of the ascetic life can be both physically and spiritually enervating. Ascetic practices are *methods,* not goals. This is an important qualification, not only for historical asceticism, but also for a 'new asceticism.'"
14. Cf. Vincent L. Wimbush, "Renunciation Towards Social Engineering (An Apologia for the Study of Asceticism in Greco-Roman Antiquity)," *Occasional Papers Number 8* (Claremont, Calif.: The Institute for Antiquity and Christianity/The Claremont Graduate School, 1986).
15. Cf. Dorinne K. Kondo, *Crafting Selves: Power, Gender, and Discourses of Identity in a Japanese Workplace* (Chicago/London, 1990).
16. Even if, as in certain forms of Indian asceticism, this means ultimately only at the point of death. The phrase "personal well-being" is admittedly vague, being meant to cover a multitude of salvations.
17. What—if anything—does each of the three presenters see in the others' papers as strikingly similar to some significant aspect of his own (not forgetting, of course, the obvious differences between them)? If we were to conclude that the individual investigations have finally absolutely nothing in common with one another, the curious fact would still remain that each presenter has nonetheless felt sufficiently sure of the term "ascetic" to use it rather freely in his particular writing. We might then simply trade definitions of asceticism as we use it, and see where that leaves us. Such a strategy, however, would only underscore how closely bound our general, or heuristic definitions—or preunderstandings—of asceticism are to the particular scholarly traditions that we variously represent, and the even more specific texts that sustain them. Hence, in my opinion, despite the postmodern truism that particularity is everything and the concomitant fear (yet

with us) of somehow backsliding into a former generation's parallelomania, it will surely be more fruitful for our conversation to risk the pleasure of finding the likenesses between our separate traditions: avenues of relatedness in those features that unite our otherwise independent interests, even if only from opposite ends of the spectrum.

18. Miles, *Fullness of Life,* p. 162: "The immediate goals of asceticism, once again, include self-understanding, overcoming of habituation and addiction, gathering and focusing of energy, ability to change our cultural conditioning, and intensification or expansion of consciousness."
19. Cf. T. N. Madan, *Non-Renunciation: Themes and Interpretations of Hindu Culture* (Delhi/New York/Oxford: Oxford University Press, 1987), pp. 1–16, esp. p. 13: "The good life is, then, above all a life of freedom from external controls: it is an inner state of maturation and grace."
20. Pinsent, p. 211.
21. Cf. S. Settar, *Inviting Death: Indian Attitude towards the Ritual Death* (Leiden: Brill, 1989), pp. 8–9: "These monks waged war against worldly desire through the weapon of self-mortification and gained victory over death. A majority of the early monks (who invited death voluntarily on the cold rocks of Katavapra) were obscure individuals who felt that nothing achieved on this earth is worth celebrating through a record. Hence they have hardly told us about themselves. Not many of them were attached to the *sangha,* not to speak of their association with society. They did not claim a high spiritual pedigree, nor a long list of disciples."
22. For the relationship between the diagnosis of disease and the perception and control of social disorder, see Turner, *Body and Society,* pp. 114, 204–226.
23. Olivelle, p. 188.
24. Ibid., p. 207.
25. Ibid.
26. If I am not mistaken, ascetic monks acted as the storm-troopers of the imperial Great Church during certain controversies of the 4th and 5th centuries CE.
27. Griffith, p. 220.
28. Ibid., p. 227.
29. Ibid., p. 228.
30. This is meant to contrast with the clothing metaphor of the Syrian ascetic putting on the fleshly robes of Christ. The Christian practice of nakedness at baptism, signifying new birth, is opposed to the Indian ascetic practice of continual nakedness, signifying yet another advance in the pursuit of a terminal death.
31. Griffith, p. 227.
32. Olivelle, p. 201.
33. Pinsent, p. 217.
34. Olivelle, p. 201.
35. See Paul Dundas, "Food and Freedom: The Jaina Sectarian Debate on the Nature of the Kevalin," *Religion* 15 (1985):161–198.
36. See Shadakshari Settar, *Inviting Death: Historical Experiments on Sepulchral Hill* (Dharwad: Institute of Indian Art History/Karnatak University, 1986); and *Pursuing Death: Philosophy and Practice of Voluntary Termination of Life* (Dharwad: Institute of Indian Art History/Karnatak University, 1990).
37. See Arthur J. Droge and James D. Tabor, *A Noble Death: Suicide and Martyrdom Among Christians and Jews in Antiquity* (San Francisco: HarperSanFrancisco, 1992), pp. 17–51.
38. Ibid., p. 29.

39. Griffith, p. 235.
40. See Olivelle, p. 201.
41. Settar, *Pursuing Death,* p. 12. Cf. Madan, *Non-Renunciation,* pp. 120–134, on types of death and their significance, esp. p. 131 on the topic of suicide.
42. Droge and Tabor, *A Noble Death,* p. 36.
43. Ibid., p. 26.
44. Ibid., p. 37.
45. Ibid., pp. 33–34.
46. See Michel de Certeau, *The Writing of History,* trans. Tom Conley (New York: Columbia University Press, 1988).
47. Cf. Miles, *Fullness of Life.*
48. Here, I am rather clearly thinking along the lines of Geoffrey Galt Harpham, *The Ascetic Imperative in Culture and Criticism* (Chicago/London: University of Chicago Press, 1987).
49. Cf. Dundas, "Food and Freedom," pp. 166–167: "There is no real controversy about the nature of *kevala* knowledge between the [Jaina] sects and, postponing an account of how it comes about, it can best be defined both as 'omniscience' in the literal sense of that knowledge which enables its possessor to know all substances in all their possible modifications including their temporal aspects and, more indirectly, 'the final consummation of moral, religious and spiritual life' or simply 'self-knowledge.'"

PART FOUR

Aesthetics of Asceticism

19

The Founding of the New Laura

Yizhar Hirschfeld

The founding of the Byzantine monastery known as the New Laura (the Nea Laura), situated about 3 kilometers south of Tekoa on the fringes of the Judean desert, was the outcome of a bitter dispute.[1]

We have various written accounts of disagreements that broke out in the monastic communities in the Judean desert. One example is the dispute between Gerasimus and members of the *laura* he had founded near the Jordan River.[2] According to the anonymous author of the biography of Gerasimus, some of the cell dwellers of the *laura* requested an improvement in their quality of life (permission to cook food in their cells and to light a lamp during night prayers), but Gerasimus rejected these requests outright. In another hagiographic source, *The Life of George of Choziba,* we hear of a great dispute that erupted at the end of the sixth century in the *laura* of Calamon, which was also near the Jordan River. This conflict concerned the elections for a new abbot following the death of the previous abbot.[3] It sparked George's departure from the *laura* of Calamon for the monastery of Choziba in Wadi Kelt (which later became the monastery of St. George), where he remained for the rest of his life. The monasteries of Euthymius and Theoctistus, which were affiliated with one another, quarreled over a large financial inheritance, a struggle that eventually resulted in a schism.[4]

But the most acrimonious, and perhaps the most protracted, of all the disputes was the one that led to the founding of the New Laura. This controversy arose shortly after Sabas founded the Great Laura in the Kidron Valley. The dramatic events that culminated in the founding of the New Laura are described in detail by Cyril of Scythopolis in *The Life of Sabas.*[5] Cyril, who lived as a monk in both the New Laura and the Great Laura, was acquainted with some of the monks who witnessed the dispute and had access to the archives of the two monasteries.[6] Another source is the fieldwork that has been carried out in recent years in the two monasteries—surveys of the Great Laura by Joseph Patrich[7] and a survey of the New Laura by the author.[8] The archaeological evidence supplements Cyril's testimony and makes it possible for the first time to present a clear and comprehensive picture of the events that led to the founding of the New Laura.

[I wish to thank Leah Di Segni and Joseph Patrich, friends and colleagues, who read the manuscript of this paper and made numerous important remarks.]

This paper is divided into three sections. The first part is devoted to the background of the crisis in the Great Laura and the second to the events that led to the founding of the New Laura. In the third section, the archaeological remains of the New Laura are described and discussed.

The Opposition to Sabas in the Great Laura

I suggest that the dispute which caused the schism at the Great Laura concerned the ascetic way of life within the *laura*. One group, under the leadership of Sabas, favored the physical enlargement of the *laura* and the construction of additional monasteries in the area; and this idea was indeed implemented at a later date. The opposing group favored the continuance of a frugal lifestyle with few possessions, and with each member residing in a cell. Such a conflict is apparent in the advanced stages of most ascetic movements. A passage in Peter Levy's *The Frontiers of Paradise* (1987), relates to this problem:

> A monastery . . . becomes an artificial world within which one may practice poverty and humility, though the world itself is not poor. The paradoxes and tensions have been set up from which monasticism will suffer ever afterwards.[9]

In the Great Laura, this discord developed into an open clash.

In order to fully grasp the way of life that existed in the Judean desert *lauras*, we have to go back to the time of Chariton, who founded the first three *lauras* in the area in the first half of the fourth century.[10] Chariton instructed his monks in the *laura* of Pharan to be frugal, eat sparingly, pray seven times a day at set hours, and spend the rest of their waking hours studying psalms or reading holy books while working at simple handicrafts (weaving baskets or twining rope).[11] The ideal of a monk in contemplation within his cell is clearly stated by the writer of the biography of Chariton: "Chariton laid down the precept that the monks must not emerge frequently from their cells but should stay at home as much as possible and adhere with all their might to tranquillity, the mother of all virtues."[12]

And indeed, the formula that developed in the *lauras* of the Judean desert was a regimen of communal prayers and meals on Saturday and Sunday and a solitary life in individual cells, consisting principally of prayer and meditation, the rest of the week. Later, in 428 CE, Sabas's teacher Euthymius modeled his *laura* in Mishor Adummim on the *laura* of Pharan.

The lauritic lifestyle advocated by Chariton and Euthymius collided with Sabas's views. Although he began as a hermit and founded his monastery in the Kidron Valley as a typical *laura,* Sabas spent most of his life promoting its expansion and the establishment of additional monasteries. Unlike Euthymius, he was not an inspired intellectual, neither as a theologian nor as a teacher for the monks.[13] On the other hand, he was an outstanding builder and organizer. His strong aptitude in these areas became apparent as early as the founding of the Great Laura.

The *laura* was built on the steep cliffs of the Kidron Valley, deep in the Judean desert. At first Sabas lived there alone, in a cave accessible only with the aid of a rope. In 483 CE, after he had been there for five years, seventy monks gathered around him. This can be seen as the founding of the Great Laura.[14] Sabas provided each of the monks with a small cell and cave. At the same time, he launched his building activities with the construction of the communal sections of the *laura.* At the northern end of the canyon-like valley, a tower was built to mark the territory of the *laura* and to establish the monks' claim on the property.[15] Then Sabas built a small chapel at the center of the *laura.* When the population of the *laura* grew, the communal buildings had to be expanded. For this purpose, Sabas adapted a large cave in the Kidron Valley for use as a church. The monastery's water problem was miraculously solved when Sabas discovered a small spring, which yields water to this day. By this time, the population of monks had increased to a hundred fifty. Numerous cells were built along either side of the crevice, and pack animals were purchased "to support the laura and serve those living in it."[16]

Above the cave church, Sabas built himself a tower in which "he would stay for the office and the rest of the administration."[17] His fame spread, and numerous admirers arrived at the monastery. The donations he received were used for construction and maintenance.[18]

Even after the cave church was consecrated in 490 CE, the expansion of the Great Laura continued. In the same year, Sabas's mother died, leaving him a sizable inheritance. Sabas used these funds to construct two hospices: one within the Great Laura and the other in Jericho.[19] Two years later, with the aid of his monks, Sabas established a new monastery—the cenobium of Castellion, about 3 kilometers northeast of the Great Laura. Construction took eight months, and the monastery was consecrated in October 492 CE.[20]

One year later Sabas founded the "Small Cenobium," as it was called by the monks; it was actually an integral part of the Great Laura.[21] In 494 CE he was appointed archimandrite (superior of an Eastern rite monastery, equivalent to an abbot in Western monasticism) of all lauritic monks in Palestine. That year, two monks named Theodulus and Gelasius, architects from Isauria in Asia Minor, arrived at the monastery. Sabas took advantage of their skills and proceeded to complete the Great Laura.[22] At first, a bakery and an infirmary were constructed. A large, elaborate church dedicated to Mary was built over them. Between the church and the cave church, a paved forecourt was created (Sabas's tomb was later placed in the forecourt). Near the church building, large cisterns were dug and plastered. The culmination of this construction effort was the consecration of the new church in 501 CE.

Sabas could not have carried out these projects without the support of his monks in the Great Laura. According to Cyril, the monks played an active part in the work. He notes that John Hesychast, one of the most prominent monks in the Great Laura in the sixth century, helped the builders of the hospice early in his career by "supplying them with stones and other building materials."[23] Sabas sent one monk to Jericho with pack animals to bring back timber beams.[24]

The work was particularly difficult in the harsh climate of the desert. Cyril writes about this problem in his description of the construction of the monastery of Castellion. After Easter, he reports, Sabas arrived at the site together with a group of monks from his monastery "and began to clear the place and to build cells from the material he found there."[25] The arduous labor continued for eight months. By midsummer, Sabas and the monks were exhausted and ill. Then, however, food and supplies were sent by Marcian, the archimandrite of the Jerusalem diocese and abbot of a monastery named for him near Bethlehem.[26]

After the completion of the monastery of Castellion and its consecration on 23 November 492, Sabas appointed one of the monks to lead the monastery and, with additional monks from the community, to settle it. In other words, not only did his monks assist in the building of the monastery, but they also helped populate it.[27]

Sabas's intensive building activity could not leave his monks unaffected. They were impelled to leave their cells; to carry out physical, occasionally strenuous, work; and to be dependent upon the church establishment in Jerusalem. As a result, opposition to Sabas at the Great Laura began early on in its existence. At first, his adversaries dared not openly oppose him. According to Cyril, the patriarch at that time was Martyrius, who "had known the great Euthymius and had a great love for [Sabas]."[28] After the death of Martyrius in 486 CE, Sabas's opponents from the Great Laura asked the new patriarch, Sallust, to appoint a new abbot. They did not recognize Sabas's leadership, accused him of extreme rusticity (he was born in a village in Cappadocia) and claimed that he was incapable of leading a community of a hundred fifty monks. But Sallust gave Sabas his full backing, even calling him to Jerusalem and ordaining him a priest in the presence of his opponents.[29]

Joseph Patrich maintains that it was this abhorrence of Sabas's rustic background by highly educated, intellectual monks in the *laura* that was the primary reason for the opposition that arose.[30] But this interpretation is not a sufficient explanation of the bitter antagonism toward Sabas. We need to have a more substantial reason for such a rebellion.

Cyril describes Sabas's opponents as people "who were fleshly in thought."[31] He may have meant that they did not see the spiritual value of Sabas's activity and were concerned with themselves alone. But it should be remembered that these monks were among the hermits who had joined Sabas in the early days of the Great Laura, and had believed he was Euthymius's disciple and thus the heir to Chariton's asceticism.[32] These hopes had turned out to be short-lived. Sabas's determination to build and develop the *laura* did not meet with their approval.

In spite of Sabas's appointment to the priesthood and the patriarch's unlimited support of him, this opposition intensified. According to Cyril, the action that most aroused the ire of Sabas's opponents was the founding of the monastery of Castellion, the first of his cenobia.[33] They viewed it as the embodiment of Sabas's aspirations as a builder. By the time the Church of the Virgin Mary was consecrated in 501 CE, the number of Sabas's opponents had grown to forty.

He decided to leave the monastery, and settled near Beit She'an-Scythopolis.[34] After establishing a cenobium there, Sabas returned to the Great Laura, but found that by then he had sixty opponents. Failing to win back their loyalty, he left once again and settled in Emmaus-Nicopolis, where he established another cenobium.[35] Meanwhile, his opponents spread the rumor that Sabas had been devoured by lions near the Dead Sea and asked the current patriarch, Elias, to appoint a new abbot for the Great Laura.[36] Elias refused, and waited until mid-September, when all the abbots traditionally gathered in Jerusalem to commemorate the dedication of the Church of the Holy Sepulcher. On that occasion, in 506 CE, Sabas came to Jerusalem. Elias, who was personally acquainted with him since they had both been disciples of Euthymius, ordered him to return to the Great Laura. He even presented Sabas with a written order that all the monks accept his leadership.

The Founding of the New Laura

Sabas's return to the Great Laura and the reading of the patriarch's order in the church infuriated his opponents. Rather than accept his style of monasticism, they gathered their belongings and prepared to leave the *laura*. Cyril reports that some of them "took axes, shovels, spades, and levers and, ascending to [Sabas's] tower, demolished it to the foundations in fierce rage, and threw its boards and stones down into the gorge."[37] The destruction of Sabas's cell was not a random act. It was a symbolic means of conveying disappointment in Sabas's leadership and in his concept of monasticism. This event was the climax of the dispute that divided the Great Laura.

Following the destruction of the tower, the dissenters left the monastery and went to the Old Laura of Chariton near Tekoa, where they asked permission to join that community. It can be assumed that the ascetic way of life in the Old Laura still conformed to Chariton's rules and, therefore, suited the dissenters from the Great Laura. But Aquilinus, the head of the Old Laura at the time, refused their request, for reasons that he kept to himself.[38] It can be assumed that Aquilinus did not wish to help monks who opposed Sabas. The dissenters "withdrew to the gorge south of Tekoa, where they found water and traces of cells once built by the Aposchists." Cyril reports that "they stayed, built themselves cells, and named the site the New Laura."[39]

The name signified their desire to return to the original lauritic way of life.[40] They settled in the abandoned cells,[41] but according to Cyril they had no possessions and no church, and so they celebrated Communion in the Church of the Prophet Amos in neighboring Tekoa.[42]

At this point, the story of the founding of the New Laura takes a surprising turn. According to Cyril, Sabas decided to come to the aid of the dissenters in a gesture of conciliation. "He took the animals of the [Great Laura] and Castellion, loaded them with provisions, and set off to visit them."[43]

When Sabas arrived, he was given a cool reception. According to Cyril, his opponents said to each other, "See, here comes the squinter."[44] Nevertheless, he was accepted, and they cooperated with him. Sabas went to Jerusalem and met with the patriarch, Elias, who assigned the New Laura to his charge as archimandrite and gave him a libra of gold to pay for construction.[45] Construction of the New Laura was carried out quickly, as related by Cyril: "So the godly old man [Sabas] returned to them with skilled workmen and all the requisites and, spending five months with them, built them a bakery and church, which he furnished and then consecrated in the sixty-ninth year of his life [507 CE]."[46] Another old monk, John, was appointed to head the *laura*. He had been among the first monks in the Great Laura and apparently was a loyal supporter of Sabas.[47]

The founding of the New Laura was, then, a solution that satisfied both camps. This is the only way to explain the cooperation between Sabas and his opponents in spite of the discord that had brought about their departure from the Great Laura. Now the two camps were physically separated but under one leader, Sabas. The monks of the New Laura could lead their lives according to the old and accepted manner, a frugal, solitary, and contemplative existence in their cells. On the other hand, Sabas and his followers in the Great Laura were freed of the opposition that had constricted their actions.

After the founding of the New Laura, Sabas had the opportunity to strive "to make the desert into a city," a goal that Cyril mentions several times.[48] In four years (508–511), he founded no fewer than four monasteries, one after the other. The first was the monastery of the Cave (Spelaion), which was a cenobium intended for experienced monks, similar in purpose to the monastery of Castellion.[49] The remains of the monastery of the Cave were discovered in Bir el-Qattar, 3.5 kilometers northeast of the Great Laura (Mar Saba).

Sabas employed a team of monks to build it, including the two master builders Theodolus and Gelasius. The financing was provided by the patriarch Elias and by Marcian, a priest from the Church of the Holy Sepulcher in Jerusalem who also headed the staff of monks in the Church of Zion in Jerusalem. According to Cyril, Marcian "made frequent visits to our sainted father Sabas, bringing him many offerings."[50] This information sheds light on the dynamics that permitted Sabas to build on a scale previously unknown in the Judean desert. On the one hand, he was helped by the monks of the Great Laura, who were employed at various construction tasks; and, on the other, his connections with the ecclesiastical establishment were useful to him in his fund-raising efforts.

One year after the founding of the monastery of the Cave, Sabas established another cenobium, later named after its first abbot, John Scholarius.[51] It was built atop Mount Muntar, the highest hill in the Judean desert (586 meters above sea level), about 4 kilometers north of the Great Laura. Not long afterward, Sabas founded the *laura* of Heptastomos (the Seven Cisterns).[52]

The remains of this *laura* were discovered in Khirbet Jinjas, 4.5 kilometers northwest of the Great Laura. The fourth monastery he founded during that period was the cenobium of Zannus. According to Cyril, it was built about 15 stadia (2.8 km.) west of the Great Laura.[53] Its archaeological remains at el-Bourj show that it was a relatively small cenobium.

Sabas's prestige and leadership extended far beyond his official status as a monk and archimandrite of the lauritic monks and the hermits. On the two trips he made to Constantinople, once during the reign of the emperor Anastasius (in 511–512) and a second time under Justinian (531), Sabas represented the Church of Jerusalem and the whole Christian population of Palestine.[54]

Upon his return from his second trip, Sabas founded his last monastery, the *laura* of Jeremias on the eastern slopes of Mount Muntar.[55] This *laura* is not included in Cyril's list of Sabas's projects,[56] but the manner in which it was founded and the degree of his personal involvement place it among "his" monasteries. Geographically, it is also connected to the entire group of Sabas's monasteries clustered near the Great Laura, with the exception of the New Laura.[57]

The Remains of the New Laura

The New Laura was built far away from the Great Laura (16.5 km. to the south), and its remains reflect the monks' concept of ascetic life in the *laura*.

The remains were discovered and identified in 1982 by the survey team for the map of Herodium, headed by this author.[58] They are situated in Wadi el-Jihar, 2.5 kilometers south of Tekoa, and occupy a slope with a height differential of over 300 meters. The site, known in Arabic as Bir el-Wa'ar (the Rugged Cistern), is rocky and dissected by many rockfalls.[59] Two ancient approaches lead to the monastery: one descending from Tekoa to Wadi el-Jihar and then rising gradually to the site, and the other descending to the site from Khirbet el-Kanub, a route connecting the monastery with the Hebron region.

The monastery is a typical *laura:* it has a nucleus; surrounding monks' cells and cultivated plots and various installations within a radius of about 400 meters; and a central path connecting the buildings of the nucleus with the cells.[60]

Careful examination of both Cyril's description of the New Laura and its archaeological remains reveals that it was simple and modest. Cyril mentions only two elements: the bakery and the church, the basic elements essential to every *laura.*[61] To better understand how modest the New Laura was, we can compare it with the Great Laura, which had three churches, a small cenobium, a hospice, a hospital, a bakery, and other facilities. In addition, Cyril mentions that the New Laura was built in only five months, as opposed to the Great Laura, which took over fifteen years.

The archaeological evidence, too, attests to its simplicity. The core buildings comprise two separate complexes: the church complex and another complex 150 meters to the west. The church complex includes a small chapel built on a natural rock step adjacent to the cliffs. The western complex is larger and consists of buildings with several rooms, cisterns, and agricultural plots arranged around an interior courtyard. This compound was probably the service area, including the bakery.

Around the core of the *laura,* the remains of more than forty cells were found and surveyed. There are no natural caves in the cliff on which the New Laura rests; hence, all the cells of the *laura* were built without making use of natural enclosures (unlike the Great Laura, where there was extensive use of natural caves).[62]

Most of the monks' cells are of uniform plan: a cistern, a room nearby, and a terraced plot. One example is a cell that lies about 200 meters south of the core buildings of the *laura.* It is almost square (6.3 m. × 7 m.). The walls are 0.7 meters thick, producing an interior area of 35.3 square meters. South of the cell is a small cistern (2m. × 3.5 m., with a depth of 2.2 m.), and to the northwest is an agricultural terrace. The other cells have an average size of 20.7 square meters. The sim-

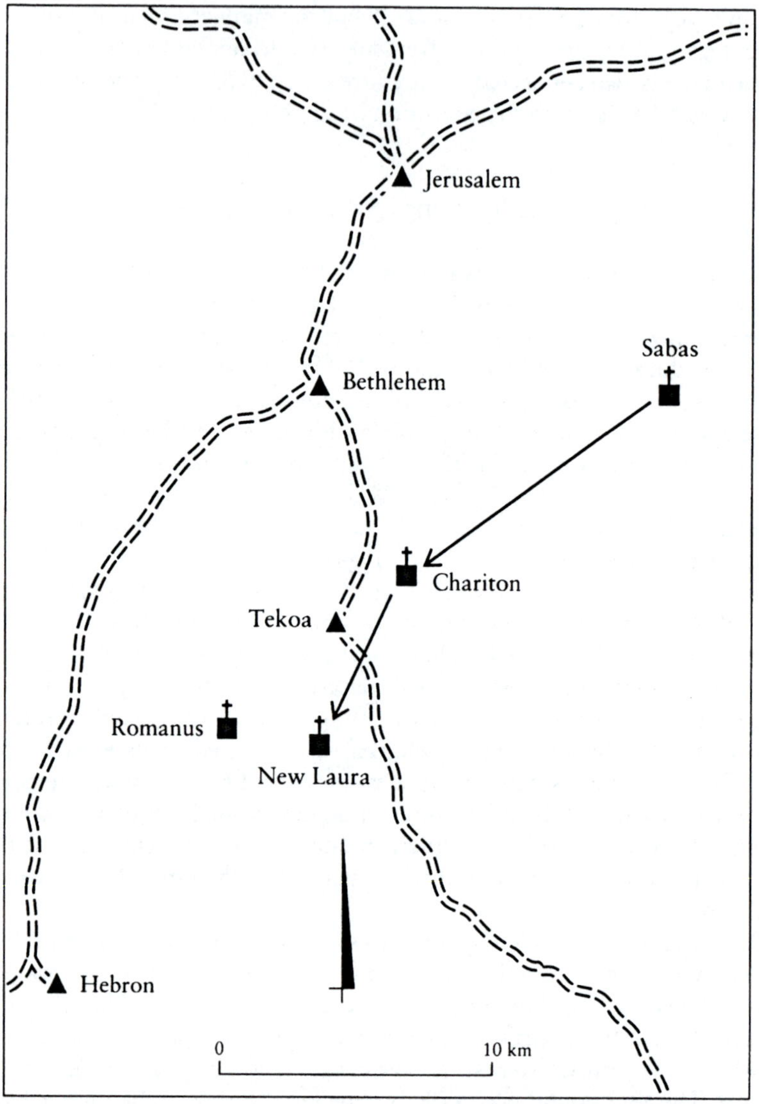

The course of the founders of the New Laura from the Great Laura of Sabas, via the Old Laura of Chariton.

plicity of the cells of the New Laura also contrasts with the much more sophisticated cells of the Great Laura.[63]

After Sabas's death in 532 CE, the Origenist dispute broke out in its full intensity, dividing the monks of the Judean desert for more than two decades (532–555).

Aerial view of the Great Laura of Sabas, looking north.

During this dispute, the New Laura was notorious as the center of Origenism. Four years after Sabas's death, forty monks left the Great Laura for the New Laura. Thus two camps emerged: the orthodox camp, whose center was the Great Laura, and the Origenist camp, whose center was the New Laura.[64]

Several scholars have suggested that the founders of the New Laura were Origenists.[65] However, in the first years of its existence there was no connection between the founders of the New Laura and the Origenist creed. The split in the Great Laura that led to the founding of the New Laura centered around practical matters concerning the monastic way of life. On the other hand, it seems reasonable that the emergence of the New Laura as the center of Origenism can be attributed to its background. Since the founding of this *laura* was the consequence of the opposition to Sabas, the community was a potential opponent of Sabas's successors in the Great Laura as well. Although Cyril does not mention this explicitly, it might be suggested that lying beneath the theological surface of the Origenist controversy was the conflict between differing approaches to the monastic way of life that began when Sabas was alive.

After the fifth Ecumenical Synod, which was held in Constantinople in 553 CE, the Origenists were excommunicated. The supporters of Origenism in the New Laura were ordered to leave, and a year later, in the autumn of 554 CE, they were expelled from the site. They were replaced by a hundred twenty orthodox monks,

Aerial view of the Old Laura of Chariton, looking west.

among them Cyril of Scythopolis, who had been a monk in the cenobium of Euthymius since 545 CE.[66] Upon his arrival at the New Laura, Cyril began writing his hagiographies, which are our main source for the events herein described.

NOTES

1. The following abbreviations are employed for note citations: Chariton = Life of Chariton, translated by L. Di Segni, in V. L. Wimbush, ed., *Ascetic Behavior in Greco-Roman Antiquity: A Sourcebook* (Minneapolis, 1990), pp. 396–420. Cyril = Cyril of Scythopolis, *The Lives of the Monks of Palestine,* trans. R. M. Price (Kalamazoo, Mich., 1991). *V. Char.* = *Vita Charitonis,* ed. G. Garitte, "La vie premetaphrastique de S. Chariton," *Bulletin de l'Institute historique Belge de Rome* 21 (1941):16–46. *V. Cyr.* = *Vita sancti Cyriaci,* ed. E. Schwartz (Leipzig, 1939), pp. 222–235. *V. Euth.* = *Vita sancti Euthymii,* ed. E. Schwartz (Leipzig, 1939), pp. 8–85. *V. Geor.* = *Vita sancti Georgii Chozibitae auctore Antonio Chozibita,* ed. C. House, *Analecta Bollandiana* 7 (1888):95–144. *V. Ger.* = *Vita sancti Gerasimi anonyma,* ed. K. M. Koikylides, (Jerusalem, 1902). *V. Sab.* = *Vita sancti Sabae,* ed. E. Schwartz (Leipzig 1939), pp. 85–200.
2. *V. Ger.* 4.4. On the simplicity of the rules Gerasimus established for his cell dwellers, see D. J. Chitty, "The Wilderness of Jerusalem," *The Christian East* 10 (1929):78. The remains of the *laura* of Gerasimus are described by Y. Hirschfeld in "Gerasimus and His Laura in the Jordan Valley," *Revue biblique* 98 (1991):419–430.
3. *V. Geor.* 3.11.106. For the historical background of the monastery of Calamon, see

S. Vailhé, "Les laures de saint Gérasime et de Calamon," *Echos d'orient* 2 (1898–1899):112–117.

4. Cyril, *Life of Cyriacus* 6–7.248–249 (= *V. Cyr.* 6–7.226). The conflicts between the monasteries of Euthymius and Theoctistus have been described by several scholars. See S. Vailhé, "Le monastère de Saint Theoctiste (410)," *Revue de l'orient chrétien* 3 (1898):72–73; ibid., "Saint Euthyme le Grand, moine de Palestine (376–473)," *ROC* 13 (1908):257–258; R. Génier, *Vie de saint Euthyme le Grand (377–473)* (Paris, 1909), pp. 292–293; D. Chitty, "Two Monasteries in the Wilderness of Judaea," *Palestine Exploration Fund, Quarterly Statement* (1928):136. Another case of twin monasteries splitting was that of the two monasteries of Elias, near Jericho. According to Cyril, one of them was later transferred to the ownership of a group of wealthy eunuchs and named "The Monastery of the Eunuchs." See Cyril, *Life of Sabas* 69, pp. 180–181.
5. Cyril, *Life of Sabas* 36.131–133 (= *V. Sab.* 36.122–123). See also S. Vailhé, "Les monasteres de Palestine," *Bessarione* 4(1898–1899):199–201; M. Marcoff and D. J. Chitty, "Notes on Monastic Research in the Judean Wilderness, 1928–9," *Palestine Exploration Quarterly* 61 (1929):171–174.
6. For Cyril's biography, see A. J. Festugière, *Cyrille de Scythopolis, vie de Saint Euthyme* (Paris, 1962), pp. 9–16; B. Flusin, *Miracle et histoire dans l'oeuvre de Cyrille de Scythopolis* (Paris, 1983), pp. 12–32; Y. Hirschfeld, "Wandering Desert Monk," *Eretz Magazine* 15 (1989):18–33.
7. J. Patrich, "The Monastic Institutions of Saint Sabas: An Archaeological-Historical Study," Ph.D. dissertation, Jerusalem, 1989 (Hebrew). This research, which is the most complete and up-to-date, deals with all of Sabas's monasteries in the Kidron Valley.
8. Y. Hirschfeld, *Archaeological Survey of Israel: Map of Herodium (108/2)* (Jerusalem, 1985), pp. 54–56 (English summary of pp. 99–105).
9. P. Levy, *The Frontiers of Paradise: A Study of Monks and Monasteries* (London, 1987), p. 50. The paradoxes of the monastic movement are well presented by E. W. McDonnell, "Monastic Stability: Some Socio-Economic Considerations," in A. E. Laiov-Thomadakis, ed., *Charanis Studies: Essays in Honor of Peter Charanis* (New Jersey, 1980), pp. 115–150 (esp. pp. 118–119).
10. For the monasteries of Chariton, see Y. Hirschfeld, "The Life of Chariton in Light of Archaeological Research," in V. L. Wimbush, ed., *Ascetic Behavior in Greco-Roman Antiquity: A Sourcebook* (Minneapolis, 1990), pp. 425–447.
11. *Life of Chariton* 16.406–407 (= *V. Char.* 16.28).
12. Ibid. The first *laura* of Chariton—Pharan—became a model for the monks of the Judean desert. The slogan "laura on the model of Pharan" had been used by Cyril twice in the *Life of Euthymius* 9.12 (= *V. Euth.* 9.16) and 16.22 (= *V. Euth.* 16.26).
13. See Patrich (above, note 7), pp. 59–143; J. Binns, "Cyril of Scythopolis and the Monasteries of the Palestinian Desert," Ph.D. dissertation, London, 1989, pp. 156–186; and E. Schwartz, *Kyrillos von Skythopolis* (Leipzig 1939), pp. 374–375.
14. Cyril, *Life of Sabas* 16.108 (= *V. Sab.* 16.99–100). The sudden growth of the Great Laura might be understood in the context of the events that were transpiring in the Judean desert. Sabas founded his *laura* in 483 CE, one year after the dedication of the rebuilt cenobium of Euthymius, which replaced the *laura;* see Chitty (above, note 4), p. 136. We can suppose that after the conversion of the *laura* of Euthymius into a cenobium, some of the monks who did not want to live a communal life left the monastery. Cyril says that when the Great Laura was founded, many of the hermits in the area joined Sabas. It might be suggested that some, if not many, of the hermits came from the monastery of Euthymius. According to Flusin (above, note 6), pp. 141–142,

this was the regular process in the Judean desert monasticism. Nevertheless, the rapid growth of Sabas's *laura* shows the enthusiastic response of the monks to the challenge he offered them.

15. Cyril, *Life of Sabas* 16.109 (= *V. Sab.* 16.100). The tower was an essential element among the monasteries of the Judean desert. See Y. Hirschfeld, *The Judean Desert Monasteries in the Byzantine Period* (New Haven and London, 1992), pp. 171–176.
16. Cyril, *Life of Sabas* 18.111 (= *V. Sab.* 18.122). For the importance of beasts of burden in monastic life, see W. N. Zeisel, *An Economic Survey of the Early Byzantine Church* (Princeton, 1975), p. 322.
17. Cyril, *Life of Sabas* 18.111 (= *V. Sab.* 18.102). A towerlike cell was known in other *lauras* in the Judean desert. See Hirschfeld (above, note 15), p. 173.
18. Cyril, *Life of Sabas* 18.112 (= *V. Sab.* 18.102). Another example of spending donations on buildings to enlarge the monastery can be found in Cyril, *Life of Euthymius* 10.16 (= *V. Euth.* 10.21) on the beginning of the monastery of Theoctistus.
19. More details concerning the hospice are given in Cyril, *Life of John Hesychast* 6–7.225 (= *V. John Hes.* 6–7.206). In his second year in the Great Laura (492 CE), John was in charge of the hospice. The kitchen of the hospice is mentioned in Cyril, *Life of Sabas* 40.140 (= *V. Sab.* 40.130) and 48.148 (= *V. Sab.* 48.137–138). For the functions of the hospice in the monasteries, see V. Corbo, "L'ambiente materiale della vita dei monaci di Palestina nel period bizantino," Orientalia Christiana Analecta 153 (Rome, 1958), p. 243.
20. Cyril, *Life of Sabas* 27.119–121 (= *V. Sab.* 27.110–112). For references to the history and research of the monastery of Castellion, see Y. Hirschfeld, "List of the Byzantine Monasteries in the Judean Desert," in G. C. Bottini et al., eds., *Christian Archaeology in the Holy Land: New Discoveries* (Jerusalem, 1990), pp. 33–34.
21. Cyril, *Life of Sabas* 28.122 (= *V. Sab.* 28.113). For more details, see Hirschfeld (above, note 20), pp. 34–35.
22. Cyril, *Life of Sabas* 32.126 (= *V. Sab.* 32.117).
23. See above, note 19.
24. Cyril, *Life of Sabas* 26.118 (= *V. Sab.* 26.109).
25. See above, note 20.
26. For details on Marcian and his monastery near Bethlehem, see S. Vailhé, "Les monasteres de Palestine," *Bessasione* 4 (1898–1899):195–196.
27. J. Patrich, "The Sabaite Monastery of the Cave (Spelaion) in the Judean Desert," *Liber Annuus* 41(1991):431–432.
28. Cyril, *Life of Sabas* 18.112 (= *V. Sab.* 18.103). Martyrius founded his monastery before Euthymius's death (473 CE). See Cyril, *Life of Euthymius* 32.48 (= *V. Sab.* 32.51). For the impressive remains of the monastery of Martyrius, see Hirschfeld (above, note 20), pp. 20–22. After his ordination as patriarch in 478 CE, Martyrius was involved in the construction of the monastery of Euthymius. This is mentioned in a comment of Cyril's that has been preserved in a Georgian version of the *Life of Cyriac,* see G. Garitte, "La version georgienne de la vie de S. Cyriaque par Cyrille de Scythopolis," *Le Muséon* 75 (1962):415 (with Latin translation). A French translation is provided by Flusin (above, note 6), p. 41. This shows Martyrius's personal involvement in the monastic life in the Judean desert.
29. Cyril, *Life of Sabas* 19.113 (= *V. Sab.* 19.104). For the refusal of Sabas to be ordained see Flusin (above, note 6), p. 149; Binns (above, note 13), 247; and Zeisel (above, note 16), p. 322.
30. Patrich (above, note 7), p. 178. See also Binns (above, note 13), pp. 246–248.

31. Cyril, *Life of Sabas* 19.112 (= *V. Sab.* 19.103). According to Flusin (above, note 6), p. 52, Cyril's description of the opposition to Sabas was influenced by the description of the opposition to Pachomius, in his monasteries in Egypt. For the rebellion in Pachomius's monasteries, see P. Rousseau, *Pachomius: The Making of a Community in Fourth-Century Egypt* (Berkeley, 1985), pp. 157–158, 186–189.
32. Cyril's phrase: "laura on the model of Pharan" (*V. Euth.* 9.12; 16.22) reflected the importance of Chariton and his *lauras*, even as late as the sixth century.
33. Cyril, *Life of Sabas* 33.127 (= *V. Sab.* 33.118).
34. Sabas's withdrawal is reminiscent of the withdrawal of his master, Euthymius, after the Council of Chalcedon. See Cyril, *Life of Euthymius* 27.41 (= *V. Euth* 27.44–45).
35. Cyril, *Life of Sabas* 35.129–130 (= *V. Sab.* 35.120). The location of Sabas's monastery near Emmaus-Nicopolis has not been ascertained, nor has that of the monastery near Beit Shean-Scythopolis.
36. Cyril, *Life of Sabas* 35.130 (= *V. Sab.* 35.121).
37. Cyril, *Life of Sabas* 36.132 (= *V. Sab.* 36.123).
38. The heads of all the *lauras* in the Jerusalem diocese, including the abbot of the Old Laura, were subordinate to the leadership of Sabas, who was archimandrite. See Chitty (above, note 4), pp. 109–110.
39. Cyril, *Life of Sabas* 36.132 (= *V. Sab.* 36.123).
40. In ancient times, the word "new" expressed the desire for renewal—for example, Constantinople was named "New Rome."
41. Cyril reports that the abandoned cells were built by the "Aposchists" (*V. Sab.* 36.123). The "Aposchists" were the schismatics who rejected Chalcedon and gained the "Monophysites." See Festugière (above, note 6), p. 101, note 88. The Nea Laura's founders settled in the abandoned cells of the Aposchists, not in the monastery of Romanus as has been suggested by most scholars, for example J. Binns, in his *Commentary to Cyril*, p. 213, note 44. The remains of the monastery of Romanus were discovered in Khirbet er-Rube'ia, 4 kilometers northwest of the site of the New Laura—see Y. Hirschfeld, "The Judean Desert and Samaria, Survey of Monasteries—1987," *Excavations and Surveys in Israel* 7–8 (1988–1989):102–104.
42. For the remains at Tekoa, see J. Escobar, "Estudio de los restos Arqueologicos de Tecoa," *Liber Annuus* 26 (1976):5–26.
43. Cyril, *Life of Sabas* 36.132 (= *V. Sab.* 36.123).
44. Ibid. It is not impossible that the fact that Sabas had a physical blemish prevented him from being ordained in the first years of his abbacy. I wish to thank Leah Di Segni for pointing out this idea.
45. One *libra* of gold was 72 solidi. The average daily wage of a worker in the sixth century was one third of a solidus. See C. Mango, *Byzantine Architecture* (Milan, 1974), p. 27.
46. Cyril, *Life of Sabas* 36.132–133 (= *V. Sab.* 36.123–124).
47. Vailhé (above, note 26), p. 208 provides all the known names of the heads of the Nea Laura, starting with John, who was the abbot from 508 to 515.
48. Cyril writes, ". . . for it was necessary that this desert be colonized through [Sabas]." See *Life of Sabas* 6.98 (= *V. Sab.* 6.90). In another place, he writes: ". . . in [Sabas's] eagerness to make the desert into a city." See Cyril, *Life of Sabas* 37.135 (= *V. Sab.* 37.126). For the phrase, "colonization of the desert," see Flusin (above, note 6), p. 185.
49. Cyril, *Life of Sabas* 37.135–136 (= *V. Sab.* 37.126–127). For the history and the remains of the monastery of the Cave (Spelaion), see Patrich (above, note 27).
50. For the financial support of the monasteries in the Judean desert, see Hirschfeld (above, note 15), pp. 102–103.

51. For the historical remains of the monastery of Scholarius, see Hirschfeld (above, note 20), pp. 39–40.
52. For the *laura* of Heptastomos, see ibid., pp. 40–41.
53. For the monastery of Zannus, see ibid., pp. 41–42.
54. See S. Vailhé, "La laure de saint Sabas," *Echos de Notre Dame* 5 (1897):136–137; Schwartz (above, note 13), p. 183; Patrich (above, note 7), pp. 287–295; Binns (above, note 13), p. 170.
55. For the *laura* of Jeremias, see Hirschfeld (above, note 20), pp. 47–49, and J. Patrich, "The Sabaite Laura of Jeremias in the Judean Desert," *Liber Annuus* 40 (1990):295–311.
56. Cyril, *Life of Sabas* 58.168 (= *V. Sab.* 58.158).
57. Sabas's monasteries were organized like a confederation, see G. Rezac, "Le diverse forme di unione fra i monasteri orientali," Orientalia Christiana Analecta 153 (Rome, 1958), pp. 107–117.
58. Y. Hirschfeld, *Archaeological Survey of Israel: Map of Herodium (108/2)* (Jerusalem, 1985), pp. 54–56.
59. The name Bir el-Wa'ar ("The Rugged Cistern") was given by the local inhabitants to the huge cistern in the center of the site.
60. For the characteristic features of the lauritic monastery, see Hirschfeld (above, note 15), pp. 18–33.
61. These elements—the church and the bakery—are mentioned in the description of the *laura* of Euthymius in Mishor Adummim. See Cyril, *Life of Euthymius* 15.20 (= *V. Euth.* 15.24).
62. Patrich (above, note 7), p. 71, for the use of caves in the Great Laura.
63. The remains of the cells in the Great Laura have been described in detail by J. Patrich, "Hermitages of the Great Laura of St. Sabas," in D. Jacoby and Y. Tsafrir, eds., *Jews, Samaritans, and Christians in Byzantine Palestine* (Jerusalem, 1988), pp. 131–160.
64. Cyril, *Life of Sabas* 84.198–199 (= *V. Sab.* 84.189–190). The best discussion concerning the Origenist controversy is Father Diekamp, *Die origenistischen Streitischen im sechsten Jahrhundert und des fünfte allgemeine Conzil,* (Münster, 1899). See also L. Duchense, *L'église au VI siècle* (Paris, 1925), pp. 165–175; Flusin (above, note 6), pp. 76–83; Binnes (above, note 13), pp. 252–265.
65. F. M. Abel, *Histoire de la Palestine* (Paris, 1952), p. 352; Festugière (above, note 6), p. 20. It is suspected that Cyril intended to connect the appearance of Nonnus, who later became the leader of the Origenists in the New Laura, with the withdrawal of Paul, the *laura*'s abbot. See Cyril, *Life of Sabas* 36.133 (= *V. Sab.* 36.124).
66. Cyril, *Life of Sabas* 90.208 (= *V. Sab.* 90.199).

20

Dreaming the Body: An Aesthetics of Asceticism

Patricia Cox Miller

Dim and Dazzling Bodies

In an essay entitled "Dim Body, Dazzling Body," Jean-Pierre Vernant argues that for Greeks of the archaic period the human body was conceptualized as a dim version of the dazzling bodies of the gods.[1] The human body was perceived by means of a comparative method in which it could be discerned by "deciphering all the signs that mark the human body with the seal of limitation, deficiency, incompleteness, and that make it a sub-body." Further, "this sub-body cannot be understood except in reference to what it presupposes: corporeal plenitude, a super-body, the body of the gods."[2] Judged according to the standards of this divine super-body, the human body is perceived as "ephemeral," "inconstant," "vulnerable to the vicissitudes of time flowing without return," with death as "a witness to its fragility."[3]

This perception of the body as the sign of human misfortune, however, does not conform to the Platonic—and, later, Cartesian—dichotomous model of human composition that splits the person into a positive soul or mind housed in a negative body construed as a prison or a mechanistic object in space. As Vernant says, "man's misfortune is not that a divine and immortal soul finds itself imprisoned in the envelope of a material and perishable body, but that his body is not fully one"[4]—that is, for the archaic Greeks, the problem is that the human body is not fully a body.

It seems to me that this archaic employment of a comparative standard for construing human identity, as well as this model's use of the image of a divine, dazzling body as the privileged signifying ground of that dim human identity, was characteristic of early Christian asceticism as well. I would like to entertain the idea that, in the Christian asceticism of late antiquity, the body was perceived to be

[Some of the material in this essay appeared originally in Patricia Cox Miller, *Dreams in Late Antiquity: Studies in the Imagination of a Culture* (Princeton: Princeton University Press, 1994).]

problematic, not because it was a body, but because it was not a body of plenitude. Although Christian theologians from Origen of Alexandria to Gregory of Nyssa had embraced the dichotomous Platonic view of the composition of the human person, they could not devalue the body to the level of prison completely if they were to affirm the positive valuation of the created world in the biblical book of *Genesis,* one of the central texts for anthropological speculation. Further, as Brown has observed, "Through the Incarnation of Christ, the Highest God had reached down to make even the body capable of transformation."[5]

Thus, when the body was viewed with despair and disgust, when it was altered by various practices of mutilation, this was not because of its sheer materiality as part of the physical world, but rather because it functioned as a signifier of a lack that was not only spiritual but also corporeal. "The disfigured was figured as desirable," as Harpham has remarked,[6] not only in opposition to classical canons of beauty now conceptualized as pagan demonism, but also as an act of defiance against the muted speech of the sub-body. In this way, asceticism can be understood as an attempt to manipulate the dim body so as to drive it as close as possible toward that corporeal vitality that is the mark of its exemplar. Asceticism, that is, attempts to control the play of the body as signifier; it attempts to reimagine how the body can be read, and what it can say.

The body of plenitude signified an existence that would defy the constraints of time and space. Hence, ascetic Christians typically used metaphors of light to convey what this exemplary self would be like. The face of Abba Pambo shone like lightning, for example, and Abba Sisoes' face shone like the sun.[7] In the glare of such brilliance, theologians like Gregory of Nyssa caught a glimpse of the dazzling plenitude of Adam, exemplar of an original humanity once lost but retrieved by Christ as the sign of human destiny. Totally lacking in the shadows that give perceptual contour to the dim bodies of historical existence, Adam's body "had been unimaginably different from our own," as Brown has explained. "It had been a faithful mirror of a soul which, itself, mirrored the utterly undivided, untouched simplicity of God. . . . It was like the diaphanous radiance of a still midday sky."[8]

Urging the dim body toward the flash of its corporeal plenitude, ascetic thinkers "lived perched between particularity and grandeur."[9] I would extend this statement by Brown by suggesting that the ascetic view of the human body oscillated between two modes of visual perception that can be aligned with the two views of the body: one that marks its dimness or particularity and the other its dazzle or grandeur. In her recent book *Saints and Postmodernism,* Edith Wyschogrod has described Maurice Merleau-Ponty's analysis of the two ways in which objects are constructed in visual perception. "He claims that two primary factors govern perceiving, first, the horizon factor, the idea that objects are not seen by themselves but are picked out against a background, and, second, the wholeness factor, the idea that each object is perceptually discriminated as a totality."[10] Merleau-Ponty discussed these two modes of perceiving by using the example of looking at a house. From the perspective of the horizon factor, "'I see the house next door from a certain angle, but it would be seen differently from the right bank of the Seine, or from the inside or from an airplane.' . . . The house is given against a backdrop which both stations and limits it, a visual horizon against which it comes forward or recedes and can be distinguished from other objects."[11] The second factor governing perception, the wholeness factor, is abstract in that it "suspends the actual spatial and temporal conditions of perception."[12] In this way of perceiving, the focus is not on the figure-and-ground character of the visual field but on the object itself. The house is not given all at once, yet the observer claims to see the whole by an act of visual inference. This is what Merleau-Ponty described as "the house seen from nowhere."[13]

Wyschogrod concludes by observing that "the phenomenon of the horizon as well as the multifaceted character of entities is integral to perception because human beings *are* their bodies. The view from nowhere and the inference to wholeness reflect perception's attempt to transcend the limitations of embodiment."[14] The problem, however, is that the human body is not a visible object like a house: "the body is not an object like others because one cannot distance oneself from one's own body so that it can give itself as a totality. I myself am that body."[15]

Viewed from the perspective of Merleau-Ponty's description of the two operations of visual perception, the ascetic imagination of the super-body is precisely an attempt to view the body from nowhere, to give the body a totality by a paradoxical act of visual inference, paradoxical because the ascetic is the body that one is trying to see. When ascetics deride the body, they are viewing it from the perceptual perspective of the horizon; the dim body is the body seen in relation to its background or context—the context of historical time, the context of a body that seems fragmented into a congeries of its own needs and desires, often described by ascetic thinkers in terms of bestiality. What I am suggesting is that asceticism constitutes an attempt to abandon the horizon and to see from nowhere. Metaphors of light as evocations of the true body were so useful because one cannot see light, just as one cannot see one's own body whole; the lightning flash in the face of a desert father marks the point of turning in what Brown described as the perch between particularity and grandeur, in which foreground and background are dissolved in a change to the perceptual mode that suspends space and time in an inference of wholeness.

How is the movement between these two perceptual operations effected, particularly when one is the object that one wishes to perceive? Since literal visual perception could not present the body of plenitude, many ascetic thinkers relied on strong acts of visual imagination to carry them from the dim body to the body from nowhere. In the case of the two ascetic theologians who will be discussed in this essay, the dazzling body was approached by way of dreams, which functioned as mediating perceptual operations that negotiated the gap between the particularizing view from the horizon and the abstracting view of the inference to wholeness.

The Ascetic Dreams of the Two Gregorys

> Then shall I see Caesarius himself, no longer in exile, but brilliant, glorious, heavenly, such as in my dreams I have often beheld you, pictured thus by my desire, if not by the very truth.[16]

> It seemed [in the dream] that I was holding in my hands the relics of martyrs, and there flowed from them such a bright beam of light, like that from a spotless mirror placed facing the sun, that my eyes were blinded by its brilliance.[17]

These two dreamers, Gregory of Nazianzus and Gregory of Nyssa, were prominent Christian theologians whose lives spanned the greater part of the fourth century CE. Although both were bishops and participated publicly in ecclesiastical affairs, both preferred the contemplative quiet of their country estates in their native Cappadocia.[18] The two Gregorys are notable for their contributions to Christian ascetic theory and to the development of a Platonized theology whose goal was the mystical union of the soul with God.[19] But they were also dreamers, and it is to their dreams that this essay will look as clues to the ways these two men understood themselves in the context of their ascetic theological perspectives.

In the cultural and religious milieu in which these Cappadocians lived, described by Peter Brown as "a stern, ceremonious Christianity, firmly rooted in the continued life of great households," the ascetic embrace of sexual renunciation was a dramatic gesture that threatened noble, landowning families, such as those the Gregorys belonged to, with social extinction.[20] This "drift toward a social void,"[21] which thoroughly altered the defining characteristics of the human person as a social being, was matched by a similar drift, in the Gregorys' theology, toward a kind of metaphysical void, in which the heretofore defining characteristics of an individual's sense of self-identity were altered theologically by the goal of emptying the self in a beatific vision of, or union with, God.[22]

Thus both asceticism and theology contributed to a destabilizing of the identity of the person, whose constitution became problematic in the thought of both Gregorys. For both, "the present constitution of the human person represented a nadir of uncertainty";[23] as Gregory of Nyssa observed, "the life of man is at present subjected to abnormal conditions."[24] As Brown has explained, in the view of the Cappadocians, "Men and women were poised between an original, lost prototype of human nature, created by God *in His own image,* and revealed to the visible world in the shimmering 'angelic' majesty of Adam, and a fullness of humanity that would come about, through the restoration of Adam's first state, at the Resurrection."[25] Part of the dilemma posed by this condition of being poised between two paradigmatic states of human being at its fullest lies in finding a means for expressing perceptions of the human that are not tainted by the fallen condition in which human life is lived. It is in the context of this perceptual dilemma that the dreams of the two Gregorys assume their importance.

We meet our first dreamer in the midst of one of life's most poignant experiences, the moment when one struggles to come to terms with the death of a beloved person. The dreamer is Gregory of Nazianzus, who wrote a funeral oration for his younger brother Caesarius after his death in 369 CE.[26] It was in this oration that Gregory reported the passage above in which he reveals that he had dreamed of his brother following his death. Gregory places the oneiric visions of his brother in the eschatological context of his own death, when he too will be in that beatific state signified by paradise. By his own report, his dreams of his brother appear to have mirrored the paradisal existence that he believes his dead brother now to be enjoying, and that he, too, longs for. The oneiric picture of the brilliant Caesarius is a construction of the human person that Gregory wishes to appropriate for himself; thus the dreams of his brother are as much about Gregory as they are about his brother.

There is an oddity about Gregory's conviction that these dreams reflected the resurrected body in all its glory. Earlier in the funeral oration for Caesarius, he described human life, the life of the living, as a day of mirrors and enigmas in which it is possible to see only a slender rivulet of the light that streams from God.[27] In one of his poems, he welcomes death as a release from the earthbound condition of human knowing, in which truth is apprehended "as if in a mirror reflected on the water's surface."[28] Because the human mind cannot contain the lightning flash of direct knowing, it must unhappily make do with a kind of impressionistic knowledge that is itself composed of images that easily slip away.[29] Given this view of the mediated state of human consciousness, how can Gregory's view of his dreams of his brother's shining form be understood? Were these dreams among those slender rivulets of light that somehow shine through the enigmatic mirroring of ordinary human knowing, or were they, too, only faint impressions of a truth that can never be fully disclosed to a living person?

Gregory attributed the epistemological dilemma in which he found himself in large part to the sheer physicality of the human condition. The thick covering of the flesh is an obstacle to the full disclosure of divine truth.[30] His goal was to press toward the life above, "deserting the earth while we are still upon the earth"; but the body formed a constant roadblock on that upward path.[31] So strong was the theologically induced prejudice against physical being-in-the-world under which Gregory labored that, in one of his long autobiographical poems, he characterized the body and physical life with bestial metaphors. Life in the world is life lived in "the mighty maw of the dragon," where one's spirit is "the prey of Belial."[32] Bitter serpents biting, jackals swarming and snarling, wild animals with tusks, the sepia fish with its poisonous black vomit, herds of swine, lions, bears, the entrails of Jonah's monster: all these describe what it is like to live in a body.[33] The body impairs our gaze upon the holy. In a striking story, now using vegetative rather than bestial images, Gregory tells of an incident in his life when he was idly toying with a twig: "I drove a thorn into my eyeball and made it all bloody."[34] The bloodied eye quickly becomes for Gregory a metaphor for the bloodied vision of human life, where insight is damaged by physicality.

One of the reasons why the body damages insight is that the sign of the flesh is differentiation; embodied life is a life in which difference reigns in such divisions as male and female, slave and free, and so on.[35] Original unity has been fragmented, and this shows itself in language as well. As Gregory laments, "It is difficult to conceive God, but to define him in words is an impossibility."[36] As a tool of life in the flesh, words can be just as misleading, for seeming to say something "real," as the body, which seems real in its own tangible way. Yet it is all an illusion. Using dream as a negative metaphor, Gregory of Nazianzus wrote in one oration that "we are unsubstantial dreams, impalpable visions, like the flight of a passing bird

. . . a flower that quickly blooms and quickly fades."[37] And, in another discourse, he observed that, apart from sin and paradise, all else is a "dream-vision, making sport of realities, and a series of phantasms which lead the soul astray."[38]

Given Gregory's view of the embodied condition of human life as, on the one hand, illusory, and, on the other, all too bestially physical, his report of his dreams of his brother Caesarius is intriguing. Gregory reports that he has seen a brilliant and heavenly Caesarius in his dreams, a figure "pictured thus by my desire, if not by the very truth." Yet, what Gregory saw in dreams was not the real body of his dead brother but a phantasmal body, an oneiric body constructed by desire. However, this body of oneiric fantasy was a picture of Caesarius no longer in exile: this was a paradisal body. The dream body was, somehow, no longer the alien body of earthly exile but a body in truth, a heavenly body. On the other hand, Gregory's phrase, "pictured thus *by my desire,* if not by the very truth," suggests that the dream body is a fabrication of the dreamer's own desire, a picture that fills a lack in his life. Yet this reading is tempered by the phrase that follows, "pictured by my desire, *if not by the very truth,*" a phrase that suggests that the dreams may well image that paradigmatic other world of Adamic existence.

Still, Gregory's phrasing leaves his understanding of the status of these dreams undecidable. Did his dreams of Caesarius show the very truth, or were they constructions of his desire that only approximated the truth? The dreams were visions of a brilliant body signifying paradisal existence—but they can also be seen as examples of the ascetic paradox of the return of the rejected body as sign.[39] From Gregory's perspective, when his brother was alive in his physical body, he was in exile, and the mark of exile was precisely the body. In the dreams, the body returns, but now it speaks a paradisal language of that perfected heavenly otherness that aided the reformulation of the identity of the dreamer. I emphasize the dreams' role in reformulating the identity of the dreamer, because these dreams were not about Caesarius; they were about what Gregory does and shall see. They picture in imaginal terms what Gregory is not but deeply desires to be: no longer in exile.

Leaving Gregory of Nazianzus in exile for the moment, I will turn to the other Gregory, Gregory of Nyssa, whose dream of the dead body of his sister Macrina also participates in the ascetic paradox of the signifying return of the body.

The time was 379 or 380 CE, some ten years after Gregory of Nazianzus had dreamed of his brother.[40] Gregory of Nyssa was on the road with the intent of visiting his sister at the community of celibate women that she had established on the family estate at Annesi. He had not seen Macrina for many years, and when he was only one day's travel away from her convent, he had a worrisome dream. In his biography of his sister, he wrote,

> I saw in dream a vision that made me apprehensive for the future. It seemed that I was holding in my hands the relics of martyrs, and there flowed from them such a bright beam of light, like that from a spotless mirror placed facing the sun, that my eyes were blinded by its brilliance. This vision occurred three times during that night, and although I was not able to interpret clearly the enigma of the dream, I nonetheless sensed some sorrow for my soul. . . .[41]

While traveling the next day, Gregory learned that Macrina was seriously ill; in fact, when he arrived, she was laid out on the ground, dying.[42]

Despite the severity of her physical condition, which Gregory compares with the disease-ravaged body of Job, Macrina "refreshed her body as though with dew" and conversed with Gregory about the destiny of the soul.[43] Finally she suggested that her brother get some rest to recover from his long journey; Gregory, however, could not sleep. He wrote, "What I had seen seemed to unravel the enigma of the dream. The sight set before me was in truth the remains of a holy martyr, the remains of one who had been dead to sin, but shining with the presence of the Holy Spirit."[44] In his dream, Gregory had seen himself holding relics of martyrs, fragments of dead bodies that gleam brilliantly, charged with the power of the religious devotion that had once animated them. Upon beholding his dying sister, he understood that the dream referred to her: the relics were her glowing bones. Thus the dream not only predicted her death but also showed her translation to heavenly status in a transformed body, fragmentary though it was. The spell of this dream also influenced the way in which Gregory saw his sister after her death. After her body was prepared for burial, it was covered by a dark cloak; yet, Gregory reports, "she shone even in that dark clothing, no doubt because the divine power added such grace to her body that, just as in the vision in my dream, beams of light seemed to shine out from her beauty."[45] Like Gregory of Nazianzus's dreams of his brother, Gregory of Nyssa's dream of his sister allowed him to see through a dead body to a body that was lively in another register.

Gregory knew that there was something special about his older sister. In his biography of her, he reports that his mother, Emmelia, had had a dream about Macrina when her labor pains began. In the dream, repeated, like Gregory's, three times, an angelic figure addressed the child as Thekla; upon awakening, Emmelia knew that the dream prefigured the reality into which her child would live, and Thekla became Macrina's secret name.[46] Thekla, a legendary figure whose cult was widespread in Asia Minor by the fourth century, was a patron saint of the ascetic life, especially among women.[47] Thus Emmelia's dream was a mirror of the ascetic vocation of her daughter, herself a mirror of the great Thekla, just as Gregory's dream mirrored the beatific result of that vocation.

Brown has remarked that, for Gregory, Macrina's body was "the untarnished mirror of a soul that had caught, at last, the blinding light of the *katharotēs,* the radiant purity, of God."[48] Yet despite all of his metaphors of light, Gregory seems reluctant to let Macrina's body disappear in a blaze of glory. He insists that her dead body is a sign of that paradigmatic radiance that marks the true identity of the human, but the body is still there as a sign. While she was alive, he wrote of Macrina that "it was as if an angel had providentially taken human form, an angel with no attachment to or affinity for life in the flesh"; Macrina had not become ensnared by the passions of the flesh.[49] He further describes her life as one poised on the boundary between human life and bodiless nature.[50] In Gregory's view, so close had Macrina come to that drastic transformation of identity from the human to the angelic that she appears to have achieved what Gregory of Nazianzus described as deserting the earth while still on it. As a shimmering object that mediated the gap between the paradigmatic worlds of Adam and the resurrection, Macrina's body provided a glimpse of the transformation that all might hope for. Her body was thus a formal analogue to Gregory's dream, itself a mediatorial vehicle that initiated Gregory, briefly, into a form of consciousness in which fleshly eyesight is blinded by beatific perception. Indeed, Macrina's body and Gregory's dream can hardly be separated, since it was the dream that had given him eyes to see the truth of his sister's body.

When he was not dreaming, however, Gregory's view of bodies was not usually so generous. In his essay *On the Making of the Human Being,* Gregory tries to envision the human person as a harmonious blend of spiritual and physical parts. Using the metaphor of a musician playing a lyre, he explains that as long as the lyre, the body, is ruled by the mind, the musician, the body can be viewed positively; it is only when the mind debases itself in following physical desires that the notion of flesh assumes a negative connotation.[51] Nonetheless, our bodies are not like the body of the archetypal Adam before the Fall, a body untouched by the brutish physicality that characterizes the bodies of the human beings now.[52] For Gregory, it was difficult to maintain the distinction between thoughts of the flesh and the flesh itself because the tug of the senses was capable of dragging the mind down to bodily concerns so easily. In his treatise *On Virginity,* the distinction tends to collapse as he describes human physicality as earthly wretchedness and, like Gregory of Nazianzus, he uses a metaphor of injured eyesight to depict the sense of estrangement that the body inflicts on us.[53] And, where Gregory of Nazianzus had used bestial images, Gregory of Nyssa uses images of dirt: the filth of the flesh now covers what was once a divine image, Adam, who in his original state looked freely upon the face of God and mirrored that brilliance.[54]

Yet, despite this rather alarming view of human physicality, Gregory's real despair centered not on the literal body but on the fall of human beings into time. As Brown has persuasively argued, Gregory thought that for the archetypal Adam, time had been infinitely openended, whereas now time was measured by a person's lifetime, with death marking the end.[55] Whereas Adam could have lived clearsightedly into a future with no end, human beings after Adam were condemned to a lifetime of anxieties regarding the future. To stave off those anxieties, especially anxieties about death, human beings placed their hopes—and also their sense of identity—on their bodies, in the form of marriage and children: "the most distinctive trait of a humanity caught in 'tainted' time," Brown writes, was "the obsession with physical continuity."[56] This kind of continuity was not satisfying, because it implied that a person's sense of self was rooted in the particulars of concrete history, producing a materialistic model of perception rather than a spiritual one.[57]

The glowing body of his virginal sister was so important to Gregory because it was a sign that a momentous shift in the constitution of the human person with respect to time was possible. Time understood as a series of lurching movements from one sensuous gratification to the next could be voided by taking off the torn garment of the historically constituted self.[58] What kind of person emerged from this divestment? Gregory's picture of Macrina offers some clues. Both in the *Life of Macrina* and in the essay *On the Soul and Resurrection,* which is structured as the dialogue that occurred between Gregory and Macrina as she lay dying, Macrina is presented as one for whom the grounds for the apprehension of meaning have shifted so dramatically away from tangible and personal concerns that she has become a living abstraction, her earthly being absorbed almost completely into theological ideas about the soul.[59] At the very moment of her painful dying, she is pictured as conversing theologically in a manner appropriate to Gregory's construction of her as a near angel. For some, this would be a scene of terrible poignancy, but not for Gregory; this represents his view of the person at its finest. In Gregory's presentation of his sister, it is hard to recognize her as a self with an identity in any conventional sense of the word, for, as Stephen Crites has remarked, "angels do not have biographies."[60]

Were it not for his dream of Macrina, Gregory's construction of her as an image of the human person whose self has become a kind of no-self would be uncompromising in its austerity. Gregory's ascetic theology tended toward the production of a view of the person that was radically ahistorical. However, in the dream, she still has a body, and even though it is a body distilled to its structural form, its bones, it nonetheless functions as a signifying vestige of Macrina's identity as a recognizable human individual—recognizable, however, in a perceptual mode that suspends time and space in an inference of dazzling wholeness.

Gregory seems to have been consistent in his attempt to view martyrs' relics as sites for the transition from personal to impersonal images of human identity. In his *Encomium on St. Theodore,* he wrote about relics that "those who behold them embrace, as it were, the living body in full flower, they bring eye, mouth, ear, all the senses into play, and there, shedding tears of reverence and passion, they address the martyr their prayers of intercession as though he were present."[61] Bones, clearly, can be just as sensuous as a real body, but the difference between the two is that relics are signifiers of a person who is both absent and present at once, or perhaps one should say, a person who is neither absent nor present. It was in this mediatorial gap between absence and presence, the gap expressed by Gregory's phrase "*as though* he were present," that the body continued to function as a magnet for expressing views of identity in an ascetic context.

It is significant that Gregory chose to reveal the relic-like state of his sister by narrating his dream. Like relics, and like the almost angelic identity of the accomplished ascetic, dreams are neither ploddingly historical nor transparently spiritual; rather, they mediate that sense of time that is no-time by using images. In fact, such an oneiric image had set Gregory himself on that path out of conventional historical time on which Macrina had traveled so far. In a panegyric to the Forty Martyrs, a group of soldiers who were killed during the Roman persecution of Christians in the early fourth century, Gregory recalls attending a festal occasion in their honor. Instead of keeping watch during the vigil, Gregory fell asleep. He dreamed that the Forty Martyrs rushed at him threateningly, shaking switches at him and admonishing him for his inattention to his religious duty.[62] For Gregory, this dream was a turning point; he set himself to follow the contemplative life unswervingly. It appears that this dream enabled Gregory to forge a new sense of his own identity, an identity in which the qualifying words "his own" would slowly, he hoped, drop away.

It is curious that Gregory placed so much emphasis on the significations of his dreams, since in his theory of dreaming he is ambivalent about their epistemological value. When viewed as products of physiological processes, they are fantastic nonsense, but when the mind is allowed a role in their production, their enigmatic images can be trusted to yield a glimmer of the timeless truth of human desire.[63] Perhaps this recourse to dreams is not surprising, since Gregory of Nyssa, like Gregory of Nazianzus, had difficulty finding a language appropriate to the expression of the ascetic vision of the self that was not tainted by the illusory world of history and time.

In the context of the autobiography of an ascetic life, dreaming became an important language for the articulation of an other perception of the self. Gregory of Nyssa's mystical theology, too, appears to have fallen under the spell of the dream. In the kind of theological language that attempts to express the linguistic analogue to the glowing bones of Macrina, the oxymoron predominates as the privileged vehicle of meaning. Such oxymorons as sober drunkenness and luminous darkness appear frequently in his mystical writings, but Gregory also created a new oxymoron, waking sleep, which has been considered among the most important of his expressions of the mystical life.[64] Just as dreams contributed to the emptying out of the conventionally understood self, so paradoxical linguistic constructions use words against themselves to express a view of the human being in those ecstatic moments of contemplative seeing in which temporality gives way to the timeless expanses of eternity. As Jean Daniélou has observed, the oxymoron waking sleep contains a negative element,[65] but it is one that is nonetheless revelatory of a transformed sense of human identity.

Having rejected any kind of literal grounds for constructing a view of human identity, Gregory turned to paradox and dream, both imaginal discourses that enabled the literal to return as sign. There was still a self to signify, even if that self was recognizable not in conventional biographical terms but in oneiric image and linguistic paradox. In his willingness to allow such images to function as mirrors of identity, Gregory was unlike his ascetic colleague Evagrius, for whom images, and especially the images of dreams, were usually signs of a soul whose mirror was spotted by passionate involvements.[66] Envisioning the true human being as one who had divested the inner self of such attachments to history, Evagrius appears to have rejected any autobiographical impulse whatsoever. He had crossed the boundary on which Gregory was poised into a radical emptying of the self into a vast but peaceful nothing that is very different from the glowing bones of Macrina's angelic transformation.[67]

Like Gregory of Nyssa, Gregory of Nazianzus was more willing than Evagrius to imagine that dreams had a useful role to play in the transformation of the person. In fact, Gregory of Nazianzus was an enthusiastic dreamer. Despite his occasional literary use of dream as a negative metaphor denoting the illusory qualities of embodied life,[68] Gregory often looked to actual dreams as vehicles of meaning and as windows through which one might look for images of authentic senses of human identity. By Gregory's report, he was the child of dreamers—perhaps it was from his mother and father that he derived his own trust in dreams.

Gregory's father had not been a Christian when he married, a situation that caused increasing distress for his wife, a committed member of the church.[69] With prayers and reproaches, she urged him to convert. In his funeral oration for his father, Gregory records the following dream.

> My father's salvation was aided jointly by his reason, which gradually accepted the healing remedy, and jointly by the vision of dreams, a benefit which God often bestows on a soul worthy of salvation. What was the vision? He thought that he was singing, what he had never done before, although his wife often prayed and made supplication, these words from the psalms of David: "I rejoiced at the things that were said to me, we shall go into the house of the Lord" [*Ps.* 121.1]. The psalm was strange and with its singing came desire. When his wife heard it, having now gained her prayer, she seized the opportunity, interpreting the vision most happily and truthfully.[70]

Thus was Gregory's father convinced to become a catechumen. It is interesting that this converting dream is viewed by Gregory as the climactic moment that brought a gradual process of reasoning to fruition. In this passage, dreams are constructed as divine gifts that enable a person to see the nature of his true identity.

Gregory's mother was not only skilled in the interpretation of dreams, as the above passage suggests; she was a great dreamer herself. The dreams that Gregory attributes to her all concern himself. Like Macrina's mother Emmelia, Gregory of Nazianzus's mother Nonna had an oneiric premonition about her son-to-be. As Gregory explains, Nonna was anxious to provide the family with a son, and prayed that her wish might be fulfilled. His account of this dream, which forms part of one of his autobiographical poems, continues:

> God granted the favor, and in her great desire, failing not in loving prayer, she actually anticipated it. There came to her a gracious foretaste, a vision containing the shadow of her request. My likeness and my name appeared clearly to her, the work of a dream by night. Then I was born to them, the gift of God the giver if worthy of the prayer: if not, it was because of my own shortcomings.[71]

This dream of himself as a divinely promised child seems to have been important to Gregory's understanding of himself, for he repeats it, using different terminology, in another autobiographical poem.

> When I was delivered from my mother's womb, she offered me to you [God]. Ever since the day she had yearned to nurse a manchild on her knee, she imitated the cry of the holy Anna. "O King Christ, that I might have a boy for you to keep within your fold. May a son be the flourishing fruit of my birth pangs." And you, O God, granted her prayer. There followed the holy dream which gave her the name. In due time you gave a son. She dedicated me as a new Samuel (if I were worthy of the name) in the temple.[72]

Described as shadows that nevertheless speak clearly, these dreams are clearly holy in Gregory's view. They give a sense of his mother's character, but more especially they give a sense of Gregory's view of himself. He derives not only his name but his very being from dreams, in which he is constructed religiously as possessed of a prophetic scriptural persona (a new Samuel). While he constantly gives voice to doubts about whether his life has conformed to that oneiric picture of himself, the dreams of his mother seem to function as images of reassurance. They are the nodal points upon which his autobiographical identity is constructed. The ascetic Gregory, dedicated from birth to the priesthood, did not shrink from autobiographical writing. Yet the poetic form in which he cast his autobiographical reminiscences, as well as the dreams recorded there that express the essence of his identity, match each other in their construction of the human person by means of images, images that mediate the gap between literal history and spiritual desire. Again, the ascetic self finds its anchor in allusive poetic forms that provide a mediating ground for understanding that self.

For Gregory, the salvific function of dreams was one of their most notable characteristics. Like generations of dreamers and dream theorists before him, he accepted without question the cultural construction of dreams that emphasized their predictive and healing value. In a section of the funeral oration for his father in which he narrates miraculous occurrences in the lives of both his parents in which he was himself involved, Gregory recorded several dreams that adhere to the Greco-Roman view of this role of dreams. Gregory remembers a time when he was sailing from Alexandria, Egypt to Greece. The ship, caught in a storm, was in danger of capsizing, and all aboard were fearful for their lives. Gregory was fearful not only for life literally but also spiritually, since he had not yet been baptized. His parents, he continues, suffered with him, because they had seen his predicament in a dream: "they brought help from land, calming the waves by prayer, as afterwards we learned upon reckoning the time when I returned home. This was also revealed to me in a salutary sleep which I at length experienced when the storm abated a little."[73] As if the double dream of his parents and his own reciprocal dream were not enough, Gregory reveals that this event had yielded a third dream:

> Another of my fellow voyagers, a boy very well disposed and dear to me and deeply concerned for me, under the circumstances, thought he saw my mother walk upon the sea and seize the ship and with no great effort draw it to land. And this vision was believed, for the sea began to grow calm, and we quickly arrived at Rhodes, without experiencing any great distress in the meantime.[74]

Here Gregory's mother assumes the form of an autonomous dream figure, familiar from writers as disparate in time and temperament as Homer and Augustine,[75] who saves her son in a dream just as she had oneirically conceived him. Once again, Gregory feels himself to have been saved by dreams for his religious vocation, since he concludes this story by noting that "we promised ourselves to God if we were saved, and, on being saved, we gave ourselves to him."[76]

In the same section of this oration, Gregory records a final dream of his mother in which he himself plays the salvific role. Telling of a time when Nonna was seriously ill, Gregory says that God healed her by sending the following dream:

> She thought she saw me, her darling—for not even in dreams did she prefer any other of us—come up to her suddenly in the night with a basket of purest white bread, and after blessing and signing it with the cross according to my custom, feed and comfort her, and that she then recovered her strength.[77]

Recovering the next day, Nonna thought that her son had actually administered the Eucharistic food to her during the night. Gregory, however, equates the dream with reality—"this vision of the night was a thing of reality."[78] For him, it was the oneiric act that had healed, not a literal one. Having once spent time in a monastery on the grounds of the incubatory cultic center of St. Thekla in Seleucia, Gregory would probably have been familiar with the Christian appropriation of Asclepian oneiric therapy.[79] It is certain, at least, that he viewed his own oneiric persona as having had a healing effect on his mother's body.

It is significant that, even with regard to the dreams that drew on conventional cultural associations of dreams with prediction and healing, Gregory was most interested in their images as mirrors of spiritual identity. He looked to the imaginal language of dreams as an autobiographical resource. Oneiric discourse was useful, especially in the context of Gregory's asceticism, because it was a discourse in which an other self was projected on the screen of consciousness. Dreams could reflect an autobiographical I that was distanced from the I of messy historical entanglements. In his own life, Gregory located the mess of history not only in the fact of having a body, but also in his entanglements in ecclesiastical affairs, most notably the bitter battles with Arian Christians during his brief stint as bishop of Constantinople in 379–381 CE.[80] Perhaps it is no wonder that Gregory dreamed of a time when he would be like his brother Caesarius, glowingly free of the turmoil of this life.

There is one more autobiographical dream of Gregory's that I wish to present. A return to his ascetic understanding of the body as sign will provide a context for what was undoubtedly the most spectacular of all his dreams. In the passage of his funeral oration for Caesarius that concludes with his dreams of his brother, Gregory engaged in theological speculation about the resurrected body. He wrote that, at death, the soul is released from the body, a darkening element that had functioned as a hard prison, binding the wing of the intellect with fetters.[81] Once aloft, the soul "enters into the possession of the blessedness reserved for it such as it has already conceived in imagination"—including especially the oneiric imagination with which this section concludes.[82] Gregory continues:

> Shortly afterwards, [the soul] takes up its own related flesh, united with which it meditated on heavenly topics, from the earth which both gave it and was entrusted with it, and, in a way which God knows who bound them together and separated them, [the flesh] is joint heir with [the soul] of supernal glory.
>
> And just as such a soul shared its sufferings because of its natural union with its flesh, so also it shares its own joys with it, having assumed [the flesh] wholly into itself and having become with it one spirit and mind and good, life having absorbed the mortal and transitory element.[83]

Gregory, whose theology was geared toward the recovery by the human being of its divine image,[84] condemned one kind of body, the imprisoning body of earth, only to petition heavenly pleasure through the sign of that very body, now transformed, now related. But his only access in the present to that imagined theological body of bliss was through the imagistic discourse of the bodies of his dreams.

In his writing, Gregory frequently indicated his longing for access to the language of God, the proper language of human beings from which they have been separated.[85] Again and again, the sign of that separation is the body, which makes human life so weak and ponderously earthbound.[86] Gregory described his rejection of life in the world as bishop of Constantinople and his subsequent return to ascetic seclusion as follows: "I was running to reach God; thus I climbed the mountain and penetrated the cloud, going inside away from matter and material things, concentrating on my inner self as much as possible; but when I looked, I caught a view only of God's back, and that scarcely."[87] Giving a negative turn to the biblical scene in which Moses is permitted to see God's back (*Ex.* 33.20–22), Gregory felt this sight to be a mark of deprivation, not blessing as in Moses' case. This knowledge, he says, exists like a shadow in water—yet his description of this moment of mystical approach shows the strength of his desire to be other, to be remade and allowed expression in another form of identity.

"I am connected with the world below, and likewise with God; I am connected with the flesh, and likewise with the spirit."[88] When he was not dreaming, Gregory felt himself to be split between two discourses, and it made him feel estranged from his own true idiom. The following passage from one of his long autobiographical poems makes this feeling of estrangement clear:

> So came I then into this life below
> Molded of mire—ah, me—of that low synthesis
> That dominates us or barely yields to our control.
> But still I take it as a pledge of what is best—
> My very birth!
>
> No right have I to carp.
> But at my birth, I immediately became an alien
> In alienation best.
> For unto God I'm given as some lamb, some sacrificial calf,
> Offering noble and adorned with mind.[89]

Picturing himself as molded of mire and of mind, Gregory feels that he was an alien at birth. Intriguing in the light of Gregory's description of himself is a statement by the contemporary philosopher and psychologist Jacques Lacan: "A certificate tells me that I was born. I repudiate this certificate: I am not a poet, but a poem. A poem that is being written, even if it looks like a subject."[90] Lacan's denial of the subject—that is, his repudiation of a substantially constituted self—along with his view of the self as a poem in the making, sounds very much like Gregory's poetically phrased autobiographical desire, expressed from within the depths of his alienation, to be rewritten in terms of the other.

Indeed, following his most significant dream in terms of his ascetic desire, Gregory reported that he had sensed the death of himself as a subject: "I died to the world and the world to me, and I am become a living corpse as devoid of strength as a dreamer. Since that day my life is elsewhere."[91] The dream that follows is the dream that led Gregory to reconceive his identity in ascetic terms. It forms part of one of his autobiographical poems.

> Two women appeared to me, brilliant in clothing shining with light, virgins, and they came close to me. Both were beautiful but neglectful of the usual adornments of women—no jewelry, no cosmetics, no silk, nothing of those things invented by men for the appearance of women in order to excite passion. Veils shrouded their heads in shadows; their eyes were lowered to the ground, their cheeks colored with the rosy tint of modesty; they were like dewy rosebuds, their lips silent. It was a great joy to contemplate them, since I was sure they were more-than-human. Because I had charmed them, they gave me kisses with their lips, as though I were a beloved child. I asked who they were, and they replied, Chastity and Wisdom, who lead humans close to Christ, rejoicing in the celestial beauty reserved for virgins. "Come child," they said, "unite your spirit to ours and bring your flaming torch to join ours so that we can take you across the sky and place you in the splendor of the Trinity." With these words they raised themselves into the sky and I watched as they flew.[92]

Along with his mother's dream about his birth, this dream was a foundational sign of Gregory's sense of himself. He remarks in his "Epitaph for Himself" that "a fervent aspiration for purity was in me aroused by a vision of the night; of all these things Christ was the author."[93] The dream showed Gregory that his life was a poetic text being written, not by himself, but by that divine other in whose image he desired to be remade.

This, then, was the dream that placed Gregory's life elsewhere. In the autobiographical poem in which this dream is recorded, Gregory commented on his experience of the dream that his heart was ravished by the beauty of its radiant virginity.[94] From the vantage point of his later years, he looked back and saw that this dream had been the beginning of his profession of asceticism.[95] Into the midst of what he characterized as a hostile life came a dream of the soul's desire, tantalizing in its call to transformation. The oneiric images of Chastity and Wisdom are analogues of the oneiric image of his brother Caesarius as mirrors of the self-identity that Gregory thought was appropriate for an ascetic. Like the oneiric Caesarius, they are recognizably human—they have bodies and names—yet they are also more than human in their mirroring of an altered sense of what constitutes human being.

Unlike the image of Caesarius, however, the two female images of this dream, with their flaming torches and dewy lips, carry a strong erotic charge that makes their use as ascetic signifiers rather ironic. Gregory's association of these two images with rosebuds is a key to their erotic construction, since the rose was preeminently the flower of Aphrodite, patron of sensuous physical love.[96] Thus this dream, with its erotic female images that are taken to signify the ascetic self, would seem to be the return, with a vengeance, of the rejected body as sign. However, as Geoffrey Harpham has observed, "asceticism is essentially a meditation on, even an enactment of, desire. . . . While asceticism recognizes that desire stands between human life and perfection, it also understands that desire is the only means of achieving perfection, and that the movement toward ideality is necessarily a movement of desire."[97] Thus the erotic images of Gregory's dream can be understood as signs that articulate the ascetic desire for the movement toward ideality to which Harpham refers. Further, the rose was often used by Christians as a symbol both of martyrdom and of virginity.[98] And, the magically transformative quality of the rose is well attested in Apuleius's *The Golden Ass,* in which the hero Lucius regains his humanity from his descent into bestial nature by eating a rose.[99] Like the fictional Lucius, the human Gregory also hoped for transformation, and the rosy-figured images of his dream fueled his ascetic desire for release from the bestial body of his temporal self. These oneiric images, with their erotically chaste character, are appropriate vehicles for the paradoxical sense of self that developed in the thought of ascetics like Gregory.

Gregory patterned the rest of his life on the basis of this dream. Yet he was not healed. In the dream, the women flew away, leaving him ravished by "such slight *genii* in such pale air."[100] His conventionally constituted identity had been shattered by the dream but, while the poetic form of his autobiographical writings suggests that he did come to see himself as a poem being written by that desired other, he remained distant from the self of his desire—except in his dreams.

It is no wonder that the two Gregorys dreamed. In dreams, those oneiric spaces on the border between the physical and the spiritual, they found a language that made expressions of ascetic self-identity possible. Like the mythic Narcissus, wondering at the watery depths of his own reflection, the Gregorys were grappling with a fundamental human question, "Who am I?" Dreams were a medium for their reflections on this question, and they used them to explore that most difficult of identities, the ascetic self. What they found in their explorations was not a unitary, epistemologically certifiable self, but something more unsettling that only an imaginative act of visual perception could articulate.

NOTES

1. Jean-Pierre Vernant, "Dim Body, Dazzling Body," in *Fragments for a History of the Human Body,* ed. Michel Feher (New York: Zone, 1989), 1:18–47.
2. Ibid., p. 23.
3. Ibid., pp. 24–25.
4. Ibid., p. 25.
5. Peter Brown, *The Body and Society: Men, Women, and Sexual Renunciation in Early Christianity* (New York: Columbia University Press, 1988), p. 31.
6. Geoffrey Galt Harpham, *The Ascetic Imperative in Culture and Criticism* (Chicago: University of Chicago Press, 1987), p. 27.
7. Benedicta Ward, trans., *Sayings of the Desert Fathers* (Kalamazoo: Cistercian Publications, 1975), p. 197, #12 (Pambo); pp. 214–215, #14 (Sisoes).
8. Brown, *The Body and Society,* p. 294.
9. Peter Brown, "The Saint as Exemplar in Late Antiquity," in *Saints and Virtues,* ed. John Stratton Hawley (Berkeley: University of California Press, 1987), p. 14.
10. Edith Wyschogrod, *Saints and Postmodernism: Revisioning Moral Philosophy* (Chicago: University of Chicago Press, 1990), p. 16.
11. Ibid.
12. Ibid., p. 18.

13. Ibid., p. 16.
14. Ibid.
15. Ibid., p. 17.
16. Gregory of Nazianzus, *Orations* 7.21 (*PG* 35.784B), trans. in *A Select Library of Nicene and Post-Nicene Fathers of the Christian Church*, 2d series, 7:237.
17. Gregory of Nyssa, *Vita Sanctae Macrinae* 15.15–19 (*PG* 46.976B), ed. Pierre Maraval, Sources chrétiennes 178 (Paris, 1971), p. 193.
18. For biographical information on Gregory of Nazianzus, see Donald F. Winslow, *The Dynamics of Salvation: A Study in Gregory of Nazianzus,* Patristic Monograph Series 7 (Cambridge, Mass.: The Philadelphia Patristic Foundation, Ltd., 1979), pp. 1–21, and Denis Molaise Meehan, trans., *Saint Gregory of Nazianzus: Three Poems,* The Fathers of the Church 75 (Washington, D.C.: The Catholic University of America Press, 1987), pp. 1–21; on Gregory of Nyssa, see Jean Daniélou, "Le mariage de Grégoire de Nysse et la chronologie de sa vie," *Revue des Études Augustiniennes* 2 (1956):71–78.
19. The classic study of Gregory of Nyssa's mystical theology is by Jean Daniélou, *Platonisme et Théologie Mystique: Doctrine Spirituelle de Saint Grégoire de Nysse* (Paris: Aubier, 1944); for Gregory of Nazianzus, see Winslow, *Dynamics of Salvation,* pp. 73–97, 179–199, and Brooks Otis, "The Throne and the Mountain: An Essay on St. Gregory Nazianzus," *Classical Journal* 56 (1961):146–165.
20. Brown, *The Body and Society,* p. 285.
21. Ibid., p. 293.
22. For Gregory Nazianzus's idea of *theiosis* (union with God), see the detailed discussion by Winslow, *Dynamics of Salvation,* pp. 179–199; for Gregory of Nyssa's idea of *theōria,* mystical vision or contemplation, see Daniélou, *Platonisme et Théologie Mystique,* pp. 134–135, 148–163, 175–177, 197–200.
23. Brown, *The Body and Society,* p. 293.
24. *Or. catechetica* 5.45 (*PG* 45.24B), trans. in Brown, *The Body and Society,* p. 293.
25. Brown, *The Body and Society,* pp. 293–294.
26. On Caesarius, see Gregory Nazianzus, *De rebus suis* 2.1.1.165–229 (*PG* 37.982A–987A).
27. *Or.* 7.17 (*PG* 35.776C), trans. *NPNF* 7:235.
28. *Niobuli filii ad patrem* 2.2.4.85 (*PG* 37.1512A), trans. Winslow, *Dynamics of Salvation,* p. 170.
29. *Or.* 45.3 (*PG* 36.625C–628B).
30. *Or.* 28.4 (*PG* 36.32A), trans. *NPNF* 7:290.
31. *Or.* 7.20 (*PG* 35.780BC), trans. *NPNF* 7:236.
32. *De rebus suis* 2.1.1.344–345 (*PG* 37.996), trans. Meehan, p. 36.
33. Ibid., lines 4 (lion), 5 (Jonah's monster), 21 (wild beasts), 183 (jackals), 191–192 (tusked animal), 235 and 619 (serpents), 498 (sepia fish), 585 (swine), 617 (bear) (*PG* 37.969–970, 971, 984, 987–988, 1007, 1013, 1016, trans. Meehan, pp. 25, 31, 33, 41, 44, 45).
34. Ibid., lines 330–32 (*PG* 37.995), trans. Meehan, pp. 35–36.
35. *Or.* 7.23 (*PG* 35.785C), trans. *NPNF* 7:237.
36. *Or.* 28.4 (*PG* 36.29C), trans. *NPNF* 7:289.
37. *Or.* 7.19 (*PG* 35.777C–D), trans. *NPNF* 7:235.
38. *Or.* 18.42 (*PG* 35.1041B), trans. *NPNF* 7:268.
39. For a discussion of the theme of ascetic use of the body as signifier in the writings of

Jerome, a contemporary of the two Gregorys, see Patricia Cox Miller, "The Blazing Body: Ascetic Desire in Jerome's Letter to Eustochium," *Journal of Early Christian Studies* 1 (1993):21–34.

40. For a discussion of the date of Gregory's visit with his sister, see Pierre Maraval, trans. and ed., *Grégoire de Nysse: Vie de Sainte Macrine,* Sources chrétiennes 178 (Paris, 1971), pp. 57–67.
41. *Vita Sanctae Macrinae* 15.14–21 (*PG* 46.976A–B), ed. Maraval, p. 193.
42. Ibid., 15.23–17.3 (*PG* 46.976B–D), ed. Maraval, pp. 193–97.
43. Ibid., 17.9–18.22 (*PG* 46.977B–C), ed. Maraval, pp. 197–201.
44. Ibid., 19.11–15 (*PG* 46.980A), ed. Maraval, p. 203.
45. Ibid., 32.8–12 (*PG* 46.992C–D), ed. Maraval, p. 247.
46. Ibid., 2.21–34 (*PG* 46.961B), ed. Maraval, pp. 145–149; such annunciatory dreams were common in late antiquity; for a list of parallels of dreams sent to pregnant women, see Maraval, *Vie de Sainte Macrine,* p. 146, note 1.
47. On the cult of St. Thekla in Asia Minor, see Gilbert Dagron, *Vie et Miracles de Sainte Thècle* (Bruxelles: Société des Bollandistes, 1978), pp. 55–79, and Maraval, *Vie de Sainte Macrine,* p. 146, note 2.
48. Brown, *The Body and Society,* p. 300.49.
49. *Vita Sanctae Macrinae* 22.27–31 (*PG* 46.981D–984A), ed. Maraval, p. 215.
50. Ibid., 11.34–35 (*PG* 46.972A), ed. Maraval, p. 179. On Gregory's idea of the *methorios,* the boundary, see Jean Daniélou, "*Methorios:* La notion de confins chez Grégoire de Nysse," *Recherches des Sciences Religieuses* 49 (1961):161–187.
51. *De hominis opificio* 8.4–12.14 (*PG* 44.144D–164D). See also Gregory's *De virginate* (*PG* 46.376D–381B), where it is the thought of the flesh, rather than the body itself, that is problematic.
52. See *De hom. op.* 16.7, 9 (*PG* 44.181A–C) and 12.9 (*PG* 44.161C).
53. *De virg.* 12.4 (*PG* 46.369D–372A); see Brown, *The Body and Society,* pp. 300–301.
54. *De virg.* 11–12 (*PG* 46.363B–375C), trans. by Virginia Woods Callahan, *Saint Gregory of Nyssa: Ascetical Works,* The Fathers of the Church (Washington, D.C.: The Catholic University of America Press, 1967), pp. 41–46.
55. Brown, *The Body and Society,* p. 297.
56. Ibid., p. 298.
57. See *De virg.* 20 (*PG* 46.397B–400D) and *De anima et resurrectione* (*PG* 46.12A–B), trans. Callahan, pp. 198–199.
58. *De an. et res.* (*PG* 46.158B), trans. Callahan, p. 266.
59. *Vita Sanctae Macrinae* 17.21–30; 18.1–22; 22.1–40 (*PG* 46.977A–B, 981A–985A), ed. Maraval, pp. 199–201, 213–217.
60. Stephen Crites, "Angels We Have Heard," in James B. Wiggins, ed., *Religion as Story* (New York: Harper and Row, 1975), p. 41.
61. *Encomium in Sanctum Theodorum* (*PG* 46.740B), trans. by Peter Brown, *Society and the Holy in Late Antiquity* (Berkeley: University of California Press, 1982), p. 7.
62. *In quadraginta martyres* (*PG* 46.785A–B).
63. For Gregory's oneiric theory, see his *De hom. op.* 13 (*PG* 44.165B–173B).
64. See the discussion by Daniélou, *Platonisme et Théologie Mystique,* pp. 274–284.
65. Ibid., p. 281.
66. For a thorough discussion of Evagrius's views of dreams, see F. Refoulé, "Rêves et Vie Spirituelle d'après Évagre le Pontique," *La Vie Spirituelle Supplément* 14 (1961):470–516, esp. pp. 488–497; see also Evagrius's *Praktikos* 55 (*PG* 40.1247A): "Natural

processes which occur in sleep without accompanying images of a stimulating nature are, to a certain measure, indications of a healthy soul. But images that are distinctly formed are a clear indication of sickness. You may be certain that the faces one sees in dreams are, when they occur as ill-defined images, symbols of former affective experiences. Those which are seen clearly, on the other hand, indicate wounds that are still fresh"; see also 64 (*PG* 40.1231A [#36 in *PG*]): "The proof of *apatheia* is had when the spirit begins to see its own light, when it remains in a state of tranquility in the presence of the images it has during sleep . . ."; and 65 (*PG* 40.1231B [#37 in *PG*]): "The spirit that possesses health is the one which has no images of the things of this world at the time of prayer" (trans. by John Eudes Bamberger, *Evagrius Ponticus: The Praktikos and Chapters on Prayer* (Kalamazoo: Cistercian Publications, 1981), pp. 31, 33–34).

67. See *Praktikos* 33–39 (*PG* 40.1231A–C) on *apatheia,* trans. Bamberger, pp. 25–26.
68. See p. 284 above re. Gregory of Nazianzus's use of dream as negative metaphor.
69. *Or.* 18.11 (*PG* 35.997B–D).
70. *Or.* 18.12 (*PG* 35.1000A–B), trans. by Leo P. McCauley in *Funeral Orations by Saint Gregory Nazianzen and Saint Ambrose,* The Fathers of the Church 22 (New York: Fathers of the Church, Inc., 1953), p. 128.
71. *De vita sua* 2.1.11.70–81 (*PG* 37.1034–1035), trans. Meehan, p. 79.
72. *De rebus suis* 2.1.1.425–432 (*PG* 37.1001–1002), trans. Meehan, p. 39.
73. *Or.* 18.31 (*PG* 35.1024B–1025A), trans. McCauley, pp. 144–145.
74. *Or.* 18.31 (*PG* 35.1025A), trans. McCauley, p. 145.
75. For discussion, see Patricia Cox Miller, "'A Dubious Twilight': Reflections on Dreams in Patristic Literature," *Church History* 55 (1986):160–161.
76. *Or.* 18.31 (*PG* 35.1025A), trans. McCauley, p. 145.
77. *Or.* 18.30 (*PG* 35.1023A), trans. McCauley, p. 144.
78. Ibid.
79. Gregory retreated to the center of St. Thekla in order to avoid being ordained bishop of the small church at Sasima to which his friend Basil of Caesarea had appointed him. See *De vita sua* 2.1.11, lines 547–549 (*PG* 37.1067A), trans. Meehan, p. 92. On the connection between Asclepian oneiric therapy and St. Thekla, see Dagron, *Vie et Miracles de Sainte Thècle,* pp. 95–108.
80. See Gregory's *De se ipso et de episcopis* 2.1.12 (*PG* 37.1166–1227), trans. Meehan, pp. 49–74, and *De vita sua* 2.1.11.562–1871 (*PG* 37.1068–1160), trans. Meehan, pp. 93–128.
81. *Or.* 7.21 (*PG* 35.781B–C), trans. McCauley, p. 22.
82. *Or.* 7.21 (*PG* 35.781C).
83. *Or.* 7.21 (*PG* 35.781C–784A).
84. The following observation by Winslow, *Dynamics of Salvation,* p. 88, is a good indicator of Gregory's position: "The *theosis* of Christ's human nature is not the disappearance of his humanity or the total absorption of the lower into the higher . . . rather, it is the participation of the human nature in the divine, a participation so complete, so intimate and interpenetrating, that to call the 'deified' human nature 'God' is not a semantic trick but a description of reality."
85. See Notes 36–38 above re. Gregory's laments about the inadequacy of human language to express truth about God.
86. See *Or.* 28.3 (*PG* 36.29A–C), trans. *NPNF* 7:289.
87. *Or.* 28.3 (*PG* 36.29A), trans. *NPNF* 7:289.

88. *Or.* 7.23 (*PG* 35.785B), trans. McCauley, p. 24.
89. *De vita sua* 2.1.11.82–90 (*PG* 37.1035–1036), trans. by Otis, "The Throne and the Mountain," p. 150.
90. Jacques Lacan, *The Four Fundamental Concepts of Psycho-analysis,* ed. Jacques-Alain Miller, trans. Alan Sheridan (New York: W. W. Norton, 1978), p. viii. I thank Professor David L. Miller of Syracuse University for bringing this quotation to my attention.
91. *De rebus suis* 2.1.1.202–204 (*PG* 37.985), trans. Meehan, pp. 31–32.
92. *De animae suae calamitatibus carmen lugubre* 2.1.45.229–266 (*PG* 37.1369–1372), here adapted from a translation by Carmen-Marie Szymusiak-Affholder, "Psychologie et histoire dans le rêve initial de Grégoire le théologien," *Philologus* 15 (1971):302–303.
93. *Epitaphium sui ipsius* 2.1.92.5–6 (*PG* 37.1447–1448), trans. by Winslow, *Dynamics of Salvation,* p. 14.
94. *De animae suae calamitatibus carmen lugubre* 2.1.45.265–266 (*PG* 37.1372).
95. *De animae suae calamitatibus carmen lugubre* 2.1.45.230 (*PG* 37.1369). See the discussion by Szymusiak-Affholder, "Psychologie et histoire," p. 309.
96. See Charles Joret, *La Rose dans l'Antiquité et au Moyen Âge* (Paris: Émile Bouillon, 1892), pp. 47–50.
97. Harpham, *The Ascetic Imperative,* p. 45.
98. See Suzanne Poque, "Des roses du printemps à la rose d'automne," *Revue des Études Augustiniennes* 17 (1971):155–169, on martyrdom; Martine Dulaey, *Le Rêve dans la Vie et la Pensée de Saint Augustin* (Paris: Études Augustiniennes, 1973), pp. 222–23, on virginity.
99. Apuleius, *The Golden Ass* 11.13, ed. and trans. J. Gwyn Griffiths, *Apuleius of Madauros: The Isis-Book (Metamorphoses,* Book XI*)* (Leiden: E. J. Brill, 1975), p. 85.
100. The phrase in quotation is from "A Primitive Like an Orb," by Wallace Stevens, in *The Collected Poems of Wallace Stevens* (New York: Alfred A. Knopf, 1975), p. 440.

21

Mirabai as Wife and Yogi

John Stratton Hawley

At first glance, Mirabai seems the most popular and accessible figure among the *bhakti* poet-saints of North India. In contrast to the poems of Tulsidas or Surdas, the compositions attributed to Mira are loose in construction, almost folkish; they lend themselves easily to song. This quality of directness and informality has something to do with gender. Mira is the only woman in the family of major North Indian *bhakti* poets, and Indian women are usually less well educated than their male counterparts. No wonder, then, that Mira's modes of speech seem on the whole closer to those of the mass than theirs. Some of the same circumstances may account for her box-office success, too. The Indian film industry has produced no fewer than ten movies about Mira, while her nearest competitors among male saints have earned at most three or four.[1] And when the creators of the Amar Chitra Katha comic-book series crossed the shallow ford that separates myth and legend from hagiography, their first subject was Mirabai—book number 36. Kabir followed as number 55, Tulsi as number 62, and it was not until number 137 that they got around to Sur.[2]

Yet, for all her accessibility, there is a dark, enigmatic side to Mira. To begin with, it is much harder in Mira's case than in that of her male rivals to have any confidence that she actually composed a substantial portion of the poetic corpus attributed to her. A poem in praise of Mira appears in the *Bhaktamal* of Nabhaji, a hagiographical anthology composed in about 1600 CE, where she takes a natural place alongside the likes of Kabir, Tulsi, and Sur.[3] But when one searches among manuscripts of roughly the same period for poems bearing her oral signature, the disappointment is great. Only two Mira poems have been found in manuscripts dating before the beginning of the eighteenth century, a far smaller number than one finds for any male saints of comparable stature. If one were to judge things solely by the manuscript evidence, in fact, Mira's efflorescence would seem best dated to the nineteenth century. It may not be accidental that the critical edition upon which most modern assessments of Mira are based—that of Parasuram Caturvedi—contains only the scantiest scholarly apparatus and no reference at all to the manuscripts upon which it is based.[4] When Kalyansimh Sekhavat went in search of Mira's poetry in the manuscript libraries of her native Rajasthan, the earliest examples he was able to find dated to the latter half of the eighteenth century, and even these were notably sparse. There were plenty of poems—he was able to add a whole new volume to the *Mira-Brhatpadavali* published posthumously on the basis of the collection made by Harinarayan Sarma—but only a handful predated 1800 CE. The rest were either more recent or, like those collected by Sarma, bore no date at all.[5]

When one speaks of the poetry of Mirabai, then, there is always an element of enigma. In what follows we will take a Vulgate approach, using the collections mentioned above, but that means there must always remain a question about whether there is any real relation between the poems we cite and an historical Mira. And in a certain sense we will compound the situation. Our aim here is to highlight an aspect of Mira's *œuvre* that is somewhat enigmatic in its own right: poems in which she departs from the received wisdom that is expressed in other *bhakti* compositions by depicting Krishna not as a debonair lover but as a yogi. Indeed, Mira sometimes pictures herself, though a married woman, as a yogini ready to take her place at the side of her beloved yogi in a new form of marriage. Our purpose will be to see how the tradition of Mirabai elaborated this unusual vision of a female ascetic and then, as if thinking better of the matter, withdrew.

The Poetry of Mira

Some of the most haunting compositions in the Mirabai corpus are those in which she calls out to Krishna as a yogi. The basic experience is one of abandonment:

Yogi, day and night I watch the road,
That difficult path where feet refuse to go—
    so blocked, so steep, so overgrown.
A yogi came to town. He roamed around
    but didn't find the love in my mind,
And I was a girl of such simple ways
    that I had no way to make him stay.
Now it's been many days that I've watched
    for that yogi, and still he hasn't come:
The flame of loneliness is kindled inside me—
    inside my body, fire.
Either that yogi is no longer in this world
    or else he's gone and forgotten me,
So what am I to do, my friend? Where am I to go?
    I've lost my eyes to tears.
Yogi, the pain of you has burrowed inside me:
    see that I am yours and come
To Mira, a desperate, lonely woman.
    The life in me, without you, writhes.[6]

In this poem Mira is the *virahini,* the desperate, lonely woman separated from her lover, and his absence is so painful that she imagines Krishna as a yogi, a wanderer entirely cut off from the settled life of home and town. Images of interiority punctuate the poem and cast the light of contrast on Krishna's elusiveness. In other poems the effects of Krishna's absence are even more vividly portrayed. In one poem addressed to her yogi, Mira explains that her suffering has made his absence seem a lifetime: it has caused her hair to turn white.[7] The shadow of death hangs over other poems, too. In perhaps the best known poem in the corpus, Mira represents herself not as old and wizened but as an incipient *satī* (an Indian widow who burned herself on her husband's funeral pyre):

Don't go, yogi, don't go,
don't go,
I fall, a slave, at your feet.
The footpath of love is ever so strange,
so please: show me the road.
I'll build myself a pyre of aloes and sandalwood—
come: light it yourself,
And after the fire has turned to ash,
cover yourself with the cinders.
To her clever Mountain Lifter Lord, Mira says:
merge my light
with yours.[8]

A score of compositions ring further changes on the same theme, and in quite a few Mira defines her own response in the same way that she depicts Krishna's absence: if he is a yogi, she vows to be a yogini. In one example that recalls the *satī* theme, we think we hear her say that she is adopting the signs of widowhood—she takes off her jewelry and shaves her head—but these turn out to be signs of a different life, a mendicant yoga in which she will search out her beloved:

My dark one has gone to an alien land.
He's left me behind,
he's never returned,
he's never sent me a single word,
So I've stripped off my ornaments,
jewels and adornments,
cut the hair from my head.
And put on holy garments,
all on his account,
seeking him in all four directions.
Mira: unless she meets the Dark One, her Lord,
she doesn't even want to live.[9]

There are times when Mira envisions her yoga as something sedentary, a life of isolation in a cave:

Your secret, yogi, I have still not found.
I've sat in a cave,
taken a yogic pose,
and trained my thoughts on Hari
With beads around my neck,
a bag of beads in my hand,

and body smeared with ash.
Mira's Lord is Hari, the indestructible.
Fate is written on my forehead,
and that is what I've found.[10]

Even in the meditative attitude Mira here describes, there is something restless. The last line is affirmative in form but opaque in content: what does she mean by her fate? And the first line, a refrain that is quoted at intervals as the poem is sung, is negative—an expression of continuous, unending search. It is no surprise, then, that Mira characteristically represents her yoga not as a static, meditative art but as a discipline of life that keeps her always on the move, wandering for Krishna's sake.

Two poems are translated here to illustrate such a mood. In the first Mira depicts her life of peregrination as the only possible alternative to death, which she also contemplates. In the second she sees it quite the other way around, as a sort of walking death that can only be ended by meeting her Mountain Lifter. In both poems, and especially in the second, where she addresses not only Krishna but a companion, we meet the oscillation of focus that is so familiar in compositions attributed to Mira. The crisp voice of autobiography has been slurred, perhaps, by hagiography. Here are two poems of journeying:

After making me fall for you so hard,
where are you going?
Until the day I see you, no repose:
my life, like a fish washed on shore,
flails in agony.
For your sake I'll make myself a yogini.
I'll hurl myself to death
on the saw of Kashi.
Mira's Lord is the clever Mountain Lifter
and I am his,
a slave to his lotus feet.[11]

Dark one, listen compassionately
to me, for I am your slave.
The hope of seeing you has made me lose my mind
and my body is besieged by your absence.
For you, I'll make myself a yogini,
wandering town to town looking for you,
looking in every grove.
Ash on my limbs and an antelope skin
pulled up to my Neck, my friend:
that's how I'll burn my body to ash for him.
I've still not found the indestructible Ram, my friend,
so I'll wander forest to forest shrieking,
crying all the time.
But let that Mountain Lifter come
and meet his servant Mira

and he'll wipe away her sadness,
he'll beat the drum of happiness,
The thrill of peace will fill her breast—
my breast—and this back and forth
will wipe itself away: I'll stay
at your feet, your slave.[12]

The note of hope on which the last poem ends is expanded in a group of poems in which the specter of a yogic life is merged with the happier vision of life in the presence of Krishna. Here Mira imagines herself not as a wanderer in search of Krishna but as a wanderer at his side. In doing so she concocts an unorthodox mixture of home and homelessness that has precedent only in a few extreme tantric groups and in the mythology of Parvati and Siva. Thoughts of Siva occupy her at least obliquely as she begins:

Oh, the yogi—
my friend, that clever one
whose mind is on Siva and the Snake,
that all-knowing yogi—tell him this:

"I'm not staying here, not staying where
the land's grown strange without you, my dear,
But coming home, coming to where your place is;
take me, guard me with your guardian mercy,
please.
I'll take up your yogic garb—
your prayer beads,
earrings,
begging-bowl skull,
tattered yogic cloth—
I'll take them all
And search through the world as a yogi does
with you—yogi and yogini, side by side.

My loved one, the rains have come,
and you promised that when they did, you'd come too.
And now the days are gone: I've counted them
one by one on the folds of my fingers
till the lines at the joints have blurred
And my love has left me pale.
my youth grown yellow as with age.

Singing of Ram
your servant Mira
has offered you an offering:
her body and her mind."[13]

It is but a small step from here to poems in which yoga and marriage, those impossible bedfellows, meet in an explicit way. In the following composition, consider the alternation between the bride's red sari and pearl-parted hair on the one hand and the ascetic's saffron robe and dishevelled coiffure on the other. Is this merely ambivalence, or is Mira saying that with Krishna yoga and marriage are tantamount to the same thing?

Go to where my loved one lives,
    Go where he lives and tell him
        if he says so, I'll color my sarı red;
        if he says so, I'll wear the godly yellow garb;
        if he says so, I'll drape the part in my hair with pearls;
        if he says so, I'll let my hair grow wild.
Mira's Lord is the clever Mountain Lifter:
    listen to the praises of that king.[14]

We have already explored one context for a poem such as this: Mira's visions of a life of yoga. There are others in which the marriage theme comes out explicitly—a second context for poems in which yoga and marriage are wed. Characteristically, however, Mira's visions of being married to Krishna have a certain subjunctive aspect, as will be evident in the following examples. In the first, Mira's marriage to Krishna is the stuff of dreams, and in the second, she approaches it not as realized fact but as something for which she longs:

Sister, I had a dream that I wed
    the Lord of those who live in need:
Five hundred sixty thousand people came
    and the Lord of Braj was the groom.
        In dream they set up a wedding arch;
        in dream he grasped my hand;
        in dream he led me around the wedding fire
        and I became unshakably his bride.
Mira's been granted her mountain-lifting Lord:
    from living past lives, a prize.[15]

I have talked to you, talked,
    dark Lifter of Mountains,
About this old love,
    from birth after birth.
Don't go, don't.
    Lifter of Mountains,
Let me offer a sacrifice—myself—
    beloved,
        to your beautıful face.

Come, here ın the courtyard.
    dark Lord,
The women are singing auspicious wedding songs;
My eyes have fashioned
    an altar of pearl tears,
And here is my sacrifice:
    the body and mind

Of Mira,
the servant who clings to your feet,
through life after life,
a virginal harvest for you to reap.[16]

Both yoga and marriage are striking visions of how a woman might establish a relation with Krishna, since both go beyond the orthodox view of what such a liaison ought to entail. This is the *parakiva* pattern established by the *gopīs* of Braj, according to which women drawn to Krishna must abandon their husbands and all the familial solidarity to which their mates provide access if they answer the call of the divine. Mira seems to reject the view that life with Krishna must be an illicit liaison and to posit marriage instead. Not only that, she often combines this deviant vision with another—the specter of a woman who is a yogi. On more than one occasion she says that she wears the forehead mark and necklace of a yogi as if they were bangles—the essential jewelry of a married woman[17]—and by doing so suggests that the love of Krishna is a force strong enough to fuse even logical opposites such as these. Her attraction to the company of other lovers of Krishna—*bhaktas* and yogis whose itinerancy meant that they were almost invariably men—is then also, by extension, a sort of marriage. When she answers for this unseemly behavior to her worldly husband, the *rana* (king) of Mewar, she merely revels in the scandal:

This bad name of mine, oh king,
is something sweet to me.
Let them blame me, let them praise:
I'll stubbornly go my way.
I met the Lord's people in chainlike lanes—
why leave my stubborn ways?
Wisdom I learned in the gathering of the good—
so the evil ones saw.
Mira's Lord is the clever Mountain Lifter—
evil ones: go roast in a stove.[18]

Early Lives of Mira

Scandal such as this is certainly the keynote in the early hagiography of Mira. The point of departure in the hymn to Mira framed by Nabhaji in his *Bhaktamal*, our earliest source, is her notorious disdain for the bonds that tie a woman to the family into which she marries. Nabhaji makes allusion to the well-known incident in which Mira survives an attempt on her life that is initiated by the *rana*, a figure who could be interpreted as being either Mira's husband or her father-in-law. (Priyadas's commentary on the *Bhaktamal* seems to suggest the latter.) Whoever he was, the *rana*'s sense of jealousy and humiliation is easy to understand, for Mira had put the claims of Krishna ahead of the man whom Indian teaching regards as her *patidev* (husband-god). Here is Nabhaji:

Mira unravelled the fetters of family;
she sundered the chains of shame to sing
of her mountain-lifting Lover and Lord.
Like a latter-day *gopī*, she showed the meaning
of devotion in our devastated age.
She had no fear. Her impervious tongue
intoned the triumphs of her artful Lord.
Villains thought it vile. They set out to kill her,
but not even a hair on her head was harmed,
For the poison she took turned elixir in her throat.
She cringed before none: she beat love's drum.
Mira unravelled the fetters of family;
she sundered the chains of shame to sing
of her mountain-lifting Lover and Lord.[19]

A century after Nabhaji, in 1712 CE, Priyadas, a devotee of Caitanya living in Brindavan, composed an additional set of verses to explain the meaning of the *Bhaktamal.* His *Bhaktirasabodhini* draws out the theme of Mira's scandalous behavior even more clearly. Priyadas makes it clear that when Mira, princess of Merta, was married to the son of another royal Rajput family—later tradition said it was the house of Mewar—she mouthed the requisite marriage mantras but in her heart she dedicated them to Krishna, not her earthly groom. When young Mira came to live in her in-laws' house, similarly, she refused to bow to her mother-in-law and honor her in-laws' family goddess, believing that either act would compromise her loyalty to Krishna. Before long, says Priyadas, Mira was spending most of her time with wandering mendicants and religious enthusiasts—the *sādhu sang* (company of the saints) who were "attached to the will of Syam," that is, Krishna.[20] It was this pattern of inattention to family mores as well as Mira's open flouting of the expectation that a Rajput woman's place is in the home that led to the incident in which her in-laws tried to poison her. It failed. Mira dutifully drank the poison, since it had been sent as an offering at Krishna's feet, but once the liquid reached her throat it actually became "immortal nectar from his feet" (*caranamrt*). Not only did Mira survive, she found that she sang more beautifully than ever.[21]

Priyadas reports other episodes that also illustrate Mira's indifference to the conjugal duties ordained for a woman by Hindu standards set forth in codes such as *The Laws of Manu.* The conflict between love of Krishna and obedience to her husband is further elaborated in a story in which Mira is heard whispering sweet nothings to a strange man behind her bedroom door. The *rana*—again it is unclear whether this is Mira's father-in-law or her husband—races forward to defend the family honor. Sword in hand, he demands to be admitted to her chamber, but when he is, he freezes like a picture on the wall, for he finds that she is merely conversing with Krishna, the image she worships.[22]

This time it is an imagined tryst, but other vignettes in the *Bhaktirasabodhini* show that Mira really does have more intimate contacts with her other family—the ragtag company of devotees—than she does with her own. There is, for instance, an account of how a lecherous man in their number develops a carnal attachment to Mira. Her response is to welcome his advances, provided that they be displayed in the company of all Krishna's followers, and this threat of ultimate sharing jolts the man into a change of heart: his misplaced ardor is transformed into true devotion.[23] Other stories in the *Bhaktirasabodhini* tell how Mira ultimately left her family altogether and adopted the wandering life to which her poems say she aspired. Her first destination was Brindavan, where she visited Jiv Gosvami,[24] and her last was Dvaraka, where she merged her body with Krishna's. She died by entering the image enshrined in his temple there. Priyadas reports that before this event occurred, Brahmins sent by the *rana* attempted to dissuade her from her extreme practices, calling her home. In this way he continues to highlight the tension between her life among those who wander for Krishna's sake and the life she would have led as a member of a noble Rajput family—right up to the end.[25]

In his account, then, the idea of Mira's marriage to Krishna appears explicitly, and something closely resembling a yogic pattern of life is often attributed to her, if not directly named. Both motifs serve to underscore the disparity between religious commitments and the demands of everyday *dharma* (caste duties and obligations)—the same sort of tension that emerges so strongly in poems attributed to Mira herself. In fact, the line separating poetry by Mira and poetry about her is a faint one at best. Many of the poems said to have been composed by Mira are in effect expositions of her life story. Though voiced in the first person, they function as additions to the corpus of her hagiography. Therefore it is not surprising that poems by Mira display an unusual ease of transition between first- and third-person utterances.[26] The poetry and hagiography of Mira, then, form a unified if somewhat unruly body of literature, and they agree in presenting her as a rebel, a woman who defied traditional patterns of womanhood to serve Krishna. She is his yogini and his wife, eternally virgin, eternally ready to mate with him, ever separate from the life of home and family that keeps the world on its course.[27]

Modern Permutations

Both in poetry and in story, then, the "canonical" figure of Mirabai presents us with a radical image of *bhakti* womanhood, an ideal that seems to challenge a woman's *dharma* at its most fundamental points.[28] In fact, this Mira evidently is too radical. As her fame increased, the offense implied in her *bhakti* asceticism must have been ever more pointedly felt, with the result that portrayals of Mira in the modern day yield a more complicated picture. As an impressionistic survey will show, Mira now comes in many more shades of gray than Nabhaji or Priyadas would have thought possible. There are settings—in the pilgrimage cities of Brindavan and Benares, for example—where we get some semblance of the old Mira, but there are other contexts in which she seems to have changed almost beyond recognition.

Suppose we begin our survey by following Mira's footsteps to Brindavan. There we find a Mira temple that has become an important stopping point on the route of many pilgrims. It is said to mark the place where the Rajput princess stayed when she came to visit Jiv Gosvami, and indeed it lies only a small distance from the temple of Radha Damodar, where Jiv lived. The temple to Mira was constructed in the middle of the nineteenth century—not earlier, be it noted—by the chief minister of the state of Bikaner, in northwest Rajasthan, and its special claim to fame, aside from the location itself, is that it houses a *salagram* stone that is said to have been produced from a snake sent by Mira's in-laws to poison her.

The story of this snake was apparently not known to Priyadas, though it obviously echoes his own account of how the *rana* tried to poison Mira. It may well have come into existence after Priyadas's lifetime and is a common feature of Mira's biography as told today.[29] The story states that the *rana* of Mewar attempted to poison Mira not only with a glass of *caranamrt* but with a live snake, which he sent to her in a basket. The result was similar: the poison turned into its opposite when exposed to Mira's faith. As the initial *caranamrt* was transformed into *caranamrt* of quite a different kind, so the black cobra was transformed into a black *salagram* stone, an object universally revered in Vaisnava worship. In the temple of Mira at Brindavan, it is said, one has a chance to see that very stone.

So far there is nothing to challenge or qualify the traditional message of the Mira story, only a further variation on the theme of her opposition to ordinary conceptions of marital obligation. The arrangement of the deities displayed in the Mira temple also seems to accord with the teachings of the *Bhaktamal* and the *Bhaktirasabodhini.* Krishna is in the center, with Radha at his left hand and Mira at his right. Radha's position is more or less dictated by Brindavan tradition: she is at Krishna's left because she is recognized to be *vamangani* (the left-hand side of his body), that is, his primary consort. Mira is exalted by being given a corresponding place at Krishna's right, and the symmetry is appropriate from the point of view of a theologian such as Nabhaji. Nabha, we recall, portrayed Mira as "a latter-day *gopī*" who "showed the meaning of devotion in our devastated age."[30] Her role parallels that of Radha, who served as the paradigm for all the *gopī*s in Krishna's own time. Nothing is actually said about marriage here—in regard to either Radha or Mira—but similar sets of images, such as those that show Visnu flanked by Bhudevi and Niladevi, do imply a marital bond, which suggests the strength of the tie between Krishna and Radha and Mira. The arrangement of figures on the altar at Brindavan's Mira temple seems an appropriate way of acknowledging Mira's conception of herself as married to Krishna.

The other side of Mira—her identity as a yogini—comes out in another pilgrimage city mentioned in the lore of Mira: Benares. Several poems in the Caturvedi collection make reference to that city, and to a particular item within it: the *karavat* (saw) that was embedded in a well near the famous temple of Visvanath. Pilgrims who wished to end their days in Benares and reap the karmic benefits of dying in such a place would jump down the well and be cut in two as they fell—or perhaps they were pushed by greedy pilgrim guides who would then rob the corpses of any jewelry, as some aver.[31]

To judge by the sampling now available in printed editions of Mira's poetry, Benares holds an ambivalent place in the Mira tradition. On the one hand it is criticized as a place where external practice, even suicide, is apt to obscure the importance of interior devotion.[32] On the other hand, as one sees in reference to the deadly saw, it is held up as the place that sets the standard for ascetic rigor.[33] In consonance with its rather distant and uncertain role in Mira's poetry, it is fitting that Benares makes a good deal less of Mira than Brindavan does. What place she has, however, is an appropriate one, for she makes her entry in search of one of the *nirguna sants*. Of all the representatives of medieval *bhakti* in North India, such *sants* come closest to living *vairagya* (a life of renunciation) such as yogis embrace.

The *sant* with whom Mirabai is associated is Ravidas, the leatherworker poet who lived in Benares in the late fifteenth or early sixteenth century.[34] Mira is said by Ravidas's followers to have sought initiation from him, and sections from a number of poems attributed to her are quoted in support of that thesis.[35] Historically it may have been a story in the *Bhaktirasabodhini* that gave rise to the tradition linking Mira with Ravidas, for we read in the section of the *Bhaktirasabodhini* describing him that Ravidas was once visited by a certain Queen Jhali of Cittor, the former capital of Mewar in southwestern Rajasthan. Cittor is the city that represents the most extreme expression of Rajput heroic ideals, for both men and women, so it is not surprising that over the course of time the legendry of Mira, that paragon of courage, gravitated in the direction of Cittor. It came to be accepted that Cittor was the home of the family into which she married, and once that tradition was established it would be then but a small step to forgetting the identity of Queen Jhali and putting Queen Mira in her place.[36] Indeed, the word *jhali* (queen) is almost generic, so Mira filled the role as well as any.

As with Brindavan, there is nothing in Mira's connection with Benares that challenges the traditional estimate of who she was. If Brindavan served as a natural locale for representing Mira's marriage to Krishna, Benares was a logical place to associate with her peripatetic asceticism. Indeed, Ravidas himself is often pictured as someone who wandered the subcontinent, so Mira must have seemed an apt pupil. It is true that many people deny the validity of the connection between Mira and Ravidas. For a Rajput woman to adopt an Untouchable as a guru seems at least as bad to many Vaisnavas as Mira's dalliance with traveling *sādhus* (Hindu holy men, ascetic and mendicant) seemed to her own much maligned in-laws, and one must grant that the purity of her devotion to Krishna makes the situation a little implausible. Ravidas speaks of Hari in his poetry—even Kabir does that—but neither could rightly be classed as a Krishnaite poet. From Mira's side, perhaps, a better case could be made. There are strands in the poetry attributed to her that ought to make a place for a guru such as Ravidas: her reverence for the divine Name, for example, and her frequent praise for "the company of the good."[37] Whatever one may think of the likelihood of such a guru–pupil alliance, one can readily see how it serves to fill a hagiographical lacuna, one that relates particularly to the yogic side of Mira's personality. In someone's eyes, at least, the act of providing a guru for Mira must have been seen as giving credence to her own claim to be a yogi. There is nothing in the poems attributed to her that requires such an idea, but it is a commonplace assumption that every yogi (or yogini) needs an initiating guru, someone to chart out the ascetic path at its outset. Whether Ravidas's fulfilling of that perceived need added more to Mira's stature or to his own depends upon the group with whom one is speaking.

In Rajasthan it would seem that Ravidas was the one to gain, and indeed the story has little currency there. Lindsey Harlan's recent interviews with Rajput women of Mewar show that in their perception the ascetic streak in Mira can stand on its own. According to them, Mira was a one-of-a-kind phenomenon made possible by the ideals of bravery long cultivated in Rajput tradition.[38] This is what made it possible for her to stand alone, defying social criticism and the cruelty of the family into which she had married. It was Rajput bravery, too, that gave Mira the courage to adopt an alternate family, the one defined by devotion to Krishna, even if its members consisted of *sādhus* and yogis, as Harlan's Rajput women affirm.[39] That Mira became functionally a yogini is a matter of no great offense to these modern-day Rajput women, but an unusually vivid expression of Rajput courage.

What is problematic, however, is Mira's marriage, since marital obligations are at the core of what these women consider to be the meaning of a woman's life. Mira is so successful as an embodiment of one Rajput ideal—brave independence of action—that her slighting of another—*pativrata* (devotion to one's husband)—presents an even greater challenge than it otherwise would. The present generation of Rajput women cannot have been the first to face this problem, as is shown by the existence of a fundamental reorganization in the mythology of Mira that appears to have taken place around the end of the nineteenth century. Its results are assumed when these women speak about their *bhakti* heroine. It may well be that this shift in the story of Mira was necessitated by the fact that Mira had become such a widely revered figure in North India. The scandalous element in her legend could no longer be tolerated in the form in which it had been received: some way had to be found to lessen the shock of her disobedience to her husband.

At the beginning of the nineteenth century, when James Tod served the British crown in Rajasthan, the prevailing notion seems to have been that Mirabai was married to Rana Kumbha, perhaps the greatest hero of Mewari legend.[40] This had the virtue of confirming her heroism by coupling it with his, but it must have made her conjugal disloyalty seem all the harder to accept. Furthermore, and in part because of the existence of Tod's own work, it came to be realized that there was a chronological problem involved: Rana Kumbha's dates significantly preceded those of the man whom tradition had come to recognize as Mira's father. In consequence, apparently, the role of being Mira's husband was assigned to Kumbha's grandson, the sixteenth-century prince Bhojraj.[41]

This solved the historical problem, but it left the moral dilemma untouched: how could Mira be allowed to insult a figure so honored in the collective memory of Mewar with her unusual sense of marital priorities? The answer was found by proposing that after Bhojraj died, at a relatively young age, Mira was set upon by his evil brother, a second *rana* named Vikramajit. This man could be held responsible for the cruelty shown to Mira, while both the honor and virtue of Bhojraj remained unscathed. With her husband dead at an early age, furthermore, Mira's devotional version of widowhood made sense—or, as one might equally see it—her devotional substitution for *satī*. She certainly owed nothing to her husband's heinous brother, so her insistent marriage to Krishna was emptied of its scandal, at least once Bhojraj had died.

This is the form of the Mira story that is now accepted across Rajasthan, and it must help considerably in enabling modern Rajput women to emulate Mira obliquely, as Harlan says they do.[42] She is their heroine for *bhakti* though not for the conduct of their own marriages.

The device of shortening Mira's marriage goes some way toward muting her offense to conjugal *dharma,* though in traditional Rajasthani culture she herself would in some measure be regarded as responsible: a wife's auspicious power should keep her husband alive.[43] In elite Indian culture one need not worry about lingering superstitions of *satī,* but even so there remains a sense of unease about Mira's marital situation. One sees this particularly in instructional literature, where Mira now plays a standard role. Take, for example, the Amar Chitra Katha comic-book version of Mira's life, where the logic of justifying Mira's domestic behavior has been pushed yet a step further. There it is claimed that Mira was an ideal Hindu wife.[44] This seemingly impossible assertion is wonderfully worked out on the page. In an initial frame, which is represented in full color, the reader sees Mira bowing at the feet of an enthroned Bhojraj. This is the panel for which we have the caption, "Mira was an ideal Hindu wife and was loved by her husband." The next frame, however, reveals a different Mira. The caption at the top says, "But as soon as her household duties were over, Mira would turn to her divine husband—her Gopala—whom she had brought with her [from Merta]." The figure we see just below is a silhouetted black-and-white Mira performing an *arati* offering before a shadowed Krishna. (See figure 1.) This way of representing the matter puts everything in good proportion: *dharma* comes first, then *bhakti,* and there is no hint of a contradiction between them. Fortunately nothing need be said to an underage readership about any uncomfortable dilemmas that may have arisen in the royal bedroom as Mira insisted on defending her virginity before Bhojraj.

This is one extreme, then. In the Amar Chitra Katha version the *rana* is split into a good and an evil half, with the result that in the first part of her married life Mira is construed as a paragon of family virtue—the episode in which she defies her mother-in-law at the threshold is forgotten—while in the second half she is placed in the position of being able to protest rightly against the advances of a wicked ruler and retreat to the kingdom of Krishna. Her virtue is doubly saved.

But that, after all, is a comic book, and one has a right to expect a certain fairy-tale touch. What happens when Mira is held up as a model for children in real life? This too is a genuine possibility, and the place in which it most obviously occurs is an educational complex in Pune: St. Mira's School for Girls and, for graduates of it and other schools, St. Mira's College. Both institutions were established by a Sindhi visionary, T. L. Vaswani, who propounded what he called a "Mira Movement in Education."[45] Vaswani was celibate, but his interest in education and social reform marked him as a *sādhu* of the distinctly modern school, and he took the figure of Mira as his patron—or rather matron—saint. In fact, it was he himself

Figure 1. Two panels from Kalama Chandrakant, *Mirabai* (Amar Chitra Katha no. 36 [Bombay: India Book House, n.d.], p. 4). (*Reproduced with permission*)

who defined her status by adopting the English term saint, as in a book called simply *Saint Mira.*[46]

It was part of Vaswani's aim to adopt for Hindu society some of the standards that typically emerged in convent schools (most of which, needless to say, also had saints in their names) and the image of Mira seemed to provide a way to do so. To Sadhu Vaswani, she was the queen saint who exemplified the virtues of purity, prayer, simplicity, and service, and images of her that appear in his books and in the schools he founded bear a startling likeness to certain depictions of that other paragon of virtue, the Virgin Mary. One much reproduced portrait, for example, is clearly a Hindu adaptation of Fra Angelico's *Annunciation.* (See figure 2.) The connection is a fascinating one, for Jesus' mother also caused a certain amount of marital embarrassment: the *Gospel of Matthew* reports that when Joseph first learned of Mary's pregnancy he was prepared (in a nice way, of course) to divorce her.[47] And Mary's example seems to have paved Mira's way in years since, too. It is possible nowadays to find images of Mira that represent her in a Madonna-like maternal pose. (See figure 3.) The child, of course, is none other than Krishna, her erstwhile lover and yogi.

All this serves as an enthralling example of intercultural experimentation, and perhaps it was more than anything the simple domination of Mira in the female hagiography of North India that created the need for such bold innovations. The more important she became, the more she had to be able to encompass—not just

Figure 2. Large painting of Mirabai on the wall of the "sanctuary" (assembly) room at St. Mira's School for Girls, Pune. (*Photograph by the author, 1985*)

the call of *bhakti* but the pull of familial and social responsibility. Oddly, the curriculum at St. Mira's College lays particular stress on the idea of being well-rounded. There is no question but that each of the graduates of St. Mira's College is expected to marry. Hence domestic science forms a required part of the curriculum and the whole thrust is to provide an education uniquely tailored to the life of a woman, including a woman's special charge to teach morals to her children. All this must sound like a travesty of the traditional Mira, but there is another side to the education at the institutions dedicated to St. Mira. The sense is also clearly conveyed that one's service as a human being ought to extend beyond the bounds of one's family, even one's community. To the extent that Mira broke beyond the bonds of tradition, forging new meanings for marriage and appropriating for women aspects of a life that had been assumed to be the exclusive preserve of man, she really does serve as a surprisingly good exemplar for this sort of school. And when one must think of fending off the demonic strength of outsiders such as the Muslims and the British, what could be better than the example of Mira's defiant Rajput heroism?[48]

It appears that if a saint is great enough, and only loosely confined by the textual tradition with which she is associated, there is plenty of room for further growth.

Figure 3. Mirabai with the infant Krishna. Poster produced by Brijbasi and Co., Delhi. (*Photograph courtesy of Diane Coccari*)

It is fascinating to see that even when the specifics of the case have changed to the point of reversal, the central message in Nabhaji's stanza on Mirabai continues to shine through. It is Mira's courage that matters most—her fearlessness. There are two ways to read events that have occurred in the hagiography of Mira over the last hundred years: either as a dilution of the strength that once was there or as a further complication of an already multifaceted and in some ways difficult image. The sober historian would probably have to choose the former, but for the hagiographer there is something attractive in the latter. It creates the possibility of seeing Mira as fearless even in the face of her own tradition.

NOTES

1. A listing of such films is provided in Kusum Gokarn, "Popularity of Devotional Films (Hindi)," National Film Archive of India Research Project 689/5/84. This study is available at the National Film Archive in Pune.
2. Kamala Chandrakant, *Mirabai;* Dolly Rizvi, *Kabir;* Suresh Chandra Sharma, *Tulsidas;* Pushpa Bharati, *Soordas* (all Bombay: India Book House, n.d.).
3. Nabhaji, *Sri Bhaktamal,* with the *Bhaktirasabodhini* commentary of Priyadas (Lucknow: Tejkumar Press, 1969), pp. 712–713. I shall cite from the Tejkumar Press edition for both Nabhaji and Priyadas. Recent critical work on the *Bhaktamal* is contained in the following: Narendra Jha, *Bhaktamal: Pathanusilan evam Vivecan* (Patna: Anupam Prakasan, 1978); Gilbert Pollet, "Eight Manuscripts of the Hindi *Bhaktamala* in England," *Orientalia Pouvaniensia Periodica* 1 (1970):203–222; and Pollet, "The Mediaeval Vaisnava Miracles as Recorded in the Hindi 'Bhakta Mala,' " *Le Muséon* 80

(1967):475–487. The texts established by Jha differ very little from those given in the Tejkumar Press edition.

4. Parasuram Caturvedi, ed., *Mirabai ki Padavali* (Allahabad: Hindi Sahitya Sammelan, 1973).
5. Kalyansimh Sekhavat, ed., *Mira-Brhatpadavali,* vol. 2 (Jodhpur: Rajasthan Oriental Research Institute, 1975); Harinarayan Sarma, *Mira-Brhatpadavali,* vol. 1 (Jodhpur: Rajasthan Oriental Research Institute, 1968).
6. Caturvedi, *Mirabai* 44.
7. Caturvedi, *Mirabai* 97.
8. Caturvedi, *Mirabai* 46. The phrase *giradhar nagar* (clever Mountain Lifter) is the standard way of naming Krishna in Mira's poems. It refers to the episode in which he lifted Mount Govardhan so that the inhabitants of the Braj region, his boyhood home, could take shelter from ravaging rains sent against them by the god Indra.
   With this poem, and in the case of many translated here, I am indebted to the editorial hand of Mark Juergensmeyer. In some instances he is at least as much responsible for these translations as I.
9. Caturvedi, *Mirabai* 68. The phrase "holy garments" translates *bhagava bhekh,* which means literally "God's clothes" and presumably refers to the sort of clothing ascetics wear. The "Dark One" is *syam,* an epithet of Krishna.
10. Caturvedi, *Mirabai* 188. Hari is a title of Krishna or Viṣṇu. The word *hajariyo,* here translated "bag of beads," refers to a sewn bag worn over the hand to conceal beads that help meditators count the number of prayers or mantras in a given sequence. It is a common Hindu belief that one's fate is written on one's forehead at birth by the god Brahma.
11. Caturvedi, *Mirabai* 49. The word *lagan,* which occurs near the beginning of the poem, can have the sense of "affection, love, infatuation" or the more formal meaning "marriage." The latter meaning is appropriate because marriages are arranged to occur at times governed by particularly auspicious astrological configurations (*lagan*). In translating, a middle course is chosen—"fortunate match"—and it is hoped that the overtones of marriage, a topic that concerns us especially here, are not lost. The phrase "like a fish washed on shore" does not occur in the original but is implied by the general usage of the verb *talaphi talaphi* (flails) in the *bhakti* literature of medieval North India.
12. Caturvedi, *Mirabai* 94. The phrase "an antelope skin pulled up to my neck" translates two words: *gale mrgachala.* Apparently Mira means that she will maintain some privacy by covering the front of her body with an antelope or deer skin, which yogis often sit on but sometimes use as loin cloths. The mention of Ram rather than Hari or Krishna is notable, but nothing out of the ordinary in poems attributed to Mira.

    This composition presents the translator with a difficulty in that it is sometimes addressed to Krishna, sometimes to the poet's female companion (as implied by the particle *ri*). Similarly, Mira sometimes seems to speak of herself in the first person, sometimes in the third. These shifts of focus are easily tolerated in the original but seem to call for some clarification in English, hence the provision of a double possessive adjective ("her . . . my") in the final verse, where the original requires neither.
13. Caturvedi, *Mirabai* 117. The snake mentioned early in the poem is Ses (Sesa), associated with Viṣṇu. The catalogue of yogic paraphernalia presented here is particularly suggestive of the Nath Yogis, in that allusion is made to the *mudara* (bone earrings) characteristic of that group. On variants in the text, see J. S. Hawley, "Images of Gender in the Poetry of Krishna," in Caroline Walker Bynum et al., eds., *Gender and Religion: On the Complexity of Symbols* (Boston: Beacon Press, 1986), p. 255, note 54.

14. Caturvedi, *Mirabai* 153.
15. Caturvedi, *Mirabai* 27. In a traditional Hindu wedding, the bridegroom leads the bride around a Vedic *homa* fire built beneath a pavilion constructed in the courtyard of the bride's house. A decorative arch is often erected in front of the doorway to welcome guests—most important, the bridegroom and his party.
16. Caturvedi, *Mirabai* 51. The "altar of pearl tears" refers to the *cauk* (altar) laid out on the floor of the bride's courtyard, beneath the pavilion, to serve as a focus of the wedding ceremony. Here various offerings and sacrifices are made into the Vedic fire, according to ancient prescriptions. The vocative *sajan,* translated "beloved," could also be rendered "husband"; it is appropriately used in both contexts.
17. Caturvedi, *Mirabai* 25 and 80.
18. Caturvedi, *Mirabai* 33. The *angithi* (stove) with which the poem concludes is a brazier into which pieces of wood or charcoal are stuffed as fuel. This is the fate to which Mira metaphorically assigns those who criticize her actions.
19. Nabhaji, *Bhaktamal,* pp. 712–713.
20. Priyadas in Nabhaji, *Bhaktamal,* p. 717. In modern Hindi the term *sādhu* has come to refer specifically to a religious mendicant. Here, however, it is translated as "saint" because the term's meaning was not restricted to ascetics in medieval Hindi. The gloss provided by the text itself—concerning obedience to Syam's will—also suggests this interpretation.
21. Priyadas in Nabhaji, *Bhaktamal,* pp. 718–719.
22. Priyadas in Nabhaji, *Bhaktamal,* p. 719.
23. Priyadas in Nabhaji, *Bhaktamal,* p. 720.
24. Priyadas in Nabhaji, *Bhaktamal,* p. 721.
25. Priyadas in Nabhaji, *Bhaktamal,* p. 722.
26. In relation to this point, see also John Stratford Hawley, "Author and Authority in the *Bhakti* Poetry of North India," *The Journal of Asian Studies* 47, no. 2 (1988):269–290.
27. See especially Caturvedi, *Mirabai* 55 and 71. English translations of these poems, along with all others in the Caturvedi edition, appear in A. J. Alston, *The Devotional Poems of Mirabai* (Delhi: Motilal Banarsidass, 1980).
28. For a further and somewhat more qualified consideration of this point, see J. S. Hawley, "Mortality Beyond Morality in the Lives of Three Hindu Saints," in Hawley, ed., *Saints and Virtues* (Berkeley: University of California Press, 1987), pp. 66–72.
29. It also makes its appearance in a number of poems attributed to Mira, for example, Caturvedi, *Mirabai* 39 and 41.
30. Nabhaji, *Bhaktamal,* p. 713.
31. Caturvedi, *Mirabai* 49 and 195. For information on the general lore of the saw at Benares, I am indebted to a conversation with James C. Lochtefeld (November 1987), Krishna Caitanya Bhatt (January 1988), and several citizens of Benares (January 1988). Also relevant is Lochtefeld's "Suicide in the Hindu Tradition: Varieties, Propriety and Practice," master's thesis, University of Washington, 1987.
32. Caturvedi, *Mirabai* 195.
33. Caturvedi, *Mirabai* 49.
34. On this general theme, see J. S. Hawley and Mark Juergensmeyer, *Songs of the Saints of India* (New York: Oxford University Press, 1988), pp. 6, 12–13, 21–22, 177.
35. Candrikaprasad Jijnasu lists eight such couplets in his *Sant Pravar Raidas Sahab* (Lucknow: Bahuvacan Kalyan Prakasan, 1984), p. 37. The best known of these is the third, to which S. M. Pandey makes reference in his "Mirabai and Her Contributions to the Bhakti Movement," *History of Religions* 5, no. 1 (1965):57–58. To the best of my

knowledge, none of these verses appears in Caturvedi's edition, where one finds only a general approbation of life with the *sants* (e.g., Caturvedi, *Mirabai* 30).

36. For the full story, see Hawley and Juergensmeyer, *Songs of the Saints of India,* p. 13. Another attempt to reconcile Jhali and Mira may be found in Jijnasu, *Sant Pravar Raidas Sahab,* p. 36.
37. On the former topic, which is the less common of the two, see Caturvedi, *Mirabai* 140, 199, and 200, and Sekhavat, ed., *Mira-Brahatpadavali,* vol. 2, nos. 68, 279, 351, 352.
38. Lindsey Beth Harlan, "The Ethic of Protection among Rajput Women: Religious Mediations of Caste and Gender Duties," Ph.D. dissertation, Harvard University, 1987, p. 276.
39. Harlan, "Ethic of Protection," p. 273.
40. James Tod, *Annals and Antiquities of Rajasthan,* vol. 1 (Delhi: Motilal Banarsidass, 1971), pp. 337–338; cf. S. S. Mehta, *A Monograph on Mirabai, the Saint of Mewad* (Bombay: author, n.d.), pp. 56, 65.
41. See Har Bilas Sarda, *Maharana Sanga* (Ajmer: Scottish Mission Industries, 1918), pp. 95–96. The matter is reconsidered in, for example, Kalyansimh Sekhavat, *Mirabai ka Jivanvrtt evam Kavya* (Jodhpur: Hindi Sahitya Mandir, n.d.), pp. 45–46.
42. Harlan, "Ethic of Protection," p. 280.
43. In some versions of the Mira legend, this motif of *sri* and *satī* is transposed to a point later in her life. In an elaboration of the accounts of her ascetic wanderings, it is said that Mira, responding to the attempts made on her life by Rana Vikramajit, deserted Cittor and returned to her native Merta. In consequence of the withdrawal of her auspicious energy from Cittor, the city suffered a series of military defeats. See, for example, Mehta, *Mirabai,* pp. 71–72.
44. Candrakant, *Mirabai,* p. 4; cf. also p. 11.
45. T. L. Vaswani, *The Call of Mira Education* (Poona: Mira, n.d.). See also (anon.), *Sadhu Vaswani Mission and its Activities* (Poona: Sadhu Vaswani Mission, n.d.).
46. T. L. Vaswani, *Saint Mira* (Poona: St. Mira's English Medium School, n.d.). I am not sure at what point in the evolution of Vaswani's thought he began to use the English designation "saint" in referring to Mira. His first Mira school, established in Hyderabad (in present-day Pakistan) in 1933, had Sindhi as its medium of instruction.
47. *Matthew* 1.19.
48. Vaswani, *Saint Mira,* pp. 36–38.

22

Understanding Asceticism—Testing a Typology

Response to the Three Preceding Papers

Walter O. Kaelber

Our effort to better understand asceticism might, I suggest, be rewarded if we begin with two interrelated objectives. Our first objective would be to extract from the concrete illustrations presented in these papers a number of cross-cultural, even universal, themes and issues pertaining to asceticism. Our second objective would then be to provide other concrete illustrations and examples of these themes from different religious traditions, thus demonstrating that these themes are indeed cross-cultural, perhaps even universal. We would thus move from the concrete and particular to the universal and then back to the particular; now, however, being able to comprehend those varied particulars in a far larger and more meaningful context.

If we might be so bold, I would propose even a third objective. In addition to suggesting that these themes are often universal, we might also demonstrate how these themes or patterns vary from tradition to tradition. And then we might, as a fourth objective, inquire as to why these variations occur in exactly the ways they do. Quite clearly, our investigations would be not only multicultural in perspective but also multidisciplinary in method. Particularly in our efforts to understand why variations occur within a basic pattern, disciplines such as history, sociology, anthropology, economics, even psychology and others might be employed.

Given the constraints of time, I will confine myself here to the first three of these objectives. After attempting to identify a number of cross-cultural themes and issues illustrated in the foregoing three papers I request your help in supplementing the concrete illustrations provided by their authors and in this response. Attempts to explain why variations in basic patterns occur will be not only welcomed but also applauded.

I wish, then, to explore with you three themes or issues related to asceticism. I will also succeed, I hope, in demonstrating the interrelationship of these themes. The themes are (1) The ascetic's vision of wholeness, plenitude, and perfection, (2) The ascetic's erotic life, and (3) The ascetic's relation to culture.

The Ascetic's Vision of Wholeness, Plenitude, and Perfection

Mira and the Gregorys, as an essential part of their ascetic endeavors, construct ideal images of themselves. Mira does this through her poetry; the Gregorys accomplish a similar end through their dreams. As Professor Miller suggests, many ascetic thinkers rely on strong acts of visual imagination, enabling them to attain a level of self-perception and self-conception unconstrained by the limitations of conventional perspective.

I believe that this is true as much for Mira as it is for the Gregorys. In her poetic vision, Mira attains completeness, wholeness, bringing together the opposites of yogini and wife. She is able to transcend the limitations imposed by reality through the poetic vision. In this vision she is able to construct what Professor Hawley terms a new form of marriage. In her ideal self-conception, Mira is relatedly able to bring together a sedentary, domestic condition and a condition of wandering and homelessness. As a yogini she is both the devoted lover and the perpetual wanderer. Yoga does not separate her from love and companionship; it rather unites her with her yoga mate, Krishna. In Mira's ideal vision, yoga and marriage are tantamount to the same thing. Quite appropriately for my purposes, Professor Hawley observes that Mira's marriage to Krishna is the stuff of dreams. In one of her poems, Mira says: "In dream he [namely, the god Krishna] grasped my hand; in dream he [the god] led me round the wedding fire." Through poetic vision and dream, Mira is able to transform herself into an ideal characterized by wholeness; she is coordinately freed from imperfection and limitation.

Through dream, the Gregorys are able to accomplish the same end. The limitations of the body, the imperfections of the body and the sorrows which those imperfections bring are overcome with the attainment of a body of bliss. But as Professor Miller notes, that body, the transformed body, the body of bliss, is possible only through poetic vision and dream. Rather than reiterate specific examples of this theme, permit me to pose a question. Is the ideal body, the body of bliss, available only in a private dream? Is the transformation to plenitude or perfection possible only in an individual's vision?

Professor Miller made reference to Jean-Pierre Vernant's thesis that for the Greek of the archaic period the problem is not that the body is necessarily evil but that the human body is not fully a body. The ideal is a body of plenitude, a divine body, a body so transformed that it is freed from the vicissitudes of time and their corrosive effects.

What immediately come to mind for me here are the many examples from Hindu, Buddhist, and Jain mythology of earthly, even human, but nonetheless, glorious bodies. Already at birth the bodies of such individuals demonstrate the thirty-two great marks of the superman. Gregory of Nyssa has a vision of Adam's body. Quoting Peter Brown as does Professor Miller: "It was like the diaphanous radiance of a still midday sky." What comes to mind here are the *tīrthaṅkara*s (saints) of Jainism, who have bodies raised to perfection and absolute purity. By leading a life of extreme asceticism they reduce and ultimately end the flow of karmic substance into the body. So pure are the bodies that they glow with an alabaster luster; even their blood has turned a milky white.

Significantly, what is involved here is not an individual's private vision, but rather a shared, a communal mythology. Nonetheless, it remains a vision. When I consider the complex phenomenon of yoga, however, what strikes me is the evident attempt to translate this vision, this idealized self-conception into a concrete, earthly, flesh and blood reality. Through yogic practice the body is transformed into what some traditions refer to as a "body of diamond," a body possessed of superhuman powers, resilient to the ravages of time.

Although led by a vision, the yogi works to make the vision reality. It is perhaps interesting in this context to consider the conservative monks of Mr. Hirschfeld's *laura*. These monks objected to the expansion of the *laura* and the threat of a greater worldliness. No doubt the vision of themselves as monks in that more opulent environment was not congruent with their idealized self-image. They attempted to actualize their ideal self-conception not only through what they envisioned as their ideal but also through evident protest and opposition to movements and practices threatening that ideal self-conception.

The Ascetic's Erotic Life

The libidinal, erotic aspect of asceticism is quite evident in the visions of both Gregory of Nyssa and Mira. Of particular significance in this context is Gregory's dream of the two beautiful virgins, shining with light. After planting kisses upon him, they say: "Unite your spirit to ours and bring your flaming torch to join ours." In this context, it is instructive to recall that in one of her poems Mira also uses the imagery of light in an erotic context, asking her beloved Krishna to merge his light with hers. In Gregory's vision, the ascetic and the erotic are beautifully merged. Although this fusion of the erotic and the ascetic might well be ironic, as Professor Miller suggests, it is hardly unique to Gregory; indeed, the fusion is quite universal in one form or another. This Professor Miller very rightly observes in her quotation from Geoffrey Harpham regarding the inextricable relation between asceticism and the desire for perfection (see p. 295).

But perhaps the link between the ascetic and the erotic goes beyond the desire for perfection. This might be worth exploring here, if only briefly. The erotic dimension of Mira's poetic visions hardly needs to be further illustrated. As suggested, it is precisely the practice of yoga which unites Mira with her lover in a new form of marriage. Although Mira remains the perpetual virgin, she is simultaneously erotic. This fusion of the ascetic and the erotic should, of course, hardly surprise us. What makes the case of Mira unusual is not that she longs for a god who is both ascetic and erotic; what is unusual is that the god is Krishna rather than Siva. The union of the ascetic and the erotic is fundamental to Siva's very being as Wendy Doniger demonstrates in her now classic work on Siva (*Siva, the Erotic Ascetic* [1973, 1981]).

Professor Hawley refers to yoga and marriage as those "impossible bedfellows," and, indeed, such is often the case. But as Professor Hawley then so clearly demonstrates, the impossible is, of course, quite possible in the case of Mira. Permit me to suggest that there are even instances in the Hindu tradition where the two are presented as coexisting without paradox or contradiction and where the union need not be termed "ironic."

Consider the principal Upaniṣads as an illustration. These texts, written approximently 600 BCE, have, I believe, been seriously misunderstood in this particular regard. The general consensus among scholars is that, according to the Upaniṣads, in order to attain knowledge of ultimate reality one must renounce one's condition as a householder. Having so renounced society, one is now free to practice yoga and meditation in the wilderness. It is true that such a position is clearly evident in the much later literature, but it is not characteristic of the Upaniṣads. Without presenting detail here, permit me to suggest that in numerous Upaniṣadic passages, the practice of yoga is by no means incompatible with the married state.

Relatedly, I believe that when one considers early Hinduism in particular, a definite distinction must be drawn between asceticism in general and renunciation of the world, in particular, such renunciation entailing the abandonment of all reproductive kinship ties as well as traditional ritual. It is important to observe that in the early Hindu or Vedic period, particularly in the Brāhmaṇas, asceticism is an integral element of the ritual process. Ascetic behavior is most evident during the *dīkṣā,* a ritual that serves as the initiatory consecration into the sacrificial scenario. Fasting, confinement to a hut, breathing restraints, abstaining from sex, and other ascetic practices characterize the three day period of consecration and purification.

During this period of asceticism or *tapas,*[1] a magical heat is accumulated within the sacrificer. In Sanskrit *tapas* refers also to the heat itself: thus, to both the practice of asceticism and product of that practice. *Tapas* flows through the ascetic, endowing him with an extraordinary power. Significantly for our purposes, the power of *tapas* is an erotic power; it is a power of fertility. This is particularly clear at the fertility ritual known as the *Pravargya.* It is clear at this rite that the fertility of the fields and the procreative powers of the sacrificer are impossible without evident ascetic endeavor.

Moreover, in the word *tapas* itself, the heat of ascetic effort and the heat of sexual arousal and performance are fused. The heat, or *tapas,* generated through asceticism and the heat, or *tapas,* generated through desire and sexual action are by no means unrelated.

The Vedic sacrificer has a clearly androgynous quality. Through the ritual, and in an act of unilateral procreation, the sacrificer generates and gives birth to a second or spiritual self. I believe that already here we can see the seeds of a later notion in Hindu thought. The later ascetic often has an idealized self-conception, as suggested earlier, in which fragmentation is left behind for plenitude and wholeness. That wholeness can be dramatically represented in a self-image of bisexuality. I suggest that the renunciation of sexuality might often be seen not as producing someone that is asexual, but rather someone that is bisexual. The objective here is not to diminish the body and its powers but to attain a body of plenitude. Hindu thought suggests that semen retained is semen strengthened. Through abstinence, the ascetic generates power within. It is asceticism that generates a body of plenitude.

When considering the fusion of the erotic and the ascetic, one should pay, I believe, particular attention to the Tantric tradition. Here, indeed, sexual postures and yogic postures become one and the same. The generation, retention, and return of semen become techniques to facilitate insight and realization.

The Ascetic's Relation to Culture

To help us apprehend and comprehend asceticism as a socio-cultural phenomenon with socio-historical consequences, permit me to suggest—for heuristic purposes only—a five-fold typology. This typology, although influenced by the work of H. Richard Niebuhr, is adapted to very different purposes than was his. Somewhat in the Weberian sense, these five categories or forms of asceticism should be seen as ideal types. They are (1) asceticism against culture, (2) asceticism of culture, (3) asceticism beyond culture, (4) asceticism and culture in paradox, and (5) asceticism as transformer of culture. Permit me to stress, before I begin, that because a given ascetic phenomenon might well trace out more than one orientation and trajectory, it could most certainly—for heuristic purposes—be classified under more than one category. This can help us to appreciate and contour what scientists term the "robustness" of the phenomenon. I shall later attempt to illustrate this by using Mira as an example.

We begin with a form of asceticism that challenges, opposes, or rejects the mainstream culture, that culture often referred to by scholars as "the world." This orientation is invariably accompanied by flight or withdrawal from a realm that is perceived as evil, or as illusion, or as entangling, depending upon the given tradition. Such an orientation, therefore, invariably entails self-conscious nonparticipation in cultural institutions such as family life, economic life, political life, and even conventional, mainstream religion.

Ascetic protest against mainstream culture and its practices almost invariably prompts the ascetic to adopt some extreme form of behavior. The ascetic practice can, therefore, often be seen as an intentional language of protest and opposition. The practice is thus fully comprehensible only when one understands what form of behavior the ascetic practice opposes. This has been very well illustrated in Patrick Olivelle's work on both the Hindu hermit and the Hindu *saṃnyāsin,* or world renouncer.[2] For much of Hinduism, culture is synonymous with village; both the hermit and the renouncer leave the village for the forest or wilderness; unlike cultural man, the hermit eats uncultivated food: fruits, roots, and herbs growing in the wild. Unlike cultural man, he stores no food. He wears bark and skin: garments not produced by technology. Like an animal and unlike cultural man, he lets his hair and nails grow.

In a related fashion, as Olivelle observes, the *saṃnyāsin* roams restlessly, thereby posing a constant challenge to the virtue of stability. The life of Mira, of course, immediately comes to mind here. In an even more extreme fashion, the Hindu renouncer is advised to behave like a child or a fool, a madman, or a drunkard. Quoting Olivelle: "This oft-repeated description indicates the renouncer's negation of three important areas of cultured behavior: rationality, morality, and purity."[3] At least in its initial form, Hindu renunciation must be seen as anticultural. The particular ascetic practice is comprehensible only in terms of the cultural practice it self-consciously seeks to challenge. Ascetic practice may, therefore, frequently be seen as an intentional language of protest. The words of Professor Miller are appropriate in this context: "The ascetic embrace of sexual renunciation was a dramatic gesture that threatened noble, landowning families." If our suggestion is taken seriously, it then appears that almost any form of extreme behavior that deviates from the cultural norm may serve as language of challenge or protest. Recalling Professor Olivelle's paper, it is clear that both shaving your head, as do the Buddhist monks, and never cutting your hair at all, a practice of many Hindu ascetics, both represent a symbolic rejection of mainstream cultural practices and values.

As is well illustrated in Yizhar Hirschfeld's excellent presentation (pp. 267–280), monks will very frequently—as part of their ascetic statement—confine themselves for extended periods of time to their cells. Indeed, as the paper makes clear, monks may be much moved to protest if efforts are made to impose upon them more spacious accommodations or greater contact with the world beyond the *laura*. On the other hand, as is made clear in Professor Hawley's presentation, the ascetic may wander constantly. From our present perspective, the extreme constriction of one's space functions as a language of anticultural protest as much as does perpetual wandering with no confinement at all.

Considering other examples, the ascetic may differentiate himself or herself either by remaining perpetually silent or by chanting and reciting continually. The ascetic may nurture, cleanse, or purify the body inordinately, or not only neglect his body but abuse it in countless ways. The ascetic may overcome the human norm either by abstaining from sex or by making sex a significant part of the ascetic routine.

Viewing this first form of asceticism from a social perspective, it is important to consider the trajectory of this challenging orientation. This form of asceticism frequently contains within itself the seeds of its own reassimilation into the mainstream culture. The trajectory may proceed under the impact of what Weber termed routinization, generating a functionally integrated subculture of its own or even be reintegrated into the cultural mainstream which it sought to leave behind and which it now changes and reforms. Olivelle's term for this later process is "domestication," a term I find particularly apt in the development of the Mira hagiography.

Our second form—the asceticism of culture—isolates asceticism as a mainstream cultural institution. Here the ascetic may function paradigmatically as a cultural hero with no or minimal conflict between worldly and ascetic institutions. The ascetic may be perceived as the pinnacle of cultural achievement and mainstream values. What comes to mind here is again Mira, but certainly not the Mira of her own poetry; it is rather the comic-book Mira. Here she clearly functions as mainstream paradigm. The challenge which her ascetic-erotic life posed to domestic values is minimized, even neutralized, if each is put in its proper place, as the comic-book attempts to do.

In the case of the asceticism of culture, ascetic institutions, even so-called otherworldly institutions and structures may be afforded great prestige by the society at large. Ritual or cult-based asceticism may be seen as falling into this category. The orthodox asceticism that accompanied the Vedic sacrifice, particularly at the *dīkṣā*, is a conspicuous example. Whereas the Hindu ascetic left urban life for the wilderness, Sabas, as Mr. Hirschfeld tells us, wished to turn the wilderness or desert into a city!

The ascetic of culture may effect significant social change. But clearly the trajectory of such change will differ markedly from that of an inherently anticultural orientation. One reason for such a difference is suggested by Niebuhr. Whereas an ascetic of the first type regards all worldly institutions with equal suspicion or hostility, an ascetic of the second type—because of his acceptance of and acceptance by the culture—is in a position of making value judgments regarding the varied aspects of worldly life. They are not all equal in his eyes. I believe it is quite possible to understand the intentions and efforts of Sabas from this perspective.

In addition to the distinguishable trajectories traced out by these two ascetic orientations, we must also be attentive to the process through which asceticism of the first type becomes asceticism of the second type through assimilation or domestication. Conversely, asceticism of culture may trace a trajectory eventuating in asceticism against culture. This is in many ways precisely how Heesterman understands the origin of renunciation in Hinduism. According to Heesterman, renunciation emerges as a necessary and logical consequence of the needs posed by orthodox, ritual asceticism. The autonomy that the brahman priest of the sacrificial world sought could be realized only in the complete autonomy of the renouncer. Hence, for Heesterman, the brahman priest, the paradigm of mainstream culture, through the inherent dynamic of his own quest for complete autonomy becomes the renouncer, the paradigm of anticulture.

Our third form, namely asceticism above or beyond culture, is an orientation that perceives ascetic goals as being both continuous and discontinuous with worldly aims and values. The more mundane aims and values are not so much rejected as transcended. Worldly endeavor and value may serve as a preliminary for attaining those ends which the ascetic seeks, but the ascetic goals are finally attained only by leaving those worldly endeavors behind. Here renunciatory asceticism is perceived as being in opposition to the world; but that opposition is itself institutionalized. Tension between the mundane and the transcendent is not eliminated or even reduced, as it would be in the asceticism of culture. It is, rather, accepted.

I believe that no better illustration of this orientation could be found than the classical life-stage system of Brāhmanic India. During the first portion of one's life, the values of wordly success, sensual pleasure, and moral virtue are enshrined. But with renunciation, the individual turns his back upon those values in order to pursue liberation or a transcendent consciousness. The fourth value, namely *mokṣa* (liberation), is discontinuous with the first three. It may even be seen as being in opposition to them. And yet the life-stage system institutionalizes all four values as well as the opposition between the first three and the fourth. Liberation, attained in the fourth life stage, is hence both the culmination of cultural achievement and its rejection. One is reminded here of Niebuhr's statement regarding the protest of Thomistic monasticism against the secular church: "This protest has now been incorporated into the church without losing its radical character."[4]

Our fourth typological category is one in which ascetic renunciation occurs not in flight from the world but rather within the world itself. The essence of this fourth type is, therefore, paradox. It is interesting in this context to consider the *Bhagavad-Gita*. The *Gita*—in response to the radical renunciation of its day—opposes all flight from socio-cultural involvement. The warrior Arjuna, as an instrument of the divine, must lead his forces in battle and vanquish the foe. He many not retreat in a posture of samnyasic nonviolence. The *Gita* demands not renunciation of action, but rather renunciation in action. And precisely here lies the paradox. Although they must be ever active in the world—just as the Lord Viṣṇu is ever active in sustaining the world—the *Gita* frees humans from any concern regarding the fruits or consequences of such action. As Heesterman suggests, the fusion of worldly and renunciatory life is achieved at the price of a paradox; the devotee fully engages in worldly activity, but does not engage himself or herself.

Our fifth, and last, category is the ascetic as transformer of culture; indeed the ascetic as social engineer. Although worldly institutions are perceived from this orientation as flawed or worse, the ascetic does not flee them; nor is he or she disengaged in his or her actions. Further, he or she is quite clearly concerned with the fruits or consequences of action. The ascetic's quest for personal transformation is inseparably tied to a necessary transformation of the socio-cultural world. He or she, therefore, acts and intentionally seeks to reconstruct that world. The ascetic may thus be seen as a social engineer. I believe it would be most instructive to consider Gandhi in this context. But I will not do so here. I rather wish to consider Mira.

Mira's wandering with holy men, or *sādhus*, was a clear threat to domestic life. Quoting again a poem by Nabhaji: "Mira unravelled the fetters of family." As Professor Hawley observes: "It was this pattern of inattention to family mores as well as Mira's open flouting of the expectation that a Rajput woman's place is in the home that led to the incident in which her in-laws tried to poison her" (p. 308). In so much of Mira's own poetry—and in the poetry about her—the tension or opposition between mainstream, domestic morality on the one hand, and ascetic wandering and challenge on the other, is central.

But the modern pictures of Mira often seek to minimize, even eliminate, this tension and opposition. We have seen this in the comic-book view of her. Ultimately Mira is so completely domesticated, to use Olivelle's term, that she can function as a cultural paradigm of mainstream values. But legend and hagiography have taken Mira even further. With the Mira Movement in Education, as Professor Hawley clearly demonstrates, she becomes the saintly embodiment of purity, courage, and service beyond the bounds of family and even community. With her impact upon the social values and social behavior of the young women in the Mira schools, she no longer represents a challenge to society; she now rather offers a challenge to serve society. She has been transformed from anticultural ascetic to disciplined, yet courageous, social servant. In being so transformed, she serves as the ascetic model for constructive, mainstream social change.

NOTES

1. Cf. my book *Tapta Mārga: Asceticism and Initiation in Vedic India* (Albany: State University of New York Press, 1989) for more comprehensive discussion.
2. Cf. Patrick Olivelle, "Contributions to the History of Saṃnyāsa," *Journal of the American Oriental Society* 101 (1981); and "Renouncer and Renunciation in the *Dharmaśātras,*" in *Studies in Dharmaśātra,* ed. R. W. Lariviere (Calcutta: Firma KLM Privat Limited, 1984).
3. Patrick Olivelle, "Village vs. Wilderness: Ascetic Ideals and the Hindu World," in *Monastic Life in the Christian and Hindu Traditions,* eds. Austin B. Creel and Vasudha Narayanan, Studies in Comparative Religion 3 (Lewiston, N.Y.: The Edwin Mellen Press, 1990), p. 14.
4. H. Richard Niebuhr, *Christ and Culture* (Harper & Row, 1956), p. 129.

23

The Significance of Food in Hebraic-African Thought and the Role of Fasting in the Ethiopian Church

Ephraim Isaac

No one would question that food is absolutely central to human existence. The processes of eating, digesting, and nutrition represent fundamental biological necessities of life. These processes promote other related functions of life such as growth and movement. But food is not only an essential and basic biological or economic necessity. It is also a fundamental ingredient of religious life and human thought.

From the view of many religions food is the foremost, blessed gift of the creator for the sustenance of life. The *Book of Genesis* expresses this view simply stating that the creator gave people "every plant that yields seed that is upon the face of the earth and every tree with seed in its fruit" (*Gn.* 1.29).

In biblical, as in many African traditions, religious life revolves around agriculture. The sacred seasons and the calendar are built around it. Tilling the ground and herding cattle are the two oldest professions mentioned in the Bible (*Gn.* 4.2). The creator emerges *par excellence* as the first gardener who makes "every tree that is pleasant to the sight and good for food" to grow (*Gn.* 2.9).

Most biblical gifts to friends as well as religious and political officials are solemn gifts of food. The Psalmist sings "[every creature, O Lord,] will look to you to give them their food in due season; when you give it to them, they gather it up; when you open your hand they are filled with good things" (*Ps.* 104.27–28).

The song of the Psalmist echoes the hymn to the Aton, which is in perfect accordance with the well-known ancient Egyptian spiritual view of food. Food is the essence of life, and sacrifice for the fertility of the earth is a cardinal element of Egyptian religion. According to the Memphite theology, food and the human soul, Ka, were among the first orders of creation.[1] The Egyptians could not conceive of life, even after death, without food in the normal form.[2] The tomb food offerings to the Ka and the burial of large numbers of utensils containing food and drink, a custom common among many African peoples, confirm this view.

For the Egyptians agriculture, as well, could not prosper without divine supervision: "If you plough and there is growth in the field, God causes it to be plenty in your hand." Ptah made all and from Ptah "came forth foods, provisions, divine offerings, and all good things." From Re flows "life, prosperity, health . . . bread, beer. . . ."[3] In a land where there was hardly any rain, the Nile—which brought the water upon which the agricultural life of the people depended—played a dominant role in the religious thought and practice of the Egyptians. The fundamental unity of the Egyptian festivals sprang precisely from the religious character of the seasonal agricultural practices. The celebration of the fertility of the soil is a dimension of this, exemplified in the festival of the goddess Bast, whose feast at Bubastis—vividly described by Herodotus (*Hist.* 2.60)—was purportedly attended by about seven hundred thousand people.

The ancient Greeks inhibited the free citizen from performing the so-called menial tasks. In particular, after Greece became a slave society and native-born Greek gentlemen became landlords, the aristocratic philosophers, especially Plato and Aristotle, propounded the view that the tillers of the soil also should be slaves (Aristotle, *Politics* 30a.25ff.; cf. Plato, *The Republic* 806.de). The earlier Greek traditions, however, attest to the fact that agricultural work, a basic economic activity, was regarded highly. Hesiod even claimed that farmers receive the favor of the gods.[4]

For the ancient Israelites, food was an essential component of the bond of true fellowship with divine and human beings, respectively; and the refusal to eat at someone's table signified hostility. According to some scholars, the rejection of the pig's flesh (*Lv.* 11.7) by the Israelites resulted from the sacrificial use of that animal by their Canaanite enemies. A meal was not only an expression of social fellowship but also a sign of moral and spiritual union. Such was the case when Moses and the elders ate and drank as they beheld God (*Ex.* 24.11; cf. *Gn.* 19.3); when the pact between Jacob and Laban was accompanied by a ceremonial meal (*Gn.* 31.54; cf. 26.30); and the Israelite–Gibeonite alliance was concluded with a similar meal (*Jos.* 9.3–15).

The wearing of special garments at certain meals (*Is.* 61.3; *Eccl.* 19.18), the obligation to say blessings over wine and bread before a meal or grace after it, as well as the respective blessings over other foodstuff (*Berakhot* 6.1; *Berakhot* 48b; *Soṭah* 10a) and similar other customs, point to the communal moral and spiritual values of food and meals. It has even been suggested that the root of the Hebrew *b*ᵉ*rit* (covenant) is *bārah* (to eat); and Geez *mesah* (meal, lunch) has definite etymological relation to *maseha,* (to anoint), a religious royal function (cf. *Ps.* 23.5). *Malaḥ* (salt) which makes food tasty, symbolizes permanent covenant (*Nm.* 18.19; 2 *Chr.* 13.5; *Ez.* 4.14).

The religious significance of food among the peoples of Ethiopia is widely recognized by those who have studied the cultures of the various nationalities. C. R. Hallpike, an anthropologist who worked among the Cushitic Konso, correctly observes that food has such an important religious significance for them that "[the bestowal of food is] a symbol of blessing between the physical order of society and the social order itself." Moreover, beer is "the prime substance used in libations" and other religious rituals. Hallpike further notes that as among the ancient Israelites, "refusing to eat with, or to accept food from, a class of persons is a clear indication of social and ritual distance. . . .Commensuality is an indication of social and ritual equality."[5] For most Ethiopian peoples, whether they are speakers of the Cushitic or Semitic languages, these observations hold true, as they do for ancient Jews and other peoples. In Ethiopia, people of different faiths such as the Christians and the Moslems would not touch any meat not slaughtered by a fellow believer. And the real sign of intimacy among members of the same household or circle of friends is direct mutual hand feeding or *gursa,* the giving or acceptance of food from the hand of one directly to the mouth of another respectively. Even the round shape of the common meal table called *masob,*[6] similar to the ancient Jewish dining table, indicates solidarity among the dining family members or guests.

The sanctity of food among the various Ethiopian peoples is further exemplified by the attitude toward cattle among the Nilotic Nuer. In refuting those who have intimated that the cow is venerated by the Nuer, E. E. Evans-Pritchard rightly agrees that

> there is . . . no evidence at all that cattle are venerated or in themselves are in any way regarded as guardian spirits, and in so far as it may be true to say that Nuer religion "is centered in the cow" or that their attachment to cattle "may also be called religious," in so far, that is, that we may legitimately speak . . . of "die sakrale Stellung des Rindes," it is for a different reason.

But this different reason is not only because of the sacrificial role of cattle, as he intimates, but also because cattle constitute the main source of the food of the people, the milk on which they depend for sustenance.[7]

The various forms of religious rituals and liturgies, including Jewish and Christian ones, have their origin in the practice of sacrifice. The Passover Seder (Mishnah, *Pesaḥ* 10), the commemoration of the Israelite liberty from Egyptian slavery, as well as the sacred meal of the Qumran covenant community (1QSa 2.17.22), the symbol of hope and longing for the coming Heavenly Kingdom, and the Christian Eucharist (*anaphora,* "offering" in Eastern Christendom), related to the Passover as a meal of redemption (*Mk.* 14.22ff.), acquire their theological significance from the ancient Hebraic-biblical sacrificial meals.[8]

Food in Hebraic-biblical thought finds its ultimate expression in the apocalyptic idea of the eschatological meal or the messianic banquet, the feast in the coming Kingdom of Heaven (*Is.* 25.6, 55.1–5, 65.13; *Ps.* 22 (23).5; *Prv.* 9.1–6; *3 En.* 62.14; *2 Bar.* 29.5–8; Mishnah *Avot* 3.20). In the beginning of creation paradise was the Garden of Eden, full of delightful edible fruit trees and plants, including the Tree of the Knowledge of Good and Evil; and at the end of time the Kingdom of Heaven will be the banquet hall of eternal meal "a feast of fat things" (*Is.* 25.6). The grandiose nature of this banquet is envisioned in the type of food reserved for the occasion: whereas fruits, légumes, milk, honey, lamb, beef, bread, and wine are most frequently mentioned as popular foods in the Bible, the huge creatures behemoth and leviathan are given in the Pseudepigrapha (*3 En.* 60.7; *2 Bar.* 29.4; *4 Ezr.* 6.52).

In the Ethiopian church, as in all other Christian churches, the Eucharist has come to take on purely spiritual meanings, losing its original physical *Sitz im Leben* of the communal meal (*koinōnia, 1 Cor.* 10.16). Nevertheless, the Ethiopian church does retain what resembles an observance of communal meals held in the church courtyards after regular worship service. At one time, such a meal, served on both Saturdays and Sundays, was set forth as a liturgical banquet. It involved the formal blessings over the wine and the bread which the people consumed, as in a Passover meal, and not unlike the Essene or early Christian eschatological meal.[9] In the fifteenth century the emperor Zar'a Ya'qob (1434–1464) restricted or prohibited such a formal ritual meal, but the ceremonial meals survive still today in many traditional churches.

Food is a special divine gift. Its absence, therefore, in the form of hunger, drought, and famine represent unusual and severe divine punishment (*Is.* 51.19; *Jer.* 14.13–18; *Am.* 4.6) especially during the apocalyptic woes of the end of time (*Mk.* 13.8). The destruction of crops by blight or locust (*Am.* 4.9), the ravaging of the land by warfare (*Is.* 1.7, 3.1,7), and particularly the absence of rain signal the withdrawal of divine favor (*Hg.* 1.10–11) or manifest direct divine punishment.

The earth yields food because of rain. Hence, its absence calls for a solemn occasion of prayers and fasting in both biblical and rabbinic Judaism (*Jgs.* 10.26; *I Kgs.* 18.12ff.; *Neh.* 9.1; *Jl.* 1.13, 2.12; *Zec.* 7.5; Mishnah, *Ta'anit*). According to *Ta'anit,* if no rain has fallen on or before Marcheswan 17, a light fast of three days, accompanied by washing and anointing, is ordered. Continued drought calls for prayers and fasts of higher intensity, ashes to be sprinkled on public streets, on the ark, and on the head of the Nasi and Ab-beth din.

It is well known to students of African religions that rain has deep religious and emotional significance. One anthropologist points out that "rain . . . come[s] from God and [is] therefore [a] manifestation of him . . ." for the Nuer.[10] Another writes of the Konso that ". . . Seldom do they merely say 'it is raining' but 'God is raining.' . . . They believe that God, Wa[q]a, withholds the rain from towns which are disturbed by too much internal quarreling, and the localized nature of rainfall lends some plausibility to this most important religious belief."[11] While such ideas can lead to a false interpretation of the understanding of the divine nature by these Ethiopian peoples, one should not underestimate the theological significance of rain in African thought.

Food has been regarded as central in the religious thinking of diverse peoples since time immemorial. It represents not only the present sustenance of life but also the very meat of eternal life. So, why is fasting, the negation of food, also part of the religious tradition of so many peoples?

Some historians of religion think that fasting inevitably and naturally grew out of the custom of leaving food and drink for the dead, so that they, and not the living, might make use of them.[12] This hypothesis does not seem to be very convincing, and requires a clear proof that there is not enough food for the living and the dead to share. Furthermore, it overlooks the fact that since time immemorial people feasted, not fasted, at burial ceremonies and held other memorial feasts (for instance, the Ethiopian *tazkar* and the Jewish *zikaron* meals) in honor of the dead. Religious fasts also precede, not follow, funeral sacrifices.

Other historians of religion hold the view that fasting grew "out of the desire in primitive man to bring on at will certain abnormal nervous conditions favorable to the seeing of visions and dreams believed to give direct access to the spiritual world."[13] This view dates from the seventeenth century, when Jesuit missionaries who worked in "New France" claimed that the natives fasted because they believed that "fasting makes their sights extraordinarily acute" and enables them to see distant or absent things, and that dreams helped them to see the whereabouts of the elks or enemies that they sought. Following these missionaries, Levy Bruhl argues that "when a dream was desired, fasting was the ordinary means of supplication" and that "if the Huron does not succeed in seeing in dreams a herd of elks or deer, it is because, in spite of his fasting, the mystic essence of these animals remains hostile to him."[14]

The problem with this hypothesis is that people do see dreams not only when the body is exhausted by hunger but also when it is fully satiated. Numerous visions seen by the prophets in the biblical books do not seem to have occurred in the context of fasting. Unusual dreams also take place after overeating, and certain foods and herbs are believed equally to induce extraordinary visions, not unlike modern-day consciousness-expanding drugs and hallucinogens. According to the Ethiopian tradition found in the *Kebra Nagast,* the night King Solomon slept with the Queen of Sheba after an elaborate spicy meal, he saw in a dream how the glory of ancient Israel departed for the land of Ethiopia in the form of the sun.[15]

A third hypothesis has it that fasting is "nothing more than a preparation for the sacramental eating of holy flesh."[16] Such an assertion of a preparatory formula is somewhat far-fetched, but the view deserves a closer examination. The great Jewish fast of Yom Kippur was accompanied by sacrificial rites (*Lv.* 16.1–34). The abstention from eating certain foods at *Pesaḥ* (Passover) may have a similar provenance. In the Christian tradition of the pre-Easter Lent, there is a connotation of a sacrificial feast preceded by fasting; in the Ethiopian church, the *gahad* of Christmas and the *gahad* of Epiphany, held on the eves of the feasts respectively; the fast of the Dormition of Mary; and others. The most notable feasts and fasts of the Ethiopian church in the established calendar are determined in relation to the time of the Jewish *Pesaḥ* or the Christian Easter, both of which carry sacrificial significance. A case can easily be made for the rhythmic cycle of fasts and feasts.[17]

The historian of religion, Gerardus van der Leeuw, wrongly attaches too much significance to mystical and divinatory origins to feasts; but he is right in asserting that festivals are not intended to be merely recreational.[18] The origin of feasts must be in the solemn seasons of sacrificial rites and the eating of ritual meals. They may be associated with certain events in the experience of the individual, from birth to death (birth, *Gn.* 40.20; marriage, *Jub.* 14.10) or the life of the society, from agriculture to warfare and victory (sowing and harvesting, *Jgs.* 9.27; *Ru.* 2.14; *1 Sm.* 13.23; sheep shearing, *1 Sm.* 25.11). They may also be associated with certain cosmic occurrences such as the beginning and end of the rainy seasons. Fasting was associated with the religious festival of Isis (Herodotus, *Hist.* 2.40).[19]

However, the eating of holy flesh or sacrificial meals, and the common fast–feast rhythmic counterpoint do not adequately or fully explain the origin of fasting.

Certain fasts happen to be expressions of mourning and calamity (*Ezr.* 8.21–23; *Neh.* 1.4; *4 Esd.* 3.6; *1 Mc.* 3.47; *2 Mc.* 13.2; *Dn.* 9.3); certain others of repentance and sorrow (*Jl.* 1.14, 2.12; *Jn.* 3.5); and still certain others of discipline, piety, and meritorious life (*Ps.* 35.13, 69.10; *Tb.* 12.8; *Testaments of the Twelve Patriarchs: Rb.* 1.10; *Sm.* 3.4; *Jd.* 15.4). Neither can one explain the origins of the pious fastings on Mondays and Thursdays (*Ta'anıt* 12a; *Lk.* 18.12; *Jdt.* 8.6) or on Wednesdays and Fridays for the early Christians (*Didache* 8.1) and present day Ethiopian Christians (cf. the Friday abstinence in Eastern and Catholic churches) on the ground of the fast–feast cycle.

The difficulty in understanding the ultimate purpose and origin of fasting arises out of the complexities of understanding the religious world view. By its very nature, the religious world view contains an internal dichotomization or contradiction. It works like a pendulum that swings from one extreme end to the other about a central focal point. Is religion a system of divine obligation with service orientation (*relegare,* "to bind," following Lactantius) or the state of a reflective and contemplative relationship with the divine and a total detachment from the world (*relegere,* "to gather," following Cicero)?

Whichever it is, religion has a force which, at one end of the pendulum, can divine the realm of phenomena into two mutually irreducible polar elements, such as the division of reality into matter and mind with their attendant spacio-temporal and subsistence forms (metaphysical/ ontological dualism), or the division of the universe into two opposing forces or principles, one good and one evil (Zoroastrian/ cosmic dualism). At the other extreme, the force of religion can unite the sacred and the profane into one single reality or creator–creation, combining the laws of humanity and nature into one single harmonious principle (as in the Hebrew Bible and certain African monistic traditions.)

These positions are essentially variations on or expressions of the human attempt at understanding the world and ultimate reality: all of the great religions of the world manifest pendulating characteristics from one polarity to the other. But generally different religions tend to pull habitually toward one or the other end of the pendulum.

Hebraic and certain African traditional religions, including ancient Egyptian, are in general homo-socio-centric and put emphasis on the unity between the divinity and creation (the material world). They make little or no distinction between the sacred and the secular, but this is not to be confused with pantheistic thought. All things are sacred and all aspects of cultural and social life are permeated by religious ideas. On the other hand, Hindu/Buddhist and ancient Greek philosophical thought in general tend to divorce the sacred from the secular, the material world from the spiritual, unity being achieved either by the abnegation of matter or its absorption into the mind. For the former, the needs of both the soul and the body are spiritual, hence food and procreation are aspects of the religious panorama. The latter, however, idealize asceticism and regard animal food and procreation as inherently evil, if at all possible to be avoided.

Asceticism is based on the *a priori* assumption that sensuous, bodily, and worldly matters, contrasted with spiritual ones, are either non-real,[20] or the source of evil,[21] or simply evil itself.[22] Eastern asceticism teaches self-denial to achieve liberation from the body through spiritual life (*mokṣa*) ultimately ending in total freedom from worldly existence and rebirth in the knowledge of Brahma or through the annihilation of the passion which attracts *karma,* a subtle form of matter, to free the soul from bondage (Jainism). Western asceticism teaches liberation through the life of reason and philosophy (Plato); through an austere life (Neo-Platonism); or through a total repression of fleshly desires and renouncing the world through mental (*gnōsis*) and spiritual life (gnosticism).

From the point of view of biblical and certain African religions, material food is central to the physical and spiritual life equally. The future/life after death itself becomes an eternal banquet with God. From the point of view of Eastern religions, however, material food is secondary to human existence: for the essence of a person, the soul, does not need it. The end or ultimate goal of life is pure spiritual existence, a *nirvāṇa* or state of nonbeing.

Buddha considered the body evil, but rejected extreme asceticism. However, his idea of the renunciation of the world led his disciples directly into instituting various rules of fasting (more severe for the monks than for the laity). The Mahayana consider fasting as a means of rebirth in higher grades.[23] In the West, even before the time of Plato, the Pythagoreans of the sixth century BCE criticized excessive bodily desires and recommended their repression to free the soul in search of knowledge, or virtue, as the Cynics put it several centuries later.[24] The Dionysian or Orphic cults also taught the avoidance of animal food and practice of self-maceration.[25] It is interesting to note the irony whereby Epicureanism has come to be equated in popular minds with sensuous eating: in fact, "eat, drink, and be merry, for tomorrow you shall die" was an ascetic maxim.[26] Even the somewhat socially conscious Stoics were not free from elements of ascetic thinking. They too considered emotion an accomplice of what they termed "irrational desire"[27] (an idea that still plagues the Western mind). The maxim "Man is an alien in his own world" succinctly summarizes the antimaterialistic philosophy of life of the Hellenistic world.

The early church inherited the ascetic philosophy of life either directly through Greek philosophical ideas or indirectly from oriental religions through syncretistic Manichaeanism or Gnosticism. Many early church leaders like Athanasius,[28] Chrysostom,[29] Gregory of Nyssa,[30] Augustine,[31] and Ambrose,[32] considered bodily desire low and recommended its suppression as much as possible to achieve Christian virtues. Some of the heroes of the early church like Antony, the anchorite founder of Christian asceticism, Pachomius, the father of organized monasticism, Black Moses, and other desert monks believed that their way of life was good and virtuous and pleasing to God. The extremist Simeon the Stylite would rather sit on his desert pillar contemplating and enjoying the worms eating his wounds caused by the ropes by which he tormented himself rather than eating victuals himself.[33]

Fasting in the early church was no doubt associated with these early ascetic tendencies, and with the belief that it exalted the spiritual faculties at the expense of the lower bodily ones. In his treatise, *De jejuniis* (of Fasting) Tertullian propounded the ascetic concept that fasting originated in the command given by God in the Garden of Eden not to eat certain fruit trees: *Acceperunt Adam Deo legem non gustandi de arbore agnitionis boni et mali, moritūrus si gustasset. . . .* In reference to the fasting of forty days and forty nights by Jesus in the desert, when he was tempted by Satan to make bread from stone, Tertullian says: *Docuit etiam adversus diriora daemonia jejuniis praeliandum. . . .*[34] The fasting mentioned for catechumen by Justin Martyr (*Apol.* 2.93), Clement of Alexandria (*Strom.* 7.877), and Eusebius (*Hist. eccl.* 5.24) move along the same ascetic-penitential axis. The *Shepherd of Hermas* (3.5) advises the one who fasts to give an equal amount of the food abstained from to the poor widow or orphan, a meritorious action; however, he regards it still as nonvirtuous.

Asceticism has deep roots in Eastern and Hellenic religions, primarily because of their general leaning towards the negative (in respect to body and matter) pole of the religious pendulum. However, it does find its manifestation even in the Hebraic-biblical and African religious life. Biblical-Hebraic and certain African religious ideas incline toward the same negative point of the pendulum, inasmuch as Eastern and Hellenic thought also incline toward the positive pole. The Egyptian teaching against greed[35] and the biblical "man does not live by bread alone" (*Dt.* 8.3) are rather commonsensical and rational maxims of life, but some interpret them as manifestations of ascetic tendencies. Better examples of ascetic ideas are found in later Egyptian religious developments: the practice of the priests of Isis who, as Plutarch described, did not eat fish and garlic because they are "unnecessary and luxurious articles of diet" (*De Is. et Os.* 5ff.). Similarly, we learn from Apuleius, the Roman writer, in his moving description of the Mysteries of Isis, that abstinence from meat and wine and luxurious foods were part of the requirement for the initiates to mysteries (*Metam.* 11). Among the Jews, Samson (*Jgs.* 13.4, 7) and John the Baptist (*Mt.* 3.4) appear to have led ascetic lives at least to some degree.

The distant origin of fasting may certainly be found in the negative attitude toward the world, the philosophy that the body should not be pampered by food and drink and that all desires should be checked. Nevertheless, it is wrong to ascribe ascetic reasons only for fasting as it developed historically.

Biblical fasts (*som,* complete abstinence from food; *cn'a,* afflict oneself; or *anah nefesh,* afflict one's soul), whether private or public remain in fact nonascetic. They are connected with mourning (seven day fast for the death of Saul and Jonathan, *1 Sm.* 31.13; *2 Sm.* 1.12), prayers for compassion (David fasting for Bathsheba's first child, *2 Sm.* 12.16–23), wartime (*1 Sm.* 14.24; *Jgs.* 20.26; *2 Chr.* 20.3), or penitence (repentance for Ninevites, *Lk.* 11.32; of Israel, *Jl.* 2.12–13). We have also considered above the fasts for rain. There are also fasts associated with divine revelation (Moses receiving the law, *Ex.* 34.28; Saul meeting the soul of Samuel, *1 Sm.* 28.30). The fixed public fasts are described as meritorious and pious disciplines, particularly such observances as Yom Kippur and the Monday and Thursday fasts of later times (*Ta'anit* 12a; *Mt.* 6.16ff.; *Lk.* 8.12; *Didache* 8.1). There are also commemorative fasts connected with great national tragedy, including the averted ones (Av 9; Adar 13; fast of Esther: *Est.* 4.16). The nonascetic character of Jewish fasts is explicitly asserted in the command that the four yearly fasts (or the fourth, fifth, seventh, and tenth months) should be "a season of joy, gladness, and cheerful feasts" (*Zec.* 8.19; *Ta'anit* 2.1).[36]

Ethiopian church fasts, including Lent, should also be classified with the fasts of penitential, meritorious, disciplinary acts. The fasts of the *Didascalia,* like the fasts promulgated in the *Fetha Nagast*[37] and incorporated into the Ethiopian church calendar, are directly related to the nonascetic biblical, Jewish, and early church fasts in respect to their origin. Like these biblical, Jewish, and early church fasts, they are rooted in the desire for meritorious living, a position consistent with the ethical emphasis of the Hebrew Bible, rather than in the idea of true bodily mortification.

To be sure, various theological expositions and even some official church declarations present a rather ascetic rationale for fasting. One such exposition declares:

> The Church, in her earliest days, recognized the necessity of her children to "chastise the body and bring it under subjection," as St. Paul advises. The body is ever striving for mastery over the spirit; besides the external sources of temptation, "the world," we have always another source with us which is a part of our nature. This is the reason for mortification. Self-denial in lawful things enables us to turn with great earnestness to spiritual things. It is on these grounds that the Ethiopian Church has strictly adhered to the injunctions of the *Didascalia* and enjoined on the faithful the longest and most austere fasts in the world.[38]

Obviously, this is a simple statement of the ascetic position; and in some sense it does agree with certain ideas in the New Testament (*1 Thes.* 5. 22; *1 Pt.* 2.11).

Nevertheless, with the exception of the fasting habits of the hermitical *bahtawi* (loners) there is little, if any, ascetic feature to Ethiopian fasting. The *bahtawi* of Ethiopia are the true modern heirs of ancient Christian ascetics. As their name designates, they live alone in remote forests or deserts. They hardly eat the normal daily quantity of food, but occasionally feed on small amounts of wild herbs, nuts, and plants.[39]

The Ethiopic *Didascalia (the Apostolic Constitution),* the authority cited in the above quotation, does not, in fact, present the ascetic rationale of fasting. On the contrary, it explicitly teaches a penitential form of fasting with the assertion, "And let them examine the one who has sinned and if he would abandon his evil way and confess his sins and repent, let them bring him into the church and command him to fast in accordance to the degree of the sins that he had committed: two weeks, or three weeks, or five weeks, or seven weeks."[40] In the same work, little, if any, consideration is given to the fasts that have been ordained for Wednesday and Friday, the fourth and the sixth days of the week, the days Jesus was arrested and crucified respectively, as explained in the *Didascalia.*[41] The only semblance of an ascetic rationale of fasting in the *Didascalia* is in the prohibition to fast on the Sabbaths, an implication that one should not retreat from bodily pleasure (feasting) to bodily mortification (fasting) on days of joy.

Ethiopian fasting varies in rigor from the most severe ones during Passion Week to the lighter Christmas fast. In either case, they are the most rigorous fasts known in any Christian church.[42] Those who observe fasting must in all cases abstain from drinking milk, eating dairy products, eggs, meats, and all animal food; smoking is generally prohibited, but beer and wine may be consumed in moderation. All cereals, vegetables, fruits, and dry foods are allowed; fish, not known to be such a common food in Ethiopia, may also be eaten.

The rules of fasting in the Ethiopian church do not only involve abstinence from eating certain foods, but also total fasts during certain periods. Thus, no meal may be eaten, particularly the clergy and the very pious, before the conclusion of church services on fasting days, that is, about three o'clock in the afternoon. Because it is a very long season (fifty-six days), Lent, one fast that is almost universally observed by Ethiopian Christians, allows those who fast to have breakfast on Saturdays and Sundays after nine o'clock in the morning. During the period following it, from Easter-Passover to Pentecost (fifty days), the Wednesday to Friday fasts are abrogated. It should also be noted that important Christian festivals such as Christmas, Timqat (Baptism-Epiphany), and the like supersede the Wednesday to Friday fasts if they happen to fall on those particular days. The strictness with which one keeps fasting varies of course from one individual to the other; whereas strictness and faithfulness are unequivocally expected from the clergy as their total duty and exemplary responsibility, these are left as matter of conscience and reputation for the laity.

The most staggering fact about Ethiopian fasting is the sheer number of days that are prescribed for it; about 250 days for the clergy (priests, deacons, and church officials, but particularly monks and nuns) and about 180 days for the laity, that is, all adults above the age of thirteen. In other words, there are more fast days than normal food consumption days during the year.[43] The obligatory days of fastings do not still take into account the number of days of private penitential fasts (from seven to forty days, or even one year), the fasting of bishops at their installations, not to mention the perennial ascetic fasts of the *bahtawi.*

The question has been raised whether seasons of famine and the scarcity of food might have contributed to the rise and development of fasting. Historically, we find little evidence to substantiate such a contention. In the New Testament, Paul twice uses the *nesteuō, nesteia* (the common expression for fasting in the Septuagint and the New Testament) in the sense of hunger, perhaps implying possible fasting because of the lack of food (2 *Cor.* 6.5, 11.27). According to *Genesis* (41.46–57), in times of plenty food should be set aside for the periods of famine; but we do not know whether people had to fast to save food, or to abstain from eating certain foods for such purposes. Additionally, our records are silent about any relationship between fasting and obesity in the historic past.

Whatever the religious merits of fasting may be, its disciplinary value for eating in the present day should not be dismissed out of hand. Questions are being continually raised about what can be done regarding world food shortage. Moreover, the possible bio-psychological value of fasts for those who suffer from overeating and obesity should not be underestimated. Naturally, above everything, the importance of the health of the person who fasts is of paramount importance. But it seems that recent scientific opinions are no longer so certain about the absolute value of eating fats and animal products as they used to be as recently as twenty years ago.

In Ethiopia, the eating habits of the people and their nutritional status is affected by the custom of fasting in a very decisive way. The studies available to us do not prove in any way that the health of the people is affected adversely by the bio-cultural phenomenon of fasting. It does appear that suckling infants may be getting less adequate calories and other nutrients that animal food provide, since their mothers do not have available to them a full diet, even though they themselves, like pregnant women, are not required to fast.[44]

In general, Ethiopian fasting foods consisting of cereals, legumes, potatoes, kale, fenugreek, safflower, oilseeds, sunflower, flax, nug (niger), mustard, and other allowed foods and drinks like *tala* (beer) and *tai* seem to provide a broad and not unhealthy menu. Indeed some modern nutritional experts can possibly learn something from the Ethiopian experience, since as a rule the Ethiopians are not an obese people.

For Ethiopia itself, a country where famine was so recently ravaging the land and where agricultural methods are being slowly updated, fasting, if done under proper medical supervision, may turn out to be not only of religious but also of biological and economic benefit. It can be a means of controlling the excessive consumption of food. Already fasting does subconsciously serve as a type of check and balance in food consumption in a society in which people also engage in numerous weekly, monthly, and yearly festivals of feasts.[45] Where such a large number of people abstain from the rarer foods for so many days of the year, the days of fasting outnumbering the days of indulgence, there are obviously other economic and biological benefits. Imagine the number of cattle, sheep, and goats (the permitted animals), as well as chickens, which rest during the greater portion of the year, and can multiply to replenish the species instead of being slaughtered ceaselessly with adverse economic effect.

NOTES

1. See H. Frankfort, *Kingship and the Gods* (Chicago: University of Chicago Press, 1948), chapter 2; and K. Sethe, *Dramatische Texte zu alteaegyptischen Mysterienspielen* (Leipzig, 1928), pp. 1ff.
2. S. Morenz, *Egyptian Religion,* trans. A. E. Keep (Ithaca: Cornell University Press, 1960), pp. 183ff.
3. *Ancient Egyptian Literature,* trans. M. Lichtheim (Berkeley: University of California Press, 1973), 1:66, 43, 55.
4. *Works and Days,* trans. H. G. Evelyn-White, Loeb Classical Library (Cambridge: Harvard University Press, 1926). Some esteem for farmers is evident later at least in the writings of Euripides, Aristophanes, and Xenophones. However, Robert Schlaifer claims that "the prejudice against workers, which had arisen first in the states ruled by exploiting aristocracies, where it extended to all forms of manual labor, had in the other states of Greece, although restricted to banausic occupations, spread so rapidly during the fifth century that by 400 B.C. it was and remained universal." *Harvard Studies in Classical Philology* 47 (1936):171–176.

   In both biblical and later Judaism all classes of labor were ascribed a high measure of dignity (*Avot* 1.10, 3.18, 4.3). But the story of Cain's descendants (*Gn.* 4.16–22) hints that probably it was once believed that, unlike agriculture which the Creator had taught humans, other types of industrial and commercial works were taught by fallen angels (*Gn.* 4.17–22). The Ethiopic *Apocalypse of Enoch* states that Azazel, the leader of the fallen angels taught people "the arts of making swords and knives, shields and breastplates; and he showed to their chosen ones the art of making bracelets, decorations, the shadowing of the eye with antimony, ornamentation, the beautifying of the eyelids, all types of precious stones, all coloring tinctures, and alchemy" (8.1; translation mine).

5. C. R. Hallpike, *The Konso of Ethiopia* (Oxford: Oxford University Press, 1972), pp. 291f. This anthropologist's contention that "[a] link between beer, women, and fertility is provided by the concept of menstrual blood" and that "beer is red except for a small amount made from white millet) . . ." is rather an exaggeration. Of course, beer does have a religious ritual function in many cultures—for example, the ancient Sumerians' beer-brewing goddess Ninkasi, known also as "the lady who fills the mouth." But the link is not in the color of beer. Louis F. Hartman and A. L. Oppenheim, "On Beer and Brewing Technques in Ancient Mesopotamia," *Journal of the American Oriental Society* 70 (1950): Supplement 10.
6. *Masob* in Ge'ez or classical Ethiopic from the root *wasaba,* to double, to combine, or to unite, which I prefer to *sawaba,* to make round; but cf. Aramaic *s-b-b,* to go around, turn, as root for to recline for eating; *Ber.* 6.6; *Pes.* 10.1; *Prv.* 26.15; *Mk.* 7.8, 14.20.
7. E. E. Evans-Pritchard, *Nuer Religion* (Oxford: Oxford University Press, 1956), pp. 248ff.
8. J. Jeremias, *The Proclamation of Jesus,* trans. J. Bowden (New York: Charles Scribner's Sons, 1971), pp. 1ff. Cf. also Hans-Josef Klauck "Lord's Supper," trans. D. Ewert, *Anchor Bible Dictionary,* ed. D. N. Freedman (New York: Doubleday, 1992), 4:362ff.
9. E. Isaac, *A New Text-Critical Introduction to Maṣḥafa Berhan: With a translation of Book 1,* (Leiden: E. J. Brill, 1973), pp. 45ff.
10. E. E. Evans-Pritchard, *Nuer,* p. 125.
11. Hallpike, *Konso,* pp. 23f.
12. This is part of the theme in H. Spencer's *The Principles of Sociology* (New York: D. Appleton, 1882), vol. 1.
13. E. B. Tylor, *Primitive Culture: Researches into the Development of Mythology, Philosophy, Religion, Language, Art and Custom,* 3d ed. (London: J. Murray, 1891), vol. 1.
14. L. Lévy-Bruhl, *Primitive Mentality,* trans. L. A. Clare (London: George Allen & Unwin Ltd., 1923), pp. 162ff.
15. *Kebra Nagast: Die Herrlichkeit der Könige,* Ethiopic text, ed. C. Bezold (München: G. Franz, 1905), p. 25.
16. This is a major theme developed by W. Robertson Smith, *The Religion of the Semites: The Fundamental Institutions* (New York: Meridian Books, 1956; originally published 1889).
17. See O. Neugebauer, *Ethiopic Astronomy and Computus* (Vienna: Verlag der Osterreichischen Akademie der Wissenschaften, 1979), pp. 9, 45ff., 135, 147–149.
18. G. van der Leeuw, *Religion in Essence and Manifestation* (New York: Harper and Row, 1963), 2:388ff.
19. Participation in the Christian Eucharist in both the Eastern and Roman Catholic churches is preceded by a fast, although this rule is thought by some to have been instituted only after the fourth century. Cf. T. F. Angelin, *The Eucharistic Fast* (Washington, D.C.: Catholic University Press, 1941).

20. In the Vendanta thought *maya* (illusion, unreality) is the material cause of the universe. *The Upaniṣads,* ed. and trans. Swami Nikhilananda (London: George Allen & Unwin, 1953), pp. 40ff., 43, 126; H. Zimmer, *Philosophies of India* (Cleveland: The World Publishing Co., 1951), pp. 19, 27, 111ff.; *Krishna: Myths, Rites, and Attitudes,* ed. M. Singer (Honolulu: East-West Center Press, [1966]), pp. 7, 47–56, 189. Cf. also the Platonic theory of forms, *Republic,* trans. F. M. Cornford (Oxford: Oxford University Press, 1945), pp. 506ff.; *Symposium,* trans. W.R.M. Lamb, Loeb Classical Library (Cambridge: Harvard University Press, 1924), pp. 201ff.; *Timaeus,* trans. F. M. Cornford, in *Plato's Cosmology* (New York: Harcourt, Brace, 1937), p. 51.
21. So in Neo-Platonic thought. See *Enneads,* trans. G. H. Turnbull, in *The Essence of Plotinus* (New York: Longmans, 1934), 3.12–15, 5.9, 7.16.
22. So in Gnosticism. See Irenaeus of Lyons, *Adversus haereses,* ed. W. W. Harvey (Cambridge: Cambridge University Press, 1857), 1.24.1; Tertullian, *De carne,* 5; *Corpus Hermeticum,* eds. A. D. Nock and A. J. Festugière, 2 vols. (Paris: Sociète d'edition "Les Belles Letters," 1960), 6:4; *The Paraphrase of Shem,* trans. F. Wisse, in *The Nag Hammadi Library,* ed. J. M. Robinson, rev. ed. (San Francisco: HarperSanFrancisco, 1988), 7:1ff.
23. Cf. *Buddhist Scriptures,* trans. E. Conze (London: Penguin Books, 1959), pp. 105, 123.
24. Diogenes Laertius, *The Life of Pythagoras,* trans. R. D. Hicks, Loeb Classical Library (Cambridge: Harvard University Press, Cambridge, 1924), 5; 8.30; W.K.C. Gutherie, *Orpheus and Greek Religion* (New York: Norton, 1966), p. 200.
25. Jane Harrison, *Prolegomena to the Study of Greek Religion* (Cambridge: Cambridge University Press, 1908), pp. 454ff., 473ff.
26. Letter to Menoeceus, trans. C. Bailey, in *Epicurus: the Extant Remains* (Oxford: Oxford University Press, 1926), pp. 127ff.
27. Epictetus, *Discourse,* trans. G. Long (New York: U.S. Book Co., n.d.), pp. 20f., 144, 147; Cicero, *De Finibus,* trans. H. Rackham, Loeb Classical Library (Cambridge: Harvard University Press, 1914), 4:21ff.; 2:45ff.
28. See his works the *Life of St. Antony* and *Letters to the Monk Amun.*
29. Ivo Auf der Maur, *Mònchtum und Glaubensverkündigung in den Schriften des hl. Johannes Chrysostomos* (Freibourg: Schwiz Universitäts Verlag, 1959).
30. *Gregory of Nyssa: Ascetical Works* (Washington, D.C.: Catholic University Press, 1967).
31. Although there are no specific works on asceticism that I am aware of, his writings such as the *Confessions* (8.10.13), *Libero arbitrio* (2.3.8), and others have ascetic statements.
32. See his *De officiis, De viduis,* and others; but most of his ascetical writings focus on sexual asceticism or virginity.
33. P. Resch, *La Doctorine ascétique des premieres maîtres Egyptiens du guatrième siècle* (Paris: Beauchesne, 1931); Marcel Viller, *Askese und Mystic in der Väterzeit,* rev. and trans. K. Rahner (Freiburg im Breisgau: Herder, 1939); H. von Campenhausen, *Die Askese im Urchristentum* (Tübingen: J.C.B. Mohr, 1949).
34. J. Schummer, *Die altchristliche Fastenpraxis, mit besonderer Berücksichtigung der Schriften Tertullians* (Münster: Aschendorff, 1933).
35. "Do not be greedy in the division, Do not covet more than your share . . ." or "Be generous as long as you live, What leaves the storehouse does not return; It is the food to be shared which is coveted. . . ." *Ancient Egyptian Literature* 1:69, 72.
36. The Islamic fasts, including Ramadan (thirty days, Q. 2.180ff.) and the pilgrim's fasts (three and seven days respectively going and returning, Q. 2.193) and the fasts of oath-

breakers and murderers (Q. 5.91, 4.94) would fall into the category of nonascetic fasts. Cf. also K. Wagtendonk, *Fasting in the Koran* (Leiden: E. J. Brill, 1968).

37. *Il Fetha Nagast,* ed. and Italian trans. by I. Guidi, 2 vols. (Rome, 1897, 1899), 1:15. Cf. also *Corpus Juris Abessinorum Textum Aethiopicum Arabicumque ad Manuscriptorum Fidem cum Versione Latina,* ed. J. Bachmann (Berlin: F. Schneider & Co., 1889).
38. Aymro Wondemagegnehu & Joachim Motovu, eds., *The Ethiopian Orthodox Church* (Addis Ababa: Ethiopian Orthodox Church Mission, 1970), p. 63.
39. It is interesting that it was an Ethiopian *bahtawi* Gabra Krestos or Abdul Masih as he is called in Egypt, a troglodyte (cave-dweller) of the Libyan desert, who led the ascetic revival in the contemporary Egyptian church. This has been reported in the Egyptian press widely, but I learned the story from the older monks of the Ethiopian Orthodox church in Jerusalem who knew him personally. Abdul Masih lived there for many years before he left for the Egyptian desert, where he became a popular ascetic role model. I was also told that among his followers or those he inspired is Pope Shinuda, the present patriarch of the Coptic church.
40. My translation from the text of *The Ethiopic Didascalia, or the Ethiopic version of the Apostolical Constitutions, Received by the Church of Abyssinia,* ed. Thomas Pell Platt (London: Oriental Translation Fund of Great Britain, 1834), p. 36. Cf. also J. M. Harden, *The Ethiopic Didascalia* (London: Society for the Promoting of Christian Knowledge, 1920), p. 29.
41. J. M. Harden, op. cit., pp. 127, 136.
42. One of the reasons for the Western Christian missionaries' criticism of the Ethiopian church is its tradition of fasts. These missionaries felt that the church put too much emphasis on deeds rather than on faith.
43. It should, however, be noted that the number of feast days is also as high as the number of fast days. Not to mention Saturday and Sunday and the great feast days of St. John or the New Year (about September 11), Feast of Masqal or the Holy Cross (about September 27), Temqat or Holy Baptism/Epiphany (about January 19), Fasika/Pesaḥ or Tensa'e/Resurrection/Easter (early spring), there are monthly feasts of protective angels and patron saints—Abbo (5th day of the Ethiopian month), Sellasse/Trinity (7th), Michael (12th), Raphael (13th), Kidana Mehrat/Covenant of Mercy/Mary (16th), Gabriel (19th), St Mary (21st), St George (23rd), Savior of the World (27th), Egzi'abher/Lord (29th). There is a rhythmic relationship between fasts and feasts.
44. K. E Knutsson and R. Selinus, "Fasting in Ethiopia," *The American Journal of Clinical Nutrition* 23 (1970):956–969.
45. Ibid.

24

Simeon the New Theologian: An Ascetical Theology for Middle-Byzantine Monks

Gregory Collins

In the life and teaching of Simeon the New Theologian (949–1022), Byzantine ascetical and mystical theology achieved its most intense penetration of the Christian Mystery.[1] Simeon wrote at a time when the Byzantine church was relatively free of dogmatic disputes and doctrinal conflicts.[2] The great Trinitarian and Christological debates of the late patristic era, although a constant source of interest in Byzantine religious life, had long since ceased to divide the "Great Church." Belief had crystallized and hardened into dogmatic definitions and conciliar formulations and an identifiable "Orthodox" identity had emerged in the Byzantine church. In dogmatic theology, the Cappadocian model of the Trinity reigned supreme; in Christology, the Chalcedonian dyophysite understanding of Christ, interpreted in an Alexandrian way, stressed the unity of the two natures in the person of the Incarnate Word. It provided a high Christology of redemption through deification.[3] The synthesis of these traditions, a blend of Alexandria, Antioch and Rome, had been achieved by John of Damascus in his work, "On the Orthodox Faith."[4] It was a faith that was still common to both branches of the Great Church, Latin and Greek, for despite the initial rumblings over the Nicene Creed's "Filioque" in the Carolingian period, the unity of the church was as yet unsundered.[5] Orthodoxy presented a coherent, confident and intelligible faith content that was heir to the best of the late antique philosophical heritage and the tradition of the fathers.

This was not simply a cerebral or intellectual system. On the contrary, Byzantine Christianity also acknowledged the centrality of the aesthetic as a theological category. As a result of the victory of the iconodules in the prolonged disputes over icons, the image had been enshrined at the heart of theology and piety.[6] In addition, worship itself—the never-to-be-forgotten context of all patristic or Byzantine theological reflection—was understood increasingly within this aesthetic and iconographic ethos.[7] Such was the climate in which Simeon elaborated his understanding of the ascetical life for the Byzantine monastic world in Constantinople.

It was not only the dogmatic, liturgical and iconographic traditions of Byzantium, however, that had developed and become systematized. The ascetical and mystical tradition, too—a tradition closely aligned with monasticism—had also achieved a set form. There was general agreement on the sources, goals and structures of monastic life.

Sources

For the middle Byzantine period, the Egyptian and Syrian monastic heritage remained normative. Transmitted in the many florilegia, anthologies, paterika, and collections of apophthegmatic wisdom so beloved of Byzantine monks, it was this desert tradition that set the agenda and defined the goals for Byzantine ascetics.[8] Antony, Arsenius, and the other heroes of the desert represented the hesychastic tradition, which was not simply some esoteric movement that later prevailed at Mount Athos but was the very life breath of the original monastic impulse.[9] By its emphasis on silence, solitude, withdrawal, meditation and incessant prayer, obedience to a spiritual father, and purity of heart, the desert literature served as a continual reminder to the monastic movement that its real ends were not social, economic or political, but ultimately eschatological. The same is equally true for the monastic movements of the West.[10] It is impossible to grasp the significance of asceticism in Byzantine society if this maximalist mentality is not understood.

Goals

St. John Climacus had defined the Christian in his "Ladder of Divine Ascent" as one who imitates Christ,[11] and St. Maximus the Confessor had explained that practical charity expressed through the service of others was the path through which this could be achieved.[12] There were, however, several interpretations of the ultimate goal of the Christian ascetic life. Those of a less speculative bent might define it as the memory of God, whether in eremitic or cenobitic life.[13] Others, in the tradition of Evagrius, might see it as a life of inner prayer, in which prayer is identified with a contemplative state, free of images and ideas, a movement into the purified mind, to contemplate the light of the Godhead.[14] Others again could see it in terms of the theories proposed by Gregory of Nyssa, and the anonymous writer of the so-called Macarian homilies.[15] For these two, the goal of the ascetic life was a mystical union with God through a kind of inner affectivity, a purified and refined sensorium for the divine.[16] This might be understood in either a Gregorian or a Macarian way. For the former, the mind is carried beyond itself, through ecstasy, into a dark communion with the unknowable Godhead that floods the senses of the soul with experience of its presence. For the latter, the heart is fixed in experience of the divine indwelling, at the core of itself. Each of these traditions was to receive further refinements and additions in the reflections of succeeding writers, and in practice, they tended to intermingle and to coalesce.[17]

St. Maximus, in particular, was to inject a fresh transfusion of Christian life into the emerging system. As an Aristotelian, he emphasized the reality of created nature, and the efficacy of secondary causality;[18] as a Chalcedonian theologian he insisted that the Incarnate Word must be at the centre of all piety; and as a monk, he taught clearly the primacy of charity in the pursuit of the Christian ideal. However, despite the nuances, the basic unity was assured by the time of Simeon, so that one can really talk of an Orthodox ascetical and mystical tradition rather than merely outline different traditions, or streams of thought.

Structures

The common heritage passed on from the desert ensured that the modes of ascetic endeavour were also matters of agreement by the beginning of the eleventh century. Climacus again set out how ascetic lifestyles could be organized,[19] but there were a multitude of ways in which individual ascetical behaviour could find expression.[20] It is worth observing that while later Byzantine monasticism, in its organized forms, might look askance at the diversity of monastic life in the Western world,[21] in its individual expressions it was always open to personal needs and even idiosyncrasies.

Within its organized forms, however, there were basically the three possibilities outlined by Climacus. There was the pure eremetical tradition, with its quest for solitude.[22] There was the regular life of the *koinobion,* a form of life that reached its greatest development at Constantinople and on Mount Athos at, and after, the time of Simeon.[22] In these monasteries work, common prayer and service to the community kept alive the reality of communion at the heart of the church.[23] Finally there was the life of the small group, whether one defines it as semieremitical, or semicenobitic.

Either way, it is forced and artificial to insist upon too strong a contrast between hesychastic and cenobitic modes of life. *Hēsychia* was not only a physical state, but an inner attitude. There was a tradition of inner and unceasing prayer in the great communal houses, as well as in the hesychasteria.[24] Indeed, it is quite wrong to identify the cenobitic house as the home of *praxis,* and the hermitage as the place of *thēoria.* In each of the lives, there was a *praxis* and a *thēoria* appropriate to each, and *hēsychia,* as purity of heart, was demanded in the common life, as much as in the cell of the recluse. There would not be much monastic life at all, if this fundamental attitude was missing, whether one was working in a Constantinopolitan monastic hospice, or practicing monologistic prayer as a hermit in Bithynia.[25] Simeon's works are a particularly valuable reminder that hesychasm is an interior value as much as an actual state of life.

There was agreement too on the basic ascetical practices that form and structure the monastic day, even if the intensity or quantity of these, (or their modality, as in the question of work) naturally varied, depending on whether the life was communal or solitary. Fasting, watching, long prayers (whether liturgical or private);[26] obedience; work; guarding of the mind; corporeal exercises (prostrations); celibacy: these were the practices designed to subjugate the flesh, calm the mind, and create inner space in the heart for union with God. Such has always been the Eastern

Christian manner of conceiving the Christian and monastic life, since Antony sought the silence of the desert, and since the "Sons of the Covenant" aimed at the maximum expression of their faith.[27] Such it is today in the Orthodox East. Such it was in eleventh-century Constantinople when the "New Theologian" preached asceticism to his monks.

Simeon brought three distinctive qualities to bear in his reception of this tradition. First he was a mystic and theologian whose keen intelligence was able to unite dogma and prayer in a compelling spiritual vision that was existential rather than merely theoretical and speculative.[28] Second, he had a refined spiritual sensibility, which favoured affective and imaginative language, the language of the heart rather than the intellect.[29] Third, like St. John of the Cross, he was a mystical poet, whose language tended naturally toward the hymn and the doxology; because of these three gifts his theology has a personal flavor that is almost unique in the Christian East. Simeon preached from his own experience, and witnessed to what he had seen.[30] Hence it is not always possible to infer that his experiences were normative for the Byzantine tradition. He was a mystical genius, and like all great men of the Spirit, he stands out from the tradition which produced him, while at the same time reflecting its concerns.[31]

That said, his works offer us a powerful theological vindication of Christian asceticism. They throw open a window upon the world of the Byzantine cloister, and allow us to penetrate the consciousness of one convinced ascetic, as he articulates principles that govern his *praxis* and unveils the experience to which they led.

In this paper I shall examine a central theme in Simeon's teaching. This theme is that of the personal experience of the paschal mystery through the practice of asceticism. It is central because the death and Resurrection of Christ is central in the Orthodox understanding of the Christian faith. Simeon, in his theology, shows how the Resurrection passes from the historical and liturgical dimensions into that of personal spiritual experience, in such a way that the ascetic participates in Christ's mysteries and makes them his own.

The Goal of Christian Asceticism: The Mystical Experience of the Resurrection

In his "Centuries" on the spiritual life, which are in some ways the most systematic expositions of his teaching, Simeon outlined the purpose of all Christian asceticism:[32] "There is a death before death, and a resurrection of souls before the resurrection of bodies. It is a fact, a power, an experience, a truth."[33] He describes there how the divine wisdom awakens the sleeping soul, which recognizes God as it awakes, and is carried away in love towards God. In the two preceding sentences, he presents ascetical activity as a crucifixion to the world, by means of which the monk becomes corpse-like in the face of its pleasures and allurements. Asceticism detaches the senses from the everyday world, without removing the monk from it, in order to allow inner sensation to blossom. The idea that one must lull, or even kill, the external senses to facilitate the growth of the spiritual senses had a long history in Eastern Christian monastic spirituality.[34] Simeon goes on to discuss the delicate problem of the relation between human effort and divine grace.

> There are the things which we contribute and there are the things given us from on high by God. To the extent that we are purified by holy toils and labours, we are illumined by the light, so are we purified in tears. On the one hand we bring our own resources, and on the other we receive the gift from on high.[35]

In the following section he discusses the problem of why spiritual experience does not necessarily happen, even when there has been great apparent purity of monastic observance. Presumably this was a difficulty that Simeon often faced when dealing with his monks. It cannot have been easy to live under such a maximalist *hēgoumenos* (monastic superior), who made few concessions to human weakness.[36] He stresses that impurity of intention such as lack of faith, or pride, makes ascetical observances unacceptable to God. Without humility, they are little better than the offering of Cain—and they will end in the same way.[37] It is clear that Simeon's main concern is with spiritual asceticism, and inner purity.[38] These "chapters" have helped us to outline the main features of his teaching:

1. There is an inner experience of the Resurrection. This comes about through the union of grace and human effort.
2. Not all ascetical activity is acceptable to God, but only asceticism that is based on humility. Hence it is important to know what humility is, and how to pursue it.

The Experience of the Resurrection

In his thirteenth catechetical instruction, preached during the paschal season, Simeon gives the fullest possible description of how the monk can participate in the Resurrection of Christ.[39] He begins by asserting the priority of inner activity over outer works. God, he says, sees the disposition with which a work is performed, and accepts it accordingly, even if it is less austere than that of works performed by other monks. It is the intention that really counts. Because of this, those who have not been so fervent as they might in Lent are not to become too discouraged. He has already launched into his main theme—that the Resurrection occurs in the heart of the monk. He enumerates the episodes of Christ's Passion, death, and exaltation. But he insists that it is not sufficient to accept these as historical occurences, or even simply to believe in them in a formal or detached way. Like Paul, he had little interest in knowing Christ after the flesh.[40] Rather, these mysteries were undergone by Christ, precisely so that the believer could enter them through faith, a lively faith vivified by works,[41] and thus participate mystically in them. As a result of the *sacrum commercium* of the Incarnation, all that belongs to Christ is to be communicated to his faithful followers. But how is this to happen? We have already seen that asceticism is to make the monk like a living corpse, but here Simeon is even more explicit. The body becomes like a tomb in which the soul experiences the Resurrection:

> But if you will, let us look and examine carefully what is the mystery of that resurrection of Christ our God which takes place mystically in us at all times, if we are willing, and how Christ is buried in us as in a tomb and how he unites himself to our souls, and rises again and raises us with himself.[42]

Simeon invokes the liturgical worship of the church to justify this, pointing to the *semeron/hodie* principle which is found in all the historic rites of Christendom. In this case he points to the text from the Byzantine office that proclaims, "Having beheld the resurrection of Christ," rather than, "Having believed." It is a matter of experience, an experience of direct illumination by the Holy Spirit, "For the light-bringing coming of the Spirit shows forth to us as in early morning, the Master's resurrection, or rather it grants us to see the risen one himself."[43] The Trinitarian structure of mystical experience is here assumed. Elsewhere he insisted that all illumination is always an experience of the Three-in-one: the Father as Source, and the Logos and Pneuma as his manifesting messengers. Simeon's theology is strongly biblical and traditional, in its emphasis on the action of the economic Trinity.[44] Here too it terminates in the One who is the Source of all things:

> When this happens to us through the Spirit, he raises us up from the dead and gives us life. He grants us to see him who is immortal and indestructible . . . to know him who raises us up and glorifies us with himself as all the divine scriptures testify.[45]

Such, then, is the spiritual logic of the discourse. Living faith, that reveals itself in works accomplishes the work of ascetic detachment. In response, God awakens the heart through the illumination of the Spirit, and inner perception.[46] The coming of this knowledge is the simultaneous experience of Christ rising in the soul and of his leading the ascetic to the vision of God. Moreover, Christ himself, by the Spirit, creates the inner sensorium that enables the soul to receive this knowledge, for "Those to whom Christ has given light as he has risen, to them he has appeared spiritually, he has been shown to their spiritual eyes."[47] The whole of Simeon's theology, hinging as it does on illumination by the Spirit, spiritual sensation, and communion with the Trinity, is present in this paschal homily. Since however, the initial step, and constant foundation is ascetical activity, we must give further consideration to the content and meaning of asceticism.

The Asceticism of the Beatitudes

In the second catechetical discourse, Simeon presented his ascetical teaching in the context of a meditation on the Beatitudes as the basic manifesto of the Christian life.[47] It begins with the strongest possible ascetical exhortation: "Whoever desires to find God, let him deny himself. . . ."[48] It goes on to counsel any of his monks who may be experiencing tedium or disappointment in the ascetical struggle:

> Reject the thought that suggests to you, "Why must you endure so much trouble, such untimely wretchedness? You have already spent a year, two or three at it, and have found no profit in it. My brother be not trapped by this snare, nor betray your own salvation! Rather press on with greater zeal and courage, in the practice of the virtues. . . ."[49]

He presents the image of the suffering Christ as the best motive for continuing the fight. Asceticism must be driven by the sense of Christ—what he elsewhere calls, in technical terminology, "the memory of Christ"[50]—if it is not to run out of steam. Christ is the substitute for all that the ascetic has abandoned. However, it is necessary to have a true understanding of who Christ really is.

> Christ—as you hear this, do not heed the simplicity of the word, or the brevity of the expression. Rather, join with me in thinking of the glory of the Godhead which is beyond thought and understanding.[51]

But as usual, his intention is not simply to excite the emotions and affections of his hearers. He wants to move them to follow Christ, and to reproduce the pattern of his life. He wants them to hasten to meet him, ". . . to find Christ and see him as he is, in his beauty and attractiveness."[52]

For Simeon, this beauty is most revealed in the Cross. He was captivated by the *kenōsis* (self-emptying) of Christ: his voluntary self-abasement in the economy of salvation. He confesses that he is at a loss for words in the presence of this mystery. The usual human response to misery and degradation is to avert the eyes and pass by on the other side of the road, but the Son of God freely elected to enter such conditions in order to assert his solidarity with suffering mankind, ". . . to become the father, the friend the brother of those rejected ones."[53] Such ineffable goodness calls forth the exclamation: "What stupendous riches of his great goodness! What an ineffable condescension on the part of our Master and our God!"[54]

Faced with this unconditional kenotic love, the only worthy response can be to return love in kind. Hence the love of Christ induces love in those who choose to follow him. This means that kenotic love is demanded of the disciple. It is not one path among others, but the very essence of the Christian way. In the light of this, the self-abandonment of the monk cannot be seen as solipsism, or selfishness. Byzantine monasticism was, in fact, usually aware of its responsibilities to society at large. Despite the rhetoric of separation from the world, it was in constant contact with it at the level of intercession, guidance, and the provision of welfare.[55]

Simeon knew well that the world is better defined as a set of attitudes, than things and places.[56] Hence, it is in this light that he presents the Beatitudes as a program for following Christ. They are not simply moral directives given to ensure a correct standard of behavior, nor are they promises to be fulfilled only in the next world. On the contrary they represent an inaugurated eschatology, which is made known through ascetical behavior and mystical perception. The Kingdom of God is to come in this life, by the living of the Beatitudes; by practicing them, the seal[57] of the Spirit, long obscured by sin, is to be revealed, and baptismal grace is to be made active.

Simeon comments on each of the Beatitudes and shows how this seal is to be manifested. The first is that of poverty freely chosen for the sake of the Kingdom. Like modern biblical scholars, he was not deceived by the words poor in spirit, into believing that this Beatitude counseled only an interior attitude of poverty, without reference to actual dispossession.[58] His asceticism demanded both realities: actual lack of possessions and inner freedom from desiring them. Only in this way can the perception of the Kingdom in inner experience be assured and realized.[59] Given the opulence and decadence of many Byzantine communities in this period, it is clear that Simeon was adopting a consciously prophetic role in witnessing to the need for real poverty.[60] He demanded a complete renunciation of soft living, wealth, and worldiness. The real proof that the ascetic has achieved such poverty comes when actual revulsion for the visible world is felt.

This immediately presents a problem, since the next Beatitude praises those who mourn! However, how can one mourn if one is no longer attached to things? Simeon interprets the Lord's instruction in two ways. Naturally, he hears it from within the classical monastic tradition of the East, which had a whole literature on the virtue of *penthos* and its place in monastic life. The core of this tradition was that the ascetic mourned not for the sufferings of the Lord, nor for his own, but chiefly out of concern for his salvation.[61] *Penthos* came from the realization that one's sins were liable to exclude one from the kingdom of God for ever. Simeon, however, adds a peculiar and subtle nuance of his own, one that is very important in understanding his teaching on humility and grace. What he says deserves to be quoted in full:

> When the faithful man who always pays strict attention to the commandments of God, performs all that the divine commandments enjoin, and directs his mind toward their sublimity, that is, to a conduct and purity that are above reproach, he will discover his own limitations. He will find that he is weak and lacks the power to attain to the height of the commandments, indeed that he is very poor, that is, unworthy to receive God and give him thanks and glory, since he has as yet failed to attain any good of his own.[62]

Simeon emphasizes here an essential trait of any asceticism that dares to call itself Christian. It is not heroic effort that gives access to God but precisely the opposite. In failing to live up to the supreme commandment of love, the monk realizes existentially that he is a sinner, and realizes further that this consciousness in itself is the very thing that opens up the treasury of God's mercy.

The words of Dom André Louf, a modern monastic author, himself a great master in the lived tradition that Simeon represents, can serve as a lucid commentary here:

> Asceticism can be reduced to an entirely human effort at generosity. It ends then in a Spartan or Nietzschean kind of straitness, where all the disposable energies are put at the service of a sought ideal. In such a context, asceticism can nourish only a more or less subtle pride . . . by his asceticism, the monk does not so much test his own strength as learn by experience that, since it is marked by sin, it will constantly let him down . . . all ascetic effort will lead him, with only brief respites, to a death-point where the old man in him will refuse to concur, and will collapse before what it sadly feels to be impossible and absolutely beyond its strength. Monastic asceticism

> is then an asceticism of the poor. It drives the monk in his weakness and his sin into a corner, while throwing him back at the same moment into the arms of mercy and of the strength that God alone can grant him.[63]

Simeon handles this central paradox of the Christian faith with great subtlety. He sees that two consequences flow from it: "One who thus reasons with himself in the perception of his soul, will indeed mourn with that sorrow which is truly most blessed, which will receive comfort and make the soul meek."[64]

Thus humility is a permanent interior *epiclēsis* (invocation) that perpetually invokes the action of the Spirit on the heart. The descent of the Spirit in turn, leads to further communion with the mystery of the Trinity. It leads to the communication of wisdom, and the transformation of sorrow into joy. Moved by this experience the soul hungers and thirsts for justice. Anger is extinguished by the flood of spiritual tears, and the heart is progressively purified by this increase in gentleness and humility. Since purity of heart is the very condition of the vision of God, union with him follows as a natural consequence.[66] The fire thus lit in the soul is kept continually alight by the life of virtue, whose good works are the combustible material used by the Spirit for the inner fire.

The Final Goal

Simeon's ascetical practice and mystical experience of the Resurrection begins with an irreducibly personal and individual impulse. It cannot end there, however, if it be authentically Christian. The ever deepening experience of communion with the Father through perception of Christ, in the power of the Spirit, is a reality which is transforming in its social consequences. Through the ascetical uncovering of the seal of the Spirit and the primordial baptismal energies that lie latent in the heart, the monk allows the love of God to permeate his being and inundate his surroundings. The transforming virtues enumerated by Simeon are of a characteristically social nature: love of enemies and prayer for them, rejoicing in difficulties, seeing the faults of others as if they were one's own, and ultimately giving one's life for the brethren.[67] Ascetical *praxis* and mystical experience are thus never purely individualistic, for communion in the Trinity is the source that creates a new community—the community based on the Beatitudes. The cyclical nature of Christian asceticism is thus made evident. It ascends to communion with God through its voluntary imitation of the kenotic descent accomplished in the mystery of redemption, and in this paschal way, passes into transforming communion with the Spirit. Pascha, in the objective order of salvation history, must always lead to Pentecost; but Pentecost is the empowering of the Christian (and the monk, who is, in truth, only a representative Christian), for the creation of a new humanity that manifests itself through charity and goodness. For this Byzantine mystic, asceticism is the key that opens the heart to the action of the Spirit's grace, but the Spirit is the key that unlocks the bosom of God and the exalted Christ who rests upon it.[68]

This is not the final end, for that is an end without end. As Simeon says, asceticism and mysticism is the anticipation here below of what will come to perfect fruition in the hereafter. It is the pledge and promise of eternal life. To attain to this end, we are exhorted to hasten on the way:

> Let us run, let us pursue, until we have laid hold of something that is permanent and does not flow away . . . let us endeavour to find him who is present everywhere and when we have found him let us hold him fast and fall at his feet and embrace them in the fervour of our souls.[69]

In the anticipation of the future that ascetical activity promises, it is the vision of Christ in the power of the Spirit that calls us upwards:

> . . . let us endeavour to see him and contemplate him even in this life. For if we are found worthy sensibly to see him here, we shall not die . . . let us not wait to see him in the future, but strive to contemplate him now, since John the Theologian tells us, "We know that we have God in our hearts from the Spirit which we have received from him."[70]

This paper has been categorized with other papers under the theme "Aesthetics of Asceticism." This is most appropriate in discussing Byzantine ascetical theory in general, and that of Simeon in particular. The word *aisthēsis* has had a long and respected (if at times rather controversial) pedigree in the history of the spiritual traditions of the Christian East. In this concluding section I would like to suggest some reflections that flow from the aesthetic nature of Simeon's teaching. They can be presented in three theses.

1. Ascetical activity is a matter of experience, of an actual praxis which involves the performance of conscious activities in the Christian life. This is the logic of the Beatitudes, and it leads to purification of the heart by invoking the action of the Spirit. Thus there is a perfect harmony between divine grace and human activity. Naturally the priority falls upon the former; but it is the conscious activity of the latter that allows it to have free rein in the heart. Simeon and the tradition for which he stood represented a creative asceticism, in which one works at the divine art of refashioning his life in accordance with the paradigm which is the Incarnate Christ. It is the passage from the human being as defiled and defaced icon to the human being as the radiant likeness of Christ.[71]

2. In this transforming movement, there is a real *aisthēsis* in the soul, a spiritual experience that is analagous to the certainty and immediacy of sense perception, and this brings with it the experience of fullness in the heart, or *plērophoria.*[72] This is the gift of the creative Spirit who endows the soul with inner senses in response to its asceticism.[73] Thus the aesthetic of the ascetic is an interior feeling that results from the crucifixion of the senses through self-denial and radical conversion. Nothing could be more wrong than to imagine that Byzantine spirituality postulated a vague inner experience of sweetness and spiritual exuberance. It was as demanding as the most stark chapters of St. John of the Cross. There can be no inner *aisthēsis* without the most kenotic *askēsis*.

3. Finally, *aisthēsis* pertains to the world of form, to the totality that is received in the senses and that awakens the heart to the mystery of beauty, goodness, and

truth. Byzantine and modern Orthodox spirituality inherited and preserved this fundamentally Neo-Platonic optic, but transformed it from within. By baptizing it into the church and clothing it with the vesture of Christian monasticism, it allowed the light of Thabor, the transfiguring radiance so beloved of Eastern Christian mysticism, to penetrate it to its very depths. It attached it to the Crucified One, and in that way enabled it to undergo the passive purgation of the paschal mystery. The discovery of this Christian aesthetic, an aesthetic of the disfigured Christ as promise of the transfigured Christian, as a category in theology, is especially associated with the last half of our century.[74] But it was fully present in Byzantium and in Simeon, its greatest mystic. Imitation of Christ, and the way of the Beatitudes, leads to the reformation of the deformed heart in the "in-formation" of the senses of the soul, by the deifying grace of the Spirit. Hence, imitation passes through its paschal initiation to the Pentecostal perfection of the pure heart—itself the radiant image of the form of God, who humbled himself and came down. In this ascetical theology, there is a whole program for Christian and monastic life (a fundamentally Johannine program) as witness, through participation in, and manifestation of, the mystery of Christ. On the great night of the Pascha, the Greek church sings, "Come and receive light from the unquenchable light." Such is the ascetic—and aesthetic—vision of the New Theologian.

NOTES

1. For a useful introduction to Simeon's life and works, see B. Krivochéine, *Dans la lumière du Christ: Saint Syméon le Nouveau Théologien, 949–1022, vie, spiritualité, doctrine* (Chevetogne, 1980).
2. See J. Meyendorff, *The Byzantine Legacy in the Orthodox Church* (New York, 1982).
3. On "deification," see G. Mantzarides, *The Deification of Man, St. Gregory Palamas and the Orthodox Tradition* (New York, 1984).
4. For the Greek text, see Migne, *PG* 94.521–1228; there is an English translation by F. H. Chase, in the series *Fathers of the Church: Saint John of Damascus, Writings* (Washington, 1958).
5. See the recent work by A. Nichols, *Rome and the Eastern Churches* (Edinburgh, 1992), pp. 188–230.
6. Otto Demus, *Byzantine Mosaic Decoration* (London, 1947).
7. H. J. Schulz provides a masterful commentary in, *The Byzantine Liturgy* (New York, 1986).
8. The standard introduction to the subject of *florilegia* and *paterika* remains M. Richard, "Florilèges Grecs," *Dictionnaire de spiritualité* (Paris, 1964), 5.475–512.
9. On Hesychasm, see I. Hausherr, *The Name of Jesus* (Michigan, 1978) and, *La Méthode d'oraison hésychaste* (Rome, 1927). See also, "L'hésychasme: Étude de spiritualité," *Orientalia Christiana Periodica* 22 (1956):5–285.
10. See the comments by J. Winandy. "Benedictine Spirituality," in, *Some Schools of Catholic Spirituality*, ed. J. Gautier (New York, 1959), pp. 18–24. The whole monastic revival in the eleventh-century West (Cistercians, Carthusians, and Camaldolese) betrays this influence.
11. See *PG* 88; for an English translation, see, Lazarus Moore, *Saint John Climacus, The Ladder of Divine Ascent* (London, 1959).
12. The basic texts are in *PG* 90.912–956, 960–1080. There are excellent translations in

the series, *Ancient Christian Writers* ed. Polycarp Sherwood, *St. Maximus the Confessor: The Ascetic Life and the Four Centuries on Charity* (London, 1955).

13. On this see, Irenée Hausherr, *The Name of Jesus,* pp. 158–180.
14. For the texts of Evagrius, on prayer and ascetical theory, see the Greek *Philokalia* 1 (Athens, 1957–1963); see also, *Traité Pratique ou Le Moine,* eds. and trans. A. and C. Guillaumont, Sources chrétiennes 170 (Paris, 1971). There is a good English translation and informative introduction in J. E. Bamberger, *Evagrius: The Praktikos and 153 Chapters on Prayer* (Spencer, Mass., 1970). For commentary, see I. Hausherr, *Les leçons d'une contemplatif: Le traité de l'oraison d'Evagre le Pontique* (Paris, 1960); also A. Louth, *The Origins of the Christian Mystical Tradition, from Plato to Denys* (Oxford, 1981), pp. 100–113.
15. Texts can be found in H. Dörries, E. Klostermann, and M. Kroeger, *Die 50 Geistlichen Homilien des Makarios* (Berlin, 1964). There is an old, but useful translation by A. J. Mason, *Fifty Spiritual Homilies* (London, 1921). See also, Louth, op. cit., pp. 113–131.
16. This expression comes from H. Urs von Balthasar, *The Glory of the Lord: A Theological Aesthetics,* vol. 1, *Seeing the Form* (Edinburgh, 1982), pp. 365–417. See also the very important article by K. Rahner, "Le début d'une doctrine des cinq sens spirituels chez Origène," *Révue d'ascétique et mystique* 13 (1932):113–145. There is also a superb study of spiritual sensation in Simeon's works, in B. Fraigneau-Julien, *Les sens spirituels et la vision de Dieu selon Syméon le Nouveau Théologian* (Paris, 1985). This is, in some ways, one of the best general introductions to Byzantine spiritual theology. It provides much more than its title suggests.
17. See the unpublished thesis by E. M. Collins, submitted to the Queen's University of Belfast in 1991, "Prayer and Mystical Theology in Eleventh-Century Byzantium," pp. 4–15, 87–108, 136–144.
18. On Maximus, see, L. Thunberg, *Man and the Cosmos* (New York, 1985).
19. Moore, op. cit., p. 56.
20. One thinks naturally of "stylites" and other ascetical heroes who continued to appear at the fringes of the Byzantine church. On the phenomenon of the "Holy Man," see *The Byzantine Saint,* ed. S. Hackel (Birmingham, 1981).
21. While it is true that Byzantine monasticism never developed the kind of diversified mendicant structures that emerged in the medieval West, it is equally true that the material available to us from cenobitic texts illustrates a great diversity of services rendered to society by the monastic order; however, it remained essentially monastic, and an "order" rather than a series of orders.
22. This tradition has tended to receive most attention from historians of spirituality.
23. The proposed translation of Byzantine cenobitic *typika* (rules and regulations for liturgical rites and ceremonies) by the Dumbarton Oaks Institute will highlight the importance of the cenobitic life in Byzantium. In addition, the forthcoming Belfast translation of, and commentary on, the texts emanating from the important Evergetis monastery will enlarge the scholarly horizon in this area.
24. See Collins, op. cit., with reference to the material from Simeon the New Theologian and the Evergetis monastery, pp. 55–71, 75–87.
25. Although there were tensions between the cenobitic and hesychastic ideals, particularly in the formative period of Athonite life, it is impossible to establish any real cleavage between them.
26. Again, Byzantine (and modern Orthodox) monastic praxis has never really suffered from the division between individual piety and liturgical prayer that has tended to appear at

certain periods in the history of Western Christianity. This is particularly clear in the evidence from the middle-Byzantine period; see Collins, op. cit., pp. 87–111.

27. It is important not to neglect the Syrian and Palestinian roots of the Byzantine tradition by overemphasizing the importance of Egypt.
28. The whole of Simeon's preaching and teaching tended to inculcate the necessity of experience.
29. Without ascribing canonical status to labels, it is legitimate to locate him within the broadly "Macarian" tradition of interior sensibility; but of course he did not escape the influence of Evagrius either, especially as this was mediated through the writings of Issac of Nineveh.
30. In this he bears comparison with St. Bernard of Clairvaux and the whole trend toward subjectivity interiority that emerged in the medieval West.
31. It is interesting to observe the rather guarded reception of Simeon's works in the period after his death. On this, see, I. Hausherr, "Paul Evergétinos, a-t-il connu Syméon le Nouveau Théologian?" *Orientalia Christiana Periodica* 23 (1957):58–79.
32. For the Greek text, with French translation see, J. Darrouzès, *Chapitres théologiques, gnostiques et pratiques,* Sources chrétiennes 51 (Paris, 1957); I have quoted from the English translation by P. McGuckin, *Symeon the New Theologian: The Practical and Theological Chapters and The Three Theological Discourses* (Michigan, 1982).
33. McGuckin, op. cit., p. 82.
34. See Rahner, "Le début . . ."
35. McGuckin, op. cit., p. 82.
36. We know that on one occasion his monks rioted in their church!
37. McGuckin, op. cit., pp. 82–83.
38. Despite their insistence on ascetic practices, we must never forget that this demand for interior purification is a constant hallmark of the Byzantine tradition.
39. Critical Greek text, and French translation, by B. Krivochéine, *Catéchèses,* Sources chrétiennes 96, 104, 113 (Paris, 1963–1965); quotations here are from the English translation by J. de Catanzaro, *Symeon the New Theologian: The Discourses* (London, 1980).
40. *2 Cor.* 5.16–17.
41. De Catanzaro, op. cit., p. 182.
42. Ibid., p. 182.
43. Ibid., p. 184.
44. See *Catechesis* 24, in de Catanzaro, op. cit., pp. 261–267, and the three discourses on theology (i.e., on the Trinity), in J. Darrouzes, *Traités théologiques et éthiques,* Sources chrétiennes, 122, 129 (Paris, 1966–1967); English translation in McGuckin, op. cit.
45. De Catanzaro, op cit., p. 184.
46. For a balanced discussion of "perception" in Simeon's works, see P. Miquel, "La conscience de la grâce selon Syméon le Nouveau Thélogian, *Irénikon* 42 (1969):314–342.
47. De Catanzaro, op. cit., p. 184.
48. Ibid., p. 47.
49. Ibid., pp. 47–48.
50. McGuckin, op. cit., p. 33; see also I. Hausherr, *The Name of Jesus,* p. 160. In general the emphasis on remembering God indicates a move away from the starkly intellectual spirituality of Evagrius. It was a democratization of the doctrine of incessant prayer.
51. De Catanzaro, op. cit., p. 48.
52. Ibid., p. 49.
53. Ibid., p. 50.
54. Ibid.

55. See D. J. Constantelos, *Byzantine Philanthropy and Social Welfare* (New Jersey, 1968).
56. See *Catechesis* 5, in de Catanzaro, op. cit., pp. 109–111. See also his discussion of the equality of vocations, in McGuckin, op. cit., p. 91. There is a clear recognition there, that the spiritual life is a set of inner attitudes essentially independent of place.
57. The notion of the Spirit's baptismal gift as a "seal" was a regular feature of patristic preaching. See G.W.H. Lampe, *The Seal of the Spirit* (London, 1951); also McGuckin, op. cit., p. 123, on how Simeon related this to incessant prayer.
58. See the perceptive comments of Dom Lucien Régnault in, "The Beatitudes in the Apophthegmata Patrum," *Eastern Churches Review* 6.1 (1974):23.
59. This was always the ultimate goal for Simeon.
60. It is difficult to assess how seriously we should take Simeon's denunciations of the Byzantine monastic world. For a good discussion of the whole area of decline and renewal in the eleventh century, see J. Thomas, *Private Religious Foundations in the Byzantine Empire* (Washington, 1987). On Simeon's own articulation of his prophetic ministry, see, de Catanzaro, op. cit., pp. 347–358, which is something of an "apologia."
61. The standard study remains that of I. Hausherr, *Penthos, The Doctrine of Compunction in the Christian East* (Michigan, 1982).
62. De Catanzaro, op. cit., p. 52.
63. Dom André Louf, "Repentance and Experience of God," *Monastic Studies* 9 (1972), Louf is particularly sensitive to the Lutheran critique of monastic asceticism in the light of the gospel.
64. De Catanzaro, op. cit., p. 52.
65. Ibid., pp. 52–53.
66. Ibid., p. 53.
67. Ibid., p. 54.
68. For an example of the Holy Spirit as the "key" that opens the "door" (Christ) to the "house" (the Father), see the *Catechesis* 33, in, de Catanzaro, op. cit., pp. 339–346.
69. De Catanzaro, op. cit., p. 57.
70. Ibid., p. 58.
71. For a good summary of this doctrine, see the relevant sections in Thomas Spidlik, *La spiritualité de l'orient chrétien* (Rome, 1978).
72. An interesting discussion of this term can be found in the article by Miquel, cited above; see also *idem* on Pseudo-Macarius, "Les caractères de l'expérience spirituelle selon le pseudo-Macaire," *Irénikon* 4 (1966):497–514.
73. See Rahner, op. cit.; and also Fraigneau-Julien, op. cit. For an explicit reference in Simeon's works, see McGuckin, op. cit., pp. 63–64.
74. Naturally one thinks of the theological work of H. Urs von Balthasar; but see also P. Evdokimov, *L'art de l'icone: Théologie de la beauté* (Bruges-Paris, 1970). There is also a very good discussion of the icon and its role in theological aesthetics in T. Spidlik, "L'icone, manifestation du monde spirituel," *Gregorianum* 61/3 (1980):539–554.

25

Asceticism and the Compensations of Art

Geoffrey Galt Harpham

Within the broad range of practices that can be called ascetical, the creation and reception of art plays a crucial role. One of its primary functions has been in the area of what has since been called "self-fashioning" (Greenblat) or "self-forming" (Foucault). The contemporary emphasis on performance in contemporary ethnography, gender studies, drama, and literary theory also characteristically suggests an ascetic genealogy. For the performing subject is a disciplined subject, one trained, often by long and tedious practice, to produce a certain kind of display. So while performance sounds more like a hobby and less like a necessity—more like a choice or preference and less like a blood passion—its capacity to hone itself through discipline reflects its ideological and historical affiliation with those practices of self-denial, or self-fashioning, that arose as testimonials of grace and faith within early Christian asceticism. Within those ascetic practices, the task of converting oneself from the flawed, fallible, failing, and flailing thing that one is, to the rigid monument to the Way that one would like to be, requires a practice of framing, planning, and construction—a practice that fulfills the requirements for what we have, since Kant, learned to call aesthetic creation. Surprisingly, perhaps, the ancient violences of desert Christianity turn out to accord pretty well with the distinctively modern category of art.

I am beginning with two premises. The first is that aesthetics is not merely a modern name for an aspect of asceticism, but constitutes asceticism's specifically modern form—its modernity. The second is that asceticism brings pressure to bear upon the very concept of art precisely insofar as art is modern.

Taking the last first, we could point to the manifestly ascetic quality of that touchstone of the modern conception of the aesthetic, disinterestedness. In addition to being one name for a general quality of detachment that characterizes the relation of the artifact to the world and to the perceiver, disinterestedness also characterizes the mode of being of the creative artist, especially the modern creative artist. For modern art characteristically emerges at the expense of the artist, who suffers privation in order to prepare himself for creation; who mutilates himself in the act of creation; who surrenders himself in the execution; and who cuts himself off from selfhood in sending the work out into the world. Nietzsche was not alone in seeing castration at the core of art's modernity; others, including Flaubert, Mallarmé, Conrad, Gide, and Kafka, made the connection as well. In the discourse of the aesthetic, modernity rearticulates in a secular vocabulary the traditional religious concern with self-negation, self-overcoming, self-alienation, self-transcendence as ways of achieving a pure presentness, an openness to being. As Donald Kuspit writes, modernity can be seen as "that point of view which sees art as the mastery of purity," purity being the ascetic virtue *par excellence*.[1] Moreover, within the ascetic aesthetic, practices and concepts that originally emerged within an intensely religious context, as its most extreme expression, survive essentially undisturbed the utter loss of that context—survive, indeed, precisely because modernity marks the loss of that context. The modern religion of art institutes an ascetic devotion not to religion, but to a kind of anti-religion. The practice is primary, surviving and sustaining any set of meanings that may be attached to it.

To see art as an instance of ascetic practices of self-formation is to clarify the sheer violence of the modern work of art. To see asceticism on the model of art is, however, to awaken to the genuine freedom of ascetic discipline, a freedom that converges on the blank page; the empty canvas; the conductor's upraised baton; the next (undiscovered, improvised) step—the freedom to make what one will out of what one has, or is.

For early Christian ascetics, the imitability of their practices was crucial. An ascetic performance was wasted if it did not possess some display value, and, thus, some conversional power to inspire others to similar performances. One modern form of this power is realized, I believe, in aesthetic criticism. While in *The Ascetic Imperative in Culture and Criticism*[2] I rehearsed the versions of asceticism instantiated by every school of criticism I could think of as though they were all substantially individuated, I now believe that criticism can be divided into two essential forms, which we could call "cenobitic" and "eremitic" based upon the fundamental relation established between critic and text. For simplicity's sake, I will begin by referring to a single text, Terry Eagleton's *Criticism and Ideology*. At the end of his first chapter, Eagleton outlines two options for criticism. In an older model, criticism acts as midwife to the text, a humbly self-effacing practice that represents itself as smoothing the passage from text to reader. Such a practice invariably winds up becoming authoritarian, acting as "repressive father, who cuts short the erotic sport of sense between text and reading, binding with the briars of its metasystem the joyfully pluralist intercourse of meanings between them."[3] This account invokes, all unconsciously to be sure, certain aspects of cenobitism, which are redoubled in the protocols of scholarship itself: those elaborate conventions of citation, close reading, research, and attention to evidence that are collectively designed to neutralize, regulate, or castrate the subjective reader by promoting the claims of the Other—the other author; the other reader; the other scholar; the textual other; the historical other.

In the second, preferred (eremitic) sense, however, criticism does not "redouble the text's self-understanding" or seek to "collude with its object in a conspiracy of eloquence. Its task is to show the text as it cannot know itself, to manifest those conditions of its making . . . about which it is necessarily silent. . . . To achieve such a showing, criticism must break with its ideological prehistory, situating itself outside the space of the text on the alternative terrain of scientific knowledge"

(Eagleton, *Criticism and Ideology,* pp. 42–43). This empowering break, in which criticism ascends the pillar in the glaring desert sun of science—displaying a truth of the text that, without such a gesture of wild self-denial on the part of the critic, would remain invisible in a world of ideology and tradition—is still castration; for, once again, it is a heroic leap to knowledge because it is a leap away from the critic's self-interest.

If Eagleton's first critical option entails a spirit of collective humility, the second is a practice of solitude and austerity. Eagleton would, I imagine, vigorously resist this assimilation of science with asceticism, since science for him means a rejection of religion and its manifold idealities, myths, and ideological fantasies. But he might be chastened by reading the third essay of *On the Genealogy of Morals,* in which Nietzsche begins by establishing science as modernity's best hope of stamping out asceticism altogether and ends by conceding that science is the purest form of asceticism yet discovered. Indeed, the way Eagleton casts the problem, it is ascetic through and through, for it urges that we choose not what we might want—the feminine gratifications of midwifery, conspiracy, eloquence, and repetition—but rather what is necessary, the sterner task of breaking with history, the task of scientific knowledge. But Eagleton is not alone here. Others—the libertines and libertarians of literary theory, whether operating according to the Rule of Roland, the Rule of Jacques, the Rule of Julia—urge a break with a tradition they depict as ascetic, involving self-effacement, humility, and anonymity, in favor of values and practices of self-fulfillment, *jouissance,* dissemination, play, sport, and a general renunciation of renunciation.

In the newer discipline of cultural studies, the model of initiation is not close reading, but ethnographic fieldwork, with its intense personal involvement in the subject, as opposed to the remote, removed perspective of the scholar. The antiascetic point, as practitioners such as Dwight Conquergood, Clifford Geertz, and Renato Rosaldo insist, is that cultural studies is an embodied practice rather than a practice of alienation, and distance. The larger point I would make in response to this is that, whatever the choice, something is renounced and something embraced; and therefore desire is always both gratified and negated. In the case of cultural studies, scholarly authority is earned by what Conquergood calls in a forthcoming book "time in the field"—by the surrender of the comforts and pleasures of the library, the office, the study; and the immersion in the ethnographic site, with its exposure, bad food, disease, and boredom, not to mention the hostility of the invaded subjects. It is always possible to depict a scholarly practice as either pleasurable or unpleasurable, fulfilling or castrating, because all such practices operate by the law of compensation—denial of something, gratification of something else. Scholarly practices, in particular, provide a conspicuous instance of ascetic imperative that simply cannot be avoided, any more than it can be perfectly realized. Scholars and critics in particular seem to prefer, out of professional obligation, castration's compensations to the pleasures of pleasure.

Not coincidentally, what unites aesthetic works and their criticism is, I believe, precisely this ascetic law of denial and compensation. Asceticism is a structure of compensation, in which something is granted—"treasure in heaven"—in return for something being given up—"all that thou hast" (*Lk.* 18.22). Peter Brown and Carolyn Walker Bynum have argued that what is literally, and most painfully, being given up in early Christian asceticism is food rather than a more obvious candidate, sex. Call me a traditionalist, but I want to insist—especially with respect to the modern form of asceticism, aesthetics and its criticism—on the primacy of sex. I begin by suggesting that both art and criticism compensate for the surrender of physical sexuality by providing imaginative gratifications that have their own attractiveness. Freud argued that beauty (by which I would understand both its creation and its reception) represented a sublimation of sexuality, a rerouting of transgressive energies along socially acceptable lines; and while this seems a decidedly modern view of the matter, I would argue that we can in fact locate the germ of sublimation, the beginnings of a modern understanding, in ascetic art and its cultural interpretation.

As one among countless examples, I want to focus on a picture by Sassetta (c.1400–1450), one of a series depicting the life of St. Antony (see figure 1). In this

Figure 1. *The Meeting of Saint Anthony and Saint Paul,* c.1440, tempera on panel. *(Samuel H. Kress Collection, National Gallery of Art, Washington, D.C., reproduced with permission)*

image, the meeting between Antony and Paul the Hermit (died c.347), sometimes called Paul of Thebes, is efficiently depicted, using the spatial narrative style common to the time. The compensation I am hunting for does not withhold itself, for the meeting between the two saints represents a momentary relief from the intense solitude suffered by each; their holy embrace provides, in fact, not only an affirmation of the worthiness of the ascetic life, but an astonishing interval of sensation, an unrepeatable break amid the unrelieved decades of self, or rather of denial of self. The image represents an especially holy moment in the lives of wholly holy men.

I want to dwell on, or in, the peculiar arch formed by Paul and Antony's embrace. Perhaps its most immediate formal function is to repeat the arch of the cave immediately behind them, Paul the Hermit's home. Doing so, they manage to suggest in human form the rock rolled back from the tomb, and thus the Resurrection, and thus the compensatory treasure in heaven that will be enjoyed by those who deny the flesh and live in the spirit. There is a certain formal precedent for such embraces, which generally carry the same message of compensation. The late twelfth-century Flemish painting of Mary and Elizabeth shown in figure 2, for example, stages an even more elaborate display of symmetry, indicated not only by the loving embrace of the two women, pregnant with Jesus and John the Baptist, but by such incidental features as the crossing of the feet, a feature it holds in common with the Sassetta.

But to the viewer suffering the trials of life the embrace may have (and has had) different meanings than for Antony and Paul, or for Elizabeth and Mary. The case for giving up all, for living in the world but not of it, may seem, from some points of view, less than persuasive. One recalls Huck Finn's account of *The Pilgrim's Progress* as "a story about a man who left his wife and children, it didn't say why." The surrender of food, sex, and the metaphorical extensions thereof may seem a harsh price to pay even for heaven's booty, distant and immaterial. The most salient and persuasive element of the story of Antony may be not the decades of fasting and solitude that preceded and followed the embrace, but the embrace itself, which suggests the principle of reward, of human contact not as transgression of the principle of sacrifice, but enfolded within the sacrifice itself.

A closer look at Sassetta's painting itself suggests that this enfolding, and the careful negotiation of intervals, serve as a structural principle of the composition itself. The dominant form of the painting is, surely, the arch; and it is replicated everywhere—not only in Paul's cave, but in the route of the road, the forms of the mountains, the shapes of the trees, the very clusters of leaves—as if their embrace replicated and brought into the human world not only a principle of affection, fellow feeling, but also a principle of natural form. Even the colors of Antony's and Paul's robes repeat the colors found in the right and left sides of the cave. The feeling is thus thoroughly naturalized. Still, one cannot help noticing that the position of the embrace itself is highly unnatural in the sense that it is clumsy, almost impossibly awkward, bad for ageing backs. Why do they assume this queer posture?

Is it only in order to create an arch? Or might there be some other, negative motivation? In the case of Elizabeth and Mary, the interval between the bodies

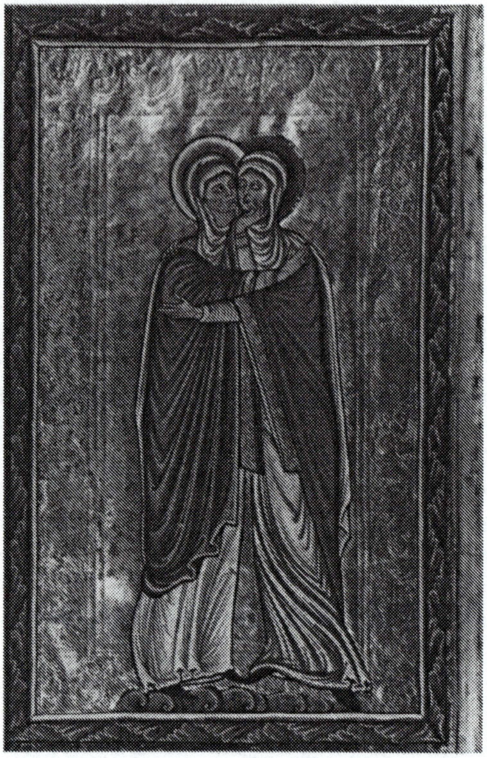

Figure 2. Flemish, 12th Century. *(Reproduced with permission of the British Library)*

leaves room for pregnant bellies to swell, and thus foregrounds the fertility of the two women. There may be something of that convention in this composition—with fertility being applied metaphorically to men who bear the Word within them. But I see another possibility in addition to this: that the unnatural posture, depicted by an artist manifestly grappling with the rigors of pictorial realism, is motivated by the necessity of creating a gap or space between bodies, a gap that would preserve, in the face of a certain transgressive threat, the interval, and so maintain the holy character of the embrace. The law of the holy embrace is clear: the genitals cannot touch, for such a touch would represent not just compensation but overcompensation. The very avoidance of genital contact through an unnatural posture permits the equally unnatural placement of the hands on the buttocks. And so, in representing a natural embrace as an amplification and reinforcement of a natural principle, and a natural principle of form, the artist has created two forms of the unnatural, the physical posture and the homosexual touch.

The unnatural act hinted at by the holy embrace would, I have no doubt, have been almost perfectly invisible to the anticipated audience for the painting. It may, for all I know, have remained invisible to everyone who had ever seen the painting until I did a few months ago, (after years of looking at it on my office wall). So heavily coded as orthodox and natural is the image that the possibility of an unnatural act occurring, or about to occur, before our eyes seems more monstrous than . . . than a centaur. The efficient resolution with which the mind censors, screens, and represses has, however, the effect of permitting a transgressive desire for human, bodily contact—which might have seemed to a prospective ascetic not unnatural but perfectly natural, given the radical deprivation of the ascetic life—to thrive on the margins, in the corners, unchecked by the vigilant eye. Repressed instincts, Freud tells us, flourish in the dark, "ramifying like a fungus."

The status of nature in the composition is, I think one would have to admit, a bit wobbly. What can we make of the centaur, colored like nothing else in the painting? The centaur represents a compromise between the human and the animal, and this one in particular provides a formal completion of the wedge in the center of the picture created by the grove of trees; in fact, two of the tree trunks seem to represent his hind legs. The central, centering centaur is still, however, radically out of place in any natural, or naturalistic, setting. The human (the centaur suggests) is both natural and unnatural. In an ascetic context, this possibly means that the human is bound to the flesh but may, through the grace of God, transcend its animal nature. Asceticism thus embraces both a principle of affection that is entirely in keeping with nature, and a counter-principle of deprivation that entails a repudiation of nature. The unnaturalness of ascetic practices and ideology may thus license a view of discipline itself as unnatural. And this would mean, for those still following, that ascetic restraint falls into the category of an unnatural act—precisely the implication I am drawing from the human arch in Sassetta's painting.

Now if we turn to Paul, we note that, like the entrance to his cave, he is halo-colored, implying through the medium of color a perfect sanctity both in himself and in his domicile. Especially in light of the pictorial convention we saw in the painting of Elizabeth and Mary, this cave might represent the source of Paul's fertility, the confinement that issues in holiness, a metaphorical womb as well (as noted earlier) as a tomb. This would confirm, for modern skeptics, what might seem to be the hidden agenda of the ascetic *fuite du monde,* a return to prenatal wholeness. But, more pertinently in the present context, we must note that it is precisely the refusal of the womb that constitutes the demand for compensation, and thus drives the entire ascetic program. The womb must be denied, or converted, before one can honorably return to it.

But no conversion converts without remainder, without creating fresh opportunities and needs for further conversion. This truism is borne out, I believe, by the deep grooves on the top of the cave entrance, which mark it not as feminine-vaginal but rather as masculine-anal. The womb is converted by being naturalized. But it is naturalized by being masculinized, which is to say, unnaturalized. The natural form of the cave is made available for human purposes by being routed through the masculine, a two-stage conversion that renders the cave an object of desire, an object to desire instead of the womb: one lives in a cave instead of with a woman. This is, to the ascetic, a natural desire that takes natural form, the form of the cave, repeated in the embrace of the two men. But life in a cave also represents a renunciation of natural desire, a will to desire the nonnatural, the unnatural, to have an unnatural desire, the very type of which is anal intercourse. The cave—or anus—is the natural and human site of gender conversion or transformation. (Here I am reminded of Eve Kosofsky Sedgwick's comment that the phrases "to use a woman like a man" and "to use a man like a woman" both designate the same act.) Let me explain, if I can. Antony sets out for his object of desire, Paul, a feminized man associated with the cave, a caveman. But on achieving his destination, Antony himself is feminized, his identity almost literally eclipsed by Paul, his head disappearing. Paul is also transformed: from a position of subordination to the greater and dominant Antony, he becomes a dominant figure, masculinizing the cave. In the holy embrace, it is Antony who is the midwife to holiness, rather than a flamboyant, charismatic eremite, while Paul emerges into a startling visibility. In terms used by Patricia Cox Miller, Antony represents, at the culminating moment, the dim body while Paul suggests a dazzling "glorified body" (pp. 281ff.). The suggestively colored robe carried by Antony, a gift of his future biographer Athanasius, enigmatically contains the entire drama in its folds. Increasingly tumescent in each stage of his pilgrimage, the phallic robe nearly envelopes Antony at the end, but envelops him—is it too scandalous to suggest this? Can we still speak of scandal here?—as a womb, as the sign of Antony's completed gender transformation. Fittingly, this robe will serve, as Jerome informs us in his *Life of Paul,* as Paul's shroud, the terminus of his short but complicated journey as well.

Here I confess that I have arrived at the navel of my dream, where my own analysis plunges into the unknown, and I feel powerless fully to reclaim the logic that constituted this representation, to abstract the architecture, the theory, from the image, which is also the un-imageable, even the unimaginable. I wonder, in fact, if the cave, the structural and conceptual center of the painting, might not indicate in its depths the essence not only of asceticism but, as a form to which no concept could be fully answerable or adequate, of the aesthetic itself, the formless origin of form. Here I sense a kind of theoretical nausea in the presence, or absence, of something I can neither assimilate nor truly reject. And with this nausea comes a nostalgia for simpler messages, more legible images.

One of these has been thoughtfully provided by Mr. Wimbush in the form of the program for this conference (see figure 3). It is not an old image protected by centuries of alienation, but a recent one, painted in the Coptic Orthodox Church in Los Angeles by a master of contemporary Coptic Art, Dr. Isaac Fanous Youssef, in 1990.[4] Dr. Youssef represents Antony the Great in splendid, centered, isolation, holding a scroll to express his devotion to the Word. Rolling down, the scroll extends all the way to Antony's center, stopping at precisely the point where the bottom of the scroll might plausibly suggest an erect penis. The life of the Word, I infer, is fulfilling in ways all men can understand, with the Word standing in, or standing up, for desire, arousal, expectation. Whether the bottom of the scroll represents a Lacanian phallic signifier or something else, perhaps a phallic signified, I cannot determine, but the coincidence of Word with phallus seems incontestable. Antony's centrality is, moreover, established by pictorial elements to his right and

Figure 3. *Saint Anthony the Great,* egg tempera on gesso. *(Reproduced with permission of Father Antonious L. Henein)*

left that echo the same general idea. On his right, he greets Paul, his hands flung back in surprise or delight, while Paul reaches forward—why? toward what? On Antony's left, a pair of lions, an icon of the peaceability and solidarity of asceticism, lie down not with lambs, but with each other—two strictly symmetrical male lions, soon to bury Paul in Antony's robe, cheek to jowl, buttressing—again, in the natural world—the otherwise unnatural homoerotic element already indicated on the other side. The lake behind them reinforces the theme of mirroring. If symmetry and mirroring are themselves at least potentially homoerotic in import, then even the very word "abba" participates, weirdly enough, in this message of brotherly compensations. The raven, whose function in the narrative of Paul and Antony is simply to bring some bread, seems involved in a more ambiguous and aggressive mission here, diving like a kamikaze pilot into the trumpet of some extraordinary, Daliesque plant.

The primary function of such homosexual signals is, I want to emphasize, not to inject a missing principle into asceticism so as to make it attractive; nor is it to disclose a secret, traumatic kernel that lies at the heart of ascetic piety. They may in fact do both these, but their primary function is to make clear what would otherwise be terribly unclear, the conundrum of how desire, the guilty party in transgression, may be turned on itself, enlisted in the service of the Other and directed not to self-gratification but to self-denial. Desire must fold back upon itself in a spirit of apparent antagonism and actual realization; it must choose objects of desire that are not, in the old sense, desirable at all, and find its fulfillment there. But how? How are we to understand this essential negation, this negation of the essence of desire, which is the essence of ourselves—much less this desire for negation, a desire that seems so infernally complex, so unnatural? Gregory Collins's paper provides a rapid series of illustrations of the way this desire is managed. In three phrases—quoted, sanctioned, official phrases—asceticism is "a kind of generosity, a Spartan kind of straitness"; "asceticism must be penetrated by humility"; and "Christ is buried in us as in a tomb, and rises in us and is transfigured" (pp. 348ff.). These sentences raise mystery to sublimity, so that my understanding rests in a state of quiet apprehension of something beyond my powers to decipher. But insofar as I seek to understand, I attend to, and am bewildered by, the meaning. I cannot comprehend the literal sense of this Spartan straitness, this penetration, this burial of one man in another, this rising, this transfiguration. I am confused, I do not understand . . . unless—I do. But if I do, I perform a rapid, even instantaneous gesture of cancellation, because the conjunction between the mysteries of faith and the groaning, heaving processes of homosexual fornication is so grotesque, impossible, ridiculous that it could not be admitted. Thus, the homoerotic serves as an explanatory model in the material world of desire for faith, one that illuminates without defiling because it is so altogether defiled that its function is never actually admitted.

It cannot be admitted, at least, within the ideology of asceticism. For one of the main points of that ideology concerns the distinction between the spirit and the flesh, a distinction that actually *permits* the homosexual embrace to serve as a model for piety. I am not using ideology here in the older Marxist sense of false consciousness, but rather in the more contemporary sense of a structurally unconscious and flexible armature of concepts that govern not only attitudes and ideas, but perception itself. The Slovenian philosopher Slavoj Zizek insists on the unconsciousness of ideology as the feature that enables its functioning. Ideology, he says, is a form of knowledge whose form is not knowledge; we "do it but don't know it," it is "in us more than ourselves."[5] In this understanding of ideology, we can actually grasp the true importance of the homoerotic as the form in desire of ideology itself. For within what theoreticians of gender have called the psycho-social regime of compulsory heterosexuality—the silent premise that normal sexuality is and ought to be hetero—the homosexual Other within stands as a primary and primordial form of something in us more than ourselves, something we do, if we do, without knowing it.

I seem to have strayed far from the original subject of the spirit of asceticism in the modernity of art. But not really. For, as I have just indicated, there are excellent reasons why homosexuality in ascetic art goes unrecognized, and even why this nonrecognition should confirm its status as art. For if art, in the post-Kantian world, is defined by the disinterestedness that attends its reception, then a representation of a banished form of sexuality is preeminently something to be "disinterested" in. As the love that dare not speak its name, homosexuality bears the burden of love generally in an ascetic context, the burden of nonrecognition, invisibility, denial. The banished form of a banished category, a form whose banishment could be generally understood and endorsed, a structurally banished form, a form to which banishment is proper, homosexuality represents the banishment of human sexuality *per se,* a banishment not the least bit less effective for its literal nonappearance—since that is what banishment is all about.

Even modern critics interested in the body promote a restriction of erotic possibilities that reinforces this banishment. I am thinking here chiefly of Bynum, who argues throughout *Fragmentation and Redemption* that, in the Middle Ages, "bodiliness" as such was associated with woman, who thus entered into an especially intimate relation with the incarnate Christ. Bynum's admirable sensitivity to the fluidity of gender distinctions during this time casts a very bright light on what seem to us to be aberrant attributions of female characteristics to men and vice versa. But when she discusses Jesus as mother, Jesus as the issue of a female genealogy, Bynum begins to close off rather than to open up possibilities of identification and desire. And when, in an historicist spirit, she cautions against importing contemporary notions of sexuality into a medieval context in which other concerns (such as food) may have been more determinant, then I begin to sense what Eagleton called a conspiracy of eloquence. That is, by cautioning that medieval people did not define themselves in terms of sexual orientation, and worried more about whether their desires came from God or from Satan than about what kind of desires they had, Bynum, perhaps inadvertently, limits one of the primary kinds of imitation of Christ, the kind we would today call homosexual.

I am, of course, all too aware of the controversial character of such readings, especially in a climate of extreme sensitivity concerning clerical homosexual pedophilia, a sensitivity stoked as well as described by such books as Jason Berry's *Lead Us Not Into Temptation: Catholic Priests and the Sexual Abuse of Children.*[6] It is not, I believe, altogether beside the point that, by Mr. Berry's estimate, 20 percent of American Catholic clergy are gay. For what this means is that a life of sacrifice and renunciation (of sexual intercourse) continues to appeal to those who might be most responsive to the necessarily indirect and coded signals of homoeroticism—or to indirection and code generally. In the face of Mr. Berry's statistic, I must insist that the compensations I am speaking of are aesthetic, which is to say imaginary, but also, and more important, unconscious. There is, if not a decisive theoretical difference, a world of worldly difference between a conscious, bodily act and an inarticulate, unconscious imaginative sensation.

I realize that I am perhaps working here with a somewhat less definite and restrictive account of asceticism than that employed by many people at this gathering. But one of my own implicit points is that history repeats itself, above all in the illusion of doing something new; and that asceticism is one name for that repetition. Although predicated on repetition, asceticism yet stands for the new, the perpetually modern, the break. Historians, inclined to be immersed in the specificity of their materials, can easily lose track of, or sympathy with, such concepts. Out of an ascetic imperative to be faithful to "the facts," they can blind themselves to the possibility of an ongoing, self-renewing, self-discovering asceticism—just as theoreticians, wary of relapsing into a pretheoretical and therefore deluded empiricism, can deny themselves the wealth of riches embedded in what they might regard as the dark prehistory of modernity. My argument here about the survival of asceticism in art and criticism presumes that asceticism is not a transcendental event but an historical constant; it is the most comprehensive name of the ways in which we understand and refashion ourselves, the ways in which we formulate our ideal conceptions while accommodating our all too human needs.

Lastly, I would like to caution against the meliorism that might be thought a natural accompaniment of such universalizing. To see asceticism everywhere, including gentler forms of moderation such as aesthetic representation, is not to restrict asceticism to those gentler forms, even though they may be more palatable, more easily discussed in society. For if moderate forms of asceticism have any transfiguring function at all, it is because they summon up and borrow from the spectacle and violence of those other, more radical modes of self-overcoming—those documented so lavishly and compellingly in hagiography that the ancient stories are read and repeated even today by people struck with wonder at the principles that might be exemplified by such mysterious forms. A disintoxicated asceticism represents a castration of castration, a repression of repression. As scholars, we are repressed enough already; we cannot afford to repress the truth that our repression is supposed to enable us to divine.

NOTES

1. "The Unhappy Consciousness of Modernism," in Ingeborg Hosterey, ed., *Zeitgeist in Babel* (Bloomington and Indianapolis: Indiana University Press), p. 50.
2. Chicago and London: University of Chicago Press, 1987.
3. *Criticism and Ideology: A Study in Marxist Literary Theory* (London: Verso, 1976).
4. An obviously rather different interpretation of the image can be seen in the booklet (*Understanding the Icon of Saint Anthony the Great,* 1993) written by Father Antonious L. Henein, Priest of the Holy Virgin Mary Coptic Orthodox Church, Los Angeles.
5. See *The Sublime Object of Ideology* (London: Verso, 1991).
6. New York: Doubleday, 1993.

26

Sensuality and Mysticism—The Islamic Tradition

Response to the Three Preceding Papers

Peter J. Awn

The challenge every respondent faces is to analyze cogently and succinctly the common themes articulated by the three authors. I have to admit honestly that I have failed miserably in this effort since there is, I believe, very little in common among these three papers. Methodologically and thematically, they are worlds apart, ranging from a phenomenological study of food, through a careful analysis of textual sources relating to Simeon's understanding of asceticism, ending with a sophisticated (and highly speculative) analysis of psycho-sexual themes in iconographic images of ascetics.

Having admitted my failure, I have decided nevertheless to pursue an issue that does strike me as important and that relates tangentially to the papers and the common theme under discussion, namely, the place of sensuality in mysticism. Since my main interest is Islamic mysticism (Sufism), I will focus my comments upon this tradition and, I trust, will highlight some areas of interesting contrast with what we have heard today.

As one of the presenters expressed, rather exasperatedly, why do American academics focus so obsessively on sexual issues in religion? This for me is exactly the point. The Christian ascetical and mystical tradition has not, in my opinion, expressed in any integral way the link between mysticism and sensuality. On the contrary, the Christian attitude is characterized by an unresolved ambivalence towards the sensual. So our obsession is not with sex as such, but with the ambivalent attitude toward sensuality apparent in the writings of Christian ascetics and the iconography in which they are depicted. And, as the discussion of iconography suggested, much of the sensuality is sublimated and hidden behind ambiguous images. One cannot help but be reminded of Bernini's extraordinary sculpture of St. Teresa of Avila. Does it depict her experience of ecstasy or sexual orgasm? The answer, of course, is both, or rather that the experience is immersed in both the spiritual and the sensual.

In the Islamic mystical tradition there is a greater willingness to give pride of place to sensuality, sometimes to the dismay of the broader Muslim population. Moreover, the highlighting of sensuality was occasionally linked to a tradition of antinomian mysticism.

A classic exponent of the sensual in mysticism is the early Sūfī Abū Sa'īd ibn Abī l'Khayr (died 1049 CE). During his early training in the mystical life, Abū Sa'īd pursued violent ascetical practices. He is said to have hung upside down in a pit at night, reciting the Qur'ān. He shunned the pleasures of the world, ate almost nothing, and was reduced to skin and bones.

Yet after Abū Sa'īd attained *ma'rifah (gnōsis)* his attitude toward the physical world changed. At least publicly, he no longer vaunted his violent asceticism but immersed himself in the sensual delights of human life. He dressed opulently, and his Sūfī convent was noted for its fine cuisine. "The true saint," said Abū Sa'īd, "goes in and out amongst the people, and eats and sleeps with them, and buys and sells in the market, and marries and takes part in social intercourse, and never forgets God for a single moment."[1]

In the tradition of Abū Sa'īd, union, or *gnōsis,* so transforms mystics that they are no longer subject to the power of the world. Their lives are governed by a new law, a law articulated for the Gnostics by the Divine Being with whom they are now in union. And it is this understanding of the consequences of *gnōsis* that leads easily to antinomian Sufism. Abū Sa'īd, for example, never performed the pilgrimage to Mecca, an obligation incumbent on all Muslims. Apparently, he looked on the pilgrimage with contempt as a quasi-pagan ritual.

> "Why have I not performed the Pilgrimage? It is no great matter that thou shouldst tread under thy feet a thousand miles of ground in order to visit a stone house. The true man of God sits where he is and the *Bayt al-Ma'mūr* (the celestial archetype of the Ka'ba) comes several times in a day and night to visit him and perform the circumambulation above his head. Look and see!" All who were present looked and saw it.[2]

The essential link between the spiritual and sensual is not restricted to the lives and teachings of a few Sūfīs, but permeates many aspects of Sufism. True, there were always contrary currents, warning of the dangers of abandoning oneself to sensual pleasure. Nevertheless, there is within the Sūfī tradition a well-established strain that attempts to integrate sensuality and the higher states of mystical union. This tradition culminates, perhaps, in one of the most controversial practices ever to develop in Sufism, the "Contemplation of the Beardless." The practice was based on the insight, articulated by Plato in the *Symposium,* that the contemplation of human beauty leads one to the contemplation of Beauty itself. And the ultimate exemplar of human beauty is the young male on the cusp between androgyny and sexual maturity, innocence and sensuality, feminine passivity and masculine aggressivity. The recognition of the male–male model for mystical union led to the inclusion of in the pantheon of great mystical lovers two historical men, the great conqueror Maḥmūd of Ghazna (died 1031 CE) and his beloved companion Ayāz. While in no way do I wish to imply that this was somehow accepted as the norm, it is remarkable that any same-sex relationship would be integrated into the poetry and prose of the high mystical tradition.

Finally, this normalization of the linkage between the sensual and the spiritual resulted in the inclusion, in some of the most highly regarded mystical works, of sections that, when first encountered by Europeans, were shocking in the extreme. This discomfort led Reynold Nicholson, in his translation of Jalāl al-Dīn Rūmī's masterpiece, *The Masnavī,* to translate the problematic material into Latin, not English!

But Nicholson was no prude. It would be shocking to any Christian scholar of mysticism to encounter Rūmī's discussion of the consequences of a lack of moderation in the sensual and, by extension, the spiritual life. He illustrates this truism by the story of the maidservant who spied on her mistress who had trained a donkey to have sex with her. The maid was inflamed with passion for the donkey, but what she did not realize was that her mistress had taken pains to fashion a gourd to place around the donkey's penis to prevent herself from being disemboweled during intercourse. One day, when her mistress was away, the maidservant, overcome by desire, enticed the donkey to sleep with her and, in the midst of her ecstasy, was disemboweled and killed. While the dangers of excess and the absolute need for moderation are common themes in the works of both Muslim and Christian spiritual writers, one would never, I believe, find such virtue illustrated in the Christian tradition by a ribald and thoroughly sensual tale like that of Rūmī. For this is an area in which Christian and Muslim attitudes are significantly different. And it is this issue that perhaps would be of interest to all three of our distinguished presenters and our other colleagues.

NOTES

1. In Reynold A. Nicholson, trans. *Studies in Islamic Mysticism* (Cambridge: Cambridge University Press, 1921; reprint edition, 1967), p. 55.
2. Ibid., p. 62.

PART FIVE

Politics of Asceticism

27

Asceticism and the Moral Good: A Tale of Two Pleasures

J. Giles Milhaven

In the present essay I write primarily as philosopher, secondarily as historian. My overriding aim is to stimulate constructive discussion of a certain value question: what pleasures are worth having for themselves? The question is pertinent to certain contemporary value discussion, particularly some led by feminists; and yet the discussers have not brought out the question so openly, lucidly, and fruitfully as they might; or so it seems to me.

To make clearer and more concrete this value question, I ponder, in the present essay, moments of the history of the question in the asceticism of the West. The question of worthwhile pleasures comes readily to mind when one ponders the phenomenon of human asceticism; for every ascetic experiences pleasure that he or she does not strive to eliminate or lessen. Every ascetic experiences some pleasure that he or she strives to gain and hold. If he does not strive for this pleasure as an end in itself, one at least prizes, cherishes and enjoys it when it comes. Augustine exemplifies this vividly, as Margaret Miles demonstrates:

> My earlier readings were not wrong. Augustine's astoundingly accurate description of *concupiscentia* as a repetition compulsion, a frantic pursuit of frustratingly elusive pleasure, does reveal the totalitarian scope of his anxiety. His tortured efforts to gather a philosophical basis for establishing a Christian anthropology are a prominent feature of the *Confessions*. His interest in asceticism as a method for maintaining the vividness and freshness of the Christian life, his search for a style of dealing with other human beings not characterized by "eating one another up, as people do with their food," a style he will come to call "loving the neighbor in God": these and other interests accurately characterize Augustine's authorship. Yet I now understand each of them to be aspects of an interest even more consuming and ardent, that of analyzing how to get—and keep—the greatest degree of pleasure.[1]

So, too, Benedicta Ward reminds us, the desert fathers had their joy in the everlasting arms of loving God:

> There are as many stories of the true joy of these men as there are of their tears. As he was dying Benjamin said, "be joyful at all times, pray without ceasing and give

> thanks for all things." Their faces shine with light, they are known for their courtesy, their joy, their welcome to visitors, their care for one another.[2]

The word "asceticism" has been transmitted down the centuries, to reacquire today the original meaning which *askeō* has in Homer: to work materials, to form by art.[3] Our modern word includes also what *askeō* and *askēsis* had come to mean by Plato's time: to practice, exercise and train so as to make oneself fine or beautiful in a specific way. Paul, speaking before the Roman governor, says: " . . . I . . . do my best to keep (*asko . . . ekein*) a clear conscience at all times before God and man" (*Acts* 24.16, Jerusalem Bible).

In the actual use of the word "asceticism," the practice so designated differs as much as does the fine self, the virtuous or excellent person, at whom it is aimed. The asceticism of Marcus Aurelius differs from that of a Cynic contemporary, that of Jerome the younger from the older. The asceticism of Benedict differs from that of the desert fathers, that of Ignatius Loyola from that of Francis of Assisi. One speaks even of the asceticism of the artist, the scientist, and the athlete; or the asceticism of the impoverished single parent.

Still, the word "asceticism" has kept, more or less, its common meaning. One part of what it usually means is a consistent, rigorous renunciation of certain pleasure. I say certain pleasure because ascetics have their own pleasures, most obviously the pleasures of self-mastery, God's presence, the pleasure of serving God, the pleasure of anticipating union with God, or the pleasure at repentance of a sinner. We have the direct report of the moments of rapture of Desert Fathers and of Augustine and Monica. In every day of the final week of the *Spiritual Exercises* of Ignatius of Loyola, the exerciser, upon rising from sleep, exerts himself to rejoice in the great joy of Christ *(exhilarescere de tanto gaudio et laetitia Christi Domini Nostri)*. He thinks of things, such as Paradise, that move him to pleasure, hilarity and spiritual joy *(res quae movent ad delectationem, hilaritatem et laetitiam spiritualem, ut de Paradiso)*. In his *Rules for Discernment of Spirit,* Ignatius assures the soul struggling to lead a good life that true joy and consolation *(veram laetitiam et gaudium et consolationem spiritualem)* will belong to it whenever it feels and follows the movement of the good spirit.[4] One may dispute whether individuals whom we identify as practicing some asceticism intend and seek their pleasures. We all agree that those whom we describe as practicing some asceticism, do, while foregoing certain kinds of pleasure, openly enjoy other kinds, show no shame or guilt or discomfort with these kinds of pleasure, and make no attempt to diminish them; nor do we expect them to.

There is no inconsistency in every ascetic's renouncing one kind of pleasure while freely enjoying another kind of pleasure. But it confronts us with two questions if we wish to understand any given ascetic. What kind of pleasure does this ascetic strive to eliminate or keep to a minimum in his or her life? What kind of pleasure does he or she unabashedly enjoy as a fruit of this austerity? If we understand only one of these two pleasures, we do not understand the asceticism.

St. Paul does not contradict himself but makes good sense when he declares:

> I have become all things to all men, that I might by all means save some. I do it for the sake of the gospel, that I may share its blessings. Do you know that in a race all

> the runners compete, but only one receives the prize? So run that you may obtain it. Every athlete exercises self-control in all things. They do it to receive a perishable wreath, but we an imperishable. Well, I do not run aimlessly, I do not box as one beating the air, but I pommel my body and subdue it, lest after preaching to others I myself should be disqualified. *1 Cor. 9.22–27, Revised Standard Version*

But what kind of pleasure is yielded Paul by the prize he wants to win? What kind of pleasure does he forego resolutely in order to gain the prize? These two questions are integral to understanding his asceticism, as they are to understanding the asceticism of every ascetic.

In the present essay, I attempt a view from a stratospheric time satellite. I premise, at least as a working hypothesis, that in good part the same basic asceticism has been endorsed by the intellectual establishment of Western civilization for at least the last twenty-five hundred years. I attempt to aim at this dominant asceticism the two questions stated above. (I focus on Greco-Roman and Christian phases of the premodern period. I am not competent to appraise the Judaic and Islamic.) Has the intellectual establishment not consistently championed an asceticism that denigrates and combats one given kind of pleasure while openly, indeed righteously, voluptuating in another kind of pleasure? And, is it not, on the whole throughout this history, the same kind of pleasure that is denigrated and combated by the reigning tradition, and the same other kind that is righteously relished by the tradition? If so, what is the one pleasure consistently opposed? What is the other pleasure consistently exalted?

This two-sided question, as I have stated it so far, is an old, overworked question of historians of Western religious thought. But historians and ethicists have recently converged to expand this question. The new dimension of the question is: has not in Western thought a countercurrent surfaced often that urges a contrary appraisal of these two pleasures? Thinkers of this countercurrent extol the traditionally scorned pleasure. They claim that this pleasure, at its best, makes up a part of the best human lives. Such pleasure was a supreme constituent of moral good. Some of the contemporary historians and ethicists to whom I refer press this historical question of fact with a philosophical question of value explicitly or implicitly in mind. Is not the countercurrent basically right? Is not this kind of pleasure, that has been scorned by the traditional establishment, while prized recurrently by a few, in truth something of great human value?

The ethical historians and historical ethicists of whom I speak argue that this generally neglected, counterculturally prized pleasure is erotic pleasure. By erotic pleasure they mean a pleasure that is often sexual and more often not sexual. Sexual pleasure is, though perhaps not the best form of this pleasure, an apt example and model for this kind of pleasure lauded persistently with in the counterculture, which recognizes it at least by metaphor and by open analogy.

It is not news that the Western intellectual establishment has depreciated consistently sex and its pleasure. It is not ethical pioneering to claim that sexual pleasure can be of much higher value than the Western tradition concedes. It is, however, novel, revolutionary for morality and spirituality to argue, as do Carter Heyward,

Mary Hunt, Audre Lorde, Beverly Harrison, and others, that good sex can be a sound paradigm for good human living in general, and that this erotic paradigm is helpful and necessary in today's moral discussion and debate.[5]

Harrison, Heyward, Lorde, and Hunt raise a promising ethical question. What precise traits of good sex characterize all good moral living? In answering the question, these contemporary theologians or philosophers of the erotic have crossed the frontier, but so far as I have read them, can yet go further. Since I have read far from all of what they have to say on the subject, I am not criticizing them. I am trying to respond constructively to what I have read by them. Their analysis, their phenomenological description, of the erotic precisely as human value and as like the sexual is enriching, but limited. They say little that is specific or exact, for instance, of what characterizes both the good sexual pleasuring that lovers seek and other good human pleasurings. How specifically are the pleasures of a good parent erotic? Or those of a good teacher? Or those of Mother Teresa, caring for the destitute?

As I say, the answer I have found in contemporary thinkers goes forward, but only so far. Their illuminating analysis calls for expansion. For such expansion it helps to turn to our Western past and to stalwart individual counterculturers, women of the Middle Ages, who in their time evoked outright the best human life not as sexual but as in some ways like making love. I have made a start at this in my book, *Hadewijch and Her Sisters: Other Ways of Loving and Knowing.*

In the present essay I press beyond my book and listen further to a woman mystic and theologian, a Beguine living in the Low Countries of Europe in the early thirteenth century. Her name is Hadewijch.[6] She describes what she experienced as the best living for all humans, that is, her supreme union with Divine Love. She describes that union more explicitly, systematically and radically in erotic terms than any Christian author that I have found up to her time. In this present essay, I put to Hadewijch questions that I did not press in the book. I ask about the nature of the pleasures ascetically renounced by Hadewijch in her pursual and gain of the supreme union and, more intensively, about the nature of the supreme pleasure that she seeks and enjoys in this supreme union.

In the present essay, we must turn first to one of the generators of our ethical mainstream. What does Plato say of pleasure? We hear Plato deprecate and scorn the kind of pleasure that Hadewijch extols and glories in. We listen to Plato in the *Philebus,* where he offers his most extended, evaluative analysis of human pleasure. Then, for a countering description of the best human pleasure as erotic pleasure, we could listen to Plotinus or Pseudo-Dionysius, or any of innumerable Christian commentators on the *Song of Songs,* from Origen in the third century on. But, what if we move from Plato's *Philebus* all the way to the thirteenth century and listen to Hadewijch as she glories in having enjoyed a kind of pleasure that is similar to the kind of pleasure which Plato looked down upon?

From our time satellite we cannot help noting a peculiarity, perhaps minor yet puzzling: the pleasure respectively scorned and gloried in is not only identified as sexual or like the sexual. Both praisers and scorners identify it also as like eating and drinking! If they are not hung up only on sex, then what are the objectors objecting to?[7] And, in the opposing thought, why so recurrent and free a metaphor for union with Christ of both banqueting and making love? What is going on?

In any case, I suggest that Plato's and Hadewijch's disagreement on the nature of the best human pleasure exemplifies a tension constant in Western ethics, Western value judgments, and Western spirituality for twenty-five hundred years, and still taut and central today (as Harrison, Heyward, Lorde, and Hunt bring out). I offer now from the *Philebus* of Plato and from the writings of Hadewijch a bit of textual evidence of the truth of this suggestion. I aspire only to make it an attractive working hypothesis for further historical study.

I press what is ultimately a question of value, the question of what makes good human living. Inasmuch as the historical picture that I propose turns out to be correct, has perhaps the Western intellectual establishment something to learn about the good human life and in it the best kind of pleasure? Is it perhaps true that the two kinds of pleasure, one scorned and the other exalted by dominant Western tradition, are indeed, as a recurrent counterculture has maintained, both of great, absolute human value? Are not both great human goods in themselves? Might this value question be surfacing in present day value questions, like those, for example, urged by some feminists? If so, might the story of answers to this question in the West over the last twenty-five hundred years be illuminating? What might follow in contemporary ideals and spiritualities if the minority's affirmative answer to these questions should be true? What kind of asceticism might blossom?

In the *Philebus*[8] Plato affirms several things about pleasure.

1. Not all pleasure is evil. There is human pleasure that is good in itself, as there is human knowing that is good in itself. In the *Philebus,* as in other dialogues, Plato seeks to identify the good human life or, as he puts it, "the good" (e.g., 11B) of human life. The good is what, if a human being should have it in his or her life, ensures that he or she neither wants nor needs anything else. Their satisfaction is complete (60C). Knowing is essential to good human life but by itself does not suffice. It does not constitute completely good human life. Good human life consists of pleasure as it consists of knowing (for example, *Philebus* 60, 63B–64A).

2. Human pleasure that is good in itself arises out of good human knowing. Human pleasures are good if they are true pleasures. Pleasures are true in that they are determined by the individual's knowing or true judgment (for example, 38A–40E). Such pleasures are indeed good in themselves (for example, 63B–64A); and this intrinsic goodness derives principally from the knowing with which they are thus related (63E, *oikeias hēmin*). Correspondingly, these pleasures are the pleasures associated with (38A, *meta*), in (40C, in the dative case), that attach to (51B, *peri*), are peculiar to (51CD, *oikeias* and *sumphutous*) the reality known: such as beautiful colors, or what one has learned. This is why, on the one hand, the best pleasures have their own intrinsic goodness, and, on the other hand, this goodness is less than, inferior to that of any human knowing as also of right opinion (66BC, 60A–D). This thesis shapes the rest of the answer that Plato gives in Socrates' voice to the single question dominating the dialogue and his debate with Philebus.

3. The best, the truest, of the true pleasures, derive their intrinsic goodness from the superior knowing, the knowing by reason, and from what is thereby known. They share in the beauty known, in its truth, identity, proportion, measure, and form. In sharing in this beauty, the pleasures share in being, not becoming. They share in what is, that which exists in reality, ever unchanged (58A, 58D–59C, 61DE). They share in the *bebaion* (fixity) and *ceilikrin* (purity, truth, perfect clarity) of what is known. The pleasure in knowing such reality and in such reality known is the best kind of pleasure.

All this fits with themes of Plato orchestrated in other dialogues. If in the *Philebus* Plato still held to be true what he wrote in earlier dialogues, he understood the good human life described in the *Philebus* to be union with the divine, in knowing the divine and in taking pleasure in the divine. This seems likely, since the traits of the reality known listed above are what characterize the divine, ultimate reality in his other dialogues. In any case, what Socrates in the *Philebus* works explicitly from beginning to end to establish is what characterizes the good human life. The *Philebus* offers Plato's most extensive and systematic exposition of what pleasure makes part of good human life and what pleasure does not do so. He builds, I submit, an intellectual position which has dominated Western thought, both religious and secular, down the ages.

4. What, then, in the *Philebus,* constitute the inferior pleasures of human life? It follows from points 2 and 3 that all other pleasures are inferior to the best pleasures in that the inferior pleasures are, first, pleasures not determined by knowing, that is, not taken in knowing or in anything known, at least not in intellectual or rational knowing or anything so known. Neither are they determined by true opinion of what is; for true opinion has a share in some properties of knowing.

Some inferior pleasures are by human nature necessary or useful, such as the basic pleasures of eating and drinking. Plato means here not pleasures of taste, but the simple pleasures of eating when hungry and drinking when thirsty. These natural pleasures often have goodness by virtue of their connection with a higher good, such as intellectual activity; as they help enable it by encouraging good health. But these lower pleasures are not good in themselves. Wise people do not seek necessary or useful pleasures for themselves, whereas they seek the pleasure of wisdom for itself and the pleasure of a virtuous life for itself.

The basic pleasures of food and drink, though natural and necessary, are not the best pleasures of human life because the pleasures of food and drink are determined by and taken in not so much a knowing of something (even relatively) permanent, but by the perception of a process of physical replenishment (for example, 51B, 66C; cf. 31B–32B, 34C–35C, 62E). The basic human pleasure of eating and drinking is not the pleasure of a resultant full stomach. It is the pleasure of the stomach's being filled as one eats, of one's desire for replenishment being satisfied (for example, 34C–35C, 35E). It is not the pleasure of any resultant satisfaction as one rises from the meal and walks away. As Plato words it, the thirsty, hungry person takes pleasure in his lack's being filled, not in his resultant fullness.

More generally and significantly, the pleasures of eating and drinking and other kindred pleasures are inferior in being, second, pleasure taken, not in anything stable, but in a process. Not in anything that is, but in something coming to be (54A–55A). More accurately, these lower pleasures (lower than pleasures in beautiful sight and sound) are taken in the coming to be of something. Once the something comes to be, it no longer gives pleasure. These lower pleasures, therefore, are radically different from pleasure in eternal beauty, or in physical beauty, or in the fact that something is.

Furthermore, the inferiority of such lower pleasures lies in that they occur, third, with pain, particularly the pain of need *(endeia)*. Thirst and hunger are kinds of painful need. Pain such as thirst or hunger occurs when harmony is dissolved in us living beings and nature is thereby disrupted (31B–32B, esp. 31Dff.). The pleasure is had inasmuch as and while harmony is being restored to the individual's nature. In the process of restoration, pleasure joins and eventually replaces the pain (31D; cf. 31E–32B, 32E).

Pleasures mixed with pain are obviously inferior to unmixed pleasures (51A–52B, 53B–C, 66B). Unlike the mixed pleasure of sating hunger, the unmixed pleasure of learning, a pleasure belonging only to the very few (52B), does not normally arise out of pain or with pain. There is not even discomfort or distress in our nature when we forget what we know, though, on occasion, the consideration of practical consequences may cause discomfort or distress. But there is always discomfort or distress when the effect of the food and drink wears off, and we once more feel needy desire for food and drink. Significantly, when we do not feel the pain of hunger and thirst but eat and drink anyway, we feel little pleasure.

Plato makes two points here.

1. We have such inferior pleasures only when we first feel pain.
2. These inferior pleasures are, from beginning to end, mixed with pain.

The pleasure thus depends on pain in two respects. Conversely, the pleasure of knowing something involves no pain, neither before the pleasure nor in its rise and continuance. Nor is our returning to know something dependent upon our feeling pain at its absence. When we desire to gain new knowledge or to return to knowledge already gained, our strong, effective desire is serene, not painful. Serene, too, is the pleasure of actually knowing.

Examples of inferior pleasure, necessary or useful, are not only the pleasures of eating when hungry and drinking when thirsty. They are also the pleasures of getting warm when chilled, getting cooled when overheated, being scratched when itchy (32A–32D, 51CD). Plato does not say explicitly in the *Philebus* that sexual pleasure, "the pleasure of love," (pleasure *peri t'aphrodisia;* 65C–66A) is a necessary or useful pleasure, nor whether it arises upon perceiving a physical process. But he treats sexual pleasure as similar to, while inferior to, the pleasures of eating and drinking.

Let me propose a concrete phenomenon of Plato's favored example of inferior pleasure, that of eating and drinking. Phenomenology can illumine further his philosophical position and our philosophical question concerning kinds of pleasure. I use here Plato's more common phrasing and speak of the pleasure of eating and drinking, not as pleasure in perceiving that I am being filled, nor even more simply as pleasure in being filled, but most simply as pleasure that the process of being filled is taking place. This remarkable phrasing reflects how little distinct for Plato are the pleasures, and perception, of hungry eating and thirsty drinking.

My enjoyment of breakfast this morning, Plato would say, was simply my emptiness being filled. That is: my conscious emptiness being consciously filled. Coming to the breakfast table I feel pain in my innards, an urgent lack, need, emptiness, disharmony, disunity. As I drink my juice and eat my cereal, pleasure arises and grows within me: a growing of satisfaction, fullness, harmony. At the same time, I have other kinds of pleasure. I take pleasure in that I am eating a healthy breakfast: simply orange juice and Muesil. I have mild pleasures of taste but not great, as I do not particularly like the taste of either orange juice or Muesli. As I eat, I reflect on this present essay. I have worked long and hard on it and am pleased at the insights with which I have brought it to its present form.

This pleasure, satisfaction, harmonizing, filling, according to Plato is nothing except the process of eating. When I stand up from the table and head for the door, I am indeed full, and I know it; but I no longer have much, if any, of the pleasure I had in eating the breakfast. My fullness gives scarcely any pleasure. My being filled was it all. But if I reflect again on my insights and resulting essay, then I have pleasure as fresh and strong as I had when reflecting on them during breakfast. On the other hand, my actual production of the essay gave me, at the time, relatively little pleasure, compared to my pleasure now at its finished state.

My pleasure in eating was simply a becoming, a coming to be. Once I finally came to be what I was coming to be, that pleasure ceased. This kind of pleasure is not in being this or that, but in coming to be this or that. This is why the fact that it is based on perception, a kind of "knowing," adds little value. The perception is only minimally a knowing. I perceive a coming-to-be, of the physical being filled. This is Plato's analysis; and I submit, that he is correct about the facts of experience here, so far as he goes. I submit, too, that this analysis is true, too, so far as it goes, of sexual making love and orgasm and other pleasures that Plato and the Western mainstream deemed similarly inferior, whether or not necessary or useful. Once I climax, a pleasure of this kind ceases, though it is perhaps replaced by other kinds of pleasure. The pleasure is only in the climaxing and its momentary sensation. I have published two phenomenologies of similar, nonsexual pleasure, in which my description is similar to, and my value judgment contrary to, that of Plato.[9]

We have, therefore, the two kinds of contrasting pleasure that, I submit, conflict in thought and culture down into the waning twentieth century. Inferior human pleasures are inferior to pleasures good in themselves in three ways. The inferior pleasure is determined by no knowing or true judgment, except, at best, by dim, tactile perception; and is thus, in contrast to true pleasures, dark and opaque. It is pleasure taken in, and sharing in, sheer becoming and not in being. It takes place only along with pain, particularly the pain of *endeia* (need), and is thus not serenely pure pleasure.

But Plato bares further differences between the two pleasures. The inferior human pleasures are also often inferior to pleasures good in themselves in that, fourth, the inferior pleasures can be and often are *sphodr-* (great, intense) or most intense pleasures (63DE, 52CD; cf. 65E–66A, 44D–45E). The higher pleasures, true pleasures, are not great or intense (52CD). The higher pleasures can, however, be *hēdion* (more pleasant) (53AB) as well as more satisfying than the greatest, most intense pleasures; and they contribute to a more peaceful, as well as more beautiful, life (53BC, 65D–66E, 63E–64A).

The greatest pleasures are bodily (45A), but Plato does not argue their inferiority simply on the basis of their bodiliness as bodiliness. He continues to analyze our experience of great, intense pleasures. The greatness and intensity of a felt pleasure constitute a basic inferiority because, as with the natural pleasures of food and drink, intense pleasure involves pain along with the pleasure (46A–47B, 50Eff.). It is telling that pleasure is intenser and greater for the ill when they are replenished than it is for the healthy. The greater desire and need of the ill make their pleasure greater and more intense. So, too, the profligate has the greatest, most intense pleasure. The greatest pleasures of all are had when body and soul are bad (44D–45E, 46A–47B).

The greatest and most intense pleasures are inferior, too, because of their consequences. The consequences arise because of a more personal inferiority that the pleasures cause: the soul is passively overcome by the pleasures and, in turmoil, is deprived of the exercise of genuine knowing. Reason and intelligence object to the presence of such pleasures because they "put countless obstacles in our way, disturbing with frenzy the souls in which we dwell, and prevent us from ever coming to existence and as to our offspring they utterly ruin them in most cases, so careless and forgetful do they make us" (63DE). The pleasures overcome the rationally judging and deciding individual.

The felt greatness and intensity of pleasures spring from another, yet more fundamental, intrinsic inferiority. A pleasure can be great and intense only to the extent that it lacks limit (*apeir-;* 28A, 31A) and measure (*metr-;* 65C–66A, 52C). Pleasure lacks limit and measure to the extent that it lacks form, beauty, being (as opposed to becoming), goodness and intelligibility. It lacks these things to the extent that it is not determined by rational knowing and the being that is so known. Positively, these pleasures that can be great and intense approach being sheer pleasure, pleasure as such.

No actual pleasure can be sheer pleasure; for all reality is to some extent, however minimal, constituted by the particular limit and measure with which cosmic intelligence fashions it. But all pleasures, conspicuously those connected with becoming and pain and open to being great and intense, are of themselves unlimited and unmeasured; for pleasure as such is unlimited and unmeasured (28A, 31A, 32D, 60DE, 63D, 65C–66A).

Once again I believe Plato is right concerning the facts, so far as he goes. With this kind of pleasure, our experience is twofold: (1) our pleasure, that is, our feeling pleasure, and (2) our knowing, our awareness of, the pleasure, of ourselves feeling pleasure. We first feel the pleasure and then we know we feel it. In feeling intense pleasures, we are aware of a sweeping, though not complete, absence of limit, measure, form, permanence, and intelligibility. Subsequently, we recognize how little aware we were of anything while we were feeling this pleasure intensely. We were aware only and barely of the pleasure and the feeling of pleasure becomes quickly dim in memory. Of the most intense pleasure, such as that of orgasm, Plato's description of extreme pleasure is almost the whole story. He who feels extreme pleasure feels it "without any true opinion that he felt it, without any recognition whatever of the character of his experience, without even a momentary memory of it" (60DE).

To keep such inferior pleasure at a minimum is a main thrust of Platonic asceticism. The Platonic ascetic seeks only the true pleasures of which Socrates spoke, and all pleasures that attend upon virtues in general and follow them around in their divinity. The pleasures sought are determined principally by intelligent knowing and share in the goodness of beauty and the beauty known: clear, unchanging being. These pleasures are linked with pertinent knowing to make up a mixture as beautiful and *astasiastoten* (peaceable) as can be (63E–64A).

5. Plato, in distinguishing the two kinds of pleasures, is as lucid, consistent, and profound as he is elsewhere. But the traits with which we have just heard him identify inferior pleasure characterize what, from his own time fairly steadily on down to our time, will be identified in countercultural thought as supremely good pleasure. This counterthinking about pleasure picks up mass and momentum, as I recalled above, from Plotinus and Origen onward. The supreme union of the individual with God, whether in passing mystical experience here below, or in eternal bliss hereafter, is identified as similar to the pleasure of sexual lovers. This erotic union with God is, I submit, described with those traits that Plato in the *Philebus* attributed to lower pleasures such as in sex and eating, and because of which traits he considered them to be lower pleasures. The erotic union with God is also, I submit (and am about to illustrate with Hadewijch), described by this countercultural tradition with traits patently true of much human sexual pleasure, yet omitted by Plato in his operative description of sexual pleasure. The historical contrast between Plato and these later erotic thinkers sets up the ethical question that concerns me. Which of them is right? Is or is not this erotic kind of pleasure, whether had in eating or sex or myriad other forms, truly good in itself in human life? When it is good in itself, what are exactly its traits?

In the present essay my ambition is only to make this ethical question, this value question, more concrete, by offering a few bits of historical documentation of the two contrasting answers. Having advanced some documentation in Plato's *Philebus,* I turn now to the mystical theologian, Hadewijch, a Beguine of the Low Countries in Europe in the early thirteenth century. Listen to her. In the present essay, I draw on and advance my report of her thought in my book, *Hadewijch and Her Sisters: Other Ways of Loving and Knowing.*

The letters, poems, and accounts of visions composed by Hadewijch come to over three hundred pages in English translation. In them she describes her asceticism over and over. More often her asceticism, as she conceives and practices it, fits into the spirituality of Platonizing Christian theologians of the preceding twelfth century, such as Bernard of Clairvaux and the Victorines. Hadewijch is, for instance, ascetic according to the general traits of asceticism that we noted above: she actively over the years makes herself a virtuous or excellent person. The excellence she claims for herself is usually the excellence Plato and, in general, the Western tradition attributes to the virtuous person. I have outlined above the properties of this excellence, that is, the good life, urged by Plato.

A number of times, however, Hadewijch claims a different excellence. At times what she affirms of herself can make sense in traditional, Platonizing Christian spirituality; but the fact that she does affirm it—indeed, emphasizes and gives it central importance—is unusual in that spirituality and jars with its wonted expression. Concluding the fourteenth and last Vision, Hadewijch records:

> The Voice said to me: "O strongest of all warriors! You have conquered everything and opened the closed totality, which never was opened by creatures who did not know, with painfully won and distressed love, how I am God and Man! O heroine, since you are so heroic, and since you never yield, you are called the greatest heroine. It is right, therefore, that you should know me perfectly.
>
> *Vision 14, 172ff., trans. Columba Hart*

Similarly, immediately before she is taken into the second, final stage of supreme union with God, she hears the divine voice crying loudly about her:

> ". . . Behold this is my bride, who has passed through all your honors with perfect love, and whose love is so strong that, through it, all attain growth." And he said, "Behold, Bride and Mother, you like no other have been able to love me as God and Man. . . . you like no other have superhumanly suffered much among men. You shall suffer everything to the end with what I am, and we shall remain one. Now enjoy fruition of me, what I am, with the strength of your victory. . . ." *Vision 10, 54ff.*

This achievement, her perfect love, comes about through her superbly strong, free will (for instance, in Vision 1, 60ff., 177ff., 288ff.; Vision 11, 98ff., 174ff.; Letter 2, 63ff.; cf. also Letter 22, 39ff.).

The affirmations of the preceding paragraph do not logically contradict the dominant Christian ideals of the time. One can argue that these mainstream ideals imply the possible truth of such affirmations. But how many Christians of her time and earlier made such affirmations? How many reported that God proclaimed their strength of self, perfect love, and conquest of everything? Hadewijch's exultant reporting of God's exaltation of herself conveys, I believe, a sense of her individual self in its strength and depth that surpasses the tradition felt and expressed by many others, particularly women, of her time. In other passages, to be discussed shortly, Hadewijch affirms herself even more strongly. She makes clear that she has in achieving their final supreme union conquered even Divine Love itself while Divine Love conquered her. Her affirmation of self is an affirmation of self in equally mutual relating with God, Divine Love. I will sketch this mutuality shortly. So high a prizing of so equal a mutuality is, to my knowledge, unparalleled in prior Western theology and spirituality.

Hadewijch is ascetic also in that she forgoes certain pleasures. Her forgoing of some of these pleasures is traditional in Christian asceticism. For most of her hours, God deprives her of the ecstatic joy of supreme union with him. Her occasional experience of this joy makes her general loss of it all the more agonizing. God directs her "back again into the cruel world, where you must taste every kind of death . . ." (Vision 6, 92ff.). The words of Vision 10 cited above are followed shortly by: "And I lay in this fruition half an hour; but then the night was over, and I came back, piteously lamenting my exile, as I have done all this winter."

Hadewijch forgoes, too, ordinary human pleasures in heeding her beloved's call: "If you wish to be like me in my Humanity, . . . you shall desire to be poor, miserable and despised by all men . . ." (Vision 1, 288ff.). She, like him, suffers bodily pain and all the hardships proper to the human condition except sin alone, while her will, like his, overflows "with charity for men through the whole world (Vision 1, 307ff., 341ff.; cf. Vision 8, 79ff.). All men forsake her because of her perfect love and because she is living in God's will (Vision 1, 364ff.).

But two kinds of pleasure that Hadewijch at times forgoes make her, again, unusual in the Western tradition. Her *untrouw* (unfaith) (in, for example, Poem in Couplets 10, 75–98; Vision 13, 179ff.; Letter 8, 27ff.; cf. Letter 1, 56ff.) in loving leads her to discard, for the moment, the comforts of both humility and reason, particularly the comfort of faith in God's providential love, a faith that reason maintains. Hadewijch cries out to God regarding God's declared love for her: "I don't believe you!" as she loves him all the more. It is, as we shall see, by this unfaith that she conquers Divine Love and effects their supreme union.

For the rest of the present essay, we will concentrate, not on the fine person that Hadewijch makes herself nor on the pleasures she forgoes, but rather on what was stated earlier to be a third facet of any asceticism: the pleasure of the life that the ascetic prizes and seeks above all. For Hadewijch, as, indeed, for Plato, this prized, desired life is a certain union with God. For Hadewijch, as for Plato, the nature of this supreme union determines the nature of the pleasure that it gives. But Hadewijch identifies differently from Plato the nature of this highest, most satisfying union with God. She differs from him radically on the nature of its pleasure, the best pleasure a human being can have. Hadewijch resembles her contemporary, Thomas Aquinas, in systematically constructing novel theology while passing over its novelty.

What, according to Hadewijch, is this supreme union of the human being with God? It is, she and Plato agree, what the blest enjoy continuously after death and she and a few others experience occasionally in this earthly life (for example, Vision 5, 59ff., 63ff.). Hadewijch often describes this supreme union in general terms and without distinguishing between stages of experience. At times, however, she distinguishes two successive stages (Vision 6, *passim* and particularly 22ff., 67ff., 76ff.; Vision 13, 252ff.; Vision 14, 145ff.).

The first stage is in the spirit. "Spirit" in medieval Dutch, *gheeste,* has more of an intellectual cast than it does in English, while still having a richer, more affective meaning than intellect or reason would convey. This stage is a Platonic kind of sublime contemplation, which is or includes a transcendent *redennen* (reasoning) (Vision 6, 67ff., 76ff.; Vision 9, 65ff., Vision 13, 128ff.), a seeing of God's divine beauty. The seeing, accompanied often by a hearing of God's words, causes great pleasure as well as other emotions in the onlooking, listening Hadewijch. Hadewijch echoes here, at times word for word, both Plato and Platonizing thinkers of the century before her such as Richard and Hugh of St. Victor, William of St. Thierry, and Bernard of Clairvaux.

Hadewijch reports exultantly that, on occasion, she passed out of this first stage of union with God into further union, out of the spirit. To describe in the present essay this second stage, I draw principally on accounts in Hadewijch's recorded visions, particularly 1, 3, 5–7, 9–14; I use only at random her letters, stanzaic poems, and poems in couplets. This second, last stage of the final union is different from, and in many aspects contrary to, the first stage of her union and thus to Plato's representation of the best human life, characterized in the *Philebus* and identified in other dialogues of Plato with union with God. For both Plato and Hadewijch, this best human life brings satisfying pleasure, but the pleasure that Hadewijch finds here, in the final stage, is the opposite of what Plato finds. The pleasure that Hadewijch finds in final union with the Divine verifies rather Plato's analysis, in the *Philebus,* of inferior human pleasure. The pleasure Hadewijch finds in supreme union with the Divine is like an inferior pleasure, as Plato describes it, both in that out of which Hadewijch's pleasure arises, and in the pleasure itself.

To characterize this second stage, Hadewijch has learned concepts and words from thinkers before her. The twelfth-century Christian Platonists who influenced Hadewijch had already departed from Plato in attributing to the very summit of supreme union with God some properties similar to those in Hadewijch's second stage. Even more so did earlier, more systematically neoplatonic Christian thinkers such as Pseudo-Dionysius, not to mention Plotinus himself. I refer once more to the countercultural prizing and theological projection of the erotic in some of this earlier theology. I refer also to not completely overlapping developments in negative theology, typified by Pseudo-Dionysius.[10] But, to my knowledge, no synthesis of any other Christian thinker by the mid-thirteenth century offered so categorically, extensively or systematically what Hadewijch presents in her theological account of this culminating union, as I outline it below.[11] On the other hand, much that is novel in her picture appears in subsequent Christian accounts of mystical experience, though its effect upon mainstream theology and ethical statement of the highest values of human life is small. In any case, I raise (but do not tackle in this essay) the questions of Hadewijch's advance over prior Christian Platonists and neo-Platonists and of her anticipation of later Christian mystical theologians. I undertake only to contrast Hadewijch describing this second, final stage of supreme union with God with Plato, discoursing in the *Philebus* on the best human life.

Let us listen further to Hadewijch telling of the second, final stage of her occasional, blissful union with God, her union with God out of the spirit. I follow the practice of Hart, her translator into English, of retaining Hadewijch's use of pronouns for God. When Hadewijch speaks of God as "Love" (*Minne,* feminine gender), she uses feminine pronouns. When she speaks of God as "God" or "Christ" or "Father," she uses masculine pronouns.

The pleasure of this second, culminating stage of Hadewijch's final union differs from the pleasure of the good life described in Plato's *Philebus* in two respects. It differs in that out of which the pleasure arises and in the pleasure itself. Let us look at particulars. For our purpose, it makes no difference whether in the following statements of Hadewijch she speaks of only the second, final stage of union with God or of both first and second stage together, since in both cases she describes the second stage. I do not address in this essay, though I do in my book, how Hadewijch describes the union out of the spirit in bodily terms and asserts nevertheless that it occurs out of the body.

In the immediate antecedent of the final blissful union, for example, Hadewijch reaches the pleasuring union (even the first stage, in the spirit) out of intense, painful, desire for it (Vision 1, 307ff.; Vision 4, 1ff.; Vision 6, 1ff.; Vision 8, 112ff.; Vision 11, 134ff.; Vision 14, 1ff.). She reports also on occasion, as in Vision 7, quoted below, what not infrequently characterizes desire for pleasure in real life—and what Plato did not mention. The intense desire is mutual. Hadewijch's desire is reciprocated.

> My heart and my veins and all my limbs trembled and quivered with eager desire and, as often occurred with me, such madness and fear beset my mind that it seemed to me I did not content my Beloved, and that my Beloved did not fulfil my desire, so that dying I must go mad, and going mad I must die. On that day my mind was beset so fearfully and so painfully by desirous love that all my separate limbs threatened to break, and all my separate veins were in travail. . . . *Vision 7, 1ff.*

> . . . he came himself to me, took me entirely in his arms, and pressed me to him, and all my members felt his in full felicity, in accordance with the desire of my heart and my humanity. *Vision 7, 64ff.*

> . . . I have never experienced Love in any sort of way as repose; on the contrary, I found Love a heavy burden and disgrace. For I was a human creature, and Love is terrible and implacable, devouring and burning without regard for anything. The soul is contained in one little rivulet; her depth is quickly filled up; her dikes quickly burst. Thus with rapidity the Godhead has engulfed human nature wholly in itself. *Vision 11, 121ff.*

> . . . such great horror as I continually was from Love, and still continually am.
> *Vision 14, 52ff.*

Hadewijch recounts how this pleasuring union arises out of her control and with a certain passivity on her part. Hadewijch is thrown (Vision 12, 1ff.) into the union and lies in it. The Angel calls out to the Lord, ". . . *transport* her wholly within yourself" (Vision 6, 22ff.). She reports, "But then wonder *seized* me . . . and through this wonder I came out of the spirit . . ." (76ff.). "But Love came and *embraced* me; and I came out of the spirit and remained lying until late in the day, *inebriated* with unspeakable wonders" (Vision 9, 65ff.). "The Voice *embraced* me with an unheard-of wonder, and I *swooned* in it, and my spirit failed me to see or hear more (Vision 10, 70ff.). "And I *lay* in that fruition half an hour; but then the night was over, and I came back, piteously lamenting my exile, as I have done all this winter" (Vision 13, 252ff.).

She falls into the union, that is, into the bottomless, swirling abyss, the profound whirlpool with hidden storms as it engulfs and swallows her; and she lies there for half an hour (symbolic time measurement of Apocalypse; Vision 1, 236ff., 246ff., 383ff.; Vision 12, 1ff., 152ff.; Vision 13, 252ff.; cf. Vision 11, 1ff., 72ff.).

Similarly, "I *fell* out of the spirit—from myself and all I had seen in him—and, wholly *lost, fell* upon the breast, the fruition, of his Nature, which is Love. There I remained, *engulfed and lost* . . ." (Vision 6, 76ff.; similarly Vision 12, 1ff., 172ff.). Note her horror of the abyss, its being terrifying (Vision 12, 105ff.), her fear of it (Vision 12, 172ff.).

In her visions Hadewijch generally felt "*such an attraction of my spirit inwardly that I could not control myself outwardly* in a degree sufficient to go among persons; it would have been impossible for me to go among them" (Vision 1, 1ff.). Hadewijch's supreme pleasure entails what Plato fears and despises: the individual is passively swept into and overcome by pleasures and is unable to act rationally.

Although Hadewijch moves into the supreme, final, blissful union overpowered by needy desire and with a certain passivity and loss of control on her part, she still affirms several times that she has the very desire that takes over her and puts her out of her control only because she wills so freely, so strongly to so desire. God recognizes, indeed applauds, that the convergence of Hadewijch's free will and fierce desire gained her the final fruition of God (Vision 11, 98ff.; cf. 174ff.; Vision 14, 52ff.).

By the greatness of her willed, loving desire, Hadewijch conquers Divine Love and gains thereby the full pleasuring union (see Stanzaic Poem 38, 7–8, 53–59; 39, 88–90; 40, 21–24). Even of the first stage of union, that of reason and humility, Mary says to Hadewijch, ". . . you vanquished Love and made Love one" (Vision 13, 228ff.). In the final, supreme stage, Hadewijch completes her conquest: Divine Love Herself cannot stay away from Hadewijch's challenging, passionate love (Vision 13, 179ff., 228ff.) with its sweet, irresistible unfaith, disbelief, in Love's love for Hadewijch (Poem in Couplets 10, 75–98; Vision 13, 179ff.; Letter 8, 27ff.; cf. Letter 1, 56ff.). At the same time Divine Love is conquering Hadewijch and her love by drawing Hadewijch powerfully to herself. Thus the supreme union of Hadewijch with God arises out of a powerful, fierce, intimate mutuality, interdependent and interactive, of her and the Divine.

All four of these traits (or sets of traits) that lead into the final union of Hadewijch with God are the opposite of Plato's picture of the movement toward the basic pleasure of good human life, as seen in the *Philebus*.

Hadewijch differs from Plato also in what she identifies to be the pleasure of the very final stage. Hadewijch most often identifies her union with God as an enjoying. She uses words of *ghebruk*-stem (e.g., Vision 12, 140ff.; Vision 13, 252ff.) throughout the recorded Visions. *Ghebruk-*, like Thomas Aquinas's *fruitio* and the modern Dutch *geniet-* (with which the modern Dutch translators of Hadewijch, Bladel, Spaapen, and Mommaers translate ghebruk-), means basically a pleasuring possessing, an enjoying having.[12] In a given context, both facets of the word's meaning, that is, both having and enjoying, may be prominent; or one may be in the foreground with the other only implied. Hart translates *ghebruk-* more commonly as "fruition" but at times as "enjoying" (as in Letter 12, 53ff.). Often where Hart translates the *ghebruk-* union of God and Hadewijch as "fruition," concomitant assertions of "sweetness" (see Letter 27, 44ff.; Letter 1, 4ff.) and of mutual "contenting" and "satisfying" (see Vision 7, 1ff.; Letter 7) make it clear that for Hadewijch the fruition is an enjoying, a pleasuring.

The human being's final union with God is an enjoying of God: "to be one with God in fruition" (Vision 1, 1ff., 246ff.). This is "that highest fruition of wonder beyond reason . . . ," to be enjoyed eternally (Vision 5, 63ff.; note God's explanatory words when Hadewijch comes again to herself and into the spirit). Hadewijch's account of the second stage of her supreme union with God differs from Plato's in her centering on its being her enjoyment of God. Plato almost always, as in the *Philebus,* typifies good human living as union in which knowing is central. Similarly does Hadewijch depict consistently her first stage of supreme union. But she depicts the second stage almost exclusively, not as knowing, but simply as pleasure. Is this merely a difference in selective highlighting? I would like first to show how Hadewijch's further picture of this supreme union agrees with, or does not clearly depart from, Christian Platonists who, from Origen up through Hadewijch's times, described to some extent the supreme human union with God in erotic images, terms, and even concepts.

Hadewijch follows the neoplatonic tradition as well as do Bernard of Clairvaux and his followers in that, in the supreme union, she made Love one (Vision 13, 128ff.). She becomes Divine Love. God enabled her to "be Love as I am Love" (Vision 3, 1ff.; Vision 7, 14ff., "to be God with God,"—though this may include the first, spiritual stage; similarly, see Vision 14, 145ff.). Eventually nothing any longer remains to her of herself (Vision 7, 94ff.). She is "lost here to myself and all persons." Yet this is not loss but gain: for now "one is not less than he himself is . . ." (Vision 14, 145ff.). I suggest that there is no pantheism in these statements but simply a momentary, complete experiential identification with Love. In her conscious experience she is nothing but Divine Love.[13]

In this supreme union, Hadewijch has "fruition *of me as the Love who I am*" (twice in Vision 3, 1ff.). Though Hadewijch has in the spirit already "seen" who He is (Vision 6, 22, 40, 43ff.), has seen and understood "the entire fruition of his nature in Love" (67ff.), and although all devout believers can have a certain fruition of God, this final stage, this enjoying of God as Love, is having fruition of God's fruition, enjoying God's own enjoying. The reality of Love is primarily Love's fruition of, pleasure in, enjoyment of, complete satisfaction with Herself (Letter 12, 53ff.; 6, 19ff.; 22, 102ff.; 21, 1ff.). Hadewijch becomes that enjoyment, *ghevoel-* (feels) it fully. She enjoys Love with Love's own enjoyment. This enjoyment yields a new knowledge: as she says, she knows how Love enjoys Herself.

But—and here again Hadewijch seems to me to depart from even eroticizing Christian thinkers up to her time—Divine Love is also desire, a "never-contented Beloved" (Letter 16, 14ff.). Divine Love desires to have fruition of creatures.

Hadewijch's becoming perfectly one with Love is not only Hadewijch's finding fruition in God. It is also God's finding fruition in her. When "the soul thinks of nothing else but kissing him and being with him, this is God's life and pleasure" (Poem in Couplets 12, 63–68; cf. 51–52, 79–87). Love finds here her fruition of herself, Love, as well as her fruition of Hadewijch. Their union is a satisfying of Love's desire as well as a satisfying of Hadewijch's desire (Letter 20, 1ff.; Letter 18, 63ff.), as is also indicated by their mutual conquest of each other that brings about this full union. God says to Hadewijch that after her death "we shall live with one life, and one love will satisfy the hunger of us both" (Letter 31, 1ff.; cf. Poem in Stanzas 12, 21–30). Hadewijch's sheer pleasure is thus also her satisfying of Divine Love, and vice versa. As Hadewijch puts it, both God and she are abysses. She satisfies herself, finds full pleasure, and passes into her liberty in the abyss that is He. He satisfies himself, finds full pleasure and passes into his freedom in the abyss that is she (Letter 18, 63ff.). Hadewijch desires the blessed repose of the saints in which God has fruition of himself (Vision 11, 134ff.).

This primal mutuality of desire and enjoyment is at least part of the sense of other formulas of Hadewijch, for example, that she and her Beloved "each wholly receive the other in . . . the passing away of the one in the other" (Vision 7, 94ff.; cf. Vision 12, 172ff.). This supreme union is ". . . to have been flowed through by the whole Godhead, and to have become totally one, flowing back through the Godhead itself" (Vision 14, 77ff.). In this union, they belong to each other, desire each other, are enough to each other (Vision 1, 391ff.; Vision 7, *passim*). Divine Love says to Hadewijch: "Go forth, and live what I am; and return bringing me full divinity, and have fruition of me as who I am" (Vision 3, 1ff.). Hadewijch compares the intimate exchange of love between God and her to ". . . the custom of friends between themselves to hide little and reveal much, what is most experienced is the close feeling of one another, when they relish, devour, drink and swallow up each other . . ." (Letter 11, 10ff.; cf. Letter 31, 1ff.). These statements apply to the final union though they may well be intended to describe also lesser unions of God and Hadewijch. In Platonic wise, the supreme ideal is participated in, in lesser degrees; the participating realities resemble, as well as depend upon, the supreme fullness.

My title for this essay can be misleading. My tale of two pleasures turns out to be a tale of three pleasures. What in the *Philebus* is seen as one kind of inferior pleasure is in human life really two kinds, depending on whether or not the pleasure is sought and enjoyed mutually. The pleasure of eating or sex is at times simply what Plato describes and no more. At other times, it is the same kind of pleasure, but now sought and enjoyed with love. That makes all the difference, and raises promising questions.

Hadewijch's picture is intricate, complex. But it is no more complex or intricate than the human analogue to which Hadewijch by explicit language and imagery compares repeatedly this divine union: two lovers making love. Hadewijch asserts a radical mutuality in the best human living, more radically mutual than any prior Western philosophical or theological account that I know. In any case, mutuality as the most fundamental model is the antithesis of Plato's dialogues and of establishment Western thought down through modern times to today. Kant, Hegel, Sartre, et al., for all their insistence on willing the good of all persons, do not make a mutuality of interdependence and interaffecting part of the rock-bottom foundation, or supreme ideal, of good human life. In the present essay I cannot develop further, historically or ethically, the revolutionary mutuality of Hadewijch's supreme human ideal. I refer the interested reader to my book for fuller presentation and documentation.

Within the limit of my essay, I can only return briefly to and present a bit further another aspect of Hadewijch's personal ideal that calls for further discussion, both historical and ethical. It is a central dimension of the kind of pleasure that Plato scorns and Hadewijch glories in. It does not necessarily entail mutuality, but it helps identify the kind of radical mutuality that Hadewijch espouses and that is highly suggestive for contemporary value thinking, as it is greatly ignored by most the exponents of this thinking.

Hadewijch breaks from Plato's representation of good human life in that this second, final stage of union is dark, "frightfully dark"; Hadewijch cannot see anything or anyone in it (Vision 1, 236ff.; Vision 11, 1ff.; Vision 12, 1ff.). She is lost (Vision 6, 1ff.). She hears nothing. Indeed of this final experience "one can never speak at all" (Vision 13, 252ff.).

In this final union with God, all the knowing, contemplating, speaking, and listening that Hadewijch had and enjoyed in the first stage have left her. This prior knowing contributes in no way to the inebriated pleasure of her supreme falling and lying, her supreme fruition with God. This pleasure fits rather the description the *Philebus* gives of pleasure undetermined by knowing that lower pleasures approached in varying degrees. Her supreme fruition, in this aspect, as in others seen above, turns Plato's hierarchy of values downside up. The kind of pleasure Plato identified as most inferior is, Hadewijch maintains, the best pleasure there is.

Though dark, this final union does include one knowing. The fruition of the union, the very enjoying, the sheer pleasure, constitutes or yields a knowing. She describes this union as ". . . without any comprehension of other knowledge, or sight, or spiritual understanding, except to be one with him and have fruition of this union" (Vision 6, 76ff.). The fruition thus seems to be not pure pleasure but to have an object, to be a peculiar, affective knowing of the object. It is a knowing in darkness, not by seeing but by divine touch (Vision 13, 179ff.) or by feeling (Vision 1, 391ff., 408ff.). Hadewijch frequently describes the supreme fruition as *ghevoel-* (feeling) not spiritual understanding (Vision 1, 246ff.). The pleasure is not self-contained but must somehow be or give an awareness of the other when it is "a fruition of [God] in feeling (this is beyond all)" (Vision 1, 364ff., 408ff.), a "feeling [God]" (Vision 1, 383ff.), a "feeling [the Son] in fruition" as he did the Father (Vision 1, 408ff.).

This unique knowing that Hadewijch gains in her supreme fruition has, therefore, a property intrinsic to the pleasures upon which Plato looked down. Plato did not deny that one enjoying sex or eating hungrily knows, either in the very enjoyment or in subsequent reflection thereof, that he had sex or a good meal and enjoyed it. But this pleasure is for Plato essentially inferior because the pleasure itself is scarcely determined by any prior knowing. It is not pleasure in anything known as good or fine. This kind of pleasure yields at most a knowledge, a dim awareness, of itself. But for Hadewijch the dark knowing of self and other that this pleasure can be or yield is a wonderful property of the best experience in human life.

With this, I close my essay and invite discussion: not only that of historians of thought but that appropriate to human beings concerned with discerning human values. I propose two questions:

1. In characterizing the supreme pleasure that they chose above all and for which they forwent other pleasures, what exactly did Plato mean in the *Philebus,* and Hadewijch mean in her visions?
2. Do you, the reader, agree or disagree with Plato or Hadewijch on the two pleasures that they contrast, according to both fact and value?

NOTES

1. Margaret R. Miles, *Desire and Delight: A New Reading of Augustine's* Confessions (New York: Crossroad, 1992), pp. 8–9.
2. Benedicta Ward, *Signs and Wonders: Saints, Miracles and Prayers from the 4th Century to the 14th* (Hampshire, Great Britain: Variorum, 1992). Ward finds an analogy in W. H. Auden's "In Memory of W. B. Yeats," where he summons the poet, "Follow, poet, follow right / To the bottom of the night; / With your unconstraining voice / Still persuade us to rejoice."
3. Liddell and Scott, *Greek-English Lexicon* (Oxford: Clarendon Press, 1948), *sub voce.*
4. Ignatius of Loyola, *Exercitia spiritualia,* 229, 329, in *Thesaurus Spiritualist Societatis Iesu* (Rome: Typis Polyglottis Vaticanis, 1948), pp. 166, 231.
5. Carter Heyward, *Touching Our Strength: The Erotic as Power and the Love of God* (San Francisco: Harper & Row, 1989); Mary Hunt, *Fierce Tenderness: A Feminist Theology of Friendship* (New York: Crossroad, 1991); Audre Lorde, *Sister Outsider* (Freedom, Calif.: Crossing Press, 1984); Beverly Harrison, *Making the Connections,* ed. Carol S. Robb (Boston: Beacon Press, 1985); Beverly W. Harrison and Carter Heyward, "Pain and Pleasure: Avoiding the Confusions of Christian Tradition in Feminist Theory," in *Christianity, Patriarchy and Abuse: A Feminist Critique,* eds. Joanne Carlson Brown and Carole R. Bohn (New York: Pilgrim Press, 1989), pp. 148–173.
6. Hadewijch, *The Complete Works,* ed. and trans. Mother Columba Hart, O.S.B. (New York: Paulist Press, 1980).
7. I probe the intellectual basis of this traditionally equal and explicitly connected depreciation of pleasures of sex, hunger, and thirst in the thought of Thomas Aquinas in the appendix to my cited book, "Appendix: Thomas Aquinas on the Pleasure of Sex and the Pleasure of Touch."
8. Plato, *Philebus,* Greek text with English translation, by Harold N. Fowler (Cambridge: Harvard Univ. Press, 1952); I profit regularly from Plato's *Philebus,* trans., with introduction and commentary, by R. Hackforth (Cambridge, England: Cambridge University Press, 1972).
9. In "Sleeping Like Spoons: A Question of Embodiment," *Commonweal* (April 7, 1989): 205–207, and in "Walking with Lewie to the Bank," delivered as part of my larger paper, "Embodied Mutuality of Pleasure and Power: One," at a four-day dialogue on Reflections on Religion, Ethics, and Reproduction in Mexico City, December 1992.

10. Cf. Paul Rorem, *Pseudo-Dionysius: A Commentary on the Texts and an Introduction to Their Influence* (Oxford University Press, 1993), pp. 237–240.
11. In my *Hadewijch and Her Sisters: Other Ways of Loving and Knowing,* I contrast in detail the picture drawn by Hadewijch with the depiction of final union by Bernard of Clairvaux and, to a much lesser extent, with that by others of her theological predecessors.
12. *Hadewijch: Brieven,* trans. F. Van Bladel and B. Spaapen (Tielt: Lannoo, 1954); *De Visioenen van Hadewijch,* trans. Paul Mommaers (Nijmegen: B. Gottmer, 1979).
13. As in Bernard of Clairvaux's account of mystical union; cf. Gilson's defense of Bernard against charge of pantheism in Etienne Gilson, *The Mystical Theology of Saint Bernard,* trans. A.C.H. Downes (New York: Sheed and Ward, 1940). But I do not find in Bernard a centering on this oneness with Love as being an enjoying of that Love.

28

Gender and Uses of the Ascetic in an Islamist Text

Fedwa Malti-Douglas

To say gender and Islam is to evoke a multiplicity of images, not the least of which is that of the patriarchal figure of Khomeini, coupled with wave patterns of veiled women. To add the ascetic dimension to this explosive combination might seem out of place. But as some of the writings of the contemporary religious revival show, nothing is strange in this universe in which the contemporary sits alongside the medieval. How does a woman articulate her religious, and, particularly, her ascetic, experience in such a context? An answer can be found in *My Journey from Unveiling to Veiling (Riḥlatī min al-Sufūr ilā al-Ḥijāb),* by the Egyptian television personality Karīmān Ḥamza.[1] One of the most popular Islamist texts, *My Journey* recounts the dramatic story of a born-again young woman who goes from a secular to a religious lifestyle and whose twentieth-century journey is juxtaposed with, and redefined by, that of a number of male medieval mystics. While asceticism has generally not been a dominant element in Islamic mysticism, or Sufism, asceticism was so important in the earliest period of the development of Sufism that these early practitioners are known in the tradition as ascetics even more than as mystics. It is primarily (though not exclusively) to members of this group of early ascetics/mystics that Karīmān Ḥamza attaches her spiritual journey.

Karīmān Ḥamza's work forms part of the by now extensive publications that emanate from the Islamist movement, a religious revival movement in the Middle East that is not just a question of street demonstrations or sermons in the local mosque. At stake is the control of various forms of cultural production, some of which, like literature and the arts, have long been in the hands of more secularized and leftist intellectuals. The transnational nature of Islamism means that its ideas and advocates know no borders. Books may be printed in Cairo and Beirut; but one is as likely to find them in bookstores in other Middle Eastern, as well as European, capitals. Karīmān Ḥamza's book can be found as easily in Egypt as in Morocco and is comfortable sitting on the shelves of religious bookstores in London and in Paris. Cassettes of the sermons of the colorful blind Egyptian *shaykh* Kishk can be had as easily in Houston as in many Arab cities.

Certainly, the religious revival in the Middle East has escaped neither the eye nor the pen of the political scientist or the religious-studies specialist. In fact, there are scholars who have compiled bibliographies of studies on the Muslim revival that to date number well over a thousand or more entries.[2]

Yet the nexus of literature and the religious revival has still to be explored. Oddly enough, this critical occultation comes about because of the unwitting collusion of different academic specialists. On the one hand, most studies of religious movements concern themselves with political and theological questions. It is, therefore, no accident that most Western authors of book-length studies on Islamism should not be cultural or literary critics.[3] On the other hand, Western specialists of Arabic and other literatures of the Middle East confine themselves to the enormous secularized literary production of the region, perceived as it is to be artistically serious and, hence, more worthy of study.

Adab islāmī (Islamic literature) is a parallel Islamic literary production that encompasses all the genres hitherto promulgated by more secularly minded intellectuals: plays, novels, shorts stories, poetry. Even the terms of the debate are clearly laid out. "Committed" literature is no longer the prerogative of one group. One must extend it, we are told, to the religiously engaged text.[4]

This Islamic literature is, of course, not neutral. It advocates a way of life, the religious way. (Statistically, in Arab countries, sales of Islamic books far outnumber those of secular ones.)[5] One of the favored modern Islamic literary genres is the autobiographical. The major figures of the Islamist movement have indulged themselves here: from the popular television preacher Muḥammad Mutawallī al-Sha'rāwī to the aforementioned *shaykh* Kishk.[6]

That gender plays a pivotal role in contemporary Islamic literature may not come as a surprise. It is one of the most consistent areas of debate. Advice on proper female behavior can be gleaned from poetry, novels, and the *fatāwā* (legal literature), akin to Dear Abby columns in which the role of adviser is held by male religious authorities.[7]

In the textual gender game, the female literary voice can be as potent as that of the male. How much more effective is the female saga of redemption when it is told in the first person by a woman otherwise doomed to perdition. This is the case of Karīmān Hamza.

By now a novelist and a television personality, Karīmān Ḥamza has penned a controversial guide on how to be a proper Muslim woman, which has earned her the ire of more conservative Muslim women writers. It is Ḥamza's saga of religious transformation, *Riḥlatī min al-Sufūr ilā al-Ḥijāb,* which is, however, most interesting, dealing as it does with issues of the body, patriarchial redefinition of the female, and religious salvation.

Karīmān Ḥamza's life could have been the dream of any young Egyptian secularized woman her age: a family that is economically comfortable, a father who is a professor of journalism at Cairo University and a successful teacher and writer, and marriage to an army officer that has produced two sons (and a daughter-to-be). To all this, add a university degree.

Yet, something is missing—religion. *My Journey From Unveiling to Veiling* is Karīmān Ḥamza's spiritual journey. Spiritual journeys are a distinct type of autobiographical text and, as such, may conform to some of the generic rules that govern autobiography. It should come as no surprise perhaps that the wealth and variety of the centuries-old Arabo-Islamic literary tradition should have given birth to this sort of testimonial. The by now classic autobiographical text by al-Ghazālī (died 505 CE), *al-Munqidh min al-Dalāl,* is one such case.[8]

But, as with other autobiographical ventures, the male voice has dominated the genre.[9] For the medieval period, woman's spiritual existence was almost always mediated through male scriptors. This is not to say that women did not participate in the religious life of the Muslim community. Far from it. Many are the famous women whose names populate the male textual tradition. Simply, in the medieval prose tradition, women were not scriptors. Their experience, spiritual or otherwise, was culled and presented by male authors.

In the modern period, the situation has changed. Women pen stories of their lives and struggles. Greater access to print for women writers means that, along with other genres, women participate in the creation of their own literary selves. They compose autobiographies. They compose prison memoirs. They compose travel texts. But, once again, it is the secularized women writers who receive critical attention.[10] This occultation of the female religious writer in the domain of Middle Eastern studies means her absence in broader collective works as well.[11]

My Journey from Unveiling to Veiling is a spiritual quest. Its primary goal is not to provide the reader with the life of its protagonist, but with only one aspect of her life, the spiritual saga. Perhaps its closest neighbor in the literature of the contemporary Muslim revival is written by a man: Mustafā Maḥmūd's *Rihlatī min al-Shakk ilā al-Imān (My Journey from Doubt to Belief).*[12] But the two stories differ, as gender dynamics alter the text. Both titles express the idea of a journey, particularly "My Journey" *(Rihlatī).* Both are journeys from one point *(min)* to another *(ilā).*

But it is the points at which the journeys begin and end that are so divergent. Mustafā Maḥmūd moves from doubt to belief, Karīmān Ḥamza, from unveiling to veiling. He draws his reader to the mental aspects of his journey, she to the vestmentary. Karīmān will exit the text as an established religious spokesperson now wearing the proper Islamic dress for women.[13] Her path is fraught with difficulties as she counters social pressure both from the male religious authorities advocating her veiling and from her secular peer group and her own upbringing advocating fashionable Western dress. But her eventual success, we understand, is worth the social and emotional struggle.[14] Indeed, for a spiritual autobiography, Karīmān Ḥamza's text speaks less of the soul than of the body. And, more striking in the work of a woman, it shows this body as defined by and for men. I have explored this aspect of Ḥamza's work elsewhere.[15] What I should like to do here is to address the issues that deal directly with the process of spiritual transformation, specifically as they relate to medieval Muslim male ascetics and mystics.

We meet Karīmān as a university student, married, and seemingly happy. She ends the text as a highly visible public persona, involved in the media.

The actual story of Karīmān's spiritual saga is embedded and hidden behind textual doors (dare we say veils?). The book is introduced by Muḥammad 'Atiyya Khamīs, the head of the Jam'iyyat Shabāb Sayyidinā Muhammad.[16] This Jam'iyya is a group which split from the Muslim Brotherhood in January 1940.[17] After this lengthy presentation, Karīmān Ḥamza introduces her own journey in a short preface-like introduction.[18] The table of contents in the back of the book is followed by some words on Karīmān Ḥamza by the religious leader, the *shaykh* Muḥammad al-Ghazālī. Men introducing women's work is certainly not a new phenomenon in modern Arabic letters, religious or secular. A man's voice validates that of a woman.[19] What is unusual here is the double presence of the male voice, both preceding and following that of the female.

Karīmān Hamza recounts her journey in the first person singular. But this is not a simple diachronic saga in which the religious experience seals the narrative. Hers is a highly complex story in which her own travails are intertextually defined and recast by intricate weavings of quotations from classical sources, in particular the Qur'ān and the *ḥadīth* (traditions of the Prophet), as well as generous selections from the works of her spiritual mentor, Dr. 'Abd al-Ḥalīm Maḥmūd. Even the first-person pronoun is not terribly stable: Karīmān's narration is enriched by the use of the first person plural at critical points in the text when she speaks in a more collective and global voice.

And what a story Karīmān will tell! "Worried. . . . Worried. . . ."[20] Thus does her saga begin. Karīmān is worried about her father's health. In ill health, he is still performing his teaching duties at Cairo University. She is afraid of losing him some day. The father's lecture comes to an end, and his daughter will accompany him to Heliopolis, where she lives next door to him. Instead of heading to this area of Cairo, however, her father instructs the driver to go to the Institute of Islamic Studies, where Karīmān will deliver some books to Dr. 'Abd Allāh al-'Arabī. The car stops in front of the "religious institute." She runs inside quickly in order to come out just as quickly. But things are not so simple. A surprise awaits her.

> The young men of the Institute look at me with an eye that is all astonishment. As though I were from another star that fell by accident on the Institute. . . . My clothes are very short, my hair descending, hanging down wild behind my back, and my small dog is in one of my hands, with the other one carrying the books. . . . Concerned, I ask about Dr. 'Abd Allāh al-'Arabī, but no one answers me. All stare at this strange creature. . . . Me.[21]

This entrance into the Institute of Islamic Studies will change Karīmān's life. But, at the moment, neither she nor the reader knows that. What we both know is that the young woman is woefully out of place in this religious institution; and this for a simple reason: her grooming is not what it should be. Her clothing is inappropriate—too short. Her hair hangs loosely behind her back. The small dog is but an unfortunate victim of this episode. On the one hand, he is a sign that the heroine is a Westernized young woman who parades her pet around the city with her. On the other, he is, as we shall see, symbolic of much more. Karīmān's inquiries remain unanswered. She is turned into a strange object, to be stared at in disbelief, as one might stare at a creature from outer space.

This state of alterity, of strangeness with which the spiritual journey begins is all important. Karīmān, as we first set eyes on her—because that is, after all, what we do as she provides her own corporal description—is a being apart. The reader has up till now only met Karīmān Ḥamza through the introductory material. And her own two-page prefatory remarks do not really introduce her. There, after the proper invocation, she modestly disclaims any pretence of writing "about Dr. 'Abd al-Ḥalīm Maḥmūd Shaykh al-Azhar al-Sharīf, that giant who made a school and founded an army of the righteous." She will establish her own personal experience. But the author does not really take the occasion to introduce herself to her reader. That will await the first page of the *Riḥla.*

Hence, when that first-person narrator reappears as the central protagonist of the spiritual journey, it is to set herself apart. She stands out from the crowd, but in a negative manner. And this crowd is male. It is their gaze that defines her. Their scopic activity begins and closes the episode. Does she possess any spirituality? Is she religious? These attributes seem almost irrelevant. The external determines the internal.

This initial state of lack with which *Riḥlatī min al-Sufūr ilā al-Ḥijāb* begins will dominate the discourse—its rectification, proper Islamic dress that covers the body, is the goal of the journey. And the most important part of the journey, as we shall see, is the call that Karīmān hears.

As Karīmān is standing, dog in hand, a *shaykh* suddenly appears. He is tall, extremely venerable, with features that bring together the modesty of the learned with "something I had not seen before. But I feel it and do not know how to express it." She tries quickly to approach this figure, but the students are faster than she is. They surround him, and she is almost unable to see him. Eventually, the entire group finds itself in a lecture hall.

> And there is the venerable *shaykh* beginning the lecture. And there I am standing, confused, in the middle of this group. Looks of disapproval surround me from every side. . . . The ultimate transgression! I sat so that I could protect myself from the glances of the students. I held my breath and the breath of my small dog, and placed the books on my knees, to protect myself with them from the disapproving, furtive glances.[22]

The section introduced by this incident is entitled "al-Liqā' al-Awwal" (The First Meeting). Karīmān and her dog have entered a forbidden territory, initially dominated by the visual and the scopic. The *shaykh* enters and the narrator describes his physical appearance. As she walks quickly toward him, the other students surround him, and she is unable to see him. Inside the lecture room she herself is surrounded by disapproving glances. When she sits, it is to protect herself from these stares. It is the same protective urge to get away from the gaze that drives her to hold her breath, to muffle that of her pet, and then to place the books on her knee.

The male gaze meets the female gaze. It is as if the narrator has seen something she should not have. After all, do not the male students surround the *shaykh* in such a way that it is difficult for her to see him? Their physical act of surrounding the venerable figure and their scopic surrounding of the narrator are expressed by verbs emanating from the same Arabic triliteral root (*ḥ-w-t*). But physically isolating and surrounding the *shaykh* is a protective act, whereas scopically isolating and surrounding the narrator is a hostile one. No one protects her. She must protect herself with her father's books. The privilege of scopic domination belongs to the men, not to the heroine.

No sooner is the domain of the visual abandoned than one enters the domain of the oral/aural. The *shaykh* begins his lecture with Islamic religious formulae, something alien to the university student. Then he continues; today he will speak about two important mystics—al-Fudayl ibn 'Iyād and Ibrāhīm ibn Adham. Al-Fudayl was born to a pious father in Khurāsān and, against his father's wishes, became a successful highway robber. He was in love with a slave girl, and one night, after attacking a caravan, he was on his way to her house. While scaling the wall, he overheard a voice from the sky addressing him: "Is it not time that the hearts of those who believe should be humbled to the Remembrance of God and the Truth which He has sent down?"[23] Every time he tried to cross the wall, the voice would repeat its message. So al-Fudayl responded: "Yes, it is time, my Lord." He descended from the wall, with his heart beating in fear and shame and his body shaking with sorrow and pain. He has heard the divine call. He also overhears some people talking about their travel plans and deciding to delay their trip until morning, because al-Fudayl will hold them up. The highway robber repents and proceeds to immerse himself in learning in order that his repentance be based on true knowledge.[24]

The second Sūfī is Ibrāhīm ibn Adham. Ibrāhīm hailed from a well-off family in Khurāsān. He was out on a hunt one day, and just as he was approaching the prey, he heard a voice saying: "Were you created for this? Or were you ordered to do this?" He stopped, looked right and left, and saw no one. The voice continued to repeat this to him. Ibrāhīm came to his senses and changed his life.[25]

The lecture ends and the students go to the *shaykh*. Karīmān "awakens" (though when she actually went into a sleeping state is not indicated) and realizes that she has heard the entire lecture. She suddenly remembers her father, runs out to the car, and apologizes to him. But he quickly informs her that he learned that his friend to whom she was to deliver the books died two days ago. She herself begins to tell him about the *shaykh*'s lecture. She repeats the story over and over, and when her father asks her who the *shaykh* is, she answers that she does not know.

From the visual world in which she is the undesirable object, Karīmān has been transported into the intellectual oral world of the *shaykh*'s lecture. The significance of this oral communication is such that the first-person female narrator exits the text, allowing the religious figure of the *shaykh* to speak for himself. He introduces the two conversions in the first person: "I will speak to you today about two great Sūfīs."[26] From the moment the lecture begins until the moment it ends and our narrator "awakens," the voice we hear is that of the *shaykh*. Karīmān's exit has been more than narratological. The voice of the lecturer has transported her into a world different from that of her everyday reality. She must awaken from this experience.

This oral aspect is crucial. Karīmān hears the *shaykh* tell the two conversion narratives. The two stories, in turn, revolve around orality/aurality. Both males hear the divine voice calling them to change their ways. And this is an insistent voice. It does not cease repeating the message. Al-Fudayl's oral experience is twice enriched. Does he not also overhear voices speaking about his activities as a highway robber? This contrast between oral and visual (with preference for the former) is familiar in Arabo-Islamic culture.[27] Distinctively, it resolves itself here into a contrast between immodest body and healing word, the visual/external being the sign of the heroine's spiritual lack.

This will turn out to be a momentous event in Karīmān's life. Karīmān spends a sleepless night. She hears the voice of the *shaykh* repeating over and over the deity's call to the two medieval mystics. Her life is laid bare before the reader, and we discover that she is indeed worried and uneasy. So much so in fact that she had spoken of this to her mother, even expressing to her a desire to die.[28] The initial worry with which the narrative opens has been redefined. To the worry over the physical ill health of the father has been added the concern over the mental ill health of the daughter. "But the words of the *shaykh* were like the finger of the professional physician, when he places his hand on an illness and prescribes the medication."[29] The spiritual malaise has been turned into a physical one, concretizing it and making possible its cure.

Should it come as a surprise then that, in the morning, Karīmān should accidentally hear that same voice while tuning to her favorite radio program on the Qur'ān? That voice is once again telling the story of a male mystic, this time Sahl ibn 'Abd Allāh al-Tustarī (died 283 CE). The identity of the voice is made when the announcer thanks him: Dr. 'Abd al-Halīm Maḥmūd. Karīmān calls her father to share her great discovery:

> and I told him, while in a quasi-dream state, what he said on the radio. . . . What is this that the *shaykh* is saying. . . . How his talk runs through my being, shaking my limbs and yielding them to the Lord, may He be exalted.[30]

What an effect the voice has on the narrator! It at once transports her into another state of consciousness and shakes her corporal entity. Its balm is mental and physical.

The father's response? He will perform the afternoon prayer with his daughter. "I returned to my bed. Happy, happy. As though I had found a treasure I had lost long ago." The identification of the mystery voice is obviously crucial. The two words, "Happy, happy" stand in opposition to the two words that opened the journey: "Worried. . . . Worried."

Karīmān has crossed an important threshold. She has listened to three narratives, all dealing with male mystics. Each narrative, in its own way, has great relevance to her own experience. The first two males, Ibrāhīm ibn Adham and al-Fudayl ibn 'Iyād, come from opposite social classes, and knew one another in Mecca.[31] Ibrāhīm died in 161 CE and al-Fudayl in 187 CE. Both are examples of the early Muslim *zuhd* (ascetic movement), which involved an individual spiritual experience, as distinct from the later phase of mysticism, in which mystics or Sūfīs attached themselves to a particular teacher and a brotherhood.

Karīmān's presentation of Ibrāhīm (it is she, after all, who has recounted the lecture) is not devoid of significance. In the contemporary setting, Ibrāhīm is a lone figure, traveling from place to place, "a tourist in the tourism of God." He contemplates creation, he battles Satan, he flees from that which is forbidden.[32] His is a lonely path. His interactions with either his contemporaries or with those who may have asked him for spiritual advice are occulted.

This twentieth-century Ibrāhīm, hence, differs from his medieval persona. Ibrāhīm ibn Adham's pre-Ḥamzian saga is perhaps one of the most enticing of that of all the mystics, reaching at times the legendary. From the earliest to the later sources on asceticism and mysticism, Ibrāhīm is there. His story shifted from Arabic to Persian and then to Turkish and even to Urdu and to Malay, along the way becoming more and more fanciful. Russell Jones argues that the Arabic sources are really the most trustworthy.[33] And of these, al-Qushayrī (died 465 CE) is, in the words of A. J. Arberry, the "author of the most famous and authoritative treatise on Sufism in Arabic."[34]

Al-Qushayrī's vision of Ibrāhīm is, in a sense, more social. Certainly, the asceticism is there, as is the piety. But the Qushayrian Ibrāhīm is a generous soul who cares both financially and emotionally for the plight of his fellow humans. To take but one example, Sahl ibn Ibrāhīm relates that he was Ibrāhīm ibn Adham's companion. Sahl became sick and Ibrāhīm ibn Adham paid the cost and when he had a craving for something, Ibrāhīm sold his donkey and spent the money on his friend. When the friend asked where the donkey was, Ibrāhīm replied: "We sold it." So his friend asked: "And on what will I ride?" Ibrāhīm ibn Adham replied: "O my brother, on my neck." And he proceeded to carry his friend.[35]

The transformation of the medieval Ibrāhīm into the contemporary one who inhabits a modern woman's religious narrative is significant. The medieval accounts show a multifaceted character, whose ascetic life is as important as—if not more important than—the actual call he receives.[36] Not so in Karīmān Ḥamza's book. In the contemporary setting, the call is primary and is in a certain sense the culmination of a previous life away from God. How interesting it then becomes to realize that 'Abd al-Ḥalīm Maḥmūd, Karīmān Ḥamza's spiritual guide, was coeditor of al-Qushayrī's work.

As for al-Fudayl ibn 'Iyād, his twentieth-century trajectory is much the same as that of his medieval contemporary.[37] His call has primacy in the modern text. His earlier life, painted by the male lecturer in the female's text, was that of debauchery. His family is presented as pious, with the father attempting in vain to guide his son on the right path. But the divine call is, of course, more powerful. Whereas Ibrāhīm is summoned to the ascetic life while hunting animals, al-Fudayl hears the divine voice while pursuing a slave girl.

The medieval intertext is, therefore, not innocent. The message inculcated by the twentieth-century teacher is quite powerful and serves to remind us that spiritual sagas do more than portray a religious transformation. This process of redefinition of the medieval male mystics will facilitate the spiritual experience of the contemporary female.

The two mystics, Ibrāhīm ibn Adham and al-Fudayl ibn 'Iyād, play similar roles in Karīmān Ḥamza's *My Journey from Unveiling to Veiling*. The call was foregrounded in their contemporary presentation and just as the call becomes of primary importance in their lives so it is also for Karīmān. But whereas the call for the two medieval figures instigated an almost instantaneous change in lifestyle, for Karīmān, the call will be but the first step on the path to salvation. Clearly, the attention to the two calls in the female contemporary account makes it clear that their purpose is to sanction her own call by ʻAbd al-Ḥalīm Maḥmūd.

True, like her medieval male predecessors, she has heard the voice. But her oral experience differs. The two men had a direct link to the deity: when called on the religious path, they could answer without intermediary. Not so in the case of the contemporary female protagonist. Her call is mediated through different male voices. The contemporary *shaykh* is but a transmitter of the original story in which the voice calls on the two males to change their ways. One of them, al-Fudayl, answers: "Yes. It is time, my Lord," a phrase that is taken out of his mouth, placed in the mouth of the venerable lecturer at the institute, and from there transported into the mouth of the female narrator, who repeats it to herself. This double mediation also occurs with the questions posed to Ibrāhīm: "Were you created for this? Or were you ordered to do this?": questions filtered through the voice of ʻAbd al-Ḥalīm Maḥmūd, only to be repeated by Karīmān.

Another important difference surfaces between the contemporary female and the medieval males. The call for Ibrāhīm and al-Fudayl represented salvation from a life away from the deity. The ascetic path will save them from eternal perdition. For Karīmān, the call is much more substantial. For her it represents salvation from physical destruction. Had she not, after all, spoken to her mother of suicide? She must be saved not only from a spiritual death but from a physical one as well. Her call has permitted her rebirth of sorts in new clothing and with a new family, the religious one.

Ibrāhīm adds an additional role to the one he shared with al-Fudayl. His presence is not simply to endorse the call but, more important, it is also a sign of vestmentary transformation. He after all shed the clothing of "arrogance and pride and wore the clothing of sincere obedience to God."[38] And this, of course, is precisely what Karīmān herself will be doing throughout her narrative. But unlike Ibrāhīm who dons his new clothing immediately, her response will be much more slow: the shedding of the Westernized clothing in favor of the Islamic dress will occupy much of the narrative. Since her salvation will culminate in the proper Islamic dress (if nothing else the title of the work tells us that), the sartorial switch will not come about easily as it did for Ibrāhīm. In fact, much of the contemporary female journey will be devoted to a step-by-step covering.

The call is, however, but one component of the religious experience, the teacher being the other. Here, again, a medieval male mystic provides the clue: Sahl ibn ʻAbd Allāh al-Tustarī.

Sahl is the mystic about whom Dr. ʻAbd al-Ḥalīm Mahmūd is speaking as Karīmān tunes to her favorite radio program on the Qur'ān. Sahl in the radio account was in need of a teacher, a *shaykh,* to help him understand his exact position vis-à-vis the right path. Sahl, therefore, differs from the two previous ascetics. He does not receive a call. And, that is in fact what the medieval accounts substantiate. Abū Muḥammad Sahl al-Tustarī was pious from early childhood. His devout uncle taught him early on to say, "God is my witness," over and over again, increasing the number of times the boy was to say this. This the young Sahl did, deriving pleasure from the experience. He was eventually sent to the *kuttāb* (Qur'ānic school), but even here he made a condition: that he would attend for an hour, only to leave after that for contemplation. He memorized the Qur'ān while still a child of six or seven. His asceticism began early in his life, when he began fasting at noon. It was at the age of thirteen that he had a problem and that is the point at which he went out in search of someone to help him cure this dilemma. He found his mentor and returned to his hometown, where he maintained his ascetic lifestyle.[39]

Once again, the medieval Sahl and his twentieth-century counterpart are not identical. In the medieval biography, Sahl's visit to the spiritual healer is embedded in an otherwise contemplative life. In one medieval account, it is simply his contemplative life that is presented.[40] In Karīmān Ḥamza's rendition, this visit to the *shaykh* is the goal of the radio message.

Like Sahl, Karīmān is afflicted with a spiritual malaise. Sahl did not need a call from the deity to pursue the ascetic life, and, at this point, neither does Karīmān. Her call has been already twice validated. Like Sahl, she will seek out her own *shaykh,* Dr. 'Abd al-Ḥalīm Maḥmūd.

Karīmān's spiritual call and her teacher came into her life through the example of medieval male ascetics. But that is not enough. The last step, Karīmān's full integration into the Islamist movement will also be heralded by another medieval male figure, this time the well-known Ṣūfī, al-Ḥārith al-Muḥāsibī (died 243 CE. He will make his guest appearance in the twentieth-century narrative toward the end of the work. Unlike Ibrāhīm, al-Fuḍayl, and Sahl, al-Ḥārith is not the subject of oral discourse. His intertextual appearance is through written discourse: a book on him authored by 'Abd al-Ḥalīm Maḥmūd and which the *shaykh* presents to his female pupil.[41]

Al-Muḥāsibī enters the Ḥamzian text after an introduction about the social and political conditions that permit such a character to flourish. The Islamic world, we read, was undergoing a battle between two forces: on the one hand, the Orthodox, at whose head was Aḥmad ibn Ḥanbal; and on the other, the Mu'tazilites, with representatives in Basra, Kufa, and Baghdad. *Shaykh* 'Abd al-Ḥalīm Maḥmūd's words go on to inform the reader that such a conflict is a natural one, from which no religion has ever escaped:

> It is the eternal conflict between the textualists and the intellectualists. It is the everlasting struggle between those who say that religion is a text which can be explained by the revelation, and language, and transmission, and those who say that religion is a text which can be explained and clarified by the intellect.[42]

Aḥmad ibn Ḥanbal (died 241 CE) is the famous legist and founder of the Ḥanbalī school, the most conservative of the four canonical schools of Islam. The Mu'tazila were "important in the history of Islamic theology . . . for initiating the discussion of Islamic dogmas in terms of Greek philosophical conceptions." The battles between the two groups were ardent ones dealing with, among other things, the createdness of the Qur'ān, with the Mu'tazilites opting for the created nature of the sacred text.[43]

Enter al-Muḥāsibī, the third fighter in this battle in the eyes of 'Abd al-Ḥalīm Maḥmūd. He took on the Mu'tazila and was himself attacked by the Orthodox. His weapons? Awe of God and knowledge. His message in Karīmān's text is one of *zuhd* (asceticism), piety, and fearfulness of God.[44]

Al-Ḥārith ibn Asad al-Muḥāsibī (died 243 CE) was, according to Arberry, "the first Sūfī author of the foremost rank whose preserved writings may truly be said to have formed to a large extent the pattern of all subsequent thought."[45] He did, in fact, have run-ins with Aḥmad ibn Ḥanbal.

But unlike the other three medieval mystics, al-Muḥāsibī and his intellectual milieu receive from the *shaykh* 'Abd al-Ḥalīm Maḥmūd an interpretation that makes them relevant for contemporary Islamic thought. "These three powers are still in conflict down to our present day, and we believe that they will continue to be." This is due to people's nature: some people are realistic and prefer a text, some are more intellectual, and some are more sensitive and lean to Sufism.[46] Karīmān's response? Long live the three orientations. "May they live in the service of God's religion, in the service of Islam." Yes, she continues, she was truthful when she declared her love for all who serve Islam, even if their paths differ, be they using intellect, or ecstasy, or text. "The difference of their ways is mercy."[47]

How interesting it then becomes to have Karīmān herself labeled "the Mystical [Television] Announcer" ("al-Mudhī'a al-Mutasawwifa"[48]) by the *Majallat al-Idhā'a wal-Tilifizyūn,* a popular illustrated Egyptian weekly that caters to a mass audience and presents various cultural and media news, extending from the secular to the religious. On the same day, Karīmān goes to the High Council for Islamic Affairs and reports the following conversation:

> —Welcome to the Mystical Announcer. . . . We
> thought you were one of the Muslim Brothers. . . .
> I said to them:
> —The truth is that I do not say that I am a Sūfī nor one of the Muslim
> Brothers. . . . I am a Muslim. . . . A Muslim and someone who professes the
> unity of God only.[49]

The dialogue continues with Karīmān arguing that she cannot possibly attribute to herself the honor of being a member of the Muslim Brotherhood, since she has not suffered all they have suffered of torture and imprisonment. When her interlocutor then replies with "Then you are a Sūfī like your *shaykh,*" Karīmān's reply is adamant: She is only a Muslim.

> Sufism is a special grade of worship, piety,
> abstention, asceticism, and sincere
> fearfulness of God. . . . And commitment. . . . And
> contentment. . . . And I am not like that. . . . I am a
> beginner, I love Islam. . . . And I love the
> Muslims only. . . . Do you not understand?[50]

This futile dialogue between the two is not so quickly resolved. First, the male speaker warns Karīmān to stay away from the Muslim Brothers, but she defends them. Then he warns her not to become a Sūfī like her *shaykh* and be one of "those of al-Ahwāl wal-Maqāmāt." She replies: "What are those of al-Aḥwāl wal-Maqāmāt? I do not understand what you mean."[51]

The *ahwāl* and *maqāmāt* are, of course, code words for the discerning reader that the subject has moved seriously into the area of mysticism. The *ahwāl* (sing. *hāl*) are the mystical states, or more properly "the *ḥāl* is spiritual mood depending not upon the mystic but upon God." The *maqāmāt* (sing. *maqām*) are the stations on the mystical path.

> The *maqām* is a stage of spiritual attainment on the pilgrim's progress to God which is the result of the mystic's personal effort and endeavors. . . . "The states," says al-Qushairī, "are gifts; the stations are earnings."[52]

These are such basic concepts in Sufism that it is difficult to believe that Karīmān does not comprehend what her interlocutor is saying. The well-versed reader will have already become aware of Karīmān's knowledge of mysticism in the earlier quote. The language she used to explain her refusal of the label of "The Mystical Announcer" is imbued with mystical terminology: for example, *wara'* (abstention), *zuhd* (asceticism), *khushū'* (fearfulness), *ridā* (contentment).[53]

Hence, Karīmān's supposed ignorance of the *aḥwāl* and *maqāmāt* is but a textual ruse, permitting her to draw out the enemy. And this she does. First he asks if she has noticed individuals in rags, dirty and smelly, in the mosques. Yes, she admits she had. These she learns are those of *al-aḥwāl*, who believe that they have a great rank with God. They speak to the angels and to the Prophets. Karīmān objects to this qualification. The dialogue becomes more and more violent as she persists in asking questions that relate to Sufism and her interlocutor persists in qualifying mystics as social marginals. When Karīmān points out that her own *shaykh* does not fit this description, the man is not assuaged. His closing argument on the Sūfīs leaves her without a counterargument: The Islamic world is drowning and both the East and the West are hurrying to swallow it up. This is happening at the same time that the mystics are not thinking about how to save Islam. Karīmān changes tactics and moves to the Muslim Brothers: why should her interlocutor be so negative about them since their way is 100 percent positive? The man is nonplussed: she is clearly one of them. He continues to rant and rave. And whereas before he had laughed like a wolf, now he speaks like a raging bull.[54] These metaphors are significant: the man has been turned into an animal, no longer in control of his emotions. Karīmān will leave the premises, but not before she has called for the revenge of God on this man, whom she perceives to be "an enemy to himself . . . to others and to Islam."[55]

What a timely debate. Its locus is perhaps as significant as its subjects. The High Council for Islamic Affairs is an organ of the Egyptian government. Of course, we read nowhere that "the man" is expressing the government's views, but his enemies are, oddly enough, the Muslim Brothers, on the one hand, and the Sūfīs, on the other. The bloody history of the Muslim Brothers with the Egyptian government goes back many years and needs no commentary. The relationship of the government with the Sūfīs has been a great deal less conflictual, but it is certainly not one of love and admiration.[56]

Karīmān tries to keep herself above the fray. However, she cannot combat the man's argument about the political ineffectiveness of the Sūfīs in defending Islam. What the dialogue makes clear is that Karīmān's perspective on Sufism is not identical to that of her interlocutor. His view, ironically enough, comes closer to the lives of the ascetics whom Karīmān called up in her text. When the man informs her that these people in rags stink, we are reminded of certain stories that have attached themselves to some of the medieval mystics, who

> . . . cared neither for their outward appearance nor their attire, and although they strictly observed the ritual purity required for prayer, Ibn Adham was proud of the huge number of lice living in his coat, and as late as 900, a maidservant of a Sufi from Baghdad exclaimed: "O God, how dirty are Thy friends—not a single one among them is clean!"[57]

Ibrāhīm ibn Adham was once asked if he had ever been happy in this world, to which he answered, "Yes, twice," one of them being when was he sitting one day and someone came along and urinated on him.[58] This anecdote is meant to explain the mystic's high character, but it can be read corporally as well, testifying in that case to a total difference to the physical entity that is the body.

What this dialogue also points to is another difference between the contemporary "Mystical Announcer" and her medieval male predecessors. The male ascetics were moving away from the ease of the world, something that Karīmān has not done. In fact, her trajectory has been, in a sense, the opposite. She has moved into the world rather than away from it, having picked up a public and visible persona. The Karīmān we met on the first pages of *My Journey from Unveiling to Veiling* was a university student like many others. The Karīmān who ends the narrative has been singularized and thrown into the public domain.

In fact, this dialogue must be juxtaposed with the initial scene in which Karīmān received the call. Both incidents are set in an official Islamic environment: the first in the Institute of Islamic Studies and the second in the High Council for Islamic Affairs. In the first, Karīmān enters with a state of lack, even her dog playing a role. The dog, as we noted earlier is not only a sign of the Westernization of the young woman. In the ascetic discourse that imbues Hamza's narrative, the dog is more than a random animal. He is associated with the baseness of the world from which an ascetic must flee, and symbolized at times man's lower nature.[59] That this dog should be present for the initial call and disappear without a trace by the end of the narrative is not accidental.

The juxtaposition of the two scenes also highlights the *shaykh* 'Abd al-Ḥalīm Maḥmūd's role. In the first, he enters the narrative as the voice that beckons the young woman to the religious path. In the second, he is there as a textual authority validating his female disciple's religious transformation. It is she who must now carry forth the message. The heated dialogue she has with the interlocutor in the offices of the High Council is embedded within selections from the *shaykh* Maḥmūd's work on al-Ḥārith al-Muḥāsibī. This will be, in fact, Maḥmūd's last appearance in Karīmān Ḥamza's book. His disappearance will signal first a textual death, as Karīmān calls forth various other religious authorities to testify to her *shaykh's* good actions. And this textual death will be followed by his physical death. He has, in a sense, performed his function in Karīmān's saga. He has helped to rectify the lack with which she began her trajectory. She is now a full member of the religious community. Interestingly enough, she is still, however, the object of the gaze. In the preconversion incident, Karīmān was the object of the male gaze and tried to hide from it. Now the "Mystical Announcer" is an even greater object of gaze, this time that of the television viewers.

Are we to interpret from all this that the ascetic intertext played no role in Karīmān's saga? On the contrary. The intertext of the medieval male mystics not only redefines the young woman's religious experience but it places it squarely in a male religious and ascetic tradition.

The verbal and textual eloquence of the males in this female's text should not dissuade us from asking about one of the most important silences and absences in Karīmān Ḥamza's *My Journey from Unveiling to Veiling:* the medieval female ascetic experience. One of the most famous early ascetics was a woman: Rābi'a al-'Adawiyya (died 185 CE).[60] Yet, she has no role to play in this contemporary account. In his introduction to *Riḥlatī min al-Sufūr ilā al-Ḥijāb,* Muḥammad 'Atiyya Khamīs singles out the importance of the gender issue in Karīmān Ḥamza's journey. He correctly notes the presence of notable women in the medieval period, beginning with the Prophet's wives.[61] Missing from his enumeration is the mystic Rābi'a. This is all the more striking since Khamīs wrote a popular biography of Rābi'a, which much like Karīmān Ḥamza's book is available on streets and in *sūgs* in the Middle East and North Africa.[62]

Is this perhaps because, for Khamīs, Ḥamza's work is an example of missionary activity?[63] In that case, the occultation of a female ascetic might be more justified. But yet the intertextual dynamics of the work are evidence that the medieval male ascetics play more than an accidental role.

Clearly, more is at stake here than mere literary categorization. What it makes us realize is that *Riḥlatī min al-Sufūr ilā al-Ḥijāb* is a complex work, the internal dynamics of which unite gender and religious and political issues. The textual validation by the male mystics is but an internal reflection of the external sandwiching of Karīmān Ḥamza's text between the introduction by Muḥammad 'Atiyya Khamīs and the epilogue by the *shaykh* Muḥammad al-Ghazālī. Much as her book is embedded between two male textual voices, so her spiritual trajectory is validated by men.[64]

NOTES

1. Karīmān Ḥamza, *Riḥlatī min al-Sufūr ilā al-Ḥijāb,* 2d ed. (Beirut: Dār al-Fath lil-Tibā'a wal-Nashr, 1986). Unless otherwise indicated, all translations are my own.
2. See, for example, *The Contemporary Islamic Revival: A Critical Survey and Bibliography,* eds. Yvonne Yazbeck Haddad, John Obert Voll, and John L. Esposito (New York: Greenwood Press, 1991).

3. See, for example, Gilles Kepel, *Le Prophète et Pharaon* (Paris: La Découverte, 1984); Bruno Étienne, *L'Islamısme radical* (Paris: Hachette, 1987); Emmanuel Sivan, *Radical Islam* (New Haven: Yale University Press, 1985).
4. See, for example, Muhammad Ra'fat Sa'īd, *al-Iltizām fī al-Tasawwur al-Islāmī lil-Adab* (Cairo: Dār al-Hidāya lil-Tibā'a wal-Nashr wal-Tawzī', 1987).
5. See, for example, Abdelhamid Bouraoui, "Note sur la production culturelle en Tunisie: Les édıteurs et leur production," in *La Dımension Culturelle du Développement* (Tunis: Centre d'Etudes et de Recherches Economiques et Sociales, 1991), pp. 217–223. It was clear at the conference at which this contribution was presented (conference on "La dimensıon culturelle du développement," held by the Centre d'Etudes et de Recherches Economiques et Sociales in Tunis in November 1988) that the Tunisian phenomenon was not peculiar to that country but was something common to the entire region.
6. Al-Shaykh Muḥammad Mutawallī al-Sha'rāwī, *Mishwār Hayātī* (Cairo: al-Mukhtār al-Islāmī lil-Nashr wal-Tawzī' wal-Tasdīr, 1988); 'Abd al-Ḥamīd Kishk, *Qissat Ayyāmī: Mudhakkirāt al-Shaykh Kishk* (Cairo: Dār al-Mukhtār al-Islāmī, 1987? 1988?). On this text, see Fedwa Malti-Douglas, "A Literature of Islamıc Revival?: The Autobiography of Shaykh Kishk," in *Cultural Transitions in the Middle East,* Social, Economic, and Polıtical Studıes of the Middle East, vol. 68, ed. Serif Mardin (Leiden: E. J. Brill, 1994).
7. The number of religious authorities who wrıte legal ınjunctions cannot be counted. Rare ıs the male religious authority who has not indulged in this.
8. See al-Ghazālī, *al-Munqidh min al-Dalāl,* ed., 'Abd al-Ḥalīm Mahmūd (Cairo: Dār al-Kutub al-Hadītha, 1965).
9. For an ıntroductıon to the Arabic autobiographical tradition, see Fedwa Malti-Douglas, *Blındness and Autobıography: al-Ayyām of Tāhā Husayn* (Princeton: Princeton University Press, 1988), pp. 3–12.
10. See Fedwa Malti-Douglas, *Woman's Body, Woman's Word: Gender and Discourse in Arabo-Islamıc Writing* (Princeton: Princeton University Press, 1991), pp. 111–178.
11. See the excellent collection, *Immaculate and Powerful: The Female in Sacred Image and Social Reality,* eds. Clarissa W. Atkinson, Constance H. Buchanan, and Margaret R. Miles (Boston: Beacon Press, 1985).
12. Mustafā Mahmūd, *Rıhlatī min al-Shakk ilā al-Imān,* 9th ed. (Cairo: Dār al-Ma'ārif, 1991).
13. As is the accepted norm with critical discussions of autobiographical texts, I shall use the first name, Karīmān, to refer to the character in the text and the full name, Karīmān Ḥamza, to refer to the historical individual or the author.
14. In her recent study, *Revealing Reveiling: Islamist Gender Ideology ın Contemporary Egypt* (Albany: State University of New York Press, 1992), Sherifa Zuhur describes the social and historical forces that lead women to veiling. She does not deal with the numerous texts written by the women Islamists themselves. The same is true for much of the work dealing with women and the religious revival. For a recent example, see Barbara F. Stowasser, "Women's Issues in Modern Islamic Thought," in *Arab Women: Old Boundaries, New Frontıers,* ed. Judith E. Tucker (Bloomington: Indiana University Press, 1993), pp. 3–28.
15. I have discussed the ımportance of the corporal in Ḥamza's narrative ın a book currently under completion.
16. Ḥamza, *Rihlatī,* pp. 5–17.
17. See Shabāb Muḥammad, *Dı'āmāt al-Da'wa: Min Tasjīlāt al-Jamā'a* (Cairo: Dār al-I'tisām, 1978), p. 65. These are the actual documents of the Jam'iyya itself. Cf. Valerie J. Hoffman-Ladd, "Polemics on the Modesty and Segregation of Women," *Internatıonal*

Journal of Middle East Studies 19 (1987):31–32, who places the break in "approximately 1939"; Sanā' al-Misrī, *Khalf al-Hijāb: Mawqif al-Jamā'āt al-Islāmiyya min Qadiyyat al-Mar'a* (Cairo: Sīnā lil-Nashr, 1989), p. 27.

18. Ḥamza, *Rihlatī*, pp. 19–20.
19. Malti-Douglas, *Woman's Body, Woman's Word*, pp. 163–164.
20. The ellipses are in the original text.
21. The ellipses are in the original text.
22. Ḥamza, *Rihlatī*, pp. 22–23. The ellipses are in the original text.
23. *Al-Qur'ān*, Sūrat al-Hadīd, verse 16. I am using Arberry's translation. See A. J. Arberry, *The Koran Interpreted* (New York: Macmillan Publishing Co., 1974), 2:259.
24. Ḥamza, *Rihlatī*, pp. 23–24.
25. Ibid., pp. 24–25.
26. Ibid., p. 23.
27. See the discussion in Fedwa Malti-Douglas, "Mentalités and Marginality: Blindness and Mamlūk Civilization," in *The Islamic World from Classical to Modern Times: Essays in Honor of Bernard Lewis*, eds. C. E. Bosworth, Charles Issawi, Roger Savory, and A. L. Udovitch (Princeton: Darwin Press, 1989), pp. 211–237.
28. Ḥamza, *Rihlatī*, p. 28.
29. Ibid., p. 29.
30. Ibid., p. 30. The ellipses are in the original text.
31. See, for example, al-Hujwīrī, *Kashf al-Mahjūb*, trans. R. A. Nicholson (Lahore: Islamic Book Foundation, 1980), p. 103; Annemarie Schimmel, *Mystical Dimensions of Islam* (Chapel Hill: University of North Carolina Press, 1975), p. 37.
32. Ḥamza, *Rihlatī*, p. 25.
33. Russell Jones, "Ibrāhīm b. Adham," *Encyclopaedia of Islam*, 2nd ed. (Leiden: E. J. Brill, 1960–).
34. A. J. Arberry, *Sufism: An Account of the Mystics of Islam* (New York: Harper & Row Publishers, 1970), p. 28. See, also, Arberry's introduction to Farīd al-Dīn 'Attār, *Muslim Saints and Mystics: Episodes from the Tadhkirat al-Auliya'* (London: Penguin Arkana, 1990), p. 5.
35. Al-Qushayrī, *al-Risāla al-Qushayriyya*, eds. 'Abd al-Ḥalīm Maḥmūd and Maḥmūd ibn al-Sharīf, (Cairo: Dār al-Kutub al-Hadītha, 1966), 1:51–53. Additional material can be had elsewhere in *al-Risāla*.
36. In addition to al-Qushayrī, see also, for example, al-Hujwīrī, *Kashf*, pp. 103–105; 'Attār, *Muslim Saints*, pp. 62–79.
37. See al-Fudayl's biography in al-Qushayrī, *al-Risāla* 1:57–59. Additional material can be had elsewhere in *al-Risāla*. See also, al-Hujwīrī, *Kashf*, pp. 97–100; Ibn Khallikān, *Wafayāt al-A'yān wa-Anbā' Abnā' al-Zamān*, ed. Ihsān 'Abbās (Beirut: Dār al-Thaqāfa, n.d.), 4:47–50; 'Attār, *Muslim Saints*, pp. 52–61.
38. Ḥamza, *Rihlatī*, p. 25.
39. Al-Qushayrī, *al-Risāla* 1:83–85. Additional material can be had elsewhere in *al-Risāla*. See also al-Hujwīrī, *Kashf*, pp. 139–140; 'Attār, *Muslim Saints*, pp. 153–160.
40. See al-Hujwīrī, *Kashf*, pp. 139–140.
41. Ḥamza, *Rihlatī*, p. 228.
42. Ibid., p. 230.
43. See W. Montgomery Watt, *Islamic Philosophy and Theology* (Edinburgh: Edinburgh University Press, 1962), pp. 58–90; for the quotation, pp. 58–59.
44. Ḥamza, *Rihlatī*, pp. 231–232.
45. Arberry, *Sufism*, p. 46. See, also, his biography in al-Qushayrī, *al-Risāla* 1:72–73, with

additional material elsewhere in *al-Risāla;* al-Hujwīrī, *Kashf,* pp. 108–109; 'Attār, *Muslim Saints,* pp. 143–145.

46. Ḥamza, *Riḥlatī,* p. 232.
47. Ibid., p. 233.
48. The term *mudhī'* (fem. *mudhī'a*) is applied to both radio and television announcers. In Karīmān's case, this is clearly a reference to her television work.
49. Hamza, *Riḥlatī,* p. 234. The ellipses are in the original text.
50. Ibid., p. 234. The ellipses are in the original text.
51. Ibid., p. 235.
52. For a discussion of the states and stations on the mystical path, see, for example, Arberry, *Sufism,* pp. 74–83; for the quotation, p. 75. See also Schimmel, *Mystical Dimensions,* pp. 98–186.
53. On some of this terminology, see Arberry, *Sufism,* pp. 74–79.
54. Ḥamza, *Riḥlatī,* pp. 235–238.
55. Ibid., p. 238. The ellipses are in the original text.
56. See, for example, Richard P. Mitchell, *The Society of the Muslim Brothers* (London: Oxford University Press, 1969); Aḥmad Rā'if, *Sarādīb al-Shaytān: Safahāt min Ta'rīkh al-Ikhwān al-Muslimīn* (Cairo: al-Zahrā' lil-I'lām al-'Arabī, 1988). See also John L. Esposito, *The Islamic Threat: Myth or Reality?* (New York and Oxford: Oxford University Press, 1992).
57. Schimmel, *Mystical Dimensions,* p. 37.
58. Al-Qushayrī, *al-Risāla* 2:496.
59. See, for example, Schimmel, *Mystical Dimensions,* pp. 67, 109, 112.
60. On this foremost medieval Muslim female mystic, see the still important study by Margaret Smith, *Rābi'a the Mystic and Her Fellow-Saints in Islam* (Cambridge: Cambridge University Press, 1928).
61. Ḥamza, *Riḥlatī,* pp. 7–12.
62. Muḥammad 'Atiyya Khamīs, *Rābi'a al-'Adawiyya* (Cairo: Dār Karam lil-Tibā'a wal-Nashr, n.d.).
63. Ḥamza, *Riḥlatī,* p. 14.
64. This recourse to the male is not a religious necessity. There are many conversion narratives by Islamist women that need no male intermediary. I am discussing these dynamics in a book currently under completion.

29

Maximus the Confessor on the Affections in Historical Perspective

Robert L. Wilken

Jonathan Edwards begins his treatise *The Religious Affections* with a citation from *1 Peter* 1.8: "Whom having not seen, ye love; in whom, though now ye see him not, yet believing, ye rejoice with joy unspeakable and full of glory." What drew Edwards to this passage were the phrases "ye love" and "ye rejoice with joy unspeakable." For Edwards, love and joy were affections, and his book was a defense of the view that true religion consisted not only in actings of the inclination and will of the soul but also in the fervent exercises of the heart. The religion that God requires has nothing to do with a state of indifference, he writes, but with ardor, with a fervent spirit and a burning heart, in short with passions of the soul. "The holy Scriptures do everywhere place religion very much in the affections; such as fear, hope, love, hatred, desire, joy, sorrow, gratitude, compassion, and zeal."[1]

Jonathan Edwards may seem a strange place to begin a discussion of Maximus the Confessor. The one was an eighteenth-century married congregationalist pastor and revivalist preacher; the other a sixth-to-seventh-century Byzantine monk, a recluse who believed that *apatheia* (freedom from passion) was the goal of the spiritual life. The true Christians, writes Maximus, are those "who pass beyond the disturbances brought about by the passions."[2] Yet, as several distinguished interpreters of Maximus have observed, Maximus did not counsel, as had the Stoics, that the passions be eradicated. Rather, Maximus speaks of transforming the passions to put them at the service of love.[3] It is perhaps more than coincidental that the two terms that Jonathan Edwards singles out, "love" and "joy," are biblical words for the two affections, desire and delight, that figure large in Maximus's presentation of the spiritual life.

Maximus begins his great work *Quaestiones ad Thalassium*, a dense book dealing with difficult texts from the Bible, with the question of whether the passions are evil in themselves or whether they become evil through their use. His answer is that, without the affections, it is not possible to hold fast to virtue and knowledge; that is, to cling to God. No doubt it is because of Maximus's penetrating grasp of the turbulent and capricious emotions that he has been venerated by spiritual and ascetical writers in the past and is today being read with keen interest. He is a sensitive interpreter of human experience, not simply a speculative thinker. As

Christoph von Schönborn observed at the Maximus symposium in 1980, Maximus has a freshness that endears him to twentieth-century readers.[4]

The topic of the passions enters Christian thought within the context of ethics or moral philosophy. In addressing the topic of the passions (or affections) Christian thinkers joined a discussion that had been going on for centuries.[5] From the outset it is apparent that they were not only well aware of positions staked out by Greek and Roman philosophers, but that, in light of the scriptures and Christian experience, they had to take sides on matters that had been debated by Greek and Roman moralists. Already in the third century, Lactantius chided the Stoics for their restrictive and one-sided view of the passions. They call "mercy, desire, and fear diseases of the soul [*morbos animi*]."[6] Desire and fear are, of course, two of the cardinal passions, and mercy (which is not) is mentioned by Lactantius because of its place in the scriptures. "Blessed are the merciful for they shall receive mercy *(misericordiam)*" (*Mt.* 5.7). Even though Lactantius offers an Aristotelian defense of the passion against the Stoics, the presence of such affections as fear, desire, sorrow, gratitude, zeal, love, and, of course, compassion (or mercy), in the Bible prompted him, as well as other Christian moralists, to rethink conventional assumptions. Though the issues were ancient, Christians came to them with new ideas and language, and, in time, a new perspective. The end toward which one aspired was no longer seen as a life of virtue, wisdom, or possession of the good but fellowship with God or divinification. When Tertullian wrote a treatise on patience, a virtue found in the scriptures but ignored by Latin moralists, he did something similar. He attributed to God, rather than to the sage, the model of virtue. "God himself," he said, "was the example of patience *(patientiae exemplum)*."[7]

The Stoics, writes Lactantius, take away from us all the "affections by the impulse of which the soul is *moved*" (cf. *Divinae institutiones* [*PL* 6.14]). As Lactantius knew well, the term "moved" came from Aristotle. In the *De motu animalium*, when discussing the movement of the soul, Aristotle had argued that all movement can be reduced to *orexis* (thought and desire).[8] Without a conception of what is to be done, we do not know what it is we are to do, but without desire, something that draws us to the object and keeps our sights fixed firmly on it, there is no possibility of movement. "The proximate reason for *movement*," writes Aristotle, "is desire."[9] Drawing on Aristotle's explanation of human action, Lactantius argued that the Stoics "deprive human beings of all the affections by whose instigation the soul is *moved*, namely desire, delight, fear, grief." These affections, he continues, have been implanted in us by God for a reason; without them it is impossible to have a moral life. His statement, "without anger there can be no virtue,"[10] though not the most felicitious, makes the point: anger, when properly used, can contribute to the virtuous life. If there is no movement toward the good (or away from evil), there can be no virtue.

For the Stoics, the goal of the sage was to be completely free of the passions, to reach a state of *apatheia*. Virtue required detachment from the unpredictable and disordered feelings that drive us.[11] Of course, some Christian thinkers, unlike Lactantius, found Stoic ethics congenial and sought to give the goal of *apatheia* a place in Christian life. Clement of Alexandria, for example, thought that *apatheia* was supported by the scriptures. Although he recognized that there is a necessary role for the passions (perhaps, better translated "appetites," or "instincts") in human life—the desire for food, for example—he refused to allow them any place in the moral life. The reason is that Christ was *apathēs,* and "after the Resurrection, the disciples learned to live in an "unwavering disposition of self-discipline."[12] It is incumbent on the one who seeks perfection—that is, the true Gnostic—to follow the example of Jesus and the apostles. The Gnostic must be free "of all passion of the soul. For knowledge leads to discipline, discipline to habit and character which issues finally in a state of *apatheia,* not *metriopatheia* (moderation of the passions)," as Clement pointedly remarks. "The fruit that comes from complete elimination of desire is *apatheia.*"[13] The Gnostic, like the apostles, he concludes, does not share even in those passions that are considered good, for example, delight, grief, and fear.[14]

These sentiments would have a powerful impact on Christian thinking during the next several centuries, especially after the rise of monasticism. The key figure here is of course Evagrius of Pontus. Because his approach to the religious life was at once theoretical as well as practical, his influence on later Christian thinkers, including Maximus, was great.[15] Evagrius believed that the chief impediment to spiritual growth were *logismoi* (thoughts), which enter the soul and distract it from contemplating God. For Evagrius, these thoughts are closely associated with the passions, chiefly desire and anger, but also with the other passions that create images of sensible objects. Through the senses, but also through memory (of things formerly known through the senses), the demons make an impression on the ruling principle, the mind. Only if one was able to silence the thoughts and fantasies that turn the soul away from its proper destiny, could one achieve *apatheia.* "Those who are no longer suceptible to such thoughts are pure and free of passion *(apatheis).*"[16] As support for his views Evagrius cited the words of the psalm: "Refrain from anger and forsake wrath" (*Ps.* 38.8).[17] For Evagrius the passions are contrary to nature and must be eradicated to free the mind from the domination of distracting images.[18]

An alternative view, closer to that of Lactantius, can be found in Gregory of Nyssa. Before Maximus, he represents the most considered criticism of the Stoic view of the affections, at least in the East. Augustine, as we shall see, was also critical of the Stoics on this point. In his treatise, *De anima et resurrectione,* Gregory asks: are the passions (desire and fear) intrinsic to the soul? That is, are they part of human nature given at creation? Gregory argues that the passions are not consubstantial with (human) nature.[19] Moses, for example, was a holy man of God who was successful in overcoming anger and desire. Yet Gregory is uneasy with the view that the affections must simply be overcome, and, as his argument moves forward, he shows that they can be useful for acquiring virtue. "In their pursuit of the good the virtuous receive not a little assistance from these affections."[20] For example, Daniel's desire (which probably means his zeal in serving God alone) was praised (*Dn.* 10.12), and Phineas's anger pleased God (*Nm.* 25.11). Further, the scriptures say that fear is the beginning of wisdom (*Prv.* 9.10) and *lupē* (godly grief) leads to salvation. The Bible teaches us "not simply to consider such things as harmful passions *(pathē)*, for if so, the passions would not have been included among things which are helpful in achieving virtue."[21]

Gregory's scriptural support for his argument is bafflingly sketchy, especially when one recalls the many texts that could have been cited in support, for example, *Psalms* 42, "As the hart longs for living waters, so yearns my soul for you, O God," or *Psalms* 63, "O God, you are my God, I seek you, my soul thirsts for you, my flesh faints for you, as in a dry and weary land where there is no water." But his point is clear. According to the scriptures, the passions aided God's saints in their pursuit of virtue. Anger, fear, desire, et al. are instruments of the soul given for the purpose of helping humans choose good and evil. If they are directed to a good end, they can be instruments of virtue; but if to an evil end, they become instruments of vice. Fear, for example, can lead to obedience and "the impulse of desire secures delight that is divine and unalloyed."[22]

Yet Gregory remains somewhat uneasy with the term *epithȳmia* (desire), for he thought it carried negative (as well as positive) overtones in the scriptures. Hence he proposes a distinction between desire and love (which, of course, in his vocabulary is a form of desire). Returning to his original statement that the passions were not part of human nature, he says that there will come a time when the *epithūmētikon* (desiring principle, sometimes called the concupiscible principle) will no longer exist, that nothing will remain to bring about movement and to arouse an *orexis* (yearning) for the good. Even when one goes beyond desire, and exists wholly in the beautiful, there must be something that binds one to the good and that, in the language of the scriptures, is the disposition to love. For love is nothing other than an *endiathetos schesis* (deep-seated relation) to that which is *katathumion* (pleasing). In the end, the soul, leaving behind desire, "clings to [the good] and mingles with it, through the movement and activity of love, fashioning itself to that which is being grasped continually and discovered." Hence, Paul writes, "love never ceases" (*1 Cor.* 13.8).[23]

Gregory, like Lactantius, retains the Aristotelian framework, that action requires movement as well as thought and that movement is only possible with desire. But he goes beyond Lactantius (and Aristotle) by interpreting desire as love.[24] For Lactantius the affections are active in avoiding evil and pursuing good; Gregory, however, is more interested in the affections as a way of establishing and maintaining the relation to God. Hence, he replaces "desire" by "love," which opens the way for a fuller appropriation of the biblical understanding of love—for example, "You shall *love* the Lord your God with all your heart and with all your soul and with all your mind" (*Mt.* 22.37).

This brings me to Maximus.[25] In the introduction to the *Quaestiones ad Thalassium*, Maximus makes clear that the passions (or affections) are central to the work and promises to address several topics. How many passions are there and of what kind? What is their origin? To what end does each aspire? In which faculty of the soul or which member of the body are they implanted? What is the meaning of the name given to each passion and its abilities? What are their hidden machinations and plots? How do some surreptitiously enter in for apparently good reasons? What are their subtleties, their pettiness, their self-importance, and what are their retreats, their feints, their obstinancy and persistence? What is the state of the soul when it is receptive to various kinds of demons, and what is the manner of their presence in us, and the great diversity and variety of the fantasies they produce in our dreams while we sleep? Are they confined to a certain part of the soul or the body, or to the soul or the body as a whole?[26]

On the basis of this passage in which the passions seem to be presented chiefly as vices (at one point he identifies them with the activity of demons), one would think that Maximus's chief effort in the *Quaestiones ad Thalassium* is to set forth the many ways in which the passions hinder genuine spiritual growth.[27] And there is much in the book that lends support to this view.[28] Yet, when one turns to the first question in the book, he surprises us by emphasizing not the evil that the passions work but the good that they make possible. He asks: "Are the passions evil in themselves or do they become evil from the way that they are used?"

Appealing to Gregory of Nyssa, he answers that the passions were not part of the original creation of human beings. This would seem to imply that the passions are intrinsically evil, the result of the Fall. Instead he stresses the positive role they play in the spiritual life.

> In the devout the passions become good when, prudently turning away from the things of the body, they concern themselves with the possession of heavenly things. For example, *desire* brings about an insatiable movement of spiritual longing for divine things, *delight* a quiet enjoyment of the activity of the mind as it is enticed by the divine gifts, *fear* unceasing diligence to avoid sin in light of the future punishment, and *distress* a scrupulous fixation on present evil.[29]

Without the passions, he continues, human beings would be unable to hold fast to virtue and knowledge and would have only an impetuous and ephemeral attachment to the good. As biblical warrant for his view, he cites *2 Corinthians* 10.5 where Paul's *logismoi* (thoughts) are understood to refer to the passions. "All these things are good when they are used by those who subject every thought [passion] to the obedience of Christ" (cf. *QThal.* 1.31–33).

Note first that Maximus explicitly mentions the four cardinal passions and that he interprets them in a thoroughly classical way. By his choice of terms, for instance, "insatiable movement" for desire and "quiet enjoyment" for delight, he allows the reader to see that there is an internal logic to the four cardinal passions. The choice of four is not arbitrary. Just as the ancient moralists spoke of four cardinal virtues—prudence, justice, courage and temperance—so they also spoke of four cardinal passions—*epithȳmia* (desire), *hēdonē* (delight), *phobos* (fear), and *lupē* (distress). In classical moral philosophy, the classification of the four passions turned on two axes: a distinction between good and bad, and a distinction between that which one possesses and that which one yearns to possess.[30] Maximus speaks of two movements—one a movement toward the good and the other a movement away from evil (desire and fear relate to that which is expected [*prosdoxomenon*])[31]—and two possessions—one suffering evil, the other enjoying the good; in Maximus's language, grief or delight over what is present *(parousia)*, that is, what one possesses. The scheme, then, is intended to be comprehensive and will serve as a framework in which to present the particulars of the ascetic life, a movement away from evil and toward God, the goal of which is the possession of God, or delight in God.[32]

Second, in spite of his statement that the passions were not part of the original creation, his final comment qualifies that assertion. Everything depends on their use, says Maximus. Parenthetically, it may be noted that Augustine came to the same conclusion about the nature of the passions. "If their love is right, these affections [he mentions the four cardinal passions] are right in them."[33] The passions are not blameworthy (not subject to praise or blame in and of themselves), but are the "inseparable accompaniments of natural inclinations." For example, just as hunger and thirst have a necessary role in sustaining human life, so also are the passions "necessary for the acquiring of virtue."[34] It is possible, then, to speak of the "right use of our natural faculties."[35]

For Maximus the passions are evidence that human beings were created with an innate capacity, a natural faculty in the soul, to delight in spiritual things. When God made human nature "he did not create with it sensual pleasure or grief (that is, the passions), but there was built into human beings a certain capacity for spiritual delight, by which, in an ineffable way, human beings would be able to enjoy God." The first human being, however, was moved by sensual things so that there "worked in him a delight that was sensual." Providentially, God set grief as a kind of opposition to delight. In other words, it was the abuse of the passions, not their existence, that led to the present lot of human beings. From the beginning, however, human nature had a capacity for delight in God. As Maximus puts it elsewhere, nothing that is natural and has been made by God is evil (Maximus's word is "impure").[36]

The affections, then, are necessary for the virtuous life. Maximus, however, wants to say more. In the response to the first question of the *Quaestiones ad Thalassium,* he says that the passions allow human beings to avoid evil, so that they might "possess and hold fast to virtue *and* knowledge." In the passage cited above where Maximus makes a similar point he only mentions *aretē* (virtue), but here, significantly, he adds *gnōsis* (knowledge).[37] In this context knowledge means knowledge of God, and for Maximus knowledge of God does not simply mean knowing something but knowledge that fashions the knower by that which is known. Such knowledge is not possible from a distance; it entails a relation. Hence, it cannot be attained without the affections, that is love that binds the knower to the object of love. He writes:

> Knowledge of divine things *without passion* does not persuade the mind to disdain material things completely, but rather resembles the mere thought of a thing of sense. . . . Just as the simple thought of human realities does not oblige the mind to disdain the divine, so neither does the simple knowledge of divine things persuade it fully to disdain human things. . . . Hence there is a need for the blessed *passion of holy love* which binds the mind to spiritual realities and persuades it to prefer the immaterial to the material and intelligible and divine things to those of sense.[38]

In conceiving of knowledge of God as participation and union with God, Maximus draws, of course, on the Holy Scriptures. In his *Commentary on the Gospel of John* Origen explained how the term "knowledge" is used in the Bible. He is commenting on *John* 8.19: "You know neither me nor my Father. If you knew me, you would know my Father also." "One should take note," he says, "that the Scripture says that those who are united to something or participate in something are said to know that to which they are united or in which they participate. Before such union and fellowship, even if they understand the reasons given for something, they do not know it." As illustrations, he mentions the union between Adam and Eve, which the Bible describes as "Adam knew his wife Eve," and *1 Corinthians* 6.16–17, the reference to union with a prostitute. This shows, he says, that knowing means being joined to or united with.[39]

In his discussion of the "use" of the passions in the spiritual life, then, it is significant that Maximus slips in the word "knowledge" alongside of "virtue." By yoking the passions to knowledge and not simply to the attainment of virtue, Maximus provides a theoretical framework that makes place for love. When knowledge is understood as participation and fellowship, love is its natural accompaniment.[40] In this Maximus shows genuine affinity with Augustine's understanding of knowledge and love. As Bernard McGinn observes: "Love and knowledge are intertwined in Augustine's mystical consciousness."[41] More specifically, there are parallels in the way the two thinkers treat the passions and the virtues. I have already cited a passage on the passions, but Augustine and Maximus make similar statements about the virtues. Maximus writes: "All these [the four cardinal virtues] are brought together in the most noble virtue of all, I mean love."[42] Likewise, Augustine interprets the cardinal virtues as forms of the love of God. Temperance is "love keeping itself entire . . . for God; fortitude is love bearing everything for the sake of God; justice is love serving God alone, . . . and prudence is love making a right distinction between what helps it towards God and what hinders it."[43]

In Augustine as well as in Maximus, love is, of course, a form of desire. In the scriptures, however, desire often carries negative overtones. For example, Paul in *1 Thessalonians* 4.5 exhorts the Thessalonians to learn how to control their bodies in holiness and honor, not *en páthei epithumías* (in the passion of desire). Hence, there was some reluctance, as by Gregory, to use the term desire without qualification. Love was a far preferable term, because it is thoroughly biblical and its field of meaning is broader. Maximus uses both terms in tandem, allowing each one to color the meaning of the other. He writes:

> "For the mind of the one who is continually with God even his desire [*epithumia*] abounds beyond measure into a divine *erōs* [*erota*] and whose entire irascible element is transformed into divine love [*agapē*]. For by an enduring participation [*metousia*] in the divine illumination it has become altogether shining bright, and having bound its passible element to itself it . . . turned it around to a never ending erōs [*erota*], completely changing over from earthly things to divine.[44]

Here, as always, Maximus is scrupulous in his choice of terms. By using desire and love in connection with *erōs,* he provides an interpretation of the passion desire in light of the biblical term for love *(agapē)*, while at the same time filling the biblical term with the echoes that are heard in desire. Of course the term *erōs*, which is not used in the New Testament, and seldom in the Old, provides the link. It is a shrewd move and one that Maximus may have learned from Pseudo-Dionysius the Areopagite. In what seems a deliberately playful passage, Pseudo-Dionysius explains how the language of love works in scripture. "Do not think," he says, "that in giving status to the term 'yearning' *(erōs)* I am running counter to scripture." For example, what does one make out of this passage from *Proverbs* about Wisdom (which for Dionysius was Christ): "Desire *(erasthēti)* her and she shall hold you; exalt her and she will extol you" (*Prv.* 4.6). The careful reader of the Bible will discover, he continues, that in places the scriptures use the term *agapē* when they mean desire or erotic love, implying that this is the case in other passages. His example comes from (the Septuagint version of) 2 *Samuel* 1.26, David's lament over Jonathan, at the end of which David speaks of the love between them. David cries out: "Your love for me was wonderful, surpassing the love of women." Here, where one would expect to find the term *erōs*, the scriptures use *agapēsis*—love having no carnal element and thus its highest form. Dionysius concludes from this: "To those listening properly to the divine things, the term 'love' is used by the sacred writers in divine revelation with the exact same meaning as the term '*erōs*.'"[45]

In the scheme of the passions, the two concupiscible passions are desire and delight. Desire, as we have seen, is transformed into the biblical love; similarly Maximus reinterprets pleasure or delight in what is possessed with the help of another biblical term, "joy." He writes: "Without virtue and knowledge [note the conjunction] it is impossible to obtain salvation. For those who are wholly devoted to God . . . the irrational powers of the soul," are tamed and assimilated. This means that "anger and desire are transformed, the one into love, the other into joy. For what is proper to joy is leaping about in a way that is fitting God *(theoprepēs)*, as great John the forerunner and herald of the truth, leaped in his mother's womb (Luke 1:41) or David king of Israel [danced with abandon] when the ark was given a resting place [in Jerusalem]." In these two instances—John leaping in the womb of Elizabeth when she heard Mary's greetings, and David dancing when the ark had found its resting place in Jerusalem—desire and longing had given way to delight, to the enjoyment of that which previously had been a matter of longing.[46]

Maximus, like other Christian writers, is more interested in the positive passions of desire and delight, than in the negative passions of fear and grief. The reason for this is that his approach to the passions is primarily theological, not moral. The goal of the Christian life is not simply to displace evil and attain virtue but to possess that which alone can bring delight, the one true God. In some passages, however, Maximus breaks down the distinction between concupiscible and irascible passions. Even anger's intensity is turned into a passion that allows one to cleave to God.

> Our reason also should therefore be moved to seek God, the force of desire should struggle to possess [him] and that of anger to hold on to him, or rather, to speak more properly, the whole mind should tend to God, stretched out as a sinew by the temper of anger, and burning with longing for the highest reaches of desire.[47]

Of course, for Maximus, as for Gregory of Nyssa, perfection is never a simple coming to rest, a standing still. Maximus, who loved paradoxical phrases, spoke of ever-moving repose or stationary movement, by which he meant that the soul that loves God is at once at rest in God and at the same time in perpetual motion drawn toward God. "All things created according to time," he writes,

> become perfect when they cease their natural growth. But everything that the knowledge of God effects according to virtue, when it reaches perfection, moves to further growth. For the end of the latter becomes the beginning of the former. Indeed, the one who by practicing the virtues keeps in check the substance of past things begins other, more divine patterns. For God never ceases from good things, just as there was no beginning of good things.[48]

One comes away from reading Maximus, as one does in reading Augustine, with the sense that the old vessels as found in the classical moral tradition have difficulty containing the new wine. Indeed Maximus's thinking on the affections moves along a path that is not unlike that of Augustine. Consider, for example, in light of Maximus's discussion of perpetual growth, a passage from Augustine's *Commentary on the First Epistle of John,* in which he describes the soul as a leather bag that stretches to make room for God.

> The whole life of a good Christian is a holy desire. However, that which you desire you do not yet see; but by desiring you become capable of being filled by that which you will see when it comes. For just as in filling a leather bag . . . one stretches the skin . . . and by stretching one makes it capable of holding more; so God by deferring that for which we long, stretches our desire; by increasing desiring stretches the mind; by stretching, makes it more capable of being filled.[49]

Other Augustinian themes—the virtues as forms of love, the conjunction of love and knowledge, cleaving to God expressed in his use of *Psalms* 73.28: *mihi adhaerere Deo bonum est* (it is good for me to draw near to God), and the notion of enjoying God—also have parallels in Maximus. Von Balthasar speculates about the possibility of contact with Augustinian ideas during Maximus's long stay in North Africa, but concludes, rightly, that Maximus is much too original for such an interpretation. "Maximus speaks less as one who has learned something from someone else, than as one who is in full control of what is distinctively his own."[50]

That is surely true. Yet it is perhaps more to the point, at least on the topic of the affections, to underscore Maximus's affinity with other Christian thinkers than his originality. The direction he pursued was set already in the third century by Lactantius (and before him by the scriptures) and explored in depth by Gregory of Nyssa and Nemesius of Emesa and, of course, by Augustine. In later centuries thinkers in both East and West, John of Damascus, Gregory Palamas, and Thomas Aquinas, built on these foundations.[51]

With this, I return to Jonathan Edwards. Whatever the differences between Edwards and Maximus—in vocation, in theological outlook, in style of argument, and in temperament—it is not insignificant that an American, a child of the Reformation, a Calvinist, a revivalist, a pastor, not an ascetic, discerned the essential point: that the religion of the Bible places religion "very much in the affections . . . and has nothing to do with a state of indifference." On the matter of the affections, Christian thinkers transcended divisions we take for granted, the differences between East and West, ancient and modern, Catholic and Protestant, monastic and lay. Ancient asceticism, at least as we come to know it in Maximus the Confessor, is perennial. What ascetics saw, others saw; and what they saw was not only for ascetics.

NOTES

1. Jonathan Edwards, *The Religious Affections* (Edinburgh, 1984), pp. 21–31.
2. *Quaestiones ad Thalassium,* eds. Carl Laga and Carlos Steel, Corpus Christianorum, Series Graeca, no. 7 (Turnhout, 1980), 55.144–145. On *apatheia* in Maximus, see E. Montmasson, "La Doctrine de l'apatheia d'après saint Maximus," *Echos d'orient* 14 (1911):36–41, and Walther Voelker, *Maximus Confessor als Meister des geistlichen Lebens* (Wiesbaden, 1965), pp. 410–423. The struggle to overcome the passions is a central theme in Maximus's writings. See Voelker, pp. 174–200.
3. See Irénée Hausherr, S.J., *Philautie: De la Tendresse pour soi à la Charité selon Saint Maxime le Confesseur* (Rome, 1952), pp. 145–146; also Lars Thunberg, *Microcosm and Mediator: The Theological Anthropology of Maximus the Confessor* (Lund, 1965), pp. 166–167; Hans Urs von Balthasar, *Kosmische Liturgie: Das Weltbild Maximus' des Bekenners* (Trier, 1988), pp. 191–193. And more recently, Paul M. Blowers, "The Substructure and Transformation of the Human Passions in Maximus the Confessor," forthcoming in *Journal of Early Christian Studies.*
4. Christoph Schoenborn, "Plaisir et Douleur dans l'analyse de S. Maxime, d'après les Quaestiones ad Thalassium," *Maximus Confessor.* Actes du Symposium sur Maxime le Confessuer Fribourg, 2–5 September 1980, eds. F. Heinzer and C. Schoenborn (Fribourg, 1982), pp. 273–284. For an illustration of Maximus's appeal to "experience," see the passage from *QThal.* 61 (*PG* 90.619D–632A), cited by Schoenborn. For further discussion of the place of experience in his thinking, see P. Miquel, "Peira: Contribution à l'étude du vocabulaire de l'expérience réligieuse dans l'oeuvre de Maxime le Confesseur," Studia Patristica, vol. 7 (Berlin, 1966), pp. 355–361.
5. For a survey of ancient views of the affections, see H. M. Gardiner et al., *Feeling and Emotion: A History of Theories* (Westport, Conn., 1970), pp. 58–118.
6. Text in *Divinarum institutionum* (Migne, *PG* 6.14–17).
7. *De patientia* 2.1.
8. Text edited by Martha Nussbaum, *Aristotle's de motu animalium* (Princeton, 1978). See *Mot. anim.* 700b18–19, pp. 38–39.
9. Ibid., 701a35.
10. *Div. inst.* 6.15.
11. On this point see Martha Nussbaum, "The Stoics on the Extirpation of the Passions," *Apeiron* 20 (1987):129–177.
12. Maximus took a quite different point of view. He said that the Logos had "not only become a full human being but also a human being fully subject to passion" (*PG* 91.1041D).
13. *Stromateis* 6.9.71, 74.
14. Clement, however, distinguishes *epithumia,* desire as an unwelcome passion, and *orexis,* a rational or well-ordered desire, and he recognizes the need for the latter in the life of virtue (*Strom.* 3.11.71). On this point, see David G. Hunter, "The Language of Desire:

Clement of Alexandria's Transformation of Ascetic Discourse," in *Semeia* 57 *(Discursive Strategies, Ascetic Piety, and the Interpretation of Religious Literature)* (1992):95–111.

15. On the influence of Evagrius on Maximus, see Marcel Viller, "Aux sources de la spiritualité de saint Maxime: Les oeuvres d'Évagre le Pontique," *Revue d'ascétique et de mystique* 11 (1930):156–184, 331–336.
16. *PG* 79.1204D.
17. *PG* 79.1205C–D. Cf. also *Lamentations* 11.10 and *1 Timothy* 2.8.
18. On this point, see Elizabeth Clark, *The Origenist Controversy* (Princeton, 1993), pp. 76–77. Evagrius, however, did have a place for love and fear of God in his spirituality. "Love," he wrote, "is the offspring of apatheia" (*Praktikos* 81). The goal of the spiritual life is not *apatheia* as such, but love (*Praktikos* 84). On this point see, Gabriel Bunge, *Evagrios Pontikos: Briefe aus der Wüste* (Trier, 1986), esp. pp. 126ff.
19. *PG* 46.50D.
20. *PG* 48.56C–57D.
21. *PG* 48.57A. In places Gregory says that the "passions" must be extirpated. When St. Paul says that "Christ alone lives in him" (*Gal.* 2.20), or "For me to live is Christ" (*Phil.* 1.11), he means that "no human or material passions live in him, neither delight, nor grief, nor anger, nor fear, nor cowardice, nor excitability, nor pride, nor rashness, impudence, ill will, nor envy, nor love of gain, nor love of glory, nor love of honor . . ." (*Commentarius in canticum canticorum* 15; W. Jaeger, *Gregorii Nysseni Opera* [Leiden, 1960], p. 440). Note, however, that this list includes many things besides the cardinal passions, and that in contrast to the cardinal passions some of these are wholly negative.
22. *PG* 48.61B.
23. *PG* 48.89A.
24. To speak of desire and love in relation to God was, of course, not unique to Christian thinkers. Similar conceptions appear in Greek thinkers; for example, Plotinus. See René Arnou, *Le désir de Dieu dans la philosophie de Plotin* (Rome, 1967). Michel Despland argues that Christian thinkers, with exceptions such as Gregory and Augustine, displaced desire in favor of will. See his *The Education of Desire: Plato and the Philosophy of Religion* (Toronto, 1985), esp. pp. 283ff.
25. For a fuller account of the history of Christian interpretation of the passions, one would have to consider the fourth-to-fifth-century bishop, Nemesius of Emesa, of the school of Antioch (Syria) who dealt with the topic at length. See *De natura hominis* 16–21 (cf. *PG* 40.504–817) and *Library of Christian Classics,* vol. 4, ed. and trans. W. Telfer (1955). This work was known to the Latin Middle Ages as a writing of Gregory of Nyssa and is cited as such by Thomas Aquinas, *De veritate* q.26a.3 ad 10m.
26. *QThal.,* introduction, p. 23, 108ff.
27. Maximus had read Evagrius. In the chapters on love he writes: "Some of the passions are of the body, some of the soul. Those of the body take their origin in the body; those of the soul from exterior things. Love and self-control cut away both of them, the former those of the soul, the latter those of the body." The same ideas are found in the same terms in Evagrius, *Praktikos* 35, as Guillaumont has show in his commentary on the *Pratikos: Évagre le pontique. Traité pratique ou le moine,* eds. A. Guillaumont and C. Guillaumont, Sources chrétiennes 171 (Paris, 1971), pp. 581–583.
28. *QThal.* 51.204–205. *QThal.* 34.20–21. Contending with the passions is a key element of the kind of literature of which the *QThal.* is a part. See Paul M. Blowers, *Exegesis and Spiritual Pedagogy in Maximus the Confessor. An Investigation of the Quaestiones ad Thalassium* (Notre Dame, 1991), pp. 13, 38, 46.

29. Gregory, *De virginate* 12.2.4–11. See also Evagrius *De diversis malignis cogitationibus* 2.29 (*PG* 79.1201C).
30. See her thorough and very insightful article, "The Stoics on the Expiration of the Passions," in *Apeiron* 20 (1987):130–177. Discussion of the distinctions is on p. 177.
31. Aristotle, *Nicomachean Ethics* 1104b9–12; Hence "moral virtue is the quality of acting in the best way in relation to pleasures and pains, and that vice is the opposite" (27–29). "The passions are: desire, anger, fear, courage, envy, joy, friendship, hatred, longing *(pothon)*, jealousy, pity and generally those states of consciousness which are accompanied by pleasure or pain" (1105b21–22). See also Nussbaum, *Mot. anim.* 8.701b33–35: "Now the origin of motion, is, as we have said, the object of pursuit *(diokton)* or avoidance *(pheukton)* in sphere of action."
32. Aristotle speaks of an "object of pursuit [*diokton*] and avoidance [*pseukton*]"; (Nussbaum, *Mot. anim.* 701b33). Maximus uses the Aristotelian term *pseugo* in *QThal.* 55.135.
33. *De civitate Dei* 14.9.
34. *QThal.* 55.133–134.
35. *PG* 91.1079B–D.
36. cf. *QThal.* 61 (*PG* 90.628A–B); *QThal.* 27.163–165.
37. The conjunction of "virtue" and "knowledge" is very frequent in Maximus. For discussion with extensive documentation, see Voelker, pp. 233ff.
38. *Quattuor centuriae caritatis* 3.66–67.
39. *Commentarium in Joannem* 8.19; 19.4.21–25.
40. On love and union, see *QThal.* 54.155–157.
41. Bernard McGinn, *The Foundations of Mysticism* (New York, 1992), 1:235.
42. *PG* 91.1249B. Also, "The end [*telos*] of the virtues is love" (*QThal.* 154.155).
43. *De moribus ecclesiae catholicae et moribus Manichaeorum* (*PL* 32.15.25).
44. *Quattuor centuriae caritatis* 2.48. Elsewhere he says that after breaking away from earthly things the mind "finally transfers its whole longing [*pothos*] to God (*Quattuor centuriae caritatis* 3.72); also, "the faculty of desire in which the divine love consists, and through which it readily affixes itself with desire to the pure godhead, and has an unwavering longing for that which is desired. There is also the irascible faculty, by which it binds itself tightly to the divine peace and draws up the movement of desire to divine love" (*QThal.* 49.75–81).
45. *Divinae nominae* (*PG* 3.11–12).
46. *Ambigua* (*PG* 91.1065D–1068A).
47. Commentary on the *Our Father* (*PG* 90.896C). *Maximus Confessor: Selected Writings*, trans. George C. Berthold (New York, 1985), p. 113.
48. Chapters on knowledge (*PG* 90.1096C). *Maximus Confessor,* pp. 134–135, slightly revised. For discussion of this point, see Paul Blowers, "Maximus the Confessor, Gregory of Nyssa, and the Concept of 'Perpetual Progress,'" *Vigiliae Christianae* 46 (1992):161; and Paul. C. Plass, "'Moving Rest' in Maximus the Confessor," *Classica et Mediaevalia* 35 (1984):177–190.
49. *Tractatus in epistolam Joannem* 4.6 (*PL* 35.2008–2009).
50. H. Urs von Balthasar, *Kosmische Liturgie: Das Weltbild Maximus des Bekenners,* 2d ed. (Einsielden, 1961), pp. 408–409.
51. See Mark D. Jordan, "Aquinas's Construction of a Moral Account of the Passions," *Freiburger Zeitschrift für Philosophie und Theologie* 33 (1986):71–97.

30

Toward a Politics of Asceticism

Response to the Three Preceding Papers

William E. Deal

The Ascetic Dimension in Religious Life and Culture conference schedule pamphlet cites conference presuppositions and objectives:

> The perdurance of asceticism within and across religious traditions and cultures suggests the need for historical, cross-cultural, and multidisciplinary perspectives. . . . Thus, the main objective of the Conference is to test whether and to what extent asceticism can be discussed across the boundaries of academic disciplines and fields, historical periods, religious traditions, sensibilities and cultures.

In light of this charge, we must ask whether there is a universal category "asceticism" that is applicable cross-culturally. Additionally, we need to consider the meaning of the construct "politics of asceticism," the category under which the papers responded to here are grouped.

To this end, I will look first at the constructs "asceticism" and "politics of asceticism." What do these terms reveal about certain kinds of religious practice and what do these terms obscure? I will then examine how the issue of the politics of asceticism gets played out in the papers to which these remarks are a response. In order to place my comments in a cross-cultural perspective, I will discuss a Japanese Buddhist example of the politics of asceticism. My concluding remarks will attempt to weave together the disparate views of asceticism presented in this paper.

In keeping with my postmodern bias, I consider my response to be one of several possible readings of these texts—I do not intend to close off the discussion about what asceticism is or means, but rather to open up debate. I am going to contrast a possible politics of asceticism with a phenomenological or typological approach to asceticism as a cross-cultural category. The politics of asceticism I will outline in a moment is not intended as a replacement to a phenomenological approach; nor am I claiming superiority for a "politics of asceticism" approach to the three papers to which I am responding. Rather, I am attempting to shift the perspective from which the material might be studied and assigned meaning.

Asceticism and the Politics of Asceticism

I will first explore the construct "asceticism" as a phenomenological category. As I have mentioned, part of the charge of this conference is to look at the extent to which asceticism can be understood as a construct understandable across cultural boundaries. What is "a" or "the" definition or description of asceticism that can or cannot cross cultural boundaries? I do not assume that everyone at this conference would define or describe asceticism in the same way—in fact, most have been unwilling to offer up any definition at all. There exists here, at least for some, a resistance to definition. I, too, am resistant to offering up a definition of asceticism, but I wonder if definitions of asceticism are not circulating by implication, anyway.

Although we do not share any necessary common definition, most of us would likely agree that there is minimally some parameter of meaning of the term that allows us to come together at this conference and presume that we are talking, somehow, about the same thing. But even this parameter of meaning suggests some fixity in terms of a conceptual boundary of meaning that certain activities do or do not fit into. After all, we would not call all activities and behaviors ascetic, although some of us might prefer a broader and others of us a narrower parameter of meaning to the term. Whatever meaning we might ultimately favor, it is most likely that our understanding will privilege meanings and significances drawn from the ascetics and ascetic texts that we deal with in our particular cultural areas. My own perspective is clearly informed by Asian traditions, particularly Japanese Shintō and Buddhist traditions.

My question, then, is this: to what extent do we imply a meaning to the concept "asceticism" just by using the term. We must, to use the term, have some notion of what asceticism is. The papers for this section suggest something about suppression of passions and sexual/bodily pleasures as at least partly constituent of the meaning of asceticism. Are there always passions and physical pleasures to be abandoned? There are, of course, other forms of asceticism that are more concerned with suppressing the illusions of the mind through ascetic practice, rather than suppressing sexuality, for example.

To the extent that we can discuss asceticism across cultures, religions, and traditions, phenomenological approaches to the problem seem fruitful, at least tentatively. Since we cannot define a singular, all-inclusive meaning to asceticism, phenomenological description would seem to be one way to access at least some of its major meanings or manifestations. Phenomenological descriptions attempt to take into account the practices and experiences of all traditions without overtly favoring one or the other as normative. Thus phenomenology strives for description only. It attempts to bracket from inquiry all attempts at explanation or all philosophical or theological questions of a phenomenon's truth or value.

A phenomenological definition or description of asceticism is provided in Walter O. Kaelber's article on asceticism in the *Encyclopedia of Religion:*

> Although the modern word *asceticism* has eluded any universally accepted definition, the term, when used in a religious context, may be defined as a voluntary, sustained,

> and at least partially systematic program of self-discipline and self-denial in which immediate, sensual, or profane gratifications are renounced in order to attain a higher spiritual state or a more thorough absorption in the sacred. Because religious man *(homo religiosus)* seeks a transcendent state, asceticism—in either rudimentary or developed form—is virtually universal in world religion.[1]

This systematic program of self-discipline and self-denial has a limited number of forms when viewed cross-culturally:

> Virtually universal are (1) fasting, (2) sexual abstinence, (3) poverty, under which may be included begging, (4) seclusion or isolation, and (5) self-inflicted pain, either physical (through such means as whipping, burning, or lacerating) or mental (e.g., contemplation of a judgment day, of existence in hell, or of the horrors associated with transmigration).[2]

Kaelber's article also mentions inner asceticism, a form of ascetic practice "consisting essentially of spiritual rather than physical discipline."[3] Glossing Weber's concept of inner-worldly asceticism, "[s]uch asceticism involves not detachment from or renunciation of any specific worldly pleasure but rather detachment from or renunciation of the world *per se*."[4] The classic Indian example of this idea comes from the Hindu text, the *Bhagavad-Gita,* in which renunciation in action is valorized over the renunciation of action.[5]

Asceticism also has specific objectives, according to Kaelber. In theistic traditions, the ascetic often seeks a personal union with the deity.[6] In nontheistic traditions, there exists "a quest for the true or essential self, which is perceived to be identical with the ground or foundation of all creation."[7] In both theistic and nontheistic traditions, "asceticism may be seen as a meritorious form of behavior, a good work, or a laudable course of action felt to ensure or facilitate a preferred condition after death."[8] Further, "acts of self-denial—particularly self-inflicted pain—may serve as a form of penance of previous misdeeds."[9] Kaelber also mentions "the use of asceticism, particularly self-inflicted pain, as a means of experiencing or reexperiencing the sufferings of either a deity or a human paradigm (i.e., a model individual)."[10]

What this typology of asceticism suggest is that no society allows free reign of expression and action, that there are always controls, restrictions, and limitations placed on what we can do with our bodies or on bodily functions and that these can be expressive of other meanings. When does self-discipline or self-denial become ascetic? It seems to me the answer is different in different cultural contexts in which acts of self-discipline and self-denial are done in relation to actions that are not conceived of as ascetic.

There are, I think, problems with this phenomenological approach. What is the explanatory value of a universal description of the term "asceticism"? Even if we could agree on asceticism as a descriptively valuable cross-cultural category, can we say that asceticism has the same import or meaning in all traditions? What do fasting, sexual abstinence, poverty, seclusion or isolation, and self-inflicted pain mean in specific contexts. I do not understand these as having the same meaning or value across cultures. Kaelber's article suggests this as well: "Viewed cross-culturally, a given ascetic form may have different, even opposite objectives."[11] Kaelber is himself suggesting a reason to look beyond universal description for the meaning(s) of asceticism.

A phenomenological view of asceticism seems to claim a universal meaning or way of conceiving of ascetic practice. This creates a normative definition of asceticism. Although this view of asceticism seems to transcend the concept itself, it is, in fact, an interpretation of asceticism grounded in the logics and concepts of the tradition out of which the term originally comes. The question still remains whether "asceticism" can be applied to the logics and concepts of traditions that do not share the same philosophical and religious foundations. In other words, can we disembody or free the term "asceticism" from its cultural and linguistic moorings?

Phenomenology explains itself as striving for description only, but descriptions and descriptive claims are also interpretive or themselves interpretations. Descriptions of ascetic practice typically favor the tradition or cultural context from which the description takes its point of departure. Family resemblances or equivalences are then discovered in other traditions that seem to affirm a meaning of asceticism. I think we need to be careful about affixing one meaning to the term "asceticism," even if we find family resemblances between traditions. Family resemblances may mask real differences in how specific behaviors are perceived or understood from within a tradition. For instance, in one tradition ascetic behavior might be viewed as operating within the religious orthopraxy. In another tradition, ascetic practice might be seen as radical, a threat to the religious status quo. Sometimes ascetics are mainstream or orthodox within a tradition, and sometimes they are minority voices protesting the corrupt ways of the dominant culture. Actually, I think we read meanings derived from our own normative tradition or perspective into the texts and traditions of others. For this conference, this reading into has largely been from the perspective of Western traditions. How for, instance, am I to make sense of ascetic practice in Japan if I start with concerns gleaned from, say, Christian late antiquity?

What if we were to shift the descriptive starting point and discuss asceticism as primarily concerned with control or suppression of certain bodily functions, so as to gain some benefit? In Japanese Shintō, ritual purification is often seen as the goal or benefit of bodily control. What would asceticism come to mean as a cross-cultural category if we understood it as control of the body in order to gain purification? When we apply universal definitions or descriptions to other traditions I fear that all we are truly measuring is the extent to which that tradition is different from the normative measure found in phenomenological configurations based on our own tradition.

Thus, a description of asceticism based on Jewish or Christian experience applied to Japan tends to obscure the distinctive aspects of Japanese religious practices. What we get is a generic, "one size fits all" asceticism. I am not saying that this is a waste of time or uninstructive, but it only points us in certain directions and certainly does not exhaust the possibilities for what we can say about asceticism. The phenomenological approach to asceticism just outlined lumps like behaviors together as having a transcendent purpose, function, or value, or as always pointed toward some transcendent goal.

One of the important reasons, then, why we cannot define asceticism in any universally satisfying way is because it is contextual, that is, asceticism has meanings within traditions and cultures, rather than as a normative description of one aspect of human behavior that can be generalized or universalized to include all cultures. Ascetic practice can be mainstream, or it can be the response of a minority group that finds in ascetic practice a way to wrest at least some control from the hegemonic grip of the dominant cultural powers. Asceticism can operate in a number of other ways as well. Asceticism is contextual as practices of bodily, emotional, and intellectual control—the ways these control issues play themselves out are different in different temporal and spatial contexts. This contextualized asceticism is in part what I think a politics of asceticism is about. We need to look at the reasons for ascetic practice, what is accomplished by it, what social, political, economic, and other relationships are shifted and altered by engaging in certain forms of behavior that are labeled ascetic.

I will turn now to the construct politics of asceticism. I have argued that a universal description or typology of asceticism stands outside of the contexts in which asceticism has meaning. This universal asceticism allows us to see only a certain part of what asceticism is about, its broad or general contours. A contextualized view of asceticism allows us to see how the specific acts of self-denial or self-discipline operate in relation to a culture's prevailing behavioral norms. The ascetic does not act outside of a historio-cultural context, therefore we cannot simply view asceticism as a universal, transcendent activity that can be understood (at least fully) out of the contexts in which it is enacted. Asceticism has meaning not as a behavior unto itself, but in relationship to behaviors that are conceived of as different from, or in opposition to, or complimentary to it. Thus, there is no essential or universal meaning to asceticism, but only its meanings in different contexts. The valuation of the relationship between different kinds of behaviors is defined within specific cultural contexts. This, I would argue, has political implications, and brings us to the construct "politics of asceticism."

What do I mean by the term "politics of asceticism?" Asceticism is not just a religious activity, but one with political implications. Stated differently, asceticism is not just a purely religious activity (whatever that might mean) because human activities always have a political aspect. Literary criticism offers insights into a definition of "politics" or "political" useful here. W.J.T. Mitchell, in his "Introduction" to *The Politics of Interpretation,* states:

> Is "politics" to be understood in a restricted sense as the actions and choices of persons in their roles as citizens and leaders, members of a polis or civil society? Or is it to be understood more broadly as the structures of belief and interest, the ideologies which permeate every level of human existence?[12]

I take "politics" in this latter sense. Similarly, Peter J. Rabinowitz provides a useful point of departure for considering the meaning of "politics":

> *Politics,* as used here, refers to the systems of power relations among groups (genders, races, nationalities, social classes, among others) in any social situation—systems that may be in part formalized (for instance, through law), but that are always in part invisible.[13]

I understand politics, then, to be about the relationships and systems of power and authority that exist within a given cultural context. A "politics of" is therefore concerned with, *inter alia,* who has control over what is acceptable speech and behavior, and who determines what is right and wrong. Ascetics are not simply engaging in spiritual practices, they are actively altering political and social relationships. Asceticism is a rhetoric of thought and action that is situated within the parameters of culturally specific religious discourses that can transform the relationships of power and authority existing within those particular contexts. Ascetic practice transforms a person's status within the web of complex social and political relationships and rearranges the power and authority brokered within these relationships in culturally significant ways.

Thus, the politics of asceticism refers to a contextualized sphere of action and interpretation, and from this the following kinds of questions emerge. What is the religious, historical, social, political, and economic context in which one becomes an ascetic or enacts a culture's version of ascetic practice? How is the behavior of ascetics different from the laity, temporal rulers, monastics, and others within their cultural context? Is ascetic practice normal or normative within the tradition in which it is performed, or is it a break from traditional modes of religious activity? That is, to what extent are ascetics "othering" themselves to some end or goal? What is being accomplished by living an ascetic lifestyle? Does becoming an ascetic or engaging in ascetic activity free one from some social or political stricture? Does it resolve a problem or cause a problem? Does it rearrange patterns of authority and power? Is it a protest? Thus, for example, a politics of asceticism might look at how bodily or emotional self-denial shifts structures of power and authority in specific contexts, or how it serves as a protest, or resolves a social problem. While we might find self-mortification practiced across different cultures, the value and meaning of such a behavior is peculiar to each specific manifestation.

A politics of asceticism, then, is concerned with the deep and complex relationship that asceticism has to political and social power—how to get, preserve, and apply it—in specific cultural contexts. It is problematic to think that there can be purely religious behavior that is completely isolated from social and political events. Regardless of motivation, religious activities like ascetic practice have an impact on the social and political life of a culture or community. Even a heartfelt reclusion alters the balance of power and relationships. If we assume that asceticism has only to do with transcendent spiritual goals, then we run the risk of overlooking how people actually lived their lives in accordance with religious ideas and how these actions, pointed at transcendent goals, nevertheless impacted social, political, and economic relationships. Indeed, I would argue, though I do not have time to develop this idea here, that ascetic discourse, grounded though it is in transcendent religious values, serves in part to legitimate certain social and political agendas.

The Politics of Asceticism: A Response to Malti-Douglas, Milhaven, and Wilken

Because the papers by Malti-Douglas, Milhaven, and Wilken were placed under the theme "politics of asceticism," I feel compelled to respond to them on the basis of this issue, rather than on some other grounds. To this end, I was interested when I read these papers how they would deal with this topic and how we would agree or differ on the parameters of a politics of asceticism. However, these particular conference papers do not directly address or engage in a sustained discussion of possible meanings of a politics of asceticism. Nevertheless, what I have termed a politics of asceticism certainly appears in or is suggested by the papers. Malti-Douglas's paper deals with gender and asceticism, and there are explicit political issues that arise from her discussion. She also provides historical context with which to locate the significance of Karīmān Ḥamza's asceticism. The Wilken and Milhaven papers are concerned with asceticism, ethics, and theology. They are, therefore, more difficult to respond to from a politics-of-asceticism perspective because they provide little of the historical context needed to relate ethical and theological issues to specific cultural contexts in which ascetic practice was enacted. Rather than try to guess contexts in which I am not expert, I will raise some questions that relate these two papers to the notion of a politics of asceticism. It should be understood that I do not mean this as a critique and that the Wilken and Milhaven papers could be compared with interesting connections drawn between them on issues of asceticism, ethics, and theology. I will not, however, attempt to do that here. My intention is to discuss some possible implications of a politics of asceticism implied in these two papers. Thus, my intention with all three papers is to ask questions of these papers in light of my understanding of a politics of asceticism. Because the papers are available in this volume I will not attempt to provide a synopsis of their content.

Malti-Douglas's paper looks at how an Egyptian Muslim woman, Karīmān Ḥamza, articulates her religious, and particularly ascetic, experience. Her autobiography narrates the story of "a born-again young woman who goes from a secular to a religious lifestyle and whose twentieth-century journey is juxtaposed with, and redefined by, that of a number of male medieval mystics" (p. 395). Malti-Douglas provides the context for understanding the politics of Karīmān Ḥamza and her identification with Islamist movements and suggests some possible contours of a theory of a politics of asceticism without explicitly making reference to such a theoretical perspective.

How does Karīmān Ḥamza understand the ascetic tradition she lives within and gains meaning from? Malti-Douglas explains that the autobiography of Karīmān Ḥamza "forms part of the by now extensive publications that emanate from the Islamist movement, a religious revival movement in the Middle East . . ." (p. 395). Malti-Douglas states the political implication of this: "At stake is the control of various forms of cultural production, some of which, like literature and the arts, have long been in the hands of more secularized and leftist intellectuals" (p. 395).

Asceticism for Karīmān Ḥamza is the asceticism of medieval male Muslim ascetics or Ṣūfīs: "The intertext of the medieval male mystics not only redefines the young woman's religious experience but it places it squarely in a male religious and ascetic tradition" (p. 408). Thus, Karīmān Ḥamza's "spiritual trajectory is validated by men" (p. 408). Malti-Douglas notes that "[t]his recourse to the male is not a religious necessity. There are many conversion narratives by Islamist women that need no male intermediary" (p. 411, fn.67). It is important to ask, as Malti-Douglas does, why the medieval female ascetic experience is missing from Karīmān Ḥamza's autobiography. What is the significance of this absence in her autobiography? How do narratives about male ascetics allow Karīmān Ḥamza to shift relationships of power and authority in her life that women's narratives would not let her do?

This question puts us squarely at the intersection of asceticism and gender. Gender is important to an understanding of asceticism because ascetic practice was a gendered experience. That is, the lives of male and female ascetics was different, and was the social and political impact of their ascetic practices. One of the reasons that asceticism is such a powerful act is that it rearranged the usual relations between men and women, thereby changing power relations as well.

It is interesting that Karīmān Ḥamza's asceticism, grounded in the theology of the Islamist movement, shifts her away from her secularized women's role (unveiled) to a religious life (veiled). Her relationship to men has certainly changed, but toward a traditional role. Malti-Douglas observes that "Karīmān Ḥamza's text speaks less of the soul than of the body. And, more striking in the work of a woman, it shows this body as defined by and for men" (p. 397). This represents a shift from her previous unveiled condition. She no longer plays the part of the modern, cosmopolitan Egyptian woman, and instead has entered the controlled world of Islamic fundamentalism. Karīmān Ḥamza's autobiography is a legitimation of the social and political relationships she has transformed by her embrace of Islam. An important feature of this legitimating discourse is that it is framed in terms of the paradigmatic hagiographies of male ascetics.

Karīmān Hamza also makes use of intertextuality—quotes from classical sources like the Qur'ān and the ḥadīth (traditions of the Prophet)—to further legitimate her new life as a worldly ascetic, the "Mystical Announcer." Ultimately, Karīmān Ḥamza's stand pits her religious awakening against the sensibilities of the Egyptian government. She stands against the Egyptian government, aligned with the Islamist movement. Thus, her ascetic lifestyle asserts pressures on the political institutions of modern Egypt. Karīmān Ḥamza's asceticism has political and social ramifications that are generalizable to a larger theory or construct of a politics of asceticism.

The purpose of Milhaven's paper is to stimulate discussion of a particular value question, a particular question of good human living. The question of good human living is connected to the phenomenon of human asceticism. Milhaven is concerned with the intersection of asceticism and ethics—nevertheless, this material suggests issues that can be framed in terms of a politics of asceticism.

Milhaven understands asceticism in part as a consistent, rigorous withdrawal from (renunciation of) certain pleasure. He uses the term "certain pleasure" because ascetics generally have their own pleasure, for example, the pleasure of self-mastery or the pleasure of anticipating union with God. The pleasures ascetics renounce and the pleasures they gain through ascetic practice are implicated in a politics of asceticism. Delineating what counts as pleasures to be embraced or avoided establishes the parameters of acceptable human activity. The meanings and significances of pleasure, once arranged or re-arranged, can be directed toward specific social ends, such as living the good life. What social and political power is brokered by embracing or denying pleasures? What ethical view is propounded and what restrictions are placed on human activity? Self-mastery, for instance, is certainly a way to wrest away the control of religious institutions and give it to the ascetic. Religious institutions are always implicated in politics because they are important brokers of power and authority in religious worlds.

Milhaven notes that the notion of rejecting one kind of pleasure and rejoicing freely in another form of pleasure confronts us with two questions if we wish to understand any given ascetic. What kind of pleasure does this ascetic strive to eliminate or keep to a minimum in his or her life? What kind of pleasure does he or she unabashedly enjoy as a fruit of this austerity? These two aspects of pleasure are intertwined according to Milhaven: "If we understand only one of these two pleasures, we do not understand the asceticism" (p. 376). Pleasures, whether to be enjoyed or eliminated, are implicated in an ethical viewpoint. There is implied here an orthopraxy, a legitimate or right way of doing things.

Milhaven's working hypothesis is that "in good part the same basic asceticism has been endorsed by the intellectual establishment of Western civilization for the last twenty-five hundred years" (p. 377). The asceticism endorsed by the intellectual establishment is the suppression of sexuality.

> Has the intellectual establishment not consistently championed an asceticism that denigrates and combats one given kind of pleasure while openly, indeed righteously, voluptuating in another kind of pleasure? And, is it not, on the whole throughout this history, the same kind of pleasure that is denigrated and combatted by the reigning tradition, and the same other kind that is righteously relished by the tradition? If so, what is the one pleasure consistently opposed? What is the other pleasure, consistently exalted? (p. 377).

This other pleasure is erotic pleasure and represents a countercurrent to the intellectual establishment. In this instance, sex is not something to renounce, but is esteemed as paradigmatic for good human living.

> It is not ethical pioneering to claim that sexual pleasure can be of much higher value than the Western tradition concedes. It is, however, novel, revolutionary for morality and spirituality to argue . . . that good sex can be a sound paradigm for good human living in general, and that this erotic paradigm is helpful and necessary in today's moral discussion and debate (pp. 377–378).

A dominant discourse of Western tradition is being overturned by a new notion of asceticism. The old and new asceticisms are not, therefore, simply about transcendent values, but are implicated in modes of social and political control. Thus, this ethical reframe has a political dimension: in what specific contexts would this erotic paradigm for good living be valued? How would the embrace of such an ethic shift social and political relationships? Who gets to say what pleasures are suppressed or valued? We might imagine a debate between liberal humanists and the religious right over such matters—power is at stake! Certainly, overturning Western intellectual hegemony has political implications and redirects much of the tradition to an alternate view.

Milhaven frames this debate over good living in terms of the views of Plato and Hadewijch. Milhaven's concern is ethical rather than historical, the question of what makes good human living.

> Is it perhaps true that the two kinds of pleasure, one scorned and the other exalted by dominant Western tradition, are indeed, as a recurrent counterculture has maintained, both of great, absolute human value? (p. 379).

Milhaven is concerned with a normative ethical question. From the perspective of a politics of asceticism, the question is not whether both pleasures are of great, absolute human value, but what power relationships get shifted if both are now valued. The fact that Milhaven looks at feminist writers to seek a ground for the value of sexuality as paradigm for the good suggests a political agenda: women are rectifying or shifting the concept of the good into new patterns which contradict mainstream Western views on this matter. The context of twentieth-century feminism as a ground for new interpretations of pleasure represents a shifting of, or addition to, the meaning of asceticism. Is an ascetic of erotic pleasure possible?

Milhaven does ask political questions when he addresses issues of the new ascetic paradigm: "How does this countercultural thought counter? Wherein precisely is it erotic?" We find a politics also in his contrasting of Hadewijch to Plato. Hadewijch centers on her enjoyment of God during the supreme union. She identifies final supreme human living as pleasuring possession and union. She also uses notions of mutuality of desire and enjoyment, for instance in the image of the divine union as two lovers making love. Hadewijch describes the final union as dark—she cannot hear or see anything or anyone in it, nor can she speak of this experience. This is pleasure "scarcely determined by any prior knowing" (p. 393), which recalls the characterization by Plato of the lower pleasures, like the pleasures of eating or sex. Milhaven explains, that no prior knowing, in Hadewijch's account, determines her supreme fruition with God. This supreme fruition, that is, Hadewijch's union with God, "turns Plato's hierarchy of values downside up" (p. 392). Plato's inferior pleasure is Hadewijch's superior pleasure. In light of this, we might ask whether a politics of asceticism always turns the dominant hierarchy of values downside up, using the cultural storehouse of images and values, but radically reinterpreting them which in turn shifts relationships of power and authority and knowledge?

Wilken's paper is concerned with the history of the Christian interpretation of the passions/affections. Christian interpretations fall into two basic camps: those who say the passions lead one to God, and those who say they lead one to evil. Maximus at first appears to say that "the passions hinder genuine spiritual growth." But, as Wilken points out, Maximus also "surprises us by emphasizing not the evil that the passions work but the good that they make possible" (p. 416). Maximus states:

> In the devout the passions become good when, prudently turning away from the things of the body, they concern themselves with the possession of heavenly things. For example, *desire* brings about an insatiable movement of spiritual longing for divine things . . . (p. 416).

For Maximus, then, without passions human beings would be unable to hold to virtue and knowledge—passions are "necessary for the acquiring of virtue." There is, therefore, a "right use of our natural faculties" (p. 417).

There is a politics at work here. Maximus writes that true Christians are those "who pass beyond the disturbances brought about by the passions" (p. 412). Maximus claims to know the truth of the passions, which provides him with a source of power and authority, and the ability to claim to know what is right and wrong. This is political because it gives him access to sources of power and notions of truth.

Wilken states that Maximus's "approach to the passions is primarily theological, not moral" (p. 419). From a politics of asceticism perspective, we can ask how directing the goal of human life to God and not simply to the good is implicated in concrete human affairs? Thus, Maximus needs to be understood not just in terms of the philosophical or theological tradition through which he argues his view of the passions, but also in terms of the social, political, and economic realities of his day. His views need not be taken only as disembodied theological musings, but expressive of contemporaneous struggles for power and authority, for assertions of the correct cosmology and the ethical actions lived in accord with his conception of ultimate reality.

What I have sought to do in this brief response to Malti-Douglas, Milhaven, and Wilken is to ask questions concerning how the asceticisms of Karīmān Ḥamza, Hadewijch, and Maximus allow them to shift and transform the political, social, and religious alignments of their specific historical contexts. At stake for these ascetics is not just a vision of ultimate reality and how humans should live in accord with it, but the rearrangement of social and political relationships and the power and authority brokered within these relationships. I will turn next to an example of ascetic practice taken from the Japanese Buddhist tradition in order to further illustrate the ramifications and meanings of a politics of asceticism.

The Politics of Asceticism: A Japanese Buddhist Example

There are numerous accounts of Japanese Buddhist ascetics and the austere lives they led in quest of salvation. In the Heian period (794–1185), monks such as Genshin retired to remote sub-temples of the Tendai school Enryakuji temple complex on Mount Hiei in order to further their religious practice. Accounts of the Heian period *hokke hijiri* (Lotus ascetics) describe their retirement into remote forests and secluded mountains in order to concentrate on ascetic rituals based on the *Lotus Sutra* (*Hokekyō*), an important Mahayana Buddhist scripture, and Tendai school Buddhist thought. Ascetic practice was meant to lead one to Perfect

Enlightenment or birth in the Pure Land of Amida Buddha. The *Hokke genki,*[14] a mid-eleventh century collection of "Miraculous Tales of the Lotus Sutra," depicts the ideal of the *hokke hijiri* or *jikyōsha* (upholder of the *Lotus Sutra*).[15]

The *Hokke genki* portrays the *hokke hijiri* as contemporary bodhisattvas whose ideal is expressed in the *Lotus Sutra,* chapter 14: "Anrakugyō hon" ("Comfortable Conduct"). This chapter, prominent in the *Hokke genki,* portrays the Buddha describing a bodhisattva as one who retires from the world: "[*a bodhisattva*] ever loves to sit in *dhyāna,* improving and collecting his thoughts in a quiet place."[16] This reclusive ground for religious action is especially appropriate for those living in what the *Lotus Sutra* calls the latter evil age, that is, a period after the extinction of the Buddha when it is difficult to understand and practice the Dharma. It is evident that the *Hokke genki* viewed the *hijiri* as situated in this latter evil age in the description, in Tale 8, of the monk Myōtatsu as "the guardian of the Correct Law *(shōbō)* in these degenerated times *(jokuse).*"[17]

Although Lotus ascetics usually had training as traditional monks, they came to eschew the institutional centers of the Buddhist monastic hierarchy for a life of extreme *shugyō* (ascetic practice) in secluded mountains and forests. Their practice centered on the *dokuju* (recitation) of the *Lotus Sutra,* performed with a repentant heart, and meant to cleanse one of sin and desire. This was said to result in liberation from the samsaric cycle of birth-death-rebirth, thereby ensuring a final birth into an enlightened state or into one of the paradises of the Buddhas and bodhisattvas, most notably the Pure Land of Amida Buddha. Besides salvation, chanting the *Lotus Sutra* was thought to direct power to numerous other goals and benefits, such as the curing of illness, expiating of sins, quelling the destructive forces of nature, causing aristocrats to mend their evil ways, and revealing one's past karmic state.

The *Hokke genki* portrays the *hijiri* as moral exemplars who are devoted to their religious practice. *Hijiri* are described as merciful, compassionate, diligent in religious practice, honest, pure, and brilliant. Although these ascetics avoid any sustained relationships with other people, they nevertheless provide clothing to the poor and medicine to the sick. The *hijiri* themselves are depicted as wearing tree bark or leaves as clothing, so that the literal donation of the clothes off their backs serves to punctuate their great compassion and selflessness toward others, especially toward the poor and socially disadvantaged. Given the overall tenor of the *Hokke genki,* it is not hard to imagine that this behavior is meant to contrast with that of the aristocrats, bureaucrats, and institutional monks who have riches but keep it for themselves. The ascetics clearly look and act differently from most people, whether aristocrats or farmers. This, of course, serves to contrast their different values and lifestyle, and to express physically their disaffection and disapproval of the prevailing values. But *hijiri* are also different because of their spiritual acumen that requires their special lifestyle to realize. So great are their spiritual accomplishments that the *Hokke genki* describes them as bodhisattvas.[18]

In short, the *Hokke genki* presents an image of the Lotus ascetics as desiring to live a holy life, purified through ascetic practice from the profane world in order to seek salvation or enlightenment. From a phenomenological perspective, these ascetic monks fit Kaelber's generic definition, cited earlier, of asceticism as "a voluntary, sustained, and at least partially systematic program of self-discipline and self-denial in which immediate, sensual, or profane gratifications are renounced in order to attain a higher spiritual state or a more thorough absorption in the sacred." Like ascetics in other religious contexts, the Lotus ascetics engaged in such practices as fasting, sexual abstinence, and seclusion.

But there is a political agenda that gets lost if we do not examine the *hokke hijiri* in context. These ascetics perceived the large Buddhist institutions, such as the great Tendai monastery on Mount Hiei, to be more concerned with worldly gain and court intrigue than spiritual growth and salvation. They expressed open antipathy toward traditional Buddhist institutions, those largely associated with state rituals, and with aristocratic court families and the ruling elite. The increasing shift away from state Buddhism and aristocratic Buddhism toward popular Buddhist practice is usually regarded as one of the central developments of Heian period Buddhism. The *hokke hijiri* represent an important development that is neither aristocratic nor popular, but rather a third form of Heian Buddhist religiosity: monks who, at least in the ideal, abandon the institutional Buddhist structure for a life of solitude away from the monastery, the court, and the towns and villages. The *hijiri* did not exchange the monastery for lay life or for a less rigorous form of religious practice, a feature of popular Buddhism developing in this period. Rather, they embraced a life more rigorous than that experienced by monastic Buddhists.

The *hokke hijiri,* by their very retreat into the recesses of the mountains, were responding to and symbolically expressing criticism of the existing institutions of Heian Buddhism. In so doing, they implicitly defined themselves in opposition to these institutions. The act of retiring to the deep mountains was a means of setting themselves apart from more traditional and conventional monks. For these ascetics, being in society, or being in the world, came to include not only the bustle of the capital and the austerity of agricultural life, but also life at monastic institutions like Mount Hiei. Thus, *hijiri* came to define themselves by setting themselves apart from the mainstream of Heian period Buddhist life. They were social protesters who lived out their protest through their alternative lifestyle.

Thus, the *hokke hijiri* defined themselves in opposition to the formal, hierarchical structure of Heian society. One of the many ways in which the *hokke hijiri* expressed their rejection of traditional structures and norms, of the community, was by valuing the ideal of the solitary ascetic, assiduous in his religious practice conducted within the confines of remote mountains. The recluse's very lifestyle was destructive of the mechanisms of control inherent in the social hierarchy. The *hokke hijiri,* as depicted in the *Hokke genki,* were especially contemptuous of the traditional institutional centers of Heian religious life, and the social hierarchy they promoted. The *Hokke genki,* Tale 44, relates the story of a former Mount Hiei monk. This monk states the reason why he shunned this mountain in favor of a remote hermitage: "Mount Hiei is filled with the hot fire of bribery by donors and believers and I cannot bear the vulgar smell of the various priests in the mountain."[19] The ultimate success of the *hijiri*'s protest is perhaps best measured by the fact that they laid important foundations for the development of later Kamakura period Buddhist traditions, and, ironically, for their own institutionalization in the religious form known as *shugendō*.

Directing the power of the *Lotus Sutra* to the goal of one's own salvation extricated the possibility of enlightenment from the tight grasp of traditional Buddhist institutions. By so doing, the very context in which salvation could be realized had been shifted. At the same time, the number of those authorized to utilize and control *Lotus Sutra* symbols had been greatly increased, thus diminishing the control of traditional Buddhist institutions in people's lives and minimizing the importance of traditional monks. In short, the powers of the universe no longer rested solely in the hands of a select few.

The practice of chanting the *Lotus Sutra* provided the *hijiri* with a conduit to the power of the universe. Recitation, then, was an act of control: the *hijiri* controlled the world through ritual performance, directing power to a number of goals. Gaining control of the universe allowed *hijiri* to also gain control of their immediate world. The performance of the *Lotus Sutra* through its recitation was thus a critically important component to the innovations the *hijiri*, in the *Hokke genki*, were advocating: *hijiri* control of Buddhist symbols, *hijiri* superiority over priests and aristocrats, and *hijiri* control of their own salvation.

Recitation, in distinction to the other practices, was clearly a shift away from the elaborate, labor intensive rituals associated with Tendai and the Buddhist practices of the imperial court. Recitation was particularly suited to the ascetic life in which mobility and simplicity dictated against extensive rituals requiring a large number of ritual implements for their proper enactment. Chanting the *Lotus Sutra* did not require special ritual implements, one did not even need a copy of the *Lotus Sutra* itself. The ascetic was said to carry the *Lotus Sutra* in his or her heart and mind, and was consequently not tethered to any specific place or group of people in order to practice. The *hijiri*'s altar was the place where he or she chose to chant. Thus, the need for action expressive of the *hijiri* cosmology and lifestyle was distilled into the simple practice of chanting the *Lotus Sutra*. The human act of recitation bound the ideal of the ascetic lifestyle with the legitimating symbol of the *Lotus Sutra*. The power of the *Lotus Sutra* was released through recitation and then directed to the human concerns of the *hijiri*. Recitation was therefore both an act of propagation, participating in the dissemination of the Dharma as taught by the *Lotus Sutra*, and a ritual practice directed toward one's spiritual well-being.

The *Hokke genki* makes it clear that the *hijiri* are superior to both the aristocrat and the traditional monk. Tale 14 suggests that aristocrats are analogous to venomous serpents: a fearsome serpent takes the form of a "person dressed in courtly attire of the fifth rank"[20] in order to converse with the *hijiri*. The serpent/aristocrat relates how, having heard this ascetic recite the *Lotus Sutra*, his evil thoughts have turned toward good. The ascetic reflects upon this unusual incident:

> Even a poisonous serpent developed a good mind by listening to the [recitation of the *Hokekyō*]. Certainly the people of later generations will benefit by it. They should know that unless faith is put in the *Lotus Sutra*, one will soon fall into the mud of sufferings and be mired in it for a long time.[21]

The serpent symbolizes the aristocrats. We are told, if indirectly, that even aristocrats can be changed if they hear the recitation of the *Lotus Sutra.* Undoubtedly this veiled rhetoric was a way for the *Hokke genki* to critique court life without saying so explicitly. In fact, we see here an important device through which the *Hokke genki* advocated change. The text never says the world must be changed now, but rather, more subtly, suggests that if we do not change our attitudes and lifestyles, we will pay the inevitable karmic consequences. The *Hokke genki* also recounts tales in which traditional priests are too impure of thought to associate with ascetics in pure and sacred places.

The practices of the Lotus ascetics were concerned with winning enlightenment or salvation, but they also rearranged relationships of power and authority, shifting emphasis away from the cultural dominance of aristocrats and the Buddhist monastic hierarchy to the ideals of the *hokke hijiri.* From a more personal, spiritual perspective, asceticism allowed one to sever the attachments to daily life that create evil karma and are a hindrance to the practice of the Buddhist path and, therefore, spiritual advancement in this life and the next. But these ascetic activities directed toward spiritual benefit also provided those disenfranchised from the dominant sources of power and authority to find in ascetic activity decisive and effective actions that gained them some control over the production of cultural and religious meaning in this period. Importantly, because ascetic practice was within the orthopraxy of traditional Japanese Buddhism, it utilized a means of shifting social and political relationships in culturally recognizable and acceptable ways, even if the interpretations made of texts like the *Lotus Sutra* were clearly at odds with the ruling hegemony. Asceticism allowed for the transformation of power, authority, and its relationships without throwing the social and political order into chaos or giving carte blanche to any political or religious comer. Therefore, asceticism was not only important for the spiritual advancement that might result, but because it rearranged social, political, and religious power and authority. The rhetoric of the *Hokke genki* attempts to legitimate the ascetic practices of the *hokke hijiri,* asserting their spiritual superiority, and thereby distinguishing them from the dominant powers of the day.

Thus, the ascetic practices of the *hokke hijiri* need to be situated in their Heian social and political context. Asceticism is not isolable as singular or pure religious activity. Whatever the motive, asceticism was done in relation to other culturally significant and meaningful activities. Spiritually, taking up the ascetic life meant renunciation of the world, but, more concretely, one also renounced relationships and religious and political office. We might think of the generalized Buddhist notion of renouncing the world as a lofty spiritual goal, but it also had a very specific impact on the institutions of Heian Buddhism and the ruling aristocracy. Asceticism allowed the *hokke hijiri* to rearrange and repattern the many complex social and political relationships of daily life and the power that was brokered within these relationships.[22]

The Politics of Asceticism and the Politics of Interpretation

I want to conclude with a brief discussion of another politics—the politics of interpretation—which is implicated in any discussion of a politics of asceticism. Following Steven Mailloux, I am interested in "the sociopolitical context in which interpretation takes place."[23] For Mailloux, a politics of interpretation is concerned with "how an interpretive act took place within the context of power relations in a historical community."[24] Thus, "interpretation takes place in a political context and each interpretive act relates directly to the power relations (whether of nation, family, gender, class, or race) involved in that context."[25] No matter what the text being read, "[i]n different ways, reading treaties, explicating poems, and interpreting scripture all involve arguments over such topics as textual meaning, authorial intention, past readings, historical contexts, and interpretive methods. All involve the rhetorical politics of interpretation."[26] Thus, an understanding of the politics of interpretation is necessary for an understanding of the politics of asceticism.

Using the term politics of asceticism is also to partake of the politics of interpretation. I have argued that a politics of asceticism refers to a contextualized sphere of action and interpretation, and that ascetic activity has a direct impact on the religious, historical, social, political, and economic contexts in which one becomes an ascetic or enacts a culture's version of ascetic practice. There is not one essential meaning to asceticism, especially not as a descriptive, potentially cross-cultural category. To fix the meaning of the term is to pass judgment on the value of one kind of behavior. It is to prize or belittle those who do or do not do ascetic practice. Within a tradition, this can be normative: "you do it wrong, we do it right."

When we are talking about a politics of asceticism we are also staking out a theoretical ground that privileges certain views and questions, and obscures others. My view of asceticism, for instance, outlines my theoretical, or political, stance toward this body of material and allows me to ask certain questions. But the question I can ask, my politics of asceticism, is embedded not only in my own interpretive politics, but also in at least four other possible layers of politics contextualized within this conference: (1) the politics embedded in the ascetics and ascetic texts studied in the papers; (2) the politics of the paper writers; (3) the politics of this response; and (4) the politics of this conference.

The first layer is the politics embedded in the ascetics and ascetic texts studied in the papers. How do Hadewijch, Maximus, and Karīmān Ḥamza interpret the ascetic traditions they live within and gain meaning from? What are the social and political contexts in which these ascetics operate? What historical precedents do they follow, and which do they change or alter in order to effect religious change? How do they interpret their tradition's past? Are we reading texts written by these individuals, or texts about them written by followers or later biographers? What was the cultural milieu of these text writers? What social and political agenda were at stake? What meanings about the world do these texts inherit from a general cultural storehouse of ideas and images, and what new meanings do these texts construct?

The second layer, the politics of the papers' authors, raises issues around how they interpret these traditions. How do the various authors legitimate their viewpoint and claims? What kinds of analogies and rhetorical devices do they use to make their points? Further, what constructs of asceticism and the politics of asceticism do the authors use? What do the interpreters assume about the intentions of authors or compilers of the texts they study? Is it assumed that ascetics have purely spiritual motives or that they can also be motivated by worldly, mundane considerations? There are also issues of academic conventions; for instance, what a paper should be like.

The third layer, the politics of this response, is concerned with how I interpret the papers. What are the implications of my finding similarities or differences in the papers? For instance, if we find similarities we might argue for asceticism as a universal category. If we locate the differences we might argue for asceticism as culture bound. What does this do to the notion that asceticism is primary or important in explicating religiosity in all traditions? Why do I find the politics of asceticism a more useful theoretical perspective than a phenomenological view? We might also want to ask what the politics of my interpretation of the politics of asceticism is about. What are my biases? What is my personal or professional relationship to the authors? To what extent might the authors feel I have reduced their meanings, or misinterpreted their ideas? I have sought to direct our discussion along certain lines, but my own politics of interpretation may seem to conflict at times with those of the authors represented.

The fourth and final layer is the politics of this conference. I have already noted that one of the objectives of this conference is to consider the extent to which asceticism can be considered a universal category for studying certain kinds of religious phenomena. By stating the agenda in this way, what has been illuminated by looking for universals, or at least their possibility, and what has been thrust into the conceptual shadows by such a theoretical starting point? Has this conference tried to find some central ground for understanding all human religiosity? Does this conference suggest that this is even possible?

Mailloux observes that "interpretive theories are not foundational but rhetorical, establishing no permanent grounding or guiding principles guaranteeing correct interpretation but certainly providing much rhetorical substance for interpretive debate."[27] In light of this observation and the questions raised by the different layers of a politics of interpretation, where does this leave us in terms of whether the politics of asceticism is a universal category? All of the different versions of asceticism—as world-affirming or world-negating, as promoting or denying pleasures and passions, as suppressing or valorizing bodily functions—are constructs. These different ascetical constructs have meaning in the contexts in which they are enacted. Plato's or Antony's asceticism is meaningless in, say, a Buddhist context in which the body is valued and understood differently, where the body/soul dichotomy is differently conceived, and where the goal of bodily control or mastery is different.

But the politics of asceticism is also a construct. It does not provide us with a meta-view unimplicated or unencumbered by our own biases and perspectives. We need to ask, therefore whether the politics of asceticism can serve as a cross-cultural category. Does a politics of asceticism allow us to treat asceticism in some new or more insightful or simply different way across traditions? If asceticism must be seen in context, is it a construct that translates in any meaningful way across cultures? The answer is no if we attempt a universal definition or description of the term. But, if we seek, for instance, to understand how different people and cultures have constructed the meaning of bodily control, then there is great value in looking at the different ways, across cultures, such constructions have been made, and how these constructions have been implicated in the structures of power and authority operating in those particular contexts.

NOTES

1. Walter O. Kaelber, "Asceticism," in *The Encyclopedia of Religion,* ed. Mircea Eliade (New York: Macmillan Publishing Company, 1987), 1:441.
2. Ibid., 442
3. Ibid.
4. Ibid.
5. Ibid.
6. Ibid.
7. Ibid.
8. Ibid., 443
9. Ibid.
10. Ibid.
11. Ibid.
12. W.J.T. Mitchell, "Introduction," in *The Politics of Interpretation,* ed. W.J.T. Mitchell (Chicago: University of Chicago Press, 1983), pp. 1–2.
13. Peter J. Rabinowitz, *Before Reading: Narrative Conventions and the Politics of Interpretation* (Ithaca: Cornell University Press, 1987), p. 5.
14. The editions of the *Hokke genki* consulted are, in Japanese, Inoue Mitsusada and Ōsone Shōsuke, eds., *Ōjōden-Hokke genki,* Nihon shisō taikei 7 (Tokyo: Iwanami Shoten, 1982), hereafter abbreviated *OHG;* and, in English translation, Yoshiko Kurata Dykstra, trans., *Miraculous Tales of the Lotus Sutra from Ancient Japan: The Dainihonkoku hokekyō kenki of the Priest Chingen* (Ōsaka: Intercultural Research Institute, The Kansai University of Foreign Studies, 1983), hereafter abbreviated *MTLS.*
15. For a discussion of the etymology of the term *hijiri,* see Maruyama Kiyoko, *Genji monogatari no bukkyō: Sono shūkyōsei no kōsatsu to gensen to naru kyōsetsu nitsuite no tankyū* (Tokyo: Sōbunsha, 1985), pp. 99–119.
16. Leon Hurvitz, trans., *Scripture of the Lotus Blossom of the Fine Dharma* (New York: Columbia University Press, 1976), pp. 209–210.
17. *MTLS,* p. 38; *OHG,* p. 63/517.
18. For instance, Tales 22 and 74.
19. *MTLS,* p. 71.
20. Ibid., p. 44.
21. Ibid., with revisions based on *OHG,* p. 71/520.
22. For a detailed discussion of the Lotus ascetics, see William Deal, "Ascetics, Aristocrats, and the Lotus Sutra: The Construction of the Buddhist Universe in Eleventh Century Japan," Ph.D. dissertation, Harvard University, 1988.

23. Steven Mailloux, "Interpretation," in *Critical Terms for Literary Study,* eds. Frank Lentricchia and Thomas McLaughlin (Chicago: University of Chicago Press, 1990), p. 127.
24. Ibid.
25. Ibid.
26. Ibid.
27. Ibid., p. 133.

31

Renunciation and Gender Issues in the Śrī Vaiṣṇava Community

Vasudha Narayanan

While the fertility of a woman is usually celebrated by the Hindu tradition (as is suggested by the title of Bumiller's book *May You be the Mother of a Hundred Sons*),[1] her ascetic practices and piety have largely been ignored by many normative Sanskrit codes of law *(dharma śāstra)* as well as by two centuries of Western scholarship that has relied on these texts for information on Hindu culture. South Indian women poets like Āṇṭāḷ (Goda), Kāraikkāl Ammaiyār, and Akka Mahādevi did not lead the ideal married life prescribed by the codes of law. Āṇṭāḷ did not want to get married and consider her husband as God; she wanted God as her husband. Through her words and actions, Āṇṭāḷ presents an alternative lifestyle to what Manu, the first-century law giver, perceived to be the role of women; she showed contempt at the idea of marrying a human being and instead, gathered her friends and observed rites to obtain the lord.

My study will focus on the complex politics of gender, marriage, and renunciation in the Śrī Vaiṣṇava tradition of Hinduism. I focus on one community in Hinduism, because (1) no one is a generic Hindu: almost all Hindus identify themselves as a member of a particular sectarian community or social caste; and (2) the history of the Hindu tradition(s) spans about three millennia and the literature is vast. By focusing on one community, which includes members of all castes, and by drawing upon its literature and practices, it is possible to have a deeper understanding of the religious roles of women than by scanning materials from hundreds of communities written over several centuries. Specifically, I will examine two different events which the Śrī Vaiṣṇava community holds as paradigmatic and see how these are worked out in the salvific process of a human being. These two paradigmatic events are (1) Āṇṭāḷ's marriage with Viṣṇu, whom she perceives as the supreme lord and (2) the rejection of a householder's life by Rāmānuja, the most important Śrī Vaiṣṇava teacher. Rāmānuja rejects married life so that he may become a renunciant or *(sannyāsi)*. In departing from the perceived norm of Hindu tradition in some critical ways, these paradigmatic events map an alternative political and religious construction of gender and social caste in asceticism.

The Śrī Vaiṣṇava tradition of South India became organized around the time of its fifth, and most important teacher, Rāmānuja (c.1017–1137 CE). The Śrī Vaiṣṇava community emphasizes exclusive devotion to the lord Viṣṇu and the

Goddess Śrī (Lakṣmī) and believes that it is their grace that leads a human being to salvation. Like many of the other Hindu traditions, it accepts the authority of the Sanskrit Vedas, the epics, the Purāṇas, and—what is relevant to us today—the codes of law known as the *dharma śāstras*. These *dharma śāstra* texts were compiled between 200 BCE and about 300 CE. In addition to these, the Śrī Vaiṣṇava community also claims that the poems of twelve Tamil poet-saints known as the Āḻvārs are revealed and equivalent to the Vedas. The Āḻvārs lived between the seventh and ninth centuries CE. The word *āḻvār* is traditionally derived from the Tamil root *āḻ* (deep), and the title was given to eleven men and one woman who are said to have been immersed deep in the love of Viṣṇu. The acceptance of the Āḻvārs as paradigmatic devotees is a significant stance taken by the community in the tenth and eleventh centuries CE, because they came from all castes and one of them was a woman. The only woman Āḻvār, Āṇṭāḷ, insisted that her bridegroom was the lord himself and composed two poems expressing her passion for the lord. The Śrī Vaiṣṇava community has thus had a heritage of being liberal in the eleventh century CE; a community that venerated a woman who refused to get married, and in a sense, defied social norms.

In this paper, I make a distinction between the words "ascetic" and "renunciant." The word "renunciant" will be used for the Sanskrit word *sannyāsi* (female: *sannyāsini*): to refer to those people who have renounced the world formally, and who have performed their own funeral rites to mark the social and legal death of their earlier identities. The Sanskrit word *sannyāsa* literally means "putting or throwing down, laying aside, resignation, abandonment, renunciation of the world, profession of asceticism, abstinence from food."[2] This ceremony releases them from the commitments and obligations of their earlier personalities and they enter a new (and final) stage of life described in the Hindu texts of law. The word "ascetic" will be used in a more general fashion, to include but not be limited to renunciants. Many women, especially widows or abandoned wives, and occasionally even married women, accept ascetic practices, and in form and content (celibacy, fasting, etc.) their lifestyle may be similar to that of the renunciant. Thus married women may adopt ascetic practices for certain weeks or months to increase domestic happiness. However, they are not initiated into a separate stage of life, that of a *sannyāsi*-renunciant who has rejected the *dharma* (duties) incumbent on a person in worldly life; rather the ascetic wife or widow may simply be fulfilling the duties imposed on her by society. The renunciant's style of life that a widow adopts is still in conformity with the duty of a woman; formal renunciation denotes a rejection of such *dharma*. This is because most of the codes of law explicitly say that women (and *śūdras*, the lowest class of society) may not become renunciants and enter the last stage of life. While the practices of the widow and the female ascetic may be similar, the intent behind them puts them in very different categories in the Hindu tradition; the ascetic life of a widow indicates that she is accepting the role of a woman/wife in compliance with the *dharma śāstra;* but becoming a renunciant shows her rejection of that role and all that is associated with this life.

From this discussion it is clear that not all ascetics are renunciants. But it is worth emphasizing that not all renunciants lead ascetic-style lives. There are certain abbots of monasteries who are renunciants (*sannyāsi*s) but whose position makes them privy to honors that befit royalty. So, while the abbot who is a renunciant may be celibate and perhaps even wear ochre clothes like other *sannyāsi*s, his robes may be of the finest silk and on ceremonial occasions he may in full regalia, don a gold crown, jewels, or ornaments that have been endowed to the monastery by pious followers.[3]

Renunciation in the *Dharma Śāstra*s

The classical Hindu tradition (which begins around the second century BCE) based on texts of religious law identifies four stages of life (student, householder, forest dweller, renunciant) that male members of the upper three classes of society can go through. A renunciant formally abandoned society and performed funeral rites for himself; with the performance of these rites he made a clean cut with his earlier personality. When he entered the fourth stage, he was socially dead.[4] After this, in his new role as a renunciant *(sannyāsi),* he was to be all alone; he went to a village only to get food. He owned nothing but a begging bowl and old clothing; but he was marked by tranquility and equanimity (*Manu Smṛiti* 6.42–44). Women did not generally go through these stages of life: it has been observed that in the Hindu tradition, "a woman's religion *is* her family life."[5] Becoming a renunciant meant that the woman had a certain amount of independence and this was explicitly denied to her by many texts of the *dharma śāstra.* Manu, the (legendary) author of the first century law book that bears his name, expressed some negative views on the status of women and denied them any form of independence. He said: "By a girl, by a young woman or even by an aged one, nothing must be done independently, even in her own house. In childhood a female must be subject to her father, in youth to her husband, when her lord is dead, to her sons; a woman must never be independent" (*Manu Smṛiti* 5.147–148). He also stated that "Though destitute of virtue, or seeking pleasure elsewhere, or devoid of good qualities, a husband must be constantly worshipped as a god by a faithful wife" (*Manu Smṛiti* 5.154). While later (male) commentators on Hindu law quote Manu approvingly and a study of these works has informed many western notions of Hindu women, Manu was not necessarily considered to be prescriptive in all sectors of society. There is evidence of women poet/saints and women renunciants who do not seem to comply with the rules of Hindu *dharma* or duty. Rather than get married they spent their lives ın search of the path to salvation. Even Manu refers to female renunciants in passing, but the commentators who cannot even tolerate the idea of women becoming renunciants are quick to point out that he probably referred to Buddhist or Jain nuns. Some commentators attribute a passage to Baudhāyana, a writer of *dharma śāstra,* in which he states that some orthodox (Hindu) women were allowed to become renunciants. Significantly enough, that passage is not found in many texts.[6]

We know that in the larger Hindu tradition, that women have, and still do, become renunciants, even though the classical texts have only allowed this stage for regenerate or twice-born men. This meant men from the so-called higher classes, the priests, the warriors and the producers/merchants. Women and *śūdras* (servants) have been left out of this grouping but as the British discovered over many years, while Hindu tradition has used hyperbole in declaring the religious-legal texts to be an exposition of the Vedas, it did not mean that they actually followed all the rules. There is a sense of dissonance between scripture and practice in some areas of dharma and the role of women and *śūdras* falls in this category. Although there were probably only small numbers of women renunciants they have been mentioned in texts and scripture.[7] It is my suspicion that many of these references have been excised over the centuries.

Female (and *śūdra*) renunciants became more common in some monastic movements after the sixteenth century when Madhusūdana Sarasvati, a theologian and social reformer, opened up the orders. Some women renunciants in Benares even today undergo the *ātma śraddhā* rites (death of the self). Celibate women lead organizations like the Siddha Yoga movement; however, significantly enough, in many of these orders, the leader is called "Mā" or "Māta" (mother). One such example is the "Mother Guru" discussed by Charles White.[8] On the other hand, male renunciants who head orders of *sannyāsis* are not called "Father"; they are known by other titles like *jagad guru* (teacher of the world.)

Most of the women renunciants today are seen in northern India; very few come from the south of India. The many sociocultural reasons for this remain outside the scope of this discussion, but it is possible that harsher attitudes toward widows in some communities and in some parts of India lead them initially to adopt the lifestyle of an ascetic, and later on, as a full-fledged renunciant.

We shall now turn our attention to the Śrī Vaiṣṇava community of South India and consider their struggle with the notion of renunciation and asceticism. To some measure, this struggle came because their loyalty to the *dharma śāstra* on the one hand, and to the devotional poems of the Āḻvārs, on the other. The struggle with this the notion of *sannyāsa* is also seen because salvation is seen as a gift of grace from Viṣṇu, and not attained by any human effort. Eventually, total surrender to the lord is seen as crucial to avail oneself of this salvific grace. We shall initially consider the case of Āṇṭāḷ, who lived around the eighth century CE. She does not struggle with theological issues; her poems are full of pain and passion. It is only about two centuries after her lifetime that the Śrī Vaiṣṇava community crystallizes and members of this tradition look to her life as paradigmatic.

The First Paradigm: Āṇṭāḷ's Asceticism and Passion

While the books on *dharma* enjoin every girl to get married and venerate her husband, the biography of Āṇṭāḷ, who lived in the eighth century, presents a different scenario. She refuses to get married to a human being and longs for union with the lord. Āṇṭāḷ is the only woman poet-saint venerated by the Śrī Vaiṣṇava community. She is considered to be the foster daughter of another Āḻvār, Periyāḻvār or Viṣṇu Citta. In her two poems, the "Tiruppāvai" and the "Nācciyār Tirumoḻi," she expresses her passionate desire to marry Viṣṇu, whom she perceives in one of his incarnate forms, as Krishna, Rāma, or as the resident deity in the temple. In the "Tiruppāvai," she imagines herself as a young *gopī* (cowherd girl) in the village where Krishna grew up. She wakes up her friends very early in the morning in the month of Mārgaḻi (about Dec. 15–Jan. 13), and they all go to wake up Krishna and give him their petition: their longing to be with him and to serve him for all time. Āṇṭāḷ asks her friends to come with her to bathe; the Tamil word *nirātal* (bathing) was frequently used to indicate a sexual union in Tamil literature. Since Viṣṇu is compared to a lotus pond frequently, her intentions would be clear to those who recite the poem, and if they were not, the commentators articulate this concept quite well. In these poems she also states that she is following some practices of self-denial and discipline:

O you people of this world,
listen to what we do for our vow
We sing, praising the feet
of the supreme one who is in yogic slumber
on the great ocean of milk.
We do not eat the clear butter,
we do not drink milk.
We bathe early in the morning,
No liner for our eyes,
no flowers in our hair.
We abstain from what is not right,
we avoid idle talk. . . . *"Tiruppāvai" 2*[9]

Āṇṭāḷ states that she is not adorning herself as a young girl normally does; she does not use makeup for her eyes or wear flowers on her hair. She observes dietary restrictions, abstaining from the luxuries of eating, like the clear butter used to enhance the flavor of food, milk, etc. She has a purifying bath before the sun rises and spends her time singing the praise of the lord. She elaborates further in another poem:

As part of my vow
I eat just once a day.
I neglect my body,
it is not adorned.
My hair is tangled in knots
My lips are cracked. . . . *"Nācciyār Tirumoḻi" 1.8*[10]

This verse is from her second poem the "Nācciyār Tirumoḻi" ("The Sacred Words of the Lady"). Here, Āṇṭāḷ talks of her pallor and wasted body; she is love sick and wants to unite with the lord. She will not marry a human being, she says; she would rather kill herself:

Like the sacred offerings
that are meant to be offered

to the sky-gods
by those skilled in the Vedas
but instead become defiled
when it is eaten by a fox
that strays from the forests
into the sacrificial ground
my soft breasts dedicated to the lord
will be violated even if there is talk
that they are to be offered to human beings.
O god of love, just watch,
I shall die. *"Nācciyār Tirumoḻi" 1.5*

Later in the poem, she dreams that Viṣṇu came to her and marries her; she recounts the rituals of a wedding in eleven verses to her friend. In one of these verses she says:

Drums beat happy sounds,
conches blew.
Under a canopy
strung with pearls,
My love, Madhusudha (Viṣnu)
lord with all good qualities
came and clasped
the palm of my hand.
I saw this in my dream,
my friend. *"Nācciyār Tirumoḻi" 6.6*

The bridegroom clasping the hand of the bride was (and is) an integral feature of a Hindu wedding. Notice that the imagery has turned from one of abstention, deprivation and restraint to a joyful one of fulfilment. Āṇṭāḷ describes in considerable detail the entire wedding—rituals that are considered to be the most auspicious among human sacraments. These verses are still recited in Śrī Vaiṣṇava weddings. In other verses in "Nācciyār Tirumoḻi," she talks of her intense love, sends messengers to communicate her love to the lord and is desolate being separated from Viṣṇu. In the last set of verses, however, there is some peace. The verses are in the form of questions and answers, and to her query "Have you seen Krishna?" she gets the answer, "We have seen him here in Brindāvan."

[Krishna] is a prankster
who knows no dharma.
He whose eyebrows arch
like the bow Saranga
in his hand
handsome one
without equal
have you seen him?

He whose form is dark
whose face glows bright
like the sun that fans
on the peaks
    of the rising hills
    We have seen him
here, in Vrindavanam. *"Nāccıyār Tirumoḻı"* 14.6

Thus we get an indication that she has seen him and has attained him.

Interestingly enough, in all her biographies, the self-denial and ascetic rites that Āṇṭāḷ says she practices are ignored and the bridal elements are emphasized. The most important biography, *The Splendor of Sucession of Teachers,* was written in the thirteenth century, and Āṇṭāḷ the bride emerges from this book. *The Splendor* portrays Āṇṭāḷ as passionately in love with Viṣṇu. Her father, Periyāḻvār, does not know what to do until Viṣṇu appears in his dream and commands him to bring his daughter to the temple in the town of Srirangam. In the dream, Viṣṇu tells Āṇṭāḷ's father that he will clasp her hands and marry her there. The lord at Srirangam then sends his servants to fetch Āṇṭāḷ with all honors. Āṇṭāḷ is dressed in bridal finery and taken in a gem-studded palanquin to Srirangam; *The Splendor* says:

> The lady made garlands for the lord (ı.e., Āntāl) was wearing her . . . silk sari, flower garland and a mark made of musk on her forehead. With her large eyes which seemed to reach her ears, slim liana-like waist, full breasts, with her bracelets jingling, walkıng gracefully like a swan, ın a manner that all could see, she went in front of the Handsome Brıdegroom [the name of Vısnu at Srirangam]. She went in, saw him till her eyes were satisfied, and as ıf she were to press his feet, she climbed on the serpent bed [on whıch the Lord reclines], joined with the Lord of Ranga . . . and disappeared while [ıt seemed to others] as if she was massagıng him. All those who beheld this, including the Āḻvār's discıple, King Vallabha deva, were astonished. . . .[11]

Notice how the biography emphasizes the beauty of Āṇṭāḷ's body; every part is described in sensual and loving terms. It also makes it clear that she united with the lord, with her full physical body; and this is quite startling. The Upaniṣads and most texts in the Hindu canon speak of the physical body as contaminating and as a hindrance to liberation, but the Śrī Vaiṣṇava tradition portrays the body as quite acceptable, indeed enjoyable, to the lord. The notion of a saint physically uniting with the lord in a temple may well be a sentiment found in Tamil region, and not quite unique to the Śrī Vaiṣṇava community. In Śaiva hagiography, the saint Māṇikka vācakar is absorbed into the icon at Chidambaram. In fact, in South Indian versions of the story of the North Indian woman saint Mira (fifteenth century?), she merges into the image of the lord; she does not suffer widowhood or old age.

What kind of role model does Āṇṭāḷ provide for the women and for the Śrī Vaiṣṇava community? In Śrī Vaiṣṇava theology, Āṇṭāḷ is clearly a paradigmatic devotee and by identifying with or imitating her love, it may be possible to reach the lord. Her poems are recited by the community every morning; if the entire "Tiruppāvai" cannot be recited, at least the penultimate verse ought to be. Bhaṭṭar, a twelfth-century theologian is quoted as advising his disciple that he ought to recite the entire "Tiruppāvai" every morning and experience its emotions. If it is not possible to do that, he should then recite at least the penultimate verse, if that was not possible, he is advised to just think of the way they experienced the joy of the verses. Commentarial literature says that by the practice of some rituals, the cowherd girls got Krishna; by imitation of those ascetic practices (which constituted their *vratās,* or rites), Āṇṭāḷ reached Krishna. By making the words of Āntāḷ our words, we are extolled to be like Āṇṭāḷ, imitating her passion, emulating and appropriating her devotion.[12] In other words, we seek union with the lord through the words of Āṇṭāḷ. In a sense, all human beings become the companions of Āṇṭāḷ and share in her passion and her power.

In the later Śrī Vaiṣṇava tradition, Āṇṭāḷ invites selective emulation; human beings can identify with her and hope to achieve, however distant it may be, some of the passion she felt for the lord. Every Śrī Vaiṣṇava bride is dressed like Āṇṭāḷ and during wedding rituals, the songs of Āṇṭāḷ's wedding dream are recited. In one sense, the bride is likened to Āṇṭāḷ; but the explanation that comes through the theological texts is that all human beings ought to be like Āṇṭāḷ. While this theme of Āṇṭāḷ as a paradigmatic devotee is unquestioned, it seems to me that the Śrī Vaiṣṇava community subscribes only to selective imitation of certain features of her life. For instance, in the Śrī Vaiṣṇava community girls are not encouraged to be unmarried and dedicate their lives to the lord like Āṇṭāḷ. Her rejection of marriage and her ascetic practices are seen as suitable only for her and not to be used as a dharmic model for women.

The Second Paradigm: Rāmānuja's Renunciation of the World

The Śrī Vaiṣṇava community became organized about two centuries after the time of Āṇṭāḷ. Rāmānuja, the eleventh-century teacher venerated by the Śrī Vaiṣṇava tradition of South India, had a wife who according to all biographical accounts, was somewhat conservative and quarrelsome. When her husband invited his teacher's family home for dinner, she fed them, but proceeded to cleanse and ritually purify the house after they left, because they were of a lower caste. On another occasion, she refused to give food to hungry devotees, by lying that there was no food in the house. Later, she picked a quarrel with another teacher's wife. Annoyed, and not believing in any half-measures, Rāmānuja cried: "You have made explicit the statement that women are the abode of all sins; you are guilty of offending the devotees of the lord." He packed her off to her paternal home, and then renounced his life as a householder:

> He thought: "I shall, as the scriptures say, adopt either a mendicant or the lord as my preceptor and enter the next stage of life; I shall become a *sannyāsin* (renun-

> ciant)."... . Considering the lord to be his preceptor, he begged, "give me the *tridaṇḍā* (three staffs that are tied together), saffron robes, etc. [emblems of a renunicant/monk]." The lord gave Rāmānuja all that he requested through a priest, and asked Tirukacchi Nampi (a devotee) to escort Rāmānuja to the monastery.[13]

Rāmānuja's renunciation of the world was extremely significant to his followers; over and over again, they call him as the "king or emperor of ascetics/renouncers" (*yatirājā, yatīndra, yatisārvabhauma, yati bhūpati, yatic cakravarti,* etc.)[14] Despite the importance given to Rāmānuja's renunciation, the Śrī Vaiṣṇava tradition does not believe that becoming a *sannyasi* is important or even necessary to gain liberation. According to their theology, they are saved because of their spiritual connection with their teachers and not because of their own efforts. Many of the prominent teachers, like Vedānta Deśika in the fourteenth century, were householders; others, like Maṉavāḷa Māmuṉi in the fifteenth century, became a renunciant very late in life after being married for several years. There is also no practice of jumping stages and going directly from the stage of a celibate student to a celibate *sannyāsi,* as is seen in the case of other traditions. Rāmānuja and his cousin, Govinda Perumāḷ, were both married, but, renouncing their wives, they entered the fourth stage. Similarly, the pontiffs of the various *mathas* (monasteries) are *sannyāsi*s today, but only after having been householders for many years. The Śrī Vaisṇava tradition is strict about the rule that one should not become a renunciant unless he has already undergone the first three stages of life. They quote the *Laws of Manu* to prove their point:

> But if a twice-born man seeks Freedom when he has not studied the Vedas, and has not begotten progeny, and has not sacrificed with sacrifices, he sinks down.[15]

The third stage of life (forest dweller) was never considered important; in initation rituals today, sometimes, the person spends one night in the third stage before he is initiated as a *sannyāsi.* When a man did become initiated as a *sannyāsi,* he conducted his funeral rituals; this becomes the point when he lost his former identity and connection with the world of *dharma.* Even today, the performance of these funeral rituals is essential under the Indian law if a man is to be recognized as a renunciant. In all these rituals there is a constant emphasis on contempt for the physical body. This despising of the human body is seen in Manu's description of a *sannyāsi*'s last moments:

> He [i.e., the *sannyāsi*] should abandon this foul-smelling, tormented impermanent dwelling-place of living beings, filled with urine and excrement, pervaded by old age and sorrow, infested by illness, and polluted by passion, with bones for beams, sinews for cords, flesh and blood for plaster, and skin for the roof. When he abandons this body, as a tree abandons the bank of a river or a bird abandons a tree, he is freed from a painful shark.[16]

The tenor of this passage (which repeats the sentiments in some of the Upaniṣads) contrasts starkly with the joyous sensuality of the description of Āṇṭāḷ's physical beauty in the biographies. The monastic tradition and the philosophy of the renunciant in the Hindu tradition is based on contempt for, or at best, toleration of, the human body. This body is seen as loathsome and as an impediment to liberation from the cycle of life and death. However, even though Rāmānuja became a renunciant and even ordained many others, over the centuries renunciation became less and less popular. This decrease in popularity seems to have been gradual, but after the fourteenth century when the concept of renunciation went through a reinterpretation in one branch of Śrī Vaiṣṇavism, there has hardly been any impetus to become a formal *sannyāsi* and only a handful of religious leaders enter the fourth stage of life. In recent years this trend has continued and there seems to be no great urge to become a *sannyāsi,* even among the very learned people. In one of the subsects of Śrī Vaiṣṇavism, (the *muṉitraya vaṭakalai* sect,) a pontiff who passed away in 1989 apparently nominated six different people to succeed him. All of them were married and had families; and all of them respectfully declined the honor. Generally, in these cases, if a man is willing to become the next leader of the community, he will be initiated as a *sannyāsi* either just before or soon after the former pontiff dies.

In passing we may note that the status of a woman whose husband has become a renunciant is ambiguous at best. On the one hand, she is still socially considered to be a *sumañgali* (auspicious woman) whose husband is alive. She still continues to dress as a *sumañgali;* those of us familiar with Indian society know that in many conservative homes, the dress code of a woman may change somewhat dramatically after her husband's death. Although the wife, or ex-wife of a man who has become a sannyasi is still considered to be a *sumañgali,* because of his civil death, and because the man has performed his own funeral rites she inherits his property like a widow. Legally, because of his nonperformance of conjugal duties, she has the right to sue for divorce.

Women renunciants in the Śrī Vaiṣṇava community

Rāmānuja and some of his companions were renunciants; according to some biographical accounts, he is said to have had women renunciants as his disciples. This information is not confirmed, but does not seem unusual because there were also *śūdra* renunciants in his tradition. Since women and *śūdras* had the same rights (or lack of rights) in the *dharma śāstra*s, it seems logical that if there were *śūdra* renunciants, there were also women renunciants. Some sources say that there were about three hundred women renunciants among the immediate followers of Rāmānuja. None of them are mentioned in the more popular biographies and we know almost nothing about their lives or how they were ordained. However, we do know definitely that there were Śrī Vaiṣṇava women renunciants in Kānchipuram around thirteenth century. An inscription in the Varadaraja Perumāḷ temple in Kānchipuram states that a woman renunciant called Pēraruḷāḷaṉ koṟṟi ordered that her jewels be sold after her death and the monies were to be used for buying land for the temple.[17] Another renunciant called Tiruvattiyūr-koṟṟi donated cattle so that a lamp could be lit in the temple.[18] The Tamil word *koṟṟi* (victorious one) added to their names identifies them as a Vaiṣṇava renunciant. Apparently, these women renunciants were attached to the temple, like Rāmānuja himself had been for several years of his life. There is also an implication that they had a certain amount of financial independence and control over funds. The fact that women in the medieval ages made so many donations in their own names is itself striking; still more striking is that some of these women had renounced life and made their new names last for centuries by inscribing them on stone. Unfortunately, the tradition of female renunciation, like their names has become, literally, petrified over the centuries.

Evidently this institution of women renunciants died out—we are not sure when and in what circumstances this happened. There is no doubt about the pressures the Śrī Vaiṣṇava community and its leaders would have been under to discourage women from becoming *sannyāsinis*. The liberal reforms that Rāmānuja could pull off with his leadership and charisma may have floundered after his time. Orthoprax sections of the *smārtha* brahman community, which had great admiration of Manu and which did not tolerate reform concerning lower caste people or women, would have disapproved of women and *śūdra* renunciants. This alone may not have ended the institution of women renunciants. In the fourteenth century Moslem invasions, especially by Malik Kafur, involved the ransacking of temples. The temple at Kānchipuram, and the large Viṣṇu temple at Srirangam, which was the nerve center of the Śrī Vaiṣṇava community, were captured and rituals were disrupted. The Srirangam temple was abandoned for almost sixty years and was in a dilapidated state until the restoration efforts of the new Hindu Vijayanagar empire. It is probable that many traditions, including that of the performance of the Āḻvārs' songs, were forgotten at this time. It was obviously not the safest of times for independent women renunciants living alone; and quite possibly after the restoration of the temples the institution of female renunciation was not revived. It is against this background that we have to understand the decline of institutionalized renunciation for both men and women. The understanding of the human being's role in the salvific drama was reinterpreted with the highlighting of some images from the past and the downplaying of others. The funeral-death rites associated with world renunciation became less important and the wedding imagery was highlighted by the teachers of the fourteenth century. Rāmānuja had himself appointed several married men as his successors. These families had grown in power and they were involved in the process of redefining *sannyāsa*.

Vedānta Deśika (1268–1368), one of the prominent theologians of this time, was a married man. He quotes a verse (17.75) from a text called *Lakṣmī Tantra,*[19] according to which the words *sannyāsa, nyāsa* (to abandon, to relinquish, to place or put down, entrust, commit), *prappati* (to drop down, to surrender), *śaraṇāgati* (going for refuge), and *tyāga* (abandonment; renunciation) are all considered to be synonyms. *Prapatti* or *śaraṇāgati* is surrender to god, seeking him and his consort, the goddess Lakṣmī, as one's refuge. The words *sannyāsa* and *nyāsa* in this connection mean not only "to relinquish," and "renunciation," but also "to commit oneself," in this case, to Viṣṇu and Śrī. The lord's grace saves the human being and one only needs to surrender oneself to him. Men and women of all castes could and, according to the tradition, should surrender themselves to Viṣṇu in order to be saved; this became one of the distinctive characterestics of the Śrī Vaiṣṇava community. What this meant in theological terms was that even women and *śūdra*s were given access to salvific rituals. This becomes a unique interpretation of asceticism and renunciation; the connection between domesticity and detachment becomes an important characterestic of the Śrī Vaiṣṇava community. Max Weber made a distinction between world-rejecting asceticism and innerworldly asceticism to describe, on the one hand, the flight of the monk from the world, and on the other, the plight of a person who stayed involved in this world and yet was detached from it. Śrī Vaiṣṇava literature has a similar distinction and the new interpretation of *sannyāsa* is like Weber's innerworldly asceticism. Thus, a person may be married, but if he or she has undergone the ritual of self-surrender (*prapatti* or *sannyāsa*) he or she is known as a renunciant. The point is that a person may be involved in worldly life, but if the action is colored with the right intent and suitable detachment (reminding us of famous dictum of the Puritans, quoted by Max Weber, asking men to "soberly produce children"), the person is to be deemed a *sannyāsi* or renunciant even though he or she has not adopted the fourth stage of life. This fusion of detachment and domesticity and the laicization of the *sannyāsa* ideal downplays the importance or necessity of abandoning the world and renouncing one's family. This somewhat innovative reinterpretation of the scripture makes both males and females *sannyāsı* (renunciants) even in their married lives.

Vedānta Deśika wrote several poems and texts on the concept of *nyāsa* (renunciation). In his opening lines of "Nyāsa Daśakam" ("Ten Verses on Renunciation/Surrender"), Deśika says:

> I do not belong to myself; the burden of protecting myself is no longer mine. I shall not enjoy the consequences that may result from my actions. They belong to lord Nārāyana. Saying thus, one should entrust oneself to the lord.[20]

What Deśika says here is that he is renouncing his sense of "I"-hood and his sense that he belongs to himself. He also says that he is abandoning any effort or action to get salvation; the burden of giving salvation now belongs to the lord. He further abandons any claim to the good merit *(puṇya karma)* that is the result of this act of renunciation. This sense of renunciation, for Deśika, is seen in the word *namo* (the root of the Hindu greeting *namaste*). He interprets the word *namo* as meaning "not mine" *(na ma)*. Reflection on its meaning, he says, will remind us that we do not exist for ourselves but for the lord.[21]

Having delineated this laicized meaning of *sannyāsa,* Deśika also revives and highlights the bridal imagery that was prominent in Āṇṭāḷ's poems. In a poem called "Śaraṇāgati Dīpika" ("The Lamp of Surrender") he likens a human being to a bride, the lord to a bridegroom, and the teacher who initiates one to the Śrī Vaiṣṇava community as the father who gives away his daughter in marriage. It is important to recognize that the *śaraṇāgati* or surrender that Deśika talks about is the concept that he equated with *sannyāsa* in many texts.

> Like a father, the best of teachers give away their children (the human souls) as brides to you who are their husband. You rejoice and accept them as your brides. To enjoy the bliss [of married life] the brides serve other devotees; this is like their "thread of aupsiciousness" which is symbol of their wedded state.[22]

The thread of auspiciousness is a necklace worn by a married woman to show that she is married; this is the Hindu equivalent of the wedding ring. In this verse, Deśika says that service to other devotees is like this symbol of marriage; it marks the one who is the bride of the lord. Deśika has universalized Āṇṭāḷ's experience and wedding to all human beings, and this spiritual wedding is to be the ultimate goal for everyone. While one may consider it to be the means to salvation, it is better seen as a marker of salvation. What is important to note here is that the community has avoided the issue of making Āṇtāḷ a social or *dharmic* role model, and has instead opted to make her a theological model or a model for all people who seek liberation; she then becomes a model not just for women, but for all human beings. Āṇṭāḷ's rejection of earthly marriage and her subsequent union with the lord is seen as an unique event and as suitable only for her; on the other hand, all human beings should marry the lord as she did, but with the guidance of a spiritual teacher.

How, then, does the Śrī Vaiṣṇava community understand renunciation? Initially, at the time of Rāmānuja, there is a formal recognition of *sannyāsa* as the fourth stage of life that men of the upper three classes of society may adopt. There is also evidence that contrary to *dharma śāstra* prescriptions, both (female and male) *śūdra*s and women (of all other classes) became *sannyāsi*s and *sannyāsini*s respectively in this tradition. However, by the fourteenth century the community adds extra dimensions to the word and laicizes the ideal. Thus, theoretically, it does not become necessary for any woman, or man, to conduct their own funeral rites and become renunciants in order to get liberation. Rather, the word *sannyāsa* is equated with *śaraṇāgati*, which means "surrender to the lord," and this is described in terms of a wedding ritual. Thus the bridal imagery is highlighted in the Śrī Vaiṣṇava tradition's understanding of renunciation, and not the imagery of death and funerals. This new interpretation coincides with Moslem occupation of the temples in South India. Thus political and ritual upheaval, along with a new politically correct interpretation of *sannyāsa* within the community, leads to a decline of renunciation in general, and a total abandonment of the institution of female renunciation. Male renunciation is still held necessary if one is chosen to be the head of one of the smaller communities; but married *ācāryas* are also recognized. Although the numbers of male renunciants is small, the institution still exists; the first thing to go during a crisis was female renunciation.

The bridal imagery suggested by Āṇṭāḷ is highlighted by the community in the fourteenth century, but the tradition seems cautious of ascetic practices for women and is certainly wary of the social role model Āṇṭāḷ may provide. In the redefinition of *sannyāsa* and the highlighting of Āṇṭāḷ's life, there is selective emulation of her devotion; the specific ascetic rituals she practiced and her rejection of her social *dharma* are not followed. Her wedding with the lord is generalized as root metaphor for the whole community but she is not seen as a social or *dharmic* role model for young girls.

Finally, what is almost palpable is the new understanding of the body as beautiful and as something the lord desires. The biographical tradition of the Tamil poets emphasizes the physical nature of union with the lord and this is certainly starkly in contrast with the repugnance shown to the human body in some[23] famous Sanskrit works like the *Laws of Manu.* The notion of the "body beautiful" is retained in the wedding symbolism. By laicizing the *sannyāsa* ideal and by speaking of the body as one which the lord enjoys, the Śrī Vaiṣṇava tradition has transformed traditional Sanskrit interpretation of renunciation. In this process, it universalizes (and domesticates) the Tamil model of Āṇṭāḷ as the bride of Viṣṇu.

NOTES

1. Elisabeth Bumiller, *May You be the Mother of a Hundred Sons* (New York: Random House, 1990).
2. Meanings taken from Monier-Williams, *A Sanskrit-English Dictionary* (Oxford, Clarendon Press, 1974).
3. The glitz that accompanies the "coronation" of such an abbot has been described by Glenn Yocum in "The Coronation of a Guru: Charisma, Politics and Philosophy in Contemporary India," in *A Sacred Thread: Modern Transmission of Hindu Traditions in India and Abroad,* ed. Raymond Williams (Chambersburg: Anima Press, 1992), pp. 68–91.
4. Louis Dumont, "World Renunciation in Indian Religions," *Contributions to India Sociology* 4 (1960):33–62. See especially p. 44.
5. Julia Leslie, "Essence and Existence: Women and Religion in Ancient Indian Texts," in *Women's Religious Experience,* ed. Pat Holden (Totowa: Barnes & Noble, 1983), pp. 89–112.
6. *Manu Smṛiti* 8.363 and the notes for 363 by G. Bühler. G. Bühler, trans., *The Laws of Manu* (Delhi: Motilal Banarsidass, 1964).
7. For a summary of these references, see Catherine Ojha, "Female Asceticism: Its Tradition and Present Condition," *Man in India* 61 (1981):254–285.
8. Charles White, "Mother Guru: Jñānānanda of Madras, India," *Unspoken Worlds: Women's Religious Lives in Non-Western Cultures,* eds. Nancy A. Falk and Rita M. Gross (San Francisco: Harper & Row, 1980), pp. 22–37.
9. Āṇṭāl, "Tiruppāvai," in P. B. Aṇnangarācāriyar, *Nālāyira tivviyap pirapantam* (Kanci: V. N. Tevanātan, 1971).
10. Āṇṭāḷ, "Nācciyār Tirumoḻi," in P. B. A̱ṇṇangarācāriyar, *Nālāyira tivviyap pirapantam* (Kanci: V. N. Tevanātan, 1971).
11. Pin̲paḻakiya Perumāl Jīyar, *Ārāyirappati Guruparamparāprabhāvam, (The Splendor of the Succession of Teachers),* ed. S. Krishnasvami Ayyankar (Tirucci: Puttur Agraharam, 1975), p. 50. This is a thirteenth-century text.
12. P. B. Aṇṇangarācāriyar, ed., *Tiruppāvai, Mūvāyirappaṭi vyāk-yānam Kūtiyatu* (Kanci: P. B. Aṇṇangarācāriyar Publications, 1970).
13. *The Splendor,* pp. 173–174.
14. On the details and occurrences of these titles, see my paper "Renunciation in Saffron and White Robes," in *Monastic Life in the Christian and Hindu Traditions,* eds. Austin B. Creel and Vasudha Narayanan (Lewiston: Edwin Mellen Press, 1990), pp. 161–190.
15. *Manu Smṛiti 6.37.* Wendy Doniger and Brian Smith, *The Laws of Manu* (Penguin, 1991).
16. Doniger and Smith. op. cit., pp. 76–78.
17. 431 of 1919, quoted by K. V. Raman in *Sri Varadarajaswami Temple—Kanci: A Study of its History, Art and Architecture* (New Delhi: Abhinav Publications, 1975), p. 135.
18. 388 of 1919; quoted by K. V. Raman, op. cit.

19. Vedānta Deśika, "Rahasya Traya Sara," chapter 11 in Vedānta Deśika, *Srimad Rahasya Traya Sāram,* ed. Śrī Rāmātēcikacāriyar, 2 vols. (Kumbakonam: Oppilliyappan Sanniti, 1961).
20. Vedānta Deśika, "Nyasa Dasakam," in *Stotramāla,* ed. Śrī Rāmātēcikacāriyar, 2 vols. (Kumbakonam: Oppilliyappan Sanniti, 1970).
21. Deśika's commentary on Yāmuna's "Stotra Ratna," in *Catuḥślokibhāṣyam, Stotraratnabhāṣyam, Gadyatrayabhāsyanca,* vol. 21 (Madras: Śrī Vedānta Deśika Seventh Centenary Trust, n.d.).
22. "Śaranāgati Dīpika," in *Stotramāla,* ed. Śrī Rāmātēcikacāriyar, 2 vols. (Kumbakonam: Oppilliyappan Sanniti, 1970).
23. The earliest Sanskrit compositions, the hymns of the Vedas, depict an acceptance of the body and the prayers are for happiness in this life. It is only from the last sections of the Vedas, the Upaniṣads, that the negative images of the body begin to appear.

BIBLIOGRAPHY

Aṇṇangarācāriyar, P. B. 1971. *Nālāyira tivviyap pirapantam.* Kanci: V. N. Tevanātan.

Aṇṇangarācāriyar, P. B., ed. 1970. *Tiruppāvai, Mūvāyirappaṭi vyākyānam Kūtiyatu.* Kanci: Śrī P. B. Annangarācāriyar Publications.

Aṇṇangarācāriyar, P. B., ed. 1974. *Rāmānujagranthamāla.* Kanci: Sri P. B. Aṇṇangarācāriyar Publications.

Ayyangar, M. R. Rajagopala, trans. 1956. *Śrīmad Rahasyatrayasāra of Śrī Vedāntadeśika.* Kumbakonam: Agnihothram Ramanuja Thathachariar Publication.

Bühler, G. trans. 1964. *The Laws of Manu.* Motilal Banarsidass.

Doniger, Wendy, and Brian Smith. 1991. *The Laws of Manu.* Penguin.

Hume, Robert Ernest. 1931. *The Thirteen Principal Upanishads.* London: Oxford University Press.

Madhavacharya, Paṇdita, trans. (Hindi). Garuḍa Vāhana Paṇḍita. 1978. *Divyasūri Caritam,* eds. T. A. Sampath Kumaracharya and K.K.A. Venkatacharya. Bombay: Ananthacharya Research Institute.

Monier-Williams, Monier. 1974. *A Sanskrit-English Dictionary.* Oxford: Clarendon Press.

Narayanan, Vasudha. 1985. "Hindu Devotional Literature, the Tamil Connection." *Religious Studies Review* 12.

Narayanan, Vasudha. 1990. "Renunciation in Saffron and White Robes." In *Monastic Life in the Christian and Hindu Traditions,* eds. Austin B. Creel and Vasudha Narayanan. Lewiston: Edwin Mellen Press.

Narayanan, Vasudha. 1994. *The Vernacular Veda: Revelation, Recitation, and Ritual.* Columbia: University of South Carolina Press.

Ojha, Catherine. 1981. "Female Asceticism: Its Tradition and Present Condition." In *Man in India* 61.

Piṉpaḻakiya Perumāḷ Jīyar. 1975. *Āṛāyirappaṭi Guruparamparāprabhāvam,* ed. S. Krishnasvami Ayyankar. Tirucci: Puttur Agraharam.

Raman, K. V. 1975. *Sri Varadarajaswami Temple—Kanchi: A Study of its History, Art and Architecture.* New Delhi: Abhinav Publications.

Reddiyar, K. Venkataswami, ed. 1981. *Nālāyira tivviyap pirapantam.* Madras: Tiruvenkatatan Tirumanram.

Vedānta Deśika. *Catuḥślokibhāsyam Stotrarratnabhyāṣyam, Gadyatrayabhāsyañca.* Madras: Śrī Vendānta Deśika Seventh Centenary Trust, n.d.

Vedānta Deśika. 1961. *Srimad Rahasya Traya Sāram,* ed. Śrī Rāmātēcikācāriyar. 2 vols. Kumbakonam: Opilliyappan Sanniti.

Vedānta Deśika. 1970. "Nyasa Daskam." In *Stotramāla*, ed. Śrī Rāmātēcikācāriyar. 2 vols. Kumbakonam: Opıllıyappan Sanniti.

Vedānta Deśika. 1970. "Śaranāgatı Dīpika." In *Stotramāla*, ed. Śrī Rāmātēcikācāriyar. 2 vols. Kumbakonam: Oppillıyappan Sanniti.

White, S. J. 1980. "Mother Guru: Jnanananda of Madras, India." In *Unspoken Worlds: Women's Relıgıous Lives in Non-Western Cultures*, eds. Nancy A. Falk and Rita M. Gross. San Francisco: Harper & Row.

Yocum, Glenn. 1992. "The Cornatıon of a Guru: Charısma, Politıcs and Philosophy in Contemporary Indıa." In *A Sacred Thread: Modern Transmıssıon of Hindu Tradıtions in India and Abroad*, ed. Raymond Wıllıams. Chambersburg: Anima Press.

32

Body Politic among the Brides of Christ: Paul and the Origins of Christian Sexual Renunciation

Daniel Boyarin

According to Peter Brown, Paul's contribution to the origination of Christian valorization of sexual renunciation in both its milder and more extreme forms was almost accidental:

> What was notably lacking, in Paul's letter, was the warm faith shown by contemporary pagans and Jews that the sexual urge, although disorderly, was capable of socialization and of ordered, even warm, expression within marriage. The dangers of *porneia,* of potential immorality brought about by sexual frustration, were allowed to hold the center of the stage. By this essentially negative, even alarmist, strategy, Paul left a fatal legacy to future ages. An argument against abandoning sexual intercourse within marriage and in favor of allowing the younger generation to continue to have children slid imperceptibly into an attitude that viewed marriage itself as no more than a defense against desire. In the future, a sense of the presence of "Satan," in the form of a constant and ill-defined risk of lust, lay like a heavy shadow in the corner of every Christian church.[1]

In this essay I will be presenting quite a different reading of Paul on sexuality, one in which I will suggest that it is possible to interpret Paul in almost the precisely opposite fashion from Brown; namely, that for this first-century Jew sexuality had become so problematic that totally escaping from it—as Paul himself claimed to have done—seemed the best possible solution. Moreover, with respect to sexual anxiety, Paul was a child of his times, since the warm faith that Brown speaks of may have been valid for pagans of Paul's time, but for Jews such positive affect around sexuality seems to have become a reality only later, around the second century, and at least partly as a reaction to the sort of pessimistic view of sexuality that produced, among others, Paul himself. This sexual discourse constitutes a politics of sexuality: the struggle for power and dominance over the inclinations of the body, and in the Pauline society of the brides of Christ who no longer produced children as the fruit of death.

[I wish to thank my student Charlotte Fonrobert for her helpful comments on an earlier version of this essay.]

Sexuality and Sin in First-Century Judaism

The Palestinian Judaism of Paul's time was strongly dualist in mood and, at best, powerfully ambivalent about sexuality.[2] In *The Testaments of the Twelve Patriarchs,* a Hellenistic Jewish text from Palestine dated to sometime approximately in the late second century BCE, each human being is inhabited by a good spirit and an evil spirit. The evil spirit is explicitly defined as sexuality and opposed by a good spirit, which is antisexual: "And the spirits of error have no power over him [the genuine man], since he does not include feminine beauty in the scope of his vision."[3] "For the person with a mind that is pure with love does not look on a woman for the purpose of having sexual relations."[4] Other passages in this same text also indicate an extremely anxious affect around sexuality. The text speaks of seven good spirits that inhabit human beings. Of these, "the sixth is the spirit of taste for consuming food and drink; by it comes strength, because in food is the substance of strength. The seventh is the spirit of procreation and intercourse, with which come sins through fondness for pleasure. For this reason, it was the last in the creation and the first in youth, because it is filled with ignorance; it leads the young person like a blind man into a ditch and like an animal over a cliff. With these are commingled the spirits of error. First the spirit of promiscuity resides in the nature and the senses. A second spirit of insatiability, in the stomach."[5] The distinction between the spirit of taste for food and the spirit of procreation is striking. Although both are listed among the good spirits, the former contributes strength to the body. We would expect, therefore, that the clause on the spirit of procreation and intercourse would similarly continue with something like: by it comes the continuation of the race, because in intercourse the race is maintained. But instead we read, ". . . with which come sins through fondness for pleasure." While the spirit of taste is commingled with a spirit of insatiability, the spirit of intercourse induces sin, even before being commingled with the spirit of promiscuity. Philo, famously, expresses himself similarly. There may be no question, then, that early Palestinian Judaism had developed extremely pessimistic notions of sexuality. The clearest expression of this Palestinian Jewish negative affect around sexuality is, of course, the term יצר הרע (evil inclination) itself, a near synonym for sexual desire.[6]

In a thinking person, such judgments would inevitably have been in powerful conflict, would, indeed create a sort of double bind, with the commandment to procreate. The fact that sexuality, the יצר הרע, is the agent of the first positive commandment in the Torah, is an irony that neither Paul nor the rabbis could escape. The very efforts that the rabbis were to make a century or two later to overcome the negative encoding of sexuality and desire as, *ipso facto,* evil provide eloquent testimony to the strength and problematic element of this ideology of sex.[7] The rabbis, for their part, heavily ironized the notion of the evil instinct through paradoxical formulations, such as calling the evil instinct very good.[8] Paul, I suggest, found a different way out.

The Law as Stimulus to Sin: *Romans* 5–8

For ancient Israel, procreation as the means of continuation of God's people was the central and highest of goods and of religious values, but at the same time, for Israel by the first century, expression of sexuality produced anxiety and guilt.[9] Many Jews of the first century had a sense that they were commanded by God to do that which God considered sinful. My thesis is that Paul has, in *Romans* 5–8, and especially in the crucial chapter 7, one solution to this terrible paradox.

In *Romans* 5.12–14, Paul explicitly discusses Adam and draws a distinction between his sin and the sin of all others from Adam to Moses:

> Therefore as sin came into the world through one man and death through sin, and so death spread to all men because all men sinned—sin indeed was in the world before the law was given, but sin is not counted where there is no law. Yet death reigned from Adam to Moses, even over those whose sins were not like the transgression of Adam, who was a type of the one who was to come.

Although the wording is somewhat confusing, I think that certain very important points can yet be derived from this passage. Paul is making a distinction between sin, on the one hand, and transgression, on the other. Adam's transgression was correctly accounted to him, because he had been given a law—the law forbidding him to eat of the tree of the knowledge of good and evil.[10] Sin is separate from the law. It is not caused by the law; all humans sin and the (natural?) consequence is death, even for those for whom sin cannot be accounted, because their "sins are not [accountable because they are not] like the transgression of Adam." Adam ends up here being prototypical of two human groups: those who have the law and thereby are subject to have their transgressions accounted (Jews) and those who are affected by unaccountable sin but nevertheless die as a result of it (gentiles).[11] "Adam's sin was παράβασις obviously = 'sin accounted' since it was an act of disobedience to what he knew to be a command of God."[12] Paul wants all to realize that, even without accounting, sin itself nevertheless results in death, so that even those who have not sinned as Adam did, that is, while knowing the law, are also in exactly the same situation as those who know the law. Paul's overall theme in *Romans* that Jews and non-Jews are in exactly the same situation is thus well supported by this argument. Paul is further counteracting a Jewish argument or attitude that we have already seen him critiquing in *Romans* 2; namely, the attitude that having the law provides some sort of immunity to sin or redemption from sin. This is the source of his assertion here and below that having the law makes sin greater not lesser. "God's purpose for the law was not to distinguish Jewish righteous from gentile sinners, but to make Israel more conscious of its solidarity in sin with the rest of Adam's offspring."[13]

The only way to understand verse 20 ("Law came in to increase the trespass") in context is in reference to Adam—one man's trespass—so Adam is clearly here the type of the Jew, or human being under the law.[14] The content of this verse is interpretable in two ways, neither of which is nearly so antithetical to rabbinic theologoumena as the Reformation tradition would have it. Either it means that the knowledge of that which is forbidden increases culpability, or that having the knowledge of that which is forbidden increases the desire to sin.[15] Either way, the point is that Jews cannot claim any privilege, because they have the law. Having the law makes their salvation more difficult, not easier. Paul is fighting against a Jewish theology—held by some, not all, first-century Jews—that argues that just having the law provides a privileged place in salvation for the Jews.

The "law of sin in our members" is sex

Starting from the assumption that *Romans* 7 continues *Romans* 5, I want to propose that the entire discourse about law and commandment in this section of *Romans* has to do with sexuality. Of all the myriad interpretations that have been offered for the soliloquy of chapter 7, the one that makes the most sense to me, for all its problems, is the interpretation that the speaker of these verses is Adam. Watson has recently presented a strong argument in support of this reading. He presents a series of detailed comparisons between the speaker of *Romans* 7.7ff. and Adam:

1. Only Adam was alive before any commandment was given (v. 9).
2. The commandment not to eat of the fruit of the tree of knowledge came and gave Sin (the Serpent) an opportunity to bring death to Adam (v. 9).
3. "Sin deceived me" [ἐξηπάτησεν] is the same term that Eve uses to describe what happened to her, namely, that the Serpent "deceived me [ἠπάτησεν με]" (v. 11, cf. *Gn.* 3.13).
4. The result of the transgression is death, so "the very commandment which promised life proved to be death to me."[16]

Westerholm and other scholars had already rejected this interpretation, arguing that "You shall not covet," refers to the prohibition in the Decalogue and not to Adam.[17] Watson, however, completely circumvents this objection by interpreting the negative command involved as both the commandment to Adam not to eat of the fruit of the tree of the knowledge of good and evil and the command against desire in the Decalogue. The two are, as I shall suggest below, in a sort of type/antitype situation. He is thus not constrained to ignore the obvious allusion to the Decalogue in the chapter in order to maintain his reading that the speaker is Adam, for Adam's commandment is a type of the commandment to all—"In Adam, all have sinned."[18] This argument that Paul could appropriately use the verse of the Ten Commandments as a sort of catchword referring to Adam's sin can be further strengthened. First of all, the commandment in the Decalogue refers precisely to sexual lust. In the version in the *Book of Deuteronomy,* this is the entire content of 5.21, which reads: "Thou shalt not desire thy neighbor's wife" [οὐκ ἐπιθυμήσεις τὴν γυναῖκα τοῦ πλησίον σου]. To be sure, the verse goes on, in a separate sentence, to list other objects of one's neighbor that one should not covet as well. Furthermore, in the version in *Exodus* 20.17, where the Hebrew reads: "Thou shalt not desire thy neighbor's house or his wife," the Greek has οὐκ ἐπιθυμήσεις τὴν γυναῖκα τοῦ πλησίον σου as the first item and as a separate sentence, precisely as in the version in *Deuteronomy*. It is thus entirely plausible that Paul has the sentence "Do not desire the woman—of your neighbor" in mind when he cites οὐκ ἐπιθυμήσεις. Now, this verse of the Decalogue is the only negative commandment in the whole Torah that refers to desire and not to an action. Thus it is the very antitype as it were of the prohibition on Adam, if that prohibition is understood, as it most often was, as a prohibition against sexual desire. Furthermore, as Watson argues:

> The serpent's use of the commandment to deceive leads to sin: "Sin . . . wrought in me every kind of desire" (Rom. 7:8). . . . "Desire" means primarily sexual desire, and this may be linked with Gen. 3:7: "Then the eyes of both were opened, and they knew that they were naked; and they sewed fig leaves together and made themselves aprons." This suggests that the "sin" of v. 6 was sexual in nature, and for this reason Paul can identify the commandment of Gen. 2:17 with the commandment, 'You shall not desire,' just as he can identify the transgression of the commandment in Gen. 3:6f. with the awakening of "every kind of desire" (Rom. 7:7f.).[19]

Watson's argument can be amplified. The story that Paul tells in verses 8 and 11 ("But sin, seizing an opportunity in the commandment, produced in me all kinds of desire. Apart from the law sin lies dead. . . . For sin, seizing an opportunity in the commandment, deceived me and through it killed me.") seems most specifically intelligible as a gloss on *Genesis* 3.1–4. It was indeed the serpent (sin) in that story who by subtly manipulating the terms of the prohibition caused Eve and Adam to eat the fruit and die. "Now the serpent was more subtle that any beast of the field which the Lord God had made. And he said unto the woman, 'Yea, hath God said, Ye shall not eat of every tree of the garden?' And the woman said unto the serpent, 'We may eat of the fruit of the trees of the garden: But of the fruit of the tree which is in the midst of the garden, God hath said, Ye shall not eat of it, neither shall ye touch it, lest ye die.' And the serpent said unto the woman, 'Ye shall not surely die.'" It seems to me that this reading makes specific and sharp sense of Paul's first-person narrative. Thus, although Westerholm's objection cannot be dismissed entirely, the other strong considerations in favor of Watson's interpretation should lead us to consider it very favorably. I believe that the speaker of *Romans* 7 is indeed Adam, the same Adam of whom Paul speaks in chapter 5.

Now if we take seriously the suggestion that the speaker here is Adam and that what he is speaking of is sexual desire, I think that we must take into consideration as well the fact that Adam and Eve had been positively commanded to "Be fruitful and multiply." In my opinion, only the interpretation that Paul is speaking of sexual lust, inflamed by the positive commandment to procreate, which "sin" does indeed know how to exploit, accounts for such expressions as the "Law of Sin in my members" and all the talk here of inflamed passions.[20] Sexual desire was referred to among Jews in the first century unambiguously as the יצר הרע, the evil inclination. As David Biale has written, "For other writers of the time, sexuality was dangerous because even if it began licitly, it could, once aroused, slide all too easily into sin."[21] This is how sin has used the commandment to procreate in order to arouse sinful desire.[22]

Sin and the law

It follows that Paul would be making a much stronger statement—but also a much more localized one—about the relationship between sin and the law. If the sin of Adam and Eve was sexual—either the discovery of sexuality itself or a change in the nature of sexuality—a view that was held throughout much if not most of ancient interpretation, then it was the positive commandment to have children that led them into it, through the occasion of sin's (the serpent's) manipulations. They had been commanded to procreate but also to avoid sexual desire. No wonder that the serpent (sin) was able to exploit the commandment to cause them to sin! Within any interpretation that begins with the assumption that sexuality is sinful, as thought many Jews and Christians in late antiquity, the blessing of procreation is going to be a logical and hermeneutical conundrum, as witness the myriad difficulties of the church fathers in sorting out the sequence of events here.[23]

Adam's double bind—commanded, on the one hand, to procreate and, on the other, to avoid eating of the fruit of the tree of the (carnal) knowledge of good and evil—is the type of Jewish humanity under the flesh, commanded to procreate but not even to have lustful desires, let alone act on them. The Christian, however, having been released from procreation and thus from sexuality, can conquer desires and bear fruit for God. On this reading, Paul's references to "bearing fruit (καρποφορήσωμεν)"—whether for God, that is, spiritual fruit, in verse 4, or for death, that is, children in verse 5—are precisely an allusion to the commandment: "Be fruitful and multiply" (*Genesis* 1.28).[24]

Children as fruit for death

No matter how we understand the soliloquy of *Romans* 7, I think a strong case can be made for the interpretation that Paul's theme in this chapter is sexuality and the Christian redemption from it. Paul opens chapter 7 with the analogy of the married woman whose husband dies:

> Do you know brethren—for I am speaking to those who know the law—that the law is binding on a person only during his life. [2]Thus a married woman is bound by law to her husband as long as he lives; but if her husband dies she is discharged from the law concerning her husband. [3]Accordingly, she will be called an adulteress if she lives with another man while her husband is alive. But if her husband dies she is free from that law, and if she married another man she is not an adulteress. [4]Likewise, my brethren, you have died to the law through the body of Christ, so that you may belong to another, to him who has been raised from the dead in order that we may bear fruit for God [Revised Standard Version].

This parable, or analogy, has often been regarded as clumsy by even the most friendly of Pauline interpreters; typical is Stephen Westerholm: "The analogy is not the most perspicuous in the literature."[25] The problem with the analogy is that Paul's parable is of a woman no longer subject to the law of adultery because her husband has died; but its application is about one who is no longer married because she herself has died. There seems to be a lack of fit. This slippage between parable and application is, however, rather typical of the parabolic structure. In the parable itself, which refers to actual human life, it is the husband who must die, for otherwise his wife could not remarry. However, in the application of the parable, the Christian reality, within which, as Paul argues in chapter 6, the believer dies to one kind of life and is reborn to another, even within this world and this body, the wife through dying becomes released from her obligations to her former husband and is free to marry again. Christians, having died to their first husband, the law, are brides of Christ, married to him, in order that they may bear fruit for God. It is indeed the Christian who dies to the law—not the law which dies—but the result is equivalent to the law's having died in that the Christian is no longer an adulteress if she does not live faithfully to the law but joins herself only to Christ.

The erotic overtones of the parable are not accidental but absolutely crucial, on my reading, to the whole context; for what has died to the law is the fleshiness, the being in the flesh, which required the pursuit of an act that bore fruit not for God but for death. The choice of the marital analogy is exact, because being tied to the law meant the obligation to marry and bear children that the law enjoins in its command to be fruitful and multiply. No longer married to the law, since they have died to the flesh—meaning both the fleshly, literal meaning of the commandment and the use of the flesh that it implies and enjoins—Christians belong to him—sexually as it were, so that as his brides they bear fruit for God, spiritual children.

Romans 7.5–6 repeats this precise argument in nonparabolic language:

> ὅτε γὰρ ἦμεν ἐν τῇ σαρκί, τὰ παθήματα τῶν ἁμαρτιῶν τὰ διὰ τοῦ νόμου ἐνηργεῖτο ἐν τοῖς μέλεσιν ἡμῶν, εἰς τὸ καρποφορῆσαι τῷ θανάτῳ. νυνὶ δὲ κατηργήθημεν ἀπὸ τοῦ νόμου ἀποθανόντες ἐν ᾧ κατειχόμεθα ὥστε δουλεύειν ἡμᾶς ἐν καινότητι πνεύματος καὶ οὐ παλαιότητι γράμματος.
> [5]When we were in the flesh, our sinful passions, aroused by the law, were at work in our members to bear fruit for death. [6]But now we are discharged from the law, dead to that which held us captive, so that we serve not under the old written code but in the new life of the Spirit [Revised Standard Version].

These verses raise several questions: (1) What is the meaning of being in the flesh? (2) What is the connection between that fleshly condition and being under the law? (3) Why does the law arouse sinful passions? And (4) How is being freed of the law going to prevent the arousal of sinful passions? As Jewett remarks, "V[erse] 5 bears within itself the argument of the entire chapter," and therefore, "it becomes a decisive verse for the interpretation of σάρξ in Pauline theology."[26]

There is, in effect, a single answer to all of these questions. Paul speaks of a situation in which we were still in the flesh, which is the antithesis to having died to the law. In other words, being in the flesh is equivalent to being alive to the law. This is best understood if the flesh is taken to refer to the letter of the law together with all of its associated fleshinesses: generation and filiation. Being alive to the law, that is, serving in the old being of the letter—"Be fruitful and multiply"—arouses sinful passions in our members to bear fruit for death, that is to have children and thus to participate in the whole disaster of human mortality. In the new life of the Spirit, however, even that most fleshy commandment to procreate will be understood in its spiritual sense; namely, as a commandment to spiritual procreation, to that which bears fruit for God and not for death.

Serving under the old written code includes the positive commandment to be fruitful and multiply—the very first commandment in the Torah—as well as the first negative commandment not to desire (Paul's *midrashic* gloss, on my hypothesis, on being forbidden to eat of the fruit). Prescribed procreation leads inevitably to forbidden sexuality and the whole process to the bearing of fruit for death. It is no wonder that Paul, given this set of assumptions, will speak of the law in the second part of *Romans* 7 as presenting an impossible dilemma, indeed a double bind. Do have sex, in order to bear children, but do not have desire. Dying to the law through the body of Christ relieves one of the obligation to produce children—fruit for death—and thus frees one to bear only spiritual fruit, fruit for God.

The fruits of this interpretation: *Romans* 6 and 8

Whether or not the specifics of this interpretation of *Romans* 7 as Adam *midrash* bear fruit and multiply, it nevertheless seems to me to be a highly plausible, if not ineluctable, line of interpretation that sees Paul's focus here as on sexuality and the contrast that he is drawing between fleshly life with its be getting of children, and spiritual life where the propagation is of spiritual fruits for God. One of the ways of testing a new interpretation of a text is, of course, to observe that it renders clear other aspects of its context that were otherwise difficult to understand. Observing the thematic that I have hypothesized for chapter 7 will help us to solve several interpretive conundra in chapters 6 and 8.

The analogies between the nexus of law and desire in *Romans* 7.5–6 and the similar one of 6.12–14 are obvious, and we are justified, therefore, in seeing these verses as glossing each other.[27] Here, however, as in the parable that opens chapter 7, there seem to be the same paradoxes about who is dead and who alive:

> τοῦτο γινώσκοντες ὅτι ὁ παλαιὸς ἡμῶν ἄνθρωπος συνεσταυρώθη, ἵνα καταργηθῇ τὸ σῶμα τῆς ἁμαρτίας [6.6]
> We know that our old man was crucified with him so that the sinful body might be destroyed [Revised Standard Version].

Paul, having just argued that Christians have been crucified and died, now argues that they have been brought from death to life:

> Μὴ οὖν βασιλευέτω ἡ ἁμαρτία ἐν τῷ θνητῷ ὑμῶν σώματι εἰς τὸ ὑπακούειν ταῖς ἐπιθυμίαις αὐτοῦ, μηδὲ παριστάνετε τὰ μέλη ὑμῶν ὅπλα ἀδικίας τῇ ἁμαρτίᾳ, ἀλλὰ παραστήσατε ἑαυτοὺς τῷ θεῷ ὡσεὶ ἐκ νεκρῶν ζῶντας καὶ τὰ μέλη ὑμῶν ὅπλα δικαιοσύνης τῷ θεῷ. ἁμαρτία γὰρ ὑμῶν οὐ κυριεύσει οὐ γάρ ἐστε ὑπὸ νόμον ἀλλὰ ὑπὸ χάριν.
> [12]Do not let sin therefore reign in your mortal bodies, to make you obey their passions. [13]Do not yield your members to sin as instruments of wickedness, but yield yourselves to God as men who have been brought from death to life, and your members to God as instruments of righteousness. [14]For sin will have no dominion over you, since you are not under law but under grace [Revised Standard Version].

There are two cruxes here. The first is the apparently self-contradictory account of the relation of life to death. On the one hand, Christians are enjoined to die with Christ; on the other, they have been brought from death to life. In other words, they have participated in both the death and the resurrection of Christ. But the Christians to whom Paul is speaking are still alive, and in the same bodies they always had. Paul is speaking in the past tense of that which has already happened to Christians and not of future expectation. Secondly, how is the nonobedience to one's passions equivalent to not being under law, or even more sharply, how can sin have no dominion over you because you are not under law?

These two interpretative cruxes may both be solved according to the present line of interpretation that precisely the body of sin of which Paul speaks is the sexual body. Thus, Christians have, through the Crucifixion, died to a certain mode of living and progressed to another mode of living, both of which are, however, available in this life. I interpret this as a reference to a life that is responsible to the needs of the flesh, a fleshy life, the life of procreation, on the one hand, and a life that is dedicated to spiritual pursuits, on the other. Christians have already died to the life of the body; they are no longer engaged in the getting of children together with its messy entanglements in passion, heat, jealousy—all that later Christian writers will refer to as concupiscence—which lead to death. Rather, having been freed from all of that, they have been brought from a condition of physical death to a condition of spiritual life. This answers, moreover, the second question as well, for it is the Torah, the Jewish Law, that enjoins the procreation of children and thus directly and necessarily stirs the passions. In other words, literally by being not under law, that is, by not being obligated to procreate, the Christian is freed from the dominion of sinful passion, free to remove sexuality from her person, and thus able to free herself from being under sin.

Romans 8 continues the theme of the immortality granted those who abandon the birth-and-death cycle from which Christ, through his birth and death has freed them. The hypothesis that I have offered enables us to make sense of at least one passage that has been hardly intelligible until now, verses 9 through 13:[28]

> 12῎Αρα οὖν ἀδελφοί ὀφειλέται ἐσμὲν οὐ τῇ σαρκὶ τοῦ κατὰ σάρκα ζῆν, 13εἰ γὰρ κατὰ σάρκα ζῆτε, μέλλετε ἀποθνῄσκειν. εἰ δὲ πνεύματι τὰς πράξεις τοῦ σώματος θανατοῦτε, ζήσεσθε.
> 9But you are not in the flesh, you are in the Spirit, if the Spirit of God really dwells in you. Any one who does not have the Spirit of Christ does not belong to him. 10But if Christ is in you, although your bodies are dead because of sin, your spirits are alive because of righteousness. 11If the Spirit of him who raised Jesus from the dead, dwells within you, he who raised Christ Jesus from the dead will give life to your mortal bodies also through his Spirit which dwells in you. 12So then, brethren, we are debtors, not to the flesh, to live according to the flesh— 13for if you live according to the flesh you will die, but if by the Spirit you put to death the deeds of the body you will live [Revised Standard Version].

These verses have caused interpreters no end of trouble. Now it is particularly the last two verses that have caused the trouble. What does Paul mean by saying that

Christians are under an obligation, but not one of the flesh? Some commentators assume an otherwise totally unknown and unalluded to gnostic sect in Rome that had practiced obligatory libertinism. According to my reading, we need assume no bizarre gnostic obligations to libertinism behind this verse. If we assume that "the flesh" here means the fleshly obligations of the law, that is both their literal sense and the fact that they are concerned with the flesh, then the answer is clear. "Obligated to the flesh" in 8.12 means simply the obligation to procreate.[29] Christians have obligations, but they do not have the obligation to keep the fleshy commandments of the Torah and particularly, I think, in this context, the commandment to procreate, which Paul refers to as deeds of the body.

Adam's situation is the situation of the Jews. As Dunn and others have pointed out, "when we were in the flesh" must mean simply "in our pre-Christian state," when we considered membership in the literal Israel according to the flesh (*1 Cor.* 10.18) as decisive for salvation, propagation of the race as a central value, and when we were alive in our fleshly bodies and subject to the law, before we died to the law.[30] If you continue in that mode of existence, then you will die, "but if by the Spirit you put to death the deeds of the body [sex and procreation] you will live" (8.13). He furthermore repeats this point at the end of the letter, when he writes, "But put on the Lord Jesus Christ, and make no provision for the flesh that desires be aroused [εἰς ἐπιθυμίας]" (13.14), which ought, on my hypothesis, to be glossed: be baptized into the body of Christ and the new family of the Spirit and make no provision for physical progeny, which provision necessitates the arousal of desires! Dying to the law in baptism is functionally identical to the baptism of converts into Judaism who are also understood as having died to their old existence and been reborn to a new one, and it is precisely this understanding of baptism that Paul is employing.[31] Paul and the other (formerly Jewish) Christians are no longer in the flesh and thus freed of the consequences of being in the flesh.

Brides of Christ: *1 Corinthians* 6

The *topos* of spiritual propagation as opposed to and higher than physical procreation is well known in Paul's world. Found already in Plato's *Symposium,* it is frequently mobilized in Paul's Jewish contemporary Philo as well, most notably in his description of the life of the celibate Therapeutae. According to my reading, Paul in *Romans* 6 and 7 also opposes a physical sexuality to a spiritual, that is, allegorical, sexuality. This reading can be strengthened by noting that the same antithesis occurs in *1 Corinthians* 6.14–20:

> [14]And God raised the Lord and will also raise us up by his power. [15]Do you not know that your bodies are members of Christ? Shall I therefore take the members of Christ and make them members of a prostitute? Never! [16]Do you not know that he who joins himself to a prostitute becomes one body with her? For, as it is written, "The two shall become one." [17]But he who is united with the Lord becomes one spirit with him. [18]Shun immorality. Every other sin which a man commits is outside the body; but the immoral man sins against his own body. [19]Do you not know that

> your body is a temple of the Holy Spirit within you, which you have from God? You are not your own; [20]you were bought with a price. So glorify God in your body.

The argument in verses 15–16 seems strikingly inconsequent in that it skips from the immorality of sex with a prostitute right over to union with Christ. Moreover, the verse cited, "And the two shall become one" refers in *Genesis* altogether positively to sexual union between husband and wife. I would certainly expect to read here: "Do you know that he who joins himself to a prostitute becomes one body with her? For, as it is written, 'The two shall become one.' But he who is united with his wife becomes one flesh with her. Shun immorality."

I think that Paul is truly revealing his hand here. For him, sexuality *per se* is tainted with immorality. Paul looks forward to the becoming one flesh of *Genesis* to be entirely replaced by an allegorical becoming one spirit with Christ. He proposes that this commandment, as well as the commandment to be fruitful and multiply, be displaced by their spiritual referents of marriage to Christ and the bearing of fruits of the Spirit. Here, however, Paul makes the point indirectly, through what he does not say because immediately below he is going to recommend legitimate marital sex for those not gifted as is he with the ability to remain celibate, and who would therefore be in danger of *porneia* were they not married. Paul says as much openly in 7.1: "It is well for a man not to touch a woman"; and 7.7, "I wish that all were as I myself am. But each has his own special gift from God."[32] The value system is crystal clear. It is thus manifest from these verses that Paul does not so much oppose sex with prostitutes to legitimate sexual intercourse, but rather physical union between men and women to spiritual union between people and Christ.

But what, however, of Paul's dual insistence here on the body as members of Christ and as a temple for the Spirit? Neither of these expressions seems to reflect an ascetic contempt for the flesh. Paying close attention to this inconsequence in Paul's argument gives us another moment of access to the very special Pauline anthropology that I have explored elsewhere with reference to *1 Corinthians* 15 and *2 Corinthians* 5. As in those passages, Paul is at great pains to disable those strains of thought—perhaps proto-gnostic—that would claim that the body is of no significance and in radical Platonic fashion only to be escaped from and denied. For Paul, not only will there be a body of resurrection, the body in this life is to be honored and paid its due by keeping it pure and holy. He is very conscious of the clear and present danger involved in devaluing the flesh and its works, most notably a tilt toward a libertinism that will achieve the precise opposite of his intention. Thus he must insist that the body is temple of the Spirit and that the Christian in his or her body is a member of Christ; but precisely that membership in Christ anticipates the resurrection body, which is not a body of flesh. Paul thus distinguishes between the flesh and the body. The flesh, that is, sexuality, has been dispensed with in the Christian dispensation, precisely in order to spiritualize the body. To be sure, a legitimated marital sexuality is allowed for in Paul's system as the second-best alternative to celibacy, but the ideal is a spiritual union as bride of Christ in which he who "is united with the Lord becomes one spirit with him" and not one flesh with even his lawful wife. Indeed the connection between chapters 6 and 7 of *1 Corinthians* is now much clearer.

Works of the Flesh in *Galatians* 5–6

The same concatenation of themes occurs in *Galatians* 5–6 as in *1 Corinthians* 6; namely, the death and resurrection of Christ, which is opposed to the fleshy or sexual nature of humans:

> [16]But I say, walk by the Spirit, and do not gratify the desires of the flesh. [17]For the desires of the flesh are against the Spirit, and the desires of the Spirit are against the flesh; for these are opposed to each other, to prevent you from doing what you would. [18]But if you are led by the Spirit you are not under the law. [19]Now the works of the flesh are plain: immorality, impurity, licentiousness, [20]idolatry, sorcery, enmity, strife, jealousy, anger, selfishness, dissension, party spirit, [21]envy, drunkenness, carousing, and the like. . . . [22]But the fruit of the Spirit is love, joy, peace, patience, kindness, goodness, faithfulness, [23]gentleness, self-control, against such there is no law. [24]And those who belong to Christ Jesus have crucified the flesh with its passions and desires.

This passage, once more, presents certain striking interpretative gaps. The most obvious is the leap in verse 18 from the discourse on libertinism or licentiousness in the previous verses to being under the law. On my reading, in this passage Paul is guarding against an obvious danger of misunderstanding that his discourse arouses. *Galatians* 3.12 amounts to a disavowal of *Leviticus* 18 as the guide to Christian living. *Leviticus* 18.5 reads "He who does them lives by them," which Paul understands to mean: one who does the commandments lives by them and not by faith. But Paul argues: since we know from *Habbakuk* that the righteous live by faith, he who lives by them and not by faith is not righteous—is not justified. Christians, therefore, no longer live by them. Now what is crucial to remember is that *Leviticus* 18.5 is the introduction to the catalog of forbidden sexual connections. One could, therefore, very easily imagine Paul at the end of the letter becoming aware of the enormous danger for misinterpretation that his letter could produce. If he has, as it were, repudiated *Leviticus* 18, does it not follow that its provisions are no longer valid and sexual license is permitted? That is precisely the conclusion that some Corinthian Christians seem to have reached. It is this that Paul seeks to counter in chapters 5 and 6 of *Galatians*. It is, therefore, most attractive to read the passage just quoted as carrying its obvious sense in which desires and passions of the flesh are just what would be referred to in a modern use of these terms; namely, sexual desire and passion. This interpretation affords an elegant bridge over the apparent gap between verses 17 and 18, in the light of *Romans* 7. We now understand precisely the connection between the desires of the flesh, and being under the law, for it is the law that produces the desires of the flesh and thus the works of the flesh through its insistence on the bearing of children that leads inexorably to passion, and thus to licentiousness, jealousy, and the rest.

An objection has been raised to the sexual interpretation of the desires of the flesh (ἐπιθυμίαν σαρκος), because the works of the flesh (ἔργα τῆς σαρκὸς) that are itemized are not primarily works of sexual immorality. The point is well taken, of course, but not, I think, decisive. We must distinguish between the desires of the flesh and the works of the flesh, that is, the results of those desires. The desires of the flesh are indeed what they seem to be; namely, sexual desire, but the works of the flesh are the social outcome of such desire: "immorality, impurity, licentiousness, idolatry, sorcery, enmity, strife, jealousy, anger, selfishness, dissension, party spirit, envy, drunkenness, carousing, and the like." Lest this sound farfetched, the following parallel from a first-century text is unambiguous:

> But the ways of the spirit of falsehood are these: greed, slackness in the search for righteousness, wickedness and lies, haughtiness and pride, falseness and deceit, cruelty and abundant evil, ill-temper and much folly and brazen insolence, abominable deeds [committed] in a spirit of lust, and ways of lewdness in the service of uncleanness.[33]

This text provides an excellent parallel to *Galatians* 5, for here we see also how the spirit of lust leads not only to sexual immorality, but to deceit, cruelty, treachery, and even shortness of temper, a list quite similar in spirit to the works of the flesh that Paul adduces. Note also that the same concatenation of themes occurs in *1 Corinthians* 6 where Paul begins his discourse attacking civil strife and jealousy and seamlessly segues into sexual immorality. In other words, those who do not crucify their flesh with its passions and desires are those who produce a society within which not only the obvious immorality, impurity, and licentiousness occur but also idolatry and sorcery—perhaps Paul means the idolatry and sorcery of love charms—as well as enmity, strife, and jealously. Those, however, who are unmoved by *erōs* are capable of creating a society of *agapē*. Philo also provides an excellent parallel to this idea when he describes first a paradisal condition in which men spend their lives in contemplation before the creation of woman but after that, he writes,

> Love supervenes, brings together and fits into one the divided halves, as it were, of a single living creature, and sets up in each of them a desire for fellowship with the other with a view to the production of their like. And this desire begat likewise bodily pleasure, that pleasure which is the beginning of wrongs and violation of the law, the pleasure for the sake of which men bring on themselves the life of mortality and wretchedness in lieu of that of immortality and bliss.[34]

There is, therefore, no reason to discredit the obvious meaning of "gratifying desires of the flesh" as referring to sexual desire.

The theme is carried further in the continuation in *Galatians* 6 in which Paul writes, "For he who sows to his own flesh will from the flesh reap corruption; but he who sows to the Spirit will from the Spirit reap eternal life" (*Gal.* 6.8). Here we find precisely the same metaphorical opposition that Paul uses in *Romans* 7.4–5. One who sows to the flesh by having children will reap corruption; that is, the corruption of death, for flesh is mortal. One who sows to the Spirit will, however, escape corruption in eternal life. Sowing is a commonplace metaphor for sexual activity.

Thus, I think we are justified in concluding that the desires of the flesh in *Galatians* 5–6 are also to be understood as sexual. Christians are freed from sexuality. The final and ultimate fruit of the Spirit that is listed in *Galatians* 5.23 is ἐγκράτεια, and given the interpretation that I have offered, we can give this word its full technical meaning of self-control and withdrawal from sexuality.[35]

Paul the Proto-Encratite

We thus see that, at three points in his discourse, Paul repeats the same highly significant sequence of ideas that constitutes a sort of body politic among the brides of Christ. In their former state of being in the flesh, Jewish Christians had been obligated under the law. This law is a law of flesh, because with its emphasis on fleshly obligations and especially procreation, it inevitably leads to passion and desire. However, under the new dispensation afforded to Christians through baptism, which is an enactment of Christ's death and resurrection, they are born again freed of the obligation to the flesh, that obligation that produces sinful desire in the members and fruit for death. The erotic life of Christians is ideally entirely devoted to the new bridegroom, Christ, and the joining with this bridegroom results not in fruit for death but in spiritual fruit for God.

The emphasis on embodiedness involved in being Jewish, in both senses of flesh (that is, valorizing circumcision and other fleshly practices as well as concentrating on genealogical connections), implies necessarily the obligation to have children. The only solution then is to escape from the condition of being in the flesh, to die to the law and be reborn in the new life of the Spirit, which spiritualizes precisely those fleshly, embodied aspects of the Torah, once again, kinship and the performance of Jewish ritual and thus sexuality.[36] Freed from the captivity of the letter, the flesh, the commandment that actually causes us to sin, we can serve God in the freedom of the Spirit and escape from that which stirs up our members. It thus constitutes a return to the prelapsarian state in which Adam was when he lived apart from the law, that is, both the law to be fruitful and multiply and the prohibition to eat of the tree of the knowledge of good and evil. Christ and dying with Christ for the Christians constitutes, therefore, return to this state of grace and redemption from the death and the bearing fruit for death that Adam's transgression occasioned, as opposed to the bearing of spiritual fruit for God of *Romans* 7.4. "In the flesh," here, like its equivalent, "in the letter," means simply in literal Jewish existence, in Israel according to the flesh. Just as the law itself is not sin, but causes sin as an inevitable consequence of its commandment to procreate, so being in the flesh, that is, being under the law, being Jewish and thus committed to physical, Jewish continuity is not, *ipso facto,* evil but leads to sin, once more, by preventing the exit from sexuality. Although life in the Spirit is obviously superior to life in the flesh, as the allegorical is superior to the literal, "in the flesh" here has no pejorative meaning of its own, that is, it is devalued with respect to the Spirit but not figured as something morally or religiously evil in itself. It is primarily, as I am claiming throughout, a hermeneutical term. The state of remaining in the literal, concrete, fleshly situation of the old Israel does, of course, have negative consequences that Paul emphasizes, largely to disabuse Jews of any sense that the law makes them superior to the gentiles. Jews bear fruit for death, that is, they have children who will feed the death machine, while Christians bear spiritual fruit, fruit that cannot die.

Paul never once to my knowledge mentions the bearing of children as a positive event, not even as a necessary evil! A rather obvious objection that I am certain will be raised is that Paul is speaking in an extreme eschatological situation, and his views are not to be taken as characteristic of his understanding of sexuality *per se*. Now it is unquestionably the case that Paul is indeed working *in extremis*, as it were. Indeed, I would to go so far as to argue that "For the form of this world is passing away" (*1 Corinthians* 7.31) is at least in part to be understood as a further argument against procreation.[37] This does not vitiate my point at all, however, for the fact that it is precisely the function of the eschatological moment to free people from sexuality and procreation—that is, to enable them to fulfill spiritual and not physical functions of propagation—makes exactly the point about Paul's thought that I wish to make. It is not, after all, in any way a necessity of eschatological expectation that it lead to an end to sexuality and procreation. As evidence for this, I may cite two modern Jewish messianic movements, quite different from each other, both characterized by the sort of eschatological tension that marks Paul's thought and both of which engage copiously in procreative activity and place it at the center and zenith of their value systems. I am referring, of course, to the messianic Zionists of Gush Emunim and the messianic Hassidim of Lubavitch (Habad). Both groups are procreating abundantly. The law of sin, I conclude, can be very plausibly understood as the commandment to procreate from which the eschatological moment of the Crucifixion and Resurrection has ideally freed Christians.

I think that if my interpretation of these passages is acceptable, a significant revision of the history of sexuality in Christendom is in order, with the encratic Fathers much closer to Paul than has been previously allowed. The meaning of *Romans* 7 is that it was the command to be fruitful and multiply that created the inescapable dilemma of Adamic humanity, and the horns of this dilemma were only sharpened by the Jewish insistence on the centrality of the commandment, because of its role in the reproduction of the people of God. The dual effect of the Christ event is that, by providing an allegorical interpretation of Jewish existence, one in which significance and salvation are found in the promise and not in the flesh, it also provides release from the terrible double bind in which first-century Jews seem to have found themselves. Commanded to procreate, for only thus could the holy seed be continued, they were plagued by a constant anxiety and sense of sinfulness about the performance of that very commandment. Paul, in one fell swoop, removes the sword of Damocles by telling them that the physical continuation of Jewish peoplehood is no longer necessary. In this end time after the death and resurrection of Christ, Israel itself is no longer according to the flesh, defined by genealogy, but has been replaced by the community of the faithful baptized. The physical command to be fruitful and multiply and thus bear fruit for death has also been replaced by the command to bear spiritual fruit for Christ, fruit that will never die. When Paul is read in this way the encratic forms of Christianity are legitimate (if less compromising) heirs to a vitally important part of Paul's thought.

NOTES

1. Peter Brown, *The Body and Society: Men, Women and Sexual Renunciation in Early Christianity,* Lectures on the History of Religions 13 (New York: Columbia University Press, 1988), p. 55.
2. Some of the material in this subsection is adapted from Daniel Boyarin, *Carnal Israel: Reading Sex in Talmudic Culture,* The New Historicism: Studies in Cultural Poetics 25 (Berkeley and Los Angeles: University of California Press, 1993), chapter 2. See also Daniel Boyarin, "'Behold Israel according to the flesh': On Anthropology and Sexuality in Late Antique Judaism," *Yale Journal of Criticism* 5.2 (Spring 1992):25–55.
3. H. C. Kee (trans. and introduction), *Testaments of the Twelve Patriarchs, the Sons of Jacob the Patriarch,* in James H. Charlesworth, ed., *The Old Testament Pseudepigrapha* (Garden City, N.Y.: Doubleday, 1983), 1:803.
4. Ibid., p. 827. Note here as well the notion of pure love that is so similar to Paul's agapic love as in *Galatians* 5.22.
5. Ibid., pp. 782–783.
6. For comparison of *Romans* 7 to the Jewish doctrine of the יצר הרע, see Hans Joachim Schoeps, *Paul: the Theology of the Apostle in the Light of Jewish Religious History,* trans. Harold Knight (Philadelphia: Westminster, 1961), p. 185.
7. See *Carnal Israel,* chapter 2.
8. See Ibid., chapter 6 for development of this point.
9. See David Biale, *Eros and the Jews from Biblical Israel to Contemporary America* (New York: Basic Books, 1992), pp. 39–40.
10. One could say that "law" sometimes functions for Paul semantically as מצוה (commandment) does in rabbinic Hebrew.
11. This obviates the sort of difficulty that Dunn runs into, because he does not understand "law" here to mean the law given to Adam (p. 292). Furthermore, if the interpretation of Watson that the speaker of *Romans* 7 is Adam be accepted (see below), then "I was once alive apart from the law" is also no problem (*pace* James D. G. Dunn, *Romans* [Dallas, Tex.: Word Books, 1988], p. 291), because Adam is speaking about the time before he was commanded not to eat of the tree of knowledge of good and evil! Sin was in the world even then, but it had not yet come into the world in the sense of being accounted.
12. Dunn, *Romans,* p. 276.
13. Ibid., p. 286.
14. I wish to dispel one possible source of confusion here. I am *not* claiming that when Paul refers to Adam as the type of the one who is to come, that this means the Jew or humanity under the law. As attractive as this interpretation would be for understanding verse 20, Dunn is clearly correct that it is excluded by verse 15, which seeks to draw a contrast between type and antitype, such that it is obvious that the antitype is Jesus and nothing else. Nevertheless, I am arguing, Adam is being *used* (if not mentioned) as the type of transgressor under the law and thus of the Jews, a point which is crucial for interpreting *Romans* 7. Quite incidentally to my argument here but important to understanding *Romans* 5 is the realization that an argument of *de minore ad maiore* (קול וחומר) from

sin to grace or from punishment to mercy is a *very* common one in rabbinic texts. I accordingly completely disagree with Dunn (op. cit., p. 293) who regards verses 15–17 as a qualifying afterthought of the comparison of Adam to Christ. I think, given the constant use of this type of argument throughout the chapter, Paul is saying here exactly what he wants to say. If through Adam's sin all are punished (the quality of judgment), how much more so that through the free gift (the quality of mercy) will all be redeemed. Retroverted back into Hebrew and without the Christology, this could be a sentence in any *midrash*!

15. For the latter in rabbinic tradition compare the rabbinic dictum that "Anyone who is greater than his fellow [in Torah], has a greater desire to sin than his fellow" discussed at length in *Carnal Israel,* chapter 2.
16. See Francis Watson, *Paul, Judaism, and the Gentiles* (Cambridge: Cambridge University Press, 1986).
17. Stephen Westerholm, *Israel's Law and the Church's Faith: Paul and his Recent Interpreters* (Grand Rapids: Wm. B. Eerdmans Publishing Co., 1988), p. 59. See also Moo, "Israel and Paul," p. 124, who writes, "How could Paul feature Adam's experience in a discussion about a law that he presents as entering the historical arena only with *Moses?*" I think his objection is, however, no objection, because Adam is certainly presented as having had at least one commandment which he transgressed in chapter 5, and he is the *type* of Israel in this respect. We do not need to appeal to a putative Jewish notion (not attested anywhere that I know of) that Adam received the Torah, only to realize that, as Paul says explicitly, Adam's small set of commandments—"Be fruitful," and "Do not eat of the fruit"—had the same function as the Torah. Moo also concedes "the great attraction of the Adamic interpretation. 'Life' and 'death' can be accorded their full theological meanings, referring, respectively, to Adam's state before and after his disastrous confrontation with the divine commandment, and the springing to life of the previous inactive sin can be regarded as a fitting description of the role of the serpent in the garden," but claims, "However, we have seen that, whatever its virtues, the Adamic view cannot satisfactorily be reconciled with the central concern of the text—the Mosaic *torah*" (op. cit., p. 125). I claim, however, that this Adamic interpretation is eminently reconcilable with the notion that Paul is talking about the Mosaic torah, for the reason I have already exposed; namely, that Adam and his commands are treated in chapter 5 as the type of Israel and her Torah. If the objection is taken as answered, then the attractions of the Adamic interpretation remain. I am entirely unimpressed by the arguments of Robert H. Gundry, "The Moral Frustration of Paul Before His Conversion: Sexual Lust in Romans 7:7–25," in *Pauline Studies: Essays Presented to F. F. Bruce,* eds. D. A. Hagner and J. Murray, (Grand Rapids: Wm. B. Eerdmans, 1980), pp. 228–245, in favor of the "autobiographical" interpretation. It is, on top of all the other inconsequentialities of its argument, dependent on the totally unsupportable assumption that the concept of bar mitzvah was present in the first century! I do, agree, of course with his assumption that Paul is talking about sexual desire. Since we agree on the sexual content of the chapter, the question of whether this is Paul's autobiography or a *midrash* on Adamic man becomes quite crucial indeed.
18. *Pace,* for example, Moo, "Israel and Paul," p. 123. Cf. S. Lyonnet, "'Tu ne convoiteras pas' (Rom. 7.7)," *Neotestamentica et Patristica: Eine Freundesgabe, Herrn Professor Dr. Oscar Cullmann zu seinem 60. Geburtstag überreicht,* Novum Testamentum Supplementum 6 (Leiden: E. J. Brill, 1962), pp. 158–64.
19. See Watson, *Paul,* p. 152; also N. T. Wright, *The Climax of the Covenant: Christ and the Law in Pauline Theology* (Minneapolis: Fortress Press, 1992), p. 197.

20. I am in complete agreement with Wright's insistence that νόμος must mean everywhere the same "Law" both in *Romans* 7 and in *Romans* 3.27 if we are not to sap Paul's writing of any strength. I think, however, that my interpretation goes much further in establishing this than his does, for, for him, this "Law of Sin" must needs be reduced to the Torah taken over and used by sin, whereas for my reading, the Torah understood literally *is* a Torah of sin, because it commands sexuality. I agree with Wright that "Those who are 'in the Spirit,' do now submit to Torah, in the sense of its righteous decree coming true in them. They are not 'under Torah'; they are not bound by 'works of Torah'; but they 'submit to it,' in the sense of its deepest intention" (op. cit., p. 213, emphasis added) and even more that "This exegesis of νόμος in Rom. 8 would give a good viewpoint, were there time and space, from which to examine Rom. 2.13f., 2.25–9, and particularly 3.27." It is this examination that I am attempting in the book entitled *A Radical Jew: Paul and the Politics of Identity,* of which this essay will eventually form a chapter.
21. Biale, *Eros,* p. 40.
22. Francis Watson, *Paul,* p. 152.
23. See Gary Anderson, "Celibacy or Consummation in the Garden? Reflections on Early Jewish and Christian Interpretations of the Garden of Eden," *Harvard Theological Review* 82.2 (1989):121–148. See also my *Carnal Israel* and brief discussion of the rabbis below.
24. This argument would be even stronger, of course, if the Septuagint used the word "fruit" in this verse, but it does not. Since, however, the Hebrew does use the verb from the root for fruit, פרו, Paul could conceivably be either remembering the Hebrew or even alluding to another, more literal Greek rendition of the verse. Even without the verbal echo, the thematic one of bearing fruit, i.e. procreating, is clear.
25. Westerholm, *Israel's Law,* p. 206.
26. Robert Jewett, *Paul's Anthropological Terms: A Study of their Use in Conflict Settings,* Arbeiten zur Geschichte des antiken Judentums und des Urchristentums 10 (Leiden: E. J. Brill, 1971), p. 145. And I am quite convinced that Jewett himself has not understood this verse. Jewett explicitly denies any sexual meaning to this verse. Taking the desire, the ἐπιθυμία of 7–12, in good Reformation fashion, as the desire to justify oneself by works, Jewett also understands the "sinful passions working in our members to bear fruit for death," as "the sinful desire to gain righteousness by means of one's works!" (ibid., p. 146, exclamation added).
27. As Westerholm already acutely observed, chapter 7, verses 5 and 6 ("When we were in the flesh, our sinful passions, aroused by the law, were at work in our members to bear fruit for death. But now we are discharged from the law, dead to that which held us captive, so that we serve not under the old written code but in the new life of the Spirit") are an interpretative gloss on 6.12–14. In order, therefore, to understand the latter we must interpret the former—and vice-versa, of course (Westerholm, *Israel's Law,* p. 54).
28. *Pace* Jewett, *Anthropological,* p. 164.
29. Cf. Jewett's rather lame reading of this as some sort of response to gnosticism (op. cit., p. 149). See further discussion of this verse below.
30. The paradox that baptized Christians still have bodies of flesh has already been anticipated and answered by Paul in *Galatians* 2.19–20.
31. Note that baptized converts into Judaism are not considered the children of their natural parents.
32. The second of these citations makes it quite clear that in 7.1 Paul is not merely quoting

or reflecting the views of the Corinthians in order to dispute them, as some commentators have argued, but in fact agreeing with and then qualifying them. As in *Galatians* 5–6 (for which see below), Paul is always concerned lest disdain for the flesh lead paradoxically toward libertinism!

33. 1QS 4.10 *(Manual of Discipline)* in G. Vermes, *The Dead Sea Scrolls in English,* 3d ed. (New York; Penguin, 1987), pp. 65–66.
34. Philo, *On the Creation,* trans. F. H. Colson, Loeb Classical Library (London: Heinemann, 1929), 1:121.
35. Jewett's interpretation of this passage in *Galatians* is untenable, and he can make no sense of the warning about sowing, referring to it as "enigmatic" (Jewett, *Anthropological,* p. 104). After his one good insight that "flesh" for Paul means the literal flesh of circumcision (and I add procreation), he quickly reverts to Bultmannian conceptions—without even Bultmann's sublimity, "The 'flesh' is Paul's term for everything aside from God in which one places his final trust. The Jew sought to gain life through the law which offers the obedient a secure future. This element of seeking the good is an essential part of the flesh idea, and may be seen likewise in the situation of the libertinist. The flesh presents to the libertinist objects of desire which man is to satisfy (*Gal.* 5.16). These objects lure man on because of the promise inherent in them. They seem to offer man exactly what the law and circumcision offered—life" (ibid., p. 103). Jewett's interpretation is dependent on assuming that Paul is arguing that one who follows the law is in danger of libertinism, "The struggle against the flesh is centered in the cross event and with the appropriation of this event for oneself in baptism, the power of the flesh is broken. It can threaten again only if man foolishly places his faith in the flesh again, thus setting his will in line with the flesh's lures" (ibid., p. 106). But this is precisely the opposite of Paul's concern here. He is not telling the Galatians that if they ignore his preaching and get circumcised they will be prey to the lures of the flesh, but rather he is afraid that if they take in his preaching, they will misunderstand and think that the flesh is permitted to them. That is, after all, what Paul articulates explicitly as his concern in *Gal.* 5.13, "For you were called to freedom brothers, only do not use your freedom as an opportunity for the flesh." Paul does, indeed, argue in other places that keeping the law leads to sensuality but not for the reasons that Jewett adduces, rather, as I claim throughout this essay, because the law requires sexuality and all of its fruits!

Jewett engages in some of the most flagrant anachronizing I have seen in modern scholarship when he writes, "Just as the law offers man life, security and a chance to reduce God to man's control, so the sexual objects calling forth πορνεία, ἀκαθαρσία, and ἀσέλγεια offer man a moment of intense life, psychological security and a way to reduce the sexual partner to submission" (ibid., p. 104), and this is allegedly why Paul analogizes the law to sex as the flesh. Jewett has gotten so involved in his anti-Jewish and nonsensical (but typical) understanding of the Law that he forgets that sex has something to do with physical flesh, just as circumcision does. This is simply bad exegesis and bad logic. By this reasoning one could come to the conclusion that Christian faith also belongs to the realm of the flesh, since it also offers life! I submit that flesh is flesh—human flesh. As such it can be involved in the performance of commandments or it can be involved in sexuality; indeed, among the commandments, the command to have sex is the most fleshy of all. All the commandments belong to the realm of the flesh, and as such, for Paul share an inferior position. Paul has argued strenuously in the first four chapters of *Galatians* for liberation from the law because it is fleshy; he now says, in effect, that it would be most ironic, if not tragic, were this liberation to be misunderstood as an opportunity for the very flesh that it was meant to defeat. The possibility for this misunderstanding is palpable, and everything Paul says in this passage is directed against it. The whole point, Paul says, was to enter the Spirit, and therefore, since the flesh and the spirit are entirely opposed to each other in desire and in works, to understand Christian freedom from the law of the flesh as permission for the flesh would be a grievous and tragic misreading indeed, escaping a pit only to plummet into a pitfall. All the other usages of flesh in Paul are derivations from this primary meaning through the chains of association and analogy that I discuss throughout the book of which this will eventually be a chapter.

36. I think Dunn is, therefore, for once absolutely wrong when he writes, "The ἐν ᾧ obviously refers to the law (as most recognize), not to the 'old man,' or the 'being in the flesh' just described." According to my interpretation, these are precisely the same thing!
37. See also Paula Fredriksen, "Judaism, the Circumcision of Gentiles, and Apocalyptic Hope: Another Look at Galatians 1 and 2," *Journal of Theological Studies* 42.2 (October 1991):532–564, 533, note 4.

33

Athanasius of Alexandria and the Ascetic Movement of His Time

Charles Kannengiesser

Athanasius of Alexandria, the most famous church leader in the Roman empire of the fourth century CE, is also the first authority in the Christian church who recognized the importance of monasticism for the Christian way of life.[1] In a public statement issued by the Alexandria clergy only eight years after the event, we learn that Athanasius was elected the bishop of Alexandria through a local procedure that included public acclamation. He was acclaimed, says the report, "as one of the ascetics."[2] This personal involvement of the new Alexandrian bishop in the ascetic movement was to become one of the decisive factors of his forty-five-year-long tenure of the episcopal office. From 328 to 373, Athanasius and the Egyptian ascetics in their mutual admiration for each other would change the Christian way of life. They would learn together how to reach into the spiritual roots of ancient Egypt, and to retrieve that heritage for the cosmopolitan world of the empire. It is not easy to retrace the interactions between the flourishing monastic movement along the Nile Valley during the first decades of the fourth century and the sophisticated administration of the Alexandrian bishop at the time that Athanasius entered upon his episcopal career, mainly because the sources of information in the Egyptian deserts remain silent.[3] But there is no doubt that Athanasius and the monks found themselves with a strong basis for collaboration. The young bishop was imbued with a renewed vision of the church which would push him into a new reading of sacred scripture, but also into a dangerous face-to-face showdown with the emperor. On their side the monks were tenacious in their determination to question church and empire alike, and to fight the evil in themselves day by day. The down-to-earth tenacity of monastic prayer, combined with the pastoral strategy of the educated Alexandrian, resulted in a fusion of heterogeneous cultures, out of which the powerful leader of Egyptian Christianity would become a founding figure of Christian spirituality.

To understand the reciprocity between Athanasius and the ascetic movement of his time, first it seems appropriate to explore the main aspects of Athanasius's personality with regard to his relationship with contemporary asceticism. How did he conceive his own ministry in the ascetic context of his church? How did he meet the ascetics of the deserts who seemed to challenge his authority in turning their backs on the big city? What did he contribute to their spiritual well-being amid the discomfort of voluntary privations? And how did they respond to his episcopal patronage?

As a first step, a biographical track leads here into the decisive challenges linked with Athanasius's involvement in the ascetic movement of his time. In a second stage, the historic results of this involvement need to be evaluated. Beyond Athanasius himself and the Egyptian solitaries, now reduced to dust in the shrines of Christian antiquity, what impact, if any, should one attribute to their meeting? Has the course of Western mysticism been changed because a young Alexandrian, (supposedly *too* young to become a bishop in 328),[4] chose those solitaries as his privileged audience, when he voiced his own spiritual message to the whole Christian Church?

Athanasius among the Ascetics

The questions debated among historians about the episcopal career of Athanasius are many, and they are intricate enough to lead contemporary research to numerous dead ends. The answer to one of these questions has so far eluded us: Why was Athanasius chosen to become the successor of the venerated old pontiff Alexander after the latter had passed away on 17 April 328? His death might not have taken his community by surprise, but the tensions rose quickly in the small world of the Alexandrian presbyterion, the group of priests who assisted the local bishop and who were in charge of providing his replacement. In the turbulent city of Alexandria serene coordination was never easy, a spark easily igniting mob violence. The Christian quarters of the city shared the general mood of the populous metropolis, and Alexander's legacy was far from being a peaceful one.[5]

A severe schism initiated by bishop Melitius of Scytopolis had afflicted the Alexandrian church since the last imperial persecution, which lasted from 303 to 312. Alexander had found himself confronted with it when he entered into office, and he died without any reconciliation in view. Clerical rancor is legendarily tenacious. In addition, Alexander took with him to his grave the responsibility for having created an impossible situation among the intellectual elite of his diocese. A middle-of-the-road intellectual, slow in decision making and preserved from excessive imagination, he had become unwillingly involved in the worst nightmare a pastor could fear: a fatal heresy—namely, questioning of the very foundations of the faith—that destroyed the peace of mind and the physical unity of the church body more destructively than could any schism. For over a decade the Alexandrian pontiff had tried to solve the problem created by Arius, but without success. First, his patience, mixed with a measure of respect for a contemporary probably a little older than he was, hoped to attain a mutual understanding. Then, a delaying tactic of conciliabules and public debates, instead of harmonizing the excited schools of thought among his urban congregation, pushed Alexander into the open, where the battle become public. He convoked a synod, which assembled about a hundred delegates from all the communities under his jurisdiction, essentially subordinate bishops and priests, with assistant deacons and some lay observers. The date remains uncertain, but it was probably around 318. Arius and a small group of bishops and priests who kept their allegiance to him were solemnly excluded from church communion. To the puzzlement of modern historians, the group was also very quickly banished from Alexandria, which underlines the fact that so little is known about the social and political status of the episcopal ruler in the church of Alexandria at the beginning of the fourth century.

Arius and his friends found refuge and protection among the envious competitors of Alexander, who occupied episcopal sees along the oriental coast of the Mediterranean, northward as far as Nicomedia, near the Bosphorus in the province of Bithynia. There was to be found the center of imperial powers in the eastern half of the gigantic empire. There, the high-ranking staff of the Roman army, joined with influential bureaucrats and with clerical dignitaries of various religious backgrounds, jostled to attract the attention of the almighty emperor. In 318, Licinius exercised this power. The pragmatic Licinius had agreed to an edict in Milan four years earlier, in accordance with his colleague in the West, Constantine. The western ruler enhanced his political power in playing the card of collaborating with Christian bishops in order to secure social stability in the cities of the vast territories under his control. The eastern Augustus, as those military dictators were called, kept his options free for another sort of gamble. He trusted more traditional values, favored economic prosperity, and disliked the trouble-making of Christian proselytism. Upset by the constant disputes that erupted among church leaders, he finally forbad their tumultuous gatherings. No more synods, no more noisy quarrels! He miscalculated the ambitious enterprise of Constantine, who was more than happy to don the robes of a political savior. Constantine invaded his territories, forced Licinius into battle, and killed him near Chrysopolis, in the vicinity of the Bosphorus, in September 324. Hence, a triumphant westerner, who did not speak Greek, sole ruler over East and West, was the self-appointed patron of Christianity in the empire. The competition among Greek-speaking churches intensified now that a generous distribution of imperial funds (from our remove, smacking of superstition in its zealous extravagance) added a new incentive to their aggressive call for public recognition. Constantine had the same reaction as his former rival. He disliked the noisy tensions developed between the main sees of the eastern empire because of Arius's excommunication. Despite the fact that he knew nothing about the whole controversy, Constantine believed that the Christian Godhead owed him a prompt return to peace and concord in the churches that he patronized.

Bishop Alexander discovered that his verdict was slowly prevailing among oriental bishops: a synod held during the winter of 324 in the city of Antioch ratified his condemnation of Arius. However, among the still recalcitrant colleagues was the learned Eusebius of Caesarea, whose reputation as a historian of early Christianity enjoyed universal acclaim. Alexander learned that he was most definitely embroiled in imperial politics when he heard that Constantine had ordered a general assembly of the episcopate belonging to his new eastern territories, in Ancyra, in the center of modern Turkey. In fact, the imperial synod gathered in the milder climate of the summer residence of his imperial majesty, near Nicomedia, in a small town called Nicaea. The awesome splendor of the event, celebrated by Eusebius of Caesarea in an addition to his *Church History,* overwhelmed the Christian clerics. Alexander, in particular, felt unable to enforce in his own church the full measure of the recommendations of the synodal fathers, to whose debate the emperor had given a pompous approval before inviting the whole party to a banquet. Alexander died without having reconciled the schismatic Melitians, nor could he heal the wounds caused by the exclusion of Arius from Communion. In their souls and minds, many Alexandrian Christians failed to understand the doctrinal issues at stake, and therefore disapproved the harsh treatment imposed on their fellow Christians in the Arian conviction.

A heavy burden would be imposed on any candidate who would replace Alexander. The burden could only feel heavier on the shoulders of a man who had not yet reached the canonical age of thirty when he was consecrated. Had this young assistant and secretary of Alexander been his proclaimed choice? Did a countermaneuver of the Melitians precipitate the events leading to Athanasius's election? Historians engage in endless speculation about these circumstances, as they do about many other dramatic turns in the career of the newly elected bishop.

Having briefly evoked the political and religious background against which the new head of Egyptian Christianity would exercise his hierarchical authority, we can plunge into the twilight of history by attending carefully to the direct witness of Athanasius's first steps as a public figure. Those steps lead him straight to the desert and linked him irrevocably with what Peter Brown called imaginatively the greatest youth movement of late antiquity.[6]

A historical survey is essential to any adequate evaluation of Athanasius's personal engagement into the ascetic world of his contemporaries, because his very first journeys, after his election was officially made public on 8 June 328, were to the ascetics. These contacts with the ascetics, chronicled in an index of his Festal Letters after his death in 373, can be subject to a surprising variety of interpretations by historians.

After only a few weeks in office, Athanasius started planning a first circular letter that he would address to all parishes in Alexandria, Egypt, and Libya placed under his ruling. The occasion was the traditional announcement of dates of Easter and Pentecost, complemented by a stern reminder about the days of fasting, preliminary to that Feast of Feasts, and occasionally, by some other advice prompted by circumstances. Alexander and earlier Alexandrian "popes" had also written such Festal Letters. The newly elected Athanasius would comply with that tradition. It is little less than a miracle that we possess today his very first written statement as a bishop, the long Festal Letter for Easter, 329, which happened to be celebrated that year on 6 April. Due to distances and slow distribution, the text needed to be ready several months in advance.[7]

I am not suggesting here that it is only a text-bound method that gives us the best access to a person who lives in fourth-century Alexandria, or that no other method could reconstruct the living conditions or detect the mind pattern of such a person. But I insist that the authentic words used by someone in late antiquity are at least as important for interpretation, as the hypothetical constructs of a contemporary historian. We are fortunate to possess the full text, or at least substantial citations, of almost all of the Festal Letters, written by Athanasius during the forty-five years of his episcopal ministry. A reading of the whole collection helps one to appreciate the first of these letters in its own right and to note the youthful fervour of its lyrical piety:

> My beloved, the present moment invites us to celebrate. For the sun of justice is risen for us, by unspoiled beams marking for us the day of the Feast; a feast in which we ought to be radiant by our obedience to God's will, if we do not want to miss the day, and with it the joy of the feast.

These introductory words echo the famous prayer to the raising sun of Amenophis IV, the mystical pharaoh in the seventeenth dynasty of ancient Egypt, not long before a certain Moses crossed the Red Sea with divine assistance. More precisely, they resound with the allegorical mysticism introduced into biblical commentaries by the great Origen, a Christian catechist of Alexandria and a true genius, who died in exile some forty years before Athanasius was born. Athanasius's letter for Easter, 329, is full of Origen's idealistic poetry, addressed to the very depths of the soul, and each biblical symbol redoubling the fervor of the expression. What the villagers and their parish priests in the Coptic hinterland of the Nile Valley could assimilate of such rhetorical artistry remains beyond our speculation, but they certainly understood with which bread their new pontiff had decided to nourish them. The list of recommended virtues was insistent: "Humility, lack of pride, sweetness, knowledge of the true God." The joy expressed in that letter, as well as in the later ones, was characteristic of the Easter celebration for which these letters were conceived. What is striking is the complete lack of any allusion to the difficulties faced by the Alexandrian church community as much as is the candid expression of enthusiastic piety that pervades the first of these Festal Letters.

In the immediate aftermath of Athanasius's death, on 2 May 373, a chancellor of his administration wrote an index to the Festal Letters of the deceased pontiff, with precise indications of the dates and the circumstances in which the letters had been written or distributed. Thus we learn that, in 330, Athanasius undertook a pastoral visitation of the Thebaid. The area of that name was not limited to the surroundings of ancient Thebes, south of modern Cairo, but included also the desert on both sides of the Nile Valley, a 150-mile-wide stretch of desolate stony plains toward east and west in which hermits, old and young, were experiencing a living death for the sake of their salvation. Athanasius could not repeat the trip the year after, because, as the index tells us, "he had gone to the court; there he met the great king Constantine, who had summoned him, because some enemies had denounced him, for having been introduced too young."[8] Having already spent the spring of 331 on that obligatory journey, the bishop, recovering from "great sickness," could not leave his town until 332, where "he visited the Pentapolis and sojourned in the Oasis of Ammon."[9] Again, the locations reveal the purpose of Athanasius's trip, which was to share the monastic adventure of the most severely sequested inhabitants of those remote places. In the Pentapolis, or modern Cynenaica, five ancient cities according to the name of the region, with Christian communities traditionally placed under the authority of the Alexandrian bishops, had a special value in Athanasius's eye. Again, the months he spent in covering distances of over 600 miles, through deserted areas as far as the western border of Libya and the deep Sahara to the Oasis of Ammon, were mainly dedicated to monastic groups and hermits. Two years later, in 334, "he visited the Low Country," which means the deserted areas surrounding the delta of the Nile.[10]

These onerous expeditions of Athanasius's first years in office are the most memorable events chronicled by the index. With the exception of his summons to appear at Constantine's court, in 331, they were his only absences from Alexandria, which itself required his vigilant presence. Why such a pastoral strategy? Was he motivated solely by the polemical context of his first years of office as bishop? It has been suggested that he went to the Pentapolis, because the strongest supporters of Arius (himself a Libyan by birth) came from there. It has also been suggested that he tried to rally the dispersed monks under his banner, in opposition to the schismatic Melitians, who seemed to be favored by many of them on account of common language and culture. One critic even went so far as to imagine Athanasius flying from Alexandria out of fear of the violent reactions after the irregularities which had tarnished his election; the journey was an attempt to legitimate his title among the solitaries, and to call on them to fight on his side against the schismatics and heretics who represented for him a permanent menace. All these interpretations, it seems to me, may be justified in the light of the problematic legacy taken over by Athanasius from his predecessor—but only to a certain point. The young bishop's own writings dating from those years, oppose a wall of silent prayer and intense spirituality to any hypothetical constructs which would focus exclusively on the world of ecclesiastical politics.

The treatise *On the Incarnation*[11] reveals the inner maturity and the real core of Athanasius's concerns, reflecting his dedication to the ascetic experiment being pursued in the deserts of his vast diocese. The essay may be assumed to have been written during the years preceding his first exile to the West (335–337). In the essay the bishop records his own inner contemplation during his visits to the monastic settlements of Egypt and Libya immediately preceding its composition. The doctrinal focus of *On the Incarnation of the Divine Logos* is not only the Christian belief in Jesus as God incarnate, but even more so, the experience of a vital renewal of the ordinary believer made possible by that divine Incarnation. The fight against evil, as exemplified by the suffering and the death of Jesus, is now shared by all believers. The believers' transformed being, through the salvation secured by Jesus, reintegrates them into the full possession of their pristine likeness with the divine Logos. In the mundane realities of daily life it is this common faith, not the ecstatic vision of an intellectual élite as conceived by Origen, that is at work in the renewal of the individual Christian believer.

Athanasius's lifelong teaching will stress divine salvation, realized in the day-to-day endeavor of ordinary Christians, eager to embody in their own lives their likeness to the Logos, which is the perfect "Image" of God. One can easily identify this theme throughout Athanasius's writings. For a correct appreciation of that Athanasian doctrine par excellence, one should not overlook the monastic overtones, which keep it linked with the author's own spiritual maturing in the desert. If the bishop's encounters with Pachomian monks were occasions for reciprocal enrichment, as related in the anecdotes of the *Lives* of Pachomius,[12] it can only be due to deep personal affinities and to a common understanding of adult faith. In any case, the Festal Letters of 333–334 and *On the Incarnation* are a clear testimony of a pastor's determination not to be distracted by bureaucracy and church politics, but on the contrary, to be dedicated to a creative appropriation of mystical values.

On his return from two years in banishment at Trier, the Alexandrian bishop would write the longest of all his Festal Letters. Except for an isolated mention of the heretic Arians in the final section, Festal Letter X of 337 is pervaded by Athanasius's contemplative fervor glorifying the suffering savior, and by his own joy of being reunited with his people.[13] Back home, the bishop undertook the task of responding to one of the most challenging requests of his monastic friends. He explained to them what it meant for him to oppose the doctrine of Arius, which had been formally condemned at the imperial synod of Nicaea in 325. He did it in his own terms, not with the fireworks of polemical rhetoric, but with a pastoral pedagogy which tirelessly stressed how to interpret scripture against the rationalistic claims of the Arians. Most important, we are morally certain that the work—for all times considered Athanasius's masterpiece—was addressed first of all to the monks. The same would be true of most of his later writings.

After the letter-essay entitled *On the Death of Arius,* Athanasius would use the years of his third exile, those five years (356–361) that he spent in hiding among the solitaries and the communities of the desert, composing one work after another at the demand of his monastic friends. These works include the letter *On His Flight,* the set of doctrinal letters *On the Divinity of the Spirit,* and the world-famous *Life of Antony.* Even when writing for lay people, as in his *Letter to Marcellinus on the Psalms,*[14] he taught the characteristic virtues of Egyptian monasticism: silent prayer and patience, a relaxed and stable self-confidence in faithful dedication, a constant discernment of spirits. When he calmed a young monk's concern because of nocturnal pollution, his advice was given in the tone characteristic of the spiritual guide of the desert.

The literary career of Athanasius, improvised as it was in responding to pastoral demands, is his most concrete link with the ascetic movement of his time. Beyond the monastic population of several thousand men in the regions under his jurisdiction, he reached out, through the *Life of Antony,* to communities of monks in the West, impossible to locate more precisely.[15] Already his exiles, first in Trier (335–337), then in Rome (339–346), had offered him the possibility to advertise the new Christian way of life inaugurated by Antony, Pachomius, and their numerous disciples. His enthusiastic descriptions provided a durable frame for western imitators. Even in 385, the rhetor Augustine, at the height of the moral crisis of his Christian conversion, heard with wonder from an eyewitness how monasticism attracted young men in the area of Trier. Additional reports, directly inspired by the *Life of Antony,* would complement Augustine's own discovery of the letters of the apostle Paul, at that crucial moment of his quest for a truly spiritual self-identification. This was so much the case that, after having been baptized and urged to accept clerical status in his African homeland, he claimed to be called by God to the monastic experiment, and then asked the bishop of Hippo for a leave of absence—a monastic retreat.

It is no surprise to hear modern experts, stating that the *Life of Antony,* translated a first time into Latin before or just after Athanasius's death, became, after the Christian Bible, the first Christian bestseller in antiquity. An old Syrian version appeared soon after, others followed. The pattern of that very first biography of a Christian saint became a paradigm for Christian hagiography for the centuries to come. With the treatise *On the Incarnation,* it is still in print today. It shall serve as my starting point for some conclusions about the ascetical legacy of Athanasius.

The Ascetical Legacy of Athanasius

My short biographical outline offered only a few glimpses into the relationship between Athanasius and the ascetics of his time in the desert areas of Egypt. Other forms of asceticism were practiced in the Christian neighborhoods surrounding the urban residence of the bishop. The tradition of the sanctification by ritual blessings of girls and women in the church communities of the fourth century was already well established. This made attacks against virgins especially odious in the violent days of street mobs. Widows enjoyed an apostolic prestige in the community because they were mentioned in some writings of the New Testament. Educated laypeople could devote part of their time to charitable activities and observe a discipline of daily readings in the Bible, or of prayers at regular hours. The *Letter to Marcellinus,* possibly addressed to a layman, would suggest such a form of ascetic devotion. Sickness, as Athanasius suggested to Marcellinus and elsewhere in his Festal Letters, must have played an important role in the lives of ascetically inclined people, Christian or not. But the documents at our disposal rarely speak of such personal trials.

Spiritual resistance

The personal strength of Athanasius has always been noted as a distinctive mark of his character. Elevated on a pedestal by hagiographers or demonized by less pious critics, the bishop of Alexandria even today creates an embarrassment and a scandal, where he does not inspire utter rejection and loud disapproval. Such is the projected image of that regrettable Athanasius. One admits that he was very young when entering into office; his lack of experience could explain the allegedly uncompromising way in which he started to apply the recommendations of the imperial synod of 325 in his diocese. By force, when not by persuasion, he tried to reintegrate schismatic clerics into the ranks of his subordinate clergy. Complaints about the matter are indisputable in Melitian sources. The negative construct of the disapproving critics claims further that Athanasius felt himself from the day of his consecration invincible in the position of power. Otherwise how could one explain why he did not comply with the new mood in the imperial administration, precisely from 328 on, which favored a compromise, or even a formal reconciliation between

Arius and his hierarchical superior. The whole Arian question would have stopped to poison the political atmosphere in the eastern provinces of the empire. Much more astute and more realistic were the senior bishops of the orient, like Eusebius of Nicomedia, a born politician and a man close to the imperial court, or Eusebius of Caesera, who had his own vision of a Christian empire. These experienced leaders, with all the less aggressive bishops whom they rallied, did not abandon any of their creedal convictions when they adjusted to the Constantinian patronage. In Arius's protest against Bishop Alexander's innovative preaching, around 318 or earlier, they had recognized a familiar theological pattern, which they could accommodate to their own Origenist tradition. Even if they disapproved some extreme Arian phrases, which seemed to negate entirely the divinity of Jesus, they found it reasonable to support the condemned priest, to plead in favor of his old age, and to ask for his readmission into the communion of the Alexandrian church. So much for the political bias in the current perception of Athanasius.

To a coalition of imperial pressure and episcopal interference, Athanasius opposed a wall of silent prayer. He had received the mandate from his predecessor, who was venerated by him like a father, to remain true forever to the solemn decision taken by the Alexandrian synod of 318 or 320 (which had condemned Arius and his local advisers) and to apply the decrees of Nicaea (invested not only with the sacred authority of the emperor, but also the unanimous approval of over three hundred synodal fathers). His determination was not his own choice; it was the duty imposed on him by the universal church. There was no individual decision required of him. The tragic disruption of concord and unity inside his own faith community was a bad memory of his teens. He did not feel trapped in it by his own Christian education, nor less by his conversion to Christianity. History accelerated in such a spectacular way, when he was in his twenties, that the horizons of the church community opened into unexpected directions. For the younger generation, the dispute about Arius belonged to a past, reduced to obsolete inner tensions inside the clerical confinement of the volatile Alexandrian community. For Athanasius that dispute was not what the new people in the church were waiting for. He shared their needs by instinct, being one of them himself, and he only tried to respond to them by investing himself in their common future. They needed what martyrdom and persecutions no longer provided, the times having apparently reconciled imperial power and church life. They needed new spiritual challenges, and for their new thinking they also needed a renovated synthesis of their traditional beliefs.

We are reaching here a conclusion, which could have been stated directly out of the facts documented for us by history: the young bishop Athanasius was more attracted by the mystical experiment of the Egyptian hermits than by the new alliances offered to church politicians at the court of Constantine. His earlier writings overflow with biblical and pastoral spirituality to the point of producing a new theological synthesis, enriched by that spirituality. His essay *On the Incarnation* results from a shift of paradigm, initiated by Alexander, but decisively focused by Athanasius. Out of this paradigm shift the Christian self-understanding no longer depended on the philosophical anthropology familiar to Origen, and started affirming itself on the basis of its own spiritual roots—the Bible and the actual practice of the church community.

One of the peculiarities of the treatise *On the Incarnation* is the complete silence observed in it by the author about the crisis developing in Alexandria from circa 318 on around the controversial figure of Arius. Therefore the learned Benedictine Bernard de Montfaucon who published in 1698 the first edition of Athanasius's *Opera omnia* in Greek and Latin, decided uncritically that the treatise must have been written by Athanasius some time before the outbreak of the Arian crisis. His opinion became standard, and it is still repeated in today's handbooks. Henry Newman in the nineteenth century as well as more recent critics noted that *On the Incarnation* was linked with another apologetic essay entitled *Against the Heathen.* As the author had exploited in the latter some materials found in his own schoolbooks, modern interpreters found it reasonable to understand the double work as a scholastic exercise, dating from Athanasius's years of training, sponsored by Bishop Alexander. Unfortunately, that theory neglected the explicit mention, in the index of the Festal Letters, of Athanasius being "too young," which means at least not thirty years old, when elected as Alexander's replacement. Thus, he was not born before early June of 298; if born as early as 299, he was nineteen years old in 318, when the heat of the controversy had become explosive in Alexandria. Other scholars suggested that *On the Incarnation* was composed in 334–335, or near that date, when the still young bishop was in the process of losing his see under stormy pressure from his opponents. That revised chronology has now circulated among the experts for a whole century, but restricted to erudite footnotes. The reevaluation of the treatise, as dating from 334–335, needs still to be thought out. It would engage an exercise of mapping out the doctrinal strategy of the new pastor after his first six or seven years in office. That later dating would reveal the depth of Athanasius's theological intuition, capable of radically contradicting the Arian claim. Against the notion of a Logos, inferior to God and not essentially God himself because of his humble conduct as a man in the gospel narratives, *On the Incarnation* celebrates the incarnation of the divine Logos as the central mystery of Christian faith. Sterile polemics are replaced by a warm and nourishing message of faith, vibrant in its perception of what the faithful experience of common believers really means in the light of the divine incarnation. Thus, the Arian dispute is ignored in that essay as a dispute of the past, or as a quarrel among clerics eager to gain some political status. The author keeps it behind the silent wall of his prayer and he refuses to get embroiled into it.

Only in line with such a strategy can one give a consistent account, it seems to me, of another silence, kept by the same author in regard to Arius. When the monks insisted, after his return from the first exile in 337, that he should explain to them what anti-Arianism actually implied, he continued the kind of literary initiative we see not only in *On the Incarnation,* but also in *Oration against the Arians,* a compact written after two or three different attempts. This letter was handed down to us as Orations I and II, in which once again he focuses passionately on the central values of the Christian doctrine on God, keeping polemics at a secondary level as a backdrop for his rhetorics. But the most intriguing omission of the "polemicist-by-order" of the monks in that famous double *Oration against the Arians,* is that in the body of the work he does not make any use of a whole set of quotations from a pamphlet of Arius entitled *Thalia,* carefully quoted in the introduction. The treatise has been transmitted with those Arian quotations as a front piece ostensibly to be refuted in the ensuing arguments, but they do not reappear in the work itself. The existence of such a *Thalia* is acknowledged. Arian propaganda phrases are discussed in it, but the extracts from Arius's pamphlet themselves quoted in the introduction are totally ignored. In other words, the collection of extracts must have been handed over to the bishop when he had already composed his bulky essay, and he added his introduction to the work *post factum.*

If the present observation is correct, it adds a possibility for new insights into the personal lack of interest shown by Athanasius, at least until 339 or 340, for the past dispute with Arius. Indeed, the students of his masterwork *Oration against the Arians* have always identified its doctrinal substance as an intense and repeated effort to interpret scripture in an anti-Arian way, rather than a proper discussion of Arius's risky theory. The wall of silence, opposed here to divisive disputation, takes on the not-so-silent form of a pastoral teaching about how to read scripture in the context of the dispute.[16]

A final observation about polemics in words and deeds: the author of the double treatise *Oration against the Arians* does not hide his reluctance to respond at length to Arian arguments in such an extensive writing. The same reluctance is revealed in the many unexpected turns imposed on his career. For three full decades of his episcopacy, the pastoral project that he tried to build up in his local church would be disrupted again and again by political actions engaged against him, actions always due to the same powerful authorities who had initially opposed the anti-Arian Creed of Nicaea and then called for an invalidation of Athanasius's election. It is arguable that the victimized bishop did not wish for those setbacks, nor did he imprudently provoke them. However it is to be explained, he survived his enemies; and it was not until the last decade of his long tenure that he was on the side of the winners. Only misguided and misleading historiography in recent times could position him as a ruthless "pharaoh," hungry for power, and unfair to his opponents. It needs some coldblooded objectivity for a balanced evaluation of his endurance in surmounting one trial after another from 333 to 363. The Athanasius whom we know through his own writings deserves to be reevaluated as a man of great character. His spiritual resistance against abusive political power perdured over a lifetime. It exemplified for the first time in the Christian traditions and at the highest ecclesial level, what would become a basic feature of many spiritual revivals: the ascetic affirmation of spiritual freedom, inside the church itself, against alienating compromises of that church with political power. Already, the ascetic movement all over Egypt, and soon over other parts of the empire, opposed its silent protest against too well-established forms of urban Christianity. Athanasius sided with that movement in his fight for the truth and the continuity of his own church tradition.

Institution and charisma

Never has the problematic antimony of institution and charisma been applied with more success than in the case of Athanasius's relationship with the ascetics of his time. It is often asserted that the Alexandrian bishop aimed at a "domestication of charismatic wisdom" in tightening his hierarchial relationship with the monastic circles. Nothing seems to be more true, if one understands it as a common cause that the monks could share with their bishop. As in the political arena, to imagine an aggressive and intolerant Athanasius lording over the ascetics strains the facts. The fact is that after his earliest pastoral trips to remote desert areas, and after only a few years of administration in Alexandria, the young bishop arrived at Tyre, where he had been convoked by a hostile synod in 335, with an imposing escort of monks, many of them being former Melitians who had reconciled with the Catholic church. The *Lives* of Pachomius did not doubt the fervor with which the bishop was welcomed in the monasteries of the Koinonia. It is more consistent with our historical information to project the imagined Athanasius as "one of the ascetics," recognized as such by the latter, not a monk himself, but very close to the monastic way of life. An innate familiarity with ascetic motives and practices allowed the bishop to identify with the solitaries, and those men and women of the desert would have trusted their leader from the great city, as they would never have trusted the remote Alexander, his predecessor. A lively interaction between the ecclesiastical hierarchy and the wild world of the hermits remains one of the striking phenomena of the period: because of his closeness to the monks, Athanasius transformed episcopacy itself, first in Egyptian Christianity and later on in the universal church.

When he escaped to the West as a political refugee, in 339, the Alexandrian pope delegated his powers of jurisdiction to Serapion of Thumis, an older friend for whom he had much admiration, who had served for a long time as the superior of a monastery before being appointed bishop in a city of the Delta. We can still read a letter that the exiled bishop sent to Serapion from Rome, urging him to introduce into Egypt the forty days of Lent as observed in the West. It became a regular option for Athanasius in the course of his episcopate to choose monks for vacant or newly created sees. His *Letter to Rufinianum* illustrates, not without some dry humor, the resistance he met occasionally on the side of unwilling candidates. But the paradigm was fixed. After the ideals of Pachomian monasticism emigrated to the West, a century later, it would not take much time before a monk would be elected bishop of Rome. The Athanasian legacy to the ascetic movement of the fourth century included more than a disciplinary administration of charisma; it created for that movement a historic chance to transform the face of the church.

The *Life of Antony* illustrates what the ascetic movement received from Athanasius on the cultural level. Through that biography, which was not only the first Christian biography ever written in the style of biographies in antiquity, but which became a source of inspiration for the Christian ascetic movement as a whole, Christian asceticism received its earliest *lettres de noblesse,* its cultural authentication. The work is of such an intriguing novelty that it continues to produce divisions among its interpreters. A recent attempt to deny its Athanasian origin has failed to convince.[17]

The historical Antony would have been an object of pure speculation, like the historical Jesus, had he not written a few letters, miraculously preserved on a papyrus of the seventh century. Samuel Rubenson has analyzed the similarities and the differences between the *Vita* and the Letters. His conclusions favor a possible recognition of the historic author of the Letters in the idealized saint presented by the *Vita*. At least the latter seems respectful of Antony's ascetical habits. Out of monastic sources, channelled through an oral tradition, the *Vita* collected enough extravagant anecdotes about poor Antony fighting with evil powers to impress the Christian memory of centuries to come. It has also been argued that there is a fundamental agreement between what Antony has to say in the *Vita* and the famous *Sayings of the Desert Fathers,* which are a collection of "systematic short dialogues, parables or anecdotes connected with the early monastic movement, primarily in lower Egypt." In claiming that Antony was a hero of the anti-Arian form of orthodoxy, which he himself embodied, Athanasius did not alienate the hermit from his Coptic background. In stressing Antony's respectful devotion to the Alexandrian see, the occupant of that see put the whole ascetic movement into the perspective that was his own. It was his way of expressing gratitude to and solidarity with the monks with his deepest trust, after he had been protected and saved by them during the dangerous years of his third exile (356–363).

NOTES

1. On Athanasius, see recent encyclopedic presentations by G. C. Stead, *Encyclopedia of the Early Church* (Cambridge, 1992), 1:93–95; and C. Kannengiesser, *Encyclopedia of Early Christianity* (New York, 1990), pp. 110–112.
2. *Apologia secunda* 5, H. G. Opitz, ed., *Athanasius Werke II* (Berlin, 1934), 1:92.
3. D. J. Chitty, *The Desert A City: An Introduction to the Study of Egyptian and Palestinian Monasticism under the Christian Empire* (Crestwood, New York: St. Vladimir's Seminary Press, 1966); C. W. Griggs, *Early Egyptian Christianity from its Origins to 451 C.E.* (Leiden: Brill, 1990); D. Burton-Christie, *The Word in the Desert: Scripture and the Quest for Holiness in Early Christian Monasticism* (New York and Oxford: Oxford University Press, 1993).
4. According to the *Syriac Index of Athanasius' Festal Letters,* Sources chrétiennes 317 (Paris, 1985), pp. 228–229.
5. For the polemical context of Athanasius's episcopacy, see R.P.C. Hanson, *The Search for the Christian Doctrine of God: The Arian Controversy, 318–381* (Edinburgh: T.&.T. Clark, 1988).
6. P. Brown, *The Body and Society: Men, Women and Sexual Renunciation in Early Christianity* (New York: Columbia University Press, 1988).
7. C. Kannengiesser, "The Homilectic Festal Letters of Athanasius," in D. G. Hunter, ed., *Preaching in the Patristic Age: Studies in Honour of Walter J. Burghardt, S.J.* (New York: Paulist Press, 1989), pp. 73–100; C. Kannengiesser, *Arius and Athanasius: Two Alexandrian Theologians* (Hampshire: Variorum, 1991), p. xv.
8. See above, note 4.
9. Sources chrétiennes 317 (Paris, 1985), pp. 230–231.

10. Ibid.
11. In *St. Athanasius: Select Works and Letters,* ed. A. Robertson, Nicene and Post-Nicene Fathers, 2d series (Grand Rapids: Eerdmans, 1971).
12. A. Veilleux, trans., *Pachomian Koinonia: The Lives, Rules, and Other Writings of Saint Pachamius and His Disciples,* 3 vols. (Kalamazoo: Cistereian Publications Inc., 1981–1982).
13. R. Lorenz, *Der zehnte Osterbrief des Athanasius von Alexandrien* (Berlin and New York, 1986).
14. P. Bright, trans., "Athanasius of Alexandria: On the Interpretation of Psalms," in C. Kannengiesser, ed., *Early Christian Spirituality,* Sources of Early Christian Thought (Philadelphia: Fortress Press), pp. 56–77.
15. R. T. Meyer, trans., *St. Athanasius: The Life of Saint Antony,* Ancient Christian Writers 10 (New York: Newman Press, 1950).
16. More on the treatise *Against the Arians* in my Oxford paper of 1979: "Athanasius of Alexandria. Three Orations against the Arians. A Reappraisal," Studia Patristica 9 (Oxford, 1982); and in *Athanase d'Alexandrie évêque et écrivain* (Paris: Beauchesne, 1983).
17. R. Draguet, *La vie primitive de S. Antoine conservée en syriaque,* Corpus scriptorum christianorum orientalium 417–418 (Louvain, 1980). Denying the authenticity of the *Vita* as known has been opposed by the unanimous verdict of the experts: G. Couilleau in *Bulletin de spiritualité monastique* 2 (1984):347–348; A. Louth in *Journal of Theological Studies,* n.s. 39 (1988):504–509; L. Abramowski in *Mélanges Antoine Guillaumont* (Geneve: P. Cramer, 1988), pp. 47–56; R. Lorenz in *Zeitschrift für Kirchengeschichte* 100 (1989):77–84; and S. Rubenson in the present volume.

34

The Politics of Piety

Response to the Three Preceding Papers

Dianne M. Bazell

However enthusiastically some of us enter into comparative enterprises, we cannot help but find such projects daunting on at least two levels. On the theoretical plane, one hopes to avoid being fooled by apparent similarities into making inappropriate associations and, as a result, imposing inappropriate hermeneutical categories onto the material at hand.[1] On the practical side of things, comparative enterprises often necessitate discussion among participants of widely diverse areas of expertise, provoking either no response at all, or discussions that may on occasion appear to follow very different vectors. These considerations in mind, I will nevertheless endeavor to address, and to put into a larger and coherent framework, some of the issues raised by the previous speakers, who themselves come from such disparate fields, each removed from mine.

A good deal of attention in these comparative endeavors is given over to determining how to circumscribe the topic and how to determine what exactly falls under that rubric. And most discussions of asceticism focus on the significance that it has for the practitioner, on his or her intentions and motivations, and on the resulting success or failure. This point of view is underlined by the etymological roots of the term that has come to identify the topic: asceticism is *askēsis,* training; a discipline or set of disciplines often (but not always) involving one's body, and generally doing without things or pleasures otherwise permitted, or engaging in strenuousness not otherwise obligatory.[2] These hardships are undertaken with the intention of achieving something—personal strengthening through less dependence on bodily comfort; ritual purity; atonement; wisdom; salvation; and mystical vision of, or union with, God, however variously construed.

Thus, considerations of ascetic exercise—fasting and abstinence, celibacy, voluntary poverty and mendicancy, disciplined limitation of pleasurable sights and sounds—even if these are undertaken communally (as in, for instance, fasting for Lent, or Ramadan, or Yom Kippur) or by a designated élite have generally tended to be framed in terms of the meaning and effect that these undertakings have for and on the practicing individual. Discussions often focus on the volition and intention underlying their performance, innerworldly or otherworldly, purifying or self-immolating. Only more recently has attention been drawn to the function of ascetic practices within the society surrounding the practitioners.

It is for this reason that addressing the political aspects of ascetic practice—what I am calling here the politics of piety—is so important. For those who undertake such discipline not only embark on a path of personal achievement, but, at the same time, they take a stand in regard to their community—either accepting roles already established and institutions already formed, or, in creative protest and even rebuke, resisting them, either by subversive reinterpretation or by suggesting new forms of spiritual expression. Thus, ascetic practice may take on the tone and function at least of political gesture, if not of polemic.

On a broader scale, whole communities, too, may use specific ascetic disciplines to define themselves in relation to others, or to identify and highlight their differences—whether conceived as doctrinal or ethnic. And so the relationship between ideology, asceticism, and religious ethnicity requires further exploration.

Roles within the Community

Ascetic practice may take place within already established institutional contexts—such as monastic orders—or in response to the normal or expected or recurrent events of life—such as childbirth, occasions of individual or communal atonement, assumption of office, harvest, sacrifice, war, or death. Even so, descriptions of ascetic, disciplined life often utilize the image of separation from normal social interaction. Included among classes of such persons are monks (those who live alone), *sannyāsis* (or those who abandon, or renounce, the world); and (though they do not constitute a precise parallel) Pharisees (separate ones). Sidney Griffith has spoken in another session (see p. 223) on the Syrian *iḥîdāyâ* (single, or solitary one). Those who adopt such ways of life may describe themselves as "leaving the world" and "going into the wilderness," whether such wilderness is perceived as situated in a desert, a forest, a mountainside, an island, or a solitary cell.

The late Roman "holy man"

But even those most visibly removed from the society whose institutions and locale they have abandoned may nevertheless be understood, as Peter Brown has pointed out, as fulfilling an important, and even interactive, social function. Their very visible and literal removal from the involvements of village life actually bestows on them a disinterestedness, a platform of objectivity, if you will, equidistant from all contending parties, and hence a kind of moral authority that would otherwise be unattainable: their separation, in other words, renders them ideal adjudicants. And this moral authority functions, Brown argues, within the outlines shaped by established social institutions—in the case of the Syrian village, the protective village patron—who mediates the feuds of his protégés, avenges their wrongs if necessary, and buffers their interactions with senior officials. A figure like Simeon the Stylite should not be understood simply in terms of his physical remove from village life;

rather, the function of that very separation should be understood in terms of the needs of the society that institutionalizes it.[3]

The Hindu *sannyāsi*

It is for this reason that I would want to see further examination of the category of renunciant (one who rejects all that is associated with this life), which Vasudha Narayanan has so sharply contrasted from that of the ascetic (as one who accepts the societal roles stipulated by the *dharma śāstra*). While she has convincingly highlighted the character of these two roles in relation to each other, I would want to reconsider the relation of renunciants to the institutions that they so adamantly reject.[4] *Sannyāsa* is, after, a formal stage of life, with its own surrounding, elaborate, funereal ritual. Questioning the discourse of separation that characterizes descriptions of the renunciant, I would want to learn, in specific regional and historical contexts, within what precise terms such institutionalized liminality as *sannyāsa* is envisioned and described. I suspect that by understanding in depth, through case studies of varied locales and historical periods, the offices and their mechanisms within each society renounced, one might better comprehend what function or functions—such as adjudicating, teaching, healing, prophesying, or protecting—that a renunciant would fulfill for the community which has provided such elaborate rituals of departure, and from which the *sannyāsi* has absented himself.

That the language of ascetic renunciation may employ the terms of social binding and loosing is no better illustrated than in the bridal terms with which women and men extricate themselves from the social and sexual obligations and risks of marriage, childbearing and rearing, family provision, dependency and breadwinning, inheritance and disinheritance: *sannyāsa,* wrote Vedānta Deśika, is like a wedding necklace, the "thread of auspiciousness" worn by the bride of a lord. Deśika's near contemporary St. Catherine of Siena prayed on bended knee to the Virgin Mary for permission to have Mary's only son as a husband—"and I promise him and you," said Catherine, "that I will accept no other spouse, and I will zealously guard my virginity for him forever unimpaired."[5] Before selling his (and his father's) belongings, St. Francis of Assisi was asked if he would marry. He is reported to have replied, "I shall take a more noble and more beautiful spouse than you have ever seen; she will surpass all others in beauty and will excell all others in wisdom."[6] This spouse, first designated as the true religion, or way of life that he embraced, was later personified as Lady Poverty, to whom Francis displayed chivalric devotion.

By marrying Lord Viṣṇu, or Christ, or Lady Poverty, or, conversely, by being widowed in relation to matters of former obligation, as Paul understood his situation, those who renounce adopt the imagery of the very institutions and obligations that they are forgoing in order to describe what it is that they are doing.

And the adoption of such language reflects the fundamental role that such institutions play in construing the very terms of ascetic renunciation, even as the act of renunciation rebukes those very institutions, and even as ascetic renunciation provides a vehicle for resistance to those communal obligations.

Resistance *to* the Community

Now, ascetic practices may function as vehicles for social resistance either by serving to reject them altogether, or by enabling them to be reformed and transformed. And ascetic behavior may be analyzed both in terms of the intention of the actor and the reaction of his or her audience.

Francis and "Waldo"

That similar behavior, intended as institutional reparation, may be interpreted by others either as dangerous and heretical rebellion or as the product of divine inspiration, is perhaps no more poignantly illustrated than in the comparative cases of two figures of the late twelfth and early thirteenth centuries—a wealthy cloth merchant, Valdes (more commonly referred to as Waldo) of Lyons, and the son of a wealthy cloth merchant, Francis of Assisi, to whom I have already referred.

Both Waldo and Francis were inspired by the same passage from the *Gospel of Matthew* (19.21) that seemed to speak directly to Antony over eight centuries earlier—the words that Jesus spoke to a rich young man who sought his direction—"If you would be perfect, go, sell what you have, and give to the poor, and you will have treasure in heaven; and come, follow me." Waldo sold his property and, having provided for his wife and daughters, dispensed the proceeds to the poor and those of whom he felt he had taken unfair advantage over the course of his business career.[7] Only a few decades later, Francis sold much of his father's inventory to give to the poor, and later renounced his own inheritance. Both Francis and Waldo adopted the clothing, preaching, and begging habits of the earliest apostolic missionaries (as they interpreted their descriptions in the *Gospel of Luke* and the *Book of Acts*). It is an often remarked irony that Waldo and his followers were eventually condemned as heretics, while less than half a century later, and under a more politically astute pope, Francis and his followers were assimilated as one of the new forms of regulated life found acceptable in the Western church.[8]

The transforming dynamic of gender

Turning to the renouncers themselves, rather than to the reactions of their public, we find that similar forms of ascetic behavior reflect very different political stances, if we attend to the dynamic of gender. Professor Naryanan has provided two models of renunciation, in Rāmānuja and Āṇṭāḷ. And in this way, too, we are able to view the issue of the politics of pious renunciation with the complexity that it deserves. With respect to their political significance, *sannyāsi* and *sannyāsini,* after all, are not parallel terms. When a man such as Rāmānuja becomes a *sannyāsi,* he is adopting a role already defined and established as a possible stage of a man's life: a role of world renunciation, institutionalized by the world. When a woman enters institutions established for men but generally (if not categorically) closed to women—when, for example, a woman such as Āṇṭāḷ becomes a *sannyāsini*—such a woman is both accepting the general outline of such established social institutions and yet critiquing their terms and transforming them by her very entrance into them. Such creative transformation of social institutions is yet a different stance that can be taken and observed in the adoption of ascetic practices that on the surface seem so alike.

Paul

Ascetic practices may also figure as creative resolutions to perceived conflicts posed by the demands of a society in transition. Daniel Boyarin, in line with recent scholarship, sets Paul within the milieu of Hellenistic Judaism in which a variety of ascetic practices and ideals is evinced.[9] He views Paul's letter to the Christians in Rome as one attempt to resolve the *angst* with respect to bodily demands and pleasures felt throughout the Greco-Roman world—both Jewish and gentile—in the first century CE, on the one hand, and the divine commandment in *Genesis* to procreate, incumbent upon Jews, on the other. If being "under the law," read also in the light of Paul's concept of being "in the flesh," is understood as being under the obligation to procreate, then being "discharged to the law," "dead to its obligations," and like a widow in relation to it, entails not so much the obligation, but the freedom, to remain celibate.

While this reading of being "under the law" and "under the written code" (which Professor Boyarin characterizes as a localized one) certainly illuminates the specific passages from *Romans* 5 and 7 considered here, I find myself recalling the caveat of Wayne Meeks, that if Paul can be characterized as anything, he must be characterized as protean.[10] Recalling other passages from Paul that appear more focused on dietary regulations, observance of special days, and circumcision, one would not want to limit Paul's notion of being "under the law," even in the verses under consideration, to the commission of sexual acts and the condition of procreative obligation. One might argue that what Paul has in mind by "law" includes other obligatory aspects of the convenantal relationship between the Jewish people and God (in addition to that of procreation), as well as both Jewish and Stoic distinctions between what is incumbent upon all human beings, as human beings, and what is incumbent upon specific ethnic or national groups as a condition of membership therein.

In addition, it is possible to view the concept of being "in the flesh," which Boyarin equates with being "under the law," as irreducible to what we take to be literal sexuality alone, and the further propagation of the Jewish people. Indeed, the very concept of procreative sexuality itself may encompass a broad apprehension of the human condition that is both existential and cultural. Read existentially, the commandment of *Genesis,* as Professor Boyarin clearly argues, perpetuates the human condition of coming into being through behavior and emotions both irrational and often lacking control, of attaining maturity with demands for sustenance and discipline whose fulfillment remains fully dependent on others, of living in a state of moral inadequacy (individual and social) that is irremedial except by divine intervention, and of ending this existence in inevitable death and bodily disintegration. And this understanding, of course, highlights one aspect of asceticism that many ascetics point to, and most of the rest of us barely seem to comprehend—that ascetic discipline may in itself constitute a relief and a release, rather than a mere propaedeutic to such liberation.

Read culturally, however, one may note that adherence to the various obligations of Jewish law other than literal procreation, such as maintaining purity codes, itself effects the continuation and propagation of the Jewish people—a cultural fruitfulness, as it were, that is rendered equally irrelevant, in Paul's view, with the coming of Christ. And such a reading, linking sexuality with cultural perpetuation, would illuminate Paul's associative handling of the state of enfleshedness and the condition of legal obligation.

Athanasius

Ascetic behavior may also serve the interests of religious leaders by signaling the desired direction to be taken by those in their care. One such leader, Athanasius, a controversial figure during his own lifetime, remains so even to this day. One modern scholar has described Athanasius's character as hard, and his methods often deplorable, perhaps giving unquestioning credence to Athanasius's contemporary critics, who described him as self-aggrandizing and intrusive and guilty of myriad wrongs and improprieties—accusations recorded (one could add, to his credit) by Athanasius himself.[11] We know the risks of relying solely on the opinions of opponents in assessing the character, and even the beliefs, of any figure—modern scholars know better than to rely on Athanasius alone in coming to an understanding of the object of his doctrinal ire, Arius.

And so Charles Kannengiesser has objected to the more negative portrait of Athanasius that has assumed such prominence, by minimizing (if not rejecting outright) any political interests in his ministry and any polemical implications to his active patronage of the monastic communities in the Egyptian desert. Instead, Professor Kannengiesser argues, Athanasius met the attacks of his doctrinal opponents with only "a wall of silent prayer." Whether or not one accepts this assessment of Athanasius, whether or not one reads a polemical tone to Athanasius's portrait of Antony, whether or not one finds a sympathetic character in Athanasius, I am left to ask whether, even if one is political, is one to that extent, less pious? Are politics and piety inherently irreconcilable? Athanasius spent over five years in association with the monastic communities of Upper Egypt. And we may well ask, when is a visit more than just a visit? Does this represent prayer devoid of political will and a retreat from the political maelstrom, or does the very act of withdrawal into the monastic city itself entail an expression of episcopal leadership?

A modern analogy may be drawn to another ecclesiastical figure, also controversial, who would appear to blend politics and piety to perfection. When Pope John Paul II has paid more than a quarter of his papal excursions to destinations outside of Europe, and over a sixth of those to the African continent,[12] he is indicating something about what he thinks the direction of the church under his care will or ought to take. Moreover, he is rewarding with the favor of his public presence the source of the greatest numbers of new converts. But who would question the piety of this exertion of highest episcopal power? So, is saying that Athanasius's sojourns into the regions of the desert monks, who (according to his own reports) showed him the strongest of support and allegiance against his doctrinal (and imperial) opponents, have political implications denying their pious nature?

Distinctions *among* Communities

Ascetic behavior may also signal in another way, serving as a marker, a sign of belonging, or allegiance, to one sect rather than another, one community rather than another. And it can operate in this way intentionally, on the part of those who signal their identity to each other and to outsiders through the medium of ascetic practices, or it can be used by outside observers to identify foreigners in their midst. Certainly, at a rather superficial level, habits and tonsures distinguish monastic orders from one another—black Benedictines from white Cistercians, adherents to Roman rites from those to Celtic practices, Vaiṣṇava from Dasanami *sannyāsis*.

But ascetic disciplines can provide sharp diacritica, so to speak, delineating more fundamental doctrinal adherence, if not ethnic membership. I have spoken elsewhere about the significance that dietary restriction, and specifically the refusal to eat meat, had for both early and medieval Christians. Evidence from the earliest decades of the Christian era suggests that Christians felt the need to distinguish themselves from non-Christian Jews, on the one hand, and members of pagan groups, on the other. Paul's letters (especially to the Christian communities in Corinth and Rome) shaped the way in which the refusal to acknowledge the significance of food itself became a distinctive and idiosyncratic feature of the developing Christian movement.[13]

An ambivalent attitude persisted, so that while dietary discipline for would-be "athletes" and "soldiers" of Christ was valued and exhorted by early Christians, still, the notion that any single food substance, such as meat, might be considered unsuitable for human consumption, let alone forbidden by God, was nevertheless associated either with Jews, on the one hand, or with various dualistic groups, on the other, all of whom threatened to compete with Christians for followers.

And this ambivalence continued to manifest itself in the contradictory ways in which abstinence from meat, specifically, functioned to define both monastic orders and doctrinal allegiances throughout the Middle Ages. On the one hand, advocates of monastic reform, such as the Carthusians and the Cistercians, viewed the consumption of meat as a symptom and stimulant of dissolution, and they chastised lapses from genuine monastic discipline, frequently associated with the Cluniacs.[14] On the other hand, inquisitors of the high Middle Ages fingered precisely the practice of abstinence from meat as a telltale sign of heresy. One, Bernard Gui, recalled Augustine's descriptions of the Manichees; another, Moneta of Cremona, characterized the pious abstinence of the Cathars as "Judaizing."[15] And elsewhere, suspected heretics were tested by being forced to eat meat, on penalty of death, just as for centuries, Jews had been tested by forced pork consumption.[16] Thus, ascetic behavior that functioned in one context to indicate the most authentic discipline and rigor, in another context signaled perilous deviance from orthodoxy.

And so we can see that an examination of ascetic practices reveals a good deal more than the psychological state of certain kinds of people. There may be, as Mary Douglas has surmised, only a finite number of categories within which human beings, physically constructed as we are, may renounce. But such renunciation, however apparently similar in form, when considered with sensitivity to the terms in which it is construed, the circumstances in which it is undertaken, and even the actual parties who undertake it, may express the gamut of political postures people may take with respect to their society and its institutions, in relation to which they must, even as ascetics, always be considered: full or merely qualified acceptance, forceful direction or energetic reform, resigned or even fierce rejection. To understand the politics of piety requires more than simply an observation of just saying no.

NOTES

1. Raffaele Pettazzoni identified what he viewed as a two-pronged risk of purely phenomenological, and historically insensitive, approaches to the study of religion. On the one hand, meanings may be falsely ascribed to phenomena that, though similar in form, bear very different significance when contextual settings within traditions are ignored; on the other, fruitful comparison of disparate phenomena may be missed if attention is given only to formal appearances, and context and function are overlooked—"History and Phenomenology in the Science of Religion," in *Essays on the History of Religions* (Leiden: E. J. Brill, 1967), pp. 215–219.
2. How different the field and evidence might appear were the defining terminology derived, not from the athletic and gladiatorial arenas of late antiquity, but from traditions and contexts more conceptually focused on the maintenance of purity or on the terms of convenantal obligation or obedient submission to divine authority.
3. "The Rise and Function of the Holy Man in Late Antiquity," *Journal of Roman Studies* 61 (1971):80–101, reprinted with updated references in *Society and the Holy in Late Antiquity* (Berkeley: University of California, 1982), pp. 103–152. The author has since put forth a more modulated view of the varied quality and degree of interaction between holy men and the communities from which they emerged, as official strangers, in late Roman and early Byzantine society. (See another essay included in the same collection, "Town, Village and Holy Man," pp. 153–164.)
4. Brown makes a similar comparison between the Christian Near East and India, that "it is the non-members of these societies—holy people—who were able to set the tone of the civilization from which they had, technically, totally disengaged themselves." See "Town, Village and Holy Man," p. 154.
5. Raymond of Capua, *Vita S. Catherinae Senensis, Acta Sanctorum,* April III (Paris, 1866), pp. 853–959, 1.35. Modern (somewhat abridged and loose) English translation by Conleth Kearns, *The Life of Catherine of Siena* (Wilmington, Del.: Michael Glazier, 1980). In keeping with the interdisciplinary nature of this conference, I am identifying editions and, where possible, English translations, of sources cited.
6. Thomas of Celano, *Vita Prima,* Analecta Franciscana 10 (Quaracchi, 1941), book 1, chapter 3; English translation by Placide Hermann, in *English Omnibus of the Sources for the Life of St. Francis,* ed. Marion A. Habig (Chicago: Franciscan Herald Press, 1973).
7. *Chronicon Laudunensis,* in *Monumenta Germaniae Historica, Scriptores* 26 (Hannover, 1882), pp. 447–448.
8. Among the many who examine the similarities among medieval poverty movements, see Lester K. Little, *Religious Poverty and the Profit Economy in Medieval Europe* (Ithaca: Cornell University Press, 1983); Gordon Leff, *Heresy in the Later Middle Ages: The Relation of Heterodoxy to Dissent c.1250–1450,* 2 vols. (New York: Barnes & Noble,

1967); Malcolm Lambert, *Franciscan Poverty* (London: Society for the Preservation of Christian Knowledge, 1961).

9. See, for example, Steven D. Fraade, "Ascetical Aspects of Ancient Judaism," in *Jewish Spirituality from the Bible through the Middle Ages,* ed. Arthur Green (New York: Crossroad, 1986), pp. 253–288.
10. In *The Writings of St. Paul* (New York: W. W. Norton, 1972), pp. 435–444.
11. See W.H.C. Frend, "Athanasius as an Egyptian Christian Leader in the Fourth Century," in *Religion Popular and Unpopular in the Early Christian Centuries* (London: Variorum Reprints, 1976); *idem, The Rise of Christianity* (Philadelphia: Fortress Press, 1984), pp. 524–527; Ammianus Marcellinus *Rerum gestorum libri qui supersunt* 15.7.7, ed. Wolfgang Seyfarth (Leipzig: B. G. Teubner, 1978), English translation by J. C. Rolfe, Loeb Classical Library (Cambridge: Harvard University Press, 1982); Athanasius, *Apologia ad Constantium,* ed. Jan M. Szymusiak, *Deux Apologies à l'Empereur,* Sources chrétiennes 56 (Paris: Éditions du Cerf, 1987), pp. 86–175; English translation in *A Select Library of Nicene and Post-Nicene Fathers of the Christian Church,* ser. 2, vol. 4, pp. 238–253.
12. From a telephone conversation with Monseigneur De Andrea of the Holy See Mission, New York City.
13. Cf. *1 Cor.* 8.8–13, 10.25–29; *Rom.* 14.14–23.
14. See, for example, the criticism directed by Peter the Venerable, Abbot of Cluny, at his own priors and subpriors: On what basis, he asks, can it be claimed that a healthy monk eating meat with healthy men not be in the wrong? Such behavior opposes the Rule (of St. Benedict, chapters 36 and 39) and violates justice. See Ep. 161, in *The Letters of Peter the Venerable,* ed. Giles Constable (Cambridge: Harvard University Press, 1967).
15. Bernard Gui, *Practica inquisitorum heretice pravitatis* (Paris, 1886), 5.1.2; Moneta of Cremona, *Adversus Catharos et Waldenses libri V* (Rome, 1743), 2.5.
16. See, for example, the treatment of suspected heretics by the emperor Henry III recounted in an eleventh-century chronicle (*Monumenta Germaniae Historica, Scriptores* 5.130).

PART SIX

The Discourse Refracted

35

The Ascetic Impulse in Religious Life

A General Response

Elizabeth A. Clark

To provide a summation of and response to a set of essays so rich and diverse as these is always a problem for the hapless commentator; to provide one for essays that posit highly divergent views of what constitutes asceticism (or even its characteristic features) seems even more daunting. As several participants wryly noted at the International Conference on the Ascetic Dimension in Religious Life and Culture, members of the group on The Ascetic Impulse in Religious Life and Culture from the American Academy of Religion/Society of Biblical Literature, despite their eight years of cooperative work and their joint production of three volumes, are nonetheless unable—still!—to arrive at a definition of asceticism on which they agree, even for the limited time span and geographical area they study.

Does asceticism signal deprivation, pain, and the shrinking of the self, as some authors (for example, Edith Wyschogrod and Bruce Malina) variously imply in this volume? Or should we opt for a characterization that stresses liberation, the fulfillment of one's true nature, as Kallistos Ware herein suggests? Yet if corporeal affirmation does not attend the ascetic body here and now, but only the body of plentitude, the body seen from nowhere (in phrases derived from Patricia Cox Miller's essay), in what ways, on this reconstrual, does asceticism render a positive evaluation of the body? If, with Elizabeth Castelli, we acknowledge that the very notion of "the self" used by some commentators betokens a transhistorical reality and stands as a conceptual remnant of an older philosophical system, does its dismantling complicate, or stimulate, our investigation of asceticism?

Can we, with Leif Vaage (p. 246), name asceticism the application of a body technology, or a soteriological methodology? Do we recognize, with Dianne Bazell (p. 493), that renunciations appearing similar in form may attend differing political stances of ascetic practitioners in relation to their own societies and societal institutions? (As she puts it, "To understand the politics of piety requires more than simply an observation of just saying no" [p. 500].) The desire for definition has, over and again in these essays, been challenged by a call for more precise contextualization. Thus, even those authors—such as conference co-organizer Richard Valantasis—who are deeply interested in theory are careful to stress the social, historical, and material aspects of asceticism to which we must attend (p. 544).

Rather than cataloging similarities in ascetic practice cross-culturally, or seeking an essence of asceticism, we might (some commentators suggest) more helpfully look to structures: here, Geoffrey Galt Harpham's evaluation of asceticism as a structure of compensation, in which the ascetic practitioner both gives up and gets, is provocative, and finds resonance in Giles Milhaven's suggestion that we focus on which particular pleasures the ascetic renounces and which she or he receives in turn. Other authors furnish variations on the theme: Bruce Malina urges students of asceticism to investigate the ways in which pain becomes power; Robert Thurman, how asceticism involves a withdrawing of energies from the habitual. For Christian theology, the paradox that the ascetic gets by giving up is manifested in the ascetic's striving for that which, theologically speaking, is supposed to be provided through God's grace (a theological breakdown, as Gregory Collins noted in our discussions [p. 343]).

Another approach to asceticism claims that its central function is to critique the dominant society in which it is embedded. Various essays address this claim. As Patrick Olivelle phrases it, is ascetic creation an attempt to deconstruct social creation? Or, in the model that Walter Kaelber borrows from H. Richard Niebuhr, does asceticism represent a stand against culture? The voluntary choice of poverty and powerlessness so characteristic of ascetic renunciation often appears as a stringent critique of the dominant culture, but even here, contributors provide evidence that might challenge, or at least nuance, this assumption. Gail Corrington-Streete suggests, in discussing some ancient Western ascetics, that asceticism may represent a form of taking power, but of power over the microcosm of the body when power over the macrocosm is denied or restricted: asceticism here appears more as retreat than as challenge. Similarly, those who address Buddhist and Hindu asceticism emphasize that ascetic renunciation was an accepted part of the general culture of its practitioners and was adopted by ordinary people at various life stages (serial asceticism, we might call it). For late ancient Christianity, Averil Cameron strikingly argues that the ascetic discourse which originally stood as a challenge to ascetic values seeped into the wider culture and eventually provided the empire with a language that signaled limitation, exclusion, and hierarchy: "The Byzantine state replicated the ascetic subject," she concludes.

Another challenge to the model of asceticism as critique of hegemonic power is found in materials pertaining to women ascetics. Gillian Clark's essay (p. 33), for example, could be mined to question the critique thesis, for it was through asceticism that some women found power denied them in the larger world. Likewise, from Fedwa Malti-Douglas's analysis (p. 395) of Karīmān Ḥamza's autobiography, we might conclude that in this quite different cultural setting, asceticism once more provided a means to power otherwise denied women. Are we to think that the asceticism of males challenges the dominant power, whereas the asceticism of females supplies power hitherto denied to its practitioners? (Feminists might note that women's rise to prominence through asceticism challenges male hegemony in particular, not just societal hegemony, loosely construed.) Nonetheless, female asceticism provides an especially good illustration of Harpham's model of structures of compensation (p. 357), in which through renunciation of the domestic, other benefits—in this case, societal power—are gained.

Thus many authors and conference participants abandoned—or at least temporarily bracketed—the attempt to provide a comprehensive definition of asceticism that would hold cross-culturally. Their reluctance to do so may signal the disfavor into which typological or phenomenological analysis has fallen among scholars of religion in recent years; the emphasis has shifted to the investigation of difference. Looking to the particularity of context is thus the dominant mode of treating asceticism in this volume: as William Deal reminds his readers, asceticism has meaning only in relation to other behaviors in a culture. He argues—and many conference participants seemed to agree—that we should look chiefly to the impact of asceticism upon a culture, not to the intentions (even if we could retrieve them) of ascetic practitioners. Hence, studying asceticism would stimulate us to investigate the rhetoric of thought and action through which the ascetic seeks to transform arrangements of power and authority within a culture: here, the social, political, and economic import of ascetic behavior is at the forefront.

Harpham's and Deal's approaches to asceticism might be variously labeled psychological, on the one hand, and social, on the other—although such a simplistic differentiation fails to do justice to their subtle discussions. Indeed, throughout the conference that saw the first reading of these essays, discussants often raised the issue of binary distinctions, only to resist them. Thus, distinctions such as natural/unnatural and nature/culture were both much discussed and much critiqued. As Kallistos Ware notes (p. 91), Dom Cuthbert Butler, early in this century, distinguished a natural (that is, moderate) asceticism from an unnatural one that involved more radical discipline of the body and the infliction of pain. Yet this distinction was rejected by many discussants, and for more than one reason: in addition to acknowledging that the terms "natural" and "unnatural" are socially constructed, various authors here insist that pain stands as part of the very definition of asceticism. Moreover, the practices that Butler would presumably have labeled "unnatural," such as flagellation, were sometimes the ones that during long periods of Christian history decisively marked one's Christian commitment, as Ann Ramsey's essay (p. 576) suggests.

Does the dichotomy of nature/culture—that dichotomy so favored by structuralist anthropologists in decades past—yield better results? The answer appears to be no: different traditions and authors have evaluated the notions quite variously. From Giulia Sfameni Gasparro's essay (p. 127), we learn that some early Christian writers claim that humans fell from a pristine natural condition to a lower state of culture; here, the vision of nature at the world's beginning provides a model for its future glory at the end. Yet in Robert Thurman's discussion (p. 108) of Buddhist asceticism, we were differently instructed: in some forms of Buddhism, there is not envisioned a fall from nature into culture (negatively evaluated as sinful, as in the early Christian texts), but rather a positively valued evolution from nature, scripted as the realm of animality, to the more fully human sphere of culture. These examples suggest that the dichotomy of nature/culture may not provide such a useful tool as at first sight appears for the understanding of asceticism cross-culturally.

In contrast, most authors agree that the range of behaviors and practices that can be labeled ascetic is very wide. Thus praxis can span the spectrum from the mere decorous adherence to moderation, as John Pinsent shows for some ancient Greek philosophers, to practices of a more violent nature that signal the body's denigration: here, the body might be seen as a bag filled with filth, as in Patrick Olivelle's vivid rendition (p. 188) of some Hindu texts.

What, then, counts as asceticism? Is asceticism an exclusively religious phenomenon? No, many contributors to this volume reply. Moreover, our task at definition has been complicated by the proneness of asceticism to be coopted for its alleged reverse. Thus, for example, the same Indian religion that produced the attitudes of which Olivelle writes could see them quite transformed, as in the Śrī Vaiṣṇava community described by Vasudha Narayanan (p. 443) that celebrated the beauty of the physical body. Reversals and paradox, we gather from these essays, attend the description of asceticism at every step of the investigation. Such attention to paradox and nuance in our subject matter should not, I think, be taken as signaling our defeat as scholars of asceticism, but rather suggests the sophistication we are increasingly bringing to our topics.

The malleability of ascetic discourse and behavior is well noted in these pages in a variety of ways. For example, nonascetic materials can be appropriated for asceticism, and vice versa. Thus Robert Wilken shows (p. 412) how the classical ("pagan") virtues were appropriated for Christian ascetic discourse in the case of Maximus the Confessor; while, in contrast, an originally ascetic figure such as the Hindu heroine Mīra was domesticated from an exemplar of yogic renunciation to a proponent of home economics training for girls, as John Hawley's essay (p. 301) so engagingly shows. And as Michael Satlow suggests (p. 535), even an "ascetic" topic such as the proper regulation of diet could be directed to different ends: in Greco-Roman culture, dietetics was linked to power, while among the rabbis, to the achievement of holiness. Likewise, practices at various times considered by some to be the "heart" of ascetic technique, such as flagellation, could be analyzed under a far less pious discourse *within* the same culture, as Ann Ramsey shows (p. 576) in her discussion of the medicalization of the discourse on flagellation in early modern and modern France.

Another blurring often noted in these pages is the relation between persons and texts, and texts and behavior: who imitates whom or what? In Teresa Shaw's phrase (p. 79), are texts used to "rein in" persons (for example, Antony) and earlier texts (for example, John Cassian's "taming" of Evagrius of Pontus)? How does privileging one text over another—the *Timaeus* over the *Phaedrus,* for example—give a different resonance to ancient views on the body?, a question addressed by John Dillon (p. 86). How did an ascetic narrative such as the *Life of Antony* serve as a basis for imitation, so that subjects themselves were in effect transformed into texts? Likewise, the link between texts and behavior demands further consideration—and not only from the typical scholarly approach that investigates élite ideas but popular behavior.

Paradox, several writers remind us, seems to be closely allied with ascetic theory and practice. Take, for example, the use of erotic language and marital imagery to describe ascetic experience—imagery derived from the very institutions and obligations that the ascetic practitioner forgoes, Dianne Bazell reminds us. The blurring and transforming of gender imagery contributes to the power of ascetic discourse, adds Verna Harrison in her discussion of Philo.

Of like paradoxicality is the contrast between ascetic behavior as display and performance, over against the usual assumption that ascetic humility calls its practitioners to resist show. Here, several discussants have borrowed from cultural-studies scholarship on performance to indicate how the ascetic rehearses the shaping of a new person; thus, Geoffrey Harpham and others see repetition as an essential feature of ascetic practice. (The important role of narrative as a carrier of ascetic value might also here be underscored.) If we claim, with Robert Thurman, that asceticism involves a break from habitual practices, we might further stress that it is through the repetition of new habits that the ascetic forges a different identity. Moreover, attention to the ascetic's audience is now urged by commentators such as Averil Cameron as of key importance for our investigations: can we even speak of asceticism's existence without the audience that sees, notes, and records the ascetic's performance?

Theater images also abound in Edith Wyschogrod's essay (p. 16). She refers to asceticism as a corporeal miming of human destitution and bodily indigence, in which hunger is mimed by fasting, "sexual desire by chastity, bodily ease by self-mortification." In the very denial of the physical body, the body is brought to the fore. And since the body of plentitude of which Patricia Cox Miller writes (p. 281) is so rarely and fleetingly available to us, it is the dim, nonidealized body that becomes the theatrical stage on and through which ascetic actors create their characters.

Our increasing sophistication in regard to ascetic discourse has in part resulted from our various efforts to bring scholarly tools from elsewhere to bear upon our topic, enabling us to gain a wider perspective. The interest in performance studies I have already noted. Attention to material culture, so-called *realia,* has also complexified our views, as the labors of Yizhar Hirschfeld (p. 267) and others show us. The institutional grounding and transmission of ideas—earlier known more exclusively in its "history of ideas" garb—is emphasized in Bernard McGinn's observations (p. 58) on how monasteries served as the material carriers for ascetic ideals. The community structures that upheld the seemingly solitary practices of the ascetic are well noted by Sidney Griffith (p. 220) regarding Syrian asceticism and Jason Beduhn regarding Manichean renunciants. In general, our attention to material culture changes our notions of ascetic operations: how differently we see women's monasticism, once we appreciate (with Gillian Clark) the vast wealth that women brought with them to ascetic institutions. Likewise, a re-estimation of the educational level of early Christian ascetics, such as Samuel Rubenson (p. 49) provides for Antony, might suggest new ideas about their material supports, ancient education being so strongly tied to class. In years ahead, students of asceticism might be prompted to explore Leif Vaage's hypothesis that there must be a surplus in a society before there can be asceticism. If we accept this claim, what might it imply about the types of societies in which asceticism develops? Do they tend to be, as Vaage suggests, translocal and imperial?

Yet it is not only to the outside or religion that we necessarily turn for assistance in understanding asceticism. Within Christianity, for example, our comprehension of ascetic phenomena is enriched by considering how asceticism relates to mysticism (Bernard McGinn), to theological anthropology (Giulia Sfameni Gasparro), or to Eucharistic devotion (Gregory Collins).

Moreover, what vision of asceticism we come to advance depends greatly upon the context in which scholars put the evidence. Some of the historiographical problems that emerged from too readily accepting past wisdom have received striking coverage here. What varying interpretations arise, as Charles Kannengiesser and Samuel Rubenson ask, when we privilege one representation of Antony over another? Or how has our view of Syriac asceticism been flawed by accepting the received model that portrayed Syria as the "Wild West" of ascetic practice? Decisions about context decisively color the results of our investigations: a striking example is furnished by Daniel Boyarin, who demonstrates that when we place Paul's words on sexuality and marriage within the contemporary context of *The Testaments of the Twelve Patriarchs,* they resonate quite differently from the way they resonate when the context is supplied by rabbinic discussions of marriage stemming from several centuries later.

Where we stand in our investigations is equally important. As William Deal notes, if we took Shintō as our definitive model of asceticism rather than Christianity, we might think that asceticism's essence lay in bodily purification, not in union with God. But further: it is not only our models, it is our contexts. Each of us—this writer included—would benefit from being more attentive to the conditions under which we have produced our own versions of asceticism, for we are very differently grounded in relation to religion, ideology, and institutions. If I write of asceticism from the standpoint of an ascetic practitioner who lives in a religious community, my approach to asceticism will probably be quite different from that of those whose primary talking partners are literary theorists, members of cultural studies programs, or coparticipants in feminist reading groups. Do we borrow our models from Anglo-American social sciences (as does Bruce Malina) or from Continental theory (as do Edith Wyschogrod, Patricia Cox Miller, and Elizabeth Castelli)? To those whose daily diet is empiricist historiography, the musings of theorists may sound like pompous and obfuscating jargon—while to those who spend their hours among partisans of Lacan, Althusser, or Haraway, traditional historiography may sound naive, unproblematized, even intellectually bankrupt. In my view, the epistemological crisis occasioned by the introduction and development of theory in academies outside Europe provides the single greatest divide among scholars of the humanities for the foreseeable future. Thus, it is to be expected that the essays in this volume reveal the rifts and disjunctions in our scholarly equipment and intellectual baggage. Attending to our own situatedness as well as to the situatedness of the texts and other materials we explore is a desideratum for all future scholarship—whether cross-cultural or tradition-specific—on asceticism.

APPENDIX

Ascetica Miscellanea

36

The Battle for the Body in Manichaean Asceticism

Jason Beduhn

As distinct from most other religious movements, which contain ascetic traditions as one option of expression, Manichaeism is ascetic at its very core, and to be a Manichaean is, by definition, to be an ascetic. Unfortunately, there are none of these fascinating people around anymore, and it is the task of historians to reconstruct, as best they can, the discourse and practices of the Manichaean faith. This historical enterprise of recovery has been hampered by two related obstacles. The first is the diverse and fragmentary character of Manichaean literary remains. The second obstacle is the great liberty modern academics have taken with this material in synthesizing an artificial Manichaeism to match their own preconceptions. The quest for a unified Manichaean tradition, if such existed, must be based on careful comparison of distinct lines of tradition, with due regard for regional variation, in search of those elements that, by their ubiquity in the sources, reveal themselves to be fundamental to Manichaeism as a whole. The practice of asceticism is one such fundamental element of Manichaeism, and this paper examines the Manichaean literary tradition that authorized and interpreted the Manichaean ascetic life.

My first task, then, is to justify the attention and weight I give to the piece of Manichaean literature I call "The Battle for the Body."[1] The narrative in question has been found so far in five languages representing the full spectrum of the Manichaean mission from fourth-century Egypt to tenth-century China. It is, therefore, the best attested piece of Manichaean literature known to us from more than one linguistic region.[2] It is most commonly known from the Chinese version discovered at Tun-huang, translated into French by Paul Pelliot and Éduard Chavannes in *Journal asiatique* in 1911,[3] and since then known as the Chinese Tractate or Treatise (or by the Chinese name *Canjing*). Since its discovery and publication, parallels have been discovered among Parthian, Sogdian, and Turkish fragments recovered at Turfan in Chinese Central Asia.[4] The final piece, and the most important link, is the Coptic version, which is contained in *Kepahalaion* 38 of the Medinet Madi find from Egypt.[5]

Most modern accounts of Manichaeism begin with a cosmogony that has been stitched together from a variety of distinct sources and polished into an artificially consistent tale. This academic product may convey some of the basic themes of Manichaean expression, but does little to explain or contextualize the actual practices of Manichaean believers. The case is quite different with "The Battle for the Body," which has been largely neglected in Manichaean studies although, ironically, it shows greater consistency among its versions than do the cosmogonic accounts. "The Battle for the Body" provides the link between primordial cosmogony and experienced anthropology; its narrative is not confined to the mythic past but includes the life of the Manichaean community and events within the living bodies of individual Manichaeans.

In various forms, Manichaean cosmogony reports that, after the primordial cataclysm that brought together the totally alien and mutually inimical forces of light and darkness, God instituted measures to recover the lost fragments of his own substance from the forces of evil. The latter sought to block such recovery by the construction of a prison for the bulk of light, molding the mixed substance of good and evil into a form that deceptively resembled a divine being. This is the human body, described as an exact counterpart, limb by limb and organ by organ, to the universe. The events of the individual body recapitulate the cosmic struggles between light and darkness—this is the major theme of "The Battle for the Body."

The forces of evil create the human body from a mixture of light and darkness, but so order it that the darkness rules over and oppresses the light, keeping it enslaved to ignorance and passions. This congenital debility is the condition into which each one of us is born, and the tale of evil's formation of such body prisons is an openended myth in which we are all characters.[6] The "Battle for the Body" recounts the ongoing efforts of divine forces, working in cooperation with the awakened self within us and the Manichaean community, to reverse this infernal control of the body, and to implant a divine dominion within the specifically Manichaean body, governed by ascetic discipline and positive attitudes. The use of the present tense by the various versions of this account—or, in the case of Coptic, the habitual tense—signifies the regular, ongoing nature of these events as the personal story of every believer from generation to generation.

I have schematized the narrative common to the different versions into three scenes. Scene 1 entails the activity of the forces of evil in setting up a disordered body. In Scene 2, the Mind of Light liberates the body's light in its five characteristic forms and imprisons the evil forces in a reversal of the body's previous arrangement. This reversal coincides with the manifestation of key positive attitudes (love, trust, contentment, patience, and wisdom). The end result of these changes is a perfected and controlled body, a new mode of existence which our parallel texts call the "New Person" in which the Mind of Light supervises the "watchtowers" of the body just as other divinities are positioned at various stations of the cosmos. Military imagery is pervasive. Mani says:

> Look, then, at how great the strength and diligence of the Mind of Light is upon all the watchtowers of the body. He stands before his camp. He shuts all of the reasonings of the body to the attractions of sin. He limits them, scatters them, removes them by his will. *Kephalaion 38:100, 1–6*

But this is not an ironclad and irreversible transformation. Disturbances arise from time to time in the body, microcosmic rebellions or "prison breaks" by the evil still inherent within us, which must be put down and suppressed. Crucial symptoms are identified by which the ascetic is made aware of internal conflict. The *Listenwis-*

The Battle for the Body

Scene 1: Anthropology

Sin takes noetic *limb*, binds it in *body part*, adds its own *limb*

(Coptic)	mind	⟶	bone	+	sin-mind
(Chinese)	ether	⟶		+	dark-mind
(Coptic)	thought	⟶	nerve	+	sin-thought
(Chinese)	wind	⟶		+	dark-thought
(Coptic)	insight	⟶	artery	+	sin-insight
(Chinese)	light	⟶		+	dark-insight
(Coptic)	intellect	⟶	flesh	+	sin-intellect
(Chinese)	water	⟶		+	dark-intellect
(Coptic)	reasoning	⟶	skin	+	sin-reasoning
(Chinese)	fire	⟶		+	dark-reasoning

Scene 2: Soteriology

From *body part*, Mind of Light releases noetic *limb*, and adds *virtue*

bone	⟶	mind	+	love
nerve	⟶	thought	+	trust
artery	⟶	insight	+	contentment
flesh	⟶	intellect	+	patience
skin	⟶	reasoning	+	wisdom

Scene 3: Ladder of Affliction

Sin expels *virtue* from noetic *limb*, and produces *vice*

love	⟵	mind	⟶	hate
trust	⟵	thought	⟶	conceit
contentment	⟵	insight	⟶	lust
patience	⟵	intellect	⟶	impatience
wisdom	⟵	reasoning	⟶	doubt

senschaft by which this account organizes bodily experience bears the hallmarks of ascetic values. Certain emotions and mental states are marked off as passions that disturb the repaired bodily order and must be overcome; others are positively affirmed as manifestations of light within us, as characteristic of proper discipline and self-control. The set of negative symptoms, and their appropriate diagnosis, are organized in both the Coptic and Chinese versions into a progressive chain I call the "Ladder of Affliction," which I have schematized as Scene 3.

The Coptic version describes it like this: Rising up from the depths of the body, sin expels wisdom and causes doubt which manifests itself in boastful speech. Rising up higher, sin expels patience and produces impatience, which is manifest in the person's rejection of the counsels of his brethren. Rising up higher, sin expels contentment and, driven by desire, conceit, and pride, the person

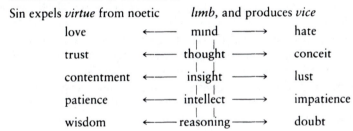

> departs from his teacher and his brethren. [He] always wishes to come and go alone. He wishes to eat and drink alone, as a solitary. [He] wishes to always walk alone. This indeed is the sign that he does not desire the company of his brethren.
>
> *Kephalaion 38:98, 18–22*

Rising up still higher, sin causes the anxiety of death to overwhelm trust in the faith and to produce conceit. Finally, reaching the highest level of the self, sin drives away love and replaces it with hate for one's teachers, religious companions—indeed, the whole Manichaean community.

At every stage, the Coptic text prescribes intervention on the part of the community. The elders and brethren (perhaps even the lay assistants: 97, 33) gather around the afflicted individual and seek to correct him with censure and edification, to calm and restore the person to his former placidity. If the afflicted individual welcomes their assistance, he can recover; rejection of their help has dire consequences:

> That man makes himself an instrument of damage: he separates from the assembly, and his end comes down to the world. The mind which existed in him scatters from him and goes up to the apostle who had sent it. He is filled with evil spirits and they occupy themselves with him, drawing him hither and thither, and he himself becomes like the worldly people—i.e., [he] will change, and will become like a bird being plucked of its feathers, and will become a man of the earth.
>
> *Kephalaion 38:99, 10–17*

The Eastern version (Chinese, with fragmentary Parthian parallels) has the same structure, matching each noetic realm with the same virtues and vices as the Western version, but moves in the opposite direction (starting at the top and moving down). Once again, the internal afflictions are manifested in "signs" or symptoms that the individual is called upon to recognize. Failure to note these symptoms leads to a progress in the moral disease. But in contrast to the Western version, the Eastern version gives only a cursory exposition of symptoms at this point of the account, and takes up the impact upon, and intervention of, other Manichaeans in a later section separate from the "Ladder of Affliction."

This separate, later section of the Eastern version actually treats the system of ascetic discipline and religious virtue more expansively than is found in the Coptic version, first of all through an extended metaphor of ten trees: five of darkness and five of light. The trees of darkness are each described by root, trunk, branch, leaf, fruit, taste, and color, which stand for (in all) thirty-five negative attitudes, such as divisiveness, negligence, laziness, hatred of superiors, contempt for others, arrogance, love of luxury, and desire for liquor and food. The trees of light in their constituent parts stand for thirty-five positive attitudes such as respect, praise of the community, vigilance, application to study, reading and recitation, obedience to disciplinary precepts, fasting, zeal, and skillful apologetics.

The Eastern version (Chinese, with both Parthian and Turkish parallels) also adds a second behavioral code, this time on an even larger scale of twelve trees, all of them good. This code of sixty categories of manifest religiosity is even more specific to life in the community of believers than the first model, and includes specific rules of personal interaction and proper deportment that give the historian important details of Manichaean practices. Here we finally find prohibitions and injunctions parallel to the specific symptoms of perversity discussed in the Coptic version, involving various forms of disrupting the assembly and the desire to depart as a solitary.

I want to emphasize the distinct handling in the literary tradition of the anthropological narrative, on the one hand, and the normative discussion of ascetic regulation, on the other. The narrative is consistent across all the versions, with only minor variants in content, some degree of compression or expansion, but clearly all going back to a common original. The ascetic regulations, on the other hand, follow independent compositional traditions. Each of these normative codes build upon the common base of experiential diagnosis that the narrative provides, and are governed by identical or nearly identical ascetic principles; but they stand as totally independent literary traditions.

From such a situation, it seems straightforward to conclude that the narrative functioned in the same capacity among fourth-century Egyptian Manichaeans as it did among tenth-century Chinese Manichaeans, and, based upon the fragmentary Parthian and Turkish parallels, among all Manichaeans in between. The "Battle for the Body" narrative is consistently linked to ascetic regulations in both Eastern and Western versions, I would suggest, because it functioned as a grounding account for the community's ascetic practices; it was, in other words, the fundamental discourse by which the practices were emplaced and authorized by the Manichaean church.

In the narrative, the Mind of Light acts out a kind of internal landscape architecture, uprooting, cutting, forming, resurfacing, enhancing the interior spaces of the body into the liberated and liberating machine so central to Manichaean ritual practice.[7] The codes of behavior are the manifest, enacted correlates of this mythology—or dare we call it a physiology?—of internal states that were considered the roots of manifest behavior. The one reinforces the other: the codes are justified by being linked to the internal battle for the body: at the same time, the truth of this invisible battle is demonstrated by the empirical manifestations of bodily order with which the codes are concerned.

Analysis of "The Battle for the Body" also provides a much needed corrective to past misconceptions of Manichaean ascetic practices. We can finally lay to rest the hypothesis that made the Manichaeans accountable for bringing eremetic asceticism to the West.[8] According to our texts, eremetic behavior is identified with the rejection of community edification and the hubris of self-sufficiency, and is a stage of the progressive erosion of discipline by evil inclinations.[9] This observation is congruent with what we know about the broader disciplinary regimen of Manichaean life. The eremetic life is inherently precluded for the Manichaean elect by, among other things, their dietary regulations, which made them passive recipients of their daily bread from a support community of auditors. The constant interaction of the ascetic elect and the less ascetic (but definitely not nonascetic!) laypeople was institutionalized in Manichaeism by stipulations put upon the lifestyle of the elect, involving daily dependence on laypeople for their shelter and the ritualized meal that provided their sole sustenance.

The ascetic Battle for the Body is intimately related to this daily ritual meal of the Manichaean elect. The meal shares the distinction with the "Battle for the Body" narrative of being attested across the geographical spectrum of our sources on Manichaeism. The entire ascetic edifice of Manichaeism is directed toward the ritual consumption of daily alms, which acquires its salvational force precisely from the successful battle to convert the bodies of the elect into divine distillaries. In Manichaeism, the body is not to be rejected as base and worthless, but to be subjugated, perfected and put into use in the process of salvation.

The question of the goal intended by ascetic practices has been repeatedly raised. This Manichaean account is explicit in its answer:

> If there is one among the pure religion-bearers who assures the prosperity of the correct law . . . and until the end does not fall back—after death their Old Person, with the dark, non-luminous force of its crowd of soldiers, will fall into hell from which it will never come out. At the same moment, the beneficent light, rousing the pure kindred of its own luminous army, will go, completely, straight into the world of light (where) that person receives joy perpetually. *Traité 554f.*

Born of a tragic intertwining of good and evil, humans can neither lay claim to inherent perfection and divinity, nor detest themselves as hopelessly perverse. Instead, they are called upon to recognize their emotional and moral turmoil as a congenital condition of human existence, and are offered a narrative within which they can situate, and come to terms with, their personal experiences. This conflict is fully situated within the body, and the "Battle for the Body" narrative linked to the Manichaean ascetic regimen offers a code, an applied *Listenwissenschaft,* by which human moral conscience and intellectual faculties may consistently promote the positive energies of the body and suppress the eruptions of negative drives, toward an end of final and complete separation.

In this way, the discourse and practices of Manichaean asceticism manipulate the raw data of bodily experience into a patterned, circumscribed and controlled identity, which serves as mediator for the spiritual needs of the world, and which ultimately will transcend the transitory and limited existence to which humans are born. Asceticism is anchored at the center of Manichaean life by being more than an exercise in humility, a mortification of bodily inconveniences, and an attenuation of earthly ties. The ascetic life embodies the subjugation of evil and demonstrates victory over the chaos, the "thrown-ness," of the human condition.

The characteristic dualism of Manichaeism—which is clearly not a simple spirit/body dichotomy—finds its practical application in a code of self-analysis and self-discipline whereby the total mass of bodily phenomena are sorted and sifted into their respective natures. As the Chinese version of "The Battle for the Body" says: "the universe is the infirmary where the luminous bodies are cured, but is at the same time the prison where the dark demons are chained" (*Traité* 515). And the composite physical body, the theater of this drama, is "the exact image, point by point, of the universe" (*Traité* 526).

NOTES

1. The Parthian version is titled "Sermon on the Light-Mind" (*Mnwhmyd Rwšn Wyfrš*), the Coptic "On the Mind of Light and the Apostles and the Saints" *(Etbe pnous novaine mn napostolos mn netouabe),* the Turkish "Book of the Two Principles" *(Iki yiltiz nom);* the title of the Chinese version is missing, but in all likelihood should be restored to "Book of the Two Principles" *(Erh tsung ching),* which Chinese sources mention frequently.
2. Two other contenders for this status are the narrative of Mani's imprisonment and demise, associated with the annual *bema* festival, and the parallel Manichaean eschatological accounts found in the Coptic *Homilies* and *Psalm-Book* and in Iranian hymns and fragments of the *Šabuhragan.*
3. "Un traité manichéen retrouvé en Chine," *Journal asiatique* 18:499–617.
4. The Parthian and Sogdian versions have now been edited by Werner Sundermann, *Der Sermon vom Licht-Nous,* Berlin Turfan Texte XVII, (Berlin: Akademic Verlag, 1992). See further W. Sundermann, "Der chinesische Traité Manichéen und der parthische Sermon vom Lichtnous," *Altorientalische Forschungen* 10 (1983):231–242; H. -J. Klimkeit & H. Schmidt-Glintzer, "Die turkischen Parallelen zum chinesischmanichäischen Traktat," *Zentralasiatische Studien* 17 (1984):82–117.
5. H. J. Polotsky and A. Böhlig, *Kephalaia* (Stuttgart, 1940), pp. 89–102.
6. The construction of the primordial human bodies of Adam and Eve are definitive for human existence, and the disordered debility of the original couple are passed down by the process of human reproduction.
7. See especially *Traité* 559ff.
8. The hypothesis is most closely associated with the work of Arthur Vööbus.
9. The Chinese version actually likens hermits to sick persons (*Traité* 573f.).

37

The Allegorization of Gender: Plato and Philo on Spiritual Childbearing

Verna E. F. Harrison

In recent scholarship, Philo of Alexandria has acquired quite a reputation for misogyny. In major studies of his gender concepts and perceptions of women, Richard Baer and Dorothy Sly have noted that in many passages he disparages women for their alleged intellectual and moral weaknesses and vices. His discussions of the intellect as symbolically male and the senses as female often make an imperceptible and perhaps unconscious transition from the allegorical to the literal level, where women in general are characterized as misled by the senses and overly attached to pleasures and material things. This raises the question whether his various allegorical uses of gender language are simply projections of an androcentric anthropology or indeed a gut-level hostility toward women. Sly's study pays close attention to the texts and their nuances and contains much significant analysis, but she appears overall to answer this question in the affirmative. My suggestion in this paper is that the place of gender in Philo's anthropology is far less monolithic and consequently far more interesting than such a reading would indicate.

Philo's statements about human ontology in the treatises *De opificio mundi (On The Creation of the World)* and the *Legum allegoriae (Allegory of the Law)* and in the *(Quaestiones et solutiones in Genesin (Questions and Answers on Genesis)* are complex and difficult to reconcile with each other. Scholars have been unable to reach consensus about the details of their meaning, but the broad picture which emerges is as follows. The ideal human person, the one made in God's image and likeness, and also the higher part of each actual human being—that is, the intellectual soul, with which the human as ideal and image is probably to be identified—transcend gender and are, as such, neither male nor female. Actual human persons, who have bodies as well as minds, are either men or women. This ontology of gender is to be distinguished from the symbolic uses of gender language in Philo's allegories. Within each human person the intellect is allegorically male while the senses are allegorically female. Because in this model the intellect, with whom the self is usually identified, is asexual in one sense and male in another sense, such interpreters as Aspegren and Sly have concluded that, for Philo, the transcendence of gender really means becoming male and negating the female.

Other prominent features of Philo's allegorical gender symbolism, however, suggest strongly that this interpretation cannot be correct. He emphasizes two positively charged feminine symbols, that of the virgin and that of the spiritual childbearer. Both of these are intrinsic components of his understanding of human wholeness and spiritual maturity and are necessary to its actualization. Like most ancient authors, he writes primarily for men from a man's point of view. It follows that he envisages the spiritually mature man as having feminine characteristics along with masculine ones; that is, men are called to become virgins, be impregnated by the divine, and bear spiritual children. Philo also recognizes that some women, such as those belonging to the ascetical Therapeutae, can exercise these positive feminine capacities, but his main focus is on men. This means that his anthropological ideal is not maleness as such but ultimately a kind of androgyny of the soul, a development of both masculine and feminine virtues and faculties within a harmonious wholeness. Baer observes that, for Philo, spiritual progress can be characterized as becoming male, becoming one, or becoming a virgin, and that these three modes of human transformation are equivalent. Aspegren and Sly have taken this to mean that Philo regards virginity as a kind of maleness, an unlikely conclusion given virginity's close link with spiritual childbearing. It is more accurate to say that Baer's equivalence involves not identity but simultaneous occurrence and interrelationship within a single process of spiritual growth. The texts suggest that becoming male, one, and virgin are three mutually supportive aspects of the same process of human transformation that occur concurrently. The soul's positive masculine and feminine faculties grow to perfection together; and thus the whole person achieves unity. This functional androgyny within the mature person, delineated in Philo's allegories, corresponds to the ontological ideal of the gender-transcending divine image and likeness in the intelligible realm. Later we will analyze how the texts support this analysis.

Philo is primarily concerned with the inner workings of the human person and how he or she can arrive at moral and spiritual growth, the contemplation of God, and union with him. In his allegories, Philo uses the male and female characters of the biblical narrative and their relationships to speak about these concerns. Although, as the literature suggests, misogyny may account for some of his emphasis on gender imagery, it comes in large part from the character of his work as combining Platonic anthropology with Jewish exegesis and spirituality. Many of the key gender concepts he develops derive from Plato. So, before considering Philo's gender allegory in more detail, it will be useful to consider male and female in Plato's anthropology, where some of the same problematics already appear. In what follows, we will look at three aspects of the Athenian philosopher's thought about gender: (1) suggestions of androgyny, (2) masculine and feminine aspects of the tripartite soul, and (3) spiritual childbearing. Then we will return to what Philo says on the same themes.

Suggestions of Androgyny

In the *Symposium,* the comic poet Aristophanes is presented as offering an entertaining account of the origin of humanity. He says that human beings were initially double what they are now, each having two faces, four arms, and four legs. In some, both halves were male, in others both were female, and in yet others one side was male and the other female. These beings were arrogant and powerful enough to attack the gods, who decided to weaken and punish them by cutting them in half, which gave rise to the kind of humans that exist now. They are wounded and incomplete beings who long to be reunited with the other halves from which they are parted, and this longing is what constitutes love. Love takes three forms corresponding to the three sexual types from which persons originally derive; namely, homoerotic attractions between women and between men, and heterosexual attraction. Aristophanes adds that the original beings that had two male halves and the corresponding homosexual men are the strongest and best humans.

Plato places this myth in the mouth of a comic poet and goes on later in the dialogue to ascribe a different and more definitive account of love's origin and character to Socrates. This suggests that he does not intend the myth to be taken with full seriousness, but it does represent something of his thought. The idea of human existence as originating in androgyny parallels a text in Philo's treatise *De opificio mundi,* which we will discuss below. Another parallel occurs in *Genesis Rabbah* where the account of Eve's creation in *Genesis* 2 is understood as God's splitting of an androgynous earth creature into two sides, one of which becomes the male Adam while the other becomes his wife. Philo may be influenced by Plato on this point, though he may also reflect Jewish traditions later compiled by the rabbis. Similarly, they may have been influenced in some indirect way by Plato. Whatever is Philo's source in the *De opificio mundi,* he is clearly aware of the *Symposium* and its myth of androgyny, since he cites it explicitly with disapproval in the treatise *De vita contemplativa (On the Contemplative Life),* paragraph 61.

The myth ascribed to Aristophanes was remembered and utilized by later thinkers for its suggestion of androgyny. Yet notice that for Plato himself the androgyny is combined with androcentrism. All three possible types of double humans are acknowledged, but the male/male variety is regarded as best. A similar picture emerges in Book V of the *Republic,* where men and women are said to be capable of exercising the same virtues and performing the same tasks with the exception of begetting and bearing children. Plato concludes from this that in the ideal state boys and girls should be given the same education so that all available human resources can be utilized to serve and strengthen the community. The presupposition here is that humans of both genders have essentially the same nature, abilities and purposes. Yet again this position is qualified in an androcentric way. Plato acknowledges that many individual women are in many ways superior to many individual men, but he adds that on the whole men are stronger and more talented than women. The equality of educational opportunity is intended to enable the exceptional women to contribute to society along with the brighter men.

Plato's androcentrism is also expressed in the preference for homosexuality, which forms the theme of the *Symposium* and the *Phaedrus*. He asserts that since men are on the whole better than women, relationships between men can enhance both partners personally, morally, and intellectually in very fruitful ways. From this perspective, a man cannot derive similar benefits from a female partner, who is useful to him only for purposes of procreation. This opinion surely reflects the limited social and cultural opportunities available to women in classical Athens. But at least Plato allows for the possibility, radical in its historical context, that with education some women could become full partners to men. However, he does not develop this possibility into an ideal of heterosexual love parallel to the ideal of homosexual love and its ascetic and mystical transformation described so eloquently in the *Phaedrus* and especially in the *Symposium*.

Masculine and Feminine Aspects of the Tripartite Soul

Book IV of the *Republic* explains how the human soul is composed of three distinct parts. The highest of these is the νοῦς (intellect), which is capable of reasoning, planning, apprehending authentic truth and contemplating ultimate reality. The second part is θυμός, a word having no satisfactory English equivalent but often translated as "spirit" or "passion." These renderings are misleading since they do not convey its meaning accurately and suggest confusion with πνεῦμα and πάθος, which name quite different concepts. Θυμός is the capacity for anger, courage, and assertiveness. It enables one to set limits on one's own behavior and that of others and to fight for justice. This faculty plays an important positive role in Plato's anthropology. When functioning properly, it is a strong ally to the intellect and controls the soul's third and lowest faculty, ἐπιθυμία (desire). Desire by itself is blind and generally misdirected toward sensual things, so it needs to be guided by intellect and controlled by assertiveness. When the soul's three parts each function as they should and abide within their hierarchical order, the result is harmony, virtue, and human wholeness.

In the *Timaeus* (69–70), a passage explaining the creation of humans by the gods, the tripartite soul is described again from a different perspective that links it to the body's physiology. The rational soul is immortal, and around it is fashioned the body as its vehicle. Within the body is formed the irrational soul, which is mortal and is the locus of strong emotions and the senses. The rational soul is placed in the head and separated by the neck from the irrational soul contained in the thorax or torso. The irrational soul is itself divided into θυμός in the chest and ἐπιθυμία in the area of the stomach and genitals. These two parts are delimited by the diaphragm, which divides the body as in a house the men's quarters are divided from the women's. This physiological arrangement corresponds to the hierarchy among the irrational soul's parts delineated in the *Republic*. The higher part, θυμός, is nearer the head so it can join reason is governing and restraining the lower part, desire, which resides in the bodily organs most associated with it.

As Sly observes, in this psychological model the assertive faculty is linked to the male and desire to the female. Although the male part ranks above the female, intellect in turn is above both of them and implicitly transcends gender altogether. Philo echoes this view in his belief that the intellect bearing God's image is beyond male and female. However, to my knowledge, he does not link the two irrational faculties with the genders. Although he sometimes mentions the Platonic tripartite soul, he usually contrasts intellect as male with desire as female, saying little about θυμός and usually ascribing its functions of governing senses and emotions to intellect itself. At this point, Philo appears more androcentric than Plato. In contrast, Clement of Alexandria and Maximus the Confessor develop a more androgynous version of Platonic psychology. They identify θυμός as male and ἐπιθυμία as female, asserting that intellect should govern both of them and thus enable the whole person to transcend their gender-based limitations. For them and for other Christian writers, such as Gregory of Nyssa, the two irrational parts of the soul are regarded as equal, and the assertive faculty no longer has the prominence and precedence ascribed to it by Plato.

The psychology described in the *Republic,* Book IV, and in the *Timaeus* confines feminine qualities to the lowest part of the soul and values them negatively. The need to control and restrain desire and sense perception is stressed. They are linked to matter while intellect is linked to the higher spiritual world. Yet in two dialogues on the subject of love, desire plays quite a different role. The *Phaedrus* pictures it as a rebellious untrained horse pulling the chariot of the soul. The intellect as charioteer has to beat it to prevent its carrying the whole vehicle away into sexual excess. Yet the same animal can become a winged steed and carry the soul up to the divine realm where it contemplates ultimate reality. In human terms, one's beloved can function either as an object of sensual pleasure or as an icon of transcendent beauty. Socrates' speech in the *Symposium* offers a more developed account of desire's spiritualization. The lover should begin by contemplating the physical beauty of a single youth, his beloved, but does not stop there. He learns that the physical beauty of all comely youths is the same, and he ceases to be attached to one alone. He moves from there to love beauty as manifest in virtuous souls, just institutions, and scientific laws to the beauty of the world in general. Finally he arrives at an apprehension of the eternal and divine beauty in itself, which transcends all other beauties that exist by participation in it. This is the ultimate goal.

Notice how desire, dismissed in the *Republic* as the lowest faculty of the soul, becomes in the *Symposium* an intrinsic aspect of the highest human activity, contemplation of the divine. Its activity now belongs to the intellect in its loftiest function, the intuitive perception of immaterial ultimate reality, which ranks above the discursive functions of reasoning, planning and controlling that also belong to it. This means that there is a tension within Plato's anthropology in regard to the role of desire and the capacities for perception and receptivity that go with it. When directed toward material things, these faculties are deceptive, so they must not be allowed to direct one's judgments, choices, and activities. They need to be channeled in more useful ways by intellect, which can apprehend a more complete picture of reality. In much of Plato's work, the rational mind has the central and highest place. It appears that the receptive faculties are rejected, though when hierarchically subordinated to intellect and θυμός they are included in the harmonious existence of the whole person. Yet in the *Symposium* desire and receptivity, though transcended in their physical form at the beginning of the spiritual journey, reemerge at the end as the highest human activities as they engage in love and contemplation of the divine. In the *Phaedrus,* love is described as against reason yet above it, as an inspired and prophetic madness that unites the soul with the gods.

This split in Plato's evaluation of desire also involves his understanding of gender. It is easy for him to identify the assertive faculty as masculine, and the same designation can be applied implicitly to the reasoning and planning intellect with which θυμός is closely allied. Sensual and material desire, then, is labeled as feminine and relegated to the lowest place, to be controlled or rejected. Yet the contemplative activity of intellect is also characterized by desire, perception, and receptivity. It is no accident that, in the *Symposium,* Socrates learns the highest mysteries of love from a wise woman, Diotima. Having reached the goal of the spiritual journey, the philosopher plays a feminine role. She is united in love to God and bears spiritual children by him, a point to which we will return.

This means that, for Plato, the masculine aspects of the human soul, θυμός and discursive intellect, are closely related to each other and can thus be clearly conceptualized and positively charged in an unambiguous way. His account of the feminine aspects is more complex and fraught with tension. These include the lower sensible desire, often negatively charged, and the highest spiritual love and contemplation. Plato tries to keep the sensible and intelligible aspects of the human person apart, but the single faculty of desire belongs to both. The *Symposium* describes how it is gradually transformed and redirected from matter toward divine beauty. In this dialogue praising homoerotic love between men, the feminine aspect of the soul is always active and positively charged. Yet its unity here is in tension with a split elsewhere in Plato's thought between the faculties exercised in sense perception and intellectual contemplation.

Notice also that though θυμός is masculine and ἐπιθυμία is feminine, the highest part of the human person, *νοῦς*, is by implication linked to both genders. Its rational and structuring activity can be regarded as masculine while its intuitive, receptive, and contemplative activity can be regarded as feminine. Plato's thought thus is capable of being developed into a truly androgynous psychology.

Plato's anthropology provides hints and allusions to gender symbolism, and these are rendered explicit and unfolded at great length in Philo's allegories. Some of their peculiarities reflect the tensions we have observed in the Athenian philosopher's psychology. The split between sensible and intelligible desire becomes for Philo a contrast between two kinds of female figures, the woman who is negatively charged and the virgin who is positively charged. The belief that the rational and contemplative activities both belong to the highest part of the soul, the *νοῦς*, finds expression in Philo's account of how spiritual progress involves at the same time becoming male, becoming a virgin, and becoming one. As a Jewish mystic in quest for an intimate relationship with the transcendent personal God, he emphasizes spiritual love, receptivity, and childbearing much more than Plato, whose treatment of these themes is largely focused in one dialogue, the *Symposium.* Thus along with his well-known androcentrism and misogyny, Philo moves toward an androgynous psychology in which the human person's feminine qualities play a large positive role. Plato's homosexuality is abandoned, in part out of faithfulness to the ethics of Torah and in part out of misogyny, so that men will not behave effeminately, but also so that the feminine aspects of spiritual life can be more fully affirmed as they are described through the allegorization of love between men and women.

Spiritual Childbearing

Alongside desire and receptivity, spiritual childbearing is an important feminine dimension of Philo's thought, and this also has its roots in Plato. In the *Thaeatetus* (150–151), Socrates describes himself as a midwife. He says that his mother was a midwife to women, but his midwifery is for men and is more important. While women are pregnant in their bodies and bear children, men are pregnant in their souls and bring forth the fruits of moral, intellectual, artistic, and civic creativity. As the female midwife is herself barren, Socrates is himself intellectually unfruitful but is able to help others bring their ideas to light and can discern whether they are genuine offspring or not.

Notice again the androcentrism. Male childbearing is linked to the intelligible realm, female childbearing only to the sensible. Notice in the *Thaeatetus* also that although men are said to become pregnant, no explanation is given of who fathers their spiritual offspring. The scenario is different in the *Symposium,* where two forms of spiritual childbearing are described. The first and lower form occurs in a homosexual relationship between a mature lover and a younger beloved. The lover serves as the youth's teacher, instructing him in virtue and knowledge, and their collaboration blossoms into a lifelong friendship and brings forth moral, intellectual, and cultural offspring. Here, the teacher functions as male and the student, though also a man, as female. When the beloved grows older and wiser, he in turn can initiate similar relationships of love and instruction with other young men, so in the end the same persons play both masculine and feminine roles. But significantly the transition from female to male represents a growth in maturity. The dimension of feminine receptivity is positively charged, but androcentrism is preserved, at least at this stage of initiation into love's mysteries.

This kind of spiritual childbearing between teacher and student will become a recurring theme among early Christian writers such as Origen and his follower Didymus of Alexandria, though for them the homosexual dimension is absent. The male/female symbolism is made explicit and is completely allegorized, so that the same persons can become either female or male depending on their spiritual development and whether they are receiving instruction or instructing others. In Philo's discussions of spiritual progress, too, the language of sexuality is completely allegorized from the outset. This contrasts with Plato, for whom the ascetical sublimation and redirection of physical *erōs* is a gradual process. As part of this process the gender language in the *Symposium,* which is initially literal, gradually becomes allegorized. As I have shown elsewhere, allegory constitutes the literary analogue of the ascetical practice itself. The tradition of love transformed into ascetical and mystical spirituality has roots in Hebrew scripture, where the relationship between God and Israel is likened to the love between husband and wife. But one of its fundamental sources is this dialogue, where Socrates, who appears to be a compelling homoerotic lover, actually proves to be a consummate ascetic, as Alcibiades' speech makes clear. Socrates has personally renounced physical *erōs* for its higher forms, yet he includes it in his theory of human transformation as the spiritual journey's starting point. Philo and the early Christian writers, on the other hand, begin the journey with a renunciation of sexual activity, which they regard as a hindrance to the ascent toward God. Plato moves through love for beautiful bodies toward ultimate beauty, while the Jewish and Christian ascetics, at least in this context, move away from it toward the ultimate. Obviously, however, the turn from the senses to the spiritual intellect is also a very Platonic move.

In the second kind of spiritual childbearing described in the *Symposium*, an intrinsic aspect of love's highest mystery, this transcendence of the sensible level is fully actualized at the journey's end. As explained above, the philosopher's soul is united in contemplation with the eternal divine beauty. This means that beyond the maleness of the teacher is a higher feminine stage of human development. As a result of her union with what is most truly real, the soul is impregnated by the divine and brings forth fruit of authentic truth and virtue. Fruit of such authenticity cannot be conceived except through this direct contact with ultimate reality, and these are the most valuable offspring of all. Philo develops this theme in terms of the virgin as mother of virtues, good thoughts and deeds that have God as their father.

Philo's Commentary

Let us now turn more directly to Philo's understanding of gender. In the treatise *De opificio mundi* 134, he says, in commenting on *Genesis* 2.7 ("God formed the human by taking clay from the earth, and breathed into his face the breath of life") that there is a vast difference between the human formed in this way and the human created earlier in the image of God (*Gn.* 1.26–27). The second one is perceptible by the senses; has various qualities; is mortal; and consists of body and soul, man and woman. The one made according to the divine image is an idea or genus or seal, perceptible by the mind, incorporeal, immortal, and neither male nor female. This language seems to be saying that the one bearing the divine image is a Platonic idea of the human existing separately in the noetic realm. However, Philo's thought in this regard is not altogether clear or consistent. Baer believes that this concept refers to the higher part within each human person, the intelligible soul, a position I find convincing. The text goes on to say that the human in *Genesis* 2.7 is formed of clay and divine breath and thus combines a mortal body and an immortal mind (135). This description of a composite being immediately follows the passage contrasting the products of the acts of creation narrated in *Genesis* 1 and 2. The immortal and mortal dimensions of humanity are identified as opposites and then combined in the actual first human person. This literary structure expresses the idea that the actual human composite combines the elements contrasted as mortal and immortal in *De opificio mundi* 134, as Baer suggests. If this interpretation is correct, Philo believes that the human person's mind transcends gender, while the body is either male or female.

A little later in the same treatise (151), the creation of Eve is linked with the origin of sin. The text begins by saying that since everything created is subject to change, the first human being also underwent a change for the worse. By itself, this statement suggests that the ontological mutability of created things as such is the cause of human involvement in evil, so maybe the woman only provides an occasion triggering what would have happened anyway. However, what follows indicates that her involvement is more serious than a chance opportunity. Philo says that she became the beginning of blameworthy life for the first human.

Next, he says that as long as the first human lived alone, he became like the world and like God and received the imprints of both in his soul, as far as he could receive them. Sly believes that for Philo the human in this original blessed condition is male, and indeed a bit later he is called ἀνήρ (153). Yet there is nothing particularly masculine about his way of life as described here. He is receptive to God and the creation, and contemplates both, so that he is imprinted with God's likeness and the likenesses of creatures. Philo is speaking of the human vocation to be microcosm as well as mediator between the world and the Creator, a concept developed further by Greek Christian writers like the Cappadocians and Maximus the Confessor. An important aspect of this vocation is openness to receive the likenesses of God and other beings into oneself and thus come to participate in them, a quality Philo often regards as feminine.

As we said earlier, a rabbinic text reports a Jewish tradition suggesting that the first human was androgynous, and with the creation of Eve, God divided its two sides, making one male and another female. In *De opificio mundi* 151–152, Philo may point to some such idea in what appears to be an allusion to Aristophanes' myth in the *Symposium.* He says that when the woman was created, Adam saw a form like and akin to his own, rejoiced, approached, and greeted her. She too saw in him a being more like herself than any other and with joy and modesty greeted him in return. Love arose between them, as if seeking to unite the divided halves of a single living being. It established in each a desire for communion with the other in order to bring into existence others like themselves. Notice how the wholeness and plenitude of the original solitary human, who enjoyed communion with God and the world around him, is broken. (One is tempted to call him anachronistically the first μοναχός.) The now incomplete halves strive to restore their primordial unity. Yet this inevitably becomes a quest for further multiplication. Philo said initially that the fall into evil was due to the changeableness of created nature; here he alludes to another related aspect of created susceptibility to corruption; namely, a tendency toward fragmentation. The next issue to arise is the presence of another human person like the self. The problematic of sexuality and a qualitative gender contrast within the human condition are at least logically subsequent to these other factors.

Philo explains that following its involvement in mutability and division, the human condition deteriorates further. The desire for union and offspring gives rise to bodily pleasure, which is the source of wrongdoing and leads humans into mortality and away from immortality and authentic happiness (152). That is, as Philo understands it, Adam and Eve immersed themselves in sensible realities instead of focusing on the noetic world and participating in it. They let the senses and the irrational parts of the soul take the lead within themselves instead of allowing the mind to govern them and engage in the activity proper to it, contemplation. This contrast between following the νοῦς and the senses is central to Philo's spirituality. In this regard the first sin has the same character as sin generally has for him.

As the narrative continues, the man represents intellect while the woman represents the senses. He errs by obeying her advice and eating the forbidden fruit. The social hierarchy between the sexes is superimposed on the psychological hierarchy that structures appropriate relationships among the faculties of the soul. In the *De opificio mundi,* strands of androcentrism and misogyny run through Philo's recounting of the story of *Genesis* 2–3, but they are woven with other kinds of fiber into a complex fabric. The theme of original androgyny is also a strong motif. This text is a good example of Philo's ambivalence and eclecticism, his creation of a rich interweaving of many threads of thought and culture.

It is important to remember that although, for him, intellect and sense are hierarchically ordered, the soul must include both in order to be fully human. Each part needs the other to function properly. When hierarchy is upset and harmony is broken, intellect and sense represented by Adam and Eve come into conflict with each other against their true nature. In the context of the psychological allegory, they are truly two halves of a single being that need to reunite. At this point the myth of androgyny and Philo's standard symbolism of mind as male and sense as female coincide. As the human brokenness that *Genesis* 3 depicts is healed, and as the person progresses spiritually, each of the soul's faculties has to be restored to its full and rightly directed activity, as unity between them is actualized. In Baer's language, this means at once becoming male through the intellect's active choice of virtue and self-control; becoming a virgin through the redirection of perception, desire, and receptivity toward the divine; and becoming one through mature harmony within the self. These three aspects of human wholeness are inseparable and mutually interdependent. Yet they remain distinct, and one cannot be reduced to another. Virginity, for example, is not the same as maleness as Sly and Aspegren suppose but remains feminine.

Baer's primary example of becoming male comes from *Quaestiones et solutiones in Genesin* 2.49, a text that actually illustrates my point. Philo asks why, in *Genesis* 7.7 and 8.18, Noah and his sons enter the ark in one group while their wives enter in another group—the men together and the women together—whereas Noah leaves the ark with his wife and his sons with their wives. His answer is that in the literal sense, the flood was a time for sorrow, vigilance, and struggle, so then it was not appropriate to enjoy pleasure and bring children into the world, but after Noah's family was saved from evil, it was fitting to procreate. An allegorical explanation follows, and that is what concerns us here. Philo says that when the soul is cleansing itself from sin, the mind should be united with its own thoughts, like

Noah with his sons, and keep itself separate from things of sense. The purpose is to ensure victory, since it is a time of war. However, once one is cleansed of sin and freed from ignorance and what is harmful, mind and sense should come together again, but in their proper hierarchical order. Masculine thoughts should not be femininzed, but the female senses should become manly by receiving seed from the masculine thoughts and thus bringing forth perceptions characterized by wisdom, prudence, justice, and courage—that is, virtue.

This text speaks of two stages in spiritual life. The first, that of ascetic struggle, is ascribed to the less mature soul that needs to be purified. It is a time of warfare, so the activities of reasoned planning, vigilence, self-control, endurance, and combat against evil must be exercised. These are the masculine virtues that Philo associates with intellect. Here mind has clearly come to include Plato's θυμός, though as usual it is not mentioned. However, this conflict within the self between mind and senses cannot be permanent and does not constitute the goal. As the person progresses to the second stage, the senses are not eradicated but transformed and redirected. The mind's masculine thoughts, having achieved victory through the military virtues, must remain as they are and not become feminized by following the senses. On the other hand, sense perception needs to become manly. This language suggests an androcentric asymmetry, as if the female is absorbed into the male. Yet that is not what the text goes on to describe. Instead there is a gender paradox. Becoming manly is said to mean receiving seed, becoming pregnant and giving birth to the virtues. What is involved is actually the fulfillment of sense's femininity, not its negation. It becomes united with mind, not displaced, and this union makes perception itself virtuous. Thus, becoming male means also becoming one as inner conflict gives way to harmony. In addition, it entails spiritual childbearing, which for Philo is an essential activity of the virgin. So becoming male involves also becoming female, in the best sense.

There is a close parallel to this text in *Legum allegoriae* 2.49–52. Philo, commenting on *Genesis* 2.24 ("For this cause shall a man leave his father and his mother, and shall cleave to his wife, and the two shall be one flesh") speaks about how human beings fall into sin. He takes this verse to mean that mind abandons God, the father of the universe, and his wisdom, the mother of all, to be enslaved to sense perception. Mind is united to sense and dissolved into it so they become one flesh and one πάθος (passion or experience). Philo remarks that it is not the woman who cleaves to the man but the man to the woman, mind to sense perception, the higher to the lower. The mode of their union is asymmetrical and reverses their proper hierarchical ordering. However, Philo adds that the opposite can also happen. Sense can follow mind, in which case it is no longer flesh but both become νοῦς (mind). He offers as an example the priest Levi, who leaves father and mother—that is, his own mind and material body—and is united to God, whom he loves. Thus, the text concludes, passion is the inheritance of the lover of passion, while God is the inheritance of one who loves him.

The contrasting examples of Adam and Levi indicate that the reader has a choice of which to follow. Thus, the human person retains all of the soul's faculties and the freedom to decide how they are to be ordered. This suggests that the mind enslaved to sense is not literally dissolved into nonexistence. Rather, it acquires the character of the sensible faculty it has chosen to follow. The whole person becomes like the part of the self that takes the lead within it. Philo's account of the other alternative supports this interpretation. When sense follows mind and thus becomes mind, what actually happens is that it desires God instead of desiring matter and the passions. This involves an attempt on Philo's part to resolve the tension implicit in Platonic anthropology. Desire is absorbed, as it were, into mind, so mind can desire God. Through spiritual progress, the soul's lowest and highest parts are made one. Notice that by being assimilated into masculine mind, sense does not lose its femininity but rather gives it to mind, which then desires God and is receptive to him. So the hierarchical subordination of female to male is not nearly so absolute as it first appears.

Notice also that Levi is said to leave his mind as well as his body to be united with God. Divine love and contemplation lead him beyond intellect. This echoes the gender reversal in the *Symposium*, where the mature person plays a male role as teacher and progresses further to a female role of receptivity to the divine. It also echoes the account of love as inspired madness in the *Phaedrus* as well as reflecting Philo's understanding of Jewish prophesy, a topic beyond the scope of this paper. But notice that this dimension of spiritual life cannot be explained within a framework that consistently subordinates feminine desire, perception, and creativity to masculine reason and self-control. Philo's spirituality is richer and more inclusive than that.

A similar parallel to the gender reversal in the *Symposium* occurs in *Quaestiones et solutiones in Genesin* 4.99, which comments on *Genesis* 24.16, a verse that speaks of Rebecca as a virgin whom no man has known. Philo begins by contrasting the bodily beauty of a young virgin girl with the more important virginity of the soul in which wisdom and virtue dwell. Then he speaks of the man who does not know her as one who has the self-control and courage to avoid corrupting the uncorrupted and resist sowing seeds of sensual pleasure in his mind. Notice again the active character of masculine virtues and the fact that, here, mind is feminine. This provides an example of the ways in which terms like wisdom, virtue, mind and soul can shift their gender in Philo's allegories, to reflect the complexities of interaction among the parts of the human soul and between the human and the divine. Another example occurs in *De fuga et inventione* 50–51, where wisdom is named as the daughter of God but the father of everything else. Similarly, all the virtues viewed as powers and activities are called perfect males. In *De Abrahamo* 99–102, virtue is again said to be male, in that it moves and organizes and initiates good words and deeds. In contrast, mind, as receptive to virtue, is called feminine. These texts cannot rightly be seen as evidence of Philo's complete androcentrism, as Sly believes, because they make wisdom and virtue male instead of female. At the same time they make mind female instead of male. Moreover, they need to be read together with many other passages where wisdom is named as mother of all and where virtue may function as wife, mother or child, depending on the context.

The definition of maleness in *Quaestiones et solutiones in Genesin* 4.99 concludes with a striking gender reversal. It says that the man who courageously resists thoughts of pleasure instead receives incorruptible and intelligible seeds of divinity from the father of all who sows them in us. The man's self is identified with his mind, which here functions as feminine. Again the point is that the mature person possesses both masculine and feminine virtues, both self-control and receptivity.

Let us now turn to Philo's concept of the virgin and its relationship to spiritual childbearing. In *Quaestiones et solutiones in Exodum* 2.3, he addresses the question of why scripture prohibits the mistreatment of widows and orphans. In the literal sense, he says, it means that there is a particular obligation to care for those who lack close relatives to provide for them. Then he suggests two deeper meanings. The first is that the soul who loves herself honors her mind as a husband who sows in her the perceiving capacities of the senses and as a father who provides her education. Notice how, in this passage, the self is identified with the female soul rather than with the male mind, as is so often the case for Philo. This suggests that he does not identify the true person or its center exclusively with its masculine parts but acknowledges psychological complexity. The second deeper meaning given in this text is that the soul free of self-love who seeks God receives from him the presence and care of a father and, as from a husband, the seeds of good thoughts, intentions, words, and deeds. This is the theme of spiritual impregnation and childbearing. Philo immediately goes on to speak of his contrast between woman and virgin, with which this theme is closely connected. He says that when men come into contact with virgins they make them women, but when souls are divinely inspired, they cease to be women corrupted by sense perception and passions and become virgins again. This means that their desire is redirected toward God, who at the same time purifies them. Their spiritual childbearing follows from this.

Philo develops these themes in several places but notably in the treatise *De cherubim* 40–52, to which we will now turn. He acknowledges that in the literal sense men and women have intercourse and produce children, but he says that allegorically the great biblical heroes Abraham, Isaac, Jacob, and Moses do not know women. Their wives, Sarah, Rebecca, Leah, and Zipporah, are virgins and are identified as virtues. It is God who begets their children, though not for himself, since he is in need of nothing, but for their husbands (40–47). Philo explains that this concept is a sacred mystery and cannot be understood by the uninitiated, to whom it should not be revealed. As mystery he may have in mind the assertion that the patriarchs' marriages are in actuality symbols of something more important; namely, the soul's virgin-motherhood and union with God. At this point there is an ascetic strand in his spirituality, and his thought appears to anticipate the Christian fathers rather than the later rabbis. The concept of the soul as virgin and mother will be developed by such writers as Gregory of Nyssa and Maximus the Confessor. For them, of course, there is a concrete human model in Mary, which is not the case for Philo. In light of this, his elaboration of the concept is quite striking.

The text goes on to say that God enters into a relationship with virgin souls, which is the opposite of what happens with human beings. As in *Quaestiones et solutiones in Exodum* 2.3, Philo says that when men unite with virgins for the procreation of children they make them women; but when God becomes intimate with a soul he makes what was a woman into a virgin again by removing her passionate desires and giving her virtues instead. The text adds that when Sarah in old age had ceased from the ways of women, she was ranked again as a pure virgin (50). This was when God as father enabled her to bear Isaac. Notice how for Philo virginity and spiritual childbearing belong together without any need for further explanation. For him they are two sides of the same coin. The positive content of virginity, for him, is receptivity to God and the corresponding creative fruitfulness. Abstinence from sensual attachments is a necessary condition for this, but in itself it is secondary. In effect, virginity is almost defined in terms of spiritual motherhood.

In *De cherubim* 52, Philo concludes his discussion by exhorting the soul, which presumably belongs to his male reader, to live as a virgin in God's house and embrace knowledge instead of holding to sense perception which feminizes and defiles it. Yet the choice offered here is actually between positive and negative kinds of femininity, which, as we have seen, is in one or another form intrinsic for Philo to human psychological and spiritual existence.

Let me conclude my discussion with a passage from the treatise *De migratione Abrahami (On the Migration of Abraham),* in which Philo speaks of his own spiritual experience. He has been discussing the perfect soul who no longer needs to struggle in acquiring virtue but is self-taught in the sense of freely receiving divine grace, a condition symbolized by Isaac. Such a soul is at rest, and God pours abundant blessings upon it. The mind no longer works at its own tasks but instead receives seed that is cultivated and watered by God. Here, agricultural language combines with the language of procreation. Philo adds that the offspring of the soul's own labor pains are usually miscarriages, but those coming from heaven are born perfect and best of all (28–33).

Clearly, receptivity to the divine and spiritual childbearing become most important at the highest stage of spiritual maturity. It even appears that the masculine virtues of struggle for self-control are no longer needed beyond a certain point, and human reason yields to what is above it. The text continues with an autobiographical passage, where Philo describes the feminine side of his own spirituality. I will quote the David Winston translation:

> I feel no shame in describing my own experience, a thing I know from its having occurred numberless times. On occasion, after deciding to follow the standard procedure of writing on philosophical doctrines and knowing precisely the elements of my composition, I have found my understanding sterile and barren and have abandoned my project without result, while reproaching my thought for its self-conceit, and struck with amazement at the might of Him that Is, on whom depend the opening and closing of the soul-wombs. At other times, I have come empty and have suddenly become full, the ideas descending like snow and invisibly sown, so that under the impact of divine possession I have been filled with corybantic frenzy and become ignorant of everything, place, people present, myself, what was said and what was written. For I acquired expression, ideas, an enjoyment of light, sharp-sighted vision, exceedingly distinct clarity of objects, such as might occur through the eyes as the result of the clearest display. *Philo of Alexandria: The Contemplative Life, the Giants, and Selections, p. 76 (Classics of Western Spirituality)*

Thus, on many occasions Philo tries to employ his controlling intellect and it proves fruitless. In humility, he is confronted with the fact that power and insight belong to God, not to himself, and that his task is to receive the divine seed, not create it. He acknowledges that his real creativity comes through self-surrender and contemplative perception. Although he prefers to emphasize the active masculine aspects of his human activity, he discovers that he has to rely on the more passive feminine aspects as well, and this brings him not oppression or mere self-effacement but instead authentic self-expression and spiritual and intellectual productivity. This autobiographical passage illustrates how Philo prefers an androcentric anthropology but is led by the requirements of the spiritual journey itself to move toward a more androgynous psychology, so that all the faculties of the human person can be fully developed and used to ascend toward God.

38

Shame and Sex in Late Antique Judaism

Michael L. Satlow

Although asceticism is a slippery phenomenon that often evades precise definition, nearly all the attempted definitions focus on individual experience and motivation. The *Encyclopedia of Religion*, for example, defines asceticism as,

> . . . a voluntary, sustained, and at least partially systematic program of self-discipline and self-denial in which immediate, sensual, or profane gratifications are renounced in order to attain a higher spiritual state or more thorough absorption in the sacred.[1]

In one respect, the focus on the individual is hardly surprising: the practice of *askēsis*, techniques of bodily control and orientation, is essentially personal.[2] Ultimately it is the individual who practices self-discipline and self-denial. The second focus on the individual, the assignment of his or her motivation, is more questionable. Individual motivations can be highly idiosyncratic and—especially in the case of ancient societies—hidden to later investigators. Marginalized in this focus is the role of the community. How are we to address the varied and often complex interactions of asceticism, the individual and the community in our investigations of asceticism? What light might a focus on the community's role and motivations in supporting ascetic practices shed on the more general study of asceticism?

Individuals do not engage in ascetic practices in a vacuum. Communal complicity is necessary. This complicity can be explicit, as in the case of communities founded upon commitment to ascetic practices, such as monasteries. More frequently, however, the relationship between an individual engaging in ascetic practices and her or his surrounding community is far more complex. Communities often provide a context and support for ascetic practices. Such support might be through the assignation to the ascetic individual of a unique role in the society, as in the case of the role of the holy man in Christianity of late antiquity.[3] Alternatively, a society might provide a language, or discourse, through which ascetic practices can be expressed and understood by all members of the community.[4] Strategies of continence and control, for example, among members of the male ruling élite of Greece and Rome in antiquity were embedded in the societal discourse, thus effectively supporting and reproducing such practices.[5]

Jewish communities in late antiquity, as reflected in rabbinic sources, both explicitly and implicitly supported a wide range of ascetic practices. The rabbis—by this term I refer to the group of men who lived between about 70 CE–500 CE in both Palestine and Babylonia who authored or contributed to what we now call the rabbinic documents—both prescribed and advised a nearly constant self-disciplinary stance. Although the modern study of rabbinic asceticism is in its infancy, it is probably safe to say that ". . . rabbinic writings express concern for the spiritual perfection of the individual and the ascetic means to that end primarily within the context of a communal, institutionalized discipline."[6] Constant vigilance not only leads to spiritual perfection of the individual, but was also necessary in order to prevent entrance to the slippery slope of transgression that leads inexorably to idolatry.[7] Like their male élite contemporaries in Rome, the Palestinian rabbis advised a system of dietetics, a regimen of strict self-control.[8] Unlike the Greek and Roman discourse, however, which linked systems of dietetics to structures of power, the rabbis linked self-control to the holy.

This admittedly insufficient thumbnail sketch of the rabbinic discourse on asceticism will serve to contextualize one example of how rabbinic discourse, asceticism, and communal institutions and goals interacted in late antiquity. As can now be inferred, for the rabbis the practice of sexual self-discipline—but not necessarily abstinence—was of the utmost importance.[9] To yield to sexual desire was tantamount to taking the first step toward apostasy.[10]

But how could the rabbis, who were for the most part at least officially juridically powerless, promote and enforce this stance?[11] One way was rhetorical: many rabbinic dicta offer advice, almost entirely to men, on how to avoid sexual temptation. The rabbis advise Torah study and consideration of eventual death and future punishment for the man troubled by sexual desire.[12] Offering carrots and sticks to their listeners and readers, the rabbis attempted to persuade people to adopt their own sexual mores.[13] This is, obviously, an élitist approach.

At the same time, within rabbinic literature one can see more popularly based strategies for controlling sexuality. That is, it appears that in some cases, it was not necessarily the rabbis who were attempting to impose an ascetic regimen on a resistant populace, but the community itself whose values and strategies were folded into rabbinic discourse. One of these communal strategies, and the one upon which I focus for the remainder of this paper, is that of sexual shame. Jewish communities in late antiquity, in both Palestine and Babylonia, institutionalized strategies of sexual shame in order to promote sexual continence and control. These strategies are assumed in the rabbinic literature, the only source through which we know of them.

Sexual Shame

Modern anthropological studies of the Mediterranean region have repeatedly observed that men were expected to control the sexuality of the women under their auspices; namely, daughters and wives.[14] Rabbinic sources reflect a similar attitude. Commenting, for example, on *Leviticus* 21.9 ("When the daughter of a priest defiles herself through harlotry, it is her father whom she profanes; she shall be put to the fire"), a Palestinian rabbi says:

> Why does Scripture say, "it is her father whom she profanes"? If they treated him as holy they now treat him as profane. If they treated him with honor they now treat him with shame. . . .[15]

This source equates profanation of a priest's daughter with his own loss of honor. In a time without a Temple, when profanation has little concrete meaning, the priest can still be profaned; that is, shamed, by his daughter. This tradition would most likely have resonated in an audience beyond the priests.

The sexual activities of a man's wife, too, could shame him. A particularly telling Palestinian source links shame to adultery:

> All those who descend to Gehenna rise [from there] except for three who descend and do not rise. And these are: one who has intercourse with a married woman; one who shames his fellow in public; and he who calls his fellow by a nickname.[16]

Without doubt, one of the reasons for this association is to (over-) emphasize the gravity of shaming another in public. Yet it is also possible that adultery, and not, for example, murder or idolatry, was chosen as the foil for a reason. Committing adultery with another man's wife is perceived as a form of public shaming: her husband is shown to be unable either to satisfy or to control her sexuality.

Support for this reading can also be found in other rabbinic traditions. One Palestinian tradition associates pride with adultery.[17] A Babylonian statement asserts that haughtiness leads to adultery.[18] This association between haughtiness and adultery is telling: it is not sexual lust or deep emotional attachment or midlife crisis that is said to lead to adultery. Rather, adultery is seen as an assertion of one's power over another man, the theft of the reproductive potential of his wife. Here is the expected "flip side" of the cuckolded husband. Underneath this tradition might lurk the assumption that the society revealed here maintains, like other ancient Mediterranean societies, a zero-sum honor code.[19] When one man takes another's wife, the cuckold must lose honor.

The threat of communal shame was also employed to help men fight what the rabbis called their *yēṣer ha-ra'* (evil desire).[20] The Palestinian Talmud, for example, records the following story:

> Once a guard of vineyards came to have intercourse with a married woman. When they were searching for a *mikvah* where they [could] immerse, passers-by came and went and the sin was averted.[21]

The fear of the public shame that would be incurred in the discovery of the adulterous liaison scares the couple from sin. One Palestinian statement forcefully assumes the power of sexual shaming:

> If a man sees that his "desire" is overpowering him, he should go to a place where no one recognizes him, dressed in black with a black cloak, and do what his heart desires and not profane God publicly.[22]

The tradition assumes that a sage who commits some kind of sexual offense in a place where he is recognized will shame all sages, thus profaning God. The solution, ironically, appears crafted to increase personal shame: who would be more obvious than a stranger dressed in black snooping about the prostitutes' quarter? What appears as a rabbinic concession is most likely yet another use of communal shame in order to fight sexual desire.

Babylonian Jews, too, used shame to help men control themselves sexually. Witness the following story:

> Certain captive women who were brought to Nehardea were taken to the home of Rav Amram the Pious. The ladder was removed before them [i.e., they were on the second story of the house and the ladder was removed to prevent the men from access to the women]. When one of them passed by [the opening to the downstairs, where the ladder usually was], light fell on the sky-light. Rav Amram the Pious took the ladder, which ten men could not raise, and raised it. He went up, and when he was half way up the ladder he forced himself to stand still, and raised his voice, "A fire at Amram's," [he shouted]. The rabbis came and they said to him, "you frightened us." He said to them, "better that you should be ashamed at Amram's house in this world than you should be ashamed of me in the world to come. . . ."[23]

Rav Amram averts falling to temptation by calling to his colleagues. The story assumes a structure of communal shaming: by calling his colleagues, Amram shames himself, thus preventing himself from acting on his desire.

For women as well as men, the threat of shame is assumed to deter unsanctioned sexual liaisons. From puberty on, a woman was socialized to be ashamed of displaying her naked body.[24] A woman, like a man, is assumed to be ashamed of having sex in a public setting. Even if a woman in one of these Jewish communities lacked this sense of shame, she risked subsequent public shaming through any act of illicit intercourse. One oft-cited rabbinic story illustrates this threat:

> One woman, from a good family, came and gathered and ate figs of the seventh year, and they made her go around in the campus. She said to him, "Please, my lord, let the king announce my sin so that all the subjects of the kingdom will not say that she is [i.e., I am] similar to an adulteress or a witch. [Let] them see figs dangling from my neck and they will know that it is for them that I am paraded thus."[25]

Adultery and public shaming of the woman were so linked that the woman in this parable thinks that when people saw her being publicly shamed they would assume that it was for her adultery. To protect her reputation, she requests that spectators be informed of the true nature of her transgression, that she ate figs in the sabbatical year. Whether or not there was a public shaming ceremony for adulteresses, this text, and many like it, create a discourse of shame whose intent, no doubt, was to promote an atmosphere in which women could be sexually controlled through the threat of shaming.[26]

In addition to these texts that indirectly promoted shame as a controlling strategy, there is evidence that women, through institutions such as gossip, themselves shamed other women into sanctioned sexual behavior. Repeatedly, a man is urged to divorce a woman whose reputation is the subject of gossip.[27] A profligate woman was seen as casting aspersions on all Jewish women,[28] and a bad reputation for a wife was to be feared.[29] Especially in the tannaitic sources, women, more than men, are the ones credited with giving bad reputations to other women.

These sources, both Palestinian and Babylonian, reflect a fairly uniform utilization of a shame/honor construct to maintain and support sexual control. Shame could police a society far better than any coercive authority. Determinations such as designating what is to be considered shameful are never imposed upon a society. Rather, it is likely that the rabbis here reflect the attitudes of the Jewish communities in which they lived.

Shame, portrayed in these rabbinic sources as an entirely public matter (in contrast to the internalized sense of shame associated with Christian writers, most notably Augustine), was used by Jewish communities in both Palestine and Babylonia to enforce sexual mores. This is hardly surprising: sexual shaming, as noted, is a characteristic of Mediterranean societies of the past and today.[30] More relevant to the present discussion are the implications of this intersection of popular values (sanctioned sexual deportment), the societal institutions that enforce them (shame), and an élitist discourse (the rabbinic discourse that links sexual self-control to the holy) for the study of asceticism.

Implications for the Study of Asceticism

This study reveals a dynamic that is significantly more complex than the common focus on the individual ascetic and the religious discourse that supports her or his practices might lead us to consider. This dynamic, I suspect, is far from unique to Jewish communities in late antiquity.[31] Three implications of this complex interaction should be emphasized.

First, considerations of motivations of ascetic behavior must consider sociological as well as individual factors. We must be sensitive not only to gradations in ascetic practices (e.g., sexual moderation vs. abstinence), but also to ascetic practices that perform religious, or transcendental, functions along with sociological ones. That is, an ascetic practice, I would contend, rarely has only a single functional goal. Codes of sexual conduct, for example, might in addition to their religious functions simultaneously serve to promote sanctioned marriages. It is not always easy to discern which function preceded which. An ascetic discourse does not guarantee the ascetic origin of a practice.

Second, not all ascetic practices and systems in antiquity (as suggested by Foucault) were élitist. Clark has shown the democratization of asceticism among the Christian fathers, a point also emphasized by Fraade for the rabbinic material.[32] Ascetic practices can also derive from and spread in popular circles, only to be more coherently systematized by the élite. Hence, a model of constant interaction and feedback might be more appropriate. Shame was a popular strategy that was assumed and used by the rabbis, who additionally developed their own more specialized discourse.

Third, individual ascetic practices are often promoted and enforced in otherwise ordinary communities. Shame, for example, helped these Jewish communities to enforce a limited continence. Every ascetic practice not only has a range of functions, but if sanctioned by the community also has attached to it a range of societal strategies that promote it.

Every society has ascetic elements in the sense that it prescribes and advises certain limits on ordinary behavior for the common good. More focus on not only the discourse but also the societal institutions that support ascetic practices will provide a more nuanced understanding of both asceticism as a universal phenomenon and of the societal and political orientations of religion itself.

NOTES

1. Walter O. Kaelber, "Asceticism," in *The Encyclopedia of Religion,* ed. Mircea Eliade (New York: Macmillan, 1987), 1:441.
2. For some comments on the connection between asceticism and bodily orientation, see Vincent L. Wimbush, "Introduction," *Semeia* 57 (1992):1–9.
3. See Peter Brown, "The Rise and Function of the Holy Man in Late Antiquity," and "Town, Village and Holy Man: The Case of Syria," reprinted in *Society and the Holy in Late Antiquity* (Berkeley: University of California Press, 1982), pp. 103–152, 153–165 (respectively).
4. Ascetic practice, by definition, cannot take place outside of the discursive structures that support it. The articles in *Semeia* 57 and 58, edited by Wimbush, explore this relationship. See especially, Leif E. Vaage, "Like Dogs Barking: Cynic Pararesia and Shameless Asceticism," *Semeia* 57 (1990):25–39.
5. Michel Foucault, *The Use of Pleasure,* vol. 2, *The History of Sexuality,* trans. Robert Hurley (New York: Viking, 1986), pp. 50–55; Vincent L. Wimbush, "*Sōphrosynē*: Greco-Roman Origins of a type of Ascetic Behavior," in *Gnosticism and the Early Christian World, In Honor of James M. Robinson,* eds. James E. Goehring et al. (Sonoma: Polebridge Press, 1990), pp. 89–102; Gail Paterson Corrington, "The Defense of the Body and the Discourse of Appetite: Continence and Control in the Greco-Roman World," *Semeia* 57 (1992):65–74.
6. Steven D. Fraade, "Ascetical Aspects of Ancient Judaism," in *Jewish Spirituality I: From the Bible through the Middle Ages,* vol. 13, *World Spirituality,* ed. Arthur Green (New York: Crossroad, 1986), p. 277. In this preliminary study of Second Temple and rabbinic asceticism, Fraade focuses on the role of the individual, especially the overzealous ascetic and his relationship to the group. See too, *idem,* "The Nazirite in Ancient Judaism (Selected Texts)," in *Ascetic Behavior in Greco-Roman Antiquity: A Sourcebook,* ed. Vincent L. Wimbush (Minneapolis: Fortress, 1990), pp. 214–215. Throughout this paper, my emphasis is on the "communal" nature of the discipline.
7. A full study of the rabbinic discourse on power and self-control is a desideratum. For illustrations of the attitude that one transgression leads to the next, see m. *Avot* 4.2. Loss of self-control is often associated with Gentiles. See y. *Sanhedrin* 10.2, 28c–28d (paralleled at b. *Sanhedrin* 106a); b. *Yevamot* 103a–103b (parallels at b. *Horayot* 10b; b. *Nazir* 23b) attributed to R. Yohanan that suggests that Sisera's fall at the hands of Jael (*Jgs.* 4.18–21) was due to his weakness after having had intercourse with her seven times. In a *baraitha* (a source attributed as tannaitic), at b. *Qiddushin* 49b Arabs are attributed with exceptional sexual desire. See also b. *Shabbat* 62b–63a.
8. On Hellenistic dietetics, see especially, Ludwig Edelstein, "The Dietetics of Antiquity," in *Ancient Medicine: Selected Papers of Ludwig Edelstein,* ed. Owsei Temkin, ed. and trans. C. Lilian Temkin (Baltimore: Johns Hopkins University Press, 1987), pp. 303–

316. Medical writers of the Roman period, like Galen and Soranus, advise detailed regimens.

9. The study of rabbinic attitudes toward abstinence has been colored by the categories and concerns of early Christianity. Most recently, see David Biale, *Eros and the Jews* (New York: Basic, 1992), pp. 33–59.
10. On the omnipresence and danger of sexual desire, see below. On the connection between sex and apostasy, in addition to the sources listed above, see b. *Ḥagigah* 15a.
11. By the rabbinic period, the Jews almost certainly lost their authority to impose the death penalty, except, perhaps, in exceptional situations. They may have had the legal power to impose flogging. This is not to say that corporeal punishments were not occasionally imposed illegally by these Jewish communities. See Origen, *Epistolae ad Africanum* 14 (*PG* 11.41); b. *Giṭṭin* 67b; b. *Bava' Qamma'* 59a–b. See further, Isaiah M. Gafni, *The Jews of Babylonia in the Talmudic Era* (Jerusalem: Zalman Shazar Center for Jewish History, 1990), pp. 99–100 (Heb.).
12. See, for examples, m. *Avot* 3.1; Daniel Boyarin, "Internal Opposition in Talmudic Literature: The Case of the Married Monk," *Representations* 36 (1991):87–113.
13. The Rabbis developed an extensive rhetoric on sanctioned sexual deportment. This rhetoric is quite complex, and often differs between rabbinic documents and Babylonian and Palestinian Rabbis: it was far from univocal. See my Ph.D. dissertation, "Talking about Sex: Rabbinic Rhetorics of Sexuality," University of Michigan, 1993.
14. Due to space considerations, I do not include here an examination of prerabbinic evidence on sexual shame. What follows is only a sketch of the role of sexual shame in late antique Judaism. The role of shame in these communities obviously was far more complex than indicated here. I am currently preparing a fuller study of the role of shame in the Judaisms and Jewish communities of late antiquity. See David D. Gilmore, "Introduction: The Shame of Dishonor," *Honor and Shame and the Unity of the Mediterranean,* ed. David D. Gilmore (Washington, D.C.: American Anthropological Association, 1987), p. 10; *idem,* "Honor, Honesty, Shame: Male Status in Contemporary Andalusia," *Honor and Shame,* pp. 90–103; Maureen Giovannini, "Female Chastity Codes in the Circum-Mediterranean: Comparative Perspectives," *Honor and Shame,* pp. 61–74; Stanley Brandes, "Reflections on Honor and Shame in the Mediterranean," *Honor and Shame,* p. 122; Bette S. Denich, "Sex and Power in the Balkans," *Women, Culture, and Society,* eds. Michelle Zimblast Rosaldo and Louise Lamphere (Stanford: Stanford University Press, 1974), pp. 254–255.
15. b. *Sanhedrin* 52a. In *MS. Munich* 95 and variants the attribution is to R. Yermiah; the printed edition reads "R. Meir taught . . ." See E. Z. Melamed, *Halachic Midrashim of the Tannaim in the Babylonian Talmud* (Jerusalem: The Magnes Press, 1988), p. 288 (Heb.).
16. b. *Bava' Metsi'a'* 58b. The order of these transgressions is different in some manuscripts.
17. b. *Soṭah* 4b. The manuscript evidence for the attribution is quite messy, but all the alternatives are Palestinian.
18. b. *Ta'anit* 7b. The printed edition reads that he will succumb to *'abērah. MS. Munich* 140 replaces this with *'ēšet 'iš.*
19. See below, and Amy Richlin, *Garden of Priapus: Sexuality and Aggression in Roman Humor* (New Haven: Yale University Press, 1983), pp. 215–219.
20. The Rabbis saw sexual desire as (1) omnipresent and (2) dangerous. Like their Greek and Roman contemporaries, the Rabbis thought that both men and women constantly craved sex. On female desire, see for example: m. *Soṭah* 3.4; b. *Qiddushin* 80b (cited in

a very different context at *Shabbat* 33b); *Soṭah* 32b; b. *Ketubbot* 65a. See further A. A. Halevi, *Arkhe ha-aggadah v'ha-halakhah* (Tel Aviv: Dvir, 1982), 3:198–207 (Heb.); Judith Romney Wegner, *Chattel or Person? The Status of Women in the Mishnah* (Oxford: Oxford University Press, 1988), pp. 153–162. On male desire: b. *Sukkah* 51b–52a (parallel at b. *Qiddushin* 30b); *Berakhot* 17a, 60b, 61a (parallel at b. *'Erubin* 18b); b. *Sanhedrin* 99b; y. *Soṭah* 3.1, 18c; *Berakhot* 4.2, 7d. See further Ephraim E. Urbach, *The Sages: Their Concepts and Beliefs,* trans. Israel Abrahams (Cambridge: Harvard University Press, 1987), pp. 471–483. On Greek and Roman perceptions of sexual desire, see especially Kenneth James Dover, *Greek Popular Morality in the Time of Plato and Aristotle* (Berkeley: University of California Press, 1974), pp. 101–102, 208–209; Juvenal 6.352–365; Livy 34.2.13–14; Richlin, *Garden of Priapus,* p. 134. The view of women as "weak" manifested itself even in Roman legal codes. See *Corpus inscriptionum indicarum* 5.37.22.5 (326); *Cahiers théologigues* 3.16.1 (331). See further Suzanne Dixon, "*Infirmitas sexus:* Womanly Weakness in Roman Law," *Tijdschrift voor Rechtsgeschiedenis* 52 (1984):343–371.

21. *Berakhot* 3.4, 6c. It is interesting to note that a somewhat parallel story at *Berakhot* 22a (attributed to a Palestinian rabbi) omits the elements of shaming from this story. (I read this source contra Ginzberg's reading. See Louis Ginzberg, *A Commentary on the Palestinian Talmud,* 3 vols. [New York: Jewish Theological Seminary of America, 1941], 2:243 [Heb.]).
22. b. *Ḥagigah* 15a; b. *Mo'ed Qaṭan* 17a; b. *Qiddushin* 40a.
23. b. *Qiddushin* 81a.
24. Ibid., 81b.
25. *Sifre Deuteronomy* 26 (ed. Finkelstein, pp. 36–37). See also *Sifre Numbers* 137 (ed. Horowitz, p. 183); b. *Yoma'* 76b. According to Fraade, the "original" version of this parable is that of *Sifre Numbers.* The differences are, however, not relevant for this discussion. See Steven D. Fraade, "Sifre Deuteronomy 26 (ad Deut. 3:23): How Conscious the Composition?" *Hebrew Union College Annual* 54 (1983):271–277; Saul Lieberman, *Greek in Jewish Palestine* (New York: Jewish Theological Seminary of America, 1942), pp. 162–164.
26. An ideal example is that of the rabbinic discourse on the *soṭah,* the suspected adulteress who, according to the Bible, is put through an ordeal. The rabbinic discussion of this ordeal—long since ceased by the time of the Rabbis—elaborates those parts of the ritual that humiliate and shame her. See for example, m. *Sóṭah* 1.4–6, 3.3; t. *Soṭah* 2.3, 3.4–5; b. *Soṭah* 8b; y. *Soṭah* 1.7, 17a, 2.1, 17d, 3.5, 19a (see also, y. *Soṭah* 1.5, 17a, 4.1, 19c).
27. m. *Soṭah* 6.1; m. *Ketubbot* 7.6.
28. *Sifre Deuteronomy* 240 (ed. Finkelstein, p. 271); b. *Sanhedrin* 50b.
29. See, m. *Yevamot* 13.1; m. *Soṭah* 3.5.
30. In addition to the anthropological sources cited above, see David Cohen, *Law, Sexuality, and Society: The Enforcement of Morals in Classical Athens* (Cambridge: Cambridge University Press, 1991); John J. Winkler, *The Constraints of Desire* (New York: Routledge, 1990); Halvor Moxnes, "Honor, Shame, and the Outside World in Romans," in *The Social World of Formative Christianity and Judaism,* eds. Jacob Neusner et al. (Philadelphia: Fortress, 1988), pp. 207–218; Bruce J. Malina, *The New Testament World: Insights from Cultural Anthropology* (Atlanta: John Knox, 1981), pp. 25–50; Elizabeth A. Clark, "Sex, Shame, and Rhetoric: En-gendering Early Christian Ethics," *Journal of the American Academy of Religion* 59 (1991):221–245.

31. In his response to the articles on asceticism published in *Semeia* 57 and 58, Harpham noted the increasing "ascetic" tendencies of our own society, especially within certain academic disciplines. Although he does not attempt to connect his observations to general modern discourses on asceticism and their histories within American Christianity, I suspect that such an inquiry would be fruitful. See Geoffrey Galt Harpham, "Old Water in New Bottles: The Contemporary Prospects for the Study of Asceticism," *Semeia* 58 (1992):135–148
32. See Elizabeth A. Clark, "Foucault, the Fathers, and Sex," *Journal of the American Academy of Religion* 56 (1988):619–641, esp. 633–637.

39

A Theory of the Social Function of Asceticism

Richard Valantasis

Over the course of the past seventy years or more, theorists in the social sciences and the humanities have explored asceticism as a vital component of sociology, social history, and hermeneutics; while historians have been exploring the role of asceticism and the place of ascetics in the societies of late antiquity and the western Middle Ages. The historical perspective has focused on the function of asceticism and the ascetic within the dominant social context, while the attention of the theorists has focused on it as an economic, social, political, and interpretative instrument within the larger cultural domain. Although at first glance the distinction seems minor, there is in fact a great difference in approach: the theorists understand asceticism as a large and pervasive cultural system; while the historians view asceticism as specific religious practices relating to social withdrawal, restriction of food, regulation of sexuality, and the formation of religious community. The larger cultural systems of the ascetical theorists locate asceticism at the center of cultural, social, and individual engagement in every sphere of cultural expression; the particular religious practices of the historian locate asceticism only in the religious or philosophical arenas.

My goal in this paper is to present the ascetical theories of the three primary ascetical theorists of this century (Max Weber, Michel Foucault, and Geoffrey Harpham) and to develop a theory of asceticism within which the social function of asceticism may be described. The three theorists presented here represent a wide diversity of interests, from economic history and the sociology of religion to social history and literary theory. Although each succeeding theorist has studied the work of the previous ones, the perspective on asceticism and the academic discourses of each has been significantly different. My own theory, presented below, will attempt to build on the contributions of each of these. I hope, thereby, to bridge the gap between ascetical theory and historical study.

Weber, Foucault, and Harpham

Max Weber's theory of asceticism, developed early in this century, treats asceticism as part of sociological theory and the history of economics. Weber's *The Protestant Ethic and the Spirit of Capitalism*[1] developed the theory of innerworldly asceticism as a means of understanding the emergence of capitalism. This initial exploration of asceticism explored the relationship between the development of the work force; the valuation of wealth and material good in the Protestant Reformation; the Protestant concept of a vocation to live in the world (as opposed to those Catholic monks who withdrew from the world); and the doctrine of predestination, which provided the opportunity for right conduct of life to prove that one is saved. In this economic study, Weber treats asceticism primarily as "methodically controlled and supervised" conduct (p. 132). Weber maintains that, for Protestants, this controlled conduct was directed specifically to living in the world, a world that consisted of daily living as the focus of Christian life and vocation. Asceticism, the controlled conduct, undertook, then, to remodel the world, so that Protestant ideals would be able to be achieved within it. The heart of the argument revolves about the remaking of the economic world through the development of theological principles that have been worked out in particular patterns of behavior. The asceticism of working in the world creates the work force; the kind of subjectivity necessary for the work force to function; and the theological justification for the sort of lifestyle to be lived.

Weber again addresses the theory of asceticism in his *Sociology of Religion.*[2] Under the heading of paths to salvation, Weber links three elements of asceticism: the particular path of salvation; particular human conduct; and the means of training in that conduct. Moving from economics to the theory of the sociology of religion, Weber locates the methodically controlled behavior specifically within the teleological path toward salvation. The particular goal of salvation, the manner of achieving sanctification, emerges from a psychic and physical regimen or discipline aimed toward controlling and creating within a person an antiinstinctual response, subordinated to the religious goal. Asceticism, here, is defined as "a methodical procedure for achieving religious salvation" (p. 164). He identifies asceticism as either world-rejecting (that is, salvation achieved through withdrawal from the world) or innerworldly (that is, salvation achieved through participation in the world while rejecting the world's institutions).

There is much about Weber's theories that is outmoded—his propensity for polarities, for example, between asceticism and mysticism, and between innerworldly and world-rejecting. Yet they establish that asceticism has wider economic and political implications; that behaviors are at the heart of ascetical activity; that those behaviors are strongly regulated and directed toward specific goals; and that ascetic behaviors set out ways of relating to other people (as, for example, by creating a work force). The link, including the economic implications and orientations toward the world, of the three elements—identified as paths of salvation, human conduct, and the means of training in that conduct—hits at the heart of ascetical theory.

Michel Foucault explores the place of asceticism in the context of ethical formation. In an interview[3] in which he explained the project of his *History of Sexuality,* Foucault distinguished four aspects of what he called "the relationship to oneself": (1) the ethical substance (that is, the part of oneself that concerns moral conduct, the material with which ethics works); (2) the mode of subjection (that is, the mode that encourages or spurs people on to relate to their moral obligations, such as revelation or divine law); (3) asceticism, or self-forming activity (that is, the changes that one makes to oneself in order to become an ethical subject); and (4) the *telos,* or goal (that is, the end toward which the ethics moves, the end result of ethical formation). Although Foucault identifies asceticism as one aspect of this process of ethical formation, he also views asceticism as the heart of the entire process of formation:

> No technique, no professional skill can be acquired without exercise; neither can one learn the art of living, the *technē tou biou,* without an *askēsis* which must be taken as a training of oneself by oneself: this was one of the traditional principles to which the Pythagoreans, the Socratics, the Cynics had for a long time attributed great importance. *History of Sexuality, vol. 1, p. 364*

In the second volume[4] of his History of Sexuality, entitled *The Use of Pleasure,* he further develops this perspective on asceticism. It is here that Foucault distinguished (p. 26) between the set of rules of moral conduct itself; the evaluation of the person based upon those rules; and the systems of formation that enable one to be a subject acting according to those rules. These different ways of constructing oneself as a subject of moral action differ according to the *telos* or the goal of the moral life that is the result of moral formation. Foucault explains:

> There is no specific moral action that does not refer to a unified moral conduct; no moral conduct that does not call for the forming of oneself as an ethical subject; and no forming of the ethical subject without "modes of subjectivation" and "ascetics" or "practices of the self" that supports them. *History of Sexuality, vol. 2, p. 28*

Foucault's system, then, proposes a system of formation that involves a goal of life encapsulated in a system of behavior, which requires formation through processes of subjectivation and ascetic practices.

Geoffrey Harpham develops a theory of asceticism in relation to contemporary structuralists, poststructuralists, and postmodern theories of literary criticism and in conversation with Mikhail Mikhailovich Bakhtin, Jacques Derrida, Michel Foucault, and other theorists of contemporary literary criticism. In his recent book, *The Ascetic Imperative in Culture and Criticism,*[5] he enlarges the arena of ascetical studies by exploring the relationship of asceticism and culture. Harpham develops the theory of asceticism as "the 'cultural' element in culture; it makes culture comparable, and is therefore one way of describing the common feature that permits communication or understanding between cultures."[6] He views asceticism as "the fundamental operating ground on which the particular culture is overlaid."[7] Harpham's work directs attention from the merely descriptive—whether of the literary strategies or of the ascetic's behavior—to the systems invoked to give meaning and to enable communication within a given culture. Harpham argues that asceticism is related to culture because asceticism is that which enables communication in a culture. He likens asceticism to the MS-DOS that enables programs to run on a computer: asceticism is the fundamental operating ground upon which culture is laid and because of which culture can function. Like Foucault, Harpham emphasizes the ethical nature of culture itself, arguing that there is an inherent level of self-denial necessary for a person to live within a culture so that the resistance to appetites and desires is at the heart of cultural integration and functioning. Asceticism, moreover, structures oppositions without collapsing them so that asceticism raises the issue of culture by creating the opposite, the anticulture. Asceticism, therefore, is always ambivalent, compromising the polarities it establishes.

Harpham defines asceticism in a tight sense as the asceticism of early Christianity, the historical ideology of a specific period, and in a loose sense as "any act of self-denial undertaken as a strategy of empowerment or gratification." Central, therefore, to any ascetical agenda is resistance. Resistance is a structural part of desire itself, not imposed from outside it; and desire is always resisted from within, since without resistance there is no desire.

A Theory of Asceticism

My own theory of asceticism begins with the important factor that Harpham's orientation omits. He correctly asserts that the basis of ascetical activity is the cultural foundations that lie behind the particularities of a given culture, like MS-DOS to a particular computer program.[8] However, the ascetical program relates not to the interaction of the two systems (deep cultural structure and cultural expression) but to the integration of an individual person, and of groups of people, into the culture itself. At the center of ascetical activity is a self who, through behavioral changes, seeks to become a different person, a new self; to become a different person in new relationships; and to become a different person in a new society that forms a new culture. As this new self emerges (in relationship to itself, to others, to society, to the world) it masters the behaviors that enable it at once to deconstruct the old self and to construct the new. Asceticism, then, constructs both the old and the reformed self and the cultures in which these selves function: asceticism asserts the subject of behavioral change and transformation, while constructing and reconstructing the environment in which that subjectivity functions.

The relationship of this subjectivity to environment is the relationship of individual to culture. Asceticism links the two by enabling the integration of individual into culture. Through asceticism, integration into a culture occurs at every level of human existence: consciously and unconsciously; voluntarily and involuntarily; somatic and mental; emotional and intellectual; religious and secular. This means that asceticism functions as a system of cultural formation; it orients the person or group of people to the immediate cultural environment and to the unexpressed, but present, systems that underlie it. Until a person or a group of people is equipped or empowered to perform within a culture, the culture remains an esoteric system into which the person or group has not been initiated. Asceticism initiates a person or group into the cultural systems that enable communication; that equip the person or group for productive living within the culture; and that empower them to live within the culture. As the primary system of formation within a culture, asceticism unlocks the otherwise closed or invisible systems of communication and rhetorical production in a culture, and hence intersects all the operative systems: larger cultural systems, social systems, and individual psychological systems.

A preliminary definition of asceticism may be advanced. Asceticism may be defined as performances designed to inaugurate an alternative culture, to enable different social relations, and to create a new identity. This definition hangs on four elements: performances, culture, relationships, and subjectivity. I will explore each one in turn.

Performances

It is not difficult to notice from the history of asceticism that it involves the performance of certain acts: fasting, withdrawal from society, silence, physical prayer, and manual labor, to name just a few. These acts function as signifiers in a semiotic system, in that they carry meaning with the context of their performance: a particular performance such as fasting bears no inherent and self-evident meaning except that which is assigned it in the system.

The method of ascetical training resembles the workshop and rehearsal method for acquiring competence in theatrical performance. Richard Schechner describes this method in this way: "The task of the workshop is to deconstruct the ready-mades of individual behavior, texts, and cultural artifacts into strips of malleable behavior material; the work of the rehearsal is to reconstruct them into a new, integral system: a performance."[9] The interiorizing and naturalizing of behavior, emotions, and every cultural expression through the deconstructive and reconstructive process, anterior to a convincing performance, emerges from the patterning of the theatrical role in its world, with its peculiar systems, relationships, and psychology. The rigorous and systematic repatterning eventually enables the actor to enter and to be the character. Asceticism, with its goal of creating new persons through patterning of behavior, operates in a similar fashion. By the systematic training and retraining, the ascetic becomes a different person molded to live in a different culture, trained to relate to people in a different manner, psychologically motivated to live a different life. Through these performances, the ascetic, like the performer who becomes able to "experience as actual" anything imaginable,[10] can experience the goal of ascetical life as the transformed life.

These performances consist of learned and repeated activity and behaviors: the ascetic learns the techniques of asceticism by repeated activity, repeated prayer, a consistently affirmed withdrawal, continuous silence, repeated physical acts of fasting, sleep deprivation, and manual labor. As these activities and behaviors are repeated, the ascetic masters them. This means that the activities and behaviors that are performed are eminently repeatable; and that they can be learned, mastered, and repeated until the ascetic achieves a certain state or quality of life. In their repetition, these acts take on the appearance of verisimilitude, they become natural activities for the monk as perceived within the ascetic culture. The verisimilitude points toward the successful creation of a larger frame of reference and of meaning that supports the ascetic manner of living.

These performances, therefore, include an element of intentionality: the behaviors intend more than mere repetition and imitation of behavior; the behaviors displace attention from themselves to a larger referential arena, and their purpose relates at once to an alternative culture and to the potential of a new subjectivity.

Culture

Clifford Geertz explains that "Culture is the fabric of meaning in terms of which human beings interpret their experience and guide their action" and that culture is "an ordered system of meaning and of symbols in terms of which social interaction takes place."[11] Negatively described, asceticism breaks down the dominant culture through performances that aim toward establishing a counter-cultural or alternative cultural milieu. Positively described, the ascetic, like an actor learning to be a character in a play, lives in a new culture created through the careful repatterning of basic behaviors and relations.

The behavior shifts the center of the culture and creates an alternative culture around this new center. The performances force the construction of a culture in which such new behavior is normative. The heavy emphasis on the location of asceticism (withdrawal, monastery, desert, pilgrimage, pillar) articulates and creates the cultural occasion for a change in cultural venue. This new culture becomes the normal or normative or true culture for those whose performance initiates them into it.

It is not necessary that the alternative culture formed through asceticism oppose the dominant culture. The counter-cultural orientation need not indicate hostility or mutual exclusion. Cultures may coinhere, and an ascetic may participate in a number of different cultures simultaneously.

Moreover, communities may, like monasteries, create a new culture without individual members of that community knowing it. The intentionality does not always rest on the individual body but may reside with the corporate body.

Relationships

Culture defines the potential, the larger systems upon which humans can call in their living: culture becomes concrete at the level of social relationships. Within this broader cultural context, Geertz explains, there are the "actually existing network of social relations" and "the ongoing process of interactive behavior." Behavior invokes the systems laid out in the culture, while the culture makes available to an individual the parameters, direction, and action of social interaction. "Culture is the fabric of meaning in terms of which human beings interpret their experience and guide their action; social structure is the form that action takes."[12] The new culture is built upon two correlative elements—new social arrangements and new subjects capable of living in the culture. Cultures enable (or prohibit) certain kinds of social structures. A new culture, therefore, must define new and different ways of relating in order to differentiate itself from other cultures and other ways of relating.

Subjectivity

The goal of ascetic performance finds its fullest expression in the articulation and construction of a new subjectivity. Both performance and culture open potential space for the creation of an alternative or new subject.

The new subjectivity is the *skopos* (guardian) that calls for the behavior and the cultural milieu. There is an element of the intentional, the deliberate, the articulation of a new goal and a new understanding of subjectivity, toward which the person moves. This teleological element is crucial and central to understanding asceticism.

The ascetic subjectivity is multivalent and multicentered in that it bears by nature at least a twoway centeredness (the old person and the ascetically reconstructed person) and possibly more, since people may participate in a number of different coinherent cultures. The various locations of the ascetic subject (social/political, geographical, philosophical, psychic) articulate or represent other centers of the ascetic subject—centers from which the entire new culture may be organized. Therefore, the ascetical location duplicates the multivalency of the emerging subject of ascetical activity.

The Social Function of Asceticism

Within this definition, asceticism performs four major social functions. First, asceticism enables the person to function within the re-envisioned or re-created world. Through ritual, new social relations, different articulations of self and body, and through a variety of psychological transformations, the ascetic learns to live within another world. To "live as an angel,"—the goal that our Orthodox monks have set for themselves—means that through their asceticism monks are enabled to function "as angels" from the beginning of their ascetical activity, or at least to begin to know what it means to "live as angels." Asceticism allows this life on the basis of a re-envisioned world.

Second, since so much of the ascetic culture relies upon narrative, biography, demonic and angelic psychology, as well as systems of theological anthropology and soteriology, asceticism provides the method for translating these theoretical and strategic concepts into patterns of behavior. The metaphoric presentation of the transfiguration of Antony in Athanasius's *Vita Antonii,* for example, does not explain how one goes about imitating Antony in order for the self to be transfigured. Asceticism patterns such theories and images into purposeful and systematic practices whose goal can be incrementally achieved. After a similar regimen of fasting, withdrawal, meditation, and conflict with demons, the ascetic may achieve the same goal as Antony, or, more precisely, the ascetic may achieve that state which a community understands as a correlative state defined by the literary presentation of Antony's life. Asceticism patterns and makes concrete such distant phenomena into purposeful behavioral patterns.

Third, the re-envisioning of the world and of human life in it requires intensive perceptual transformation. In order to achieve a different state, as visualized or pictorialized by a religion, there must be at the most basic perceptual level of the senses, and of perceptions and experience, a form of retraining geared toward the re-envisioned world. Asceticism provides the means for this retraining. It is at the level of ascetical performance that the ascetic experiences and perceives the world differently. The novice who enters a monastery must learn at the outset the differences between, for example, "eating in the world" and "eating in the monastery":

both relate to food, but the signification of the food and its eating will differ, in referent and in content, from cultural domain to cultural domain. At this most basic level, asceticism retrains the senses and perceptions of the ascetic, a retraining based upon the theological culture and its articulated goals.

Fourth, asceticism provides the means through which other domains of knowledge and understanding can be incorporated into the re-envisioned world. Scientific, historical, doctrinal, sectarian, and other kinds of issues are translated through asceticism into the other conception of the world. A good example of this is the patristic genre of the *Hexameron,*[13] a theological exposition of the days of creation, which uses the ascetical activity of exegesis to incorporate coeval scientific and medical information into the religious culture. Asceticism functions as a prism through which the light of other domains of knowledge are refracted into a new cultural environment. This refraction gives the old knowledge a new interpretative environment so that the context provides the frame of reference for understanding and meaning.

Asceticism operates through the goals that it sets up for organizing human mentation and behavior.[14] By positing a goal (or goals) toward which the individual or group is to progress as the highest good, or the more perfect state, or the most absorbed by the sacred, asceticism lays out the attaining of that goal through concrete patterning of behavior. Because asceticism operates at the level of behavior, the behavior itself often becomes the focus of attention, yet the goal is generally not known in the specific behavior, but in the state or experience the behavior is designed to effect. The goal, however, expresses the particular culture's own peculiar systems; the ascetical practices systematize the procedure for movement into the culture; and the individual finds fulfillment and nurture in the integration into the highest aspiration expressed in the goal.

My definition of asceticism, then, locates the function of asceticism in the cultural, social, and psychological frames of a culture and its counter-cultures. Asceticism initiates the practitioner into the new culture, and initiates the practitioner into the social and psychological systems that activate the culture. This theory of asceticism points our historical study of religious asceticism toward the exploration of the larger cultural complex of meanings, relationships, and subjectivities that construct the ascetic and the ascetic's performances.

NOTES

1. The full reference for this is: Max Weber, *The Protestant Ethic and the Spirit of Capitalism,* trans. Talcott Parsons (London: Unwyn Hyman, 1930).
2. Max Weber, *The Sociology of Religion,* trans. Ephraim Fishcoff [originally published in Germany by J.C.B. Mohr, 1922] (Boston: Beacon Press, 1963).
3. Michel Foucault, "On the Genealogy of Ethics: An Overview of Work in Progress," in *The Foucault Reader,* ed. Paul Rabinow [originally published in Hubert L. Dreyfus and Paul Rabinow, eds., *Michel Foucault: Beyond Structuralism and Hermeneutics,* 2d ed. (Chicago: University of Chicago Press, 1983)] (New York: Pantheon Books, 1984).
4. Michel Foucault, *The Use of Pleasure,* vol. 2, *The History of Sexuality,* trans. Robert Hurley (New York: Vintage Books, 1985).

5. Geoffrey Harpham, *The Ascetic Imperative in Culture and Criticism* (Chicago: University of Chicago Press, 1987).
6. Ibid., p. xi.
7. Ibid.
8. Ibid.
9. "Magnitudes of Performance," in *The Anthropology of Experience,* eds. Victor W. Turner and Edward M. Bruner (Urbana: University of Illinois Press, 1986), p. 345.
10. Schechner, "Magnitudes of Performance," p. 363.
11. Clifford Geertz, *The Interpretation of Cultures* (New York: Basic Books, 1973), p. 144.
12. Ibid.
13. Basil the Great, Gregory of Nyssa, and Ambrose of Milan have written such expositions of the first six days of creation in *The Book of Genesis.*
14. Michel Foucault, *Care of the Self,* vol. 3, *The History of Sexuality,* trans. Robert Hurley (New York: Vintage Books, 1988), pp. 64–68.

40

Psychophysiological and Comparative Analysis of Ascetico-Meditational Discipline: Toward a New Theory of Asceticism

William C. Bushell

In this paper I describe a number of the major psychophysiological enhancements that accompany the practice, particularly the long-term practice, of asceticism and meditation (including prayer, contemplation, etc.), with special reference to contemporary Ethiopian Orthodox Christian asceticism and to the desert Christian movement of the early centuries CE. The present description and explanation of ascetic and meditational practice (the ascetico-meditational regimen) constitutes a new theory of the functions of asceticism and altered states of consciousness (ASCs), a theory that is developed in greater depth elsewhere.[1]

In this same source I also present the first study ever undertaken of the living tradition of Ethiopian eremitic asceticism, the research for which was conducted by me in Ethiopia over the course of the period 1988–1991. Ethiopia, as is not at all well known, possesses the last remaining large-scale tradition of Christian eremitic asceticism in the world. Thousands of men and women practice rigorous ascetico-meditational discipline throughout the mountain caves (much of Ethiopia exists on an extensive highland plateau), forests, deserts, and lake islands of present-day Ethiopia. Owing to a relative absence of modernization and westernization, which, in turn, is due in part to its relative geographical and geological inaccessibility, the tradition of eremitic asceticism, which became established in this country beginning at the latest in the fourth century CE, remains to this day not only extraordinarily robust but also strikingly pristine. The contemporary forms of eremitic ascetic Christianity that survive in robust and pristine form in Ethiopia are direct descendants of the desert Christian movement of Egypt, Palestine, and Syria (third and fourth centuries onward), and in a sense preserve a kind of "window" on these traditions. However, it is important to emphasize that the genius of Ethiopian Christianity has been to preserve and continue the authentic, virtuoso eremitic traditions that have all but disappeared from most other parts of the Christian world; geographical determinism is only part of the reason for this phenomenon of preservation.

I have organized the following analysis of Christian eremitic asceticism around some key points presented by one of the premier interpreters of early Christian asceticism, Peter Brown. However, my analysis of ascetico-meditational phenomena is based on relevant data from various branches of psychophysiological and medical research, as well as on a theoretical orientation that looks at ascetico-meditational discipline as a widespread human phenomenon, and is therefore cross-cultural and comparative.

A key concept in what follows is Weber's notion of the "ideal type": as an anthropologist who conducts field research, I am well aware of the variations in behaviors that are always found "on the ground," as the anthropological term has it. Nevertheless, although people may engage in ascetico-meditational behaviors for an almost infinite variety of reasons, I believe the following analysis will demonstrate that certain specific functions, "outcomes," provide the best (functional) explanation for the *raison d'être* of these practices.

Distilling a great deal of early Christian ascetic literature, Brown explains the beliefs of these ascetics concerning the potential outcome of persistence in the rigorously observed, long-term ascetico-meditational régime. After issuing the warning that "it takes some effort of the modern imagination to recapture this aspect of the ascetic life," he explains:

> The ascetics of late antiquity tended to view the human body as an "autarkic" system. In ideal conditions it was thought capable of running on its own "heat"; it would need only enough nourishment to keep that heat alive. In its "natural" state—a state with which the ascetics tended to identify the bodies of Adam and Eve—the body had acted like a finely tuned engine, capable of "idling" indefinitely.[2]

It was "their lust for physical food" in fact, that "[destroyed . . .] the perfect physical equilibrium with which they [Adam and Eve] had first been created"; this perfect physical equilibrium had revealed a "frankly physical exuberance,"[3] moreover.

In fact, and contrary to common belief—including that of many modern medically trained persons—the Desert Fathers' beliefs regarding fasting, radical restriction of food intake, and nutrition and energy are consistent with a large body of contemporary experimental research, research that demonstrates that fasting and significant reductions in caloric intake (dietary restriction) actually may result in a broad spectrum of psychophysiological enhancements, including just those touted by the ascetic tradition.

Ascetic fasting or restriction of food intake, if done properly,[4] would result in outcomes consistent with the strikingly salutary principles of scientifically investigated fasting and what researchers have called dietary restriction, in which the constellation of potential outcomes includes: the disappearance of the pain, discomfort, and dysphoria of hunger, and their replacement with feelings of well-being, tranquillity, and even euphoria;[5] "(enhanced) efficiency of food utilization,"[6] as evinced by indices of body weight, nutritional status, and activity or energy;[7] and even general enhancement of health, as evinced by decreases in illness and retardation of aging.[8]

According to a number of recent medical (experimental) studies and case reports, the subjective feeling of hunger may, in fact, disappear or become greatly diminished in the course of fasting.[9] Moreover, fasting may even result in a range of positive affective states including tranquillity and euphoria, which in some cases has been found to be associated with elevations of opioid substances produced by the body. The finding of the combination of disappearing hunger and positive affect, replicated under experimental conditions and in the clinical setting, has not been commonly recognized, and runs counter, as do other outcomes of fasting, to commonly held notions. It must also be borne in mind that, frequently, the diminishment or disappearance of hunger is preceded by intensely uncomfortable and distressful feelings of hunger, which may in turn be accompanied by the equally unpleasant experience of dysphoria, disorientation, confusion, weakness, and fatigue (the "ascetic challenge").

Research also indicates that, under conditions of dietary restriction, the body demonstrates "enhanced efficiency of food utilization." For example, nutrients such as vitamins are more thoroughly absorbed through the intestine after the inception of dietary restriction.[10] Weight gain is proportionately greater per unit mass of food ingested under dietary-restricted conditions than under normal or *ad libitum* feeding.[11] And, of great significance for the present discussion, numerous studies have demonstrated in various species, including the human, the "paradoxical"[12] finding that restriction of food intake frequently leads to increased activity and energy.[13]

It is necessary to make emphatic the point that, again contrary to common sense, the "inverse relationship between activity and energy intake,"[14] the "pattern of diminished intake and heightened output,"[15] is a highly robust and replicated finding. Describing several study populations, including patients with compulsive eating or exercise behaviors as well as laboratory animals—the finding is not a function of psychopathology—the researcher Yates explains,

> When eating-disordered women and obligatory runners combine diet and exercise in an effort to become healthy, thin, or even younger, the pattern of diminished intake and heightened output seems to regenerate and reinforce itself and the system becomes remarkably resistant to change. The animal laboratory provides a clue as to how this process might transpire. Many studies demonstrate that the activity level of animals—especially male animals—increases as a function of food deprivation (Siegel and Steinberg 1949; Teitelbaum 1957; Cornish and Mrosovosky 1965). The longer animals are deprived the more active they become (DiBattista and Bedard 1987). . . . That the combination of diet and exercise is associated with an increase in activity is supported by a study of athletes which was completed by Richert and Hummers (1986). These researchers report that the number of hours that men spend running correlates positively and significantly with the stringency of their diets and with their abnormal attitudes toward food and eating. The more stringently they diet, the more they are involved in various activities (including running) and the more hours they spend involved in these activities.[16]

This paradoxical nature of energy balance involves not only food intake but physical activity as well, as Yates points out. Moreover, several other recent studies provide further support for the assertion of Yates and others that dietary restriction and physical exertion are associated with increased energy levels. Endurance testing showed that whereas after one week of significant dietary restriction subjects experienced a 20 percent decrease in endurance, after six weeks on the same diet subjects experienced a 55 percent increase in endurance over baseline.[17] It has also been found that poor Indian laborers work well and are symptom free although semistarved and emaciated: "Despite the undoubtedly malnourishing state of their diet they have achieved a long-term adaptation at least to the energy differential."[18] Along with this paradoxical energy- or activity-enhancing effect of the practices of fasting and physical activity, as I have discussed elsewhere,[19] deprivation or restriction of sleep may likewise lead to a paradoxical increase in energy and the reduction or disappearance of sleepiness and fatigue. Hence, it can be seen, through experimental studies of "analogues" of ascetic practices—especially fasting, religious prostrations (analogous to exercise or intensive physical activity such as manual labor), and "vigil" or voluntary sleep deprivation—that energy, rather than fatigue, is increased. Through phenomenological as well as empirical objective means, then, the Desert Fathers came to realize, as Brown characterizes it, that the human body does indeed behave as an "autarkic system" needing "only enough energy to keep (its) heat alive," reaching beyond idling, in fact, to a "frankly physical exuberance."

Surprise results to common-sense predictions regarding fasting and dietary restriction continue beyond those considered so far. Restriction of food has been demonstrated, in a significant number of studies, to be associated with enhanced immune function, decreased illness, and retardation of aging, as will be discussed shortly.

According to my interviews and observations of the ascetico-meditational practices of contemporary Ethiopian Christian ascetics, many of the latter appear to be aware, in their own "emic" terms and idiom, of the constellation of psychophysiological enhancements that are associated with the rigorous and long-term ascetico-meditational régime. Specifically regarding the practice of fasting, the latter is still rigorously observed in Ethiopian Orthodoxy generally, and by ascetics, especially hermits, in particular.[20] The hermits with whom I spoke and stayed demonstrated awareness of the range of salutory effects accompanying the fasting ascesis. One of my key informants, G-Y,[21] for example, apparently lived on approximately one cup of lentils and one cup of water per day. He explained that he had lost his ability to discriminate good- from bad-tasting foods and was completely devoid of interest in food. Fasting, combined with vigil and a strict, demanding regimen of prostrations, was also linked by these hermits with the occurrence of euphoric states, which were sometimes described paradoxically in the "delician" idiom identified by Camporesi for medieval European ascetics.[22] Such states, brought about by fasting and accompanying ascetic practice, were characterized as "delicious," "delightful," and likened to the pleasures of the banquet table.

Contemporary Ethiopian hermits also recognize that fasting specifically (and in combination with vigil and prostrations) can lead to the experience of heightened energy, which comes, they believe, in the form of the Holy Spirit. My own *manafasawi abbat* (spiritual father), a hermit with whom I was close and who taught me much about advanced ascetico-meditational discipline, described the process thus: "First, one engages in fasting and prostrations until the knees are wounded, then God sends the spirit [i.e. the Holy Spirit] to encourage. You get this with many struggles, little by little . . ." and "little by little you increase energy. . . ." Other hermits attributed the increase in strength and endurance arising from the ascetico-meditational régime to "the grace of God"—an attribution not necessarily different from the Holy Spirit—also recognizing that the energy increase was in part due to the results of ascetic dietary restriction.

This constellation of psychophysiological enhancements, associated with the long-term ascetico-meditational régime recognized by the contemporary Ethiopian ascetic tradition was similar to its predecessor of the third and fourth centuries in that it was not considered some kind of "self improvement" scheme (in contemporary Western terms). As already mentioned, such a constellation was theologically integral, central, to the entire ascetic enterprise. As Brown is at pains to emphasize, the transfiguration, transformation, of the bodies of the few great ascetics on earth signaled to the average ascetics their future inheritance at the Resurrection. Spiritual advancement may be in some sense, in some cases, measured according to physical or bodily changes, which indicated a premortem attainment by the most righteous and rigorously ascetic of what all who had truly striven for righteousness were promised. The Resurrection inheritance was to be like Adam's state before the Fall:[23] no suffering or pain, no disease, no aging, continual bliss. The "glorified bodies" of the saints were evidence of Christian eschatological and soteriological doctrine. Shortly, we shall consider just how suggestive of this glorified body certain biomedical data may be interpreted as being. Before this we must consider how both the desert ascetic and the contemporary Ethiopian ascetic traditions sought to attain to this Adamic state, partly through conquest or eradication of major obstructions to the state; that is, the passions.

The passions—which include the basic biological drives for food and so forth—obstruct the ascetico-meditational endeavor, and the goal of attaining the Adamic pre-Fall condition, in several crucial ways. First and foremost, the incessant dissatisfaction and cravings of the passions interfere with the tranquillity, peace, stillness, the unification of heart, soul, and body, necessary for spiritual advancement generally. As Isaac of Nineveh (died c.700) would say some several hundred years after the time of the Desert Fathers, echoing them, "Without tranquillity of thoughts the intellect will not be moved in hidden mysteries."[24] Brown explains:

> It was only the twisted will of fallen men that had crammed the body with unnecessary food, thereby generating in it the dire surplus of energy that showed itself in physical appetite, in anger, and in the sexual urge. In reducing the intake to which he had become accustomed, the ascetic slowly remade his body. He turned it into an exactly calibrated instrument. Its drastic physical changes, after years of ascetic discipline, registered with satisfying precision the essential, preliminary stages of the long return to an original, natural and uncorrupted state.[25]

Indeed, if we compare the fasting, dietary-restricted body to the unfasted, non-restricted one according to the evidence of the psychophysiological research cited above, what do we find? None of the commonly feared outcomes of fasting are, in fact, to be found, except during the more or less brief challenge period, before the transformation to a fasting/dietary-restriction physiology becomes established. The discomfort, pain (pangs), and dysphoria of hunger disappear, replaced by a sense of well-being and even possibly euphoria; the feared lassitude, lethargy, fatigue, and mental confusion[26] actually give way to alertness and a heightened energy; even physical health is improved. In combination with the substantial retardation of aging that occurs in most animal species and is likely to occur in humans under dietary restriction,[27] the effects of fasting alone among the ascetic practices suggest the trajectory from the nonfasted, fallen condition to the fasted Adamic condition with its absence of hunger, illness, and aging; other features, such as the absence of pain, common to both the Adamic condition and the advanced ascetico-meditational program, are soon to be discussed. Yet (and it is significant that even in animals it is the case that) it is the fallen nature that has become normal, and the prefallen one that must be sought through a radical commitment to asceticism, morality, and spiritual practice:

> The ascetic had to learn, over the long years of life in the desert, to do nothing less than to untwist the very sinews of his private will. Fasting and heavy labor were important, in their own right, in the first years of the ascetic life, and especially for young monks in their full physical vigor. They were part of a "Cold Turkey Treatment," by which the ascetic leeched out of his body his former excessive dependence on food and sexual satisfaction.[28]

Elsewhere I have described in greater depth and detail the psychoneuroendocrinological changes likely to be produced through ascetico-meditational practices.[29] An analysis of these practices based on contemporary psychophysiological research into their analogues, strongly suggests that the ascetico-meditational régime can lead to a profound mediation modulation of primary drives (the passions), and, in fact, to a complete restructuring of the conventional drive-reward architecture into an ascetic drive-reward architecture.

The significant body of evidence demonstrating that fasting leads to the diminishment or disappearance of hunger—that is, to profound modulation of the hunger drive—has already been referred to. An equally robust phenomenon associated with radical dietary restriction or fasting is the loss of libido and suppression of gonadal axis activity. Research has found that dietary restriction can lead not only to low sex drive in both sexes but also to impotence in males, "obliteration of sexual drive,"[30] regression to prepubertal and infantile gonadal hormone profiles,[31] and even, in severe cases, to testicular atrophy and complete loss of secondary sex characteristics, to the point at which clinical examination is required in order to determine gender.[32] Thus, fasting alone may lead to radical attenuation of two of the strongest primary drives, for food and sex, which, as noted by Brown, were particular concerns for the Desert Fathers.

Moreover, Brown's choice of addiction terminology to describe the attitude of the Desert Fathers, (and similarly, of contemporary Ethiopian ascetics) to the passions is not misplaced, according to a psychoneuroendocrinological analysis of conventional rewards and asceticism. It has been recently determined that the reward associated with the pleasure of eating is likely to result in part from the activation of an endogenous reward system in the central nervous system, in which opioid substances produced by the body play a major role.[33] Several important studies have shown that brain neurons that respond to feeding respond identically to the direct application of opioids,[34] while others have determined that endogenous opioids in the brain are mobilized in response to feeding.[35] The same endogenous reward pathways activated by drugs of abuse are activated by conventional rewards, such as food.[36] Obese subjects, moreover, show elevated levels of endogenous opioids.[37] Endogenous opioids are involved in other conventional rewards as well,[38] and Shippenberg has described "the existence of a tonically active endogenous opioid reward pathway, the disruption of which produces aversive states."[39] There are, then, intriguing similarities between the addictive nature of such drugs of abuse as morphine and the addictive nature of conventional rewards such as that associated with the drive for food.[40]

Of major significance, additionally, is the fact that if normal eating behavior is examined in the light of dietary-restriction research, it appears that even normal (in the sense of typical) eating behavior shows qualities of "excessiveness" (Brown's term). Whether judged from a criterion of affect, nutrition, energetics, or even health status (including morbidity and mortality), it appears that optimal functioning—in the sense of the survival and optimal health of the organism—is clearly associated with restricted rather than normal or typical diet.[41] Hence, it may be said that normal appetite exceeds the appropriate intake for optimum health, a situation also suggestive of addictive behavior.

While conventional drive rewards are apparently mediated in part by endogenous opioids, it appears to be, nevertheless, true that what we may call "ascetic rewards" are likewise endogenous opioid mediated. While obese subjects have been found to have elevated levels of endogenous opioids, anorectic patients as well as other subjects undergoing fasting have also demonstrated elevated endogenous opioid levels. Anorexia nervosa patients with elevated levels of endogenous opioids also report feelings of elation and euphoria, similar to those reported by morphine users.[42]

While the rewards of eating, overeating, and abstention all appear to be endogenous opioid mediated, it can be suggested that, based on clinical and experimental research, the endogenous opioid-mediated reward of abstention is greater than that associated with eating. Elevated levels of endogenous opioids (in blood plasma and cerebrospinal fluid) are found in both obese and anorectic subjects, while reports of euphoria are generally found with significantly greater frequency in the latter group. Moreover, the experience of reward associated with abstention from food is not only of a greater intensity but also of a greater duration: rewarding affect clusters around periods of ingestion in eating subjects, whereas rewarding affect in abstainers may last for extended durations; it is not associated with a discrete event, such as the eating of a meal. Fasting, then, changes the conventional drive-reward architecture from a consummatory to an ascetic one; the change in reward, moreover—and this is of the greatest significance—is apparently supported metabolically, energetically, and so forth, through the enhanced efficiency of food utilization arising from dietary restriction.

Moreover, the change in drive-reward architecture is not restricted to one drive:

fasting, possibly through its endogenous opioid-enhancing effects, also reduces the sex drive, as has been said. Furthermore, as I have demonstrated elsewhere,[43] all categories of ascetic practice, in their ideal-type forms, appear to result in drive reduction, possibly by directly or indirectly leading to enhanced endogenous opioid activity. Psychophysiological information about the ascetic practice of seclusion/isolation (especially in darkness) has been provided by a substantial body of clinical and experimental research into its secular analogue, sensory deprivation or as it has come to be known by its more recent terminology, "restricted environmental stimulation" or REST.[44] This research has determined that REST can lead in many subjects both to reductions in drive of both a specific (i.e., of the information drive[45]) and a general (i.e., to global states of relaxation[46]) nature, as well as apparently to increases in endogenous opioid activity.[47] The discipline of religious prostrations is analogous to forms of exercise studied in the laboratory, which latter have likewise been found associated with endogenous opioid enhancement[48] and with detachment from aversive drive.[49] Sexual asceticism or celibacy, at least if reinforced by behaviors such as fasting that results in corresponding reductions in libido, appears to lead to an endocrine *milieu intérieur* that is conducive to heightened opioid activity,[50] with its associated drive reduction and tranquillity- and euphoria-enhancing properties.

The ascetic practice of vigil, analogous to sleep deprivation (also studied under experimental and clinical conditions), would seem, based on comparison with the latter, also to result in both specific and general drive reduction, as well as, according to at least one study, increased endogenous opioid activity.[51] Finally, ascetic self-mortification practices that involve the deliberate self-infliction of pain are interpretable in terms of the principles of what pain researchers have labeled "hyperstimulation analgesia." Hyperstimulation analgesia results from deliberately induced, brief, acute, and circumscribed pain, which in turn mobilizes one or more of several endogenous analgesia systems, at least one of which is mediated through mechanisms involving endogenous opioids.[52] The result of this mobilization is analgesia, potentially euphoria, and aversive drive reduction.[53]

The net effect of the practice of the full ascetico-meditational régime is a global reduction in drives, of both consummatory and aversive categories. A key role in this reduction is probably played by the endogenous opioids, the activity of which appears to be enhanced by all categories of ascetic practice. Opioids are well known for their profound drive-reducing properties: consummatory drives, such as for food and sex, as well as aversive drives, such as those associated with pain, anxiety, fear, and dysphoria, have all been demonstrated to be profoundly modulated by various forms of opioids.[54] Opioids are also, of course, well known for their euphorigenic properties, and perhaps less well known for the potentially biphasic nature of their effects on arousal, in which they may lead to both hypo- and hyperarousal.

Ascetic practice, then, actually leads to an "uncoupling" of the (most probably endogenous opioid-mediated) experience of reward from the object of reward: paradoxically, the absence of food replaces food in the production of reward experience, resulting in a reward experience of greater intensity and duration; the absence of sexual activity and consummation produces a neuroendocrine *milieu intérieur* that is more conducive to extended and more intense experience of euphoria than is the brief euphoria associated with orgasm. Paradoxically, too, the experience of aversiveness (the pain of self-mortification practices, the fatigue associated with sleep deprivation and rigorous prostration practice, the tedium of isolation in darkness) may lead to the conquest of aversiveness, to the replacement of aversiveness with bliss. The architecture of normal drive-reward pathways is dismantled and replaced by an architecture in which reward precedes goal—is independent of goal: it is the psychoneuroendocrine, the psychophysiological, architecture of dispassion, of detachment, of *apatheia*. It is the untwisting of the very sinews of the private will. It is the régime that must be successfully pursued before the ascetic's will can be "buried in a heart that [is] as dead to self as the sterile sand of the desert": the work that must precede, or be a part of, the larger work of storming the fortress of "the heart of stone," as Brown explains.[55]

The complete change in fundamental motivational structure is required for the ascetic to progress to spiritual advancement. This process—usually long and struggle-filled—is conceived by both the Desert Fathers and their present-day spiritual sons and daughters in Ethiopia, in highly dualistic terms of a conflict between body and soul, "the mind of flesh" and the spirit. "By nature the soul is *passionless*" declared Isaac,[56] distilling the essence of the collective experience of desert Christianity as it had been transmitted through *The Lives,* and *The Sayings of the Fathers,* and other sources. According to my spiritual father and other hermits, the body likes to eat, drink, sleep in a good bed, likes luxury, and "every nice thing in this world"; the soul likes to stand, pray, prostrate, weep (i.e., to experience "the gift of tears"), give alms. Moreover, it is humble, loving, charitable, and prefers, even likes, fasting. Spiritual progress requires undistracted periods of meditation (Geez: *tamasto*) or "stillness" in Isaac's terms, for pursuit of the transformation *(metanoia)* from a being dominated by "the mind of flesh" to one dominated by the soul:

> When life's concerns do not incur on the soul from without, and she abides in her nature, then she does not require prolonged toil to penetrate into and understand the wisdom of God. For her separation from the world [i.e., through separation from the passions] and her stillness naturally move her towards the understanding of God's creatures. And by this she is lifted up toward God; being astonished, she is struck with wonder, and she remains with God. When water does not seep into the fountain of the soul from without, the natural water that springs up in her incessantly bubbles forth intuitions of God's wonders. But when the soul is found bereft of those, it is either because she has received a cause for this from some alien recollection, or because the senses have stirred up turmoil against her by means of encounters with objects. When the senses, however, are confined by stillness and not permitted to sally forth, and by its aid the soul's memories grow old, then you will see what are the soul's natural thoughts, what is the nature of the soul, and what treasures she has hidden within herself.[57]

And

> When the senses are chaste and collected, they give birth to peace in the soul and do not allow her to experience strife; and whenever the soul has no perception of any-

> thing, victory will be gained without struggle. But if the soul should grow negligent in this matter, she will not be able to remain secure; and after a perception has entered, she must fight hard to expel it from herself. However, her first state of limpid purity and natural innocence are lost. The majority of men, if not all the world, for this reason depart from the natural state and that limpid purity which is prior to the knowledge of diverse things. On this account, the more men are involved in the world, the more it is difficult for them to regain limpid purity, by reason of their knowledge of many evil things. Only one man among many can once again return to his primordial state by another means.[58]

It is true that ascetic struggle—with attendant craving, obsession, "demonic visitation"—is, in this sense, not conducive to long periods free of distraction. However, the passions can become at least relatively subjugated—a process which apparently obeys certain psychoneuroendocrinological principles in response to certain behaviors, as can be observed in analogous present-day secular contexts, under clinical and laboratory conditions, in the case of radically diminished appetite and libido in response to fasting associated with eating disorders or with voluntary fasting in normal experimental subjects.

Coinciding with the subjugation of the passions and control of the senses in the properly educated ascetic, is an increase in both the depth and the duration of *tamasto,* stillness, until the duration can allegedly be measured in numbers of days and the depth can be assessed in physiological terms of profound cataleptic trance in which vital signs become virtually undetectable. Both in the literary sources and in interviews with contemporary Ethiopian hermits, we find descriptions of prolonged hypometabolic states achieved in the seclusion of caves and huts by advanced ascetico-meditational practitioners.[59] Descriptions reveal a range of ASCs, from light trance to states in which there is complete immobility, lack of signs of consciousness, breathing, pulse, or heartbeat—in short, a deathlike appearance or condition—but one from which the ascetic may waken after anywhere from hours to weeks to months. These latter states, as I have discussed in some detail elsewhere, can be described as revealing a number of important similarities to hibernation.[60] The range of potential psychological and spiritual phenomena, to be found associated with such physiological states, has also been discussed elsewhere.[61] For present purposes I will focus specifically on the set of primarily physical features that is apparently common both to advanced ascetico-meditational practice and to the prefallen Adamic state.

Adam's prefallen condition, according to *Genesis* and its interpretations, is characterized by bliss, awe and wonder, and an absence of pain (including discomfort, fatigue, hunger) suffering, illness, aging, and death. His activity, importantly, was the ongoing contemplation of, meditation on, God's glory.[62]

In the ethos of the desert ascetics of the third and fourth centuries and of contemporary Ethiopian asceticism, there exists a belief that Adam's prefallen condition is approachable through a rigorous, uncompromising devotion to spiritual discipline focused on devotion to God, asceticism, and contemplation or meditation (which category includes stillness and *tamasto*). Significantly, the properties associated with Adam's prefallen condition are strikingly similar to properties found through clinical and experimental means to be associated with meditation and similar forms of ASCs such as self-hypnosis (and with ascetic practices or their analogues), namely, bliss and analgesia, immune enhancement and illness reduction, and even, remarkably, aging retardation/reversal.

A sizable body of case studies, along with experimental research, has demonstrated the potentially significant analgesic properties of hypnotic and self-hypnotic trance.[63] Meditation has also been found to have significant pain-reduction potential, and in fact a quite successful chronic-pain treatment program employing meditation as a primary treatment modality has produced impressive results.[64] I referred previously to the extensive review and analysis of data that has determined that ascetic practices are likely to lead directly or indirectly to the enhanced activity of endogenous opioids, which have well-known, profound analgesic properties. Among the ascetic practices, the mobilization of endogenous analgesia systems (both opioid and nonopioid) through self-mortification practices was briefly described; the principle of "hyperstimulation" analgesia, which I have theorized underlies ideal-type self-mortification practice, has been described by pain researchers as having potentially powerful analgesic applications, leading in some cases to complete eradication of longstanding painful conditions.[65] In short, this evidence shows quite clearly that meditative ASCs (including those accessed through self-hypnosis) and related ascetic practice have inherently profound analgesic properties.

Similarly, it is likely that the ascetico-meditational regimen will result in enhancements to the immune system and reductions in illness, corresponding in some measure to the disease-free nature of the original Adamic state. Such a proposition is based on evidence from clinical, experimental, and epidemiological research (1) on meditation and related means of inducing ASCs, and (2) on the analogues of ascetic practices. A number of studies have shown that states resulting from meditation, hypnosis, or other stylized forms of inducing relaxation states may be associated with enhancements of the immune system, including increases in the functioning or number of immune cells.[66] One study compared the effects of meditation-like relaxation with a control group (no relaxation), finding that relaxation resulted in significant enhancement of immune-cell functioning as well as significant reductions in antibody titers to herpes simplex virus.[67] The clinical effects of meditative ASCs have been reflected in epidemiological studies that showed reduced medical-care utilization rates in meditators as compared to nonmeditating controls, including for cancer and all infectious diseases.[68] These clinical effects have been demonstrated in a recent study that found an approximate doubling of survival rate associated with self-hypnosis (and group therapy) in breast-cancer patients.[69] There is also good reason to expect that some ascetic practices result in immune-system enhancement and prevention/cure of illness: dietary restriction has been found (robustly) to result in decreases in the incidence of illness,[70] while some kinds of endogenous opioids—which are, as has been indicated, stimulated by ascetic practices—have been found to be immunostimulators.[71] These data, primarily drawn from studies of subjects who were naive with regard to meditative (and ascetic) practices, nonetheless indicate that ascetico-meditational discipline may lead to significant immune-enhancing and illness-reducing outcomes; there is also reason to expect that long-term virtuoso practitioners of disciplines involving meditation and asceticism in isolated environments may even learn substantially to increase the magnitude of these salutary effects found in novices.

While the subject of using psychological means to reduce pain and enhance the immune system has received recent scientific (and some popular) attention, perhaps less attention has been paid to some recent important studies in aging research, studies that have a pronounced if initially unsuspected significance for the present consideration of advanced ascetico-meditational practice. Nevertheless, it is not only possible but indeed important to examine evidence that in fact suggests that advanced long-term ascetico-meditational practice may lead to more than antinociceptive and immune enhancing outcomes; it may even lead to the retardation (and reversal) of aging. While this evidence is examined in detail elsewhere, it will here be briefly reviewed. Three key points must first be made: (1) forms of aging retardation—and even aging reversal—have in fact been experimentally demonstrated in animals and humans; (2) aging retardation and reversal are phenomena claimed by most ascetico-meditational traditions to result for some virtuoso practitioners of these disciplines; and (3) there is compelling evidence that suggests that some mechanisms of aging retardation/reversal may be stimulated by ascetico-meditational practices.

Probably the most obvious antiaging pathway associated with the long-term ascetico-meditational regimen is also that most linkable to a very robust body of data. Dietary restriction has been researched in a large number of studies across a fairly wide range of species, and "has been shown to extend the species characteristic maximum life span in nearly all species so far tested, including a number of invertebrates . . ., fish, and homothermic vertebrates such as mammals";[72] such extension of life span may be "by as much as 50%."[73] Although long-term dietary-restriction studies have not yet been conducted on humans, "epidemiological observations as well as inferential data derived from physiologic alterations during long-term weight loss regimens for obesity, suggest that humans would respond to DR in a manner similar to other animals."[74]

Long-term practitioners of ascetic fasting and dietary restriction, moreover, would make an ideal human study population for aging effects of dietary restriction. Furthermore, accounts of advanced long-term ascetics often include descriptions of observable physical characteristics that indicate physiological changes associated with prolonged fasting or dietary restriction, such as abundant growth of body ("lanugo") hair.[75] "Hairy anchoritism" is a recorded phenomenon in ancient Near Eastern, Hindu, Tibetan Buddhist, as well as Oriental Christian ascetico-meditational traditions.[76]

Related to the antiaging effects of dietary restriction are those associated with suppression of the human gonadal axis, which, as already mentioned, may result from forms of restriction of dietary intake. Castration has been shown to extend life span in animal[77] and human studies (medical castration being performed on prostrate cancer patients and, formerly—and deplorably—on mentally retarded and psychotic individuals); in one human study (of castrated mentally retarded individuals), castrated subjects were found to outlive by an average of ten years a control (unoperated) group matched for mental status and date of birth.[78] Not only dietary restriction but also other ascetico-meditiational practices may, through the antigonadal properties of endogenous opioids,[79] result in what can be called hormonal or "functional castration," which may in fact be another pathway to aging retardation/reversal.[80] Moreover, descriptions of long-lived ascetics who not only appear youthful but androgynous as well can be found in at least several ascetico-meditational traditions.[81]

Many ascetico-meditational traditions report that advancement in the tradition results in the experience of profound and prolonged tranquillity and bliss. While the possible if not probable relationship between the experience of tranquillity and bliss and heightened endogenous opioid activity has already been mentioned, the possible antiaging effects of endogenous opioids have not. Several theories of aging have emphasized a major role in aging for the long-term physiological effects of stress; opioids are known to counteract the effects of stress on both phenomenological and physiological levels.[82] Moreover, some endogenous opioids, as mentioned above, have immune-enhancing properties and, additionally, may stimulate the activities of other neurohormones with antiaging effects, such as human growth hormone[83] and melatonin.[84]

The net effect of both dietary restriction and enhanced endogenous opioid activity is to lower metabolism. Since several prominent theories of aging, such as "the wear and tear theory," hold that aging results from the long-term and cumulative effects of metabolism, significant reduction of metabolism has been proposed as a potentially viable antiaging mechanism. Accounts of advanced long-term practitioners remaining in profound catalepsy-like states for prolonged periods, in extremely isolated mountain caves, only visited by a helper who periodically brings food for consumption during bouts of arousal, suggest the kind of protracted hypometabolic condition that may actually result in the radically reduced metabolic costs necessary to realize the phenomenon of aging retardation. The compelling nature of this hypothesis is increased by the likelihood that other potential antiaging mechanisms, those associated with dietary restriction, gonadal axis suppression, and the counteracting effects on stress toxicity of endogenous opioid-mediated tranquillity and bliss, may be simultaneously triggered by the ascetico-meditational regimen. It is important to note that in some ascetico-meditational traditions, an explicit association of lowered metabolism with aging retardation is actually made: for example, certain schools of Tibetan Buddhism explain the efficacy of life span–lengthening yoga by the reductions in respiratory rate that result from yogic practice.[85]

Furthermore, there are other mechanisms, involving the antiaging effects of several powerful hormones, that seem likely to be triggered by long-term ascetico-meditational practices, including growth hormone and melatonin. Prolonged states characterized by radically lowered arousal would be expected to enhance secretion of these antiaging hormones for the following reasons. Human growth hormone is normally secreted primarily during states of deep ("slow wave" or *delta*) sleep, which, as I have argued in greater detail elsewhere,[86] are likely to closely resemble states of deep meditation. Whereas normally both slow-wave sleep and secretion of human growth hormone decline radically after the age of thirty in humans,[87] the practice of deep meditation (and possibly also fasting) is likely to restore secretion of the hormone to the range of youthful levels. Remarkably, a recent study published in the *New England Journal of Medicine* demonstrated that exogenous (intravenous) administration of human growth hormone in healthy volunteers did, in fact, lead to somatic tissue changes—reversals—"equivalent to the changes in magnitude incurred during 10 to 20 years of aging."[88] These changes occurred in what is called the "lean body mass," which normally atrophies at a predictable rate during aging. As the authors of the study describe it,

> In middle and late adulthood all people experience a series of progressive alterations in body composition. the lean body mass shrinks and the mass of adipose tissue expands. The contraction in lean body mass reflects atrophic processes in skeletal, muscle, liver, kidney, spleen, skin and bone. These structural changes have been considered unavoidable results of aging.[89]

Intravenous administration of human growth hormone reversed these changes in humans. Remarkably, the *Life of Antony* contains a description of what appears to be aging retardation/reversal effects associated with the ascetico-meditational regimen of the "Father" of Christian asceticism, and these effects are strikingly similar to tissue changes described in the *New England Journal of Medicine* study on growth hormone. "Contemporaries liked to think that they sensed [the "original, natural and uncorrupted" Adamic prefallen state] in Antony, when he first emerged from his cell at the bottom of a ruined fort, after twenty years, in 305" writes Brown, who goes on to quote the *Life:*

> When they beheld him, they were amazed to see that *his body had maintained its former condition, neither fat for lack of exercise nor emaciated* from fasting and combat with demons, *but just as it was* when they had known him previous to his withdrawal [emphasis mine].[90]

Although Antony was not administering exogenous growth hormone to himself, the description suggests, in light of the evidence reviewed here and elsewhere,[91] the compelling possibility that the changes—or *absence* of changes—observable in him resulted from the stimulation of enhanced endogenous growth hormone activity by ascetico-meditational practice. The *Life* goes on to relate that Antony lived beyond the age of one hundred and that his passing represented more of a direct entrance to Paradise than a typical death. Moreover, Athanasius's description of his last years suggests other features consistent with aging retardation/reversal.

> . . . in every way [Antony] remained free of injury. For he possessed eyes undimmed and sound, and he saw clearly. He lost none of his teeth—they simply had been worn to the gums because of the old man's great age. He also retained health in his feet and hands, and generally he seemed brighter and of more energetic strength than those who make use of baths and a variety of foods and clothing.[92]

Athanasius's description of Antony's general well-being is also consistent with the results of the Rudman growth hormone studies, which demonstrated improvements in the functioning of major bodily organs (as assessed in the studies by organ mass, that is, or reversal of organ atrophy) including those responsible for primary physiological processes (such as the liver), as well as in muscle, skin, and vertebral bone. The description is also consistent with results of dietary-restriction research, particularly regarding beneficial effects on energy and the musculoskeletal system.[93] And the description of Antony's superhealthy condition is also consistent with the results of research on the antiaging properties of the hormone melatonin, the actions of which I have proposed are also enhanced through ascetico-meditational practices.

While several practices of the ascetico-meditational regimen are likely to result in increased secretion of melatonin,[94] the one with the most pronounced potential is likely to be immobilization in darkness. Recent research has shown that humans who are relatively immobile in extended periods of darkness experience increased levels of melatonin secretion.[95] Other research has demonstrated the profound antiaging effects of melatonin in humans[96] and animals.[97] Several very recent studies in particular graphically demonstrate the potentially profound antiaging effects of melatonin. The studies, conducted in Switzerland and the United States, found "striking improvement of the general state of mice" as well as a "remarkable prolongation of life associated with melatonin administration."[98] Specifically, the researchers claimed:

> . . . starting at 5 months from the initiation of melatonin administration, the body weight of the untreated mice still surviving started to decrease rapidly, and also astonishing differences in the fur and in the general conditions of the two [i.e. melatonin-receiving and control] groups *(vigor, activity, posture)* became increasingly evident. Melatonin preserved completely optimal pelage [i.e. fur coat] conditions and the body weight was maintained at the original values. . . . Furthermore, the mean survival time ± standard deviation was 931 ± 80 days in the melatonin-treated group versus 752 ± 81 days in the untreated controls. This difference is significant. . . .[99]

Although this kind of comprehensive antiaging experimental protocol has not yet been undertaken with human subjects, there are indications that melatonin has similar antiaging influences on humans.[100] Because melatonin is normally secreted in humans under conditions of darkness, and the surge of melatonin is enhanced by the reduction or elimination of bodily movement, the widespread ascetico-meditational practice of mediation in a darkened, secluded environment while remaining immobile for extended durations may well also result in antiaging effects. In fact, there is apparently an explicit connection between this specific practice and antiaging phenomena recognized by some ascetico-meditational schools, for example, in Tibetan Buddhism.[101] Also quite significant in this regard is the fact that Athanasius makes a conspicuous point of noting that Antony remained alone in his cell for a protracted period before he describes the latter's amazing youthfulness: "Nearly twenty years he spent in this manner pursuing the ascetic life by himself, not venturing out. . . ."[102]

The same constellation of ascetico-meditational practices and practice outcomes reported for Antony and some of the other Desert Fathers (as well as for individuals in other ascetico-meditational traditions) can be discerned in the contemporary Ethiopian Christian eremitic tradition. Interviews with close to one hundred brought me descriptions of (and possibly contact with) some of "the few great ascetics" of the Ethiopian tradition. I was also able to observe at first hand that the general health of a number of the ascetics seemed to reflect the putative enhancements of the ascetico-meditational regimen, although, of course, these impressionistic observations cannot qualify as strict scientific evidence. Nevertheless, I met more than one ascetic who, subsisting on a very limited diet of lentils and water, seemed to reflect a level of energy, vigor, suppleness, and healthiness that betrayed their reported ages. I also collected, from a number of helpers, fairly detailed accounts of some advanced hermits who were described as remaining in prolonged hypometabolic states (in some cases for months with brief intermittent periods of arousal). Some of these were believed to be experiencing a heavenly ascent of the soul while their bodies remained on earth, barely alive.

I found also that the ethos of the potential attainment of the prefallen Adamic state is still very much alive in the contemporary Ethiopian ascetico-meditational tradition, although such an attainment is humbly reserved in the imagination of the many "average ascetics" for the few great ones. A state of heavenly bliss, unpunctuated by pain or suffering of any kind, nor disease, injury, corruption, aging or death, testifying to the eschatological and postmortem inheritance awaiting those not fortunate, gifted, or heroically ascetic enough to achieve it in the premortem, preapocalyptic time, is still held to exist in this most extraordinary and unique surviving Christian tradition.

NOTES

1. W. C. Bushell, "Psychophysiological and Cross-Cultural Dimensions of Ascetico-Meditational Practices: Special Reference to the Christian Hermits of Ethiopia and Application to Theory in Anthropology and Religious Studies," unpublished Ph.D. dissertation, Columbia University, 1993.
2. Peter Brown, *The Body and Society: Men, Women, and Sexual Renunciation in Early Christianity* (New York: Columbia University Press, 1988), p. 223.
3. Ibid., pp. 220–221.
4. The crucial principle in nutrition research is what Walford and others have referred to as "undernutrition without malnutrition": in other words, a diet of significantly reduced caloric content, but sufficiently well-balanced in terms of necessary nutritional categories (vitamins, protein, etc.). Cf. R. Weindruch and R. L. Walford, *The Retardation of Aging and Disease by Dietary Restriction* (Springfield, Ill.: Charles C. Thomas, 1988), pp. 315f.; R. L. Walford et al., "Dietary Restriction and Aging: Historical Phases, Mechanisms, Current Directions," *Journal of Nutrition* 117 (1987):1650.
5. See Alayne Yates, *Compulsive Exercise and the Eating Disorders* (New York: Brunner/Mazel, 1991); Alayne Yates et al., "Running: An Analogue of Anorexia?" *New England Journal of Medicine* 308 (1983):251–255; A. Keys et al., *The Biology of Human Starvation* (Minneapolis: University of Minnesota Press, 1950); Gen Komaki et al., "Plasma Beta-Endorphin during Fasting in Man," *Hormone Research* 33 (1990):239–243.
6. M. A. Marrazzi and E. D. Luby, "An Auto-Addiction Opioid Model of Chronic An-

orexia Nervosa," *International Journal of Eating Disorders* 5.2 (1986):191–208.

7. P. C. Boyle et al., "Increased Efficiency of Food Utilization Following Weight Loss," *Physiology and Behavior* 21 (1978):261; Weindruch and Walford 1988; Yates 1991.
8. Roy L. Walford et al., "Dietary Restriction and Aging: Historical Phases, Mechanisms, Current Directions," *Journal of Nutrition* 117 (1987):1650; Weindruch and Walford 1988; and below.
9. See note 4.
10. For example, D. Hollander et al., "Influence of Life-Prolonging Dietary Restriction on Intestinal Vitamin A Absorption in Mice," *Age* 9 (1986):57; Weindruch and Walford 1988.
11. Boyle et al. 1978. As Weindruch and Walford (1988) describe this study: "The most severely [dietary] restricted group gained 30 grams [body weight] on 140 grams of food, the group on milder [dietary restriction] gained 21 grams on 154 grams of food, and the controls gained an average of only 2 grams after eating 156 grams of food." For similar results in humans undergoing refeeding after dietary restriction, see Marrazzi and Luby 1986.
12. S. W. Touyz et al., "Exercise Anorexia: A New Dimension in Anorexia Nervosa?" in G. D. Burrows et al., eds., *Handbook of Eating Disorders, Pt. 1: Anorexia Nervosa and Bulimia* (New York: Elsevier, 1987), pp. 143–158.
13. Ibid.; Yates 1991; Keys et al. 1950.
14. Marrazzi and Luby 1986, p. 197.
15. Yates 1991, p. 87.
16. Ibid., pp. 87–88, 89.
17. Weindruch and Walford 1988, p. 304. See E. S. Horton, "Effects of Low Energy Diets on Work Performance," *American Journal of Clinical Nutrition* 35 (1982):1228; S. D. Phinney, "The Metabolic Intereaction Between Very Low Calorie Diet and Exercise," in G. L. Blackburn and G. A. Bray, eds., *Management of Obesity by Severe Caloric Restriction* (Littleton, Mass.: P.S.G., 1985), pp. 99–105.
18. Weindruch and Walford 1988, p. 305. See J. C. Waterlow, "Metabolic Adaptation to Low Intakes of Energy and Protein," *Annual Review of Nutrition* 6 (1986):495.
19. Bushell 1993. Cf. also J. A. Horne, *Why We Sleep: The Functions of Sleep in Humans and Other Mammals* (New York: Oxford University Press, 1988), and R. E. Thayer, *The Biopsychology of Mood and Arousal* (New York: Oxford University Press 1989).
20. Bushell 1993; Karl E. Knutsson and Ruth Selinus, "Fasting in Ethiopia: An Anthropological and Nutritional Study," *American Journal of Clinical Nutrition* 23.7 (1970):969.
21. I have retained the anonymity of most interviewees in general and whenever requested.
22. Piero Camporesi, *The Incorruptible Flesh; Bodily Mutation and Mortification in Religion and Folklore* (New York: Cambridge University Press, 1988), esp. p. 27.
23. Or better in some opinions in the history of Christian dogma; on variations in the eschatological dimension of "Adam theology," see C. M. Pate, *The Glory of Adam and the Afflictions of the Righteous* (New York: Edwin Mellen Press, 1993).
24. *The Ascetical Homilies of Saint Isaac the Syrian,* trans. and ed. Holy Transfiguration Monastery (Boston, Mass.: Holy Transfiguration Monastery, 1984), p. 45.
25. Brown 1988, p. 223.
26. Not only an absence of mental-cognitive deficits has been found in some studies of fasting, but actual cognitive enhancements have also been reported: see F. G. Benedict, *A Study of Prolonged Fasting* (Washington, D.C.: Carnegie Institute, 1915); I. H. Mills and L. Medlicott, "The Basis of Naloxone Treatment in Anorexia Nervosa and the

Metabolic Responses to It," in K. M. Pırke and D. Ploog, eds., *Psychobiology of Anorexia Nervosa* (New York: Springer-Verlag, 1984), pp. 159–170; S. Fourest-Fontcave et al., "Mental Alertness in Response to Hypoglycaemia in Normal Man: The Effect of 12 Hours and 72 Hours of Fasting," *Diabete et metabolisme* 13.4 (1987):405–410.

27. See below, note 73.
28. Brown 1988, p. 224.
29. Bushell 1993; W. C. Bushell and J. P. Halper, "Possibility of Prolonged 'Cataleptic' States and Aging Retardation in Long-term Ascetico-Meditational Practitioners: Some Hypotheses," in preparation.
30. Keys et al. 1950.
31. K. M. Pirke and D. Ploog, "Biology of Human Starvation," in G. D. Burrows et al., eds., *Handbook of Eating Disorders, Pt. 1: Anorexia Nervosa and Bulimia* (New York: Elsevıer, 1987), pp. 79–104; J. Russell and P.J.V. Beumont, "The Endocrinology of Anorexia Nervosa," in G. D. Burrows et al., eds., ibid.
32. Keys et al. 1950, pp. 749f., 906.
33. On opioid substances produced by the body and their wıde range of effects, see J. H. Jaffe and W. R. Martin," Opioid Analgesics and Antagonists," in A. Goodman Gilman et al., eds., *Goodman and Gılman's The Pharmacological Basis of Therapeutics,* 8th ed. (New York: Pergamon 1990), pp. 485–521; G. A. Olson et al., "Endogenous Opiates: 1991," *Peptides* 13 (1992):1247–1287; J. E. Smith and J. D. Lane, eds., *The Neurobiology of Opıate Reward Mechanisms* (New York: Elsevier, 1983); on the specific role of endogenous opioids in food reward, see E. Rolls, "Brain Electrical Stimulation and 'Natural Reward,'" ın B. G. Hoebel and D. Novin, eds., *The Neural Basis of Feeding and Reward* (Brunswick, Maine: Haer Institute for Electrophysiological Research, 1982), pp. 321–337; H. Aou et al., "Feeding—Induced Reward in the Lateral Hypothalamus: Role of Opioid Peptides," in P. Illes and C. Farsang, eds., *Regulatory Roles of Opioid Peptides* (New York: VCH, 1987), pp. 127–139; S. J. Cooper et al., "Endorphins, Opiates, and Food Intake," in R. J. Rodgers and S. J. Cooper, eds., *Endorphins, Opiates, and Behavioural Processes* (New York: John Wiley, 1988), pp. 247–269.
34. For example, Aou et al. 1987, using primates.
35. J. Dum et al., "Activation of Hypothalamic Beta-Endorhpin Pools by Reward Induced by Highly Palatable Food," *Pharmacology and Biochemistry of Behavior* 18 (1983):443–447.
36. Cf. R. A. Wise, "Brain Neuronal Systems Mediating Reward Processes," in J. E. Smith and J. D. Lane, *Neurobiology;* S. D. Iversen, "Brain Endorphins and Reward Function: Some Thoughts and Speculations," in J. E. Smith and J. D. Lane, *Neurobiology;* G. Di Chiara et al., "Drugs of Abuse: Biochemical Surrogates of Specific Aspects of Natural Reward?" in S. Wonnacott and G. G. Lunt, eds., *Neurochemistry of Drug Dependence* (London: 1993), pp. 65–82.
37. For example, S. Balon-Perin et al., "The Effects of Glucose Ingestion and Fasting on Plasma Immunoreactive Beta-Endorphin, Adrenocorticotropic Hormone and Cortisol in Obese Subjects," *Journal of Endocrinological Investigation* 14 (1991):919–925; see revıew of studies in Olson et al. 1991, p. 1254f.
38. See note 35.
39. T. S. Shippenberg and A. Bals-Kubik, "Homeostatic Functions of Endogenous Opioids," in O. F. Almeida and T. S. Shippenberg, eds., *Neurobiology of Opioids* (New York: Springer-Verlag, 1991), p. 333.
40. See discussion in Bushell 1993.

41. See reviews of wide range of phenomena in Weindruch and Walford 1988, and B. Wu and P. Marliss, "Interorgan Metabolic Coordination during Fasting and Underfeeding: An Adaptation for Mobilizing Fat while Sparing Protein in Humans," in G. H. Anderson and S. H. Kennedy, eds., *The Biology of Feast and Famine: Relevance to Eating Disorders* (San Diego: Academic Press, 1992), pp. 220–244; and Bushell 1993.
42. Marrazzi and Luby 1986; Yates 1991, p. 75; R. Moore et al., "Naloxone in the Treatment of Anorexia Nervosa: Effect of Weight Gain and Lipolysis," *Journal of Research of the Society of Medicine* 74 (1981):129–131.
43. The following discussion is based on extensive data subjected to review and analysis in Bushell 1993.
44. On REST, see P. Suedfeld, *Restricted Environmental Stimulation: Research and Clinical Applications* (New York: Wiley, 1980); P. Suedfeld et al., eds., *Restricted Environmental Stimulation: Theoretical and Empirical Developments in Flotation REST* (New York: Springer-Verlag 1990).
45. See Bushell 1993, pp. 112f.
46. Suedfeld 1980; Suedfeld et al. 1990.
47. J. W. Turner and T. H. Fine, "Hormonal Changes Associated with Restricted Environmental Stimulation Therapy," in Suedfeld et al. 1990, pp. 71–92.
48. M. N. Janal et al., "Pain Sensitivity, Mood and Plasma Endocrine Levels in Man Following Long-Distance Running: Effects of Naloxone," *Pain* 19 (1984):13–25; M. Daniel et al., "Opiate Receptor Blockade by Naltrexone and Mood State after Acute Physical Activity," *British Journal of Sports Medicine* 26.2 (1992):111–115.
49. W. P. Morgan et al., "Facilitation of Physical Performance by Means of a Cognitive Strategy," *Cognitive Therapy and Research* 7.3 (1983):251–264.
50. The endocrine *milieu intérieur* of a celibate who is not experiencing libidinous drives—such as some patients with eating disorders—may apparently facilitate endogenous opioid activity because of a reduction in the antiopioid activities of gonadal hormones. On the absence of libidinous urges associated with dietary restriction, see D. B. Herzog et al., "Sexuality in Males with Eating Disorders," in A. E. Andersen, ed., *Males with Eating Disorders* (New York: Brunner/Mazel 1990), pp. 40–53; and, on the antiopioid properties of gonadal hormones, see L. A. Berglund et al., "Desensitization of Brain Opiate Receptor Mechanisms by Gonadal Steroid Treatments that Stimulate Luteinizing Hormone Secretion," *Endocrinology* 122 (1988):2718–2726.
51. On the drive reduction associated with sleep deprivation, see Horne 1989, pp. 56f., and D. R. Haslam, "The Incentive Effect and Sleep Deprivation," *Sleep* 6.4 (1983):362–368. On involvement of endogenous opioid activity in sleep deprivation in laboratory animals, see P. Fadda et al., "Dopamine and Opioid Interactions in Sleep Deprivation," *Progress in Neuro-Pharmacology and Biological Psychiatry* 17 (1993):269–278.
52. R. Melzack, "Prolonged Relief of Pain by Brief, Intense Transcutaneous Somatic Stimulation," *Pain* 1 (1975):357–373; R. Melzack, "Hyperstimulation Analgesia," in R. Melzack and P. Wall, eds., *Textbook of Pain* (New York, 1989); K. Lewit, "The Needle Effect in the Relief of Myofascial Pain," *Pain* 6 (1979):83–90.
53. Drive reduction and euphoria related to deliberate self-infliction of pain have been demonstrated. See, for example, R. M. Winchel and M. Stanley, "Self-Injurious Behavior: A Review of the Behavior and Biology of Self-Mutilation," *American Journal of Psychiatry* 148.3 (1991):306–317; and Bushell 1993.
54. See, for example, Jaffe and Martin 1990.
55. Brown 1988, p. 225.

56. See *The Ascetical Homilies of Saint Isaac The Syrian*, p. 17.
57. Ibid., p. 16.
58. Ibid., p. 22.
59. See description of Abba Silvanus in the *Apophthegmata patrum;* B. Ward, *The Desert Christian: The Sayings of the Desert Fathers* (New York: Macmillan, 1975), pp. 222f.; descriptions in the *Ascetical Homilies of Saint Isaac the Syrian*, pp. 271–272; some Ethiopian versions of the homilies of John Saba (Syrian mystical writer very influential on Ethiopian ascetic spirituality) claim that periods close to a year are possible. For a review of similar long-term hypometabolic states in the Buddhist, Hindu, Taoist, Sūfī, Kabbalistic, and other ascetico-meditational traditions, and for a review of interviews with Ethiopian hermits, see Bushell, 1993.
60. Bushell and Halper, in preparation; Bushell 1993. On states in humans that "resemble patterns of torpor and shallow hibernation in animals," see R. J. Berger et al., "Humans Sleeping in Cold: Thermoregulatory and Metabolic Aspects," in H. C. Heller et al., eds., *Living in the Cold: Physiological and Biochemical Adaptations* (New York: Elsevier, 1986); also, H. T. Hammel et al, "Thermal and Metabolic Responses of the Australian Aborigine Exposed to Moderate Cold in Summer," *Journal of Applied Physiology* 14.4 (1959):605–615; R. J. Berger, "Slow Wave Sleep, Shallow Torpor and Hibernation: Homologous States of Diminished Metabolism and Body Temperature," *Biological Psychology* 19 (1984):305–326. On prolonged states identified as cataleptic (of, however, unknown etiology) see Tebb and Vollum, *Premature Burial and How It May Be Prevented, with Special Reference to Trance, Catalepsy, and Other Forms of Suspended Animation* (New York, 1896).
61. Bushell 1993.
62. For references, cf. M. Fishbane, "Adam," in M. Eliade, ed., *The Encyclopedia of Religion* (New York: Macmillan, 1987), 1.27–28; significantly, Adam while in Eden is characterized as "*sunk in deep contemplation*" (my emphasis).
63. See, for review of a substantial portion of the literature up until approximately 1983, E. A. Hilgard and J. Hilgard, *Hypnosis in the Relief of Pain*, 2d ed. (New York, 1983); also D. Spiegel, "Hypnosis with Medical/Surgical Patients," *General Hospital Psychiatry* 5 (1983):265–277.
64. J. Kabat-Zinn et al., "The Clinical Use of Mindfulness Meditation for the Self-Regulation of Chronic Pain," *Journal of Behavioral Medicine* 8.2 (1985):163–190; also, W. W. Mills and J. T. Farrow, "The Transcendental Meditation Technique and Acute Experimental Pain," *Psychosomatic Medicine* 43.2 (1981):157–164.
65. It is worth quoting Melzack, one of the "deans" of contemporary pain research, on the remarkable analgesic potential of hyperstimulation analgesia as revealed in the clinical experimental research of Lewit (see above, note 52) and others. The treatment investigated involved the infliction of brief, intense, circumscribed cutaneous pain with a needle in order to mobilize endogenous analgesia systems ("the needle effect"): "The needle . . . must penetrate at the point of maximum pain. While this sounds like torture, the brief shot of pain produced by the needle resulted in striking relief of pain in 86.8% of [241] cases [of myofascial and vertebrogenic pain] and persistent relief for months or even permanently in about 50% of the cases" (Melzack, "Hyperstimulation . . .," 1989, p. 329). These data have important implications for the fundamental modulation of aversive (nociceptive) sensation and drive generally.
66. B. L. Gruber et al., "Immune System and Psychological Changes in Metastatic Cancer Patients Using Relaxation and Guided Imagery: A Pilot Study," *Scandanavian Journal of Behaviour Therapy* 17 (1988):25–46; H. R. Hall, "Imagery and Cancer," in A. A.

Sheikh, ed., *Imagination and Healing* (Farmingdale, N.Y.: Baywood, 1984); B. S. Peavey et al., "Biofeedback-Assisted Relaxation: Effects on Phagocytic Activity," *Biofeedback and Self-Regulation* 10.1 (1985):33–47; J. K. Kiecolt-Glaser et al., "Psychosocial Enhancement of Immunocompetence in a Geriatric Population," *Health Psychology* 4.10 (1985):25–41.

67. Kiecolt-Glaser et al. 1985; the immune parameter measured was natural killer-cell activity, an important function in cellular immunity. (It should be noted that the natural killer-cell activity of the experimental group was also compared to that of a "social contact" group—a group that met with the experimenters as did the relaxation group, but *without* instruction in relaxation technique—in order to attempt discrimination of the social from the specifically relaxational effects of instruction in relaxation.)
68. D. Orme-Johnson, "Medical Care Utilization and the Transcendental Meditation Program," *Psychosomatic Medicine* 49 (1987):493–507.
69. Moreover, by the termination of the study, most patients practicing self-hypnosis (and group therapy) were still alive, while most control patients had died; D. Spiegel et al., "Effect of Psychosocial Treatment on Survival of Patients with Metastatic Breast Cancer," *Lancet* 8668 (October 14, 1989):888–891.
70. Weindruch and Walford 1988; Walford et al. 1987.
71. See N. P. Plotnikoff et al., eds., *Enkephalins and Endorphins: Stress and the Immune System* (New York: Plenum, 1986); N. P. Plotnikoff et al., "Methione Enkephalin: Enhancement of T-cells in Patients with Kaposi's Sarcoma (AIDS)," *Psychopharmacology Bulletin* 22 (1986):695–697; A. J. Murgo et al., "Enhancement of Tumor Resistence in Mice by Enkephalins," in N. P. Plotnikoff et al., eds., *Stress and Immunity* (Boca Raton, Fla.: CRC Press, 1991); G.J.M. Maestroni and A. Conti, "Anti-Stress Role of the Melatonin-Immuno-Opioid Network: Evidence for a Physiological Mechanism Involving T Cell-Derived, Immuno-Reactive B-Endorphin and Met-Enkephalin Binding to Thymic Opioid Receptors," *International Journal of Neuroscience* 61 (1991):289–298; G.J.M. Maestroni and A. Conti, "Immuno-Derived Opioids as Mediators of the Immuno-Enhancing and Anti-Stress Action of Melatonin," *Acta Neurologica* 13.4 (1991):356–360.
72. Weindruch and Walford 1988, p. 5.
73. B. P. Yu, "Why Dietary Restriction may Extend Life: A Hypothesis," *Geriatrics* 44 (1989):87–90.
74. Weindruch and Walford 1988, p. 5.
75. "Striking generalized excessive long, dark lanugo hair is seen on the trunk and extremities in a nonsecondary sexual distribution" in anorexia nervosa. See L. A. Schechner and R. C. Hansen, eds., *Pediatric Dermatology,* vol. 2 (New York: Churchill Livingstone, 1988), p. 1154. This is a description very consistent with those of "hairy anchorites." The white color hair of the body often reported for "hairy anchorites" may result from the bleaching that can accompany prolonged exposure to the sun. Excessive growths of lanugo hair are also found in famine victims as well as anorexia nervosa patients.
76. See C. A. Williams, "Oriental Affinities of the Legend of the Hairy Anchorite," *University of Illinois Studies in Language and Literature* 10.2 (1925)—reviews evidence on ancient Near Eastern, Hindu, and Oriental Christian versions; also W. Y. Evans-Wentz, *Tibet's Great Yogi Milarepa* (London: Oxford University Press, 1951), p. 197—describes evidence of the phenomenon in the Tibetan Buddhist context.
77. J. F. Nelson, "Puberty, Gonadal Steroids and Fertility: Potential Reproductive Markers of Aging," *Experimental Gerontology* 23 (1988):359–367.

78. J. B. Hamilton and G. E. Mestler, "Mortality and Survival: Comparison of Eunuchs with Intact Men and Women in a Mentally Retarded Population," *Journal of Gerontology* 24.4 (1969):395–411.
79. See, for example, Jaffe and Martin 1990.
80. See Bushell 1993, and on hormonal or reversible castration, see A. Money and J. Earhardt, *Man and Woman, Boy and Girl* (New York, 1972). See also R. Santen, "Hypogonadism," in S.S.C. Yen and R. B. Jaffe, eds., *Reproductive Endocrinology*, 3d ed. (Philadelphia: Saunders, 1991), on the loss of secondary sex characteristics due to the actions of heightened endogenous opioid activity.
81. See Bushell 1993. Ethiopian Christian hermits, particularly revered figures (including saints), are often referred to expressly in "angelic" terms; angels are both youthful and androgynous. See S. Kaplan, *The Monastic Holy Man and the Christianization of Early Solomonic Ethiopia* (Wiesbaden: Franz Steiner Verlag, 1984), especially pp. 81–83. The *Chuang Tzu* referes to an aged mountain dwelling hermit "with skin like ice or snow, and gentle and shy as a young girl" (cited in J. Blofeld, *Taoism; The Road to Immortality* [Boston: Shambhala, 1985], p. 50).
82. For example, J. W. Rowe and B. R. Troen, "Sympathetic Nervous System and Aging in Man," *Endocrine Reviews* 1.2 (1980):167–179; R. M. Sapolsky, *Stress, the Aging Brain, and the Mechanisms of Neuron Death* (Cambridge, Mass.: MIT Press, 1992).
83. For example, G. Delitala et al., "Opioids Stimulate Growth Hormone (GH) Release in Man Independently of GH-Releasing Hormone," *Journal of Clinical Endocrinology and Metabolism* 69.2 (1989):356–358; Bushell 1993.
84. Maestroni and Conti, "Anti-Stress Role . . .," 1991.
85. On the interpretation of life-span extension as due to reduced respiratory rate (and hence metabolism) by a contemporary school of Tibetan Buddhist yoga, see D. Cozort, *Highest Yoga Tantra; An Introduction to the Esoteric Buddhism of Tibet* (Ithaca, N.Y.: Snow Lion Publications, 1986), p. 86. Tibetan Buddhist yoga is particularly interested in the antiaging dimensions of yoga or ascetico-meditational practice; see also H. H. Dalai Lama and J. Hopkins, *The Yoga of Tibet* (London: George Allen & Unwin, 1981); N. Norbu, *The Crystal and the Way of Light: Sutra, Tantra and Dzogchen* (New York: Routledge & Kegan Paul, 1986); G. Samuel, *Civilized Shamans: Buddhism in Tibetan Societies* (Washington, D.C.: Smithsonian Institution Press, 1993); G. H. Mullin, *Death and Dying: The Tibetan Tradition* (Boston: Arkana, 1986). Again it must be emphasized that many of the ascetico-meditational practices with antiaging effects are common to most if not all ascetico-meditational traditions.
86. Bushell 1993.
87. D. Rudman et al., "Effects of Human Growth Hormone on Body Composition in Elderly Men," *Hormone Research* 36 (Supplement 1, 1991):73–81.
88. D. Rudman et al., "Effects of Human Growth Hormone in Men Over 60 Years Old," *New England Journal of Medicine* 323.1 (1990):1–5; the results of the study were replicated in Rudman et al., "Effects of Human Growth . . ." 1991.
89. Rudman et al. 1990, p. 1.
90. Brown 1988, p. 224 (including citation from *Life of Antony*). Regarding the absence of emaciation in such a renowned faster as Antony, recall the above discussion on "the enhanced efficiency of food utilization" associated with dietary restriction.
91. Bushell 1993.
92. *Athanasius, The Life of Anthony and the Letter to Marcellinus,* trans. R. C. Gregg (New York: Paulist Press, 1980), p. 98. Recall again in the context of this passage the energy-enhancing properties of dietary restriction.

93. See above and Walford et al. 1987, and Weindruch and Walford 1988 on the antiarthritic effects of dietary restriction.
94. See sections on fasting and ascetic prostrations in Bushell 1993 for discussions of the importance of melatonin.
95. See especially T. A. Wehr, "The Durations of Human Melatonin Secretion and Sleep Respond to Changes in Daylength (Photoperiod)," *Journal of Clinical Endocrinology and Metabolism* 73 (1991):1276–1280.
96. According to the extensive review of Grad and Rozencwaig, "Treatment with melatonin restored adaptive systems which declined due to aging in . . . humans. . . ." See B. R. Grad and R. Rosencwaig, "The Role of Melatonin and Serotonin in Aging: Update," *Psychoneuroendocrinology* 18.4 (1993):283–295. See especially p. 285.
97. For example, G.J.M. Maestroni et al., "Pineal Melatonin, its Fundamental Immunoregulatory Role in Aging and Cancer," *Annals of the New York Academy of Sciences* 521 (1988):140–148.
98. Maestroni et al. 1988, pp. 146–147.
99. Ibid.
100. See Bushell 1993; R. J. Reiter, "A Brief Overview of New Areas of Pineal Research and Some Old Ones Revisited," in Y. Touitou et al., eds., *Melatonin and the Pineal Gland; From Basic Science to Clinical Application* (New York: Excerpta Medica, 1992).
101. On the implicit connection between the "dark retreat" and extended longevity in Tibetan Buddhism, see Norbu, *Crystal,* 1986, p. 156. See note 83.
102. *Life of Antony,* trans. Gregg, p. 42.

41

Flagellation and the French Counter-Reformation: Asceticism, Social Discipline, and the Evolution of a Penitential Culture

Ann W. Ramsey

This paper proposes a revision of the trend in Counter-Reformation scholarship which regards sixteenth- and seventeenth-century Catholic reform through the lens of modernization and acculturation.[1] I examine two major strands of the historiography dealing with modernization and acculturation to show how historians of the Catholic Reformation have overlooked the important reactivation of an older tradition of asceticism—flagellation and penitential piety—as the spiritual sources of the increased emphasis on social discipline in early modern Catholic piety.[2] This misreading of Catholic spirituality in the sixteenth and seventeenth centuries is of general interest, because it has helped to maintain unwelcome residues of the Whig interpretation of history. We can see this, for example, in the persistence of notions of a steady progress, from the Renaissance onward, of rationalization and secularization, leading to the ultimate triumph of civil eudemonism in the eighteenth century.

In contrast, my evidence about religious reform in Paris in the sixteenth and seventeenth centuries throws into relief the importance of flagellation and related penitential behaviors in early modern Catholicism. This makes it possible to grasp the fundamental unity of the sixteenth and seventeenth centuries, as part of the broader evolution of a much older penitential culture, which calls into question any linear progression from the Renaissance to the Enlightenment that is conceived simply as modernization or acculturation.

In addition, my conclusion will also show that the unity of the period of penitential piety is itself broken around 1700 in an unexpected way. In analyzing a debate between two French clerics in the early eighteenth century about the merits of voluntary flagellation, we can see how the rupture occurs, first at a theoretical level, through the medicalization of a formerly religious discourse about flagellation.[3] Taken together, these revisions will reveal new ways of looking at fundamental issues of continuity and discontinuity in Europe from the Renaissance to the Enlightenment. This, in turn, also highlights at least two paradoxes at the heart of modernity. The first concerns the ongoing importance, for the seventeenth century, of spiritual aspects of the ideology of *contemptus mundi* (contempt for the world) and the penitential sense of the self that recasts our understanding of the reform of popular culture (associated with modernity), by stressing its spiritual and ascetic dimensions. The second paradox, which concerns the medicalization of the religious discourse on flagellation in the eighteenth century, points toward future challenges that psychiatric explorations of the self pose for the pursuit of happiness in European culture.[4]

To contextualize these developments within the historiography, it will be useful to take a brief look at the overall evolution of the concept of the Counter-Reformation, focusing on recent permutations. I will focus on two recent groupings: first, the modernization/acculturation/reform of popular-culture literature (more secularly oriented) and, second, the Catholic reform literature (more oriented toward spirituality).

Since its appearance at the end of the eighteenth century, the idea of the Counter-Reformation has undergone an evolution from what was conceived as a purely reactive local reversal of the Reformation to what is now seen as an independent and self-subsistent broad movement of religious and cultural reform by which Catholicism made its adjustments to the modern world.[5] As some of the historiography gradually moved beyond institutional history and began to connect religious reform with broad behavioral changes, a significant number of historians began to focus on how Catholic religious reform changed popular religion and culture. The intellectual forces that combined to produce this change were the vast movement to do "social history from below" and the call for a history of mentalities—both of which emphasize the aggregate over the individual.[6] What might be termed an acculturation school emerged in early modern historiography, dominated by social and cultural, not religious, historians, who saw the Counter-Reformation as an instance of a fundamental historical problematic: the clash between learned culture and popular culture. This historiography has tended to focus very selectively on élite ideas and theories of reform and popular behaviors, mostly reactions.[7] Moreover, since such Counter-Reformation reforms have been perceived as most effective when the church allied with the increasingly absolutist state to implement them, there has often been a strong statist and, hence, secular emphasis in the acculturation literature.[8] It is time to draw some conclusions about where this literature might redirect its energies—and we will see emerge a crucial and neglected field of élite and popular penitential piety that can shape a new view of early modern Catholicism as a penitential culture.

To do this requires the reintegration of questions and perspectives that acculturation historians of the Counter-Reformation have neglected. The most important of these has to do with asking questions about élite behaviors and not just élite ideas, while at the same time looking at popular ascetic practices instead of considering asceticism as a primarily élite phenomenon. When this crucial adjustment is made, the first thing to come into focus is the importance of the practice of flagellation for leading Counter-Reformation reformers, lay as well as religious, whose spirituality and ideas of reform are discussed with little or no reference to their use of flagellation: this is most prominently true for Charles Borromeo, cardinal and archbishop of Milan, one of the primary architects of diocesan reform within the Counter-Reformation church, whose work entailed a strong desire to reform popular religion and culture. In terms of the laity, flagellation has not been seriously studied for the French *dévot* (seventeenth-century ultra-Catholic and mystic), or for the lay Marian congregations—a crucial part of Catholic renewal, led by the Jesuits, which reached beyond the élite.[9] The list of important omissions is a long one.[10] Renewed focus on institutional history, especially from the perspective of small group research, combined with the effort to integrate a true social history of the sacraments (as well as liturgical and paraliturgical behaviors, like processions and religious theater) makes a whole series of practices fall into place. These practices are interrelated parts of the penitential culture of early modern Catholicism. In France, for example, the religious revival of the sixteenth and seventeenth centuries cannot be understood apart from small institutional settings, like the confraternities of penitents and the Marian congregations that practiced flagellation. And, at crucial periods during the wars of religion (1562–1598) mass penitential processions and the popularity of the Forty Hours eucharistic devotion testify to an upsurge of popular asceticism inextricably linked to religious renewal.

Before examining some of the results of my work on penitential and ascetic practices in early Counter-Reformation Paris, I would like to comment briefly on the second, more spiritual, wing of Counter-Reformation scholarship, where primarily religious historians write on Catholic spirituality as part of an independent "Catholic reform." Some of the same problems found with the acculturation school occur here. With the tendency to focus on élites and élitist "spirituality" rather than popular piety, there is the same inclination to divorce ideas from behaviors, coupled here with a neglect of the social and cultural consequences of religious ideas and practice. An older generation of historians of French spirituality, like Antoine Adam and Henri Brémond, have much to teach contemporary cultural historians, but, in general, their insights have not been integrated into the social history of behavior and gesture in order to provide a comprehensive view of penitential culture during the Counter-Reformation.[11]

I would like to turn now to some specific problems and sources in writing the history of penitential behavior during the French Counter-Reformation of the sixteenth and seventeenth centuries. Despite much earlier work on penitential confraternities, historians have only very recently begun to analyze the profound consequences of the general upsurge of eschatological anguish at the heart of the Reformation.[12] For France, the anguish and the millenarian expectations lasted for the better part of a century. The sense of the Christian as quintessentially a penitent, punished for the sins of heresy, peaked during the final phase of a nearly forty-year period of religious and civil war. This final phase is known as the Catholic League (1585–1594) when the forces of militant Catholicism challenged the monarchy for its toleration of heresy. Militant Catholics assassinated King Henry III in 1589; held the city of Paris under their own rule for six years; and eventually forced King Henry IV to abjure his Protestantism in order to gain general recognition as king of France—only to be himself assassinated by the ultra-Catholic monk Jacques Clément in 1610.

The association of sixteenth-century militant Catholicism in France with civil disorder, treason, and regicide has had long-term negative effects on the historiography of the period and has created special difficulties in writing the history of the French Counter-Reformation. The desire to isolate the difficulties of the later sixteenth century from the great lines of French cultural and political development in *le grand siècle*—the great seventeenth century—has caused historians to see a great divide separating the disorder of the sixteenth century from the search for order in the seventeenth century. This has obscured the essential continuities in the penitential culture of the sixteenth and seventeenth centuries. Historians have overlooked the religious creativity of the civil war years and missed the sixteenth-century roots of the golden age of French spirituality in the seventeenth century.[13] While there has been some general acknowledgment of the seventeenth century as an Augustinian century, historians have so far failed to take the next step and treat behaviorally the fundamental unity of the sixteenth and seventeenth centuries as one evolving penitential religious culture, deeply rooted in an Augustinian anthropology focused on original sin and the constant need for expiatory acts.[14] While the eschatological anguish may become attenuated after 1610, and while not all schools of French spirituality in the seventeenth century make the most severe Augustinian judgment about human nature, I believe the spiritual source of "Catholic action" of the seventeenth century—the unprecedented upsurge in charity movements; the intensification of eucharistic piety; the reform of popular religion and culture, and other social projects of the *dévots* in the seventeenth century—lies in the resurgence of penitential piety in the sixteenth century.

The failure of so many historians to see these links, and the related inability to focus at all upon flagellant behavior, is directly related to the larger problem I raised at the outset: how do we conceptualize the period separating the Renaissance from the Enlightenment?[15] Many factors have worked to enforce the view of linear progress: French Republican and sometimes anti-Catholic fascination with the evolution of the state and the tendency to prioritize the political over the religious have especially contributed to difficulties in writing the history of the Counter-Reformation in the sixteenth and seventeenth centuries. Historians of spirituality, religious cultures, and asceticism need to be particularly aware of versions of these same problems in the historiographies of all nations. What seem to be very specialized concerns in religious history are actually tied closely to central conceptual issues in the discipline of history as a whole. The division of history into periods is only one reflection of the problem. As a result of the linear view, we have been left with a focus on the forces of modernity, with little sense of their connections to older gestural systems such as asceticism, both élite and popular. My point is that, in the sixteenth and seventeenth centuries, revitalization of ancient traditions of penitential piety produced, however unintentionally, modernizing effects through the emphasis on disciplined meditation, the productive use of time, processional decorum, and eucharistic and confessional discipline.[16]

I would now like to turn to some specific research issues in writing a history of the penitential culture of the French Counter-Reformation. Flagellation needs to be understood as part of a broad spectrum of penitential behaviors that were renewed, revitalized, and themselves reformed as part of the religious and (in France) political crisis of the Reformation and wars of religion. Flagellation is only one of a whole series of acts related to the *Imitatio Christi,* a focus on the Passion and revitalization of eucharistic piety that served to intensify and order religious experience during the Counter-Reformation. As some of the dangers of lay religious enthusiasm became manifest over the sixteenth century, flagellation was restricted to more carefully regulated or individual sites; and the church hierarchy expressed a strong preference for Holy Sacrament over penitential confraternities.[17] Particularly in northern France, popular religious enthusiasm was carefully redirected to parish-based confraternities like the Holy Sacrament; to more frequent use of the reiterative sacraments of the Eucharist and penance; and to new religious ceremonies such as the practice of the Forty Hours eucharistic devotion (sometimes in France called the *oratoire*). Nonetheless, lay flagellation continued to flourish in sites where it could be carefully regulated by a learned clergy; the Marian congregations founded by the Jesuits are a prime example of this; and it is generally believed that flagellation was practiced by the seventeenth century *dévot*s, although much more research is required here. I want to insist on focusing upon a whole spectrum of penitential behaviors, however; because only in this way can the strong and widespread appeal of penitential piety be grasped. Even when not directly practiced, flagellation was also the model for other forms of penitential piety. For example, in 1576 in Paris, a charity school was founded for poor orphan children known as la maison de la Charité chrestienne. In 1580, the founder, Nicolas Houel, wrote a treatise describing the school. The founding is explicitly described as an expiatory act. Moreover, among the regular activities of the children was nightly recitation of the penitential psalms, while kneeling, including the "Miserere mei" (*Psalm* 51) and "De profundis" (*Psalm* 130). As contemporaries would have immediately understood, this behavior is, in its combination of words and gesture, related to flagellation itself. Aside from the numerous monastic constitutions of the period that prescribe flagellation for the length of time it takes to say the "Miserere mei, Deus" and the "De profundis," the best known of the diocesan reformers, Carlo Borromeo, himself a flagellant, prescribed flagellation for members of his local penitential confraternity in the kneeling position while reciting the two.[18]

As a way of understanding the links between sixteenth- and seventeenth-century penitential practices, much more work can be done on the various associational settings—small groups, both clerical and lay—where penitential piety and charity work were practiced. The founding of the charitable and devotional association of the Oratory of Divine Love (St. Philip Neri, 1497) is now considered one of the hallmarks of "Catholic Reform"; yet the actual penitential practices, including flagellation, are rarely discussed. The statutes of the Oratory reveal the complex of penitential themes and behaviors that reappear in various combinations throughout the sixteenth and seventeenth centuries in both Italy and France. Charity work is combined with a series of penitential devotional practices: meditative prayer at carefully prescribed intervals during the day, meditation on the Passion, group flagellation during the Thursday assemblies, recitation of the "Miserere mei" and the "De profundis," and fasting one day a week are but some of the forms of discipline practiced. The psychological effects and cultural consequences of these behaviors are of broad social significance. There is not only a crucial disciplining of the self and control of affect for Oratory members, but also an accompanying social program to discipline behaviors during church services and in popular pastimes. Similar campaigns against blasphemy, sexual immorality, games, and undiscipline in church are taken as hallmarks of a reform of popular culture by historians of the seventeenth century, without an analysis of the matrix of penitential piety that remains the source for such reforms. In France, for example, clear links have emerged between the Parisian confraternity of Grey Penitents, active during the League; and the charitable and devotional association of the Company of the Holy Sacrament, founded in Paris in 1627. Yet again, historians focus on the charity and social reforms sought by the Company, without analysing the continuity in devotional behaviors of the élite members. Because of the secrecy practiced, evidence must often be indirect, but Molière's *Tartuffe* clearly portrays the Parisian *dévots*, among whom were founders of the Company of the Holy Sacrament, as practicing flagellation.[19]

Another important source for analyzing the small-group settings of penitential devotional practices are wills. In the legal and religious culture of sixteenth and seventeenth centuries, Paris wills are primarily religious documents, part of a strategy of salvation in which testators organize their funeral processions; request various masses and foundations for their souls; and make pious bequests to religious institutions, among them confraternities. For example, in over six hundred Parisian wills from 1590, a key year during the crisis of the Catholic League, Confraternities of the Holy Sacrament received the most number of bequests. An analysis of all the extant wills from 1630 (over three hundred) shows a marked increase in eucharistic piety. When this information is placed alongside of manuals of piety for Holy Sacrament members, in which the disciplining and penitential uses of eucharistic worship are stressed, the real social contours of a range of penitential behaviors begin to take shape.[20]

In conclusion, I would like to turn to the debate on the merits of voluntary flagellation carried out between Abbé Boileau and Abbé Jean-Baptist Thiers in their two treatises on flagellation published in 1701 and 1703, respectively. From these two works it is possible to begin to discern changing attitudes to flagellation across the seventeenth century, culminating in a radical epistemological rupture with Boileau's condemnation of voluntary flagellation as pathological sexual arousal.[21] This critical view, coming from Boileau, who was both a cleric and a doctor at the Sorbonne, as well as a medical doctor, signals, much more than any shift between the sixteenth and seventeenth centuries, the decisive rupture in the ideology of penitential piety.

Of the two authors, Abbé Thiers is the better known to historians now, because he was "rediscovered" in the late 1960s and 1970s as a ardent proponent of the reform of popular culture and religion. In works like his *Traité des jeux . . .* (Paris, 1686) and *Traité des superstitions qui regardent les sacramens* (Paris, 1679), he gave detailed accounts of the popular practices he sought to reform, thus providing crucial ethnographic data for historians of popular culture.[22] His treatise defending voluntary flagellation, however, has been completely neglected in the modern literature.[23] For our purposes, this oversight simply underscores the modernist bias in writing about the reform of popular culture and provides yet another example of how the deep spiritual connections between the reform of popular culture and the traditions of penitential piety have been missed.

Much less is presently known about our innovator Abbé Boileau. At the outset of his work, Boileau signals that he is writing from the perspective of a new genre that he calls simply *la critique,* noting that this is more suitable to the subject matter than *la science sublime de la théologie.* He thus begins on a note of radical epistemological reorientation, which reorders the boundaries of the sacred and the profane and transforms the religious understanding of the body. In this context, it is interesting to note that the edition of Boileau that I consulted contains the handwritten notation that the owner of the book had been one "Hatte, médecin [medical doctor], 1801."

Boileau argues for a new ethic on the religious uses of the body based on the key concepts of *pudeur* (sexual modesty), *bienséance* (propriety), and *superstition.* The superstition condemned by Thiers was that found in folkloric rural Christianity. Boileau, instead, redefines the concept of superstition and applies it this time to learned Christianity itself, whenever and wherever it has praised the flamboyant and highly exteriorized practice of flagellation. Boileau's model is based on the need for *la componction intérieur,* where behavior is guided by the norms of *pudeur* and *bienséance.* Although Boileau does not mention the word *civilité,* his terms *pudeur* and *bienséance* are drawn from an essentially secular discourse on *civilité* that, since the Renaissance, had been profoundly reshaping norms of behavior. It is this discourse on civility whose norms are so much more familiar and "reasonable" to us, that has helped to obscure the ongoing importance of penitential piety as a source of social discipline, especially in the seventeenth century. The great virtue of the Boileau–Thiers debate is to throw into relief the coexistence of two radically different sources of social discipline in the seventeenth century, "civility" and "penitential piety." Only in the eighteenth century did a new medical discourse of speculative and empirical anatomy and psychiatry challenge the pious understanding of flagellation and begin to assert its theoretical hegemony over the body of the believer.

NOTES

1. The material for this paper is drawn from my two books now in progress, both dealing with different aspects of the evolution of a penitential culture: *Piety in Paris, 1545–1630: The Catholic League and the Counter-Reformation* and *The Flagellant: Piety, Sexuality and Changing Ascetic Ideals in the Making of the Modern Individual, 1500–1800.*

   Modernization proponents write about a progressive adaptation of Catholicism to the modern world through institutional modernization; standardization through teaching (seminaries) and catechism; and individualization of piety, through the abandonment of communal cloistered ritual by the Jesuits and reform and suppression of extended kinship and communal aspects of lay piety. Various aspects of these indicators of modernization are discussed by H. Outram Evennett, *The Spirit of the Counter-Reformation*

(Notre Dame and London, 1970) and John Bossy, "The Counter-Reformation and the People of Catholic Europe," *Past and Present* 47 (1970):51–70. For more on the modernization thesis see note 2, below, on Wolfgang Reinhard.

Proponents of acculturation usually have in mind the imposition on the lower classes of élite standards of behavior, decorum, and religious practice. This movement is called by Peter Burke "the reform of popular culture," a phrase launched in his *Popular Culture in Early Modern Europe* (London, 1978). Other proponents of acculturation are Robert Muchembled (numerous works), but see especially *Popular Culture and Elite Culture in France, 1400–1750,* trans. Lydia Cochrane (Baton Rouge and London, 1978). For some important comments of caution in applying the concept of acculturation, see Nathan Wachtel, "L'acculturation," in *Faire de l'histoire: Nouveaux problèms,* eds. J. Le Goff and Pierre Nora (Paris, 1974) and, in the same collection, Dominique Julia, "La religion—Histoire religieuse."

For an attempt to avoid some of the most mechanistic aspects of the "imposition from above" approach in acculturation by focusing on the parish priest as cultural intermediary, see Philip T. Hoffman, *Church and Community in the Diocese of Lyon, 1500–1789* (New Haven, 1984). Newer work on early modern religious change increasingly rejects the rigid distinction between élite and popular culture, in favor of a more interactive model entailing an ongoing "negotiation of meaning" between élites and segments of the people. For this approach, see Keith P. Luria, *Territories of Grace: Cultural Change in the Seventeenth-Century Diocese of Grenoble* (Berkeley, 1991); Miri Rubin, *Corpus Christi: The Eucharist in Late Medieval Culture* (Cambridge, 1991); and Michael Mullett, *Popular Culture and Popular Protest in Late Medieval and Early Modern Europe* (London, 1987), especially "Conclusion: Social Control and Popular Culture in Early Modern Europe," pp. 156–169. For the most recent local study of the Counter-Reformation that argues for the local community's selection among the reforms proposed by élites, see Marc Forster, *The Counter-Reformation in the Villages: Religion and Reform in the Bishopric of Speyer, 1560–1720* (Ithaca and London, 1992).

One of the most important versions of the acculturation/modernization thesis comes from Jean Delumeau, *Catholicism between Luther and Voltaire,* who argues for the Christianization of an essentially still pagan countryside during the Counter-Reformation. He avoids the worst of the "imposition from above" thesis by speaking of the genuine religious hunger among the people; but many historians have challenged his idea of an essentially pagan folk religion in the countryside at the time of the Reformation and Counter-Reformation. For this debate, see John van Engen, "The Christian Middle Ages as an Historiographical Problem," *American Historical Review* 91 (June 1986):519–552. One of the most suggestive works on the relationship between acculturation and religious reform comes from Denis Richet, "Sociocultural Aspects of Religious Conflicts in Paris during the Second Half of the Sixteenth Century," in *Ritual, Religion and the Sacred, Selections from the Annales, Economies, Civilisations,* eds. Robert Forster and Orest Ranum, vol. 7 (Baltimore, 1982).

Finally, one particularly important variant on modernization/acculturation from the Middle Ages to the eighteenth century is the literature on the "civilizing process" first conceptualized by Norbert Elias in his invaluable two-volume study: *The History of Manners,* vol. 1 of *The Civilizing Process,* trans. Edmund Jephcott (New York, 1978) and vol. 2, *Power and Civility* (New York, 1982) (German original, *Über den Prozess der Zivilisation,* 2 vols. [Switzerland, 1939]). The final part of my conclusion critiques the totally secular approach taken by Elias. The most recent adaptation of Elias's work is by Marvin B. Becker, *Civility and Society in Western Europe, 1300–1600* (Bloomington and Indianapolis, 1988). He writes in terms of élites' efforts "to detach themselves from the trammels of an archaic and communal culture formerly considered normative," (p. xi). Aside from his completely secular bias, his work does not allow for the creative reappearance of the so-called archaic, which is what my emphasis on the creative evolution of the penitential culture is intended to emphasize. For Germany, see R. Po-Chia Hsia, *Social Discipline in the Reformation: Central Europe, 1550–1750* (London, 1989). The forthcoming work by Dilwyn Knox, *Disciplina: The Monastic and Clerical Origins of European Civility* (Princeton University Press) should be an important contribution to this debate.

2. This oversight is all the more striking in light of Max Weber's analysis of early modern Calvinism as a form of *innerweltliche Askese* (this-worldly asceticism). Interestingly, calling attention to the relevance of this aspect of Weber's thesis for the interpretation of Catholic piety makes it possible to continue to emphasize important parallels between Catholic and Protestant reform movements, which is one of the important contributions of the modernization school of Counter-Reformation scholarship. See, for example, Wolfgang Reinhard, "Gegenreformation als Modernisierung? Prolegomena zu einer Theorie des konfessionellen Zeitalters," *Archiv für Reformationsgeschichte* 68 (1977), and *idem,* "Reformation, Counter-Reformation, and the Early Modern State, A Reassessment," *The Catholic Historical Review* 75 (1989).
3. For a striking example of the medicalization of a formerly religious discourse on voluntary flagellation, see Abbé Boileau, *Histoire des flagellans . . .* (Amsterdam 1701), pp. 307–308:

> Anatomists observe that the loins extend as far as the three exterior muscles of buttocks, the large, the medium and the small; and that there are three internal or one large muscle which is called the muscle with three heads, or the triceps, because it originates in three places of the pubic bone: the upper, median and lower. This having been said it is absolutely unavoidable that when the loin muscles are whipped with sticks or with a whip the animal spirits are violently forced back toward the pubic bone and that they excite immodest movements because of their proximity to the genital parts: these impressions go to the brain and paint there vivid images of forbidden pleasures which fascinate the mind and with their tempting charms reduce chastity to dissipation [my translation from the French edition].

4. The classic site of this challenge is, of course, Freud's *Civilization and its Discontents* but see also the broad linkages to Foucault, Michel de Certeau, and Lacan. For two key revisions in early modern European history that are generally consonant with the notion of the evolution of a penitential culture I am proposing here, see Jean Delumeau, *Sin and Fear: The Emergence of a Western Guilt Culture 13th–18th Centuries,* trans. Eric Nicholson (New York, 1990) and French original *Le peché et la peur: La culpabilisation en occident XIIIe–XVIIIe siècle* (Paris, 1983); and, to a certain extent, Denis Crouzet, *Les guerriers de Dieu: La violence au temps des troubles de réligion, vers 1525–vers 1610,* 2 vols. (Paris, 1990), although I would not share the emphasis on a fundamental break in 1610.
5. For an historiographical overview of these changes, see especially H. Outram Evennett, *The Spirit of the Counter-Reformation* (Cambridge, 1968) and Wolfgang Reinhard, "Reformation, Counter-Reformation, and the Early Modern State, A Reassessment," *The Catholic Historical Review* 75 (1989). It may finally be time now to speak simply of the Catholic Reformation although much work remains to be done on "periodization" within that broad rubric.
6. An important exception to the emphasis on aggregate data that has the effect of drawing

a much more complex and nuanced picture of the interaction between cultural strata is Carlo Ginzburg, *The Cheese and the Worms: The Cosmos of a Sixteenth-Century Miller* (Penguin, 1982). But note also the recent criticism of Ginzburg by Neil D. Kamil, "War, Natural Philosophy, and the Metaphysical Foundations of Artisanal Thought in an American Mid-Atlantic Colony: La Rochelle, New York City, and the Southwestern Huguenot Paradigm, 1517–1730," Ph.D. dissertation, Johns Hopkins University, 1989. Kamil argues (pp. 189–192), that Ginzburg does not do enough to contextualize and historicize the peasant strata of the miller's beliefs that he studies and falls back instead on a timeless ethos of peasant cosmology.

7. Ginzburg is again an important exception here, for his focus on the intellectual system of his Firulian miller Mennochio. For the most incisive critique of the tendency to privilege élite ideas, while ignoring élite behaviors and concomitantly stressing the behaviors of subordinates rather than their ideas, see Richard Trexler, "Reverence and Profanity in the Study of Early Modern Religion," in *Religion and Society in Early Modern Europe,* ed. Kaspar von Greyerz (1984). Trexler calls for a "behavioral definition of religion" (p. 264), something that a study of actual practices of flagellation will provide.
8. Muchembled, cited in note 1, is the best instance of the "statist" bias.
9. As early as 1965, Marguerite Pecquet suggested linkages between the sixteenth-century Confraternity of the Grey Penitents and the seventeenth-century Company of the Holy Sacrament, without, however, ever exploring a "behavioral" approach to the piety practiced by these groups or mentioning flagellation: see Pecquet, "Des Compagnies de Pénitents à la Compagnie du Saint-Sacrament," *XVIIe Siècle* 69 (1965). No one seems to have followed up on her research. The most recent treatment of the *dévot* Company of the Holy Sacrament does not raise the question of flagellation at all; and Pecquet's article does not even appear in the bibliography. See Alain Tallon, *La Compagnie du Saint-Sacrament (1626–1667): Spiritualité et société* (Paris, 1990). In the most recent study of the Marian Congregations by Louis Châtellier, *The Europe of the Devout: The Catholic Reformation and the Formation of a New Society* (Cambridge, 1989), flagellation is mentioned in passing only three times (pp. 36, 120, and 151). The author once briefly mentions Jacques Gretser, a key Jesuit involved with the Marian Congregations, and cites Gretser's *De sacris et religiosis peregrinationibus* (Ingolstadt, 1606) but completely ignores Gretser's treatise on flagellation, *De spontanea disciplinarum seu flagellorum cruce* (Cologne, 1606).
10. Little work has been done on Philip Neri and all the various Oratory groups, or on Savonarola, both of whom are now taken as a crucial part of "Catholic Reform." See below, note 10, in John Olin. See also Bellintani da Salò, who brought the Capuchins to Paris in 1578, and his connections with King Henry III, who was himself a penitent.
11. In general, this literature also fails to comment at all on the place of flagellation in the Counter-Reformation. The most important recent example of this is the work of John C. Olin, whose books have been crucial in setting out the case for "Catholic Reform" in the sixteenth century. Although his edited collection includes part of a Savonarola sermon on penance and the statutes of the Oratory of Divine Love, which specifically mentions flagellation, Olin's synthetic introductory essays make no mention of the practice; nor does he comment on the central place of penitential piety in general. See John C. Olin, *The Catholic Reformation: Savonarola to Ignatius Loyola, Reform in the Church, 1495–1540* (New York, 1969) and *idem,* introductory essay, "Catholic Reform from Cardinal Ximenes to the Council of Trent," in *Catholic Reform from Cardinal Ximenes to the Council of Trent, 1495–1563* (New York, 1990). For the emerging history of gesture and the body, see, for example, Jean-Claude Schmitt, *La raison des*

gestes dans l'occident médiéval (Paris, 1990); Robert Muchembled, "Pour une histoire des gestes, XVe–XVIIIe siècle," *Revue d'histoire moderne et contemporaine* 34 (Jan.–March 1987); *The Making of the Modern Body: Sexuality and Society in the Nineteenth Century,* eds. Catherine Gallagher and Thomas Laqueur (Berkeley, 1987); *Fragments for a History of the Human Body,* eds. Michel Feher with Ramona Naddaff and Nadia Tazi (New York, 1989); and Caroline Walker Bynum, *Fragmentation and Redemption: Essays on Gender and the Human Body in Medieval Religion* (New York, 1991).

12. For the two works most responsible for the recent focus on fear and eschatological anguish, see Jean Delumeau and Denis Crouzet, cited in note 3. The literature on penitential confraternities is too vast to be cited here; but see for example, Andrew E. Barnes, "De poenitentibus civitatis Massaliae: The Counter-Reformation Religious Change and the Confraternities of Penitents of Marseille, 1499–1792," Ph.D. dissertation, Princeton University, 1983, and several of Barnes's articles: " 'Ces Sortes de Pénitence imaginaires': The Counter-Reformation Assault on Communitas," in Andrew E. Barnes and Peter N. Stearns, eds., *Social History and Issues in Human Consciousness: Some Interdisciplinary Connections* (New York, 1989); Andrew E. Barnes, "Cliques and participation: Organizational Dynamics in the Penitents Bourras," *Journal of interdisciplinary history* 19.1 (1988); *idem,* "Religious anxiety and devotional change in XVII-century French penitential confraternities," *Sixteenth-Century Journal* 19.3 (1988):389–405; *idem,* "The Wars of Religion and the Origins of Reformed Confraternities of Penitents: A Theoretical Approach," *Archives de sciences sociales de religion* 32.64/1 (1987):117–136. See also Marc Venard, "Les confréries de pénitents au XVIe siècle dans la province ecclésiastique d'Avignon," in *Mémoires de l'académie de Vaucluse,* 6e série, vol. 1 (1967); Maurice Aguhlon, *Pénitents et francs-maçons de l'ancienne Provence* (Paris, 1968); Robert A. Schneider, "Mortification on Parade: penitential processions in sixteenth- and seventeenth-century France," *Renaissance and Reformation* n.s. 10.1 (1986); and Daniel E. Bornstein, *The Bianchi of 1399: Popular Devotion in Late Medieval Italy* (Ithaca: Cornell University Press, 1993).

13. Attempts to redress this imbalance can be seen in Philip Benedict, "The Catholic Response to Protestantism: Church Activity in Rouen, 1560–1600," in *Religion and the People,* ed. J. Obelkevich (Chapel Hill: University of North Carolina Press, 1979) and, especially, Denis Richet, cited in note 1.

14. For the view of the seventeenth century as an Augustinian century, see A. D. Wright, *The Counter-Reformation: Catholic Europe and the Non-Christian World* (London: Weidenfeld and Nicolson, 1982), without, however a behavioral perspective. J. P. Gutton, *La société et les pauvres,* also speaks of an Augustinian seventeenth century. He does not, however, take the next step and treat charity works as a primarily expiatory gesture and part of a larger penitential culture.

15. My conclusion will also suggest the need to avoid characterizing the Enlightenment in monolithic terms as well; that is, there are important paradoxes at the heart of the eighteenth-century pursuit of happiness that a history of early psychiatry will help to throw into relief. For more on this argument, see note 1, *The Flagellant: Piety, Sexuality and Changing Ascetic Ideals in the Making of the Modern Individual, 1500–1800.*

16. For a more detailed argument, see my "Eucharistic Piety and Social Discipline," unpublished paper presented at the Sixteenth-Century Studies Conference, Atlanta, October 1992.

17. As study of manuals of piety for Holy Sacrament confraternities, statutes of foundation, and comments in visitation reports show, penitential and Holy Sacrament confraternities are genetically related to each other as two institutional versions of penitential piety with

an eucharistic focus. The church élite clearly preferred Holy Sacrament to penitential confraternities, because they were parish based and more easily controlled by the parish *curé.* In general, Trent sought not only to empower bishops, but also to focus all devotional life in the *cadre* of the parish.

18. See Carlo Borromeo, *Acta ecclesiae mediolanensis* (Milan, 1892), vol. 3, cols. 269–297; and Nicolas Houel, *Advertissement et declaration de l'institution de la maison de la charité-chrestienne*. . . (Paris, 1580), reproduced in Michel Félibien and G.-A. Lobineau, *Histoire de la ville de Paris* (Paris, 1725), 3:727.
19. Louis Châtellier's (see note 9) treatment of this evidence is characteristic of the way so many historians of the Counter-Reformation avoid direct discussion of flagellation. He cites the relevant lines from *Tartuffe,* "serrez ma haire avec ma discipline . . . " ("pull closed my hairshirt with my whip"), but then speaks more generally only of "rigorous mortifications."
20. See my analysis of one of these manuals of eucharistic piety by the Jesuit Amable Bonnefons, *Les devoirs du chrestien qui visite le très-saint sacrament de l'autel* (Paris, 1643), who stresses long periods of eucharistic adoration and meditative prayer, solemn processions, regular confession and communion, abstention from games and pastimes, and penitential humility, in "Eucharistic Piety and Social Discipline," cited in note 16. To give but one more example of the way wills help shed light on pentiential piety: the wills of 1630 give evidence of a confraternity in honor of Saint Charles Borromeo, heretofore unknown for Paris, which suggests the ways Borromean penitential piety was disseminated to the laity. See the December 17, 1630, will of Damoiselle Marguerite LeFevre, Minutier Central étude II, 134 (Archives Nationales, Paris) where a large bequest to this confraternity is combined with numerous charitable bequests, some to newly founded parish associations. Will data as well as penitentials, manuals of piety, and sermons may also help link Jansenist asceticism of the mid seventeenth- to sixteenth- and early seventeenth-century penitential traditions. Also, there has been little attempt to connect the Jansenist convulsionnaires of the eighteenth century with the overall evolution of ascetic and penitential practices in the sixteenth and seventeenth centuries, although there is much suggestive evidence.
21. See the long quotation from Boileau cited in note 3, above.
22. Thiers was used to advantage, for example, in two early and crucial works on early modern popular culture: N. Z. Davis, *Society and Culture in Early Modern France* (Stanford, 1965) and Yves-Marie Bercé, *Fête et révolte: Des mentalités populaires du XVIe au XVIIIe siècle* (Paris, 1976).
23. This is despite the fact that both Thiers and Boileau are cited in the bibliographies for the articles on "flagellants" in the *Dictionnaire de spiritualité* (article written by Paul Bailly) and in the *Dictionnaire du théologie catholique,* eds. A. Vacant and E. Mangenot, vol. 6 (Paris, 1920).

42

Practices and Meanings of Asceticism in Contemporary Religious Life and Culture

A Panel Discussion

Richard Valantasis, Moderator

Opening Statement and General Introductions
—*Richard Valantasis*

The unusual combination in this conference of practitioners of asceticism and historians of asceticism, as well as representatives of asceticism across religious and cultural lines, was at once a stroke of genius and a very frightening possibility, because these are groups of people who normally do not speak to one another. Those for whom ascetical texts are still determinative and important do not meet often with those for whom they are important primarily for their historical context, nor with those who find the texts' importance to lie in their contemporary application.

The following discussion fulfills two primary goals of the conference: to integrate the various domains of ascetical conversation, and to include in that conversation both scholars and practitioners. In preparation for this session, I asked the panelists (1) to observe the conference and its papers; to comment on the current direction in the study and practice of asceticism and to suggest directions for future investigation and practice; (2) to identify areas that have not been addressed in the conference (especially those relating to ascetical practices in our own various cultures), in order to explore other implications for this conference in contemporary society; and (3) to converse about the larger issues of ascetical theory and practice in our own cultures which have emerged from the papers and from our conversations.

I also suggested to the panelists that they consider some of the following questions:

1. What are some domains of contemporary activity and practice (religious or secular) that exhibit an ascetical orientation? What makes them ascetical? What are the theories and practices that support the activities?

2. What are the theories and practices that support contemporary understandings of identity and personality? How is a person trained to become a person?

3. What kinds of asceticism are necessary for the various religious expressions in our culture? In a Western Christian environment, for example, what ascetical preparation is necessary for participation in African-American, Eastern Orthodox, Protestant, Fundamentalist, liberal, conservative, Catholic, or any other category of religious association? How are these ascetical activities supported and presented to others?

4. What are the secular asceticisms in American culture (the legal system, the social welfare institutions, the penal practices, educational methods)? How are people trained to perform in those systems?

It is clear that there are in modern industrial and postmodern cultures a number of different ascetical practices; but asceticism as a subject of conversation within contemporary living has not emerged. Modern Western culture, it seems, assimilates people into various functioning systems without addressing directly the question of formation, integration, or development. This tells us that the modern period has not, as yet, assimilated asceticism as a subject to the extent that contemporary people discuss ascetical theories or practices.

Our panel, then, will address the contemporary ascetical scene. The order is straightforward: our panelists will each briefly present a position; they will have an opportunity to respond to the other panelists at the end of the presentations; and then other participants in the conference may query and respond to the discussion. The panelists are Elaine Pagels (Religion Department, Princeton University), Peter Van Ness (Union Theological Seminary), Paul Julian (a solitary monastic, New York City), Ehsan Yarshater (Center for Iranian Studies, Columbia University) and Gillian Lindt (Religion Department, Columbia University); and I am Richard Valantasis (Department of Theological Studies, Saint Louis University). We begin with Peter Van Ness.

Asceticism in Philosophical and Cultural-Critical Perspective
—*Peter H. Van Ness*

In my remarks I will briefly describe the meanings of asceticism as they occur within a radical tradition of Western philosophy. In so doing, I will broach a central concern of this conference: whether the ascetic dimension is a key for understanding religious life. Next, I will assess the cogency of the meaning ascribed to asceticism by a key figure in this radical tradition, Friedrich Nietzsche. I do so intending to differentiate between the elements of insight and hyperbole in his treatment of asceticism. Finally, informed by this radical tradition, but by no means confined to it, I will suggest a new role and rationale for the ascetic impulse in contemporary religious life. My response to the challenge of identifying the contemporary meaning of the ascetic impulse, emerging as it will from conversation with recent philosophers, will be as much philosophical advocacy as historical reportage.

It was probably the German philosopher Arthur Schopenhauer who first made asceticism a topic of modern philosophical discussion. In drawing implications of his pessimistic philosophy articulated in *The World as Will and Representation,* Schopenhauer embraced asceticism as the essence of the more sublime religions of Christianity and Buddhism and also as the practical answer to the riddle of life. Badly put, Schopenhauer thought that life was irretrievably a miserable affair and, frankly, not worth the effort. He then defined asceticism as "the denial of the will to live" and recommended it above suicide because killing oneself suffers from the inconsistency of being a willful act intended to put to conclusion efforts of human willing.[1] Recall that, for Schopenhauer, the human body was only the phenomenal manifestation of the will.

Friedrich Nietzsche called Schopenhauer his teacher, and he appreciated his teacher's trenchant condemnation of life in nineteenth-century Europe. Furthermore, Nietzsche, for the most part, accepted Schopenhauer's understanding of asceticism as the essence of Christianity and as an expression of life denial. Although perhaps for the wrong reasons, philosophers have regarded asceticism as central to the nature of religion. In the third essay of *On the Genealogy of Morals,* entitled "What is the Meaning of Ascetic Ideals?," Nietzsche identified asceticism with "a will to nothingness," noting that subscribers to the ascetic ideal would rather will nothingness than not will at all.[2] This may seem a small difference to scholars assembled here, most of whom would probably find these philosophical accounts woefully short of historical truth. For what Nietzsche saw, but Schopenhauer did not, and what historians of religion have only recently appreciated fully, is that asceticism—its ideals and practices—gains its proper meaning only when placed in a context of social conflict.

"The ascetic ideal springs from the protective instinct of degenerating life."[3] This is from Friedrich Nietzsche. The conflict that most concerned Nietzsche existed between powerful life and degenerating life, between the extraordinary individual and the mediocre masses, between the *Übermensch* and the ascetic priest. Nietzsche's pithy motto: "Dionysus versus the crucified" draws the battle line very clearly.[4] Ascetic ideals and practices are motivated, claimed Nietzsche, by feelings of *ressentiment,* and are developed as a strategy by which the weak seek to overcome the strong. Specifically, they seek to infect them with life-denying values that compromise bold assertions of power and at the same time ensure continued existence for even weak human beings, albeit in a minimal way. In this context, "Blessed are the meek" (*Mt.* 5.5) is a phrase that has sinister connotations when interpreted by Nietzsche; it smacks of decadence.

Now whatever one might think about Nietzsche's critique of asceticism and morality, one must grant that his work in this area has proved influential in helping to portray the ascetic practitioner as unhealthy and in some ways sinister. Mary Daly, together with other radical feminist philosophers who find little to admire in Nietzsche's view on women and other social issues, still voices some partial support for Nietzsche's vehement denunciation of Christianity and its ascetic traditions in her book *Pure Lust.*[5] Nietzsche, however, was not entirely negative in his remarks about asceticism; he says that philosophers, for instance, have had to adopt its forms in the past as a protective measure and as a precondition for "the highest and boldest spirituality."[6] Nietzsche also regarded spiritual self-mastery, as a form of sublimation, as crucial for any figure who wanted to give style to his or her life and who wanted to create something genuinely new. Michel Foucault, about whom we have heard a good deal already, was strongly influenced by Nietzsche in his basic categories and was also influenced by this more positive aspect of Nietzsche's views on asceticism. His portrayal of *askēsis,* in *The Uses of Pleasure,* the second volume of his *History of Sexuality,* is a profoundly Nietzschian retrieval: Foucault emphasizes the classical Greek meaning of asceticism as exercises that forge a distinctive "aesthetics of existence."[7] And this retrieval of *askēsis* is very close to the Nietzschian understanding of spiritual self-mastery.

In this tradition of thinking about asceticism there are, I think, several things to be commended and a number of things to be rejected outright. To identify the meaning of asceticism as indebted to a context of social conflict is important, as is the realization that ascetic practices can be productive of a distinctive aesthetic sensibility. The program of this conference has acknowledged the importance of this aspect of the question. Certainly an appreciation of these points makes asceticism more readily applicable to contemporary culture. What is flawed in this approach, and especially in Nietzsche's critique of asceticism, is the isolation of ascetic practices from their celebrative practices and counterparts. Historically, there has been a complementarity between ascetic practices and celebrative practices that can lay equal claim to being spiritually disciplined: silence has its counterpart in song, sitting in dance, and solitary meditation in communal worship. Nietzsche attributes ascetic practices to Christianity but denies its celebrative counterparts; indeed, the latter he reserves for pagan Greek religion. His account of asceticism is clearly tendentious, and makes asceticism, even in its more positive aspects, terribly individualistic (because Nietzsche sees no form of excellence that is genuinely communal), and it unnecessarily divorces ascetic dispositions from feelings of love. By so denying the dispositions of love with the possibility of creating things new and vital, he sees in *ressentiment* alone, and not in notions of love, the sources of asceticism in human personality.

More contemporary students of Nietzsche, like Foucault and other postmodernists, have provided a helpful corrective to Nietzsche's characteristic equation of power and excellence. For Nietzsche, powerful individuals alone are capable of creating excellence; while for Foucault, powerful institutions are among the certain enemies of genuine human excellence. This suggests a recharacterization of the context of social conflict in which asceticism should be interpreted. Asceticism, I believe, should now be understood in the context of the oppressive—and life-denying—forces exemplified by powerful, contemporary corporations, governments, churches, and professions. Increasingly, such forces advance their interests by encouraging and manipulating habitual, if not always addictive, forms of popular consumption. Sell a consumer a sufficient number of cigarettes to instill the smoking habit, and you make that person a loyal customer who buys the product again and again in an unthinking way. This has become a model of advertising success for hamburgers and video games, as well as for cigarettes and alcohol. It threatens to become a model of commercial relations. The sardonic epitome of American consumerism that William Burroughs sketched in the late fifties is today even more apt and more horrifying:

> Junk is the ideal product . . . the ultimate merchandise. No sales talk necessary . . . The junk merchant does not sell his product to the consumer, he sells the consumer to the product. He does not improve and simplify his merchandise. He degrades and simplifies his client.[8]

Consider further examples. Governments find that voters balk at increases in their taxes, and so they offer them public lotteries and casino gambling as an alternative way to support government programs. Here too, once sold on the product, the future sales come easily, almost automatically. Finally, churches are not exempt from this phenomenon. Since some church officials find that it is hard to persuade people to give time to the church and its activity because of the competition from habitual diversions like television and radio, they simply accommodate church life to the television viewing habits of the audience. Televangelism is born.

In this social context of a consumerist ethos manipulated by powerful institutions for purposes of personal habituation and cultural domination, the deliberate strategies of withdrawal that have characterized traditional asceticism can take on new forms and new meanings. The particular withdrawal that we are talking about now is from a frenetic consumerism and from conformist models of socializing. Included in the social conformity that corporations, governments, professions, and even churches foster are attitudes and practices that are racist and sexist, homophobic and xenophobic. To desist from these attitudes and practices might be understood as a type of ascetic withdrawal. Ascetic habitual regimens can undermine the pernicious habits that avid consumers surely develop and signal a path of personal and communal health. Such practices constitute a path toward personal health and communal well-being. As Kallistos Ware has recommended, such ascetic withdrawal need not be complete and permanent, rather it can be done for the purpose of a more productive reengagement with society after a period of ascetic retreat.

Unlike the models of asceticism that Kallistos Ware has emphasized, however, the variety of which I am speaking may include both traditionally religious and currently secular regimens. Holistic health practices and twelve-step programs, for instance, can be seen as ascetic in the sense of being deliberate strategies for withdrawing from unhealthy patterns of work, consumption, and recreation. In a similar manner, ecological activism of various sorts and naturalistic recreation like mountain climbing or canoeing are similarly ascetic in the sense that they are withdrawing from customary patterns of behavior on behalf of greater human vitality and greater human health. These examples illustrate a vision of ascetic values and practices that is adoptable by secular and religious persons alike. They are not, however, immune to abuse. Professional experts can be purveyors of commercial dependency too; for instance, diet doctors often do less to change people's eating habits than to establish the habit of dieting.

This conception of asceticism (though in my own writings I have preferred the phrase "spiritual discipline" or "spiritually disciplined practices" because such terms lack exclusively private connotations) offers a means by which such diverse persons and groups can resist the deadening and cheapening influences of the forces that dominate the marketplace of products and ideas in the contemporary developed Western world and, increasingly, in the world at large.[9] Indeed, the specific location of these institutional forces in nominally democratic societies and intensively consumerist economies suggests a rationale for a new form of asceticism. In nominally democratic societies like the United States, powerful social forces cannot attain social control of people through fiat or even gross intimidation. The political ethos resists that. Hence they promote habitual regimens of consumption and socialization as a means of securing social control through acceptable means. This means that regimens of spiritual discipline or ascetic behavior that seek to counter such controlling habits take on a form that is distinctly political and can be understood as a form of political resistance. And I think herein lies a rationale for certain types of ascetic behavior suited to our context, and certainly to a context that is oriented toward a progressive political agenda.

Edith Wyschogrod has advocated a postmodern asceticism as a sort of pedagogy of pain, in which persons engage in acts of self-denial as a way of making a space in their own experiences for compassionately identifying with the pain of others. Clearly, developing such a compassionate sensibility is important. My impression is that much pain is already part of our experience and is the price we pay for manic habits of consumption and fearful strategies of socialization. I recommend that we attend more to that existing pain than engender new suffering and that we seek to alleviate such pain in ourselves and others by withdrawing from the patterns of consumption and socialization that dominate contemporary society.

Asceticism understood in this fashion has a striking conclusion, and perhaps here I will end with a note that sounds as much as if it came from a dean as from a philosopher: at the very beginning of the conference Vincent Wimbush commented that Union Theological Seminary in New York City might be an improbable place for a conference on asceticism. Perhaps, if one is talking about certain traditional forms of ascetic practice, that might be true. Traditional expressions of asceticism may be rather foreign to university-related and interdenominational seminaries such as Union. Yet if one understands asceticism as withdrawal from dominant patterns of consumption and socialization, from certain sorts of behavior that are characterized by sexism and racism and other social toxins, then I think Union and kindred seminaries are not at all an inappropriate place for a conference on asceticism and contemporary culture. This place seeks to be a community, as many other contemporary religious communities do, that provides a withdrawal from these social forces and an opportunity for learning, reflection and pursuit of a spiritual life in a way that is genuinely helpful and faithful. It is that mission that many of us as Christian scholars have at Union.

Asceticism in Sociological Perspective —*Gillian Lindt*

I understand our task after four full days of deliberations as not to have yet another set of academic papers, but to provoke, in a few minutes, a set of ideas that might stimulate further discussion. So I want to underscore here that I do not have a separate paper, but want rather to suggest how one might address questions concerning the ascetic impulse in contemporary American religious life and culture from the perspective of someone who is really not a traditional historian, let alone a philosopher or a theologian. I come to the study of American culture from a socio-historical and more sociologically informed perspective.

Let me begin with certain shared data. It seems that when we talk about ascetic images in contemporary American religious life (and much of this I think would apply also to the broader contemporary Western capitalist type of society), we are reminded that there are still in our midst instances of images of asceticism that are tied to specific religious communities. They tend, however, for better or worse to be associated with those labeled (at least in the popular language) "religious conservatives." It is interesting to observe that the popular understanding of such asceticism tends to focus on items that are seen primarily in negative terms: proscriptions against smoking, movies, sexuality; on views on reproduction and rock music; among others. But beyond these primarily proscriptive religious images of asceticism, we have, increasingly, images of asceticism in popular culture that are not tied to religious constituencies at all. Although, they draw on some of the early etymology of these terms, they speak now about ascetic ideas and practices relating to renunciation in food habits, a kind of obsession one might say (at least among some groups) with diets and other contemporary forms of fasting, and emphasize strenuous physical exercise and the ascetic impulse that is reflected in the jogger's "higher self"—as one poster put it: "On a clear day, I too can run forever."

I would like to suggest that in dealing with asceticism as an impulse in contemporary religious culture, we should not altogether ignore these nonreligious manifestations, even though to many of you they may seem trivial or marginal at the outset. Let me suggest, then, some defining characteristics of these modern, contemporary religious and secular images of asceticism as they are reflected in American culture today. First of all, I have already noted that these images seem to focus disproportionately on values that are expressed in primarily negative terms (stress on renunciation, on control, on discipline), but they often do not evoke a counterpart emphasizing the pleasures that might be associated with such practices. Secondly, and very powerfully in terms of the dominant culture, images of the ascetic are frequently tied to images of the "other," seeking in effect to define for the dominant culture that which it is not. Thirdly, they seem to reflect outsiders' fascination with ideas and behavior that are perceived as not merely strange but in some sense alien, exotic, or largely inconsistent with popular understandings of the human psyche. Certainly, such topics as the flagellation practices in the Middle Ages, and even into the seventeenth century, do not evoke images with which modern Americans are typically comfortable.

It is interesting to me that much of the contemporary secular focus on ascetic practices tends to reduce that ascetic experience to an end in itself, rather than, as in many earlier religious formulations, seeing it as always and necessarily linked to a means to an end. This means that what we find here is a preoccupation with abstention from alcohol, with physical exercise, or with dieting—practices that are perceived as goods in and of themselves, and are only intermittently linked to a schema that ties them to a different or superior sense of self.

It seems to me that the pluralization and secularization of that ascetic impulse in American culture has reduced its significance as a unifying frame within which to define and interpret ascetic experiences. At least as reflected in popular culture, we have a veritable tower of Babel in which there is no overarching symbol, or set of meanings, that give unity to whatever discourse is subsumed here.

There is an obvious sociological point, which has been made by the historians present: the increased social differentiation of modern societies, accentuating as it does the importance of race, ethnicity, gender, and age, as well as religion, as constituents of personal identity, also casts doubt upon the adequacy of any model that asserts the moral good of asceticism as a paradigm for all human beings. A specific ascetic mode of human living may, as Giles Milhaven's "Tale of Two Pleasures" documents, be defined by some as truly good in itself, but it would not, by any means, at least in this modern consciousness, be seen as desirable for everyone.

I note also that any emphasis on the ascetic experience in modern times in our contemporary culture tends to view such experience as intermittent, as involving a temporary rather than a permanent change, at least in regard to practices, if not in regard to ideas. Peter Van Ness has already emphasized the notion of withdrawal, but I see this withdrawal primarily as reflecting a temporary escape from the pressures of the modern world. This escape is reflected in the ways in which people will temporarily withdraw to involve themselves in experiences such as workshops, beauty spas, seminars on the ascetic dimensions of certain kinds of art—phenomena that must be seen, then, not as a permanent withdrawal but as a means of escape, of replenishment, with a subsequent return to the mainstream of society.

In summary, it seems to me that there are two major defining characteristics of this ascetic dimension or image, as reflected in contemporary American culture. At one level, we have unquestionably witnessed a considerable increase in the range and proliferation of ascetic images, values, and ideas. The older, more religiously grounded and better-established forms continue, but they are constantly faced with and juxtaposed to deviant alternatives. In part, this trend is clearly rooted in the greater opportunities for economic expansion, opportunities also for a greater number of individuals to pursue careers that give them the luxury of becoming specialists on certain ascetic ideas and practices, whether these be careers in theology, in literature, or in art—all of these enlarge certain constituencies. At the same time we see an enlargement of a population with the requisite excess of income and leisure to devote itself to ascetic pursuits. Having said this, of course, I am immediately privileging the notion of asceticism that ties into an élite culture; therefore, I want to point out immediately that, even given the extent to which we deal with ascetic images, values, and practices in popular culture, we are still assuming certain changes regarding the disposition of time and other resources; changes are important in terms of making this asceticism a more central concern.

My second, broader, generalization is this: while, on the one hand, there is a wide range and proliferation of ascetic images and ideas, as well as practices, at the same time this diversity is accompanied by the absence, a rather marked absence, of strong institutionalization of newer ideologies and practices in what my colleague Robert Wuthnow (cf. his *Communities of Discourse: Ideology and Social Structure in the Reformation, the Enlightenment, and European Socialism* [Harvard University Press, 1989]) has called "concrete communities of discourse." What, in fact we have is a free-floating market of ascetic ideas and practices emanating from the creative minds of a whole series of inventors and purveyors. One could say that to the older, religiously grounded communities of discourse have been added those of medicine, of psychiatry, of politics, and of experts on power, as well as those of the arts, both élite and popular. This phenomenon suggests an institutional weakness in that there is a lack of shared symbols and language that make it possible for individuals to participate in these enterprises.

And that leads me to my final two conclusions about the consequences of such an understanding of contemporary ascetic images and practices. First, at one level I see an increased privatization of such ascetic experiences and a loss of their historical influence in defining a communal and shared cultural identity. This identity is a collective symbolic affirmation of the values and ends of such ascetic ideas and experiences. Even where we have such shared symbolic meanings, the constituency of those communities has typically been small and has itself had its legitimation questioned by the very polarity of such groups.

Secondly, I wonder whether, in relation to this kind of diversity and proliferation of ascetic models in the larger secular community, one does not also have to be aware of a possible trivialization of that ascetic dimension, owing to its intermittent character in the life experiences of individuals. I am struck by the fact that, while the importance may be stressed, at least in the marketplace, of new strategies and ideals of asceticism as they relate to a person's well-being and health, they are never defined in terms of actions that seriously challenge dominant values of the society or its status quo. Indeed, the very notion of a kind of temporary withdrawal, which is followed by a return to the fray, confirms that.

So, in conclusion, I would argue that, judging by contemporary American and, to some extent, Western European experiences, ascetic images and practices have indeed survived as one of many features of modern culture, both religious and secular. But I think they play a decidedly limited role in defining the central values of the dominant society of modern Western capitalism. In short, what we see is a set of muted murmurs rather than any kind of central impulse that is really redefining the fundamental values of these types of Western societies.

Asceticism in Zoroastrian Perspective —*Ehsan Yarshater*

What I am going to say is rather more descriptive than analytical because it has to do with a religion that is not usually as fully studied as other higher religions—Zoroastrianism. In passing, I will refer also to a couple of other religions, the common feature of which is that they all sprang from Persia, although their practice was not confined to that country.

The religion of Zoroastrianism was the official religion of the Persian empire for at least twelve or thirteen centuries. It was defeated, one might say, by Islam, when Persia was conquered in the seventh century, and it became overshadowed by the spread of Islam. Nevertheless, it survived both in Persia and also in India: today Zoroastrians are found in India, Persia, the United States, Canada, England, and a number of other countries.

One of the features of the Zoroastrian religion that sets it apart from the religions in the Judeo-Christian tradition, is that its practitioners not only do not believe in asceticism as a meritorious practice, but in fact they forbid it. They make a point of the enjoyment of life, while recognizing that this rejection of asceticism differentiates Zoroastrianism from other religions. In order to give you a taste of what Zoroastrians today believe, I will read to you an excerpt from the September 1992 "Newsletter of Zoroastrian Studies" in Bombay. This Zoroastrian study group is very conservative when it comes to Zoroastrian creed and practice.

> Zoroastrianism offers a cheerful optimism to its followers, with the spiritual world being an extension of the physical one in which we live. The task of a Zoroastrian is to qualitatively improve the physical world through the purposeful generation of wealth. Zoroastrianism sees no virtue in fasting, monasticism, abstinence, celibacy or any other ascetic practices as so avowedly advocated by all the other major religions of the world, whose followers believe such practices as being necessary and relevant to achieve spiritual salvation in the hereafter. However, none of these practices are recommended in the Zoroastrian faith. Zoroastrian children are made to think in their classes as to why a God would want to punish his creations through pain and suffering in this world as versus Zoroastrian belief in Ahura Mazda (that is the supreme God of the Zoroastrian) being man's best friend and therefore devoid of any wrath or anger.

Of course, it is not true that Zoroastrianism in the course of its long history has not known asceticism. It is true, however, that in its oldest texts, a set of hymns composed by Zoroaster himself most probably around 1900 BCE, there are no references to any practices that allude to asceticism or similar attitudes. In a country like Persia, which has been subject to all types of influences from other societies, it is almost certain that some Zoroastrian sects advocated asceticism. There is internal and external evidence for that. The external evidence is a Zoroastrian sect called Mazdakism, which flourished in Persia in the fifth and sixth century CE. It was populist in its approach, egalitarian in its thinking, and communistic (one might say) in its view of possessions and wealth. Its members advocated sharing the wealth of the wealthy and giving to the poor and equalizing the enjoyment of married life. Their enemies, in fact, advanced the notion that they advocated a community of women—a polemical view difficult to believe. Now these Mazdakites, in some of their texts that have reached us indirectly, showed certain tastes for limiting enjoyment of life in this world by practices that approximate asceticism. One polemical text refers to Mazdak, a leader of this religion who was in fact a revolutionary, saying that he forbids his followers to eat and drink, whereas he himself eats and drinks freely. That shows the type of attitude Mazdakism may have had.

Another external piece of evidence for variant ascetical activity in Persian religion is found in Manichaean practices. Manichaeism, as you all know, was a religion which arose in Persian territories in the third century CE. In that religion there is a very strong streak of asceticism. In fact, Manichaean believers are divided into two distinct groups: the élite and the rest of the believers, who were called hearers. The élite were forbidden to kill animals, to break branches of plants, to cut flowers, to make food, or to make clothing for themselves. And they survived in this way: they were always served by some of the hearers, who were allowed to engage in those practices and who were, nevertheless, also enjoined to despise the world and prepare for the next.

The theological hallmark of Zoroastrian religion is a dualist explanation of the universe. Unlike monotheistic religionists, Zoroastrians believe in two independent forces—good and evil, or light and darkness. It is characteristic of the Zoroastrian religion that the corporeal world, the material world, is not created by the evil forces but by the Ahura Mazda, the good god, the supreme God, as in fact a kind of defense against evil. Therefore, unlike some other religions that later became current in Persia and in the Middle East, they do not shun the good life. In fact, founding settlements, planting trees, sowing seeds, and making hearths are not only meritorious but are religious duties for the Zoroastrians. So it was quite a change when Persia turned Muslim and had to abandon this dualistic approach and believe in Allah as the one and unique God.

Asceticism in Contemporary Religious Life —*Paul Julian*

I am very grateful for the opportunity to participate in this conference. I have no academic perspective on the ascetic life, because my understanding of asceticism is mostly experiential. So it is from my own experience that I must speak about it. But I would like to thank those who have presented papers here, because they have given me a new way of examining my experiences and of understanding the history of this tradition in which I live.

In attempting to address the meaning of asceticism in contemporary religious life and culture, I must first give a brief account of the origins of my own religious life as an ascetic. For me, the ascetic life began with my own experience of several initial revelations. These revelations were not profound in themselves, but as I began to understand them in the larger context of my life and of the world in which I live, I realized their significance. I began to understand the contradiction between my own revelations and much of my previous thinking and understanding of myself and the world. I could not avoid or defer these insights; they were no longer isolated incidents. The revelations themselves had to become the new focus of my life.

The new focus revolved about trying to understand how such seemingly small revelations could have such a profound effect on my life. This led to a process of discovery of a larger meaning in my life. As I searched for external understanding of these experiences and what they meant to me and to the world around me, I was unable to find people or institutions that could address my exploration. I could not find people or institutions who understood my experience. The more I would question and search, the less others would confirm my experience. I slowly began to realize that the world, as I had come to understand it, was not truly understanding who I was. And in that realization, I also began to understand that who I was, as I had come to understand myself, was not the new self I had discovered in these experiences.

Could this be the call of the ascetics? Is this call to begin to discover oneself beyond the concepts and trappings given to them by the world? Is this the source of the ascetics' flight from the world in order to struggle with it? Could all the forms of the ascetic life to which each individual is called be unique to that individual's experiences? Could each of us, in our own and unique experiences, have a vocation to an ascetic life?

As we have struggled for a systematic definition of asceticism during this conference, we may have been continually hindered by an attempt to simplify the complex or to complicate something very simple—there is no one definition. As the ascetic begins to discover personally, through the freeing of self-identity from culture, society, nation, religion, race, and subcultures based on politics, gender, sexuality, and ideology, the ascetic is able to reenter all of these through a continuing letting go of any identification with them. This continued call to die to self and to be reborn to new self is the experience of the ascetic, as I have known it—a process of freeing oneself for one's ultimate use by God.

Asceticism and Scholarly Formation —*Elaine H. Pagels*

After that, one should hardly speak, but I am happy to be here and want to thank the conference leadership for bringing into this Protestant theological seminary this most unlikely topic and this very diverse group of people representing and embodying such a wide range of traditions. Because my work is in the early history of Christianity and not in contemporary history, I want simply to state that the way I was educated and the way many of you were educated involves a deep, passionate Protestant bias against recognizing asceticism as a fundamental part of Christian tradition.

I was actually surprised in graduate school—when I suggested at one point that the apostle Paul thought celibacy was definitely preferable to marriage—to be told by my German Lutheran professor that this was a complete misunderstanding of what Paul meant. And later, after writing *The Gnostic Gospels,* I found a scathing review by my former teacher, Professor Henry Chadwick, who said that the Gnostics were not rejected from the early Christian movement because their movement involved a contradiction of its institutionalization, but rather because the Gnostics rejected the goodness of the body and the world. I thought that his was a remarkable statement, because this was the man with whom I studied patristics. And perhaps the most prominent study we did together was on the Egyptian ascetic Origen, who was radically ascetic in his practice in life. The most liberal of those Alexandrians was Clement of Alexandria, who thought (contrary to Origen and others) that marriage was given by God and appropriate, but who certainly thought that celibacy was preferable, and ascetic marriage preferable to nonascetic marriage.

So this conference has made me aware of the difficulty, if one has been brought up in that kind of Protestant Christian environment, of actually uncovering what happens in the Christian gospels and what occurred in the early sources of this Christian tradition. This has made me very grateful to the many people in this room who have been doing that work of uncovering in the early Christian tradition. And, finally, I am grateful to people like Brother Julian because as I heard him I remembered the introduction that Thomas Merton wrote to the *Wisdom of the Desert Fathers* in which he says that the ascetic life offers the means of divesting oneself of the false, socially constructed, self to discover one's own true self in Christ.

Response to Panel Presentations —*Richard Valantasis*

In the few minutes remaining, let me perform one of my duties as moderator and identify some of the areas that may not have been addressed in our deliberations, both historical and cross-cultural. The first area concerns diversity. Although we have dealt at various times in this conference with gender, race has not been addressed directly. Many of the ascetics whom we have studied and discussed in this conference do not look like the people who have studied them and presented papers about them in this conference. We have been remiss, it seems to me, in not exploring the asceticism of people from Africa, Asia, the Middle East, South America, and indigenous America and the many other peoples who are both ascetic and not European or white American.

The second area is on a more modern front. Ascetical literature, especially Christian and Byzantine monastic literature, stresses the centrality and importance of grieving and mourning. In a time of a pandemic of HIV infection and AIDS, it seems to me that much of the language, concepts, teachings, and traditions emerging from a trans-historical and cross-cultural study of asceticism as it relates to living and dying, grieving and mourning, burying and remembering, would directly apply to this context of our contemporary society. How do we form people into those capable of living well and dying well, of living fully and grieving fully? Many of our traditions and historical subjects have in one way or another addressed these issues, and yet they remain locked in historical and cultural isolation.

Finally, I would simply identify another area (and this particularly applies to the United States): the development of a kind of depth of communication. Most of the ascetical systems that we have discussed have shown an intentionality about language and communion one with another, which we, in the age of advertising and short-segmented video newscasts, have lost. Communication, it seems, has less to do with depth than with appeal. There seems to be a need to train people through asceticism in the arts of communion, not just the arts of modern communication. Ascetical discipline is desperately needed in this arena.

General Discussion

Valantasis: Brother Paul Julian, as a practicing ascetic, you have listened primarily to scholars (some of whom may be scholar-practitioners) talking about asceticism. How do we sound to you? What comments do you have regarding the quality and depth of our conversation? Your response is particularly important because, as Elaine Pagels has pointed out, we scholars are trained to speak and see in a particular way—a way that frequently ignores asceticism.

Julian: The time and commitment involved in being an academic, and particularly a scholar of asceticism, proves to be as much of an ascetic discipline and lifestyle, I think, as any monastic life because it requires such an increment of dedication and stability. I have learned much, much more than I initially thought I would about the tradition in which I live, and there has been for me no conflict between my ascetic experience and what I have heard. In fact, the conference has affirmed much of my experience.

Valantasis: Gillian Lindt, you spoke in your conclusions about the privatization of experience and the lack of a collective symbolic language. How would you envision that privatization and lack of collective language to be addressed in terms of either the practice of religion or the study of religion? I raise this question because one of the difficulties in the conference that has emerged is the energetic resistance between traditional historical interpretation of ascetical materials, on the one hand, and more theoretical and postmodern understandings of asceticism involving an increment of suspicion about practice, on the other hand. This problem, it seems to me, is endemic to the entire academic endeavor in the twentieth century and is essential to the evaluation of asceticism in modern times. How do you see the common forging of that language operating, or what can we do?

Lindt: It is a good question, but I really do not think I have any clear answers. I would first of all say that, for all of the multivalence of symbols and images of asceticism in contemporary societies, at least in the West, it is still clear that the dominant models derive from memories and sometimes faulty applications of ascetic experiences that are rooted in religious traditions. In that sense, I would argue that a study of religions in the plural would be very important, rather than seeing asceticism as rooted in a single tradition, or even a single type of ascetic experience. Equally important, however, is the danger of the over-intellectualization of that language; therefore, the emphasis on practice and practitioners would also be important. Having said that, I am also struck by the fact that, whether we like it or not, language that once was essentially religious has now appropriated dimensions of the ascetic and taken them out of religious context. I am not sure that its heritage can necessarily be reclaimed. This response presents only one model; and we need to be prepared, at least in the immediate, foreseeable future, to have forms of communication that may be technologically facilitated, but are inhibited by the fact that we do not all speak the same language.

I want to come back to the earlier point about the importance of making the distinction between the art of communion and the art of communication. I would absolutely agree with that, but at that level of communion we resort again to smaller and more finite constituencies that entail not only to vocabularies but also to values and understandings that are not readily translatable—especially when we recognize that many of these experiences cannot be adequately represented simply in words or in written texts.

Van Ness: I would like to make an observation about the point that many forms of the ascetic impulse in contemporary culture are very individualistic. I think that, in large measure, that is true. A particular situation is exemplified here in New York City by churches, synagogues, and other religious institutions, where there is a worshiping community on the first floor that is praying and engaging in activities traditionally religious, and in some sense ascetical; there is also a twelve-step program, such as Alcoholics Anonymous, meeting in the basement; and the same institution is used for Boy Scout or Girl Scout troop meetings. To a certain extent, there are dimensions in all these activities that represent an attempt to withdraw from certain patterns of behavior characteristic of the culture of the world outside, for the sake of a greater vitality for some form or vision of human flourishing. But I do not think we have the vocabulary or the inclination to see them as any way related. The fact that all these disparate activities occur in a church indicates to me that there is some instinct or some social impulse that sees such activities as related. We do not, however, have a way of providing a social vision that connects them in a meaningful way. One way to approach that connectedness is, at least in the context of religious persons and religious leaders, to keep in tension a process of formation and education that relates to historical tradition, the elements of one's religious background, and one's religious community. This equilibrium maintains a respectful dialogue and engagement with these other sources of ascetic impulse or spiritual life in our time. It is only by living in the midst of those different, and in some ways competing and incompatible, dimensions of the ascetic impulse that there may possibly emerge a language that has some capacity for representing a broader social vision. I think a conference like this brings people together in exploration of these sorts of tensions regarding historical manifestations of asceticism in contrast to contemporary ones. It is by living in this conversation that we even have the possibility of forging some language capable of a vision that allows for human potential to act and live in more healthful ways, informed by these impulses.

Valantasis: You spoke earlier about Nietzsche's theories of domination in discourse. The languages of modern academic study are quite diverse, as is readily obvious from the conference participants: on one extreme, there is a postmodern language, and on the other a strictly historical and positivist language. The modern asceticism of the academic study of religion has yet, however to discover a means of addressing the current resistance between these extremes of academic languages, and all of the gradations between them. So there are academics who speak one language or the other, with a clear preference for one (some being conversant in more than one), but for whom the dominant mode and the will to dominate through a particular language is microcosmically representing the problem in contemporary Western culture. And we still have not found a way to be multilingual. Even though most of the people in this room are in fact extremely multilingual, we have not yet taught ourselves how to speak the languages simultaneously.

Question (from the audience): I address this question to Professors Lindt and Van Ness. Professor Lindt spoke about the partial or muted quality of much of modern ascetic practice, and Professor Van Ness has identified some rather unusual practices (canoeing and other middle-class adventuring) as ascetical. One way to define asceticism is through its ability to go beyond the point of no return, as we find, for example, in the practice of celibacy, or of going out into the desert and never returning from it. Are we not defining asceticism too broadly, so that, by including such a wide diversity of activities, we have lost the heart of it?

Lindt: I would like to take up your issue of stressing one dimension of asceticism, that of reaching the point of no return. If that were all there was to understanding the consequences of asceticism for human societies, I do not think it would have survived this long. At the same time, I grant you that there is a discrepancy between your emphasis on a kind of absolute form of withdrawal and what I understand Van Ness to be asserting; namely, the opportunity for developing and articulating a new social vision out of such experiences. I tend to side more with you in understanding (at least in the modern period) this emphasis on preoccupation with self as primary, and I have some doubts as to how we take that impetus and translate it into a broader social vision. So now my question to Van Ness is, how do we articulate such a vision out of these kinds of collective experiences of asceticism?

Van Ness: My remarks attempted to identify some elements of contemporary ascetic impulse for which I could find a rationale. I identified the removal or withdrawal with its rationale of being promoted for reengagement, and not simply reengagement of the world in the same way as before one withdrew. If the virtue of withdrawing from customary patterns of consumption or social behavior is to develop a recognition that those present patterns are harmful to others, then indeed the withdrawal can be something that is transformative and can lead to a reengagement that is very strongly motivated by ethical concern or social vision that will allow for a more healthy, peaceful, and just life together. I am not saying that these forms of secular asceticism are in fact to be understood in that way, but they represent modes of experience that can yield very valuable meanings and can enrich my own understanding of asceticism received from, for example, the Christian religious tradition. Mine is not a sociological statement so much as it is a philosophical formulation, an ascetic impulse understood in such a way that it carries great meaning and value in our contemporary context.

Question: I responded well to Paul Julian's explanation of the call to what we may understand as religious asceticism. According to the titles of most of the papers,

I gather that has been our primary point of conversation, and not the *askēsis* that is an athletic preparation for some *ergon.* As I understand religious asceticism, however, it is a response to a call to strip oneself of everything, however minor or major, that would inhibit complete response to whatever one perceives as the absolute and then to live out that response for everybody as a radical witness. Self-denial geared for that purpose is usually what we call asceticism, whether it is an asceticism simply to perfect the body or to celebrate the self or to express anger with one's society. I suppose it could be called asceticism, but not religious asceticism.

Julian: I do not think that an initial ascetical awakening needs, or my initial revelation needed, necessarily to be a religious one. I think that it is possible for a person to withdraw to the wilderness for a weekend and have such an experience that would then cause him or her to pursue an ascetical discipline in his life. Eventually that awakening may lead to a religious setting, but the experience itself can be any human experience.

Valantasis: I am not sure that I would be able to identify a religious ascetical activity in the twentieth century that was indigenous to the twentieth-century environment (with the possible exception of listening to postmodernist lectures in which the language is inverted to the point that it requires *askēsis* merely to comprehend!). This raises the question about what modern ascetical practices imitate, and whether that imitation is of a historical (or some other) pattern. Why are there not contemporary idioms of asceticism that are religious and not secular? Clearly asceticism is present in a wide diversity of contemporary cultures.

Question: This question is mostly addressed to Professor Van Ness. After the presentations, there seemed to develop a consensus that a primary distinction between Islamic asceticism and Christian asceticism turned on the notion of success and failure in the ascetic life. Generally, Sūfī ascetic practices were in contrast to very indulgent ascetic practices. Even in the Hindu tradition, there is a period when one practices rigorous asceticism, followed by one of living an indulgent, pleasurable life quite freely. I think that the general assumption at that time was that Christian ascetics do not have this periodic excess. They go to the desert never to be heard from again. I have been thinking more and more about the bipolarity that may be more generally present in asceticism than I habitually thought. It is striking to contrast deprivation and self-indulgence. Although Christian ascetics do not follow the pattern that Peter Awn presented regarding the Sūfī ascetics, perhaps Christian ascetics, as you pointed out in discussing what Nietzsche failed to observe in Christianity, through their feast days, popular piety, joy, art, and communal worship, may manifest the same bipolar asceticism so evident in Islamic asceticism.

Van Ness: I would be surprised at an understanding of asceticism in a Christian context that did not have counterparts to embodied practices of withdrawal or deprivation in communal aspects of celebration. In my own Calvinist tradition, which has not traditionally affirmed ascetic practices, Christian activities are placed in a context of a liturgical year centered around the affirmation of the Easter faith. I very much see a bipolarity when I talk about the ascetical dimensions that are held in counterpoint with celebratory dimensions. Yes, I would affirm that as a dimension of my understanding of Christian tradition.

I was trying to affirm a theme of withdrawal and reengagement. The idea of asceticism as going beyond the point of no return makes me uncomfortable. Many modern practices that I characterized as having an ascetic impulse involve people attempting to withdraw precisely in order to heal themselves, so that they may again return to their lives. Without the ascetic impulse's being connected to a larger theological or philosophical vision, asceticism does become something where you take a break and heal yourself and then return and engage in the same unhealthy and perhaps unjust social life. That is not a compelling vision for me. I would see the process as threefold: withdrawal, transformation, reengagement. The purpose is some sort of transformation designed to fulfill a goal of ethical good or religious salvation.

Question: As a monk in a modern monastery, I would like to address two matters. The first point that I would like to make is in support of Paul Julian. I believe that for modern people, and particularly for young people, the initial impulse toward the absolute is something that may not come from specifically religious or sacred things. It may come from literature or from poetry or from art or from any other medium.

I would like also to respond to a point made about the modalities of asceticism in the modern age. Karl Rahner has argued that there is nothing in tradition that is absolutely old: everything in tradition has an old dimension and a new dimension. It seems to me that modern people must creatively translate traditional models of asceticism into terms that are comprehensible to the modern world. This translation can only occur by speaking the language of the modern world, through reading modern philosophers and modern literature and art, and through attempting to express the truths of the ascetic tradition in this modern language, to make it intelligible for the world. Otherwise, it is liable to be a monastic and ecclesiastic ghetto. It is very important that a conference like this has brought together people who are Freudians, people who are social philosophers, people who are monks, people who are literary critics, all of whom should perhaps not look for conclusions but simply rejoice in the fact that contacts have been made.

Question: Ascetic impulses and self-denial are against our more natural instincts, and yet they have been strong enough to engage so many people both in history and in modern times. These impulses, in order to be useful and appropriate to our educational work, must be validated by some larger vision of the world, by a theology. The Gnostics, for instance, described the soul trapped in matter and the ascetic practices necessary to release it and thereby to achieve salvation. These ascetical practices had meaning. In our contemporary life today, that cohesive vision of the world seems lacking; and it is therefore problematic for modern people to make sense of ascetic impulses or ascetic tendencies.

Question: As a religious woman, I know that one of the most basic principles of ascetic practice is consistency. One has a practice and one does it consistently every day. It is more valuable to be consistent than to go on a retreat and to practice asceticism for a short period of time and not continue with it. There is some consensus among practitioners on this point.

Another elementary ascetical point is to be rooted in a tradition and in a context and not to move eclectically from one tradition to another. This lack of rootedness makes a jumble of world religions and encourages short-term religious practice that discourages making progress with the discipline.

Valantasis: On those words I would like to thank the participants and the panel for the discussion.

NOTES

1. Arthur Schopenhauer, *The World as Will and Representation*, 2 vols., trans. E.F.J. Payne (New York: Dover Publications, 1969), 1:383.
2. Friedrich Nietzsche, *On the Genealogy of Morals* (bound with *Ecce Homo*), trans. and ed. Walter Kaufmann (New York: Vintage Books, Random House, 1969), p. 163.
3. Ibid., p. 120.
4. Friedrich Nietzsche, *Ecce Homo* (bound with *On the Genealogy of Morals*), trans. and ed. Walter Kaufmann (New York: Vintage Books, 1969), p. 335.
5. Mary Daly, *Pure Lust: Elemental Feminist Philosophy* (Boston: Beacon Press, 1984), pp. 100–101.
6. Nietzsche, *Genealogy of Morals*, p. 108.
7. Michel Foucault, *The Uses of Pleasure*, trans. Robert Hurley, vol. 2, *The History of Sexuality* (New York: Vintage Books, 1986), pp. 12, 89–93.
8. William Burroughs, *Naked Lunch* (Secaucus, N.J.: Castle Books, 1959), p. vii.
9. For a reconception of the notion of spiritual discipline in this direction, see my *Spirituality, Diversion, and Decadence: The Contemporary Predicament* (Albany: State University of New York Press, 1992).

SELECTED BIBLIOGRAPHY

The following list is designed to help the reader continue the explorations that were begun in the essays included in this volume. The entries below have been chosen because they (1) are generally (but not absolutely) recently published (from mid-1980s); (2) contain important and often comprehensive area-specific bibliographic listings themselves; and (3) either model or in some other way contribute to the interdisciplinary, interreligious, and intercultural study of asceticism.

General Works

L'androgyne. Cahiers de l'hermetisme. Paris, 1986.

Barnhart, Bruno. "Monastic Wisdom and the World of Today." *Monastic Studies* 16 (1985): 111–138.

Black, H. *Culture and Restraint.* Chicago, 1901.

Braun, Katharin. *Asketischer Erōs und die Rekonstruktion der Natur zur Maschine.* Studien zur Soziologie und Politikwissenschaft. Oldenburg, 1987.

Chang, Chung-yuan. *Tao: A New Way of Thinking: A Translation of the "Tao Te Ching," with an Introduction and Commentaries.* New York, 1975.

Colliander, Tito. *Way of the Ascetics* (1960), translated by Katherine Ferre, introduction by Kenneth Leech. San Francisco, 1982.

Collier, Thomas. *A Doctrinal Discourse of Self-Denial.* London, 1691.

Demant, Vigo Auguste. *The Idea of a Natural Order, with an Essay on Modern Asceticism.* Philadelphia, 1966.

Devine, K. R. *A Manual of Ascetical Theology or the Supernatural Life of the Soul on Earth and in Heaven.* New York, 1902.

Dumont, Louis. *Essays on Individualism: Modern Ideology in Anthropological Perspective.* Chicago and London, 1986.

Eisenstadt, S. N., ed. *The Origins and Diversity of Axial Age Civilizations.* Albany, 1986.

Fleming, Sandford. "Ascetism and Aestheticism: Their Conflict and Reconciliation in the History of Christian Thought." Ph.D. diss., Graduate Theological Union, 1924.

Foucault, Michel. *The History of Sexuality,* vol. 1, *An Introduction,* translated by Robert Hurley. New York, 1980.

Gendolla, Peter. *Phantasien der Askese: Uber die Entstehung innerer Bilder am Beispiel der "Versuchung des heiligen Antonius."* Heidelberg, 1991.

Ghurayyib, Jurj. *Abu al-'Atahiyah fi zuhdiyatih.* Beirut, 1985.

Guibert, Joseph de. *The Theology of the Spiritual Life.* New York, 1953.

Gusmer, Charles W. *Asceticism for Contemporary People.* Sound recording. Kansas City, NCR Cassettes, 1977.

Hardman, Oscar. *The Ideals of Asceticism.* New York, 1924.

Harpham, Geoffrey Galt. *The Ascetic Imperative in Culture and Criticism.* Chicago, 1987.

Horton, P. *The Elements of the Spiritual Life: A Study in Ascetical Life.* New York, 1954.

Kaelber, Walter O. "Asceticism." In *The Encyclopedia of Religion,* edited by Mircea Eliade et al. New York, 1987.

Laing, R. D. *The Divided Self.* New York, 1965.

Laqueur, Thomas W. *Making Sex: Body and Gender from the Greeks to Freud.* Cambridge, Mass., 1990.

Marson, Eric Lawson. *The Ascetic Artist: Prefigurations in Thomas Mann's Der Tod in Venedig.* Australian and New Zealand Studies in German Language and Literature. Bern, Frankfurt, and Las Vegas, 1979.

Mazlish, Bruce. *The Revolutionary Ascetic: Evolution of a Political Type.* New York, 1976.

Miles, Margaret R. *Practicing Christianity: Critical Perspectives for an Embodied Spirituality.* New York, 1988.

Morris, Marcia A. *Saints and Revolutionaries: The Ascetic Hero in Russian Literature.* Albany, 1993.

Nisbet, Robert. *The Social Philosophers: Community and Conflict in Western Thought.* New York, 1973.

Parente, Pascal P. *The Ascetical Life.* Rev. ed. Saint Louis, 1955.

Rogers, William Elford. *Interpreting Interpretation: Textual Hermeneutics as an Ascetic Discipline.* University Park, Pa., 1994.

Rouselle, Aline. *Porneia: On Desire and the Body in Antiquity,* translated by Felicia Pheasant. Oxford, 1988.

Sabine, George H. *A History of Political Thought.* 3d ed. London, 1963.

Stout, Jeffrey. *The Flight from Authority: Religion, Morality, and the Quest for Autonomy.* Notre Dame, Ind., 1981.

Tarnas, Richard. *The Passion of the Western Mind: Understanding the Ideas That Have Shaped Our World View.* New York, 1991.

Taylor, Charles. *Sources of the Self: The Making of Modern Identity.* Cambridge, Mass., 1989.

Van Ness, Peter H. *Spirit, Diversion, and Decadence: The Contemporary Predicament.* Albany, 1992.

Wimbush, Vincent L. "*Contemptus Mundi*: The Social Power of an Ancient Rhetorics and Worldview." *Union Seminary Quarterly Review* 47. 1–2 (1993): 1–13.

Wu, Kuang-ming. *Chuang-tzu: World Philosopher at Play.* New York, 1982.

Wyschogrod, Edith. *Saints and Postmodernism: Revisioning Moral Philosophy.* Chicago, 1990.

South and Southeast Asia

Primary Sources

Carter, John Ross, and Mahinda Palihawadana. *The Dhammapada: A New English Translation with the Pali Text.* New York and Oxford, 1987.

Chapple, Christopher. *The Yoga Sutras of Patanjali.* Delhi, 1990.

Embree, Ainslee T., ed. *Sources of Indian Tradition.* 2d ed. New York, 1988.

Hirakawa, Akira. *Monastic Discipline of Buddhist Nuns* (Mahasamghika-Bhuksuni-Vinaya). Patna, 1982.

Horner, I. B. *The Book of Discipline* (Vinayapiṭika). 6 vols. London, 1938–1966.

Hume, R. E. *The Thirteen Principle Upanishads.* 2d ed. London, 1971.

Iyer, Raghavan. *The Essential Writing of Mahatma Gandhi.* Oxford, 1990.

Johnston, E. H. *Aśvaghoṣa's Buddhacarita, or, Acts of the Buddha.* Reprint. Delhi, 1992.

Koller, John M., and Patricia Koller. *A Sourcebook in Asian Philosophy.* New York, 1991.

Law, Bimala Churn. *Some Jaina Canonical Sutras.* Bombay, 1949.

Miller, Barbara Stoller. *The Bhagavad Gita.* New York, 1986.

Murcott, Susan. *The First Buddhist Women: Translations and Commentary on the Therigatha.* Berkeley, 1991.

Nanamoli, Bhikkhu. *The Path of Purification* (Visuddhimagga). 5th ed. Kandy, 1991.

O'Flaherty, Wendy Doniger. *The Rig Veda: An Anthology.* New York, 1981.

Olivelle, Patrick. *Vāsudevāśrama Yatidharmaprakāśa: A Treatise on World Renunciation.* Vienna and Delhi, 1976–1977.

Olivelle, Patrick. "Pañcamāśramavidhi: Rite for Becoming a Naked Ascetic." *Weiner Zeitschrift fur die Kunde Sudasiens* 24 (1980): 129–145.

Olivelle, Patrick. *Saṃnyāsapaddhati of Rudra Deva.* Madras, 1986.

Olivelle, Patrick. *Saṃnyāsa Upaniṣads: Hindu Scriptures on Asceticism and Renunciation.* New York and Oxford, 1992.

Prebish, Charles S. *Buddhist Monastic Discipline: The Sanskrit Prātimokṣa Sutras of the Mahāsaṃghikas and Mūlasarvāstivādins.* University Park, Pa., 1975.

Radhakrishnan, Sarvapalli. *The Principal Upaniṣads* New York, 1953.

Rani, Sharada. *Wratisasana.* New Delhi, 1961.

Sastri, Alladi Mahadeva. *Yoga Upaniṣads.* Madras, 1920.

Takakusa, J. Makoto Nagai, and Kogen Midzuno. *Buddhaghosa's Commentary on the Vinaya Pitika* (Samantapāsādikā). 7 vols. London, 1938–1947.

Secondary Sources

Abhishiktananda, Swami. *The Further Shore: Sannyasa and the Upanishads.* Delhi, 1975.

Alter, Joseph S. "The Sannyasi and the Indian Wrestler: The Anatomy of a Relationship." *American Ethnologist* 19 (1992): 317–336.

Barthakuria, Apurba Chandra. *The Kāpālikas.* Calcutta, 1984.

Bhagat, M. G. *Ancient Indian Asceticism.* New Delhi, 1976.

Bouillier, Veronique. *Naître renoncant: Une caste de Sannyasi villageois au Nepal.* Nanterre, France, 1979.

Bradford, Nicholas J. "The Indian Renouncer: Structure and Transformation in a Lingayat Community." In *Indian Religion,* edited by Richard Burghart and A. Cantlie, pp. 79–104. London, 1985.

Briggs, G. W. *Gorakhnāth and the Kānphatā Yogīs.* Delhi, 1973.

Bronkhorst, Johannes. *Two Sources of Indian Asceticism.* Bern, 1993.

Burghart, Richard. "Secret Vocabularies of the 'Great Renouncers' of the Rāmānandī Sect." In *Early Hindi Devotional Literature,* edited by W. Callewaert, pp. 17–26. New Delhi, 1980.

Burghart, Richard. "Wandering Ascetics of the Rāmānandī Sect." *History of Religions* 22 (1983): 361–380.

Caillat, Colette. "Le sadhaka śaiva à la lumiere de la discipline jaina." In *Studien zum Jainismus und Buddhismus,* edited by K. Bruhn and A. Wezler. Wiesbaden, 1981.

Carrithers, Michael. *The Buddha.* Oxford and New York, 1983.

Carrithers, Michael. *The Forest Monks of Sri Lanka: An Anthropological and Historical Study*. Delhi, 1983.

Carrithers, Michael. "Naked Ascetics in Southern Digambar Jainism." *Man* 24 (1989): 219–235.

Chakraborti, Haripada. *Asceticism in Ancient India in Brahmanical, Buddhist, Jaina, and Ajivika Societies from the Earliest Times to the Period of Sankaracharya*. Calcutta, 1973.

Chatterjee, Asoke. *Upaniṣadyoga and Patañjalayoga*. Calcutta, 1989.

Denton, Lynn Teskey. "Varieties of Hindu Female Asceticism." In *Role and Rituals for Hindu Women*, edited by J. Leslie, pp. 211–231. Rutherford, N.J., 1991.

Deo, Shantatam Chalchandra. *History of Jaina Monasticism*. Poona, 1956.

Dhavamony, Mariasusai. "The Sadhu Ideal as Realized by Hindu Saints." *Studia Missionalia* 35 (1986): 199–224.

Dumont, Louis. "World Renunciation in Indian Religions." *Contributions to Indian Sociology* 4 (1960): 33–62.

Dutt, Sukumar. *Early Buddhist Monachism* (1941–1945). New Delhi, 1984.

Dutt, Sukumar. *Buddhist Monks and Monasteries in India*. London, 1962.

Eliade, Mircea. *Yoga: Immortality and Freedom*. Princeton, 1958.

Eliade, Mircea. *Patañjali and Yoga* (1965), translated by C. L. Markmanm. New York, 1975.

Feuerstein, Georg. *Yoga: The Technology of Ecstasy*. Los Angeles, 1989.

Friedrich-Silber, Ilana. *Virtuosity, Charism, and Social Order: A Comparative Sociological Study of Monasticism in Theravada Buddhism and Medieval Catholicism*. New York, 1994.

Ghurye, G. S. *Indian Sadhus*. Bombay, 1964.

Giri, Sadananda. *Society and Sannyasi: A History of the Dasanami Sannyasis*. Varanasi, 1976.

Gosh, Indu Mala. *Ahiṃsā: Buddhist and Gandhian*. Delhi, 1988.

Gross, Rita M. "The Householder and the World-Renunciant: Two Modes of Sexual Expression in Buddhism." *Journal of Ecumenical Studies* 22 (Winter 1985): 81–96.

Gross, Robert Lewis. *A Study of Sadhus of North India*. Berkeley, 1979.

Hartsuiker, Dolf. *Sadhus: India's Mystic Holy Men*. Rochester, Vt., 1993.

Hawley, John S. "Asceticism Denounced and Embraced: Rhetoric and Reality in North Indian Bhakti." In *Monastic Life in the Christian and Buddhist Traditions*, edited by Austin B. Creel and Vasudha Narayanan, pp. 459–495. Lewiston, N.Y., 1990.

Heesterman, J. C. "Brahmin, Ritual and Renouncer." *Weiner Zeitschrift fur die Kunde Südasiens* 8 (1964): 1–31.

Henry, Patrick G., and Donald K. Swearer. *For the Sake of the World: The Spirit of Christian and Buddhist Monasticism*. Minneapolis, 1989.

Hiltebeitel, Alf., ed. *Criminal Gods and Demon Devotees: Essays on the Guradians of Popular Hinduism*. Albany, 1989.

Hinuber, Oskar von. *Sprachentwicklung and Kulturgeschichte: Ein Beitrag zur materiallen Kultur des buddhistischen Klosterlebens*. Mainz, 1992.

Holch, H. F. "Manus asketische Ideale: Ein Beitrig zu den indischen Erscheinungsformen der Askese." *Kairos* 10.3 (1968): 175–185.

Holt, John. *Discipline: The Canonical Buddhism of the Vinayapitika*. Delhi, 1981.

Ingalls, Daniel Henry Holmes. "Cynics and Pasupatas: The Seeking of Dishonor." *Harvard Theological Review* 55 (1962): 281–298.

Iyengar, B.K.S. *Light on Yoga* (1966). Rev. ed. New York, 1977.

Iyengar, B.K.S. *Light on Prāṇāyama.* New York, 1981.

Jaina, Padmanabh S. *The Jaina Path to Purification* (1979). Delhi, 1990.

Jash, Pranabananda. *History of Parivrājaka.* Delhi, 1991.

Johnson, Willard. "Death and the Symbolism of Renunciant Mysticism: Reflections on Some Indo-Aryan and Asian Rituals of Death and Dying." In *Asian Religions,* edited by Frank Reynolds, pp. 12–21. Tallahassee, 1973.

Kabilsingh, Chatsumarn. *A Comparative Study of Bhikkhuni Patimokkha.* Varanasi, 1984.

Kaelber, Walter O. *Tapta Mārga: Asceticism and Initiation in Ancient India.* Albany, 1989.

Kloppenborg, Ria. *The Paccekabuddha: A Buddhist Ascetic.* Leiden, 1974.

Kohli. S. *Yoga of the Sikhs.* Delhi, 1991.

Kotturan, George. *Ahiṃsā: Gautama to Gandhi.* New Delhi, 1973.

Leslie, Julia. "A Problem of Choice: The Heroic Sati or the Widow-Ascetic." In *Panels of the VIIth World Sanskrit Conference,* edited by Johannes Bronkhorst, pp. 46–61. New York, 1991.

Lorenzen, David N. *The Kāpālikas and Kālāmukhas: Two Lost Śaivite Sects.* Los Angeles, 1972.

MacQueen, Graeme. "The Conflict between External and Internal Mastery: An Analysis of the Khantivadi Jataka." *History of Religions* 20 (February 1981): 242–252.

Madhusudan Reddy, V. *Yoga of the Rishis.* Hyderabad, 1985.

Marcaurelle, Roger. "Śankara's Hermeneutics on Renunciation in the Gita." *Journal of Studies in the Bhagavadgita* 5–7 (1985–1987): 98–126.

Michael, R. Blake. "Laicization of the Ascetic Ideal: The Case of the Virasáivas." In *Monastic Life in the Christian and Hindu Traditions,* edited by Austin B. Creel and Vasudha Narayanan, pp. 404–441. Lewistown, N.Y., 1990.

Miller, David M., and Dorothy C. Wertz. *Hindu Monastic Culture.* Montreal, 1976.

Mishra, Yugal Kishore. *Asceticism in Ancient India.* Vaishali, 1987.

Misra, G.S.P. *The Age of Vinaya.* New Delhi, 1972.

Narayanan, Vasudha. " 'Renunciation' in Saffron and White Robes." In *Monastic Life in the Christian and Hindu Traditions,* edited by Austin B. Creel and Vasudha Narayanan, pp. 161–190. Lewiston, N.Y., 1990.

O'Flaherty, Wendy Doniger. "The Symbolism of Ashes in the Mythology of Shiva." *Purana* 8.1 (1971): 26–35.

O'Flaherty, Wendy Doniger. *Asceticism and Sexuality in The Mythology of Śiva.* London, 1973.

Ojha, Catherine. "Feminine Asceticism in Hinduism: Its Tradition and Present Condition." *Man in India* 61 (1981): 254–285.

Olivelle, Patrick. "A Definition of World Renunciation." *Weiner Zeitschrift für die Kunde Südasiens* 19 (1975): 27–35.

Olivelle, Patrick. "Ritual Suicide and the Rite of Renunciation." *Weiner Zeitschrift fur die Kunde Sudasiens* 22 (1978): 19–44.

Olivelle, Patrick. "Contributions to the Semantic History of Saṃnyāsa." *Journal of the American Oriental Society* 101 (1981): 265–74.

Olivelle, Patrick. "Renouncer and Renunciation in the Dharmaśāstras." In *Studies in Dharmaśāstra,* edited by R. Lariviere. Calcutta, 1984.

Olivelle, Patrick. *Renunciation in Hinduism: A Medieval Debate.* 2 vols. Vienna, 1986–1987.

Olivelle, Patrick. "Village vs. Wilderness: Ascetic Ideals and the Hindu World." In *Monasticism in Christian and Hindu Traditions,* edited by A. Creel and Vasudha Narayanan, pp. 125–160. Lewiston, N.Y., 1990.

Olivelle, Patrick. "From Fast to Feast: Food and the Indian Ascetic." In *Panels of the VIIth World Sanskrit Conference,* edited by Johannes Bronkhorst, pp. 17–36. New York, 1991.

Olivelle, Patrick. *The Āśrama System: The History and Hermeneutics of a Religious Institution.* New York and Oxford, 1993.

Omam, John Campbell. *The Mystics, Saints, and Ascetics of India* (1903). New Delhi, 1984.

Pachow, Wang. "A Comparative Study of the Prātimokṣa." *Sino-Indian Studies* 6 (1951), pts. 1–2.

Pande, Govind Chandra. *Śramana Tradition: Its History and Contribution to Indian Society.* Ahmedabad, 1978.

Parry, Jonathan. "Sacrificial Death and the Necrophagous Ascetic." In *Death and the Regeneration of Life,* edited by M. Bloch and J. Parry, pp. 74–110. Cambridge, 1982.

Parry, Jonathan. "The Aghorī Ascetics of Benares." In *Indian Religion,* edited by Richard Burghart and A. Cantlie. London, 1985.

Pemaratana, W. "Philosophy of Asceticism with Special Reference to Ancient India." In *Buddhism and Jainism,* edited by H. Das, S. Das, and C. Pal, pp. 258–267. Cuttuck, 1976.

Pocock, D. F. *Mind, Body, and Wealth: A Study of Belief and Practice in an Indian Village.* Oxford, 1973.

Reddy, Mahasudan. *Yoga of the Rishis.* Hyderabad, 1985.

Rueping, Klaus. "Zur Askese in indischen Religionen." *Zeitschrift für Missionswissenschaft und Religionswissenschaft* 61.2 (1977): 81–98.

Sawyer, Dana W. "The Monastic Structure of Banarsi Dandi Sādhus." In *Living Banaras,* edited by B. R. Hertzel and C. A. Humes, pp. 159–180. Albany, 1993.

Sen Sharma, Debabrata. *The Philosophy of Sādhana.* Karnal, India, 1983.

Settar, S. *Inviting Death: Historical Experiments on Sepulchral Hill.* Dharwad, India, 1986.

Sharma, H. D. *Contributions to the History of Brahmanical Asceticism.* Poona, 1939.

Shastry, Ajay Mitra. "The Bhiksu-Sūtra of Parasarya." *Journal of the Asiatic Society* 14.2–4 (1972): 52–59.

Silber, Ilana. "Dissent through Holiness: The Case of the Radical Renouncer in Theravada Buddhist Countries." In *Orthodoxy, Heterodoxy and Dissent,* edited by S. N. Eisenstadt, R. Kahane, et al., pp. 85–110. Berlin and New York, 1984.

Sinha, S., and B. Saraswati. *Ascetics of Kāshī.* Varanasi, 1978.

Skurzak, L. *Etudes sur l'origine de l'ascétisme Indien.* Wrocław, 1948.

Smith, Mary C. "Warrior Ethics in the Bhagavadgita." *Journal of Studies in the Bhagavadgita* 4 (1984): 32–46.

Sprockhoff, J. F. *Saṃnyāsa: Quellenstudien zur Askese im Hinduismus—I, Untersuchungen uber die Saṃnyāsa-Upaniṣads.* Wiesbaden, 1976.

Sprockhoff, J. F. "Āranyaka and Vānaprastha in der vedischen Literatur." *Weiner Zeitschrift fur die Kunde Sudasiens* 25 (1981): 19–90; 28 (1984): 5–43.

Sprockhoff, J. F. "Kathaśruti and Mānavaśrautasūtra. Eine Nachlese zur Resignation." *Studien zur Indologie and Iranistik* 13–14 (1987): 235–257.

Sprockhoff, J. F. "Versuch einer deutschen Ubersetzung der Kaṭhaśruti und der Kaṭharudra-Upaniṣad." *Asiatische Studien* 43 (1989): 137–163.

Sprockhoff, J. F. "Vom Umgag mit den Saṃnyāsa-Upaniṣads." *Weiner Zeitschrift für die Kunde Sudasiens* 34 (1990): 5–48.

Tambiah, Stanley J. *World Conqueror and World Renouncer.* Cambridge, 1977.

Tambiah, Stanley J. "The Buddhist Arahant: Classical Paradigm and Modern Thai Manifestations." In *Saints and Virtue,* edited by John Stratton Hawley, pp. 11–126. Berkeley, 1987.

Tatia, Nathmal. "The Interaction of Jainism and Buddhism and Its Impact on the History of Buddhist Monasticism." In *Studies in the History of Buddhism*, edited by A. Narain, pp. 321–338. Delhi, 1980.

Tatia, Nathmal. *Aspects of Jaina Monasticism*. New Delhi, 1981.

Taylor, J. L. *Forest Monks and the Nation-State: An Anthropological and Historical Study in North-eastern Thailand*. Singapore, 1993.

Thiel-Horstmann, M. "On the Dual Identity of the Nagas." In *Devotion Divine*, edited by Diana Eck and F. Mallison, pp. 255–271. Paris, 1991.

Thurman, Robert A. F. *Tsong Khapa's Speech of Gold in the "Essence of True Eloquence."* Princeton, 1984.

Tiwari, Kapil N. *Dimensions of Renunciation in Advaita Vedanta*. Delhi, 1977.

Tripathi, B. D. *Sadhus of India*. Bombay, 1978.

Tukol, T. K. *Sallekhana Is Not Suicide*. Ahmedabad, 1976.

Unbescheid, G. *Kānphatā*. Wiesbaden, 1980.

Van der Veer, Peter. "Taming the Ascetic: Devotionalism in Modern Hindu Monastic Orders." *Man* 22 (1987): 680–695.

Van Troy, J. "The Training of the Shaiva Ascetics in the Early Middle Ages." In *Christian Spirituality for India*, edited by M. Druille, pp. 103–118. Bangalore, 1978.

Varenne, Jean. *Yoga and Hindu Tradition*, translated by Derek Coltman. Chicago, 1976.

Wadley, Susan S. "Vrats: Transformers of Destiny." In *Karma: An Anthropological Inquiry*, edited by C. F. Keyes and E. V. Daniel, pp. 147–162. Berkeley, 1983.

Wijayaratna, Mohan. *Buddhist Monastic Life According to the Theravada Tradition*. Cambridge, 1990.

Williams, Cyril G. "World Negation and World Maintenance: Some Hindu Perspectives." *The Scottish Journal of Religious Studies* 8 (Autumn 1987): 85–102.

Williams, R. *Jaina Yoga: A Survey of Medieval Śrāvākācaras*. London, 1963.

Wiltshire, Martin G. *Ascetic Figures before and in Early Buddhism*. Berlin, 1990.

Woods, J. F. "The Concept of Abandonment in the System of Ramanuja." *Journal of Studies in the Bhagavadgita* 5–7 (1985–1987): 82–97.

Central and East Asia

Primary Sources

Bstan-'dzin-rgya-mtsho (Dalai Lama XIV). *Advice from Buddha Shakyamuni: An Abridged Exposition of the Bikkshu's Precepts*. Dharmasala, 1982.

Chan, Wing-tsit, trans. and comp. *A Sourcebook in Chinese Philosophy*. Princeton, 1963.

Chan, Wing-tsit, trans. and comp. *Instructions for Practical Living and Other Neo-Confucian Writings by Wang Yang-ming*. New York, 1984.

Dykstra, Yoshiko Kuirata, trans. *Miraculous Tales of the Lotus Sutra from Ancient Japan: The "Dainihonkoku hokekyo kenki" of the Priest Chingen*. Ōsaka, 1983.

Earhart, H. Byron. *Religion in the Japanese Experience: Sources and Interpretations*. Belmont, Calif., 1974.

Hirose, Nobuko. *Immovable Wisdom: The Art of Zen Strategy*. Longmead, England, 1992.

Hurvitz, Leon, trans. *Scripture of the Lotus Blossom of the Fine Dharma*. New York, 1976.

Kohn, Livia. *The Taoist Experience: An Anthology*. Albany, 1993.

Koller, John M., and Patricia Koller. *A Sourcebook in Asian Philosophy*. New York, 1991.

Lau, D. C. *Tao Te Ching*. Hong Kong, 1982.

Lhalungpa, Lobsang, P. *The Life of Milarepa.* New York, 1977.

Luk, Charles. *Taoist Yoga: Alchemy and Immortality.* London, 1970.

Mi-pham-rgya-mtsho. *Lama Mipam's Commentary to Nagarjuna's Stanzas for a Novice Monk, Together with Tsong Khapa['s] Essence of the Ocean of Vinaya.* Dharmasala, 1978.

Wile, Douglas. *Art of the Bedchamber: The Chinese Sexual Yoga Classics.* Albany, 1992.

Wong, Eva. *Cultivating Stillness* (T'ai Shang Ch'ing-ching Ching). Boston, 1992.

Yokoi Yuho. *Zen Master Dogen.* New York, 1976.

Secondary Sources

Angurohita, Pratoom. *Buddhist Influence on the Neo-Confucian Concept of the Sage.* Philadelphia, 1989.

Blacker, Carmen, *The Catalpa Bow: A Study of Shamanistic Practices in Japan.* 2d ed. London, 1986.

Blofeld, John. *The Way of Power: A Practical Guide to the Tantric Mysticism of Tibet.* London, 1970.

Bowering, Gerhard. *The Ascetic Struggle and Mystic Prayer of a Central Asian Sufi.* Tokyo, 1987.

Buswell, Robert E., Jr. *The Zen Monastic Experience: Buddhist Practice in Contemporary Korea.* Princeton, 1992.

Chang, Chung-yuan. *Tao: A New Way of Thinking: A Translation of the "Tao Te Ching," with an Introduction and Commentaries.* New York, 1975.

Collcutt, Martin. *Five Mountains: The Rinzai Zen Monastic Institution in a Medieval Japan.* Cambridge, 1981.

Deal, William E. "Ascetics, Aristocrats, and the Lotus Sutra: The Construction of the Buddhist Universe in Eleventh Century Japan." Ph.D. diss., Harvard University, 1988.

De Bary, Wm. Theodore. *Self and Society in Ming Thought.* New York, 1970.

Durckheim, Karlfried. *Hara: The Vital Centre of Man,* translated by S. von Kospoth. London, 1977.

Earhart, H. Byron. *A Religious Study of the Mount Haguro Sect of Shugendo.* Tokyo, 1970.

Eliade, Mircea. *Shamanism: Archaic Techniques of Ecstasy* (1951). Princeton, 1972.

Garrett, William R. "The Ascetic Conundrum: The Confucian Ethic and Taoism in Chinese Culture." In *Twentieth-Century World Religious Movements,* edited by W. Swatos, pp. 21–30. Lewiston, N.Y., 1992.

Goullart, Peter. *The Monastery of Jade Mountain.* London, 1961.

Havnevik, Hanna. *Tibetan Buddhist Nuns.* Oslo, 1989.

Hori Ichiro. "On the Concept of the Hijiri (Holy Man)." *Numen* 5 (April 1958): 128–160, 199–232.

Hourmant, Louis, "Ascèse, rationalité, modernité en contexte oriental: Le bouddhisme Soka Gakkai." *Social Compass* 36 (1989): 83–94.

Jan Yun-hua. "Buddhist Self-Immolation in Medieval China." *History of Religions* 4.2 (1965): 243–268.

King, Winston. *Zen and the Way of the Sword: Arming the Samurai Psyche.* New York and Oxford, 1993.

Kohn, Livia. *Taoist Meditation and Longevity Techniques.* Ann Arbor, 1989.

Lutkins, Patricia M. *Aspects of the Aesthete-Recluse Tradition in Japanese Culture.* 1990.

Maspero, Henri. *Taoism and Chinese Religion,* translated by F. A. Kierman. Amherst, Mass., 1981.

Matsunaga, Daigan. *Foundations of Japanese Buddhism.* Los Angeles, 1974–1976.

Miyake Hitoshi. "The Influence of Shugendo on the 'New Religions.' " In *Japanese Buddhism,* edited by M. Kiyota, B. Earhart, P. Griffith, et al., pp. 71–82. Tokyo and Los Angeles, 1987.

Nitobe Inazo. *Bushido: The Soul of Japan.* Rutland, Vt., 1969.

Overmyer, Daniel L. *Folk Buddhist Religion: Dissenting Sects in Late Traditional China.* Cambridge, Mass., 1976.

Porter, Bill. *Road to Heaven: Encounters with Chinese Hermits.* San Francisco, 1993.

Prip-Moller, Johannes. *Chinese Buddhist Monasteries: Their Plan and Its Function as a Setting for Buddhist Monastic Life* (1937). Hong Kong, 1967.

Renondeau, Hartmut O. *Le Shugendo.* Paris, 1965.

Rhodes, Robert F. "The Kaihogyo Practice of Mt. Hiei." *Japanese Journal of Religious Studies* 14 (June–September 1987): 185–202.

Rotermund, Hartmut O. *Die Yamabushi.* Hamburg, 1968.

Stevens, John. *The Marathon Monks of Mount Hiei.* London, 1988.

Suzuki, D. T. *The Training of the Zen Buddhist Monk* (1934). New York, 1965.

Vervoorn, Aat Emile. *Men of Cliffs and Caves: The Development of the Chinese Eremetic Tradition to the End of the Han Dynasty.* Hong Kong, 1990.

Wu, Kuang-ming. *Chuang-tzu: World Philosopher at Play.* New York, 1982.

Judaism

Boyarin, Daniel. *Carnal Israel: Reading Sex in Talmudic Literature.* Berkeley, 1993.

Bulka, Reuven P. *The Jewish Pleasure Principle.* New York, 1987.

Cohen, Shaye. "Asceticism." In *The Universal Jewish Encyclopedia.* New York, 1969

Cohn, J. "Two Studies in Classical Jewish Mysticism." *Judaism* 11 (1962): 242–248.

Fraade, Steven D. "Ascetical Aspects of Ancient Judaism." In *Jewish Spirituality: From the Bible to the Middle Ages,* edited by Arthur Green, pp. 253–288. New York, 1986.

Franck, A. *The Kabbalah: The Religious Philosophy of the Hebrews.* New Hyde Park, N.Y., 1967.

Friedman, M. "Hasidism and the Contemporary Jew." *Judaism* 9 (1960): 197–206.

Green, Arthur, ed. *Jewish Spirituality,* vol. 1, *From the Bible to the Middle Ages;* vol. 2, *From the Sixteenth Century Revival to the Present.* World Spirituality: An Encyclopedic History of the Religious Quest, vols. 13 and 14. New York, 1986, 1987.

Haberman, J. "Asceticism." In *Encyclopedia Judaica.* Jerusalem, 1971.

Halivni, David. "On the Supposed Anti-Asceticism or Anti-Naziritiam of Simon the Just." *Jewish Quarterly Review* 58 (1968): 243–252.

Halperin, David J. *Faces of the Chariot.* Tubingen, 1988.

Meijers, Daniel. *Ascetic Hasidism in Jerusalem: The Guardian-of-the-Faithful Community of Mea Shearim.* Studies in Judaism in Modern Times, vol. 10. Leiden, 1992.

Neusner, Jacob. *The Idea of Purity in Ancient Judaism.* Leiden, 1973.

Safran, A. *Die Kabbala.* Bern, 1966.

Scholem, Gerschom. *Origins of the Kabbalah.* Princeton, 1987.

Schwartz, Michael D. "Hekalot Rabbati #297–306: A Ritual for the Cultivation of the Prince of the Torah." In *Ascetic Behavior in Greco-Roman Antiquity: A Sourcebook,* edited by Vincent L. Wimbush, pp. 227–234. Minneapolis, 1990.

Urbach, E. E. "Askēsis and Suffering in Talmudic and Midrashic Sources" (Hebrew text with English summary). In *Yitzak F. Baer Jubilee Volume,* edited by S. W. Baron, pp. 48–68. Jerusalem, 1960.

Islam

Primary Sources

Cragg, Kenneth, and R. Marston Speight, eds. *Islam from Within: Anthology of a Religion.* Belmont, Calif., 1980.

Encyclopaedia of Islam. New ed. Leiden, 1954–.

Guillaume, Alfred, trans. *The Life of Muhammad: A Translation of Ishaq's "Sirat Rasul Allah."* London, 1967.

Shorter Encyclopaedia of Islam. Leiden, 1953.

Secondary Sources

Beck, Lois Grant, and Nikki R. Keddie, eds. *Women in the Muslim World.* Cambridge, Mass., 1978.

Fasting: A Divine Banquet. Islamic Concepts, 3. Teheran, 1990.

Malti-Douglas, Fedwa. *Structures of Avarice: The Bukhala' in Medieval Arabic Literature.* Leiden, 1985.

Malti-Douglas, Fedwa. *Woman's Body, Woman's Word: Gender and Discourse in Arabo-Islamic Writing.* Princeton, 1991.

Nasr, Seyyed Hossein. *Ideals and Realities of Islam.* Boston, 1972.

Qaradawi, Yusuf al-. *The Lawful and the Prohibited in Islam.* Indianapolis, 1980.

Schimmel, Annemarie. *Mystical Dimensions of Islam.* Chapel Hill, 1975.

Smith, Margaret. *Rabi'a the Mystic and Her Fellow-Saints in Islam* (1928). Cambridge and New York, 1984.

Wiebke, Walther. *Women in Islam.* Montclair, N.J., 1981.

Woodward, Mark R. *Islam in Java: Normative Piety and Mysticism in the Sultanate of Yogyakarta.* Tucson, 1989.

Greco-Roman Antiquity

Primary Sources

Brock, Sebastian P., and Susan B. Harvey, eds. and trans. *Holy Women of the Syrian Orient.* Transformation of the Classical Heritage, vol. 13. Berkeley and Los Angeles, 1987.

Chadwick, Owen. *Western Asceticism.* Library of Christian Classics. Philadelphia, 1958.

Kraemer, Ross S., ed. *Maenads, Martyrs, Matrons, Monastics: A Sourcebook on Women's Religions in the Greco-Roman World.* Philadelphia, 1988.

Wimbush, Vincent, L., ed. *Ascetic Behavior in Greco-Roman Antiquity: A Sourcebook.* Studies in Antiquity and Christianity. Minneapolis, 1990.

Secondary Sources

Bonhoeffer, A. *Die Ethik des Stoikers Epictet.* Stuttgart, 1894.

Dover, K. J. *Greek Popular Morality in the the Time of Plato and Aristotle.* Oxford, 1974.

Foucault, Michel. *The History of Sexuality,* vol. 2, *The Care of the Self,* translated by Robert Hurley. New York, 1985.

Foucault, Michel. *The History of Sexuality,* vol. 3, *The Use of Pleasures,* translated by Robert Hurley. New York, 1985.

Fuchs, Harald. *Der Geistige Widerstand gegen Rom in der Antiken Welt.* Berlin, 1938.

Goulet-Caze, Marie-Odile. *L'ascèse cynique: Une commentaire de Diogene Laerce VI 70–71.* Histoire des doctrines de l'Antiquité classique, 10. Paris, 1986.

Hadot, Pierre. *Exercices spirituels et philosophie antique.* Paris, 1981.

Hadot, Pierre. "Forms of Life and Forms of Discourse in Ancient Philosophy." *Critical Inquiry* 16 (1990): 483–505.

Hadot, Pierre. *Plotinus, or The Simplicity of Vision,* translated by Michael Chase, introduction by Arnold I. Davidson. Chicago and London, 1993.

Inwood, Brad. *Ethics and Human Action in Early Stoicism.* Oxford, 1985.

Jones, C. P. *Plutarch and Rome.* Oxford, 1971.

Leipoldt, J. *Griechische Philosophie und Fruehchristliche Askese.* Berlin, 1961.

Lohse, B. *Askese und Monchtum in der Antike und in der Alten Kirche.* Munich and Vienna, 1969.

Lutz, Cora E. *Musonius Rufus: "The Roman Socrates."* New Haven, 1947.

MacMullen, Ramsay. *Enemies of the Roman Order: Treason, Unrest, and Alienation in the Empire.* Cambridge, Mass., 1966

Meredith, A. "Asceticism—Christian and Greek." *Journal of Theological Studies* 27 (1976): 313–332.

Nietzsche. Friedrich Wilhelm. *On the Genealogy of Morals* (1967). New York, 1989.

North, Helen F. *Sōphrosynē: Self-Knowledge and Self-Restraint in Greek Literature.* Cornell Studies in Classical Philology, vol. 35. Ithaca, 1966.

Nussbaum, Martha C. *The Therapy of Desire: Theory and Practice in Hellenistic Ethics.* Princeton, 1994.

Parker, Robert. *Miasma: Pollution and Purification in Early Greek Religion.* Oxford, 1983.

Randall, John Hermann. *Hellenistic Ways of Deliverance and the Making of the Christian Synthesis.* New York, 1970.

Rist, John M. *Stoic Philosophy.* Cambridge, 1969.

Rist, John M., ed. *The Stoics.* Berkeley, 1978.

Swain, Joseph Ward. *The Hellenic Origins of Christian Asceticism.* New York, 1916.

Veyne, Paul, ed. *A History of Private Life,* vol. 1, *From Pagan Rome to Byzantium,* translated by Arthur Goldhammer. Cambridge, Mass., 1987.

Whitchurch, I. G. *The Philosophical Bases of Asceticism in Platonic Writings and in the Pre-Platonic Tradition.* New York and London, 1923.

Wicker, Kathleen O. "The Ascetic Marriage in Antiquity." *Bulletin of the Institute for Antiquity and Christianity* 15 (1988): 10–13.

Wimbush, Vincent L. *Renunciation towards Social Engineering: An Apologia for the Study of Asceticism in Greco-Roman Antiquity.* Occasional Papers of the Institute for Christianity and Antiquity, 8. Claremont, Calif., 1986.

Wimbush, Vincent L. "*Sōphrosynē:* Greco-Roman Origins of a Type of Ascetic Behavior." In *Gnosticism and the Early Christian World,* edited by James E. Goehring et al., pp. 89–102. Sonoma, Calif., 1990.

Black Ascetics in Greco-Roman Antiquity

Primary Sources

Wicker, Kathleen O. "Ethiopian Moses (Collected Sources)." In *Ascetic Behavior in Greco-Roman Antiquity: A Sourcebook,* edited by Vincent L. Wimbush, pp. 329–348. Minneapolis, 1990.

Secondary Sources

Courtes, Jean Marie. "The Theme of 'Ethiopians' in Patristic Literature." In *The Image of the Black in Western Art: From the Early Christian Era to the Age of Discovery,* edited by Jean Devisse, vol. 2.1, translated by William Granger Ryan. New York, 1979.

Frost, Peter. "Attitudes toward Blacks in the Early Christian Era." *Second Century* 8 (1991): 1–11.

Snowden, Frank. *Blacks in Antiquity: Ethiopians in the Greco-Roman Experience.* Cambridge, Mass., 1970.

Snowden, Frank, Jr. *Before Color Prejudice: The Ancient View of Blacks.* Cambridge, Mass., 1983.

Vercoutter, J., et al., eds. *The Image of the Black in Western Art,* vol. 1, *From the Pharaohs to the Fall of the Roman Empire.* New York, 1976.

Wimbush, Vincent L. "Ascetic Behavior and Color-ful Language: Stories about Ethiopian Moses." *Semeia* 58 (*Discursive Formations, Ascetic Piety and the Interpretation of Early Christian Literature,* edited by Vincent L. Wimbush) (1992): 81–92.

Early Christianity

Brown, Peter. *The Body and Society.* New York, 1988. Note: This work should be consulted for an extensive bibliographic listing up to 1987.

Primary Sources

Chadwick, Owen. *Western Asceticism.* Library of Christian Classics. Philadelphia, 1958.

Doran, Robert. *The Lives of Symeon Stylites.* Kalamazoo, 1992.

Driscoll, J. *The "Ad Monachos" of Evagrius Ponticus: Its Structure and a Select Commentary.* Rome, 1991.

Kraemer, Ross S., ed. *Maenads, Martyrs, Matrons, Monastics.* Minneapolis, 1988.

Price, R. M. *Cyril of Scythopolis: The Lives of the Monks of Palestine.* Kalamazoo, 1991.

Vivian, Tim. *History of the Monks of Upper Egypt and the Life of Onnophrius by Paphnutius.* Kalamazoo, 1993.

Wimbush, Vincent L., ed. *Ascetic Behavior in Greco-Roman Antiquity: A Sourcebook.* Studies in Antiquity and Christianity. Minneapolis, 1990.

Secondary Sources

Bitel, Lisa M. *Isle of the Saints: Monastic Settlement and Christian Community in Early Ireland.* Ithaca, 1990.

Boswell, John. *Same-Sex Unions in Premodern Europe.* New York, 1994.

Brakke, David Bernhard. "St. Athanasius and Ascetic Christians in Egypt." Ph.D. diss., Yale University, 1992.

Brown, Peter. *The Body and Society: Men, Women, and Sexual Renunciation in Early Christianity.* New York, 1988.

Burton-Christie, Douglas. *The Word in the Desert: Scripture and the Quest for Holiness in Early Christian Monasticism.* New York and Oxford, 1993.

Cameron, Averil. *Christianity and the Rhetoric of Empire.* Berkeley, 1990.

Clark, Elizabeth A. *The Origenist Controversy: The Cultural Construction of an Early Christian Debate.* Princeton, 1992.

Cooper, Kate. "Concord and Martyrdom: Gender, Community, and the Uses of Christian Perfection in Late Antiquity." Ph.D. diss., Princeton University, 1993.

Countryman, L. William. *Dirt, Greed and Sex: Sexual Ethics in the New Testament and Their Implications for Today.* Philadelphia, 1988.

Dechow, Jon F. *Dogma and Mysticism in Early Christianity: Epiphanius of Cyprus and the Legacy of Origin.* Macon, Ga., 1988.

Goehring, J. E. "The World Engaged: The Social and Economic World of Early Egyptian Monasticism."

In *Gnosticism and the Early Christian World,* edited by J. E. Goehring et al., pp. 134–144. Sonoma, Calif., 1990.

Harvey, Susan Ashbrook. *Asceticism and Society in Crisis: John of Ephesus and the Lives of the Eastern Saints.* Berkeley, 1990.

Hirschfeld, Yizhar. *The Judean Desert Monasteries in the Byzantine Period.* New York, 1992.

Markus, R. A. *The End of Ancient Christianity.* Cambridge, 1991.

McGinn, Bernard, et al., eds. *Christian Spirituality: Origins to the Twelfth Century.* World Spirituality: An Encyclopedic History of the Religious Quest, vol. 16, New York, 1989.

Meeks, Wayne A. *The Origins of Christian Morality; The First Two Centuries.* New Haven and London, 1993.

Miles, Margaret R. *Desire and Delight: A New Reading of Augustine's Confessions.* New York, 1992.

Regnault, Lucien. *La vie quotidienne des pères du désert en Égypte au IVe siècle.* Paris, 1990.

Rouselle, Aline. *Porneia: On Desire and the Body in Antiquity.* Oxford, 1988.

Rousseau, Philip. "Christian Ascetics and the Early Monks." In *Early Christianity,* edited by I. Hazlett, pp. 112–122. Nashville, 1991.

Rubenson, Samuel. *The Letters of St. Anthony.* Lund, 1990.

Salisbury, Joyce E. *Church Fathers, Independent Virgins.* London, 1991.

Theissen, Gerd. *Social Reality and the Early Christians: Theology, Ethics, and the World of the New Testament,* translated by Margaret Kohl. Minneapolis, 1992.

Trexler, Richard C. *Naked before the Father: The Renunciation of Francis of Assisi.* New York, 1989.

Valantasis, Richard. *Spiritual Guides of the Third Century: A Semiotic Study of the Guide-Disciple Relationship in Christianity, Neoplatonism, Hermetism, and Gnosticism.* Harvard Dissertations in Religion, 27. Minneapolis, 1991.

Van den Hoek, Annawies. *Clement of Alexandria and His Use of Philo in the Stromateis: An Early Christian Reshaping of a Jewish Model.* Leiden, 1988.

Wengst, Klaus. *Humility: Solidarity of the Humiliated,* translated by John Bowden, 1988.

Wimbush, Vincent L. *Paul the Worldly Ascetic: Response to the World and Self-Understanding According to 1 Corinthians 7.* Macon, Ga., 1987.

Wimbush, Vincent L., ed. *Semeia* 57 and 58: *Discursive Formations, Ascetic Piety and the Interpretation of Early Christian Literature.* Atlanta, 1992.

Women

Primary Sources

Brock, Sebastian P., and Susan Ashbrook Harvey, eds. *Holy Women of the Syrian Orient.* Transformation of the Classical Heritage, vol. 13. Berkeley and Los Angeles, 1987.

Kraemer, Ross S., ed. *Maenads, Martyrs, Matrons, Monastics: A Sourcebook on Women's Religions in the Greco-Roman World.* Philadelphia, 1988.

Wimbush, Vincent L., ed. *Ascetic Behavior in Greco-Roman Antiquity: A Sourcebook.* Minneapolis, 1990.

Secondary Sources

Beck, Lois Grant, and Nikki R. Keddie, eds. *Women in the Muslim World.* Cambridge, Mass., 1978.

Burrus, Virginia. *Chastity as Autonomy: Women in the Stories of the Apocryphal Acts.* Lewiston, N.Y., 1987.

Bynum, Caroline Walker. *Holy Feast and Holy Fast: The Religious Significance of Food to Medieval Women.* Berkeley and Los Angeles, 1987.

Cameron, A., and A. Kuhrt, eds. *Images of Women in Late Antiquity*. Detroit, 1983.

Cantarella, Eva. *Pandora's Daughters: The Role and Status of Women in Greek and Roman Antiquity*, translated by Maureen B. Fant. Baltimore and London, 1987.

Clark, Elizabeth A. *Ascetic Piety and Women's Faith: Essays on Late Ancient Christianity*. Lewiston, N.Y., 1986.

Clark, E., and H. Richardson, eds. *Women and Religion: A Feminist Sourcebook of Christian Thought*. New York, 1977.

Cooper, Kate. "Concord and Martyrdom: Gender, Community, and the Uses of Christian Perfection in Late Antiquity." Ph.D. diss., Princeton University, 1993.

Corrington, Gail P. "Anorexia, Asceticism, and Autonomy: Self-Control as Liberation and Transcendence." *Journal of Feminist Studies in Religion* 2 (1986): 51–61.

Elm, Susanna K. "The Organization and Institutions of Female Asceticism in Fourth-Century Cappadocia and Egypt." D.Phil. thesis, University of Oxford, 1987.

Hallett, Judith P. *Fathers and Daughters in Roman Society: Women and the Elite Family*. Princeton, 1984.

Hickey, Ann E. *Women of the Roman Aristocracy as Christian Monastics*. Ann Arbor, 1987.

King, Karen, L., ed. *Images of the Feminine in Gnosticism*. Studies in Antiquity and Christianity. Minneapolis, 1990.

Kraemer, Ross S. "The Conversion of Women to Ascetic Forms of Christianity." *Signs* 6.2 (1980): 298–307.

Lang, K. C. "Images of Women in Early Buddhism and Christian Gnosticism." *Buddhist and Christian Studies* 2 (1965): 95–105.

Malaty, T. Y. "Early Monasticism among Women in the Coptic Church." *Coptic Church Review* 1 (1980): 168–172.

Malti-Douglas, Fedwa. *Woman's Body, Woman's Word: Gender and Discourse in Arabo-Islamic Writing*. Princeton, 1991.

Ruether, Rosemary. R., and E. McLaughlin, eds. *Women of Spirit: Female Leadership in the Jewish and Christian Traditions*. New York, 1979.

Sharma, Arvind, ed. *Women in World Religions*. McGill Studies in the History of Religions. Albany, 1987.

Sharma, Arvind. *Religion and Women*. McGill Studies in the History of Religions. Albany, 1994.

Sharma, Arvind, ed. *Today's Woman in World Religions*. McGill Studies in the History of Religions. Albany, 1994.

Smith, Margaret. *Rabi'a the Mystic and Her Fellow Saints in Islam: Being the Life and Teachings of Rabi'a-'Adawiyya al-Qaysiyya of Basra Together with Some Accounts of the Place of Women Saints in Islam*. Cambridge and New York, 1984.

Torjesen, Karen Jo. *When Women Were Priests: Women's Leadership in the Early Church and the Scandal of Their Subordination in the Rise of Christianity*. New York, 1993.

Wiebke, Walther. *Women in Islam*. Montclair, N.J., 1981

Wire, Antoinette C. *The Corinthian Women Prophets: A Reconstruction through Paul's Rhetoric*. Minneapolis, 1990.

Medieval and Modern Europe

Boswell, John. *Same-Sex Unions in Premodern Europe*. New York, 1994.

Brundage, James A. *Law, Sex, and Christian Society in Medieval Europe*. Chicago and London, 1987.

Bugge, John. *Virginitas: An Essay in the History of a Medieval Ideal*. The Hague, 1975.

Chartier, Roger, ed. *A History of Private Life*, vol. 3, *Passions of the Renaissance,* translated by Arthur Goldhammer. Cambridge, Mass., and London, 1989.

Davis, K. R. *Anabaptism and Asceticism: A Study in Intellectual Origins*. Scottdale, Pa., 1974.

Delumeau, Jean. *Sin and Fear: The Emergence of a Western Guilt Culture: Thirteenth–Eighteenth Centuries,* translated by Eric Nicholson. New York, 1990.

Duby, Georges, ed. *A History of Private Life,* vol. 2, *Revelations of the Medieval World,* translated by Arthur Goldhammer. Cambridge, Mass., and London, 1988.

McGinn, Bernard, et al., eds. *Christian Spirituality: Origins to the Twelfth Century*. World Spirituality: An Encyclopedic History of the Religious Quest, vol. 16. New York, 1985.

Raitt, Jill, et al., eds. *Christian Spirituality: High Middle Ages and Reformation*. World Spirituality: An Encyclopedic History of the Religious Quest, vol. 17. New York, 1985.

Weinstein, Donald, and Rudolph M. Bell. *Saints and Society: The Two Worlds of Western Christendom, 1000 to 1700.* Chicago, 1986.

INDEX

Lightning Source UK Ltd.
Milton Keynes UK
UKOW03f0156241014

240479UK00011BA/266/P

9 780195 151381